SHELLY CASHMAN SERIES®

INTRODUCTORY

Microsoft® Office 365® & OFFICE 2019

SANDRA E. CABLE | STEVEN M. FREUND | ELLEN F. MONK
SUSAN L. SEBOK | MISTY E. VERMAAT

Cengage

SHELLY CASHMAN SERIES®

Australia • Brazil • Canada • Mexico • Singapore • United Kingdom • United States

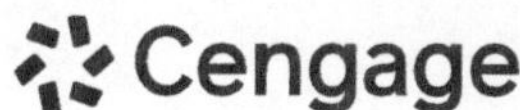

Shelly Cashman Series® Microsoft® Office 365® & Office 2019 Introductory
Sandra E. Cable, Steven M. Freund, Ellen F. Monk, Susan L. Sebok, Misty E. Vermaat

SVP, GM Skills & Global Product Management: Jonathan Lau

Product Director: Lauren Murphy

Product Assistant: Veronica Moreno-Nestojko

Executive Director, Content Design: Marah Bellegarde

Director, Learning Design: Leigh Hefferon

Associate Learning Designer: Courtney Cozzy

Vice President, Marketing—Science, Technology, and Math: Jason R. Sakos

Senior Marketing Director: Michele McTighe

Marketing Manager: Timothy J. Cali

Director, Content Delivery: Patty Stephan

Senior Content Manager: Anne Orgren

Digital Delivery Lead: Laura Ruschman

Designer: Lizz Anderson

Cover image(s): Sergey Kelin/ShutterStock.com (Ocean), nikkytok/ShutterStock.com (Crystal), PARINKI/ShutterStock.com (Marble), Erika Kirkpatrick/ShutterStock.com (Driftwood), Vladitto/ShutterStock.com (Skyscraper), Roman Sigaev/ShutterStock.com (Clouds)

Mac Users: If you're working through this product using a Mac, some of the steps may vary. Additional information for Mac users is included with the Data files for this product.

Disclaimer: This text is intended for instructional purposes only; data is fictional and does not belong to any real persons or companies.

Disclaimer: The material in this text was written using Microsoft Windows 10 and Office 365 Professional Plus and was Quality Assurance tested before the publication date. As Microsoft continually updates the Windows 10 operating system and Office 365, your software experience may vary slightly from what is presented in the printed text.

Library of Congress Control Number: 2018966288

Student Edition ISBN: 978-0-357-02643-4
K12 ISBN: 978-0-357-11944-0
Looseleaf available as part of a digital bundle

Cengage
200 Pier 4 Boulevard
Boston, MA 02210
USA

Cengage is a leading provider of customized learning solutions with employees residing in nearly 40 different countries and sales in more than 125 countries around the world. Find your local representative at **www.cengage.com.**

To learn more about Cengage platforms and services, visit **www.cengage.com**.

Printed at CLDPC, USA, 05-22

Microsoft® Office 365® & OFFICE 2019

INTRODUCTORY

Brief Contents

Microsoft® Office 365® & OFFICE 2019

INTRODUCTORY

Contents

MODULE TWO

Creating a Research Paper

MODULE THREE

Creating a Business Letter

Microsoft **PowerPoint 2019**

MODULE ONE

Creating and Editing Presentations with Pictures

MODULE TWO

Enhancing Presentations with Shapes and SmartArt

MODULE THREE
Inserting WordArt, Charts, and Tables

Microsoft Excel 2019

MODULE ONE
Creating a Worksheet and a Chart

MODULE TWO

Formulas, Functions, and Formatting

MODULE TWO
Querying a Database

MODULE THREE
Maintaining a Database

Getting to Know Microsoft Office Versions

Cengage is proud to bring you the next edition of Microsoft Office. This edition was designed to provide a robust learning experience that is not dependent upon a specific version of Office.

Microsoft supports several versions of Office:

- **Office 365:** A cloud-based subscription service that delivers Microsoft's most up-to-date, feature-rich, modern productivity tools direct to your device. There are variations of Office 365 for business, educational, and personal use. Office 365 offers extra online storage and cloud-connected features, as well as updates with the latest features, fixes, and security updates.
- **Office 2019:** Microsoft's "on-premises" version of the Office apps, available for both PCs and Macs, offered as a static, one-time purchase and outside of the subscription model.
- **Office Online:** A free, simplified version of Office web applications (Word, Excel, PowerPoint, and OneNote) that facilitates creating and editing files collaboratively.

Office 365 (the subscription model) and Office 2019 (the one-time purchase model) had only slight differences between them at the time this content was developed. Over time, Office 365's cloud interface will continuously update, offering new application features and functions, while Office 2019 will remain static. Therefore, your onscreen experience may differ from what you see in this product. For example, the more advanced features and functionalities covered in this product may not be available in Office Online or may have updated from what you see in Office 2019.

For more information on the differences between Office 365, Office 2019, and Office Online, please visit the Microsoft Support site.

Cengage is committed to providing high-quality learning solutions for you to gain the knowledge and skills that will empower you throughout your educational and professional careers.

Thank you for using our product, and we look forward to exploring the future of Microsoft Office with you!

Using SAM Projects and Textbook Projects

SAM and *MindTap* are interactive online platforms designed to transform students into Microsoft Office and Computer Concepts masters. Practice with simulated SAM Trainings and MindTap activities and actively apply the skills you learned live in Microsoft Word, Excel, PowerPoint, or Access. Become a more productive student and use these skills throughout your career.

If your instructor assigns SAM Projects:

1. Launch your SAM Project assignment from SAM or MindTap.
2. Click the links to download your **Instructions file**, **Start file**, and **Support files** (when available).
3. Open the Instructions file and follow the step-by-step instructions.
4. When you complete the project, upload your file to SAM or MindTap for immediate feedback.

To use SAM Textbook Projects:

1. Launch your SAM Project assignment from SAM or MindTap.
2. Click the links to download your **Start file** and **Support files** (when available).
3. Locate the module indicated in your book or eBook.
4. Read the module and complete the project.

Open the Start file you downloaded.

Save, close, and upload your completed project to receive immediate feedback.

IMPORTANT: To receive full credit for your Textbook Project, you must complete the activity using the Start file you downloaded from SAM or MindTap.

1 Creating and Modifying a Flyer

Objectives

After completing this module, you will be able to:

- Start and exit Word
- Enter text in a Word document
- Adjust margins
- Check spelling and grammar as you work in a document
- Save a document
- Format text, paragraphs, and document elements
- Undo and redo commands or actions
- Insert and format a picture
- Add a page border
- Change document properties
- Open and close a document
- Correct errors and revise a document
- Cut, copy, and paste text
- Print a document
- Use Word Help

What Is Word?

Microsoft Word, or Word, is a full-featured word processing app that allows you to create professional-looking documents and revise them easily. With Word, you can create business, academic, and personal documents, including flyers, research papers, letters, memos, resumes, reports, mailing labels, and newsletters.

Word has many features designed to simplify the production of documents and add visual appeal. Using Word, you easily can change the shape, size, and color of text. You also can include borders, shading, tables, pictures, charts, and other objects in documents. While you are typing, Word performs many tasks automatically. For example, Word detects and corrects spelling and grammar errors in several languages. Word's thesaurus allows you to add variety and precision to your writing. In addition to formatting text as you type, such as headings, lists, fractions, borders, and web addresses, Word includes a great deal of predefined text and many predefined objects and document types. Word also provides tools that enable you to create webpages and save the webpages directly on a web server.

To illustrate the features of Word, this book presents a series of projects that use Word to create documents similar to those you will encounter in business and academic environments.

Introduction

To convey a message or announcement to employees or staff members, campus or school students, or the community or public, you may want to create a flyer. You then can post the flyer in a location targeted to your intended audience, such as on an employee bulletin board or in an office cubicle, at a kiosk, or on a hallway wall. You may also see flyers on webpages, on social media, or in email messages.

Project: Flyer with a Picture

Businesses create flyers to gain attention for a message or an announcement. Flyers, which usually are a single page in length, are an inexpensive means of reaching an audience. Many flyers, however, go unnoticed because they are designed poorly.

The project in this module follows generally accepted design guidelines and uses Microsoft Word to create the flyer shown in Figure 1–1. This colorful, eye-catching flyer is intended to convey proper handwashing techniques to food service employees at a campus or school cafeteria. The flyer, which will be hung above every sink in the kitchen and restroom areas, contains a digital picture of an employee washing his hands. The headline on the flyer is large and colorful to draw attention into the text. The body copy

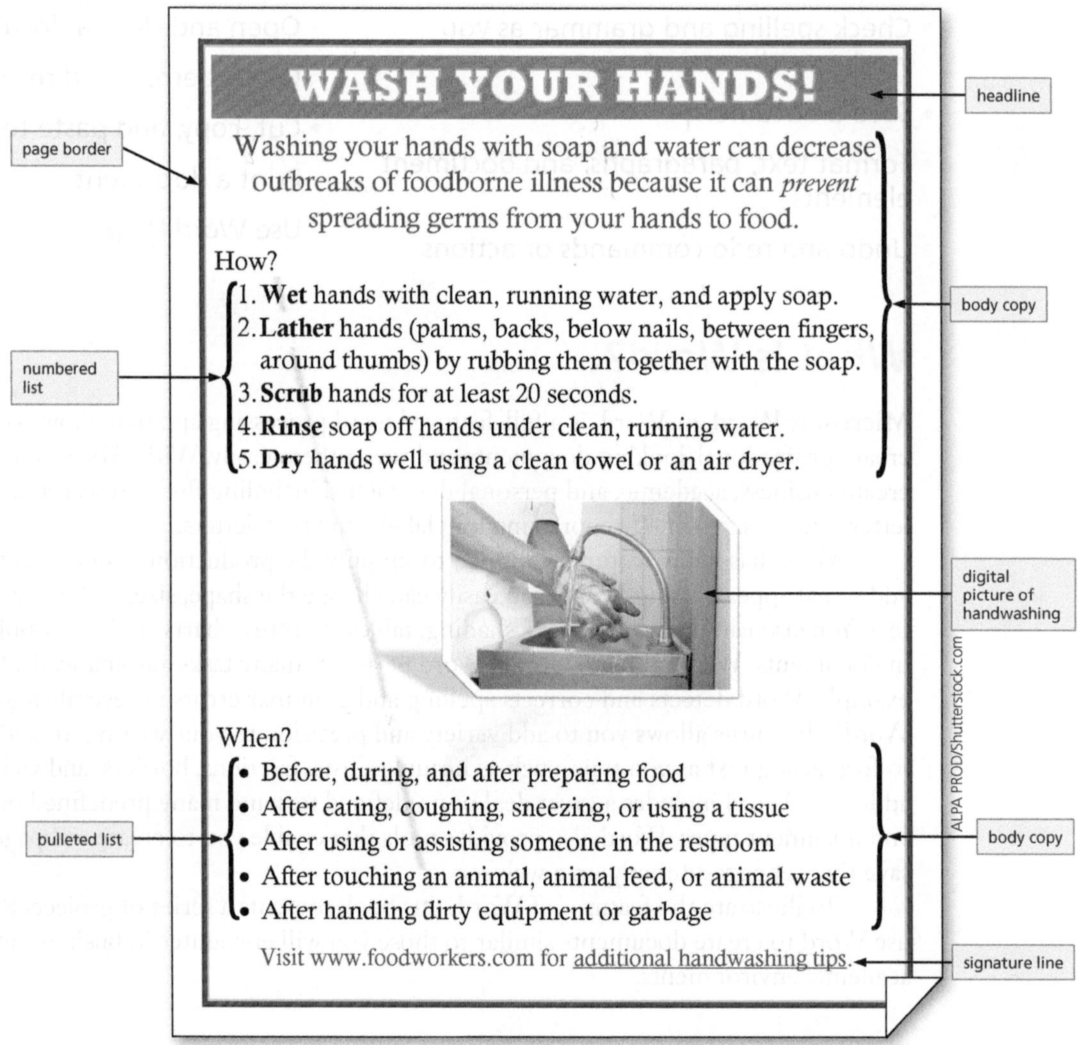

Figure 1–1

below the headline briefly describes the purpose of handwashing, along with a numbered list that highlights how to wash hands and a bulleted list that concisely describes when to wash hands. The signature line of the flyer identifies a website that employees can visit for additional handwashing tips. Some words in the flyer are in a different color or further emphasized so that they stand apart from the rest of the text on the flyer. Finally, the page border nicely frames and complements the contents of the flyer.

In this module, you will learn how to create the flyer shown in Figure 1–1. You will perform the following general tasks as you progress through this module:

1. Start and use Word.
2. Enter text in a document.
3. Format the text in the flyer.
4. Insert and format a picture in the flyer.
5. Enhance the layout of the flyer on the page.
6. Correct errors and revise text in the flyer.

Starting and Using Word

To use Word, you must instruct the operating system (i.e., Windows) to start the app. The following sections start Word, discuss some elements of the Word window, and perform tasks to specify Word settings.

If you are using a computer or device to step through the project in this module and you want your screen to match the figures in this book, you should change your screen's resolution to 1366 × 768.

BTW
Resolution
For information about how to change a computer's resolution, search for 'change resolution' in your operating system's help files.

To Start Word and Create a Blank Document

The following steps, which assume Windows is running, start Word and create a blank document based on a typical installation. ***Why?*** *You will use Word to create the flyer in this module.* You may need to ask your instructor how to start Word on your computer or device.

1

- **sam** Click the Start button on the Windows taskbar to display the Start menu.

Q&A What is a menu?
A **menu** contains a list of related items, including commands, apps, programs, and folders. Each **command** is a menu item that performs a specific action, such as saving a file or obtaining help. A **folder** is a named location on a storage medium that usually contains related documents.

- If necessary, scroll through the list of apps on the Start menu until the Word app name appears (Figure 1–2).

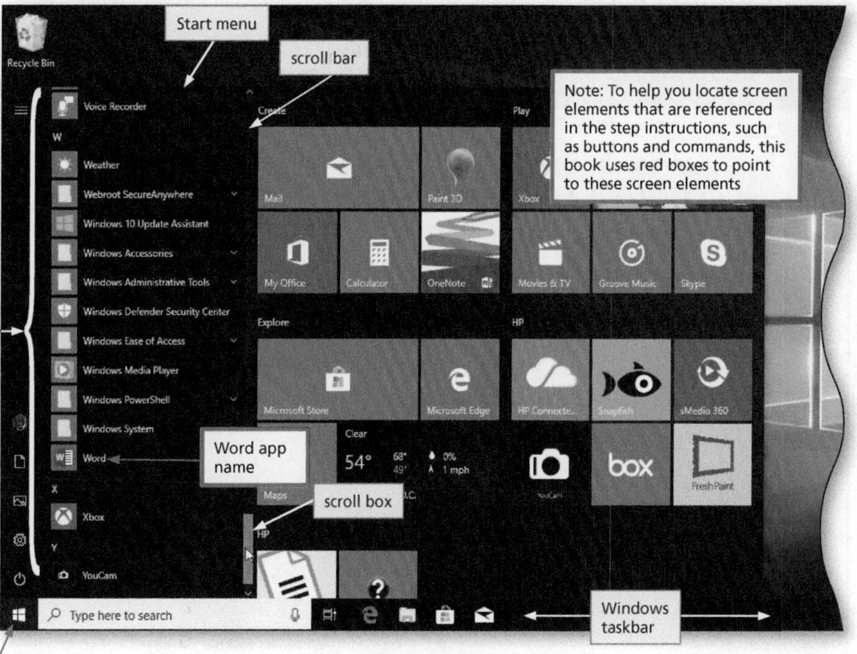

Figure 1–2

Q&A What if my Word app is in a folder?
Click the appropriate folder name to display the contents of the folder.

- Click Word on the Start menu to start Word and display the Word start screen (Figure 1–3).

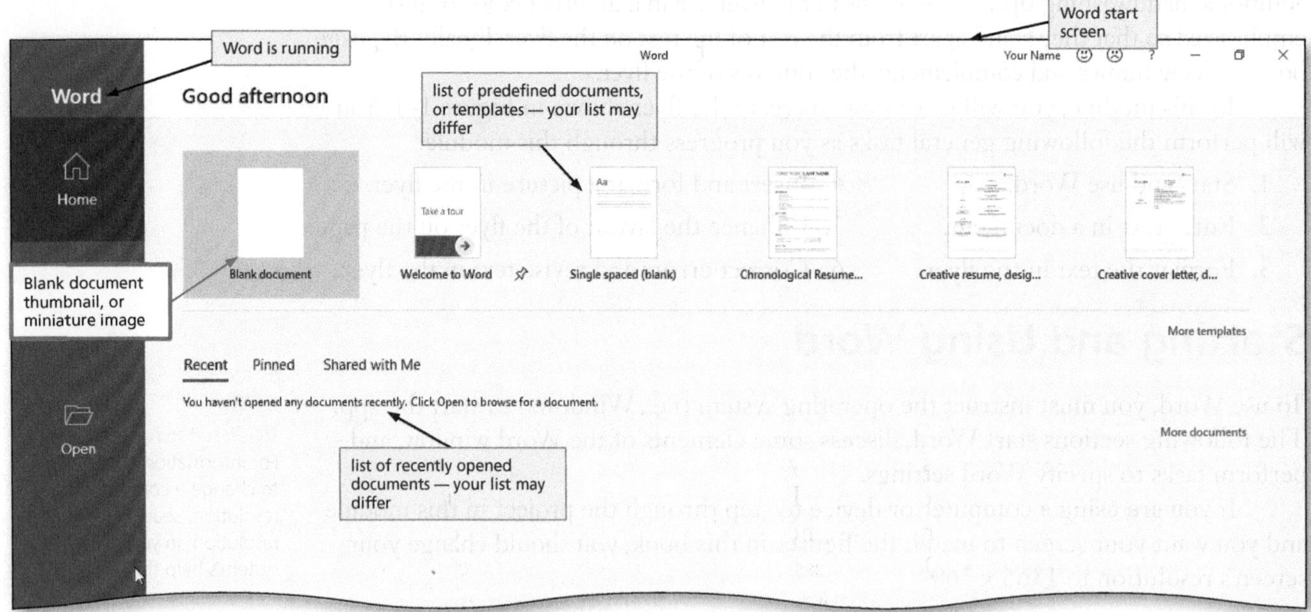

Figure 1–3

- Click the Blank document thumbnail on the Word start screen to create a blank document in the Word window (Figure 1–4).
- If the Word window is not maximized, click the Maximize button next to the Close button on the title bar to maximize the window.

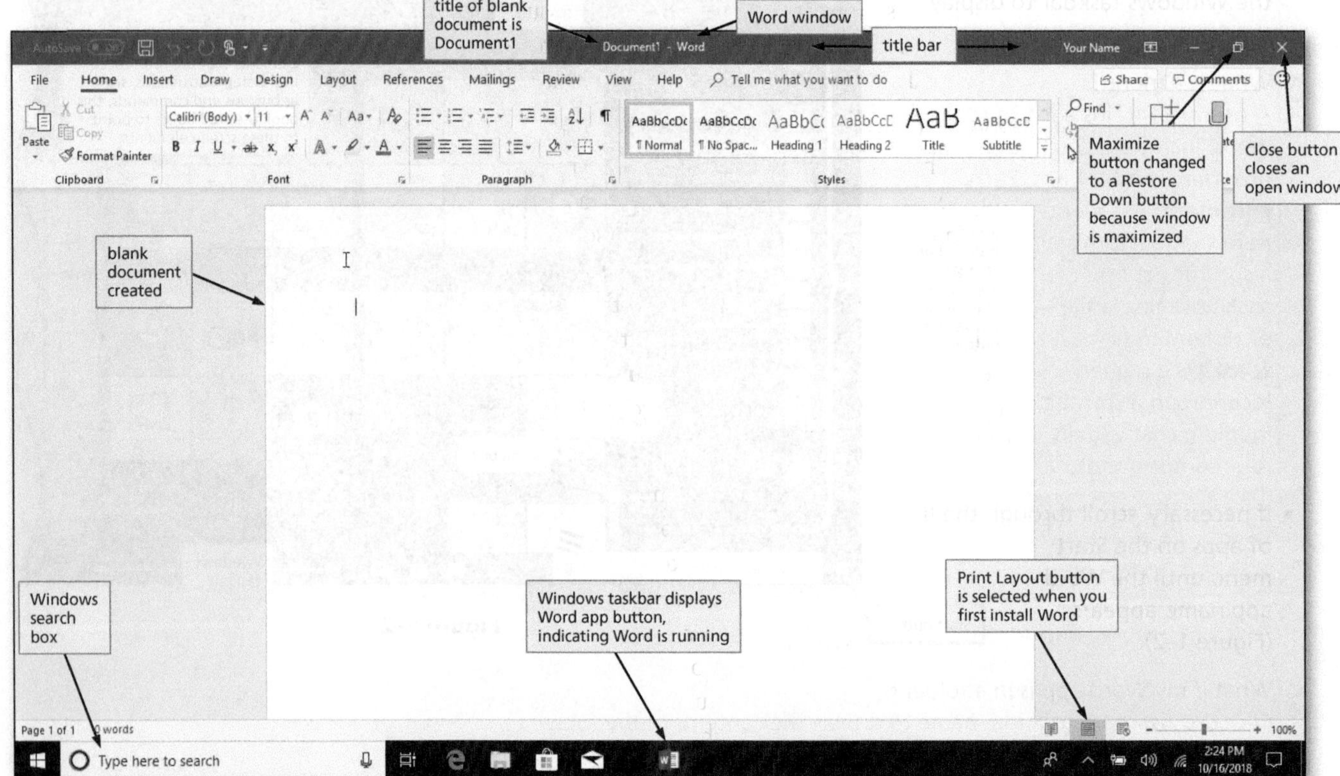

Figure 1–4

Q&A | What is a maximized window?
A maximized window fills the entire screen. When you maximize a window, the Maximize button changes to a Restore Down button.

- **If the Print Layout button is not selected, click it so that your screen layout matches Figure 1–4.**

Q&A | What is Print Layout view?
The default (preset) view in Word is **Print Layout view**, which shows the document on an image of a sheet of paper in the document window.

Other Ways

1. Type app name in Windows search box, click app name in results list
2. Double-click Word icon on desktop, if one is present

The Word Window

BTW
The Word Window
The modules in this book begin with the Word window appearing as it did at the initial installation of the software. Your Word window may look different depending on your screen resolution and other Word settings.

The Word window consists of a variety of components to make your work more efficient and documents more professional. These include the document window and several other elements, depending on the task you are performing: scroll bar(s), status bar, ribbon, Tell Me box, Quick Access Toolbar, Mini toolbar, shortcut menus, KeyTips, and Microsoft Account area. Most of these are common to other Microsoft Office apps; others are unique to Word. The following sections briefly describe these elements; others are discussed as they appear in the Word window.

You view or work with a document on the screen through a **document window**, which is a window within Word that displays all or part of an open document (Figure 1–5). In the document, the **insertion point** is a blinking vertical line that appears when you click in the document and indicates where new text, pictures, and other objects will be inserted. As you type, the insertion point moves to the right, and when you reach the end of a line, it moves down to the beginning of the next line. The **pointer** is a small symbol on the screen that becomes different shapes depending on the task you are performing in Word and the pointer's location on the screen. You move the pointer with a pointing device, such as a mouse or touchpad. The pointer in Figure 1–5 is the shape of an I-beam.

Scroll Bar You use **scroll bars**, which appear at the right and bottom edges of the document window, to view documents that are too large to fit on the screen at once. At the right edge of the document window is a vertical scroll bar. If a document is too wide to fit in the document window, a horizontal scroll bar also appears at the bottom of the document window. On a scroll bar, the position of the **scroll box** reflects the location of the portion of the document that is displayed in the document window; you can drag the scroll box, or click above or below it, to scroll through or display different parts of the document in the document window. A **scroll arrow** is a small triangular up or down arrow that is located at each end of a scroll bar; you can click the scroll arrows to scroll through the document in small increments.

Status Bar The **status bar**, located at the bottom of the document window above the Windows taskbar, presents information about the document, the progress of current tasks, and the status of certain commands and keys; it also provides controls for viewing the document, such as zoom controls. As you type text or perform certain commands, various indicators and buttons may appear on the status bar.

The left side of the status bar in Figure 1–5 shows the current page followed by the total number of pages in the document, the number of words in the document, and an icon to check spelling and grammar. The right side of the status bar includes buttons and controls you can use to change the view of a document and adjust the size of the displayed document.

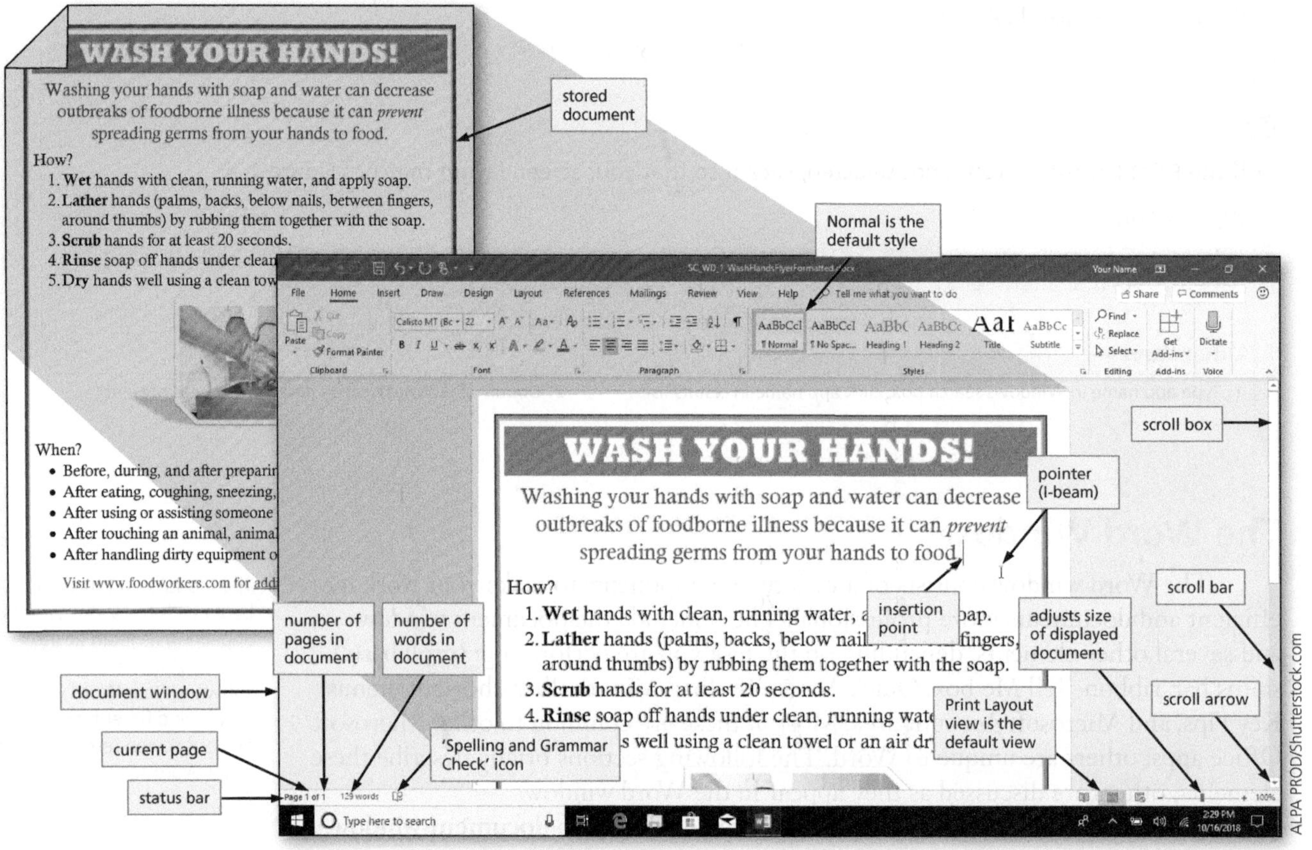

ALPA PROD/Shutterstock.com

Figure 1–5

Ribbon The **ribbon**, which is a horizontal strip located near the top of the Word window below the title bar, is the control center in Word that contains tabs of grouped commands that you click to interact with Word (Figure 1–6a). Each **tab** contains a collection of groups, and each **group** contains related commands. The ribbon provides easy, central access to the tasks you perform while creating a document.

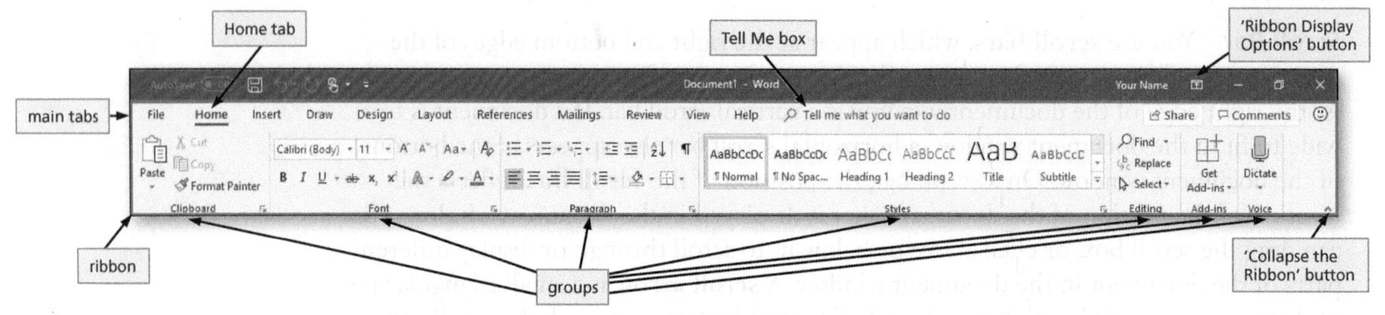

Figure 1–6a

BTW

Pointer

If you are using a touch screen, the pointer may not appear on the screen as you perform touch gestures. The pointer will reappear when you begin using the mouse.

When you start Word, the ribbon displays several main tabs, also called default or top-level tabs (i.e., File, Home, Insert, Draw, Design, Layout, References, Mailings, Review, View, and Help). (Note that depending on the type of computer or device you are using, the Draw tab may not appear.) The **Home tab**, also called the primary tab, contains the more frequently used commands. The tab currently displayed is called the **active tab**.

To display more of the document in the document window, some users prefer to minimize the ribbon, which hides the groups on the ribbon and displays only the main tabs (Figure 1–6b). To minimize the ribbon, click the 'Collapse the Ribbon' button or click the 'Ribbon Display Options' button on the title bar and then click Show Tabs on the menu. To use commands on a minimized ribbon, sometimes called a simplified ribbon, click the tab that you wish to expand. To expand the ribbon, double-click a tab, click the 'Pin the ribbon' button on an expanded tab, or click the 'Ribbon Display Options' button on the title bar and then click 'Show Tabs and Commands' on the menu.

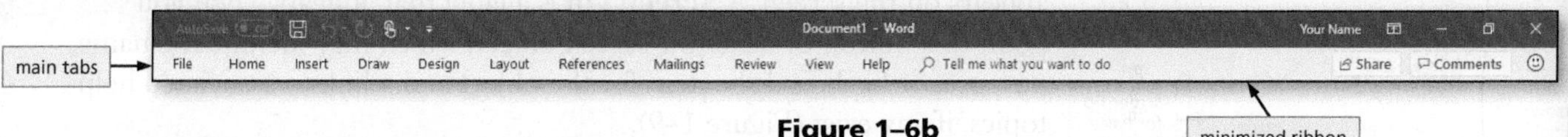

Figure 1–6b

Each time you start Word, the ribbon appears the same way it did the last time you used Word. The modules in this book, however, begin with the ribbon appearing as it did at the initial installation of the software.

In addition to the main tabs, Word displays other tabs, called **tool tabs** or contextual tabs, when you perform certain tasks or work with objects such as pictures or tables. If you insert a picture in the document, for example, the Picture Tools tab and its related subordinate Format tab appear, collectively referred to as the Picture Tools Format tab (Figure 1–7). When you are finished working with the picture, the Picture Tools Format tab disappears from the ribbon. Word determines when tool tabs should appear and disappear based on tasks you perform. Some tool tabs, such as the Table Tools tab, have more than one related subordinate tab.

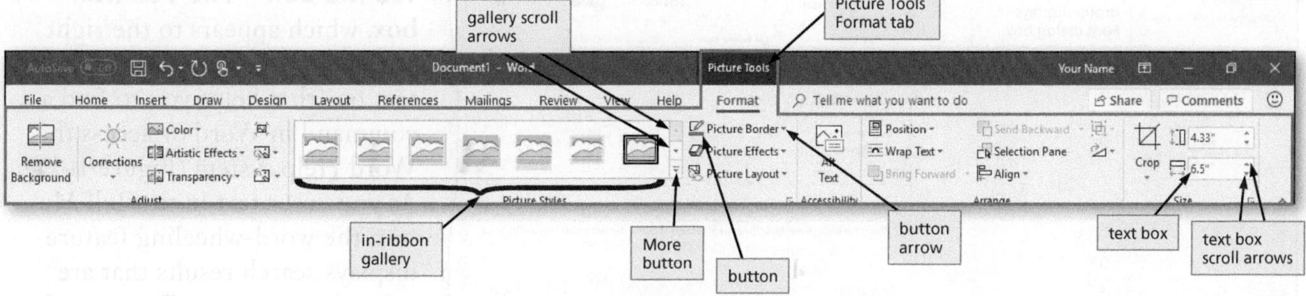

Figure 1–7

Items on the ribbon include buttons, boxes (text boxes, check boxes, etc.), and galleries (shown in Figure 1–7). A **gallery** is a set of choices, often graphical, arranged in a grid or in a list that you can browse through before making a selection. You can scroll through choices in an in-ribbon gallery by clicking the gallery's scroll arrows. Or, you can click a gallery's More button to view more gallery options on the screen at a time.

Some buttons and boxes have arrows that, when clicked, also display a gallery; others always cause a gallery to be displayed when clicked. Most galleries support **Live Preview**, which is a feature that allows you to point to a gallery choice and see its effect in the document — without actually selecting the choice (Figure 1–8).

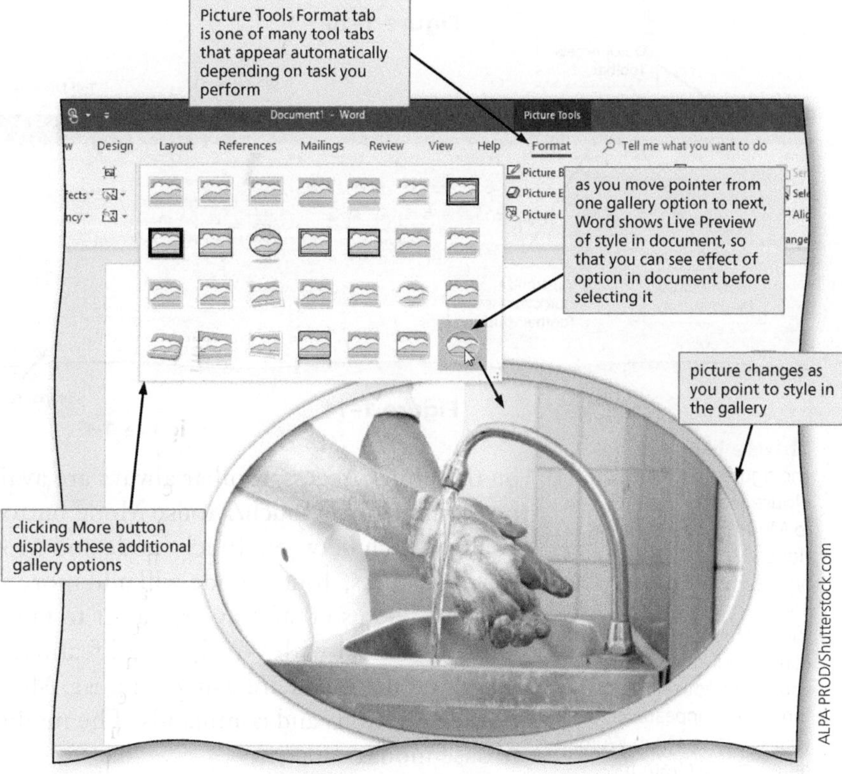

Figure 1–8

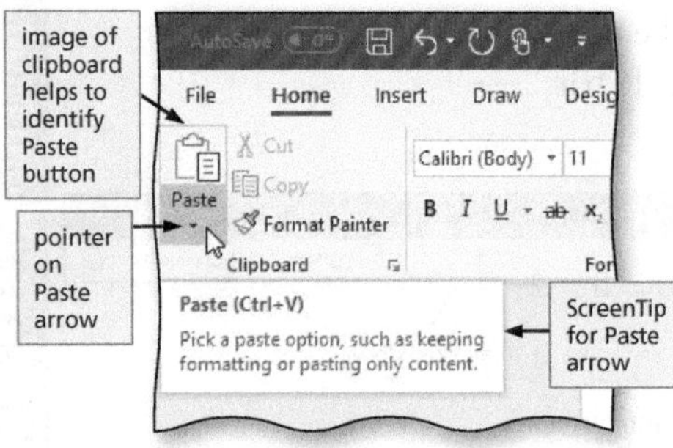

Figure 1–9

Some commands on the ribbon display an image to help you remember their function. When you point to a command on the ribbon, all or part of the command glows in shades of gray, and a ScreenTip appears on the screen. A **ScreenTip** is a label that appears when you point to a button or other on-screen object, which may include the name, purpose, or keyboard shortcut for the object and a link to associated help topics, if any exist (Figure 1–9).

Some groups on the ribbon have a small arrow in the lower-right corner, called a **Dialog Box Launcher**, that when clicked, displays a dialog box or opens a pane with additional options for the group (Figure 1–10). When presented with a dialog box, you make selections and must close the dialog box before returning to the document. A **pane**, in contrast to a dialog box, is a window that can remain open and visible while you work in the document and provides additional options.

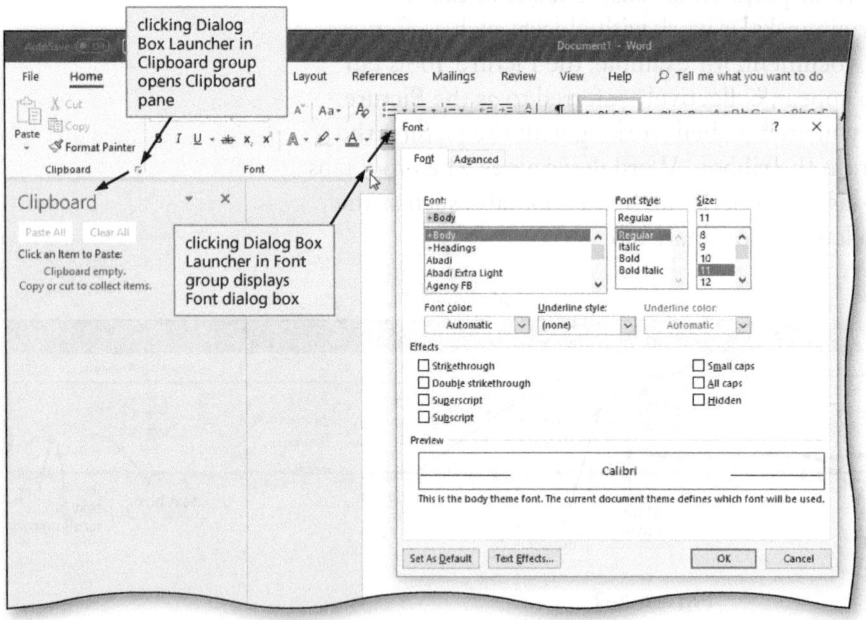

Figure 1–10

Tell Me Box The **Tell Me box**, which appears to the right of the tabs on the ribbon, is a text box that helps you to find a command in Word or access the Word Help system (Figure 1–11). As you enter text in the Tell Me box, the word-wheeling feature displays search results that are refined as you type. For example, if you want to insert a picture in a document, you can type the text “insert picture” in the Tell Me box and then select the appropriate command.

Figure 1–11

Quick Access Toolbar The **Quick Access Toolbar**, located initially (by default) above the ribbon at the left edge of the title bar, is a customizable toolbar that contains buttons you can click to perform frequently used commands (shown in Figure 1–11). The commands on the Quick Access Toolbar always are available, regardless of the task you are performing. The Touch/Mouse Mode button on the Quick Access Toolbar allows you to switch between Touch mode and Mouse mode. If you primarily are using touch gestures, Touch mode will add more space between commands on menus and on the ribbon so that they are easier to tap. While touch gestures are convenient ways to interact with Word, not all features are supported when you are using Touch mode. If you are using a mouse, Mouse mode will not add the extra space between buttons and commands. The modules in this book show the screens in Mouse mode.

BTW

Mouse Mode

The figures in this book use Mouse mode. To switch to Mouse mode, click the ‘Touch/Mouse Mode’ button on the Quick Access Toolbar and then click Mouse on the Touch/Mouse Mode menu. If you are using Touch mode, you might notice that the function or appearance of your touch screen in Word differs slightly from this module’s presentation.

You can add other commands to or delete commands from the Quick Access Toolbar so that it contains the commands you use most often. To do this, click the 'Customize Quick Access Toolbar' button on the Quick Access Toolbar and then select the commands you want to add or remove. As you add commands to the Quick Access Toolbar, its length may interfere with the document title on the title bar. For this reason, Word provides an option of displaying the Quick Access Toolbar below the ribbon on the Quick Access Toolbar menu.

Each time you start Word, the Quick Access Toolbar appears the same way it did the last time you used Word. The modules in this book, however, begin with the Quick Access Toolbar appearing as it did at the initial installation of the software.

BTW
Turning Off the Mini Toolbar
If you do not want the Mini toolbar to appear, click File on the ribbon to open Backstage view, click Options in Backstage view, if necessary, click General (Options dialog box), remove the check mark from the 'Show Mini Toolbar on selection' check box, and then click OK.

Mini Toolbar and Shortcut Menus The **Mini toolbar**, which appears next to selected text, contains the most frequently used text formatting commands (which are those commands related to changing the appearance of text in a document). If you do not use the Mini toolbar, it disappears from the screen. The buttons, arrows, and boxes on the Mini toolbar vary, depending on whether you are using Touch mode or Mouse mode. To use the Mini toolbar, move the pointer into the Mini toolbar.

All commands on the Mini toolbar also exist on the ribbon. The purpose of the Mini toolbar is to minimize hand or mouse movement. For example, if you want to use a command that currently is not displayed on the active tab, you can use the command on the Mini toolbar — instead of switching to a different tab to use the command.

A **shortcut menu**, which appears when you right-click an object, is a list of frequently used commands that relate to the right-clicked object. When you right-click selected text, for example, a shortcut menu appears with commands related to text. If you right-click an item in the document window, Word displays both the Mini toolbar and a shortcut menu (Figure 1–12).

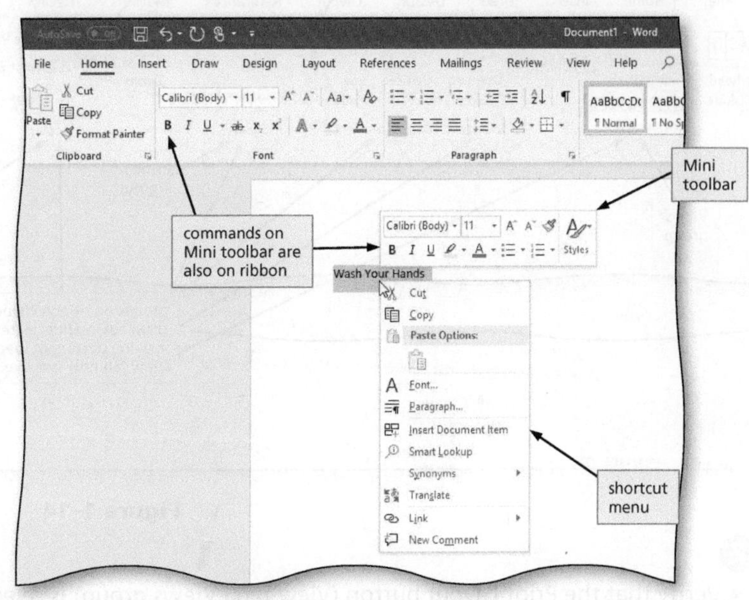

Figure 1–12

KeyTips If you prefer using the keyboard instead of the mouse, you can press ALT on the keyboard to display **KeyTips**, which are labels that appear over each tab and command on the ribbon (Figure 1–13). To select a tab or command using the keyboard, press the letter or number displayed in the KeyTip, which may cause additional KeyTips related to the selected command to appear. For example, to select the Bold button on the Home tab, press ALT, then press H, and then press 1. To remove the KeyTips from the screen, press ALT or ESC until all KeyTips disappear, or click anywhere in the Word window.

Microsoft Account Area In the Microsoft Account Area (shown in Figure 1–13), you can use the Sign in link to sign in to your Microsoft account. Once signed in, you will see your account information.

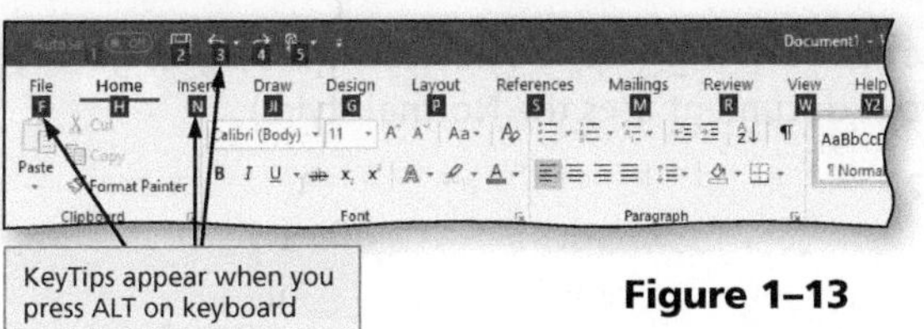

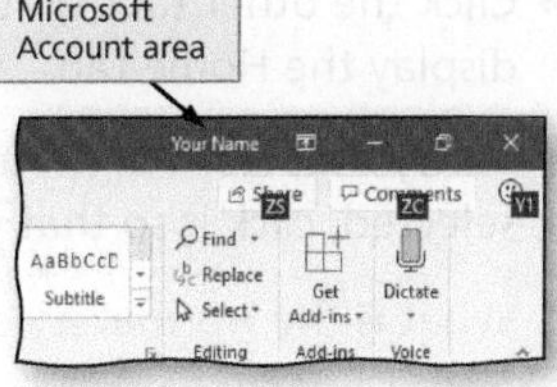

Figure 1–13

To Display a Different Tab on the Ribbon

When you start Word, the ribbon displays 11 main tabs: File, Home, Insert, Draw, Design, Layout, References, Mailings, Review, View, and Help. (Note that depending on the type of computer or device you are using, the Draw tab may not appear.) The tab currently displayed is called the active tab. To display a different tab on the ribbon, you click the tab. The following step displays the View tab, that is, makes it the active tab. ***Why?*** *When working with Word, you may need to switch tabs to access other options for working with a document or to verify settings.*

- Click View on the ribbon to display the View tab (Figure 1–14).

Q&A Why did the groups on the ribbon change?
When you switch from one tab to another on the ribbon, the groups on the ribbon change to show commands related to the selected tab.

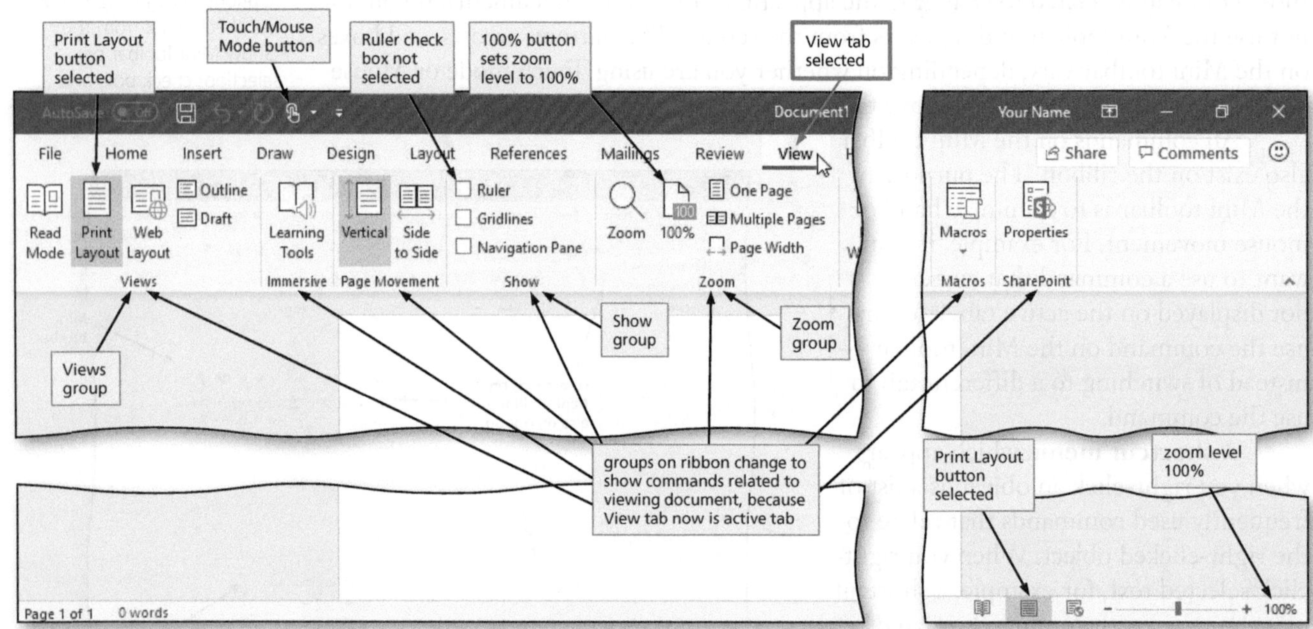

Figure 1–14

- Verify that the Print Layout button (View tab | Views group) is selected. (If it is not selected, click it to ensure the screen is in Print Layout view.)
- Verify that the zoom level is 100% on the status bar. (If it is not, click the 100% button (View tab | Zoom group) to set the zoom level to 100%.)
- Verify that the Ruler check box (View tab | Show group) is not selected. (If it is selected, click it to remove the selection because you do not want the rulers to appear on the screen.)

Experiment

- Click the other tabs on the ribbon to view their contents. When you are finished, click Home on the ribbon to display the Home tab.
- Verify that Normal (Home tab | Styles group) is selected in the Styles gallery (shown in Figure 1–5). (If it is not selected, click it so that your document uses the Normal style.)

Q&A What is the Normal style?
When you create a document, Word formats the text using a particular style. The **Normal style** is the default style that is applied to all text when you start Word.

- If you are using a mouse, verify that you are using Mouse mode so that your screens match the figures in this book by clicking the Touch/Mouse Mode button on the Quick Access Toolbar (shown in Figure 1–5) and then, if necessary, clicking Mouse on the menu (if your Quick Access Toolbar does not display the Touch/Mouse Mode button, click the Customize Quick Access Toolbar button on the Quick Access Toolbar and then click Touch/Mouse Mode on the menu to add the button to the Quick Access Toolbar).

To Adjust the Margins

Word is preset to use standard 8.5-by-11-inch paper, with 1-inch top, bottom, left, and right margins. The flyer in this module uses .5-inch top, bottom, left, and right margins. ***Why?*** *You would like more text to fit from left to right and top to bottom on the page.*

When you change the default (preset) margin settings, the new margin settings affect every page in the document. If you wanted the margins to affect just a portion of the document, you would divide the document into sections (discussed in a later module), which enables you to specify different margin settings for each section. The following steps change margin settings.

1

- Click Layout on the ribbon to display the Layout tab.
- Click the Margins button (Layout tab | Page Setup group) to display the Margins gallery (Figure 1–15).

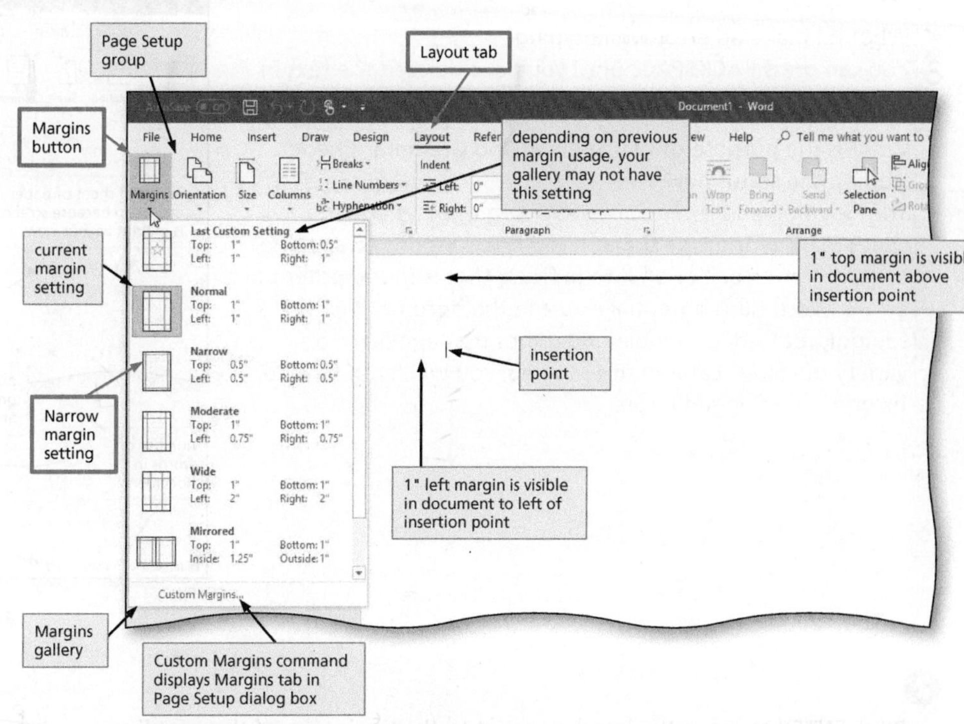

Figure 1–15

2

- Click Narrow in the Margins gallery to change the margins to the specified settings (Figure 1–16).

Q&A What if the margin settings I want are not in the Margins gallery?
You can click Custom Margins in the Margins gallery and then enter your desired margin values in the top, bottom, left, and right boxes in the Page Setup dialog box.

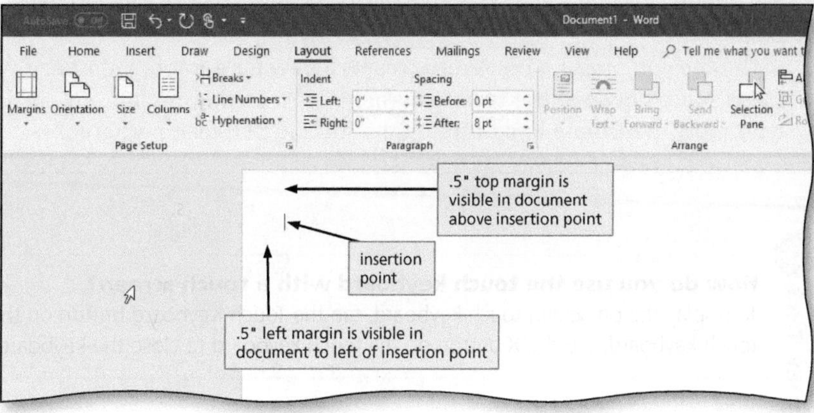

Figure 1–16

Other Ways

1. Position pointer on margin boundary on ruler; when pointer changes to two-headed arrow, drag margin boundary on ruler

BTW
Character Widths
Many word processing documents use variable character fonts, where some characters are wider than others; for example, the letter w is wider than the letter i.

Entering Text in a Document

The first step in creating a document is to enter its text. With the projects in this book, you enter text by typing on the keyboard. By default, Word positions text you type at the left margin. In a later section of this module, you will learn how to format, or change the appearance of, the entered text.

To Type Text

To begin creating the flyer in this module, type the headline in the document window. ***Why?*** ***The headline is the first line of text in the flyer.*** The following steps type the first line of text in the document.

- Type **`Wash Your Hands!`** as the headline (Figure 1–17).

Q&A What if I make an error while typing?
You can press BACKSPACE until you have deleted the text in error and then retype the text correctly.

What is the purpose of the 'Spelling and Grammar Check' icon on the status bar?
The 'Spelling and Grammar Check' icon displays either a check mark to indicate the entered text contains no spelling or grammar errors, or an X to indicate that it found potential errors. Word flags potential errors in the document with squiggly, dotted, or double underlines that appear in a variety of colors. Later in this module, you will learn how to fix or ignore flagged errors.

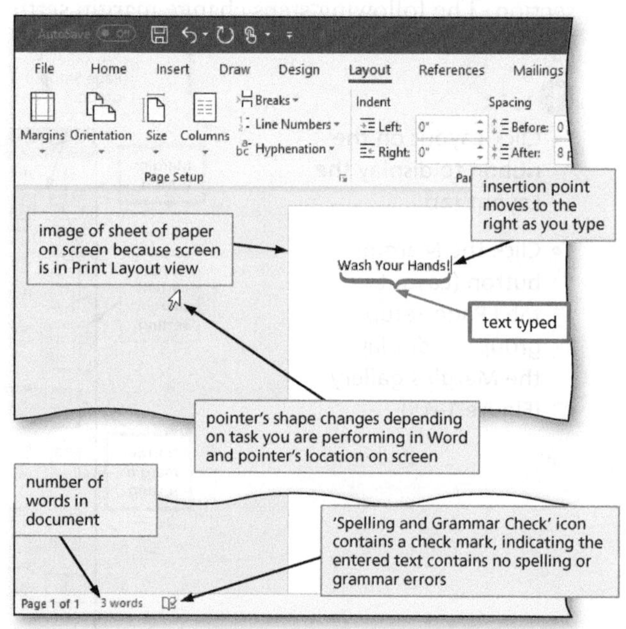

Figure 1–17

- Press ENTER to move the insertion point to the beginning of the next line (Figure 1–18).

Q&A Why did blank space appear between the headline and the insertion point?
Each time you press ENTER, Word creates a new paragraph and inserts blank space between the two paragraphs. Later in this module, you will learn how to increase and decrease the spacing between paragraphs.

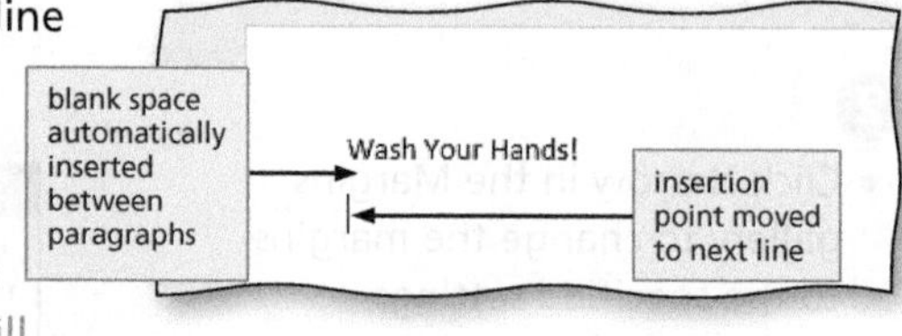

Figure 1–18

CONSIDER THIS

How do you use the touch keyboard with a touch screen?
To display the on-screen touch keyboard, tap the Touch Keyboard button on the Windows taskbar. When finished using the touch keyboard, tap the X button on the touch keyboard to close the keyboard.

To Change the Zoom to Page Width

The next step in creating this flyer is to enlarge the contents that appear on the screen. ***Why?*** *You would like the text on the screen to be larger so that it is easier to read.* The document currently displays at a zoom level of 100% (shown in Figure 1–14). With Word, you can change the zoom to page width, which zooms (enlarges or shrinks) the image of the sheet of paper on the screen so that it is the width of the Word window. The following step changes the zoom to page width.

- Click View on the ribbon to display the View tab.
- Click the Page Width button (View tab | Zoom group) to display the page the same width as the document window (Figure 1–19).

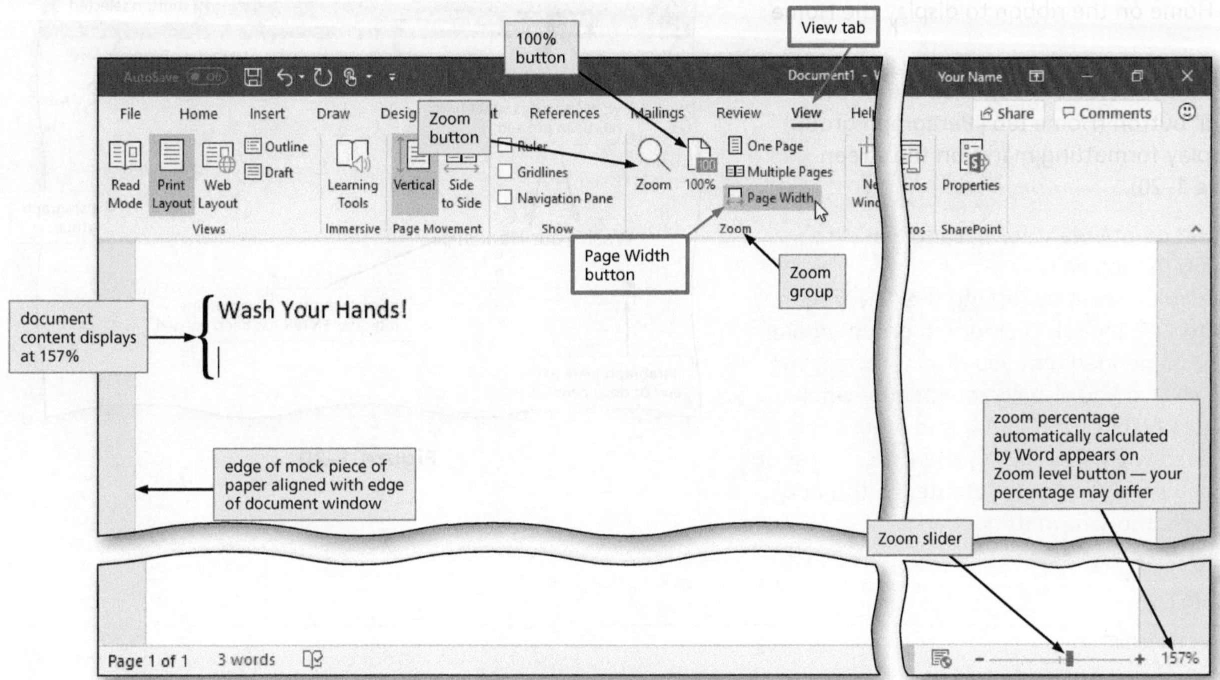

Figure 1–19

Q&A

If I change the zoom, will the document print differently?
Changing the zoom has no effect on the printed document.

What are the other predefined zoom options?
Through the View tab | Zoom group or the Zoom dialog box (Zoom button in Zoom group), you can zoom to one page (an entire single page appears in the document window), many pages (multiple pages appear at once in the document window), page width, text width, and a variety of set percentages. Whereas changing the zoom to page width places the edges of the page at the edges of the document window, changing the zoom to text width places the document contents at the edges of the document window.

What if I wanted to change the Zoom back to 100%?
You could click the 100% button (View tab | Zoom group) or drag the zoom slider until 100% appears on Zoom level button.

Other Ways

1. Click Zoom button (View tab | Zoom group), click Page width (Zoom dialog box), click OK

To Display Formatting Marks

You may find it helpful to display formatting marks while working in a document. ***Why?*** *Formatting marks indicate where in a document you pressed ENTER, SPACEBAR, and other nonprinting characters.* A **formatting mark** is a nonprinting character that appears on the screen to indicate the ends of paragraphs, tabs, and other formatting elements. For example, the paragraph mark (¶) is a formatting mark that indicates where you pressed ENTER. A raised dot (·) shows where you pressed SPACEBAR. Formatting marks are discussed as they appear on the screen.

Depending on settings made during previous Word sessions, your Word screen already may display formatting marks (shown in Figure 1–20). The following step displays formatting marks, if they do not show already on the screen.

- Click Home on the ribbon to display the Home tab.
- If it is not selected already, click the 'Show/Hide ¶' button (Home tab | Paragraph group) to display formatting marks on the screen (Figure 1–20).

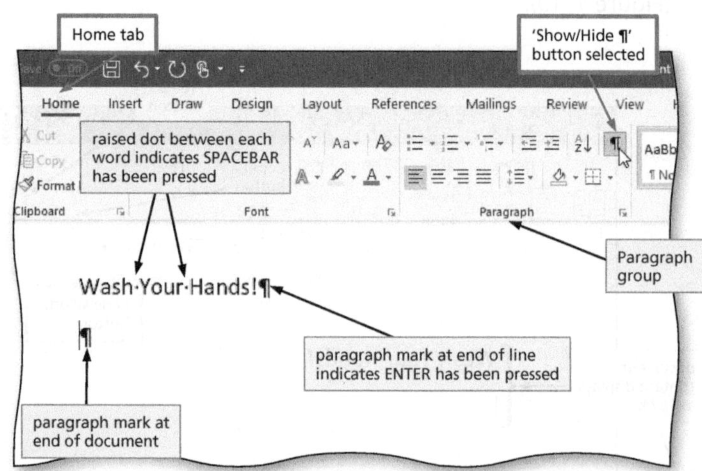

Figure 1–20

Q&A What if I do not want formatting marks to show on the screen?

You can hide them by clicking the 'Show/Hide ¶' button (Home tab | Paragraph group) again. It is recommended that you display formatting marks so that you visually can identify when you press ENTER, SPACEBAR, and other keys associated with nonprinting characters. Most of the document windows presented in this book, therefore, show formatting marks.

Other Ways

1. Press CTRL+SHIFT+*

BTW

Formatting Marks

With some fonts, the formatting marks will not be displayed properly on the screen. For example, the raised dot that signifies a blank space between words may be displayed behind a character instead of in the blank space, causing the characters to look incorrect.

Wordwrap

Wordwrap allows you to type words in a paragraph continually without pressing ENTER at the end of each line. As you type, if a word extends beyond the right margin, Word also automatically positions that word on the next line along with the insertion point.

Word creates a new paragraph each time you press ENTER. Thus, as you type text in the document window, do not press ENTER when the insertion point reaches the right margin. Instead, press ENTER only in these circumstances:

1. To insert a blank line(s) in a document (as shown in a later set of steps)
2. To begin a new paragraph
3. To terminate a short line of text and advance to the next line
4. To respond to questions or prompts in Word dialog boxes, panes, and other on-screen objects

To Wordwrap Text as You Type

The next step in creating the flyer is to type the body copy. ***Why?*** *In many flyers, the body copy text appears below the headline.* The following steps illustrate how the body copy text wordwraps as you enter it in the document, which means you will not have to press ENTER at the end of the line.

- Type the first sentence of the body copy: **Washing your hands with soap and water can decrease outbreaks of foodborne illness because it can prevent spreading germs from your hands to food.**

Q&A Why does my document wrap on different words?
The printer connected to a computer or device is one factor that can control where wordwrap occurs for each line in a document. Thus, it is possible that the same document could wordwrap differently if printed on different printers.

- Press ENTER to position the insertion point on the next line in the document (Figure 1–21).

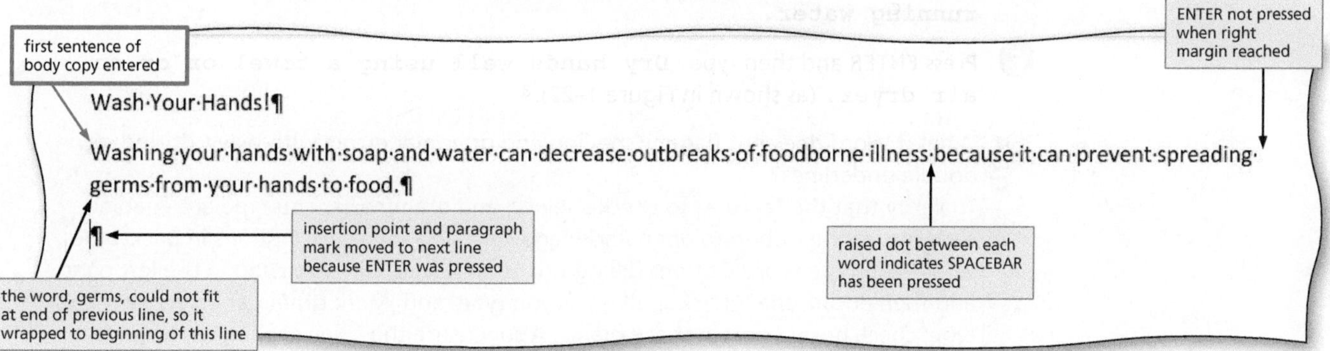

Figure 1–21

Spelling and Grammar Check

As you type text in a document, Word checks your typing for possible spelling and grammar errors. If all the words you have typed are in Word's dictionary and your grammar is correct, as mentioned earlier, the Spelling and Grammar Check icon on the status bar displays a check mark. Otherwise, the icon shows an X. In this case, Word flags the potential error(s) in the document window with a red, green, or blue underline.

- A red wavy underline means the flagged text is not in Word's dictionary (because it is a proper name or misspelled).
- A blue double underline indicates the text may be incorrect grammatically, such as a misuse of homophones (words that are pronounced the same but that have different spellings or meanings, such as one and won).
- A gold dotted underline indicates that Word can present a suggestion for more concise writing or different word usage.

A flagged word is not necessarily misspelled or grammatically incorrect. For example, many names, abbreviations, and specialized terms are not in Word's main dictionary. In these cases, you can instruct Word to ignore the flagged word. As you type, Word also detects duplicate words while checking for spelling errors. For example, if your document contains the phrase, to the the store, Word places a red wavy underline below the second occurrence of the word, the.

BTW
Automatic Spelling Correction
As you type, Word automatically corrects some misspelled words. For example, if you type recieve, Word automatically corrects the misspelling and displays the word, receive, when you press the SPACEBAR or type a punctuation mark. To see a complete list of automatically corrected words, click File on the ribbon to open Backstage view, click Options in Backstage view, click Proofing in the left pane (Word Options dialog box), click the AutoCorrect Options button, and then scroll through the list near the bottom of the dialog box.

To Enter More Text with Spelling and Grammar Errors

BTW
Zooming
If text is too small for you to read on the screen, you can zoom the document by dragging the Zoom slider on the status bar or by clicking the Zoom Out or Zoom In buttons on the status bar. Changing the zoom has no effect on the printed document.

When entering the following text in the flyer, you will intentionally make some spelling and grammar errors, because the next set of steps illustrate checking spelling and grammar as you work in a document. The following steps enter text in the flyer that contains spelling and grammar errors. Later in this module, the text you enter here will be formatted as a numbered list.

1. With the insertion point positioned as shown in Figure 1–21, type **How?**
2. Press ENTER and then type **Wet hands with clen, running water, and apply soap.**
3. Press ENTER and then type **Lather hands (palms, backs, below nails, between fingers, around thumbs) by rubbing them together with the soap.**
4. Press ENTER and then type **Scrub hands fore at least 20 seconds.**
5. Press ENTER and then type **Rinse soap off of hands under clean, running water.**
6. Press ENTER and then type **Dry hands well using a towel or or an air dryer.** (as shown in Figure 1–22).

Q&A
What if Word does not flag my spelling and grammar errors with wavy, dotted, or double underlines?
To verify that the features to check spelling and grammar as you type are enabled, click File on the ribbon to open Backstage view and then click Options in Backstage view. When the Word Options dialog box is displayed, click Proofing in the left pane and then ensure the 'Check spelling as you type' and 'Mark grammar errors as you type' check boxes contain check marks. Also, ensure the 'Hide spelling errors in this document only' and 'Hide grammar errors in this document only' check boxes do not contain check marks. Click OK to close the Word Options dialog box.

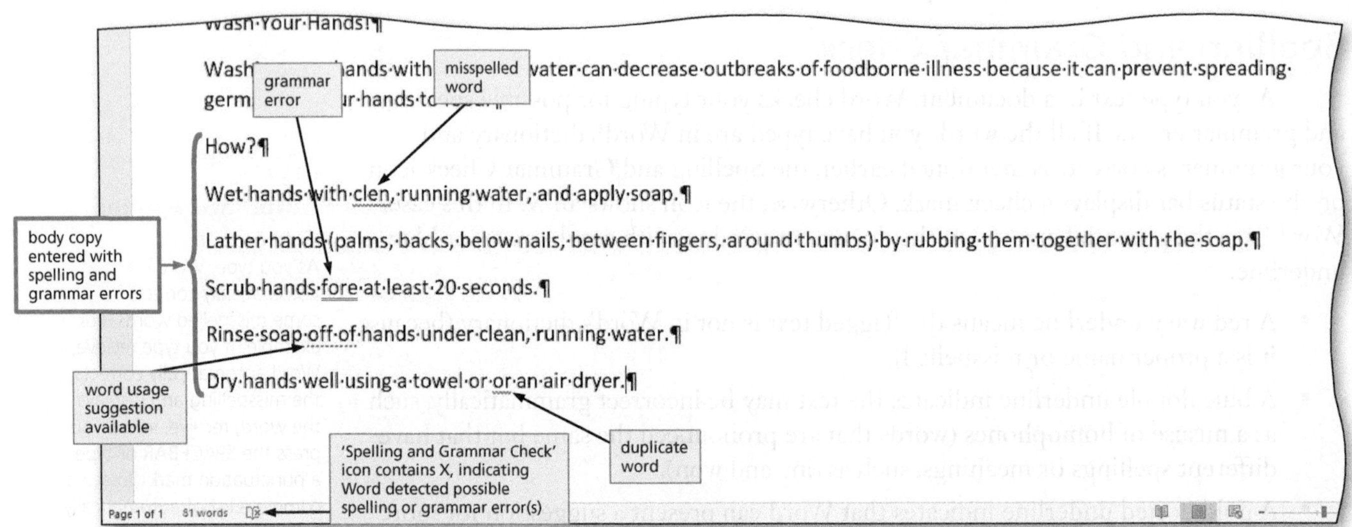

Figure 1–22

To Check Spelling and Grammar as You Work in a Document

Although you can check an entire document for spelling and grammar errors at once, you also can check flagged errors as they appear on the screen while you work in a document. The following steps correct the spelling and grammar errors entered in the previous steps. ***Why?*** *These steps illustrate Word's features that check spelling and* *grammar as you type. If you are completing this project on a computer or device, your flyer may contain additional or different flagged words, depending on the accuracy of your typing.* If your screen does not flag the text shown here, correct the errors without performing these steps.

1

- Right-click the word flagged with a red wavy underline (clen, in this case) to display a shortcut menu that presents a list of suggested spelling corrections for the flagged word (Figure 1–23).

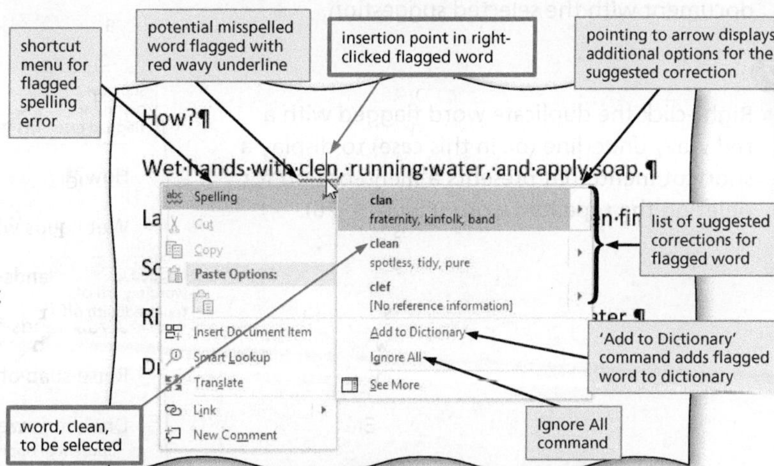

Figure 1–23

Q&A What if, when I right-click the misspelled word, my desired correction is not in the list on the shortcut menu?
You can click outside the shortcut menu to close the shortcut menu and then retype the correct word.

What if a flagged word actually is, for example, a proper name and spelled correctly?
Click Ignore All on the shortcut menu to instruct Word not to flag future occurrences of the same word in this document. Or, click 'Add to Dictionary' to add it to Word's dictionary so that it is not flagged in the future.

2

- Click the desired correction (clean, in this case) on the shortcut menu to replace the flagged misspelled word in the document with a correctly spelled word.

3

- Right-click the text flagged with a blue double underline (fore, in this case) to display a shortcut menu that presents a suggested grammar correction for the flagged word (Figure 1–24).

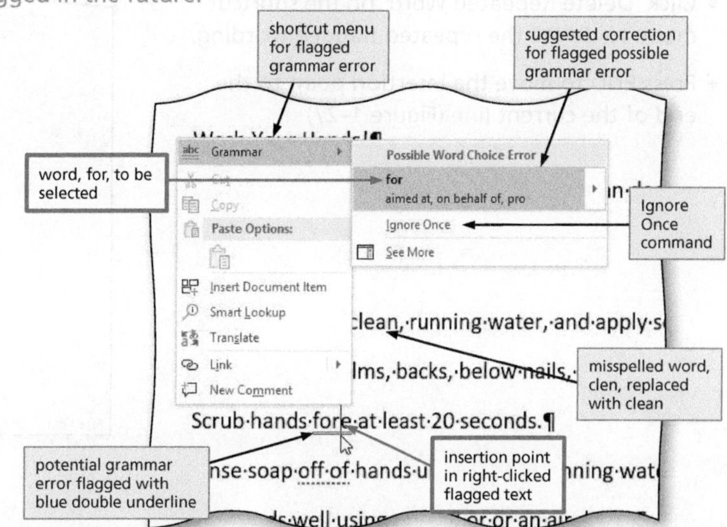

Figure 1–24

Q&A What if a flagged text is not a grammar error?
Click Ignore Once on the shortcut menu to instruct to ignore flagged text.

4

- Click the desired correction (for, in this case) on the shortcut menu to replace the flagged grammar error in the document with the selected suggestion (shown in Figure 1–27).

5

- Right-click the text flagged with a gold dotted underline (off of, in this case) to display a shortcut menu that presents suggested wording options for the flagged text (Figure 1–25).

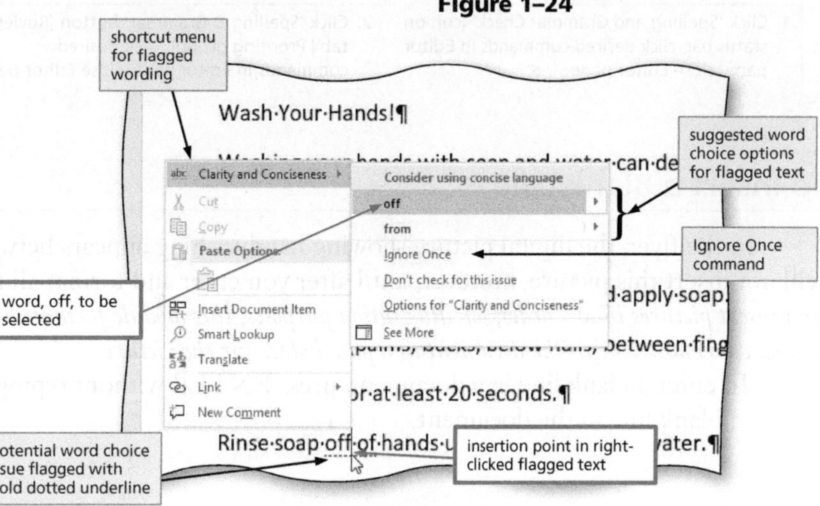

Figure 1–25

- Click the desired word choice (off, in this case) on the shortcut menu to replace the flagged wording issue in the document with the selected suggestion.

- Right-click the duplicate word flagged with a red wavy underline (or, in this case) to display a shortcut menu that presents a menu option for deleting the repeated word (Figure 1–26).

Figure 1–26

- Click 'Delete Repeated Word' on the shortcut menu to delete the repeated flagged wording.
- Press END to move the insertion point to the end of the current line (Figure 1–27).

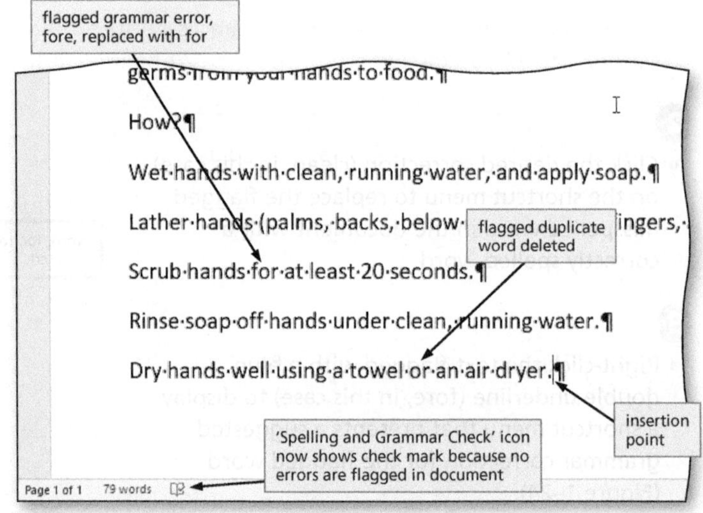

Figure 1–27

Other Ways

1. Click 'Spelling and Grammar Check' icon on status bar, click desired commands in Editor pane, close Editor pane
2. Click 'Spelling & Grammar' button (Review tab | Proofing group), click desired commands in Editor pane, close Editor pane
3. Press F7, click desired commands in Editor pane, close Editor pane

To Insert a Blank Line

In the flyer, the digital picture showing handwashing appears between the two lists in the body copy. You will not insert this picture, however, until after you enter and format all text. ***Why?** Although you can format text and insert pictures in any order, for illustration purposes, this module formats all text first before inserting the picture. Thus, you leave a blank line in the document as a placeholder for the picture.*

To enter a blank line in a document, press ENTER without typing any text on the line. The following step inserts a blank line in the document.

1

- With the insertion point at the end of the last line of text on the page (shown in Figure 1–27), press ENTER to position the insertion point on a blank line below the last line of text on the page.
- With the insertion point on a blank line, press ENTER to insert a blank line in the document above the insertion point; if necessary, scroll to see the insertion point (Figure 1–28).

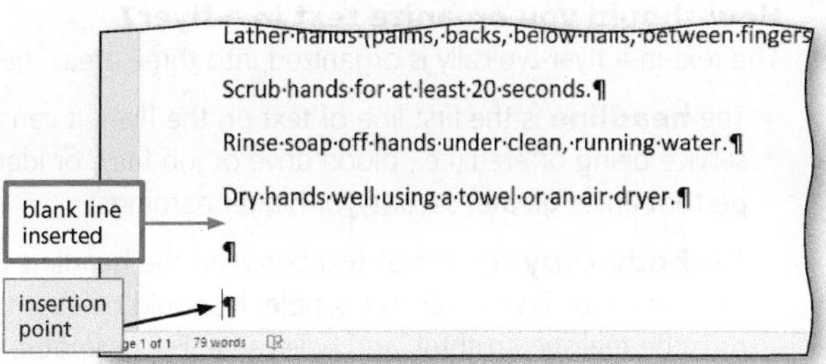

Figure 1–28

To Enter More Text

In the flyer, the text yet to be entered includes the remainder of the body copy, some of which will be formatted as a bulleted list, and the signature line. The following steps enter the remainder of text in the flyer.

1. With the insertion point positioned as shown in Figure 1–27, type `When?` and then press ENTER.
2. Type `After eating, coughing, sneezing, or using a tissue` and then press ENTER.
3. Type `Before, during, and after preparing food` and then press ENTER.
4. Type `After using or assisting someone in the restroom` and then press ENTER.
5. Type `After touching an animal, animal feed, or animal waste` and then press ENTER.
6. Type `After handling dirty equipment or garbage` and then press ENTER.
7. Type the signature line in the flyer (Figure 1–29): `Visit www.foodworkers.com for additional handwashing tips.`

Q&A Why is the text www.foodworkers.com the color blue and underlined?
Word recognized the text as a web address and automatically changed its appearance to look and function like a web link. Later in this project, you will change its appearance and function back to regular text.

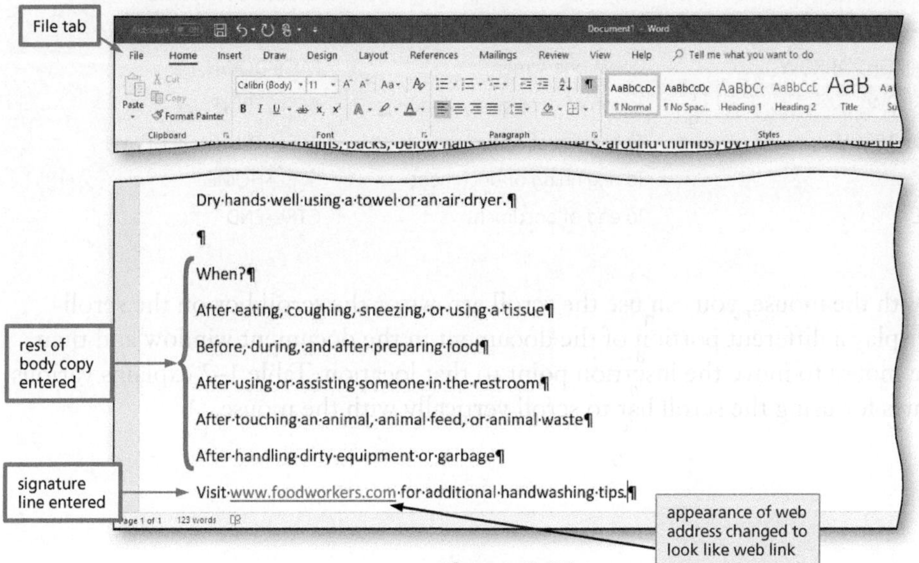

Figure 1–29

BTW

The Ribbon and Screen Resolution

Word may change how the groups and buttons within the groups appear on the ribbon, depending on the computer or mobile device's screen resolution. Thus, your ribbon may look different from the ones in this book if you are using a screen resolution other than 1366 × 768.

CONSIDER THIS

How should you organize text in a flyer?

The text in a flyer typically is organized into three areas: headline, body copy, and signature line.

- The **headline** is the first line of text on the flyer. It can contain a message (i.e., wash your hands), name the product or service being offered (i.e., blood drive or job fair), or identify the benefit that will be gained (such as a convenience, better performance, greater security, or higher earnings).
- The **body copy** consists of text between the headline and the signature line. This text highlights the key points of the message in as few words as possible. It should be easy to read and follow. While emphasizing the positive, the body copy must be realistic, truthful, and believable. For ease of reading, the body copy often contains a numbered list and/or a bulleted list and a picture or other graphical object.
- The **signature line**, which is the last line of text on the flyer, may contain contact information, reference additional information, or identify a call to action.

BTW
Minimize Wrist Injury
Computer users frequently switch among the keyboard, the mouse, and touch gestures during a word processing session; such switching strains the wrist. To help prevent wrist injury, minimize switching. For instance, if your fingers already are on the keyboard, use keyboard keys to scroll. If your hand already is on the mouse, use the mouse to scroll. If your fingertips already are on the touch screen, use your finger to slide the document to a new location (or use touch gestures to scroll).

Navigating a Document

You view only a portion of a document on the screen through the document window. At some point when you type text or insert objects (such as pictures), Word probably will scroll the top or bottom portion of the document off the screen. Although you cannot see the text and objects once they scroll off the screen, they remain in the document.

You can use touch gestures, the keyboard, or a mouse to scroll to a different location in a document and/or move the insertion point around a document. If you are using a touch screen, simply use your finger to slide the document up or down to display a different location in the document and then tap to move the insertion point to a new location. When you use the keyboard, the insertion point automatically moves when you press the desired keys. Table 1–1 outlines various techniques to navigate a document using the keyboard.

Table 1–1 Moving the Insertion Point with the Keyboard

Insertion Point Direction	Key(s) to Press	Insertion Point Direction	Key(s) to Press
Left one character	LEFT ARROW	Up one paragraph	CTRL+UP ARROW
Right one character	RIGHT ARROW	Down one paragraph	CTRL+DOWN ARROW
Left one word	CTRL+LEFT ARROW	Up one screen	PAGE UP
Right one word	CTRL+RIGHT ARROW	Down one screen	PAGE DOWN
Up one line	UP ARROW	To top of document window	ALT+CTRL+PAGE UP
Down one line	DOWN ARROW	To bottom of document window	ALT+CTRL+PAGE DOWN
To end of line	END	To beginning of document	CTRL+HOME
To beginning of line	HOME	To end of document	CTRL+END

With the mouse, you can use the scroll arrows or the scroll box on the scroll bar to display a different portion of the document in the document window and then click the mouse to move the insertion point to that location. Table 1–2 explains various techniques for using the scroll bar to scroll vertically with the mouse.

Table 1–2 Using the Scroll Bar to Scroll Vertically with the Mouse

Scroll Direction	Mouse Action	Scroll Direction	Mouse Action
Up	Drag the scroll box upward.	Down one screen	Click anywhere below the scroll box on the vertical scroll bar.
Down	Drag the scroll box downward.	Up one line	Click the scroll arrow at the top of the vertical scroll bar.
Up one screen	Click anywhere above the scroll box on the vertical scroll bar.	Down one line	Click the scroll arrow at the bottom of the vertical scroll bar.

To Save a Document for the First Time

While you are creating a document, the computer or mobile device stores it in memory. When you **save** a document, the computer or mobile device places it on a storage medium such as a hard drive, USB flash drive, or online using a cloud storage service such as OneDrive, so that you can retrieve it later. A saved document is referred to as a **file**, which contains a collection of information stored on a computer, such as a document, photo, or song. A **file name** is a unique, descriptive name that identifies the file's content and is assigned to a file when it is saved.

When saving a document, you must decide which storage medium to use:

- If you always work on the same computer and have no need to transport your projects to a different location, then your computer's hard drive will suffice as a storage location. It is a good idea, however, to save a backup copy of your projects on a separate medium in case the file becomes corrupted or the computer's hard drive fails. The documents created in this book are saved to the computer's hard drive.
- If you plan to work on your documents in various locations or on multiple computers or mobile devices, then you should save your documents on a portable medium, such as a USB flash drive. Alternatively, you can save your documents to an online cloud storage service, such as OneDrive.

The following steps save a document in the Documents library on your computer's hard drive. ***Why?*** *You have performed many tasks while creating this project and do not want to risk losing the work completed thus far.* Accordingly, you should save the file.

1

- Click File on the ribbon (shown in Figure 1–29) to open Backstage view (Figure 1–30).

What is the purpose of the File tab on the ribbon, and what is Backstage view?
The File tab opens **Backstage view**, which contains a set of commands that enable you to manage documents and options for Word. As you click different commands along the left side of Backstage view, the associated screen is displayed on the right side of Backstage view.

What if I accidentally click the File tab on the ribbon?
Click the Back button in Backstage view to return to the document window.

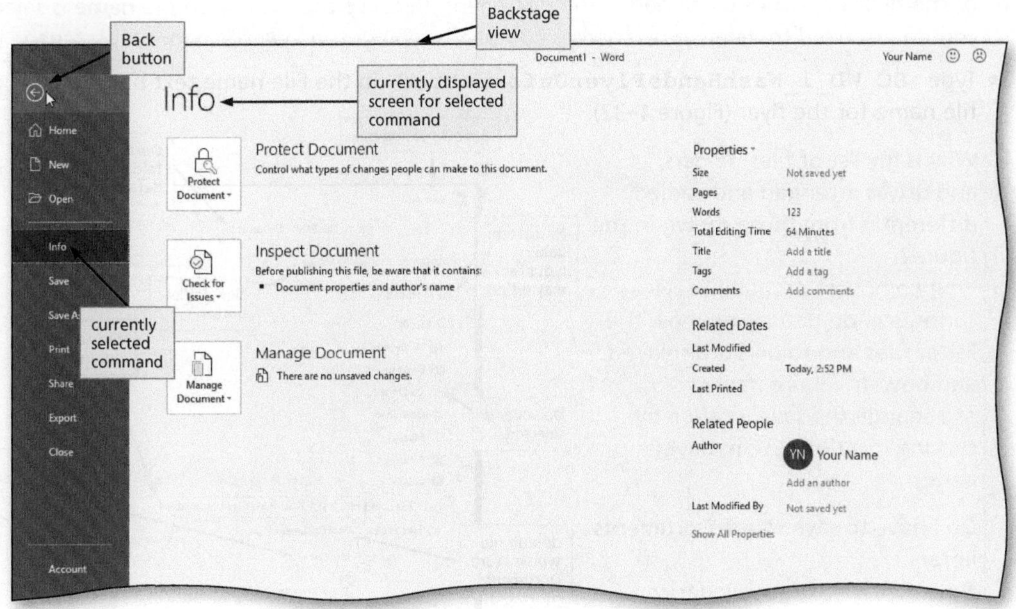

Figure 1–30

- Click Save As in Backstage view to display the Save As screen.
- Click This PC in the Save As screen to display the default save location on the computer or mobile device (Figure 1–31).

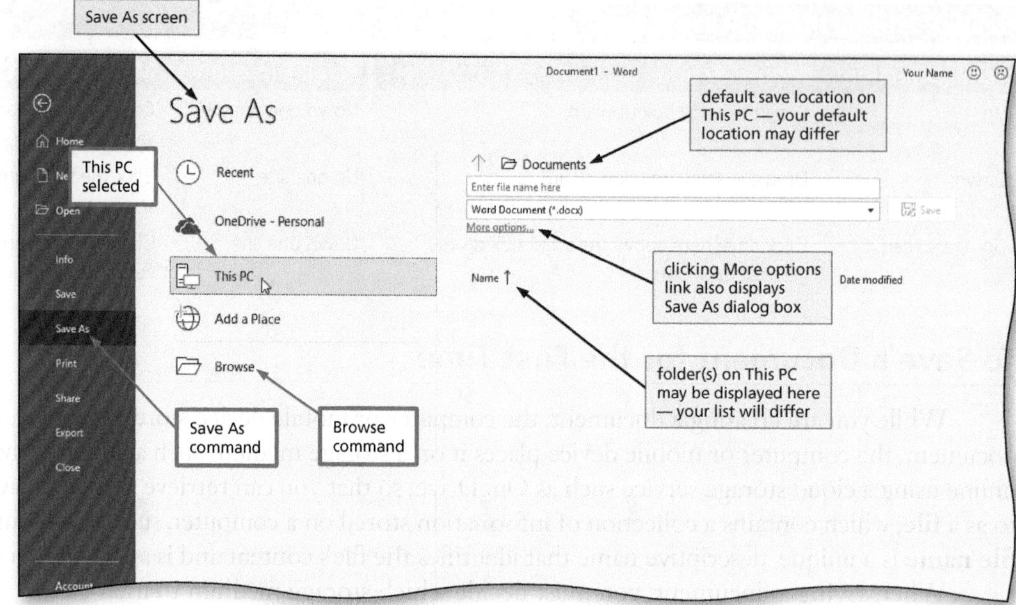

Figure 1–31

Q&A Can I type the file name below the default save location that displays in the Save As screen?
If you want to save the file in the default location, you can type the file name in the text box below the default save location and then click the Save button to the right of the default save location. These steps show how to display the Browse dialog box, in case you wanted to change the save location.

What if I wanted to save to OneDrive instead?
You would click OneDrive in the Save As screen.

- Click Browse in the Save As screen to display the Save As dialog box.

Q&A Why does a file name already appear in the File name box in the Save As dialog box?
Word automatically suggests a file name the first time you save a document. The suggested name usually consists of the first few words contained in the document. Because the suggested file name is selected in the File Name box, you do not need to delete it; as soon as you begin typing, the new file name replaces the selected text.

- Type `SC_WD_1_WashHandsFlyerUnformatted` in the File name text box (Save As dialog box) to specify the file name for the flyer (Figure 1–32).

Q&A Why is my list of files, folders, and drives arranged and named differently from those shown in the figure?
Your computer or mobile device's configuration determines how the list of files and folders is displayed and how drives are named. You can change the save location by clicking locations in the Navigation pane.

Do I have to save to the Documents library?
No. You can save to any device or folder. You also can create your own folders by clicking the New folder button shown in Figure 1–32.

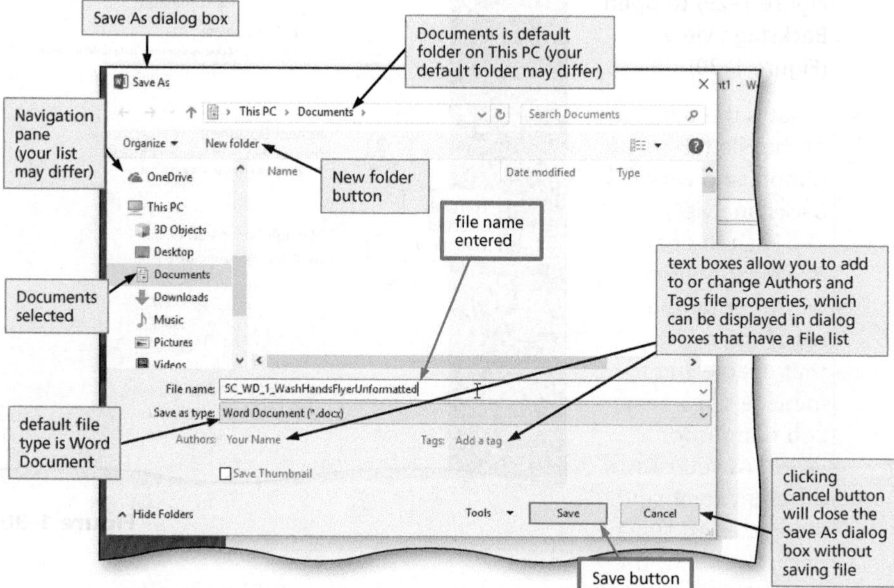

Figure 1–32

Q&A

What characters can I use in a file name?
The only invalid characters are the backslash (\), slash (/), colon (:), asterisk (*), question mark (?), quotation mark ("), less than symbol (<), greater than symbol (>), and vertical bar (|).

What are all those characters in the file name in this project?
Some companies require certain rules be followed when creating file names; others allow you to choose your own. While you could have used the file name 'Wash Hands Flyer Unformatted' with spaces inserted for readability, the file names in this book do not use spaces and all begin with SC (for Shelly Cashman) and WD (for Word) followed by the module number and then a descriptor of the file contents, so that they work with SAM, if you are using that platform as well.

4

- **Click Save to save the flyer with the file name, SC_WD_1_WashHandsFlyerUnformatted, to the default save location (Figure 1–33).**

Q&A

How do I know that Word saved the document?
While Word is saving your file, it briefly displays a message on the status bar indicating the amount of the file saved. When the document appears after saving, the new file name will be displayed in the title bar.

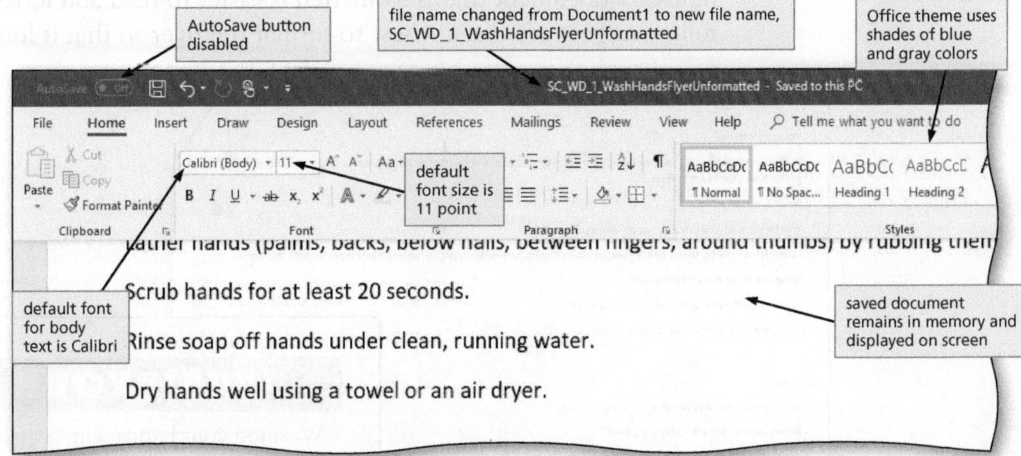

Figure 1–33

Why is the AutoSave button disabled on the title bar?
If you are saving the file on a computer or mobile device, the AutoSave button on the title bar may be disabled. If you are saving the file on OneDrive, the AutoSave button may be enabled, allowing you to specify whether Word saves the document as you make changes to it. If AutoSave is turned off, you will need to continue saving changes manually.

Other Ways

1. Press F12, type file name (Save As dialog box), navigate to desired save location, click Save

CONSIDER THIS

How often should you save a document?
It is important to save a document frequently for the following reasons:

- The document in memory might be lost if the computer or mobile device is turned off or you lose electrical power while Word is running.
- If you run out of time before completing a project, you may finish it at a future time without starting over.

BTW
File Type
Depending on your Windows settings, the file type .docx may be displayed on the title bar immediately to the right of the file name after you save the file. The file type .docx identifies a Word 2019 document.

Formatting Paragraphs and Characters

With the text for the flyer entered, the next step is to **format**, which is the process of changing the appearance of text and objects. A paragraph encompasses the text from the first character in the paragraph up to and including its paragraph mark (¶). **Paragraph formatting** is the process of changing the appearance of a paragraph on-screen and in print. For example, you can center or add bullets to a paragraph. Characters include letters, numbers, punctuation marks, and symbols. **Character formatting** is the process of changing the way characters appear on the screen and in print. You use character formatting to emphasize certain words and improve readability of a document. For example, you can color, italicize, or underline characters. Often, you apply both paragraph and character formatting to the same text. For example, you may center a paragraph (paragraph formatting) and underline some of the characters in the same paragraph (character formatting).

Although you can format paragraphs and characters before you type, many Word users enter text first and then format the existing text. Figure 1–34a shows the flyer in this module before formatting its paragraphs and characters. Figure 1–34b shows the flyer after formatting its paragraphs and characters. As you can see from the two figures, a document that is formatted is easier to read and looks more professional. The following sections discuss how to format the flyer so that it looks like Figure 1–34b.

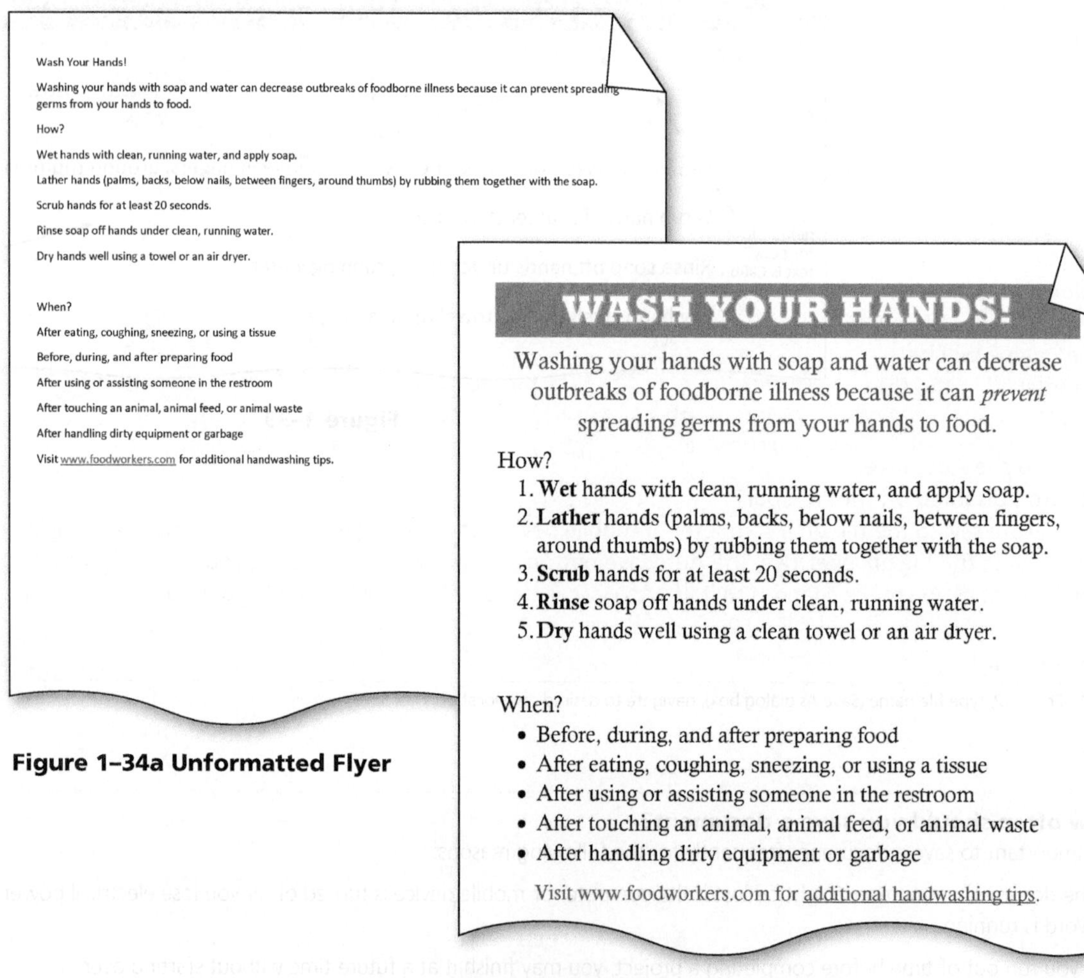

Figure 1–34a Unformatted Flyer

Figure 1–34b Formatted Flyer

Figure 1–34

BTW
Microsoft Updates
The material in this book was written using Microsoft Word 2019 and was quality assurance tested before the publication date. As Microsoft continually updates Office 2019 and Office 365, your software experience may vary slightly from what is seen in the printed text.

Font, Font Sizes, and Themes

Characters that appear on the screen are a specific shape and size. The **font**, or typeface, defines the appearance and shape of the letters, numbers, and special characters. In Word, the default font usually is Calibri (shown in Figure 1–33). You can leave characters in the default font or change them to a different font. **Font size** specifies the size of the characters, measured in units called points. A single **point**, which is a unit of measure for font size, is about 1/72 of one inch in height. The default font size in Word typically is 11 (shown in Figure 1–33). Thus, a character with a font size of 11 is about 11/72 or a little less than 1/6 of one inch in height. You can increase or decrease the font size of characters in a document. A **style** is a named collection of character and paragraph formats, including font, font size, font styles, font color, and alignment, that are stored together and can be applied to text to format it quickly, such as Heading 1 or Title.

A **document theme** is a coordinated combination of formats for fonts, colors, pictures, and other objects. Word includes a variety of document themes to assist you with coordinating these visual elements in a document. The default theme fonts are Calibri Light for headings and Calibri for body text. By changing the document theme, you quickly can give your document a new look. You also can define your own document themes.

CONSIDER THIS

How do you know which formats to use in a flyer?

In a flyer, consider the following formatting suggestions.

- **Increase the font size of characters.** Flyers usually are posted on a bulletin board, on a wall, or in a window. Thus, the font size should be as large as possible so that your audience easily can read the flyer. To give the headline more impact, its font size should be larger than the font size of the text in the body copy.
- **Change the font of characters.** Use fonts that are easy to read. Try to use only two different fonts in a flyer; for example, use one for the headline and the other for all other text. Too many fonts can make the flyer visually confusing.
- **Change the paragraph alignment.** The default alignment for paragraphs in a document is **left-aligned**, that is, flush at the left margin of the document with uneven right edges. Consider changing the alignment of some of the paragraphs to add interest and variety to the flyer.
- **Highlight key paragraphs with numbers or bullets.** A numbered paragraph is a paragraph that begins with a number. Use numbered paragraphs (lists) to organize a sequence. A bulleted paragraph is a paragraph that begins with a dot or other symbol. Use bulleted paragraphs to highlight important points in a flyer.
- **Emphasize important words.** To call attention to certain words or lines, you can underline them, italicize them, or bold them. Use these formats sparingly, however, because overuse will minimize their effect and make the flyer look too busy.
- **Use color.** Use colors that complement each other and convey the meaning of the flyer. Vary colors in terms of hue and brightness. Headline colors, for example, can be bold and bright. Signature lines should stand out but less than headlines. Keep in mind that too many colors can detract from the flyer and make it difficult to read.

To Change the Document Theme

The current default document theme is Office, which uses Calibri and Calibri Light as its font and shades of grays and blues primarily (shown in the Styles group in Figure 1–33). Calibri and Calibri Light are **sans serif fonts**, which are fonts that do not include short decorative lines at the upper and lower ends of their characters. Other fonts such as Calisto MT are **serif fonts**, which are fonts that have short decorative lines at the upper and lower ends of their characters (shown in Figure 1–36). The following steps change the document theme to Slate for the flyer in this module, which uses the Calisto MT font and shades of browns and oranges primarily. ***Why?*** *Some organizations specify document themes that all employees should use when creating printed and online documents. Studies have shown that sans serif fonts are easier to read on the screen and serif fonts are easier to read in print.*

- Press CTRL+HOME to display the top of the flyer in the document window.
- Click Design on the ribbon to display the Design tab.
- Click the Themes button (Design tab | Document Formatting group) to display the Themes gallery (Figure 1–35).

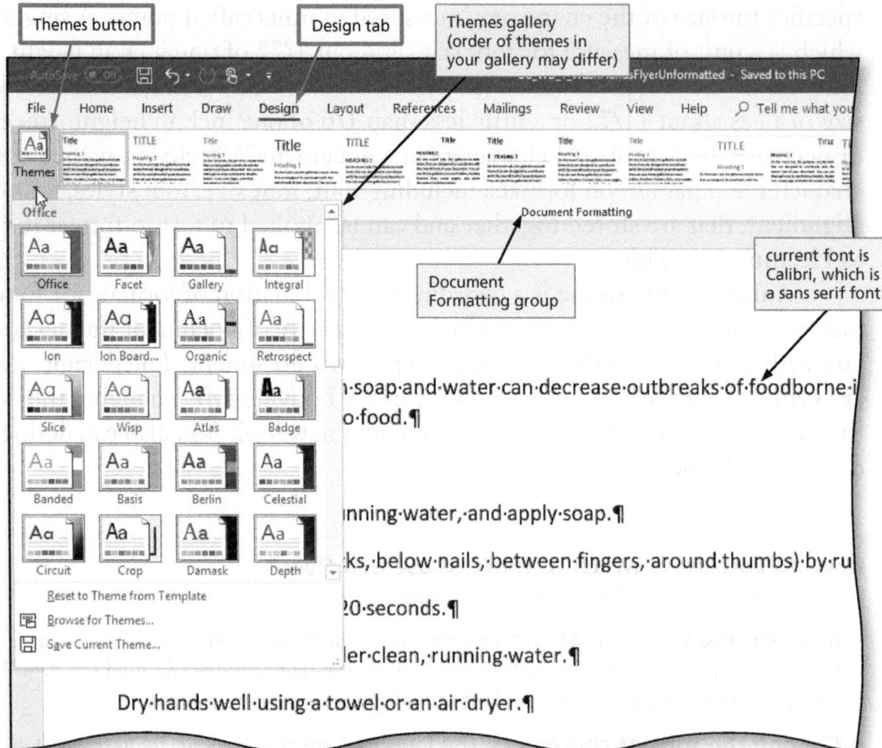

Figure 1–35

- Scroll to and then point to Slate in the Themes gallery to display a Live Preview of that theme applied to the document (Figure 1–36).

Experiment

- Point to various themes in the Themes gallery to display a Live Preview of the various themes applied to the document in the document window.

Q&A

What is Live Preview?
Recall from the discussion earlier in this module that Live Preview is a feature that allows you to point to a gallery choice and see its effect in the document — without actually selecting the choice.

Can I use Live Preview on a touch screen?
Live Preview is not available on a touch screen.

Figure 1–36

- Click Slate in the Themes gallery to change the document theme.

To Center a Paragraph

The headline in the flyer currently is left-aligned. ***Why?*** *Word, by default, left-aligns text, unless you specifically change the alignment.* You want the headline to be **centered**, that is, positioned evenly between the left and right margins, or placeholder edges, on the page. Recall that Word considers a single short line of text, such as the one-word headline, a paragraph. Thus, you will center the paragraph containing the headline. The following steps center a paragraph.

- Click Home on the ribbon to display the Home tab.
- Click somewhere in the paragraph to be centered (in this case, the headline) to position the insertion point in the paragraph to be centered (Figure 1–37).

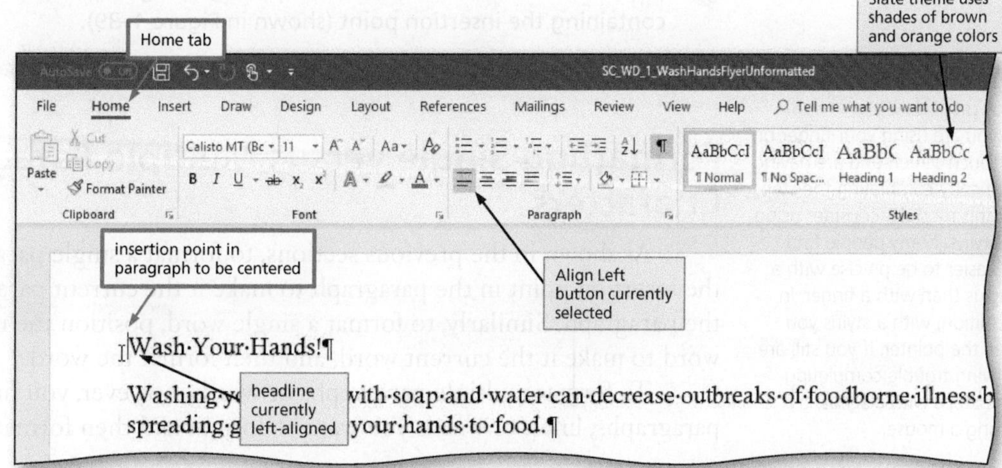

Figure 1–37

- Click the Center button (Home tab | Paragraph group) to center the paragraph containing the insertion point (Figure 1–38).

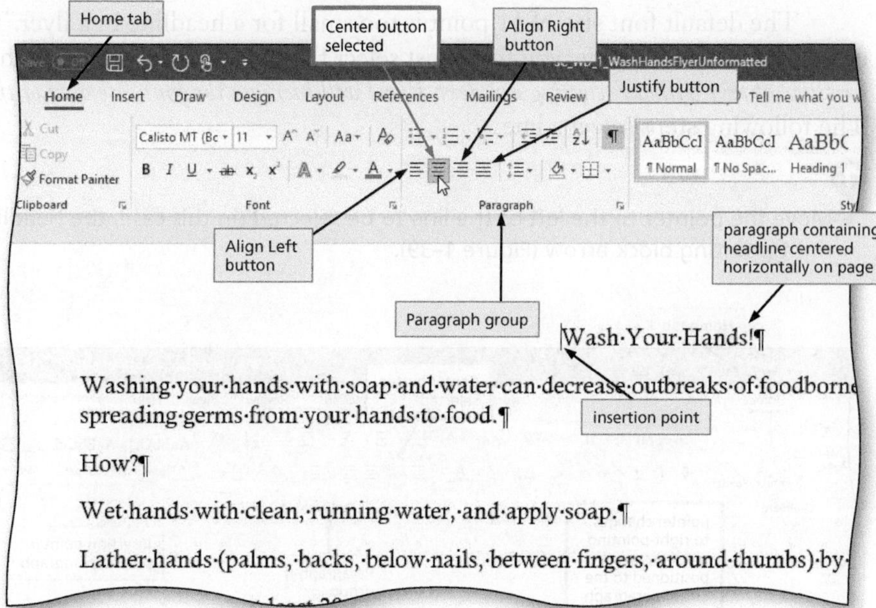

Figure 1–38

Q&A

What if I want to return the paragraph to left-aligned?

You would click the Center button again or click the Align Left button (Home tab | Paragraph group).

What are other ways to align a paragraph?

A **right-aligned** paragraph appears flush at the right margin of the document with uneven left edges. You right-align a paragraph by clicking the Align Right button (Home tab | Paragraph group). A **justified** paragraph means that full lines of text are evenly spaced between both the left and right margins, like the edges of newspaper columns, with extra space placed between words. You justify a paragraph by clicking the Justify button (Home tab | Paragraph group).

Other Ways

1. Right-click paragraph (or if using touch, tap 'Show Context Menu' button on Mini toolbar), click Paragraph on shortcut menu, click Indents and Spacing tab (Paragraph dialog box), click Alignment arrow, click Centered, click OK
2. Click Paragraph Dialog Box Launcher (Home tab or Layout tab | Paragraph group), click Indents and Spacing tab (Paragraph dialog box), click Alignment arrow, click Centered, click OK
3. Press CTRL+E

To Center Another Paragraph

The second paragraph in the flyer (the first paragraph of body copy) also is centered. The following steps center the first paragraph of body copy.

1. Click somewhere in the paragraph to be centered (in this case, the second paragraph on the flyer) to position the insertion point in the paragraph to be formatted.

2. Click the Center button (Home tab | Paragraph group) to center the paragraph containing the insertion point (shown in Figure 1–39).

BTW

Touch Screen

If you are using your finger on a touch screen and are having difficulty completing the steps in this module, consider using a stylus. Many people find it easier to be precise with a stylus than with a finger. In addition, with a stylus you see the pointer. If you still are having trouble completing the steps with a stylus, try using a mouse.

Formatting Single versus Multiple Paragraphs and Characters

As shown in the previous sections, to format a single paragraph, simply position the insertion point in the paragraph to make it the current paragraph and then format the paragraph. Similarly, to format a single word, position the insertion point in the word to make it the current word, and then format the word.

To format multiple paragraphs or words, however, you first must select the paragraphs, lines, or words you want to format and then format the selection.

To Select a Line

The default font size of 11 point is too small for a headline in a flyer. To increase the font size of the characters in the headline, you first must select the line of text containing the headline. ***Why?*** *If you increase the font size of text without selecting any text, Word will increase the font size only of the word containing the insertion point.* The following steps select a line.

- Move the pointer to the left of the line to be selected (in this case, the headline) until the pointer changes to a right-pointing block arrow (Figure 1–39).

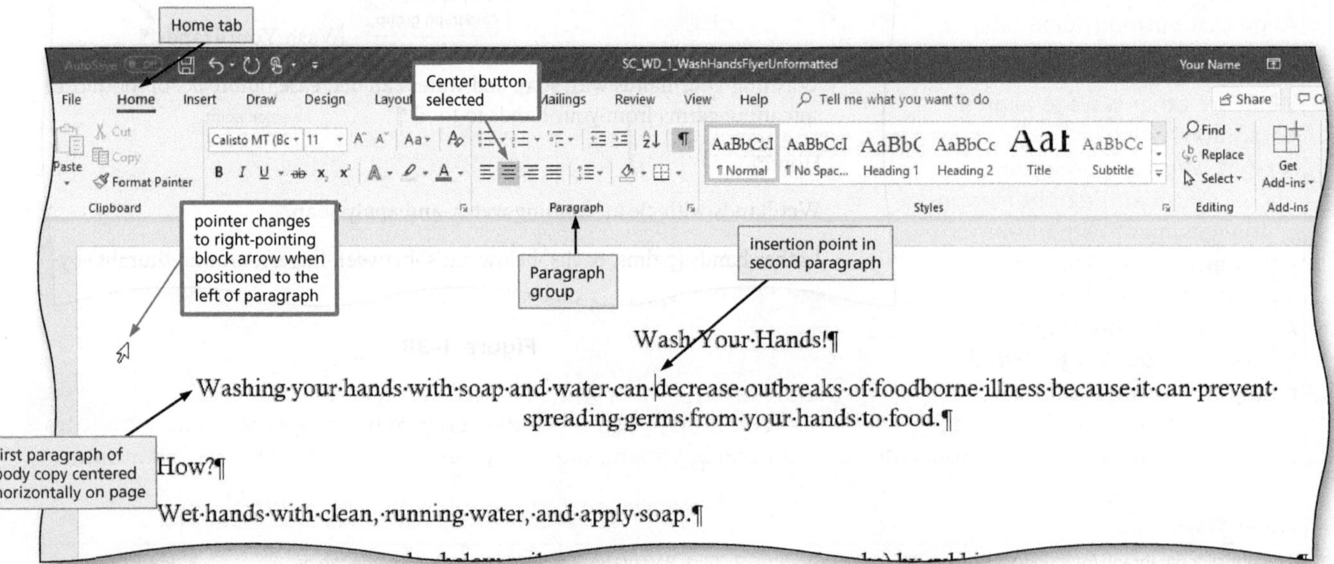

Figure 1–39

2

- While the pointer is a right-pointing block arrow, click the mouse button to select the entire line to the right of the pointer (Figure 1–40).

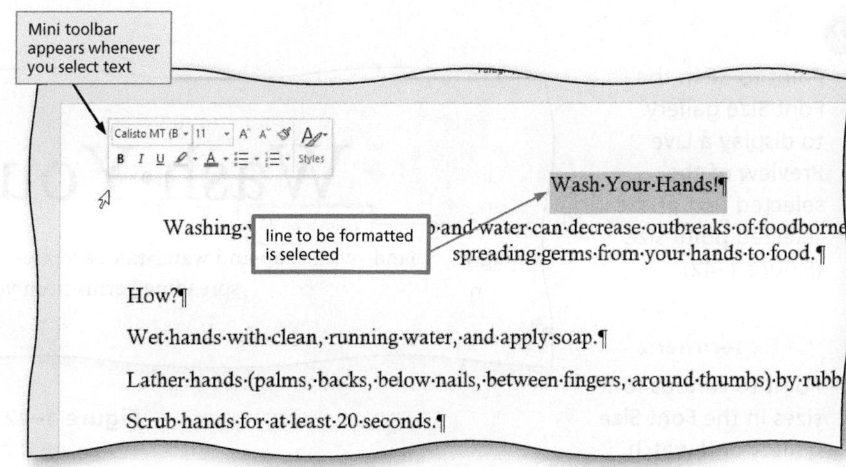

Figure 1–40

What if I am using a touch screen?
You would double-tap to the left of the line to be selected to select the line.

Why is the selected text shaded gray?
If your screen normally displays dark letters on a light background, which is the default setting in Word, then selected text is displayed with a light shading color, such as gray, on the dark letters. Note that the selection that appears on the text does not print.

Other Ways

1. Drag pointer through line
2. With insertion point at beginning of desired line, press CRTL+SHIFT+DOWN ARROW

To Change the Font Size of Selected Text

The next step is to increase the font size of the characters in the selected headline. ***Why?*** *You would like the headline to be as large as possible and still fit on a single line, which in this case is 36 point.* The following steps increase the font size of the headline from 11 to 36 point.

1

- With the text selected, click the Font Size arrow (Home tab | Font group) to display the Font Size gallery (Figure 1–41).

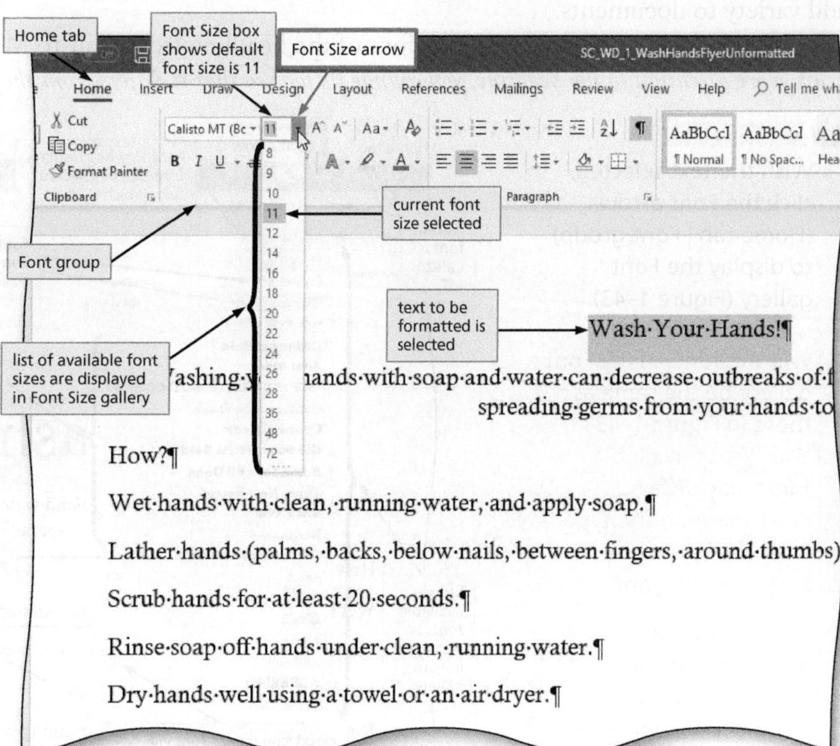

Figure 1–41

Q&A

What is the Font Size arrow?
The Font Size arrow is the arrow to the right of the Font Size box, which is the text box that displays the current font size.

Why are the font sizes in my Font Size gallery different from those in Figure 1–41?
Font sizes may vary depending on the current font and your printer driver.

What happened to the Mini toolbar?
Recall that the Mini toolbar disappears if you do not use it. These steps use the Font Size arrow on the Home tab instead of the Font Size arrow on the Mini toolbar.

- Point to 36 in the Font Size gallery to display a Live Preview of the selected text at the selected point size (Figure 1–42).

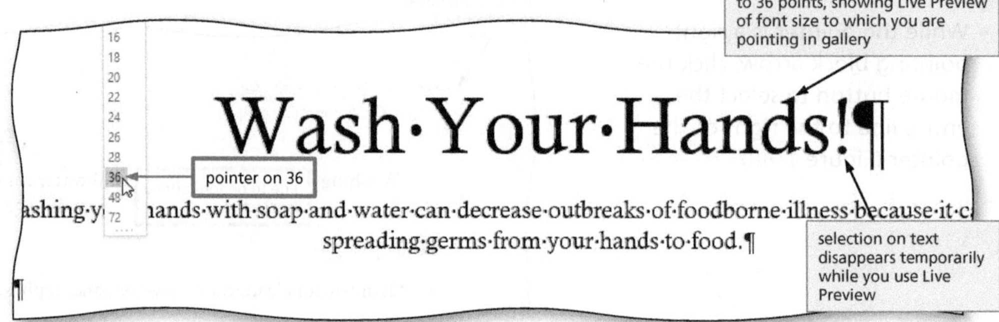

Figure 1–42

Experiment

- Point to various font sizes in the Font Size gallery and watch the font size of the selected text change in the document window.

- Click 36 in the Font Size gallery to increase the font size of the selected text.

Other Ways

1. Click Font Size arrow on Mini toolbar, click desired font size in Font Size gallery
2. Right-click selected text (or, if using touch, tap 'Show Context Menu' button on Mini toolbar), click Font on shortcut menu, click Font tab (Font dialog box), select desired font size in Size list, click OK
3. Click Font Dialog Box Launcher (Home tab | Font group), click Font tab (Font dialog box), select desired font size in Size list, click OK
4. Press CTRL+D, click Font tab (Font dialog box), select desired font size in Size list, click OK

To Change the Font of Selected Text

The default font when you install Word is Calibri. The font for characters in this document is Calisto MT because earlier you changed the theme to Slate. Many other fonts are available, however, so that you can add variety to documents.

The following steps change the font of the headline from Calisto MT to Rockwell Extra Bold. ***Why?*** *To draw more attention to the headline, you change its font so that it differs from the font of other text in the flyer.*

- With the text selected, click the Font arrow (Home tab | Font group) to display the Font gallery (Figure 1–43).

Q&A **Will the fonts in my Font gallery be the same as those in Figure 1–43?**
Your list of available fonts may differ, depending on the type of printer you are using and other settings.

What if the text no longer is selected?
Follow the steps described earlier to select a line and then perform Step 1.

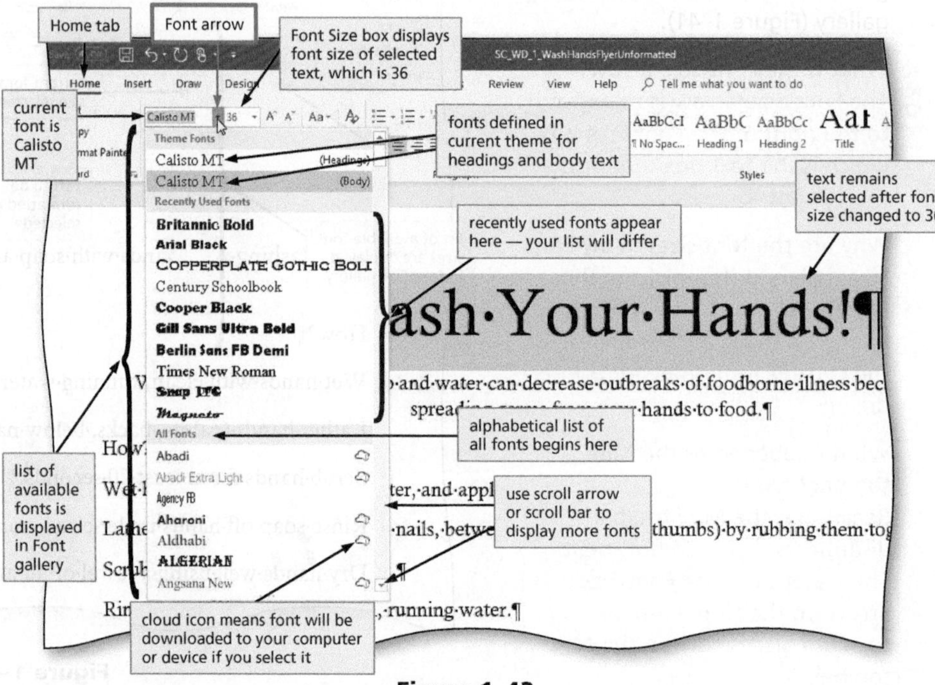

Figure 1–43

2

- If necessary, scroll through the Font gallery to display 'Rockwell Extra Bold' (or a similar font).
- Point to 'Rockwell Extra Bold' (or a similar font) to display a Live Preview of the selected text in the selected font (Figure 1–44).

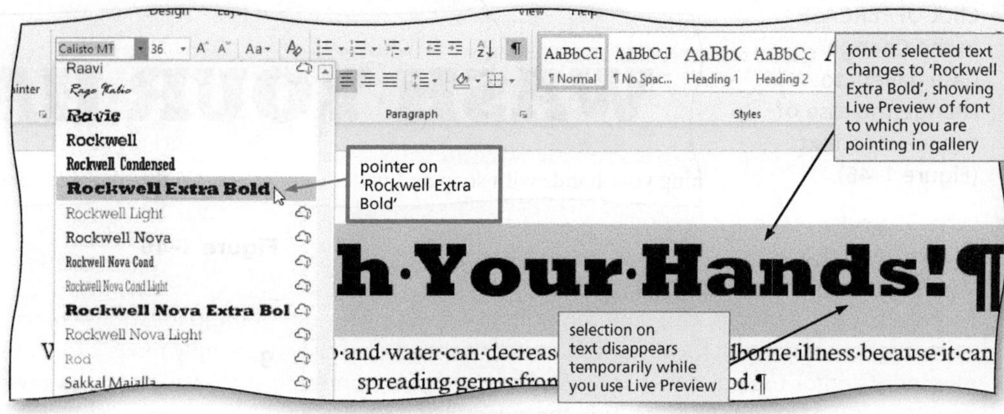

Figure 1–44

Experiment

- Point to various fonts in the Font gallery and watch the font of the selected text change in the document window.

3

- Click 'Rockwell Extra Bold' (or a similar font) in the Font gallery to change the font of the selected text.

Q&A If the font I want to use appears in the Recently Used Fonts list at the top of the Font gallery, could I click it there instead?
Yes.

Other Ways

1. Click Font arrow on Mini toolbar, click desired font in Font gallery
2. Right-click selected text (or, if using touch, tap 'Show Context Menu' button on Mini toolbar), click Font on shortcut menu, click Font tab (Font dialog box), select desired font in Font list, click OK
3. Click Font Dialog Box Launcher (Home tab | Font group), click Font tab (Font dialog box), select desired font in Font list, click OK
4. Press CTRL+D, click Font tab (Font dialog box), select desired font in Font list, click OK

To Change the Case of Selected Text

The headline currently shows the first letter in each word capitalized, which sometimes is referred to as initial cap. The following steps change the headline to uppercase. ***Why?*** *To draw more attention to the headline, you would like the entire line of text to be capitalized, or in uppercase letters.*

1

- With the text selected, click the Change Case button (Home tab | Font group) to display the Change Case gallery (Figure 1–45).

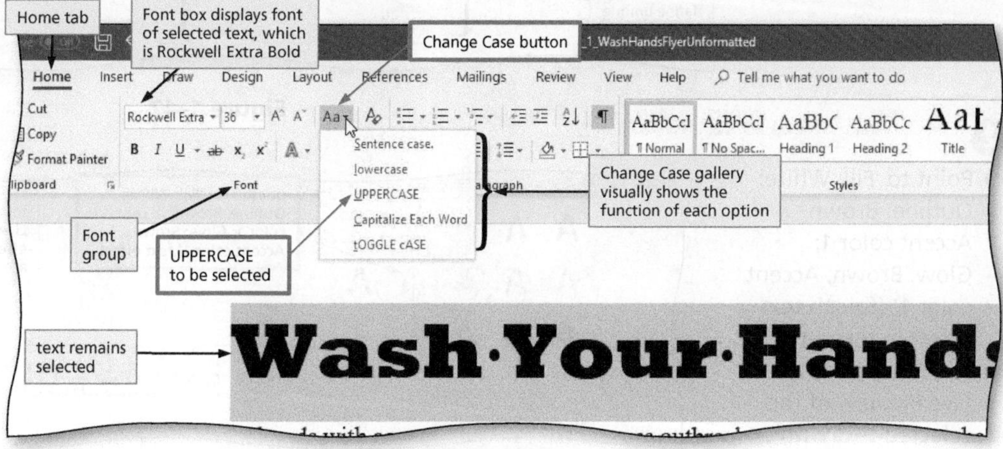

Figure 1–45

- Click UPPERCASE in the Change Case gallery to change the case of the selected text (Figure 1–46).

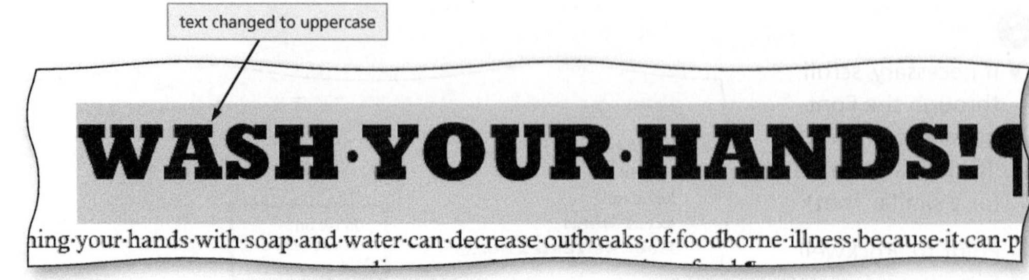

Figure 1–46

Q&A What if a ruler appears on the screen or the pointer shape changes?
If you are using a mouse, depending on the position of your pointer and locations you click on the screen, a ruler may appear automatically or the pointer's shape may change. Simply move the mouse and the ruler should disappear and/or the pointer shape will change. If you wanted to show the rulers, you would select the Ruler check box (View tab | Show group). To hide the rulers, deselect the Ruler check box (View tab | Show group).

Other Ways

1. Right-click selected text (or, if using touch, tap 'Show Context Menu' button on Mini toolbar), click Font on shortcut menu, click Font tab (Font dialog box), select All caps in Effects area, click OK
2. Click Font Dialog Box Launcher (Home tab | Font group), click Font tab (Font dialog box), select All caps in Effects area, click OK
3. Press SHIFT+F3 repeatedly until text is desired case

To Apply a Preset Text Effect to Selected Text

Word provides many text effects to add interest and variety to text. The following steps apply a preset text effect to the headline. ***Why?*** *You would like the text in the headline to be even more noticeable.*

- With the text selected, click the 'Text Effects and Typography' button (Home tab | Font group) to display the Text Effects and Typography gallery (Figure 1–47).

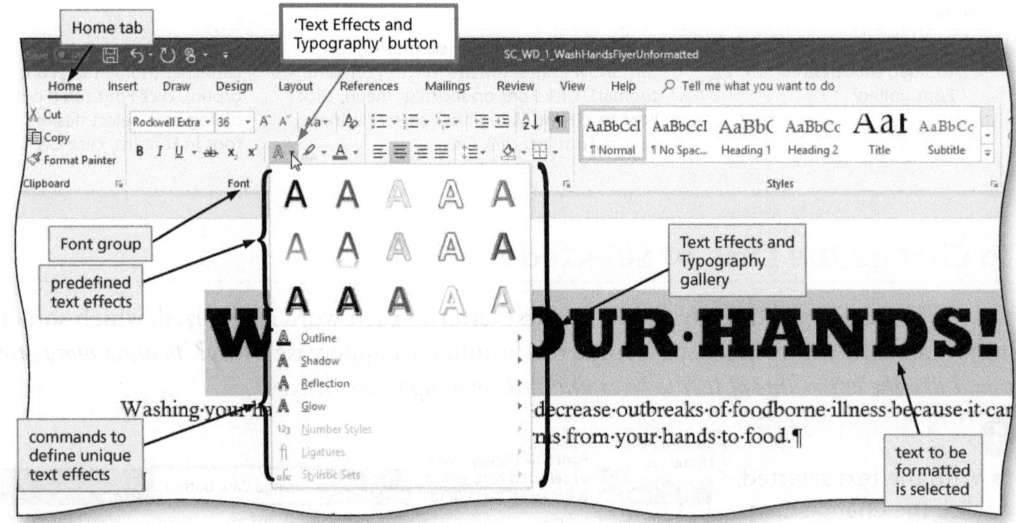

Figure 1–47

2

- Point to 'Fill: White; Outline: Brown, Accent color 1; Glow: Brown, Accent color 1' (fourth text effect in second row) to display a Live Preview of the selected text with the selected text effect (Figure 1–48).

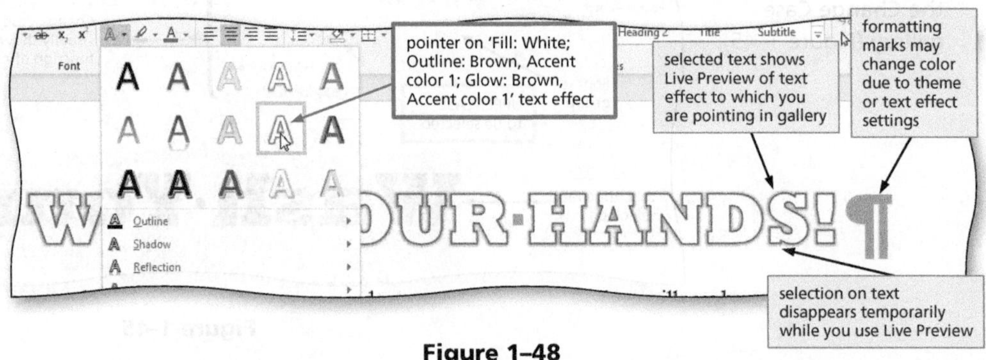

Figure 1–48

Experiment

- Point to various text effects in the Text Effects and Typography gallery and watch the text effects of the selected text change in the document window.

3

- Click 'Fill: White; Outline: Brown, Accent color 1; Glow: Brown, Accent color 1' to change the text effect of the selected text.

4

- Click anywhere in the document window to remove the selection from the selected text.

Other Ways

1. Right-click selected text (or, if using touch, tap 'Show Context Menu' button on Mini toolbar), click Font on shortcut menu, click Font tab (Font dialog box), click Text Effects button, expand Text Fill or Text Outline section and then select the desired text effect(s) (Format Text Effects dialog box), click OK, click OK
2. Click Font Dialog Box Launcher (Home tab | Font group), click Font tab (Font dialog box), click Text Effects button, expand Text Fill or Text Outline section and then select desired text effect (Format Text Effects dialog box), click OK, click OK

To Shade a Paragraph

Shading is the process of applying a background color or pattern to a page, text, table, or other object. When you shade a paragraph, Word shades the area from the left margin to the right margin of the current paragraph. To shade a paragraph, place the insertion point in the paragraph. To shade any other text, you must first select the text to be shaded. For example, to shade a word, you would select the word before performing these steps.

This flyer uses a shading color for the headline. ***Why?*** *To make the headline of the flyer more eye-catching, you shade it.* The following steps shade a paragraph.

1

- Click somewhere in the paragraph to be shaded (in this case, the headline) to position the insertion point in the paragraph to be formatted.
- Click the Shading arrow (Home tab | Paragraph group) to display the Shading gallery (Figure 1–49).

Q&A What if I click the Shading button by mistake?
Click the Shading arrow and proceed with Step 2. Note that if you are using a touch screen, you may not have a separate Shading button.

Why does my Shading gallery display different colors?
Your theme colors setting may display colors in a different order.

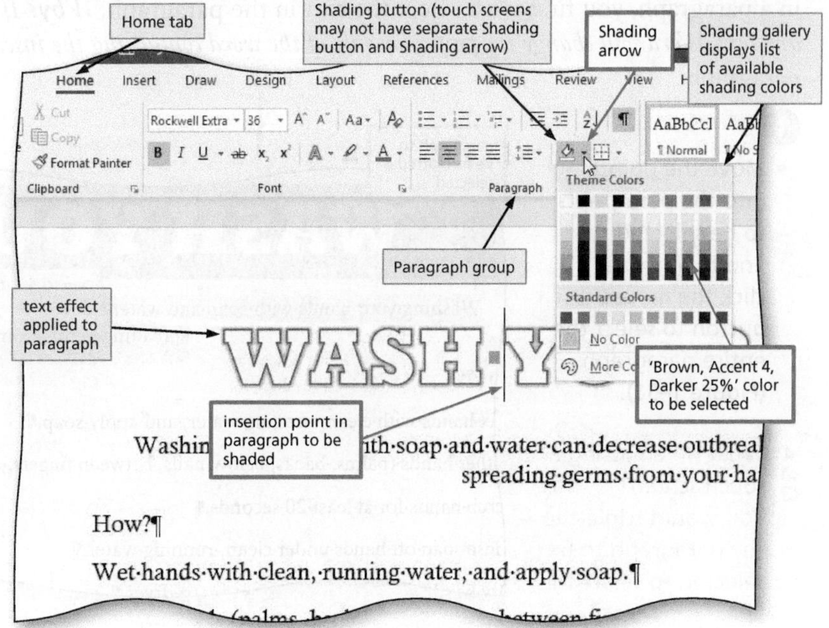

Figure 1–49

Experiment

- Point to various colors in the Shading gallery and watch the shading color of the current paragraph change.

- Click 'Brown, Accent 4, Darker 25%' (eighth color in fifth row) to shade the current paragraph (Figure 1–50).

Q&A What if I apply a dark shading color to dark text?
When the font color of text is Automatic, the color usually is black. If you select a dark shading color, Word automatically may change the text color to white so that the shaded text is easier to read.

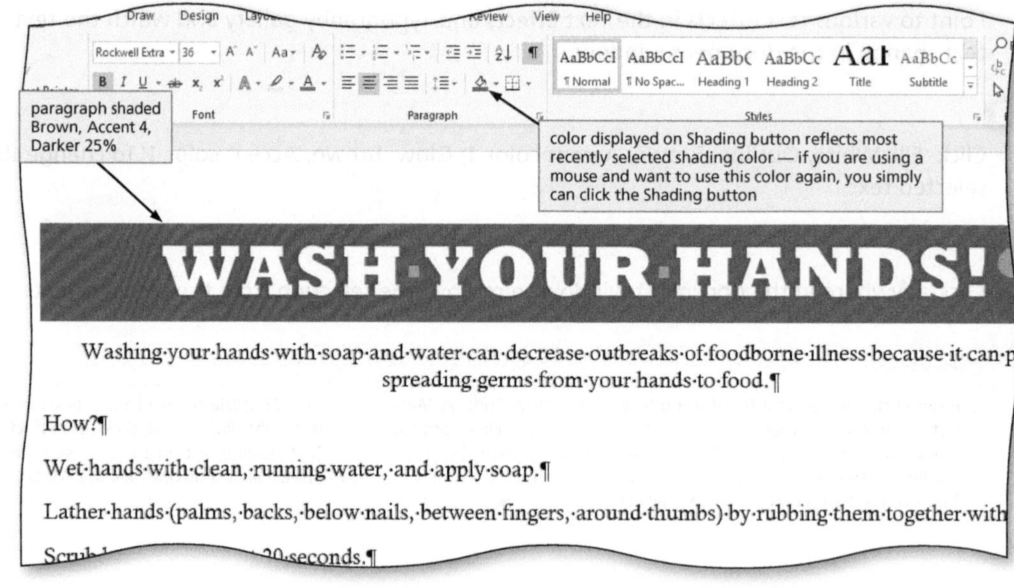

Figure 1–50

Other Ways

1. Click Borders arrow (Home tab | Paragraph group), click 'Borders and Shading', click Shading tab (Borders and Shading dialog box), click Fill arrow, select desired color, click OK

To Select a Paragraph

The next step is to change the color of the paragraph below the headline. To format all the characters in a paragraph, you first must select the text in the paragraph. ***Why?*** *If you change the font color without selecting any text, Word will change the font color only of the word containing the insertion point.* The following step selects a paragraph.

- Move the pointer into the paragraph to be selected and then triple-click the mouse button to select the entire paragraph (Figure 1–51).

Q&A What if I am using a touch screen?
You would triple-tap the paragraph to be selected to select the line.

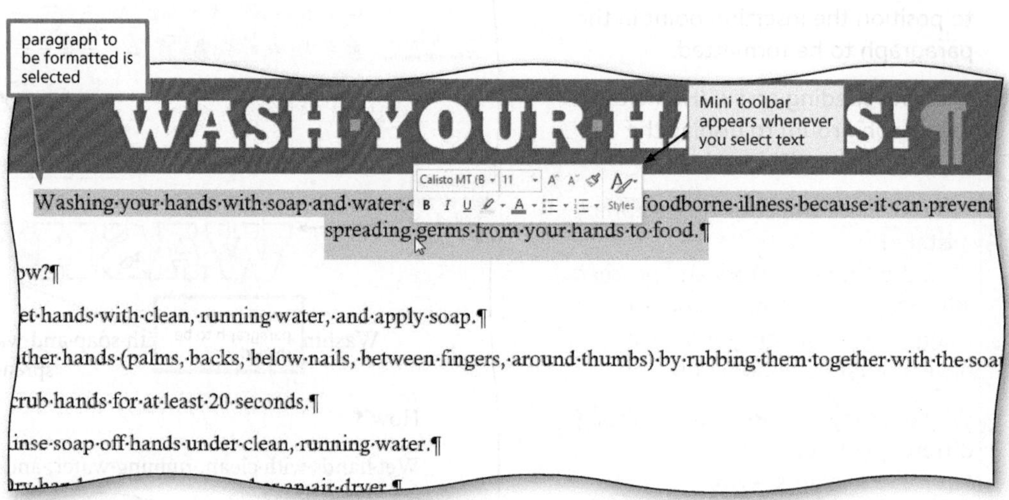

Figure 1–51

Other Ways

1. Move pointer to left of paragraph until pointer changes to right-pointing arrow and then double-click
2. With insertion point at beginning of first character in paragraph, press CRTL+SHIFT+DOWN ARROW until paragraph is selected

To Change the Font Color of Selected Text

The following steps change the color of the selected paragraph. ***Why?*** *To emphasize the paragraph, you change its color.*

1

- With the paragraph selected, click the Font Color arrow (Home tab | Font group) to display the Font Color gallery (Figure 1–52).

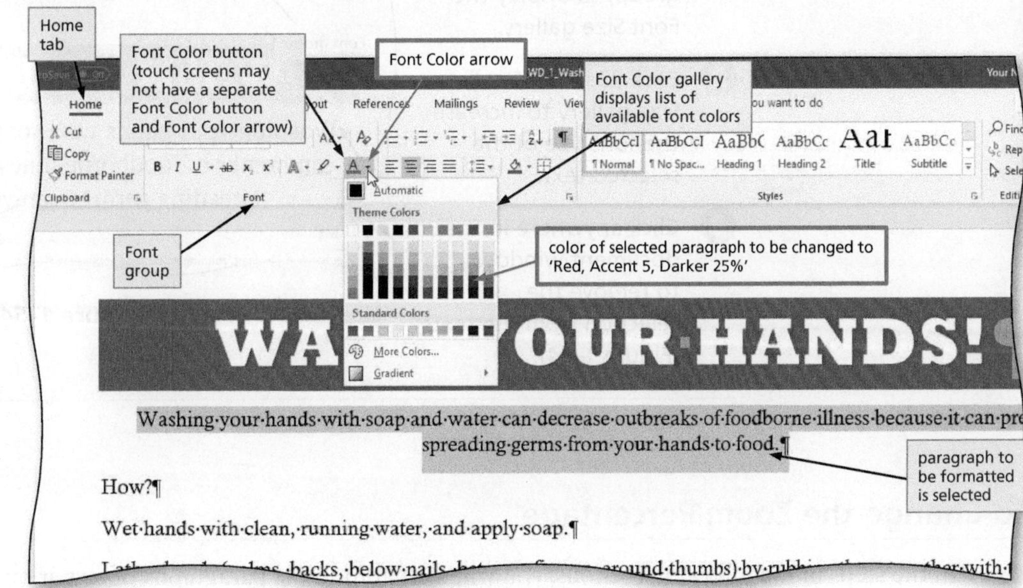

Figure 1–52

Q&A What if I click the Font Color button by mistake?
Click the Font Color arrow and then proceed with Step 2. Note that you may not have a separate Font Color button if you are using a touch screen.

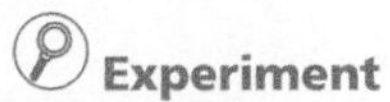

Experiment

- If you are using a mouse, point to various colors in the Font Color gallery and watch the color of the current word change.

2

- Click 'Red, Accent 5, Darker 25%' (ninth color in fifth row) to change the color of the selected text (Figure 1–53).

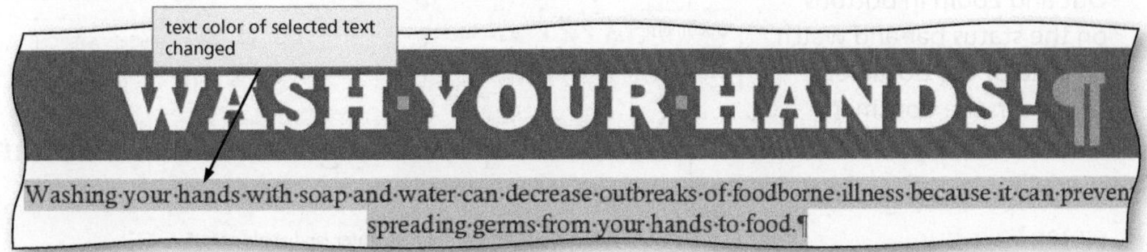

Figure 1–53

Q&A How would I change the text color back to black?
You would select the text or position the insertion point in the word to format, click the Font Color arrow (Home tab | Font group) again, and then click Automatic in the Font Color gallery.

Other Ways

1. Click Font Color arrow on Mini toolbar, click desired color	2. Right-click selected text (or, if using touch, tap 'Show Context Menu' button on Mini toolbar), click Font on shortcut menu, click Font tab (Font dialog box), click Font color arrow, click desired color, click OK	3. Click Font Dialog Box Launcher (Home tab | Font group), click Font tab (Font dialog box), click Font color arrow, click desired color, click OK

To Change the Font Size of Selected Text

The font size of characters in the currently selected paragraph is 11 point. To make them easier to read from a distance, this flyer uses a 22-point font size for these characters. The following steps change the font size of the selected text.

1. With the text selected, click the Font Size arrow (Home tab | Font group) to display the Font Size gallery.
2. Click 22 in the Font Size gallery to increase the font size of the selected text.
3. Click anywhere in the document window to remove the selection from the text (Figure 1–54).

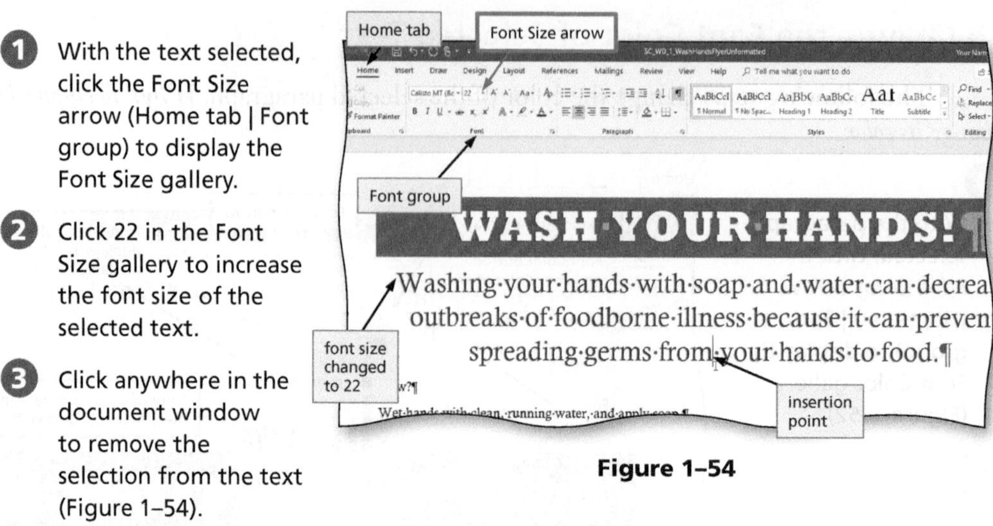

Figure 1–54

To Change the Zoom Percentage

In the steps in the following sections, you will format multiple paragraphs of text at once that currently cannot all be displayed in the document window at the same time. The next task is to adjust the zoom percentage. ***Why?*** *You want to be able to see all the text to be formatted in the document window.* The following step zooms the document.

1.

Experiment

- Repeatedly click the Zoom Out and Zoom In buttons on the status bar and watch the size of the document change in the document window.

Q&A What if I am using a touch screen?

Repeatedly pinch (move two fingers together on the screen) and stretch (move two fingers apart on the screen) and watch the size of the document change in the document window.

- Click the Zoom Out or Zoom In button as many times as necessary until the Zoom level button on the status bar displays 120% on its face.
- Scroll if necessary to display all text beginning with the word, How?, to the signature line (Figure 1–55).

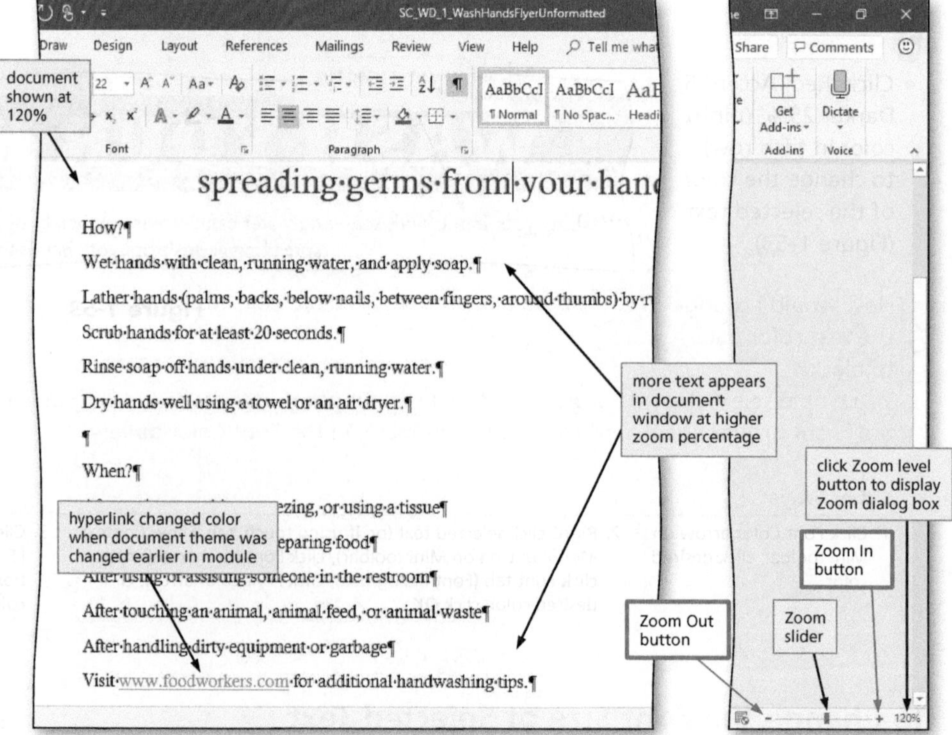

Figure 1–55

Other Ways

1. Drag Zoom slider on status bar
2. Click Zoom level button on status bar, select desired zoom percent or zoom type (Zoom dialog box), click OK
3. Click Zoom button (View tab | Zoom group), select desired zoom percent or zoom type (Zoom dialog box), click OK

To Select Multiple Lines

The next formatting step for the flyer is to increase the font size of the characters from the word, How?, to the last line of body copy above the signature line. ***Why?*** *You want this text to be easier to read from a distance.*

To change the font size of the characters in multiple lines, you first must select all the lines to be formatted. The following steps select multiple lines.

- Scroll, if necessary, so that all text to be formatted is displayed on the screen.
- Move the pointer to the left of the first paragraph to be selected until the pointer changes to a right-pointing block arrow (Figure 1–56).

Q&A What if I am using a touch screen?
You would tap to position the insertion point in the text to select.

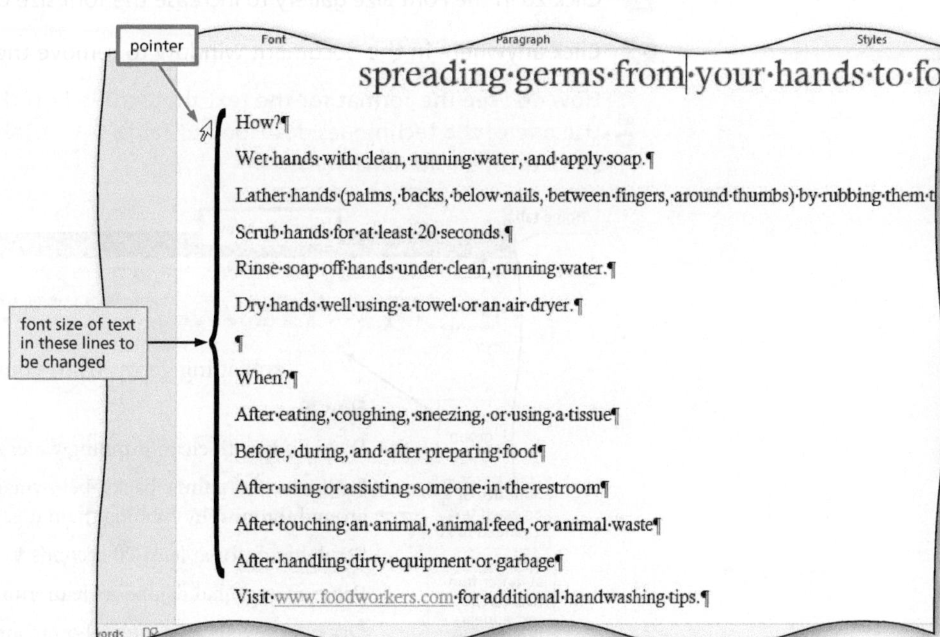

Figure 1–56

2

- While the pointer is a right-pointing block arrow, drag downward to select all lines that will be formatted (Figure 1–57).

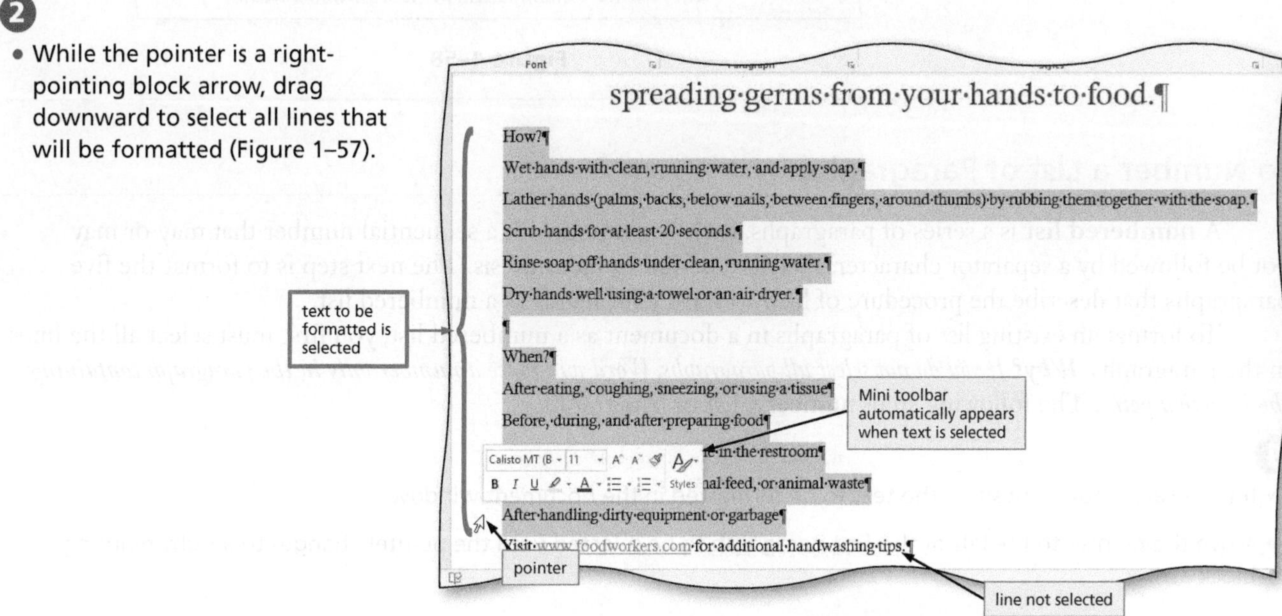

Figure 1–57

Other Ways

1. With insertion point at beginning of desired line, press SHIFT+DOWN ARROW repeatedly until all lines are selected

To Change the Font Size of Selected Text

The characters in the selected text currently are 11 point. To make them easier to read from a distance, this flyer uses a 20-point font size for these characters. The following steps change the font size of the selected text.

1. With the text selected, click the Font Size arrow (Home tab | Font group) to display the Font Size gallery.
2. Click 20 in the Font Size gallery to increase the font size of the selected text (Figure 1–58).
3. Click anywhere in the document window to remove the selection from the text.

Q&A How do I see the format for the text that scrolled off the screen?
Use one of the techniques described in Table 1–1 or Table 1–2 earlier in this module to scroll through the document.

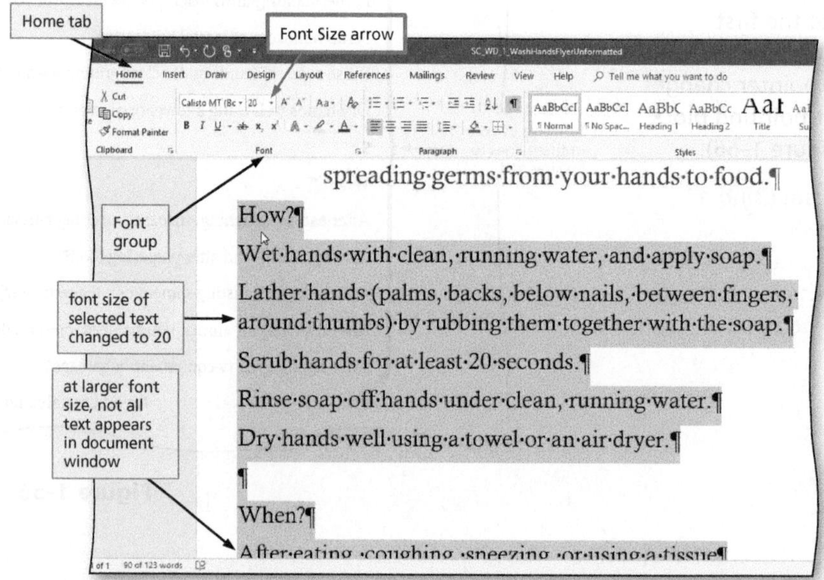

Figure 1–58

To Number a List of Paragraphs

A **numbered list** is a series of paragraphs, each beginning with a sequential number that may or may not be followed by a separator character, such as a period or parenthesis. The next step is to format the five paragraphs that describe the procedure of how to wash your hands as a numbered list.

To format an existing list of paragraphs in a document as a numbered list, you first must select all the lines in the paragraphs. ***Why?*** *If you do not select all paragraphs, Word will place a number only in the paragraph containing the insertion point.* The following steps number a list of paragraphs.

- If necessary, scroll to position the text to be formatted in the document window.
- Move the pointer to the left of the first paragraph to be selected until the pointer changes to a right-pointing block arrow.

- Drag downward until all paragraphs that will be formatted as a numbered list are selected (Figure 1–59).

Q&A What if I am using a touch screen?
Tap to position the insertion point in the text to select and then drag the selection handle(s) as necessary to select the text that will be formatted. When working on a touch screen, a **selection handle** is a small circle that appears below the insertion point as you drag with a fingertip to select text.

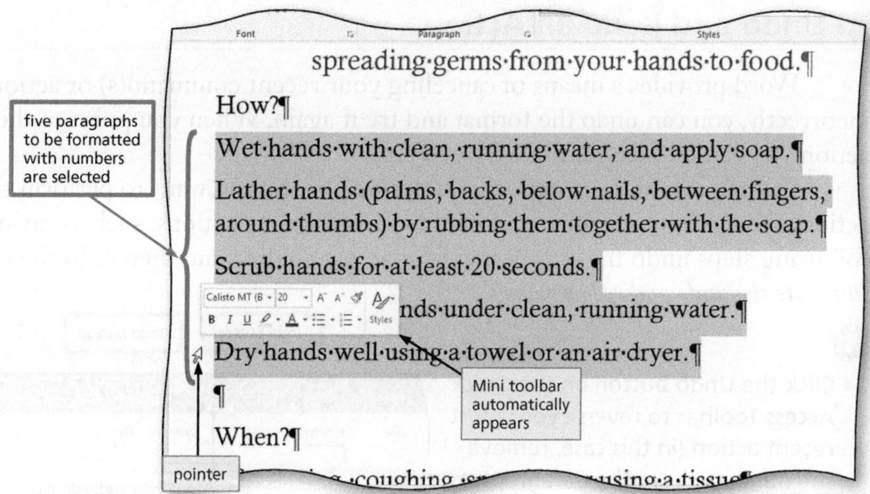

Figure 1–59

2

- Click the Numbering button (Home tab | Paragraph group) to place a number followed by a period at the beginning of each selected paragraph (Figure 1–60).

Q&A Why does my screen display a Numbering gallery?
If you are using a touch screen, you may not have a separate Numbering button and Numbering arrow. In this case, select the desired bullet style in the Numbering gallery.

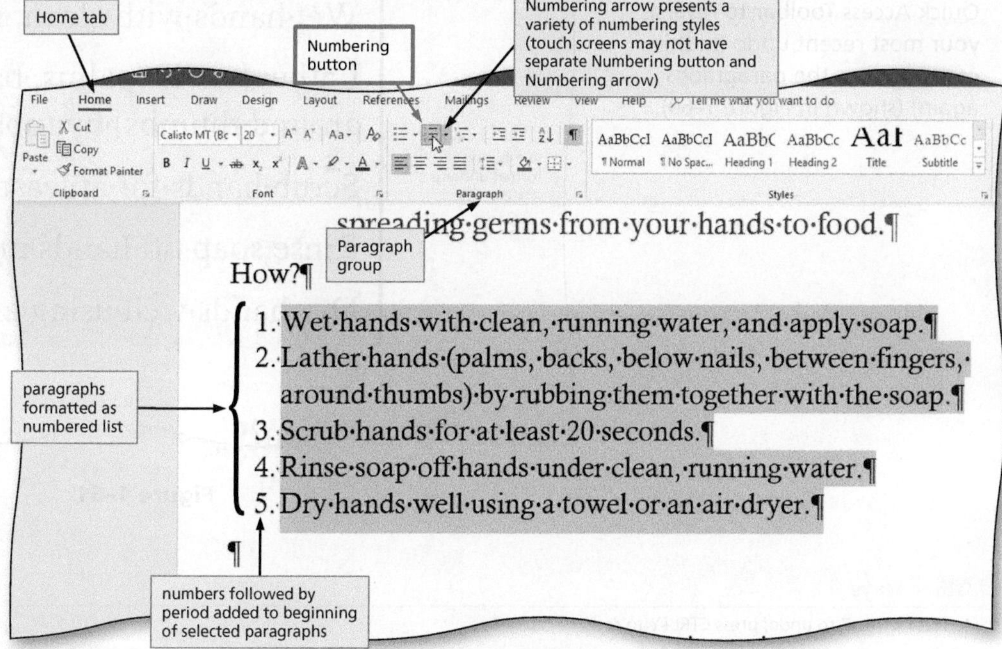

Figure 1–60

What if I accidentally click the Numbering arrow?
Press ESC to remove the Numbering gallery from the screen and then repeat Step 2.

How do I remove numbering from a list or paragraph?
Select the list or paragraph and then click the Numbering button again, or click the Numbering arrow and then click None in the Numbering Library.

Other Ways

1. Click Numbering button on Mini toolbar

To Undo and Redo an Action

Word provides a means of canceling your recent command(s) or action(s). For example, if you format text incorrectly, you can undo the format and try it again. When you point to the Undo button, Word displays the action you can undo as part of a ScreenTip.

If, after you undo an action, you decide you did not want to perform the undo, you can redo the undone action. Word does not allow you to undo or redo some actions, such as saving or printing a document. The following steps undo the numbering format just applied and then redo the numbering format. ***Why?*** *These steps illustrate the undo and redo actions.*

- Click the Undo button on the Quick Access Toolbar to reverse your most recent action (in this case, remove the numbers from the paragraphs) (Figure 1–61).

- Click the Redo button on the Quick Access Toolbar to reverse your most recent undo (in this case, number the paragraphs again) (shown in Figure 1–60).

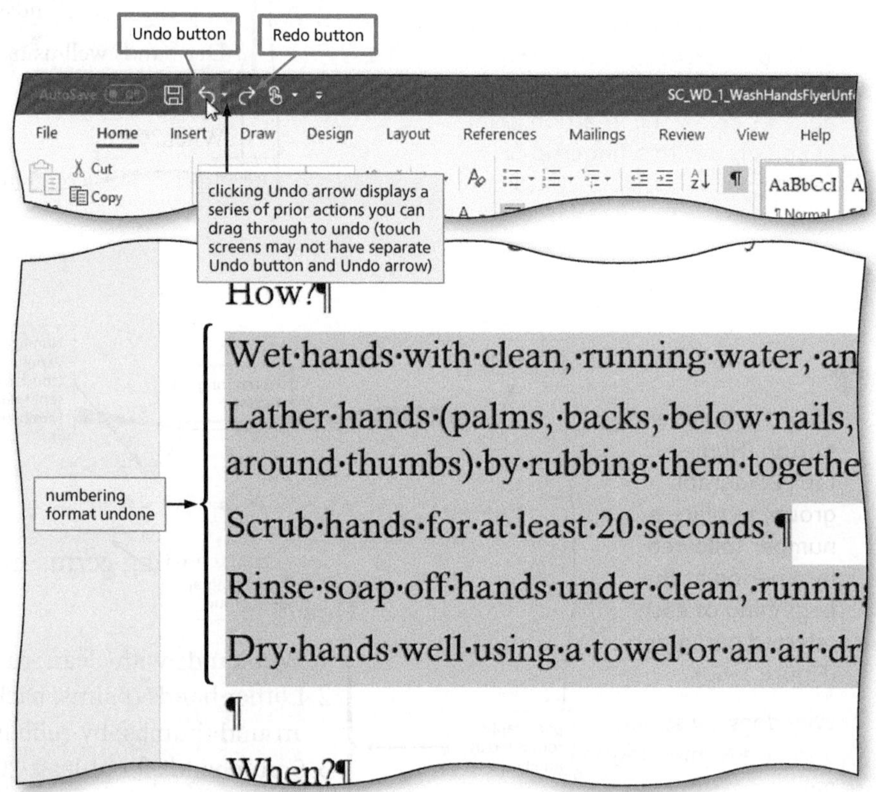

Figure 1–61

Other Ways

1. Press CTRL+Z to undo; press CTRL+Y to redo

To Bullet a List of Paragraphs

A **bulleted list** is a series of paragraphs, each beginning with a bullet character, such as dot or check mark. The next step is to format the five paragraphs that describe when to wash your hands as a bulleted list.

To format a list of paragraphs as a bulleted list, you first must select all the lines in the paragraphs. ***Why?*** *If you do not select all paragraphs, Word will place a bullet only in the paragraph containing the insertion point.* The following steps bullet a list of paragraphs.

- If necessary, scroll to position the text to be formatted in the document window.
- Move the pointer to the left of the first paragraph to be selected until the pointer changes to a right-pointing block arrow.

- Drag downward until all paragraphs that will be formatted with a bullet character are selected (Figure 1–62).

Q&A What if I am using a touch screen?
Tap to position the insertion point in the text to select and then drag the selection handle(s) as necessary to select the text that will be formatted.

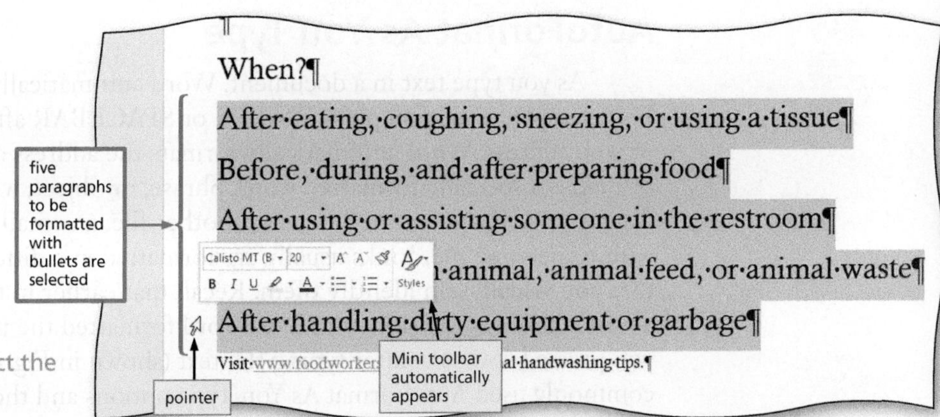

Figure 1–62

- Click the Bullets button (Home tab | Paragraph group) to place a bullet character at the beginning of each selected paragraph.
- Click anywhere in the document window to remove the selection from the text (Figure 1–63).

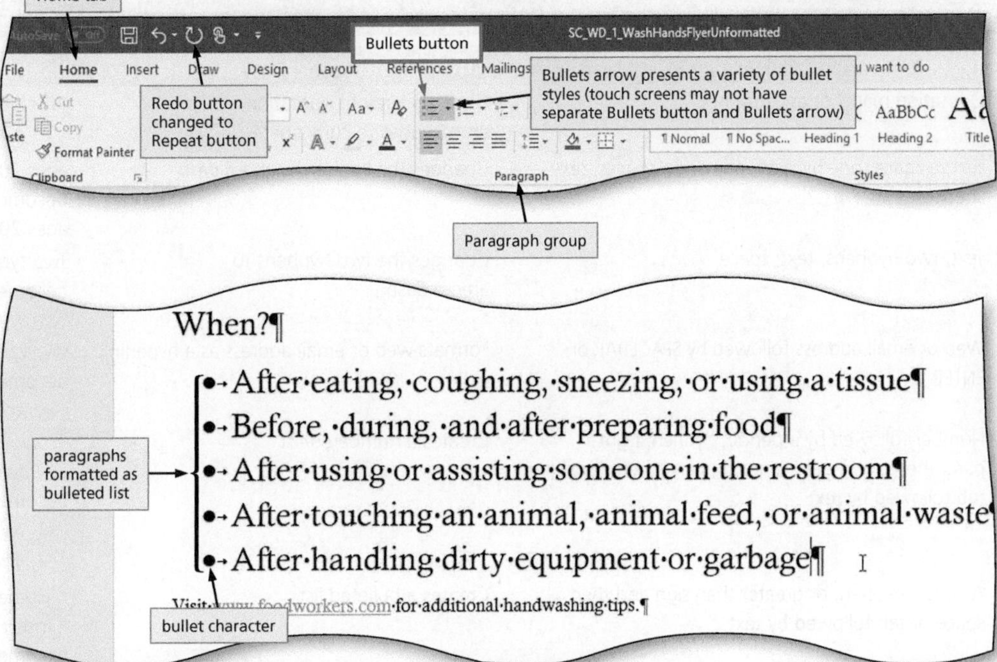

Figure 1–63

Q&A Why does my screen display a Bullets gallery?
If you are using a touch screen, you may not have a separate Bullets button and Bullets arrow. In this case, select the desired bullet style in the Bullets gallery.

What if I accidentally click the Bullets arrow?
Press ESC to remove the Bullets gallery from the screen and then repeat Step 2.

How do I remove bullets from a list or paragraph?
Select the list or paragraph and then click the Bullets button again, or click the Bullets arrow and then click None in the Bullets Library.

Why did the appearance of the Redo button change?
It changed to a Repeat button. When it is a Repeat button, you can click it to repeat your last action. For example, you can select different text and then click the Repeat button to apply (repeat) the bullet format to the selected text.

Other Ways

1. Click Bullets button on Mini toolbar

AutoFormat As You Type

As you type text in a document, Word automatically formats some of it for you. For example, when you press ENTER or SPACEBAR after typing an email address or web address, Word automatically formats the address as a hyperlink. A **hyperlink**, or link, is a specially formatted word, phrase, or object, which, when clicked or tapped, displays a webpage on the Internet, another file, an email window, or another location within the same file. Links usually are formatted in a different color and underlined so that you visually can identify them. Recall that earlier in this module, when you typed a web address in the signature line, Word formatted the text as a hyperlink because you pressed SPACEBAR after typing the text (shown in Figure 1–64). Table 1–3 outlines commonly used AutoFormat As You Type options and their results.

Table 1–3 Commonly Used AutoFormat As You Type Options

Typed Text	AutoFormat As You Type Feature	Example
Quotation marks or apostrophes	Changes straight quotation marks or apostrophes to curly ones	"the" becomes “the”
Text, a space, one hyphen, one or no spaces, text, space	Changes the hyphen to an en dash	ages 20-45 becomes ages 20–45
Text, two hyphens, text, space	Changes the two hyphens to an em dash	Two types--yellow and red becomes Two types—yellow and red
Web or email address followed by SPACEBAR or ENTER	Formats web or email address as a hyperlink	www.cengage.com becomes www.cengage.com
Number followed by a period, hyphen, right parenthesis, or greater than sign and then a space or tab followed by text	Creates a numbered list	1. Word 2. PowerPoint becomes 1. Word 2. PowerPoint
Asterisk, hyphen, or greater than sign and then a space or tab followed by text	Creates a bulleted list	* Home tab * Insert tab becomes • Home tab • Insert tab
Fraction and then a space or hyphen	Condenses the fraction entry so that it consumes one space instead of three	1/2 becomes ½
Ordinal and then a space or hyphen	Makes part of the ordinal a superscript	3rd becomes 3rd

To Remove a Hyperlink

The web address in the signature line of the flyer should be formatted as regular text; that is, it should not be a different color or underlined. ***Why?*** *Hyperlinks are useful only in online documents, and this flyer will be printed instead of distributed electronically.* The following steps remove a hyperlink format.

1

- Right-click the hyperlink (in this case, the web address) to display a shortcut menu (or, if using a touch screen, press and hold the hyperlink and then tap the 'Show Context Menu' button on the Mini toolbar) (Figure 1–64).

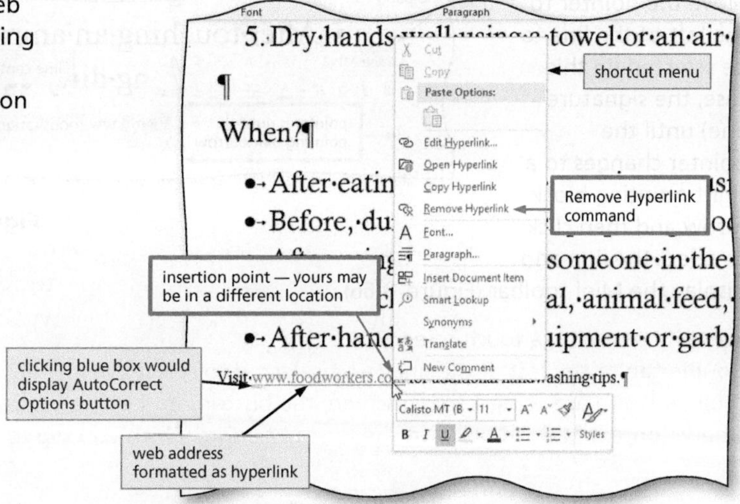

Figure 1–64

2

- Click Remove Hyperlink on the shortcut menu to remove the hyperlink format from the text; if the text remains colored and underlined, change the color to Automatic and remove the underline (Figure 1–65).

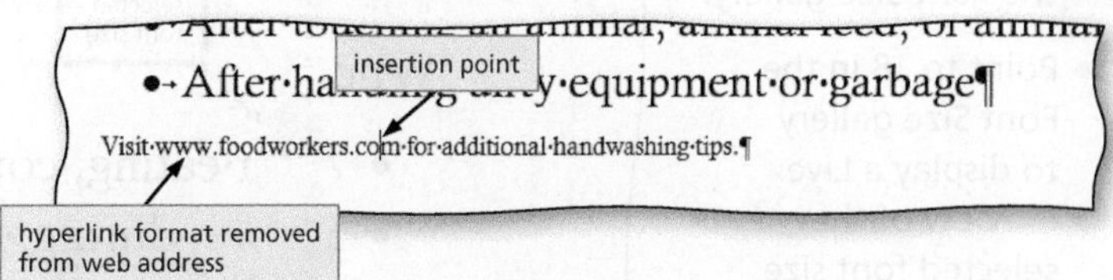

Figure 1–65

Q&A Could I have used the AutoCorrect Options button instead of the Remove Hyperlink command?

Yes. Alternatively, you could have pointed to the small blue box at the beginning of the hyperlink (if it is visible), clicked the AutoCorrect Options button, and then clicked Undo Hyperlink on the AutoCorrect Options menu.

Other Ways

1. With insertion point in hyperlink, click Link button (Insert tab | Links group), click Remove Link button (Edit Hyperlink dialog box)

To Center Another Paragraph

In the flyer, the signature line is to be centered to match the paragraph alignment of the headline. The following steps center the signature line.

1. Click somewhere in the paragraph to be centered (in this case, the signature line) to position the insertion point in the paragraph to be formatted.
2. Click the Center button (Home tab | Paragraph group) to center the paragraph containing the insertion point (shown in Figure 1–66).

To Use the Mini Toolbar to Format Text

Recall that the Mini toolbar automatically appears based on certain tasks you perform. ***Why?*** *Word places commonly used buttons and boxes on the Mini toolbar for your convenience. If you do not use the Mini toolbar, it disappears from the screen.* All commands on the Mini toolbar also exist on the ribbon.

The following steps use the Mini toolbar to change the font size and color of text in the signature line of the flyer.

- Move the pointer to the left of the line to be selected (in this case, the signature line) until the pointer changes to a right-pointing block arrow and then click to select the line and display the Mini toolbar (Figure 1–66).

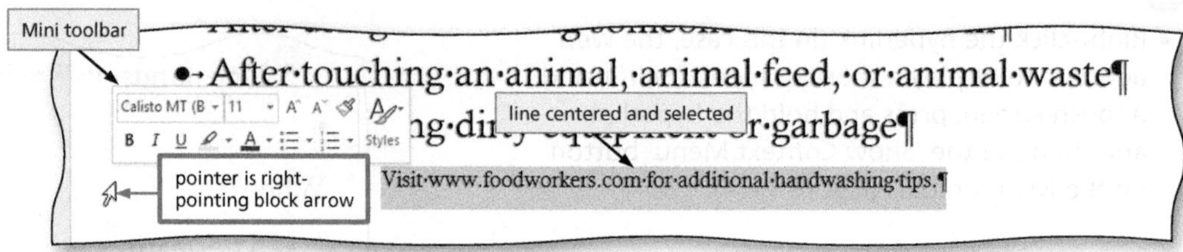

Figure 1–66

Q&A

What if I am using a touch screen?

Double-tap to the left of the line to be selected to select the line and then tap the selection to display the Mini toolbar. If you are using a touch screen, the buttons and boxes on the Mini toolbar differ. For example, it contains a 'Show Context Menu' button at the far-right edge, which you tap to display a shortcut menu.

- Click the Font Size arrow on the Mini toolbar to display the Font Size gallery.
- Point to 18 in the Font Size gallery to display a Live Preview of the selected font size (Figure 1–67).

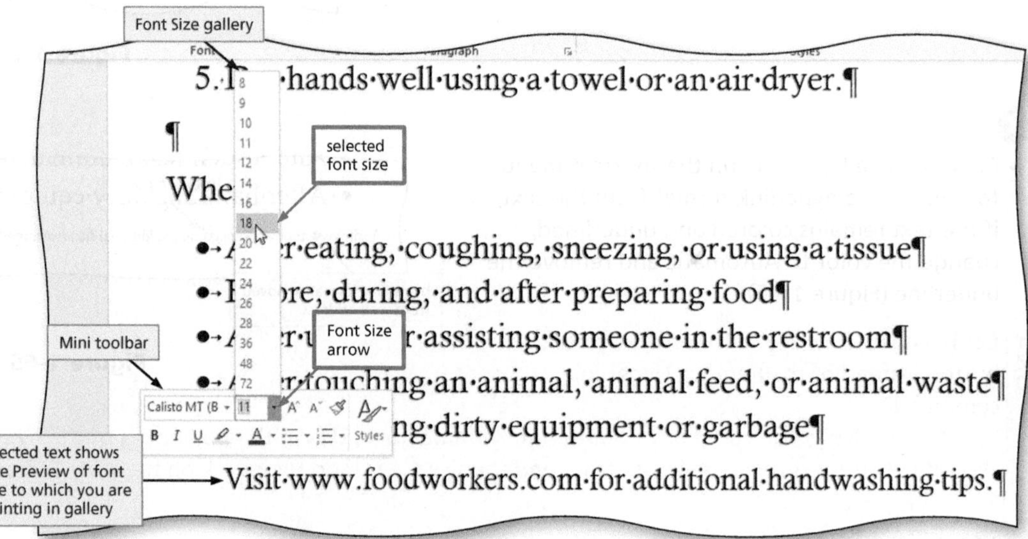

Figure 1–67

- Click 18 in the Font Size gallery to increase the font size of the selected text.

- With the text still selected and the Mini toolbar still displayed, click the Font Color arrow on the Mini toolbar to display the Font Color gallery.
- Point to 'Red, Accent 5, Darker 25%' (ninth color in the fifth row) to display a Live Preview of the selected font color (Figure 1–68).

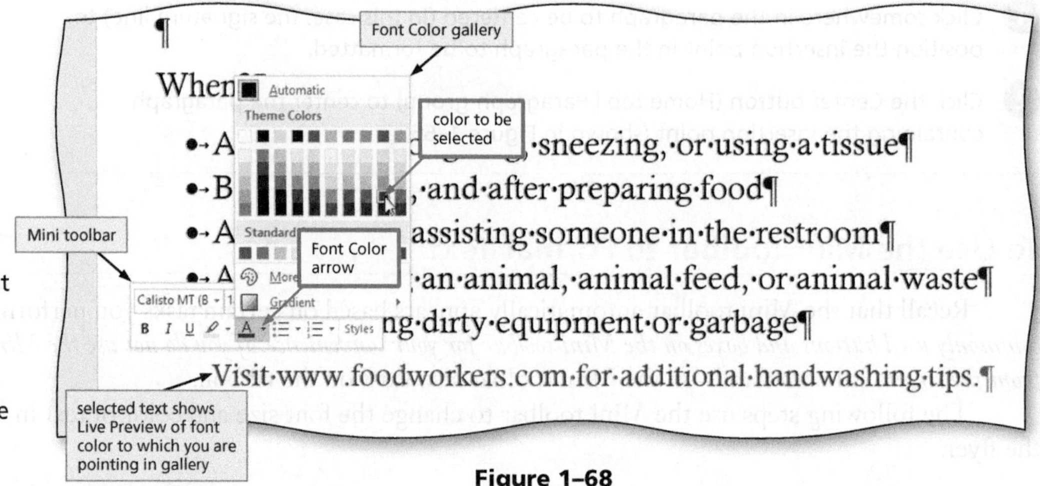

Figure 1–68

- Click 'Red, Accent 5, Darker 25%' to change the color of the selected text (shown in Figure 1–69).
- Click anywhere in the document window to remove the selection from the text.

To Select a Group of Words

The words, additional handwashing tips, in the signature line of the flyer, are underlined to further emphasize them. To format a group of words, you first must select them. ***Why?*** *If you underline text without selecting any text first, Word will underline only the word containing the insertion point.* The following steps select a group of words.

- Position the pointer immediately to the left of the first character of the text to be selected, in this case, the a in the word, additional (Figure 1–69).

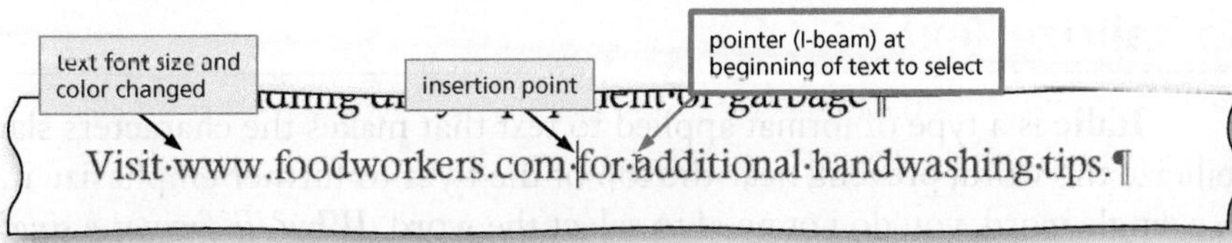

Figure 1–69

Q&A Why did the shape of the pointer change?
The pointer's shape is an I-beam when positioned in unselected text in the document window.

- Drag the pointer through the last character of the text to be selected, in this case, the s in the word, tips (Figure 1–70).

Q&A Why did the pointer shape change again?
When the pointer is positioned in selected text, its shape is a left-pointing block arrow.

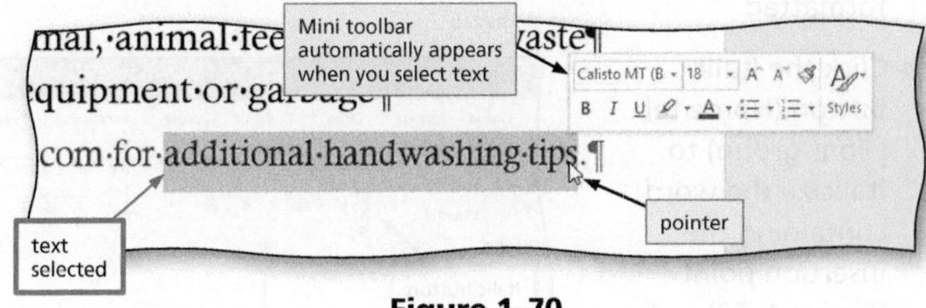

Figure 1–70

Other Ways

1. With insertion point at beginning of first word in group, press CTRL+SHIFT+RIGHT ARROW repeatedly until all words are selected

To Underline Text

Underlined text prints with an underscore (_) below each character, including spaces. In the flyer, the text, additional handwashing tips, in the signature line is underlined. ***Why?*** *Underlines are used to emphasize or draw attention to specific text.* The following step formats selected text with an underline.

- With the text selected, click the Underline button (Home tab | Font group) to underline the selected text (Figure 1–71).

Q&A What if my screen displays an Underline gallery?
If you are using a touch screen, you may not have a separate Underline button and Underline arrow. In this case, select the desired underline style in the Underline gallery.

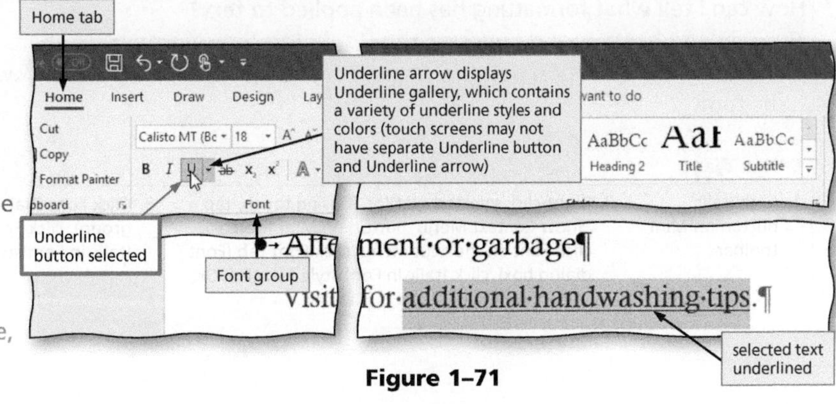

Figure 1–71

Q&A

If a button exists on the Mini toolbar, can I click that instead of using the ribbon?
Yes.

How would I remove an underline?
You would click the Underline button a second time, or you immediately could click the Undo button on the Quick Access Toolbar or press CTRL+Z.

Other Ways

1. Click Underline button on Mini toolbar	2. Right-click text (or, if using touch, tap 'Show Context Menu' button on Mini toolbar), click Font on shortcut menu, click Font tab (Font dialog box), click Underline style box arrow, click desired underline style, click OK	3. Click Font Dialog Box Launcher (Home tab | Font group), click Font tab (Font dialog box), click Underline style arrow, click desired underline style, click OK	4. Press CTRL+U

To Italicize Text

Italic is a type of format applied to text that makes the characters slant to the right. The next step is to italicize the word, prevent, near the top of the flyer to further emphasize it. If you want to format the characters in a single word, you do not need to select the word. ***Why?*** *To format a single word, you simply position the insertion point somewhere in the word and apply the desired format.* The following step italicizes a word.

- If necessary, scroll to the top of the document in the document window.
- Click somewhere in the word to be italicized (prevent, in this case) to position the insertion point in the word to be formatted.
- Click the Italic button (Home tab | Font group) to italicize the word containing the insertion point (Figure 1–72).

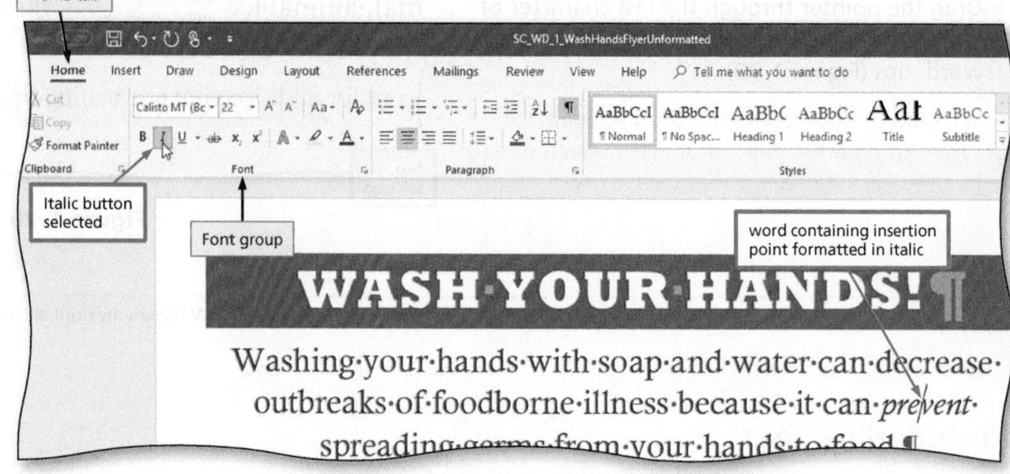

Figure 1–72

Q&A

How would I remove an italic format?
You would click the Italic button a second time, or you immediately could click the Undo button on the Quick Access Toolbar or press CTRL+Z.

How can I tell what formatting has been applied to text?
The selected buttons and boxes on the Home tab show formatting characteristics of the location of the insertion point. With the insertion point in the word, prevent, the Home tab shows these formats: 22-point Calisto MT italic font.

Other Ways

1. Click Italic button on Mini toolbar	2. Right-click selected text (or, if using touch, tap 'Show Context Menu' button on Mini toolbar), click Font on shortcut menu, click Font tab (Font dialog box), click Italic in Font style list, click OK	3. Click Font Dialog Box Launcher (Home tab | Font group), click Font tab (Font dialog box), click Italic in Font style list, click OK	4. Press CTRL+I

To Select Nonadjacent Text

The next step is to select the first word in every paragraph in the numbered list (Wet, Lather, Scrub, Rinse, Dry) and bold them. ***Why?*** *You want to emphasize these words further.* Word provides a method of selecting nonadjacent items, which are items such as text, pictures, or other objects that are not immediately beside one another. When you select nonadjacent items, you can format all occurrences of the selected items at once. The following steps select nonadjacent text.

- If necessary, scroll to display the entire numbered list in the document window.
- Select the first word to format (in this case, double-click the word, Wet) (Figure 1–73).

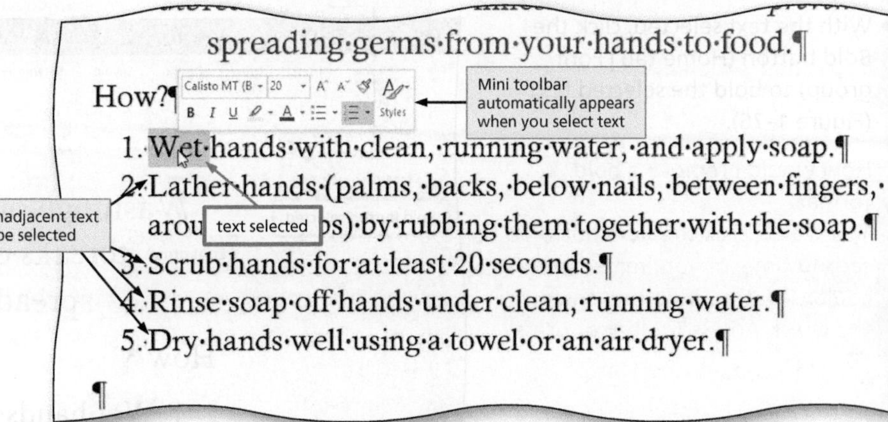

Figure 1–73

- While holding down CTRL, select the next word to format (in this case, double-click the word, Lather), which selects the nonadjacent text (Figure 1–74).

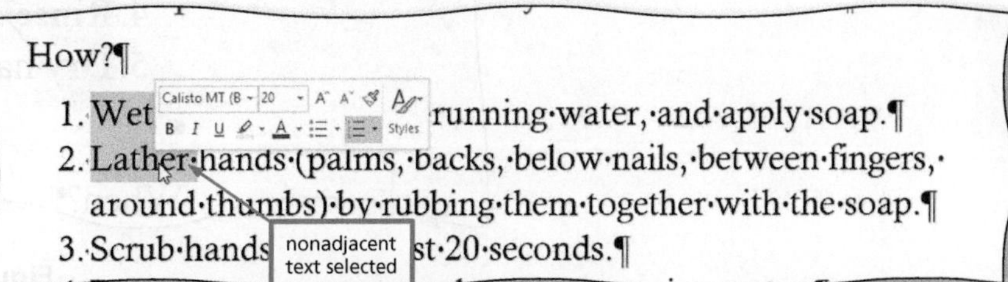

Figure 1–74

- While holding down CTRL, select the remaining nonadjacent text (that is, the words, Scrub, Rinse, Dry), as shown in Figure 1–75.

Q&A Do I follow the same procedure to select any nonadjacent item?
Yes. Select the first item and then hold down CTRL while selecting the remaining items.

What if my keyboard does not have a key labelled CTRL?
You will need to format each item individually, one at a time.

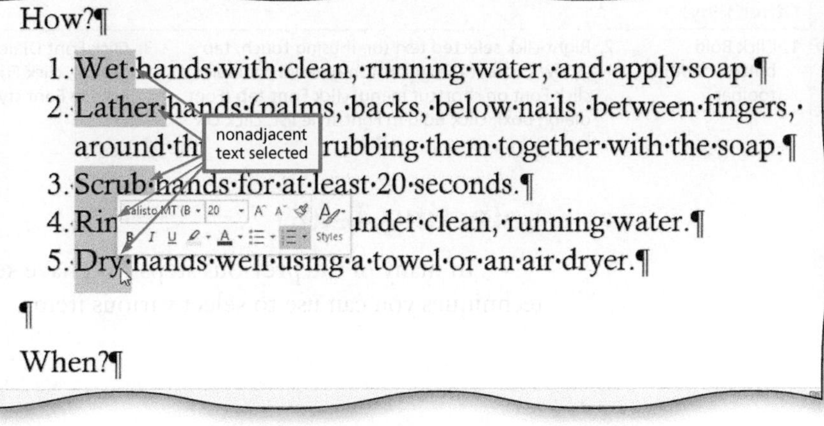

Figure 1–75

To Bold Text

Bold is a type of format applied to text that makes the characters appear somewhat thicker and darker than those that are not bold. The following steps format the selected text in bold characters. ***Why?*** *To further emphasize this text, it is bold in the flyer.* Recall that if you want to format a single word, you simply position the insertion point in the word and then format the word. To format text that consists of more than one word, as you have learned previously, you select the text first.

- With the text selected, click the Bold button (Home tab | Font group) to bold the selected text (Figure 1–76).

Q&A How would I remove a bold format?
You would click the Bold button a second time, or you immediately could click the Undo button on the Quick Access Toolbar or press CTRL+Z.

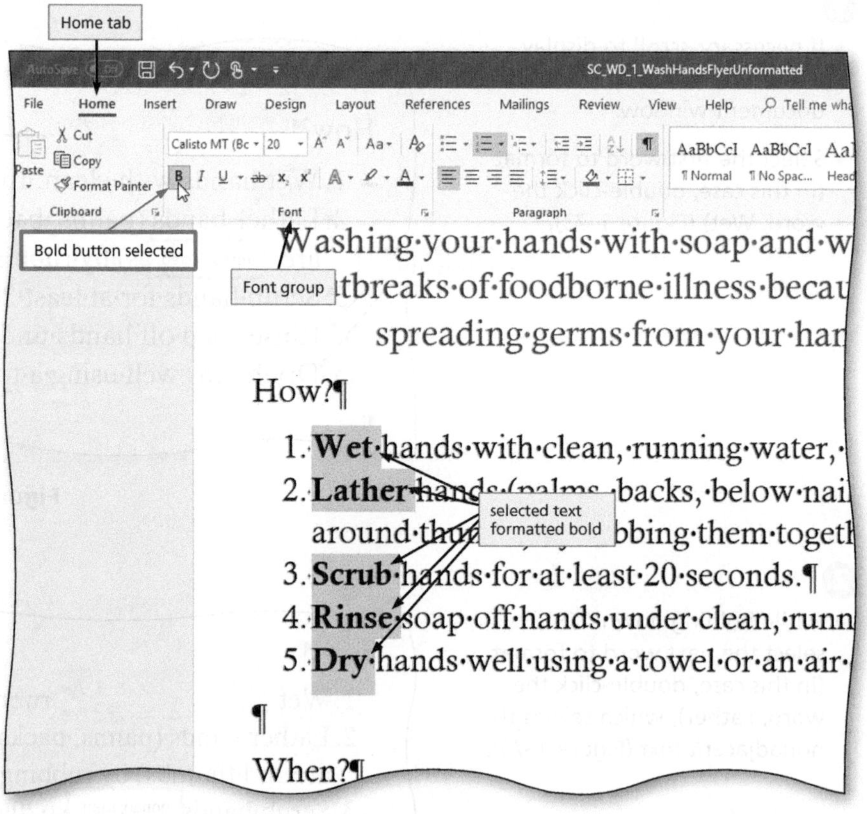

Figure 1–76

- Click anywhere in the document window to remove the selection from the screen.

Other Ways

1. Click Bold button on Mini toolbar	2. Right-click selected text (or, if using touch, tap 'Show Context Menu' button on Mini toolbar), click Font on shortcut menu, click Font tab (Font dialog box), click Bold in Font style list, click OK	3. Click Font Dialog Box Launcher (Home tab | Font group), click Font tab (Font dialog box), click Bold in Font style list, click OK	4. Press CTRL+B

Selecting Text

In many of the previous steps, you have selected text. Table 1–4 summarizes the techniques you can use to select various items.

Table 1–4 Techniques for Selecting Text

Item to Select	Touch	Mouse	Keyboard (where applicable)
Block of text	Tap to position insertion point in text to select and then drag selection handle(s) to select text.	Click at beginning of selection, scroll to end of selection, position pointer at end of selection, hold down SHIFT, and then click; or drag through the text.	
Character(s)	Tap to position insertion point in text to select and then drag selection handle(s) to select text.	Drag through character(s).	SHIFT+RIGHT ARROW or SHIFT+LEFT ARROW
Entire Document		Move pointer to left of text until pointer changes to right-pointing block arrow and then triple-click.	CTRL+A
Line	Double-tap to left of line to be selected.	Move pointer to left of line until pointer changes to right-pointing block arrow and then click.	HOME, then SHIFT+END or END, then SHIFT+HOME
Lines	Tap to position insertion point in text to select and then drag selection handle(s) to select text.	Move pointer to left of first line until pointer changes to right-pointing block arrow and then drag up or down.	HOME, then SHIFT+DOWN ARROW or END, then SHIFT+UP ARROW
Paragraph	Tap to position insertion point in text to select and then drag selection handle(s) to select text.	Triple-click paragraph; or move pointer to left of paragraph until pointer changes to right-pointing block arrow and then double-click.	CTRL+SHIFT+DOWN ARROW or CTRL+SHIFT+UP ARROW
Paragraphs	Tap to position insertion point in text to select and then drag selection handle(s) to select text.	Move pointer to left of paragraph until pointer changes to right-pointing block arrow, double-click, and then drag up or down.	CTRL+SHIFT+DOWN ARROW or CTRL+SHIFT+UP ARROW repeatedly
Picture or other object	Tap the graphic.	Click the object.	
Sentence	Tap to position insertion point in text to select and then drag selection handle(s) to select text.	Press and hold down CTRL and then click sentence.	
Word	Double-tap word.	Double-click word.	CTRL+SHIFT+RIGHT ARROW or CTRL+SHIFT+LEFT ARROW
Words	Tap to position insertion point in text to select and then drag selection handle(s) to select text.	Drag through words.	CTRL+SHIFT+RIGHT ARROW or CTRL+SHIFT+LEFT ARROW repeatedly

To Save an Existing Document with a Different File Name

You might want to save a file with a different file name. For example, you might start a homework assignment with a data file and then save it with a final file name for submission to your instructor, saving it to a location designated by your instructor.

The following steps save the SC_WD_1_WashHandsFlyerUnformatted file with a different file name.

1. Click File on the ribbon to open Backstage view.
2. Click Save As in Backstage view to display the Save As screen.
3. Type **`SC_WD_1_WashHandsFlyerFormatted`** in the File name box, replacing the existing file name (Figure 1–77).
4. Click the Save button in the Save As screen to save the flyer with the new name in the same save location.

BTW
Organizing Files and Folders
You should organize and store files in folders so that you easily can find the files later. For example, if you are taking an introductory technology class called CIS 101, a good practice would be to save all Word files in a Word folder in a CIS 101 folder.

Q&A What if I wanted to save the file to a different location?
You would click Browse or click the More options link in the Save As screen to display the Save As dialog box, navigate to the desired save location, and then click Save in the dialog box.

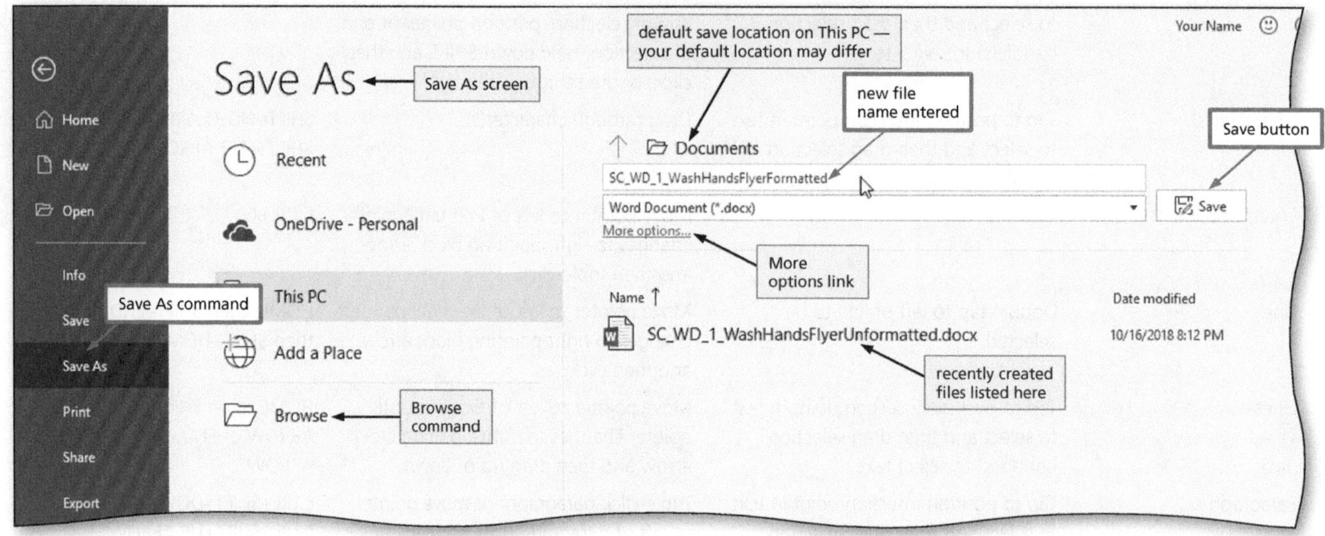

Figure 1–77

Break Point: If you want to take a break, this is a good place to do so. You can exit Word now. To resume later, start Word, open the file called SC_WD_1_WashHandsFlyerFormatted.docx, and continue following the steps from this location forward.

Inserting and Formatting a Picture in a Word Document

With the text formatted in the flyer, the next step is to insert a digital picture in the flyer and format the picture. Flyers usually contain a picture or other object to attract the attention of passersby. In the following sections, you will perform these tasks:

1. Insert a digital picture into the flyer.
2. Reduce the size of the picture.
3. Change the look of the picture.

CONSIDER THIS

How do you locate a picture to use in a document?

To use a picture in a Word document, the image must be stored digitally in a file. Files containing pictures are available from a variety of sources:

- The web has pictures available, some of which are free, while others require a fee.
- You can take a picture with a digital camera or smartphone and **download** it, which is the process of transferring (copying) a file (such as a picture) from a server, computer, or device (such as a camera or phone) to another computer or device.
- With a scanner, you can convert a printed picture, drawing, diagram, or other object to a digital file.

If you receive a picture from a source other than yourself, do not use the file until you are certain it does not contain a virus. A **virus** is a computer program designed to copy itself into other programs with the intention of causing mischief, harm, or damage to files, programs, and apps on your computer, usually without the user's knowledge or permission. Use an antivirus program or app to verify that any files you use are virus free.

To Center a Paragraph

In the flyer, the digital picture showing handwashing should be centered on the blank line between the numbered list and the bulleted list. The blank paragraph below the numbered list currently is left-aligned. The following steps center this paragraph.

1. Click somewhere in the paragraph to be centered (in this case, the blank line below the numbered list) to position the insertion point in the paragraph to be formatted.

2. Click the Center button (Home tab | Paragraph group) to center the paragraph containing the insertion point (shown in Figure 1–78).

To Insert a Picture from a File

The next step in creating the flyer is to insert a digital picture showing handwashing in the flyer on the blank line below the numbered list. The picture, which was taken with a digital camera, is available in the Data Files. Please contact your instructor for information about accessing Data Files.

The following steps insert a picture, which, in this example, is located in a folder in the Data Files folder. ***Why?*** *It is good practice to organize and store files in folders so that you easily can find the files at a later date.*

sam If your instructor wants you to submit your work as a SAM Project for automatic grading, you must download the Data Files from the assignment launch page.

1

- If necessary, position the insertion point at the location where you want to insert the picture (in this case, on the centered blank paragraph below the numbered list).
- Click Insert on the ribbon to display the Insert tab (Figure 1–78).

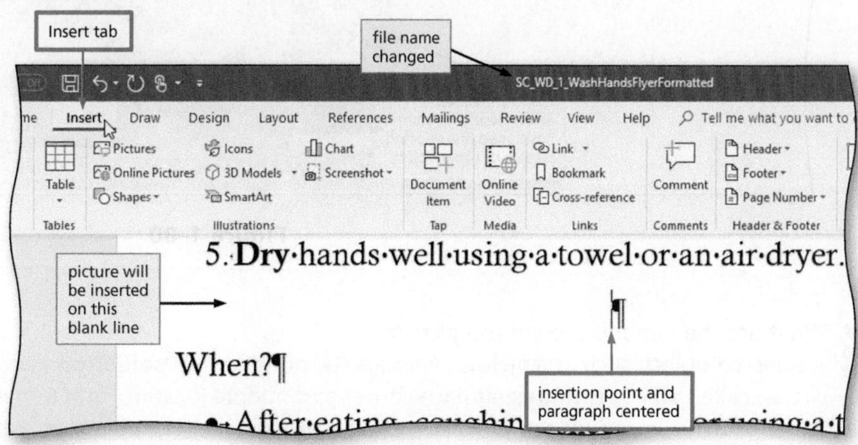

Figure 1–78

- Click the Pictures button (Insert tab | Illustrations group) to display the Insert Picture dialog box.

- In the Insert Picture dialog box, navigate to the location of the digital picture (in this case, the Module folder in the Data Files folder).
- Click Support_WD_1_WashingHands to select the file (Figure 1–79).

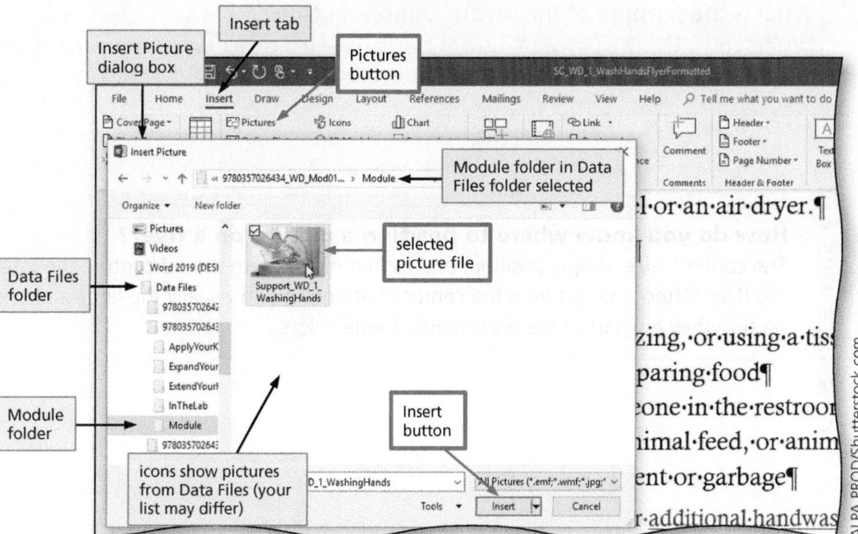

Figure 1–79

- Click the Insert button (Insert Picture dialog box) to insert the picture at the location of the insertion point in the document (Figure 1–80).

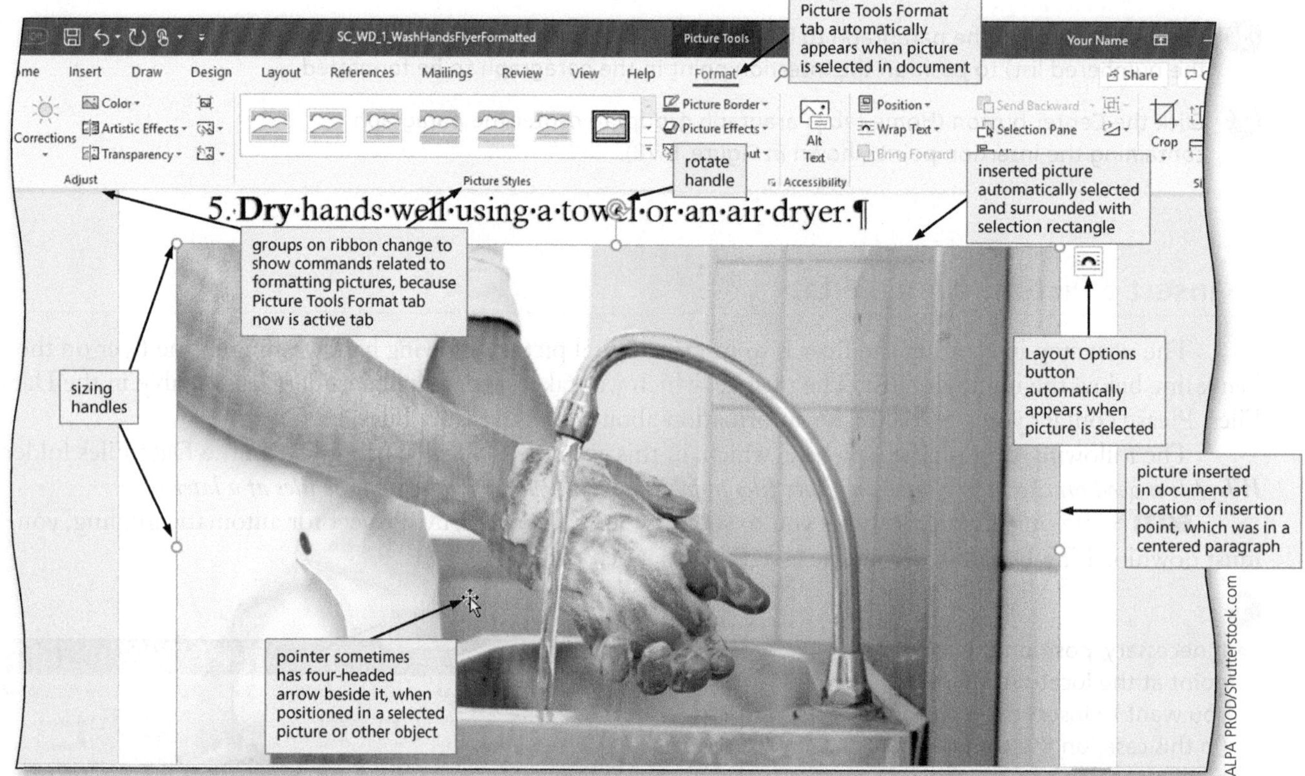

Figure 1–80

Q&A

What are the symbols around the picture?

A selected object, such as a picture, appears surrounded by a **selection rectangle**, which is a box that has small circles, called **sizing handles**, at each corner and middle location, and a rotate handle; you drag the sizing handles to resize the selected object. When you drag a picture or other object's **rotate handle**, which is the small circular arrow at the top of the selected object, the object moves in either a clockwise or counterclockwise direction.

What is the purpose of the Layout Options button?

When you click the Layout Options button, Word provides options for changing how the selected picture or other object is positioned with text in the document.

CONSIDER THIS

How do you know where to position a picture on a flyer?

The content, size, shape, position, and format of a picture should capture the interest of your audience, enticing them to read the flyer. Often, the picture is the center of attention and visually the largest element on a flyer. If you use colors in the picture, be sure they are part of the document's theme colors.

To Change the Zoom to One Page

Earlier in this module, you changed the zoom to page width so that the text on the screen was larger and easier to read. In the next set of steps, you want to see the entire page (as an image of a sheet of paper) on the screen at once. ***Why?*** *The large size of the picture caused the flyer contents to spill to a second page. You want to resize the picture enough so that the entire flyer fits on a single page.* The following step changes the zoom to one page so that an entire page can be displayed in the document window at once.

- Click View on the ribbon to display the View tab.
- Click the One Page button (View tab | Zoom group) to change the zoom to one page (Figure 1–81).

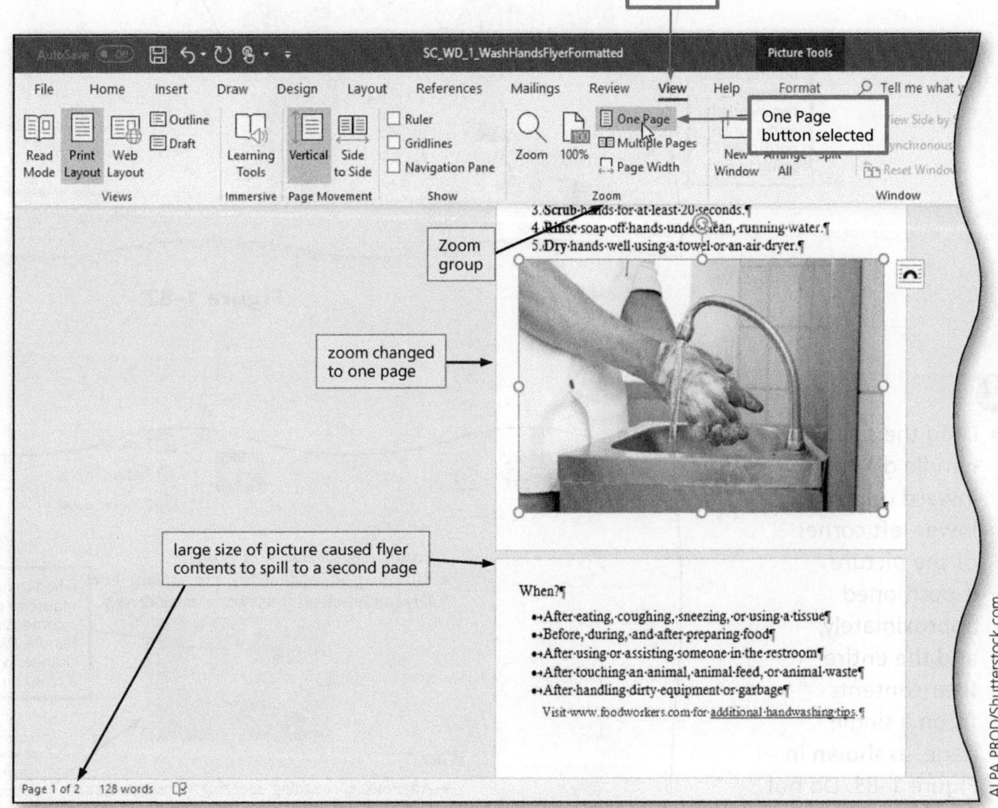

Figure 1–81

Other Ways

1. Click Zoom button (View tab | Zoom group), click Whole page (Zoom dialog box), click OK

To Resize an Object Proportionally

When you **resize** an object, such as a picture, you increase or decrease its size. The next step is to resize the picture so that it is smaller in the flyer. ***Why?*** *You want the picture and all the text on the flyer to fit on a single sheet of paper.* The following steps resize a selected object (picture).

- Be sure the picture still is selected.

Q&A What if the object (picture) is not selected?
To select a picture, click it.

- If necessary, click Picture Tools Format on the ribbon to display the Picture Tools Format tab.

- Point to the lower-left corner sizing handle on the picture so that the pointer shape changes to a two-headed arrow (Figure 1–82).

Figure 1–82

- Drag the sizing handle diagonally inward until the lower-left corner of the picture is positioned approximately, and the entire flyer contents fit on a single page, as shown in Figure 1–83. Do not release the mouse button at this point.

Q&A What if I am using a touch screen?
Drag a corner of the picture, without lifting your finger, until the picture is the desired size.

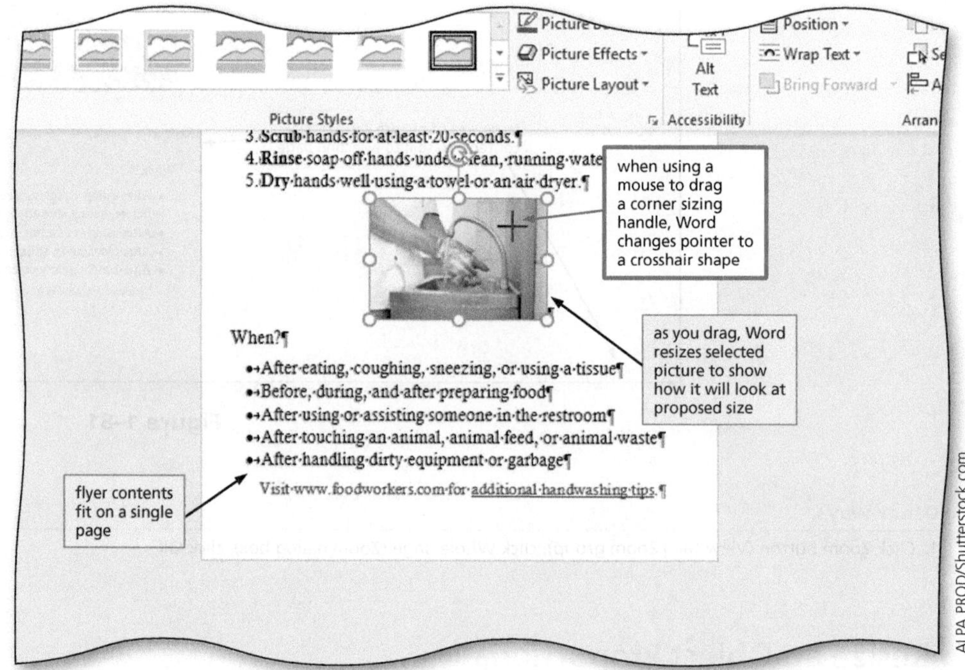

Figure 1–83

- Release the mouse button to resize the picture, which, in this case, should have a height of about 2" and a width of about 3" (shown in Figure 1–84).

Q&A How can I see the height and width measurements?
Look in the Size group on the Picture Tools Format tab to see the height and width measurements of a currently selected graphic (shown in Figure 1–84). If necessary, click the Picture Tools Format tab on the ribbon to display the tab.

What if the object (picture) is the wrong size?
Repeat Steps 1, 2, and 3, or enter the desired height and width values in the Shape Height and Shape Width boxes (Picture Tools Format tab | Size group).

Q&A What if I want to return an object (picture) to its original size and start again?
With the object (picture) selected, click the Size Dialog Box Launcher (Picture Tools Format tab | Size group), click the Size tab (Layout dialog box), click the Reset button, and then click OK.

Other Ways

1. Enter height and width of selected object in Shape Height and Shape Width boxes (Picture Tools Format tab | Size group)
2. Click Size Dialog Box Launcher (Picture Tools Format tab | Size group), click Size tab (Layout dialog box), enter desired height and width values in boxes, click OK

To Apply a Picture Style

Word provides more than 25 picture styles. ***Why?*** *Picture styles enable you easily to change a picture's look to a more visually appealing style, including a variety of shapes, angles, borders, and reflections.* The flyer in this module uses a style that applies a snip corner shape to the picture. The following steps apply a picture style to a picture.

1

- Ensure the picture still is selected and that the Picture Tools Format tab is displayed on the ribbon (Figure 1–84).

Q&A What if the picture is not selected?
To select a picture or other object, click it.

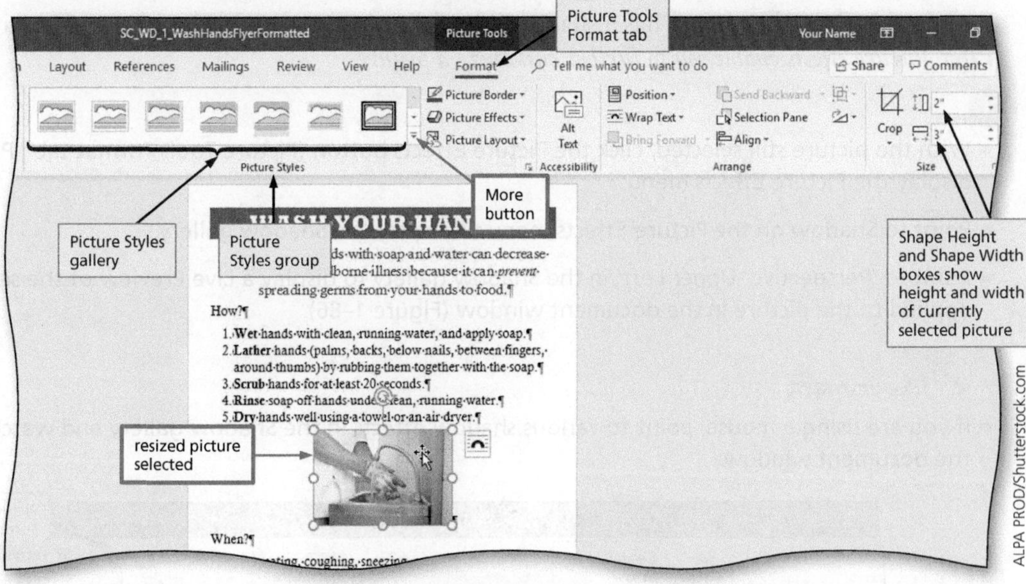

Figure 1–84

2

- Click the More button in the Picture Styles gallery (Picture Tools Format tab | Picture Styles group) to expand the gallery.
- Point to 'Snip Diagonal Corner, White' in the Picture Styles gallery to display a Live Preview of that style applied to the picture in the document (Figure 1–85).

Experiment

- Point to various picture styles in the Picture Styles gallery and watch the style of the picture change in the document window.

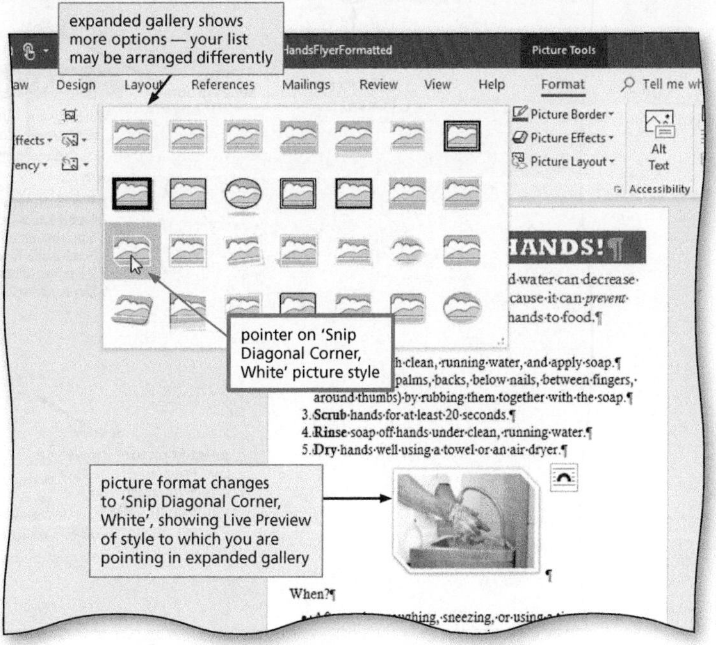

Figure 1–85

- Click 'Snip Diagonal Corner, White' in the Picture Styles gallery (first style in third row) to apply the style to the selected picture.

Q&A What if the flyer contents spill to a second page?
Reduce the size of the picture.

Other Ways

1. Right-click picture, click Style button on Mini toolbar, select desired style

To Apply a Picture Effect

Word provides a variety of picture effects, such as shadows, reflections, glows, soft edges, bevels, and 3-D rotations. The difference between the effects and the styles is that each effect has several options, providing you with more control over the exact look of the image.

In this flyer, the picture has a shadow. The following steps apply a picture effect to the selected picture. ***Why?*** *Picture effects enable you to further customize a picture.*

- With the picture still selected, click the Picture Effects button (Picture Tools Format tab | Picture Styles group) to display the Picture Effects menu.
- Point to Shadow on the Picture Effects menu to display the Shadow gallery.
- Point to 'Perspective: Upper Left' in the Shadow gallery to display a Live Preview of the selected shadow effect applied to the picture in the document window (Figure 1–86).

Experiment

- If you are using a mouse, point to various shadow effects in the Shadow gallery and watch the picture change in the document window.

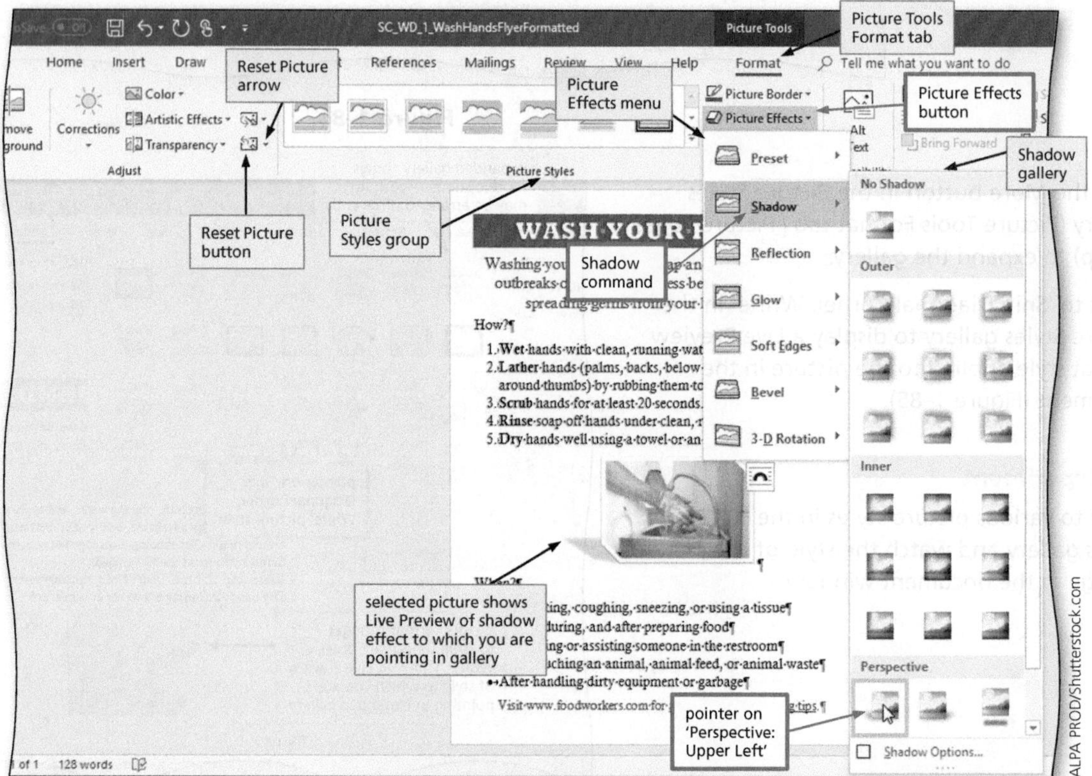

Figure 1–86

2

- **Click 'Perspective: Upper Left' in the Shadow gallery to apply the selected picture effect.**
- **Click somewhere in the document other than the picture and notice the Picture Tools Format tab disappears from the screen when the picture is not selected (shown in Figure 1–87).**

Q&A

How would I redisplay the Picture Tools Format tab?
Click the picture to select it and the Picture Tools Format tab will reappear.

What if I wanted to discard formatting applied to a picture?
You would click the Reset Picture button (Picture Tools Format tab | Adjust group). To reset formatting and size, you would click the Reset Picture arrow (Picture Tools Format tab | Adjust group) and then click 'Reset Picture & Size' on the Reset Picture menu.

Other Ways

1. Right-click picture (or, if using touch, tap 'Show Context Menu' button on Mini toolbar), click Format Picture on shortcut menu, click Effects button (Format Picture pane), select desired options, click Close button
2. Click Picture Styles Dialog Box Launcher (Picture Tools Format tab | Picture Styles group), click Effects button (Format Picture pane), select desired options, click Close button

Enhancing the Page

With the text and picture entered and formatted, the next step is to look at the page as a whole and determine if it looks finished in its current state. As you review the page, answer these questions:

- Are the colors appropriate for the message?
- Does it need a page border to frame its contents, or would a page border make it look too busy?
- Is the spacing between paragraphs and the picture on the page adequate? Do any sections look as if they are positioned too closely to the items above or below them?

You determine that you would like to change the text and shading colors and that a graphical, color-coordinated border would enhance the flyer. You also notice that the flyer would look better proportioned if it had a little more space above and below the picture. The following sections make these enhancements to the flyer.

CONSIDER THIS

What colors should you choose when creating documents?
When choosing color, associate the meaning of the color with your message:

- Red expresses danger, power, or energy and often is associated with sports or physical exertion.
- Brown represents simplicity, honesty, and dependability.
- Orange denotes success, victory, creativity, and enthusiasm.
- Yellow suggests sunshine, happiness, hope, liveliness, and intelligence.
- Green symbolizes growth, healthiness, harmony, and healing and often is associated with safety or money.
- Blue indicates integrity, trust, importance, confidence, and stability.
- Purple represents wealth, power, comfort, extravagance, magic, mystery, and spirituality.
- White stands for purity, goodness, cleanliness, precision, and perfection.
- Black suggests authority, strength, elegance, power, and prestige.
- Gray conveys neutrality and, thus, often is found in backgrounds and other effects.

To Change Theme Colors

A **theme color** in Word is a named set of complementary colors for text, background, accents, and links in a document. With more than 20 predefined theme colors, Word provides a simple way to coordinate colors in a document.

In the flyer, you will change the theme colors. ***Why?*** *You want the colors in the flyer to represent healthiness, healing, integrity, and trust, which are conveyed by shades of greens and blues. In Word, the Blue II theme color uses these colors.* The following steps change theme colors.

- Click Design on the ribbon to display the Design tab.
- Click the Colors button (Design tab | Document Formatting group) to display the Colors gallery.
- Point to Blue II in the Colors gallery to display a Live Preview of the selected theme color (Figure 1–87).

Experiment

- Point to various theme colors in the Colors gallery and watch the colors change in the document.

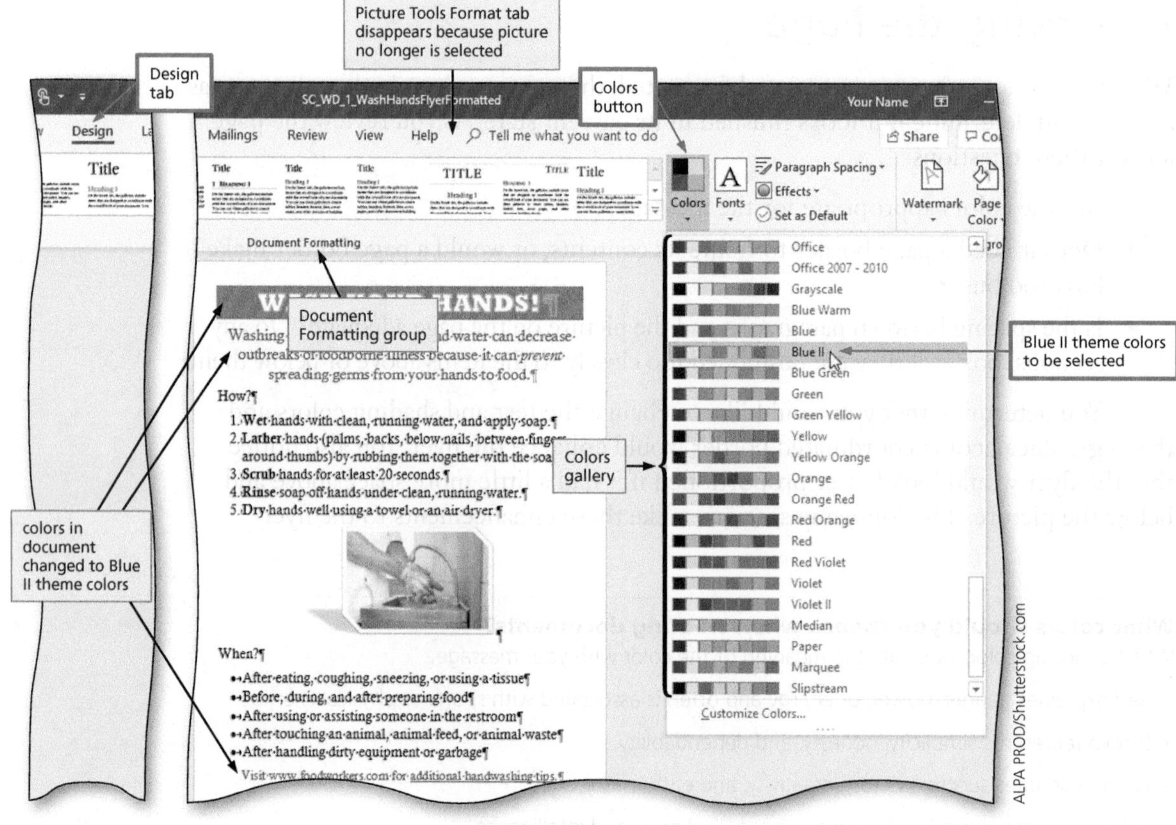

Figure 1–87

- Click Blue II in the Colors gallery to change the document theme colors.

Q&A What if I want to return to the default theme colors?
You would click the Colors button again and then click Office in the Colors gallery.

To Add a Page Border

In Word, you can add a border around the perimeter of an entire page. The flyer in this module has a blue-green border. ***Why?*** *This border color complements the color of the flyer contents.* The following steps add a page border.

1

- Click the Page Borders button (Design tab | Page Background group) to display the Borders and Shading dialog box (Figure 1–88).

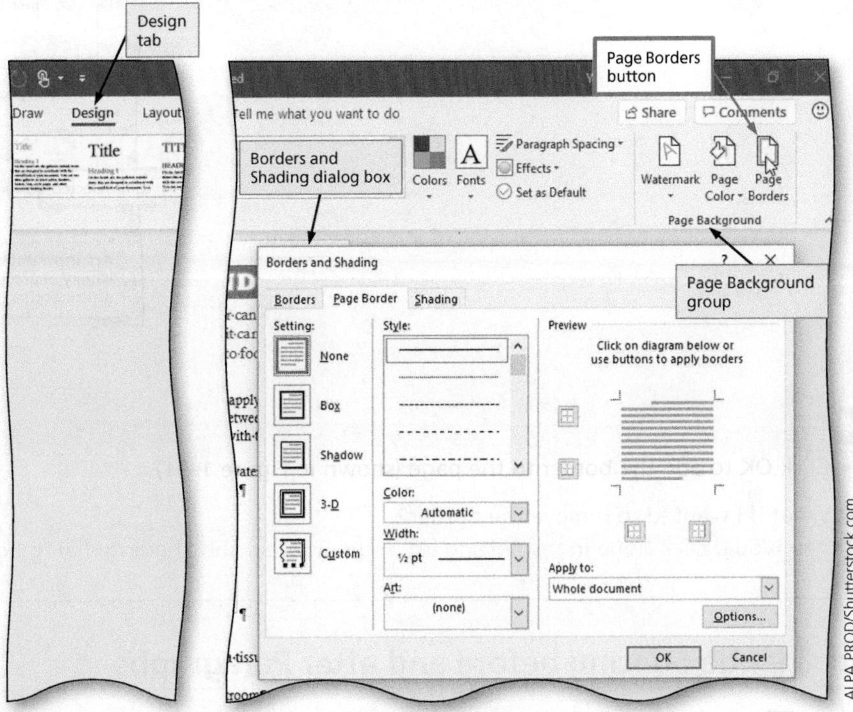

Figure 1–88

2

- Click Box in the Setting list to select the border setting.
- Scroll to, if necessary, and then click the third border style from the bottom of the Style list (Borders and Shading dialog box) to select the border style.
- Click the Color arrow to display a color palette (Figure 1–89).

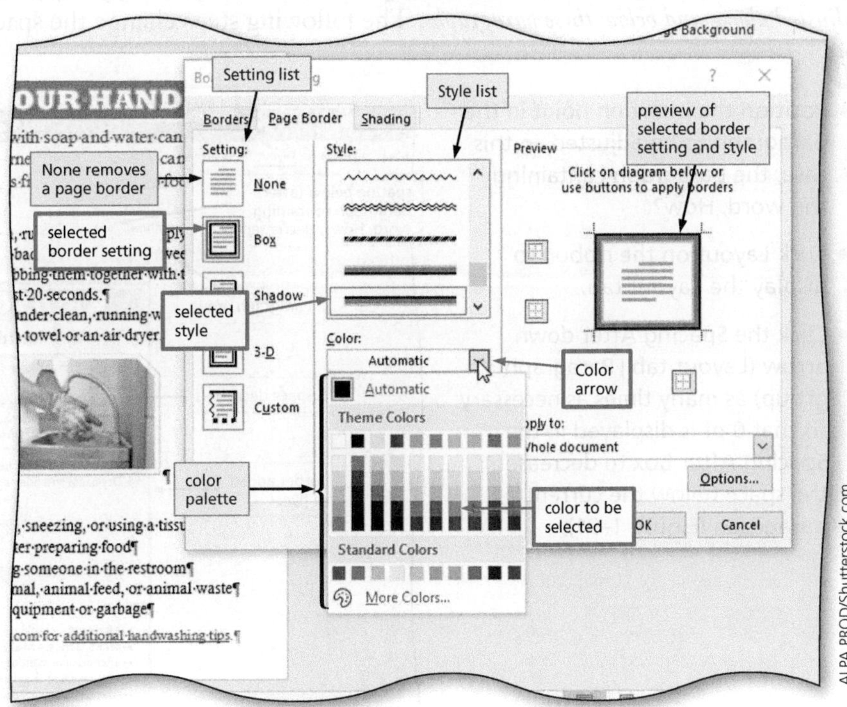

Figure 1–89

• Click 'Turquoise, Accent 3, Darker 25%' (seventh color in fifth row) in the color palette to select the color for the page border (Figure 1–90).

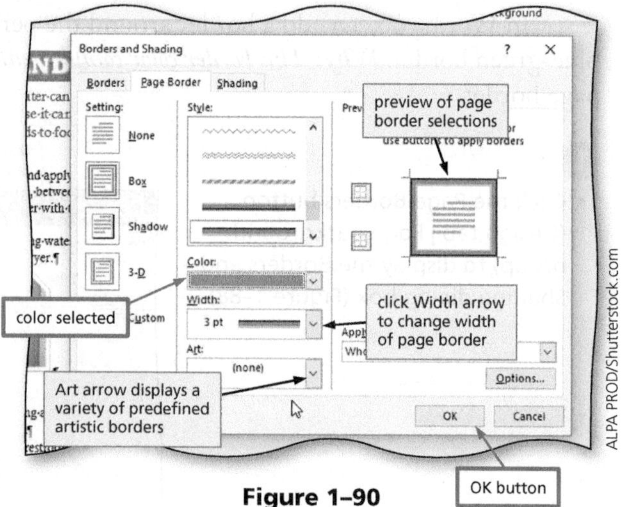

Figure 1–90

• Click OK to add the border to the page (shown in Figure 1–91).

Q&A What if I wanted to remove the border?
You would click None in the Setting list in the Borders and Shading dialog box.

To Change Spacing before and after Paragraphs

The default spacing above (before) a paragraph in Word is 0 points and below (after) is 8 points. In the flyer, you want to decrease the spacing below (after) the paragraphs containing the words, How? and When?, and increase the spacing above (before) the signature line. ***Why?*** *The flyer spacing will look more balanced with spacing adjusted above and below these paragraphs.* The following steps change the spacing before and after paragraphs.

• Position the insertion point in the paragraph to be adjusted, in this case, the paragraph containing the word, How?.

• Click Layout on the ribbon to display the Layout tab.

• Click the Spacing After down arrow (Layout tab | Paragraph group) as many times as necessary so that 0 pt is displayed in the Spacing After box to decrease the space below the current paragraph (Figure 1–91).

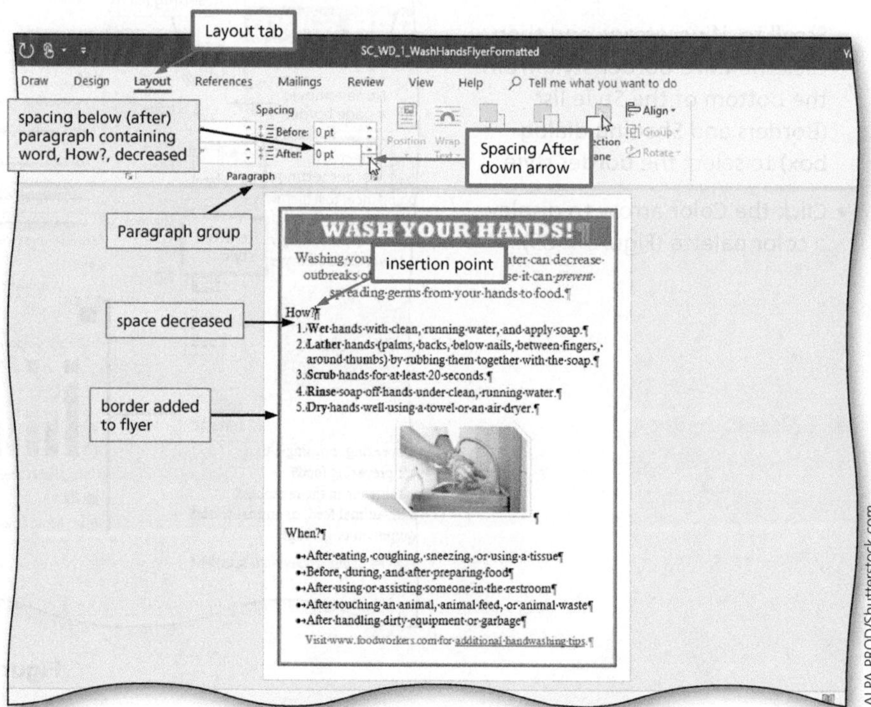

Figure 1–91

ALPA PROD/Shutterstock.com

2

- Position the insertion point in the next paragraph to be adjusted, in this case, the paragraph containing the word, When?.
- Click the Spacing After down arrow (Layout tab | Paragraph group) as many times as necessary so that 0 pt is displayed in the Spacing After box to decrease the space below the current paragraph.
- Position the insertion point in the paragraph to be adjusted, in this case, the paragraph containing the signature line.
- Click the Spacing Before up arrow (Layout tab | Paragraph group) as many times as necessary so that 12 pt is displayed in the Spacing Before box to increase the space above the current paragraph (Figure 1–92).
- If the text flows to two pages, reduce the spacing above and below paragraphs as necessary so that the entire flyer fits on a single page.

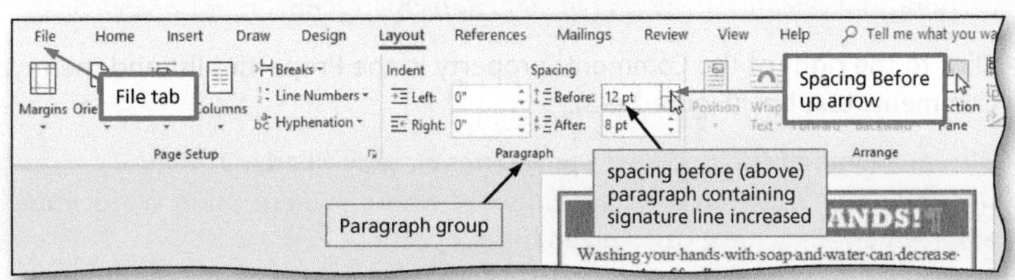

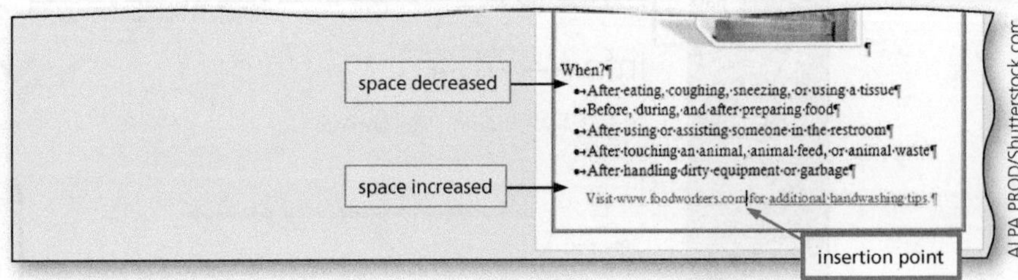

ALPA PROD/Shutterstock.com

Figure 1–92

Other Ways

1. Right-click paragraph (or, if using touch, tap 'Show Context Menu' button on Mini toolbar), click Paragraph on shortcut menu, click Indents and Spacing tab (Paragraph dialog box), enter spacing before and after values, click OK
2. Click Paragraph Dialog Box Launcher (Home tab or Layout tab | Paragraph group), click Indents and Spacing tab (Paragraph dialog box), enter spacing before and after values, click OK

To Change the Document Properties

Word helps you organize and identify your files by using **document properties**, which are the details about a file, such as the project author, title, and subject. For example, a class name or document topic can describe the file's purpose or content.

Document properties are valuable for a variety of reasons:

- You can save time locating a particular file because you can view a document's properties without opening the document.
- By creating consistent properties for files having similar content, you can better organize your documents.
- Some organizations require Word users to add document properties so that other employees can view details about these files.

The more common document properties are standard and automatically updated properties. **Standard properties** are associated with all Microsoft Office files and include author, title, and subject. **Automatically updated properties** include file system properties, such as the date you create or change a file, and statistics, such as the file size.

You can change the document properties while working with the file in Word. When you save the file, Word will save the document properties with the file. The following steps change the comment document property. ***Why?*** *Adding document properties will help you identify characteristics of the file without opening it.*

- Click File on the ribbon (shown in Figure 1–92) to open Backstage view and then, if necessary, click Info in Backstage view to display the Info screen.

Q&A | **What is the purpose of the Info screen in Backstage view?**
The Info screen contains commands that enable you to protect a document, inspect a document, and manage versions of a document, as well as view and change document properties.

- Click to the right of the Comments property in the Properties list and then type `CIS 101 Assignment` in the Comments text box (Figure 1–93).

Q&A | **Why are some of the document properties already filled in?**
Depending on previous Word settings and where you are using Word, your school, university, or place of employment may have customized the properties.

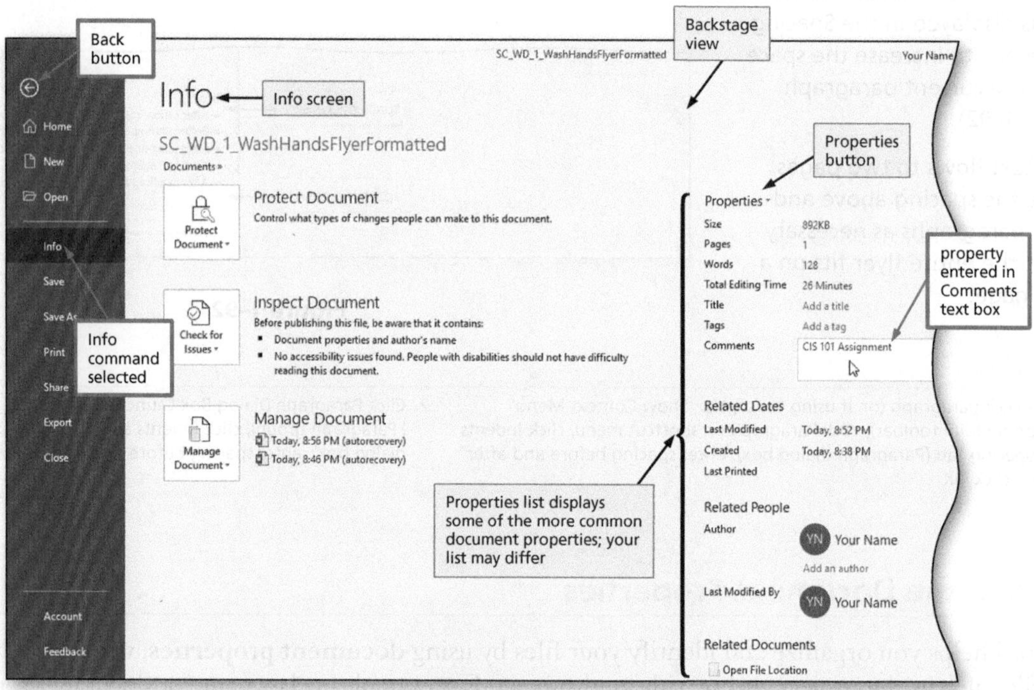

Figure 1–93

- Click the Back button in the upper-left corner of Backstage view to return to the document window.

Q&A | **What if the property I want to change is not displayed in the Properties list?**
Scroll to the bottom of the Info screen and then click the 'Show All Properties' link to display more properties in the Properties list, or click the Properties button to display the Properties menu, and then click Advanced Properties on the Properties menu to display the Summary tab in the Properties dialog box. Type your desired text in the appropriate property text boxes. Click OK (Properties dialog box) to close the dialog box and then click the Back button in the upper-left corner of Backstage view to return to the document window.

To Save an Existing Document with the Same File Name

Saving frequently cannot be overemphasized. ***Why?** You have made modifications to the document since you last saved it. Thus, you should save it again.* Similarly, you should continue saving files frequently so that you do not lose the changes you have made since the time you last saved the file. You can use the same file name, such as SC_WD_1_WashHandsFlyerFormatted, to save the changes made to the document. The following step saves a file again with the same file name in the same save location.

- Click the Save button on the Quick Access Toolbar to overwrite the previously saved file (SC_WD_1_WashHandsFlyerFormatted, in this case) in the same location it was saved previously (Documents library) (Figure 1–94).

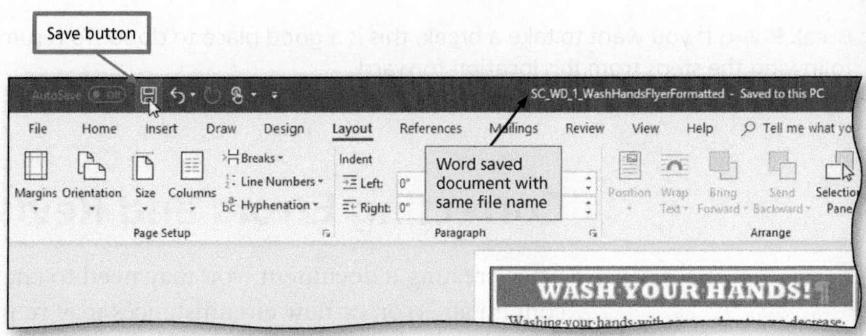

Figure 1–94

Other Ways	
1. Press CTRL+S	2. Press SHIFT+F12

To Close a Document

Although you still need to make some edits to this document, you want to close the document at this time. ***Why?*** *You should close a file when you are done working with it or wish to take a break so that you do not make inadvertent changes to it.* The following steps close the current active Word document, SC_WD_1_WashHandsFlyerFormatted.docx, without exiting Word.

- Click File on the ribbon to open Backstage view (Figure 1–95).

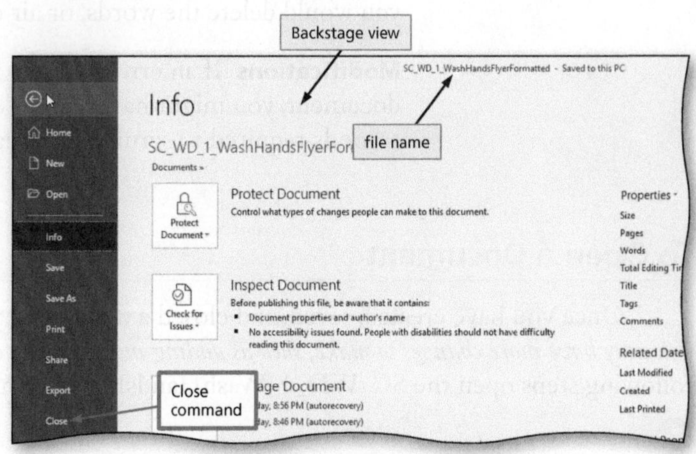

Figure 1–95

- Click Close in Backstage view to close the currently open document (SC_WD_1_WashHandsFlyerFormatted.docx, in this case) without exiting Word (Figure 1–96).

Q&A What if Word displays a dialog box about saving?
Click Save if you want to save the changes, click Don't Save if you want to ignore the changes since the last time you saved, and click Cancel if you do not want to close the document.

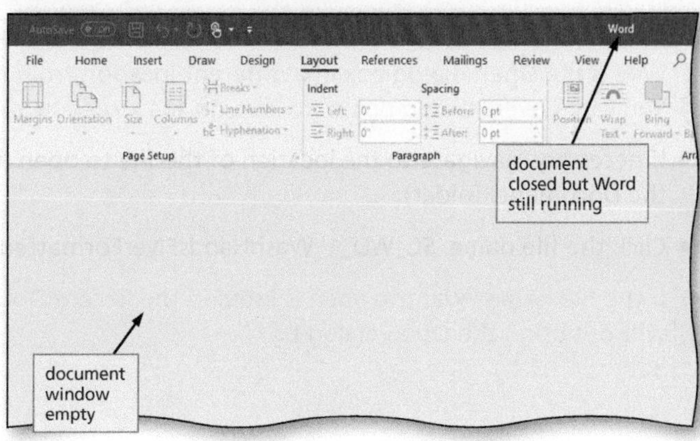

Figure 1–96

Other Ways
1. Press CTRL+F4

Break Point: If you want to take a break, this is a good place to do so. To resume later, start Word and continue following the steps from this location forward.

Correcting Errors and Revising a Document

After creating a document, you may need to change it. For example, the document may contain an error, or new circumstances may require you to add text to the document.

Types of Changes Made to Documents

The types of changes made to documents normally fall into one of the three following categories: additions, deletions, or modifications.

Additions Additional words, sentences, or paragraphs may be required in a document. Additions occur when you omit text from a document and want to insert it later. For example, you may want to add an email address to the flyer.

Deletions Sometimes, text in a document is incorrect or no longer is needed. For example, you may discover that air dryers are no longer used to dry hands. In this case, you would delete the words, or air dryer, from the flyer.

Modifications If an error is made in a document or changes take place that affect the document, you might have to revise a word(s) in the text. For example, the number of seconds required to scrub hands may change.

To Open a Document

Once you have created, saved, and closed a document, you may need to retrieve it from storage. ***Why?*** *You may have more changes to make, such as adding more content or correcting errors, or you may want to print it.* The following steps open the SC_WD_1_WashHandsFlyerFormatted.docx file.

- Click File on the ribbon to open Backstage view.
- If necessary, click Open in Backstage view to display the Open screen.
- Click Browse to display the Open dialog box.

Q&A Why is the Open dialog box in a different location from my screen?
You can move a dialog box anywhere on the screen by dragging its title bar.

- If necessary, navigate to the location of the file to open (in this case, SC_WD_1_WashHandsFlyerFormatted.docx in the Documents folder).
- Click the file name, SC_WD_1_WashHandsFlyerFormatted, to select the file (Figure 1–97).

Q&A If the file name I want to open is listed in the Recent Documents list, can I click the file name to open the document without using the Open dialog box?
Yes.

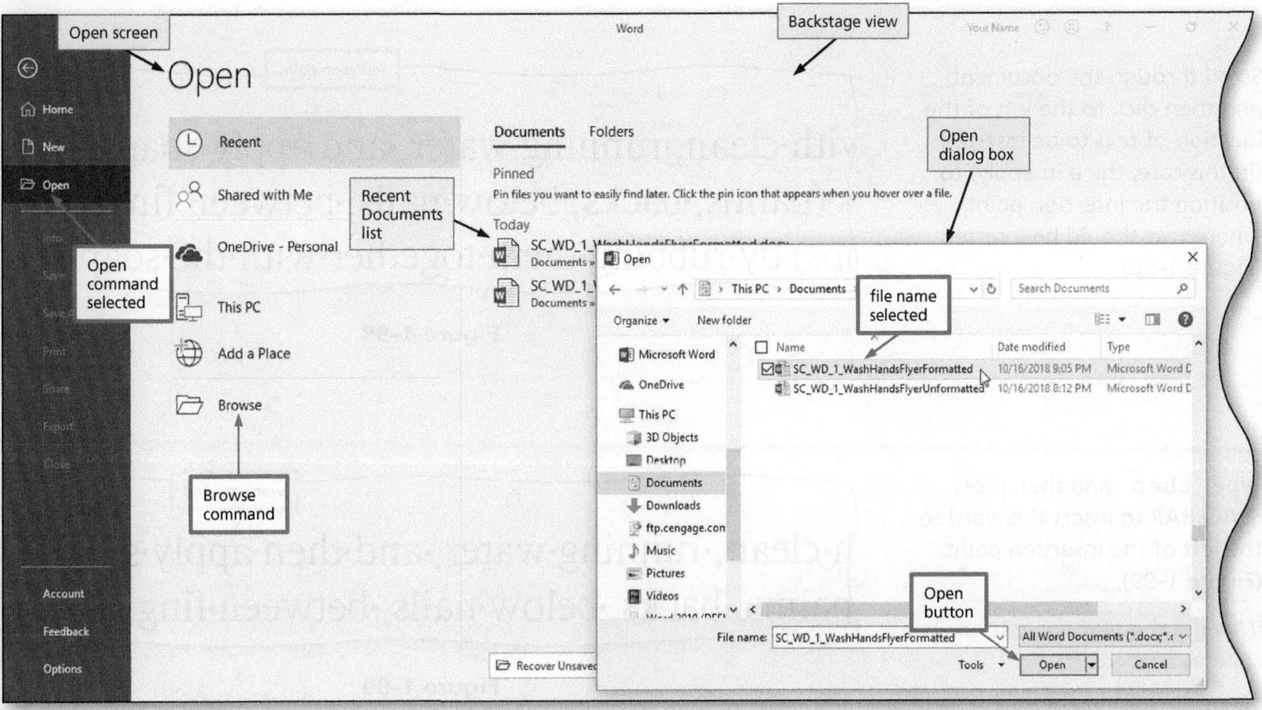

Figure 1–97

2

- Click the Open button (Open dialog box) to open the selected file and display its contents in the document window (shown in Figure 1–98). If necessary, click the Enable Content button.

Other Ways

1. If file appears in Recent Documents list, click file name
2. Press CTRL+O
3. Navigate to file in File Explorer window, double-click file name

To Change the Zoom to Page Width

Because the document contents are small when displayed on one page, the following steps zoom page width again.

1 Click View on the ribbon to display the View tab.

2 Click the Page Width button (View tab | Zoom group) to display the page the same width as the document window.

To Insert Text in an Existing Document

Word inserts text to the left of the insertion point. The text to the right of the insertion point moves to the right and downward to fit the new text. The following steps insert the word, then, to the left of the word, apply, in the numbered list in the flyer. ***Why?*** *These steps illustrate the process of inserting text.*

1

- Scroll through the document and then click to the left of the location of text to be inserted (in this case, the a in apply) to position the insertion point where text should be inserted (Figure 1–98).

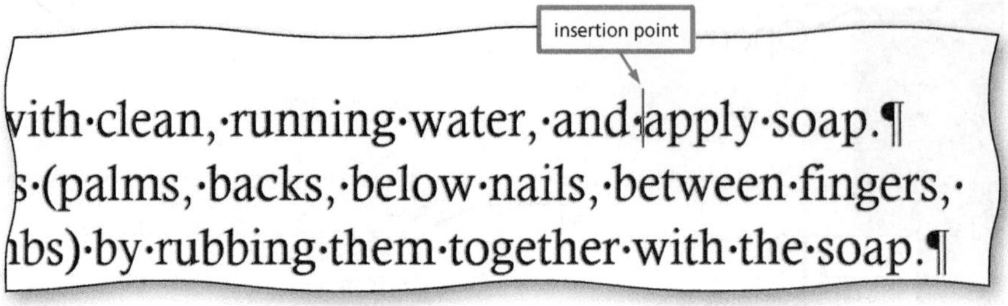

ALPA PROD/Shutterstock.com

Figure 1–98

2

- Type **then** and then press SPACEBAR to insert the word to the left of the insertion point (Figure 1–99).

ALPA PROD/Shutterstock.com

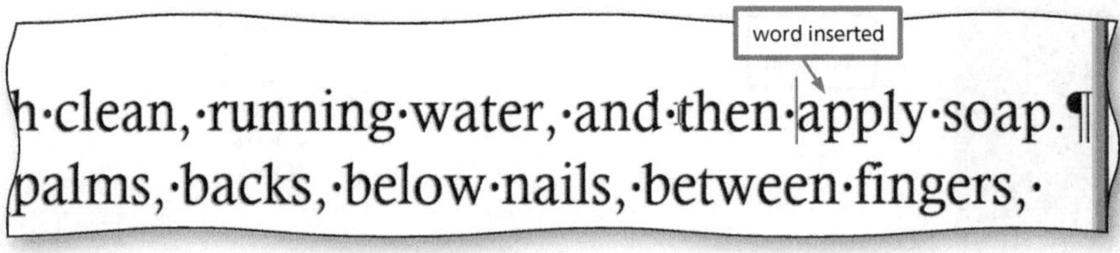

Figure 1–99

Q&A Why did the text move to the right as I typed?
In Word, the default typing mode is **insert mode**, which means as you type a character, Word moves all the characters to the right of the typed character one position to the right.

BTW
Delete versus Cut
When you press DELETE, the deleted text is not placed on the Office Clipboard. If you want deleted text to be placed on the Office Clipboard, use the Cut button (Home tab | Clipboard group).

Cutting, Copying, and Pasting

The **Office Clipboard** is a temporary storage area in a computer's memory that lets you collect up to 24 items (text or objects) from any Office document and then paste these items into almost any other type of document. The Office Clipboard works with the copy, cut, and paste commands:

- To **copy** is the process of selecting text or an object and placing a copy of the selected items on the Office Clipboard, leaving the item in its original location in the document.
- To **cut** is the process of removing text or an object from a document and placing it on the Office Clipboard.
- To **paste** is the process of placing an item stored on the Office Clipboard in the document at the location of the insertion point.

To Delete or Cut Text

It is not unusual to type incorrect characters or words in a document. As discussed earlier in this module, you can click the Undo button on the Quick Access Toolbar or press CTRL+Z to undo a command or action immediately — this includes typing. Word also provides other methods of correcting typing errors.

To delete an incorrect character in a document, simply click next to the incorrect character and then press BACKSPACE to erase to the left of the insertion point, or press DELETE to erase to the right of the insertion point.

To cut a word or phrase, you first must select the word or phrase. The following steps select the word, then, which was just added in the previous steps, and then cuts the selection. ***Why?*** *These steps illustrate the process of selecting a word and then cutting selected text.*

- Click Home on the ribbon to display the Home tab.
- Double-click the word to be selected (in this case, then) to select the word (Figure 1–100).

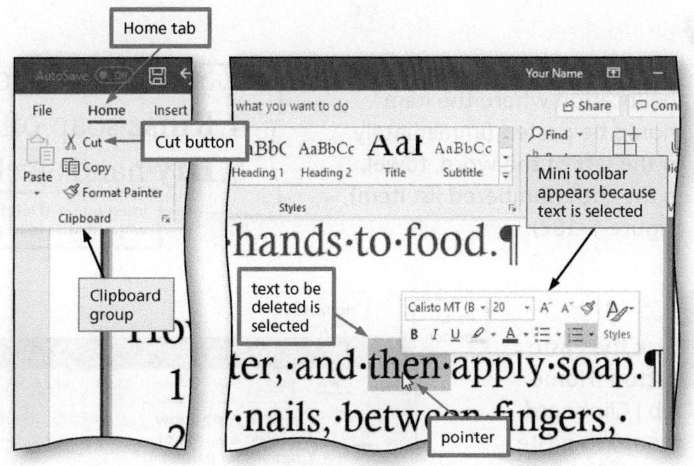

Figure 1–100

- Click the Cut button (Home tab | Clipboard group) to cut the selected text (shown in Figure 1–98).

Q&A What if I am using a touch screen?
Tap the selected text to display the Mini toolbar and then tap the Cut button on the Mini toolbar to delete the selected text.

Other Ways

1. Right-click selected item, click Cut on shortcut menu
2. Select item, press BACKSPACE to delete to left of insertion point or press DELETE to delete to right of insertion point
3. Select item, press CTRL+X or DELETE

To Copy and Paste

In the flyer, you copy a word from one location (the first numbered list item) to another location (the fifth numbered list item). ***Why?*** *The fifth numbered item is clearer with the word, clean, inserted before the word, towel.* The following steps copy and paste a word.

- If necessary, scroll so that all the numbered list items appear in the document window.
- Select the item to be copied (the word, clean, in this case).
- Click the Copy button (Home tab | Clipboard group) to copy the selected item in the document to the Office Clipboard (Figure 1–101).

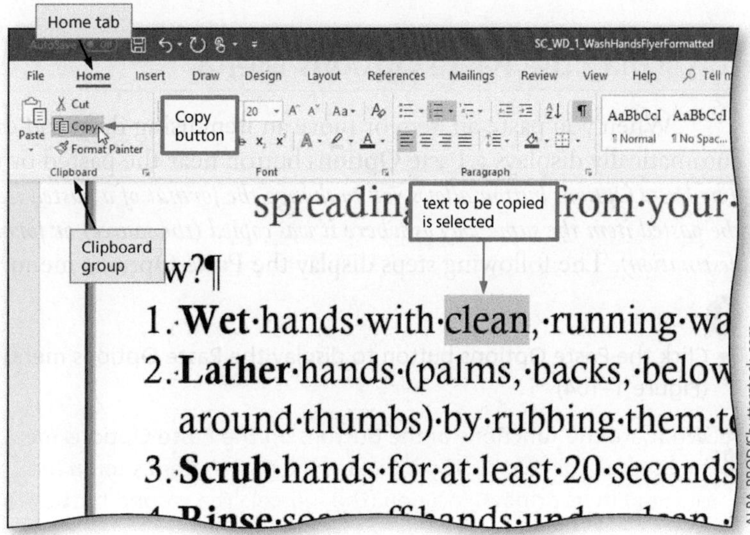

Figure 1–101

- Position the insertion point at the location where the item should be pasted (immediately to the left of the word, towel, in the fifth numbered list item) (Figure 1–102).

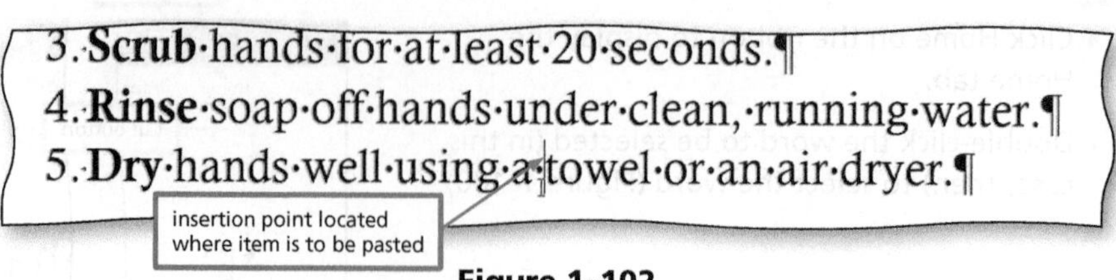

Figure 1–102

- Click the Paste button (Home tab | Clipboard group) to paste the copied item in the document at the location of the insertion point (Figure 1–103).

Q&A What if I click the Paste arrow by mistake?
Click the Paste arrow again to remove the Paste menu and repeat Step 3.

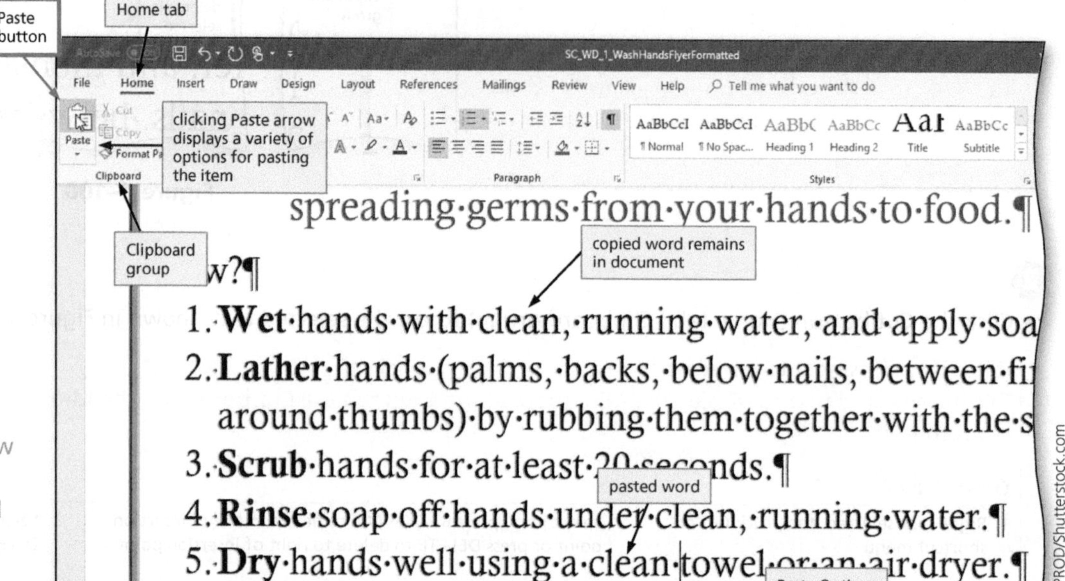

Figure 1–103

Other Ways

1. Right-click selected text (or, if using touch, tap 'Show Context Menu' button on Mini toolbar), click Copy on shortcut menu (or, if using touch, tap Copy on Mini toolbar), right-click where item is to be pasted, click 'Keep Source Formatting' in Paste Options area on shortcut menu (or, if using touch, tap Paste on Mini toolbar)
2. Select item, press CTRL+C, position insertion point at paste location, press CTRL+V

To Display the Paste Options Menu

When you paste an item or move an item using drag and drop (discussed in the next section), Word automatically displays a Paste Options button near the pasted or moved text (shown in Figure 1–103). ***Why?*** *The Paste Options button allows you to change the format of a pasted item. For example, you can instruct Word to format the pasted item the same way as where it was copied (the source) or format it the same way as where it is being pasted (the destination).* The following steps display the Paste Options menu.

- Click the Paste Options button to display the Paste Options menu (Figure 1–104).

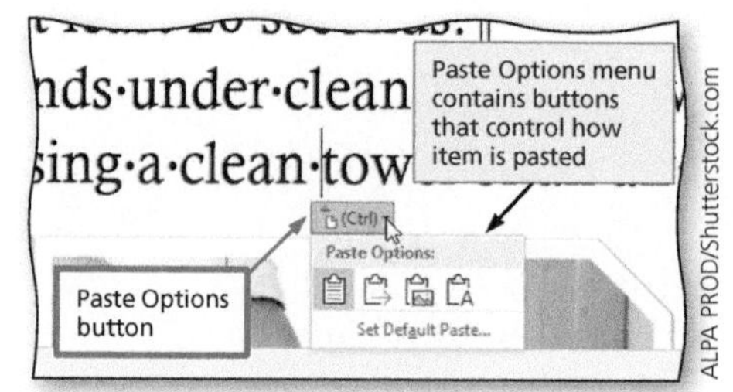

Figure 1–104

Q&A What are the functions of the buttons on the Paste Options menu?
In general, the left button indicates the pasted item should look the same as it did in its original location (the source). The second button formats the pasted text to match the rest of the item where it was pasted (the destination). The third button pastes the item and a picture, and the fourth button removes all formatting from the pasted item. The 'Set Default Paste' command displays the Word Options dialog box. Keep in mind that the buttons shown on a Paste Options menu will vary, depending on the item being pasted.

2

- Click anywhere to remove the Paste Options menu from the window.

Other Ways

1. Press CTRL or ESC (to remove the Paste Options menu)

To Move Text

If you are moving text a short distance, instead of using cut and paste, you could use drag and drop. With **drag and drop**, you move an item by selecting it, dragging the selected item to a new location, and then dropping, or inserting, it in the new location.

The following steps use drag and drop to move text. ***Why?*** *While proofreading the flyer, you realize that the body copy would read better if the first two bulleted paragraphs were reversed.*

1

- Scroll to, if necessary, and then select the text to be moved (in this case, the second bulleted item).
- With the pointer in the selected text, press and hold down the mouse button, which displays a small dotted box with the pointer (Figure 1–105).

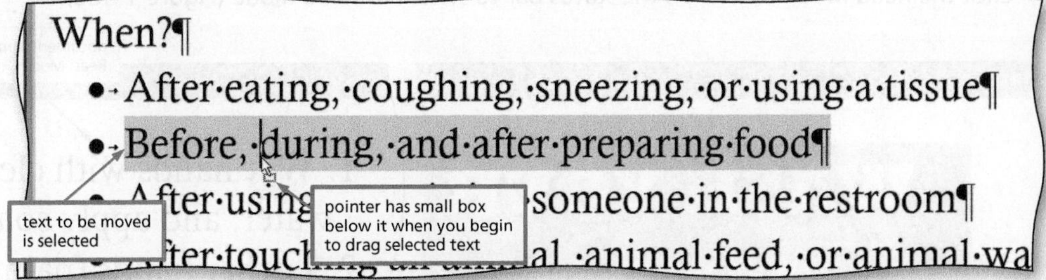

Figure 1–105

2

- Drag the insertion point to the location where the selected text is to be moved, as shown in Figure 1–106.

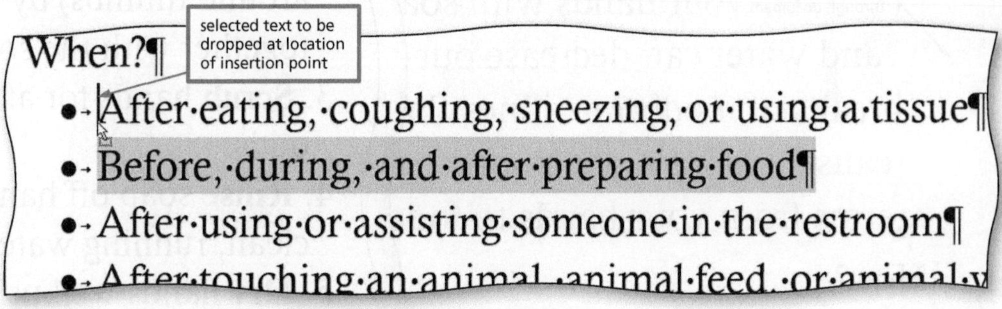

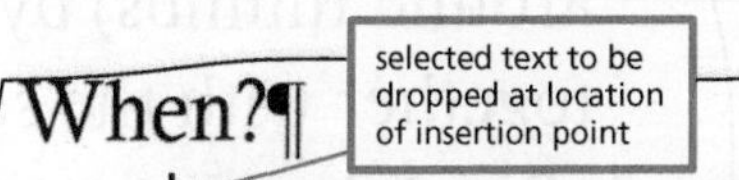

Figure 1–106

3

- Release the mouse button to move the selected text to the location of the dotted insertion point (Figure 1–107).

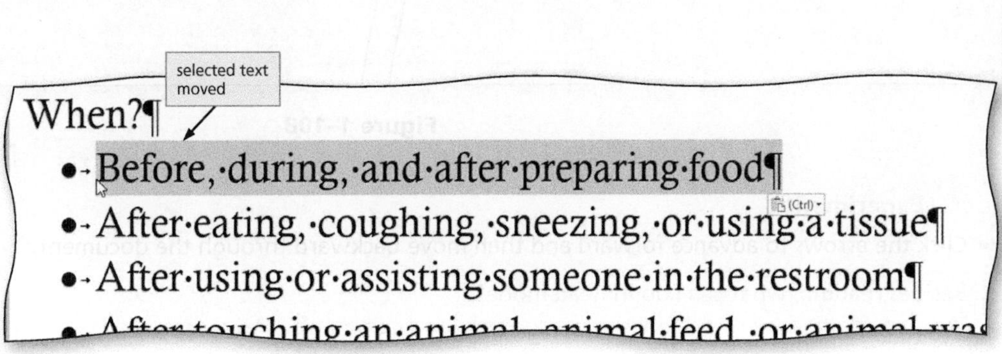

Figure 1–107

Q&A What if I accidentally drag text to the wrong location?

Click the Undo button on the Quick Access Toolbar or press CTRL+Z and try again.

Q&A Can I use drag and drop to move any selected item?
Yes, you can select words, sentences, phrases, pictures, or any object and then use drag and drop to move them.

- Click anywhere in the document window to remove the selection from the bulleted item.

Q&A What if I am using a touch screen?
If you have a stylus, you can follow Steps 1 through 3 using the stylus. If you are using your finger, you will need to use cut and paste, which was described earlier in this section.

To Switch to Read Mode

Some users prefer reading a document on-screen instead of on paper. ***Why?*** *If you are not composing a document, you can switch to* ***Read mode****, which is a document view that makes the document easier to read by hiding the ribbon and other writing tools so that more content fits on the screen.* The following step switches from Print Layout view to Read mode.

- Press CTRL+HOME to position the insertion point at the top of the document.
- Click the Read Mode button on the status bar to switch to Read mode (Figure 1–108).

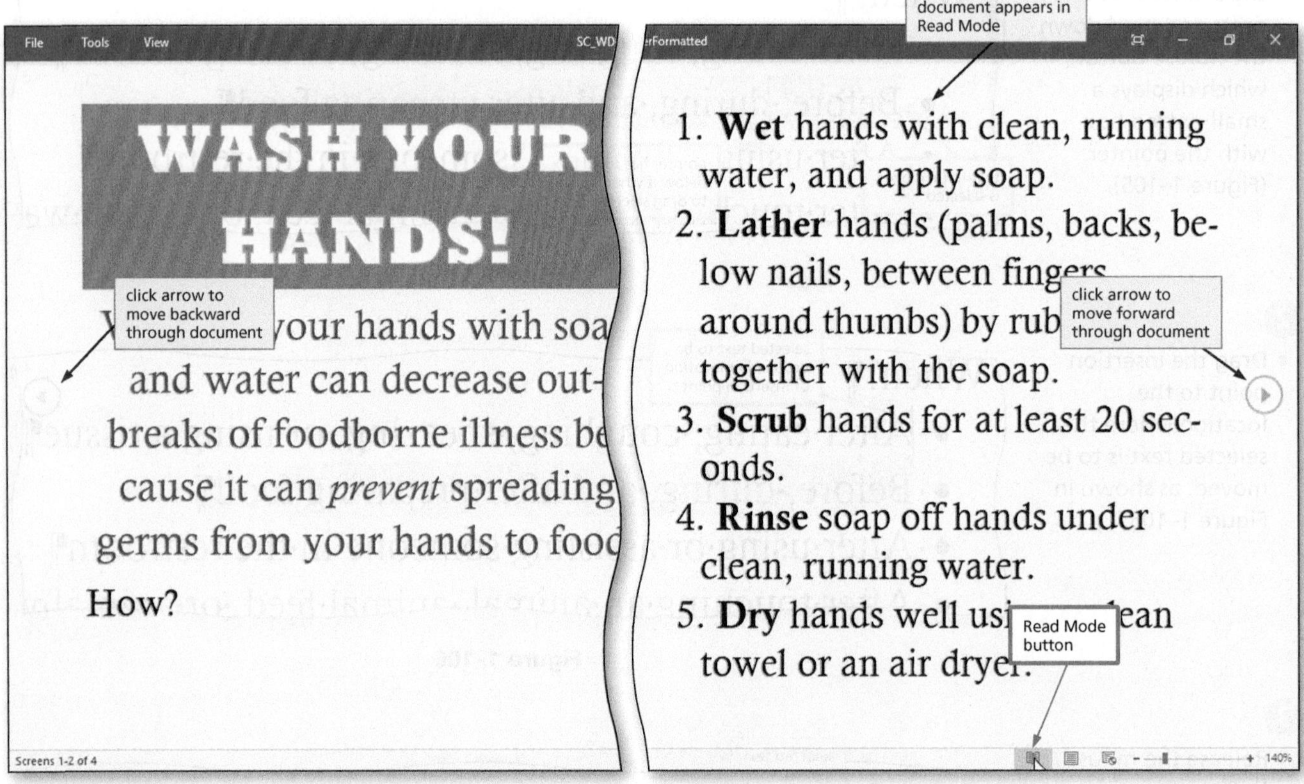

Figure 1–108

Experiment

- Click the arrows to advance forward and then move backward through the document.

Q&A Besides reading, what can I do in Read mode?
You can zoom, copy text, highlight text, search, add comments, and more.

Other Ways

1. Click Read Mode button (View tab | Views group)

To Switch to Print Layout View

The next step switches back to Print Layout view. ***Why?*** *If you want to show the document on an image of a sheet of paper in the document window, along with the ribbon and other writing tools, you should switch to Print Layout view.* The following step switches to Print Layout view.

- Click the Print Layout button on the status bar to switch to Print Layout view (Figure 1–109).

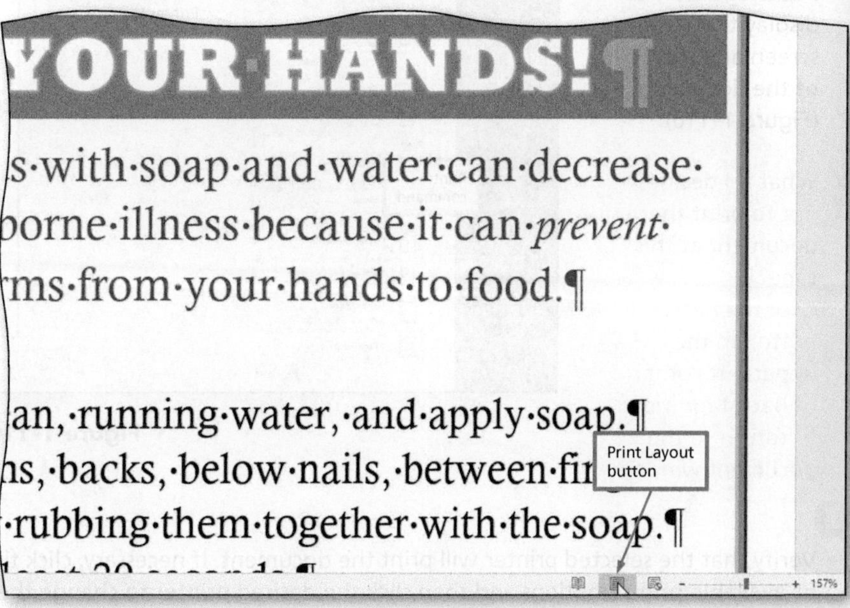

Figure 1–109

Other Ways

1. Click Print Layout button (View tab | Views group)
2. In Read Mode, click View on the ribbon, click Edit Document

To Save a Document with the Same File Name

It is a good practice to save a document before printing it, in the event you experience difficulties printing. The following step saves the document again on the same storage location with the same file name.

1 Click the Save button on the Quick Access Toolbar to overwrite the previously saved file (SC_WD_1_WashHandsFlyerFormatted, in this case) in the same location it was saved previously (Documents library).

Q&A Why should I save the flyer again?
You have made several modifications to the flyer since you last saved it; thus, you should save it again.

BTW
Conserving Ink and Toner
If you want to conserve ink or toner, you can instruct Word to print draft quality documents by clicking File on the ribbon to open Backstage view, clicking Options in Backstage view to display the Word Options dialog box, clicking Advanced in the left pane (Word Options dialog box), scrolling to the Print area in the right pane, placing a check mark in the 'Use draft quality' check box, and then clicking OK. Then, use Backstage view to print the document as usual.

To Print a Document

After creating a document, you may want to print it. ***Why?*** *You want to see how the flyer will appear on a printed piece of paper.* The following steps print the contents of the document on a printer.

- Click File on the ribbon to open Backstage view.
- Click Print in Backstage view to display the Print screen and a preview of the document (Figure 1–110).

Q&A What if I decide not to print the document at this time?
Click the Back button in the upper-left corner of Backstage view to return to the document window.

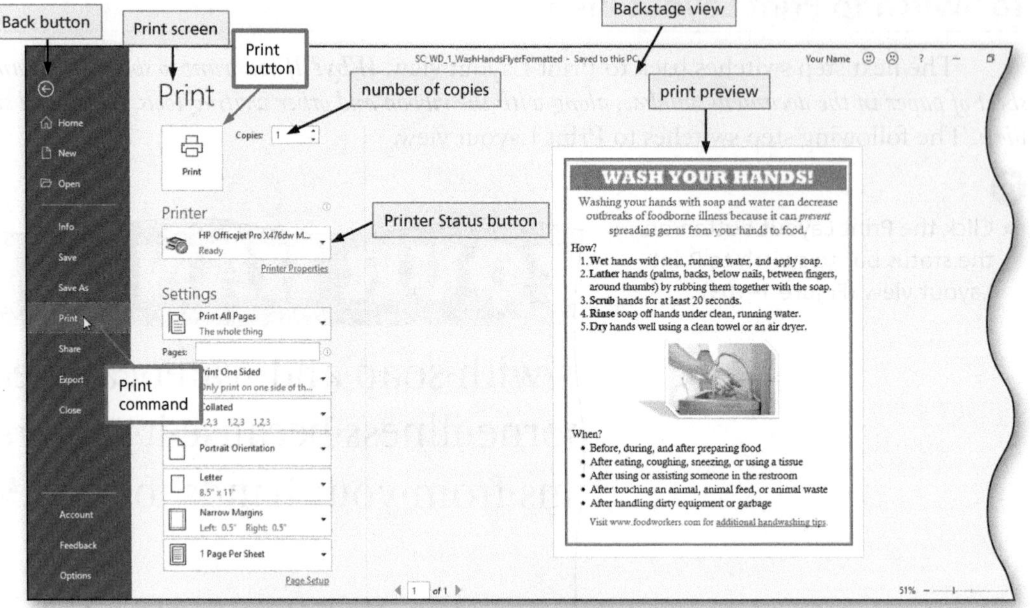

Figure 1–110

- Verify that the selected printer will print the document. If necessary, click the Printer Status button to display a list of available printer options and then click the desired printer to change the currently selected printer.

Q&A How can I print multiple copies of my document?
Increase the number in the Copies box in the Print screen.

3

- Click the Print button in the Print screen to print the document on the currently selected printer.
- When the printer stops, retrieve the printed document (shown in Figure 1–1).

Q&A What if one or more of my borders do not print?
Click the Page Borders button (Design tab | Page Background group), click the Options button (Borders and Shading dialog box), click the Measure from arrow and click Text, change the four text boxes to 15 pt, and then click OK in each dialog box. Try printing the document again. If the borders still do not print, adjust the boxes in the dialog box to a number smaller than 15 point.

Do I have to wait until my document is complete to print it?
No, you can print a document at any time while you are creating it.

Other Ways

1. Press CTRL+P

BTW
Printing Document Properties
To print document properties, click File on the ribbon to open Backstage view, click Print in Backstage view to display the Print screen, click the first button in the Settings area to display a list of options specifying what you can print, click Document Info in the list to specify you want to print the document properties instead of the actual document, and then click the Print button in the Print screen to print the document properties on the currently selected printer.

Using Word Help

At any time while you are using Word, you can use Word Help to display information about all topics associated with Word. You can search for help by using the Tell Me box or the Help pane.

To Use the Tell Me Box

If you are having trouble finding a button, box, or other command in Word, you can use the Tell Me box to search for the task you are trying to perform. As you type, the Tell Me box will suggest commands that match the search text you are entering. ***Why?*** *You can use the Tell Me box to access commands quickly that you otherwise may be unable to find on the ribbon or to display help about a command in the Help pane.* The following steps find information about margins.

1

- Type **margins** in the Tell Me box and watch the search results appear.
- Point to (or click, if necessary) Adjust Margins on the Tell Me menu to display the Margins gallery (Figure 1–111).

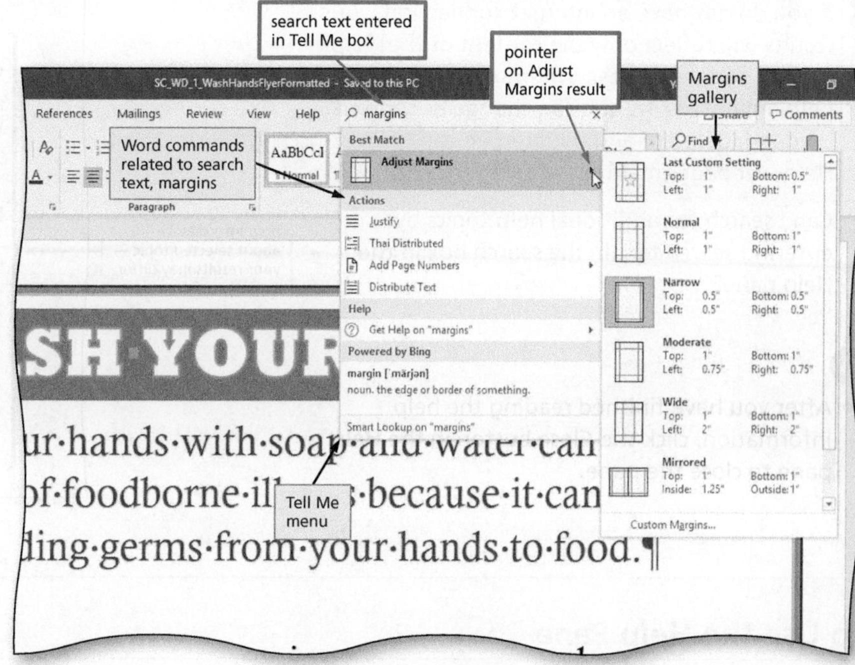

Figure 1–111

Does this Margins gallery work the same as the one I used earlier in this module to change the margins?
Yes, it is the exact same Margins gallery. You can select an option in the gallery to apply that command to the document.

2

- Point to 'Get Help on "margins"' on the Tell Me menu to display a submenu displaying the various help topics about the entered search text, margins (Figure 1–112).

Q&A What is a submenu?
A **submenu** is a list of additional commands associated with the selected command on a menu. If you point to an arrow on a menu, Word displays submenu.

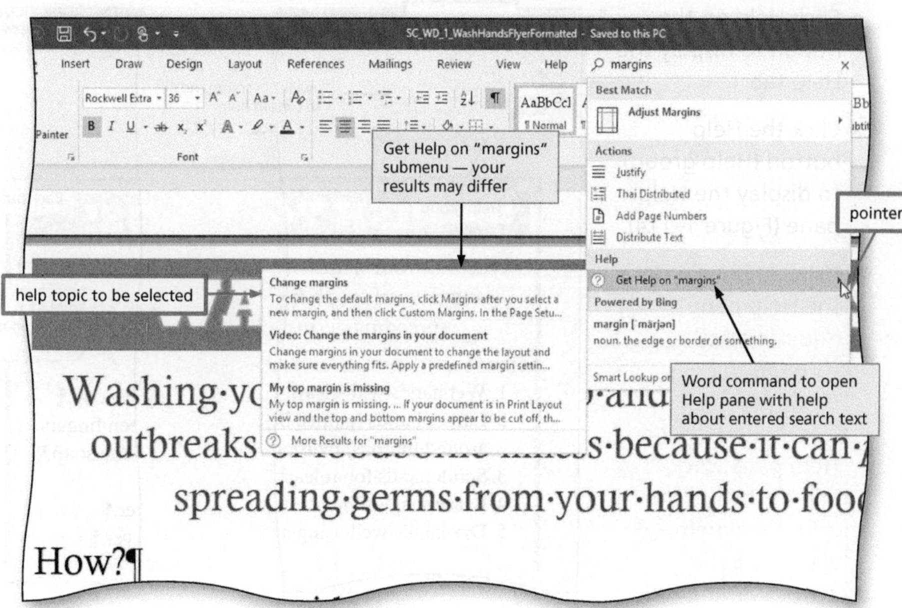

Figure 1–112

3

- Click the first help topic displayed on the submenu to open the Help pane, which displays a help topic about the selected command (Figure 1–113).

Q&A Why do my search results differ?
If you do not have an Internet connection, your results will reflect only the content of the Help files on your computer. When searching for help online, results also can change as content is added, deleted, and updated on the online Help webpages maintained by Microsoft.

Can I search for additional help topics by entering search text in the search box in the Help pane?
Yes.

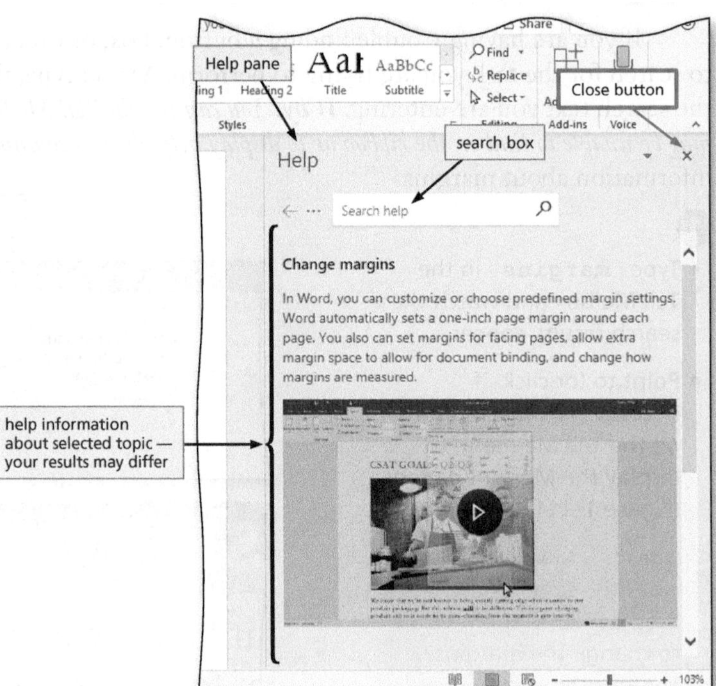

Figure 1–113

4

- After you have finished reading the help information, click the Close button in the Help pane to close the pane.

To Use the Help Pane

The following steps display the Help pane. ***Why?*** *You may not know the exact help topic you are looking to find, so you want to navigate the Help pane.*

1

- Click Help on the ribbon to display the Help tab.
- Click the Help button (Help group) to display the Help pane (Figure 1–114).

Q&A How do I navigate the Help pane?
You can scroll through the displayed information in the Help pane, click any of the links to additional help, click the Back button on the Help pane to return to a previously displayed screen, or enter search text in the search box.

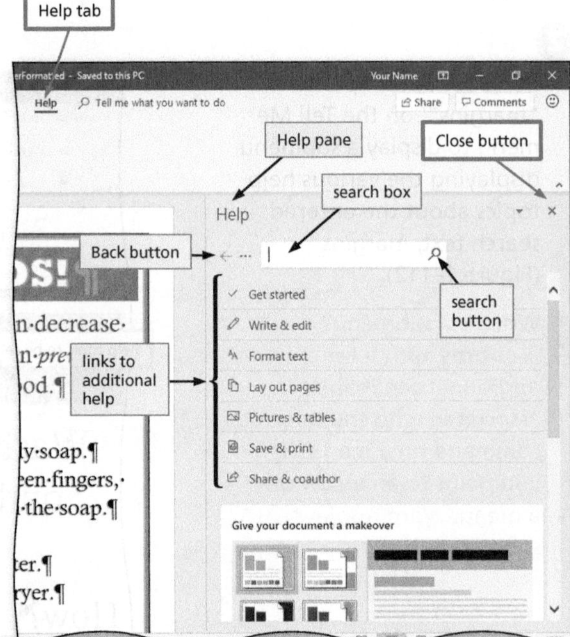

Figure 1–114

Does the search box in the Help pane work the same as the Tell Me box?
Yes. In the same way that you entered search text in the Tell Me box, you would enter search text in the search box in the Help pane and then press ENTER or click the search button to display a list of Help topics that match the entered search text.

2

- **When you are finished with the Help pane, click its Close button to close the pane.**

Other Ways

1. Press F1

Obtaining Help while Working in Word

You also can access Help without first using the Tell Me box or opening the Help pane and initiating a search. For example, you may be unsure about how a particular command works, or you may be presented with a dialog box that you are not sure how to use.

If you want to learn more about a command, point to its button and wait for the ScreenTip to appear, as shown in Figure 1–115. If the Help icon and 'Tell me more' link appear in the ScreenTip, click the 'Tell me more' link (or press F1 while pointing to the button) to open the Help pane and display a help topic associated with that command.

Dialog boxes also contain Help buttons, as shown in Figure 1–116. Clicking the Help button or pressing F1 while the dialog box is displayed opens a help window in your browser, which will display help contents specific to that dialog box, if available.

BTW
Word Help
At any time while using Word, you can find answers to questions and display information about various topics through Word Help. Used properly, this form of assistance can increase your productivity and reduce your frustrations by minimizing the time you spend learning how to use Word.

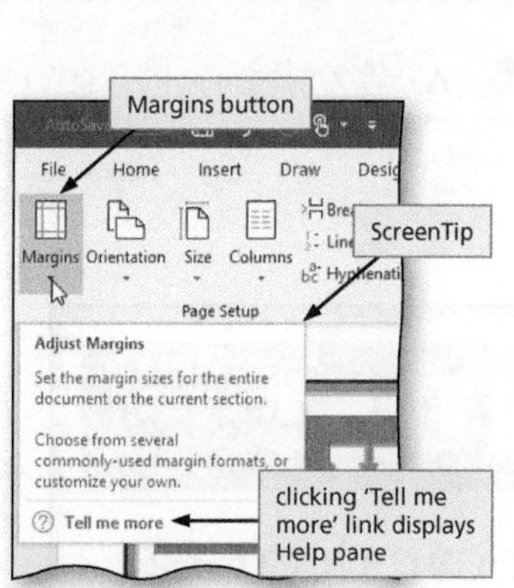

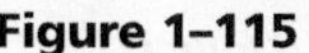

Figure 1–115

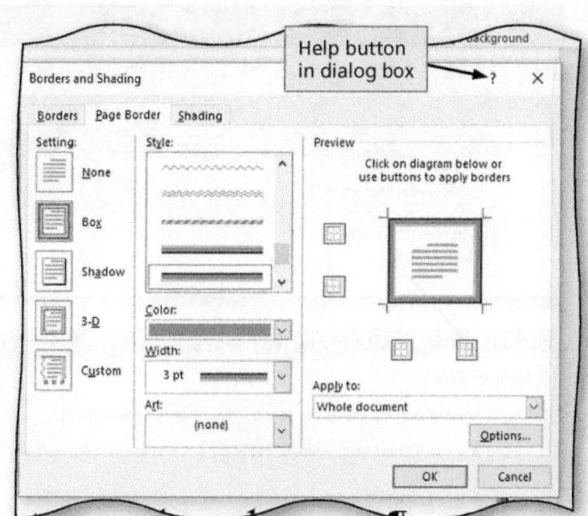

Figure 1–116

To Sign Out of a Microsoft Account

If you are using a public computer or otherwise wish to sign out of your Microsoft account, you should sign out of the account from the Accounts screen in Backstage view. Signing out of the account is the safest way to ensure that no one else can access online files or settings stored in your Microsoft account. If you wanted to sign out of a Microsoft account from Word, you would perform the following steps.

1. Click File on the ribbon to open Backstage view and then click Account to display the Account screen.

2. Click the Sign out link, which displays the Remove Account dialog box. If a Can't remove Windows accounts dialog box appears instead of the Remove Account dialog box, click OK and skip the remaining steps.

Q&A Why does a Can't remove Windows accounts dialog box appear?
If you signed in to Windows using your Microsoft account, then you also must sign out from Windows, rather than signing out from within Word. When you are finished using Windows, be sure to sign out at that time.

3 Click the Yes button (Remove Account dialog box) to sign out of your Microsoft account on this computer.

Q&A Should I sign out of Windows after removing my Microsoft account?
When you are finished using the computer, you should sign out of Windows for maximum security.

4 Click the Back button in the upper-left corner of Backstage view to return to the document window.

BTW
Office Suite
Word is part of the Microsoft Office 365 suite; other apps in the suite include Microsoft PowerPoint, Microsoft Excel, Microsoft Access, and Microsoft Outlook. Apps in a suite, such as Microsoft Office, typically use a similar interface and share features.

To Exit Word

You saved the document prior to printing and did not make any changes to the project. The following step exits Word. ***Why?*** *The SC_WD_1_WashHandsFlyerFormatted.docx project now is complete, and you are ready to exit Word.*

1

- Click the Close button in the upper-right corner of the Word window to Exit Word.
- sam If a Microsoft Word dialog box is displayed (Figure 1–117), click Save to save changes before exiting.

Q&A When I exited Word, a dialog box did not display. Why not?
If you made changes to your document since you last saved it, the dialog box shown in Figure 1–117 will appear when you exit Word. If you want to save changes before exiting, click Save; if you do not want to save changes, click Don't Save; if you change your mind and do not want to exit Word, click Cancel to return to the document in the document window.

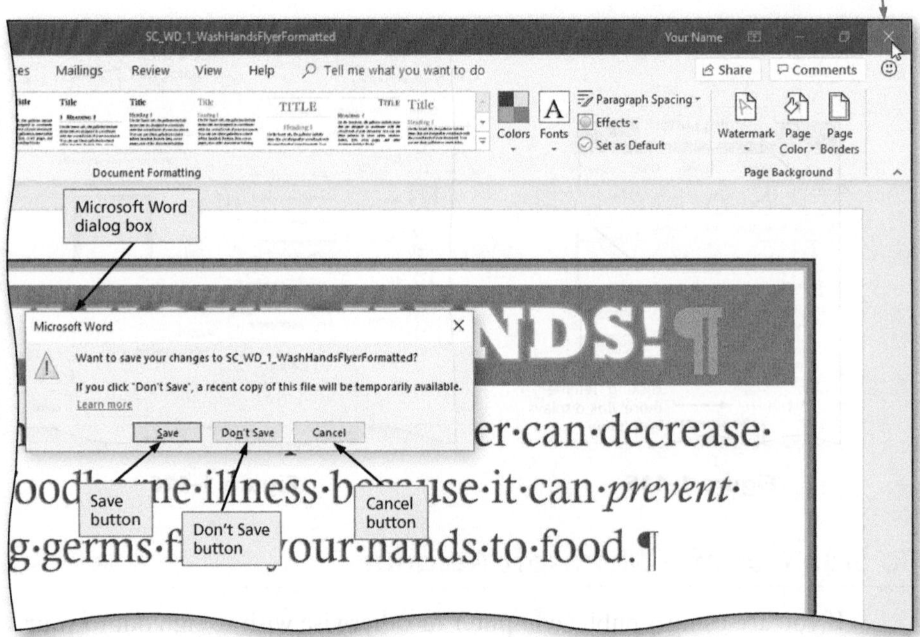

Figure 1–117

Other Ways

1. Right-click Microsoft Word button on Windows taskbar, click Close Window on shortcut menu

Summary

In this module, you learned how to start and use Word, enter text in a document, correct spelling and grammar errors as you work in a document, format paragraphs and characters, insert and format a picture, add a page border, adjust paragraph and page spacing, revise a document, print a document, and use Word Help.

CONSIDER THIS

What decisions will you need to make when creating your next flyer?

Use these guidelines as you complete the assignments in this module and create your own flyers outside of this class.

1. Choose the text for the headline, body copy, and signature line, using as few words as possible to make a point.
2. Format various elements of the text.
   a) Select appropriate font sizes for text in the headline, body copy, and signature line.
   b) Select appropriate fonts for text in the headline, body copy, and signature line.
   c) Adjust paragraph alignment, as appropriate.
   d) Highlight key paragraphs with bullets or numbers.
   e) Emphasize important words.
   f) Use color to convey meaning and add appeal.
3. Find an eye-catching picture(s) that conveys the overall message and meaning of the flyer.
4. Establish where to position and how to format the picture(s) so that it grabs the attention of passersby and draws them into reading the flyer.
5. Determine whether the flyer needs enhancements, such as a graphical, color-coordinated border, or spacing adjustments to improve readability or overall appearance.
6. Correct errors and revise the document as necessary.
   a) Post the flyer on a wall and make sure all text and images are legible from a distance.
   b) Ask someone else to read the flyer and give you suggestions for improvements.
7. Determine the best method for distributing the document, such as printing, sending via email, or posting on the web or social media.

BTW

Distributing a Document

Instead of printing and distributing a hard copy of a document, you can distribute the document electronically. Options include sending the document via email; posting it on cloud storage (such as OneDrive) and sharing the file with others; posting it on social media, a blog, or other website; and sharing a link associated with an online location of the document. You also can create and share a PDF or XPS image of the document, so that users can view the file in Acrobat Reader or XPS Viewer instead of in Word.

Apply Your Knowledge

Reinforce the skills and apply the concepts you learned in this module.

Modifying Text and Formatting a Document

Note: To complete this assignment, you will be required to use the Data Files. Please contact your instructor for information about accessing the Data Files.

Instructions: Start Word. Open the document, SC_WD_1-1.docx, which is located in the Data Files. The flyer you open contains an unformatted flyer that announces a blood drive for Lightwing Center for Outpatient Care. The manager of medical services, who created the text in the unformatted flyer, has asked you to modify the text in the flyer, format its paragraphs and characters, and insert a picture to create the formatted flyer shown in Figure 1–118.

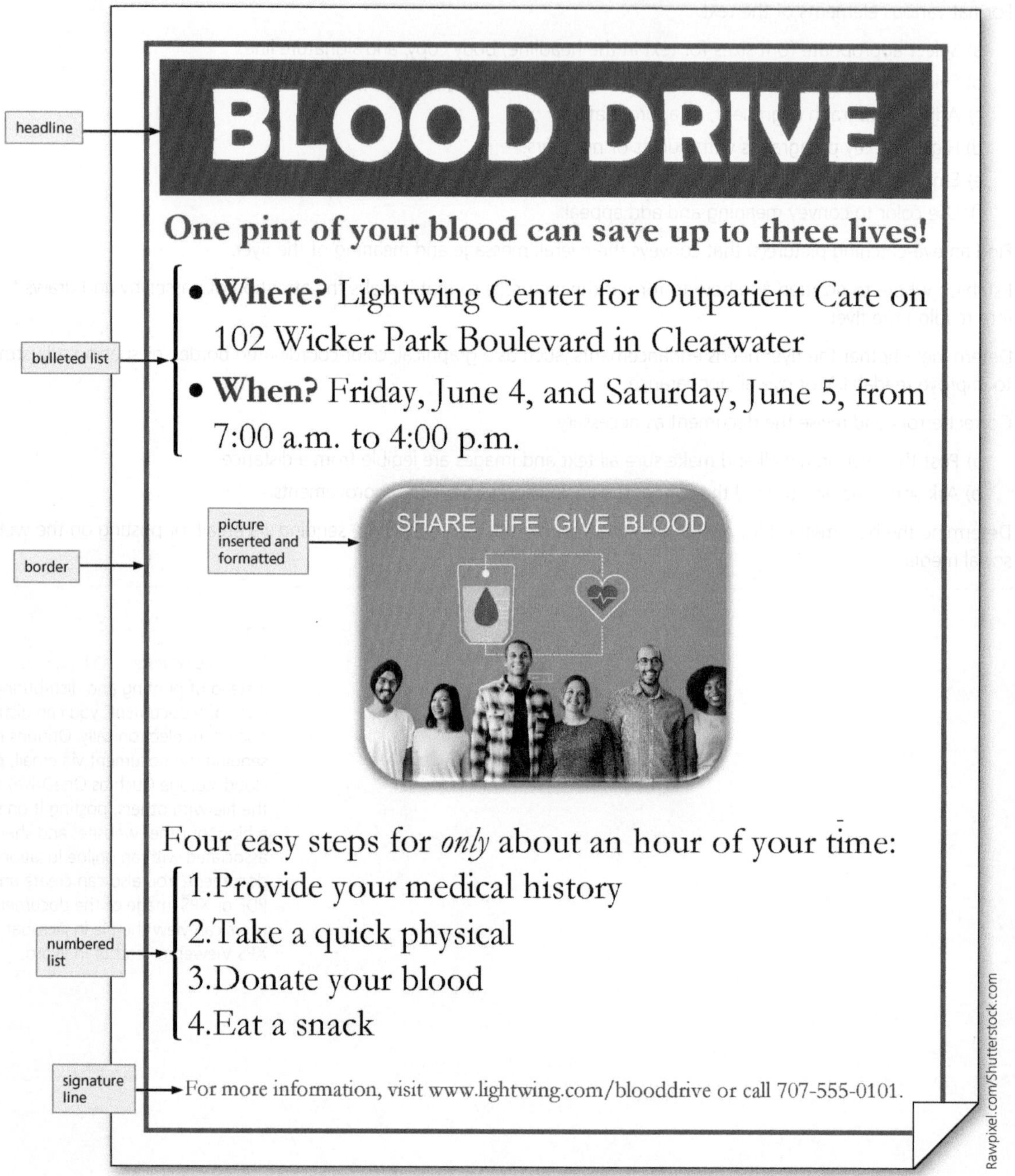

Figure 1–118

Perform the following tasks:

1. Display formatting marks on the screen.
2. Click File on the ribbon, click Save As, and then save the document using the new file name, SC_WD_1_BloodDriveFlyer.
3. Review each spelling (red wavy underline), grammar (blue double underline), and word choice (gold dotted underline) suggestion in the document by right-clicking the flagged text and then clicking the appropriate correction on the shortcut menu. Use the Ignore All command if the name of the medical center, Lightwing, is flagged because it is a proper name and spelled correctly.
4. Delete the second question mark after the text, When??, so that only one question mark follows the word.
5. Delete the word, single, in the line of text below the headline.
6. Insert the word, call, to the left of the phone number in the signature line (so that it reads: ...or call 707-555-0101).
7. Change the word, Sunday, to the word, Saturday, in the fourth line.
8. If requested by your instructor, change the phone number in the flyer to your phone number.
9. Change the document theme to Organic.
10. Change the margins to Narrow (that is, .5" top, bottom, left, and right margins).
11. Center the headline, the first paragraph of body copy below the headline, and the signature line in the flyer.
12. Change the font size of all the body copy text between the headline and signature line to 26 point.
13. Select the second and third paragraphs of body copy in the flyer and format the selected paragraphs as a bulleted list (that is, the paragraphs that begin with the words, Where? and When?).
14. Select the four paragraphs immediately above the signature line and format the selected paragraphs as a numbered list.
15. Change the font and font size of the headline to 72-point Berlin Sans FB Demi, or a similar font. Change the case of the text in the headline to uppercase letters. Apply the preset text effect called 'Fill: White; Outline: Green, Accent color 1; Glow: Green, Accent color 1' to the entire headline. Shade the text in the headline Gold, Accent 6, Darker 25%.
16. Change the theme colors to Red Violet.
17. Change the font color of the first line (paragraph) of body copy below the headline to Red, Accent 6, Darker 25%. Bold the text in this line.
18. Cut the word, Park, in the first bulleted paragraph. Paste the cut word in the same paragraph before the word, Boulevard, so the address reads: 102 Wicker Park Boulevard.
19. Copy the word, your, before the word, time, in the line above the numbered list. Paste the copied word before the word, blood, in the first paragraph of body copy below the headline, so that it reads: One pint of your blood can save up to three lives! Click the Paste Options button that appears before the pasted text and then click Merge Formatting on the Paste Options menu so that the pasted text has the same formats as the location of the insertion point.
20. Remove the hyperlink format from the web address in the signature line. If the text is still colored and underlined, change the color to Automatic and remove the underline.
21. Select the last paragraph on the page (the signature line) and then use the Mini toolbar to change the font size of the text in this paragraph to 16 point and its font color to Blue, Accent 4, Darker 50%.

Continued >

Apply Your Knowledge *continued*

22. Switch the second and third paragraphs in the numbered list. That is, select the 'Take a quick physical' numbered paragraph and use drag and drop to move it so that it is the second numbered paragraph (and then the 'Donate your blood' numbered paragraph will be the third numbered paragraph).
23. Select the words, three lives, in the first paragraph of body copy below the headline and underline these words. Undo this change and then redo the change.
24. Select the text, Where?, in the first bulleted paragraph and then select the nonadjacent text, When?, in the second bulleted paragraph. Bold the selected text. Change the font color of this same selected text to Blue, Accent 4, Darker 50%.
25. Italicize the word, only, in the paragraph above the numbered list.
26. Change the zoom to One Page, so that the entire page is visible in the document window.
27. Insert the blood drive picture so that it is centered on the blank line below the bulleted list. The picture is called Support_WD_1_GiveBlood.jpg and is available in the Data Files. Resize the picture proportionally so that it is approximately 2.8" × 3.53". Apply the Bevel Rectangle picture style to the inserted picture. Add the 'Glow: 8 point; Blue, Accent color 4' picture effect to the inserted picture.
28. Add a page border to the flyer using these formats: Setting: Box; Style: first style in list; Color: Blue, Accent 4, Darker 25%; Width 3 pt.
29. Change the spacing after the paragraph above the numbered list to 0 points. Change the spacing before the signature line to 18 points.
30. The entire flyer should fit on a single page. If it flows to two pages, resize the picture or decrease spacing before and after paragraphs until the entire flyer text fits on a single page.
31. Change the zoom to text width, then page width, then 25%, then 100% and notice the differences.
32. If requested by your instructor, enter the text, Blood Drive Flyer, as the comments in the document properties. Change the other document properties, as specified by your instructor.
33. Save the document again with the same file name.
34. Print the document. Switch to Read Mode and browse pages through the document. Switch to Print Layout view.
35. Close the document. Exit Word.
36. Submit the revised document, shown in Figure 1–118, in the format specified by your instructor.
37. If this flyer were announcing a company picnic instead of a blood drive, which theme colors would you apply and why?

Extend Your Knowledge

Extend the skills you learned in this module and experiment with new skills. You may need to use Help to complete the assignment.

Modifying Text, Lists, and Picture Formats and Adding Page Borders

Note: To complete this assignment, you will be required to use the Data Files. Please contact your instructor for information about accessing the Data Files.

Instructions: Start Word. Open the document called SC_WD_1-2.docx, which is located in the Data Files. The document contains a flyer that communicates phone tips for customer service representatives at Trustland Insurance. You will enhance the look of the flyer shown in Figure 1–119.

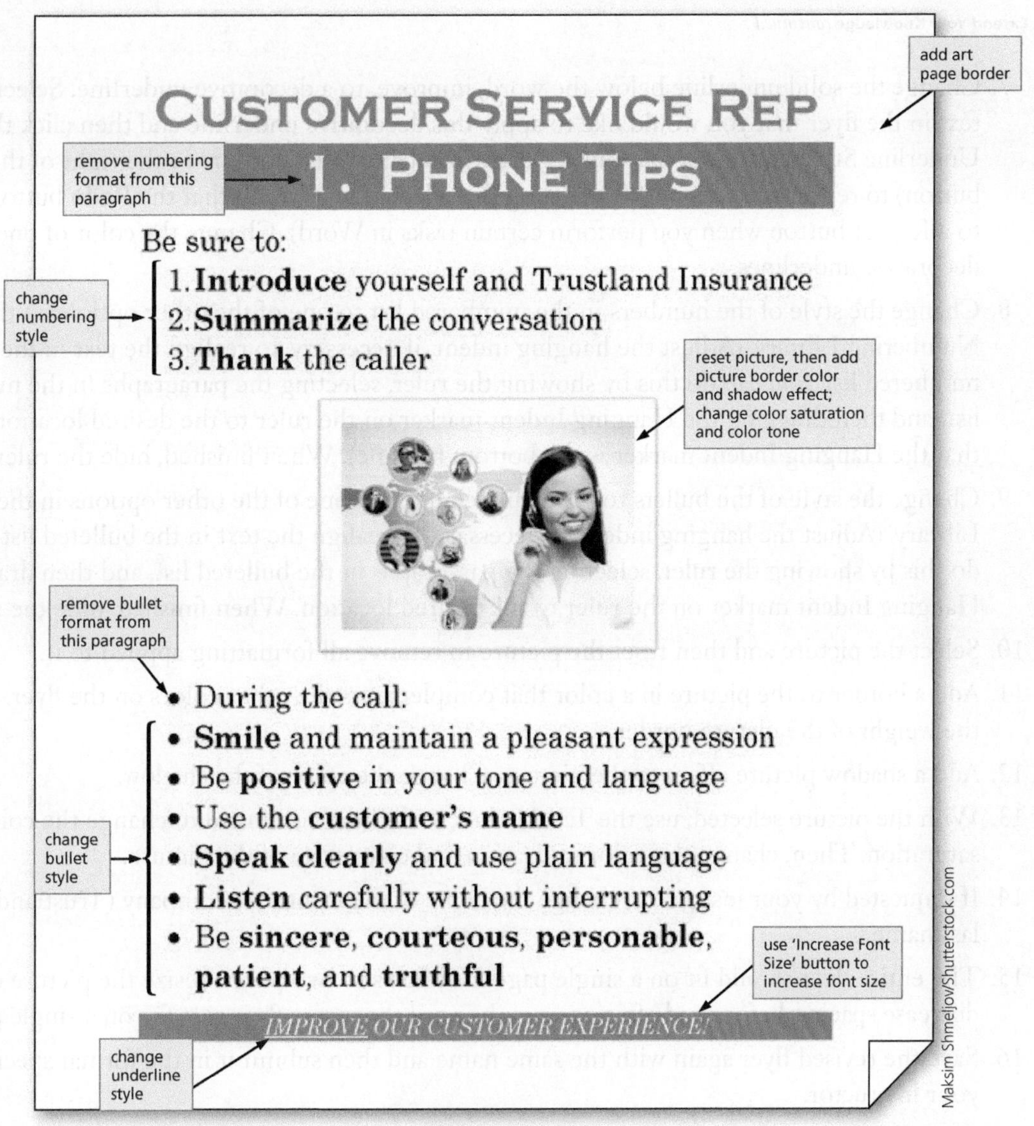

Figure 1–119

Perform the following tasks:

1. Use Help and the Tell Me box to learn about the following: remove bullets from a paragraph, remove numbers from a paragraph, grow font, shrink font, art page borders, decorative underlines, bulleted list formats, numbering formats, hanging indents, picture border shading, picture border color, shadow picture effects, and color saturation and tone.
2. Click File on the ribbon, click Save As, and then save the document using the new file name, SC_WD_1_PhoneTipsFlyer.
3. Remove the numbering format from the second line of the headline, so that it reads: Phone Tips.
4. Remove the bullet format from the paragraph immediately below the picture, so that it reads: During the call:.
5. Select the paragraph containing the signature line, IMPROVE OUR CUSTOMER EXPERIENCE!, and use the 'Increase Font Size' button (Home tab | Font group) to increase its font size.
6. Add an art page border to the flyer. If the border is not in color, add color to it if the border supports color.

Continued >

Extend Your Knowledge *continued*

7. Change the solid underline below the word, improve, to a decorative underline. Select more text in the flyer that you would like to apply this decorative underline and then click the Repeat Underline Style button on the Quick Access Toolbar (which appears to the right of the Undo button) to repeat the action of formatting the selected text (recall that the Redo button changes to a Repeat button when you perform certain tasks in Word). Change the color of one of the decorative underlines.
8. Change the style of the numbers in the numbered list to one of the other options in the Numbering Library. (Adjust the hanging indent, if necessary, to realign the text in the numbered list. You can do this by showing the ruler, selecting the paragraphs in the numbered list, and then dragging the Hanging Indent marker on the ruler to the desired location (note that the Hanging Indent marker is the bottom triangle). When finished, hide the ruler.)
9. Change the style of the bullets to in the bulleted list to one of the other options in the Bullet Library. (Adjust the hanging indent, if necessary, to realign the text in the bulleted list. You can do this by showing the ruler, selecting the paragraphs in the bulleted list, and then dragging the Hanging Indent marker on the ruler to the desired location. When finished, hide the ruler.)
10. Select the picture and then reset the picture to remove all formatting applied to it.
11. Add a border to the picture in a color that complements the other colors on the flyer. Change the weight of the picture border.
12. Add a shadow picture effect to the picture. Change the color of the shadow.
13. With the picture selected, use the Tell Me box to find the command to change the color saturation. Then, change the color saturation and color tone of the picture.
14. If requested by your instructor, change the name of the insurance company (Trustland) to your last name.
15. The entire flyer should fit on a single page. If it flows to two pages, resize the picture or decrease spacing before and after paragraphs until the entire flyer text fits on a single page.
16. Save the revised flyer again with the same name and then submit it in the format specified by your instructor.
17. In this assignment, you changed the numbering and bullet formats on the numbered and bulleted lists. Which numbering style and bullet character did you select and why?

Expand Your World

Create a solution that uses cloud or web technologies by learning and investigating on your own from general guidance.

Using Word Online to Create a Flyer with a Picture

Note: To complete this assignment, you will be required to use the Data Files. Please contact your instructor for information about accessing the Data Files.

Instructions: You will use Word Online to prepare a flyer. As a career services specialist at Cengage College, you will create a flyer announcing an upcoming job fair to be held on campus. Figure 1–120 shows the unformatted flyer. You will enter the text and insert the picture in Word Online and then use its tools to enhance the look of the flyer.

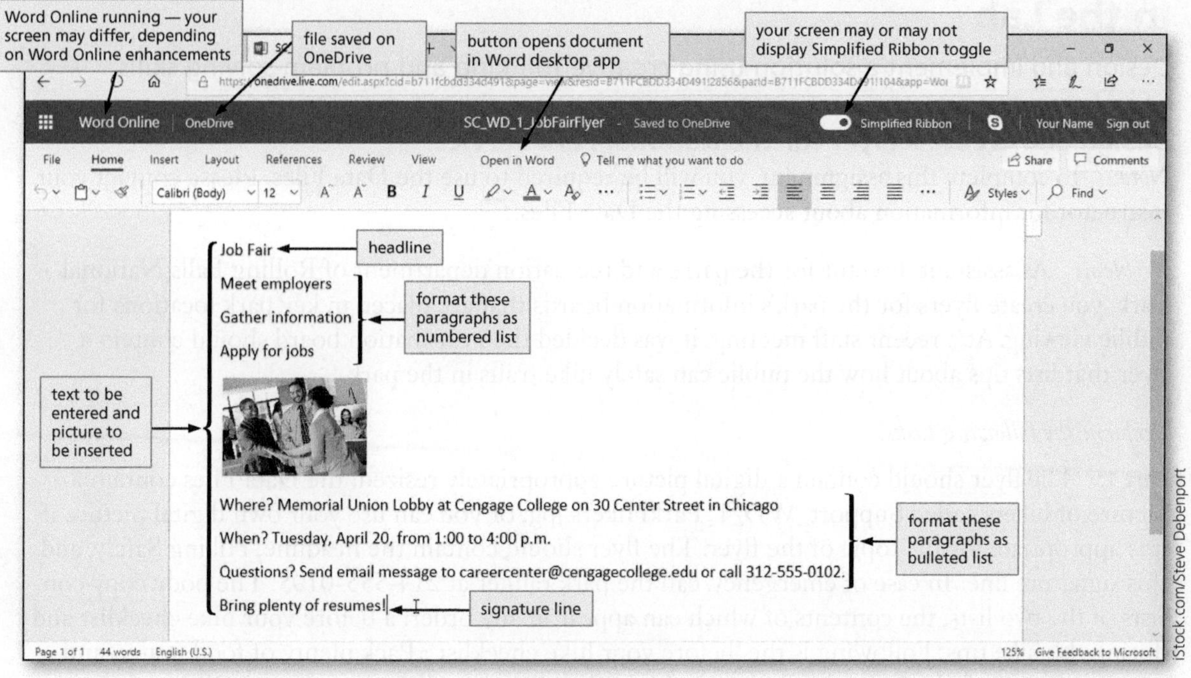

Figure 1–120

Perform the following tasks:

1. Start a browser. Search for the text, Word Online, using a search engine. Visit several websites to learn about Word Online. Navigate to the Word Online website. You will need to sign in to your OneDrive account.
2. Create a new blank Word document using Word Online. Name the document SC_WD_1_JobFairFlyer.
3. Notice the differences between Word Online and the Word desktop app you used to create the project in this module.
4. Enter the text in the flyer, shown in Figure 1–120, checking spelling and grammar as you work in the document.
5. Insert the picture called Support_WD_1_JobFair.jpg, which is located in the Data Files, below the numbered list.
6. Use the features available in Word Online, along with the concepts and techniques presented in this module, to format this flyer. Be sure to change the document margins, font and font size of text, center a paragraph(s), bold text, italicize text, color text, and underline text. Apply bullets and numbering to paragraphs as indicated in the figure. Resize the picture and apply a picture style. Adjust spacing above and below paragraphs as necessary. The flyer should fit on a single page.
7. If requested by your instructor, replace the email address in the flyer with your email address.
8. Save the document again. Click the button to open the document in the Word desktop app. If necessary, sign in to your Microsoft account when prompted. Notice how the document appears in the Word desktop app.
9. Using either Word Online or the Word desktop app, submit the document in the format requested by your instructor.
10. Exit Word and Word Online. If necessary, sign out of your OneDrive account and your Microsoft account in Word.
11. What is Word Online? Which features that are covered in this module are not available in Word Online? Do you prefer using Word Online or the Word desktop app? Why?

In the Lab

Design and implement a solution using creative thinking and problem-solving skills.

Design and Create a Flyer for the National Park Service

Note: To complete this assignment, you will be required to use the Data Files. Please contact your instructor for information about accessing the Data Files.

Problem: As assistant director for the parks and recreation department of Rolling Falls National Park, you create flyers for the park's information boards that are placed in key park locations for public viewing. At a recent staff meeting, it was decided the information board should contain a flyer that lists tips about how the public can safely hike trails in the park.

Perform the following tasks:

Part 1: The flyer should contain a digital picture appropriately resized; the Data Files contain a picture of hikers called Support_WD_1_ParkHikers.jpg, or you can use your own digital picture if it is appropriate for the topic of the flyer. The flyer should contain the headline, Hiking Safely, and this signature line: In case of emergency, call the park ranger at 214-555-0105. The body copy consists of the two lists, the contents of which can appear in any order: a before your hike checklist and during the hike tips. Following is the 'before your hike checklist': Pack plenty of food, water, and supplies. Bring a fully charged cell phone with backup battery, a battery-powered GPS, and two-way radios for all members of the hiking party. Bring binoculars or a telephoto camera lens to view wildlife from a safe distance. Check weather conditions and dress appropriately. Tell others when you plan to leave and which trail(s) at Rolling Falls National Park that you will be hiking. Following is the 'during the hike tips': Do not litter. Stay on official park trails and follow all park signs. Make noise while hiking. Do not approach, feed, or touch wildlife. Keep a distance of 100 feet between you and larger wildlife and a distance of 50 feet from smaller wildlife. Stay alert and watch your surroundings.

Use the concepts and techniques presented in this module to create a new blank document and format this flyer. Be sure to check spelling and grammar, accepting and ignoring suggested spelling and grammar changes as appropriate. When finished, save the flyer with the file name SC_WD_1_SafeHikingFlyer. Submit your assignment and answers to the Part 2 critical thinking questions in the format specified by your instructor.

Part 2: You made several decisions while creating the flyer in this assignment: where to place text, which margin settings and document themes to use, how to format the text (i.e., font, font size, paragraph alignment, bulleted paragraphs, numbered paragraphs, underlines, italics, bold, color, etc.), which picture to use, where to position the picture, how to format the picture, and which page enhancements to add (i.e., theme colors, borders, and spacing before/after paragraphs, etc.). What was the rationale behind each of these decisions? When you proofread the document, what further revisions did you make and why?

2 Creating a Research Paper

Objectives

After completing this module, you will be able to:

- Describe the MLA documentation style for research papers
- Modify a style
- Change line and paragraph spacing in a document
- Use a header to number pages of a document
- Apply formatting using keyboard shortcuts
- Modify paragraph indentation
- Insert and edit citations and their sources
- Add a footnote to a document
- Insert a page break
- Create a bibliographical list of sources
- Find text and replace text
- Use the thesaurus
- Check spelling and grammar at once
- Look up and research information
- Work with comments in a document

Introduction

In both business and academic environments, you will be asked to write reports. Business reports range from proposals to cost justifications to five-year plans to research findings. Academic reports focus mostly on research findings.

A **research paper** is a document you can use to communicate the results of research findings. To write a research paper, you learn about a particular topic from a variety of sources (research), organize your ideas from the research results, and then present relevant facts and/or opinions that support the topic. Your final research paper combines properly credited outside information along with personal insights. Thus, no two research papers — even if they are about the same topic — will or should be the same.

Project: Research Paper

When preparing a research paper, you should follow a standard documentation style that defines the rules for creating the paper and crediting sources. A variety of documentation styles exists, depending on the nature of the research paper. Each style requires the same basic information; the differences in styles relate to requirements for presenting the information. For example, one documentation style uses the term, bibliography, for the list of sources, whereas another uses the term, references, and yet a third prefers the term, works cited. Two popular documentation styles for research papers are the

BTW
APA Documentation Style
In the APA style, a separate title page is required instead of placing the name and course information on the paper's first page. Double-space all pages of the paper with one-inch top, bottom, left, and right margins. Indent the first word of each paragraph one-half inch from the left margin. In the upper-right margin of each page, including the title page, place a running head that consists of the page number preceded by a brief summary of the paper title.

MLA and APA styles. The **MLA (Modern Language Association of America)** style defines a set of formatting and content guidelines for publications and student research papers in the humanities and other fields, whereas the **APA (American Psychological Association)** style defines a set of formatting and content guidelines for publications and student research papers in the social and behavioral sciences. This module uses the MLA documentation style because it is used in a wider range of disciplines.

The project in this module follows research paper guidelines and uses Word to create the short research paper shown in Figure 2–1. As communications associate at a local outpatient care center, you communicate with and educate patients about a variety of health issues. You also are a part-time student who has been assigned a research paper. You decide to combine your work and school interests and compose a short research paper about health concerns of using technology. Your supervisor has expressed interest in incorporating the information in your paper for use in a patient brochure.

This paper, which discusses repetitive strain injuries and hearing loss, follows the MLA documentation style. Each page contains a page number. The first two pages present the name and course information (student name, instructor name, course name, and paper due date), paper title, an introduction with a thesis statement, details that support the thesis, and a conclusion. This section of the paper also includes references to research sources and a footnote. The third page contains a detailed, alphabetical list of the sources referenced in the research paper. All pages include a header at the upper-right edge of the page.

In this module, you will learn how to create the research paper shown in Figure 2–1. You will perform the following general tasks as you progress through this module:

1. Change the document settings.
2. Create the header, which will appear on each page of the research paper.
3. Type the research paper text with citations.
4. Create an alphabetical works cited page.
5. Proofread and revise the research paper.
6. Work with comments in the research paper.

MLA Documentation Style

The research paper in this project follows the guidelines presented by the MLA. To follow the MLA documentation style, use a 12-point Times New Roman or similar font. Double-space text on all pages of the paper using one-inch top, bottom, left, and right margins. Indent the first word of each paragraph one-half inch from the left margin. At the right margin of each page, place a page number one-half inch from the top margin. On each page, precede the page number with your last name.

The MLA documentation style does not require a title page. Instead, place your name and course information in a block at the left margin beginning one inch from the top of the page. Center the title one double-spaced line below your name and course information.

In the text of the paper, place author references in parentheses with the page number(s) of the referenced information. The MLA documentation style uses in-text **parenthetical references** to reference sources used in a research paper instead of noting each source at the bottom of the page or at the end of the paper. In the MLA documentation style, notes are used only for optional content or bibliographic notes.

If used, content notes elaborate on points discussed in the paper, and bibliographic notes direct the reader to evaluations of statements in a source or provide a means for

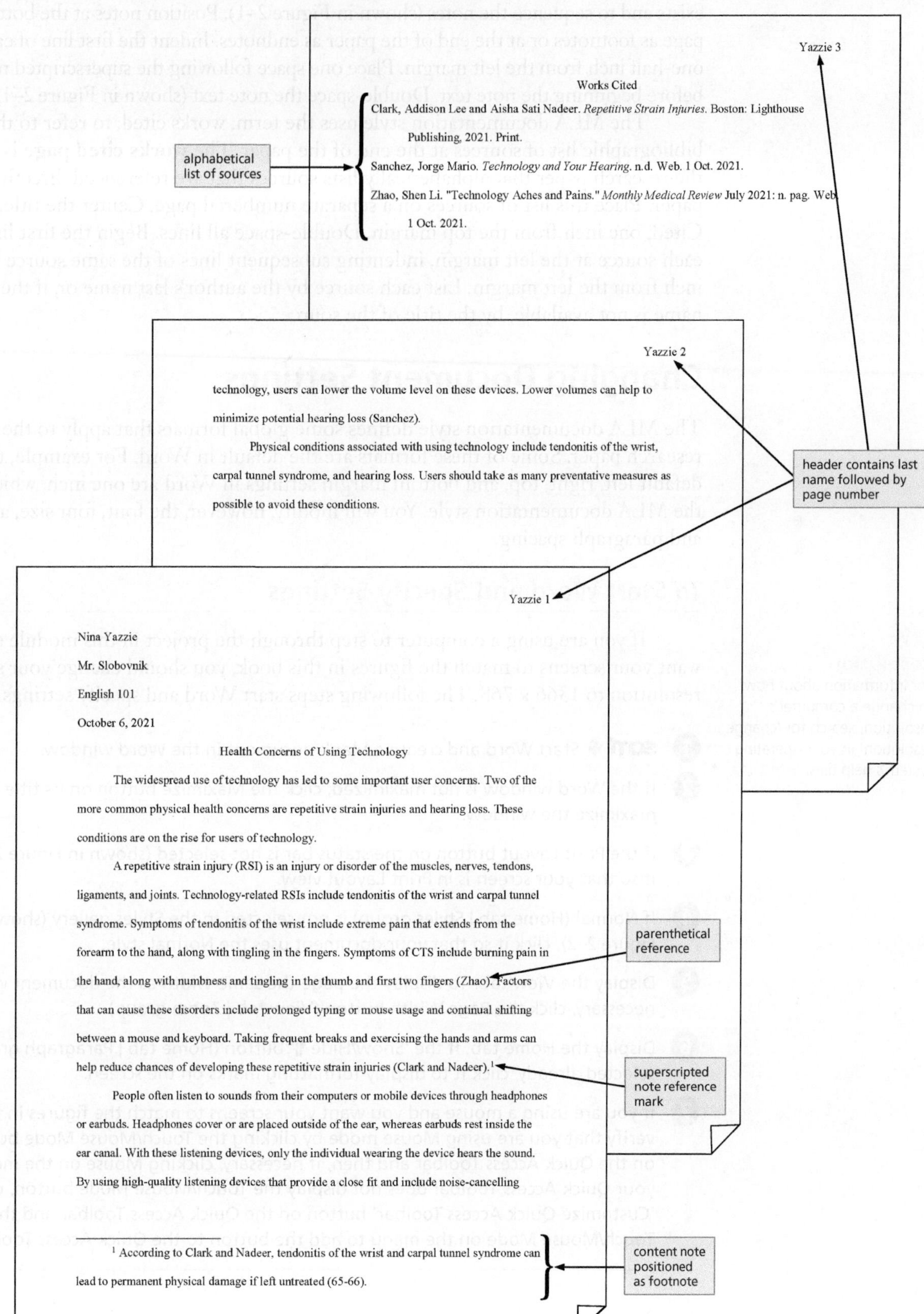

Yazzie 3
Works Cited
Clark, Addison Lee and Aisha Sati Nadeer. *Repetitive Strain Injuries.* Boston: Lighthouse Publishing, 2021. Print.
Sanchez, Jorge Mario. *Technology and Your Hearing.* n.d. Web. 1 Oct. 2021.
Zhao, Shen Li. "Technology Aches and Pains." *Monthly Medical Review* July 2021: n. pag. Web. 1 Oct. 2021.
alphabetical list of sources
Yazzie 2
technology, users can lower the volume level on these devices. Lower volumes can help to minimize potential hearing loss (Sanchez).
Physical conditions associated with using technology include tendonitis of the wrist, carpal tunnel syndrome, and hearing loss. Users should take as many preventative measures as possible to avoid these conditions.
header contains last name followed by page number
Yazzie 1
Nina Yazzie
Mr. Slobovnik
English 101
October 6, 2021
Health Concerns of Using Technology
The widespread use of technology has led to some important user concerns. Two of the more common physical health concerns are repetitive strain injuries and hearing loss. These conditions are on the rise for users of technology.
A repetitive strain injury (RSI) is an injury or disorder of the muscles, nerves, tendons, ligaments, and joints. Technology-related RSIs include tendonitis of the wrist and carpal tunnel syndrome. Symptoms of tendonitis of the wrist include extreme pain that extends from the forearm to the hand, along with tingling in the fingers. Symptoms of CTS include burning pain in the hand, along with numbness and tingling in the thumb and first two fingers (Zhao). Factors that can cause these disorders include prolonged typing or mouse usage and continual shifting between a mouse and keyboard. Taking frequent breaks and exercising the hands and arms can help reduce chances of developing these repetitive strain injuries (Clark and Nadeer).[1]
People often listen to sounds from their computers or mobile devices through headphones or earbuds. Headphones cover or are placed outside of the ear, whereas earbuds rest inside the ear canal. With these listening devices, only the individual wearing the device hears the sound. By using high-quality listening devices that provide a close fit and include noise-cancelling
[1] According to Clark and Nadeer, tendonitis of the wrist and carpal tunnel syndrome can lead to permanent physical damage if left untreated (65-66).
parenthetical reference
superscripted note reference mark
content note positioned as footnote

Figure 2–1

identifying multiple sources. Use a superscript (raised number) both to signal that a note exists and to sequence the notes (shown in Figure 2–1). Position notes at the bottom of the page as footnotes or at the end of the paper as endnotes. Indent the first line of each note one-half inch from the left margin. Place one space following the superscripted number before beginning the note text. Double-space the note text (shown in Figure 2–1).

The MLA documentation style uses the term, works cited, to refer to the bibliographic list of sources at the end of the paper. The **works cited page** is a page in the research paper that alphabetically lists sources that are referenced directly in the paper. Place this list of sources on a separate numbered page. Center the title, Works Cited, one inch from the top margin. Double-space all lines. Begin the first line of each source at the left margin, indenting subsequent lines of the same source one-half inch from the left margin. List each source by the author's last name or, if the author's name is not available, by the title of the source.

Changing Document Settings

The MLA documentation style defines some global formats that apply to the entire research paper. Some of these formats are the default in Word. For example, the default left, right, top, and bottom margin settings in Word are one inch, which meets the MLA documentation style. You will modify, however, the font, font size, and line and paragraph spacing.

To Start Word and Specify Settings

BTW
Resolution
For information about how to change a computer's resolution, search for 'change resolution' in your operating system's help files.

If you are using a computer to step through the project in this module and you want your screens to match the figures in this book, you should change your screen's resolution to 1366 × 768. The following steps start Word and specify settings.

1. sam Start Word and create a blank document in the Word window.
2. If the Word window is not maximized, click the Maximize button on its title bar to maximize the window.
3. If the Print Layout button on the status bar is not selected (shown in Figure 2–2), click it so that your screen is in Print Layout view.
4. If Normal (Home tab | Styles group) is not selected in the Styles gallery (shown in Figure 2–2), click it so that your document uses the Normal style.
5. Display the View tab. To display the page the same width as the document window, if necessary, click the Page Width button (View tab | Zoom group).
6. Display the Home tab. If the 'Show/Hide ¶' button (Home tab | Paragraph group) is not selected already, click it to display formatting marks on the screen.
7. If you are using a mouse and you want your screens to match the figures in the book, verify that you are using Mouse mode by clicking the Touch/Mouse Mode button on the Quick Access Toolbar and then, if necessary, clicking Mouse on the menu. (If your Quick Access Toolbar does not display the Touch/Mouse Mode button, click the 'Customize Quick Access Toolbar' button on the Quick Access Toolbar and then click Touch/Mouse Mode on the menu to add the button to the Quick Access Toolbar.)

Styles

When you create a document, Word formats the text using a particular style. A **style** is a named collection of character and paragraph formats, including font, font size, font styles, font color, and alignment, that are stored together and can be applied to text or objects to format them quickly. The default style that is applied to all text in Word is called the **Normal style**, which most likely uses an 11-point Calibri font. If you do not specify a style for text you type, Word applies the Normal style to the text. In addition to the Normal style, Word has many other built-in, or predefined, styles that you can use to format text. Styles make it easy to apply many formats at once to text. You can modify existing styles and create your own styles. Styles are discussed as they are used in this book.

To Modify a Style

The MLA documentation style requires that all text in the research paper use a 12-point Times New Roman or similar font. If you change the font and font size using buttons on the ribbon, you will need to make the change many times during the course of creating the paper. ***Why?*** *Word formats various areas of a document based on the Normal style, which uses an 11-point Calibri font. For example, body text, headers, and bibliographies all display text based on the Normal style.*

Thus, instead of changing the font and font size for various document elements, a more efficient technique is to change the Normal style for this document to use a 12-point Times New Roman font. ***Why?*** *By changing the Normal style, you ensure that all text in the document will use the format required by the MLA.* The following steps change the Normal style.

1

- Right-click Normal in the Styles gallery (Home tab | Styles group) to display a shortcut menu related to styles (Figure 2–2).

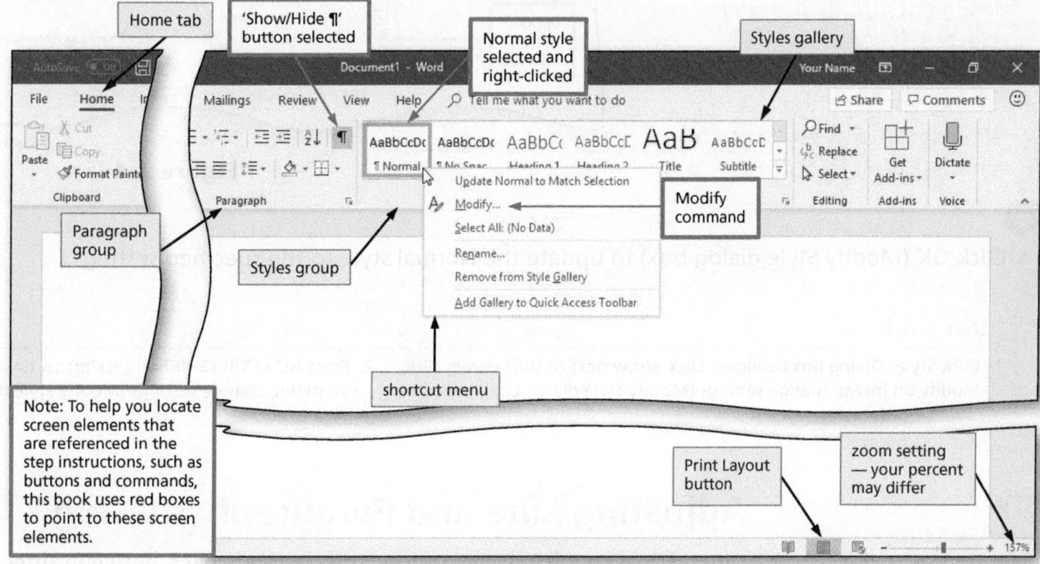

Figure 2–2

2

- Click Modify on the shortcut menu to display the Modify Style dialog box (Figure 2–3).

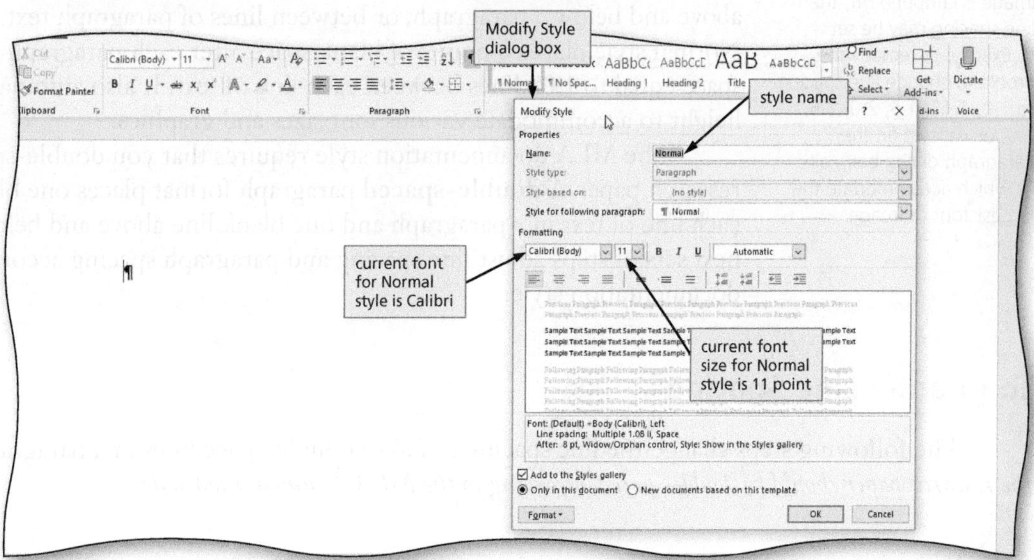

Figure 2–3

- Click the Font arrow (Modify Style dialog box) to display the Font list. Scroll to and then click Times New Roman in the list to change the font for the style being modified.
- Click the Font Size arrow (Modify Style dialog box) and then click 12 in the Font Size list to change the font size for the style being modified.
- Ensure that the 'Only in this document' option button is selected (Figure 2–4).

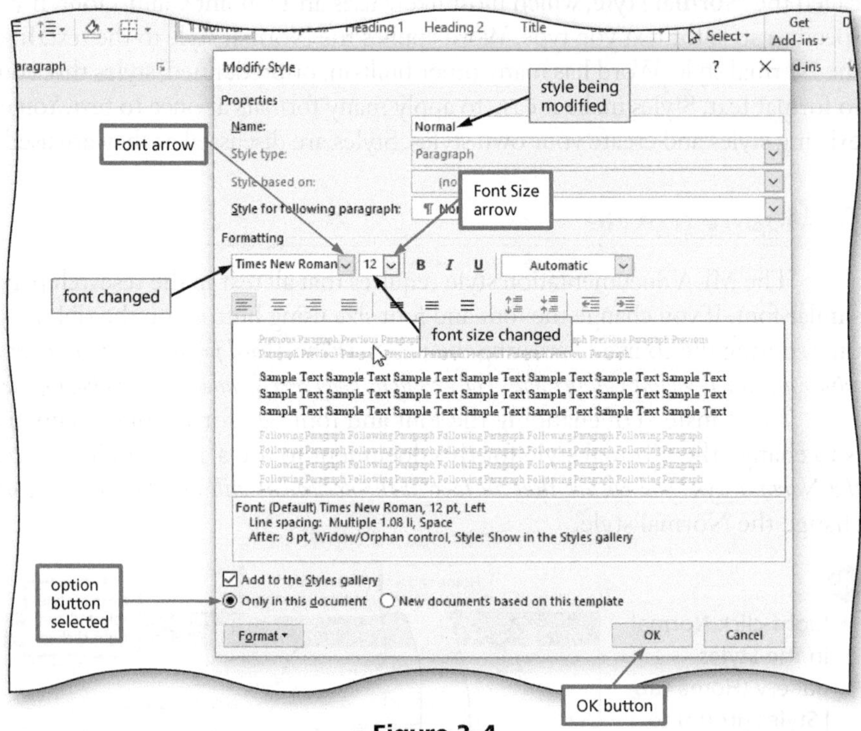

Figure 2–4

Q&A Will all future documents use the new font and font size?
No, because the 'Only in this document' option button is selected. If you wanted all future documents to use a new setting, you would select the 'New documents based on this template' option button.

- Click OK (Modify Style dialog box) to update the Normal style to the specified settings.

Other Ways

1. Click Styles Dialog Box Launcher, click arrow next to style name, click Modify on menu, change settings (Modify Style dialog box), click OK
2. Press ALT+CTRL+SHIFT+S, click arrow next to style name, click Modify on menu, change settings (Modify Style dialog box), click OK

Adjusting Line and Paragraph Spacing

Line spacing is the amount of vertical space between lines of text in a paragraph. **Paragraph spacing** is the space, measured in points, that appears directly above and below a paragraph, or between lines of paragraph text. By default, the Normal style places 8 points of blank space after each paragraph and inserts a vertical space equal to 1.08 lines between each line of text. It also automatically adjusts line height to accommodate various font sizes and graphics.

The MLA documentation style requires that you double-space the entire research paper. A **double-spaced** paragraph format places one blank line between each line of text in a paragraph and one blank line above and below a paragraph. The next sets of steps adjust line spacing and paragraph spacing according to the MLA documentation style.

BTW
Line Spacing
If the top of a set of characters or a graphical image is chopped off, then line spacing may be set to Exactly. To remedy the problem, change line spacing to 1.0, 1.15, 1.5, 2.0, 2.5, 3.0, or At least (in the Paragraph dialog box), all of which accommodate the largest font or image.

To Change Line Spacing

The following steps change the line spacing to 2.0 to double-space lines in a paragraph. ***Why?*** *The lines of the research paper should be double-spaced, according to the MLA documentation style.*

1

- Click the 'Line and Paragraph Spacing' button (Home tab | Paragraph group) to display the Line and Paragraph Spacing gallery (Figure 2–5).

Q&A What do the numbers in the Line and Paragraph Spacing gallery represent?
The options 1.0, 2.0, and 3.0 set line spacing to single, double, and triple, respectively. Similarly, the 1.15, 1.5, and 2.5 options set line spacing to 1.15, 1.5, and 2.5 lines. All of these options adjust line spacing automatically to accommodate the largest font or graphic on a line.

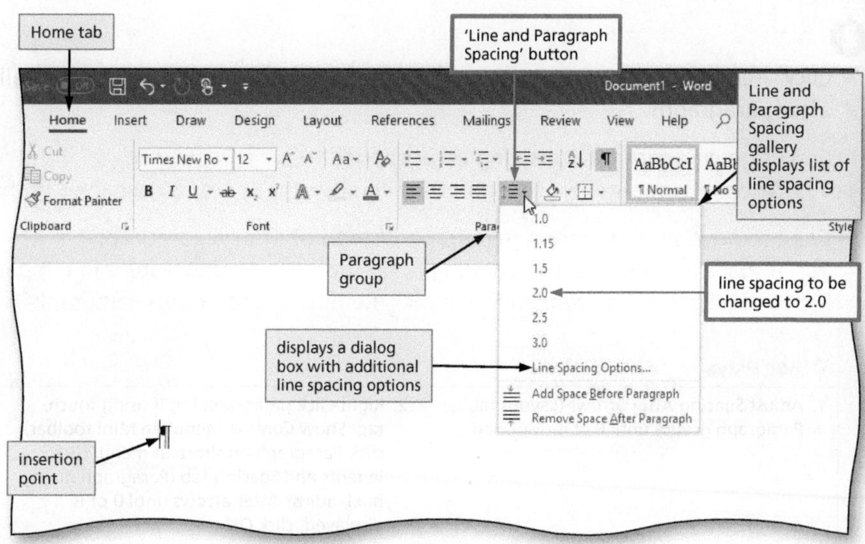

Figure 2–5

2

- Click 2.0 in the Line and Paragraph Spacing gallery to change the line spacing at the location of the insertion point.

Q&A Can I change the line spacing of existing text or the entire document?
Yes. Select the text first or select the entire document, and then change the line spacing as described in these steps. To select the entire document, click the Select button (Home tab | Editing group) and then click Select All on the Select menu or press CTRL+A.

Other Ways

1. Right-click paragraph (or, if using touch, tap 'Show Context Menu' on Mini toolbar), click Paragraph on shortcut menu, or click Indents and Spacing tab (Paragraph dialog box), click Line spacing arrow, select desired spacing, click OK
2. Click Paragraph Dialog Box Launcher (Home tab or Layout tab | Paragraph group), click Indents and Spacing tab (Paragraph dialog box), click Line spacing arrow, select desired spacing, click OK
3. Press CTRL+2 for double-spacing

To Remove Space after a Paragraph

The following steps remove space after a paragraph. ***Why?*** *The research paper should not have additional blank space after each paragraph, according to the MLA documentation style.*

1

- Click the 'Line and Paragraph Spacing' button (Home tab | Paragraph group) to display the Line and Paragraph Spacing gallery (Figure 2–6).

Q&A Why does a check mark appear to the left of 2.0 in the gallery?
The check mark indicates the currently selected line spacing.

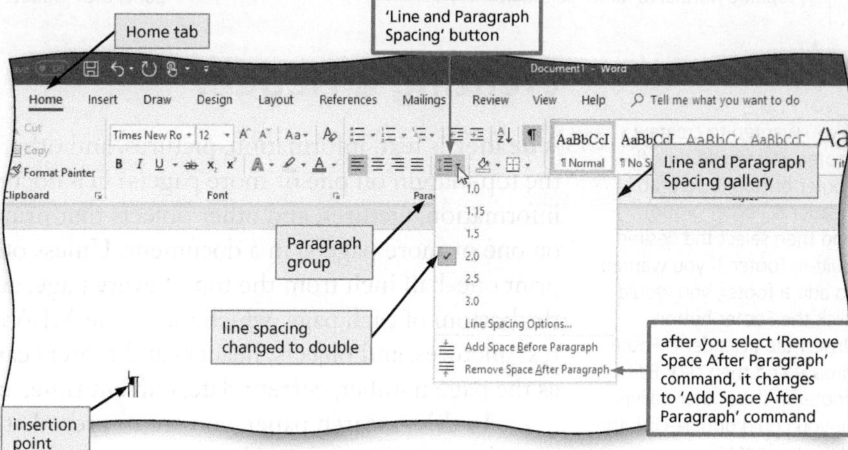

Figure 2–6

- Click 'Remove Space After Paragraph' in the Line and Paragraph Spacing gallery so that no blank space appears after paragraphs.

Q&A

Can I remove space after existing paragraphs?
Yes. Select the paragraphs first and then remove the space as described in these steps.

Can I remove space before a paragraph instead of after a paragraph?
Yes. If space exists before the paragraph, position the insertion point in the paragraph to adjust, click the 'Line and Paragraph Spacing' button, and then click 'Remove Space Before Paragraph' in the Line and Paragraph Spacing gallery.

Other Ways

1. Adjust Spacing After arrows (Layout tab | Paragraph group) until 0 pt is displayed
2. Right-click paragraph (or, if using touch, tap 'Show Context Menu' on Mini toolbar), click Paragraph on shortcut menu, click Indents and Spacing tab (Paragraph dialog box), adjust After arrows until 0 pt is displayed, click OK
3. Click Paragraph Dialog Box Launcher (Home tab or Layout tab | Paragraph group), click Indents and Spacing tab (Paragraph dialog box), adjust After arrows until 0 pt is displayed, click OK

To Update a Style to Match a Selection

To ensure that all paragraphs in the paper will be double-spaced and do not have space after the paragraphs, you want the Normal style to include the line and paragraph spacing changes made in the previous two sets of steps. The following steps update the Normal style. ***Why?*** *You can update a style to reflect the settings of the location of the insertion point or selected text. Because no text has been typed in the research paper yet, you do not need to select text prior to updating the Normal style.*

1

- Right-click Normal in the Styles gallery (Home tab | Styles group) to display a shortcut menu (Figure 2–7).

- Click 'Update Normal to Match Selection' on the shortcut menu to update the selected (or current) style to reflect the settings at the location of the insertion point.

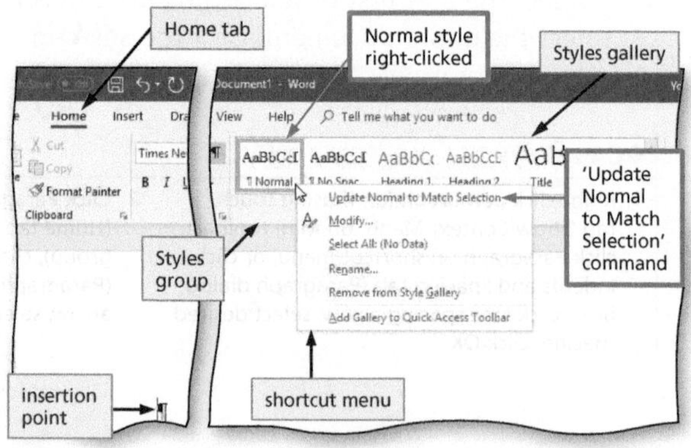

Figure 2–7

Other Ways

1. Click Styles Dialog Box Launcher, click arrow next to style name, click 'Update Normal to Match Selection'
2. Press ALT+CTRL+SHIFT+S, click arrow next to style name in Styles pane, click 'Update Normal to Match Selection'

BTW
Footers
If you wanted to create a footer, you would click the Footer button (Insert tab | Header & Footer group) and then select the desired built-in footer. If you wanted to edit a footer, you would click the Footer button (Insert tab | Header & Footer group) and then click Edit Footer in the Footer gallery, or you could double-click the dimmed footer.

Creating a Header

A **header** is text, information, pictures, and other objects that print in an area above the top margin on one or more page(s) in a document. Similarly, a **footer** is text, information, pictures, and other objects that print in an area below the bottom margin on one or more page(s) in a document. Unless otherwise specified in Word, headers print one-half inch from the top of every page, and footers print one-half inch from the bottom of each page, which meets the MLA documentation style. In addition to text, pictures, and objects, headers and footers can include document information, such as the page number, current date, current time, and author's name.

In this research paper, you are to precede the page number with your last name placed one-half inch from the upper-right edge of each page. The procedures in the following sections enter your name and the page number in the header, as specified by the MLA documentation style.

To Insert a Header

The following steps insert a blank built-in header. ***Why?*** *To enter text in the header, you instruct Word to insert a header, which you will edit.*

- Click Insert on the ribbon to display the Insert tab.
- Click the Header button (Insert tab | Header & Footer group) to display the Header gallery (Figure 2–8).

Experiment

- Click the down scroll arrow in the Header gallery to see the available built-in headers.

Q&A How would I enter a footer in a document?
You would click the Footer button (Insert tab | Header & Footer group) and select the desired footer in the list. To edit a footer, you would click the Footer button (Insert tab | Header & Footer group) and the click Edit Footer in the Footer gallery.

How would I remove a header from a document?
You would click Remove Header in the Add a Header gallery. Similarly, to remove a footer, you would click Remove Footer in the Add a Footer gallery.

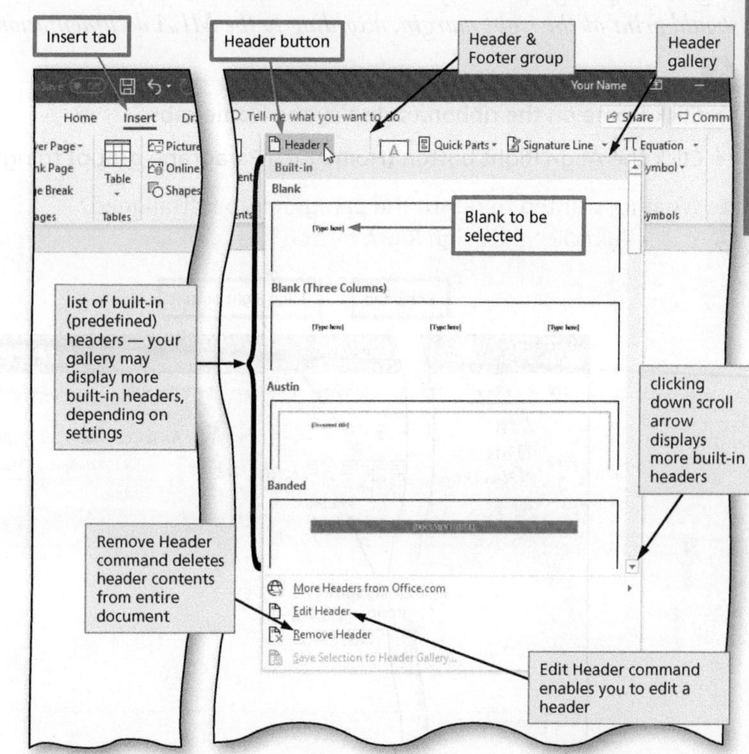

Figure 2–8

- Click Blank in the Header gallery to switch from the document text to the header and insert placeholder text in the header (Figure 2–9).

Q&A What is placeholder text?
Placeholder text is default text that indicates where text can be typed.

How do I remove the Header & Footer Tools Design tab from the ribbon?
When you are finished editing the header, you will close it, which removes the Header & Footer Tools Design tab.

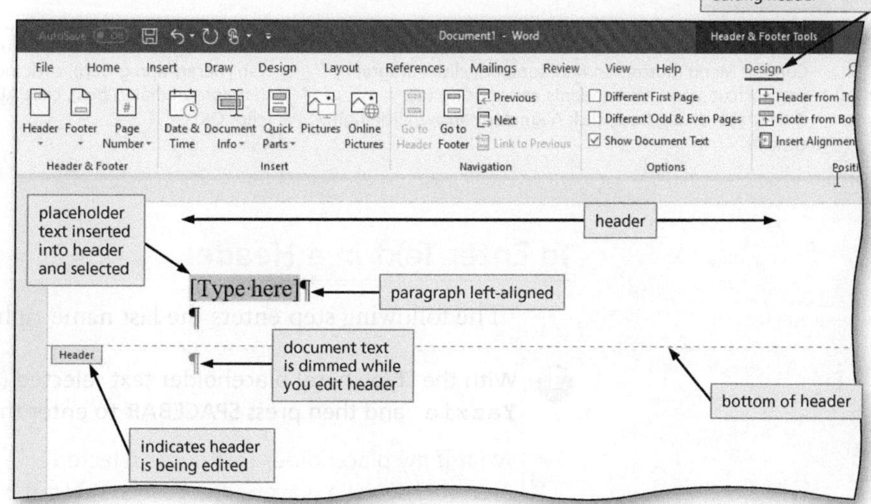

Figure 2–9

Other Ways

1. Double-click dimmed header
2. Right-click header in document, click Edit Header button that appears

To Right-Align a Paragraph

The paragraph in the header currently is left-aligned (shown in Figure 2–9). The following step right-aligns this paragraph. ***Why?*** *Your last name and the page number in the header should print* ***right-aligned****; that is, they should print at the right margin, according to the MLA documentation style.*

- Click Home on the ribbon to display the Home tab.
- Click the Align Right button (Home tab | Paragraph group) to right-align the current paragraph (Figure 2–10).

Q&A What if I wanted to return the paragraph to left-aligned?
You would click the Align Right button again, or click the Align Left button (Home tab | Paragraph group).

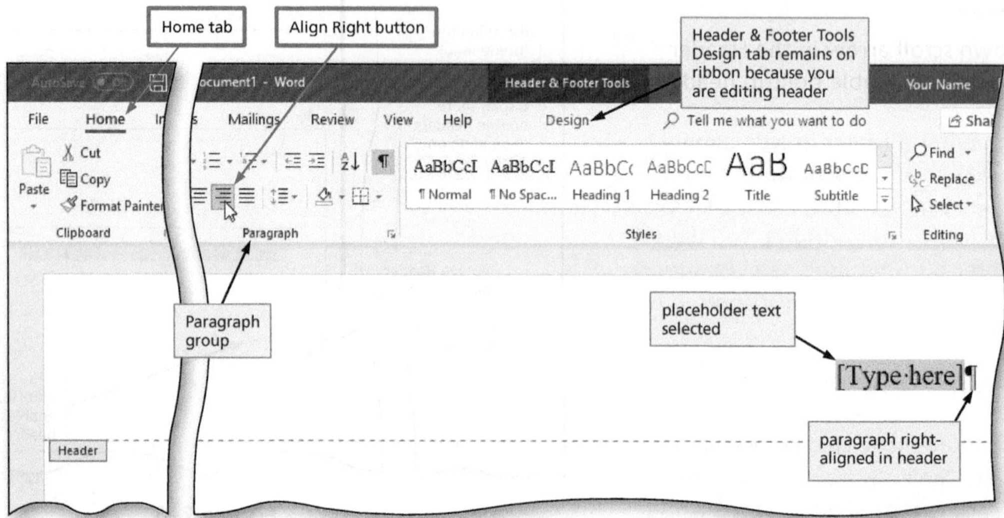

Figure 2–10

Other Ways

1. Right-click paragraph (or, if using touch, tap 'Show Context Menu' button on Mini toolbar), click Paragraph on shortcut menu, click Indents and Spacing tab (Paragraph dialog box), click Alignment arrow, click Right, click OK
2. Click Paragraph Dialog Box Launcher (Home tab or Layout tab | Paragraph group), click Indents and Spacing tab (Paragraph dialog box), click Alignment arrow, click Right, click OK
3. Press CTRL+R

To Enter Text in a Header

The following step enters the last name right-aligned in the header area.

1 With the [Type here] placeholder text selected (as shown in Figure 2–10), type **`Yazzie`** and then press SPACEBAR to enter the last name in the header.

Q&A What if my placeholder text is not selected?
Drag through the placeholder text to select it and then perform Step 1.

To Insert Page Numbers

The following steps insert a page number at the location of the insertion point and in the same location on all subsequent pages in the document. ***Why?*** *The MLA documentation style requires a page number following the last name in the header.*

1

- Click Header & Footer Tools Design on the ribbon to display the Header & Footer Tools Design tab.
- Click the Page Number button (Header & Footer Tools Design tab | Header & Footer group) to display the Page Number menu.

Q&A Why does my button name differ from the name on the face of the button in the figure?
The text that appears on the face of the button may vary, depending on screen resolution.

- Point to Current Position on the Page Number menu to display the Current Position gallery (Figure 2–11).

Experiment

- Click the down scroll arrow in the Current Position gallery to see the available page number formats.

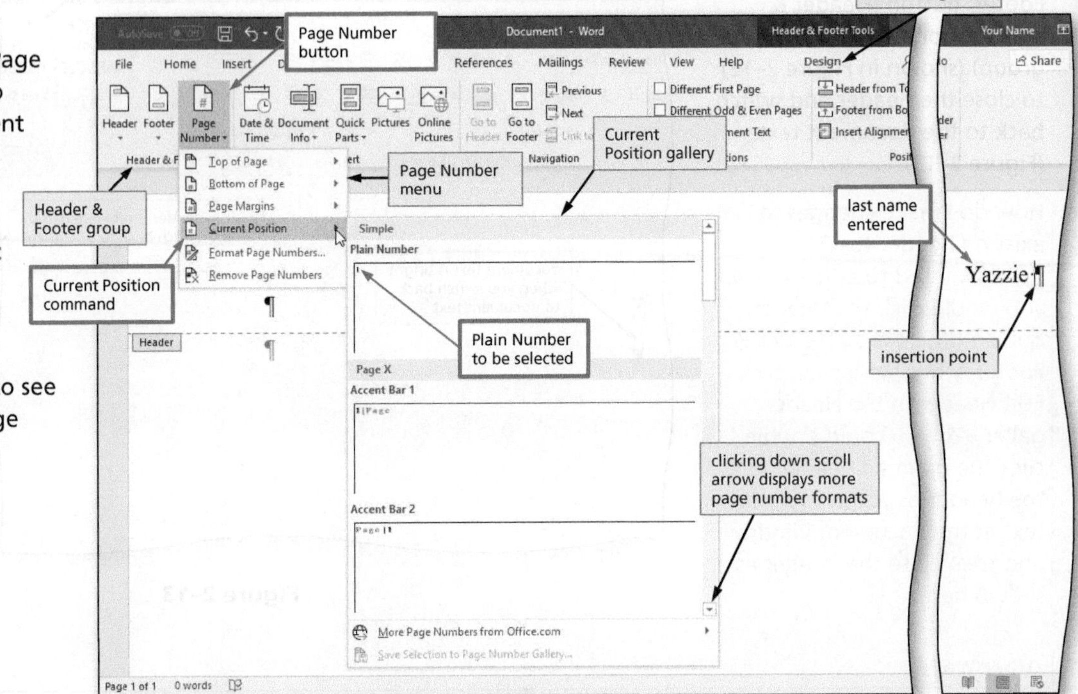

Figure 2–11

2

- If necessary, scroll to the top of the Current Position gallery.
- Click Plain Number in the Current Position gallery to insert an unformatted page number at the location of the insertion point (Figure 2–12).

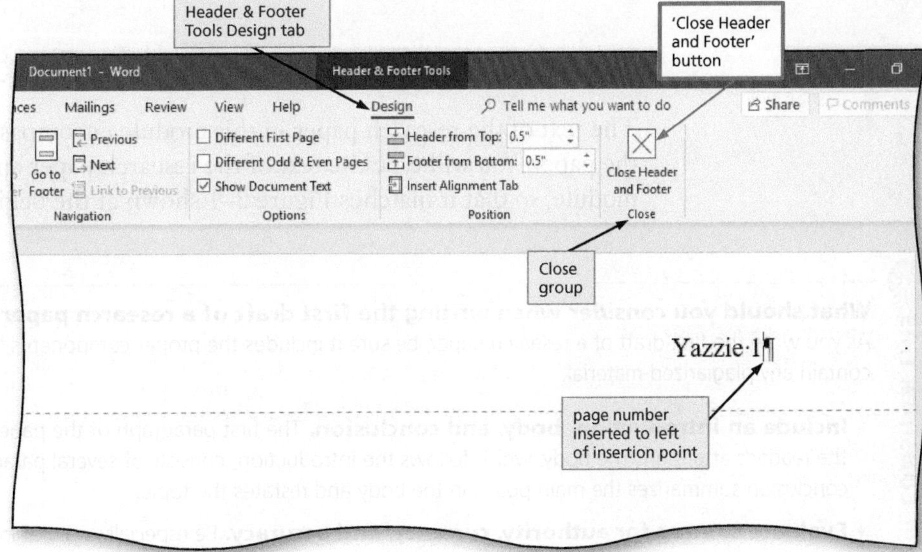

Figure 2–12

Other Ways

1. Click Page Number button (Insert tab | Header & Footer group)
2. Click Quick Parts button (Insert tab | Text group or Header & Footer Tools Design tab | Insert group), click Field on Quick Parts menu, select Page in Field names list (Field dialog box), select desired format in Format list, click OK

To Close the Header

The next task is to close the header and switch back to the document text. ***Why?*** *You are finished entering text in the header.* The following step closes the header.

1

- Click the 'Close Header and Footer' button (Header & Footer Tools Design tab | Close group) (shown in Figure 2–12) to close the header and switch back to the document text (Figure 2–13).

Q&A How do I make changes to existing header text?
If you wanted to edit a header, you would click the Header button (Insert tab | Header & Footer group) and then click Edit Header in the Header gallery, or you could double-click the dimmed header, edit the header as you would edit text in the document window, and then close the header as shown here.

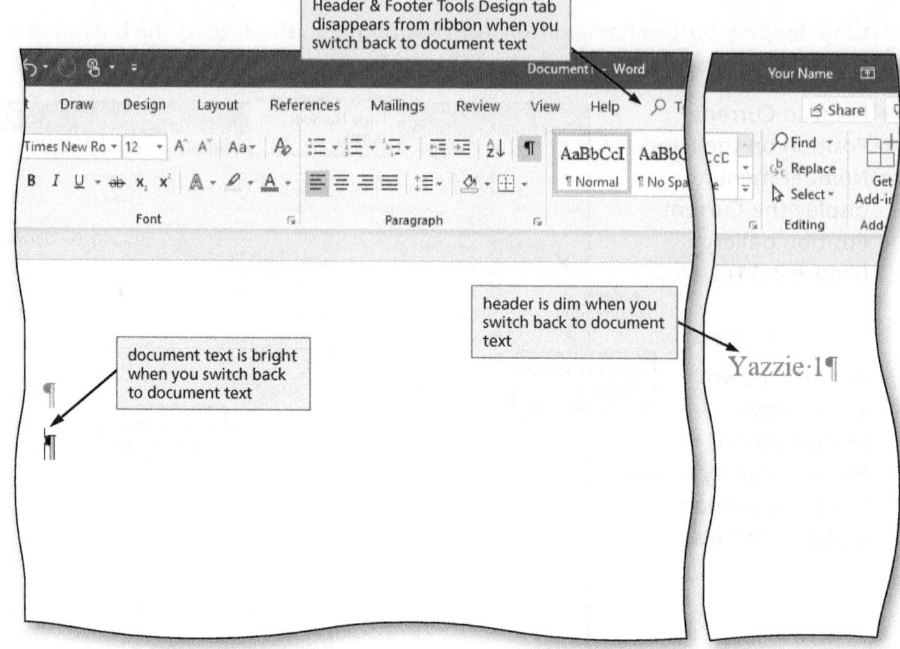

Figure 2–13

Other Ways

1. Double-click dimmed document text

Typing the Research Paper Text

The text of the research paper in this module encompasses the first two pages of the paper. You will type the text of the research paper and then modify it later in the module, so that it matches Figure 2–1 shown at the beginning of this module.

CONSIDER THIS

What should you consider when writing the first draft of a research paper?

As you write the first draft of a research paper, be sure it includes the proper components, uses credible sources, and does not contain any plagiarized material.

- **Include an introduction, body, and conclusion.** The first paragraph of the paper introduces the topic and captures the reader's attention. The body, which follows the introduction, consists of several paragraphs that support the topic. The conclusion summarizes the main points in the body and restates the topic.
- **Evaluate sources for authority, currency, and accuracy.** Be especially wary of information obtained on the web. Any person, company, or organization can publish a webpage on the Internet. When evaluating the source, consider the following:
  - Authority: Does a reputable institution or group support the source? Is the information presented without bias? Are the author's credentials listed and verifiable?
  - Currency: Is the information up to date? Are dates of sources listed? What is the last date revised or updated?
  - Accuracy: Is the information free of errors? Is it verifiable? Are the sources clearly identified?

- **Acknowledge all sources of information; do not plagiarize.** Sources of research include books, magazines, newspapers, the Internet, and more. As you record facts and ideas, list details about the source: title, author, place of publication, publisher, date of publication, etc. When taking notes, be careful not to **plagiarize**, that is, do not copy or use someone else's work and claim it to be your own. If you copy information directly, place it in quotation marks and identify its source. Not only is plagiarism is unethical, but it is considered an academic crime that can have severe punishments, such as failing a course or being expelled from school.

  When you summarize, paraphrase (rewrite information in your own words), present facts, give statistics, quote exact words, or show a map, chart, or other object, you must acknowledge the source. Information that commonly is known or accessible to the audience constitutes common knowledge and does not need to be acknowledged. If, however, you question whether certain information is common knowledge, you should acknowledge it — just to be safe.

To Enter Name and Course Information

As discussed earlier in this module, the MLA documentation style does not require a separate title page for research papers. Instead, place your name and course information in a block at the top of the page, below the header, at the left margin. The following steps enter the name and course information in the research paper.

1. With the insertion point positioned as shown in Figure 2–13, type `Nina Yazzie` as the student name and then press ENTER.
2. Type `Mr. Slobovnik` as the instructor name and then press ENTER.
3. Type `English 101` as the course name and then press ENTER.
4. Type `October 6, 2021` as the paper's due date and then press ENTER (Figure 2–14).

Q&A Why did the word, October, appear on the screen as I began typing the month name?
Word has an AutoComplete feature, where it predicts some words or phrases as you are typing and displays its prediction in a ScreenTip. If the AutoComplete prediction is correct, you can press ENTER (or, if using touch, tap the ScreenTip) to instruct Word to finish your typing with the word or phrase that appears in the ScreenTip.

BTW
Date Formats
The MLA style prefers the day-month-year (6 October 2021) or month-day-year (October 6, 2021) format.

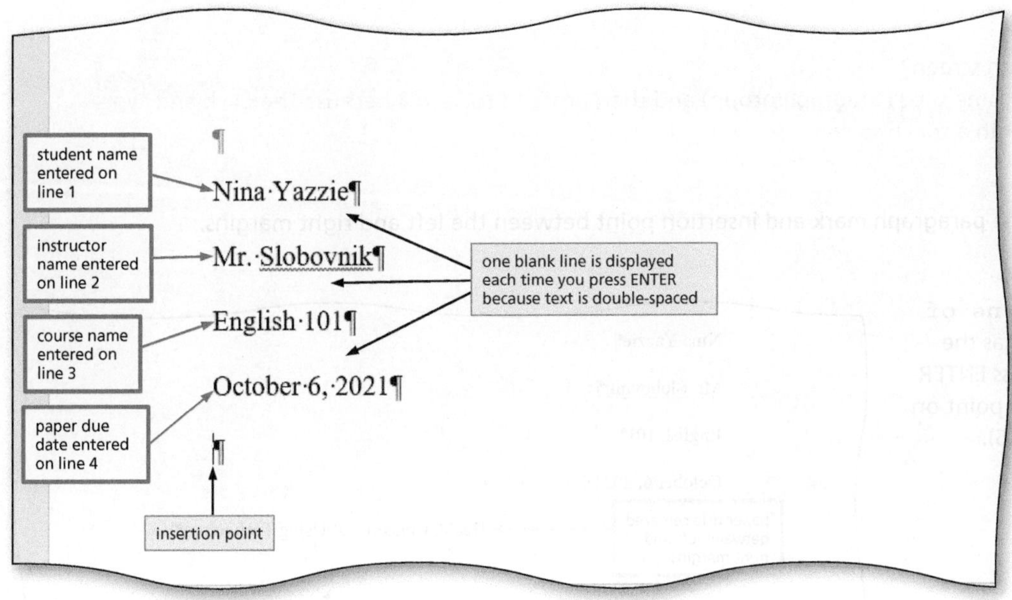

Figure 2–14

To Click and Type

The next task is to enter the title of the research paper centered between the page margins. In Module 1, you used the Center button (Home tab | Paragraph group) to center text and pictures. As an alternative, if you are using a mouse, you can use Word's Click and Type feature to format and enter text, pictures, and other objects. ***Why?*** *With **Click and Type**, you can double-click a blank area of the document and Word automatically formats the item you type or insert based on the location where you double-clicked.* The following steps use Click and Type to center and then type the title of the research paper.

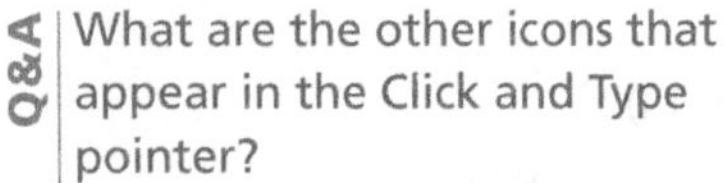

Experiment

- Move the pointer around the document below the entered name and course information and observe the various icons that appear with the I-beam.
- Position the pointer in the center of the document at the approximate location for the research paper title until a center icon appears below the I-beam (Figure 2–15).

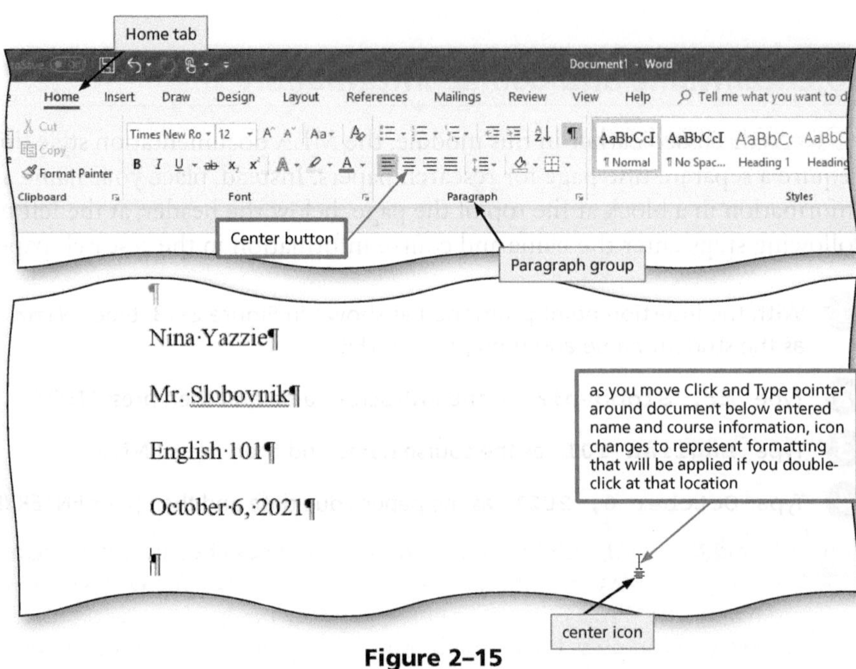

Figure 2–15

Q&A What are the other icons that appear in the Click and Type pointer?
A left-align icon appears to the right of the I-beam when the Click and Type pointer is in certain locations on the left side of the document window. A right-align icon appears to the left of the I-beam when the Click and Type pointer is in certain locations on the right side of the document window.

What if I am using a touch screen?
Tap the Center button (Home tab | Paragraph group) and then proceed to Step 3 because the Click and Type feature does not work with a touch screen.

- Double-click to center the paragraph mark and insertion point between the left and right margins.

- Type **`Health Concerns of Using Technology`** as the paper title and then press ENTER to position the insertion point on the next line (Figure 2–16).

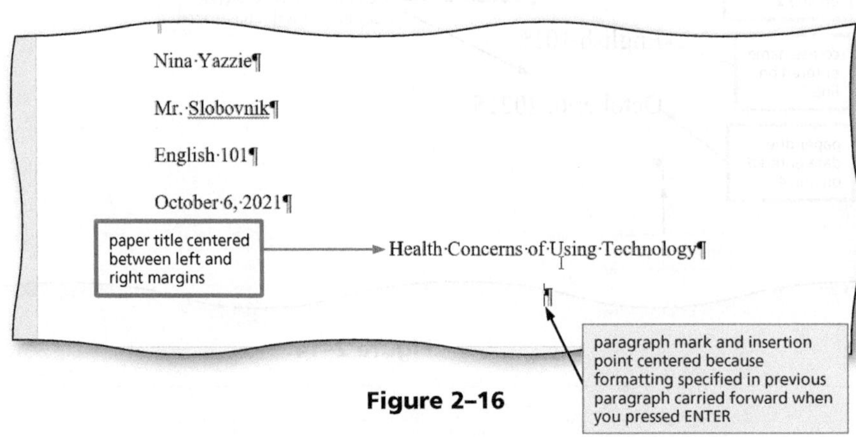

Figure 2–16

Keyboard Shortcuts for Formatting Text

Word has many **keyboard shortcuts**, sometimes called shortcut keys or keyboard key combinations, which are a key or combination of keys you press to access a feature or perform a command, instead of using a mouse or touch gestures. Many users find keyboard shortcuts a convenience while typing. Table 2–1 lists the common keyboard shortcuts for formatting characters. Table 2–2 lists common keyboard shortcuts for formatting paragraphs.

Table 2–1 Keyboard Shortcuts for Formatting Characters

Character Formatting Task	Keyboard Shortcut	Character Formatting Task	Keyboard Shortcut
All capital letters	CTRL+SHIFT+A	Italic	CTRL+I
Bold	CTRL+B	Remove character formatting (plain text)	CTRL+SPACEBAR
Case of letters	SHIFT+F3	Small uppercase letters	CTRL+SHIFT+K
Decrease font size	CTRL+SHIFT+<	Subscript	CTRL+EQUAL SIGN
Decrease font size 1 point	CTRL+[	Superscript	CTRL+SHIFT+PLUS SIGN
Double-underline	CTRL+SHIFT+D	Underline	CTRL+U
Increase font size	CTRL+SHIFT+>	Underline words, not spaces	CTRL+SHIFT+W
Increase font size 1 point	CTRL+]		

Table 2–2 Keyboard Shortcuts for Formatting Paragraphs

Paragraph Formatting	Keyboard Shortcut	Paragraph Formatting	Keyboard Shortcut
1.5 line spacing	CTRL+5	Justify paragraph	CTRL+J
Add/remove one line above paragraph	CTRL+0 (ZERO)	Left-align paragraph	CTRL+L
Center paragraph	CTRL+E	Remove hanging indent	CTRL+SHIFT+T
Decrease paragraph indent	CTRL+SHIFT+M	Remove paragraph formatting	CTRL+Q
Double-space lines	CTRL+2	Right-align paragraph	CTRL+R
Hanging indent	CTRL+T	Single-space lines	CTRL+1
Increase paragraph indent	CTRL+M		

To Format Text Using a Keyboard Shortcut

The paragraphs below the paper title should be left-aligned, instead of centered. Thus, the next step is to left-align the paragraph below the paper title. When your fingers already are on the keyboard, you may prefer using keyboard shortcuts to format text as you type it.

The following step left-aligns a paragraph using the keyboard shortcut CTRL+L. (A notation such as CTRL+L means to press the letter L on the keyboard while holding down CTRL.)

1. **Press CTRL+L to left-align the current paragraph, that is, the paragraph containing the insertion point (shown in Figure 2–17).**

Q&A Why would I use a keyboard shortcut instead of the ribbon to format text?
Switching between the mouse and the keyboard takes time. If your hands are already on the keyboard, use a keyboard shortcut. If your hand is on the mouse, use the ribbon.

BTW

Keyboard Shortcuts

To see a complete list of keyboard shortcuts in Word, press F1 to open the Help pane, type `keyboard shortcuts` in the Search box in the Word Help pane, press ENTER, and then click the 'Keyboard shortcuts for Microsoft Word on Windows' link. To create a Word document with all keyboard shortcuts, click the 'Word for Windows keyboard shortcuts' link near the top of the Help pane to open a View Downloads window, click the Open button in the View Downloads window to start Word and create a Word document with all keyboard shortcuts, and then, if necessary, click the Enable Editing button. You can print or save the Word document. When finished, exit Word and then close the Help pane.

2 Save the research paper on your hard drive, OneDrive, or other storage location using the file name, SC_WD_2_TechnologyHealthConcernsPaper.

Q&A Why should I save the research paper at this time?
You have performed many tasks while creating this research paper and do not want to risk losing work completed thus far.

To Display the Rulers

According to the MLA documentation style, the first line of each paragraph in the research paper is to be indented one-half inch from the left margin. Although you can use a dialog box to indent paragraphs, Word provides a quicker way through the **horizontal ruler**, which is a ruler that appears below the ribbon in the document window in Print Layout and other views. Word also provides a **vertical ruler** that appears along the left edge of the document window in Print Layout view. The following step displays the rulers. ***Why?*** *You want to use the horizontal ruler to indent paragraphs.*

- If necessary, scroll the document so that the research paper title is at the top of the document window.
- Click View on the ribbon to display the View tab.
- If the rulers are not displayed, click the Ruler check box (View tab | Show group) to place a check mark in the check box and display the horizontal and vertical rulers on the screen (Figure 2–17).

Q&A What tasks can I accomplish using the rulers?
You can use the horizontal and vertical rulers, usually simply called **rulers**, to indent paragraphs, set tab stops, change page margins, adjust column widths, and measure or place objects.

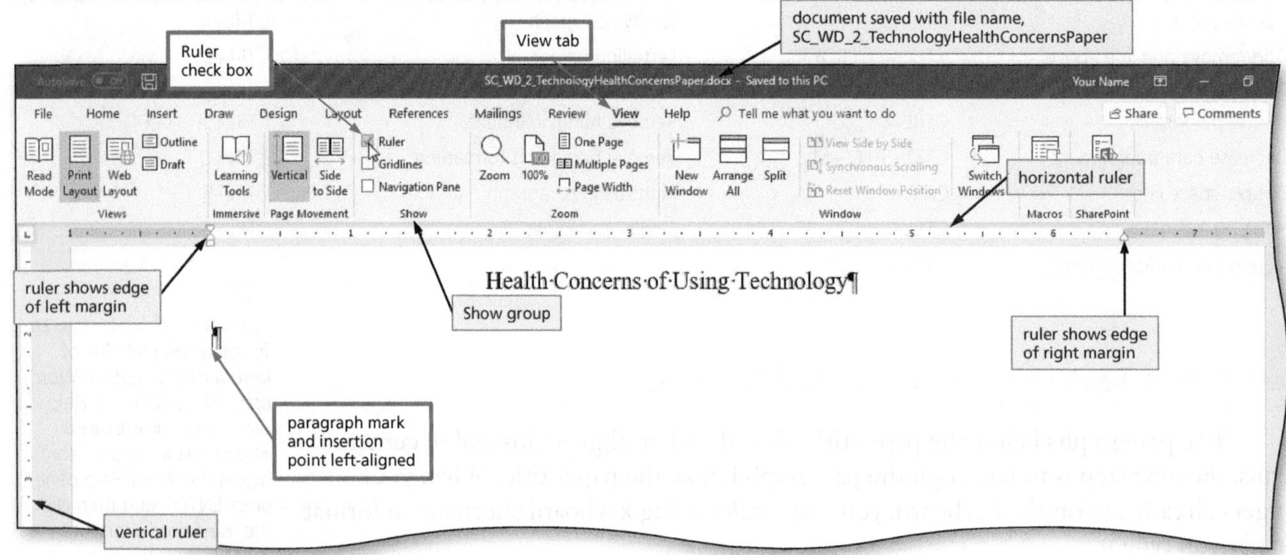

Figure 2–17

To First-Line Indent Paragraphs

If you are using a mouse, you can use the horizontal ruler to indent just the first line of a paragraph, which is called a **first-line indent**. The left margin on the ruler contains two triangles above a square. The 'First Line Indent' marker is the top triangle at the 0" mark on the ruler (shown in Figure 2–18). The bottom triangle, which is the Hanging Indent marker, is discussed later in this module. The small square at the 0" mark is the Left Indent marker. The Left Indent marker allows you to change the entire left margin, whereas the 'First Line Indent' marker indents only the first line of the paragraph.

The following steps first-line indent paragraphs in the research paper. ***Why?*** *The first line of each paragraph in the research paper is to be indented one-half inch from the left margin, according to the MLA documentation style.*

1

- With the insertion point on the paragraph mark below the research paper title, point to the 'First Line Indent' marker on the ruler (Figure 2–18).

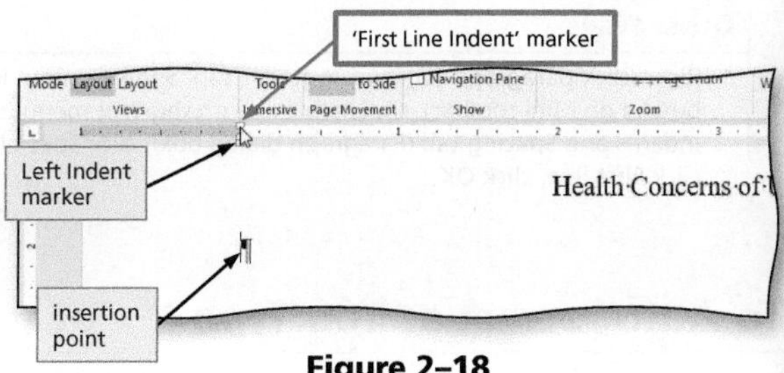

Figure 2–18

2

- Drag the 'First Line Indent' marker to the .5" mark on the ruler to display a vertical dotted line in the document window, which indicates the proposed indent location of the first line of the paragraph (Figure 2–19).

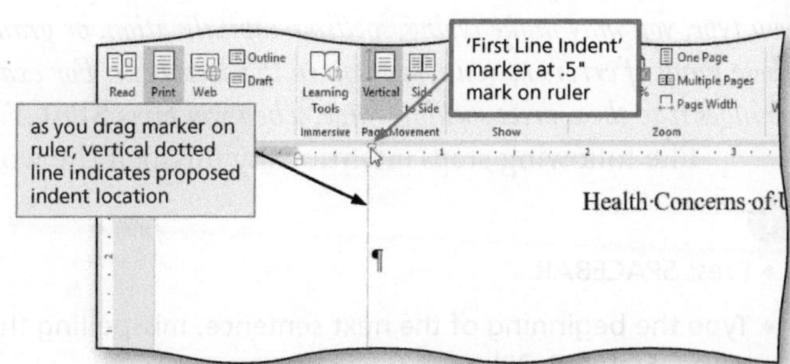

Figure 2–19

3

- Release the mouse button to place the 'First Line Indent' marker at the .5" mark on the ruler, or one-half inch from the left margin (Figure 2–20).

Q&A What if I am using a touch screen?
If you are using a touch screen, you cannot drag the 'First Line Indent' marker and must follow these steps instead: tap the Paragraph Dialog Box Launcher (Home tab or Layout tab | Paragraph group) to display the Paragraph dialog box, tap the Indents and Spacing tab (Paragraph dialog box), tap the Special arrow, tap First line, and then tap OK.

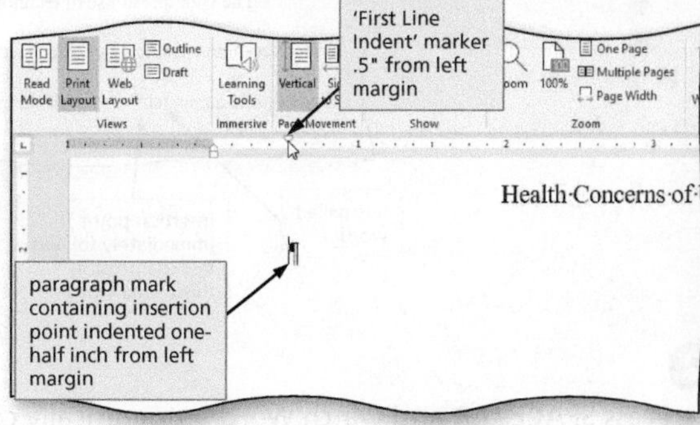

Figure 2–20

4

- Type **The widespread use of technology has led to some important user concerns. Two of the more common physical health concerns are repetitive strain injuries and hearing loss.** and notice that Word automatically indents the first line of the paragraph by one-half inch (Figure 2–21).

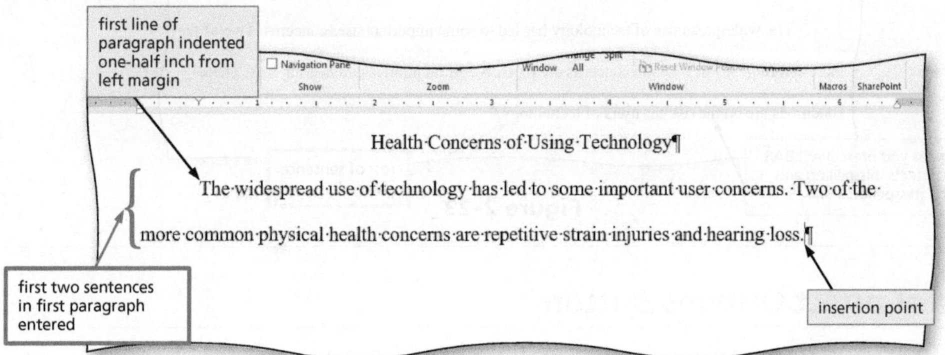

Figure 2–21

Q&A Will I have to set a first-line indent for each paragraph in the paper?
No. Each time you press ENTER, paragraph formatting in the previous paragraph carries forward to the next paragraph. Thus, once you set the first-line indent, its format carries forward automatically to each subsequent paragraph you type.

Other Ways

1. Right-click paragraph (or, if using touch, tap 'Show Context Menu' button on Mini toolbar), click Paragraph on shortcut menu, click Indents and Spacing tab (Paragraph dialog box), click Special arrow, click First line, click OK
2. Click Paragraph Dialog Box Launcher (Home tab or Layout tab | Paragraph group), click Indents and Spacing tab (Paragraph dialog box), click Special arrow, click First line, click OK

To AutoCorrect as You Type

Word has predefined many commonly misspelled words, which it automatically corrects for you. ***Why?*** *As you type, you may make typing, spelling, capitalization, or grammar errors. Word's* ***AutoCorrect*** *feature automatically corrects these kinds of errors as you type them in the document. For example, if you type the characters, ahve, Word automatically changes it to the correct spelling, have, when you press* SPACEBAR *or a punctuation mark key, such as a period or comma.*

The following steps intentionally misspell the word, the, as teh to illustrate the AutoCorrect feature.

- Press SPACEBAR.
- Type the beginning of the next sentence, misspelling the word, the, as follows: **`These conditions are on teh`** (Figure 2–22).

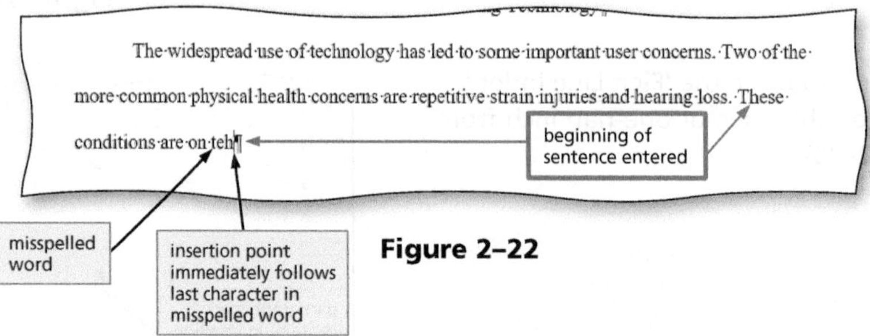

Figure 2–22

- Press SPACEBAR and watch Word automatically correct the misspelled word.
- Type the rest of the sentence (Figure 2–23): **`rise for users of technology.`**

Q&A What if I do not want to keep a change made automatically by Word?

If you notice the automatically corrected text immediately, you can press CTRL+Z or click the Undo button on the Quick Access Toolbar to undo the automatic correction. If you do not notice it immediately, you can undo a correction through the AutoCorrect Options button shown in the next set of steps.

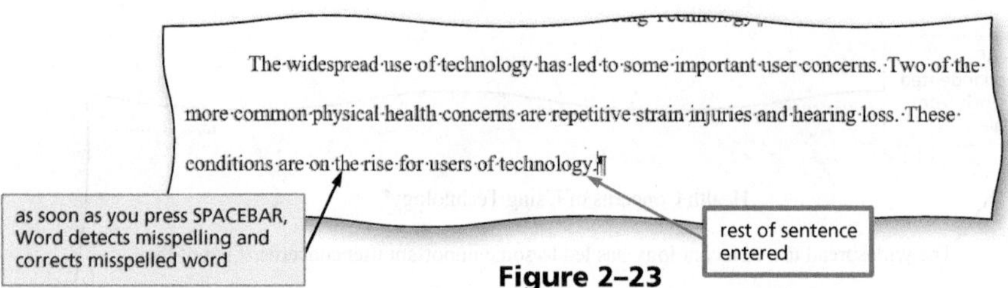

Figure 2–23

To Use the AutoCorrect Options Button

The following steps illustrate the AutoCorrect Options button and menu. ***Why?*** *If you are using a mouse, when you position the pointer on text that Word automatically corrected, a small blue box appears below the text. If you point to the small blue box, Word displays the AutoCorrect Options button. When you click the* ***AutoCorrect Options button****, which appears below the automatically corrected text, Word displays a menu that allows you to undo a correction or change how Word handles future automatic corrections of this type.*

- Position the pointer in the text automatically corrected by Word (the word, the, in this case) to display a small blue box below the automatically corrected word (Figure 2–24).

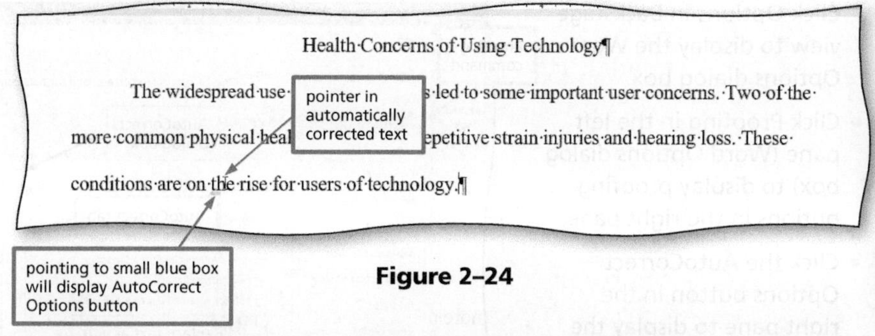

Figure 2–24

- Point to the small blue box to display the AutoCorrect Options button.
- Click the AutoCorrect Options button to display the AutoCorrect Options menu (Figure 2–25).
- Press ESC to remove the AutoCorrect Options menu from the screen.

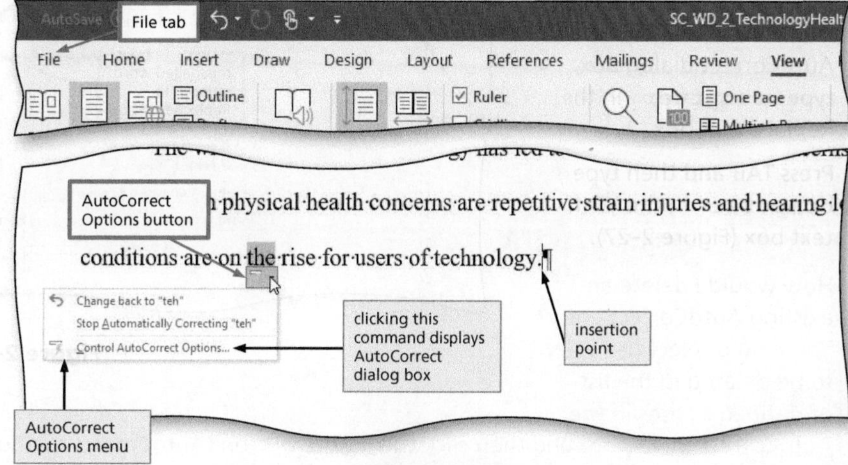

Figure 2–25

Q&A Do I need to remove the AutoCorrect Options button from the screen?

No. When you move the pointer, the AutoCorrect Options button will disappear from the screen. If, for some reason, you wanted to remove the AutoCorrect Options button from the screen, you could press ESC a second time.

To Create an AutoCorrect Entry

The next steps create an AutoCorrect entry. ***Why?*** *In addition to the predefined list of AutoCorrect spelling, capitalization, and grammar errors, you can create your own AutoCorrect entries to add to the list. For example, if you tend to mistype the word computer as comptuer, you should create an AutoCorrect entry for it.*

- Click File on the ribbon (shown in Figure 2–25) to open Backstage view (Figure 2–26).

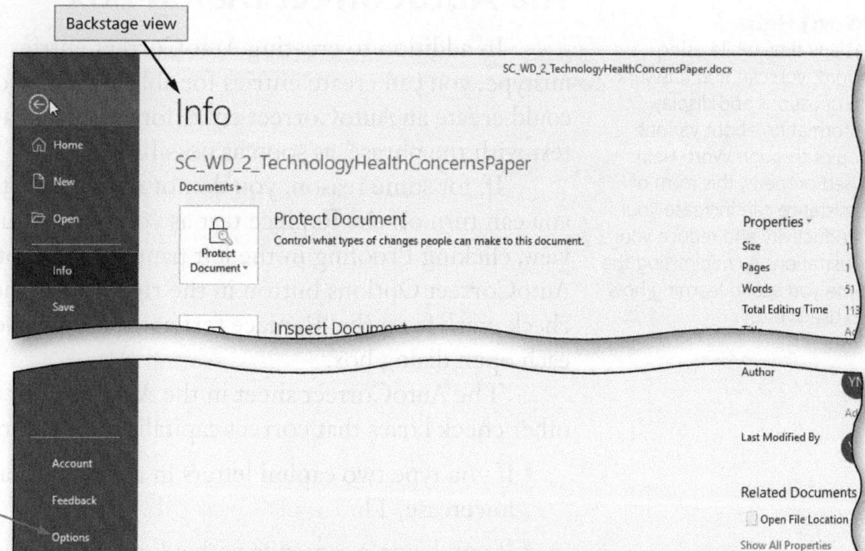

Figure 2–26

- Click Options in Backstage view to display the Word Options dialog box.
- Click Proofing in the left pane (Word Options dialog box) to display proofing options in the right pane.
- Click the AutoCorrect Options button in the right pane to display the AutoCorrect dialog box.
- When Word displays the AutoCorrect dialog box, type **comptuer** in the Replace text box.
- Press TAB and then type **computer** in the With text box (Figure 2–27).

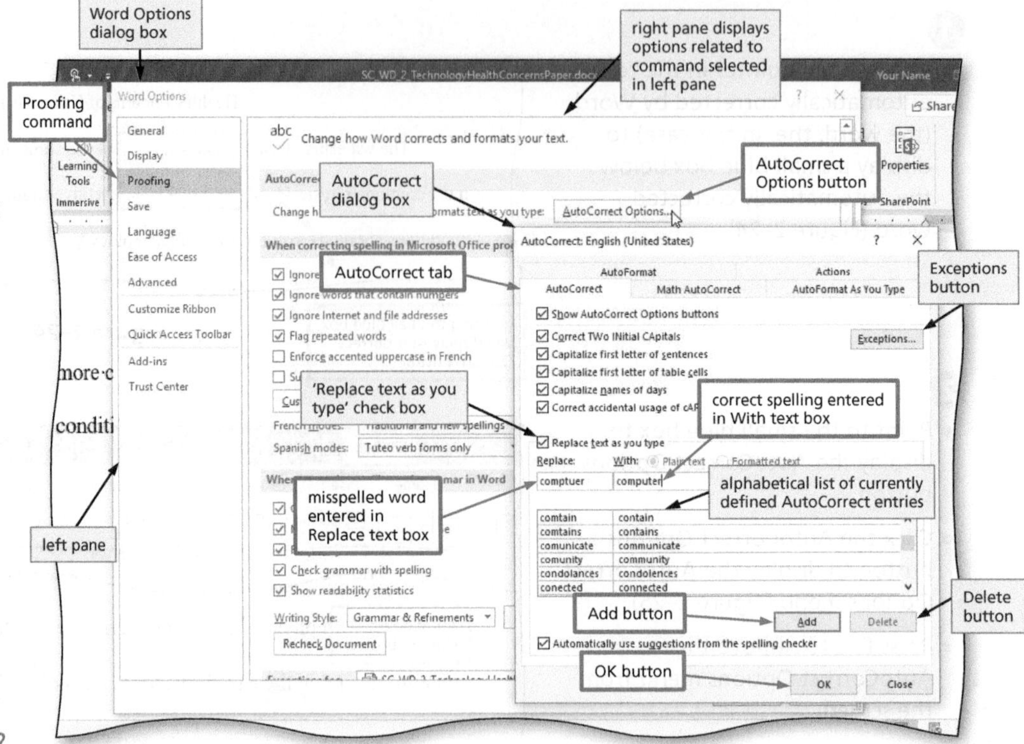

Figure 2–27

Q&A How would I delete an existing AutoCorrect entry?
You would select the entry to be deleted in the list of defined entries in the AutoCorrect dialog box and then click the Delete button (AutoCorrect dialog box).

- Click the Add button (AutoCorrect dialog box) to add the entry alphabetically to the list of words to correct automatically as you type. (If your dialog box displays a Replace button instead, click it and then click the Yes button in the Microsoft Word dialog box to replace the previously defined entry.)
- Click OK (AutoCorrect dialog box) to close the dialog box.
- Click OK (Word Options dialog box) to close the dialog box.

BTW
Word Help
At any time while using Word, you can find answers to questions and display information about various topics through Word Help. Used properly, this form of assistance can increase your productivity and reduce your frustrations by minimizing the time you spend learning how to use Word.

The AutoCorrect Dialog Box

In addition to creating AutoCorrect entries for words you commonly misspell or mistype, you can create entries for abbreviations, codes, and so on. For example, you could create an AutoCorrect entry for asap, indicating that Word should replace this text with the phrase, as soon as possible.

If, for some reason, you do not want Word to correct automatically as you type, you can turn off the Replace text as you type feature by clicking Options in Backstage view, clicking Proofing in the left pane (Word Options dialog box), clicking the AutoCorrect Options button in the right pane (shown in Figure 2–27), removing the check mark from the 'Replace text as you type' check box, and then clicking OK in each open dialog box.

The AutoCorrect sheet in the AutoCorrect dialog box (Figure 2–27) contains other check boxes that correct capitalization errors if the check boxes are selected:

- If you type two capital letters in a row, such as TH, Word makes the second letter lowercase, Th.
- If you begin a sentence with a lowercase letter, Word capitalizes the first letter of the sentence.

- If you type the name of a day in lowercase letters, such as tuesday, Word capitalizes the first letter in the name of the day, Tuesday.
- If you leave CAPS LOCK on and begin a new sentence, Word corrects the typing and turns off CAPS LOCK.

If you do not want Word to perform any of these corrections automatically, simply remove the check mark from the appropriate check box in the AutoCorrect dialog box.

Sometimes, you do not want Word to AutoCorrect a particular word or phrase. For example, you may use WD. as a code in your documents. Because Word automatically capitalizes the first letter of a sentence, the character you enter following the period will be capitalized (in the previous sentence, it would capitalize the letter a in the word, as). To allow the code, WD., to be entered into a document and still leave the AutoCorrect feature turned on, you would set an exception. To set an exception to an AutoCorrect rule, click Options in Backstage view, click Proofing in the left pane (Word Options dialog box), click the AutoCorrect Options button in the right pane, click the Exceptions button (Figure 2–27), click the appropriate tab in the AutoCorrect Exceptions dialog box, type the exception entry in the text box, click the Add button, click the Close button (AutoCorrect Exceptions dialog box), and then click OK in each of the remaining dialog boxes.

To Enter More Text

The next task is to continue typing text in the research paper up to the location of the in-text parenthetical reference. The following steps enter this text.

1. With the insertion point positioned at the end of the first paragraph in the paper, as shown in Figure 2–25, press ENTER to start a new paragraph and then type the following text: **A repetitive strain injury (RSI) is an injury or disorder of the muscles, nerves, tendons, ligaments, and joints. Technology-related RSIs include tendonitis of the wrist and carpal tunnel syndrome. Symptoms of tendonitis of the wrist include extreme pain that extends from the forearm to the hand, along with tingling in the fingers. Symptoms of CTS include burning pain in the hand, along with numbness and tingling in the thumb and first two fingers**

2. Press SPACEBAR (Figure 2–28).

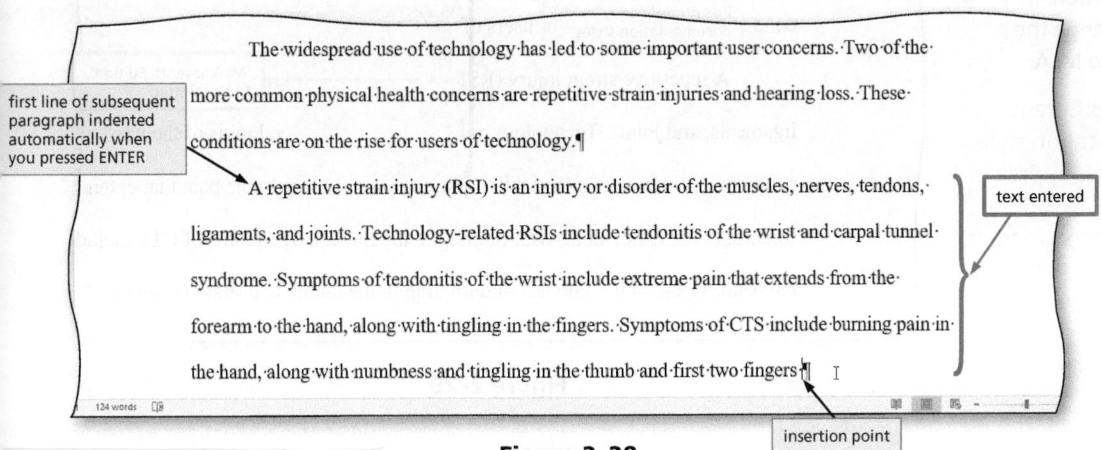

Figure 2–28

BTW

Spacing after Punctuation

Because word processing documents use variable character fonts, it often is difficult to determine in a printed document how many times someone has pressed the SPACEBAR between sentences. Thus, the rule is to press the SPACEBAR only once after periods, colons, and other punctuation marks.

Citations

Both the MLA and APA guidelines suggest the use of in-text parenthetical references (placed at the end of a sentence), instead of footnoting each source of material in a paper. These parenthetical references, called citations in Word, guide the reader to the end of the paper for complete information about the source.

Word provides tools to assist you with inserting citations in a paper and later generating a list of sources from the citations. With a documentation style selected, Word automatically formats the citations and list of sources according to that style. The process for adding citations in Word is as follows:

1. Change the documentation style, if necessary.
2. Insert a citation placeholder.
3. Enter the source information for the citation.

You can combine Steps 2 and 3, where you insert the citation placeholder and enter the source information at once. Or, you can insert the citation placeholder as you write and then enter the source information for the citation at a later time. While creating the research paper in this module, you will use both methods.

BTW
The Ribbon and Screen Resolution
Word may change how the groups and buttons within the groups appear on the ribbon, depending on the computer or mobile device's screen resolution. Thus, your ribbon may look different from the ones in this book if you are using a screen resolution other than 1366 × 768.

To Change the Bibliography Style

The first step in inserting a citation is to be sure the citations and sources will be formatted using the correct documentation style, called the bibliography style in Word. ***Why?*** *You want to ensure that Word is using the MLA documentation style for this paper.* The following steps change the specified documentation style.

- Click References on the ribbon to display the References tab.
- Click the Style arrow (References tab | Citations & Bibliography group) to display the Style gallery, which lists predefined documentation styles (Figure 2–29).

- Click 'MLA Seventh Edition' in the Style gallery to change the documentation style to MLA.

Q&A What if I am using a different edition of a documentation style shown in the Bibliography Style gallery?
Select the closest one and then, if necessary, perform necessary edits before submitting the paper.

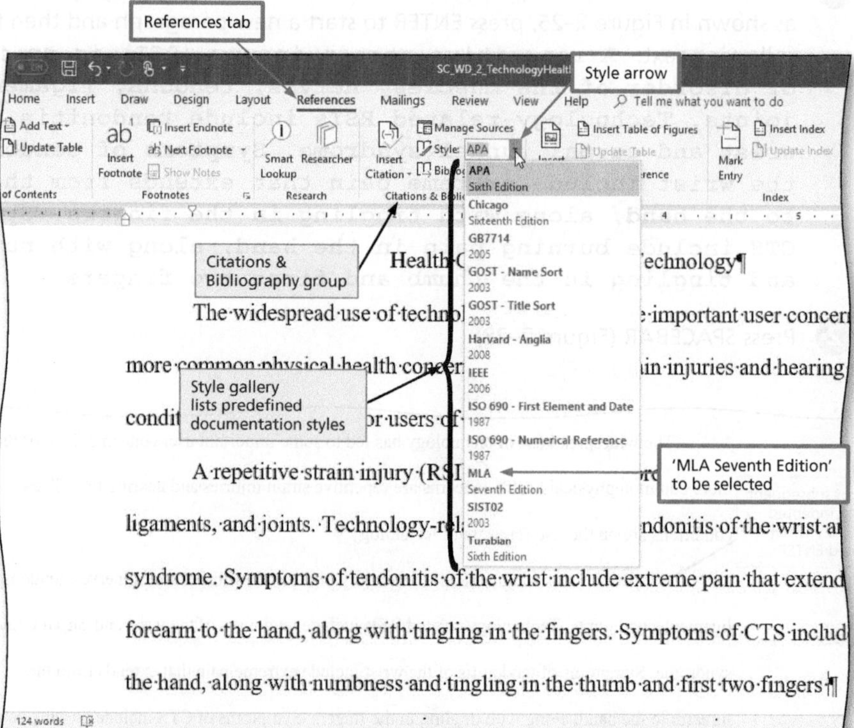

Figure 2–29

CONSIDER THIS

What details are required for sources?
During your research, be sure to record essential publication information about each of your sources. Following is a sample list of types of required information for the MLA documentation style.

- Book: full name of author(s), complete title of book, edition (if available), volume (if available), publication city, publisher name, publication year, and publication medium
- Magazine: full name of author(s), complete title of article, magazine title, issue number (if available), date of magazine, page numbers of article, publication medium, and date viewed (if medium is a website)
- Website: full name of author(s), title of website, publication date (if none, write n.d.), publication medium, and date viewed

To Insert a Citation for a New Source

With the documentation style selected, the next task is to insert a citation at the location of the insertion point and enter the source information for the citation. You can accomplish these steps at once by instructing Word to add a new source. The following steps add a new source for a magazine (periodical) article on the web. ***Why?*** *The material preceding the insertion point was summarized from an online magazine article.*

- With the insertion point at the location for the citation (as shown in Figure 2–28), click the Insert Citation button (References tab | Citations & Bibliography group) to display the Insert Citation menu (Figure 2–30).

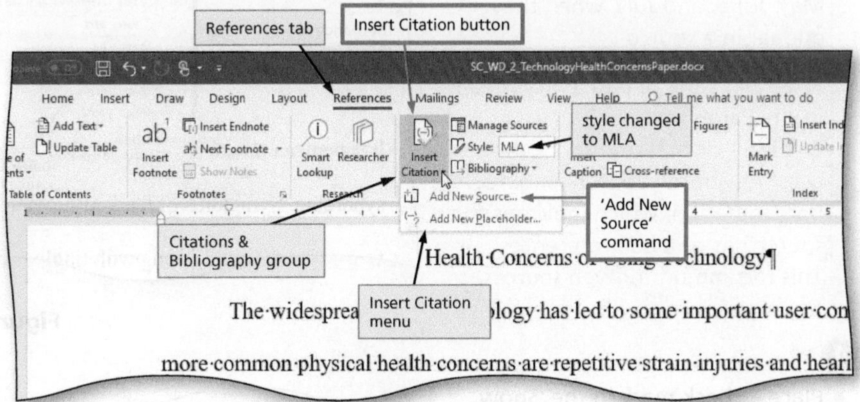

Figure 2–30

- Click 'Add New Source' on the Insert Citation menu to display the Create Source dialog box (Figure 2–31).

Q&A **What are the Bibliography Fields in the Create Source dialog box?**
A **field** is a code that serves as a placeholder for data whose contents can change. You enter data in some fields; Word supplies data for others. In this case, you enter the contents of the fields for a particular source, for example, the author name in the Author field.

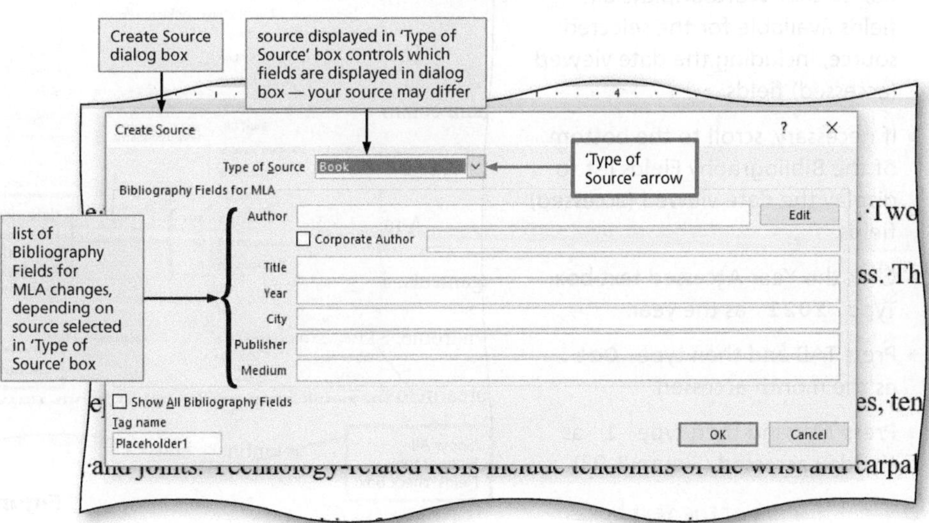

Figure 2–31

Experiment

- Click the 'Type of Source' arrow and then click one of the source types in the list, so that you can see how the list of fields changes to reflect the type of source you selected.

3

- If necessary, click the 'Type of Source' arrow (Create Source dialog box) and then click 'Article in a Periodical', so that the list shows fields required for a magazine (periodical).
- Click the Author text box. Type `Zhao, Shen Li` as the author.
- Click the Title text box. Type `Technology Aches and Pains` as the article title.
- Press TAB and then type `Monthly Medical and Review` as the periodical title.
- Press TAB and then type `2021` as the year.
- Press TAB and then type `July` as the month.
- Press TAB twice and then type `n. pag.` as the number of pages.
- Press TAB and then type `Web` as the medium (Figure 2–32).

Q&A Should the month names ever be abbreviated?

The MLA documentation style abbreviates all months, except May, June, and July, when they appear in a source.

What does the n. pag. entry mean in the Pages text box?

The MLA documentation style uses the abbreviation n. pag. for no pagination, which indicates the source has no page references. This is common for web sources.

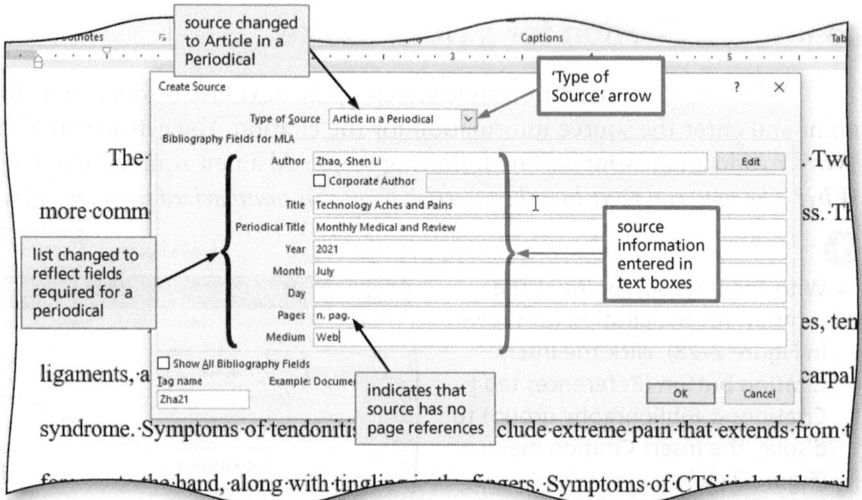

Figure 2–32

- Place a check mark in the 'Show All Bibliography Fields' check box so that Word displays all fields available for the selected source, including the date viewed (accessed) fields.
- If necessary, scroll to the bottom of the Bibliography Fields list to display the date viewed (accessed) fields.
- Click the Year Accessed text box. Type `2021` as the year.
- Press TAB and then type `Oct.` as the month accessed.
- Press TAB and then type `1` as the day accessed (Figure 2–33).

Figure 2–33

Q&A What if some of the text boxes disappear as I enter the fields?

With the 'Show All Bibliography Fields' check box selected, the dialog box may not be able to display all fields at the same time. In this case, some may scroll up off the screen.

- Click OK to close the dialog box, create the source, and insert the citation in the document at the location of the insertion point.
- Press END to move the insertion point to the end of the line, if necessary, which also deselects the citation.
- Press the PERIOD key to end the sentence (Figure 2–34).

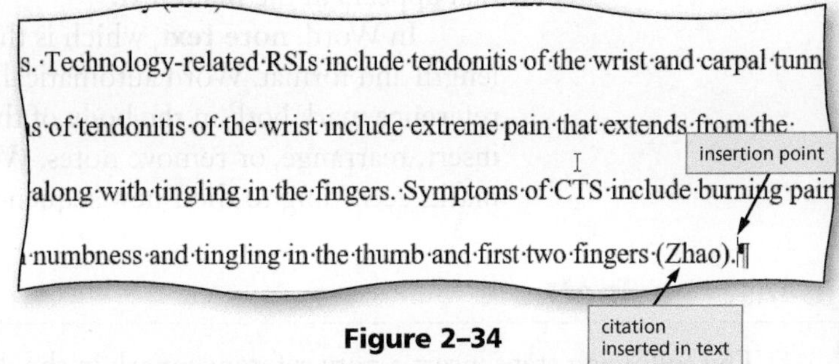

Figure 2–34

To Enter More Text

The next task is to continue typing text in the research paper up to the location of the footnote. The following steps enter this text.

1. Press SPACEBAR.
2. Type the next sentences (Figure 2–35): **`Factors that can cause these disorders include prolonged typing or mouse usage and continual shifting between a mouse and keyboard. Taking continual breaks and exercising the hands and arms can help reduce chances of developing these repetitive strain injuries.`**
3. Save the research paper again on the same storage location with the same file name.

Q&A Why should I save the research paper again?
You have made several modifications to the research paper since you last saved it; thus, you should save it again.

BTW
Organizing Files and Folders
You should organize and store files in folders so that you easily can find the files later. For example, if you are taking an introductory technology class called CIS 101, a good practice would be to save all Word files in a Word folder in a CIS 101 folder.

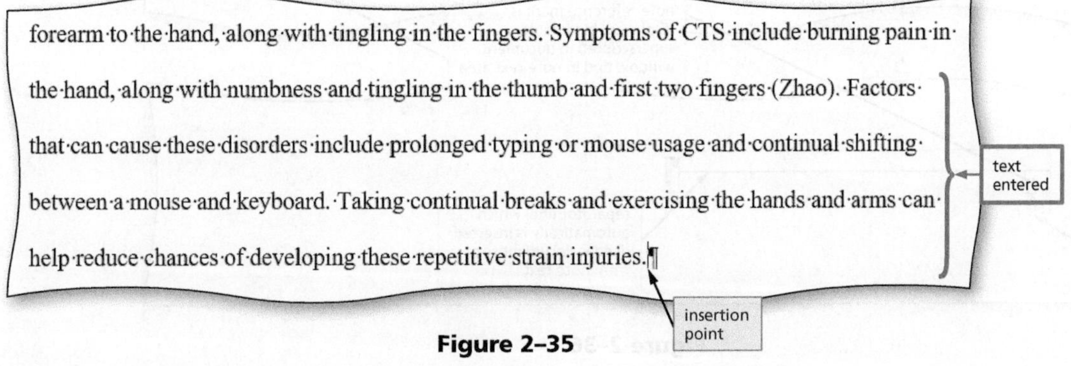

Figure 2–35

Footnotes

As discussed earlier in this module, notes are optional in the MLA documentation style. If used, content notes elaborate on points discussed in the paper, and bibliographic notes direct the reader to evaluations of statements in a source or provide a means for identifying multiple sources. The MLA documentation style specifies that a superscript (raised number or letter) be used for a **note reference mark** to signal that additional information is offered in a note that exists either as a footnote or endnote. A **footnote**, which is located at the bottom of the page on which the note reference mark appears, is text that provides additional information or acknowledges sources for text in a document. Similarly, an **endnote** is text that provides additional information or acknowledges sources for text in a document but is located at the end of a document (or section) and uses the same note reference mark that appears in the main text.

In Word, **note text**, which is the content of footnotes or endnotes, can be any length and format. Word automatically numbers notes sequentially by placing a note reference mark both in the body of the document and to the left of the note text. If you insert, rearrange, or remove notes, Word renumbers any subsequent note reference marks according to their new sequence in the document.

To Insert a Footnote

The following steps insert a note reference mark in the document at the location of the insertion point and at the location where the footnote text will be typed. ***Why?*** *You will insert a content note elaborating on the seriousness of tendonitis and carpal tunnel syndrome, which you want to position as a footnote.*

- With the insertion point positioned as shown in Figure 2–35, click the Insert Footnote button (References tab | Footnotes group) to display a note reference mark (a superscripted 1) in two places: (1) in the document window at the location of the insertion point and (2) at the bottom of the page where the footnote text will be positioned, just below a separator line (Figure 2–36).

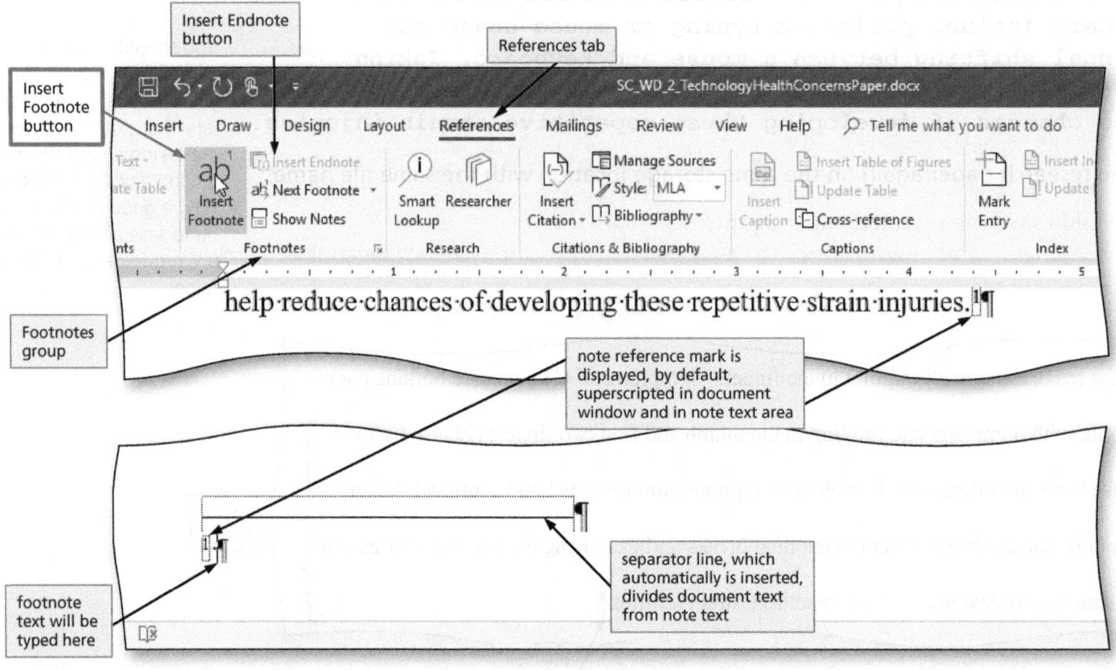

Figure 2–36

Q&A

What if I wanted notes to be positioned as endnotes instead of as footnotes?

You would click the Insert Endnote button (References tab | Footnotes group), which places the separator line and the endnote text at the end of the document, instead of the bottom of the page containing the reference.

- Type the footnote text up to the citation (shown in Figure 2–37): **`According to Clark and Nadeer, tendonitis of the wrist and carpal tunnel syndrome can lead to permanent physical damage if left untreated`** and then press SPACEBAR.

Other Ways

1. Press ALT+CTRL+F

To Insert a Citation Placeholder

Earlier in this module, you inserted a citation and its source at once. In Word, you also can insert a citation without entering the source information. ***Why?*** *Sometimes, you may not have the source information readily available and would prefer to enter it at a later time.*

The following steps insert a citation placeholder in the footnote, so that you can enter the source information later.

- With the insertion point positioned as shown in Figure 2–37, click the Insert Citation button (References tab | Citations & Bibliography group) to display the Insert Citation menu (Figure 2–37).

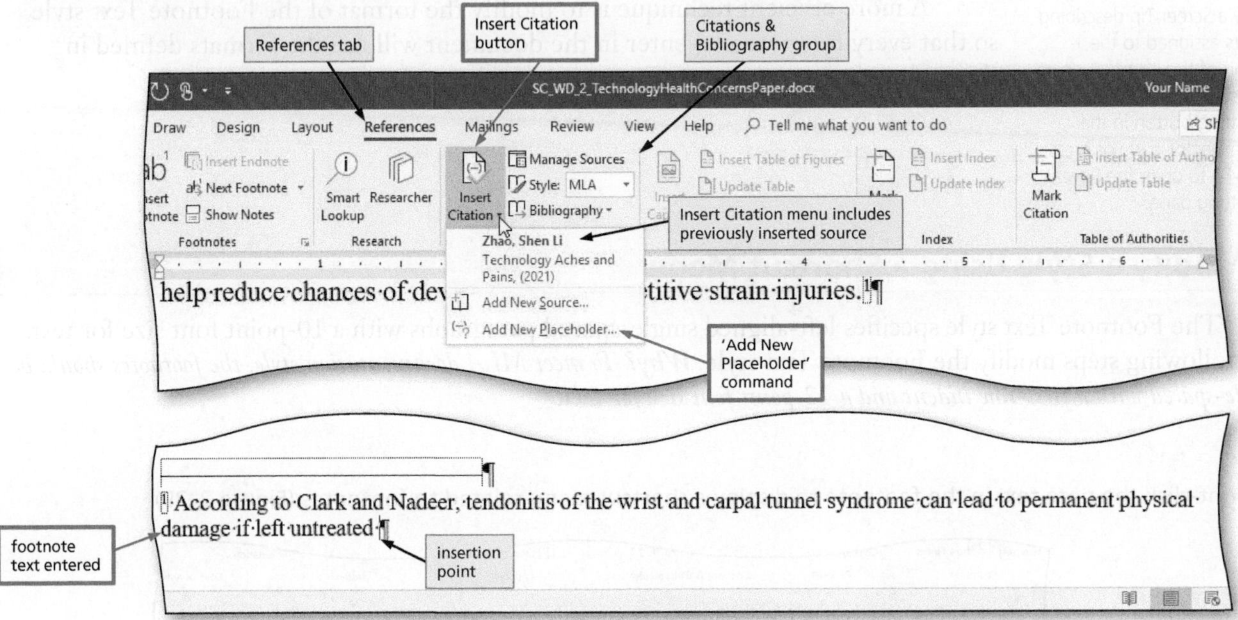

Figure 2–37

- Click 'Add New Placeholder' on the Insert Citation menu to display the Placeholder Name dialog box.
- Type `Clark` as the tag name for the source (Figure 2–38).

Q&A What is a tag name?
A tag name is an identifier that links a citation to a source. Word automatically creates a tag name when you enter a source. When you create a citation placeholder, enter a meaningful tag name, which will appear in the citation placeholder until you edit the source.

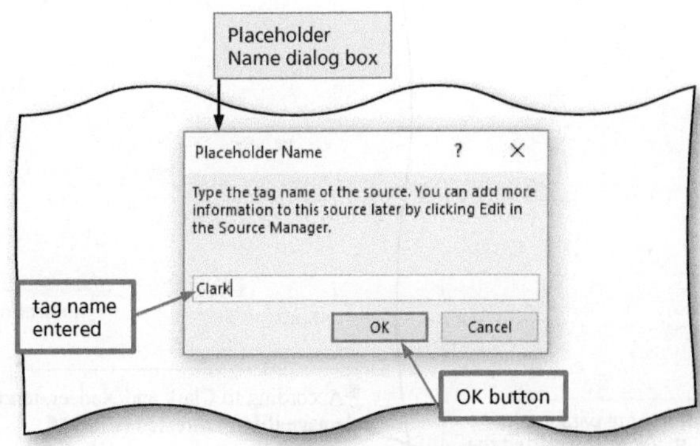

Figure 2–38

- Click OK (Placeholder Name dialog box) to close the dialog box and insert the entered tag name in the citation placeholder in the document (shown in Figure 2–39).
- Press the PERIOD key to end the sentence.

Q&A What if the citation is in the wrong location?
Click the citation to select it and then drag the citation tab (on the upper-left corner of the selected citation) to any location in the document.

BTW
Style Formats
To see the formats assigned to a particular style in a document, click the Styles Dialog Box Launcher (Home tab | Styles group) and then click the Style Inspector button in the Styles pane. Position the insertion point in the style in the document and then point to the Paragraph formatting or Text level formatting areas in the Style Inspector pane to display a ScreenTip describing formats assigned to the location of the insertion point. You also can click the Reveal Formatting button in the Style Inspector pane or press SHIFT+F1 to open the Reveal Formatting pane.

Footnote Text Style

When you insert a footnote, Word formats it using the Footnote Text style, which does not adhere to the MLA documentation style. For example, notice in Figure 2–37 that the footnote text is single-spaced, left-aligned, and a smaller font size than the text in the research paper. According to the MLA documentation style, notes should be formatted like all other paragraphs in the paper.

You could change the paragraph formatting of the footnote text to first-line indent and double-spaced and then change the font size from 10 to 12 point. If you use this technique, however, you will need to change the format of the footnote text for each footnote you enter into the document.

A more efficient technique is to modify the format of the Footnote Text style so that every footnote you enter in the document will use the formats defined in this style.

To Modify a Style Using a Shortcut Menu

The Footnote Text style specifies left-aligned single-spaced paragraphs with a 10-point font size for text. The following steps modify the Footnote Text style. ***Why?*** *To meet MLA documentation style, the footnotes should be double-spaced with a first-line indent and a 12-point font size for text.*

- Right-click the note text in the footnote to display a shortcut menu related to footnotes (Figure 2–39).

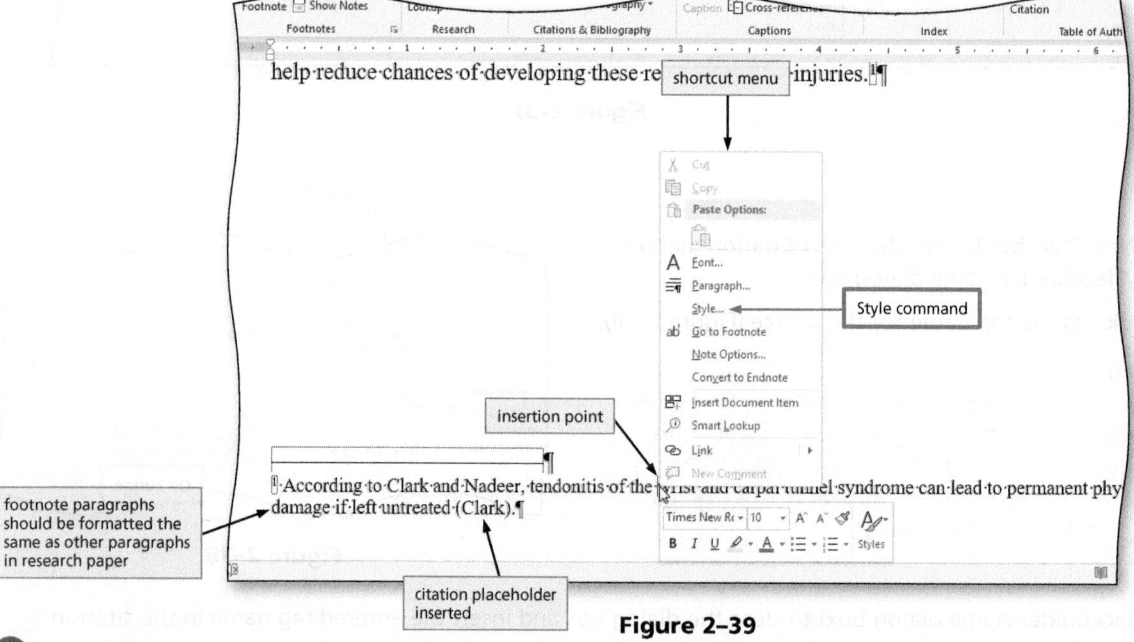

Figure 2–39

2

- Click Style on the shortcut menu to display the Style dialog box. If necessary, click the Category arrow, click All styles in the Category list, and then click Footnote Text in the Styles list to select the style to modify.
- Click the Modify button (Style dialog box) to display the Modify Style dialog box.
- Click the Font Size arrow (Modify Style dialog box) to display the Font Size list and then click 12 in the Font Size list to change the font size.
- Click the Double Space button to change the line spacing.

- Click the Format button to display the Format menu (Figure 2–40).

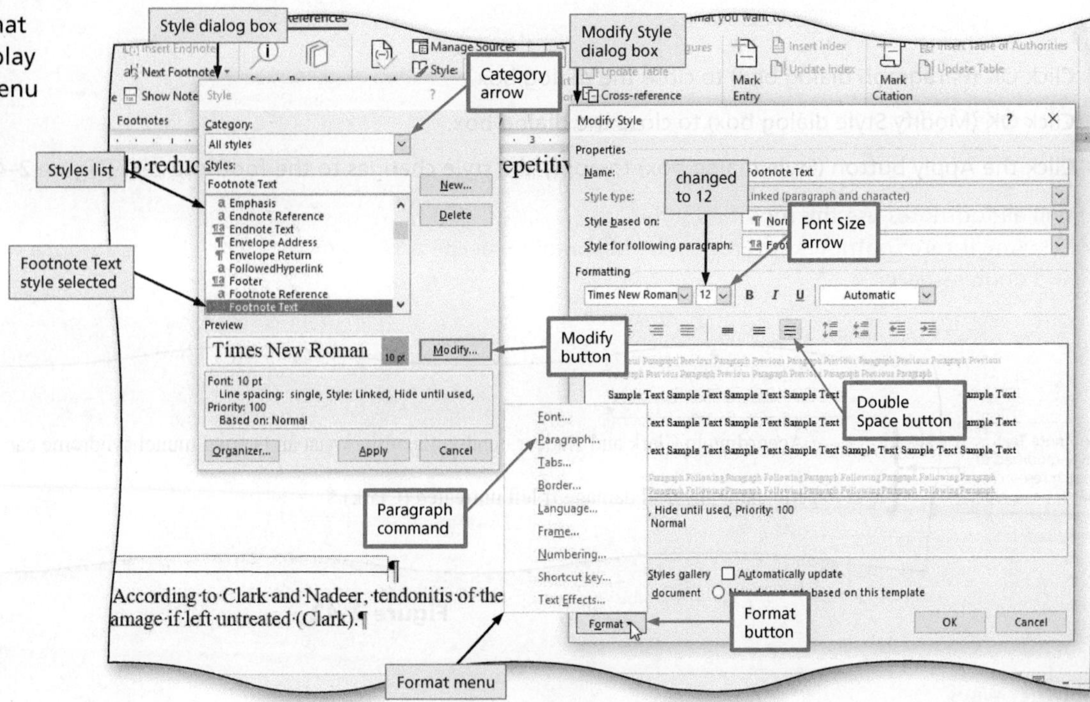

Figure 2–40

3

- Click Paragraph on the Format menu (Modify Style dialog box) to display the Paragraph dialog box.
- Click the Special arrow in the Indentation area (Paragraph dialog box) and then click First line (Figure 2–41).

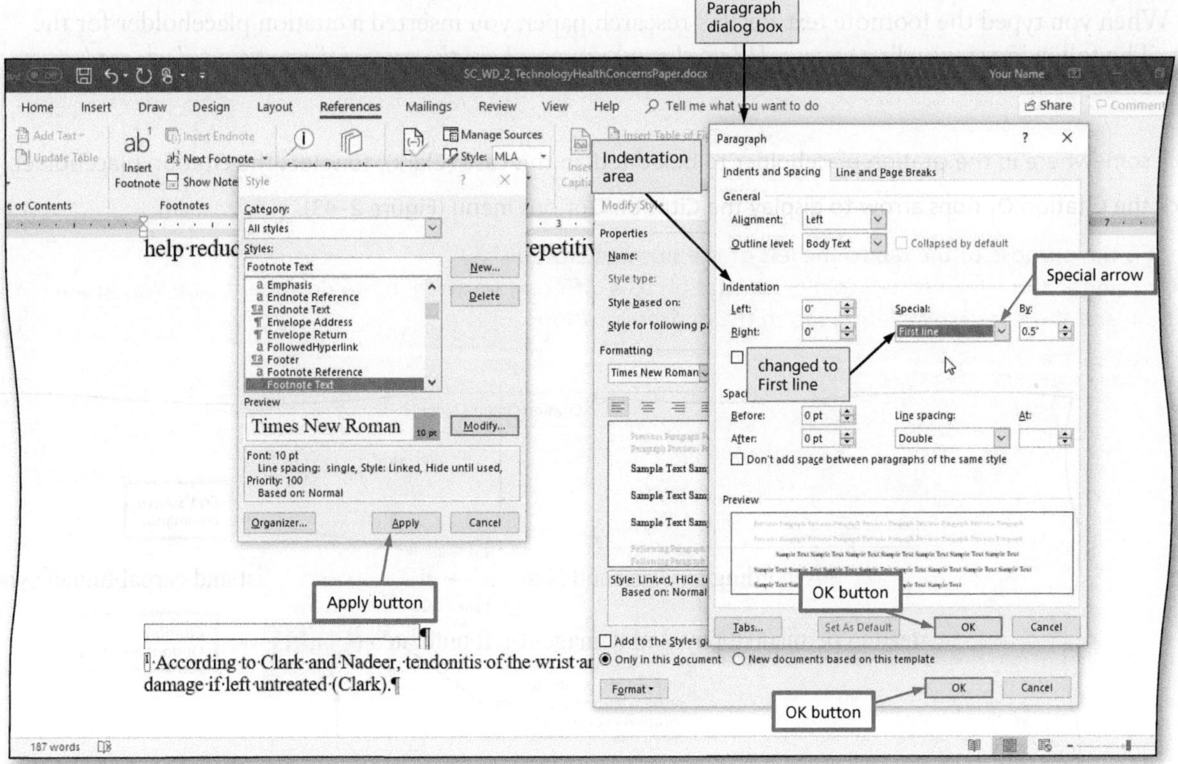

Figure 2–41

- Click OK (Paragraph dialog box) to close the dialog box.
- Click OK (Modify Style dialog box) to close the dialog box.
- Click the Apply button (Style dialog box) to apply the style changes to the footnote text (Figure 2–42).

Q&A Will all footnotes use this modified style?
Yes. Any future footnotes entered in the document will use a 12-point font with the paragraphs first-line indented and double-spaced.

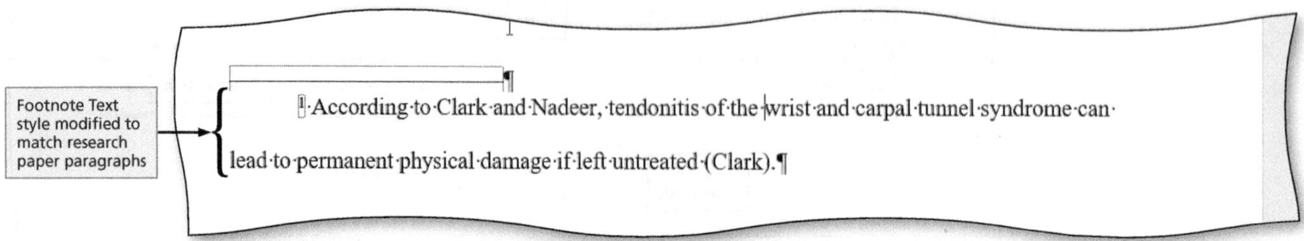

Figure 2–42

Other Ways

1. Click Styles Dialog Box Launcher (Home tab | Styles group), point to style name in list, click style name arrow, click Modify, change settings (Modify Style dialog box), click OK
2. Click Styles Dialog Box Launcher (Home tab | Styles group), click Manage Styles button in pane, select style name in list, click Modify button (Manage Styles dialog box), change settings (Modify Style dialog box), click OK in each dialog box

To Edit a Source

When you typed the footnote text for this research paper, you inserted a citation placeholder for the source. The following steps edit a source. ***Why?*** *Assume you now have the source information and are ready to enter it.*

- Click somewhere in the citation placeholder to be edited, in this case (Clark), to select the citation placeholder.
- Click the Citation Options arrow to display the Citation Options menu (Figure 2–43).

Q&A What is the purpose of the tab to the left of the selected citation?
If, for some reason, you wanted to move a citation to a different location in the document, you would select the citation and then drag the citation tab to the desired location.

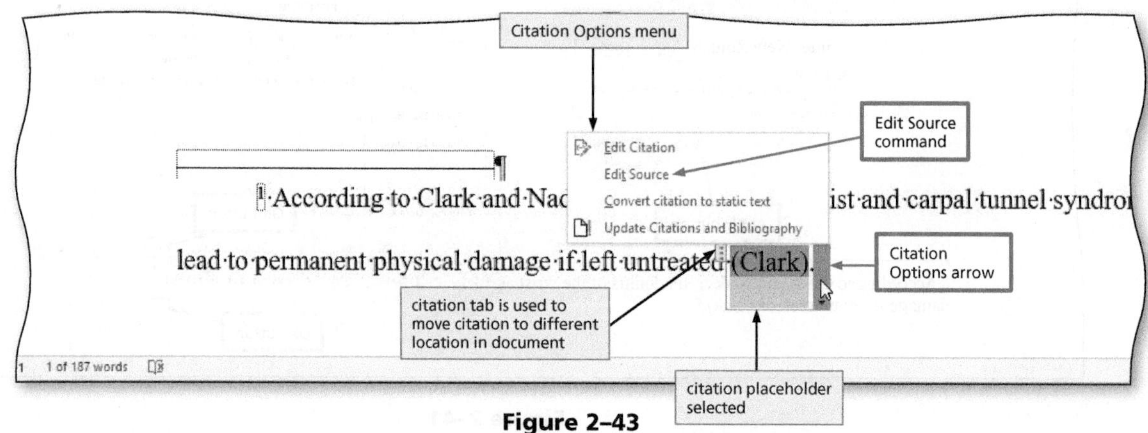

Figure 2–43

2

- Click Edit Source on the Citation Options menu to display the Edit Source dialog box.
- If necessary, click the 'Type of Source' arrow (Edit Source dialog box) and then click Book, so that the list shows fields required for a book.
- Because this source has two authors, click the Edit button to display the Edit Name dialog box, which assists you with entering multiple author names.
- Type **`Clark`** as the first author's last name; press TAB and then type **`Addison`** as the first name; press TAB and then type **`Lee`** as the middle name (Figure 2–44).

What if I already know how to punctuate the author entry properly?

You can enter the name directly in the Author box.

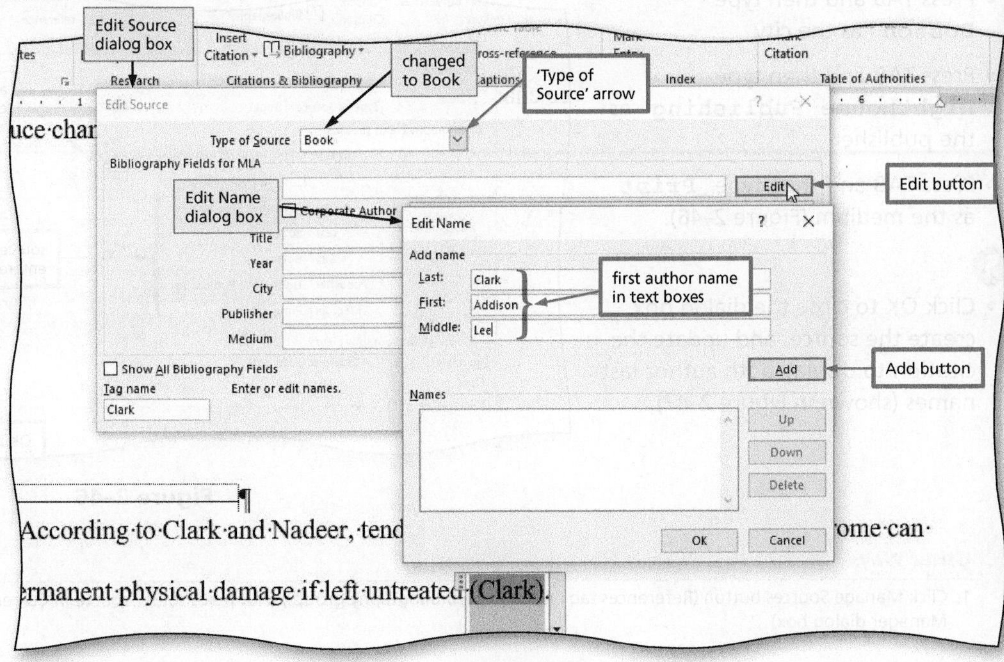

Figure 2–44

3

- Click the Add button (Edit Name dialog box) to add the first author name to the Names list.
- Type **`Nadeer`** as the second author's last name; press TAB and then type **`Aisha`** as the first name; press TAB and then type **`Sati`** as the middle name.
- Click the Add button (Edit Name dialog box) to add the second author name to the Names list (Figure 2–45).

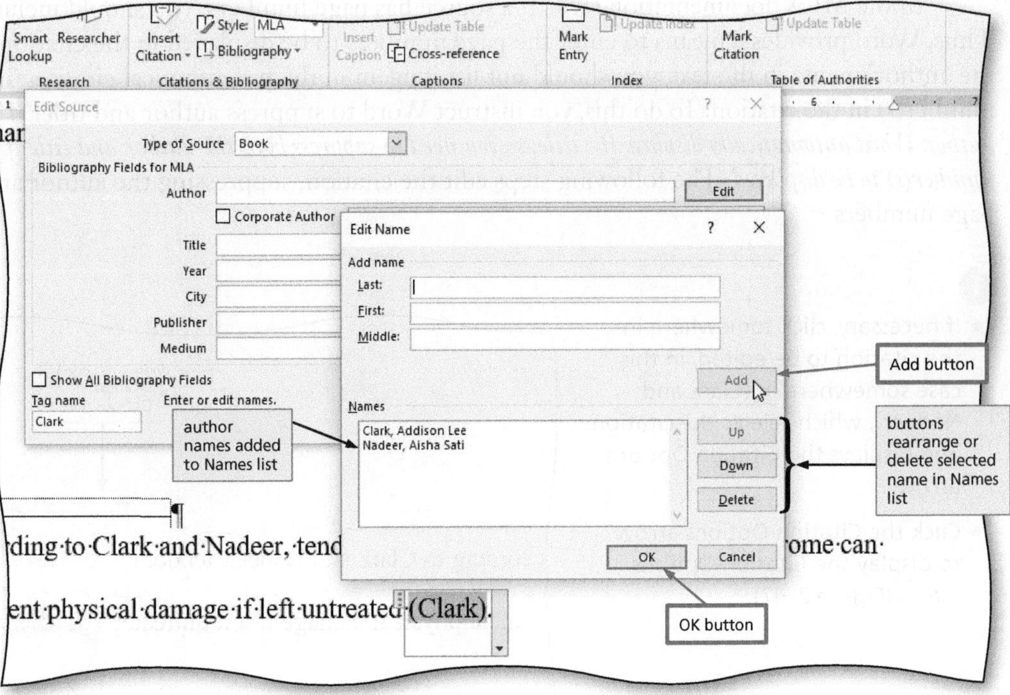

Figure 2–45

- Click OK (Edit Name dialog box) to add the author names that appear in the Names list to the Author box in the Edit Source dialog box.
- Click the Title text box (Edit Source dialog box). Type **Repetitive Strain Injuries** as the book title.
- Press TAB and then type **2021** as the year.
- Press TAB and then type **Boston** as the city.
- Press TAB and then type **Lighthouse Publishing** as the publisher.
- Press TAB and then type **Print** as the medium (Figure 2–46).

- Click OK to close the dialog box, create the source, and update the citation to display both author last names (shown in Figure 2–47).

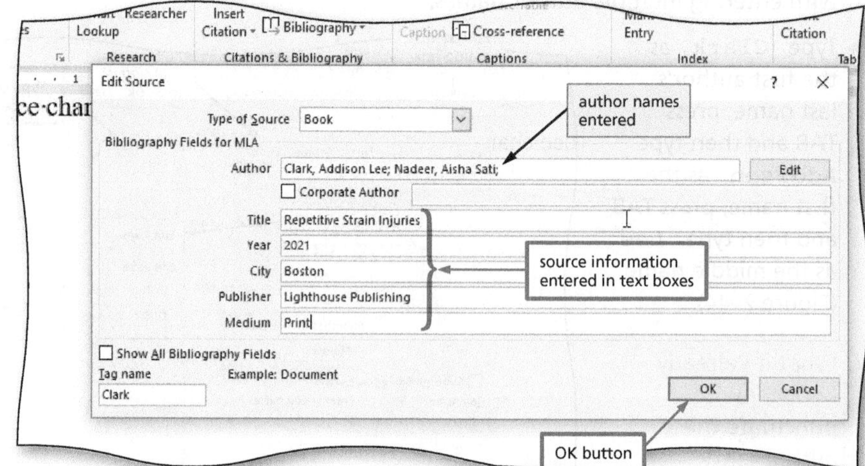

Figure 2–46

Other Ways

1. Click Manage Sources button (References tab | Citations & Bibliography group), click placeholder source in Current List, click Edit button (Source Manager dialog box)

To Edit a Citation

In the MLA documentation style, if a source has page numbers, you should include them in the citation. Thus, Word provides a means to enter the page numbers to be displayed in the citation. Also, if you reference the author's name in the text, you should not list it again in the parenthetical citation. Instead, just list the page number(s) in the citation. To do this, you instruct Word to suppress author and title. ***Why?*** *If you suppress the author, Word automatically displays the title, so you need to suppress both the author and title if you want just the page number(s) to be displayed.* The following steps edit the citation, suppressing the author and title but displaying the page numbers.

- If necessary, click somewhere in the citation to be edited, in this case somewhere in (Clark and Nadeer), which selects the citation and displays the Citation Options arrow.
- Click the Citation Options arrow to display the Citation Options menu (Figure 2–47).

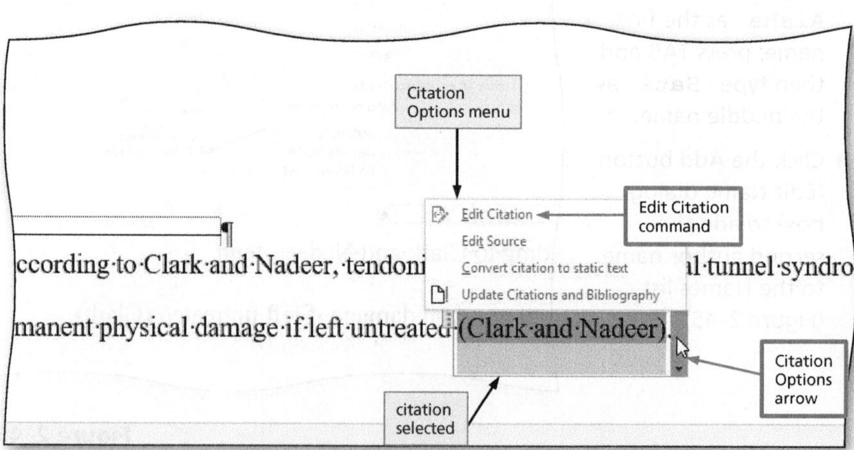

Figure 2–47

- Click Edit Citation on the Citation Options menu to display the Edit Citation dialog box.
- Type `65–66` in the Pages text box (Edit Citation dialog box).
- Click the Author check box to place a check mark in it.
- Click the Title check box to place a check mark in it (Figure 2–48).

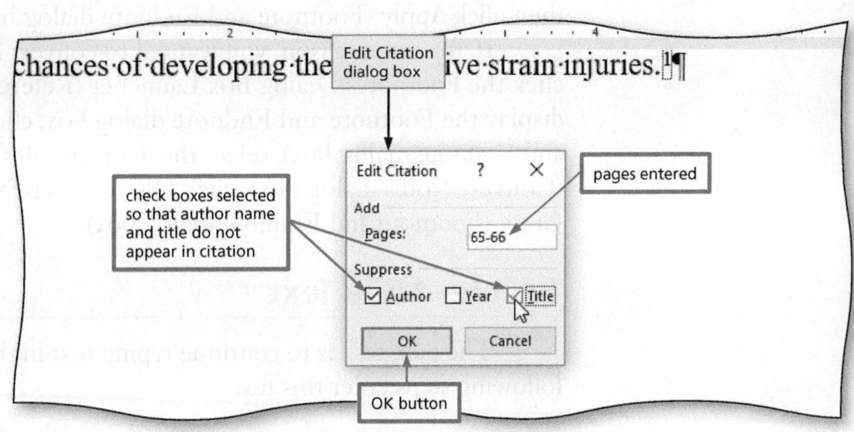

Figure 2–48

- Click OK to close the dialog box, remove the author names from the citation in the footnote, suppress the title from showing, and add page numbers to the citation.
- Press END to move the insertion point to the end of the line, which also deselects the citation (Figure 2–49).

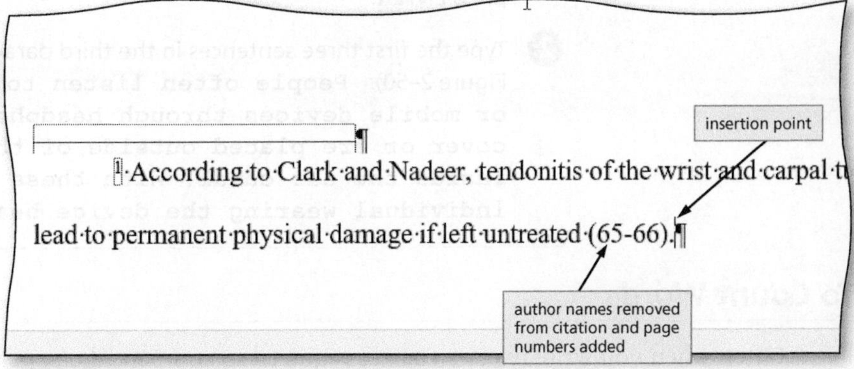

Figure 2–49

Working with Footnotes and Endnotes

You edit footnote text just as you edit any other text in the document. To delete or move a note reference mark, however, the insertion point must be in the document text (not in the footnote text).

To delete a note, select the note reference mark in the document text (not in the footnote text) by dragging through the note reference mark and then click the Cut button (Home tab | Clipboard group). Or, click immediately to the right of the note reference mark in the document text and then press BACKSPACE twice, or click immediately to the left of the note reference mark in the document text and then press DELETE twice.

To move a note to a different location in a document, select the note reference mark in the document text (not in the footnote text), click the Cut button (Home tab | Clipboard group), click the location where you want to move the note, and then click the Paste button (Home tab | Clipboard group). When you move or delete notes, Word automatically renumbers any remaining notes in the correct sequence.

If you are using a mouse and position the pointer on the note reference mark in the document text, the note text is displayed above the note reference mark as a ScreenTip. To remove the ScreenTip, move the pointer.

If, for some reason, you wanted to change the format of note reference marks in footnotes or endnotes (i.e., from 1, 2, 3 to A, B, C), you would click the Footnotes Dialog Box Launcher (References tab | Footnotes group) to display the Footnote and Endnote dialog box, click the Number format arrow (Footnote and Endnote dialog box), click the desired number format in the list, and then click Apply button.

If, for some reason, you wanted to change a footnote number, you would click the Footnotes Dialog Box Launcher (References tab | Footnotes group) to display the

BTW

Footnote and Endnote Location

You can change the location of footnotes from the bottom of the page to the end of the text by clicking the Footnotes Dialog Box Launcher (References tab | Footnotes group), clicking the Footnotes arrow (Footnote and Endnote dialog box), and then clicking Below text. Similarly, clicking the Endnotes arrow (Footnote and Endnote dialog box) enables you to change the location of endnotes from the end of the document to the end of a section.

Footnote and Endnote dialog box, enter the desired number in the Start at box, and then click Apply (Footnote and Endnote dialog box).

If, for some reason, you wanted to convert footnotes to endnotes, you would click the Footnotes Dialog Box Launcher (References tab | Footnotes group) to display the Footnote and Endnote dialog box, click the Convert button (Footnote and Endnote dialog box), select the 'Convert all footnotes to endnotes' option button (Convert Notes dialog box), click OK (Convert Notes dialog box), and then click Close (Footnote and Endnote dialog box).

To Enter More Text

The next task is to continue typing text in the body of the research paper. The following steps enter this text.

1. Position the insertion point after the note reference mark in the document and then press ENTER.

2. Type the first three sentences in the third paragraph of the research paper (shown in Figure 2–50): **`People often listen to sounds from their computers or mobile devices through headphones or earbuds. Headphones cover or are placed outside of the ear, whereas earbuds rest inside the ear canal. With these auditory devices, only the individual wearing the device hears the sound.`**

To Count Words

Often when you write papers, you are required to compose the papers with a minimum number of words. The minimum requirement for the research paper in this module is 275 words. You can look on the status bar and see the total number of words thus far in a document. For example, Figure 2–50 shows the research paper has 231 words, but you are not sure if that count includes the words in your footnote. The following steps display the Word Count dialog box. ***Why?*** *You want to verify that the footnote text is included in the count.*

1

- Click the Word Count indicator on the status bar to display the Word Count dialog box.
- If necessary, place a check mark in the 'Include textboxes, footnotes and endnotes' check box (Word Count dialog box) (Figure 2–50).

Q&A Why do the statistics in my Word Count dialog box differ from those in Figure 2–50?
Depending on the accuracy of your typing, your statistics may differ.

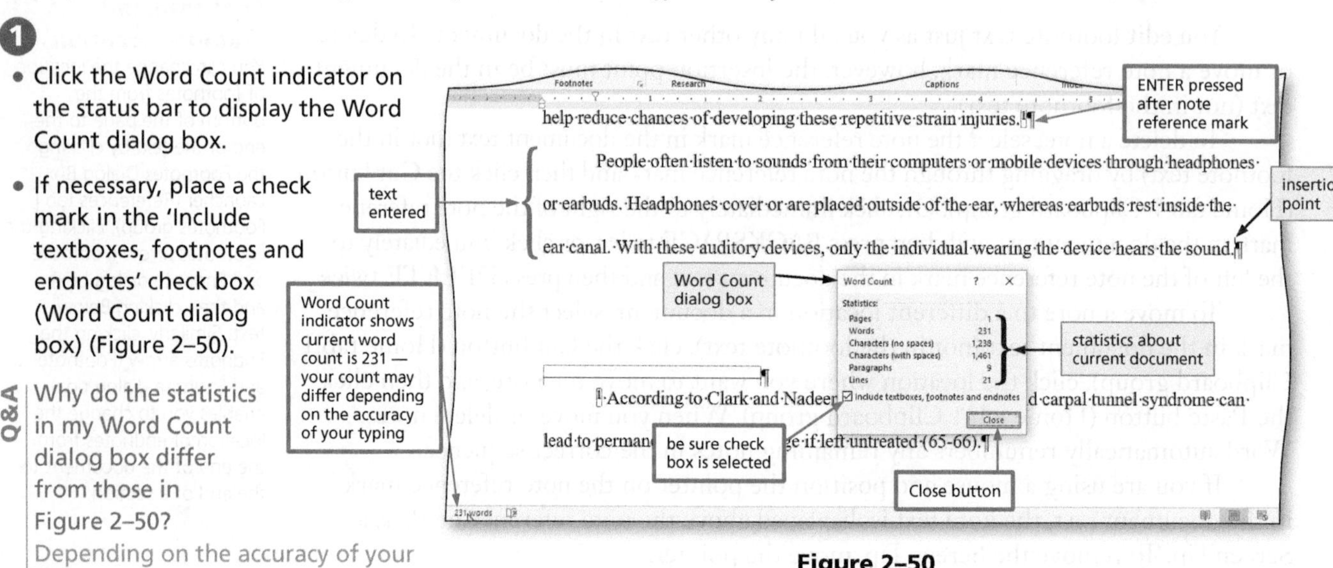

Figure 2–50

2

- Click the Close button (Word Count dialog box) to close the dialog box.

Q&A Can I display statistics for just a section of the document?
Yes. Select the section and then click the Word Count indicator on the status bar to display statistics about the selected text.

Other Ways

1. Click Word Count button (Review tab | Proofing group)
2. Press CTRL+SHIFT+G

Automatic Page Breaks

As you type documents that exceed one page, Word automatically inserts page breaks at the bottom of a page, called **automatic page breaks** or **soft page breaks,** when it determines the text has filled one page according to paper size, margin settings, line spacing, and other settings. If you add text, delete text, or modify text on a page, Word recalculates the location of automatic page breaks and adjusts them accordingly.

Word performs page recalculation between the keystrokes, that is, in between the pauses in your typing. Thus, Word refers to the automatic page break task as **background repagination.** An automatic page break will occur in the next set of steps.

BTW
Page Break Locations
As you type, your page break may occur at different locations depending on Word settings and the type of printer connected to the computer.

To Enter More Text and Insert a Citation Placeholder

The next task is to type the remainder of the third paragraph in the body of the research paper. The following steps enter this text and a citation placeholder at the end of the paragraph.

1. With the insertion point positioned at the end of the third sentence in the third paragraph, as shown in Figure 2–50, press SPACEBAR.
2. Type the rest of the third paragraph: `By using high-quality auditory devices that provide a close fit and include noise-cancelling technology, users can lower the volume level on these devices. Lower volumes can help to minimize potential hering loss` and then press SPACEBAR.

Q&A

Why does the text move from the second page to the first page as I am typing?
Word, by default, will not allow the first line of a paragraph to appear by itself at the bottom of a page (an **orphan**) or the last line of a paragraph to appear by itself at the top of a page (a **widow**). As you type, Word adjusts the placement of the paragraph to avoid orphans and widows.

Why is the word, hering, misspelled?
Later in this module, you will use Word's check spelling and grammar at once feature to check the entire document for errors.

3. Click the Insert Citation button (References tab | Citations & Bibliography group) to display the Insert Citation menu. Click 'Add New Placeholder' on the Insert Citation menu to display the Placeholder Name dialog box.
4. Type `Sanchez` as the tag name for the source.
5. Click OK (Placeholder Name dialog box) to close the dialog box and insert the tag name in the citation placeholder.
6. Press the PERIOD key to end the sentence (shown in Figure 2–51).

To Hide and Show White Space

With the page break and header, it is difficult to see the entire third paragraph at once on the screen. With the screen in Print Layout view, you can hide white space, which is the space that is displayed at the top and bottom of pages (including headers and footers) and also the space between pages. The following steps hide white space, if your screen displays it, and then shows white space. ***Why?*** *You want to see as much of the third paragraph as possible at once, which spans the bottom of the first page and the top of the second page.*

- Position the pointer in the document window in the space between pages so that the pointer changes to a 'Hide White Space' button (Figure 2–51).

Q&A What if I am using a touch screen?
Proceed to step 2.

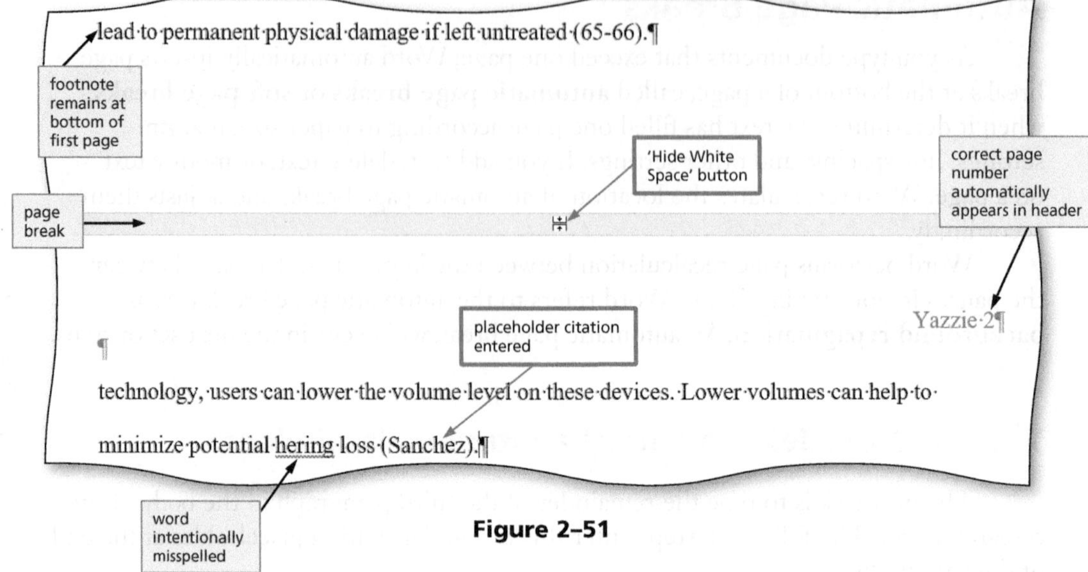

Figure 2–51

- Double-click while the pointer is a 'Hide White Space' button to hide white space.
- If necessary, scroll so that both pages appear in the document window at once.

Q&A What if I am using a touch screen?
Double-tap in the space between pages.

Does hiding white space have any effect on the printed document?
No.

- Position the pointer in the document window on the page break between pages so that the pointer changes to a 'Show White Space' button (Figure 2–52).

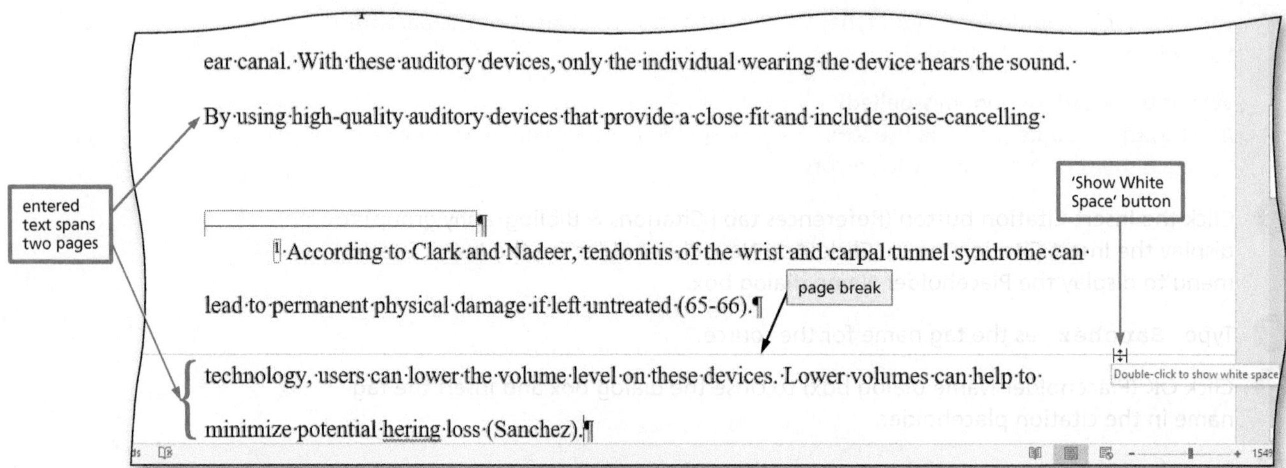

Figure 2–52

- Double-click while the pointer is a 'Show White Space' button to show white space.

Q&A What if I am using a touch screen?
Double-tap the page break.

Other Ways

1. Click File on ribbon, click Options in Backstage view, click Display in left pane (Word Options dialog box), remove or select check mark from 'Show white space between pages in Print Layout view' check box, click OK

To Edit a Source

When you typed the third paragraph of the research paper, you inserted a citation placeholder, Sanchez, for the source. You now have the source information, which is for a website, and are ready to enter it. The following steps edit the source for the Sanchez citation placeholder.

1. Click somewhere in the citation placeholder to be edited, in this case (Sanchez), to select the citation placeholder.
2. Click the Citation Options arrow to display the Citation Options menu.
3. Click Edit Source on the Citation Options menu to display the Edit Source dialog box.
4. If necessary, click the 'Type of Source' arrow (Edit Source dialog box); scroll to and then click Web site, so that the list shows fields required for a Web site.
5. Click the Author text box. Type `Sanchez, Jorge Mario` as the author.
6. Click the 'Name of Web Page' text box. Type `Technology and Your Hearing` as the webpage name.
7. Click the Year Accessed text box. Type `2021` as the year accessed.
8. Press TAB and then type `Oct.` as the month accessed.
9. Press TAB and then type `1` as the day accessed.
10. Press TAB and then type `Web` as the Medium (Figure 2–53).

Q&A Do I need to enter a web address (URL)?
The latest MLA documentation style update does not require the web address in the source.

11. Click OK to close the dialog box and create the source.

BTW
Touch Screen Differences
The Office and Windows interfaces may vary if you are using a touch screen. For this reason, you might notice that the function or appearance of your touch screen differs slightly from this module's presentation.

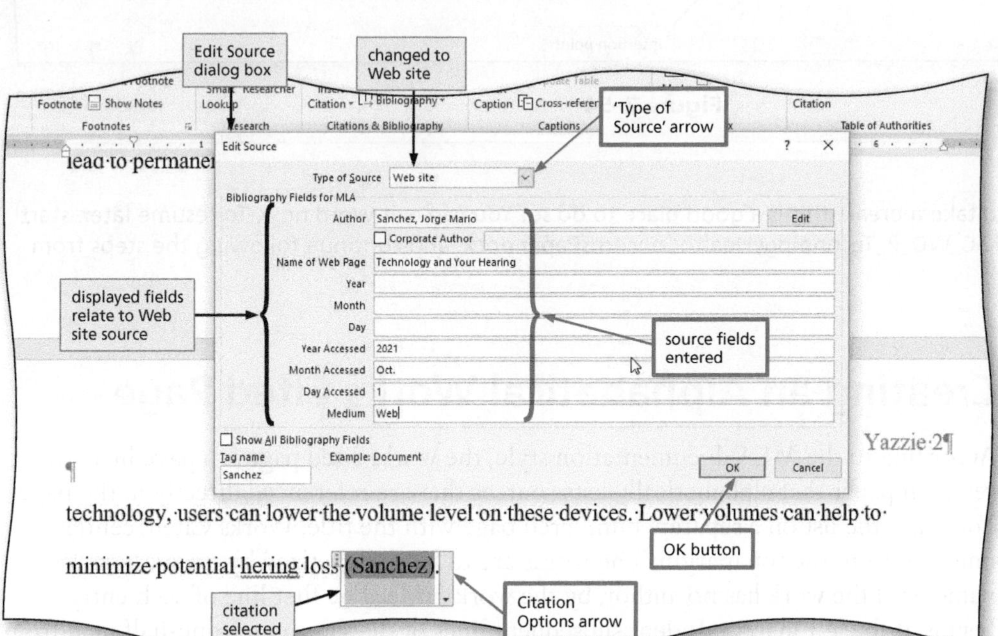

Figure 2–53

To Enter More Text

The next task is to type the last paragraph of text in the research paper. The following steps enter this text.

1. Press END to position the insertion point at the end of the third paragraph and then press ENTER.
2. Type the last paragraph of the research paper (Figure 2–54): **`Physical conditions associated with using technology include tendonitis of the wrist, carpal tunnel syndrome, and also hearing loss. Users should take as many preventative measures as possible to avoid these conditions.`**

   Q&A Why do the words, and also, have a gold dotted underline below them?
   The gold dotted underline indicates that Word can present a suggestion for more concise writing or different word usage. Later in this module, you will use Word's check spelling and grammar at once feature to check the entire document for flagged text.

3. Save the research paper again on the same storage location with the same file name.

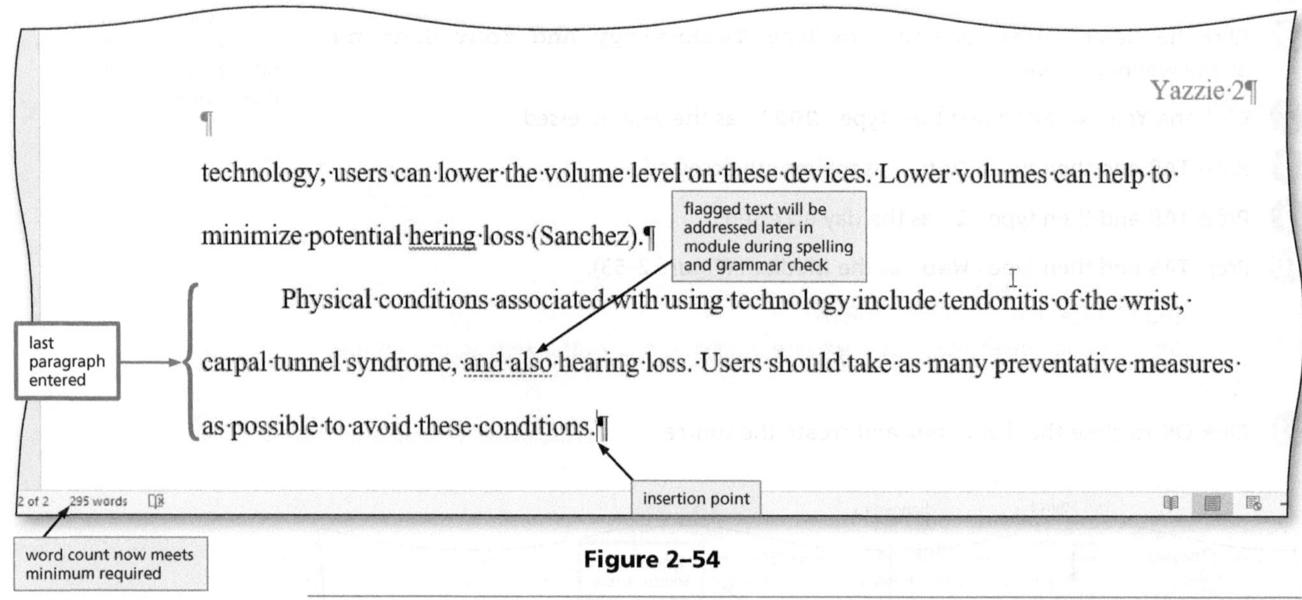

Figure 2–54

Break Point: If you want to take a break, this is a good place to do so. You can exit Word now. To resume later, start Word, open the file called SC_WD_2_TechnologyHealthConcernsPaper.docx, and continue following the steps from this location forward.

Creating an Alphabetical Works Cited Page

According to the MLA documentation style, the works cited page is a page in a research paper that alphabetically lists sources that are referenced directly in the paper. You place the list on a separate numbered page with the title, Works Cited, centered one inch from the top margin. The works are to be alphabetized by the author's last name or, if the work has no author, by the work's title. The first line of each entry begins at the left margin. Indent subsequent lines of the same entry one-half inch from the left margin.

CONSIDER THIS

What is a bibliography?

A **bibliography**, also called a bibliographical list, is an alphabetical list of sources referenced in a paper. Whereas the text of the research paper contains brief references to the source (the citations), the bibliography lists all publication information about the source. Documentation styles differ significantly in their guidelines for preparing a bibliography. Each style identifies formats for various sources, including books, magazines, pamphlets, newspapers, websites, television programs, paintings, maps, advertisements, letters, memos, and much more. You can find information about various styles and their guidelines in printed style guides and on the web.

To Insert a Page Break

The next step is to insert a manual page break following the body of the research paper. ***Why?*** *According to the MLA documentation style, the works cited are to be displayed on a separate numbered page.*

A **manual page break**, or **hard page break**, is a page break that you force into the document at a specific location so that the text following the break begins at the top of the next page, whether or not the previous page is full. Word never moves or adjusts manual page breaks. Word, however, does adjust any automatic page breaks that follow a manual page break. Word inserts manual page breaks immediately above or to the left of the location of the insertion point. The following step inserts a manual page break after the text of the research paper.

- Verify that the insertion point is positioned at the end of the text of the research paper, as shown in Figure 2–54.
- Click Insert on the ribbon to display the Insert tab.
- Click the Page Break button (Insert tab | Pages group) to insert a manual page break immediately to the left of the insertion point and position the insertion point immediately below the manual page break (Figure 2–55).

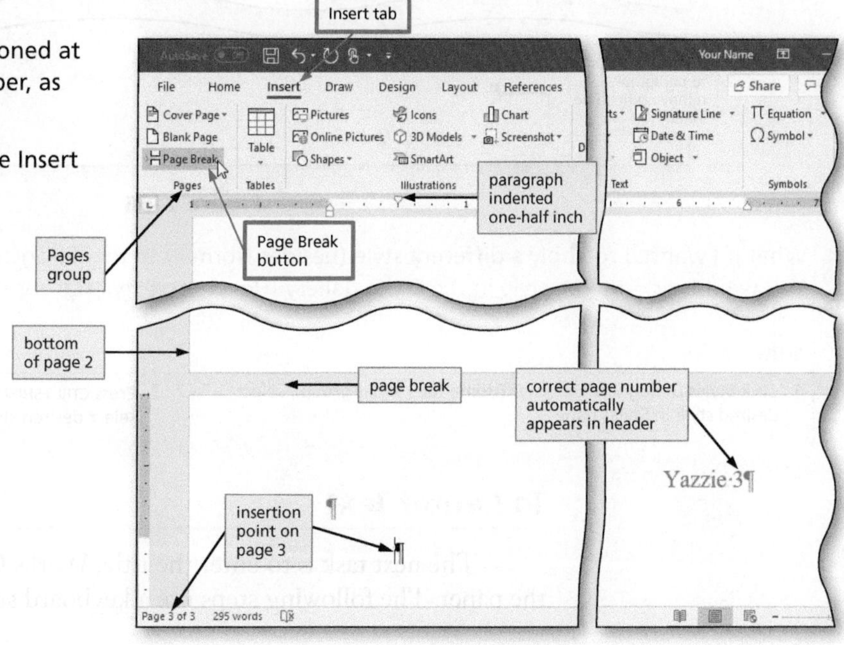

Figure 2–55

Other Ways

1. Press CTRL+ENTER

To Apply a Style

The works cited title is to be centered between the margins of the paper. If you simply issue the Center command, the title will not be centered properly. ***Why?*** *It will be to the right of the center point because earlier you set the first-line indent for paragraphs to one-half inch.*

To properly center the title of the works cited page, you could drag the 'First Line Indent' marker back to the left margin before centering the paragraph, or you could apply the Normal style to the location of the insertion point. Recall that you modified the Normal style for this document to 12-point Times New Roman with double-spaced, left-aligned paragraphs that have no space after the paragraphs.

To apply a style to a paragraph, first position the insertion point in the paragraph and then apply the style. The following step applies the modified Normal style to the location of the insertion point.

- Click Home on the ribbon to display the Home tab.
- With the insertion point on the paragraph mark at the top of page 3 (as shown in Figure 2–55) even if Normal is selected, click Normal in the Styles gallery (Home tab | Styles group) to apply the Normal style to the paragraph containing the insertion point (Figure 2–56).

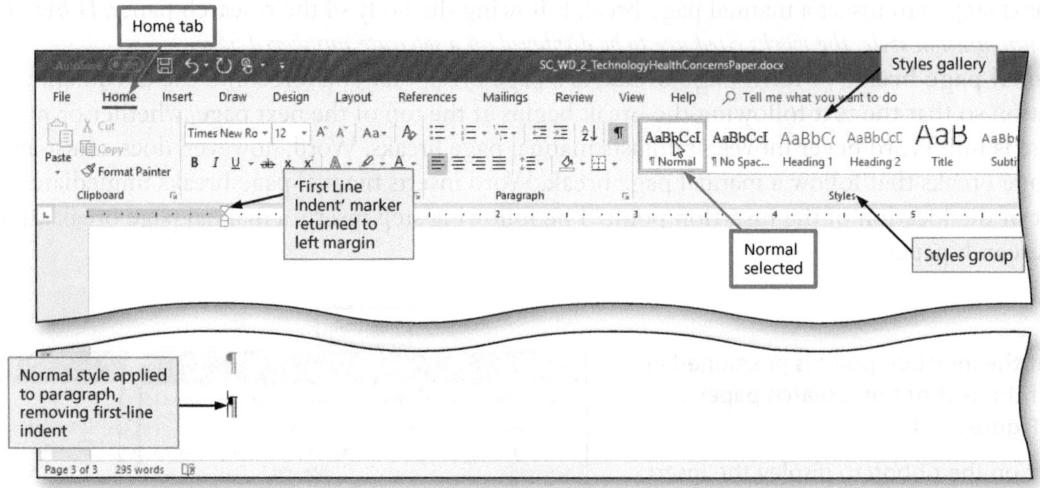

Figure 2–56

Q&A

What if I wanted to apply a different style (besides Normal) to the paragraph?

You would click desired style in the Styles gallery (Home tab | Styles group) to apply a style to the current paragraph.

Other Ways

1. Click Styles Dialog Box Launcher (Home tab | Styles group), select desired style in Styles pane
2. Press CTRL+SHIFT+S, click Style Name arrow in Apply Styles pane, select desired style in list

To Center Text

The next task is to enter the title, Works Cited, centered between the margins of the paper. The following steps use a keyboard shortcut to format the title.

1. Press CTRL+E to center the paragraph mark.
2. Type **Works Cited** as the title.
3. Press ENTER.
4. Press CTRL+L to left-align the paragraph mark (shown in Figure 2–57).

To Create a Bibliographical Reference List

While typing the research paper, you created several citations and their sources. The next task is to use Word to format the list of sources and alphabetize them in a bibliographical list. ***Why?*** *Word can create a bibliographical list with each element of the source placed in its correct position with proper punctuation, according to the specified style, saving you time looking up style guidelines. For example, in this research paper, the book source will list, in* *this order, the author name(s), book title, publisher city, publishing company name, and publication year with the correct punctuation between each element according to the MLA documentation style.* The following steps create an MLA-styled bibliographical list from the sources previously entered.

1

- Click References on the ribbon to display the References tab.
- With the insertion point positioned as shown in Figure 2–57, click the Bibliography button (References tab | Citations & Bibliography group) to display the Bibliography gallery (Figure 2–57).

Q&A Will I select the Works Cited option from the Bibliography gallery?

No. The title it inserts is not formatted according to the MLA documentation style. Thus, you will use the Insert Bibliography command instead.

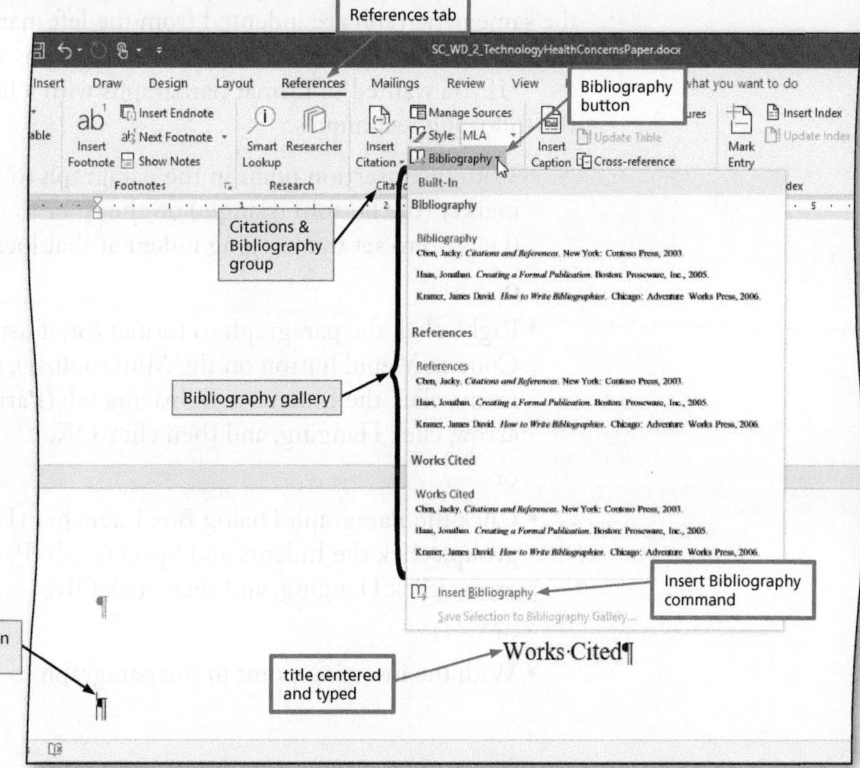

Figure 2–57

2

- Click Insert Bibliography in the Bibliography gallery to insert a list of sources at the location of the insertion point.
- If necessary, scroll to display the entire list of sources in the document window (Figure 2–58).

Q&A What is the n.d. in the second work?

The MLA documentation style uses the abbreviation n.d. for no date (for example, no date appears on the webpage).

What if my list is not double-spaced and has extra spacing after each paragraph?

You skipped a step earlier in this module. Select the entire bibliography, change line spacing to double, and remove space after the paragraph.

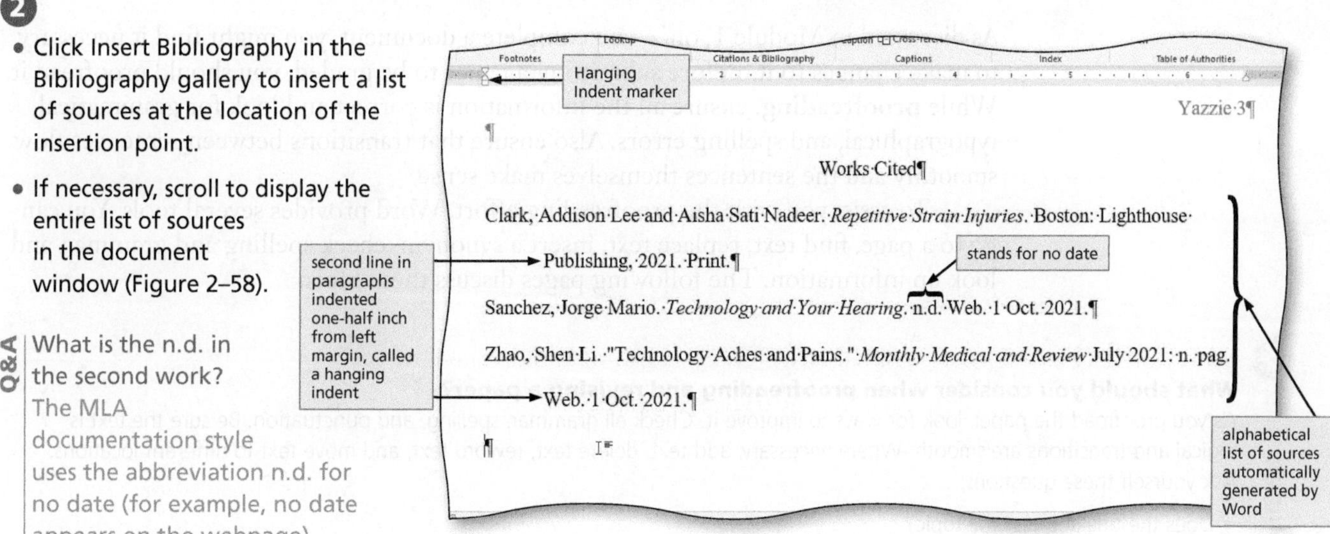

Figure 2–58

- Save the research paper again on the same storage location with the same file name.

To Format Paragraphs with a Hanging Indent

Notice in Figure 2–58 that the first line of each source entry hangs to the left of the rest of the paragraph; this type of paragraph formatting is called a **hanging indent** because the first line of the paragraph begins at the left margin and subsequent lines in the same paragraph are indented from the left margin. The Bibliography style in Word automatically formats the works cited paragraphs with a hanging indent.

If you wanted to format paragraphs with a hanging indent, you would use one of the following techniques.

- With the insertion point in the paragraph to format, drag the Hanging Indent marker (the bottom triangle) on the ruler to the desired mark on the ruler (i.e., .5") to set the hanging indent at that location from the left margin.

  or

- Right-click the paragraph to format (or, if using a touch screen, tap the 'Show Context Menu' button on the Mini toolbar), click Paragraph on the shortcut menu, click the Indents and Spacing tab (Paragraph dialog box), click the Special arrow, click Hanging, and then click OK.

  or

- Click the Paragraph Dialog Box Launcher (Home tab or Layout tab | Paragraph group), click the Indents and Spacing tab (Paragraph dialog box), click the Special arrow, click Hanging, and then click OK.

  or

- With the insertion point in the paragraph to format, press CTRL+T.

Proofreading and Revising the Research Paper

As discussed in Module 1, once you complete a document, you might find it necessary to make changes to it. Before submitting a paper to be graded, you should proofread it. While **proofreading**, ensure all the information is correct and look for grammatical, typographical, and spelling errors. Also ensure that transitions between sentences flow smoothly and the sentences themselves make sense.

To assist you with the proofreading effort, Word provides several tools. You can go to a page, find text, replace text, insert a synonym, check spelling and grammar, and look up information. The following pages discuss these tools.

CONSIDER THIS

What should you consider when proofreading and revising a paper?

As you proofread the paper, look for ways to improve it. Check all grammar, spelling, and punctuation. Be sure the text is logical and transitions are smooth. Where necessary, add text, delete text, reword text, and move text to different locations. Ask yourself these questions:

- Does the title suggest the topic?
- Is the thesis clear?
- Is the purpose of the paper clear?
- Does the paper have an introduction, body, and conclusion?
- Does each paragraph in the body relate to the thesis?
- Is the conclusion effective?
- Are sources acknowledged correctly?

To Edit a Source Using the Source Manager Dialog Box

While proofreading the paper, you notice an error in the magazine title; specifically, the word, and, should be removed. If you modify the contents of any source, the list of sources automatically updates. ***Why?*** *Word automatically updates the contents of fields, and the bibliography is a field.* The following steps delete a word from the title of the magazine article.

- Click the Manage Sources button (References tab | Citations & Bibliography group) to display the Source Manager dialog box.
- Click the source you wish to edit in the Current List, in this case the article by Zhao, to select the source.
- Click the Edit button (Source Manager dialog box) to display the Edit Source dialog box.
- In the Periodical Title text box, delete the word, and, from the title (Figure 2–59).

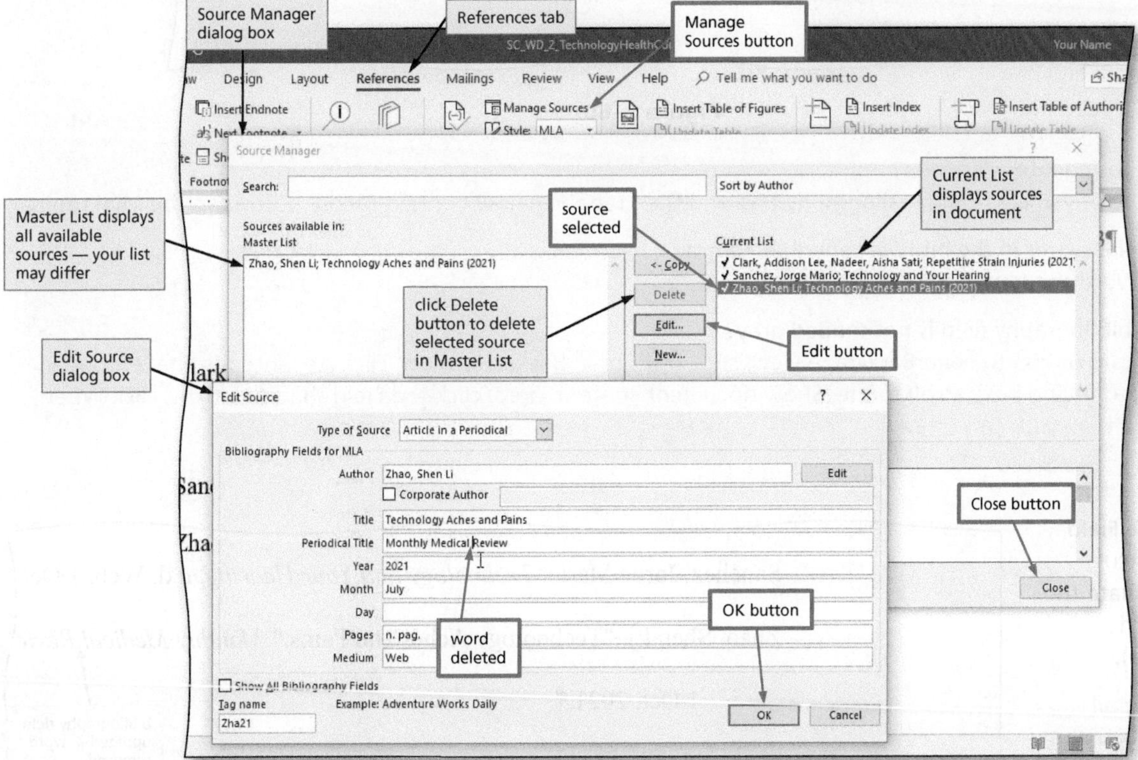

2

- Click OK (Edit Source dialog box) to close the dialog box.
- If a Microsoft Word dialog box appears, click Yes to update all occurrences of the source.
- Click the Close button (Source Manager dialog box) to update the list of sources and close the dialog box.

Q&A How would I delete an existing source?

You would select the source in the Master List and then click Delete (Source Manager dialog box). If the source is not listed in the Master List, click the source in the Current List and then click Copy (Source Manager dialog box) to copy the source from the Current List to the Master List.

To Update a Field (the Bibliography)

Depending on settings, the bibliography field may not automatically reflect the edited magazine title. Thus, the following steps update the bibliography field. ***Why?*** *Because the bibliography is a field, you may need to instruct Word to update its contents.*

- Right-click anywhere in the bibliography text to display a shortcut menu related to fields (Figure 2–60).

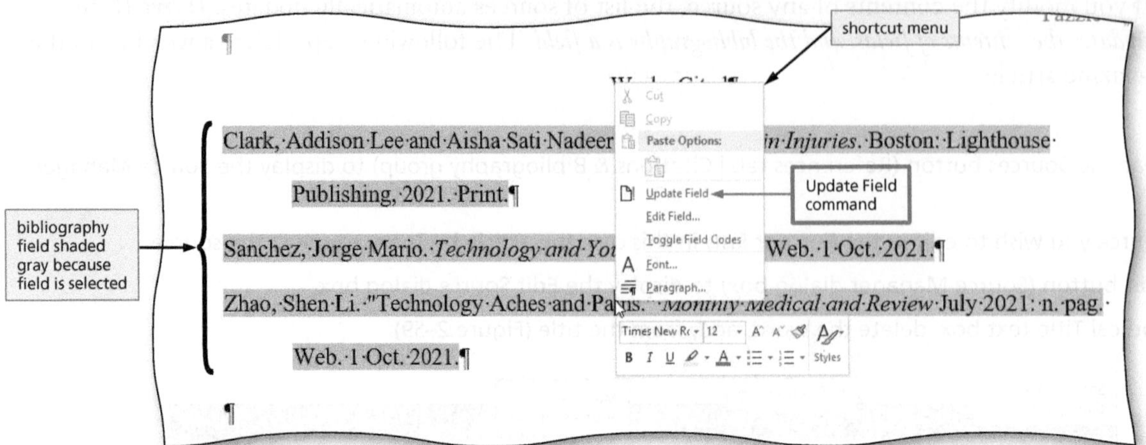

Figure 2–60

Q&A

What if I am using a touch screen?
Press and hold anywhere in the bibliography text and then tap the 'Show Context Menu' button on the Mini toolbar.

Why are all the words in the bibliography shaded gray?
By default, Word shades selected fields gray.

What if the bibliography field is not shaded gray?
Click File on the ribbon to open Backstage view, click Options in Backstage view, click Advanced in the left pane (Word Options dialog box), scroll to the 'Show document content' area, click the Field shading arrow, click When selected, and then click OK.

- Click Update Field on the shortcut menu to update the selected field (Figure 2–61).

Q&A

Can I update all fields in a document at once?
Yes. Select the entire document and then follow these steps.

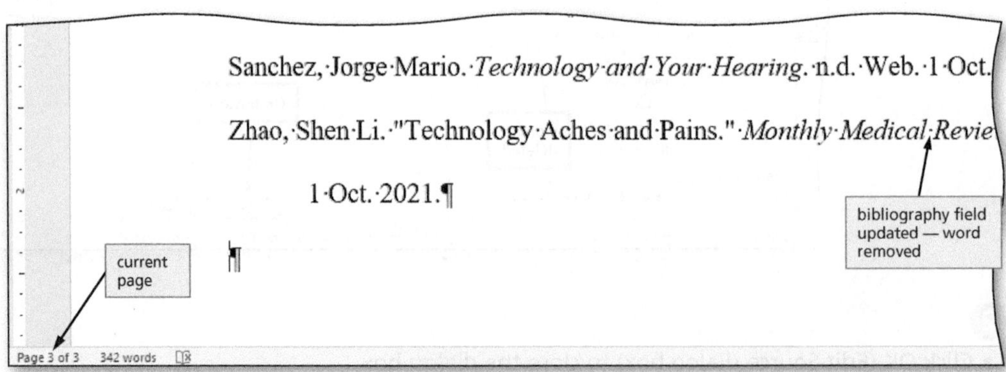

Figure 2–61

Other Ways

1. Select the field, press F9

To Convert a Field to Regular Text

If, for some reason, you wanted to convert a field, such as the bibliography field, to regular text, you would perform the following steps. Keep in mind, though, once you convert the field to regular text, it no longer is a field that can be updated.

1. Click somewhere in the field to select it, in this case, somewhere in the bibliography.
2. Press CTRL+SHIFT+F9 to convert the selected field to regular text.

To Open the Navigation Pane

The next task in revising the paper is to modify text on the first page of the document. ***Why?*** *You want to insert another citation on the first page.* You could scroll to the desired location in the document or you can use the Navigation Pane to browse through pages in a document. The following step opens the Navigation Pane.

1

- Click View on the ribbon to display the View tab.
- Place a checkmark in the Navigation Pane check box (View tab | Show group) to open the Navigation Pane on the left side of the Word window.
- If necessary, click the Pages tab in the Navigation Pane to display thumbnails of the pages in the document (Figure 2–62).

Q&A What is the Navigation Pane?
The Navigation Pane is a window that enables you to browse through headings in a document, browse through pages in a document, or search for text in a document.

How do I close the Navigation Pane?
You click the Close button in the upper-right corner of the Navigation Pane, or remove the checkmark from the Navigation Pane check box (View tab | Show group).

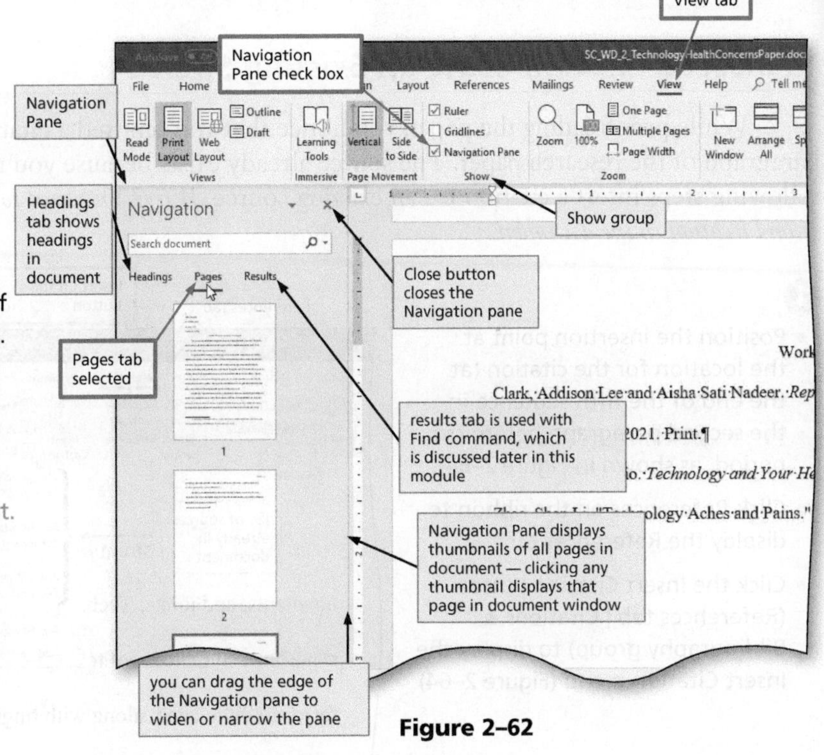

Figure 2–62

To Go to a Page

The next task in revising the paper is to insert a citation on the first page of the document. ***Why?*** *You overlooked a citation when you created the paper.* The following steps display the top of the first page in the document window using the Navigation Pane.

1

- With the Navigation Pane open in the document window, if the Pages tab is not selected, click it to select it.

Q&A What if the Navigation Pane is not open?
Repeat the previous set of steps.

- Scroll to, if necessary, and then click the thumbnail of the first page in the Navigation Pane to display the top of the selected page in the top of the document window (Figure 2–63).

2

- Click the Close button in the Navigation Pane to close the pane.

Q&A What if I wanted to use the Go To dialog box instead of the Navigation Pane to go to a page?
You would click the Find arrow (Home tab | Editing group) to display the Find menu, click Go To on the Find menu to display the Go To dialog box, click the Go To tab (Find and Replace dialog box), enter the desired page number in the text box, and then click the Go To button to display the desired page in the document window.

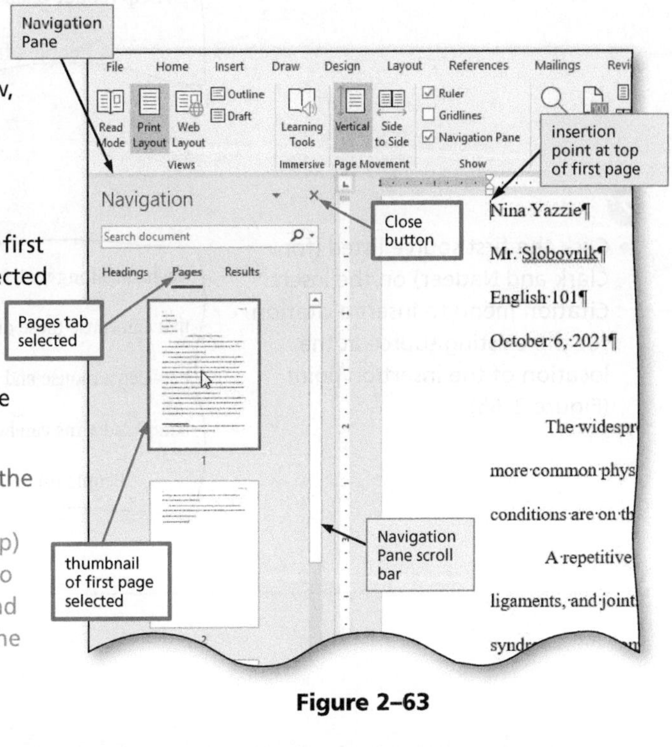

Figure 2–63

Other Ways

1. Click Find arrow (Home tab | Editing group), click Go To on Find menu, click Go To tab (Find and Replace dialog box), enter page number, click Go To button
2. Click Page Number indicator on status bar, click Pages tab in Navigation Pane, click thumbnail of desired page (Navigation Pane)
3. Press CTRL+G, enter page number (Find and Replace dialog box), click Go To button

To Insert a Citation Using an Existing Source

While proofreading the paper, you notice that you omitted a citation that should appear in the second paragraph of the research paper. The source already exists because you referenced it in the footnote. The following steps insert a citation for an existing source. ***Why?*** *You want to insert a citation for an existing source in a second location in the document.*

- Position the insertion point at the location for the citation (at the end of the fifth sentence in the second paragraph before the period, as shown in Figure 2–64).
- Click References on the ribbon to display the References tab.
- Click the Insert Citation button (References tab | Citations & Bibliography group) to display the Insert Citation menu (Figure 2–64).

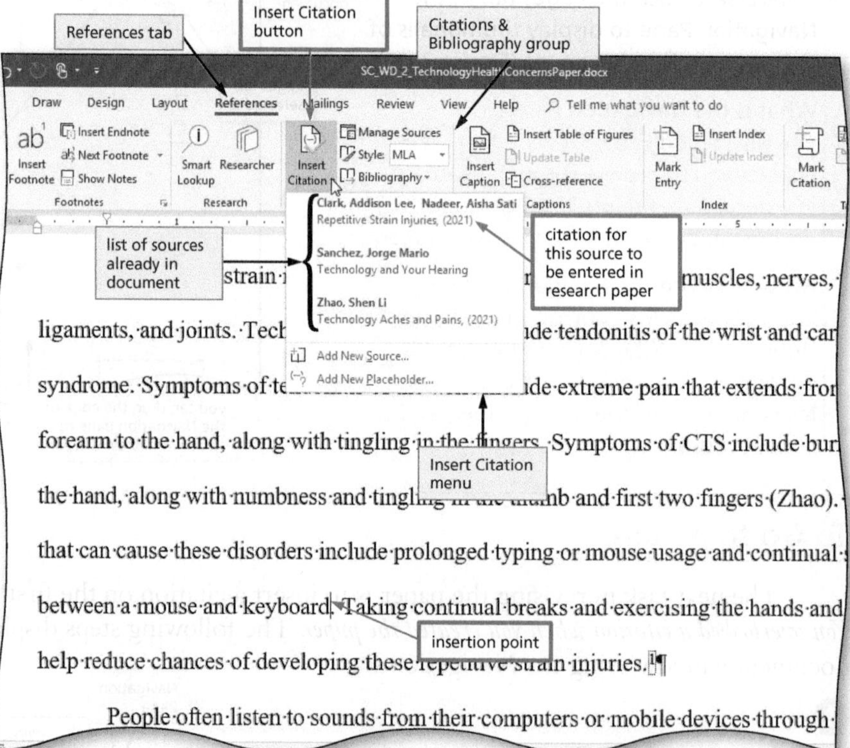

Figure 2–64

- Click the first source listed (for Clark and Nadeer) on the Insert Citation menu to insert a citation for the existing source at the location of the insertion point (Figure 2–65).

existing citation entered at location of insertion point

the·hand,·along·with·numbness·and·tingling·in·the·thumb·and·first·two·fingers·(Zhao).·Factors·that·can·cause·these·disorders·include·prolonged·typing·or·mouse·usage·and·continual·shifting·between·a·mouse·and·keyboard·(Clark·and·Nadeer).·Taking·continual·breaks·and·exercising·the·hands·and·arms·can·help·reduce·chances·of·developing·these·repetitive·strain·injuries.¶

People·often·listen·to·sounds·from·their·computers·or·mobile·devices·through·headphone

Figure 2–65

To Move a Citation

The citation just entered is not in the correct location. The following steps move a citation in a document. ***Why?*** *You want to move the citation to the end of the next sentence.*

- Click somewhere in the citation to be moved to select it.
- Position the pointer on the citation tab until the pointer changes to a left-pointing block arrow (Figure 2–66).

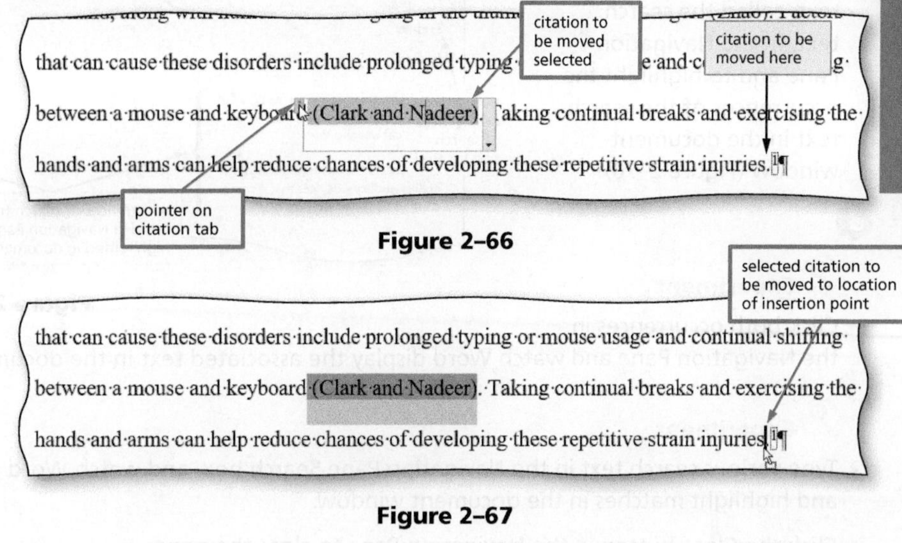

Figure 2–66

- Drag the citation tab, which changes to an insertion point as you drag, to the location where the selected citation is to be moved (Figure 2–67).

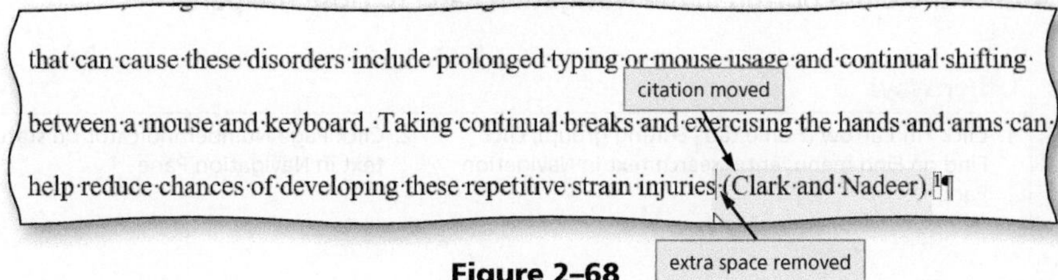

Figure 2–67

- When you release the mouse button, the citation moves to the location of the dragged insertion point.
- Click outside the citation to deselect it. If necessary, delete the extra space to the left of the moved citation (Figure 2–68).

that·can·cause·these·disorders·include·prolonged·typing·or·mouse·usage·and·continual·shifting·
between·a·mouse·and·keyboard.·Taking·continual·breaks·and·exercising·the·hands·and·arms·can·
help·reduce·chances·of·developing·these·repetitive·strain·injuries·(Clark·and·Nadeer).¶

citation moved

extra space removed

Figure 2–68

To Find Text

While proofreading the paper, you would like to locate all occurrences of the word, auditory. ***Why?*** *You are contemplating changing occurrences of this word to the word, listening.* The following steps find all occurrences of specific text in a document.

- Click Home on the ribbon to display the Home tab.
- Click the Find button (Home tab | Editing group) to open the Navigation Pane.

Q&A Why did the Find menu appear?
You clicked the Find arrow. Press ESC and repeat Step 1.

What if I am using a touch screen?
Tap the Find button (Home tab | Editing group) and then tap Find on the menu.

- If necessary, click the Results tab in the Navigation Pane, which displays a Search box where you can type text for which you want to search (Figure 2–69).

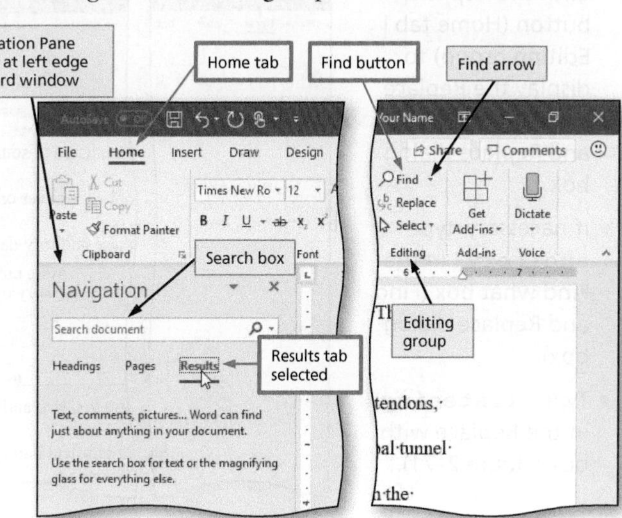

Figure 2–69

- Type **auditory** in the Navigation Pane Search box to display all occurrences of the typed text, called the search text, in the Navigation Pane and to highlight the occurrences of the search text in the document window (Figure 2–70).

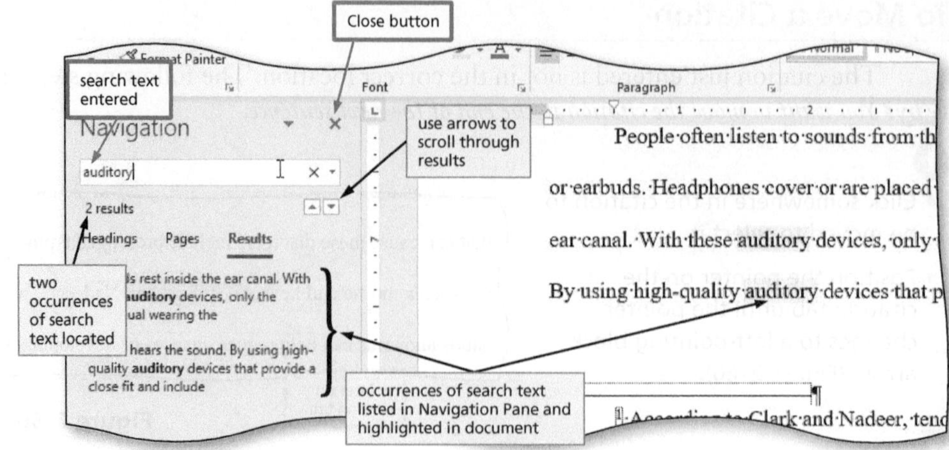

Figure 2–70

Experiment

- Click both occurrences in the Navigation Pane and watch Word display the associated text in the document window.

Experiment

- Type various search text in the Navigation Pane Search box, and watch Word list matches in the Navigation Pane and highlight matches in the document window.
- Click the Close button in the Navigation Pane to close the pane.

Other Ways

1. Click Find arrow (Home tab | Editing group), click Find on Find menu, enter search text in Navigation Pane
2. Click Page Number indicator on status bar, enter search text in Navigation Pane
3. Press CTRL+F, enter search text in Navigation Pane

To Replace Text

You decide to change all occurrences of the word, auditory, to the word, listening. ***Why?*** *The term, listening devices, is more commonly used than auditory devices.* Word's find and replace feature locates each occurrence of a word or phrase and then replaces it with text you specify. The following steps find and replace text.

1

- Click the Replace button (Home tab | Editing group) to display the Replace sheet in the Find and Replace dialog box.
- If necessary, type **auditory** in the Find what box (Find and Replace dialog box).
- Type **listening** in the Replace with box (Figure 2–71).

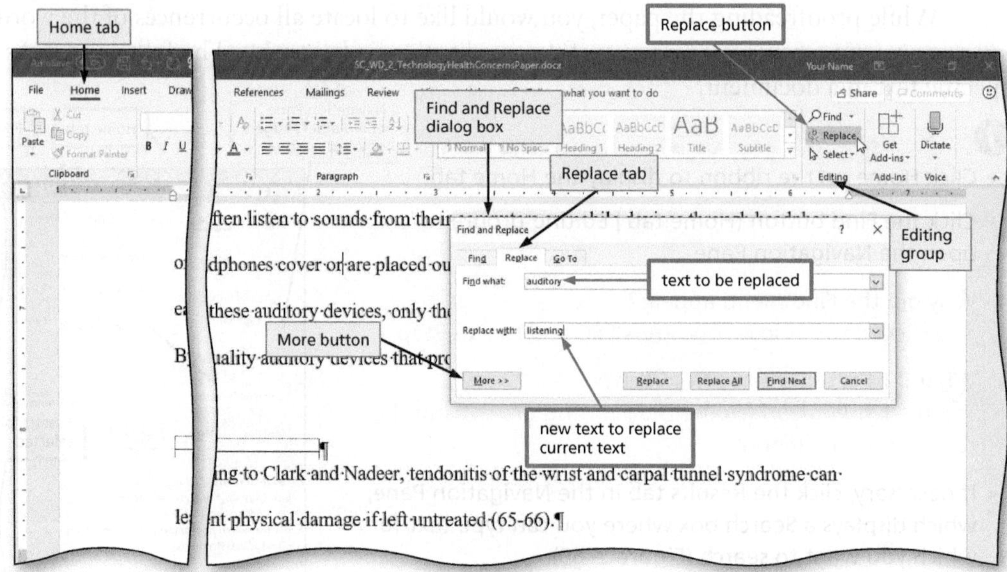

Figure 2–71

2

- Click the Replace All button to instruct Word to replace all occurrences of the Find what text with the Replace with text (Figure 2–72). If Word displays a dialog box asking if you want to continue searching from the beginning of the document, click Yes.

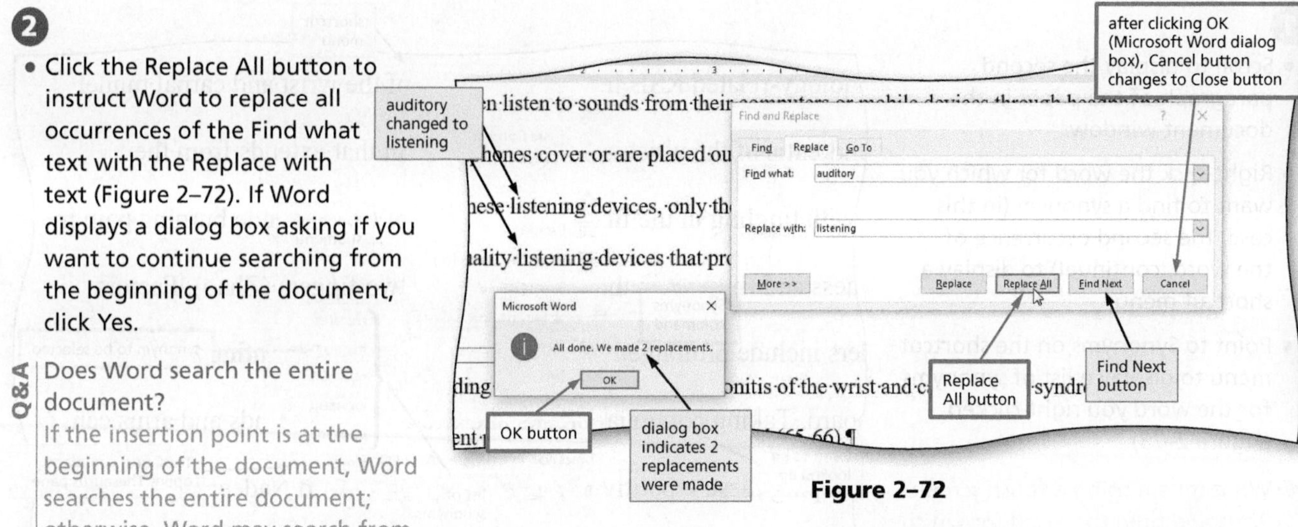

Figure 2–72

Q&A Does Word search the entire document?
If the insertion point is at the beginning of the document, Word searches the entire document; otherwise, Word may search from the location of the insertion point to the end of the document and then display a dialog box asking if you want to continue searching from the beginning. You also can search a section of text by selecting the text before clicking the Replace or Replace All button.

3

- Click OK (Microsoft Word dialog box) to close the dialog box.
- Click the Close button (Find and Replace dialog box) to close the dialog box.

Other Ways

1. Press CTRL+H

Find and Replace Dialog Box

The Replace All button (Find and Replace dialog box) replaces all occurrences of the Find what text with the Replace with text. In some cases, you may want to replace only certain occurrences of a word or phrase, not all of them. To instruct Word to confirm each change, click the Find Next button (Find and Replace dialog box) (shown in Figure 2–72), instead of the Replace All button. When Word locates an occurrence of the text, it pauses and waits for you to click either the Replace button or the Find Next button. Clicking the Replace button changes the text; clicking the Find Next button instructs Word to disregard the replacement and look for the next occurrence of the Find what text.

If you accidentally replace the wrong text, you can undo a replacement by clicking the Undo button on the Quick Access Toolbar or by pressing CTRL+Z. If you used the Replace All button, Word undoes all replacements. If you used the Replace button, Word undoes only the most recent replacement.

BTW
Finding Formatting and Special Characters
To search for formatting or a special character, click the Find tab or Replace tab in the Find and Replace dialog box and then click the More button (Find and Replace dialog box) (shown in Figure 2–71). To find formatting, use the Format button in the Find dialog box. To find a special character, use the Special button. To specify search options, place a check mark in the desired option in the Search Options area.

To Use the Thesaurus

In this project, you would like a synonym for the word, continual, in the second paragraph of the research paper. ***Why?*** *When writing, you may discover that you used the same word in multiple locations or that a word you used was not quite appropriate, the former of which is the case here.* In these instances, you will want to look up a **synonym**, or a word similar in meaning, to the duplicate or inappropriate word. A **thesaurus** is list of alternate word choices. Word provides synonyms and a thesaurus pane for your convenience. The following steps find a suitable synonym.

- Scroll to display the second paragraph of the paper in the document window.
- Right-click the word for which you want to find a synonym (in this case, the second occurrence of the word, continual) to display a shortcut menu.
- Point to Synonyms on the shortcut menu to display a list of synonyms for the word you right-clicked (Figure 2–73).

Q&A What if I am using a touch screen?
Press and hold the word for which you want a synonym, tap the 'Show Context Menu' button on the Mini toolbar, and then tap Synonyms on the shortcut menu.

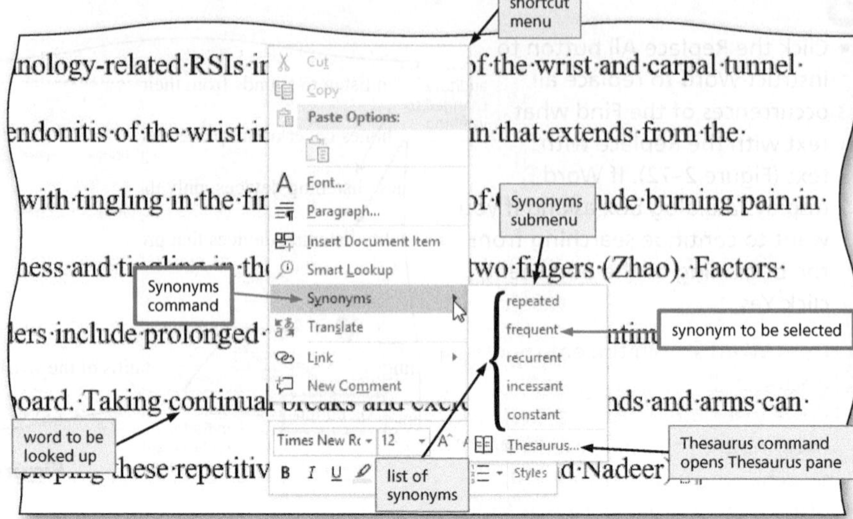

Figure 2–73

- Click the synonym you want (in this case, frequent) on the Synonyms submenu to replace the selected word in the document with the selected synonym (Figure 2–74).

se·these·disorders·include·prolonged·typing·or·mouse·usage·and·continual
ouse·and·keyboard.·Taking·frequent·breaks·and·exercising·the·hands·and·a
hances·of·developing·these·repetitive (Clark·and·Nadeer).
word, continual, changed to frequent

Figure 2–74

Q&A What if the synonyms list on the shortcut menu does not display a suitable word?
You can display the thesaurus in the Thesaurus pane by clicking Thesaurus on the Synonyms submenu. The Thesaurus pane displays a complete thesaurus, in which you can look up synonyms for various meanings of a word.

Other Ways

1. Click Thesaurus button (Review tab | Proofing group)
2. Press SHIFT+F7

To Check Spelling and Grammar at Once

As discussed previously, Word checks spelling and grammar as you type and flags possible spelling or grammar errors with different types of underlines, depending on the potential error type. The following steps check spelling and grammar in the entire document at once. ***Why?*** *Some users prefer to wait and check their entire document for spelling and grammar errors at once rather than checking as they type.*

Previously in this module, you entered the word, hearing, misspelled intentionally as hering and entered the words, and also, to illustrate the use of Word's check spelling and grammar at once feature. If you are completing this project on a computer or mobile device, your research paper may contain different misspelled words, depending on the accuracy of your typing.

- Press CTRL+HOME because you want the spelling and grammar check to begin from the top of the document.
- Click Review on the ribbon to display the Review tab.
- Click the 'Spelling & Grammar' button (Review tab | Proofing group) to begin the spelling and grammar check at the location of the insertion point, which, in this case, is at the beginning of the document; when Word identifies a potential spelling error, it opens the Editor pane with suggestions for the flagged text (Figure 2–75).

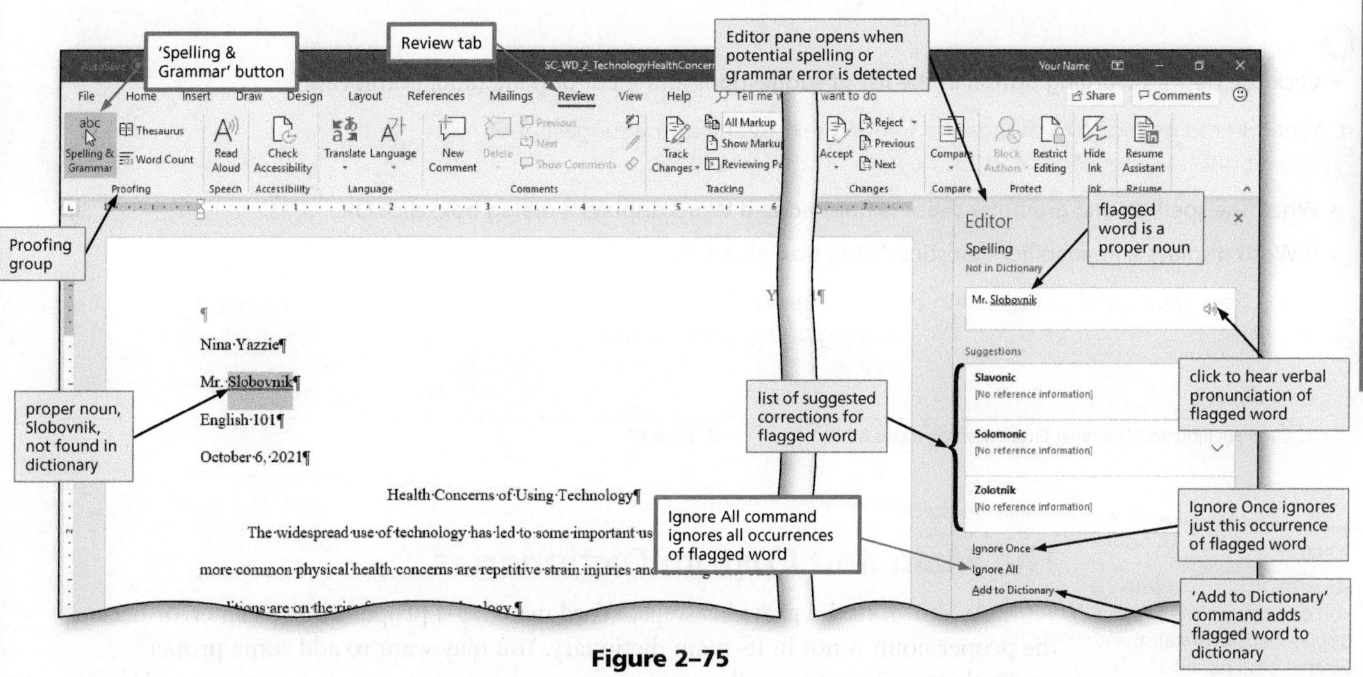

Figure 2–75

- Because the first occurrence of flagged text is a proper noun and spelled correctly (Slobovnik), click Ignore All in the Editor pane to ignore this and future occurrences of the flagged proper noun and then continue the spelling and grammar check until the next potential error is identified or the end of the document is reached; in this case, it identifies the potential misspelled word, hering.

3

- Click the arrow to the right of the desired suggestion (hearing) to display a suggestion menu for the desired suggestion (Figure 2–76).

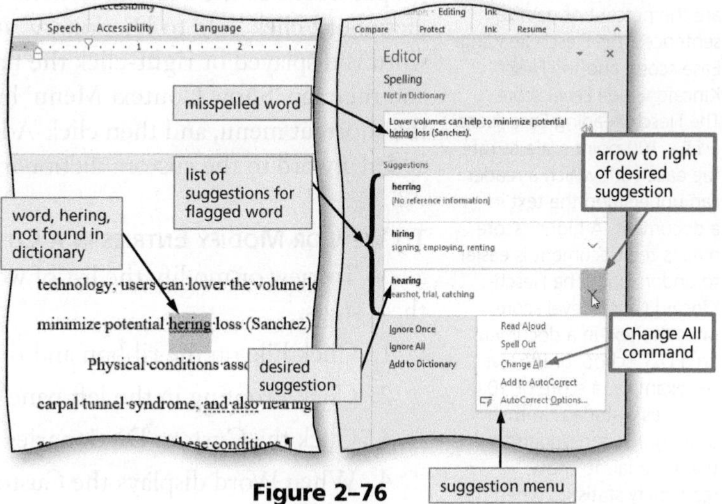

Figure 2–76

4

- Click Change All on the suggestion menu to change the flagged word, and any other exact misspellings of this word, to the selected suggestion and then continue the spelling and grammar check until the next error is identified or the end of the document is reached, which in this case is a suggestion to change the words, and also, to more concise language (Figure 2–77).

Q&A How would I change just the flagged text (and not all occurrences of the misspelled word)?

You would click the desired suggestion instead of the arrow to the right of the suggestion.

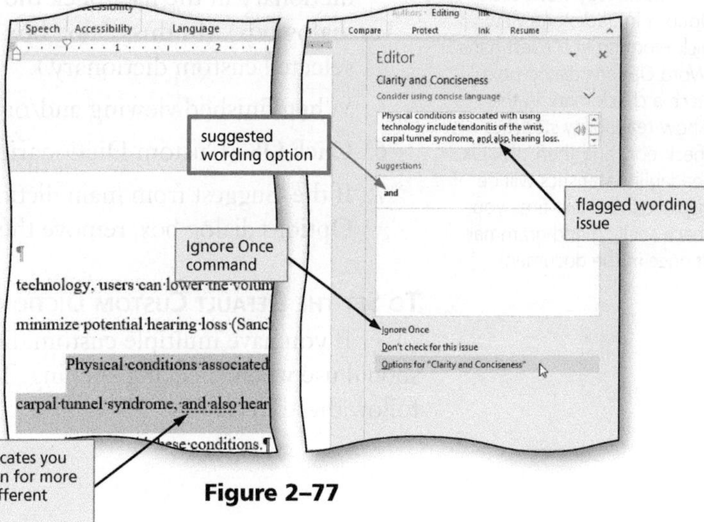

Figure 2–77

- Click the desired wording option in the list of suggestions in the Editor pane (and, in this case).

Q&A What if I did not want to change the flagged text to any of the suggestions?
You would click Ignore Once at the bottom of the Editor pane.

- When the spelling and grammar check is finished and Word displays a dialog box, click OK.
- If Word displays a Readability Statistics dialog box, click OK.

Q&A Can I check spelling of just a section of a document?
Yes, select the text before starting the spelling and grammar check.

Other Ways

1. Click 'Spelling and Grammar Check' icon on status bar
2. Press F7

BTW
Readability Statistics
You can instruct Word to display readability statistics when it has finished a spelling and grammar check on a document. Three readability statistics presented are the percent of passive sentences, the Flesch Reading Ease score, and the Flesch-Kincaid Grade Level score. The Flesch Reading Ease score uses a 100-point scale to rate the ease with which a reader can understand the text in a document. A higher score means the document is easier to understand. The Flesch-Kincaid Grade Level score rates the text in a document on a U.S. school grade level. For example, a score of 10.0 indicates a student in the tenth grade can understand the material. To show readability statistics when the spelling check is complete, open Backstage view, click Options in Backstage view, click Proofing in the left pane (Word Options dialog box), place a check mark in the 'Show readability statistics' check box, and then click OK. Readability statistics will be displayed the next time you check spelling and grammar at once in the document.

The Main and Custom Dictionaries

As shown in the previous steps, Word may flag a proper noun as an error because the proper noun is not in its main dictionary. You may want to add some proper nouns that you use repeatedly, such as a company name or employee names, to Word's dictionary. To prevent Word from flagging proper nouns as errors, you can add the proper nouns to the custom dictionary. To add a correctly spelled word to the custom dictionary, click 'Add to Dictionary' at the bottom of the Editor pane when the flagged word is displayed or right-click the flagged word (or, if using touch, press and hold and then tap 'Show Context Menu' button on the mini toolbar), point to Spelling on the shortcut menu, and then click 'Add to Dictionary' on the submenu. Once you have added a word to the custom dictionary, Word no longer will flag it as an error.

To View or Modify Entries in a Custom Dictionary

To view or modify the list of words in a custom dictionary, you would follow these steps.

1. Click File on the ribbon and then click Options in Backstage view.
2. Click Proofing in the left pane (Word Options dialog box).
3. Click the Custom Dictionaries button.
4. When Word displays the Custom Dictionaries dialog box, if necessary, place a checkmark next to the dictionary name to view or modify and then select the dictionary in the list. Click the 'Edit Word List' button (Custom Dictionaries dialog box). (In this dialog box, you can add or delete entries to and from the selected custom dictionary.)
5. When finished viewing and/or modifying the list, click OK in the dialog box.
6. Click OK (Custom Dictionaries dialog box).
7. If the 'Suggest from main dictionary only' check box is selected in the Word Options dialog box, remove the checkmark. Click OK (Word Options dialog box).

To Set the Default Custom Dictionary

If you have multiple custom dictionaries, you can specify which one Word should use when checking spelling. To set the default custom dictionary, you would follow these steps.

1. Click File on the ribbon and then click Options in Backstage view.
2. Click Proofing in the left pane (Word Options dialog box).
3. Click the Custom Dictionaries button.
4. When the Custom Dictionaries dialog box is displayed, place a checkmark next to the desired dictionary name and then select the dictionary name in the list. Click the Change Default button (Custom Dictionaries dialog box).
5. Click OK (Custom Dictionaries dialog box).
6. If the 'Suggest from main dictionary only' check box is selected in the Word Options dialog box, remove the checkmark. Click OK (Word Options dialog box).

To Save and Print the Document

The following steps save and print the document.

1. **sam** Save the research paper again on the same storage location with the same file name.
2. If requested by your instructor, print the research paper.

BTW

Conserving Ink and Toner

If you want to conserve ink or toner, you can instruct Word to print draft quality documents by clicking File on the ribbon to open Backstage view, clicking Options in Backstage view to display the Word Options dialog box, clicking Advanced in the left pane (Word Options dialog box), scrolling to the Print area in the right pane, placing a check mark in the 'Use draft quality' check box, and then clicking OK. Then, use Backstage view to print the document as usual.

To Recover Unsaved Documents (Draft Versions)

If you accidently exit Word without saving a document, you may be able to recover the unsaved document, called a draft version, in Word. If you wanted to recover an unsaved document, you would perform these steps.

1. Start Word and create a blank document in the Word window.
2. Open Backstage view and then, if necessary, click Info to display the Info screen. If the autorecovery file name appears below the Manage Document list, click the file name to display the unsaved file in the Word window.

   or

   Open Backstage view and then, if necessary, click Open to display the Open screen. Scroll to the bottom of the Recent Documents list and then click the 'Recover Unsaved Documents' button to display an Open dialog box that lists unsaved files retained by Word. Select the file to recover and then click Open to display the unsaved file in the Word window.

   or

   Open Backstage view and then, if necessary, click Info to display the Info screen. Click the Manage Document button to display the Manage Document menu. Click 'Recover Unsaved Documents' on the Manage Document menu to display an Open dialog box that lists unsaved files retained by Word. Select the file to recover and then click Open to display the unsaved file in the Word window.
3. To save the document, click the Save As button on the Message Bar.

To Delete All Unsaved Documents (Draft Versions)

If you wanted to delete all unsaved documents, you would perform these steps.

1. Start Word and create a blank document in the Word window.
2. Open Backstage view and then, if necessary, click Info to display the Info screen.
3. Click the Manage Document button to display the Manage Document menu.
4. If available, click 'Delete All Unsaved Documents' on the Manage Document menu.
5. When Word displays a dialog box asking if you are sure you want to delete all copies of unsaved files, click Yes to delete all unsaved documents.

To Use Smart Lookup

If you are connected to the Internet, you can use the Smart Lookup pane to search through various forms of reference information, including images, on the web and/or look up a definition of a word. The following steps use the Smart Lookup pane to look up information about a series of words. ***Why?*** *Assume you want to see some images and know more about the words, headphones or earbuds.*

1

- Select the words you want to look up (in this case, headphones or earbuds).

Q&A What if I wanted to look up a single word?
You would position the insertion point in the word you want to look up.

- Click References on the ribbon to display the References tab.
- Click the Smart Lookup button (References tab | Research group) to open the Smart Lookup pane (Figure 2–78).

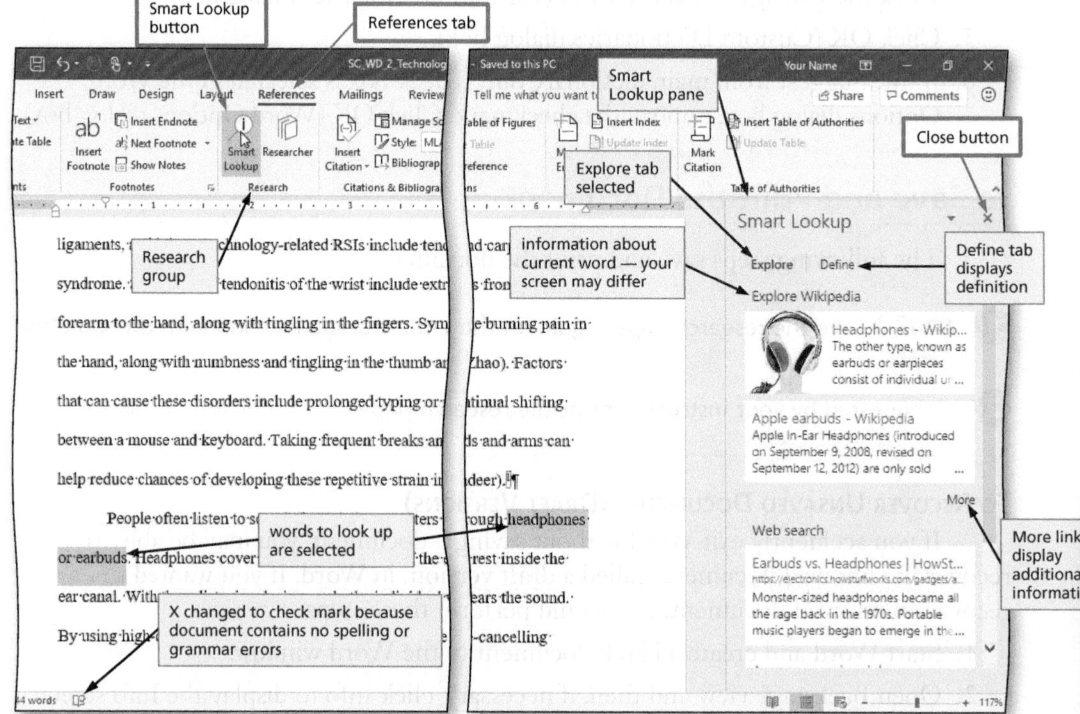

Figure 2–78

Q&A What if Word asks if I want to turn on intelligent services?
Select the option to turn on intelligent services.

Why does my Smart Lookup pane look different?
Depending on your settings, your Smart Lookup pane may appear different from the figure shown here.

 **Experiment**

- With the Explore tab selected in the Smart Lookup pane, scroll through the information that appears in the Smart Lookup pane. Click the Define tab in the Smart Lookup pane to see a definition of the first selected word. Click the Explore tab to redisplay information from the web about the selected text. Click one of the More links in the Smart Lookup pane to view additional information. If a Back button appears at the top of the Smart Lookup pane, click it to return to the previous display.

2

- Click the Close button in the Smart Lookup pane to close the pane.
- Click anywhere in the document window to deselect the text.

To Use Researcher

If you are connected to the Internet, you can use the Researcher pane to search through various forms of reference information on the web and locate sources for research papers from within Word. The following steps use the Researcher pane to look up information about carpal tunnel syndrome. ***Why?*** *Assume you want to see additional sources for this topic.* Note that the Researcher is only available to Office 365 installations. If you do not have Office 365, read these steps without performing them.

1

- Click the Researcher button (References tab | Research group) to open the Researcher pane (Figure 2–79).

Q&A Why does my Researcher pane look different?
Depending on your settings, your Researcher pane may appear different from the figure shown here.

Experiment

- With the Find Sources tab selected in the Researcher pane, scroll through the information and images that appear in the pane.

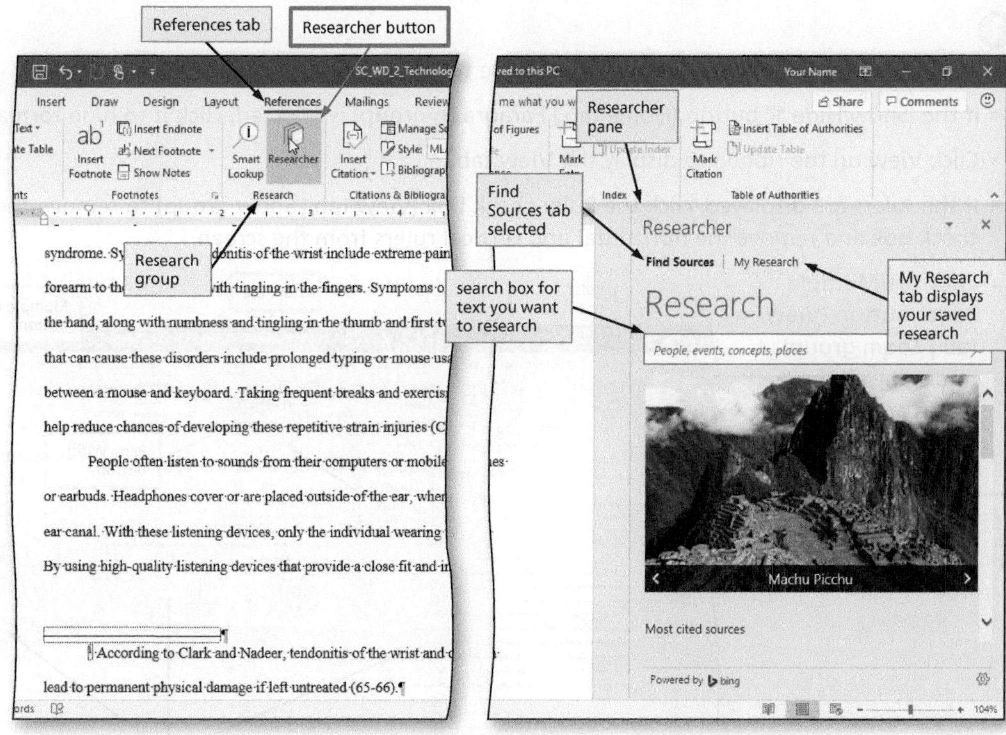

Figure 2–79

2

- Type **`carpal tunnel syndrome`** in the search box in the Researcher pane and then press ENTER to display topics and sources related to the search text (Figure 2–80).

Experiment

- With the Find Sources tab selected in the Researcher pane, scroll through the topics and sources that appear in the pane. Point to the + symbols on the right edge of the topics and sources and read their function. Click one of the topics and read its information. Drag through text in the topic and notice the submenu with the 'Add and Cite' command, which allows you to add the text in your document at the location of the insertion point and cite its source. Click the Back button at the top of the Researcher pane to return to the previous display. Click one of the sources and read its information. Click the Back button to return to the previous display.
- Click the Close button in the Researcher pane to close the pane.

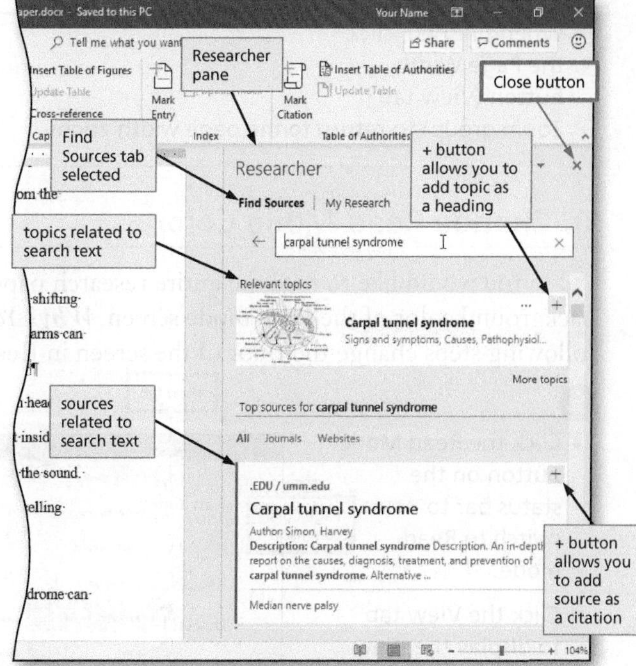

Figure 2–80

Q&A Can I use the information in my paper that I add from the Researcher pane?
When using Word to insert material from the Researcher pane or any other online reference, be careful not to plagiarize.

To Change the Zoom to Multiple Pages

The following steps display multiple pages in the document window at once. ***Why?*** *You want to be able to see all pages in the research paper on the screen at the same time. You also hide formatting marks and the rulers so that the display is easier to view.*

- Click Home on the ribbon to display the Home tab.
- If the 'Show/Hide ¶' button (Home tab | Paragraph group) is selected, click it to hide formatting marks.
- Click View on the ribbon to display the View tab.
- If the rulers are displayed, click the Ruler check box (View tab | Show group) to remove the checkmark from the check box and remove the horizontal and vertical rulers from the screen.
- Click the Multiple Pages button (View tab | Zoom group) to display all three pages at once in the document window (Figure 2–81).

Q&A Why do the pages appear differently on my screen?
Depending on settings, Word may display all the pages as shown in Figure 2–81 or may show the pages differently.

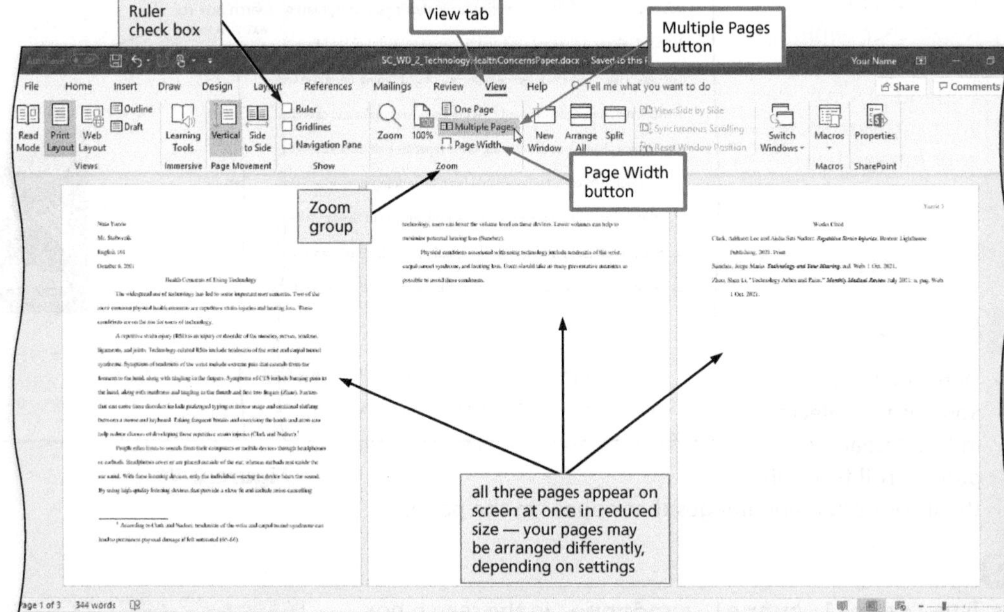

Figure 2–81

- When finished, click the Page Width button (View tab | Zoom group) to return to the page width zoom.

To Change Read Mode Color

You would like to read the entire research paper using Read mode but would like to change the background color of the Read mode screen. *Why? You prefer a softer background color for reading on the screen.* The following steps change the color of the screen in Read mode.

1

- Click the Read Mode button on the status bar to switch to Read mode.
- Click the View tab to display the View menu.
- Point to Page Color on the View menu to display the Page Color submenu (Figure 2–82).

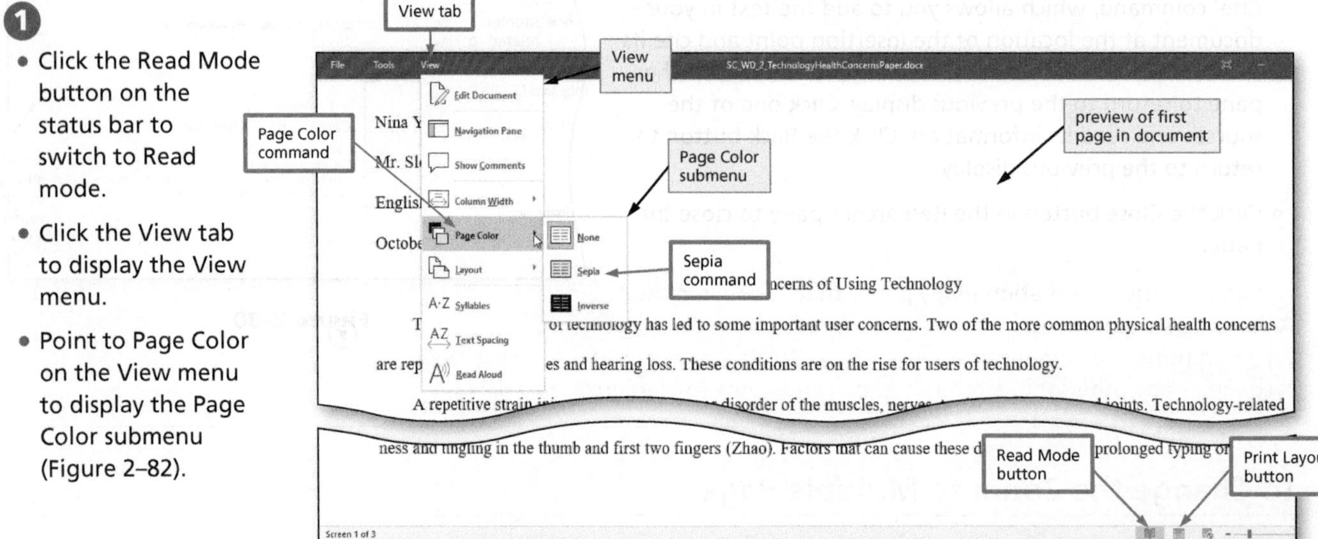

Figure 2–82

- Click Sepia on the Page Color submenu to change the color of the Read mode screen to sepia (Figure 2–83).

- When finished, click the Print Layout button (shown in Figure 2–82) on the status bar to return to Print Layout view.

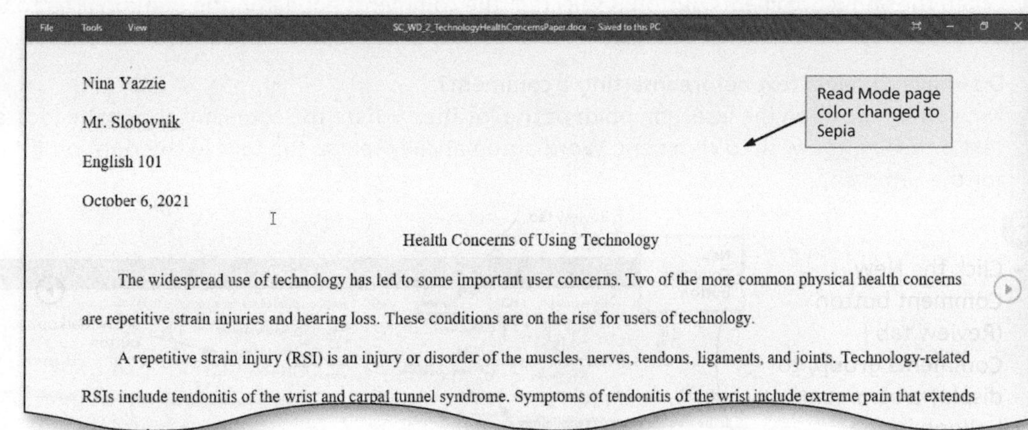

Figure 2–83

Working with Comments in a Document

Word provides tools, such as comments, that allow users to collaborate on a document. A **comment** is a note that an author or reviewer adds to a document. Reviewers often use comments to communicate suggestions, tips, and other messages to the author of a document. Comments do not affect the text of the document.

To Insert a Comment

After reading through the paper, you have two comments for the originator (author) of the document related to the patient brochure that will be created from content in the research paper. The following steps insert a comment in the document. ***Why?*** *You insert a comment, which creates a note for the author of the document.* Because you want the comment associated with several words, you select the text before inserting the comment.

- Select the text to which the comment applies (in this case, in the last sentence of the second paragraph).
- Click Review on the ribbon to display the Review tab.
- If the 'Display for Review' box (Review tab | Tracking group) does not show Simple Markup, click the 'Display for Review' arrow (Review tab | Tracking group) and then click Simple Markup on the Display for Review menu to instruct Word to display a simple markup.

Q&A What is Simple Markup?
Simple Markup is a less cluttered view of comments and other collaboration elements than All Markup.

- If the Show Comments button (Review tab | Comments group) is not selected, click it to select it (Figure 2–84).

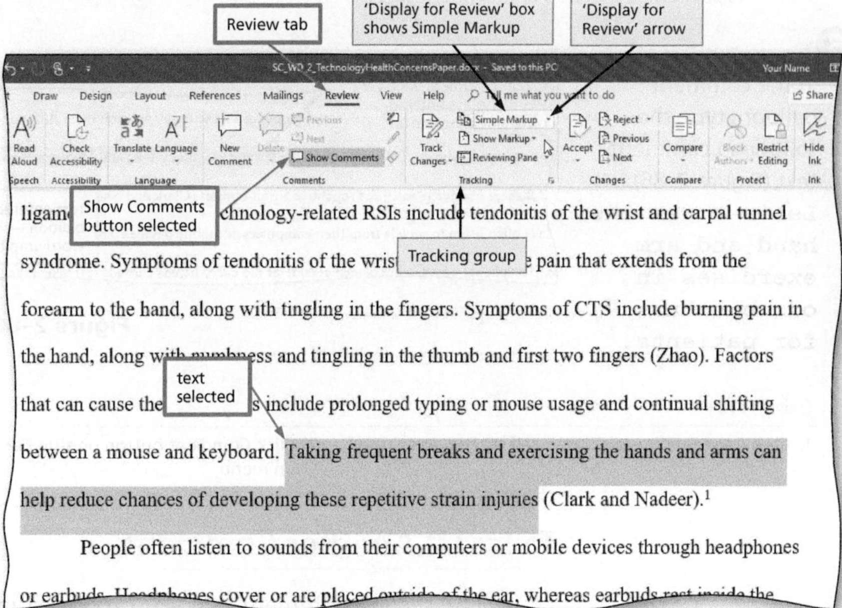

Figure 2–84

Q&A What is the purpose of the Show Comments button?
When the Show Comments button is selected, the comments appear in the markup area to the right of the document. When it is not selected, comments appear as icons in the document.

Do I have to select text before inserting a comment?
No, you can position the insertion point at the location where the comment should be located. If you do not select text on which you wish to comment, Word automatically selects the text to the right or left of the insertion point for the comment.

- Click the New Comment button (Review tab | Comments group) to display a comment balloon in the markup area in the document window.
- Change the zoom so that the entire document and markup area are visible in the document window (Figure 2–85).

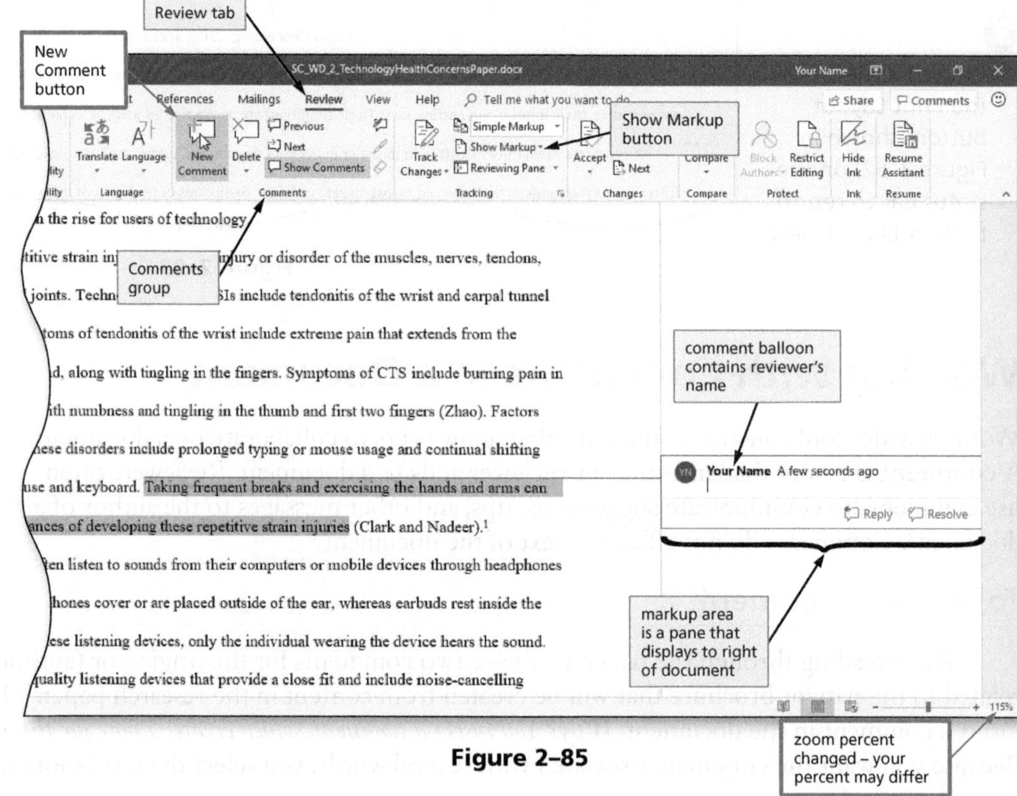

Figure 2–85

Q&A What if the markup area does not appear with the comment balloon?
The balloons setting has been turned off. Click the Show Markup button (Review tab | Tracking group) and then, if a checkmark does not appear to the left of Comments on the Show Markup menu, click Comments. If comments still do not appear, click the Show Markup button again, point to Balloons on the Show Markup menu, and then click 'Show Only Comments and Formatting in Balloons' on the Balloons submenu, which is the default setting.

- In the comment balloon, type the following comment text (Figure 2–86): **Let's cover the hand and arm exercises in our brochure for patients.**

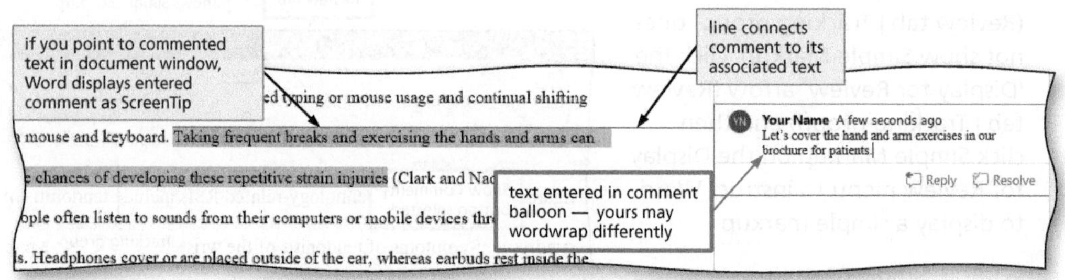

Figure 2–86

Other Ways

1. Click Comment button (Insert tab | Comments group)
2. Click Comment button on title bar, click New Comment on menu
3. Press CTRL+ALT+M

To Insert Another Comment

The second comment you want to insert in the document refers to a topic for the brochure. The following steps insert another comment in the document.

1. Select the text to which the comment applies (in this case, the last sentence of the fourth paragraph).
2. Click the New Comment button (Review tab | Comments group) to display another comment balloon in the markup area in the document window.
3. In the new comment balloon, type the following comment text (Figure 2–87): **`Let's stress this point in our brochure for patients.`**

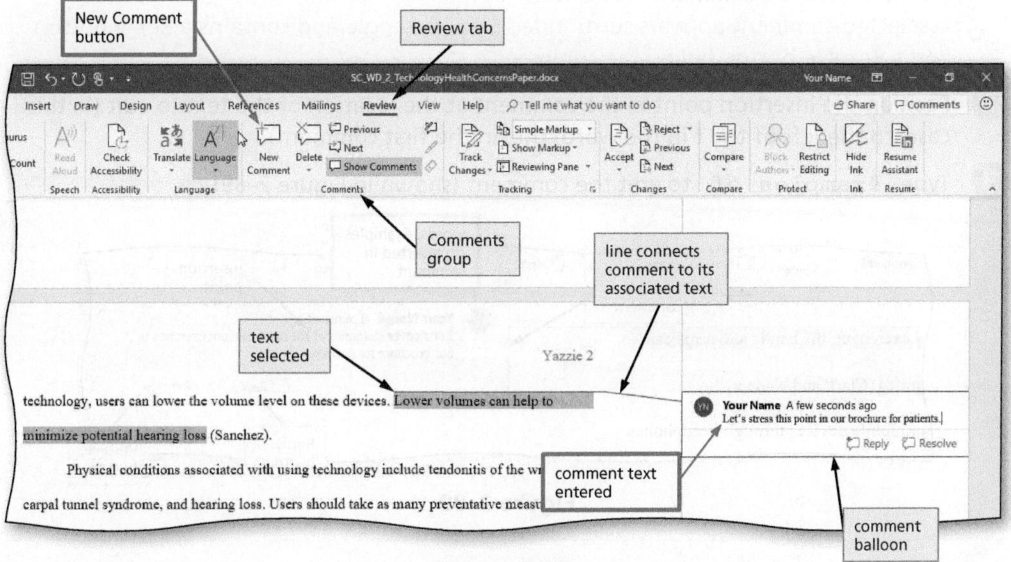

Figure 2–87

To Go To a Comment

The next step is to display the previous comment. ***Why?*** *You could scroll through the document to locate a comment by reading them as they appear in the markup area, but it is more efficient to use the Review tab.* The following step displays the previous comment in the document.

1.
- Click the Previous button (Review tab | Comments group), which causes Word to locate and select the previous comment in the document (Figure 2–88).

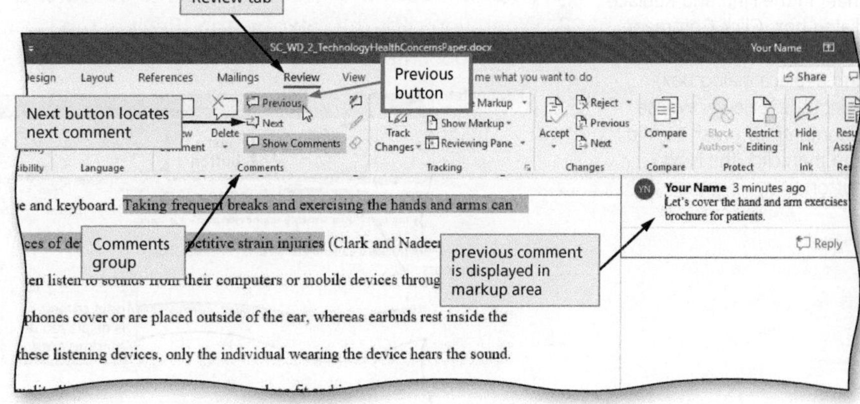

Figure 2–88

Q&A What if I wanted to see the next comment, instead of the previous comment, in a document?
You would click the Next button (Review tab | Comments group) instead of the Previous button.

What if I wanted to move from one comment to the next in a document from the beginning of the document?
You would position the insertion point at the top of the document, and then click the Next button (Review tab | Comments group) repeatedly until you have seen all comments in the document.

Other Ways

1. Click Find arrow (Home tab | Editing group), click Go To, click Comment in Go to what area (Find and Replace dialog box), click Next button
2. Press CTRL+G, click Comment in Go to what area (Find and Replace dialog box), click Next button

To Edit a Comment in a Comment Balloon

You modify comments in a comment balloon by clicking inside the comment balloon and editing the same way you edit text in the document window. In this project, you insert the words, examples of, in the first comment. The following steps edit a comment in a balloon.

1. Click the comment balloon to select it.

Q&A How can I tell if a comment is selected?
A selected comment appears surrounded by a rectangle and contains a Reply button and a Resolve button below the comment.

2. Position the insertion point in the comment at the location of the text to edit (in this case, to the left of the t in the word, the, in the first comment).

3. Type **examples of** to edit the comment (shown in Figure 2–89).

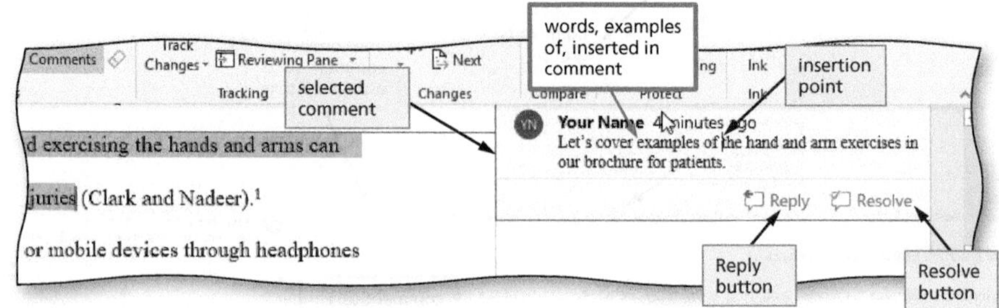

Figure 2–89

To Go to a Comment

The next step is to display the next comment because you want to reply to it. The following step displays the next comment in the document.

- Click the Next button (Review tab | Comments group), which causes Word to locate and select the next comment in the document (Figure 2–90).

Q&A What if I reach the last comment in a document?
When you click the Next button (Review tab | Comments group), Word moves to the top of the document and displays the first comment in the document.

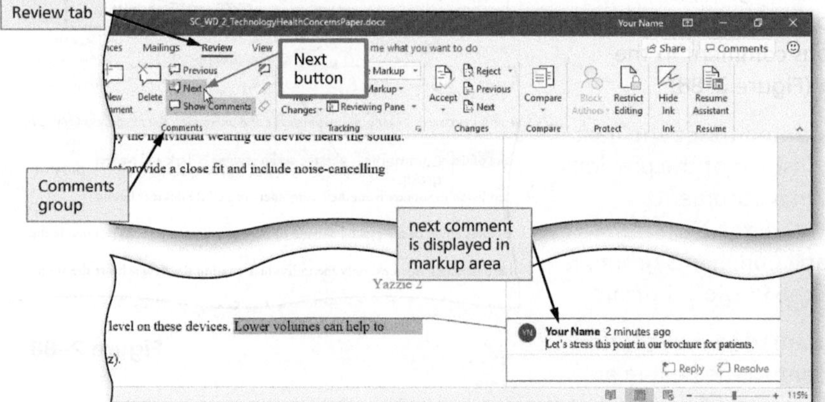

Figure 2–90

BTW
Locating Comments by Reviewer
You can find a comment from a specific reviewer through the Go To dialog box. Click the Find arrow (Home tab | Editing group) and then click Go To or press CTRL+G to display the Go To sheet in the Find and Replace dialog box. Click Comment in the Go to what list (Find and Replace dialog box). Select the reviewer whose comments you wish to find and then click the Next button.

To Reply to a Comment

Sometimes, you want to reply to an existing comment. ***Why?** You may want to respond to a question by another reviewer or provide additional information to a previous comment you inserted.* The following steps reply to the comment you inserted on the second page of the document.

1

- If necessary, click the comment to which you wish to reply so that the comment is selected (in this case, the second comment).

2

- Click the Reply button in the selected comment to display a reply comment for the selected comment.

3

- In the new indented comment, type the following comment text: `Excellent idea!` (Figure 2–91).

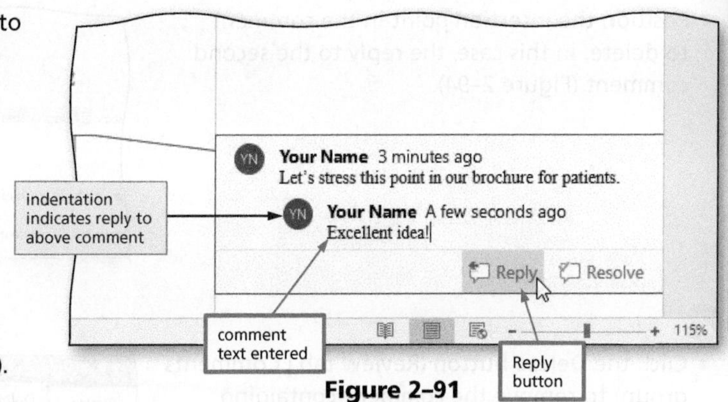

Figure 2–91

Other Ways

1. Right-click comment (or, if using touch, tap 'Show Context Menu' button on Mini toolbar), click 'Reply To Comment' on shortcut menu

To Hide and Show Comments

The next step is to hide all comments in the document. ***Why?*** *You would like to view the document without the markup area on the screen but do not want to delete the comments at this time.* The following steps hide comments and then show them.

1

- If the Show Comments button (Review tab | Comments group) is selected, click it to deselect it, which hides comments in the document (Figure 2–92).

Q&A What happened to the markup area?
When the Show Comments button is not selected, the markup area is hidden and comments appear as icons in the document.

Are the hidden comments deleted from the document?
No.

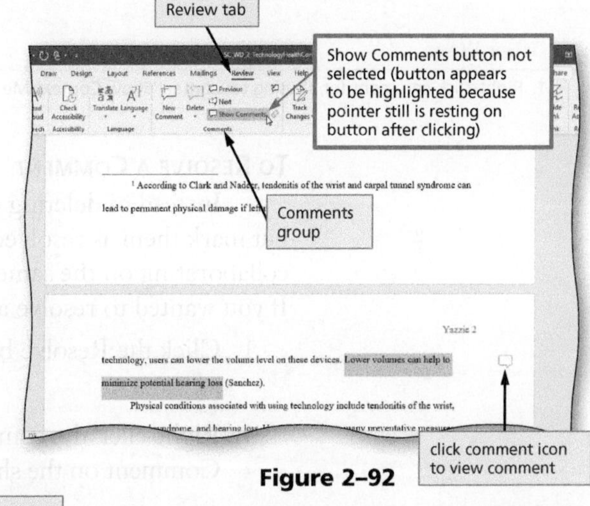

Figure 2–92

2

- Click the comment icon to display the associated comment (Figure 2–93).

3

- Click the comment icon again, or click the comment Close button, to hide the comment.
- Click the Show Comments button (Review tab | Comments group) to show comments again, which redisplays the comments in the markup area (as shown in Figure 2–91).

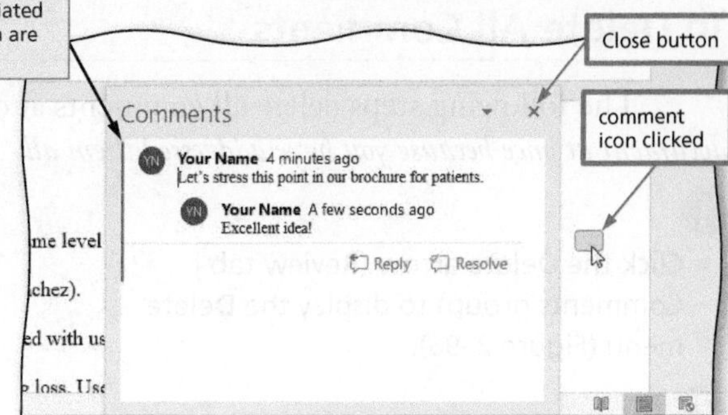

Figure 2–93

To Delete a Comment

The following steps delete a comment. ***Why?*** *You have read the comment and want to remove it from the document.*

- Position the insertion point in the comment to delete, in this case, the reply to the second comment (Figure 2–94).

Figure 2–94

- Click the Delete button (Review tab | Comments group) to remove the comment containing the insertion point from the markup area (Figure 2–95).

Q&A What if I accidentally click the Delete arrow?
Click Delete on the Delete menu.

If the insertion point was in a comment that contained a reply, would the reply also be deleted?
Yes.

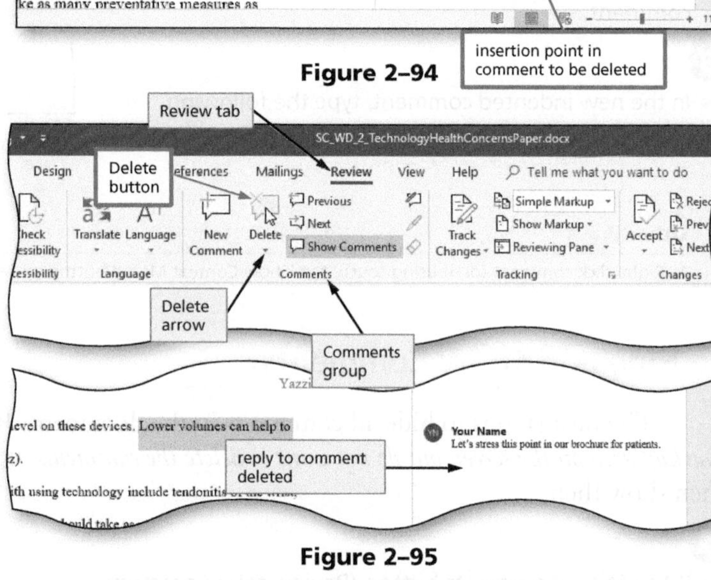

Figure 2–95

Other Ways

1. Right-click comment (or, if using touch, tap 'Show Context Menu' button on Mini toolbar), click Delete Comment on shortcut menu

To Resolve a Comment

Instead of deleting comments, some users prefer to leave them in the document but mark them as resolved. This is especially useful when multiple users are collaborating on the same document. When you resolve a comment, it changes color. If you wanted to resolve a comment, you would perform one of the following steps.

1. Click the Resolve button in the comment balloon.

or

1. Right-click the comment to display a shortcut menu and then click Resolve Comment on the shortcut menu.

To Delete All Comments

The following steps delete all comments at once. ***Why?*** *Assume you now want to delete all the comments in the document at once because you have addressed them all.*

- Click the Delete arrow (Review tab | Comments group) to display the Delete menu (Figure 2–96).

2

- Click 'Delete All Comments in Document' on the Delete menu to remove all comments from the document, which also closes the markup area.

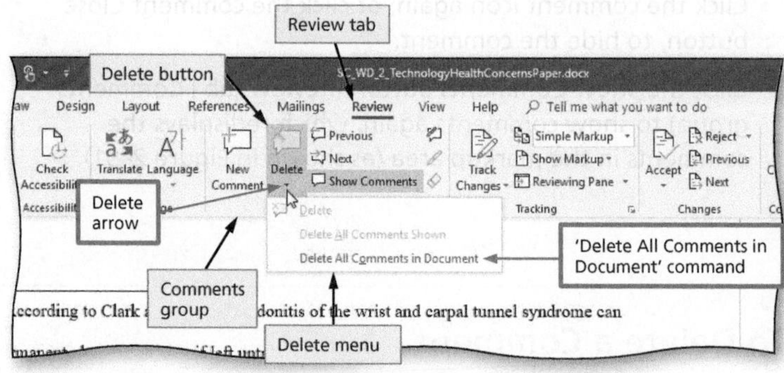

Figure 2–96

TO USE THE DOCUMENT INSPECTOR

Word includes a Document Inspector that checks a document for content you might not want to share with others, such as comments or personal information. Before sharing a document with others, you may want to check for this type of content. If you wanted to use the Document Inspector, you would do the following:

1. Open Backstage view and, if necessary, click Info in Backstage view to display the Info screen.
2. Click the 'Check for Issues' button in the Info screen to display the Check for Issues menu.
3. Click Inspect Document on the Check for Issues menu to display the Document Inspector dialog box. Select the check boxes for which you would like to check the document.
4. Click the Inspect button (Document Inspector dialog box) to instruct Word to inspect the document.
5. Review the results (Document Inspector dialog box) and then click the Remove All button(s) for any item that you do not want to be saved with the document.
6. When finished removing information, click the Close button to close the dialog box.

To Exit Word

You are finished with this project. The following step exits Word.

 Exit Word.

Summary

In this module, you learned how to modify styles, adjust line and paragraph spacing, use headers to number pages, insert and edit citations and their sources, add footnotes, create a bibliographical list of sources, update a field, go to a page, find and replace text, check spelling and grammar, look up information, and work with comments.

CONSIDER THIS: PLAN AHEAD

What decisions will you need to make when creating your next research paper?

Use these guidelines as you complete the assignments in this module and create your own research papers outside of this class.

1. Select a topic.
   a) Spend time brainstorming ideas for a topic.
   b) Choose a topic you find interesting.
   c) For shorter papers, narrow the scope of the topic; for longer papers, broaden the scope.
   d) Identify a tentative thesis statement, which is a sentence describing the paper's subject matter.
2. Research the topic and take notes, being careful not to plagiarize.
3. Organize your notes into related concepts, identifying all main ideas and supporting details in an outline.
4. Write the first draft from the outline, referencing all sources of information and following the guidelines identified in the required documentation style.
5. Create the list of sources, using the formats specified in the required documentation style.
6. Proofread and revise the paper.

Apply Your Knowledge

Reinforce the skills and apply the concepts you learned in this module.

Revising Content and Working with Citations and Sources in a Document

Note: To complete this assignment, you will be required to use the Data Files. Please contact your instructor for information about accessing the Data Files.

Instructions: Start Word. Open the document, SC_WD_2-1.docx, which is located in the Data Files. The document you open contains two paragraphs of text that are notes about shopping safely online with respect to passwords and credit cards. The manager of Brayden Department Stores, who created the shopping safely online notes, has asked you to revise the document as follows: check spelling and grammar, change paragraph indentation, change line spacing, remove space before and after paragraphs, find all occurrences of a word, replace all occurrences of a word with another series of words, locate a synonym, edit the header, add a sentence, insert and edit citations and sources, delete a source, and insert a reference list. The modified document is shown in Figure 2–97.

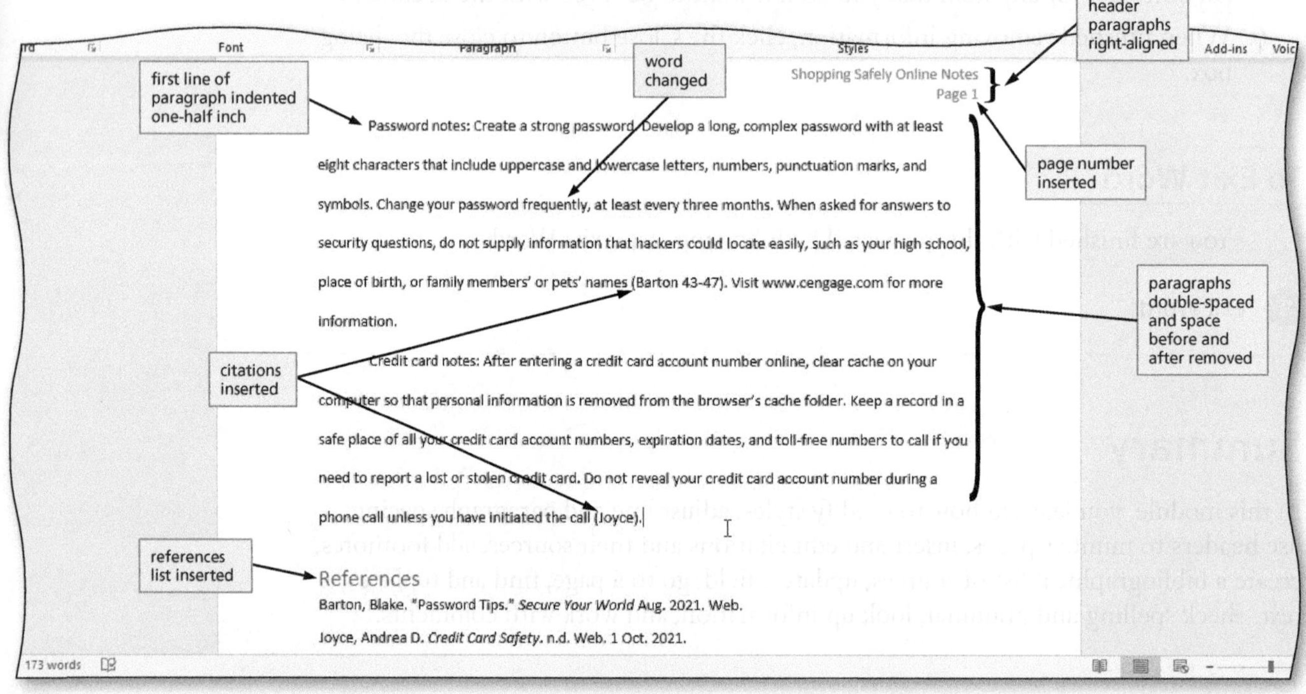

Figure 2–97

Perform the following tasks:

1. Click File on the ribbon, click Save As, and then save the document using the new file name, SC_WD_2_ShoppingSafelyOnlineNotes.
2. Check spelling and grammar at once. Correct the spelling and grammar mistakes in the document. Change all instances of the suggested spelling change of account for the misspelled word, accounte.
3. Display the ruler, if necessary. Use the ruler to indent the first line of the first paragraph one-half inch. (If you are using a touch screen, use the Paragraph dialog box.) Hide the ruler.
4. Select the entire document and change the line spacing to double. With entire document selected, remove space after paragraphs. With the entire document selected, remove space before and after paragraphs. (*Hint:* Use the 'Line and Paragraph Spacing' button again for each command.)
5. Find all occurrences of the word, password. How many are there?

6. Use the Find and Replace dialog box to replace all occurrences of the word, card, with the words, credit card. How many replacements were made?
7. Show the Navigation Pane. Use the Navigation Pane to find the word, often. Close the Navigation Pane. Use Word's thesaurus to change the word, often, to the word, frequently. What other words are in the list of synonyms?
8. Switch to the header so that you can edit it. In the first line of the header, insert the word, Online, after the word, Safely, so that it reads: Shopping Safely Online Notes.
9. In the second line of the header, insert a page number (a plain number with no formatting) one space after the word, Page.
10. If requested by your instructor, enter your first and last name on a separate line below the page number in the header.
11. Change the alignment of all lines of text in the header from left-aligned to right-aligned. Close the header and footer.
12. At the end of the Password notes paragraph. Type `Visit www.cengage.com for more information.` After you type the web address, continue typing to accept the automatic correction of the web address to a hyperlink format. Use the AutoCorrect Options button (point to the web address to display the small blue underline and then point to the blue underline to display the AutoCorrect Options button) and then undo the automatic hyperlink correction using the AutoCorrect Options button.
13. At the end of the fourth sentence in the Password notes paragraph (before the period), insert a citation using the existing source in the document for the article by Blake Barton. Edit this citation to include the page numbers 43–47.
14. At the end of the last sentence in the Credit card notes paragraph (before the period), insert a citation placeholder called Joyce. Edit the source for the placeholder, Joyce, as follows: Type of source is Web site, author is Andrea D. Joyce, name of webpage is Credit Card Safety, year accessed is 2021, month accessed is Oct., day accessed is 1, and medium is Web.
15. Delete the source for the author named Anastasia Maria Pappas. (*Hint:* Use the Manage Sources button.)
16. Press ENTER at the end of the document. Apply the Normal style to the blank line at the end of the document. Insert a bibliography using the References format in the Bibliography gallery.
17. Save the document again with the same file name.
18. Submit the modified document, shown in Figure 2–97, in the format specified by your instructor.
19. Use the Smart Lookup pane to look up the word, cache. If necessary, click the Explore tab in the Smart Lookup pane. Which web articles appeared? Click the Define tab in the Smart Lookup pane. Which dictionary was used?
20. Exit Word.
21. Answer the questions posed in #5, #6, #7, and #19. How would you find and replace a special character, such as a paragraph mark?

Extend Your Knowledge

Extend the skills you learned in this module and experiment with new skills. You may need to use Help to complete the assignment.

Working with References and Proofing Tools

Note: To complete this assignment, you will be required to use the Data Files. Please contact your instructor for information about accessing the Data Files.

Continued >

Extend Your Knowledge *continued*

Instructions: As a customer relationship coordinator at Windermere Bank and Trust, you communicate banking tips to customers. You also are a part-time student who has been assigned a research paper. You decide to combine your work and school interests and compose a short research paper about ATM safety. You will communicate your findings with bank customers.

Start Word. Open the document, SC_WD_2-2.docx, which is located in the Data Files. The document is your draft research paper. You will do the following to finish the paper: find formats and special characters, delete a footer, add another footnote to the paper, change the format of the note reference marks, convert the footnotes to endnotes, modify a style, use Word's readability statistics, work with comments, and translate the document to another language (Figure 2–98).

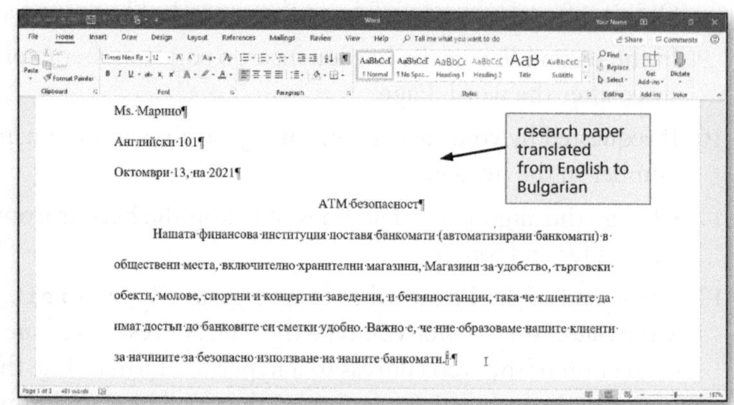

Figure 2–98

Perform the following tasks:

1. Use Help to learn more about finding formats and special characters, footers, footnotes and endnotes, readability statistics, bibliography styles, AutoCorrect, and Word's translation features.
2. Click File on the ribbon, click Save As, and then save the revised document using the new file name, SC_WD_2_SafelyUsingATMs.
3. Use the Advanced Find command on the Find menu to find the italic format in the paper and then remove the italic format. Click the No Formatting button in the Find and Replace dialog box to clear the format from the next search.
4. Use the Advanced Find command on the Find menu to find a footnote mark in the paper (which is a special character). What characters did Word place in the Find what box to search for the footnote mark? What number in the research paper is the footnote reference mark?
5. Edit the footer so that it reads: Delete this footer from the research paper. Delete the footer from the document.
6. Insert a second footnote at an appropriate place in the research paper. Use the following footnote text: **`If you suspect someone is following you, immediately walk to a populated area or business, or drive to a police or fire station.`**
7. Change the location of the footnotes from bottom of page to below text. How did the placement of the footnotes change?
8. Change the format of the note reference marks to capital letters (A, B, etc.). (*Hint:* Change the footnote number format using the Footnote and Endnote dialog box.)
9. Convert the footnotes to endnotes. Use the Navigation Pane to display each page in the document. Where are the endnotes positioned? What is the format of the note reference marks when they are endnotes?
10. Modify the Endnote Text style to 12-point Times New Roman font, double-spaced text with a hanging indent by clicking Style on the shortcut menu, clicking Endnote Text (Style dialog box), clicking the Modify button, and then selecting appropriate options in the Modify Style dialog box.

11. Insert this endnote for the first paragraph in the paper: **Our ATMs enable customers to withdraw and deposit money, transfer funds, or inquire about an account balance.**
12. Add an AutoCorrect entry that replaces the word, costomers, with the word, customers. Type the following sentence as the last sentence in the last paragraph of the paper, misspelling the word, customers, as costomers to test the AutoCorrect entry: **Taking precautions when using our ATMs can help costomers avoid becoming a target of criminal activity.** Delete the AutoCorrect entry that replaces costomers with the word, customers.
13. Display the Word Count dialog box. How many words, characters without spaces, characters with spaces, paragraphs, and lines are in the document? Be sure to include footnote and endnote text in the statistics.
14. Check spelling of the document, displaying readability statistics. What are the Flesch-Kincaid Grade Level and the Flesch Reading Ease score? How could you modify the paper to increase the reading ease score and lower the grade level?
15. If requested by your instructor, change the student name at the top of the paper to your name, including the last name in the header.
16. Change the zoom to multiple pages. How many pages are in the document?
17. Save the revised document paper again with the same name and then submit it in the format specified by your instructor.
18. Display the Info screen in Backstage view. How many draft versions of the document have been saved? How would you recover unsaved changes? If you have unsaved changes, recover them.
19. If it is not dimmed, test the Read Aloud button (Review tab | Speech group). What is the purpose of the Read Aloud button?
20. If requested by your instructor, perform these tasks:
    a. Insert this comment in the third paragraph: **Add a discussion about skimmers after this paragraph.**
    b. Insert another comment in the fourth paragraph: **Add a paragraph about reviewing bank statements after this paragraph.**
    c. Go to the first comment. Change the word, discussion, to the word, paragraph, in the first comment.
    d. Go to the second comment. Reply to the second comment with this comment text: **Also discuss reviewing transactions online.**
    e. Submit the document with comments in the format specified by your instructor.
    f. Inspect the document and review the results.
    g. Hide comments and then show comments.
    h. Delete the first comment. Resolve the second comment.
    i. Delete all comments.
21. If you have an Internet connection, translate the research paper into a language of your choice using the Translate button (Review tab | Language group), as shown in Figure 2–98. If requested by your instructor, submit the translated document in the format specified by your instructor.
22. Answer the questions posed in #4, #7, #9, #13, #14, #16, #18, and #19. Where did you insert the second footnote and why?

Expand Your World

Create a solution that uses cloud or web technologies by learning and investigating on your own from general guidance.

Using an Online Bibliography Tool to Create a List of Sources

Instructions: Assume you are attending a conference about workplace diversity and the computer or mobile device you have available at the conference does not have Word but has Internet access. As a human resources generalist at Whole Health Foods, you decide while attending this conference that you would like to educate employees about workplace diversity. You decide to use an online bibliography tool to create a list of sources that you can copy and paste into the Works Cited pages of a research paper you will create when you return to the office.

Perform the following tasks:

1. Start a browser. Search for the text, online bibliography tool, using a search engine. Visit several of the online bibliography tools and determine which you would like to use to create a list of sources. Navigate to the desired online bibliography tool.
2. Use the online bibliography tool to enter list of sources shown below (Figure 2–99):

   Chung, Kim Li, and Jordan Taylor Green. *Managing Diversity in the Workplace.* Chicago: Windy City Press, 2021. Print.

   Delhi, Rajesh. "Workplace Monthly Review." *Your Workplace.* Sept. 2021. Web. 1 Oct. 2021.

   Garlapati, Vidya. "Creating an Inclusive Workplace." *Diversity Learning.* July 2021. Web. 9 Oct. 2021.

   Hidalgo, Ronald P. *The Workplace Diversity Handbook.* Dallas: Lone Star Publishing, 2021. Print.

   Samaras, Alexander Lee. *Workplace Diversity.* Los Angeles: Sunshine Publications, 2021. Print.

   VanWijk, Fred J., and John L. Walker. "Work Team Diversity." *The Successful Workplace.* June 2021. Web. 8 Oct. 2021.

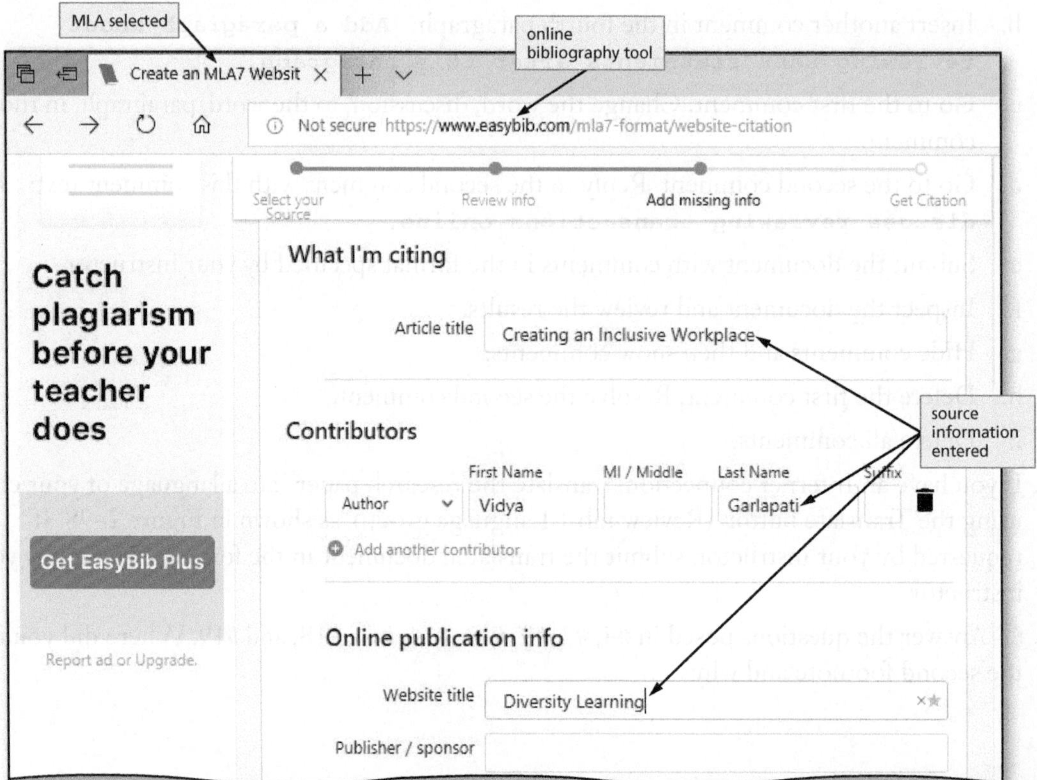

Figure 2–99

3. If requested by your instructor, replace the name in one of the sources above with your name.
4. Search for another source that discusses workplace diversity. Add that source.
5. Use the Export option in the online bibliography tool or copy and paste the list of sources into a Word document.
6. Save the document with the file name, SC_WD_2_WorkplaceDiversitySources. Submit the document in the format specified by your instructor.
7. Which online bibliography tools did you evaluate? Which one did you select to use and why? Do you prefer using the online bibliography tool or Word to create sources? Why? What differences, if any, did you notice between the list of sources created with the online bibliography tool and the lists created when you use Word?

In the Lab

Design and implement a solution using creative thinking and problem-solving skills.

Create a Research Paper about Drones

Note: To complete this assignment, you will be required to use the Data Files. Please contact your instructor for information about accessing the Data Files.

Problem: As the marketing communications coordinator for Darden Aircraft, you create a research paper about drones because you want to educate the public about them.

Perform the following tasks:

Part 1: The source for the text in your research paper is in a file named SC_WD_2-3.docx, which is located in the Data Files. Organize the notes in the text in the file in the Data Files, rewording as necessary so that you can create a research paper. Using the concepts and techniques presented in this module, along with your organized notes from the Data File, create and format a research paper according to the MLA documentation style (be sure to write an appropriate conclusion). While creating the paper, be sure to do the following:

1. Modify the Normal style to the 12-point Times New Roman font.
2. Adjust line spacing to double.
3. Remove space below (after) paragraphs.
4. Update the Normal style to reflect the adjusted line and paragraph spacing.
5. Insert an MLA-style header, and insert page numbers in the header.
6. Type the name and course information at the left margin. Use your name and course information. Center and type the title.
7. Set a first-line indent to one-half inch for paragraphs in the body of the research paper.
8. Add an AutoCorrect entry to correct a word you commonly mistype.
9. Type the body of the research paper from the notes. Change the bibliography style to MLA. As you insert citations, enter their source information. Edit the citations so that they are displayed according to the MLA documentation style.
10. At the end of the research paper text, press ENTER and then insert a page break so that the Works Cited page begins on a new page. Enter and format the works cited title and then use Word to insert the bibliographical list (bibliography).

Continued >

In the Lab *continued*

11. If your instructor requests, use the Researcher pane to obtain information from another source and include that information as a note positioned as a footnote in the paper, and enter its corresponding source information as appropriate. Update the bibliography.
12. Check the spelling and grammar of the paper at once. Add one of the source last names to the dictionary. Ignore all instances of one of the source last names. If necessary, set the default dictionary.

When you are finished with the research paper, save it with the file name, SC_WD_2_DronesPaper. Submit your assignment and answers to the Part 2 critical thinking questions in the format specified by your instructor.

Part 2: You made several decisions while creating the research paper in this assignment: how to organize the notes, what text to use for the conclusion, where to place citations, how to format sources, and which source on the web to use for the footnote text (if requested by your instructor). What was the rationale behind each of these decisions? When you proofread the document, what further revisions did you make and why?

2 Enhancing Presentations with Shapes and SmartArt

Objectives

After completing this module, you will be able to:

- Search for and download an online theme
- Insert a symbol
- Insert a hyperlink
- Convert text to SmartArt
- Edit and format SmartArt text
- Insert and resize a shape
- Apply effects to a shape
- Add text to a shape
- Apply a shape style
- Insert a picture as a shape fill
- Move an object using grids, guides, and the ruler
- Merge shapes
- Add a footer
- Add a slide transition and change effect options

Introduction

In our visually oriented culture, audience members enjoy viewing effective graphics. Whether reading a document or viewing a PowerPoint presentation, people increasingly want to see photographs, artwork, graphics, and a variety of typefaces. Researchers have known for decades that documents with visual elements are more effective than those that consist of only text because the illustrations motivate audiences to study the material. People remember at least one-third more information when the document they are seeing or reading contains visual elements. These graphics help clarify and emphasize details, so they appeal to audience members with differing backgrounds, reading levels, attention spans, and motivations.

BTW
Building Speaker Confidence
As you rehearse your speech, keep in mind that your audience will be studying the visual elements during your actual presentation and will not be focusing on you. Using graphics in a presentation should give you confidence as a presenter because they support your verbal message and help reinforce what you are trying to convey.

Project—Presentation with SmartArt and Shapes

In this module's project, you will follow proper design guidelines and learn to use PowerPoint to create the slides shown in Figures 2–1a through 2–1e. The objective is to produce a presentation for the Greenest Street Corporation that focuses on publicizing its energy conservation program for customers. Homeowners can reduce energy consumption by using such products as LED light bulbs, low-flow showerheads, and programmable thermostats. They also can manage their energy usage by reducing consumption during peak times and cycling their air conditioning compressor. The presentation shown in Figure 2–1 follows graphical guidelines and has a variety of visual elements that are clear and appealing to homeowners seeking to reduce their utility bills. For example, the shapes have specific designs and effects. They are formatted using styles and SmartArt, which give the presentation a professional look. Transitions help one slide flow gracefully into the next during a slide show.

presentation theme downloaded
Conserve Energy at Home
SAVE MONEY AND INCREASE COMFORT
shape inserted with picture fill and formatted

iStock.com/Telman Bagirov

(a) Slide 1 (Title Slide with Shape with Picture Fill)

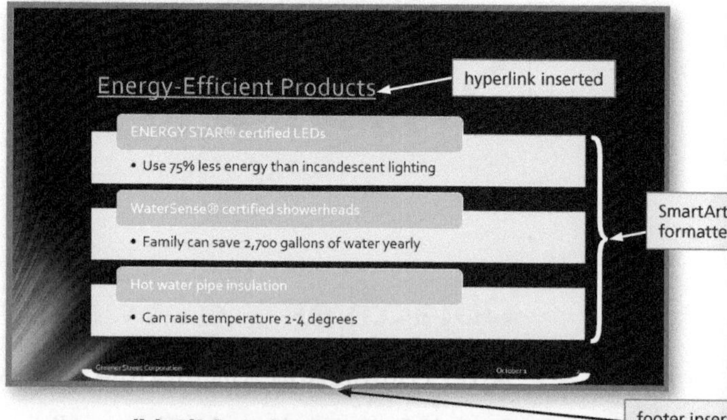

(b) Slide 2 (Formatted SmartArt)

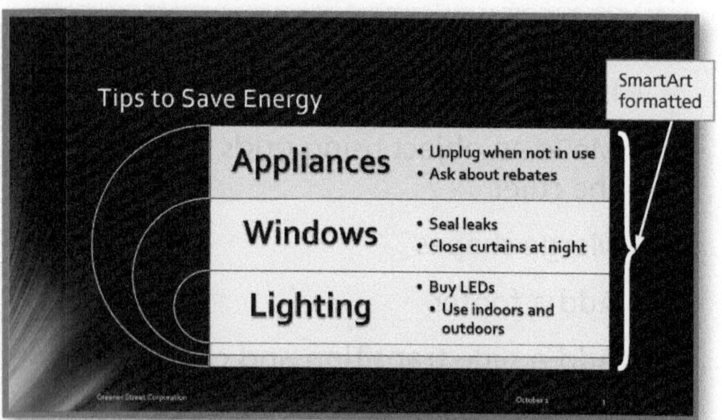

(c) Slide 3 (Formatted SmartArt)

Manage Your Energy
shape inserted with picture fill and formatted
SmartArt formatted
Hourly pricing
Peak time savings
Central AC cycling

iStock.com/malerapaso

(d) Slide 4 (Formatted SmartArt and Shape with Picture Fill)

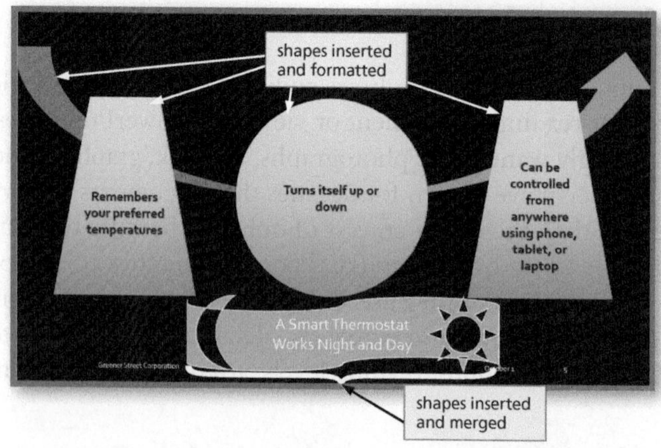

(d) Slide 5 (Shapes Inserted and Formatted)

Figure 2–1

In this module, you will learn how to create the slides shown in Figure 2–1. You will perform the following general tasks as you progress through this module:

1. Download a theme and select slides for the presentation.
2. Insert a symbol and a hyperlink.
3. Create, edit, and format SmartArt.
4. Insert and format shapes.
5. Resize and merge shapes.
6. Move shapes using grids, guides, and ruler.
7. Add a footer and a transition.

Downloading a Theme and Editing Slides

In Module 1, you selected a theme and then typed the content for the title and text slides. In this module, you will type the slide content for the title and text slides, insert and format SmartArt, and insert and format shapes. To begin creating the five slides in this presentation, you will download a theme, delete unneeded slides in this downloaded presentation, and then enter content in the slides.

BTW
Screen Resolution
If you are using a computer to step through the project in this module and you want your screens to match the figures in this book, you should change your screen's resolution to 1366 × 768.

To Search for and Download an Online Theme

PowerPoint displays many themes that are varied and appealing and give you an excellent start at designing a presentation. At times, however, you may have a specific topic and design concept and could use some assistance in starting to develop the presentation. Microsoft offers hundreds of predesigned themes and templates that could provide you with an excellent starting point. ***Why?*** *You can search for one of these ready-made presentations, or you can browse one of the predefined categories, such as business or education. The themes and templates can save you time and help you develop content.* The following steps search for a theme with an electric concept.

1

- **sam** Run PowerPoint and then point to the More themes link (Figure 2–2).

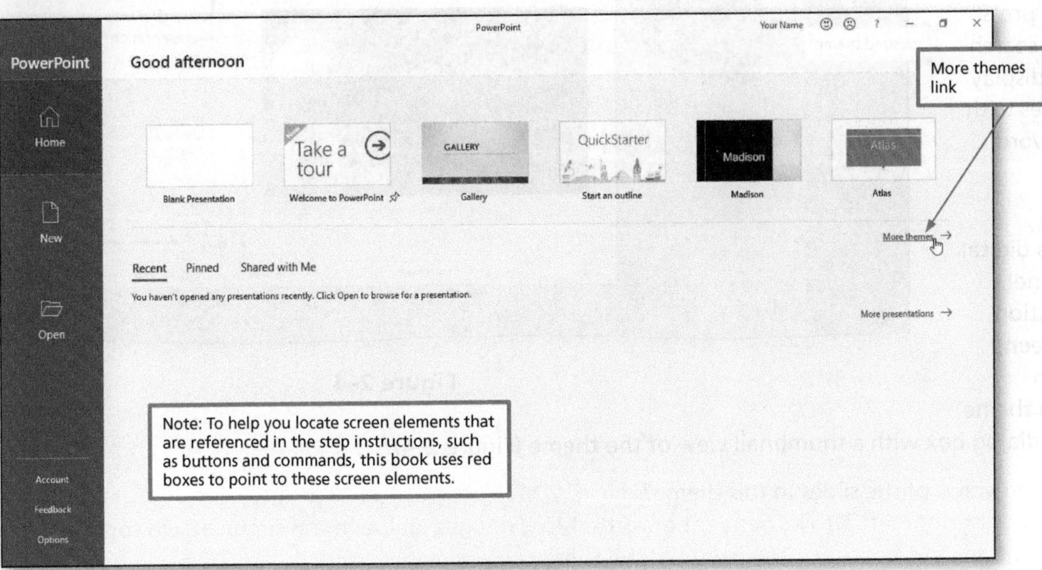

Figure 2–2

- Click the More themes link to display the New screen and then type **electric** in the 'Search for online templates and themes' box (Figure 2–3).

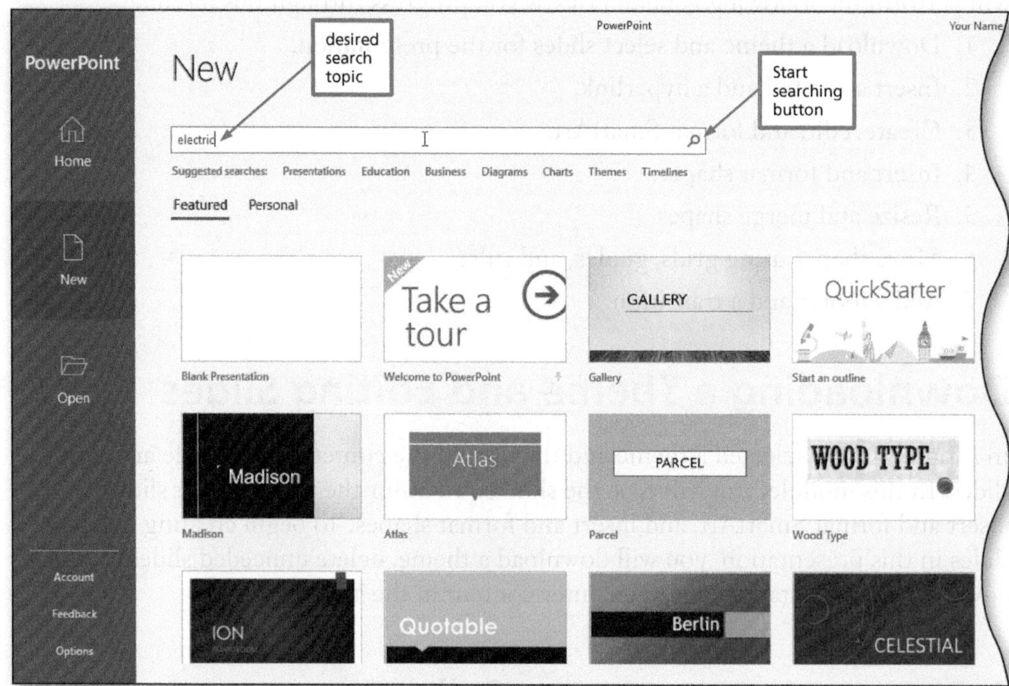

Figure 2–3

Q&A Why are my theme thumbnails displaying in a different order?
The order changes as you choose themes for presentations. In addition, Microsoft occasionally adds and modifies the themes, so the order may change.

Can I choose one of the keywords listed below the 'Search for online templates and themes' box?
Yes. Click one of the terms in the Suggested searches list to display a variety of templates and themes relating to those topics.

- Click the Start searching button (the magnifying glass) or press ENTER to search for and display all themes with the keyword, electric.
- Click the 'Business digital blue tunnel presentation (widescreen)' theme to display a theme preview dialog box with a thumbnail view of the theme (Figure 2–4).

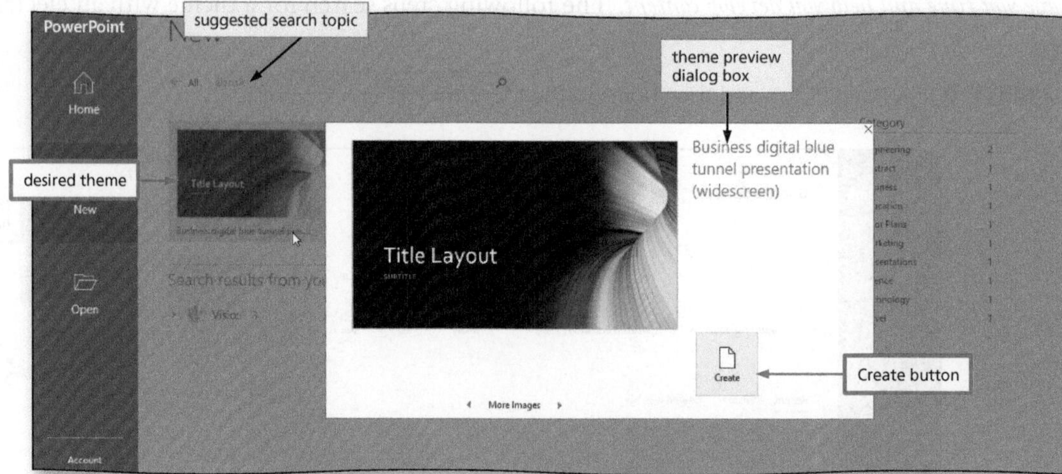

Figure 2–4

Q&A Can I see previews of the slides in this theme?
Yes. Click the right or left arrows beside the words, More Images, below the thumbnail. On some devices, a preview of all slides starts automatically after you tap the theme.

- Click the Create button to download the theme and open a presentation with that theme in PowerPoint.

To Save the Presentation

You can save the downloaded slides now to keep track of the changes you make as you progress through this module. The following steps save the file as a PowerPoint presentation.

1. Click the File tab to display the Backstage view, click the Save As tab to display the Save As gallery, click This PC in the Other Locations list, and then click the More options link to display the Save As dialog box.
2. Type `SC_PPT_2_Energy` as the file name.
2. Click Save to save the presentation to the default save location.

BTW

Organizing Files and Folders

You should organize and store files in folders so that you easily can find the files later. For example, if you are taking an introductory technology class called CIS 101, a good practice would be to save all PowerPoint files in a PowerPoint folder in a CIS 101 folder.

To Delete a Slide

The downloaded theme has 11 slides with a variety of layouts. You will use three of these different layouts in your Conserve Energy presentation, so you can delete the slides you downloaded that you will not need. ***Why?** Deleting the extra slides now helps reduce clutter and helps you focus on the layouts you will use.* The following steps delete the extra slides.

1

- Click the Slide 3 thumbnail in the Slides tab to select this slide.
- Press and hold CTRL and then click the thumbnail for Slide 4 to select both slides 3 and 4 (Figure 2–5).

Q&A Do I need to select consecutive slides?
No. You can select an individual slide to delete. You also can select nonconsecutive slides by pressing and holding CTRL down and then clicking the thumbnails of the slides you want to delete.

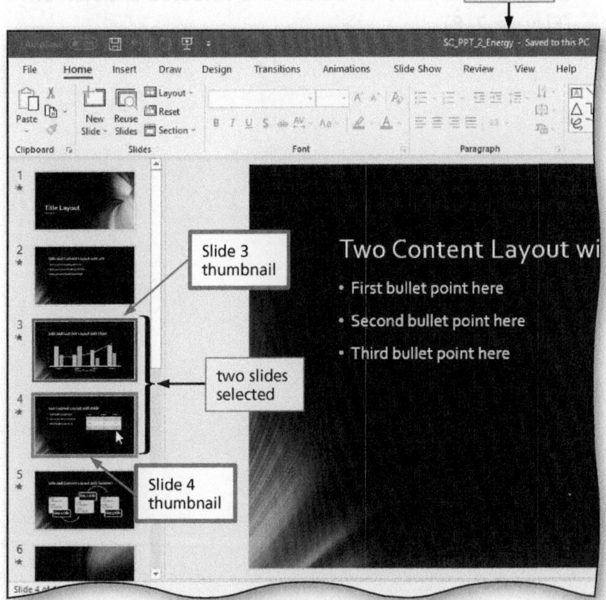

Figure 2–5

2

- Right-click either selected slide to display the shortcut menu (Figure 2–6).

3

- Click Delete Slide to delete the selected slides from the presentation.

4

- Click the Slide 4 thumbnail in the Slides tab to select this slide.
- Press and hold SHIFT, scroll down, and then click the thumbnail for Slide 9 to select slides 4 through 9.

Q&A Why did I press and hold down CTRL to select the first two slides to delete and then SHIFT to select slides 4 through 9?
Holding CTRL selects only the slides you click, whereas holding down SHIFT selects consecutive slides between the first and last selected slides.

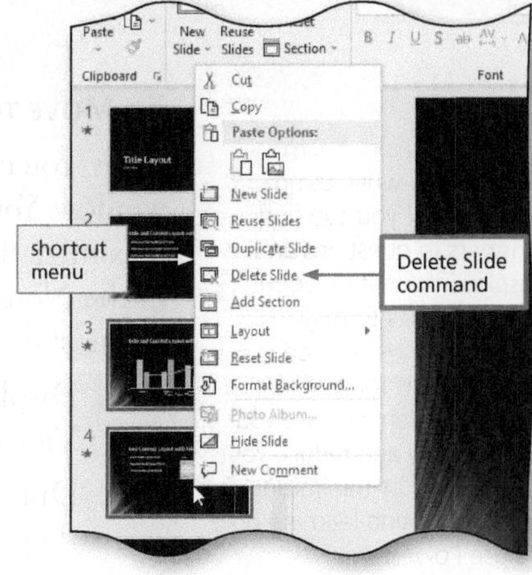

Figure 2–6

- Right-click any selected slide to display the shortcut menu (Figure 2–7).

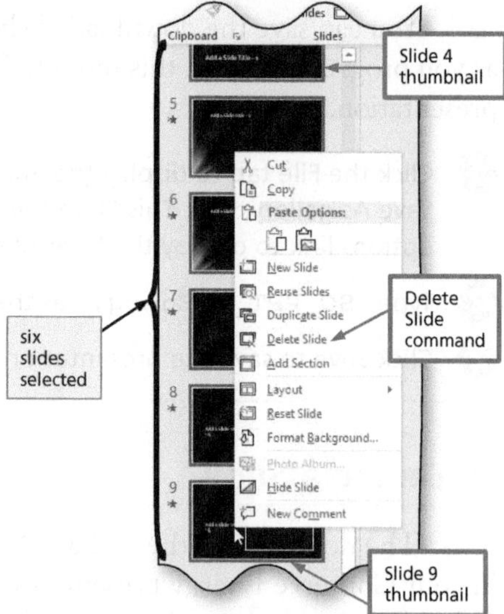

Figure 2–7

- Click Delete Slide to delete the selected slides from the presentation (Figure 2–8).

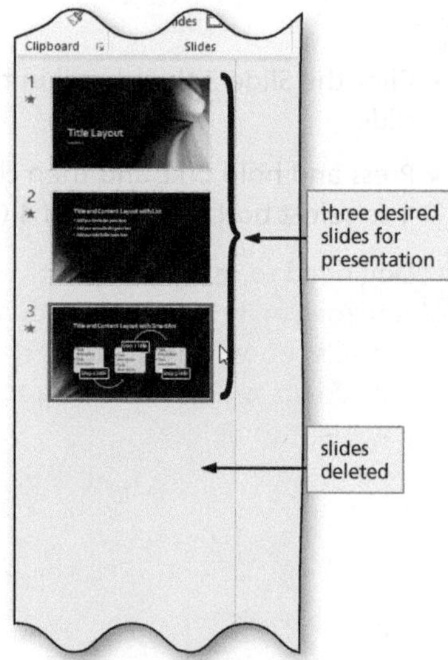

Figure 2–8

Other Ways

1. Select slide(s), press DELETE
2. Select slide(s), press BACKSPACE

BTW
PowerPoint Help
At any time while using PowerPoint, you can find answers to questions and display information about various topics through PowerPoint Help. Used properly, this form of assistance can increase your productivity and reduce your frustrations by minimizing the time you spend learning how to use PowerPoint.

To Move the Splitters in a Window

You can maximize the working space of each of the panes in the PowerPoint window. You can, for example, hide or narrow the thumbnail views of your slides to maximize the editing space in the Slide pane. You also can increase or decrease the area of the Notes pane by dragging the splitter bar up or down. To hide or decrease the size of the slide thumbnails, you would perform the following steps.

1. Display the View tab and then click the Normal button (View tab | Presentation Views group).
2. Drag the splitter bar to the left until the slide thumbnails are the desired size or they are completely hidden.

To show or increase the size of the slide thumbnails, you would perform the following steps.

1. Display the View tab and then click the Normal button (View tab | Presentation Views group).
2. Point to the splitter bar between the Slide pane and the thumbnails, and then drag the splitter bar to the right.

If the thumbnails are hidden, you will see a collapsed Thumbnails menu. To show the thumbnails, you would perform the following step.

1. Click the collapsed menu button (a downward arrow) located to the right of the word, Thumbnails.

To Create a Title Slide

Recall from Module 1 that the title slide introduces the presentation to the audience. In addition to introducing the presentation, this project uses the title slide to capture the audience's attention by using title text. The following steps create the slide show's title slide.

1. Display Slide 1, select the text in the title text placeholder, and then type `Conserve Energy at Home` as the title text.
2. Increase the font size of this title text to 80 point.

Q&A Why do I have to select the text in the placeholder before typing?
This downloaded template includes text in some of the placeholders that must be replaced with your own text.

3. Click the subtitle text placeholder, select the text in that placeholder, and then type `Save Money and Increase Comfort` as the subtitle text.
4. Increase the font size of this subtitle text to 28 point, bold this text, and then change the font color to Green (sixth color in the Standard Colors row) (Figure 2–9).

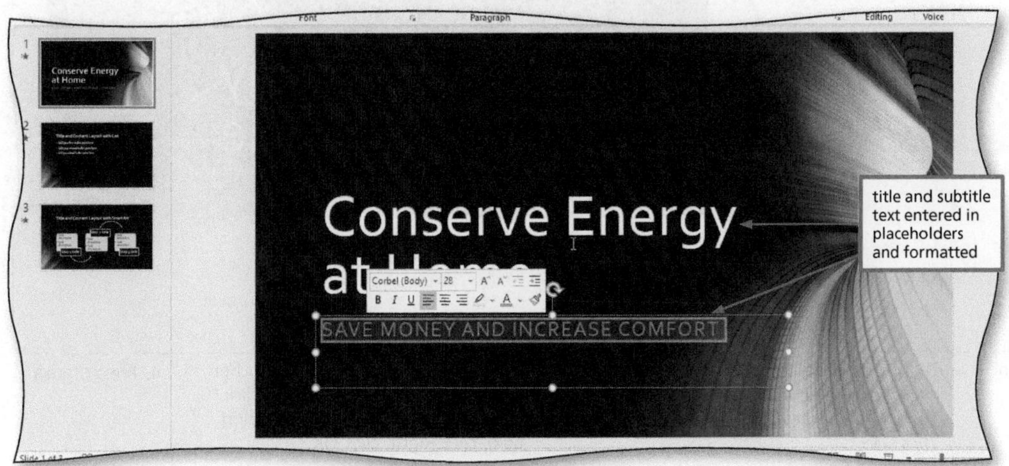

Figure 2–9

To Align a Paragraph

The PowerPoint design themes specify default alignment of and spacing for text within a placeholder. For example, the text in most paragraphs is **left-aligned**, so the first character of each line is even with the left side of the placeholder. Text alignment also can be horizontally **centered** to position each line evenly between the left and right placeholder edges; **right-aligned**, so that the last character of each line is even with the last character of each line above or below it; and **justified**, where the first and last characters of each line are aligned and extra space is inserted between words to spread the characters evenly across the line.

By default, all placeholder text in the Digital Blue Tunnel theme is left-aligned. You want the text to be right-aligned, or placed with the words Energy and Home moved to the right edge of the placeholders. ***Why?*** *You later will add a shape in the lower-right corner of the slide, so you want the text to be adjacent to this graphical element.* The following steps right-align the text in the title and subtitle placeholders on Slide 1.

- Place the insertion point anywhere in the Slide 1 title text (Figure 2–10).

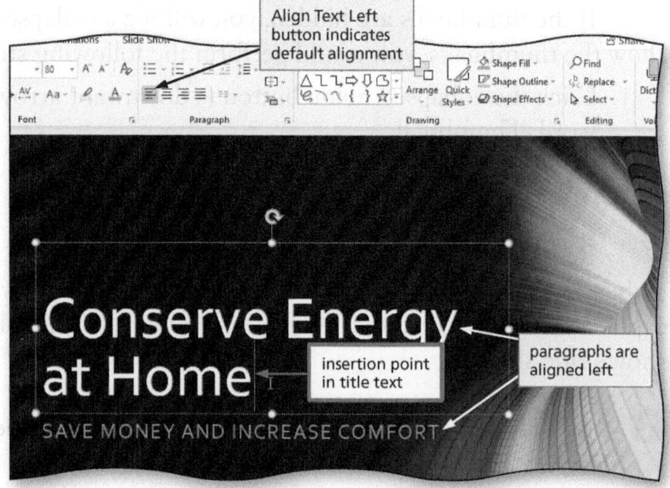

Figure 2–10

- Click the Align Right button (Home tab | Paragraph group) to right-align this paragraph.
- Place the insertion point anywhere in the subtitle text and then click the Align Right button to right-align the subtitle text (Figure 2–11).

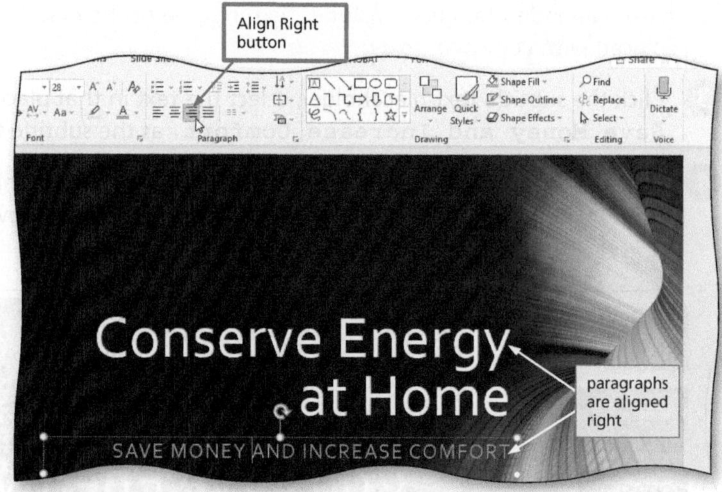

Figure 2–11

Other Ways

1. Click Align Right button on Mini toolbar
2. Right-click selected text, click Paragraph on shortcut menu, click Alignment arrow (Paragraph dialog box), click Right, click OK
3. Click Paragraph Dialog Box Launcher (Home tab | Paragraph group), click Alignment arrow (Paragraph dialog box), click Right, click OK
4. Press CTRL+R

To Create the First Text Slide

The first text slide you create in Module 2 emphasizes three energy-efficient products: certified LEDs, low-flow showerheads, and insulation for hot water pipes. The following steps create the Slide 2 text slide using the Title and Content layout.

1. Display Slide 2, select the text in the title text placeholder, and then type `Energy-Efficient Products` in the placeholder.

2. Select the text in the first bulleted paragraph ("Add your first bullet point here") and then type `ENERGY STAR certified LEDs` as the first paragraph.

3. Press ENTER, click the 'Increase List Level' button to indent the second paragraph below the first, and then type `Use 75% less energy than incandescent lighting` as the first second-level paragraph.

4. Select the text in the next bulleted paragraph ("Add your second bullet point here") and then type `WaterSense certified showerheads` as the second first-level paragraph.

5. Press ENTER, press TAB to indent the next paragraph, and then type `Family can save 2,700 gallons of water yearly` as the second second-level paragraph.

6. Select the text in the next bulleted paragraph ("Add your third bullet point here") and then type `Hot water pipe insulation` as the third first-level paragraph.

7. Press ENTER, press TAB to indent the next paragraph, and then type `Can raise temperature 2-4 degrees` as the third second-level paragraph (Figure 2–12).

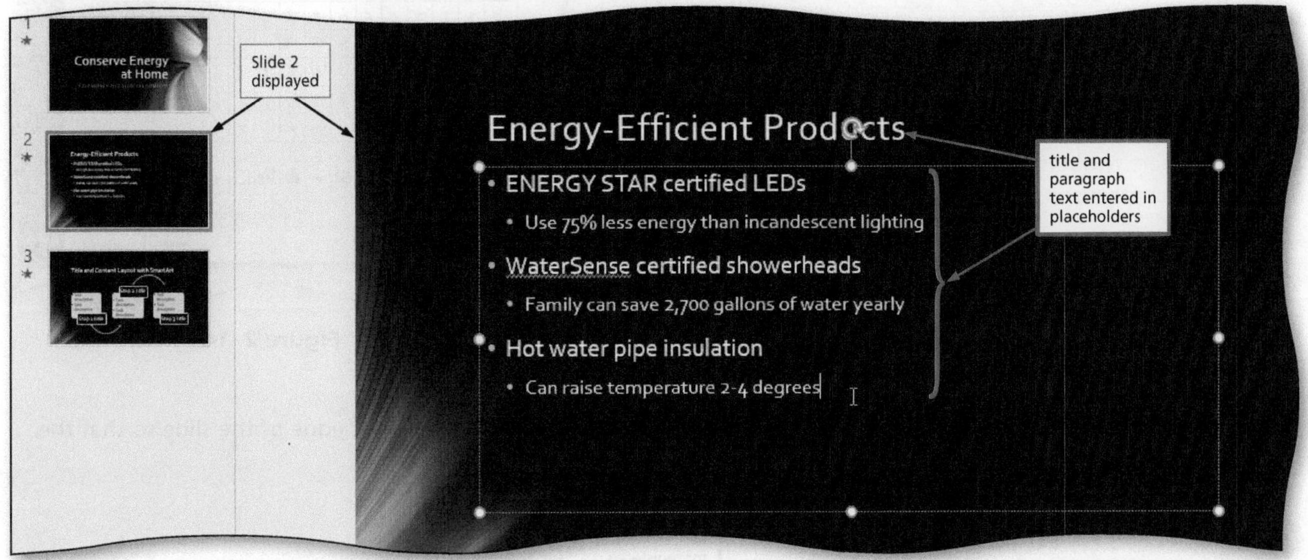

Figure 2–12

To Insert a Symbol

The terms, ENERGY STAR and WaterSense, are registered trademarks, so you should indicate this designation by inserting this trademark symbol (®). Many symbols are located in the Symbol, Webdings, and Wingdings fonts. The registered trademark symbol is located in the Symbol font. ***Why?** Many mathematical symbols, dots, and geometric shapes are found in this font.* You insert symbols by changing the font. The following steps insert a trademark symbol after the word, STAR.

BTW

Inserting Special Characters

Along with adding shapes to a slide, you can insert characters not found on your keyboard, such as the section sign (§), the copyright sign (©), and Greek capital letters (e.g., Δ, Ω, and ß). To insert these characters, click the Insert tab and then click Symbol (Insert tab | Symbols group). When the Symbol dialog box is displayed, you can use the same font you currently are using in your presentation, or you can select another font. The Webdings, Wingdings, Wingdings 2, and Wingdings 3 fonts have a variety of symbols.

- Place the insertion point directly after the letter R in STAR.
- Display the Insert tab.
- Click the Symbols button (Insert tab | Symbols group) to display the Symbols menu (Figure 2–13).

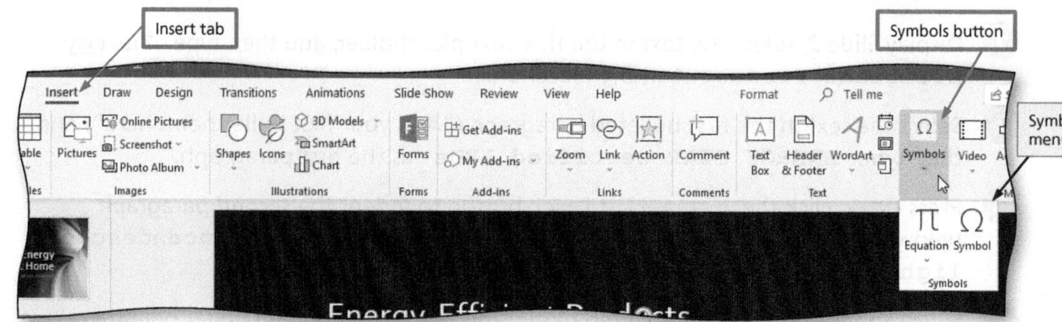

Figure 2–13

- Click the Symbol button to display the Symbol dialog box (Figure 2–14).

Q&A What if the symbol I want to insert already appears in the Symbol dialog box?
You can click any symbol shown in the dialog box to insert it in the slide.

Why does my 'Recently used symbols' list display different symbols from those shown in Figure 2–14?
As you insert symbols, PowerPoint places them in the 'Recently used symbols' list.

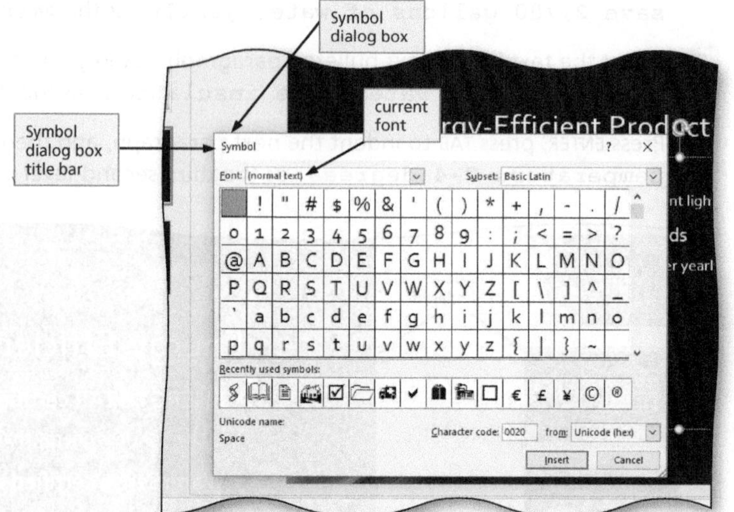

Figure 2–14

- Click the Symbol dialog box title bar and then drag the dialog box to the lower-right edge of the slide so that the bullets and first few words of the first and second first-level paragraphs are visible.

4

- If Symbol is not the font displayed in the Font box, click the Font arrow (Symbol dialog box) and then drag or scroll to Symbol and click this font.
- Drag or scroll down until the last row of this font is visible.
- Scroll down and then click the registered trademark symbol as shown in Figure 2–15. The symbol number and character code (226) appear at the bottom of the dialog box.

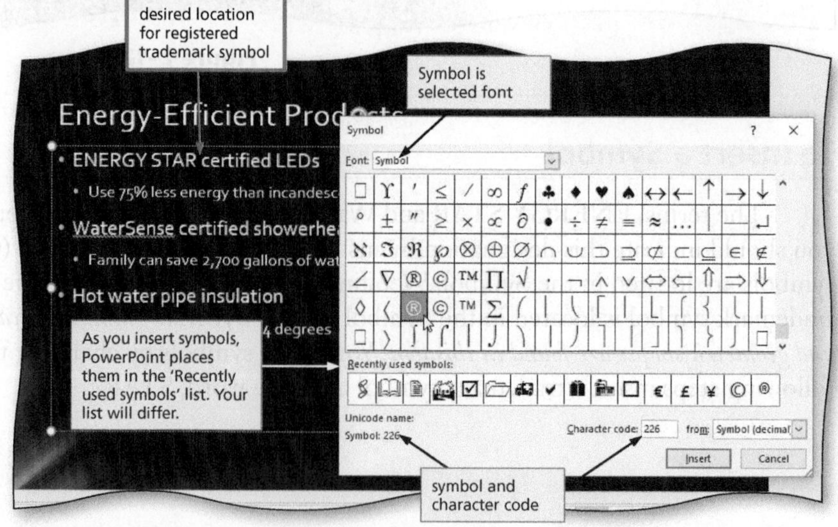

Figure 2–15

5

- Click the Insert button (Symbol dialog box) to place the registered trademark symbol after the word, STAR (Figure 2–16).

Q&A Why is the Symbol dialog box still open?
The Symbol dialog box remains open, allowing you to insert additional symbols.

6

- Click the Close button (Symbol dialog box).

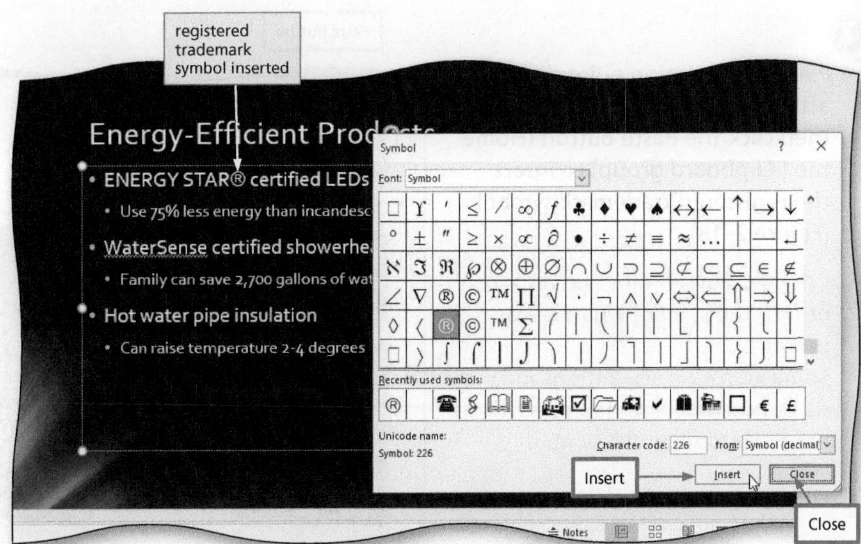

Figure 2–16

Other Ways

1. Press CTRL+ALT+R

To Copy a Symbol

To add the registered trademark after the word, WaterSense, in the second first-level paragraph, you could repeat the process you used to insert the first registered trademark. Rather than inserting this symbol from the Symbol dialog box, you can copy the symbol and then paste it in the appropriate place. ***Why?*** *This process can be accomplished more quickly with copy and paste when using the same symbol multiple times.* The following steps copy the trademark symbol after the word, WaterSense.

1

- Select the registered trademark symbol in the first paragraph, display the Home tab, and then click the Copy button (Home tab | Clipboard group) to copy the registered trademark symbol to the Office Clipboard (Figure 2–17).

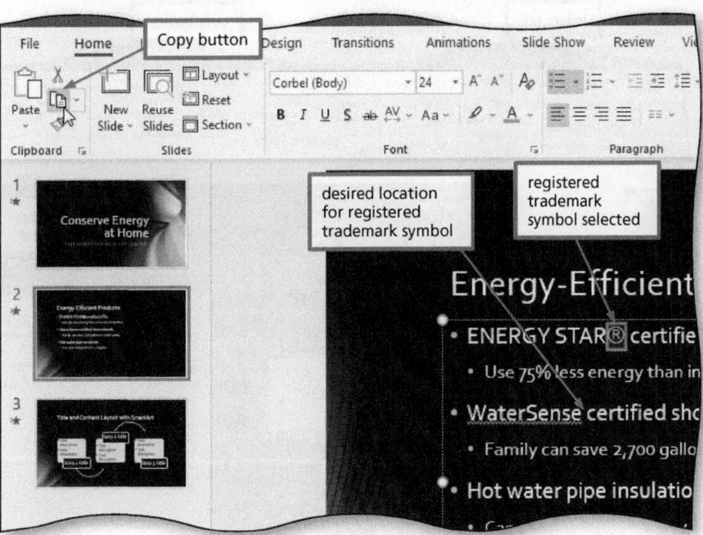

Figure 2–17

- Place the insertion point directly after the word, WaterSense, and then click the Paste button (Home tab | Clipboard group) to insert the registered trademark symbol (Figure 2–18).

Q&A Why did PowerPoint add a space before the symbol when it was pasted?

Some AutoCorrect settings may cause this to occur. If this happens, delete the space before the symbol.

Figure 2–18

To Add a Hyperlink to a Paragraph

Speakers may desire to display a webpage during a slide show to add depth to the presented material and to enhance the overall message. When presenting the Conserve Energy slide show and discussing energy tips on Slide 2, for example, a speaker could access a website to show specific products that are energy savers. One method of accessing a webpage is by clicking a hyperlink on a slide. A **hyperlink**, also called a **link**, connects a slide or slide element to a webpage, another slide, a custom show consisting of specific slides in a presentation, an email address, or a file. A hyperlink can be any element of a slide. This includes a single letter, a word, a paragraph, or any graphical image such as a picture, shape, or graph.

If you are connected to the Internet when you run the presentation, you can click each hyperlinked paragraph, and your browser will open a new window and display the corresponding webpage for each hyperlink. By default, hyperlinked text is displayed with an underline and in a color that is part of the color scheme. The following steps create a hyperlink for the title text on Slide 2. ***Why?** The title text will be a hyperlink to a webpage for more information about energy saving appliances and products.*

- With Slide 2 displaying, display the Insert tab and then select the title text, Energy-Efficient Products.
- Click the Link button (Insert tab | Links group) to display the Insert Hyperlink dialog box.
- If necessary, click the 'Existing File or Web Page' button in the Link to area (Figure 2–19).

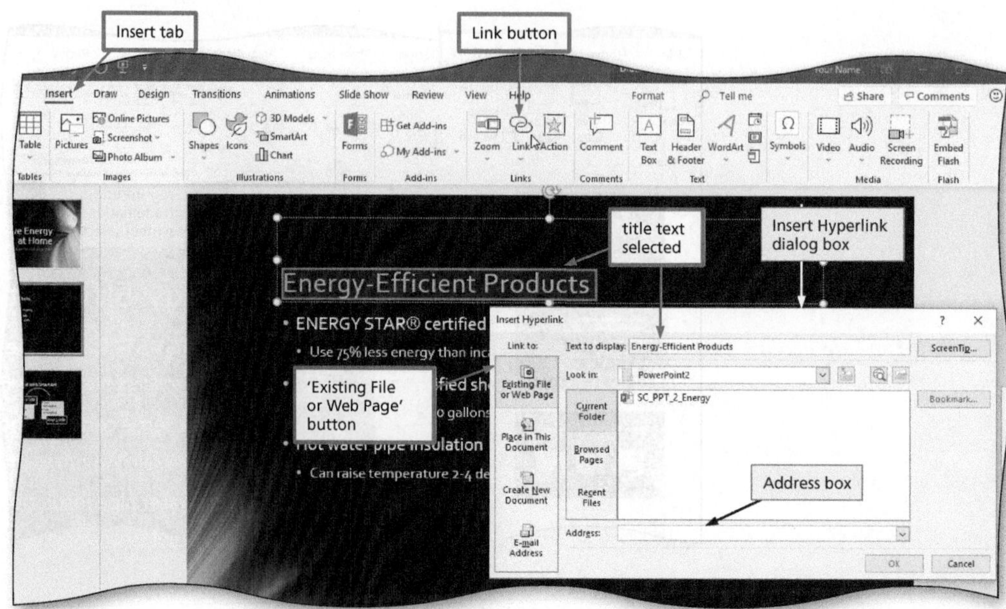

Figure 2–19

2

- If necessary, delete the text in the Address text box and then type **www.energy.gov** in the Address box (Figure 2–20).

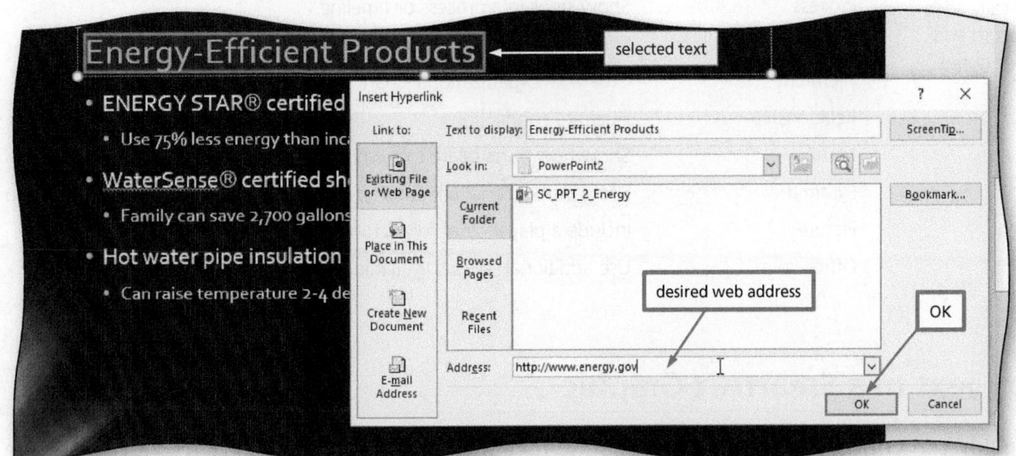

Figure 2–20

Q&A Why does http:// appear before the address I typed?
PowerPoint automatically adds this protocol identifier before web addresses.

3

- Click OK to insert the hyperlink.

Q&A Why is this paragraph now underlined and displaying a new font color?
The default style for hyperlinks is underlined text. The Digital Blue Tunnel built-in theme hyperlink color is orange, so PowerPoint formatted the paragraph to that color automatically.

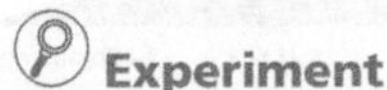

Experiment

- Press CTRL and then click the link to access the website. Then, close the browser to return to PowerPoint.

Other Ways

1. Right-click selected text, click Hyperlink, click 'Existing File or Web Page,' type address, click OK
2. Select text, press CTRL+K, click 'Existing File or Web Page,' type address, press ENTER

Creating and Formatting a SmartArt Graphic

An illustration often can help convey relationships between key points in your presentation. Microsoft Office includes **SmartArt graphics**, which are customizable diagrams that you can use to pictorially present lists, processes, and other relationships. The SmartArt layouts have a variety of shapes, arrows, and lines to correspond to the major points you want your audience to remember.

You can create a SmartArt graphic in two ways: Convert text or pictures already present on a slide to a SmartArt graphic, or select a SmartArt graphic type and then add text and pictures. Once the SmartArt graphic is present, you can customize its look. Table 2–1 lists the SmartArt types and their uses.

BTW
Ribbon and Screen Resolution
PowerPoint may change how the groups and buttons within the groups appear on the ribbon, depending on the screen resolution of your computer. Thus, your ribbon may look different from the ones in this book if you are using a screen resolution other than 1366 × 768.

BTW
Updated Layouts
Some of the items in the SmartArt Styles gallery may be updates; Microsoft periodically adds layouts to Office.com and corresponding categories.

Table 2–1 SmartArt Graphic Layout Types and Purposes

Type	Purpose
List	Show nonsequential information
Process	Show steps in a process or timeline
Cycle	Show a continual process
Hierarchy	Create an organizational chart
Relationship	Illustrate connections
Matrix	Show how parts relate to a whole
Pyramid	Show proportional relationships with the largest component at the top or bottom
Picture	Include a placeholder for pictures within the graphic
Office.com	Use additional layouts available from Office.com

To Convert Text to a SmartArt Graphic

You quickly can convert small amounts of slide text and pictures into a SmartArt graphic. Once you determine the type of graphic, such as process or cycle, you then have a wide variety of styles from which to choose in the SmartArt Graphics gallery. As with other galleries, you can point to the samples and view a live preview if you are using a mouse. The following steps convert the six bulleted text paragraphs on Slide 2 to the 'Vertical Box List' graphic, which is part of the List category. ***Why?*** *This SmartArt style is a good match for the content of Slide 2. It has three large areas for the titles and placeholders for the Level 2 text under each title.*

- With Slide 2 displaying, click the Home tab.
- Select the six bulleted list items and then click the 'Convert to SmartArt' button (Home tab | Paragraph group) to display the SmartArt Graphics gallery (Figure 2–21).

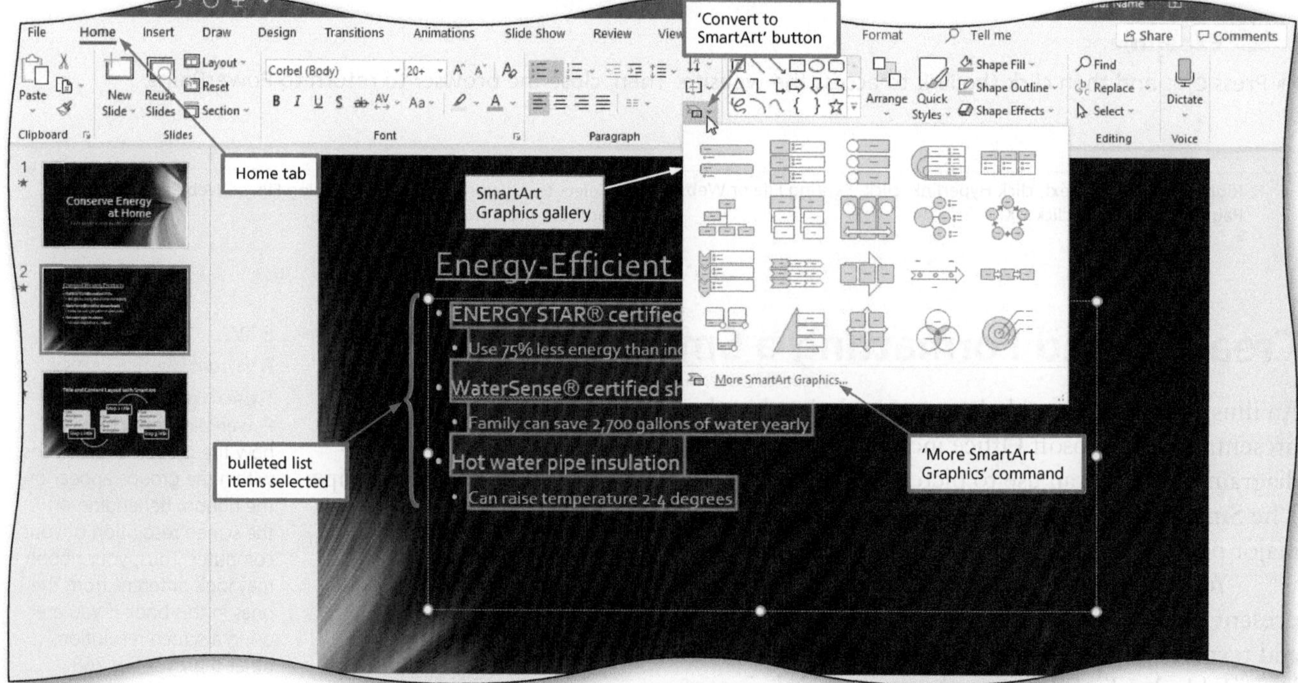

Figure 2–21

2

- Click 'More SmartArt Graphics' in the SmartArt Graphics gallery to display the Choose a SmartArt Graphic dialog box.
- Click List in the left pane to display the List gallery.
- Click the 'Vertical Box List' graphic (second graphic in second row) to display a preview of this graphic in the right pane (Figure 2–22).

Experiment

- Click various categories and graphics in the SmartArt Styles gallery and view the various layouts.

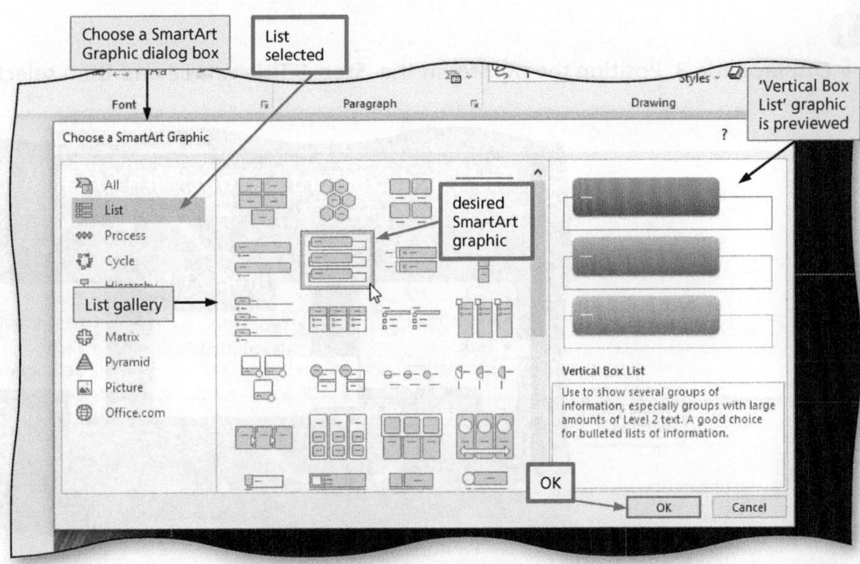

Figure 2–22

3

- Click OK (Choose a SmartArt Graphic dialog box) to apply this shape and convert the text (Figure 2–23).

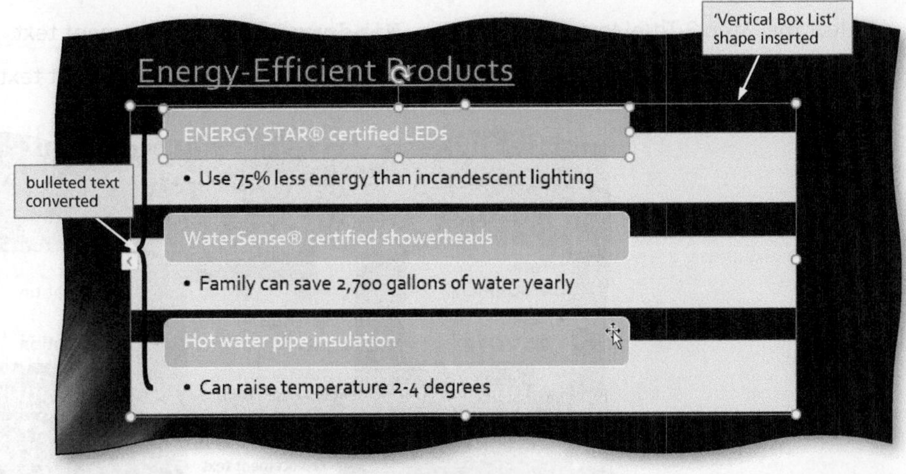

Figure 2–23

Other Ways

1. Select text, click 'Convert to SmartArt' on shortcut menu

To Edit SmartArt Shape Text

You may desire to change the text that appears in a SmartArt graphic. To do so, you can select the text and then make the desired changes. Also, if you display the Text Pane on the left side of the graphic, you can click the text you want to change and make your edits. The Digital Blue Tunnel theme included a slide with a SmartArt graphic, which is on Slide 3 of your slide deck. The SmartArt layout is Alternating Flow, which is part of the Process category. The following steps edit the sample text included in the graphic. First, you will edit the text in the three title shapes by selecting the text and then typing the replacement titles. ***Why?*** *The new title text has only one word for each shape, so it is easy simply to select the sample text and then type the replacement word.*

- Display Slide 3. Position the pointer in the 'Step 1 Title' shape and then select this text (Figure 2–24).

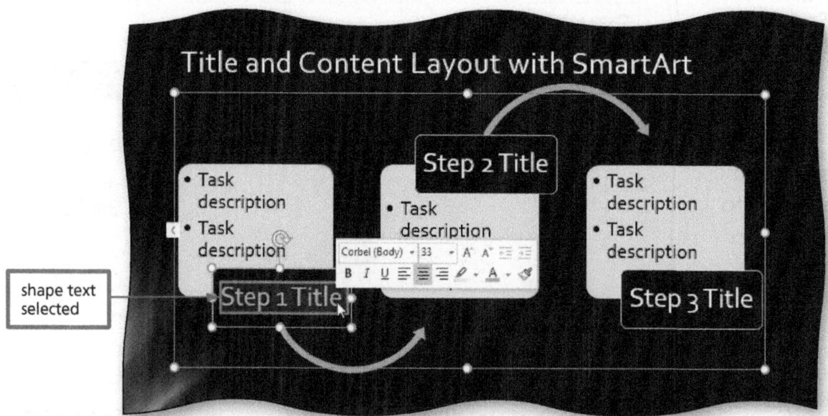

Figure 2–24

- Type **Appliances** as the replacement text for this shape.
- Select the 'Step 2 Title' text and then type **Windows** as the replacement text.
- Select the 'Step 3 Title' text and then type **Lighting** as the replacement text (Figure 2–25).

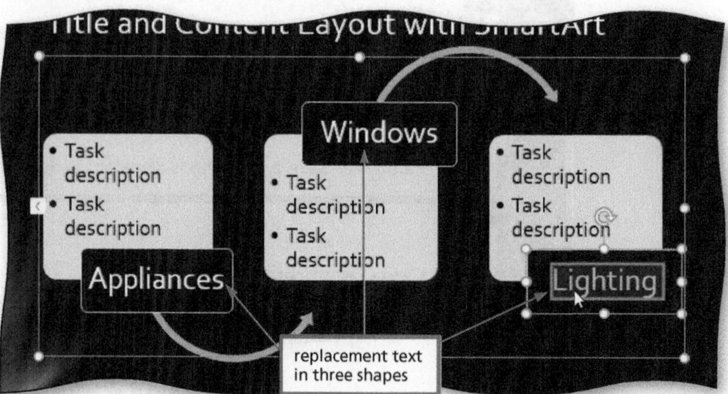

Figure 2–25

Text Pane

The **Text Pane** assists you in creating a graphic because you can direct your attention to developing and editing the message without being concerned with the actual graphic. The Text Pane consists of two areas: The top portion has the text that will appear in the SmartArt layout, and the bottom portion gives the name of the graphic and suggestions of what type of information is best suited for this type of visual. Each SmartArt graphic has an associated Text Pane with bullets that function as an outline and map directly to the image. You can create new lines of bulleted text and then indent and demote these lines. You also can check spelling. Table 2–2 shows the keyboard shortcuts you can use with the Text Pane.

Table 2–2 Text Pane Keyboard Shortcuts

Activity	Keyboard Shortcut
Indent text	TAB or ALT+SHIFT+RIGHT ARROW
Demote text	SHIFT+TAB or ALT+SHIFT+LEFT ARROW
Add a tab character	CTRL+TAB
Create a new line of text	ENTER
Check spelling	F7
Merge two lines of text	DELETE at the end of the first text line
Display the shortcut menu	SHIFT+F10
Switch between the SmartArt drawing canvas and the Text Pane	CTRL+SHIFT+F2
Close the Text Pane	ALT+F4
Switch the focus from the Text Pane to the SmartArt graphic border	ESC

To Edit SmartArt Bulleted Text

***Why?** You want to add text that shows the topic of the presentation and labels the images you will add on this slide.* The Alternating Flow graphic has three placeholders for bulleted text. The following steps edit the bulleted list paragraphs in the Text Pane and in the corresponding SmartArt shapes on Slide 3.

1

- With the Slide 3 SmartArt selected, click the Text Pane button (SmartArt Tools Design tab | Create Graphic group) or the arrow icon in the left-center edge of the graphic to open the Text Pane.
- Select the text in the first Appliances second-level paragraph in the Text Pane (Figure 2–26).

2

- Type `Unplug when not in use` as the replacement text for this second-level paragraph.
- Click the second bullet line or press DOWN ARROW to move the insertion point to the next second-level paragraph. Select the text in this paragraph and then type `Ask about rebates` as the replacement text.

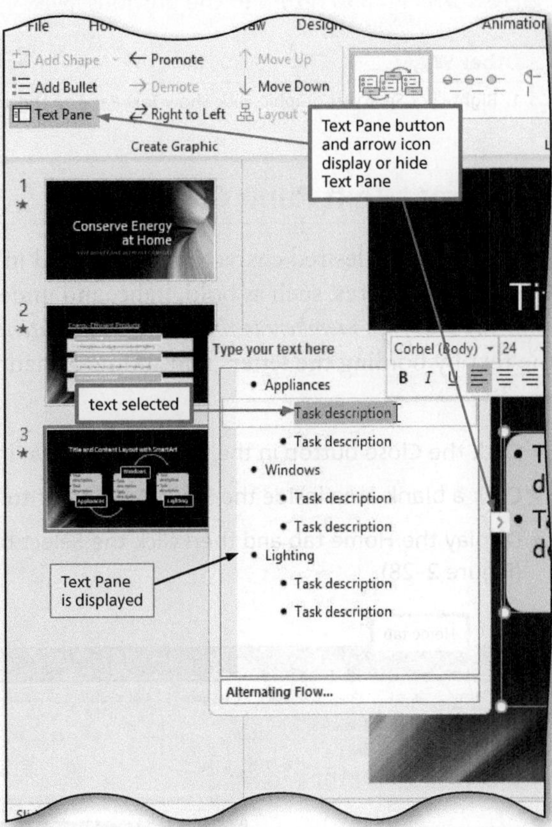

Figure 2–26

- Type **Seal leaks** as the replacement text for the first Windows second-level paragraph.
- Type **Close curtains at night in winter** as the replacement text for the second Windows second-level paragraph.

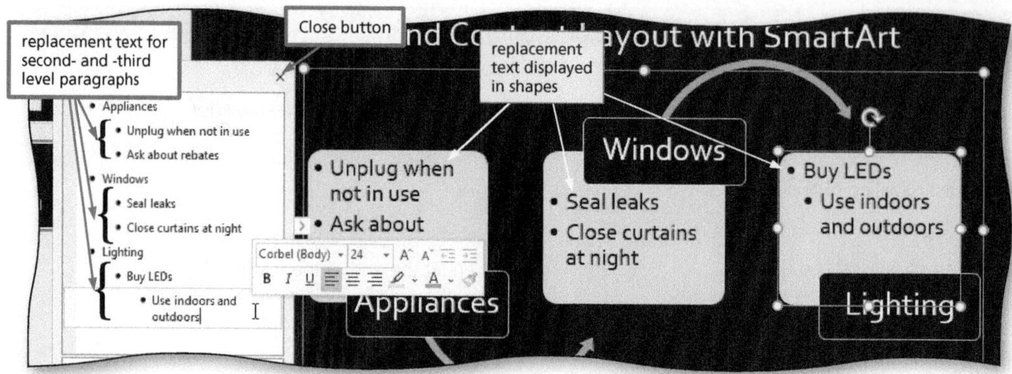

Figure 2–27

- Type **Buy LEDs** as the replacement text for the first Lighting third-level paragraph.
- Press TAB and then type **Use indoors and outdoors** as the replacement text for the Lighting third-level paragraph (Figure 2–27).

Q&A

If my Text Pane no longer is displayed, how can I get it to appear?
Click the control, which is the tab with a left-pointing arrow, on the left side of the SmartArt graphic.

I mistakenly pressed DOWN ARROW or ENTER. How can I delete the bullet paragraph I just added?
Press BACKSPACE to delete the paragraph.

I mistakenly pressed TAB to move to the next paragraph, and the current paragraph's level was changed. How can I fix it?
Press SHIFT+TAB to return to the previous level.

Other Ways

1. Right-click SmartArt graphic, click Show Text Pane on shortcut menu, enter text in Text Pane

To Format Text Pane Characters

Once the desired characters are entered in the Text Pane, you can change the font size and apply formatting features, such as bold, italic, and underlined text. ***Why?*** *Changing the font and adding effects can help draw the audience members to the varied slide content and coordinate with the visual content.* The following steps format the text by bolding the letters and adding a shadow.

- Click the Close button in the Text Pane (shown in Figure 2–27) so that it no longer is displayed.
- Click a blank area inside the SmartArt border to deselect the Lighting shapes.
- Display the Home tab and then click the Select button (Home tab | Editing group) to display the Select menu (Figure 2–28).

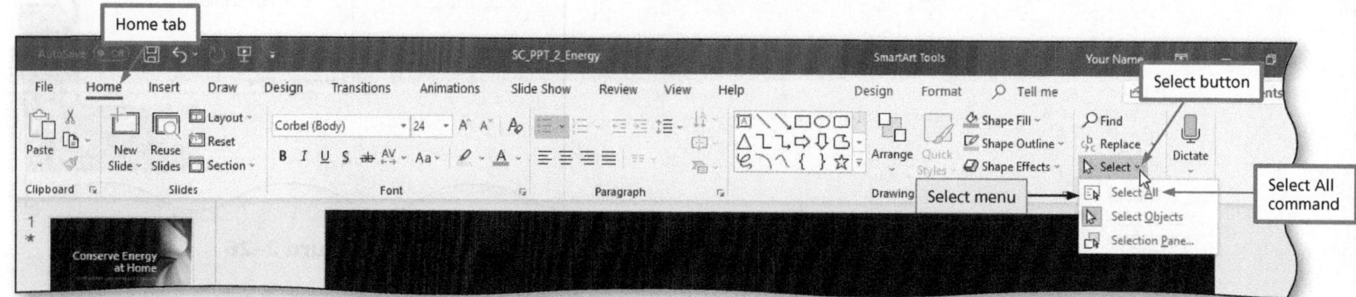

Figure 2–28

2

- Click Select All to select all six shapes in the SmartArt graphic.
- Click the Bold button (Home tab | Font group) to bold all the text.
- Click the Text Shadow button (Home tab | Font group) to add a shadow to all the SmartArt text (Figure 2–29).

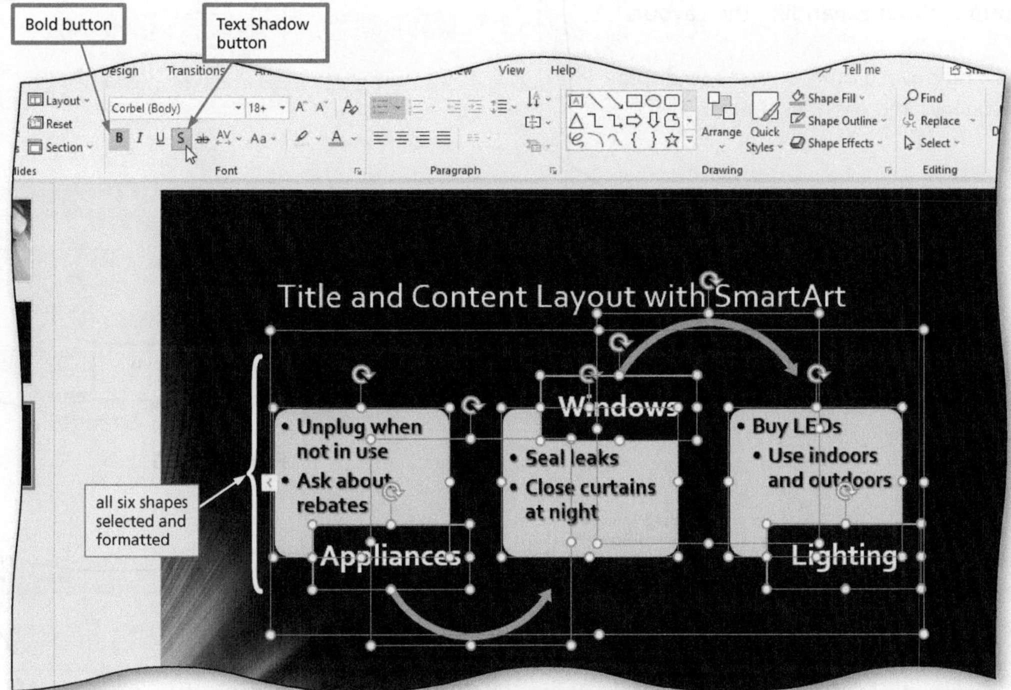

Figure 2–29

3

- Click a blank area inside the SmartArt border to deselect the shapes.

Other Ways

1. Drag through all text in Text pane, click Bold button on shortcut menu
2. Drag through all text in Text pane, click Bold button and Text Shadow button on ribbon (Home tab | Font group)

To Change the SmartArt Layout

Once you begin formatting a SmartArt shape, you may decide that another layout better conveys the message you are communicating to an audience. PowerPoint allows you to change the layout easily. Any graphical changes that were made to the original SmartArt, such as changing and formatting text, are applied to the new SmartArt layout. The following steps change the SmartArt layout to Target List. ***Why?*** *It works well with the circular background and prominently displays the three categories.*

1

- With the Slide 3 SmartArt graphic still selected, display the SmartArt Tools Design tab (Figure 2–30).

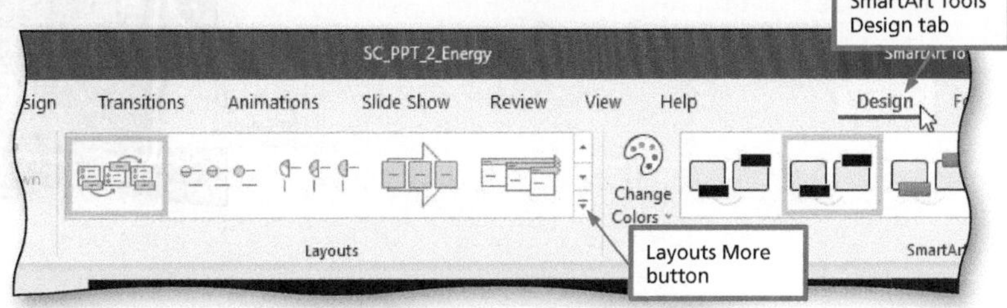

Figure 2–30

- Click the More button in the Layouts group (shown in Figure 2–30) to expand the Layouts gallery (Figure 2–31).

Q&A Can I select one of the layouts displaying in the Layouts group without expanding the Layouts gallery?

Yes. At times, however, you may want to display the gallery to view and preview the various layouts.

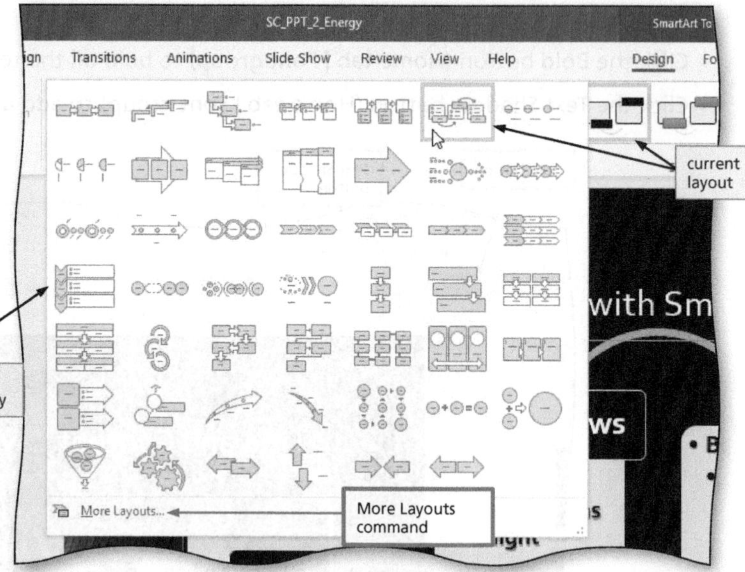

Figure 2–31

- Click More Layouts at the bottom of the Layouts gallery to display the Choose a SmartArt Graphic dialog box.
- Click List in the list of graphic categories and then click the Target List layout (last layout in ninth row) to display a picture and a description of this SmartArt layout (Figure 2–32).

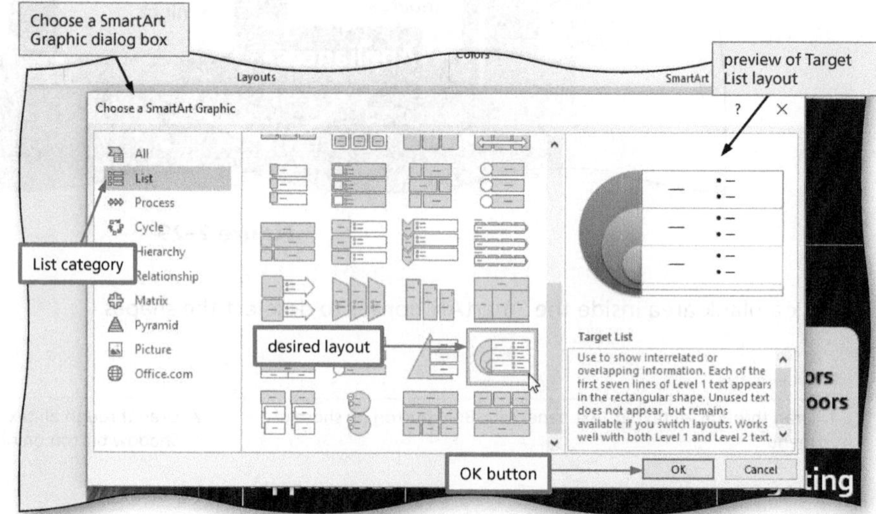

Figure 2–32

- Click OK (Choose a SmartArt Graphic dialog box) to change the layout (Figure 2–33).

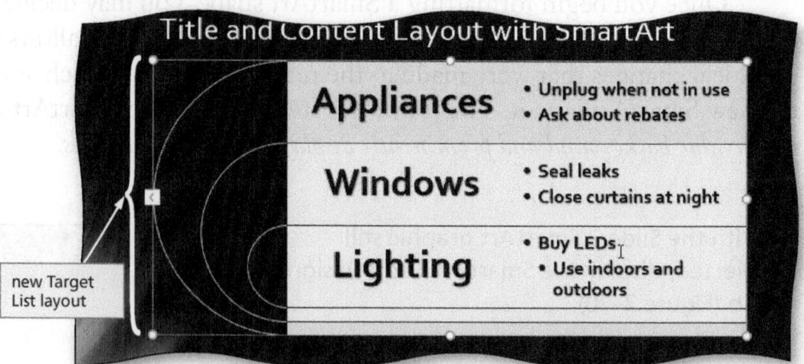

Figure 2–33

To Edit the Title Text

The Slide 3 title text placeholder has the default wording from the online template. You need to change this text to reflect the current slide content. The following step edits the title text.

1. Select the current title text and then type `Tips to Save Energy` as the replacement text (Figure 2–34).

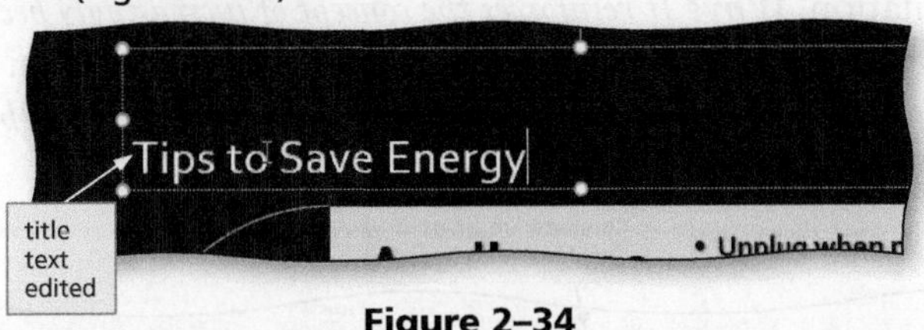

Figure 2–34

To Duplicate a Slide

If you are satisfied with the design of a slide, you may want to duplicate it and then make slight modifications. ***Why?*** *You can save time and provide a consistent design.* The following steps insert a new slide and duplicate it.

1

- With Slide 3 selected, insert a new slide with the Title and Content layout.
- With the new Slide 4 selected, click the New Slide arrow (Home tab | Slides group) to display the Digital Blue Tunnel layout gallery (Figure 2–35).

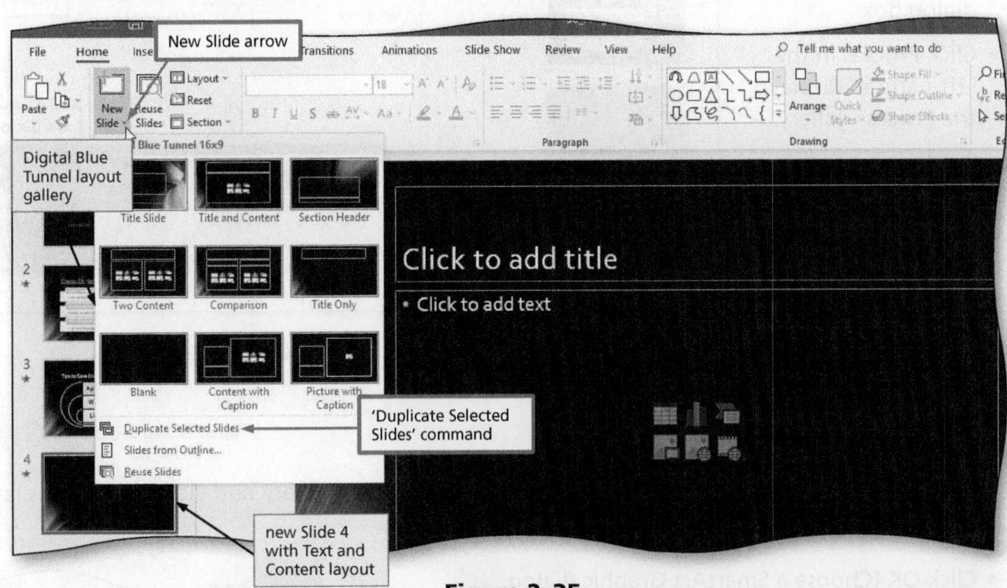

Figure 2–35

2

- Click 'Duplicate Selected Slides' in the Digital Blue Tunnel layout gallery to create a new Slide 5, which is a duplicate of Slide 4 (Figure 2–36).

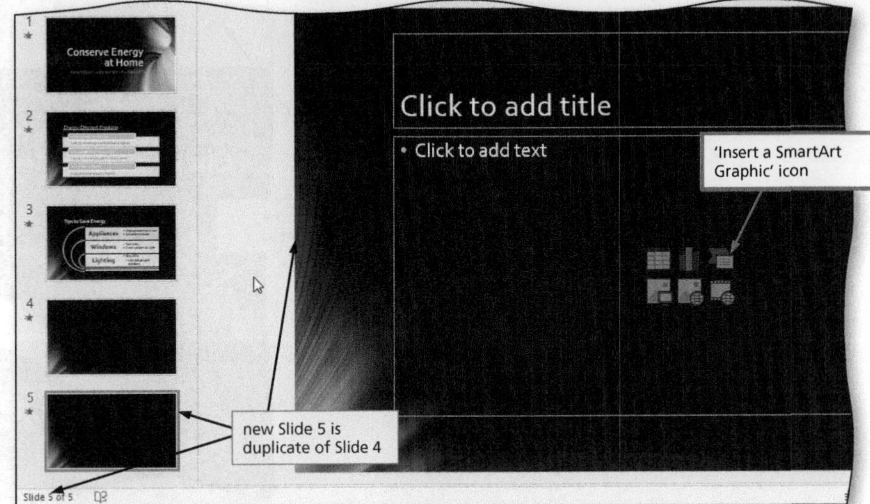

Figure 2–36

Other Ways

1. Right-click slide thumbnail in Slide pane, click Duplicate Slide

To Insert a SmartArt Graphic

Several SmartArt layouts have designs that reinforce concepts presented in a presentation. The Upward Arrow graphic is appropriate for this presentation. ***Why?*** *It reinforces the concept of increasingly becoming energy efficient, which should create interest among community residents considering participating in this effort. Later in this project you will format a slide with an upward-pointing arrow, so the two slides will complement each other.* The following steps insert the Upward Arrow SmartArt graphic.

1

- Display Slide 4 and then click the 'Insert a SmartArt Graphic' icon in the content placeholder (shown in Figure 2–36) to display the 'Choose a SmartArt Graphic' dialog box.
- Click Process in the left pane to display the Process gallery.
- Scroll down and then click the Upward Arrow graphic (second graphic in tenth row) to display a preview of this layout in the right pane (Figure 2–37).

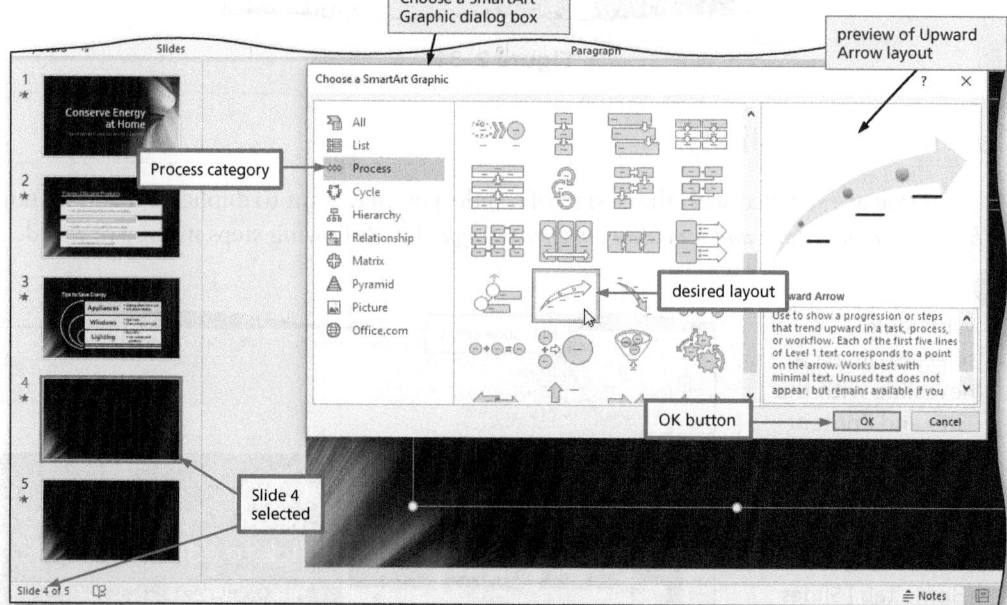

Figure 2–37

 **Experiment**

- Click various categories and graphics in the SmartArt Styles gallery and view the various layouts.

2

- Click OK (Choose a SmartArt Graphic dialog box) to insert Upward Arrow SmartArt layout on Slide 4 (Figure 2–38).

Figure 2–38

Other Ways

1. Click SmartArt button (Insert tab | Illustrations group)

To Add Text to the SmartArt Graphic

The Upward Arrow SmartArt layout has three placeholders for text. You can type a small amount of text, and PowerPoint assists with the graphic design. ***Why?*** *PowerPoint automatically adjusts the font size for text in all the placeholders as you type.* The following steps insert text into the three SmartArt placeholders.

- Click the left placeholder labeled [Text] to place the insertion point in that box (Figure 2–39).

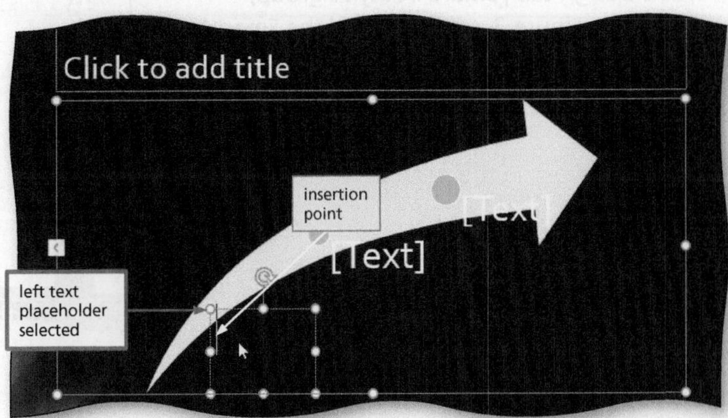

Figure 2–39

2

- Type **Hourly pricing** in the placeholder and then click the middle text placeholder.
- Type **Peak time savings** in the middle placeholder and then click the right text placeholder.
- Type **Central AC cycling** in the right placeholder (Figure 2–40).

- Click a blank area inside the SmartArt border to deselect the right placeholder.

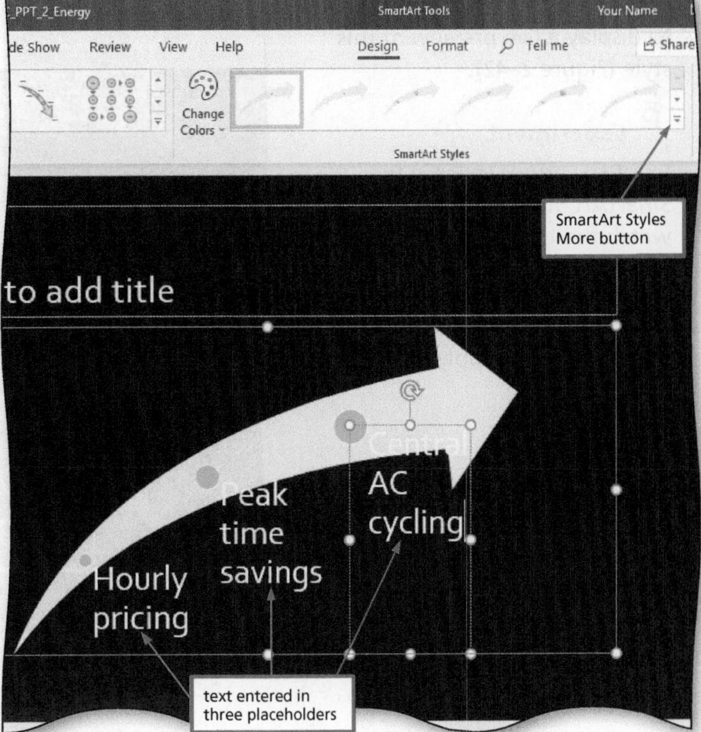

Figure 2–40

To Apply a SmartArt Style

You can change the look of your SmartArt graphic easily by applying a **SmartArt Style**, a pre-set combination of formatting options for SmartArt that follows the design theme. ***Why?*** *You can use these professionally designed effects to customize the appearance of your presentation with a variety of shape fills, edges, shadows, line styles, gradients, and three-dimensional styles.* The following steps add the Powder style to the Upward Arrow SmartArt graphic.

- With the SmartArt graphic still selected, click the SmartArt Styles More button (SmartArt Tools Design tab | SmartArt Styles group) (shown in Figure 2–40) to expand the SmartArt Styles gallery (Figure 2–41).

Q&A How do I select the graphic if it no longer is selected?
Click anywhere in the graphic.

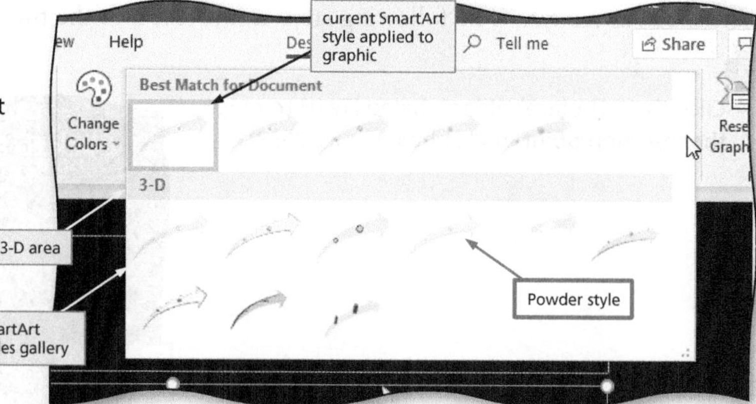

Figure 2–41

- Point to the Powder style in the 3-D area (fourth style in first 3-D row) in the SmartArt Styles gallery to display a live preview of this style (Figure 2–42).

- Point to various styles in the SmartArt Styles gallery and watch the Upward Arrow graphic change styles.

- Click Powder to apply this style to the graphic.

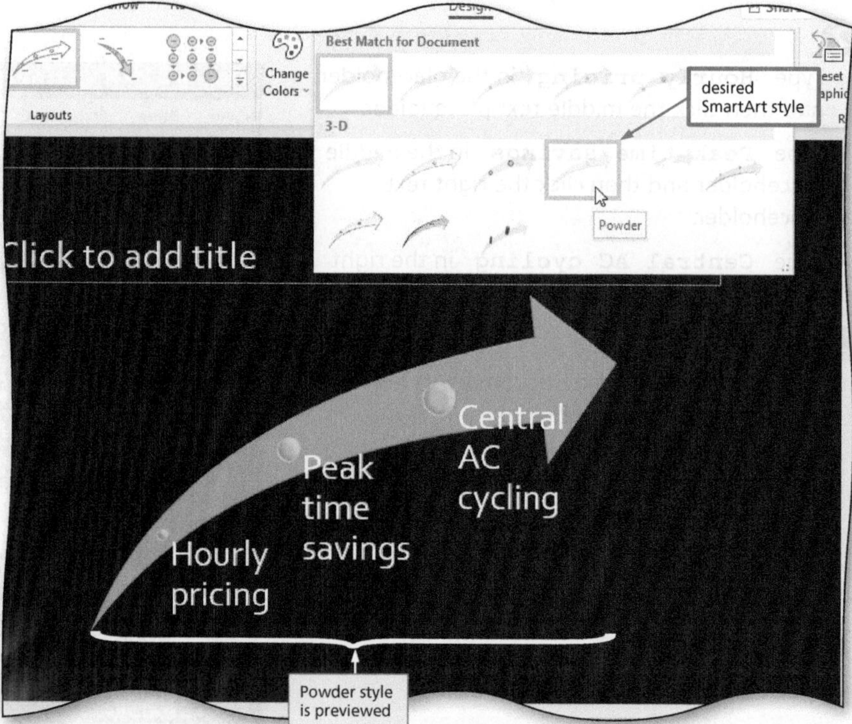

Figure 2–42

Other Ways

1. Right-click SmartArt graphic in an area other than a picture, click Style button

Inserting and Formatting a Shape

One method of getting the audience's attention and reinforcing the major concepts being presented is to have graphical elements on the slide. PowerPoint provides a wide variety of predefined shapes that can add visual interest to a slide. Diagrams with labels often help audiences identify the parts of an object. Text boxes with clear, large type and an arrow pointing to a precise area of the object work well in showing relationships between components. You also can use shapes to create your own custom artwork.

Shape elements include lines, basic geometrical shapes, arrows, equation shapes, flowchart symbols, stars, banners, and callouts. After adding a shape to a slide, you can change its default characteristics by adding text, bullets, numbers, and styles. You also can combine multiple shapes to create a more complex graphic. At times, you may be unable to find a shape that fits your specific needs. In those instances, you might find a similar shape and then alter it to your specifications.

The predefined shapes are found in the Shapes gallery. This collection is found on the Home tab | Drawing group and the Insert tab | Illustrations group. Once you have inserted and selected a shape, the Drawing Tools Format tab is displayed, and the Shapes gallery also is displayed in the Insert Shapes group.

You will add shapes to Slide 5 and then enhance them in a variety of ways. First, an oval, a trapezoid shape, and an arrow are inserted on the slide, sized, and formatted. Then, text is added to the oval and trapezoid and formatted. The trapezoid is copied, and the text is modified in this new shape. Finally, the arrow shape is formatted and moved into position.

To Insert a Shape

Many of the shapes included in the Shapes gallery can direct the viewer to important aspects of the presentation. Ovals, squares, arrows, stars, and equation shapes are among the items included in the Shapes gallery. These shapes can be combined to show relationships among the elements, and they can help illustrate the basic concepts presented in your slide show. The following steps add an oval, an arrow, and a trapezoid shape to Slide 5. ***Why?*** *Many smart thermostats have a circular design, the arrow complements the Upward Arrow SmartArt design on Slide 4, and the trapezoid has sufficient area to add text.*

- Display Slide 5 and then change the layout to Blank (Figure 2–43).

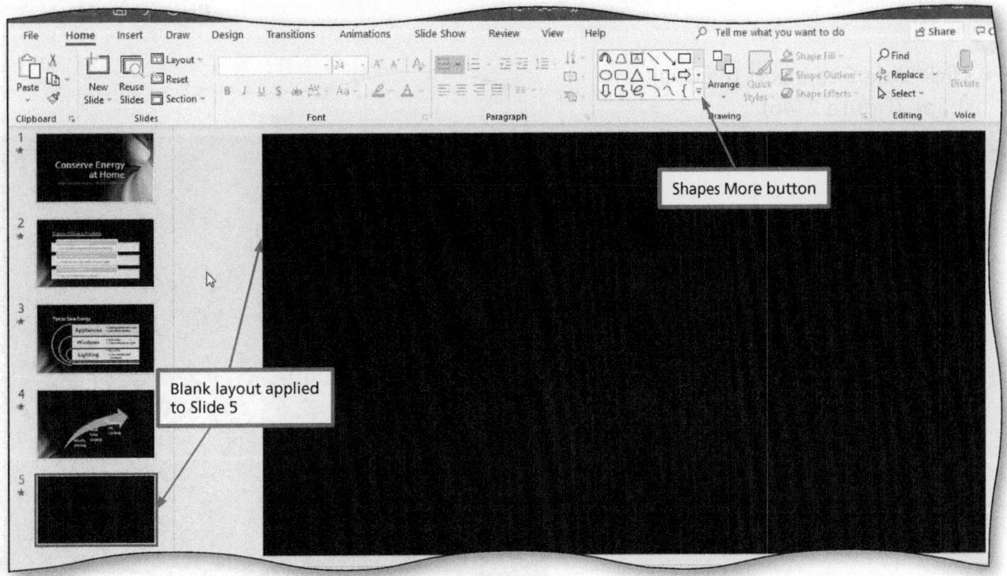

Figure 2–43

2

- Click the Shapes More button (Home tab | Drawing group) (shown in Figure 2–43) to display the Shapes gallery (Figure 2–44).

Q&A I do not see a Shapes More button and the three rows of the shapes shown in Figure 2–43. Instead, I have a Shapes button. Why?

Monitor dimensions and resolution affect how buttons display on the ribbon. Click the Shapes button to display the entire Shapes gallery.

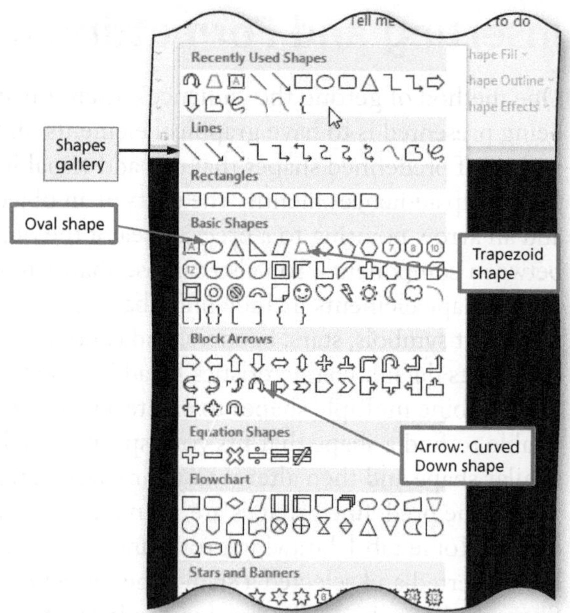

Figure 2–44

3

- Click the Oval shape (second shape in the first row of the Basic Shapes area) in the Shapes gallery.

Q&A Why did my pointer change shape?

The pointer changed to a plus shape to indicate the Oval shape has been added to the Clipboard.

- Position the pointer (a crosshair) near the center of the slide, as shown in Figure 2–45.

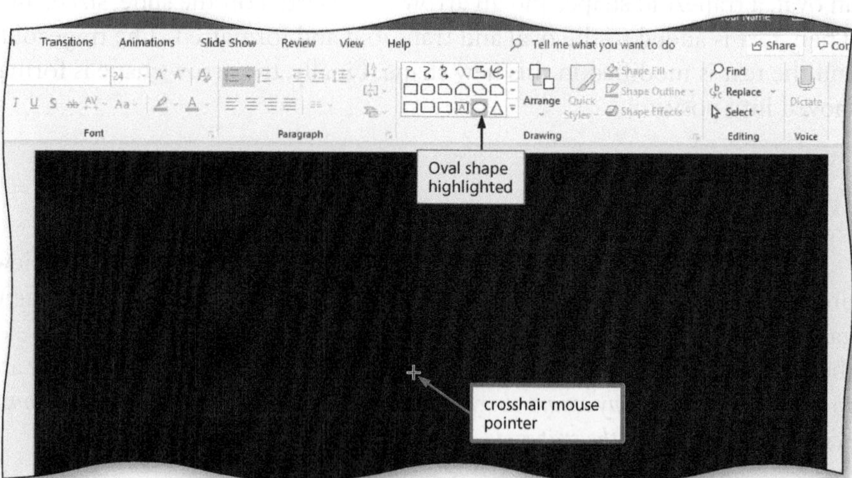

Figure 2–45

4

- Click Slide 5 to insert the Oval shape (Figure 2–46).

Q&A When I inserted the Oval shape, I selected it on the Home tab. Is the same Shapes gallery also displayed on the Drawing Tools Format tab?

Yes. The Shapes gallery is displayed on this tab once an object is inserted and selected on the slide.

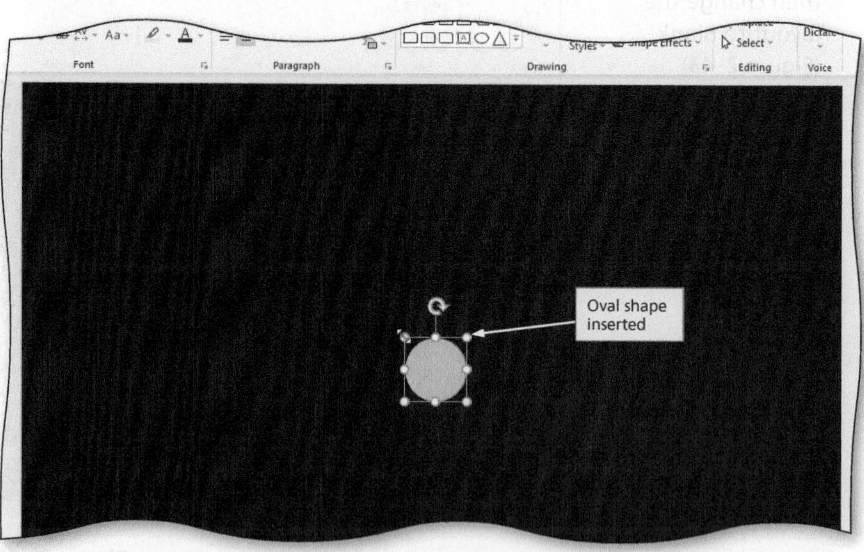

Figure 2–46

- Display the Shapes gallery again and then click the Trapezoid shape (sixth shape in the first row of the Basic Shapes area) in the gallery (shown in Figure 2–44).
- Position the pointer toward the right side of the oval and then click to insert the Trapezoid shape.

- Display the Shapes gallery again and then click the Arrow: Curved Down shape (fourth shape in the second Block Arrows row) in the gallery (shown in Figure 2–44).
- Position the pointer in the lower-left corner of the slide and then click to insert the Arrow: Curved Down shape (Figure 2–47).

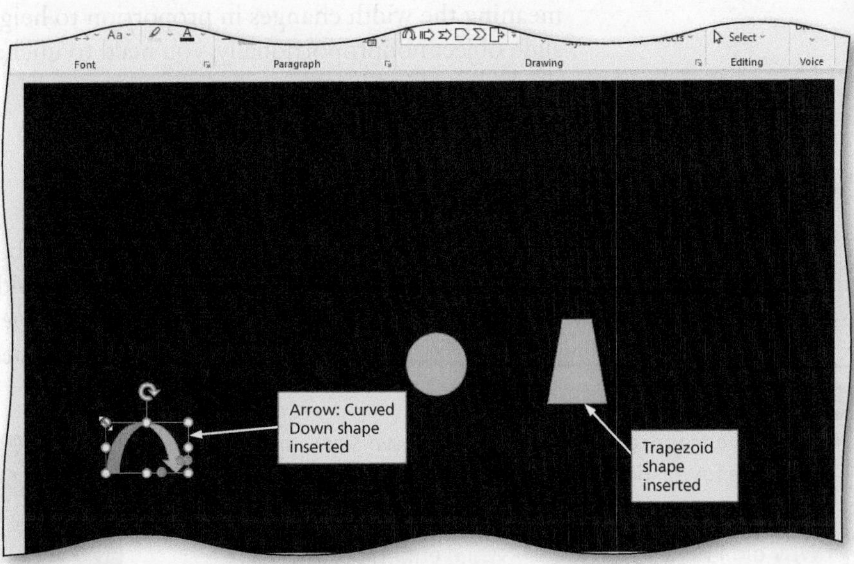

Figure 2–47

Other Ways

1. Click Shapes button (Insert tab | Illustrations group)

To Change a Shape Type

Once you insert a shape, you can change it into another shape. To change the shape type, you would do the following.

1. Select the shape you want to change and then click the Edit Shape button (Drawing Tools Format tab | Insert Shapes group).
2. Point to Change Shape and then select the desired shape.

To Delete a Shape

Once you insert a shape, you can delete it. To delete a shape, you would do the following.

1. Select the shape and then press DELETE.
2. If you want to delete multiple shapes, press CTRL while clicking the undesired shapes and then press DELETE.

Resizing Shapes

You can change the size and proportions of slide elements in two ways: proportionally and nonproportionally. To change them proportionally, you can keep the resized shape proportions identical to the original shape by pressing SHIFT while clicking a sizing handle and then dragging the pointer inward or outward to decrease or increase the size. If you do not hold down SHIFT, you can nonproportionally elongate the height or the width to draw an object that is not identical to the shape shown in the Shapes gallery. If you want to alter the shape's proportions, drag one of the sizing handles inward or outward.

You also can resize slide elements by entering exact height and width measurements in the Size group, which is located on the Drawing Tools Format tab and the SmartArt Tools Format tab. Some graphic elements are sized proportionally, meaning the width changes in proportion to height changes. If you want to alter the slide object nonproportionally, you need to uncheck the Lock aspect ratio check box in the Format Shape pane.

To Resize a Shape Proportionally

The three shapes on Slide 5 are the default sizes, and they need to be enlarged to be seen clearly and to allow text to be seen inside of them. The next step is to resize the trapezoid and oval shapes. ***Why?*** *The oval should be enlarged so that it is a focal point in the middle area of the slide, and the trapezoid needs to be large enough to contain text.* The following steps resize the Slide 5 trapezoid and oval shapes.

1

- **Select the trapezoid, press and hold down SHIFT, and then drag the lower-right corner sizing handle until the shape is resized approximately as shown in Figure 2–48.**

Q&A

Why did I need to press SHIFT while enlarging the shape?
Holding down SHIFT while dragging keeps the proportions of the original shape.

What if my shape is not selected?
To select a shape, click it.

If I am using a touch screen, how can I maintain the shape's original proportion?
If you drag one of the corner sizing handles, the object should stay in proportion.

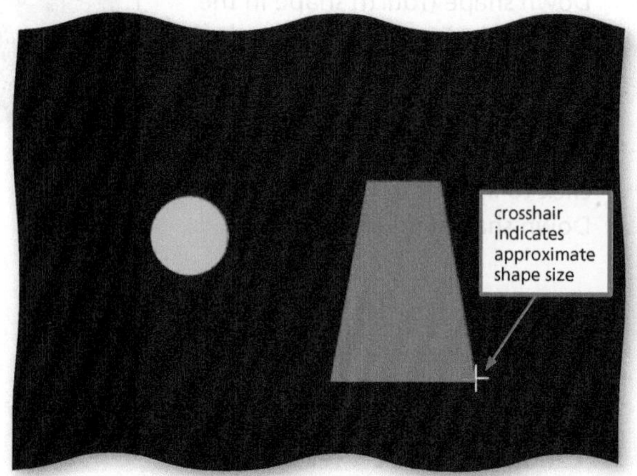

Figure 2–48

2

- **Release to resize the shape.**

3

- **Select the oval, press and hold down SHIFT, and then drag the lower-left corner sizing handle until the shape is resized approximately as shown in Figure 2–49.**

Q&A

What if I want to move the shape to a precise location on the slide?
With the shape selected, press ARROW or CTRL+ARROW to move the shape to the desired location.

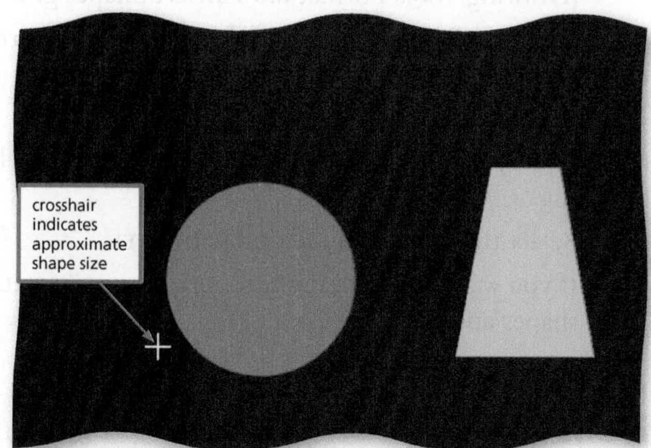

Figure 2–49

To Resize a Shape Nonproportionally by Entering an Exact Measurement

Why? *Adequate space exists on the slide to increase all the SmartArt shapes.* You can resize a slide element by dragging the sizing handles or by specifying exact measurements for the height and width. The following steps resize the arrow shape by entering an exact measurement and then check the dimensions of the resized oval and trapezoid.

1

- Select the arrow shape and then display the Drawing Tools Format tab.

Q&A How will I know the arrow shape is selected?
You will see the sizing handles around the outer edge of the shape.

- Click the Shape Height box up arrow (Drawing Tools Format tab | Size group) several times until the Height measurement is 3".
- Click the Shape Width box up arrow (Drawing Tools Format tab | Size group) several times until the Width measurement is 13.5" (Figure 2–50).

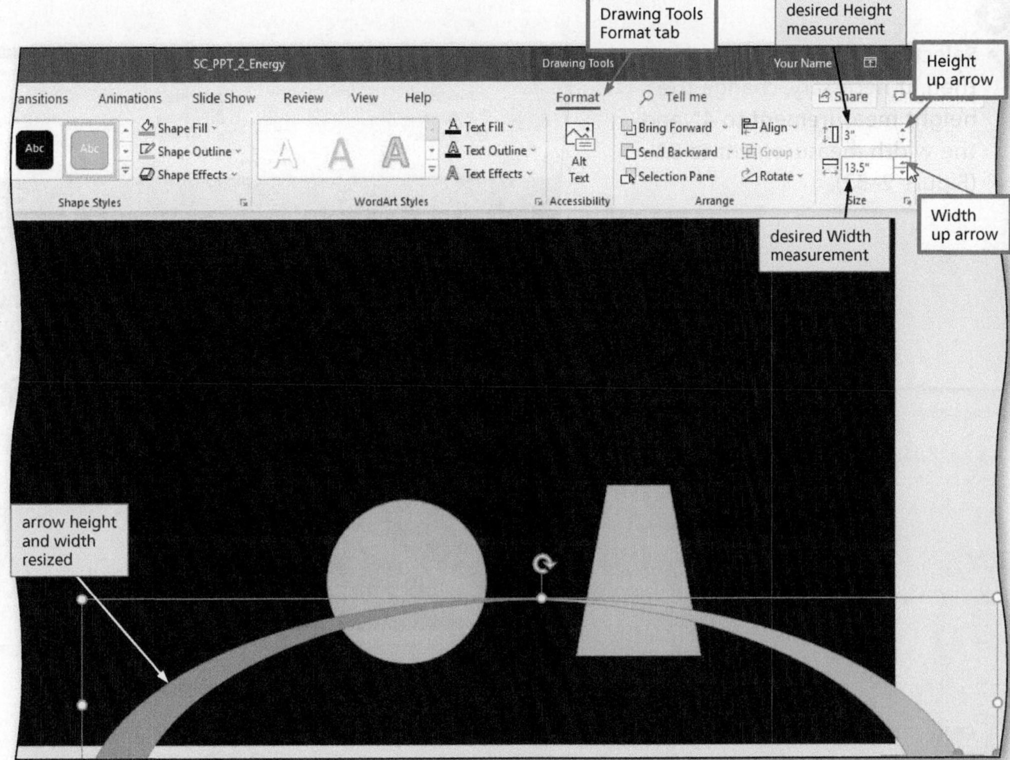

Figure 2–50

Q&A Part of the arrow is extending off the slide. Do I need to move it on the slide now?
No. You will position this arrow later in this module.

Can I just enter the Height and Width measurements I want in the Height and Width boxes?
Yes. You can replace the existing measurements with your desired sizes.

2

- Select the oval shape and then, if necessary, change the height and width measurements to 4" (Figure 2–51).

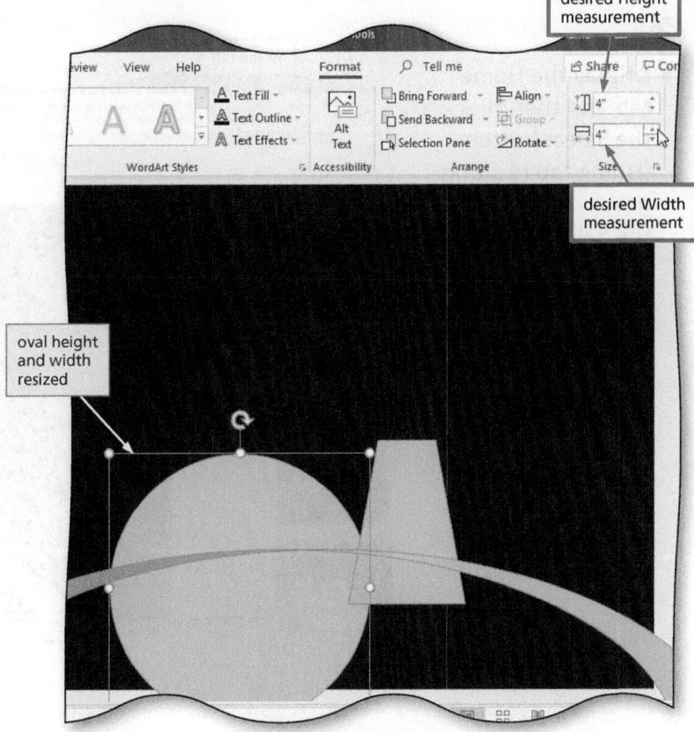

Figure 2–51

- Select the trapezoid shape and then, if necessary, change the height measurement to 4" and the width measurement to 3" (Figure 2–52).

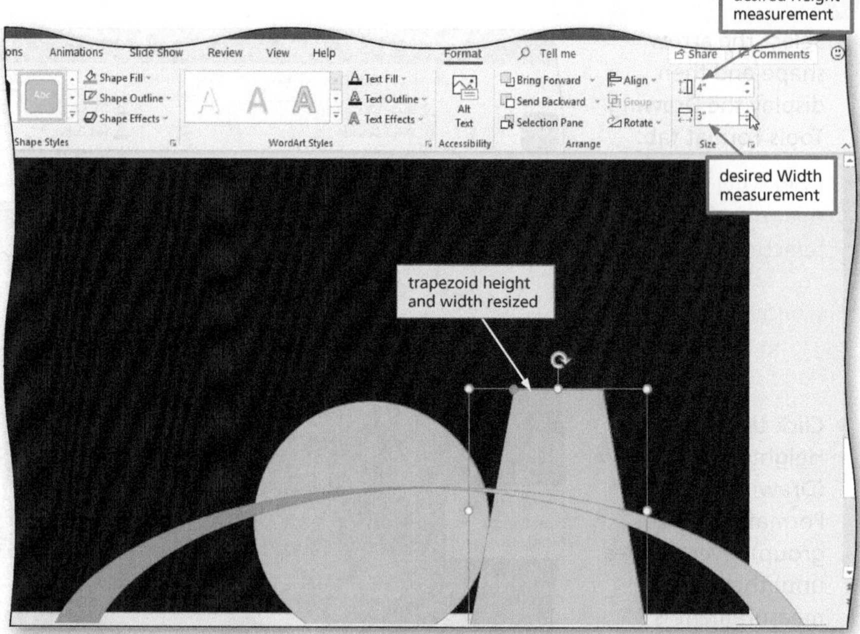

Figure 2–52

Other Ways

1. Right-click shape, click 'Size and Position' on shortcut menu, if necessary click 'Size & Properties' icon (Format Shape pane), if necessary click Size, enter shape height and width values in boxes, close Format Shape pane
2. Click Size and Position pane launcher (Drawing Tools Format tab | Size group), click Size tab, enter desired height and width values in boxes, click Close button

To Select All Slide Content

When you want to format multiple objects on a slide, one efficient method of performing this task is to select all these objects and then apply changes to them simultaneously. ***Why?*** *You want to apply the same changes to all three shapes.* The following steps select the three shapes on Slide 5.

- Display the Home tab and then click the Select button (Home tab | Editing group) to display the Select menu (Figure 2–53).

Figure 2–53

2

- Click Select All to select the three shapes on Slide 5 (Figure 2–54).

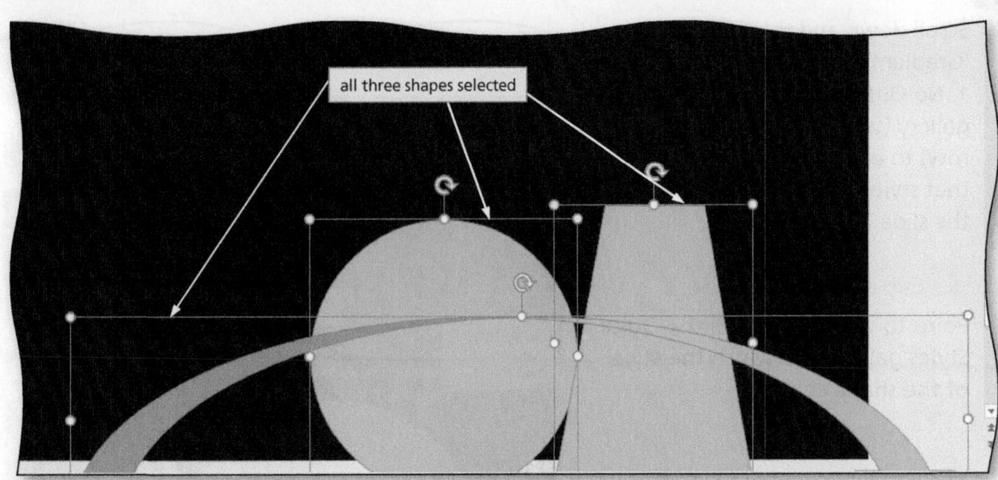

Figure 2–54

To Apply a Shape Style

The Quick Styles gallery has a variety of styles that change depending upon the theme applied to the presentation. Formatting text in a shape follows the same techniques as formatting text in a placeholder. You can change font, font color and size, and alignment. You later will add information to the oval and trapezoid shapes, but first you want to apply a shape style. ***Why?*** *The style will give depth and dimension to the object.* The following steps apply a style to the three shapes on Slide 5.

1

- With the Home tab displaying, click the Quick Styles button (Home tab | Drawing group) to display the Shape Quick Styles gallery (Figure 2–55).

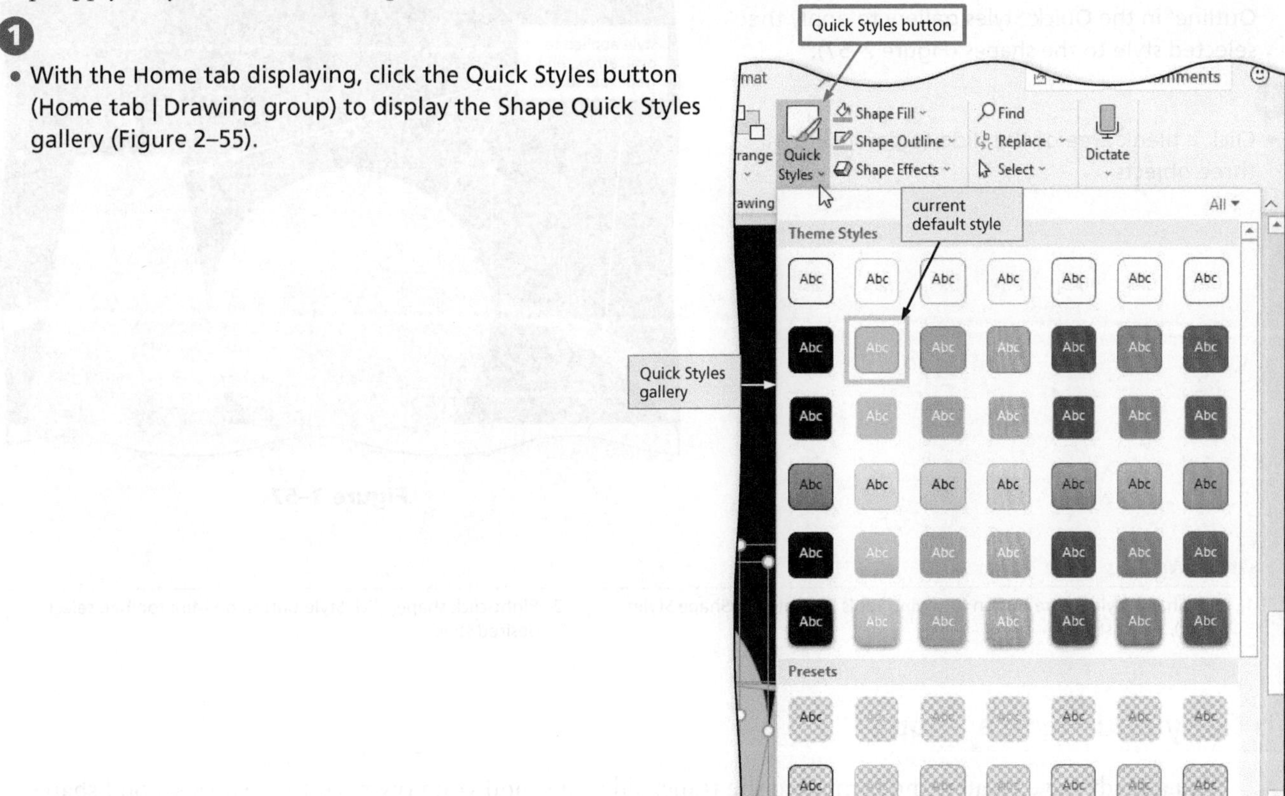

Figure 2–55

- Scroll down and then point to 'Gradient Fill - Light Blue, Accent 1, No Outline' in the Quick Styles gallery (second shape in last Presets row) to display a live preview of that style applied to the shapes in the slide (Figure 2–56).

Experiment

- Point to various styles in the Quick Styles gallery and watch the style of the shape change.

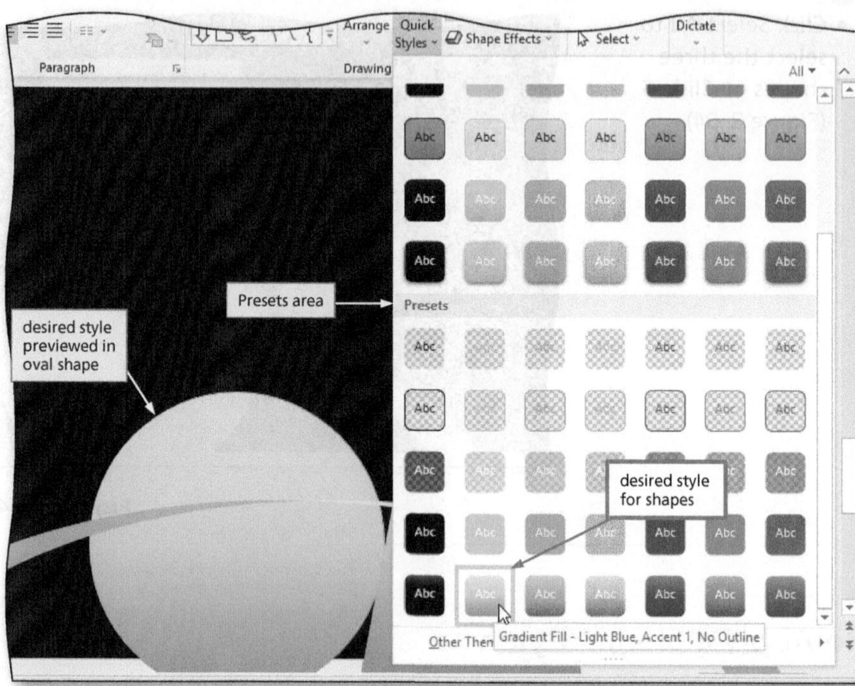

Figure 2–56

- Click 'Gradient Fill-Light Blue, Accent 1, No Outline' in the Quick Styles gallery to apply the selected style to the shapes (Figure 2–57).

- Click a blank area of the slide to deselect the three objects.

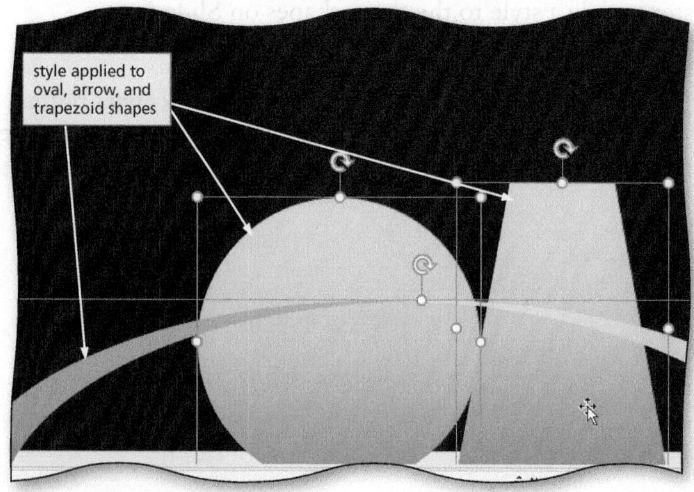

Figure 2–57

Other Ways

1. Click Shape Styles More button (Drawing Tools Format tab | Shape Styles group), select style
2. Right-click shape, click Style button on Mini toolbar, select desired style

To Copy and Paste a Shape

You already have created and formatted the trapezoid shape, and you now need to create a second shape with the same formatting. The following steps copy the trapezoid shape and then paste it on the left side of the slide. ***Why?*** *You could repeat all the steps you performed to create the first trapezoid, but it is much more efficient to duplicate the formatted shape.*

1
- Select the trapezoid shape and then click the Copy button (Home tab | Clipboard group) (Figure 2–58).

2
- Click the Paste button (Home tab | Clipboard group) to insert a duplicate trapezoid shape on Slide 5.

Figure 2–58

3
- Drag the new trapezoid shape to the left side of the slide (Figure 2–59).

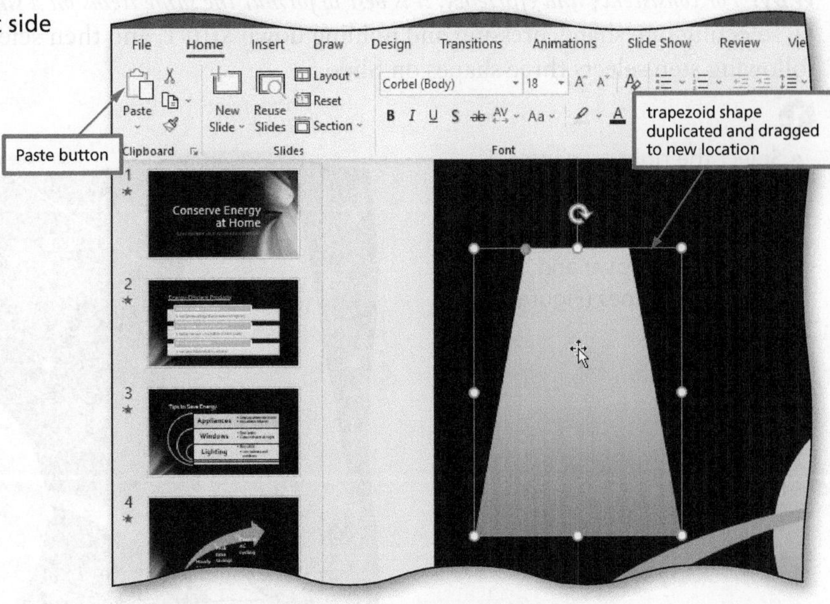

Figure 2–59

To Add Text to a Shape

The shapes on Slide 5 help call attention to the key aspects of your presentation. ***Why?*** *Your goal is to emphasize features of smart thermostats.* The next step is to add this information to Slide 5. The following steps add text to the trapezoid and oval shapes.

1
- With the left trapezoid shape selected, type **`Remembers your preferred temperatures`** to add the text in the shape.

2
- Click the oval to select it and then type **`Turns itself up or down`** to add the text in the shape.

- Click the right trapezoid to select it and then type `Can be controlled from anywhere using phone, tablet, or laptop` to add the text in the shape (Figure 2–60).

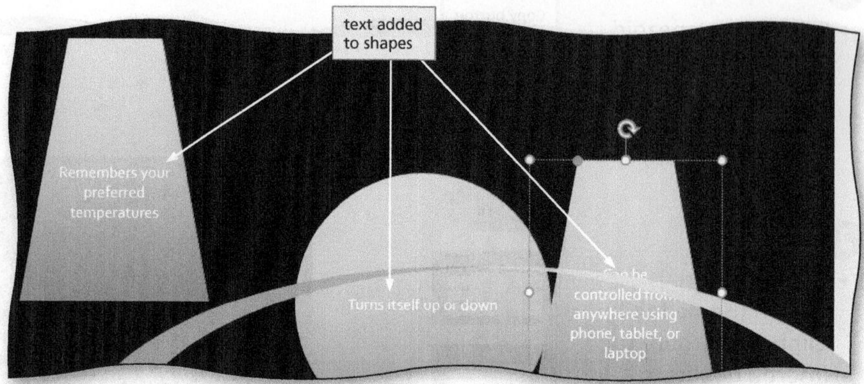

Figure 2–60

Other Ways

1. Right-click selected shape, click Copy on shortcut menu, right-click blank area, click Paste on shortcut menu
2. Select shape, press CTRL+C, press CTRL+V

To Select Shapes

The text in the three shapes can be formatted. You can select all these shapes and then change the text. ***Why?*** *For consistency and efficiency, it is best to format the same items on a slide simultaneously.* Select these objects by selecting one shape, pressing and holding down SHIFT, and then selecting the second and third shapes. The following step selects three shapes on Slide 5.

- Select the right trapezoid, if necessary.
- Press and hold down SHIFT and then click the oval and the left trapezoid shapes (Figure 2–61).

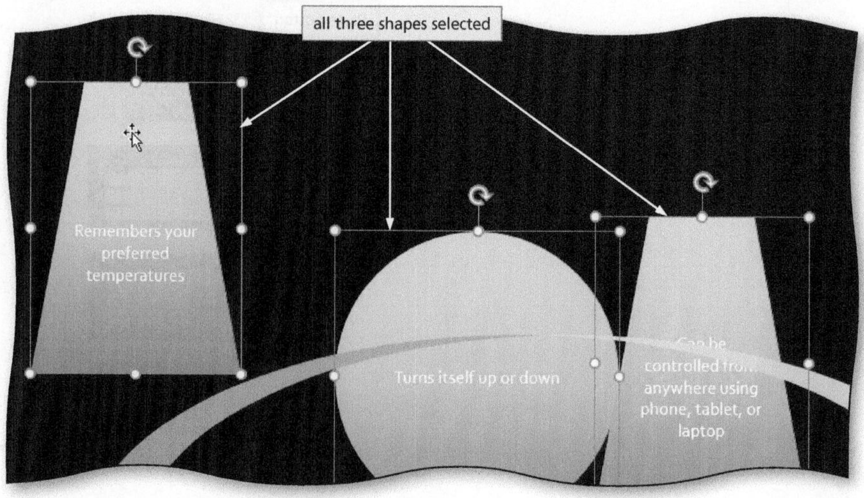

Figure 2–61

To Format Shape Text

The text in the three shapes has the default formatting, but you can enhance these letters. ***Why?*** *The size, color, and other formatting aspects will make the text more readable.* You can format shape text with the same features used to format slide placeholder text. The following step simultaneously bolds the text, adds a shadow, changes the font color to Dark Blue, and increases the font size.

1

- If necessary, display the Home tab and then click the Bold button (Home tab | Font group).
- Click the Text Shadow button (Home tab | Font group) to add a shadow to the text.
- Click the Font Color arrow and then click Dark Blue (ninth color in Standard Colors row) to change the font color to Dark Blue.
- Click the 'Increase Font Size' button to increase the font size to 20 point (Figure 2–62).

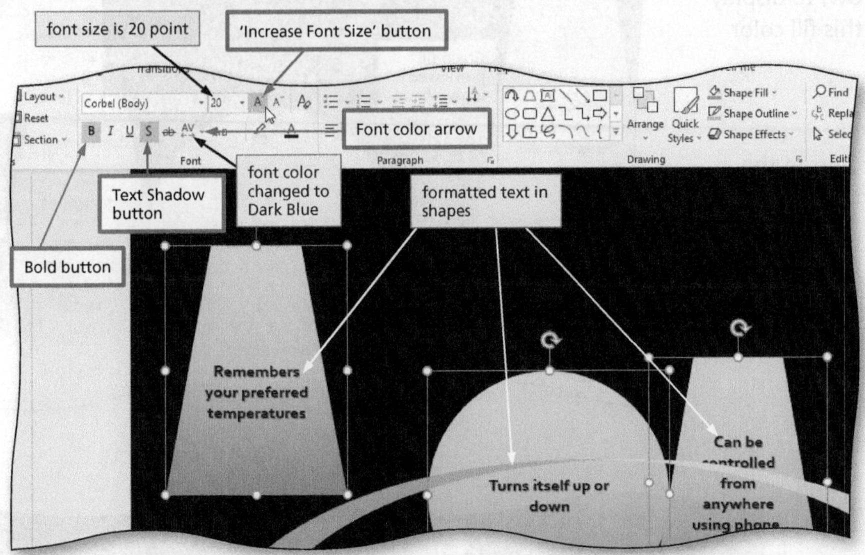

Figure 2–62

Q&A Can I make other formatting changes to the graphics' text?
Yes. You can format the text by making any of the modifications in the Font group.

If I am using a touch screen, can I modify all three rectangles simultaneously?
No. You need to repeat Step 1 for each of the shapes.

Other Ways

1. Right-click selected text, click desired text format button on Mini toolbar

To Undo Text Formatting Changes

To remove a formatting change you have made to text, such as bolding or shadowing, you would do the following.

1. Select the text and then click the button that originally applied the format. For example, to undo bolding, select the text and then click the Bold button.
2. If you apply a format and then immediately decide to remove this effect, click the Undo button on the Quick Access Toolbar.

BTW
Touch Screen Differences
The Office and Windows interfaces may vary if you are using a touch screen. For this reason, you might notice that the function or appearance of your touch screen differs slightly from this module's presentation.

To Change a Shape Fill Color

The downward arrow has the same blue formatting as the three other slide shapes. You can change the arrow's fill color to green. ***Why?*** *The color green is associated with money, conservation, and clean environments.* The following steps change the fill color of the arrow.

- Click the arrow shape to select it, and then click the Shape Fill arrow (Drawing Tools Format tab | Shape Styles group) to display the Shape Fill gallery.
- Point to Green (sixth color in Standard Colors row) to display a live preview of this fill color (Figure 2–63).

Experiment

- Point to various colors in the gallery and watch the fill color change.

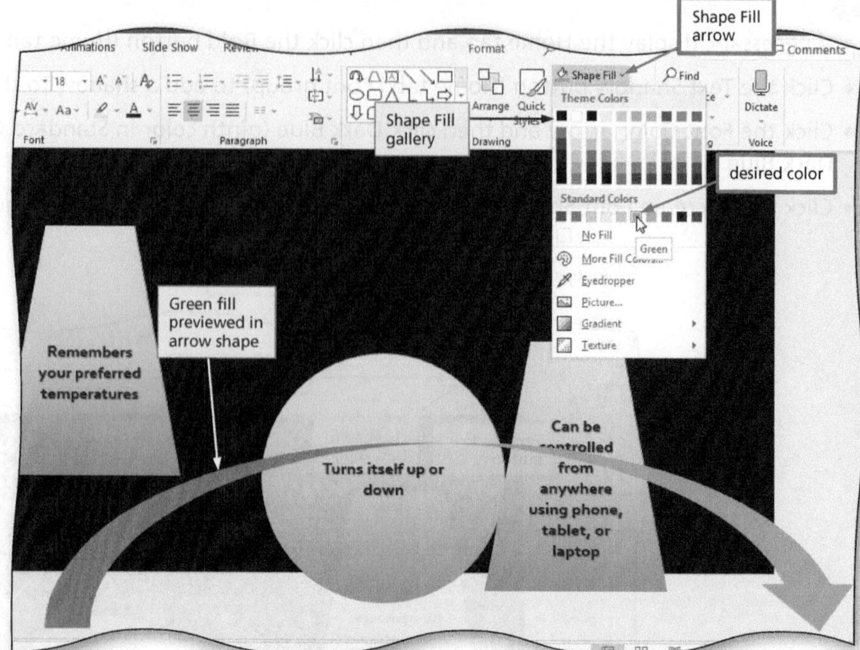

Figure 2–63

2

- Click Green to apply this color to the arrow.
- Click a blank area of the slide outside of the arrow shape to deselect this slide element (Figure 2–64).

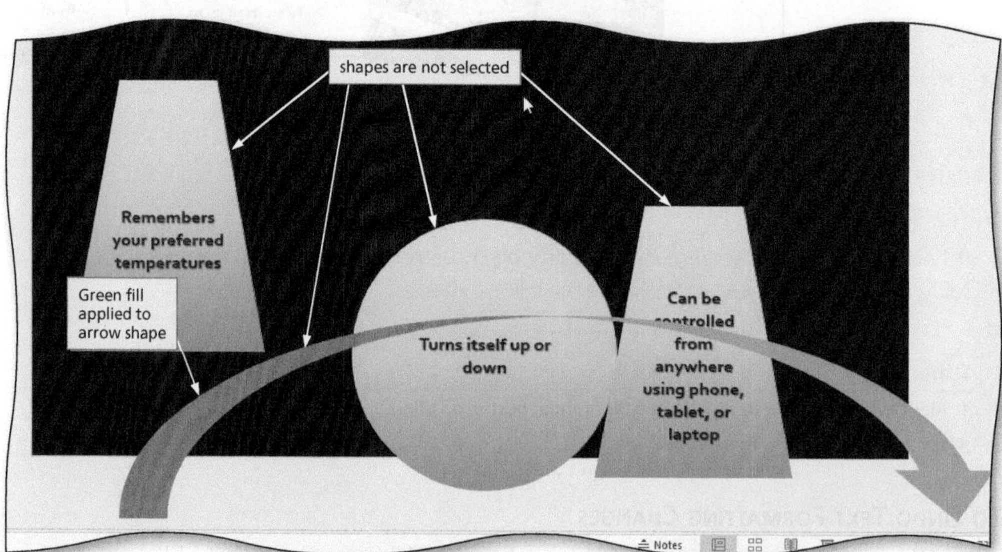

Figure 2–64

Break Point: If you wish to take a break, this is a good place to do so. Be sure the Energy file is saved and then you can exit PowerPoint. To resume later, start PowerPoint, open the file called SC_PPT_2_Energy.pptx, and continue following the steps from this location forward.

BTW

Drawing Guides and Touch Screens

If you are using a touch screen, you may not be able to change the position of the drawing guides. In addition, the measurements indicating the position of the guides are not displayed.

Positioning Slide Elements

At times you may desire to arrange slide elements in precise locations. PowerPoint provides useful tools to help you position shapes and objects on slides. **Drawing guides** are two straight dotted lines, one horizontal and one vertical. When an object is close to a guide, its corner or its center (whichever is closer) **snaps**, or aligns precisely, on top of the guide. You can drag a guide to a new location to meet your alignment requirements. Guides can be added and deleted as you develop slide content. Another tool is the vertical or horizontal **ruler**, which can help you drag an object to a precise location on the slide. The center of a slide is 0.00 on both the vertical and the horizontal rulers.

Gridlines are evenly spaced horizontal and vertical lines that help give you visual cues when you are formatting objects on a slide. You can use gridlines to help you align shapes and other objects.

BTW

Changing Rulers Measurements

The vertical and horizontal rulers display the units of measurement in inches by default. This measurement system is determined by the settings in Microsoft Windows. You can change the measurement system to centimeters by customizing the numbers format in the 'Clock, Language, and Region' area of the Control Panel. Click Region, click Additional Settings, and then choose the desired measurement system.

Aligning and Distributing Objects

If you display multiple objects, PowerPoint can **align** them above and below each other (vertically) or side by side (horizontally). The objects, such as SmartArt graphics, shapes, boxes, and other slide elements, can be aligned relative to the slide so that they display along the top, left, right, or bottom borders or in the center or middle of the slide. They also can be aligned relative to each other, meaning that you position either the first or last object in the desired location and then command PowerPoint to move the remaining objects in the series above, below, or beside it. Depending on the alignment option that you click, objects will move straight up, down, left, or right, and might cover an object already located on the slide. Table 2–3 describes alignment options.

Table 2–3 Alignment Options

Alignment	Action
Left	Aligns the edges of the objects to the left
Center	Aligns the objects vertically through the centers of the objects
Right	Aligns the edges of the objects to the right
Top	Aligns the top edges of the objects
Middle	Aligns the objects horizontally through the middles of the objects
Bottom	Aligns the bottom edges of the objects
to Slide	Aligns one object to the slide

One object remains stationary when you align objects relative to each other by their edges. For example, Align Left aligns the left edges of all selected objects with the left edge of the leftmost object. The leftmost object remains stationary, and the other objects are aligned relative to it. Objects aligned to a SmartArt graphic are aligned to the leftmost edge of the SmartArt graphic, not to the leftmost shape in the SmartArt graphic. Objects aligned relative to each other by their middles or centers are aligned along a horizontal or vertical line that represents the average of their original positions. All of the objects might move.

Smart Guides appear automatically when two or more shapes are in spatial alignment with each other, even if the shapes vary in size. To evenly space multiple objects horizontally or vertically, you **distribute** them. PowerPoint determines the total length between either the outermost edges of the first and last selected object or the edges of the entire slide. It then inserts equal spacing among the items in the series. You also can distribute spacing by using the Size and Position dialog box, but the Distribute command automates this task.

BTW

Deleting a Shape

If you want to delete a shape you have added to a slide, click that shape to select it and then press DELETE. If you want to delete multiple shapes, press CTRL while clicking the unwanted shapes and then press DELETE.

To Display the Drawing Guides

Why? Guides help you align objects on slides. Using a mouse, when you point to a guide and then press and hold the mouse button, PowerPoint displays a box containing the exact position of the guide on the slide in inches. An arrow is displayed below the guide position to indicate the vertical guide either left or right of the center. An arrow also is displayed to the right of the guide position to indicate the horizontal guide either above or below the center. The following step displays the guides.

- With Slide 5 displaying, display the View tab and then click the Guides check box (View tab | Show group) to place a checkmark in the box and display the horizontal and vertical guides (Figure 2–65).

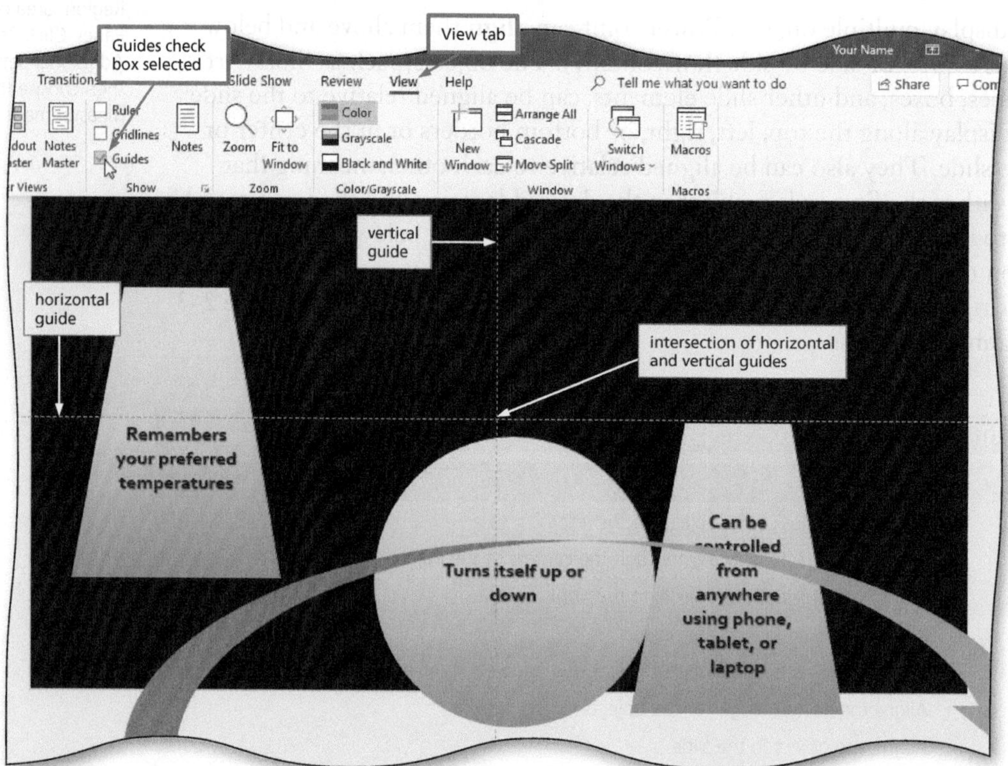

Figure 2–65

Other Ways

1. Right-click area of slide other than a placeholder or object, point to 'Grid and Guides' arrow on shortcut menu, click Guides
2. Press ALT+F9 to toggle guides on/off

BTW
Displaying the Ruler
The ruler is not available in all views, such as Slide Sorter view. If the Ruler box is grayed out, try switching to Normal view.

To Display the Ruler

The ruler is another feature to use when positioning objects. ***Why?*** *The ruler helps you align slide elements in precise location on slides.* One ruler is displayed horizontally at the top of the slide, and the other is displayed vertically along the left edge of the slide. The following step displays the ruler.

1

- With Slide 5 displaying, click the Ruler check box (View tab | Show group) to place a checkmark in the box and display the horizontal and vertical rulers (Figure 2–66).

Ruler check box selected

ruler shows vertical guide positioned at 0"

ruler shows horizontal guide positioned at 0"

Remembers your preferred temperatures

Turns itself up or down

Can be controlled from anywhere using phone, tablet, or laptop

Figure 2–66

BTW

Hiding the Vertical Ruler

To permanently hide the vertical ruler, click the File tab, click Options, click Advanced, scroll down to the Display section, and then clear the 'Show vertical ruler' box.

Other Ways

1. Right-click area of slide other than a placeholder or object, point to Ruler on shortcut menu, click Ruler

To Display the Gridlines

Why? *The gridlines give you precise visual cues when you are developing slide content.* The vertical and horizontal lines are spaced at one-inch intervals. When shapes or objects are near an intersection of the grid, they snap to this location. The following step displays the gridlines.

1

- With Slide 5 displaying, click the Gridlines check box (View tab | Show group) to place a checkmark in the box and display the horizontal and vertical gridlines (Figure 2–67).

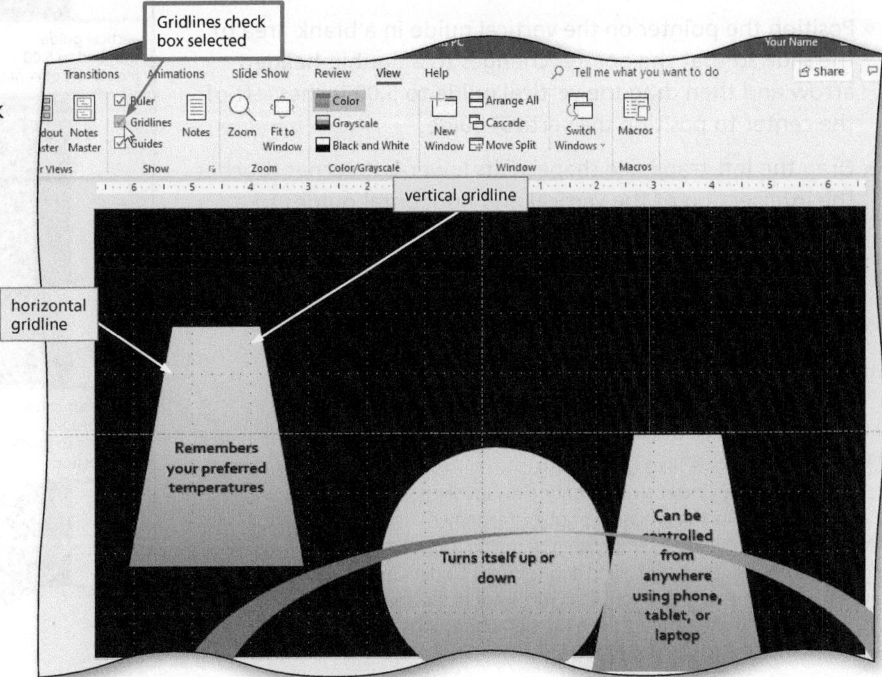

Figure 2–67

Other Ways

1. Right-click area of slide other than a placeholder or object, point to 'Grid and Guides' arrow on shortcut menu, click Gridlines

BTW
Overriding Snap-To Options
To temporarily override the snap-to options, hold down ALT while you drag the object, picture, or chart.

To Position a Shape Using Guides, Gridlines, and the Ruler

The lower edges of the three shapes on Slide 5 should be displayed in the same horizontal location. ***Why?*** *The design will look professional if they are aligned precisely near the bottom of the slide.* You can use the rulers and gridlines to help you verify the desired guide locations and where to drag an object to an exact location on the slide. The center of a slide is 0.00 on both the vertical and the horizontal rulers. The following steps position the shapes on Slide 5.

- Position the pointer on the horizontal guide in a blank area of the slide so that the pointer changes to a double-headed arrow and then drag the horizontal guide to 3.00 inches below the center. Do not release the mouse button (Figure 2–68).

Q&A Why does 3.00 display when I hold down the mouse button?
The ScreenTip displays the horizontal guide's position. A 0.00 setting means that the guide is precisely in the middle of the slide and is not above or below the center, so a 3.00 setting indicates the guide is 3 inches below the center line.

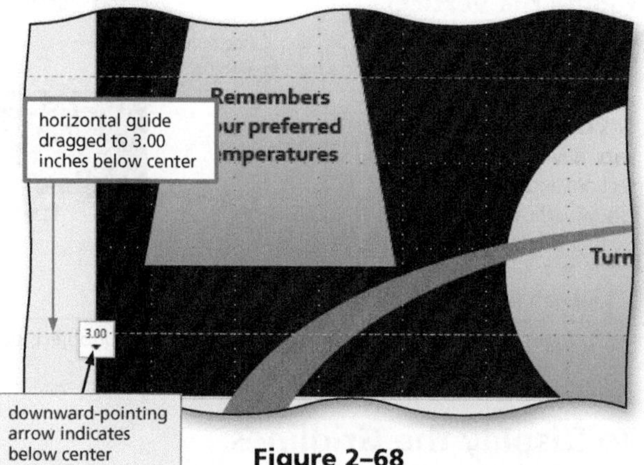

Figure 2–68

- Release the mouse button to position the horizontal guide at 3.00, which is the intended location of the shape's bottom border.
- Position the pointer on the vertical guide in a blank area of the slide so that the pointer changes to a double-headed arrow and then drag the vertical guide to 5.00 inches left of the center to position the vertical guide.
- Drag the left trapezoid shape so its lower-left corner touches the intersection of the vertical and horizontal guides to position the shape in the desired location (Figure 2–69).

Q&A Can I add guides to help me align multiple objects?
Yes. Position the pointer over one guide and then press CTRL. When you drag your pointer, a second guide appears.

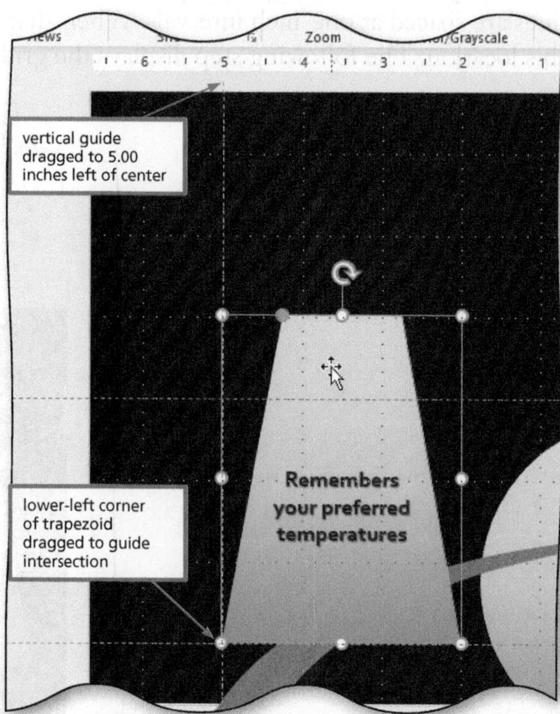

Figure 2–69

BTW
Changing Grid Measurements
You can change the increments of grid measurements, which allows you to adjust the precision of object alignment. In Normal view, right-click an empty area or margin of a slide (not a placeholder) and then click 'Grid and Guides'. Under Grid settings, enter the measurement that you want in the spacing list. If you want these settings to be the default settings for all your presentations, click 'Set as Default'.

To Position the Remaining Shapes

The bottom edges of the oval and right trapezoid shapes on Slide 4 should be positioned in the same location as left trapezoid. The horizontal guide will display in the same location, but you can move the vertical guide to help you align these objects. The rulers and gridlines will help you verify the desired guide locations. The following steps position the oval and right trapezoid shapes.

1. Drag the vertical guide to 2.00 left of the center. Select the oval shape and then position it so its lower-left corner touches the intersection of the vertical and horizontal guides.

2. Drag the vertical guide to 2.00 right of the center. Select the right trapezoid shape and then position it so its lower-left corner touches the intersection of the vertical and horizontal guides (Figure 2–70).

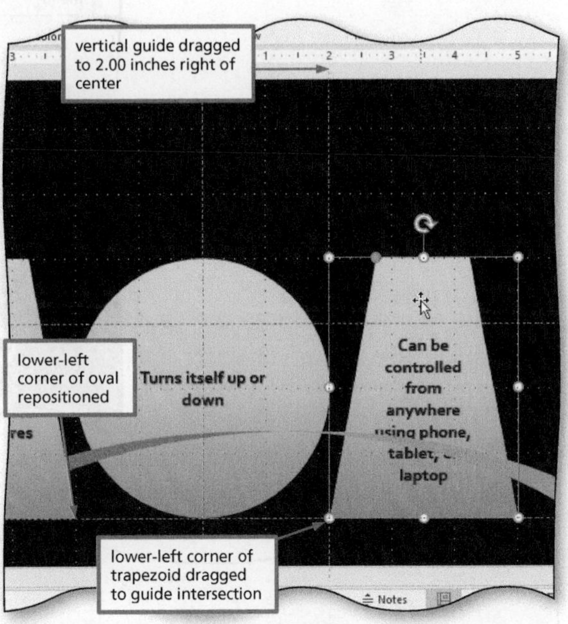

Figure 2–70

To Distribute Shapes

Now that the three Slide 3 pictures are aligned, you can have PowerPoint place the same amount of space between them. You have two distribution options: 'Align to Slide' spaces all the selected objects evenly across the entire width of the slide; 'Align Selected Objects' spaces only the middle objects between the fixed right and left objects. The following steps use the 'Align to Slide' option. ***Why?*** *This option will distribute the Slide 5 shapes horizontally to fill some of the space along the bottom of the slide.*

1.
- Select the left trapezoid, oval, and right trapezoid, display the Drawing Tools Format tab, and then click the Align button (Drawing Tools Format tab | Arrange group) to display the Align Objects menu (Figure 2–71).

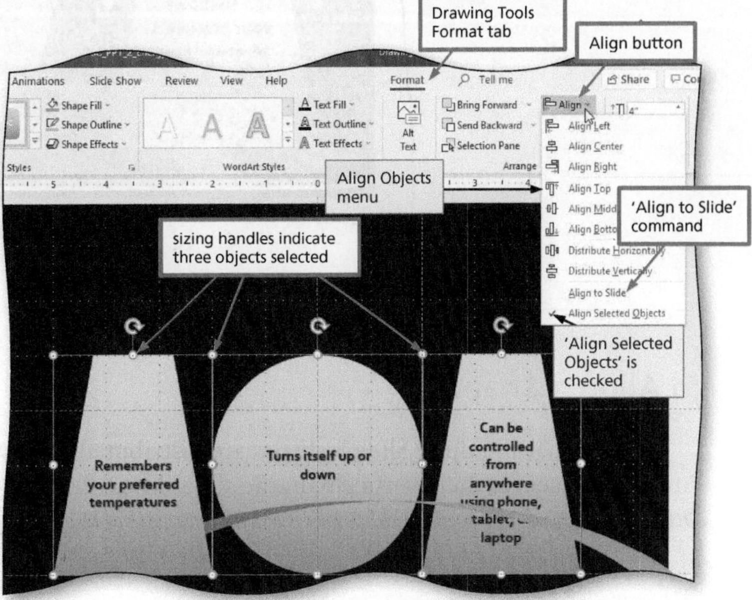

Figure 2–71

- Click 'Align to Slide' so that PowerPoint will adjust the spacing of the pictures evenly between the slide edges. Click the Align button again to display the Align Objects menu (Figure 2–72).

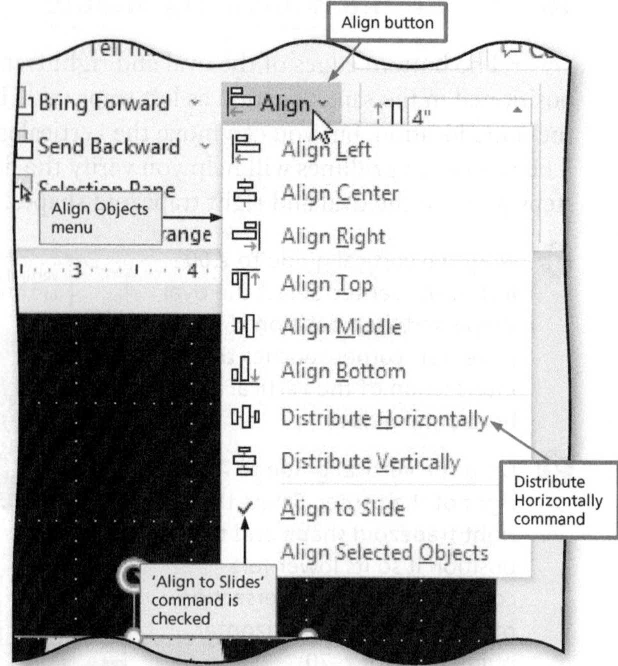

Figure 2–72

- Click Distribute Horizontally to adjust the spacing (Figure 2–73).

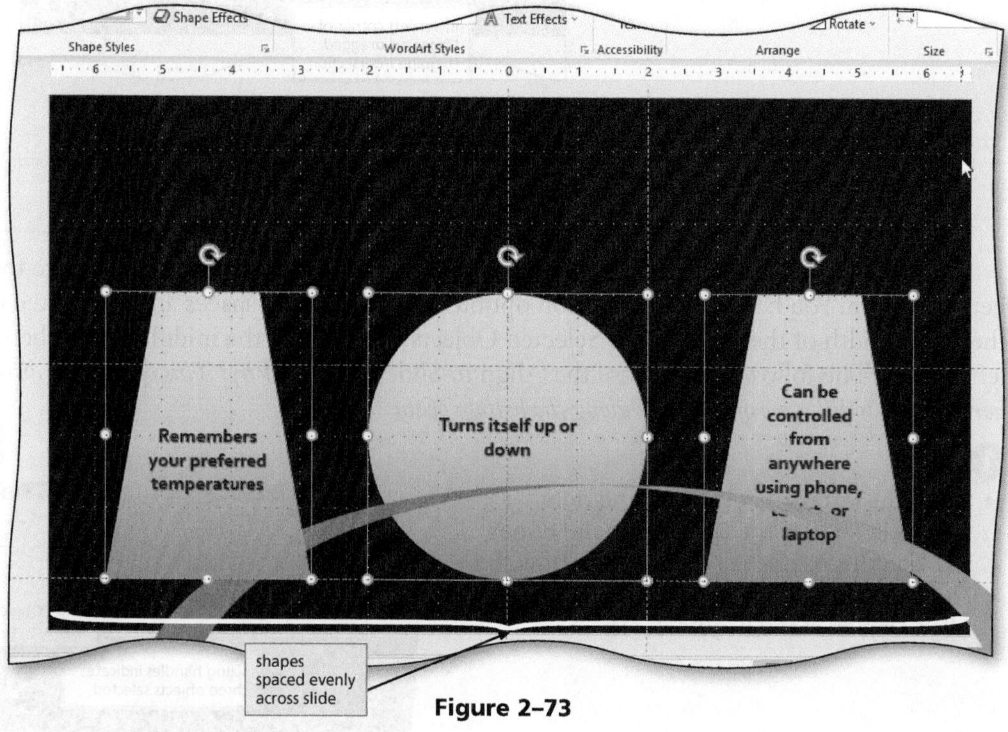

Figure 2–73

To Align a Shape

Now that the three Slide 3 shapes are distributed evenly across the width of the slide, you can have PowerPoint center them vertically in the slide. The following steps use the Align Middle option. ***Why?*** *This option will spread the Slide 5 shapes horizontally to fill some of the space in the slide.*

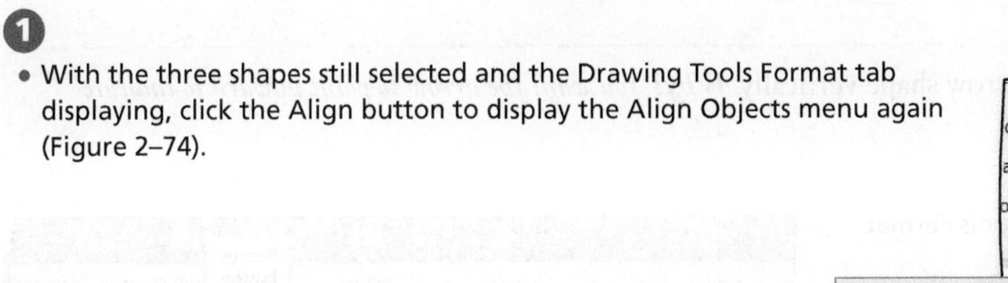

1

- **With the three shapes still selected and the Drawing Tools Format tab displaying, click the Align button to display the Align Objects menu again (Figure 2–74).**

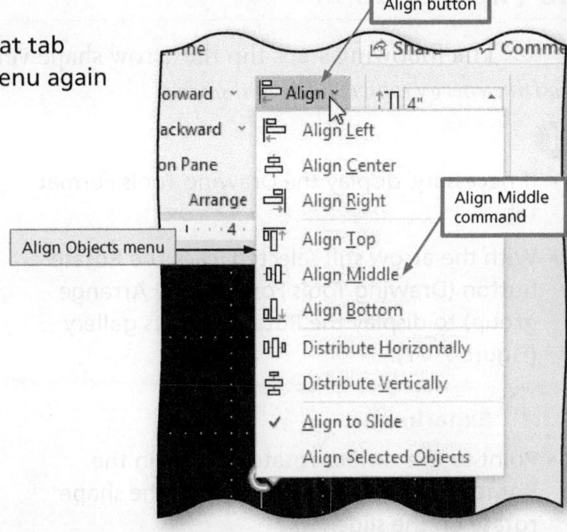

Figure 2–74

2

- **Click Align Middle to move the three shapes to the middle of the slide (Figure 2–75).**

Q&A What is the difference between the Align Middle and Align Center commands?
Align Middle places the center of each object vertically on the slide; Align Center places all the objects in the center of the slide.

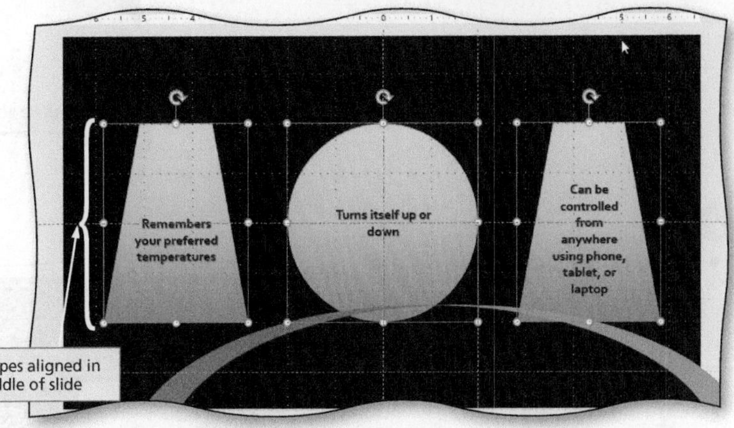

Figure 2–75

To Position the Arrow Shape

The arrow shape represents increased energy savings, so you want it to display prominently flowing under the shapes and then pointing near the top of the slide. The following step positions the arrow shape.

1 **Drag the horizontal guide to 3.00 inches above the center and the vertical guide 6.66 inches left of the center (at the left edge of the slide). Select the arrow shape and then drag it upward so its upper-left corner touches the intersection of the vertical and horizontal guides (Figure 2–76).**

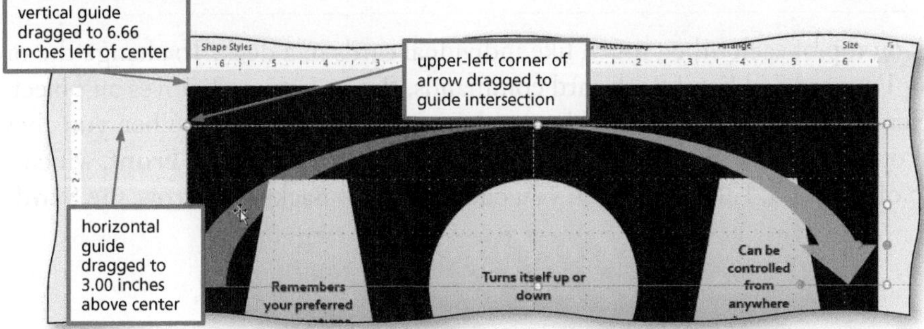

Figure 2–76

To Flip a Shape

The following steps flip the arrow shape vertically. ***Why?*** *You want the arrow to point upward to indicate positive energy conservation and savings.*

- If necessary, display the Drawing Tools Format tab.
- With the arrow still selected, click the Rotate button (Drawing Tools Format tab | Arrange group) to display the Rotate Objects gallery (Figure 2–77).

- Point to the various rotate options in the Rotate Options gallery and watch the shape rotate on the slide.

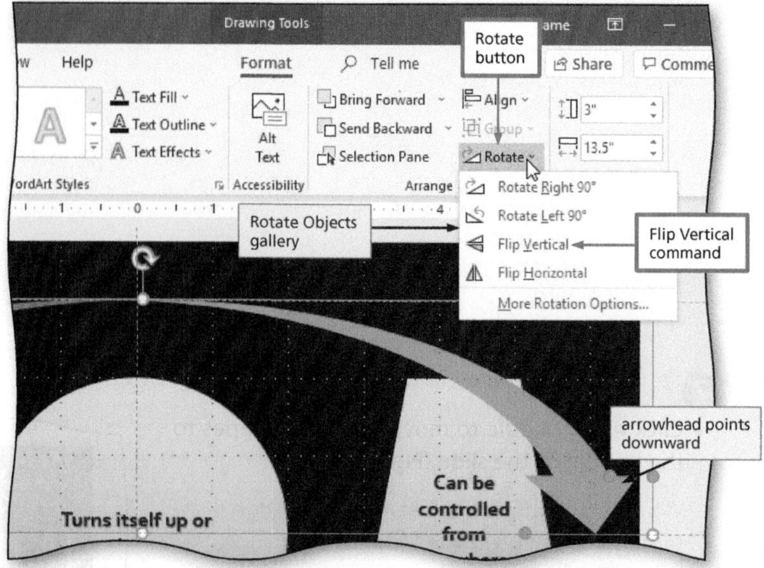

Figure 2–77

2

- Click Flip Vertical in the Rotate Options gallery, so that the arrow flips to display its mirror image and points upward (Figure 2–78).

Q&A Can I flip a graphic horizontally?
Yes, you would click Flip Horizontal in the Rotate Options gallery. You also can rotate a graphic clockwise or counterclockwise by clicking 'Rotate Right 90°' and 'Rotate Left 90°'.

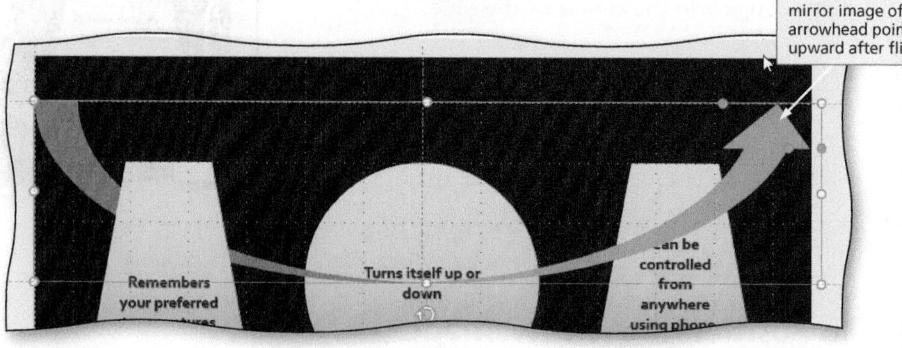

Figure 2–78

BTW
Using Text in a Shape
When you add text to a shape, it becomes part of the shape. If you rotate or flip the shape, the text also rotates or flips.

To Change the Stacking Order

The objects on a slide stack on top of each other, much like individual cards in a deck. To change the order of these objects, you use the Bring Forward and Send Backward commands. **Bring Forward** moves an object toward the top of the stack, and **Send Backward** moves an object underneath another object. When you click the Bring Forward arrow, PowerPoint displays a menu with an additional command, **Bring to Front**, which moves a selected object to the top of the stack. Likewise, when you click the Send Backward arrow, the **Send**

to Back command moves the selected object underneath all objects on the slide. The following steps move the arrow backwards so that the shapes display over it. ***Why?*** *On this slide, the arrow is on top of some of the shapes, so you no longer can see some of the text. If you send the arrow to the bottom of the stack on the slide, the letters will become visible.*

1

- With the arrow shape selected, display the Drawing Tools Format tab if necessary, and then click the Send Backward arrow (Drawing Tools Format tab | Arrange group) to display the Send Backward menu (Figure 2–79).

Q&A How can I see objects that are not on the top of the stack?
Press TAB or SHIFT+TAB to display each slide object.

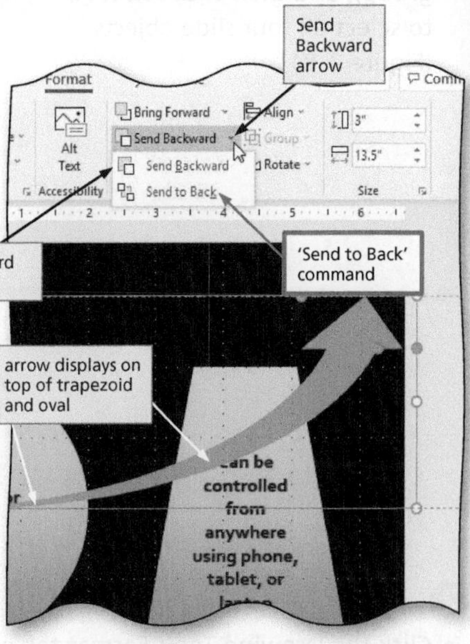

Send Backward arrow
Send Backward menu
'Send to Back' command
arrow displays on top of trapezoid and oval

Figure 2–79

2

- Click 'Send to Back' to move the arrow underneath the trapezoids and oval shapes (Figure 2–80).

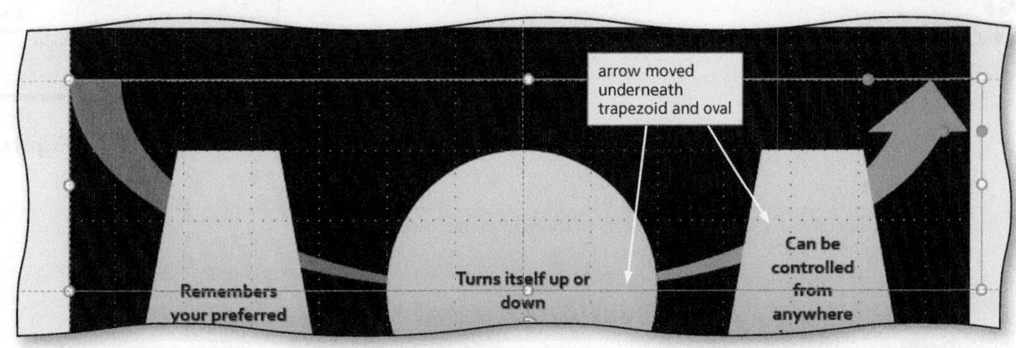

Figure 2–80

Other Ways

1. Click Send Backward arrow (Picture Tools Format tab | Arrange group), press K
2. Right-click shape, point to 'Send to Back' on shortcut menu, click 'Send to Back'

To Group Objects

If you attempt to move or size the four shapes on Slide 5, you might encounter difficulties because the multiple objects are separate objects on the slide. Dragging or sizing affects only a selected object, not the entire collection of objects, so you must use caution when objects are not grouped. You can **group** the objects so they are assembled into a single unit. ***Why?*** *When they are grouped, they cannot be accidentally moved or manipulated.* The following steps group these four objects into one object.

- Display the Home tab, click the Select button (Home tab | Editing group), and then click Select All to select all four slide objects (Figure 2–81).

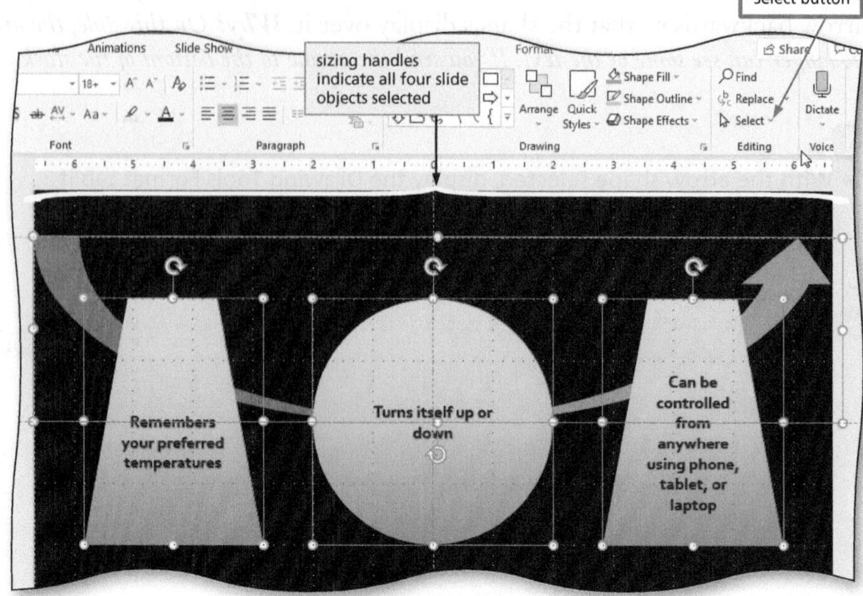

Figure 2–81

- Click the Drawing Tools Format tab and then click the Group button (Drawing Tools Format tab | Arrange group) to display the Group Objects menu (Figure 2–82).

3

- Click the Group command to combine all the shapes.

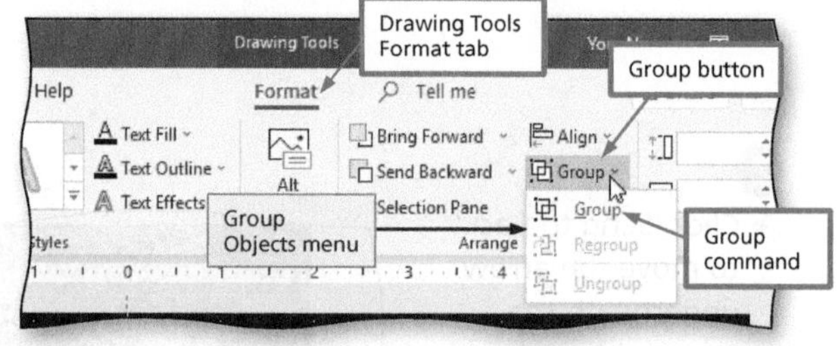

Figure 2–82

Other Ways

1. Right-click selected shapes, point to Group on shortcut menu, click Group

> BTW
> **Replacing Words with Objects**
> Consider using shapes and symbols to identify a slide's purpose instead of using text in a title placeholder. Your audience tends to remember objects rather than words when they recall slide content after a presentation has concluded.

To Insert Additional Shapes

The Slide 5 content pertains to the benefits of using smart thermostats throughout the day and night. Instead of identifying this information in a title placeholder, you want to create a unique shape with text. You first will insert three shapes: a banner (punched tape), a sun, and a moon. Then, you will arrange and format them and add text. Finally, you will merge the shapes to create one object. The following steps insert and format the three objects.

1. With the Drawing Tools Format tab displaying, click the Symbol More button (the down arrow) (Drawing Tools Format tab | Insert Shapes group) to display the Shapes gallery.

2. Insert three shapes at the bottom of the slide: the Moon shape (tenth shape in third Basic Shapes row), the Flowchart: Punched Tape (banner) shape (fourth shape in second Flowchart area row), and the Sun shape (ninth shape in third Basic Shapes row). Drag the moon to the lower-left side of the slide, the banner under the oval, and the sun to the right side of the slide.

3. Select the three new shapes, click the Shape Styles More button (the down arrow) (Drawing Tools Format tab | Shape Styles group), and then apply the Light 1 Outline, Colored Fill – Green, Accent 2 Shape Style (third style in third Theme Styles row).

4 Proportionally resize the moon to 1.5" x 0.8" and the sun to 1.5" x 1.5" and then nonproportionally resize the banner to 1.5" x 6.5".

5 Align the banner so that the left edge is 3 inches left of center (along the fourth vertical gridline) and the lower edge is 3.50 inches below center.

6 If necessary, select the moon and then click the Bring Forward button (Drawing Tools Format tab | Arrange group) to reposition the moon above the banner. Align the moon so that the right edge is 2 inches left of center (along the fifth vertical gridline from the left side of the slide) and the lower edge is 3.50 inches below center.

7 Align the sun so that the left edge is 2 inches right of center (along the fifth vertical gridline from the right side of the slide) (Figure 2–83).

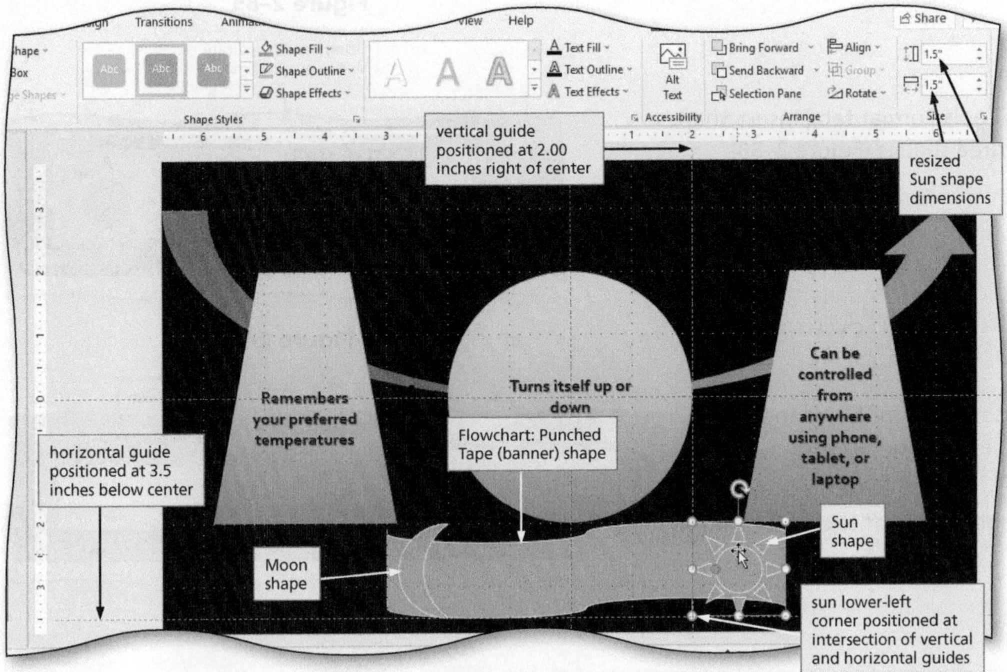

Figure 2–83

To Merge Shapes

The moon and sun overlap the banner and appear as separate items. You can combine, or merge, them into one object. ***Why?*** *The three elements will appear seamless as a unified graphical element.* The following steps merge the three shapes.

1

- Select the moon, banner, and sun shapes (Figure 2–84).

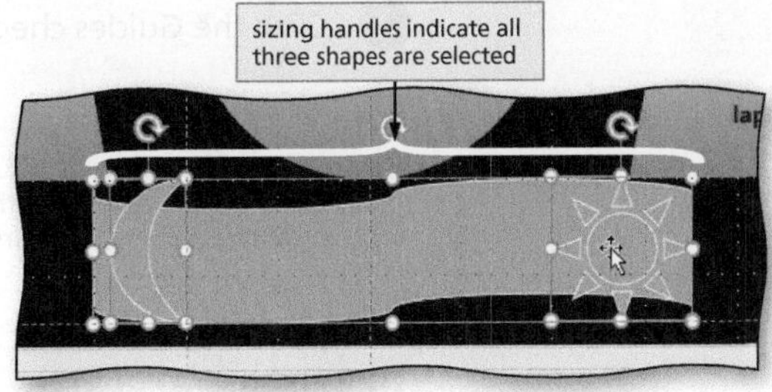

Figure 2–84

- With the Drawing Tools Format tab displaying, click the Merge Shapes button (Drawing Tools Format tab | Insert Shapes group) to display the Merge Shapes menu (Figure 2–85).

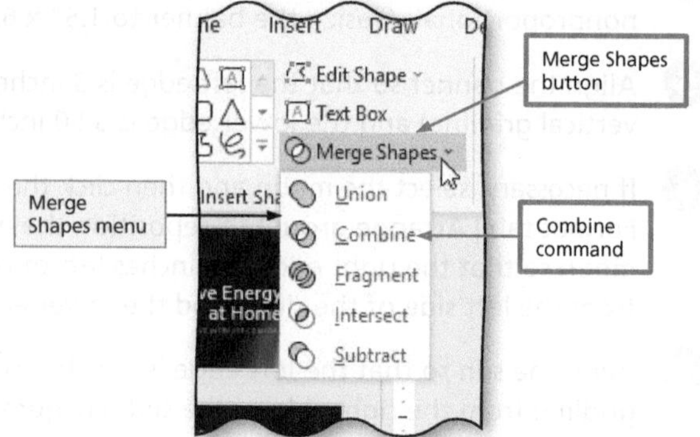

Figure 2–85

- Click Combine (Drawing Tools Format tab | Insert Shapes group) to combine the three shapes (Figure 2–86).

Q&A When would I use the Union command instead of the Combine command?
The Union command joins the shapes using the formatting of the top shape. The Combine command also joins shapes, but it deletes the area where two shapes overlap.

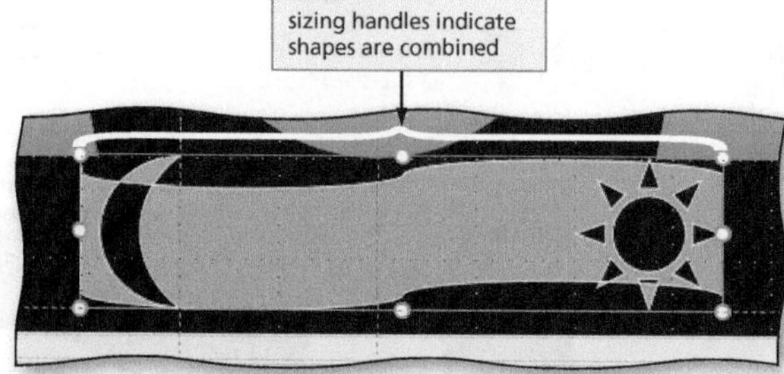

Figure 2–86

- Type **`A Smart Thermostat`** in the banner and then press ENTER. Type **`Works Night and Day`** as the second line in the shape.
- Increase the font size of both lines of text to 24 point (Figure 2–87).

Figure 2–87

To Hide the Grid and Guides

The three shapes on Slide 5 are positioned in the desired locations, so the grid and guides no longer are needed. The following steps hide the grid and the guides.

1. Display the View tab and then click the Gridlines check box (View tab | Show group) to clear the checkmark and hide the grid.
2. Click the Guides check box to clear the checkmark and hide the guides.

Other Ways

1. Right-click area of slide other than a placeholder or object, click Grid and Guides on shortcut menu, click Gridlines to turn off Gridlines or Guides to turn off Guides
2. Press ALT+F9 to toggle guides on/off

To Hide Rulers

The shapes on Slide 5 are positioned in the desired locations, so the rulers no longer need to display. The following step hides the rulers.

1 Display the View tab if necessary, and then click the Ruler check box (View tab | Show group) to remove the checkmark and hide the rulers.

Other Ways

1. Right-click area of slide other than a placeholder or object, click Ruler
2. Press SHIFT+ALT+F9 to toggle ruler on/off

To Apply a Picture Fill to a Shape

Sufficient space exists in the right size of Slide 4 to insert a shape filled with a picture. ***Why?*** *A shape and picture help to draw attention to the slide, reinforce the written message, and call attention to the conserving energy theme.* A light bulb picture coordinates with the star. You can insert a shape that has the default formatting and then add a picture. The following steps insert a shape and then apply a picture.

1

- Display Slide 4. Insert the Star: 7 Points shape (sixth shape in first Stars and Banners row).
- Proportionally resize the star shape to 3" x 3" and then use the smart guides to position the shape as shown in Figure 2–88.

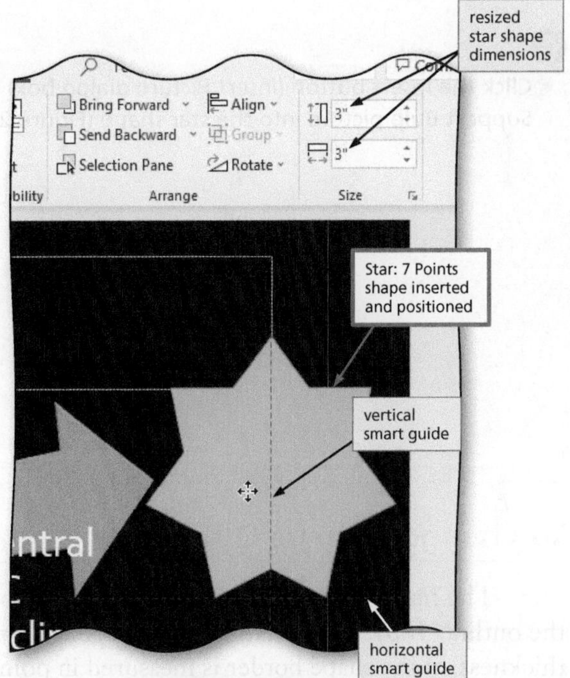

Figure 2–88

2

- With the Drawing Tools Format tab displaying, click the Shape Fill arrow (Drawing Tools Format tab | Shape Styles group) to display the Shape Fill gallery (Figure 2–89).

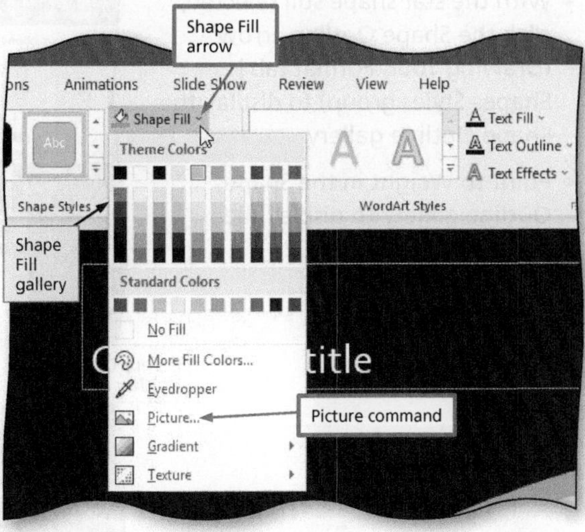

Figure 2–89

- Click Picture in the Shape Fill gallery to display the Insert Pictures dialog box, click From a File, and then navigate to the location where your Data Files are stored.
- Click Support_PPT_2_Bulb.jpg to select the file name (Figure 2–90).

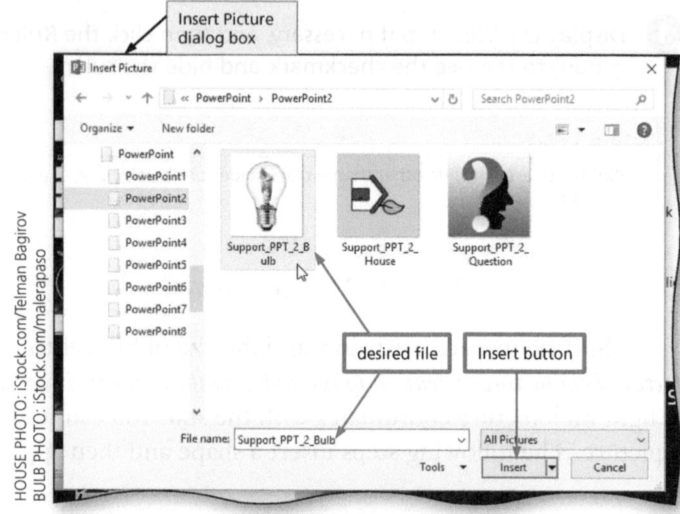

Figure 2–90

- Click the Insert button (Insert Picture dialog box) to insert the Support Bulb picture into the star shape (Figure 2–91).

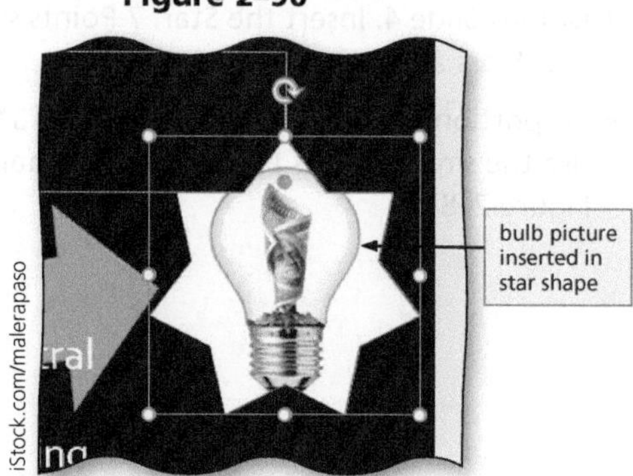

Figure 2–91

To Change a Shape Outline Weight

The first graphical change you will make to the shape border is to increase the thickness, which is called the outline. ***Why?*** *This thicker line is a graphical element that helps to call attention to the shape.* The weight, or thickness, of the shape border is measured in points. The following steps increase the outline weight.

- With the star shape still selected, click the Shape Outline arrow (Drawing Tools Format tab | Shapes Styles group) to display the Shape Outline gallery.
- Point to Weight in the Shape Outline gallery to display the Weight list (Figure 2–92).

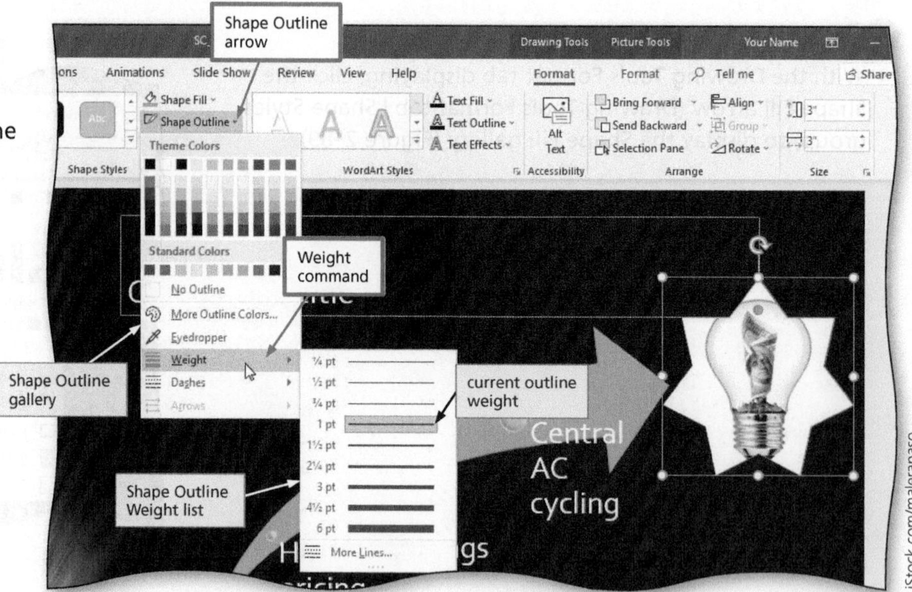

Figure 2–92

2

- Point to 6 pt to display a live preview of this outline line weight (Figure 2–93).

Experiment

- Point to various line weights on the Weight list and watch the border weights on the shape change.

3

- Click 6 pt to increase the size of the outline around the shape.

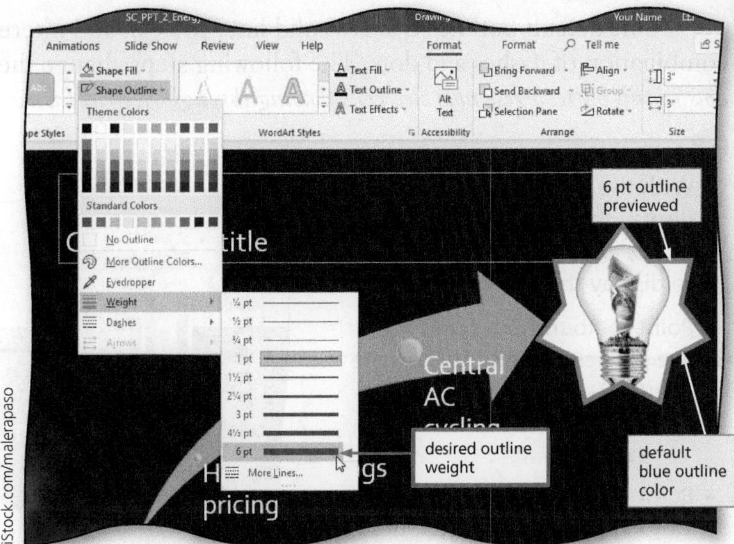

Figure 2–93

Other Ways

1. Click Shape Outline arrow (Home tab | Drawing group), click Weight
2. Right-click shape, click Outline below shortcut menu, click Weight

To Change a Shape Outline Color

The default outline color in the Digital Blue Tunnel theme is light blue. In this project, you will change the outline color to green. ***Why?*** *Green is associated with conservation and money, and that color is found in the money inside the light bulb picture and on some of the other slides in the presentation.* The following steps change the shape outline color.

1

- With the shape still selected, click the Shape Outline arrow again to display the Shape Outline gallery.
- Point to Green (sixth color in Standard Colors row) to display a live preview of that outline color on the shape (Figure 2–94).

Experiment

- Point to various colors in the Shape Outline gallery and watch the border colors on the shape change.

2

- Click Green to change the shape border color.

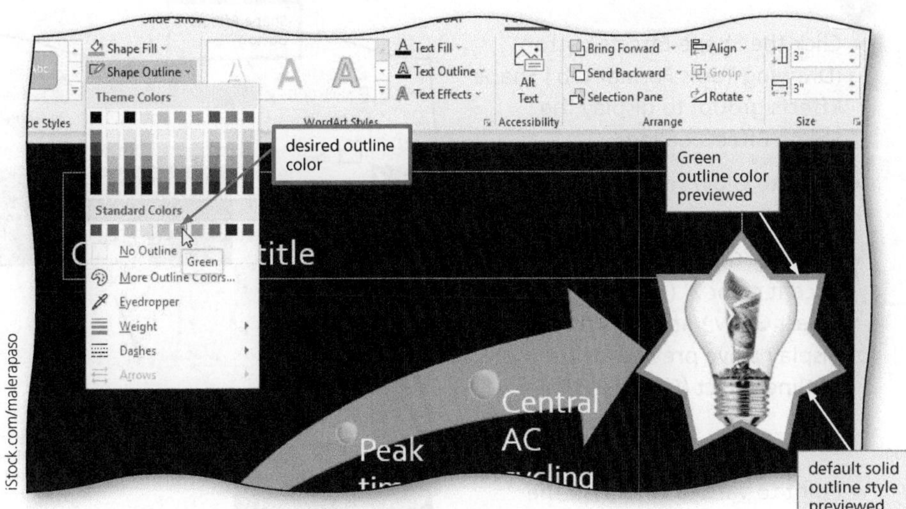

Figure 2–94

To Change a Shape Outline Style

The default outline style is a solid line. You can add interest by changing the style to dashes, dots, or a combination of dashes and dots. The following steps change the shape outline style to Round Dot. ***Why?*** *The dots in this pattern resemble electrons flowing through electrical wires.*

- With the shape still selected, display the Shape Outline gallery again, and then point to Dashes to display the Dashes list.
- Point to Round Dot to display a live preview of this outline style (Figure 2–95).

Experiment

- Point to various styles in the Shape Outline gallery and watch the borders on the shape change.

- Click Round Dot to change the shape border style.

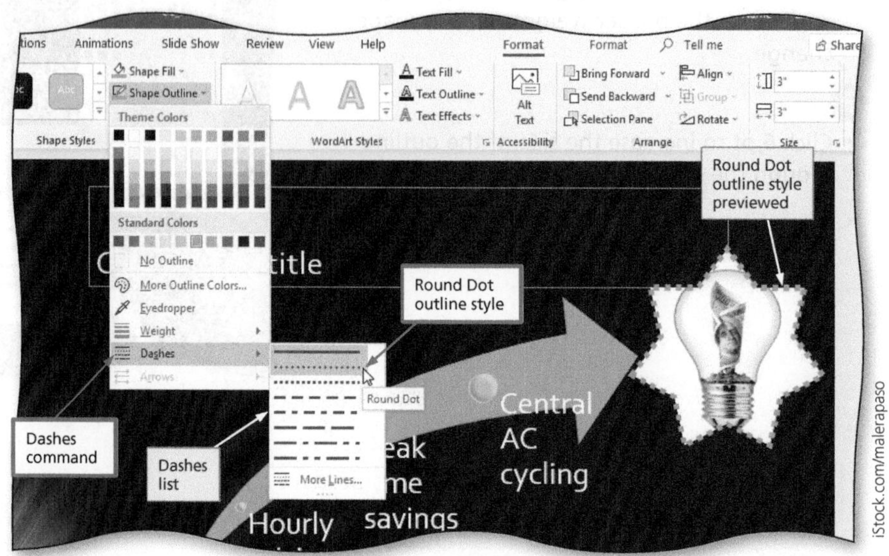

Figure 2–95

To Apply an Effect to a Shape

PowerPoint provides a variety of visual effects to add to the shape. They include shadow, glow, reflection, and 3-D rotation. The following steps apply a green glow effect to the shape. ***Why?*** *The outline color and other elements on the slides in the presentation are green.*

- Click the Shape Effects button (Drawing Tools Format tab | Shape Effects group) to display the Shape Effects gallery.
- Point to Glow to display the Glow gallery.
- Point to 'Glow: 18 point; Green, Accent color 2' (second color in last Glow Variations row) to display a live preview of this outline effect (Figure 2–96).

Experiment

- Point to various effects in the Glow gallery and watch the glow effects change on the shape.

- Click the 'Glow: 18 point; Green, Accent color 2' variation to apply the glow effect.

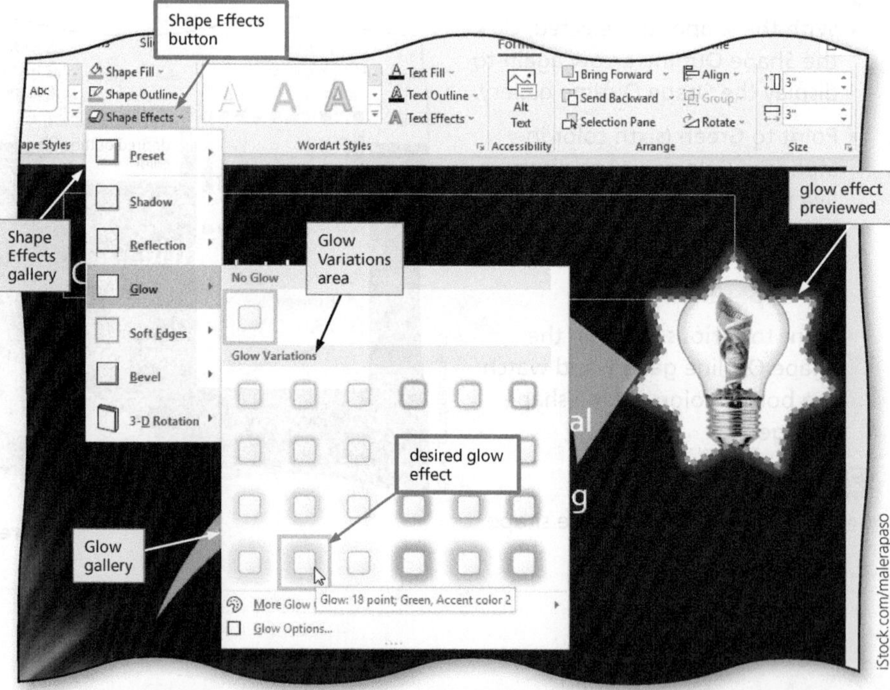

Figure 2–96

To Rotate a Shape to an Exact Value

In Module 1 you rotated a picture using the rotate handle. Similarly, you can rotate a shape using the rotate handle. You also can rotate a shape clockwise or counterclockwise in two preset values: Right 90° and Left 90°. In addition, you have the option of rotating the shape to any specific degree from 0 to 360. On Slide 4, you will rotate the star counterclockwise to the exact value of –15°. ***Why?*** *You want the outline of the star to align with the arrowhead.* The following steps rotate the star shape.

1

- With the star shape still selected, click the Rotate button (Drawing Tools Format tab | Arrange group) to display the Rotate Objects gallery (Figure 2–97).

Q&A I also see a Picture Tools Format tab. Could I use the Rotate button on this tab?

Yes. The star shape includes a picture, so you see both the Drawing Tools Format tab and the Picture Tools Format tab with similar commands in the Arrange group.

Experiment

- Point to the various rotate options in the Rotate Options gallery and watch the shape rotate on the slide.

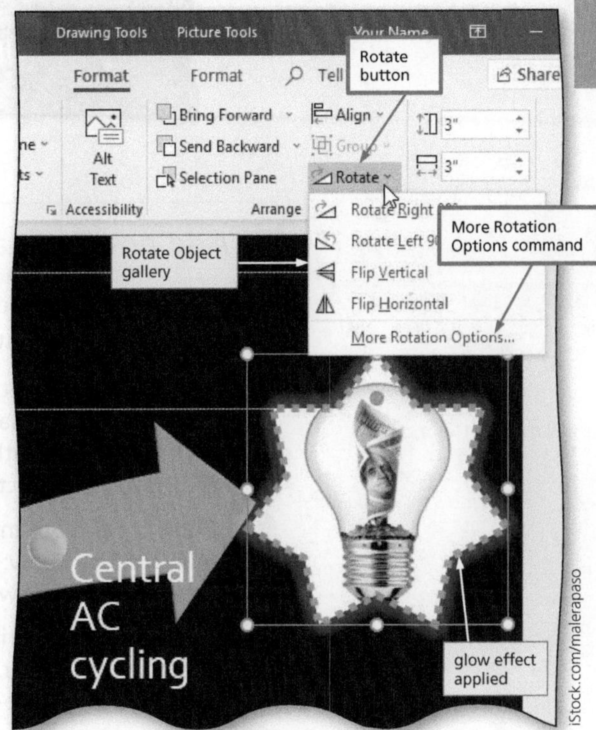

Figure 2–97

2

- Click 'More Rotation Options' in the Rotate Options gallery to display the Format Picture pane.
- Click the Rotation down arrow several times until –15° is displayed (Figure 2–98).

Q&A Why is the rotation value negative?

When you rotate a shape counterclockwise, the degrees are expressed as a negative number.

3

- Click the Close button (shown in Figure 2–98) to close the Format Picture pane.

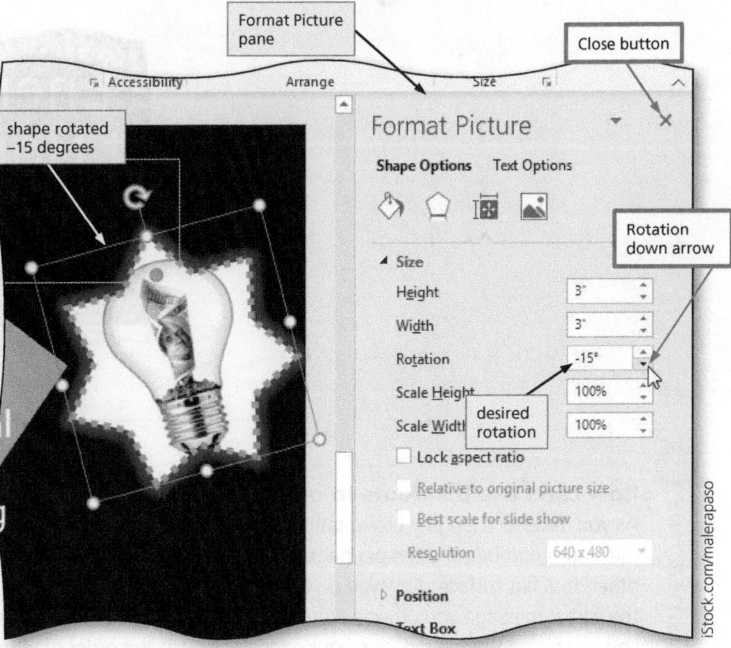

Figure 2–98

To Add a Slide Title

A final enhancement you will make to Slide 4 is to add a title. The following steps add this title to the slide.

1. Type **Manage Your Energy** in the title text placeholder (Figure 2–99).

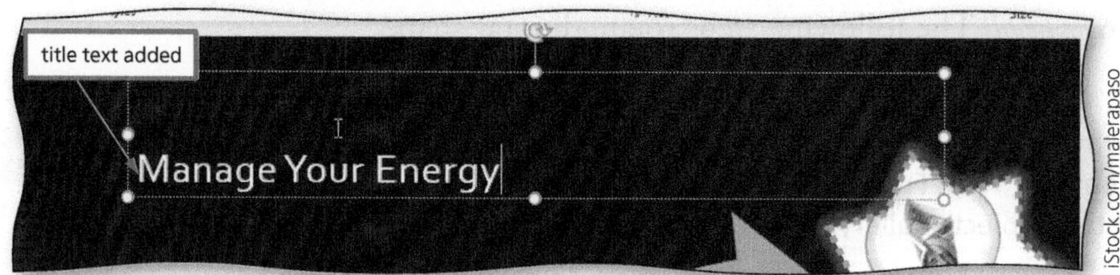

Figure 2–99

To Add and Format a Shape

The title slide does not have any added graphical elements, so you want to add a shape and then format it. The following steps add and format this shape on Slide 1.

1. Display Slide 1 and then insert the Rectangle: Top Corners Snipped (fourth shape in Rectangles area) shape. Proportionally size this shape to 2.2" x 2.2". Fill the rectangle with the picture with the file name Support_PPT_2_House.jpg, located in the Data Files. Rotate the rectangle Left 90 degrees, and then flip the picture Horizontal.
2. Add a 3 point outline to the rectangle, change the outline style to Square Dot, and then add the 'Glow: 11 point; Green, Accent color 2' glow (second variation in third Glow Variations row).
3. Display the ruler, gridlines, and guides and then position the rectangle so that the bottom-right corner is at the intersection of 6.00 right of the center and 3.00 below the center (Figure 2–100).
4. Hide the ruler, gridlines, and guides.
5. Click a blank area of the slide to deselect the shape.

Figure 2–100

CONSIDER THIS

How can I use handouts to organize my speech?

As you develop a lengthy presentation with many visuals, handouts can help you organize your material. Print handouts with the maximum number of slides per page. Use scissors to cut each thumbnail and then place these miniature slide images adjacent to each other on a flat surface. Any type on the thumbnails will be too small to read, so the images will need to work with only the support of the verbal message you provide. You can rearrange these thumbnails as you organize your speech. When you return to your computer, you can rearrange the slides on your screen to match the order of your thumbnail printouts. Begin speaking the actual words you want to incorporate in the body of the talk. This process of glancing at the thumbnails and hearing yourself say the key ideas of the speech is one of the best methods of organizing and preparing for the actual presentation. Ultimately, when you deliver your speech in front of an audience, the images on the slides or on your note cards should be sufficient to remind you of the accompanying verbal message.

Adding a Footer

Slides can contain information at the top or bottom. The area at the top of a slide is called a **header**, and the area at the bottom is called a **footer**. In general, footer content displays along the lower edge of a slide, but the theme determines where these elements are placed. As a default, no information is displayed in the header or footer. You can choose to apply only a header, only a footer, or both a header and footer. In addition, you can elect to have the header or footer display on single slides, all slides, or all slides except the title slide.

Slide numbers are one footer element. They help a presenter organize a talk. While few audience members are cognizant of this aspect of a slide, the presenter can glance at the number and know which slide contains particular information. If an audience member asks a question pertaining to information contained on a slide that had been displayed previously or is on a slide that has not yet been viewed, the presenter can jump to that slide in an effort to answer the question. In addition, the slide number helps pace the slide show. For example, a speaker could have the presentation timed so that Slide 4 is displaying three minutes into the talk.

PowerPoint gives the option of displaying the current date and time obtained from the system or a fixed date and time that you specify. In addition, you can add relevant information, such as your name, your school or business name, or the purpose of your presentation in the Footer area.

BTW

Distributing Slides

Instead of printing and distributing a hard copy of PowerPoint slides, you can distribute the slides electronically. Options include sending the slides via email; posting it on cloud storage (such as OneDrive) and sharing the link with others; posting it on social media, a blog, or other website; and sharing a link associated with an online location of the slides. You also can create and share a PDF or XPS image of the slides, so that users can view the file in Acrobat Reader or XPS Viewer instead of in PowerPoint.

To Add a Footer with Fixed Information

To reinforce the fact that Greenest Street Corporation has created this presentation, you can add this information in the Footer area. You also can add a slide number. The following steps add this text to all slides in the presentation except the title slide. ***Why?*** *In general, the footer text should not display on the title slide.*

1

- Display the Insert tab.
- Click the 'Header & Footer' button (Insert tab | Text group) to display the Header and Footer dialog box.
- If necessary, click the Slide tab to display the Slide sheet (Figure 2–101).

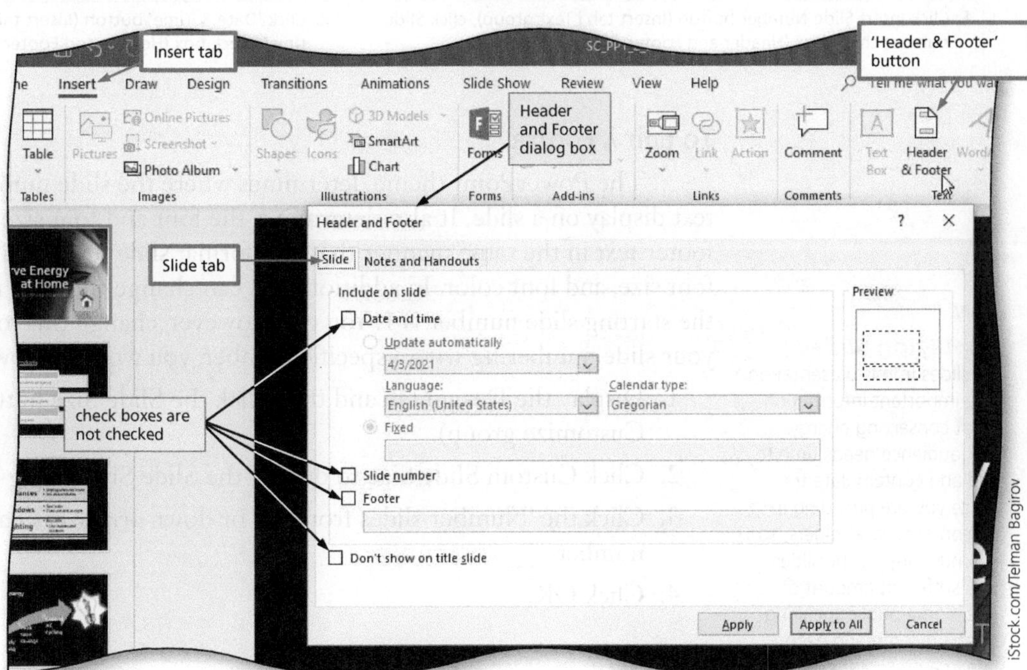

Figure 2–101

Q&A

Can I use this dialog box to add a header?

The slide theme determines the location of the placeholders at the top or bottom of the slide. The footer elements generally are displayed along the lower edge of the slide. Some themes, however, have the footer elements along the top edge, so they are considered header text.

- Click 'Date and time' to select this check box.
- If necessary, click the Fixed option button to select this option. Select the existing date, if any, and then type **October 1** in the Fixed box.
- Click Slide number to place a checkmark in the check box.
- Click Footer to place a checkmark in the box.
- Type **Greenest Street Corporation** in the Footer box.
- Click the 'Don't show on title slide' check box to place a checkmark in the box (Figure 2–102).

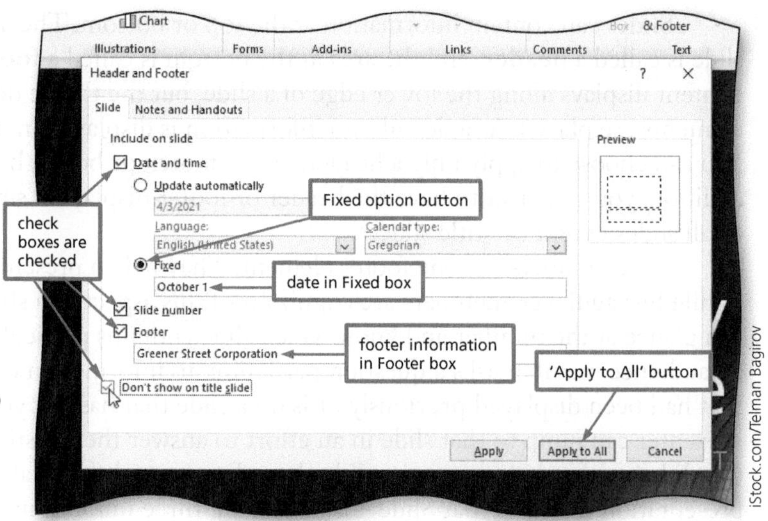

Figure 2–102

Q&A Can the footer information also appear on all the slides?
Yes. If the 'Don't show on title slide' check box is not selected, the footer will appear on all slides.

What if I want the current date and time to appear?
Click Update automatically in the 'Date and time' section.

- Click the 'Apply to All' button to display the date, footer text, and slide number on all slides except the title slide (Slide 1).

Q&A When would I click the Apply button instead of the 'Apply to All' button?
Click the Apply button when you want the header and footer information to appear only on the slide currently selected.

Other Ways

1. Click Insert Slide Number button (Insert tab | Text group), click Slide number check box (Header and Footer dialog box)
2. Click 'Date & Time' button (Insert tab | Text group), click 'Date and time' check box (Header and Footer dialog box)

To Edit a Footer

The PowerPoint theme determines where the slide numbers, date, and footer text display on a slide. It also determines the font and font size. You can format the footer text in the same manner that you format slide text, such as changing the font, font size, and font color. In addition, you can change the slide numbering. By default, the starting slide number is 1. You can, however, change this footer character. To start your slide numbering with a specific number, you would follow these steps.

1. Display the Design tab and then click the Slide Size button (Design tab | Customize group).
2. Click Custom Slide Size to display the Slide Size dialog box.
3. Click the 'Number slides from' up or down arrow to change the starting slide number.
4. Click OK.

BTW
Displaying Slides
The slides in this presentation have important information about conserving energy. Your audience needs time to read and contemplate the advice you are providing in the content placeholders, so you must display the slides for a sufficient amount of time. Some public speaking experts recommend each slide in a presentation should display for at least one minute so that audience members can look at the material, focus on the speaker, and then refer to the slide again.

Adding a Transition

PowerPoint includes a wide variety of visual and sound effects that can be applied to text or content. A **slide transition** is a special effect used to progress from one slide to the next in a slide show. Most transitions have default rotations, but you can change the direction. You also can control the speed of the transition effect and add a sound.

To Add a Transition between Slides

Why? *Transitions add interest when you advance the slides in a presentation and make a slide show presentation look professional.* In this presentation, you apply the Box transition in the Exciting category to all slides. The default rotation is From Right, so the current slide turns to the left while the new slide appears from the right side of the screen. When you change the Box rotation to From Top, the current slide moves to the bottom of the screen and the new slide appears from the top. You also change the transition speed from 1.60 seconds to 3 seconds. The following steps apply this transition to the presentation.

1

- Click the Transitions tab on the ribbon and then point to the More button (Transitions tab | Transition to This Slide group) in the 'Transition to This Slide' gallery (Figure 2–103).

Q&A Is a transition applied now?
Yes. The stars that appear on the left side of the slide thumbnails indicate a transition has been applied to all slides.

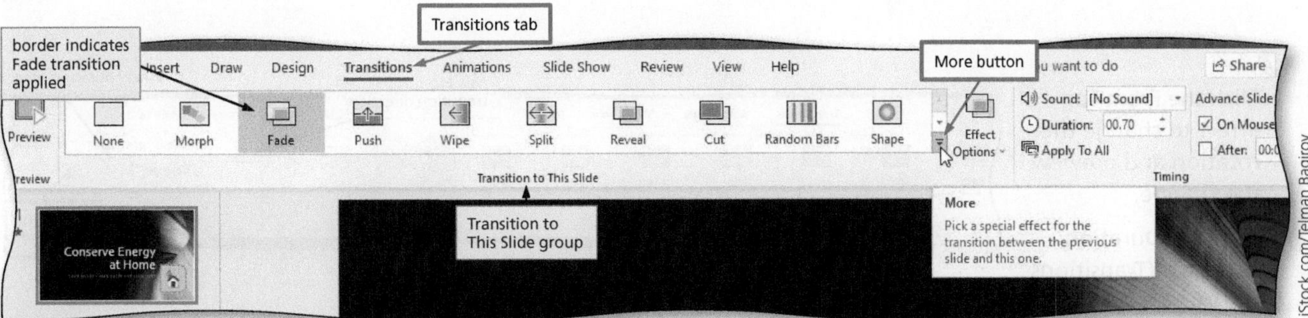

Figure 2–103

- Click the More button to expand the Transitions gallery.

Q&A Which transition is applied now?
Fade, the third slide icon in the Subtle category, is selected, which indicates this default transition from the theme has been applied.

- Point to the Box transition in the Exciting category in the Transitions gallery (Figure 2–104).

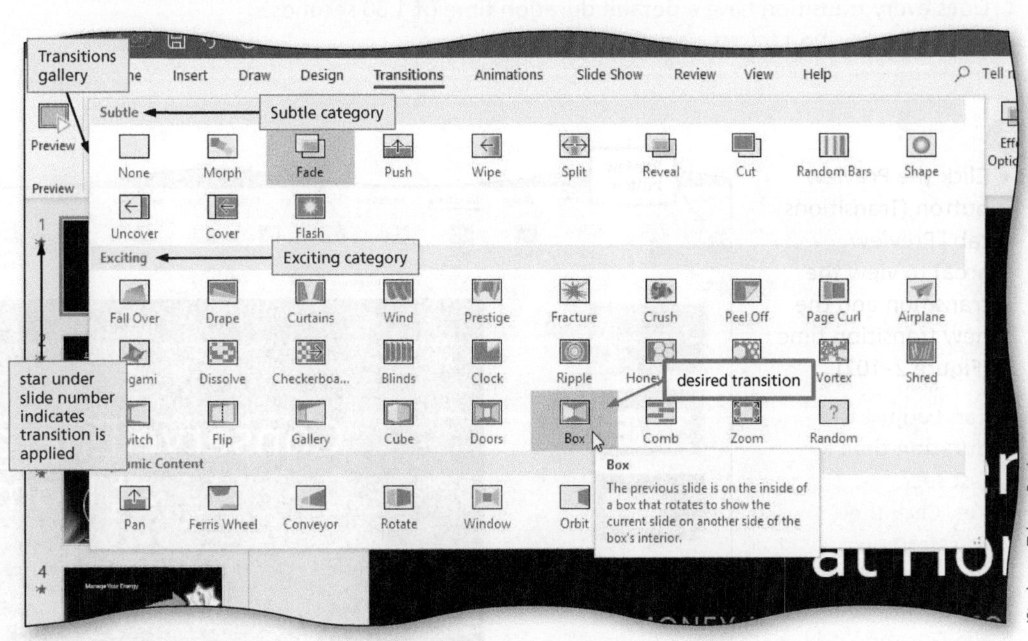

Figure 2–104

- Click Box to view a preview of this transition and to apply this transition to the title slide.

- Click the Effect Options button (Transitions tab | Transition to This Slide group) to display the Effect Options gallery (Figure 2–105).

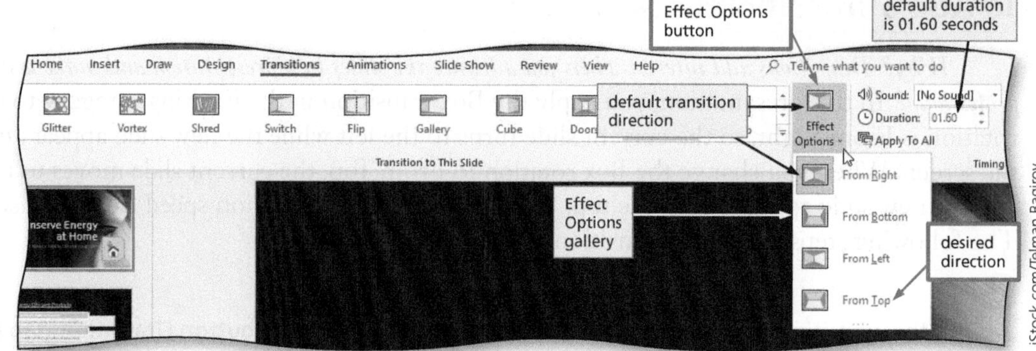

Figure 2–105

Q&A Are the same four effects available for all transitions?
No. The transition effects vary depending upon the particular transition applied.

- Click the From Top effect to change the rotation and preview the change.
- Click the Duration up arrow (Transitions tab | Timing group) six times to change the transition speed from 01.60 seconds to 03.00 seconds (Figure 2–106).

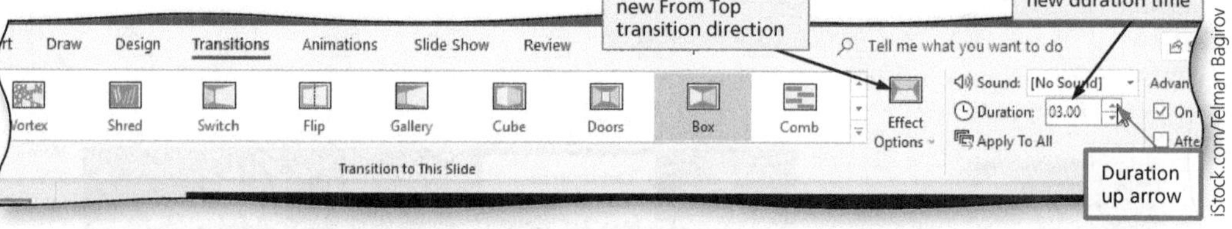

Figure 2–106

Q&A Does every transition have a default duration time of 1.60 seconds?
No. Each transition has its own default duration time.

- Click the Preview button (Transitions tab | Preview area) to view the transition and the new transition time (Figure 2–107).

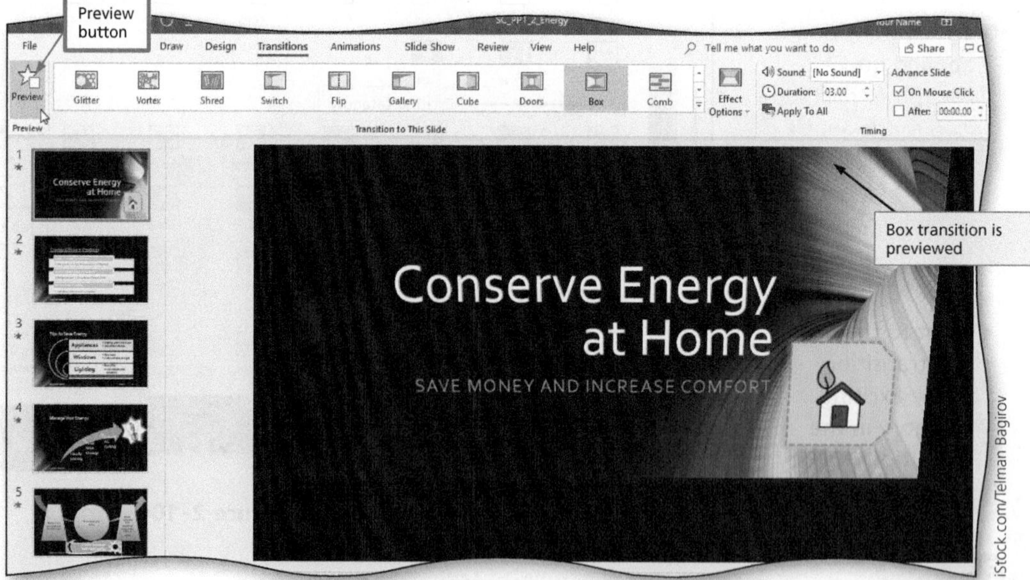

Figure 2–107

Q&A Can I adjust the duration time I just set?
Yes. Click the Duration up or down arrows or type a speed in the Duration box and preview the transition until you find the time that best fits your presentation.

7

- Click the 'Apply To All' button (Transitions tab | Timing group) to apply the Box transition and the increased transition time to Slides 1 through 5 in the presentation (Figure 2–108).

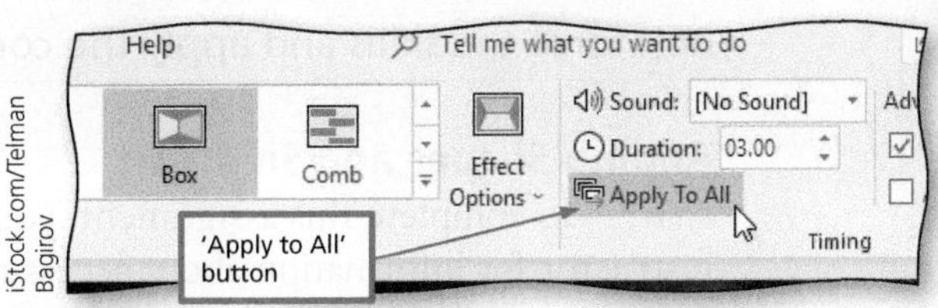

Figure 2–108

Q&A How does clicking the 'Apply to All' button differ from clicking the Apply button?
The Apply button applies the transition only to the currently displayed slide, whereas the 'Apply to All' button applies the transition to all slides.

What if I want to apply a different transition and duration to each slide in the presentation?
Repeat Steps 2 through 5 for each slide individually.

To Save and Print the Presentation

It is a good practice to save a presentation before printing it, in the event you experience difficulties printing. The following steps save and print the presentation.

1. Save the presentation again in the same storage location with the same file name.
2. Print the slides as a handout with two slides per page.

Q&A Do I have to wait until my presentation is complete to print it?
No, you can follow these steps to print a presentation at any time while you are creating it.

3. sam↑ Because the project now is complete, you can exit PowerPoint.

BTW

Conserving Ink and Toner

If you want to conserve ink or toner, you can instruct PowerPoint to print draft quality documents by clicking File on the ribbon to open Backstage view, clicking Options in Backstage view to display the PowerPoint Options dialog box, clicking Advanced in the left pane (PowerPoint Options dialog box), scrolling to the Print area in the right pane, verifying there is no check mark in the High quality check box, and then clicking OK. Then, use Backstage view to print the document as usual.

Summary

In this module, you learned how to use PowerPoint to enhance a presentation with SmartArt and formatted shapes. You searched for and downloaded an online theme; inserted a symbol and hyperlink; inserted, edited, and formatted SmartArt; resized and formatted shapes; moved objects using guides, gridlines, and the ruler; added a footer; and added a transition.

CONSIDER THIS: PLAN AHEAD

What decisions will you need to make when creating your next presentation?

Use these guidelines as you complete the assignments in this module and create your own slide show decks outside of this class.

1. Determine if an online theme can help you design and develop the presentation efficiently and effectively.
2. Identify symbols, shapes, and pictures that would create interest and promote the message being presented.
3. Develop SmartArt that emphasizes major presentation messages.
   a) Format text.
   b) Add styles.
   c) Add effects.
4. Locate shapes that supplement the verbal and written message.
   a) Size and position them aesthetically on slides.
   b) Add styles.
   c) Add and format outlines.
   d) Add a picture fill.
5. Use the guides, gridlines, and ruler to position slide elements.
6. Add a footer.
7. Add a transition.

Apply Your Knowledge

Reinforce the skills and apply the concepts you learned in this module.

Adding Shapes and SmartArt

Note: To complete this assignment, you will be required to use the Data Files. Please contact your instructor for information about accessing the Data Files.

Instructions: Start PowerPoint. Open the presentation called SC_PPT_2-1.pptx, which is located in the Data Files. The presentation you open contains four unformatted slides. You work in the Human Resources Department at Eversafe Bank, and the HR manager has asked you to prepare slides that will accompany her presentation regarding choosing a health care plan. You begin by creating these four unformatted slides. You are to add shapes and SmartArt, add a footer, and apply a transition so the slides look like Figure 2–109.

Perform the following tasks:

1. Add the Metropolitan theme to the presentation.
2. On the title slide, bold the title text and then apply a text shadow. Use your name in place of Student Name.

   If requested by your instructor, change your first name to your mother's first name on the title slide.
3. With Slide 1 still displayed, insert the Rectangle: Diagonal Corners Rounded shape located in the Rectangles area (last shape) and then resize it to a height of 3" and a width of 2.5". Insert the picture named Support_PPT_2_Question.jpg as a fill for this shape. Display the ruler, gridlines, and guides, and then align this shape so that the right edge is 5 inches right of the center and the bottom is 3.50 inches below the center, as shown in Figure 2–109a.
4. On Slide 2 (Plan and Network Types), change the fill color of the left rectangle (HMO) to Dark Red, the middle rectangle (PPO) to Blue, and the right rectangle (POS) to Purple. Resize each rectangle to a height of 4" and a width of 3.5" and then apply the 'Glow: 11 point; Aqua, Accent color 1' Glow Variation effect (first variation in third Glow Variations row). Change the font of the text in these three rectangles to Cambria and the font size to 20 point, and then bold the text. Align these three rectangles to the slide and then distribute them horizontally.
5. With Slide 2 still displayed, insert the Lightning Bolt shape (eighth shape in third Basic Shapes row). Change the fill color to Yellow and the outline weight to 3 point. Then add the 'Inside: Top Left' Shadow effect (first shadow in first Inner row).
6. Resize the lightning bolt to a height of 13" and a width of 1.5". Flip the shape horizontal. Rotate this shape Left 90 degrees. Use the smart guides to move the lightning bolt to the center of the slide. Send the lightning bolt to the back so that it is behind all three rectangles, as shown in Figure 2–109b.
7. Group the three rectangles and lightning bolt.
8. Hide the ruler, gridlines, and guides.
9. On Slide 3 ("Steps to Take"), insert a telephone symbol (symbol and character code 40) from the Wingdings font after the word, doctors, in the first first-level paragraph.
10. Convert the numbered list into the Tabbed Arc SmartArt graphic located in the Relationship category. Change the SmartArt style to Polished (first style in first 3-D row), as shown in Figure 2–109c.
11. Delete Slide 4.
12. Add slide numbers and the fixed date of **`October 2`** to all slides except the title slide. Then type **`Eversafe Bank`** as the footer text.

13. Apply the Peel Off transition in the Exciting category to all slides. Change the effect option to Right. Change the duration to 2.00 seconds.
14. Save the file with the file name, **`SC_PPT_2_Health`**, and submit the revised presentation in the format specified by your instructor. Slide Sorter view is shown in Figure 2–109d. Exit PowerPoint.
15. In Step 4 you applied many formatting styles to the rectangles. How did these styles enhance the graphics?

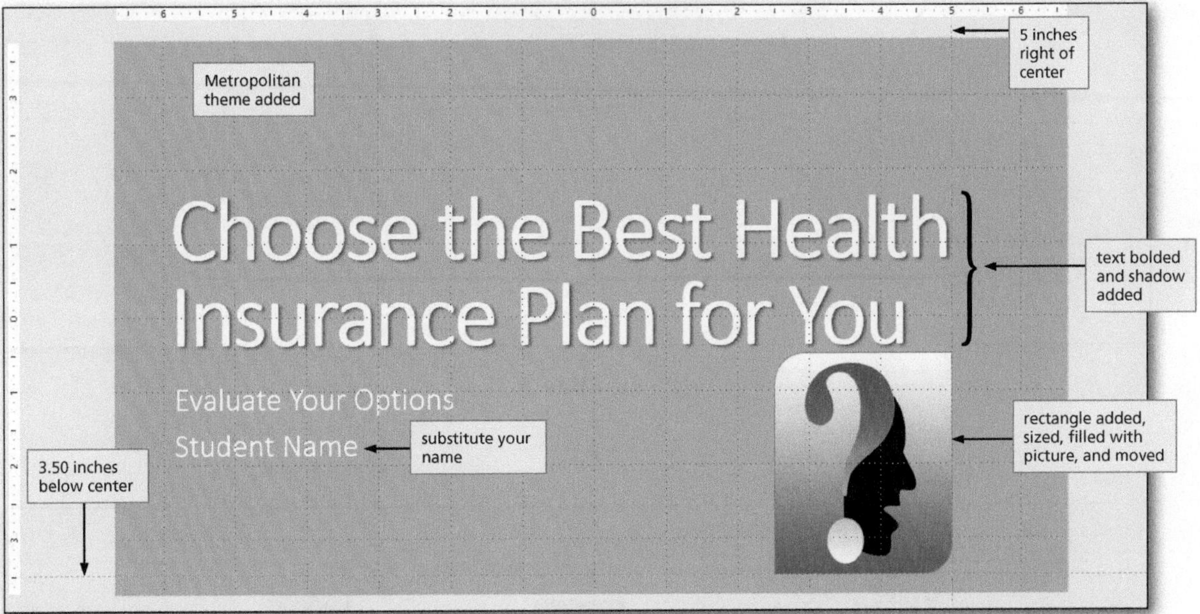

(a) Slide 1

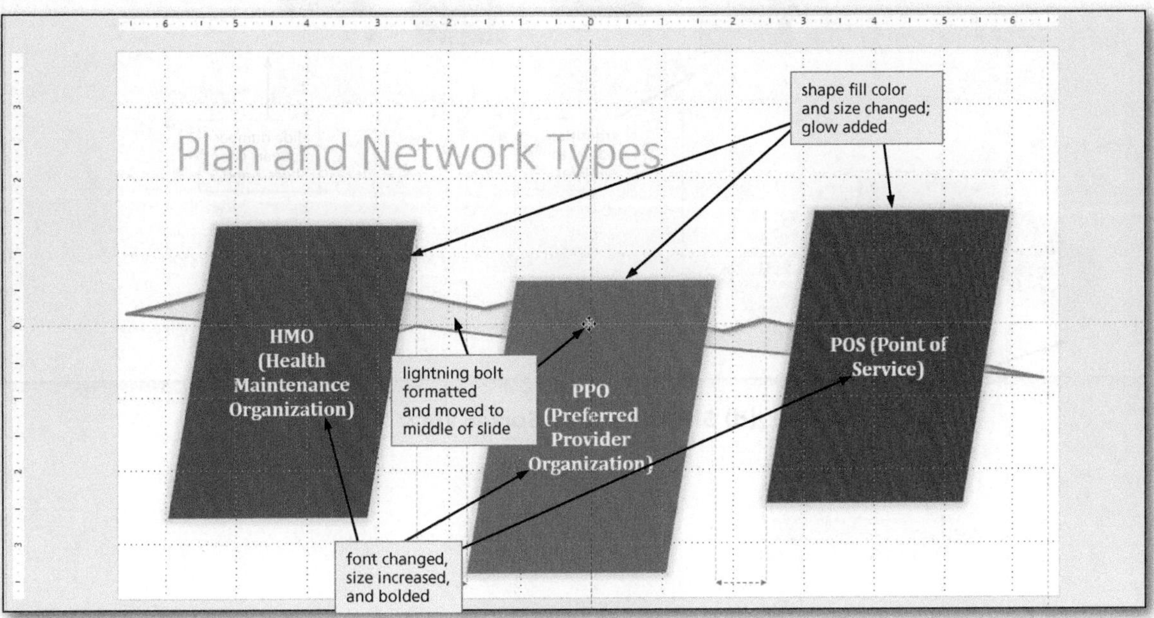

(b) Slide 2

Figure 2–109

Continued >

Apply Your Knowledge *continued*

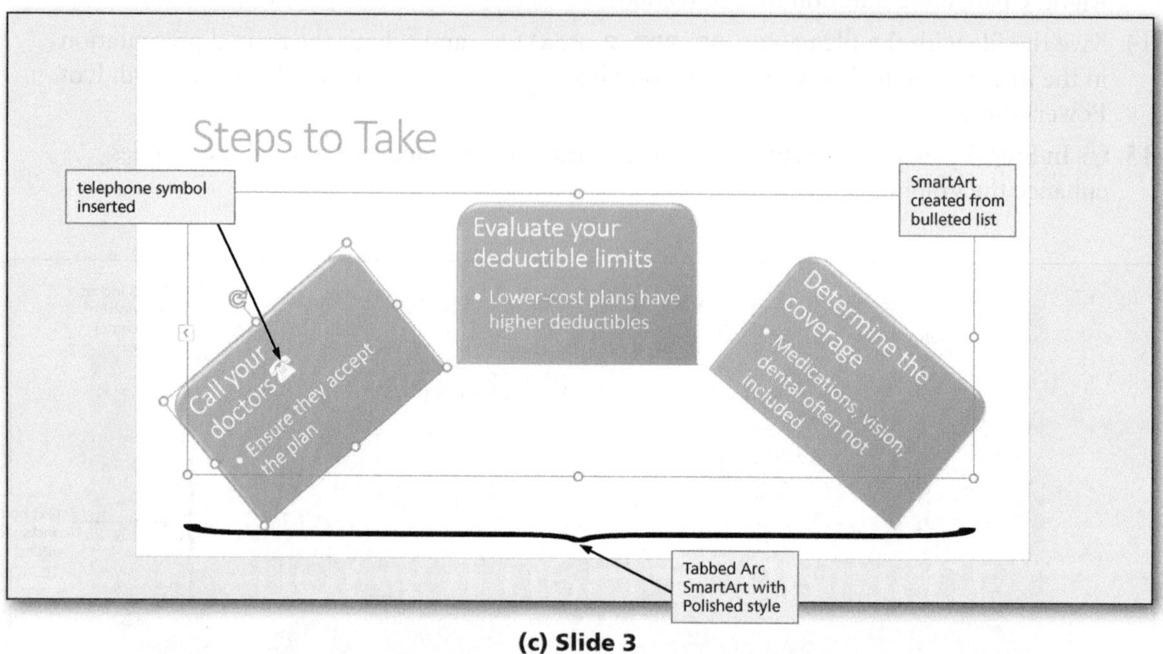

(c) Slide 3

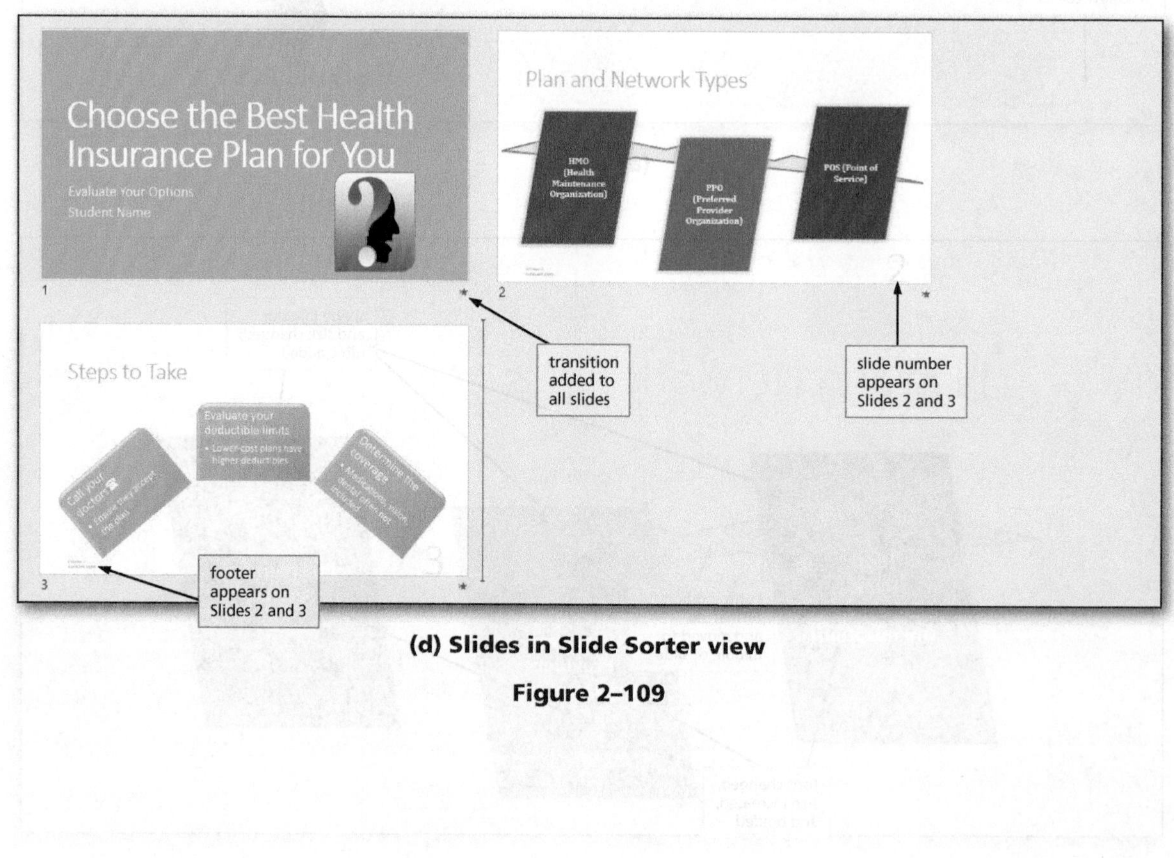

(d) Slides in Slide Sorter view

Figure 2–109

Extend Your Knowledge

Extend the skills you learned in this module and experiment with new skills. You may need to use Help to complete the assignment.

Adding Icons and SmartArt Shapes

Note: To complete this assignment, you will be required to use the Data Files. Please contact your instructor for information about accessing the Data Files.

Instructions: Start PowerPoint. Open the presentation, SC_PPT_2-2.pptx, which is located in the Data Files. You will create backgrounds including inserting a photo to create a background, apply a WordArt Style and effect, add shapes, and find and replace text to create the presentation.

Perform the following tasks:

1. On the title slide, insert the icon shown in Figure 2–110a in the ribbon shape. Inserting an icon is similar to inserting a picture from a file: you select the shape, click the Shape Fill button, and then click Picture in the Fill menu. When the Insert Pictures dialog box is displayed, click From Icons to display the Insert Icons dialog box. People is the first category, and the icon you want to insert in the shape has two adults and two children. Select this icon and then click Insert.
2. Center the title and subtitle paragraphs.

   If requested by your instructor, add your current or previous pet's name in the Slide 1 subtitle text placeholder in place of Student Name.
3. On Slide 2, insert the Bending Picture Caption SmartArt in the Picture category. Type `Use Social Media` in the left text placeholder and then type `Offer Value` in the right text placeholder.
4. Add a third picture and caption by right-clicking the right picture placeholder, pointing to Add Shape in the shortcut menu, and then clicking 'Add Shape After'. Type `Educate Clients` in the new text placeholder.
5. In the left picture placeholder, insert a laptop icon from the 'Technology and electronics' category. In the middle picture placeholder, insert a paper money icon from the Commerce category. In the right placeholder, insert a tablet icon from the Education category, as shown in Figure 2–110b.
6. Change the SmartArt layout by clicking the More button in the Layouts group and then selecting the 'Vertical Picture Accent List' in the Picture category. Apply the Bird's-Eye Scene 3-D design.
7. Reverse each picture and text placeholder by clicking the 'Right to Left' button (SmartArt Tools Design tab | Create Graphic category).
8. Align the SmartArt graphic in the middle of the slide.
9. On both slides, insert a footer with the text, **Communication is key to success** in the placeholder.
10. Apply an appropriate transition to all slides.
11. Save the presentation using the file name, `SC_PPT_2_Insurance`, and submit the revised presentation in the format specified by your instructor.
12. In this assignment, you used icons instead of shapes. How useful were these graphical elements in promoting the presentation's message? Did the new SmartArt layout and design in Step 6 enhance the presentation? Why or why not? Did reversing the picture and text placeholders in Step 7 add value to the design? Why or why not?

Continued >

Extend Your Knowledge *continued*

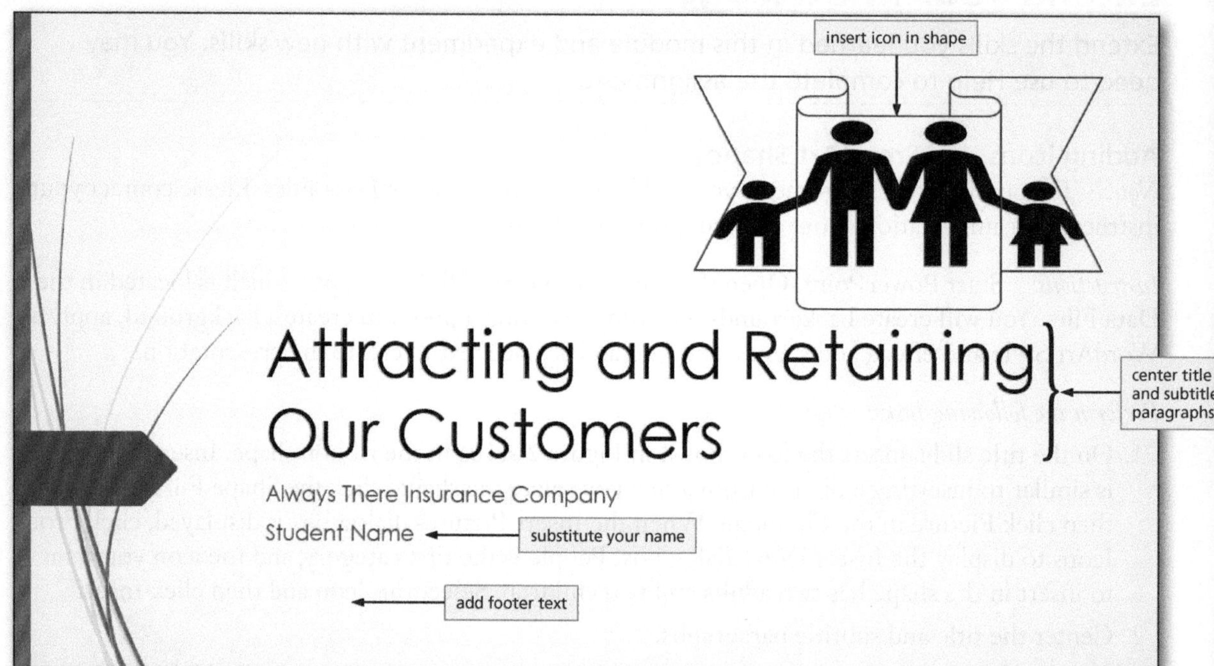

(a) Slide 1

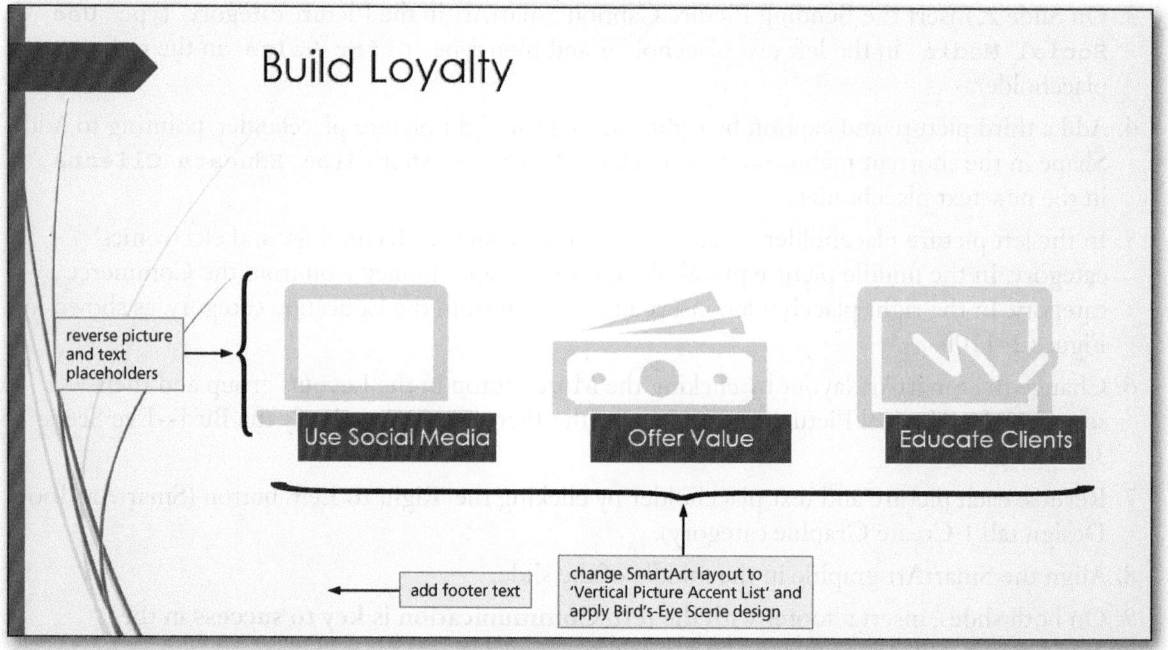

(b) Slide 2

Figure 2–110

Expand Your World

Create a solution that uses cloud or web technologies by learning and investigating on your own from general guidance.

Modifying a Presentation Using PowerPoint Online

Note: To complete this assignment, you will be required to use the Data Files. Please contact your instructor for information about accessing the Data Files.

Instructions: You are assisting the Marketing Project Manager at Always Online Telecommunications by developing slides for an upcoming seminar. The presentation concerns factors predicted to disrupt the telecommunications industry in the near future. You have created the slides in the file named SC_PPT_2-3.pptx, and you want to view and edit them using PowerPoint Online.

Perform the following tasks:

1. Run a browser. Search for the text, `PowerPoint Online`, using a search engine. Visit several websites to learn about PowerPoint Online. Navigate to the PowerPoint Online website. You will need to sign in to your OneDrive account.
2. Upload the SC_PPT_2-3.pptx file to your OneDrive account. Modify the presentation by editing the footer text to the name and address of your school in the Notes pane on Slide 1.

   If requested by your instructor, add the name of one of your high school teachers in place of the Marketing Project Manager's name on the title slide.
3. With Slide 1 still displaying, insert the Cloud shape (in the Basic Shapes category) and move it to the lower-right corner of the slide. Change the shape fill color to Light Blue and then flip the shape horizontal. Change the shape outline weight to 4½ point and then change the outline dash to Round Dot. Use the smart guides to position the shape in the location shown in Figure 2–111a.
4. On Slide 2, change the SmartArt layout to Trapezoid List and then change the style to Intense Effect (Figure 2–111b).
5. Add the Wipe transition and then change the effect option to From Left. Increase the duration to 2 seconds and then apply the transition to both slides.
6. Play the presentation from the beginning.
7. Rename the presentation using the file name, `SC_PPT_2_Telecommunications`, and submit the presentation in the format requested by your instructor.
8. How does modifying presentations using PowerPoint Online differ from modifying other presentations you have created in Module 2? Which tabs are not available when the simplified ribbon is used in PowerPoint Online? View the Home, Design, and Transitions tabs. Do you think the formatting functions, themes, and transitions are adequate to develop effective presentations? Why or why not?

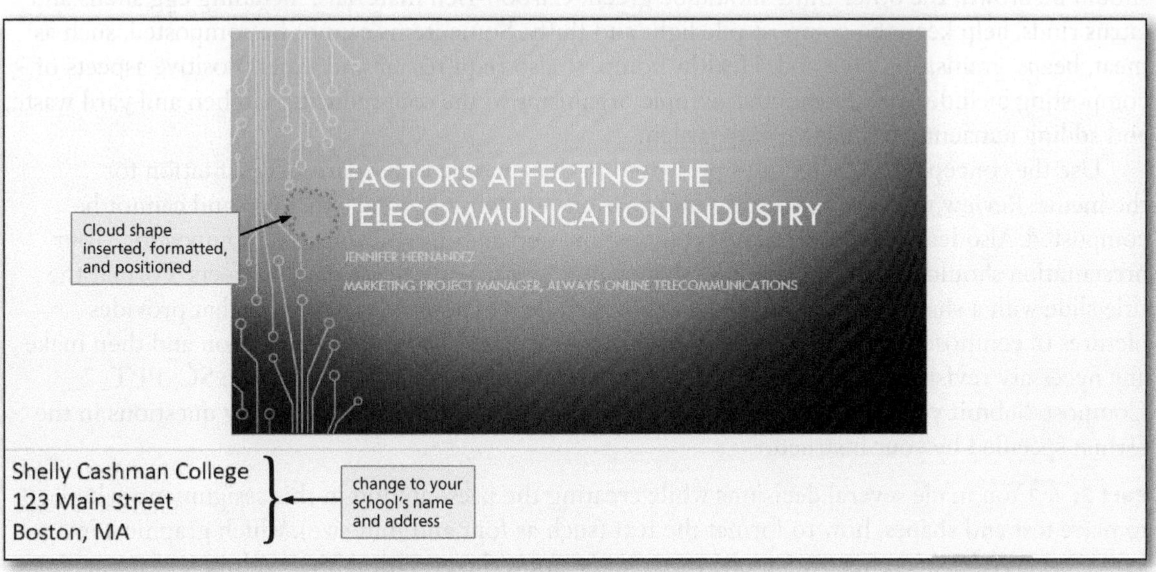

(a) Slide 1

Figure 2–111

Continued >

Expand Your World *continued*

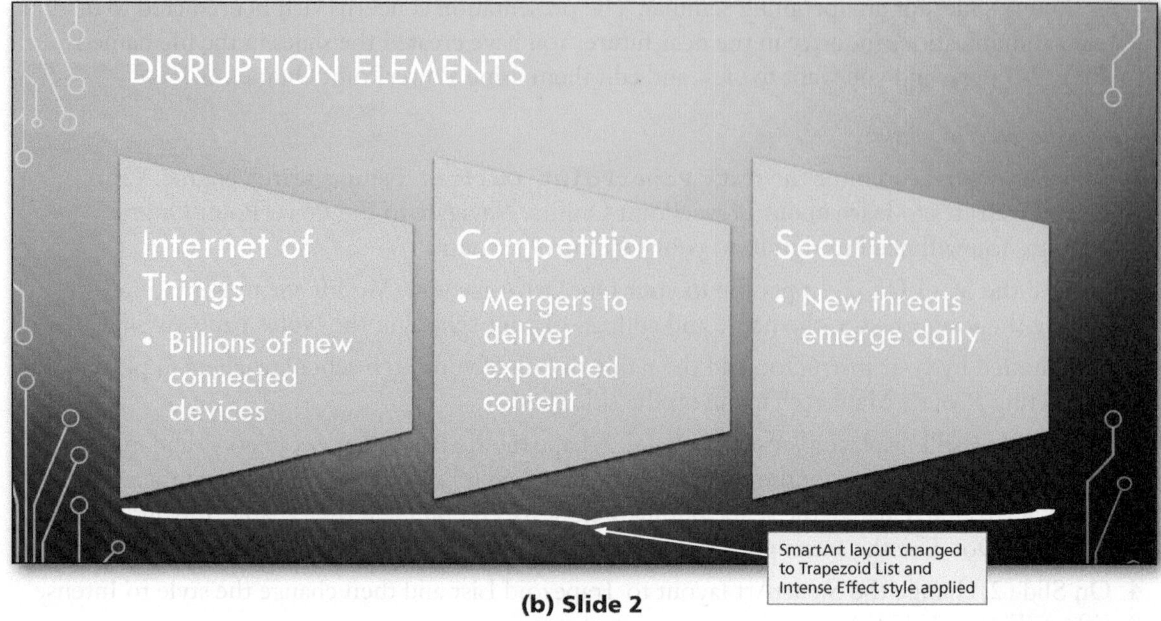

(b) Slide 2

Figure 2–111

In the Lab

Apply your creative thinking and problem-solving skills to design and implement a solution.

Design and Create a Presentation about Your City's Composting Program

Part 1: The Communications Manager in your town is promoting the new composting program for all residents. She would like you to help prepare a presentation for the local media planned for next month. You perform some research and learn that certain items can be composted, such as fruit and vegetable trimmings, coffee grounds, dry leaves, and newspaper. Two-thirds of these items should be brown; the other third should be green. Carbon-rich materials, including egg shells and citrus rinds, help keep the compost pile light and fluffy. Some items cannot be composted, such as meat, beans, grains, and plywood. Healthy compost also requires air and water. Positive aspects of composting include introducing microscopic organisms to the soil, reducing kitchen and yard waste, and adding nutrients to the lawn and garden.

Use the concepts and techniques presented in this module to prepare a presentation for the media. Review websites containing information regarding products that can and cannot be composted. Also learn about creating a compost bin and additional benefits of composting. Your presentation should include a title slide, shapes, and SmartArt with styles and effects. Format the title slide with a shape containing a picture fill. Include a hyperlink to a website that provides pictures of compost bins. Add a footer and slide transitions. View your presentation and then make any necessary revisions. When finished, save your presentation with the file name SC_PPT_2_Compost. Submit your assignment and the answers to the Part 2 critical thinking questions in the format specified by your instructor.

Part 2: You made several decisions while creating the presentation in this assignment: where to place text and shapes, how to format the text (such as font and font size), which graphical image to use, what styles and effects to apply, where to position the graphical images, how to format the graphical images, and which shapes to use to add interest to the presentation. What was the rationale behind each of these decisions? When you reviewed the document, what further revisions did you make and why? Where would you recommend showing this slide show?

3 Inserting WordArt, Charts, and Tables

Objectives

After completing this module, you will be able to:

- Insert a chart and enter data
- Change a chart style
- Insert a table and enter data
- Apply a table style
- Insert a text box
- Change text box defaults and apply preset effects
- Reuse slides from another presentation
- Insert a picture without using a content placeholder
- Crop a picture
- Change a picture color tone and softness
- Convert text to WordArt
- Change WordArt style, fill, and outline
- Animate text and change options
- Insert video

Introduction

Audiences generally focus first on the visual elements displayed on a slide. Graphical elements increase **visual literacy**, which is the ability to examine and assess these images. They can be divided into two categories: images and information graphics. Images are the pictures you have used in Modules 1 and 2, and information graphics are tables, charts, graphs, and diagrams. Both sets of visuals help audience members interpret and retain material, so they should be designed and presented with care.

BTW
Increasing Audience Retention
When audience members view graphics and listen to a speaker, they become engaged in the presentation. They tune out distractions and recall more material during a presentation when clear graphics, including WordArt, charts, and tables, are displayed visually and then explained verbally.

Project—Presentation with WordArt, a Chart, and a Table

In this module's project, you will follow proper design guidelines and learn to use PowerPoint to create the slides shown in Figures 3–1a through 3–1d. The objective is to produce a presentation for Shelly Insurance Company to help policy holders understand how quality sleep affects their overall health. Company executives have surveyed their customers and have found that one-third report they get fewer than the recommended hours of sleep each night. This lack of quality sleep is linked to many chronic diseases and conditions, including heart disease and diabetes. Different

BTW

Preparation Time

Be certain to begin developing a presentation well in advance of assignment deadlines when incorporating information graphics. Create a schedule so that you have adequate time to prepare clear visuals. Developing a presentation incorporating charts and tables generally requires extra preparation time because you need to gather data from reputable and current sources to incorporate into these visual elements.

hours of nightly sleep are recommended for various age groups, with the number of hours decreasing as people grow older. For teens and adults, naps should not exceed 20 minutes. Quality sleep has five stages that repeat every 90 to 120 minutes, with Stage 2 being the longest.

The PowerPoint presentation uses several visual elements to help audience members understand that good sleep habits can help people get a good night's sleep and awake refreshed. The title slide is enhanced with a WordArt graphic and formatted picture. The sleep habits listed on Slide 2 are reinforced with a video clip. The three-dimensional pie chart on Slide 3 depicts the five stages of the sleep cycle, and the three-column table on Slide 4 lists the number of hours of sleep various age groups should have each night.

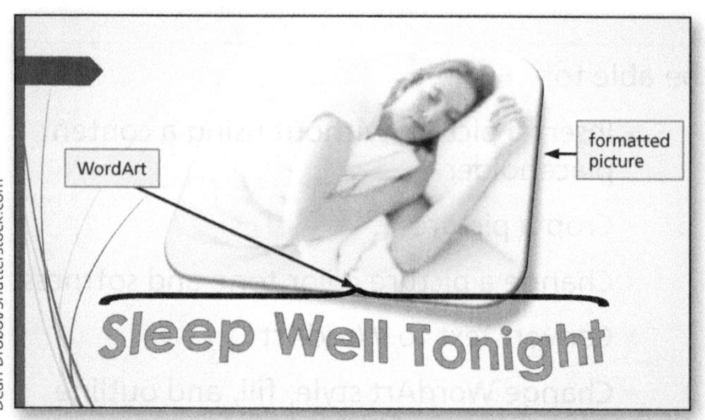

(a) Slide 1 (Title Slide with WordArt and Enhanced Photo)

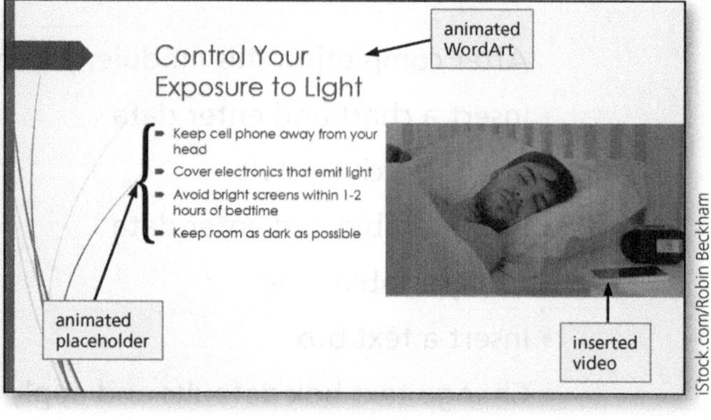

(b) Slide 2 (WordArt and Video Clip)

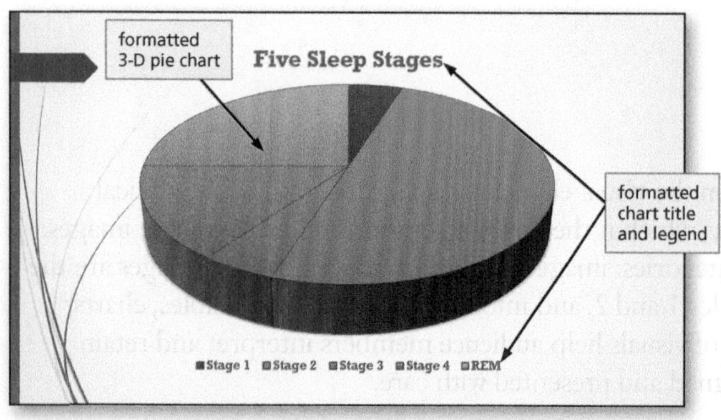

(c) Slide 3 (3-D Chart)

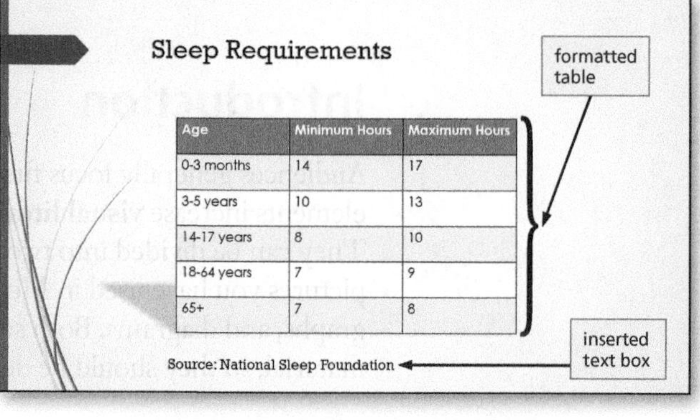

(d) Slide 4 (Three-column Table)

Figure 3–1

BTW

PowerPoint Help

At any time while using PowerPoint, you can find answers to questions and display information about various topics through PowerPoint Help. Used properly, this form of assistance can increase your productivity and reduce your frustrations by minimizing the time you spend learning how to use PowerPoint.

In this module, you will learn how to create the slides shown in Figure 3–1. You will perform the following general tasks as you progress through this module:

1. Create a chart to show proportions.
2. Format a chart by changing style.
3. Create a table to compare and contrast data.
4. Change table format and content style.
5. Insert a text box.

6. Insert slides from another presentation.
7. Crop a picture and apply effects.
8. Insert and modify wordart.
9. Add wordart styles and effects.
10. Animate text.
11. Insert video.

Adding a Chart to a Slide and Formatting

Most people cycle through five stages of sleep—1, 2, 3, 4, and REM (rapid eye movement)—approximately every 90 to 110 minutes. Stages 1 and 2 are considered light sleep, and Stages 3 and 4 are deep sleep. The brain is very active during the REM stage, when the most vivid dreams occur. The chart on Slide 3, shown earlier in Figure 3–1c, shows the proportion of the five sleep stages in the sleep cycle.

When a slide contains a content placeholder, you can click the placeholder's Insert Chart button to start creating a chart. Alternatively, you can click the Chart button (Insert tab | Illustrations group) to add a chart to any slide. A sample **Clustered Column chart** displays in the Insert Chart dialog box. This default chart type is appropriate when comparing two or more items in specified intervals, such as comparing how inflation has risen during the past 10 years. Other popular chart types are line, bar, and pie. You will use a pie chart in Slide 3.

When you select a chart type and then click OK, the sample chart is inserted in the current slide and an associated Microsoft Excel **worksheet** with sample data is displayed in a separate window. You enter data for the chart in this worksheet, which is a rectangular grid containing vertical columns and horizontal rows. Column letters display above the grid to identify particular **columns**, and row numbers display on the left side of the grid to identify particular **rows**. **Cells** are the intersections of rows and columns, and they are the locations for the chart data and text labels. For example, cell A1 is the intersection of column A and row 1. Numeric and text data are entered in the **active cell**, which is the currently selected cell surrounded by a heavy border. You will replace the sample data in the worksheet by typing entries in the cells, but you also can import data from a text file, import an Excel worksheet or chart, or paste data obtained from another program. Once you have entered the data, you can modify the appearance of the chart using menus and commands.

In the following pages, you will perform these tasks:

1. Insert a chart and then replace the sample data.
2. Change the line and shape outline weights.
3. Resize the chart and then change the title and legend font size.

To Run PowerPoint, Apply a Theme, and Save the Presentation

You can save the downloaded slides now to keep track of the changes you make as you progress through this module. The following steps save the file as a PowerPoint presentation.

1 sam Run PowerPoint. If necessary, maximize the PowerPoint window.

2 Apply the Wisp theme.

BTW

Screen Resolution

If you are using a computer to step through the project in this module and you want your screens to match the figures in this book, you should change your screen's resolution to 1366 × 768.

3. Apply the Title and Content layout.
4. Save the presentation using `SC_PPT_3_Sleep` as the file name.

BTW
Organizing Files and Folders
You should organize and store files in folders so that you easily can find the files later. For example, if you are taking an introductory technology class called CIS 101, a good practice would be to save all PowerPoint files in a PowerPoint folder in a CIS 101 folder.

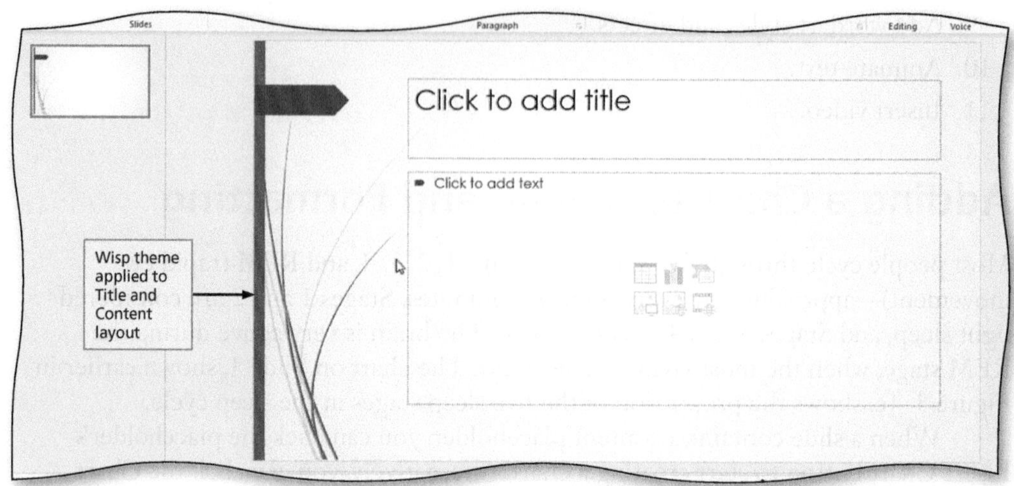

Figure 3–2

To Delete a Placeholder

When you run a slide show, empty placeholders do not display. You may desire to delete unused placeholders from a slide. ***Why?*** *Empty placeholders can be a distraction when you are designing slide content because they cover an area of the slide that can display other slide content.* The title text placeholder on Slide 1 is not required for this presentation, so you can remove it. The following steps remove the Slide 1 title text placeholder.

- Click a border of the title text placeholder so that it appears as a solid or finely dotted line (Figure 3–3). The words, Click to add title, will still be displayed.

- Press DELETE to remove the title text placeholder.

Q&A
Can I also click the Cut button (Home tab | Clipboard group) to delete the placeholder?
Yes. Generally, however, Cut is used when you desire to remove a selected slide element, place it on the Clipboard, and then paste it in another area. DELETE is used when you do not want to reuse that particular slide element.

If I am using a touch screen, how do I delete the placeholder?
Press and hold on a border of the title text placeholder and then tap DELETE on the shortcut menu to remove the placeholder.

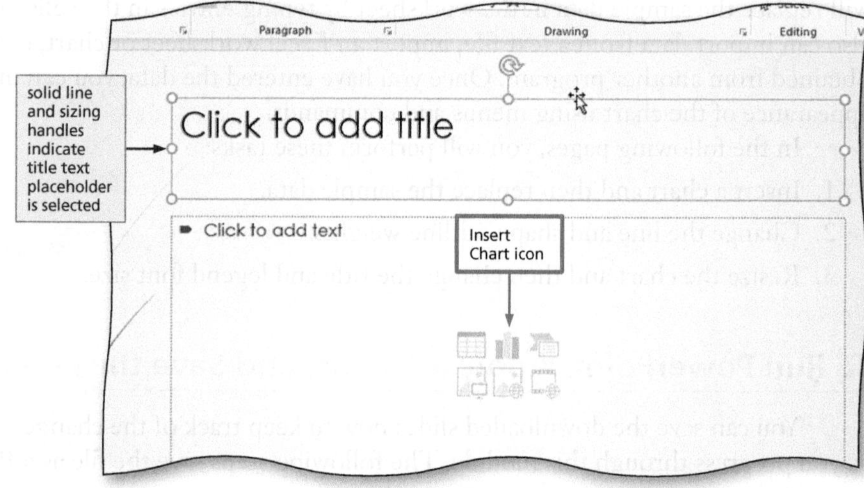

Figure 3–3

Other Ways
1. Select placeholder, press BACKSPACE

CONSIDER THIS

How can I choose an appropriate chart type?
General adult audiences are familiar with bar and pie charts, so those chart types are good choices. Specialized audiences, such as engineers and architects, are comfortable reading scatter and bubble charts. Common chart types and their purposes are as follows:

- Column — Vertical bars compare values over a period of time.
- Bar — Horizontal bars compare two or more values to show how the proportions relate to each other.
- Line — A line or lines show trends, increases and decreases, levels, and costs during a continuous period of time.
- Pie — A pie chart divides a single total into parts to illustrate how the segments differ from each other and the whole.
- Scatter — A scatterplot displays the effect on one variable when another variable changes.

In general, three-dimensional charts are more difficult to comprehend than two-dimensional charts. The added design elements in a three-dimensional chart add clutter and take up space. A chart may include a **legend**, which is information that identifies parts of the chart and coordinates with the colors assigned to the chart categories. A legend may help to unclutter the chart, so consider using one prominently on the slide.

To Insert a Chart

The first step in developing slide content for this presentation is to insert a pie chart. ***Why?*** *The pie chart is a useful tool to show proportional amounts. In this presentation, you want to show the length of time in each stage of sleep.* The following steps insert a chart with sample data into a content placeholder on Slide 1.

1

- **Click the Insert Chart icon in the content placeholder to display the Insert Chart dialog box.**
- **Click Pie in the left pane to display the Pie gallery and then click the 3-D Pie button (second chart) to select that chart type (Figure 3–4).**

Experiment

- **Point to the 3-D Pie chart to see a large preview of this type.**

Q&A Can I change the chart type after I have inserted a chart?
Yes. Click the 'Change Chart Type' button in the Type group on the Chart Tools Design tab to display the Change Chart Type dialog box and then make another selection.

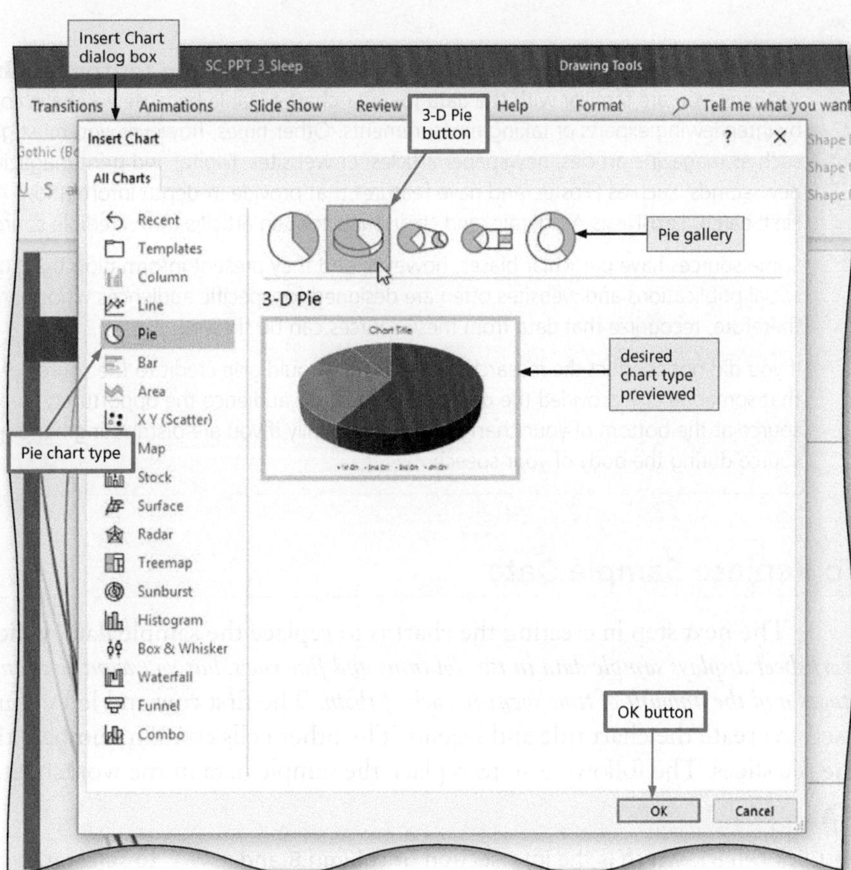

Figure 3–4

2

• Click OK (Insert Chart dialog box) to start the Microsoft Excel program and open a worksheet on the top of the Sleep presentation (Figure 3–5).

Q&A What do the numbers in the worksheet and the chart represent?
Excel places sample data in the worksheet and charts the sample data in the default chart type.

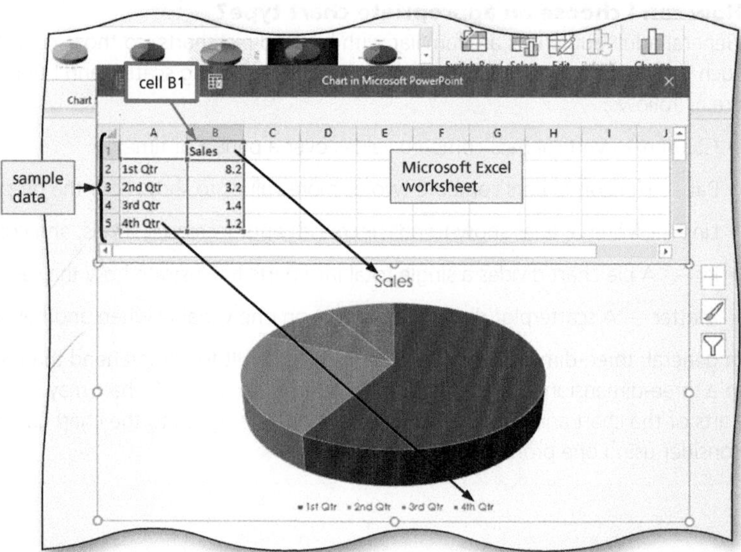

Figure 3–5

Other Ways

1. Click Chart (Insert tab | Illustrations group)

CONSIDER THIS

How do I locate credible sources to obtain information for the graphic?

At times, you are familiar with the data for your chart or table because you have conducted in-the-field, or primary, research by interviewing experts or taking measurements. Other times, however, you must gather the data from secondary sources, such as magazine articles, newspaper articles, or websites. Digital and print magazines and newspapers are available in digital newsstands, such as Flipster, and have features that provide in-depth information. Also, online databases, such as EBSCOhost, FirstSearch, LexisNexis Academic, and NewsBank contain articles from credible sources.

Some sources have particular biases, however, and they present information that supports their causes. Political, religious, and social publications and websites often are designed for specific audiences who share a common point of view. You should, therefore, recognize that data from these sources can be skewed.

If you did not conduct the research yourself, you should give credit to the source of your information. You are acknowledging that someone else provided the data and giving your audience the opportunity to obtain the same materials you used. Type the source at the bottom of your chart or table, especially if you are distributing handouts of your slides. At the very least, state the source during the body of your speech.

To Replace Sample Data

The next step in creating the chart is to replace the sample data, which will redraw the chart. ***Why?*** *The worksheet displays sample data in two columns and five rows, but you want to change this data to show the specific sleep stages and the amount of time spent in each of them.* The first row and left column contain text labels and will be used to create the chart title and legend. The other cells contain numbers that are used to determine the size of the pie slices. The following steps replace the sample data in the worksheet.

• Click cell B1, which is the intersection of column B and row 1, to select it.

Q&A Why did my pointer change shape?
The pointer changes to a block plus sign to indicate a cell is selected.

- Type **`Five Sleep Stages`** in cell B1 to replace the sample chart title (Figure 3–6).

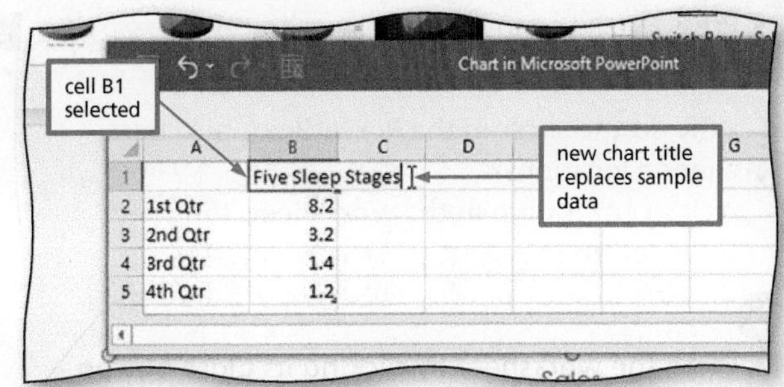

Figure 3–6

2

- Click cell A2 to select that cell.
- Type **`Stage 1`** in cell A2 (Figure 3–7).

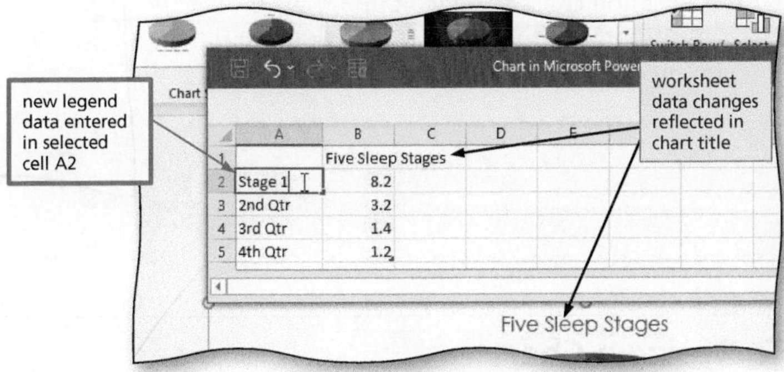

Figure 3–7

3

- Move the pointer to cell A3.
- Type **`Stage 2`** in cell A3 and then move the pointer to cell A4.
- Type **`Stage 3`** in cell A4 and then move the pointer to cell A5.
- Type **`Stage 4`** in cell A5 and then press ENTER to move the pointer to cell A6.
- Type **`REM`** in cell A6 (Figure 3–8).

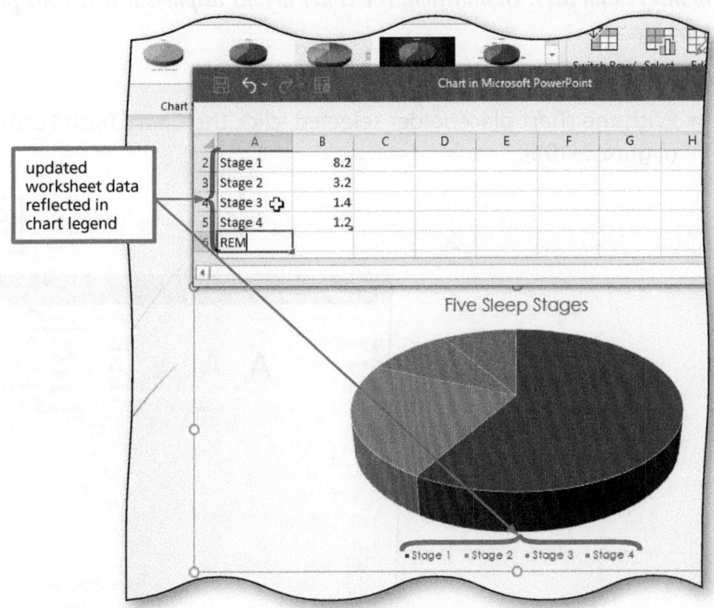

Figure 3–8

4

- Click cell B2, type 5 in that cell, and then move the pointer to cell B3.
- Type **`50`** in cell B3 and then move the pointer to cell B4.
- Type **`5`** in cell B4 and then move the pointer to cell B5.
- Type **`15`** in cell B5 and then move the pointer to cell B6.
- Type **`25`** in cell B6.

- Press ENTER to move the pointer to cell B7 (Figure 3–9).

Q&A Why do the slices in the PowerPoint pie chart change locations?
As you enter data in the worksheet, the chart slices rotate to reflect these new figures.

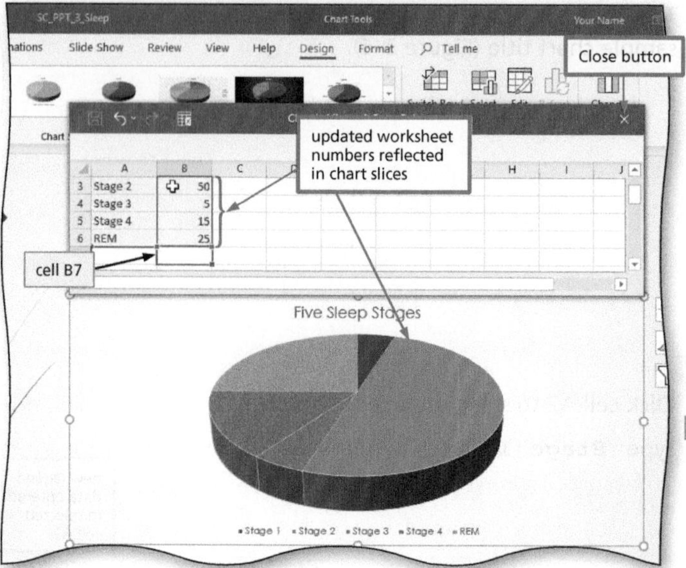

Figure 3–9

5

- Close the worksheet by clicking its Close button.

Q&A Can I open the worksheet once it has been closed?
Yes. Click the chart to select it and then click the Edit Data button (Chart Tools Design tab | Data group).

To Resize a Chart

You resize a chart the same way you resize a SmartArt graphic or any other graphical object. The following steps resize the chart to fill the slide. ***Why?*** *The slide has a large area of white space, so you are able to enlarge the chart to aid readability. In addition, the chart layout displays a title that provides sufficient information to describe the chart's purpose.*

1

- With the chart placeholder selected, click the Chart Tools Format tab to display the Chart Tools Format ribbon (Figure 3–10).

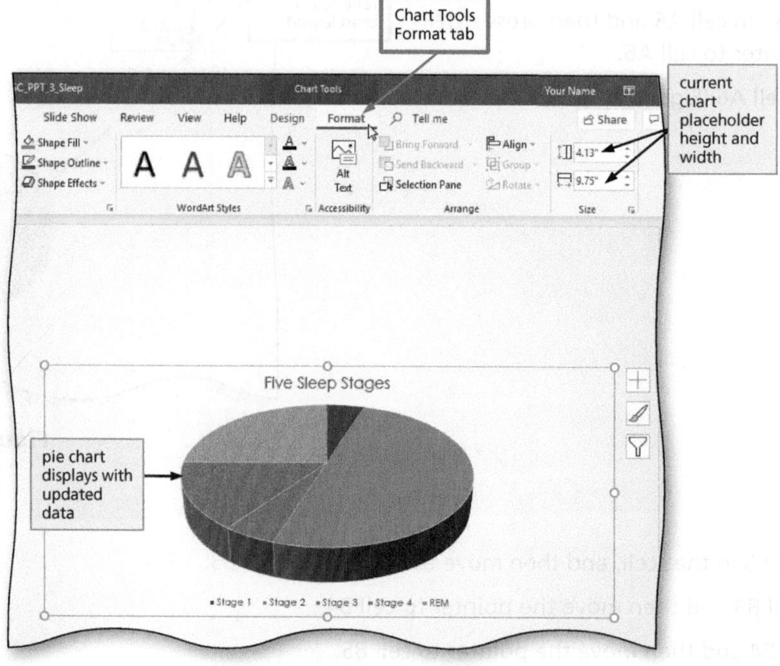

Figure 3–10

- Click the Shape Height up arrow repeatedly until 6.5" is displayed in the box.
- Click the Shape Width up arrow repeatedly until 10.5" is displayed in the box (Figure 3–11).

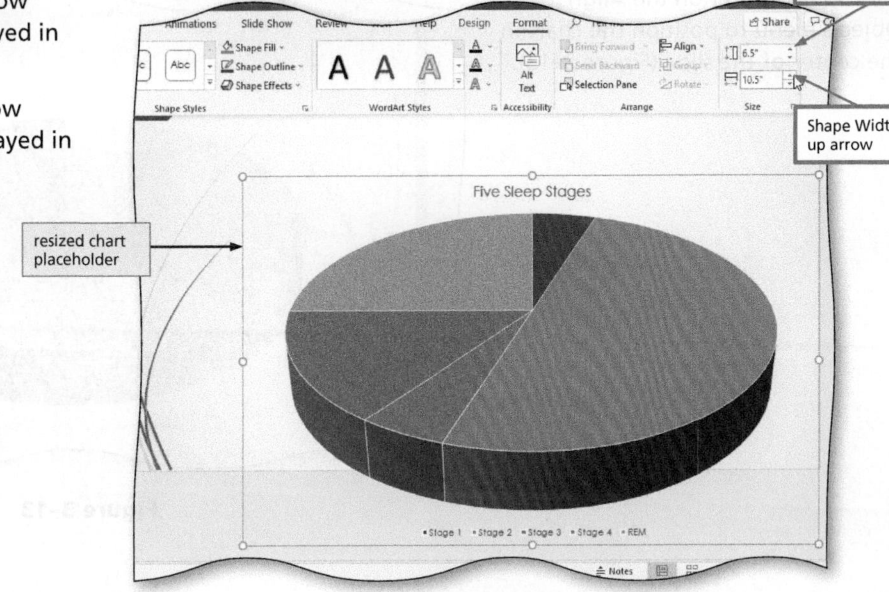

Figure 3–11

BTW
Ribbon and Screen Resolution
PowerPoint may change how the groups and buttons within the groups appear on the ribbon, depending on the screen resolution of your computer. Thus, your ribbon may look different from the ones in this book if you are using a screen resolution other than 1366 × 768.

To Align a Chart

Part of the resized chart placeholder is located below the slide, so you need to reposition it. ***Why?*** *You can move the placeholder to the center and middle of the slide so that the entire chart and legend can be seen.* The following steps align the chart.

- With the chart selected and the Chart Tools Format tab displaying, click the Align button (Chart Tools Format tab | Arrange group) to display the Align Objects menu (Figure 3–12).

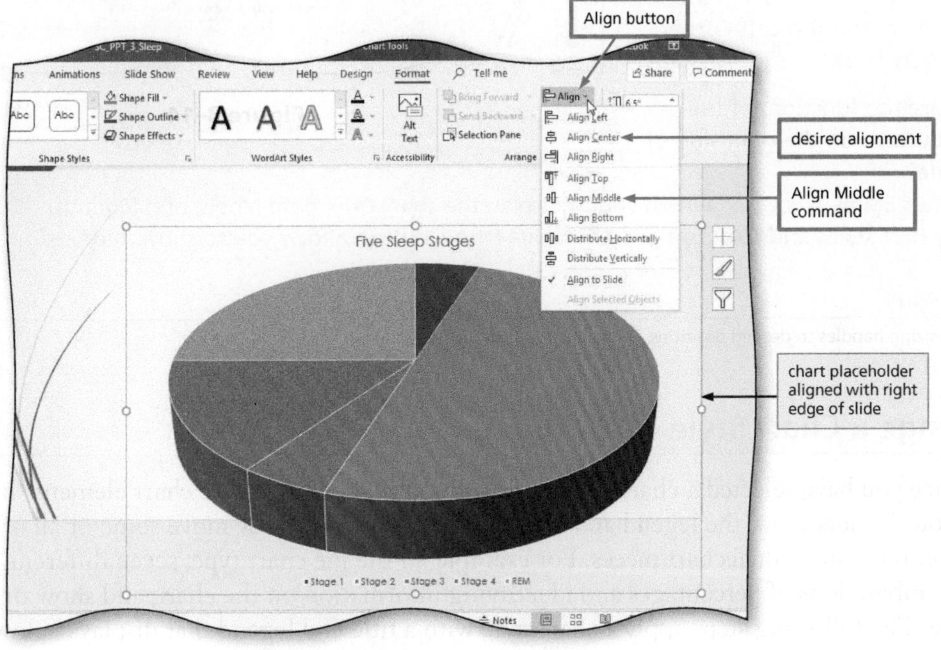

Figure 3–12

- Click Align Center on the Align Objects menu to position the chart in the center of the slide (Figure 3–13).

chart placeholder centered on slide

chart placeholder extends past bottom edge of slide

Figure 3–13

- Click Align again and then click Align Middle (shown in Figure 3–12) to position the chart in the middle of the slide (Figure 3–14).

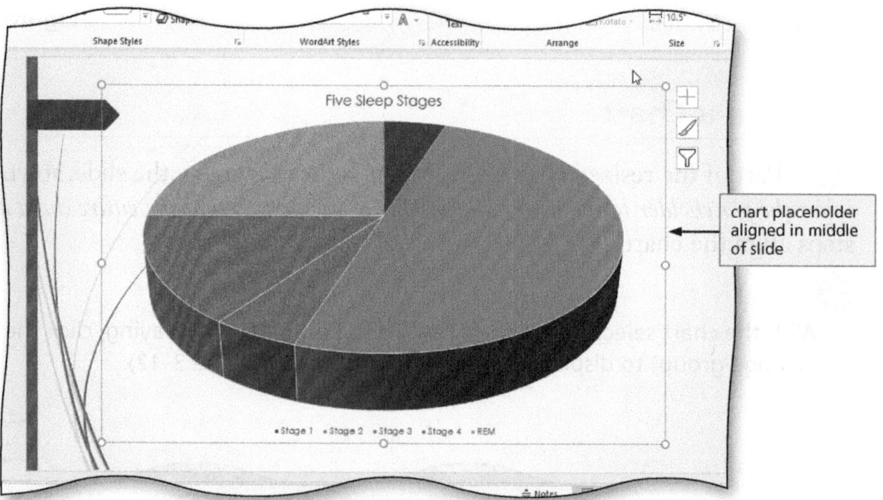

Figure 3–14

Q&A

Can I specify a precise position where the chart will display on the slide?

Yes. Right-click the edge of the chart, click 'Format Chart Area' on the shortcut menu, click 'Size & Properties' in the Format Chart Area pane, enter measurements in the Position section, and then specify from the Top Left Corner or the Center of the slide.

What are the functions of the three buttons on the right side of the slide?

The Chart Elements button allows you to display the chart title, data labels, and legends; the Chart Styles button shows chart styles and color options; the Chart Filters button allows you to show, hide, edit, or rearrange data.

Other Ways

1. Drag sizing handles to desired positions.

To Change a Chart Style

Once you have selected a chart type, you can modify the look of the chart elements by changing its style. The various layouts move the legend above or below the chart, or they move some or all of the legend data directly onto the individual chart pieces. For example, in the pie chart type, seven different layouts display various combinations of percentages and identifying information on the chart, and show or do not show the chart title. The following steps apply a chart style with a title and legend that displays below the pie slices. ***Why?*** *Your data consists of category names and percentages, so you need a layout that shows the proportion of each category along with a corresponding legend.*

1

- With the chart still selected, click the Chart Styles button (paintbrush icon) on the right side of the chart area to display the Chart Style gallery with the Style tab displayed.
- Scroll down until the fifth style (Style 5) in the Chart Style gallery is displayed and then point to this style to see a live preview on the slide (Figure 3–15).

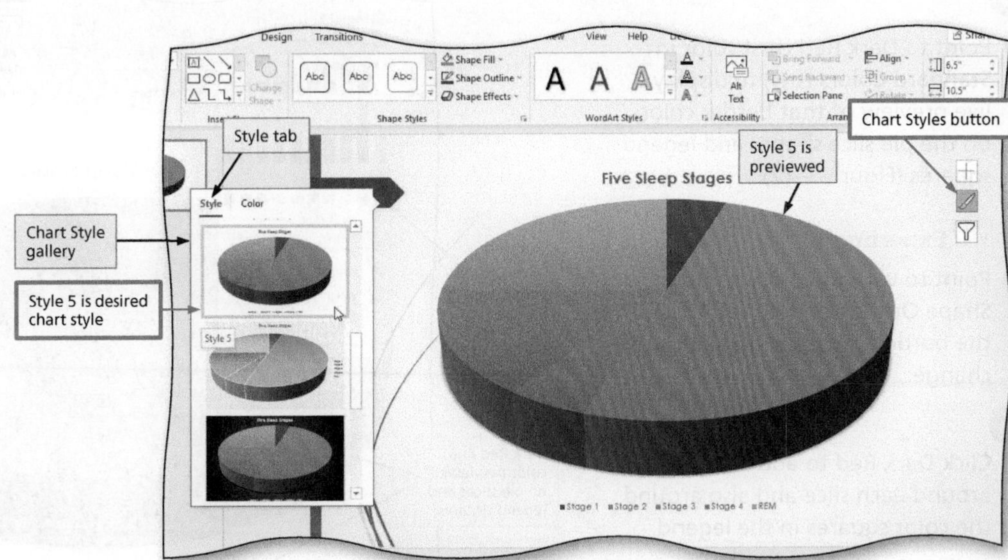

Figure 3–15

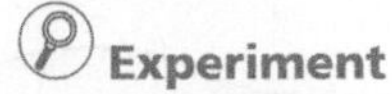

Experiment

- Point to various chart styles and watch the layouts on the chart change.

2

- Click Style 5 in the Chart Style gallery to apply the selected chart style to the chart.

3

- Click Chart Styles to hide the Chart Style gallery.

To Change the Shape Outline Color

You can change the outline color to add contrast to each slice and legend color square. The following steps change the shape outline color to Dark Red. ***Why?*** *At this point, it is difficult to see the borders around the legend squares and around each pie slice. The arrow in the upper-left corner of the slide is dark red, so you can add a similar color to the pie slices.*

1

- Click the center of the pie chart to select it and to display the sizing handles around each slice.

2

- Click the Shape Outline arrow (Chart Tools Format tab | Shape Styles group) to display the Shape Outline gallery (Figure 3–16).

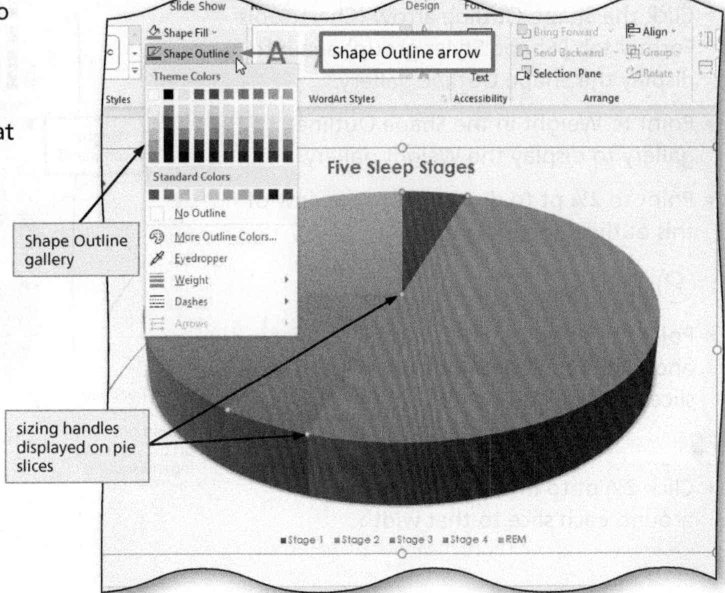

Figure 3–16

- Point to Dark Red (first color in Standard Colors row) to display a live preview of that border color on the pie slice shapes and legend squares (Figure 3–17).

Experiment

- Point to various colors in the Shape Outline gallery and watch the border colors on the pie slices change.

- Click Dark Red to add red borders around each slice and also around the color squares in the legend.

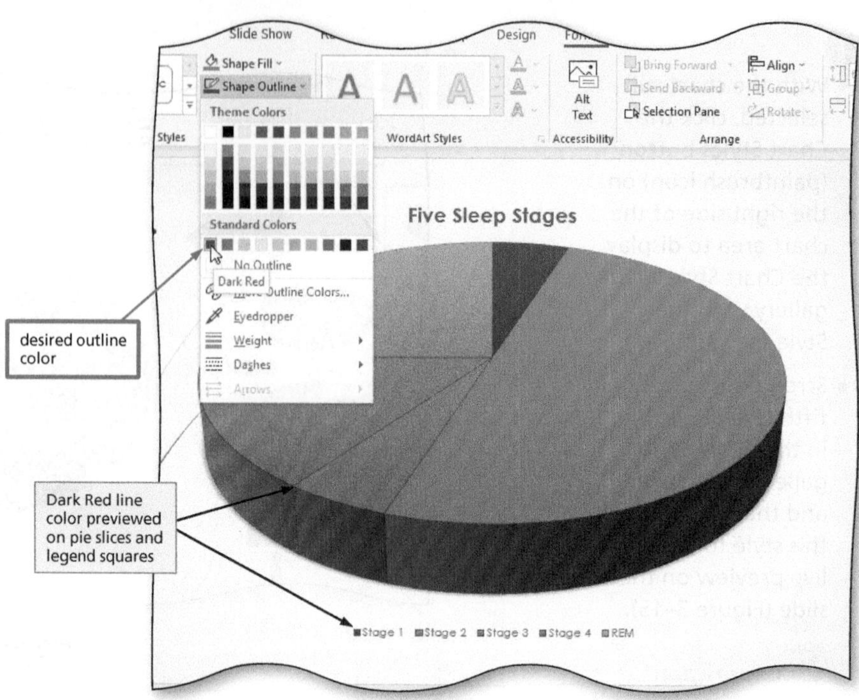

Figure 3–17

Other Ways

1. Right-click chart, Outline, click desired color

To Change the Shape Outline Weight

The chart has a thin outline around each pie slice and around each color square in the legend. You can change the weight of these lines. ***Why?*** *A thicker line can accentuate each slice and add another strong visual element to the slide.* The following steps change the outline weight.

- If necessary, click the center of the pie chart to select it and to display the sizing handles around each slice.
- Click the Shape Outline arrow (Chart Tools Format tab | Shape Styles group) again to display the Shape Outline gallery.
- Point to Weight in the Shape Outline gallery to display the Weight gallery.
- Point to 2¼ pt to display a live preview of this outline line weight (Figure 3–18).

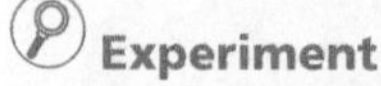

Experiment

- Point to various weights on the submenu and watch the border weights on the pie slices change.

- Click 2¼ pt to increase the border around each slice to that width.

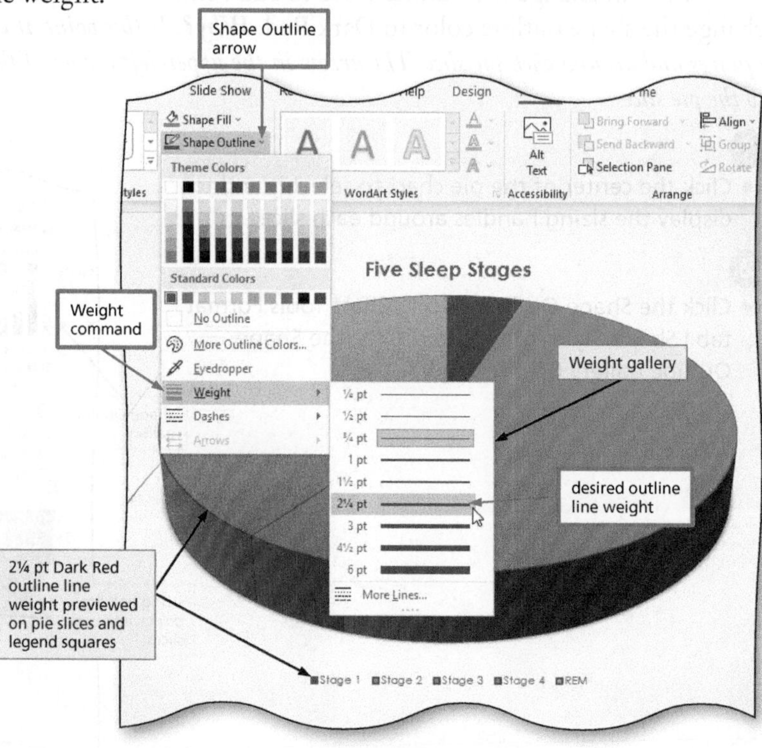

Figure 3–18

Other Ways

1. Right-click chart, click Outline button, click Weight

To Change the Title and Legend Font and Font Size

Depending upon the complexity of the chart and the overall slide, you may want to increase the font size of the chart title and legend. ***Why?*** *The larger font size increases readability.* The following steps change the font size of both of these chart elements.

- Click the chart title, Five Sleep Stages, to select the text box.
- Display the Home tab and then click the 'Increase Font Size' button (Home tab | Font group) repeatedly until the font size is 32 point.
- Change the font of the chart title to Rockwell (Figure 3–19).

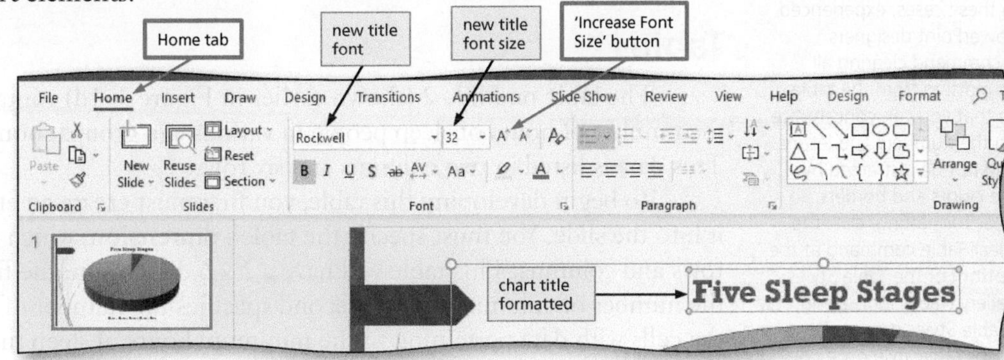

Figure 3–19

- Click one of the legends to select the legends text box.
- Click the 'Increase Font Size' button (Home tab | Font group) repeatedly until the font size of the legend text is 18 point.
- Change the legend font to Rockwell.
- Click the Bold button (Home tab | Font group) to bold the legend text (Figure 3–20).

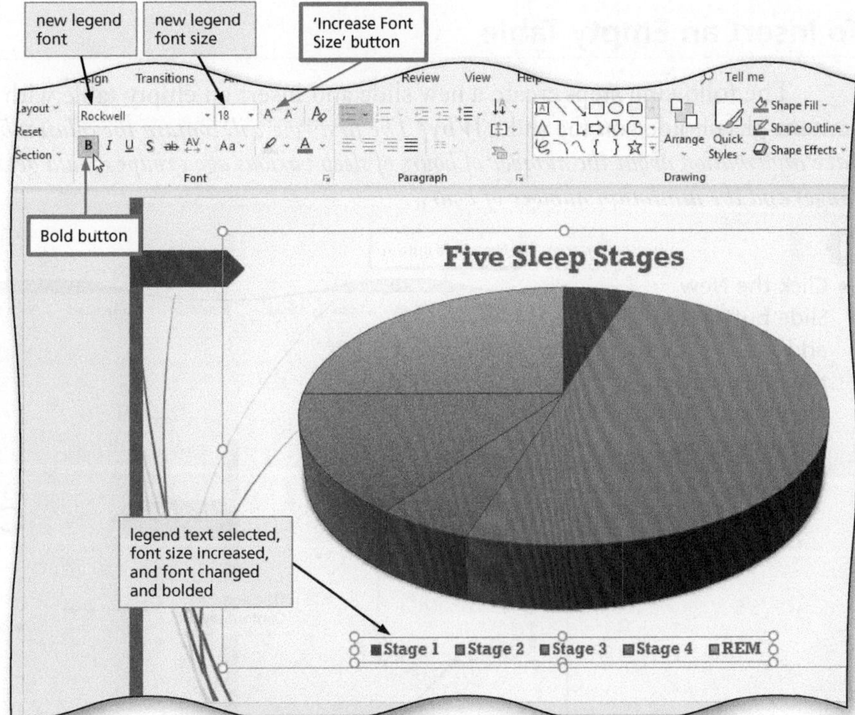

Figure 3–20

Adding a Table to a Slide and Formatting

One effective method of organizing information on a slide is to use a **table**, which is a grid consisting of rows and columns that can contain text and graphics. You can enhance a table with formatting, including adding colors, lines, and backgrounds, and changing fonts.

In the following pages, you will perform these tasks:

1. Insert a table and then enter data.
2. Apply a table style.
3. Add table borders and an effect.
4. Resize the table.
5. Insert a row and a column.

BTW

Clearing Table Formatting

Many times you may need to create large tables and then enter data into many cells. In these cases, experienced PowerPoint designers recommend clearing all formatting from the table so that you can concentrate on the numbers and letters and not be distracted by the colors and borders. To clear formatting, click the Clear Table command at the bottom of the Table Styles gallery (Table Tools Design tab | Table Styles group). Then, add a table style once you have verified that all table data is correct.

Tables

The table on Slide 2 (shown earlier in Figure 3–1d) contains information about the number of hours of sleep people in various age groups should have each night. This data is listed in two columns and six rows.

To begin developing this table, you first must create an empty table and insert it into the slide. You must specify the table's **dimension**, which is the total number of rows and columns. This table will have a 2 × 6 dimension: the first number indicates the number of columns and the second specifies the number of rows. You will fill the cells with data pertaining to the minimum hours of sleep that various age groups should have. Later in this module you will add a column to show the maximum hours recommended for each age category. Then you will format the table using a table style.

To Insert an Empty Table

The following steps create a new slide and insert an empty table with two columns and five rows into a content placeholder on the slide. ***Why?*** *The first row will contain the column headings, and the additional rows will have information about the number of hours of sleep various age groups should get. The two columns will contain the age ranges and the minimum number of hours.*

- Click the New Slide button to add a new slide to the presentation with the Title and Content layout (Figure 3–21).

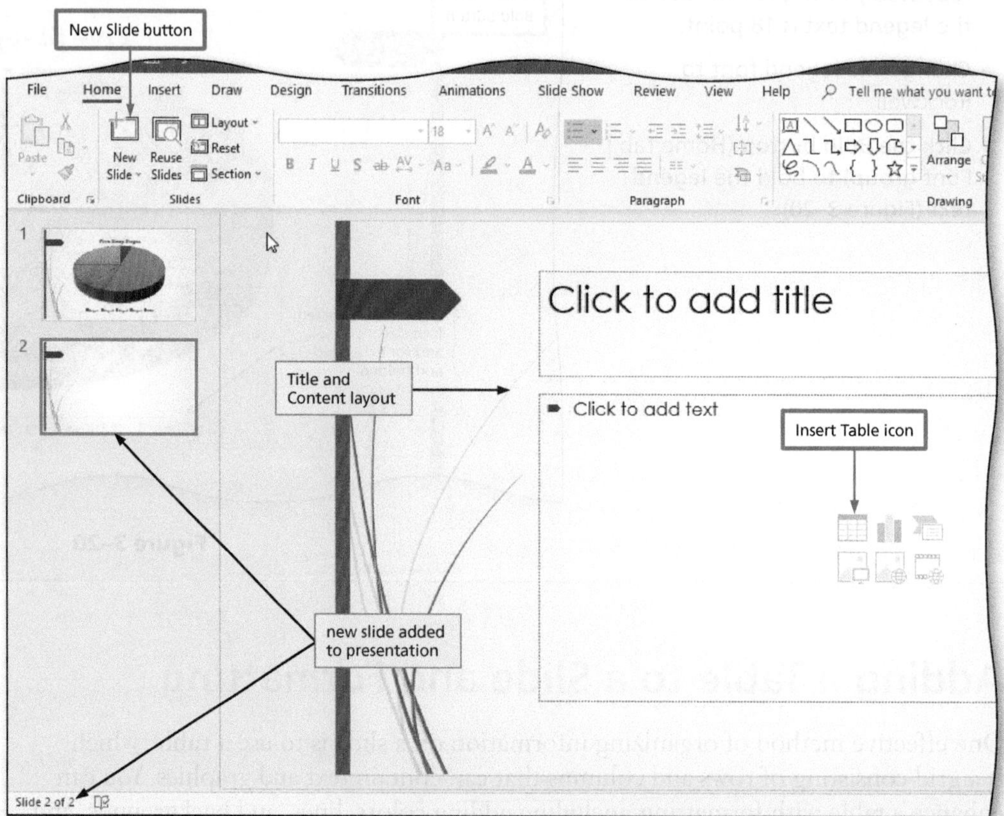

Figure 3–21

- Click the Insert Table icon in the content placeholder to display the Insert Table dialog box.
- Click the down arrow to the right of the 'Number of columns' box three times so that the number 2 appears in the box.
- Click the up arrow to the right of the 'Number of rows' box three times so that the number 5 appears in the box (Figure 3–22).

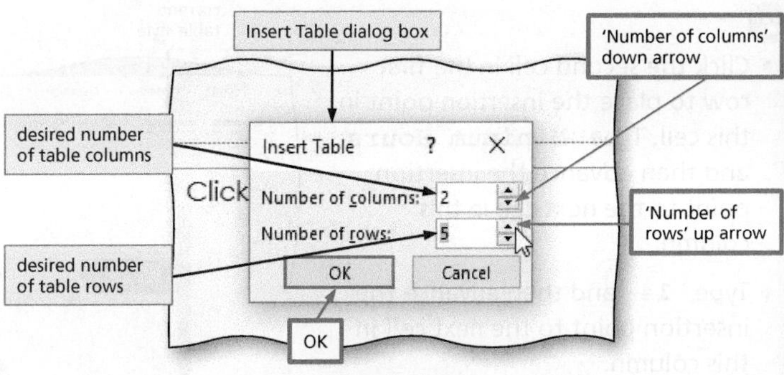

Figure 3–22

- Click OK (Insert table dialog box) to insert the table into Slide 2 (Figure 3–23).

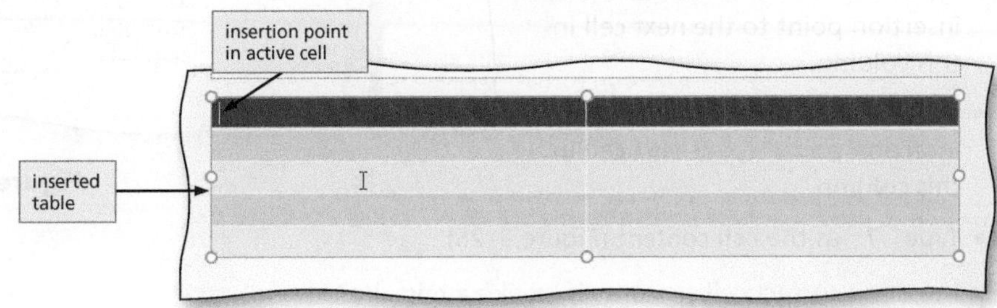

Figure 3–23

Other Ways

1. Click Table (Insert tab | Tables group), drag to select columns and rows, click or press ENTER

To Enter Data in a Table

Before formatting or making any changes in the table style, you enter the data in the table. ***Why?*** *It is easier to see formatting and style changes applied to existing data.* The second column will have the minimum hours recommended for the age groups listed in the first column. The next step is to enter data in the cells of the empty table. To place data in a cell, you click the cell and then type text. The following steps enter the data in the table.

1

- With the insertion point in the first cell in the first column, type `Age` and then click the cell below or press DOWN ARROW to advance the insertion point to the next cell in this column.
- Type `0-3 months` and then advance the insertion point to the next cell in this column.

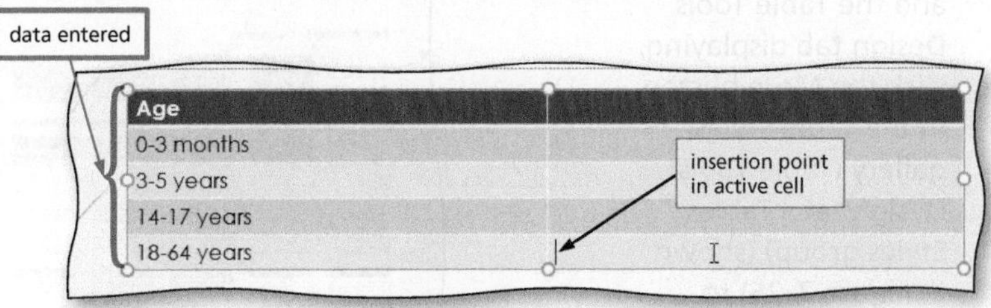

Figure 3–24

- Type `3-5 years` and then advance the insertion point to the next cell in this column.
- Type `14-17 years` and then advance the insertion point to the next cell in this column.
- Type `18-64 years` and then click the empty cell to the right or press TAB (Figure 3–24).

Q&A

What if I pressed ENTER after filling in the last cell?
Press BACKSPACE.

How would I add more rows to the table?
Press TAB when the insertion point is positioned in the bottom-right cell.

If I am using a touch screen, how do I add rows to the table?
Press and hold the bottom-right cell, tap Insert on the shortcut menu, and then tap Insert Rows Below.

BTW
Touch Screen Differences
The Office and Windows interfaces may vary if you are using a touch screen. For this reason, you might notice that the function or appearance of your touch screen differs slightly from this module's presentation.

- Click the second cell in the first row to place the insertion point in this cell. Type `Minimum Hours` and then advance the insertion point to the next cell in this column.
- Type `14` and then advance the insertion point to the next cell in this column.
- Type `10` and then advance the insertion point to the next cell in this column.
- Type `8` and then advance the insertion point to the next cell in this column.
- Type `7` as the cell content (Figure 3–25).

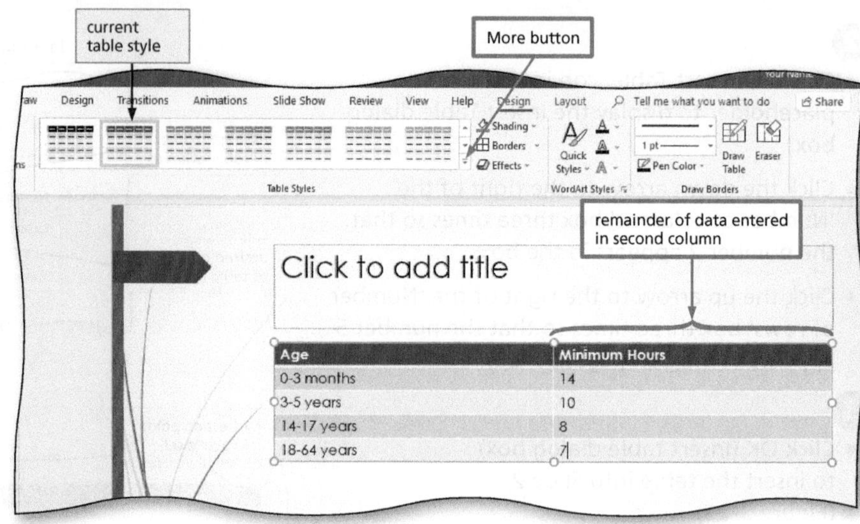

Figure 3–25

Q&A How do I correct cell contents if I make a mistake?
Click the cell and then correct the text.

To Apply a Table Style

When you inserted the table, PowerPoint automatically applied a style. Thumbnails of this style and others are displayed in the Table Styles gallery. These styles use a variety of colors and shading and are grouped in the categories of Best Match for Document, Light, Medium, and Dark. The following steps apply a table style in the Medium area to the Slide 2 table. ***Why?*** *The green styles in the Medium area use the colors appearing on the slide, so they coordinate nicely with the Wisp theme colors in this presentation.*

- With the insertion point in the table and the Table Tools Design tab displaying, click the More button in the Table Styles gallery (Table Tools Design tab | Tables Styles group) (shown in Figure 3–25) to expand the Table Styles gallery.
- Point to 'Medium Style 1 – Accent 4' in the Medium area (fifth style in first Medium row) to display a live preview of that style applied to the table (Figure 3–26).

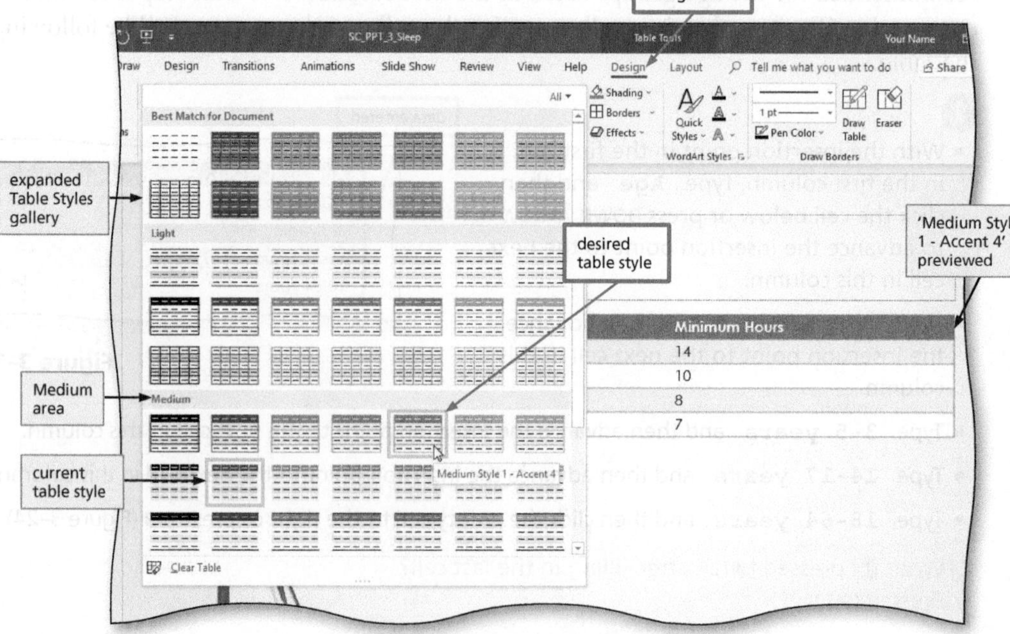

Figure 3–26

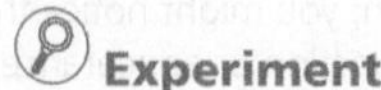

Experiment

- Point to various styles in the Table Styles gallery and watch the colors and format change on the table.

2

- Click 'Medium Style 1 – Accent 4' in the Table Styles gallery to apply the selected style to the table (Figure 3–27).

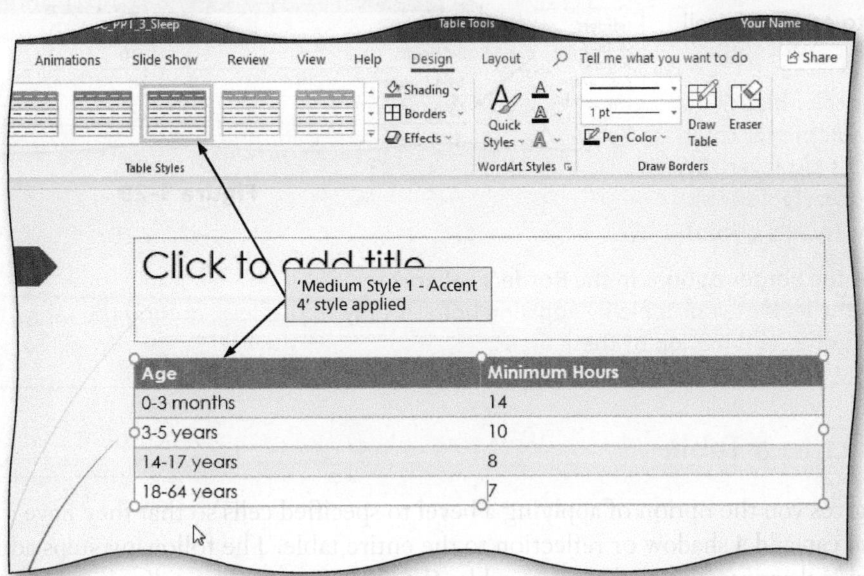

Figure 3–27

Q&A Can I resize the columns and rows or the entire table?
Yes. To resize columns or rows, drag a **column boundary** (the border to the right of a column) or the **row boundary** (the border at the bottom of a row) until the column or row is the desired width or height. To resize the entire table, drag a **table sizing handle**, the small circle that appears when you point to any corner of a table.

To Add Borders to a Table

The Slide 2 table does not have borders around the entire table or between the cells. The following steps add borders to the entire table. ***Why?*** *These details will give the chart some dimension and add to its visual appeal.*

1

- Click the edge of the table so that the insertion point does not appear in any cell.
- Click the Borders arrow (Table Tools Design tab | Table Styles group) to display the Borders gallery (Figure 3–28).

Q&A Why is the button called No Border in the ScreenTip and Borders on the ribbon?
The ScreenTip name for the button will change based on the type of border, if any, present in the table. Currently no borders are applied.

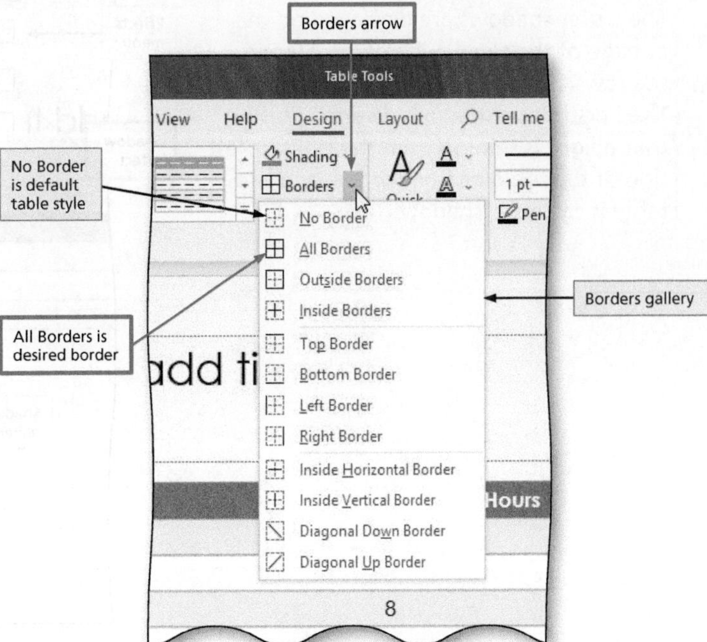

Figure 3–28

- Click All Borders in the Borders gallery to add borders around the entire table and to each table cell (Figure 3–29).

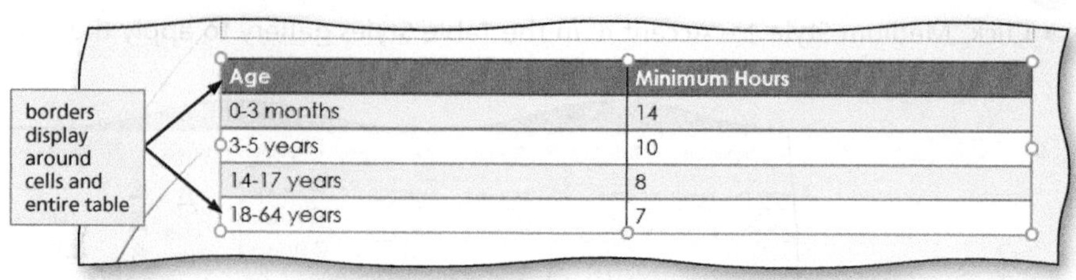

Figure 3–29

Q&A Why is the border color black?
PowerPoint's default border color is black. This color is displayed on the Pen Color button (Table Tools Design tab | Draw Borders group).

Can I apply any of the border options in the Borders gallery?
Yes. You can vary the look of your table by applying borders only to the cells, around the table, to the top, bottom, left or right edges, or a combination of these areas.

To Add an Effect to a Table

PowerPoint gives you the option of applying a bevel to specified cells so that they have a three-dimensional appearance. You also can add a shadow or reflection to the entire table. The following steps add a shadow and give a three-dimensional appearance to the entire table. ***Why?** Adding an effect will enhance the table design.*

1

- With the table selected, click the Effects button (Table Tools Design tab | Table Styles group) to display the Effects menu.

Q&A What is the difference between a shadow and a reflection?
A shadow gives the appearance that light is falling on the table, which causes a shadow behind the graphic. A reflection gives the appearance that the table is shiny, so a mirror image appears below the actual graphic.

2

- Point to Shadow to display the Shadow gallery (Figure 3–30).

Q&A How do the shadows differ in the Outer, Inner, and Perspective categories?
The Outer shadows are displayed on the outside of the table, whereas the Inner shadows are displayed in the interior cells. The Perspective shadows give the illusion that a light is shining from the right or left side of the table or from above, and the table is casting a shadow.

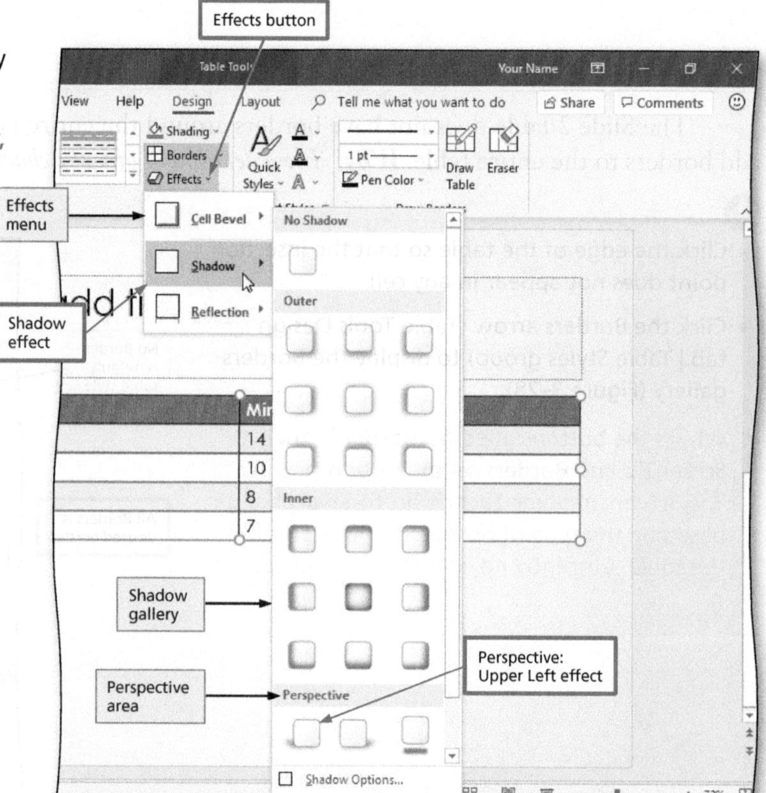

Figure 3–30

3

- Point to Perspective: Upper Left in the Perspective category (first shadow in first row) to display a live preview of this shadow (Figure 3–31).

Experiment

- Point to the various shadows in the Shadow gallery and watch the shadows change in the table.

4

- Click Perspective: Upper Left to apply this shadow to the table.

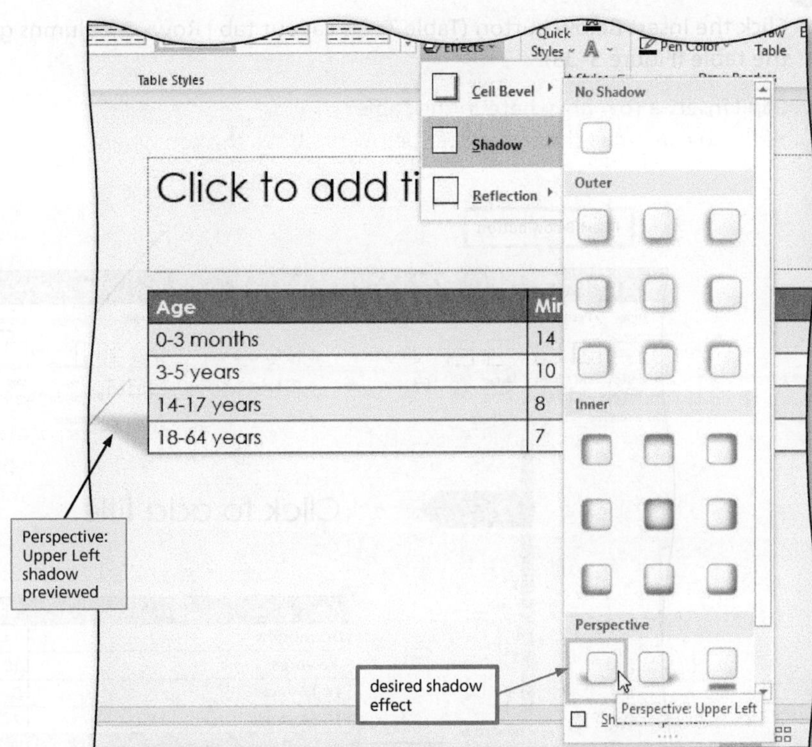

Figure 3–31

To Insert a Table Row

You can add a table row easily in any area of the chart. The following steps insert a row in the table. ***Why?*** *You want to add information pertaining to individuals who are 65 years of age or older.*

1

- With the table still selected, display the Table Tools Layout tab.
- Click the last cell in the first column (18–64 years) to place the insertion point in this cell (Figure 3–32).

Q&A Could I also have placed the insertion point in the last cell in the second column (7)?
Yes. You are going to insert the row below these cells, so either location would work.

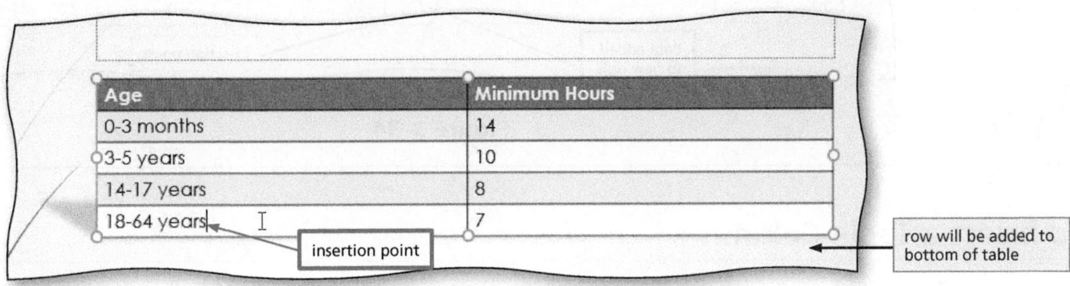

Figure 3–32

- Click the Insert Below button (Table Tools Layout tab | Rows & Columns group) to insert a new row at the bottom of the table (Figure 3–33).

Q&A Can I insert a row anywhere in the table?
Yes. You can insert the row either below or above the cell where the insertion point is positioned.

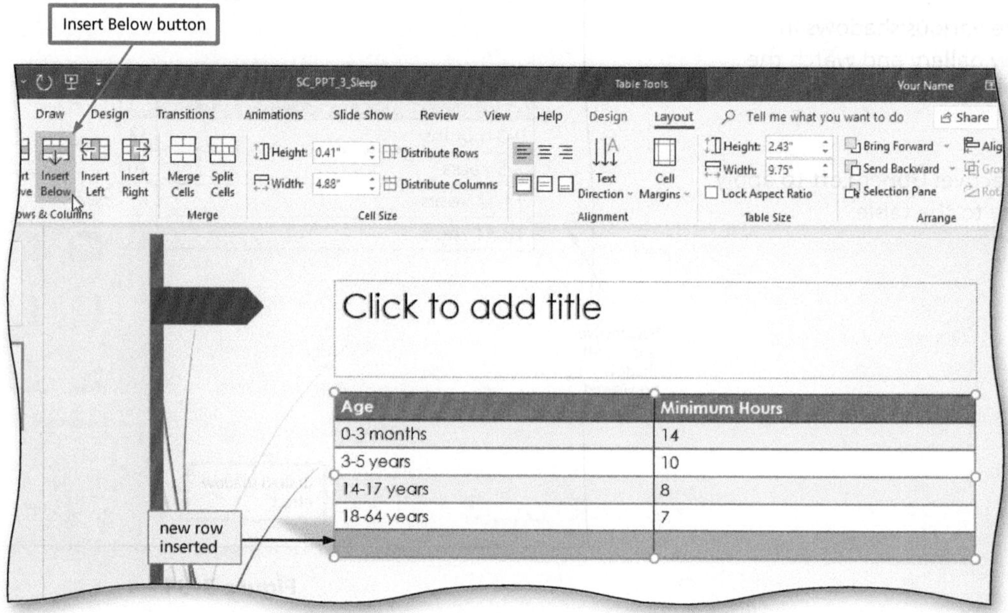

Figure 3–33

- Click the new cell in the Age column and then type **65+** in the cell.
- Type **7** in the new Minimum Hours column cell (Figure 3–34).

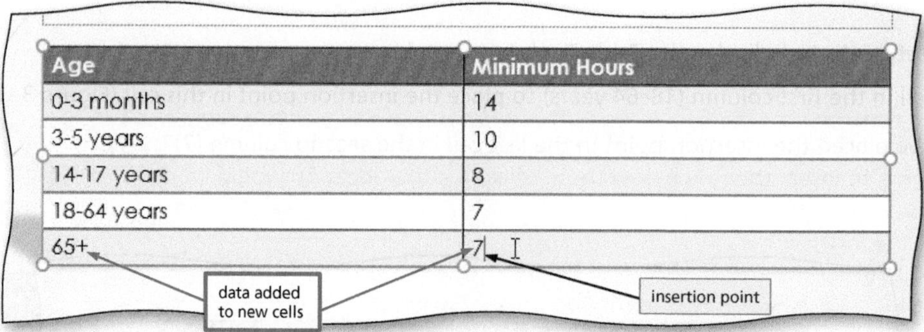

Figure 3–34

To Insert a Table Column

You add a column in a similar manner that you added a row to the table. The following steps insert a column in the table. ***Why?*** *The right table column lists the minimum hours people should sleep each night. A third column can list the maximum recommended hours.*

1

- With the insertion point still in the lower-right cell (7), click the Insert Right button (Table Tools Layout tab | Rows & Columns group) to insert a column to the right of the Minimum Hours column (Figure 3–35).

Q&A Could I have placed the insertion anywhere in the Hours column?
Yes. You are going to insert the row to the right of these cells, so any location in the column would work.

Can I insert a column anywhere in the table?
Yes. You can insert the column to the left or the right of any cell where the insertion point is positioned.

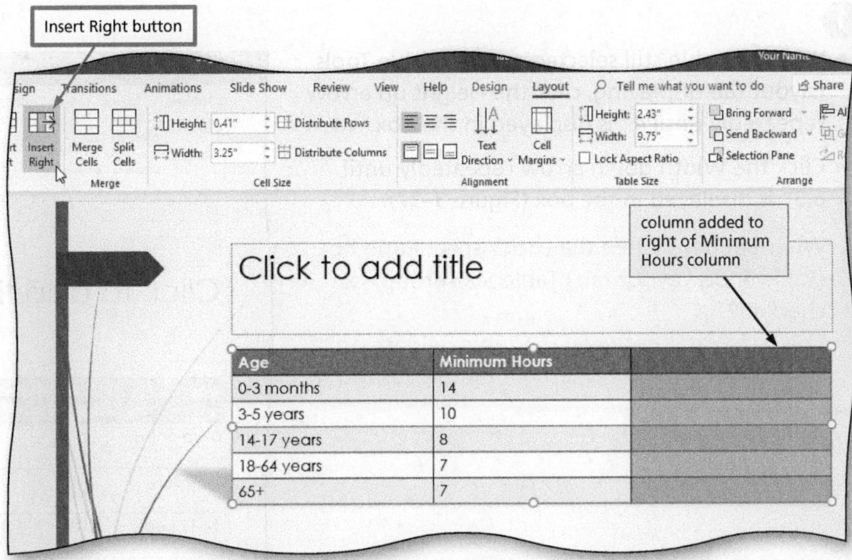

Figure 3–35

2

- Click the first cell in the new column and then type **`Maximum Hours`** as the new column heading. Advance the insertion point to the next cell in this column.
- Type **`17`** and then advance the insertion point to the next cell in this column.
- Type **`13`** and then advance the insertion point to the next cell in this column.
- Type **`10`** and then advance the insertion point to the next cell in this column.
- Type **`9`** and then advance the insertion point to the next cell in this column.
- Type **`8`** as the cell content (Figure 3–36).

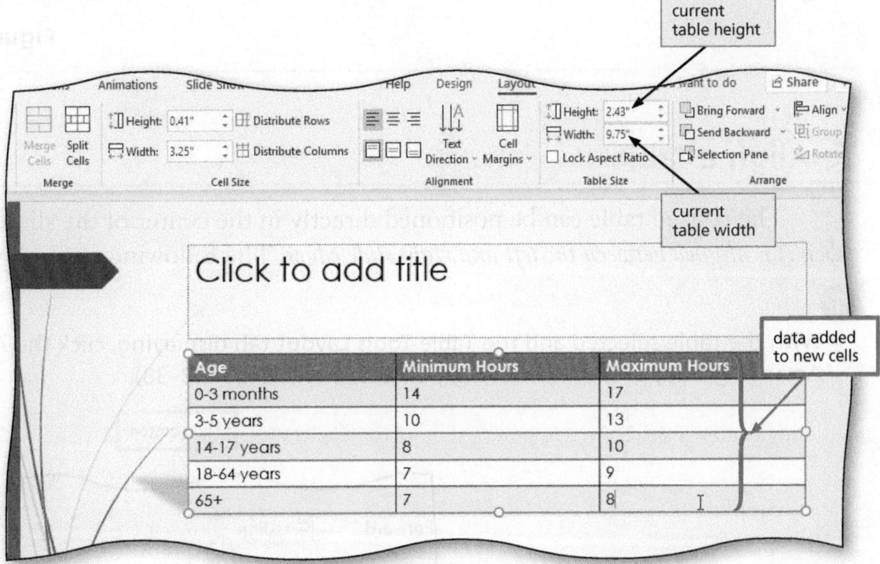

Figure 3–36

To Resize a Table

You resize a table the same way you resize a chart, a SmartArt graphic, or any other graphical object. The following steps resize the table on Slide 2. ***Why?*** *Slide 2 has much white space below the chart. If you resize the table to fill this white space, it will be more readable.*

- With the table still selected and the Table Tools Layout tab displaying, click the Height up arrow repeatedly until 4" is displayed in the box.
- Click the Width down arrow repeatedly until 6.5" is displayed in the box (Figure 3–37).

Q&A What happens when the Lock Aspect Ratio box (Table Tools Layout tab | Table Size group) is checked?
The same ratio between the table height and width is maintained when the table is resized.

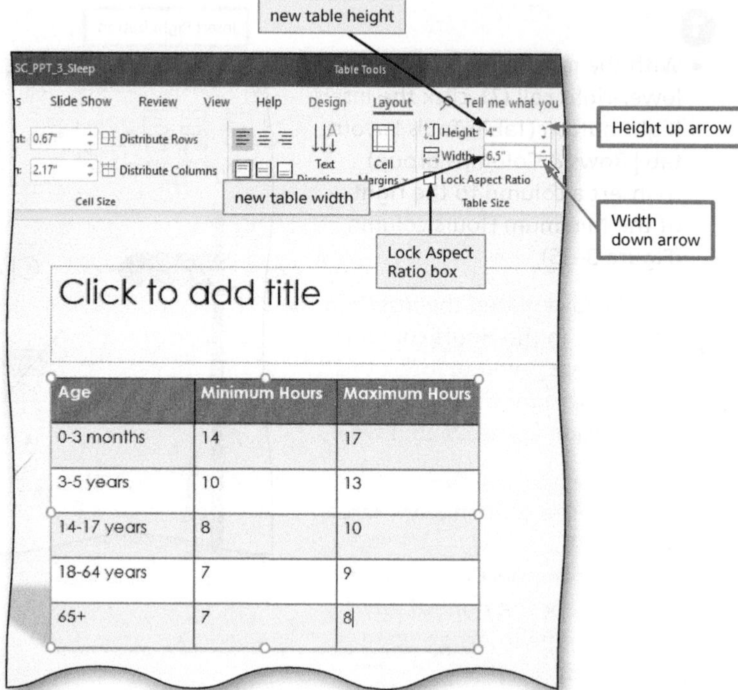

Figure 3–37

To Align a Table

The resized table can be positioned directly in the center of the slide. *Why? Your slide content looks balanced when it is aligned between the left and right slide edges.* The following steps align the table.

- With the table selected and the Table Tools Layout tab displaying, click the Align button (Table Tools Layout tab | Arrange group) to display the Align Objects menu (Figure 3–38).

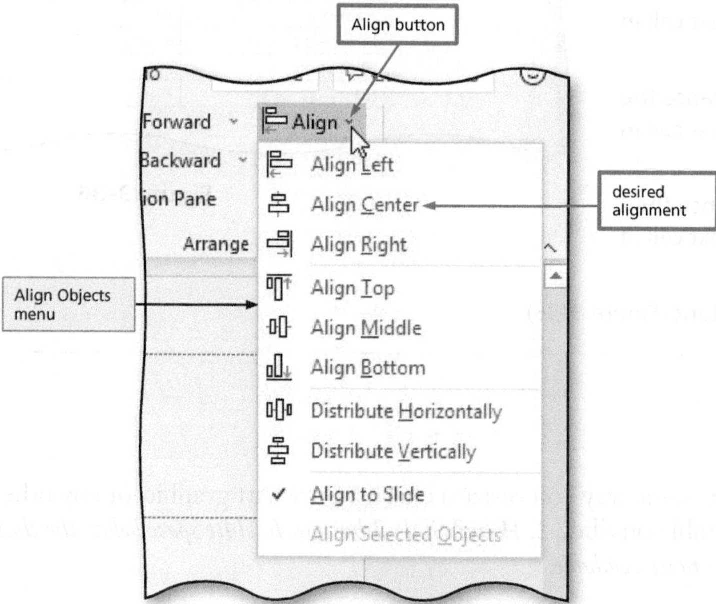

Figure 3–38

2
- Click Align Center on the Align Objects menu to position the table in the center of the slide (Figure 3–39).

Q&A Can I use the smart guides to align the table?
Yes.

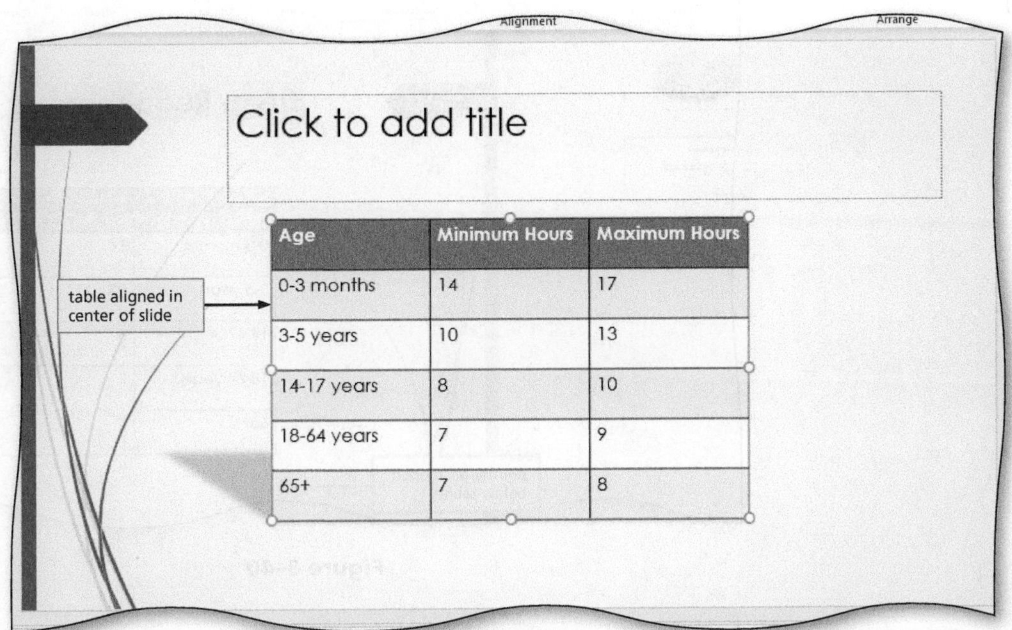

Figure 3–39

To Add a Slide Title

The slide needs a title to inform your audience about the table content. The following steps add a title to Slide 2.

1. With Slide 2 displaying, type **`Sleep Requirements`** in the title text placeholder.
2. Change the title text font to Rockwell.

Inserting and Formatting a Text Box

A text box can contain information that is separate from the title or content placeholders. You can place this slide element anywhere on the slide and format the letters using any style and effect. You also can change the text box shape by moving the sizing handles.

To Insert a Text Box and Format Text

The following steps insert a text box and add text. ***Why?*** *You want to reference the source of the table data.*

- Display the Insert tab, click the Text Box button (Insert tab | Text group), and then position the pointer below the table (Figure 3–40).

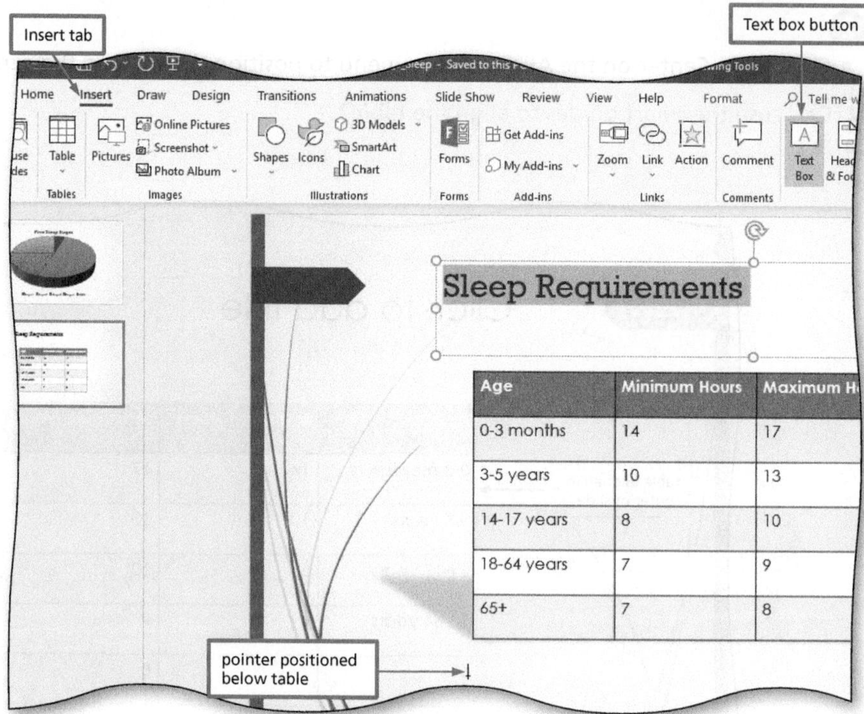

Figure 3–40

- Click below the table to insert the text box.
- Type **Source: National Sleep Foundation** in the text box (Figure 3–41).

Figure 3–41

To Format Text Box Characters

The following steps format the text box characters to coordinate the font with the title text font.

1. Select the text in the text box and then increase the font size to 20 point and change the font to Rockwell.
2. Use the smart guides to align the text box, as shown in Figure 3–42.

   Q&A Can I change the shape of the text box?
   Yes. Drag the sizing handles to the desired dimensions.

3. Click outside the text box to deselect this object.

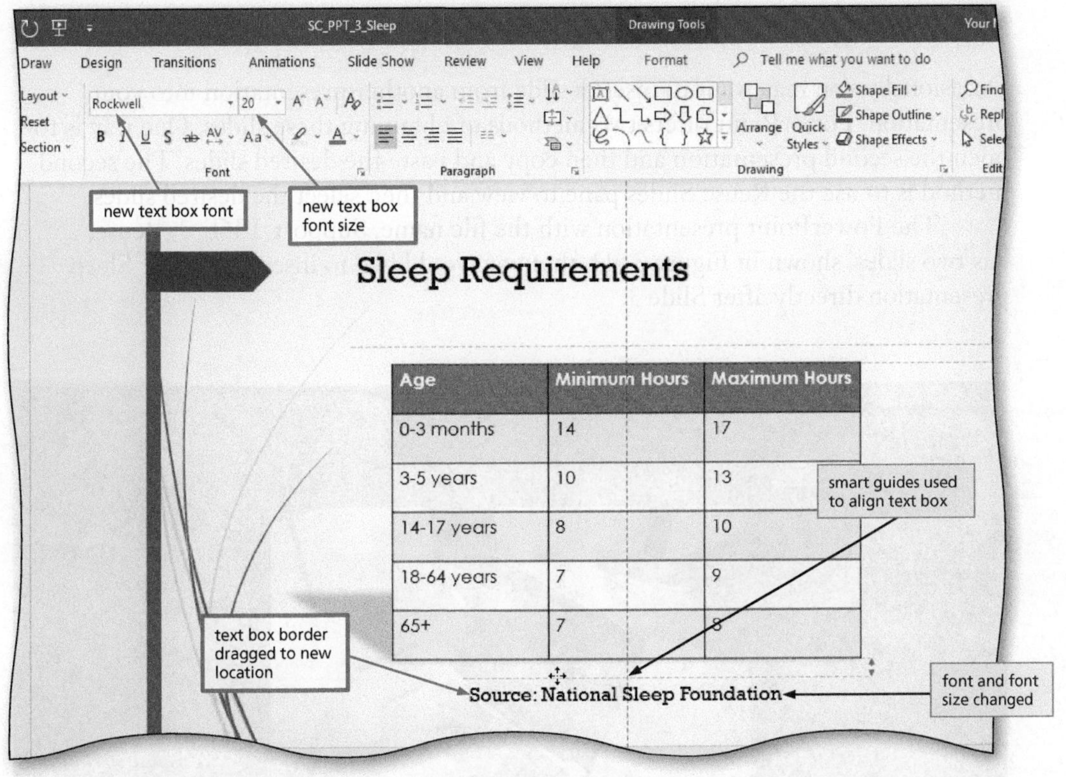

Figure 3–42

To Apply a Preset Shape Effect

Once you have inserted a text box, you can format it in a variety of ways to draw attention to slide content. You can, for example, add a fill to change the inside color of the text box. A **fill** is a color, pattern, texture, picture, or gradient applied to the interior of a shape or slide background. You also can combine multiple individual effects to create a custom design. To apply a preset shape effect to the text box, you would perform the following steps.

1. Select the text box.
2. Display the Drawing Tools Format tab and then click the Shape Effects button (Drawing Tools Format tab | Shape Styles group) to display the Shape Effects menu.
3. Select the desired effect (Shadow, Reflection, Glow, Soft Edges, Bevel, or 3-D Rotation).

To Change Text Box Defaults

You can set the formatting of the text box you inserted as the default for all other text boxes you insert into the presentation so that the text boxes have a consistent look. To change the text box defaults, you would perform the following steps.

1. Right-click the text box outline to display the shortcut menu.
2. Click 'Set as Default Text Box' on the shortcut menu.

Break Point: If you wish to take a break, this is a good place to do so. Be sure the Sleep file is saved and then you can exit PowerPoint. To resume later, start PowerPoint, open the file called SC_PPT_3_Sleep, and continue following the steps from this location forward.

Inserting and Moving Slides

Occasionally you may want to insert a slide from another presentation into your presentation. PowerPoint offers two methods of obtaining these slides. One way is to open the second presentation and then copy and paste the desired slides. The second method is to use the Reuse Slides pane to view and then select the desired slides.

The PowerPoint presentation with the file name, Support_PPT_3_Reuse, has two slides, shown in Figure 3–43, that you would like to insert into your Sleep presentation directly after Slide 3.

iStock.com/relif

Figure 3–43a (Insert and Use as Title Slide)

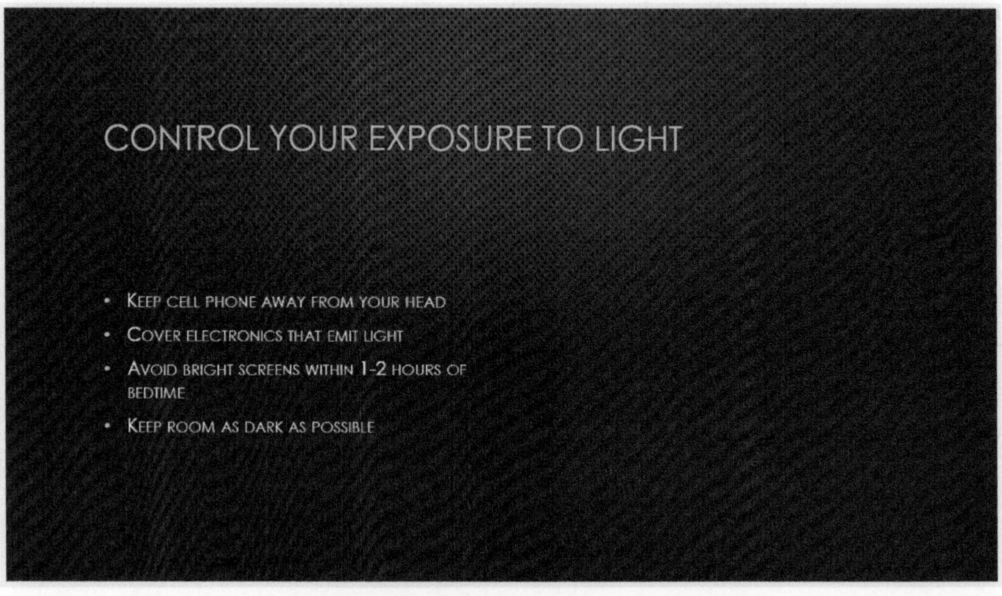

Figure 3–43b (Insert and Move to Slide 2)

To Reuse Slides from an Existing Presentation

PowerPoint converts inserted slides to the theme and styles of the current presentation, so the inserted slides will inherit the styles of the current Wisp theme. The Support_PPT_3_Reuse.pptx presentation is in your Data Files. The following steps add these two slides to your presentation and specify that you want to change the design to the Wisp formatting. ***Why?*** *One slide has a picture you can change, and the second has useful information about providing a good sleeping environment.*

1

- If necessary, display the Home tab and then click the New Slide arrow (Home tab | Slides group) to display the Wisp layout gallery (Figure 3–44).

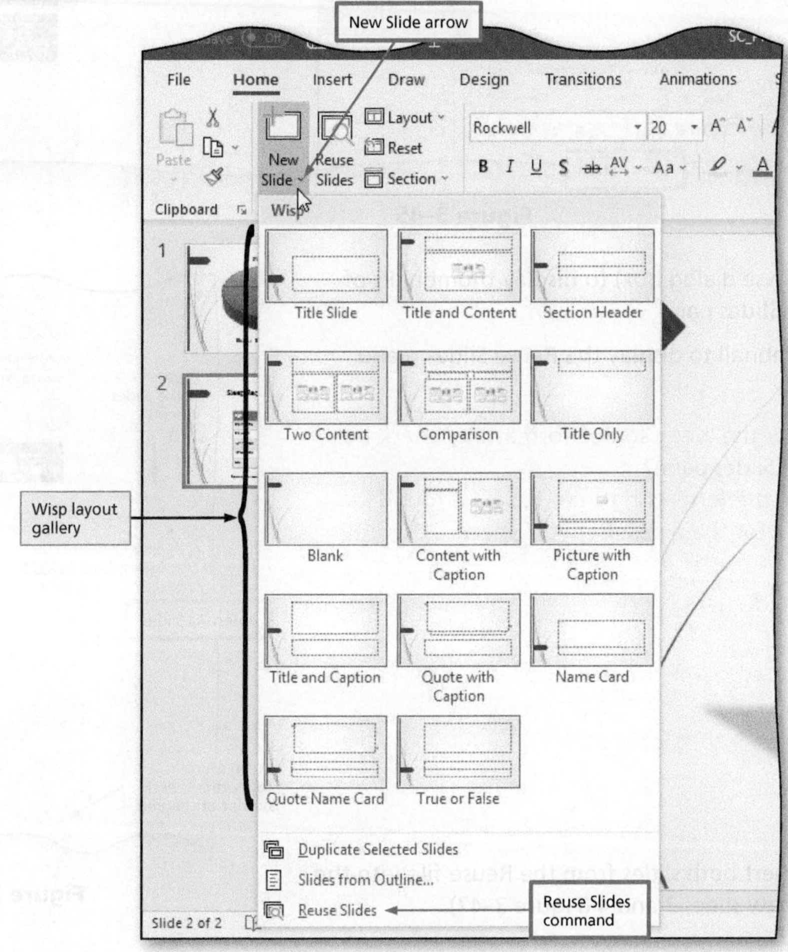

Figure 3–44

2

- Click Reuse Slides in the Wisp layout gallery to display the Reuse Slides pane.
- Click the Browse button (Reuse Slides pane) to display the Browse dialog box.
- If necessary, navigate to the location of your Data Files and then click Support_PPT_3_Reuse.pptx to select the file (Figure 3–45).

Q&A Could I have clicked the 'Open a PowerPoint File' link to display the Browse dialog box?
Yes. Either method will display the dialog box.

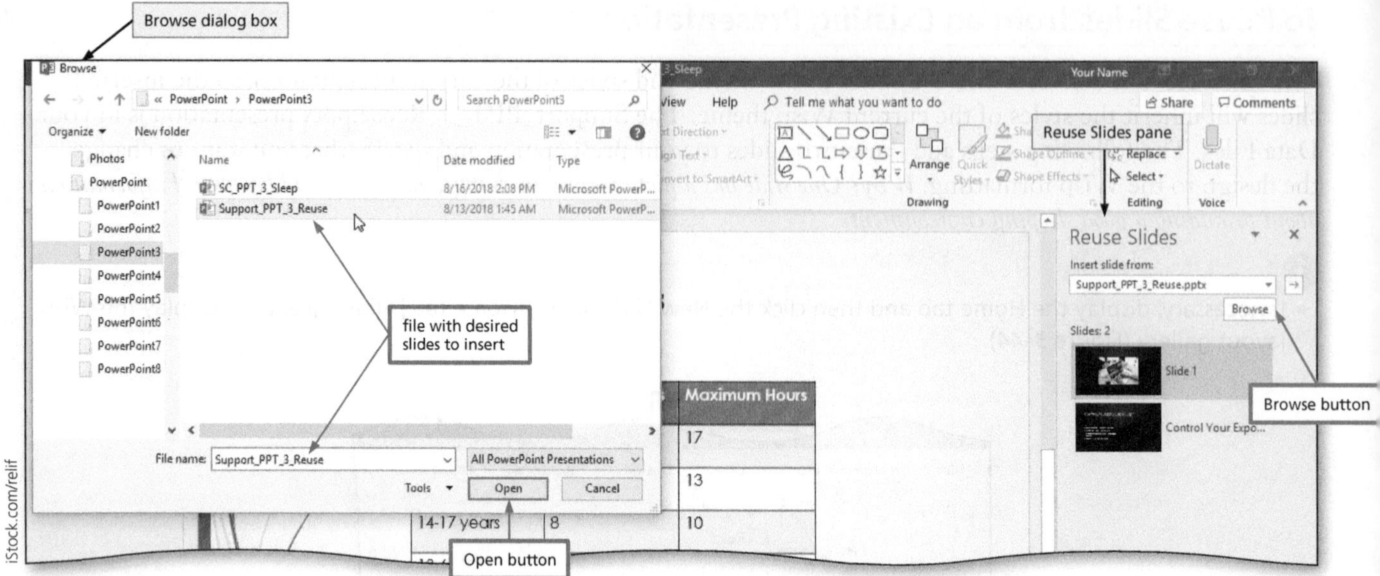

Figure 3–45

3

- Click the Open button (Browse dialog box) to display thumbnails of the two slides in the Reuse Slides pane.
- Right-click either slide thumbnail to display the Reuse Slides menu (Figure 3–46).

Q&A What would happen if I click the 'Keep source formatting' check box at the bottom of the Reuse Slides pane?

PowerPoint would preserve the formatting characteristics found in the Reuse file's Mesh theme for the slides that you insert.

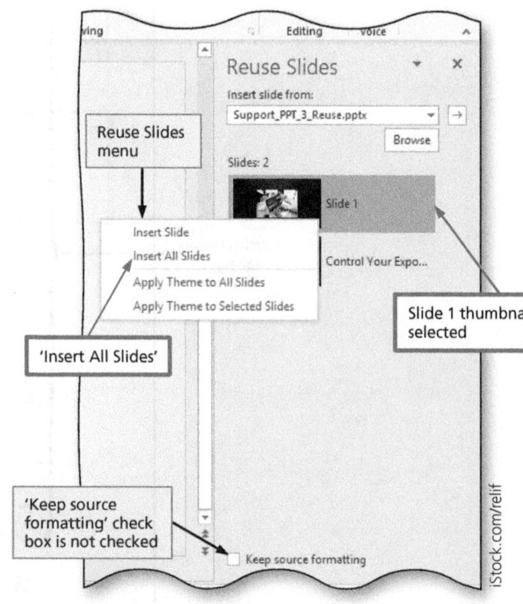

Figure 3–46

4

- Click 'Insert All Slides' to insert both slides from the Reuse file into the Sleep presentation as the new slides 3 and 4 (Figure 3–47).

Q&A Can I insert only one slide in the Insert file?

Yes. Click the thumbnail of the slide you wish to insert and then click 'Insert Slide.'

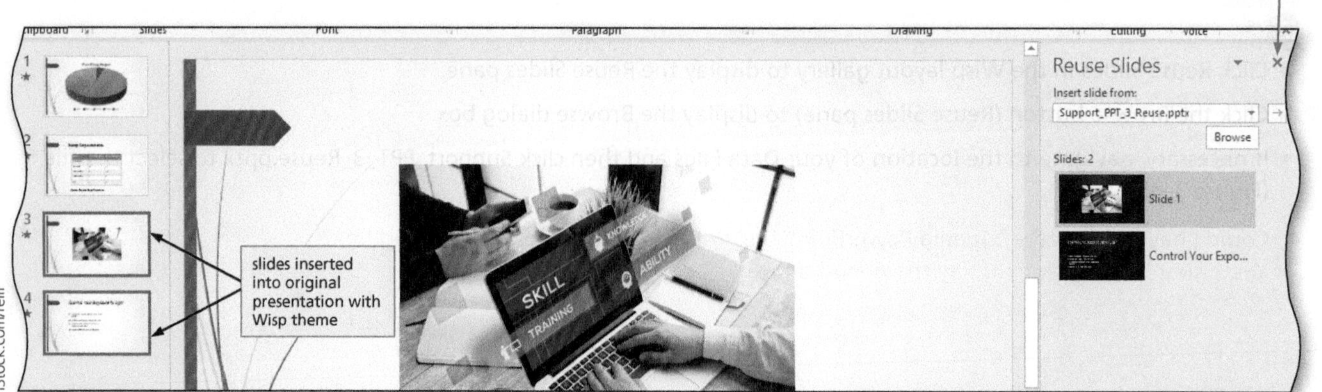

Figure 3–47

5

- Click the Close button in the Reuse Slides pane so that it no longer is displayed.

To Move a Slide in Slide Sorter View

Changing slide order is an easy process in either Slide view or Slide Sorter view. As you learned in Module 1, the drag-and-drop method allows you to click a thumbnail and drag it to a new location, and the remaining thumbnails realign to show the new sequence. You want the new slides you inserted into the Sleep file to display at the beginning of the presentation. ***Why?*** *The first slide would be an effective title slide, and the second slide presents useful information that your audience should keep in mind throughout the remainder of the presentation.* The following steps move the inserted slides to the beginning of the presentation.

1

- Click the Slide Sorter view button the right slide of the status bar to display the presentation in Slide Sorter view (Figure 3–48).

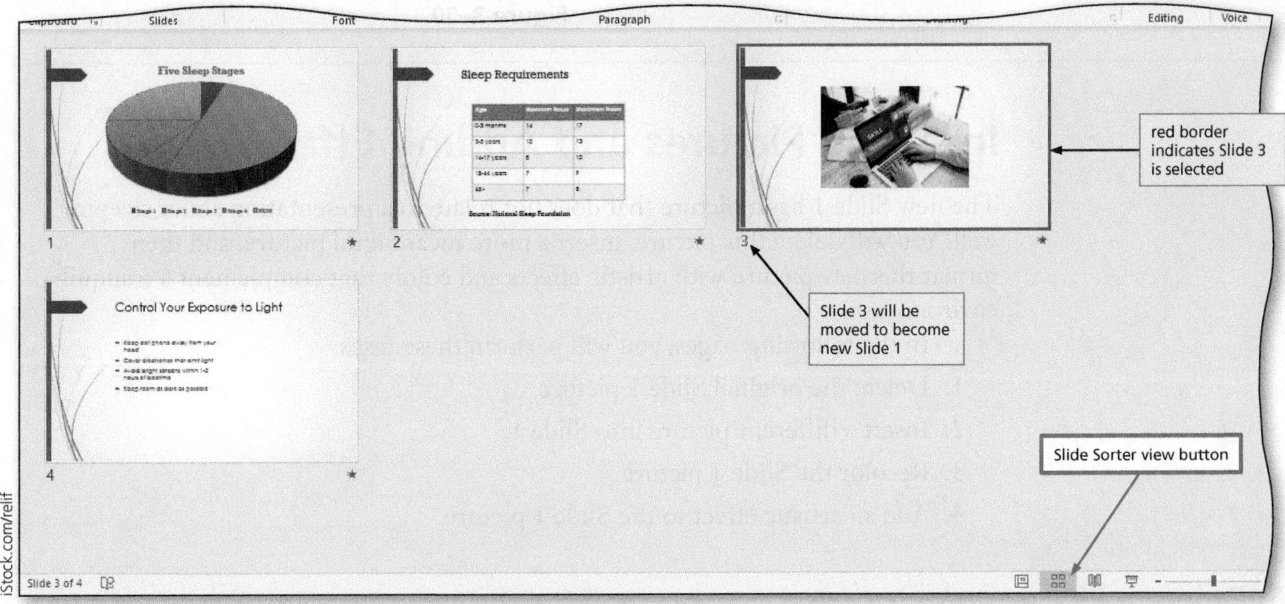

Figure 3–48

2

- Click the Slide 3 thumbnail to select it and then drag it to the left of the current Slide 1, as shown in Figure 3–48, so that it becomes the new Slide 1 (Figure 3–49).

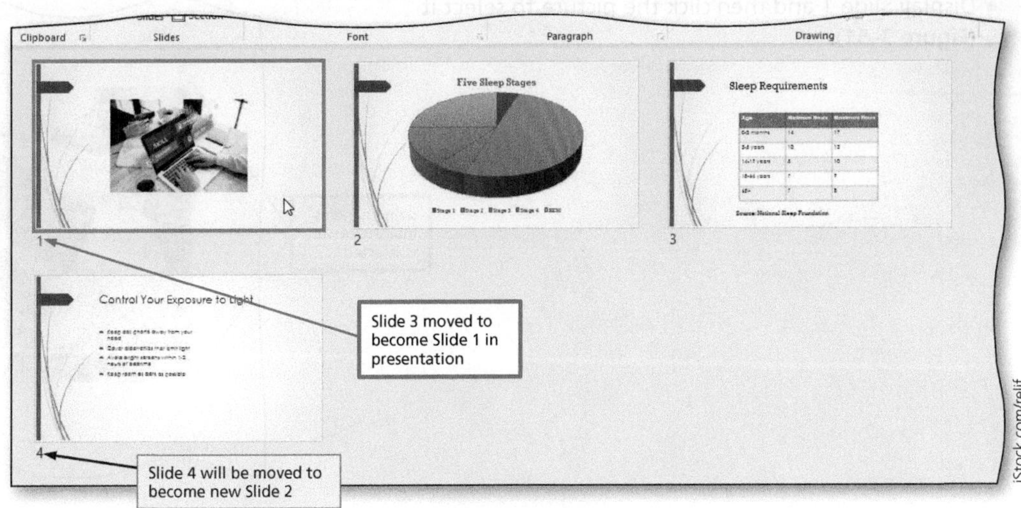

Figure 3–49

- Click the Slide 4 thumbnail and then drag it to the right of the new Slide 1 so that it becomes the new Slide 2 (Figure 3–50).

- Click the Normal view button to display the presentation in Normal view.

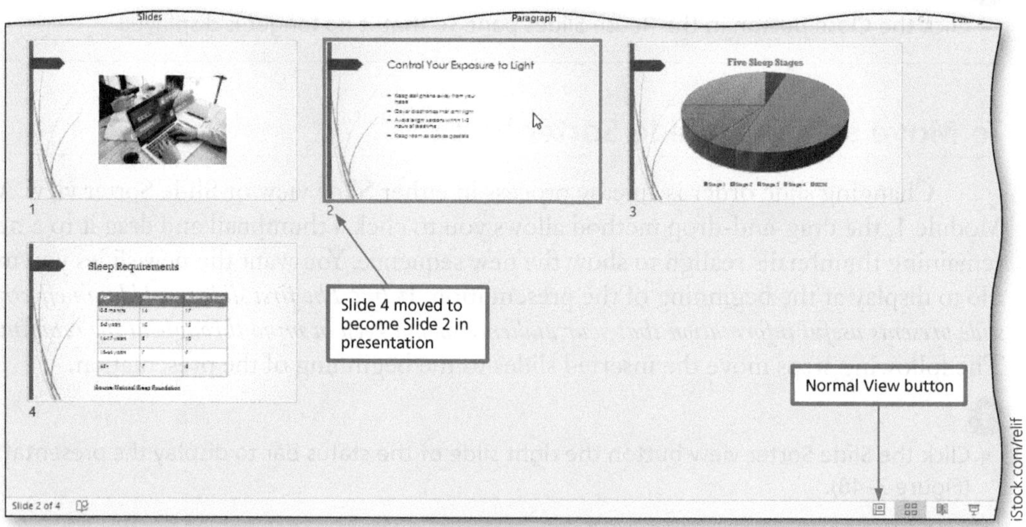

Figure 3–50

Inserting Pictures and Adding Effects

The new Slide 1 has a picture that does not relate to a presentation about sleeping well. You will delete this picture, insert a more meaningful picture, and then format this new picture with artistic effects and colors that complement a tranquil environment.

In the following pages, you will perform these tasks:

1. Delete the original Slide 1 picture.
2. Insert a different picture into Slide 1.
3. Recolor the Slide 1 picture.
4. Add an artistic effect to the Slide 1 picture.

To Delete a Picture

- Display Slide 1 and then click the picture to select it (Figure 3–51).

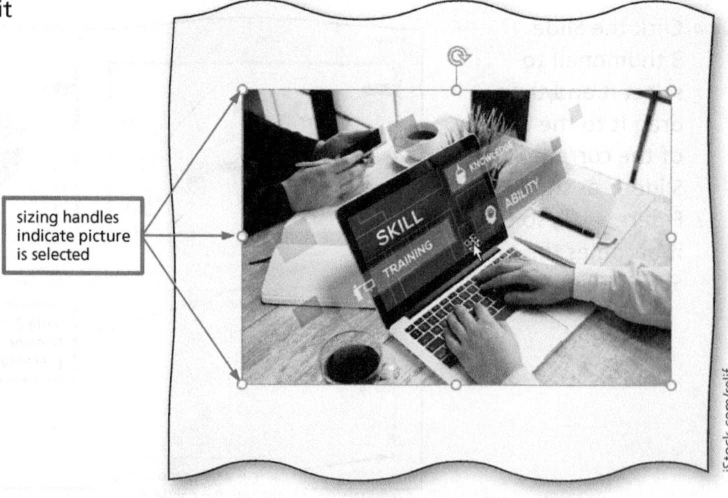

Figure 3–51

2

- Press DELETE to delete the picture.

Other Ways

1. Select picture, click Cut button (Home tab | Clipboard group)
2. Right-click picture, click Cut on shortcut menu
3. Select picture, press BACKSPACE

To Insert and Resize a Picture into a Slide without Content Placeholders

The next step in developing the title slide is to insert a different picture. The slide layout is Blank and does not have a content placeholder, so the picture will display in the center of the slide when you insert it. The picture is available in the Data Files. The following steps insert a picture into Slide 1.

1 With Slide 1 displaying, click Insert on the ribbon to display the Insert tab and then click the Pictures button (Insert tab | Images group) to display the Insert Picture dialog box.

2 If necessary, navigate to the picture location and then click Support_PPT_3_Bed.jpg to select the file.

3 Click the Insert button (Insert Picture dialog box) to insert the picture into Slide 1. Close the Design Ideas pane if it opens.

4 Resize the picture to an approximate height of 7" and width of 11.23". Use the smart guides to move the picture to the center of the slide, as shown in Figure 3–52.

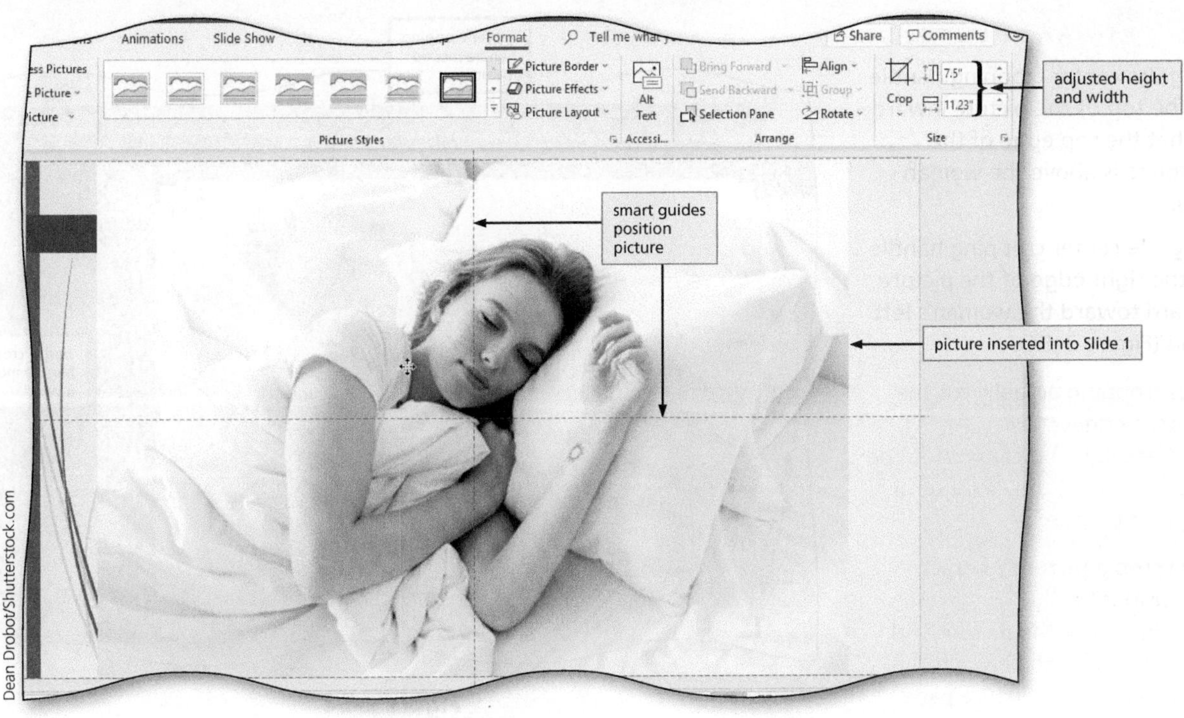

Figure 3–52

To Crop a Picture

You can remove the unnecessary elements of the picture and crop it. ***Why?*** *The picture contains much white linen, and you want to focus on the person sleeping.* When you crop a picture, you trim the vertical or horizontal sides so that the most important area of the picture is displayed. Any picture file type except animated GIF can be cropped. The following steps crop the title slide picture.

1

- With the picture selected and the Picture Tools Format tab displaying, click the Crop button (Picture Tools Format tab | Size group) to display the cropping handles on the picture.
- Position the pointer over the center cropping handle on the top of the picture (Figure 3–53).

Q&A Why did my pointer change shape?
The pointer changed to indicate you are about to crop a picture.

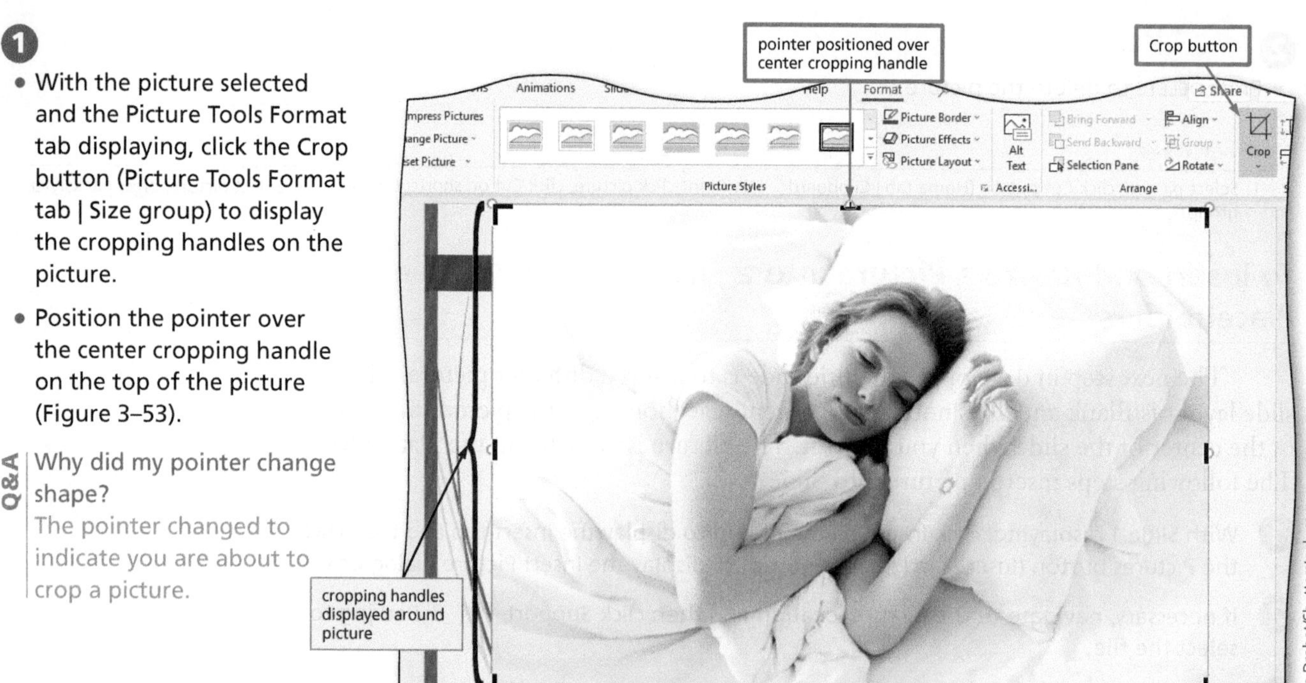

Figure 3–53

2

- Drag the center cropping handle on the top of the picture inward so that the top edge of the marquee is above the woman's head.
- Drag the center cropping handle on the right edge of the picture inward toward the woman's left hand (Figure 3–54).

Q&A Does cropping actually cut the picture's edges?
No. Although you cannot see the cropped edges, they exist until you save the file.

Can I crop a picture to exact dimensions?
Yes. Right-click the picture and then click Format Picture to open the Format Picture pane. Click the Picture icon, then Crop. Under Picture position, enter the measurements in the Width and Height boxes.

center cropping handle moved inward

center cropping handle moved inward

Dean Drobot/Shutterstock.com

Figure 3–54

3

- Click the Crop button again to crop the edges (Figure 3–55).

Q&A Can I press ESC to crop the edges?
Yes.

Can I change the crop lines?
If you have not saved the file, you can undo your crops by clicking Undo on the Quick Access Toolbar, or clicking the Reset Picture button (Picture Tools Format tab | Adjust group), or pressing CTRL+Z. If you have saved the file, you cannot undo the crop.

Figure 3–55

Other Ways

1. Right-click picture, click Crop on Mini toolbar

To Crop a Picture to a Shape

In addition to cropping a picture, you can change the shape of a picture by cropping it to a specific shape. The picture's proportions are maintained, and it automatically is trimmed to fill the shape's geometry. To crop to a specific shape, you would perform the following steps.

1. Select the picture you want to crop.
2. Display the Picture Tools Format tab and then click the Crop arrow (Picture Tools Format tab | Size group) to display the Crop menu.
3. Point to 'Crop to Shape' and then click the desired shape in the Shape gallery.

BTW
Simultaneous Cropping on Two or Four Sides
To crop equally on two sides simultaneously, press CTRL while dragging the center cropping handle on either side inward. To crop all four sides equally, press CTRL while dragging a corner cropping handle inward.

Adjusting Picture Colors

PowerPoint allows you to adjust picture colors. The Color gallery has a wide variety of preset formatting combinations. The thumbnails in the gallery display the more common color saturation, color tone, and recolor adjustments. **Color saturation** changes the intensity of colors. High saturation produces vivid colors; low saturation produces gray tones. **Color tone** affects the coolness, called blue, or the warmness, called orange, of pictures. When a digital camera does not measure the tone correctly, a **color cast** occurs, and, as a result, one color dominates the picture. **Recolor** effects convert the picture into a wide variety of hues. The more common are **grayscale**, which changes a color picture into black, white, and shades of gray, and **sepia**, which changes picture colors into brown, gold, and yellow, reminiscent of a faded picture. You also can fine-tune the color adjustments by clicking the Picture Color Options and More Variations commands in the Color gallery.

To Color a Picture

The Wisp theme enhances the tranquil message of the sleep presentation. You may want to supplement this theme by adding an effect to the picture. ***Why?** An effect adds variety to the presentation and helps enhance ordinary pictures.* The following steps recolor the Slide 1 picture to soften the predominantly white bedding.

1

- With Slide 1 displaying and the bed picture selected, click the Color button (Picture Tools Format tab | Adjust group) to display the Color gallery (Figure 3–56).

Q&A Why are the gray borders surrounding the thumbnails in the Color Saturation, Color Tone, and Recolor areas in the gallery?
The gray borders show the color saturation, tone, and recolor settings currently in effect for the image on Slide 1.

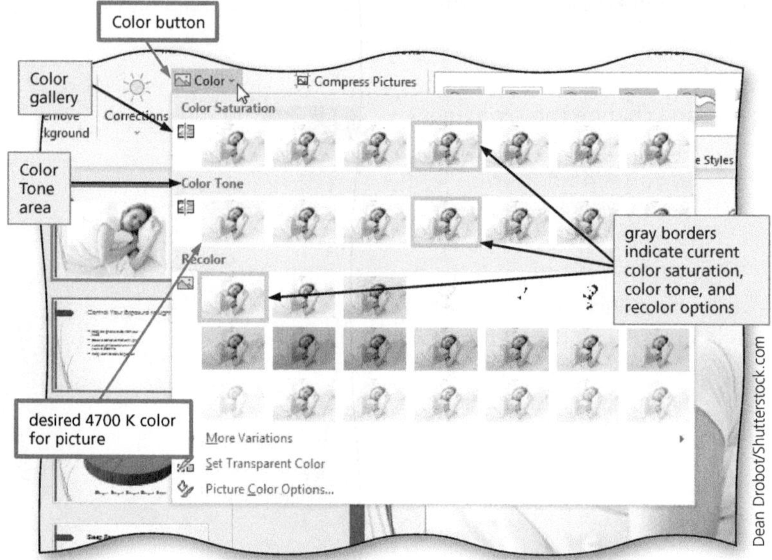

Figure 3–56

2

- Point to Temperature: 4700 K (first thumbnail in Color Tone row) to display a live preview of this adjustment on the picture (Figure 3–57).

 **Experiment**

- Point to various thumbnails in the Color Tone area and watch the colors change on the picture in Slide 1.

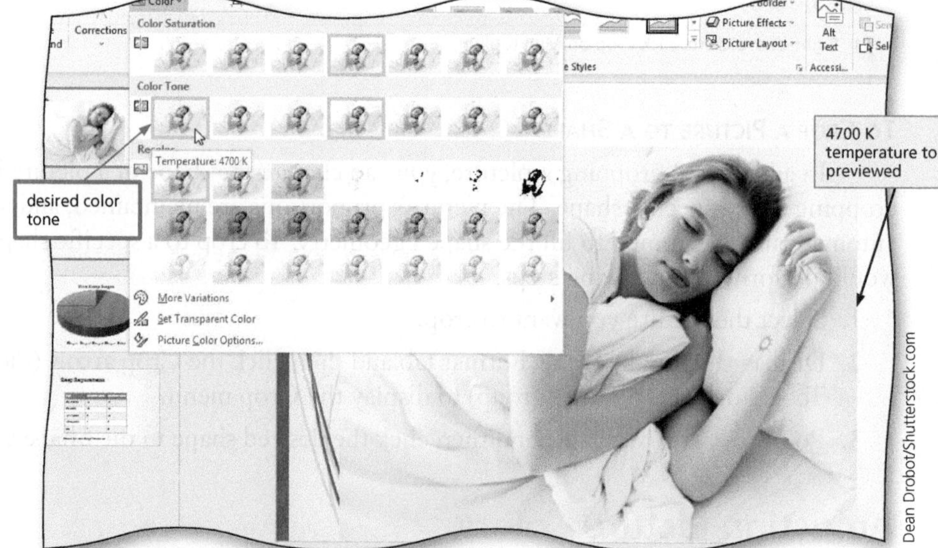

Figure 3–57

3

- Click Temperature: 4700 K to apply this saturation to the bed picture.

Q&A Could I have applied this recoloring to the picture if it had been a background instead of a file inserted into the slide?
No. Artistic effects and recoloring cannot be applied to backgrounds.

Other Ways

1. Click Format Picture on shortcut menu, click Picture icon, click Picture Color, use Temperature slider (Format Picture pane)

To Add an Artistic Effect to a Picture

Artists use a variety of techniques to create effects in their paintings. They can vary the amount of paint on their brushstroke, use fine bristles to add details, mix colors to increase or decrease intensity, and smooth their paints together to blend the colors. You, likewise, can add similar effects to your pictures using PowerPoint's built-in artistic effects. ***Why?*** *The completed Slide 1 will have both a picture and WordArt, so applying an artistic effect to the picture will provide a contrast between the two images.* The following steps add an artistic effect to the Slide 1 picture.

1

- With the bed picture still selected, click the Artistic Effects button (Picture Tools Format tab | Adjust group) to display the Artistic Effects gallery (Figure 3–58).

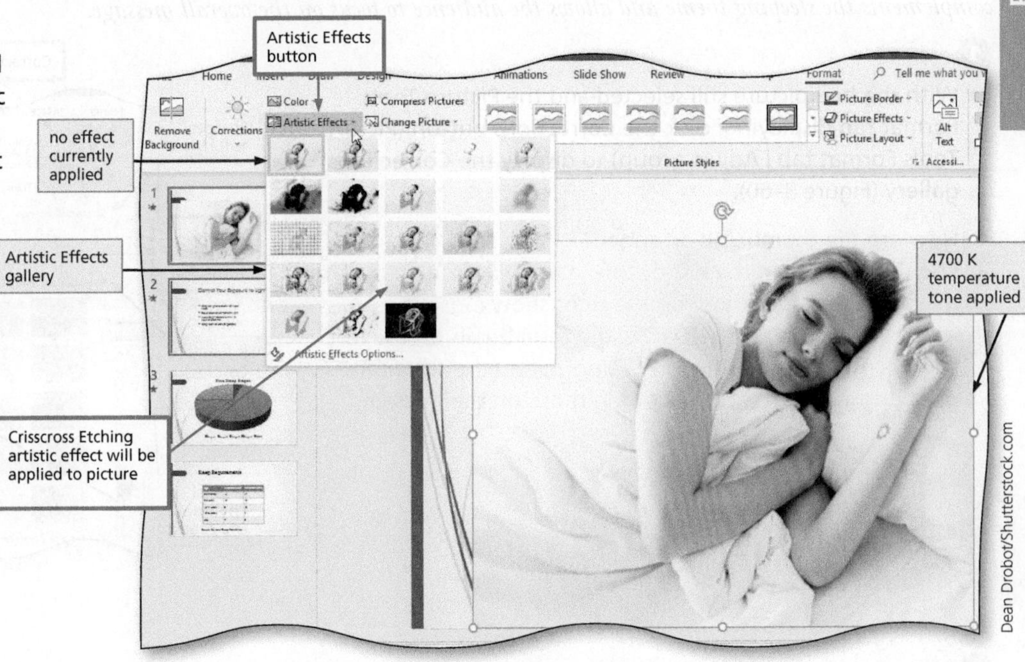

Figure 3–58

- Point to Crisscross Etching (third thumbnail in fourth row) to display a live preview of this effect on the picture (Figure 3–59).

Experiment

- Point to various artistic effects and watch the hues change on the picture in Slide 1.

- Click Crisscross Etching to apply this artistic effect to the picture.

Q&A Can I adjust a picture by recoloring and applying an artistic effect?

Yes. You can apply both a color and an effect. You may prefer at times to mix these adjustments to create a unique image.

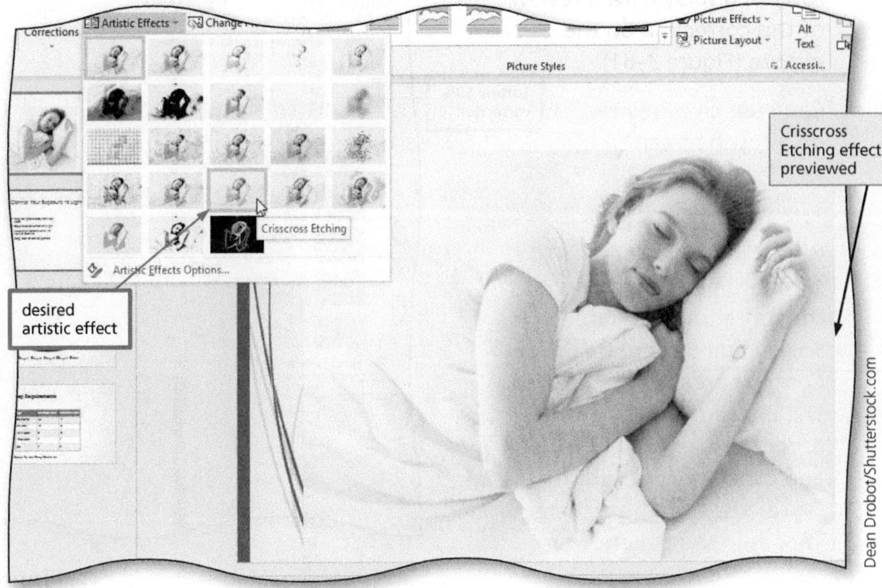

Figure 3–59

Other Ways

1. Click Format Picture on shortcut menu, click Effects icon, click Artistic Effects

To Change the Picture Softness

The Corrections tools allow you to change a picture's brightness, contrast, sharpness, and softness. A picture's color intensity can be modified by changing the brightness and contrast. **Brightness** determines the overall lightness or darkness of the entire image, whereas **contrast** is the difference between the darkest and lightest areas of the image. **Sharpness** determines the picture's clarity. These corrections are changed in predefined percentage increments. The following steps increase the picture's softness. ***Why?*** *The softness complements the sleeping theme and allows the audience to focus on the overall message.*

1

- With the bed picture still selected and the Picture Tools Format tab displaying, click the Corrections button (Picture Tools Format tab | Adjust group) to display the Corrections gallery (Figure 3–60).

Q&A How are the thumbnails arranged?
The thumbnails on the left of the Sharpen/Softness area show more softness, and those on the right show more sharpness. In the Brightness/Contrast area, the thumbnails on the left are less bright than those on the right, and the thumbnails on the top have less contrast than those on the bottom.

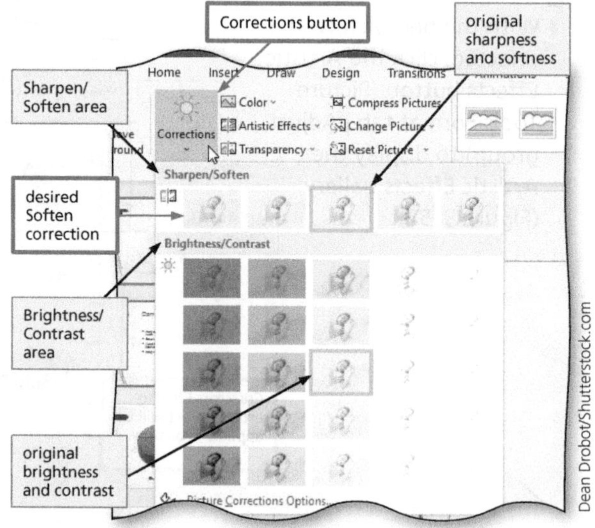

Figure 3–60

2

- Point to Soften: 50% (first thumbnail in Sharpen/Soften row) to display a live preview of this correction on the picture (Figure 3–61).

Q&A Can I use Live Preview on a touch screen?
Live Preview is not available on a touch screen.

Why is a gray border surrounding the pictures in the center of the Sharpen/ Soften and Brightness/ Contrast areas of the gallery?
The image currently has normal sharpness, brightness, and contrast (0%), which is represented by these center images in the gallery.

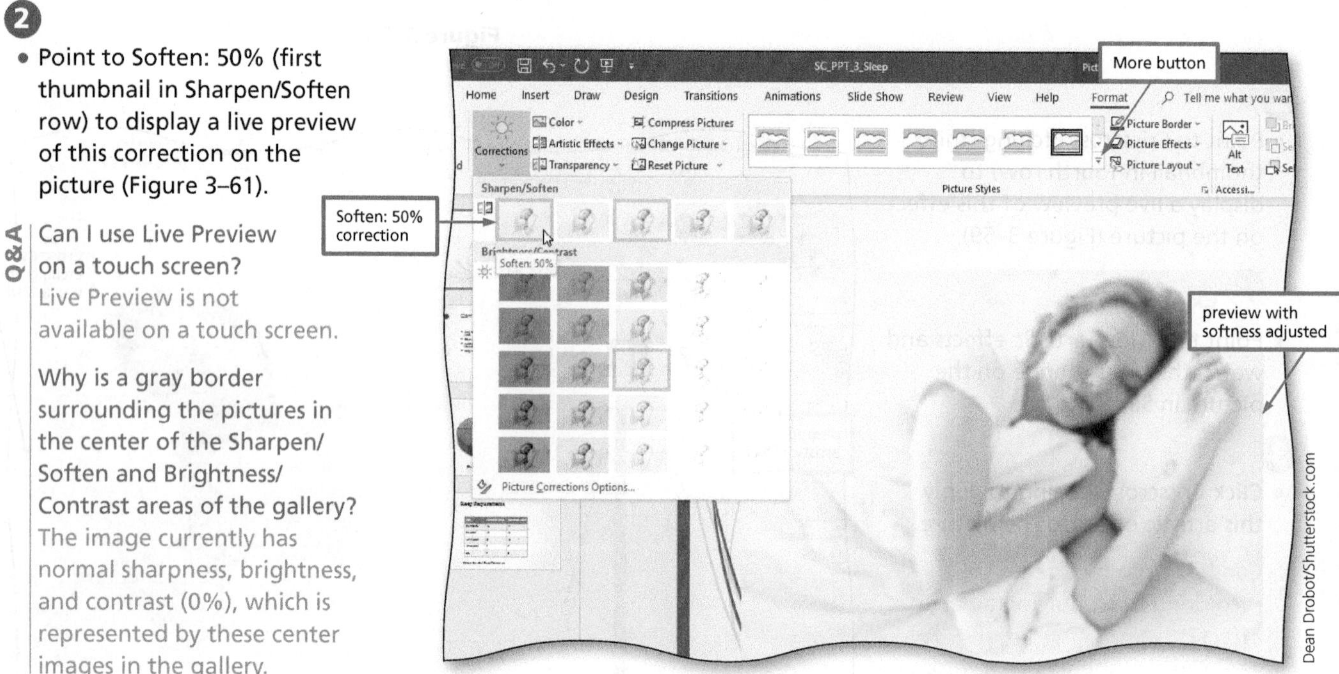

Figure 3–61

Experiment

- Point to various pictures in the Brightness/Contrast area and watch the brightness and contrast change on the picture in Slide 2.

3

- Click Soften: 50% to apply this correction to the bed picture.

Q&A

How can I remove all effects from the picture?
Click the Reset Picture button (Picture Tools Format tab | Adjust group).

Can I fine-tune any correction?
Yes. Click Picture Corrections Options and then move the slider for Sharpness, Brightness, or Contrast.

Other Ways

1. Click Picture Corrections Options (Corrections gallery), move Sharpness slider or enter number in box next to slider (Format Picture pane)

To Apply a Picture Style

A **style** is a named group of formatting characteristics. The picture on Slide 2 emphasizes the concept of sleep, and you can increase its visual appeal by applying a picture style. ***Why?*** *PowerPoint provides more than 25 picture styles that enable you easily to change a picture's look to a more visually appealing style, including a variety of shapes, angles, borders, and reflections.* You want to use a style that applies a shadow to the bed picture. The following steps apply a picture style to the Slide 1 picture.

1

- With the Slide 1 picture selected and the Picture Tools Format tab displaying, click the More button in the Picture Styles gallery (Picture Tools Format tab | Picture Styles group) (shown in Figure 3–61) to expand the gallery.
- Point to Bevel Perspective in the Picture Styles gallery (first style in last row) to display a live preview of that style applied to the picture in the document (Figure 3–62).

Experiment

- Point to various picture styles in the Picture Styles gallery and watch the style of the picture change in the document window.

2

- Click Bevel Perspective in the Picture Styles gallery to apply the style to the selected picture.

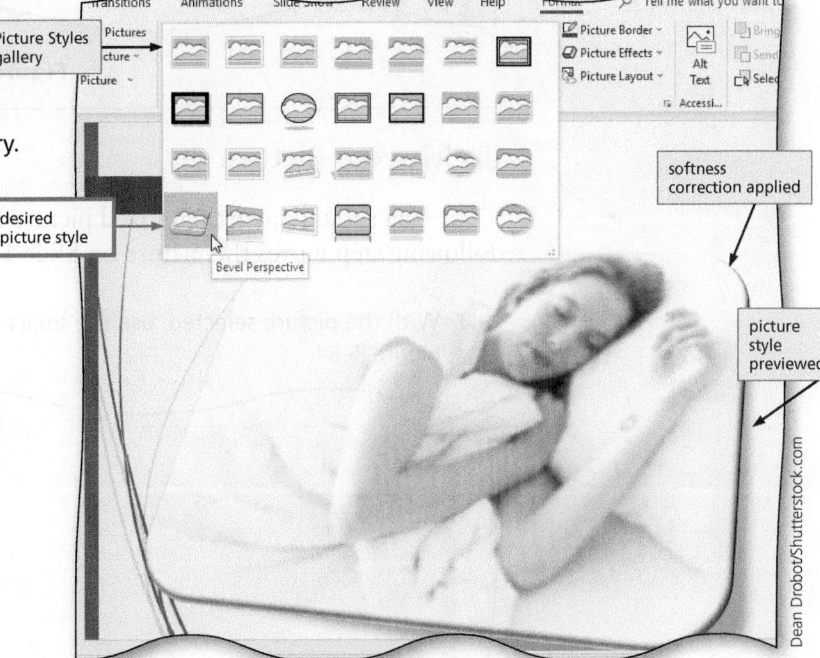

Figure 3–62

To Size a Picture

The formatted picture is too small for Slide 1, so you need to resize it. You can resize this slide element by dragging the sizing handles or by specifying exact measurements for the height and width. The following step resizes the picture by entering an exact measurement.

1 **With the picture selected and the Picture Tools Format tab displaying, click the Shape Height box down arrow until the Height measurement is 5.5" (Figure 3–63).**

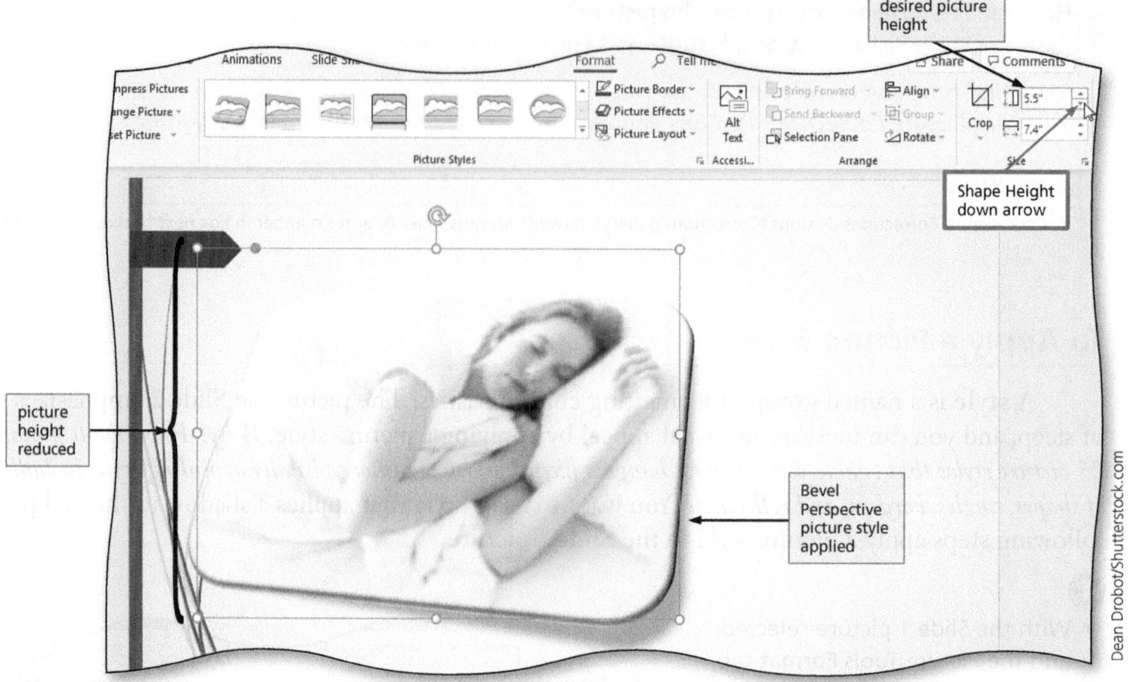

Figure 3–63

To Move a Picture

You should move the resized picture to allow space for a slide title. The following step moves the picture on Slide 1.

1 **With the picture selected, use the smart guides to position the picture as shown in Figure 3–64.**

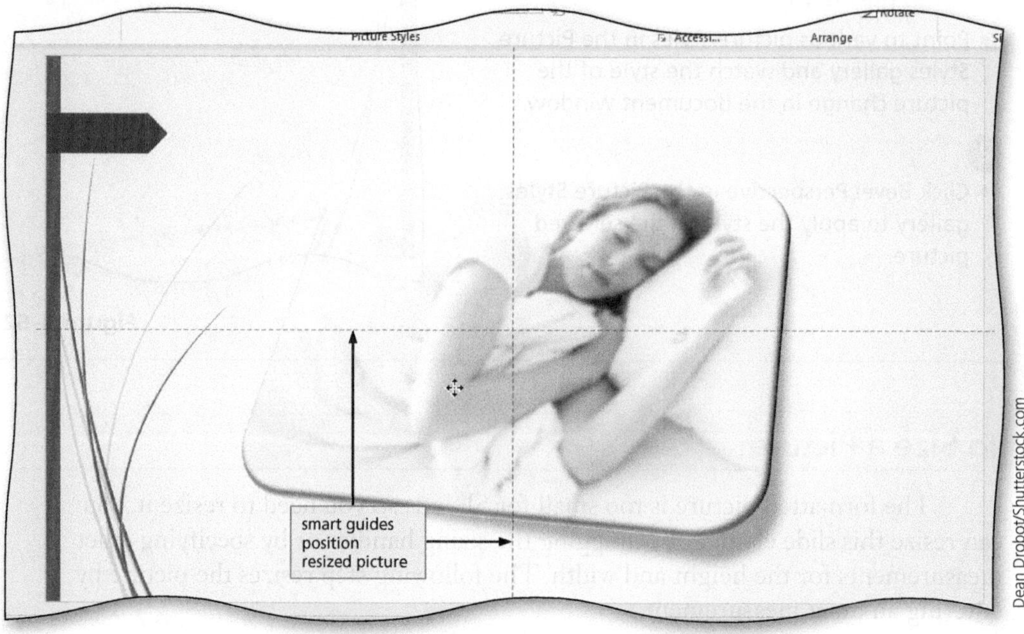

Figure 3–64

To Align Pictures

You should move the picture to the top of Slide 1 ***Why?*** *You want to add a slide title at the bottom of the slide, so you need to make room for this graphical element.* The following steps align the picture at the top of the slide.

1

- With the picture selected and the Picture Tools Format tab displaying, click the Align button (Picture Tools Format tab | Arrange group) to display the Align Objects menu (Figure 3–65).

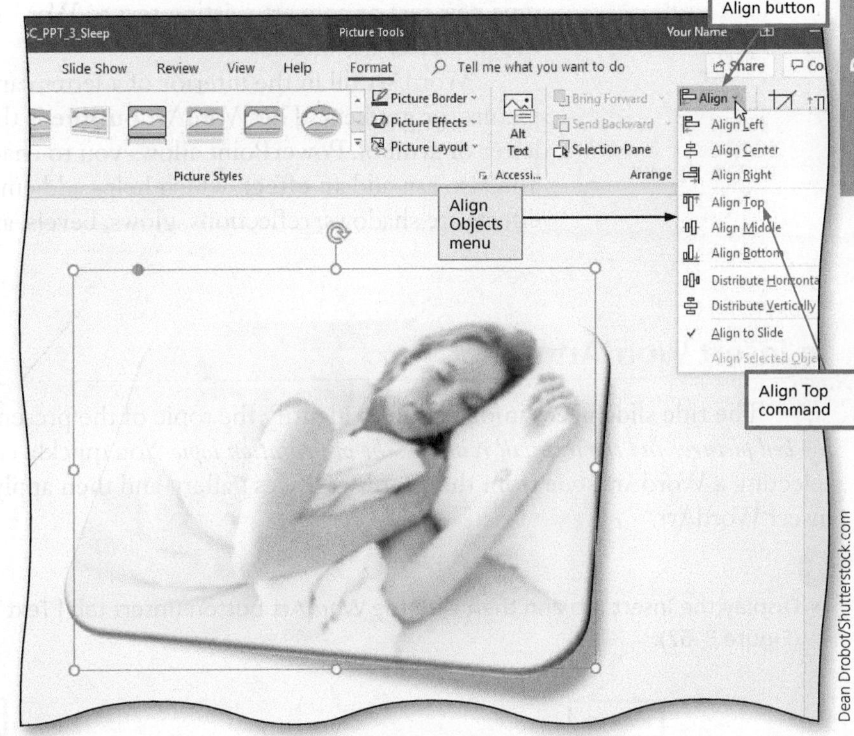

Figure 3–65

2

- Click Align Top to move the picture to the top edge of the slide (Figure 3–66).

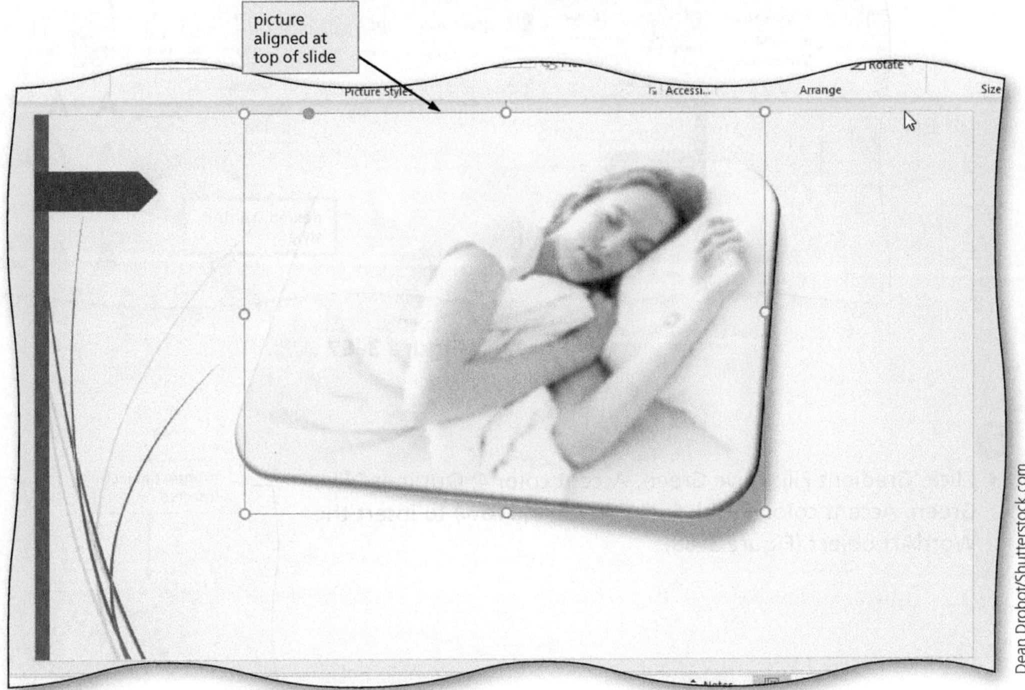

Figure 3–66

Creating and Formatting WordArt

One method of adding appealing visual elements to a presentation is by using **WordArt**, formatted decorative text. This feature is found in other Microsoft Office applications, including Word and Excel. This gallery of decorative effects allows you to type new text or convert existing text to WordArt. You then can add elements such as fills, outlines, and effects.

WordArt fill in the interior of a letter can consist of a solid color, texture, picture, or gradient. The WordArt **outline** is the exterior border surrounding each letter or symbol. PowerPoint allows you to change the outline color, weight, and style. You also can add an **effect**, which helps add emphasis or depth to the characters. Some effects are shadows, reflections, glows, bevels, and 3-D rotations.

To Insert WordArt

The title slide needs information to identify the topic of the presentation. ***Why?*** *Audience members will see the bed picture, and the text will reinforce the presentation topic.* You quickly can add a visual element to the slide by selecting a WordArt style from the WordArt Styles gallery and then applying it to some text. The following steps insert WordArt.

- Display the Insert tab and then click the WordArt button (Insert tab | Text group) to display the WordArt gallery (Figure 3–67).

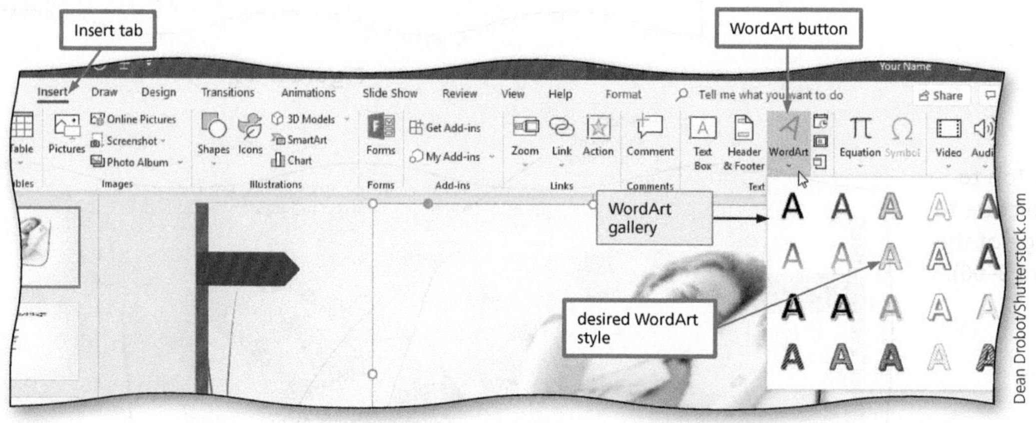

Figure 3–67

2

- Click 'Gradient Fill: Olive Green, Accent color 4; Outline: Olive Green, Accent color 4' (third style in second row) to insert the WordArt object (Figure 3–68).

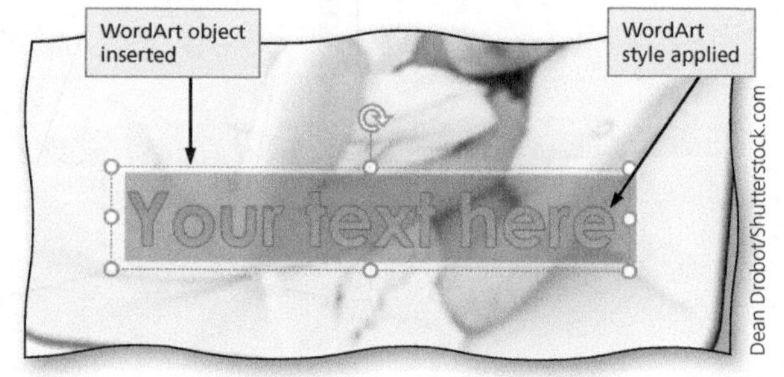

Figure 3–68

3

- Type **Sleep Well Tonight** in the object as the WordArt text (Figure 3–69).

Q&A Why did the Drawing Tools Format tab appear automatically in the ribbon?
It appears when you select text to which you could add a WordArt style or other effect.

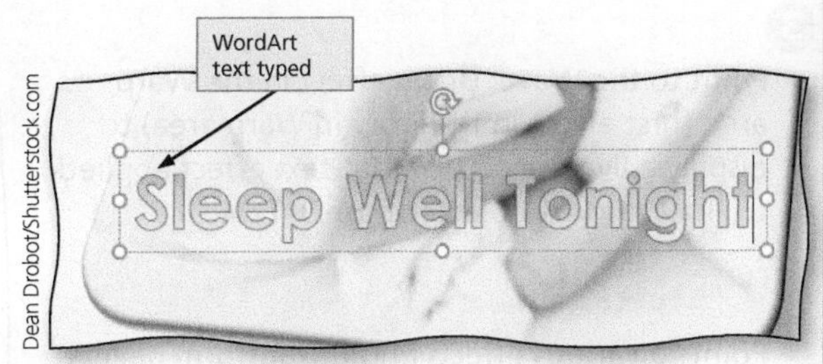

Figure 3–69

To Change the WordArt Shape

PowerPoint provides a variety of graphical shapes that add interest to WordArt text. The following steps change the Transform effect of the WordArt shape to Wave: Down. ***Why?*** *The text provides the presentation's subject, and you want to emphasize the tranquil topic further by changing the WordArt shape.*

1

- With the WordArt object still selected, click the Text Effects button (Drawing Tools Format tab | WordArt Styles group) to display the Text Effects menu (Figure 3–70).

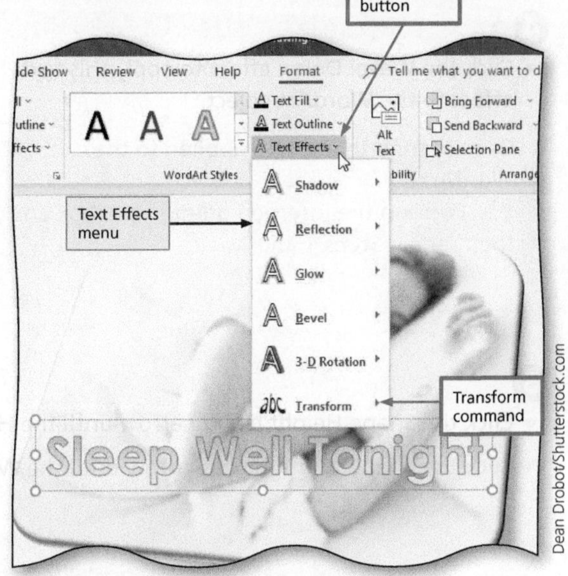

Figure 3–70

2

- Point to Transform in the Text Effects menu to display the WordArt Transform gallery (Figure 3–71).

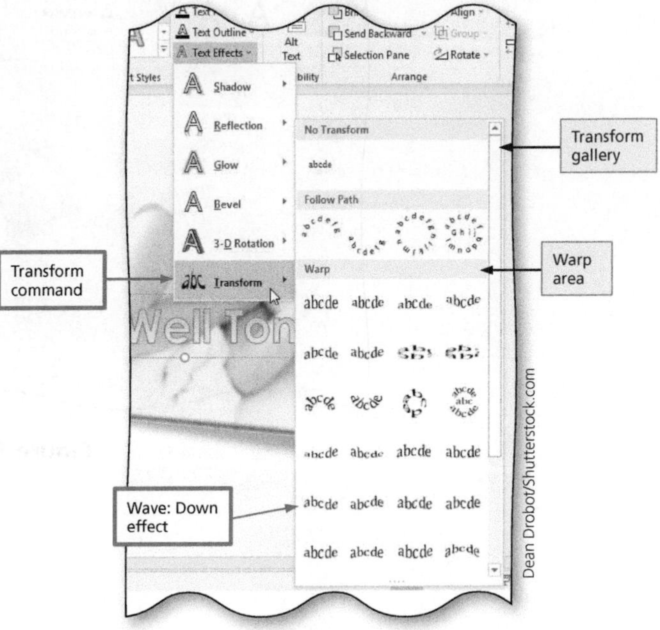

Figure 3–71

- Point to the Wave: Down effect in the Warp area (first effect in fifth row in Warp area) to display a live preview of that text effect applied to the WordArt object (Figure 3–72).

Experiment

- Point to various effects in the Transform gallery and watch the format of the text and borders change.

Q&A How can I see the preview of a Transform effect if the gallery overlays the WordArt letters?
Move the WordArt box to the left or right side of the slide and then repeat Steps 1 and 2.

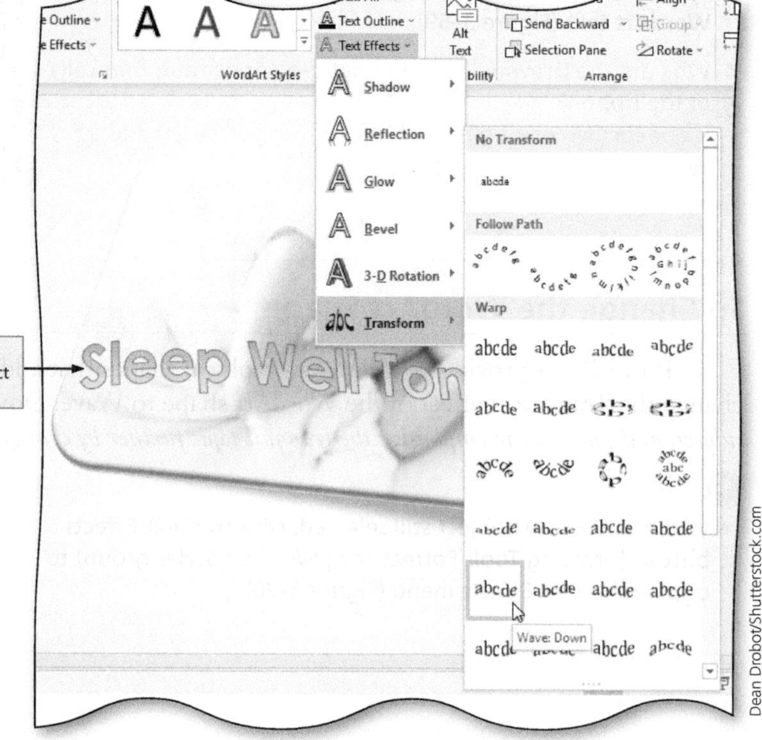

Figure 3–72

- Click the Wave: Down effect to apply this text effect to the WordArt object.

Q&A Can I change the effect I applied to the WordArt?
Yes. Position the insertion point in the box and then repeat Steps 1 and 2.

- Click the Shape Height box up arrow until the Height measurement is 1.5".
- Click the Shape Width box up arrow until the Width measurement is 10" (Figure 3–73).

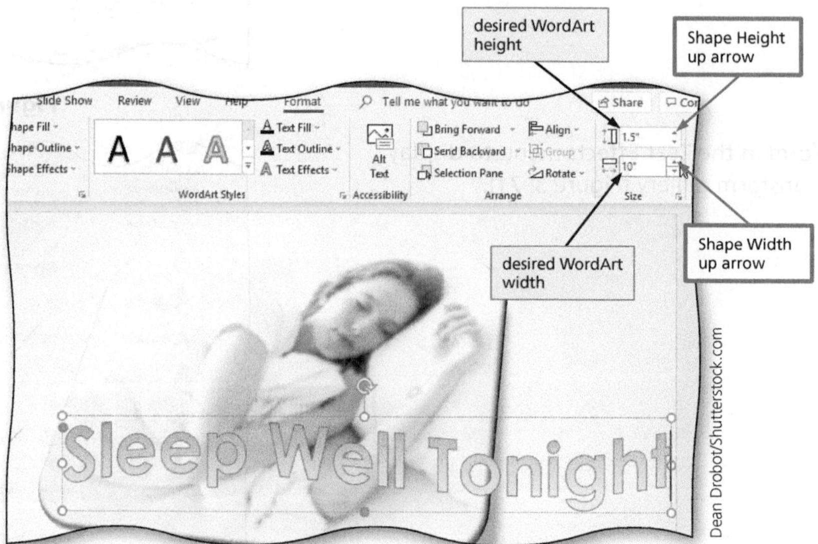

Figure 3–73

- Use the smart guides to position the WordArt as shown in Figure 3–74.

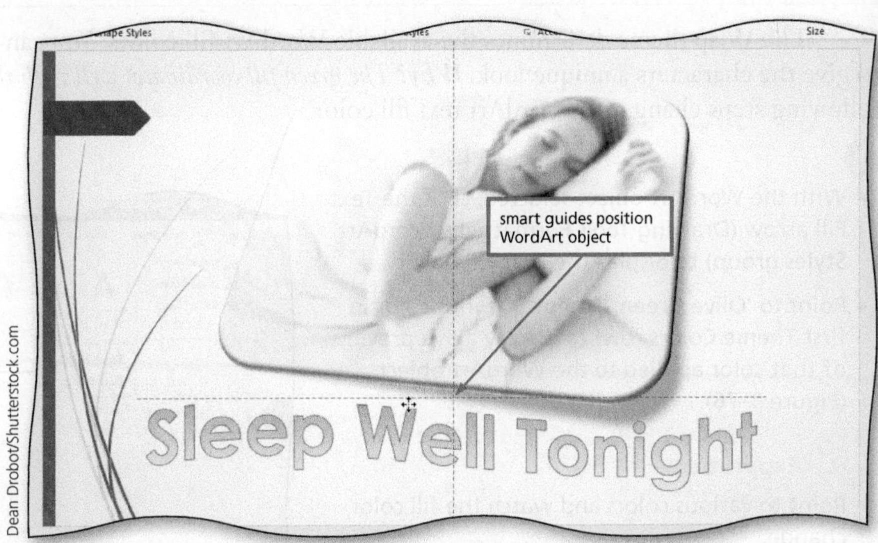

Figure 3–74

To Change the WordArt 3-D Rotation Effect

The following steps change the WordArt 3-D rotation effect. ***Why?*** *The 3-D effect is a subtle visual element that enhances the slide feature.*

1

- With the WordArt object still selected, display the Text Effects menu.
- Point to 3-D Rotation to display the 3-D Rotation gallery.
- Point to Perspective: Above (first rotation in second Perspective row) to display a live preview of this effect (Figure 3–75).

Experiment

- Point to various rotations in the gallery and watch the WordArt change.

2

- Click Perspective: Above to apply this rotation to the WordArt.

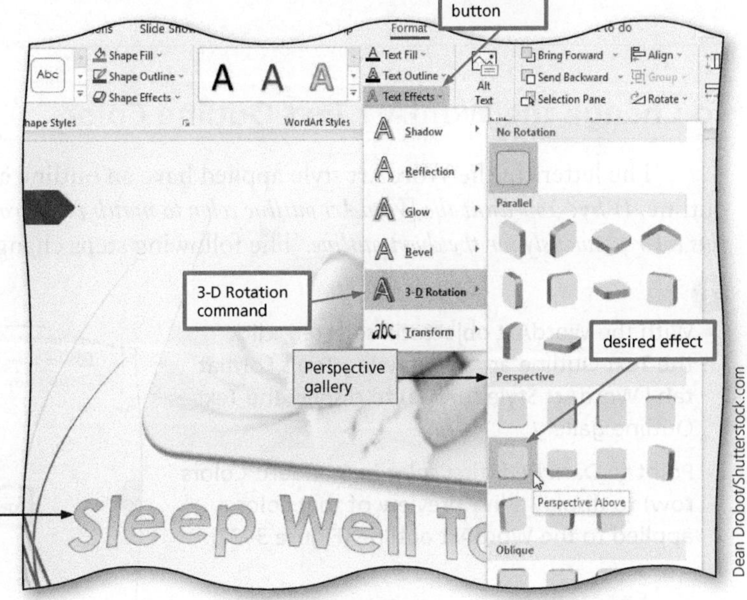

Figure 3–75

To Change the WordArt Text Fill Color

The Wisp theme determines the available WordArt fill colors. You can change the default WordArt colors to give the characters a unique look. ***Why?*** *The green fill coordinates well with the Wisp background colors.* The following steps change the WordArt text fill color.

- With the WordArt object selected, click the Text Fill arrow (Drawing Tools Format tab | WordArt Styles group) to display the Text Fill gallery.
- Point to 'Olive Green, Accent 5' (ninth color in first Theme Colors row) to display a live preview of that color applied to the WordArt object (Figure 3–76).

Experiment

- Point to various colors and watch the fill color change.

- Click 'Olive Green, Accent 5' to apply this color as the fill for the WordArt object.

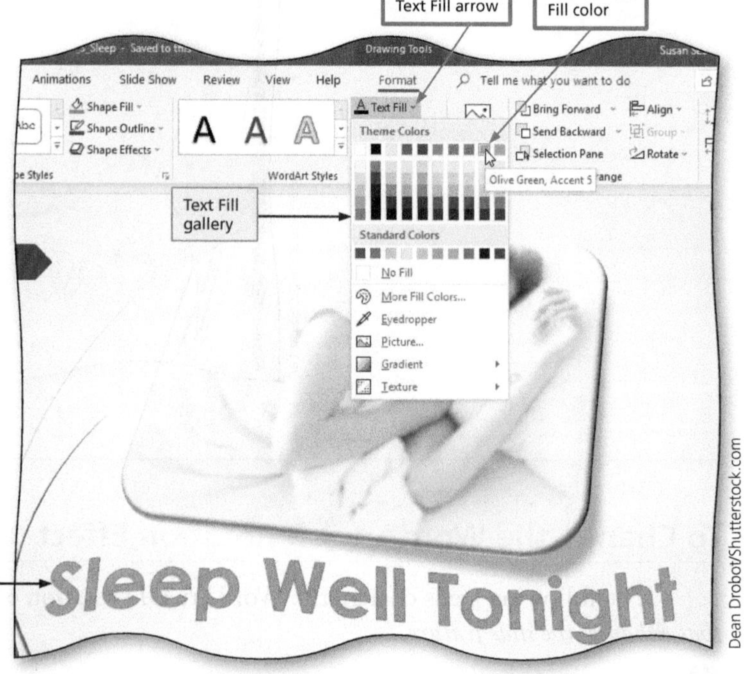

Figure 3–76

To Change the WordArt Text Outline Color

The letters in the WordArt style applied have an outline around the edges. You can change the color of the outline. ***Why?*** *You want the WordArt outline color to match the arrow in the upper-left corner of the slide, and you used this color previously for the chart outline.* The following steps change the WordArt outline color.

- With the WordArt object still selected, click the Text Outline arrow (Drawing Tools Format tab | WordArt Styles group) to display the Text Outline gallery.
- Point to Dark Red (first color in Standard Colors row) to display a live preview of that color applied to the WordArt outline (Figure 3–77).

Experiment

- Point to various colors and watch the outline color change.

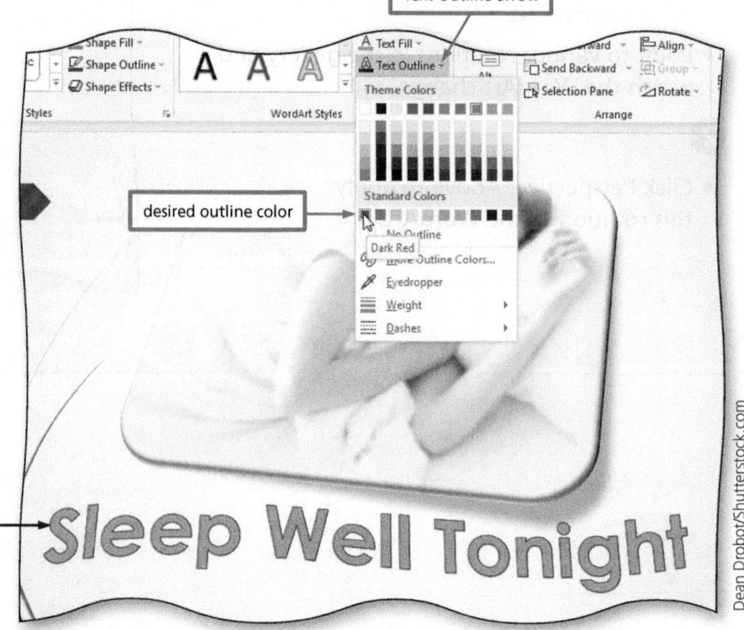

Figure 3–77

2

- Click Dark Red to apply this color to the WordArt outline.

Q&A

Can I change the outline line width?
Yes. Click the Text Outline button, point to Weight, and then click the desired line weight.

Must my text have an outline?
No. To delete the outline, click No Outline in the Text Outline gallery.

To Convert Text to WordArt

You wish to convert the title text letters to WordArt. ***Why?*** *WordArt can enhance the visual appeal of the slide.* The following steps convert the title text of Slide 2 to WordArt.

1

- Display Slide 2 and then select the title text (Control Your Exposure to Light) (Figure 3–78).

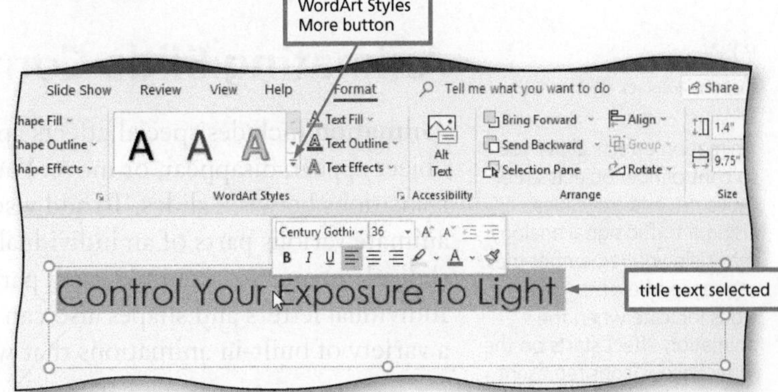

Figure 3–78

2

- If necessary, display the Drawing Tools Format tab and then click the WordArt Styles More button (Drawing Tools Format tab | WordArt Styles group) (shown in Figure 3–78) to display the WordArt Styles gallery.
- Point to 'Fill: Dark Red, Accent color 1; Shadow' (second color in first row) to display a live preview of that style applied to the title text (Figure 3–79).

Experiment

- Point to various styles and watch the text change.

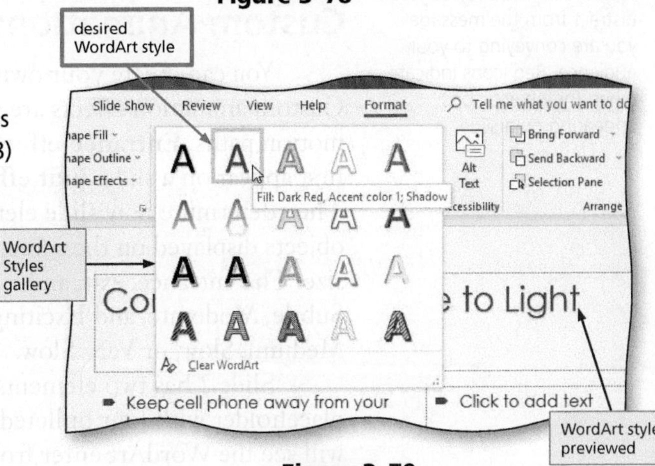

Figure 3–79

3

- Click 'Fill: Dark Red, Accent color 1; Shadow' to apply this style to the title text.

To Resize WordArt Proportionally

The WordArt object can be stretched, shrunk, or resized in two ways: using the sizing handles or changing the Size options on the Drawing Tools Format tab. To maintain the height and width proportions, press and hold SHIFT when dragging a sizing handle. Similarly, if you want to keep the proportions and also keep the center in the same location, press and hold both CTRL and SHIFT while dragging the sizing handle. On Slide 2, you want to resize the WordArt object proportionally. ***Why?*** *Moving the WordArt above the bulleted list allows extra space on the slide for the video you insert later in this module.* The following step resizes the WordArt proportionally.

- With the WordArt object still selected, press and hold SHIFT and then drag the middle sizing handle on the right side of the box inward, as shown in Figure 3–80.

Q&A Does resizing change the WordArt font size?
No. Resizing a WordArt object only resizes the box the WordArt is in. If you want to resize the WordArt characters, you would select the text and then change the font size on the Home tab of the ribbon.

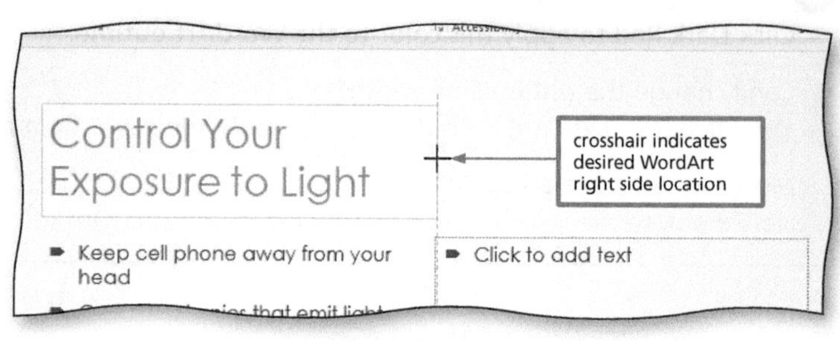

Figure 3–80

BTW
Animation Effect Icon Colors
Animation effects allow you to control how objects enter, move on, and exit slides. Using a traffic signal analogy may help you remember the sequence of events. Green icons indicate when the animation effect starts on the slide. Yellow icons represent the object's motion; use them with caution so they do not distract from the message you are conveying to your audience. Red icons indicate when the object stops appearing on a slide.

Animating Slide Content

Animation includes special effects applied to text or other objects that make the object appear, disappear, or move. You already are familiar with one form of animation: transitions between slides. To add visual interest and clarity to a presentation, you can animate various parts of an individual slide, including pictures, shapes, text, and other slide elements. For example, each paragraph on the slide can spin as it is displayed. Individual letters and shapes also can spin or move in various motions. PowerPoint has a variety of built-in animations that will fade, wipe, or fly-in text and graphics.

Custom Animations

You can create your own **custom animations** to meet your unique needs. Custom animation effects are grouped in categories: entrance, exit, emphasis, and motion paths. **Entrance effects**, as the name implies, determine how slide elements first appear on a slide. **Exit effects** work in the opposite manner as entrance effects: They determine how slide elements disappear. **Emphasis effects** modify text and objects displayed on the screen. For example, letters may darken or increase in font size. The entrance, exit, and emphasis animations are grouped into categories: Basic, Subtle, Moderate, and Exciting. You can set the animation speed to Very Fast, Fast, Medium, Slow, or Very Slow.

Slide 2 has two elements with text: the WordArt title and the content placeholder with four bulleted paragraphs. When the slide is displayed, the audience will see the WordArt enter from the top of the slide. Then, the four paragraphs will display simultaneously. In the following steps, you will perform these tasks:

1. Apply an entrance effect to the WordArt
2. Change the WordArt direction.
3. Change the animation start option.
4. Preview the animation sequence.
5. Modify the entrance timing.
6. Animate text paragraphs.
7. Change the animation sequence.

To Animate an Object Using an Entrance Effect

The WordArt will enter the slide from the top when you display this slide. ***Why?*** *The graphic is positioned above the bulleted paragraphs, so you want it to enter and then move into this location.* Entrance effects are colored green in the Animation gallery. The following step applies an entrance effect to the WordArt in Slide 2.

1

- With the WordArt on Slide 2 still selected, click Animations on the ribbon to display the Animations tab.
- Click the Float In animation in the Animation gallery (Animations tab | Animation group) to display a live preview of this animation and to apply this entrance animation to the WordArt object (Figure 3–81).

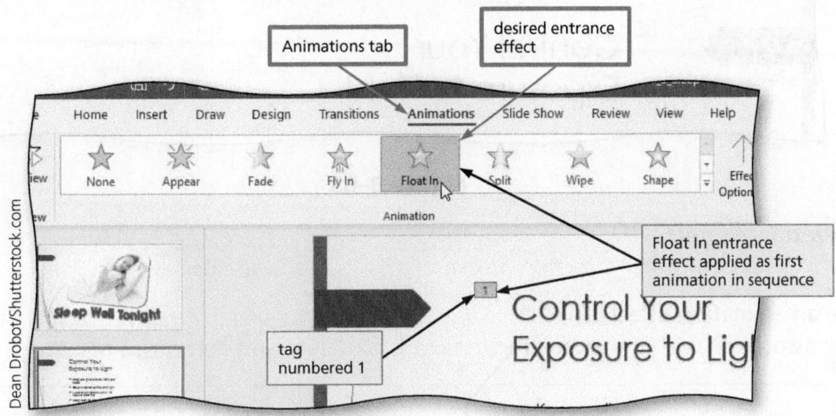

Figure 3–81

Q&A Are more entrance animations available?
Yes. Click More in the Animation gallery to see additional animations. You can select one of the 13 entrance animations that are displayed, or you can click the 'More Entrance Effects' command to expand the selection. You can click any animation to see a preview of the effect.

Why does the number 1 appear in a box on the left side of the WordArt?
The 1 is a sequence number and indicates Float In is the first animation that will appear on the slide when you click the slide.

To Change Animation Direction

You can modify an animation's direction and specify that it enters from another side or from a corner. The following steps change the WordArt entrance animation to enter from the top. ***Why?*** *By default, the WordArt appears on the slide by entering from the bottom edge, and you want it to enter from the top.*

1

- Click the Effect Options button (Animations tab | Animation group) to display the Direction gallery (Figure 3–82).

Q&A Why does a box appear around the Float Up arrow?
Float Up is the default entrance direction applied to the animation.

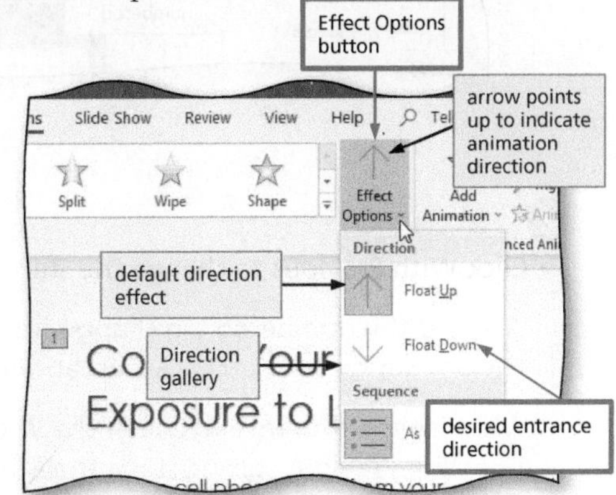

Figure 3–82

- Click the Float Down arrow to see a preview of this animation and apply this direction to the entrance animation (Figure 3–83).

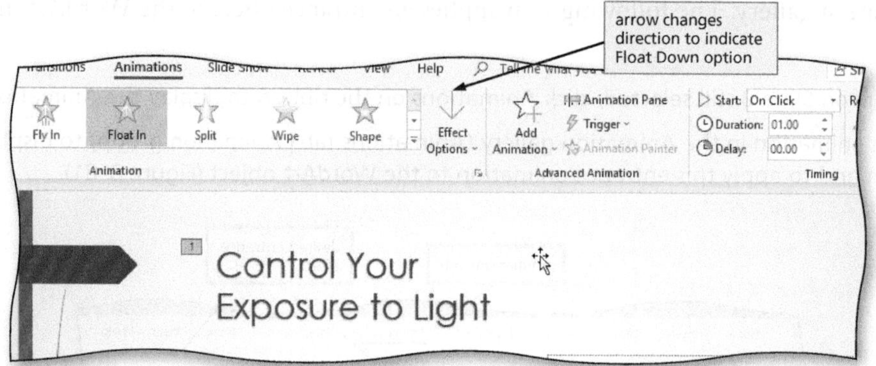

Figure 3–83

Q&A Can I change an entrance effect?
Yes. Repeat Step 1 to select another direction if several effects are available.

How can I delete an animation effect?
Click the number associated with the animation you wish to delete and then press DELETE.

To Change the Animation Start Option

The default WordArt setting is to start the animation with a click, but you can change this setting so that the entrance effect occurs automatically. The following steps change the WordArt entrance effect to automatic. ***Why?*** *You want the slide title text animation to display when the slide is displayed.*

- Click the Start arrow (Animations tab | Timing group) to display the Start menu (Figure 3–84).

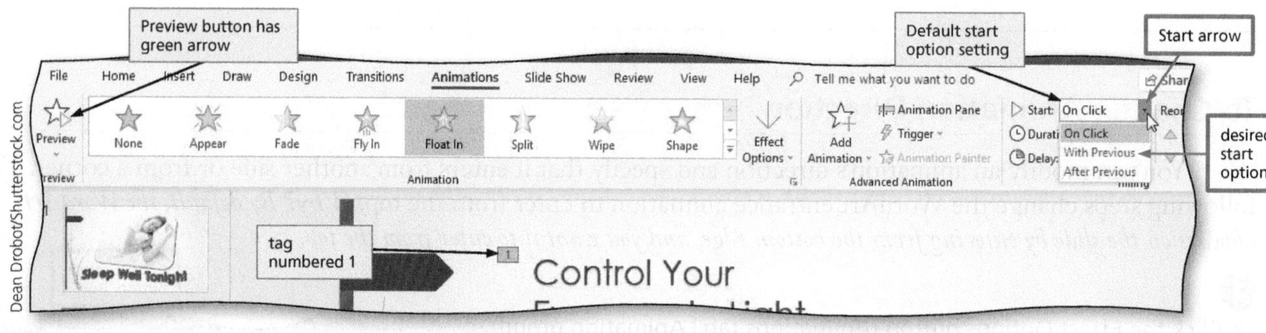

Figure 3–84

- Click With Previous to change the start option.

Q&A Why did the numbered tag change from 1 to 0?
The animation now occurs automatically without a click.

What is the difference between the With Previous and After Previous settings?
The With Previous setting starts the effect simultaneously with any prior animation; the After Previous setting starts the animation after a prior animation has ended.

To Preview an Animation Sequence

By default, the animations will be displayed when you run the presentation and click the slide. The following step runs the presentation and displays the Slide 2 animation. ***Why?*** *Although you have not completed developing the presentation, you should view the animation you have added to check for continuity and verify that the animation is displaying as you expected.*

1

- Click the Preview button (Animations tab | Preview group) to view the Slide 2 animation (Figure 3–85).

Q&A Why does a red square appear in the middle of the circle on the Preview button when I click that button?
The red square indicates the animation sequence is in progress. Ordinarily, a green arrow is displayed in the circle.

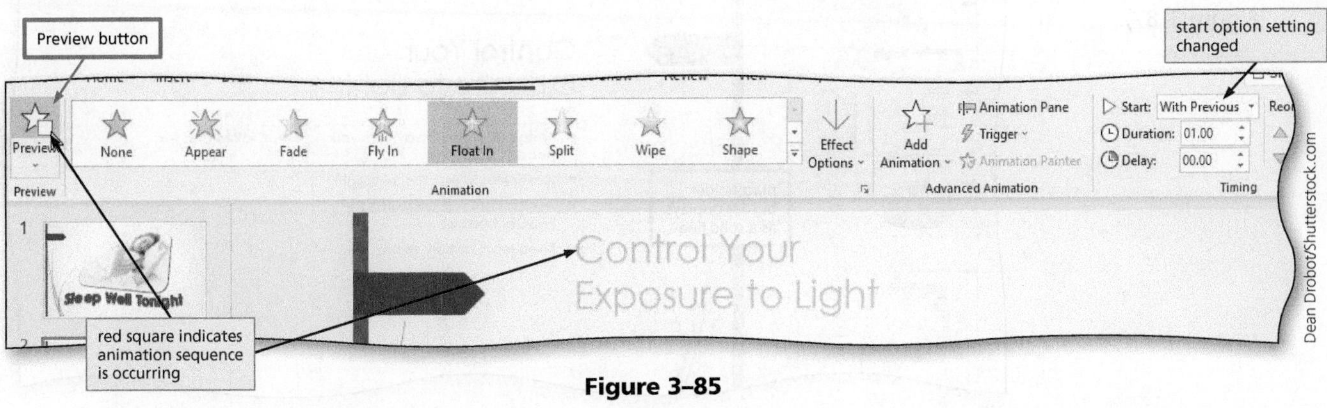

Figure 3–85

To Change the Animation Duration

The entrance animation effect is displayed quickly. To create a dramatic effect, you can change this setting so that the entrance effect occurs slowly during a specified number of seconds. The following step modifies the duration setting for the entrance animation. ***Why?*** *You want the slide title text to move down from the top of the slide slowly.*

1

- Click the Duration up arrow (Animations tab | Timing group) several times to increase the time from 01.00 second to 02.00 seconds (Figure 3–86).
- Click the Preview button to view the animation.

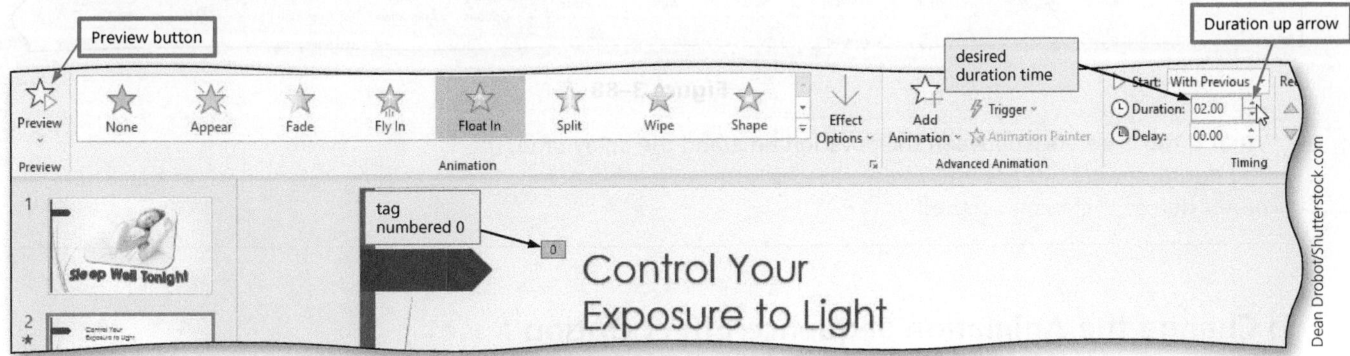

Figure 3–86

Q&A What is the difference between the duration time and the delay time?
The duration time is the length of time in which the animation occurs; the delay time is the length of time that passes before the animation begins.

Can I type the speed in the Duration box instead of clicking the arrow to adjust the speed?
Yes. Typing the numbers allows you to set a precise timing.

To Animate Text

You can animate the four bulleted paragraphs in the left Slide 2 content placeholder. ***Why?*** *For a special effect, you can display each paragraph individually during a presentation rather than have all four paragraphs appear together.* The following steps animate the bulleted list paragraphs.

- Click any bulleted list text the Slide 2 left content placeholder to select the placeholder (Figure 3–87).

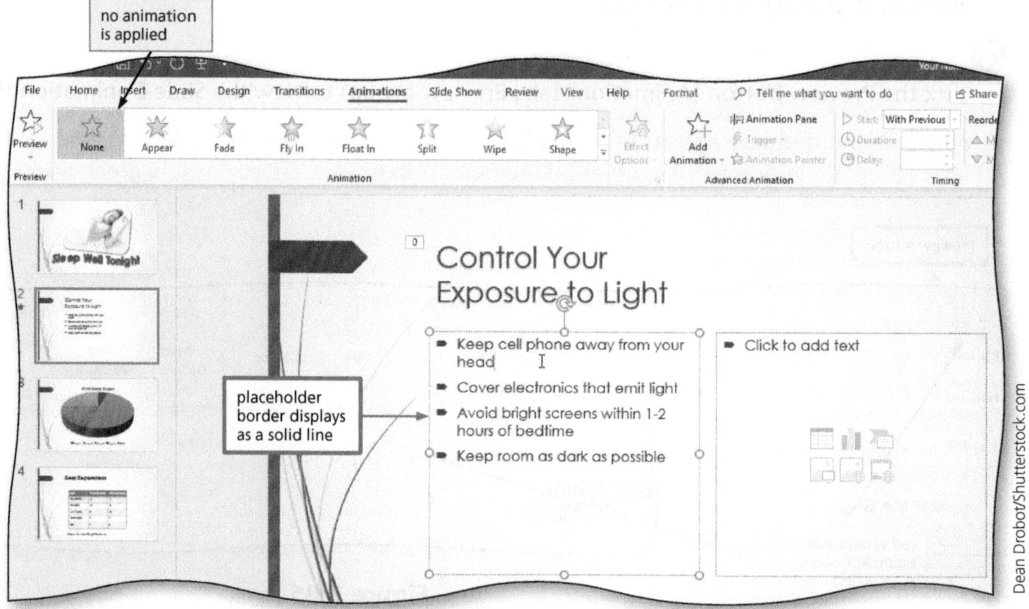

Figure 3–87

- Click the Fade entrance effect in the Animation gallery to add and preview this animation.
- Change the Duration time to 02.00 seconds (Figure 3–88).
- Click the Preview button to view the animations.

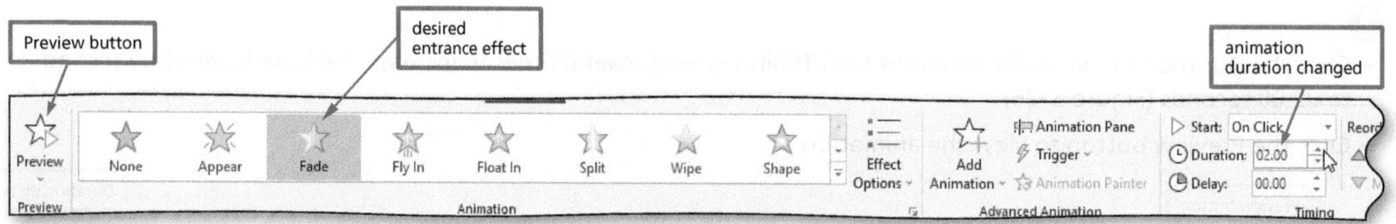

Figure 3–88

Q&A What is the difference between the duration time and the delay time?

The duration time is the length of time in which the animation occurs; the delay time is the length of time that passes before the animation begins.

To Change the Animation Sequence Effect Option

By default, each paragraph in the content placeholder enters one at a time in response to a click when you present in Slide Show view. You can modify this entrance sequence setting. ***Why?*** *You want all the paragraphs to enter the slide simultaneously.* The following steps change the sequence for the paragraphs to appear all at once.

1

- Click the Effect Options button to display the Effect Options menu (Figure 3–89).

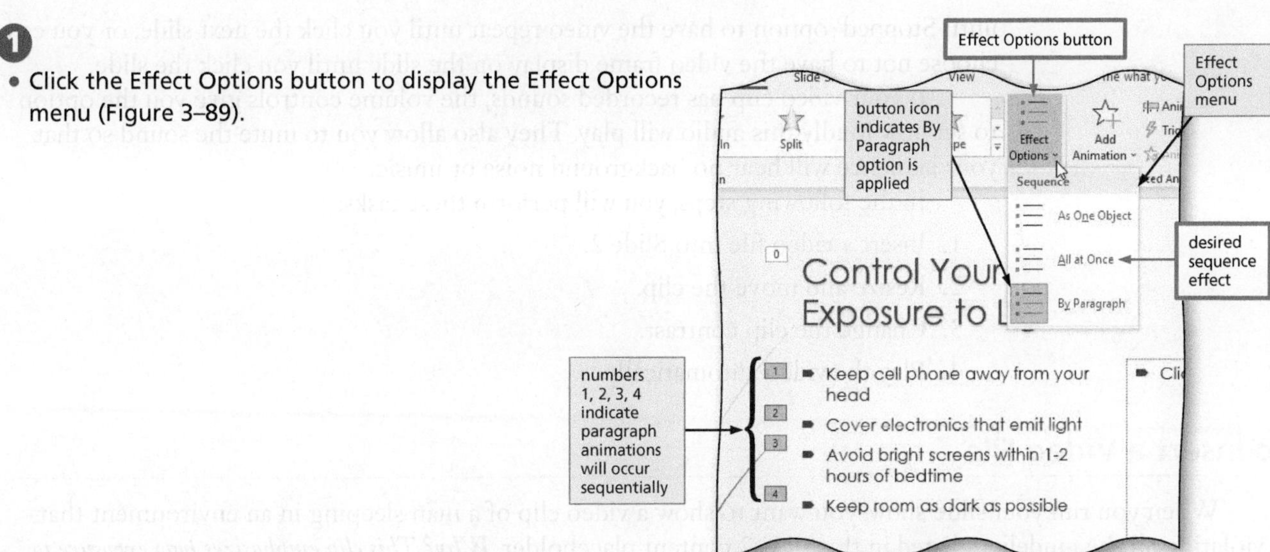

Figure 3–89

2

- Click 'All at Once' to change the sequence (Figure 3–90).

Q&A Why did the numbered tags change from 1, 2, 3, 4 to 1, 1, 1, 1?

All four paragraphs now will appear simultaneously.

- Click the Preview button to view the animations.

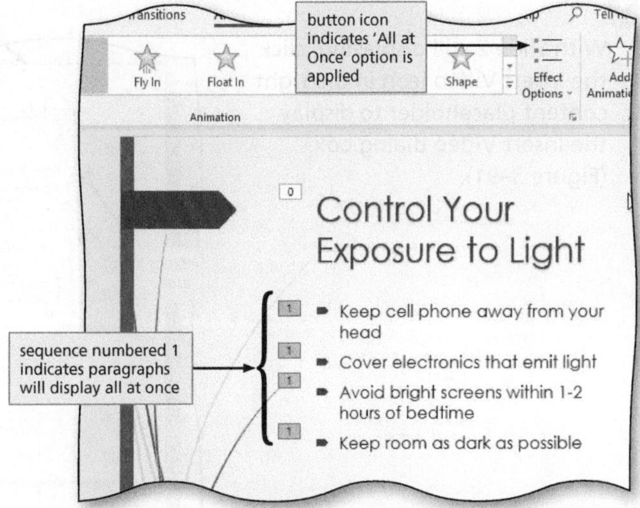

Figure 3–90

Adding Media to Slides

Media files can enrich a presentation if they are used correctly. Video files can be produced with a camera and editing software, and sound files can come from the Internet, files stored on your computer, or an audio track on a CD. To hear the sounds, you need a sound card and speakers or headphones on your system.

Once an audio or video clip is inserted into a slide, you can specify options that affect how the file is displayed and played. For example, you can have the video play automatically when the slide is displayed, or you can click the video frame when you are ready to start the playback. You also can have the video fill the entire slide, which is referred to as **full screen**. If you decide to play the slide show automatically and have it display full screen, you can drag the video frame to the gray area off the slide so that it does not display briefly before going to full screen. You can select the 'Loop

BTW
Using Codecs
Video and audio content developers use a codec (compressor/decompressor) to reduce the file size of digital media. The reduced file size helps transfer files across the Internet quickly and smoothly and helps save space on storage media. Your computer can play any compressed file if the specific codec used to compress the file is available on your computer. If the codec is not installed or is not recognized, your computer attempts to download this file from the Internet. Many codec files are available to download from the Internet at no cost.

until Stopped' option to have the video repeat until you click the next slide, or you can choose not to have the video frame display on the slide until you click the slide.

If your video clip has recorded sounds, the volume controls give you the option to set how loudly this audio will play. They also allow you to mute the sound so that your audience will hear no background noise or music.

In the following steps, you will perform these tasks:

1. Insert a video file into Slide 2.
2. Resize and move the clip.
3. Change the clip contrast.
4. Play the video automatically.

To Insert a Video File

When you run your slide show, you want to show a video clip of a man sleeping in an environment that is violating all the guidelines listed in the Slide 2 content placeholder. ***Why?*** *This clip emphasizes how exposure to light disrupts sleep.* PowerPoint allows you to insert this clip into your slide in the same manner that you insert a picture in a content placeholder. The following steps insert this video clip into Slide 2.

1

- With Slide 2 still displaying, click the Insert Video icon in the right content placeholder to display the Insert Video dialog box (Figure 3–91).

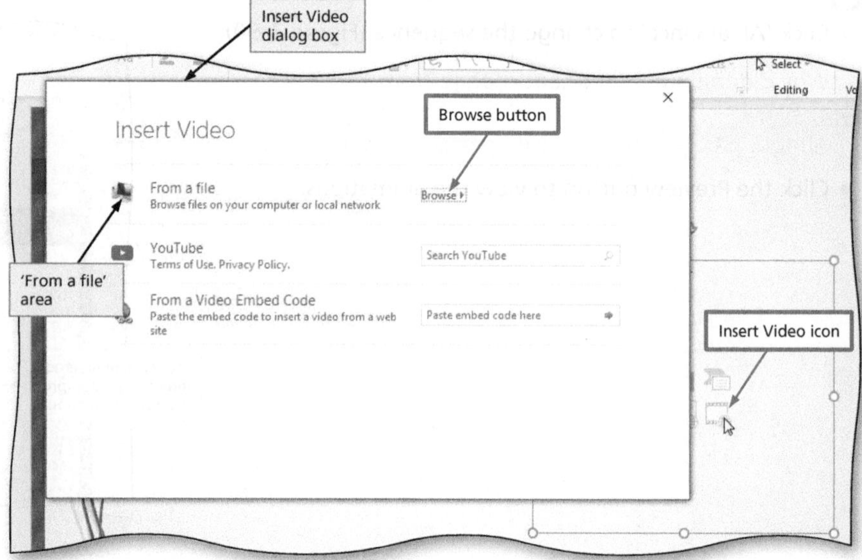

Figure 3–91

- Click the Browse button in the 'From a file' area (Insert Video dialog box) to navigate to the location where your data files are located.
- Click Support_PPT_3_Awake.mp4 to select the file (Figure 3–92).

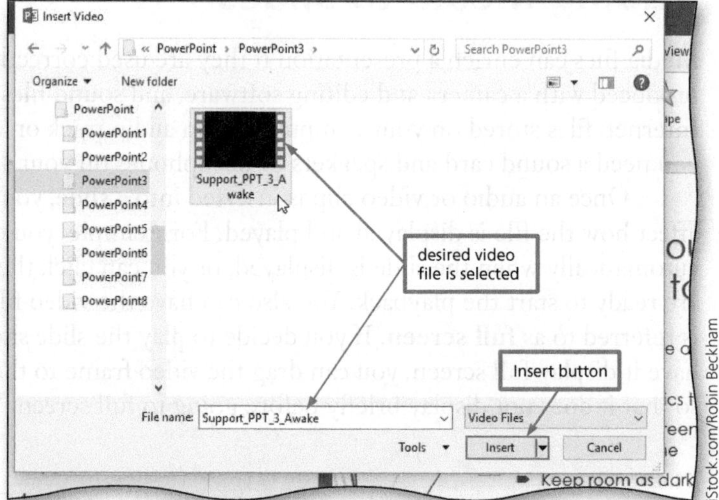

Figure 3–92

3

- Click the Insert button (Insert Video dialog box) to insert the video clip into Slide 2 (Figure 3–93).

Q&A Can I adjust the color of a video clip?
Yes. You can correct the brightness and contrast, and you also can recolor a video clip using the same methods you learned in this module to color a picture. You will adjust the contrast and brightness later in this module.

4

- Click the Play/Pause button to review the video clip.

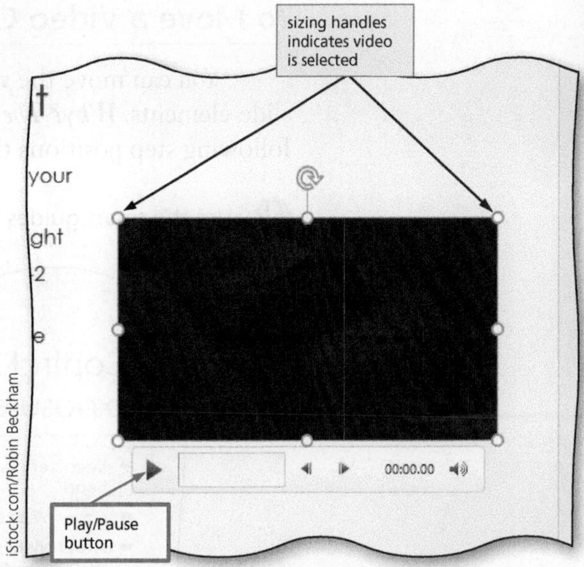

Figure 3–93

To Resize a Video Clip

You can enlarge the video clip in the same manner that you increase the size of a picture. ***Why?*** *You have sufficient white space on the slide to increase the video clip size.* The following step increases the video clip size.

1

- With the Video Tools Format tab displaying, click the Video Height up arrow several times until the height is 3.3" (Figure 3–94).

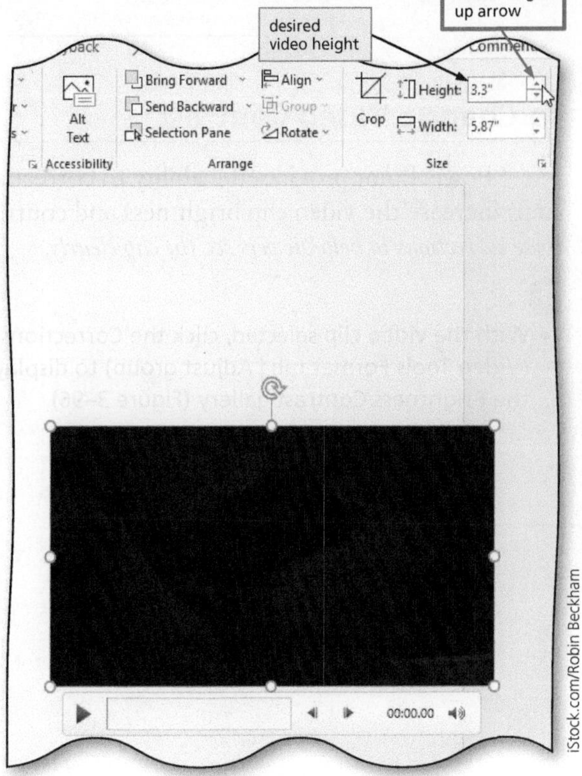

Figure 3–94

BTW
Restricting Permissions
You can allow PowerPoint users to see your presentation but not allow them to change the slide content, copy the slides, or print the presentation. To protect your presentation, click File on the ribbon to open Backstage view, display the Info tab, click Protect Presentation, click Restrict Access, and then click 'Connect to Rights Management Servers and get templates'

To Move a Video Clip

You can move the video clip upward in the same manner that you move other slide elements. ***Why?*** *The video clip size is balanced with the content placeholder.* The following step positions the video clip on the slide.

1 Use the smart guides to position the video clip, as shown in Figure 3–95.

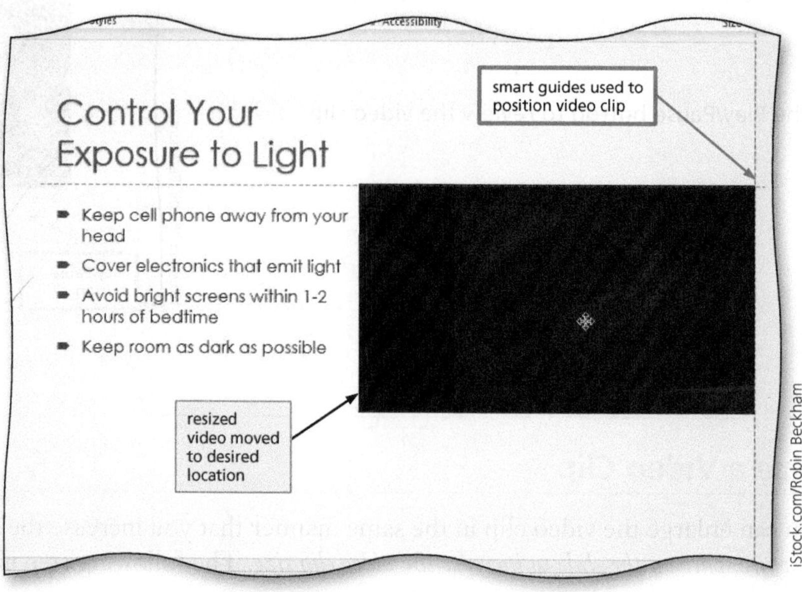

Figure 3–95

To Change Video Contrast

PowerPoint provides the ability to correct a video by changing the brightness and contrast. The following steps increase the video clip brightness and contrast. ***Why?*** *The video clip you inserted is dark, so you want to apply these corrections to help viewers see the clip clearly.*

1

- With the video clip selected, click the Corrections button (Video Tools Format tab | Adjust group) to display the Brightness/Contrast gallery (Figure 3–96).

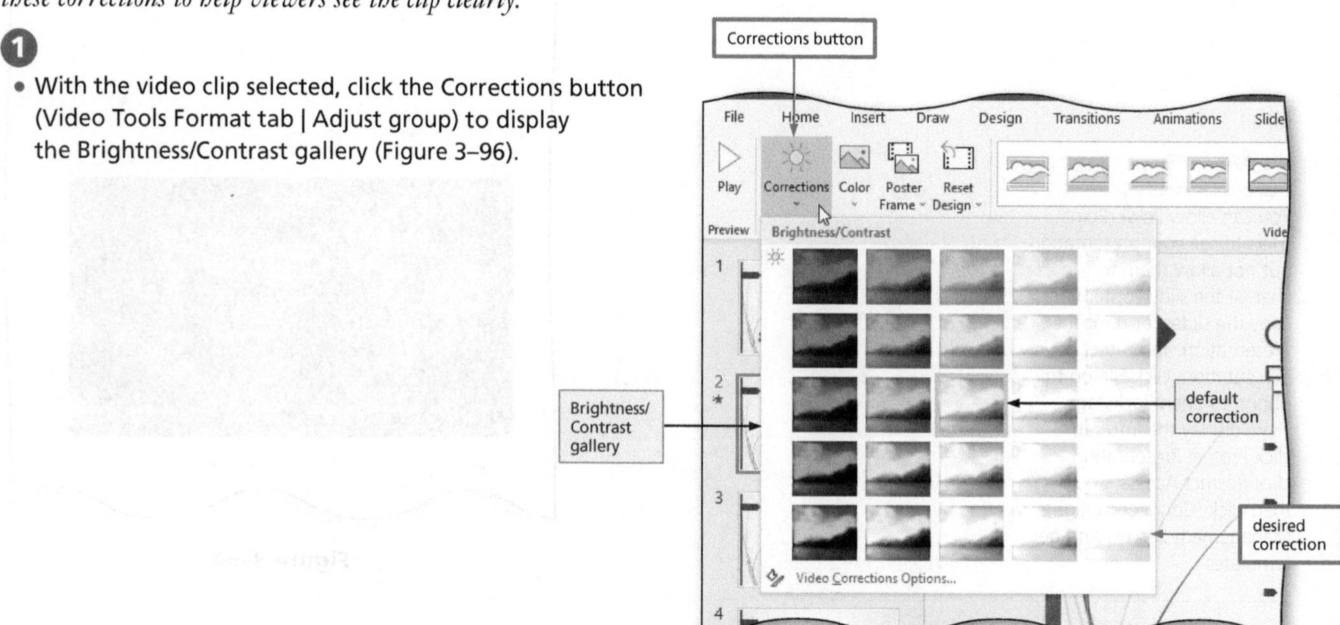

Figure 3–96

2

- Point to Brightness: +40% Contrast: +40% (last thumbnail in last row) to display a preview of this correction on the clip (Figure 3–97).

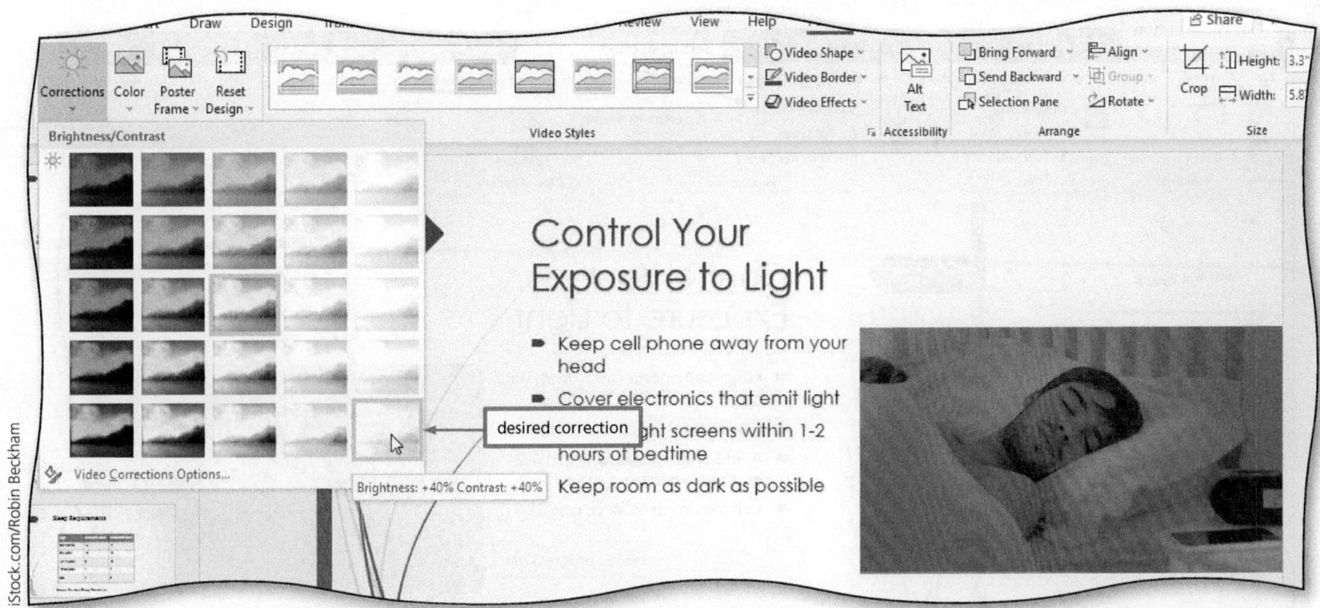

Figure 3–97

Q&A Why does the gray box display in the center of the gallery?
That setting is the default brightness/contrast setting of 'Brightness: 0% (Normal) Contrast: 0% (Normal).'

Experiment

- Point to various pictures in the Brightness/Contrast area and watch the brightness and contrast change on the video clip.

3

- Click Brightness: +40% Contrast: +40% (last thumbnail in last row) to apply this correction to the video clip.

To Play a Video File Automatically

Once the video clip is inserted, you can specify that the video plays automatically when the slide is displayed. ***Why?*** *When you are giving your presentation, you do not want to click the mouse to start the video.* The following steps play the video file automatically.

1

- With the video clip selected, display the Video Tools Playback tab.
- Click the Start arrow (Video Tools Playback tab | Video Options group) to display the Start menu (Figure 3–98).

Q&A What does the When Clicked On option do?
The video clip would begin playing when the presenter clicks the video frame during the slide show.

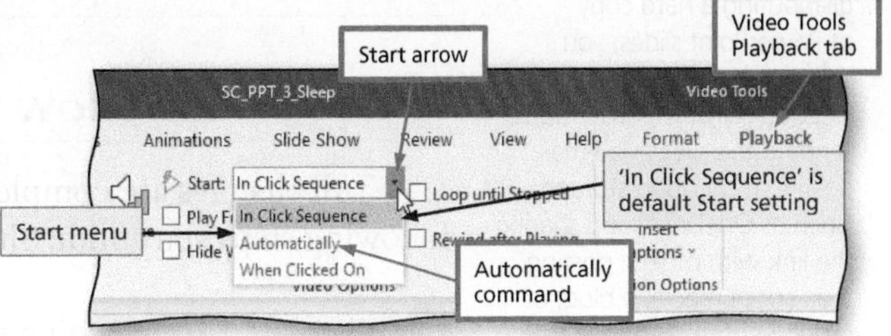

Figure 3–98

- Click Automatically to have the video clip play automatically when the slide is displayed.
- Click the Play button (Video Tools Playback tab | Preview group) to preview the video (Figure 3–99).

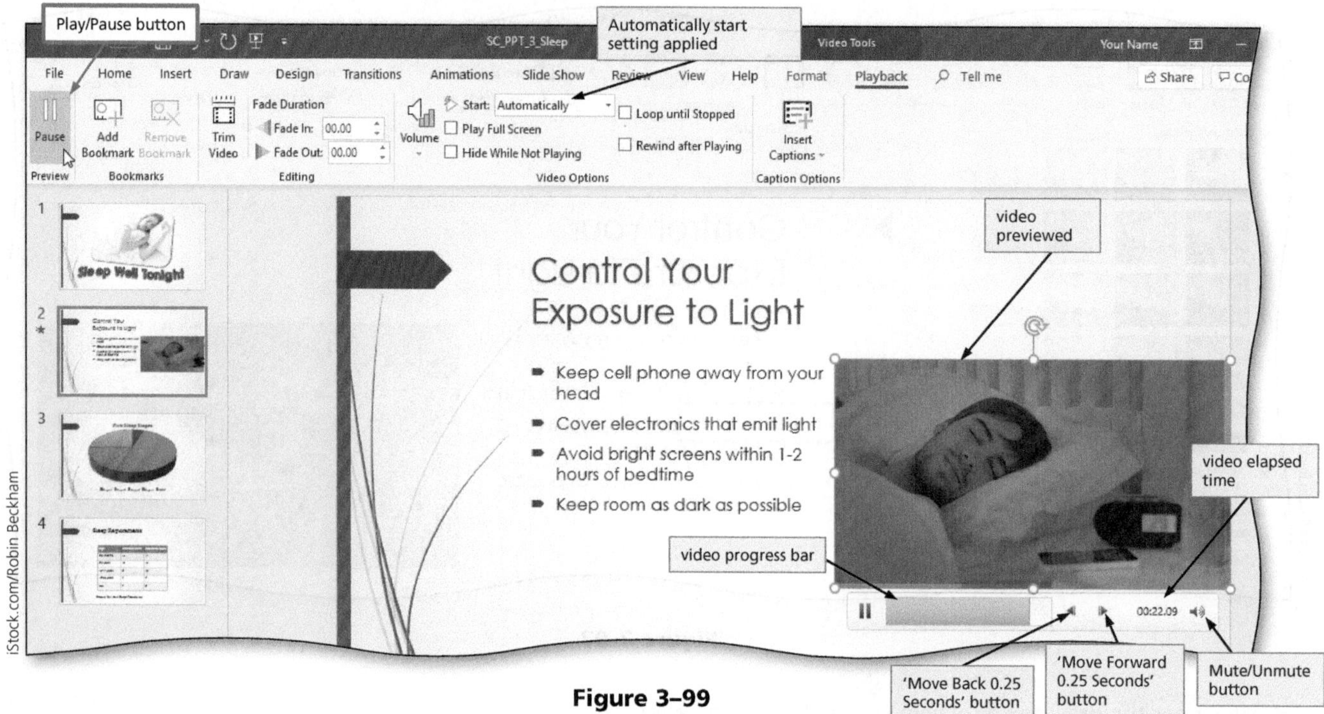

Figure 3–99

Q&A Why did the Play button change to Pause when the video was playing?
The button changes to allow you to stop the preview if desired.

BTW
Printing Document Properties
PowerPoint 2019 does not allow you to print document properties. This feature, however, is available in other Office 2019 apps, including Word and Excel.

BTW
Distributing Slides
Instead of printing and distributing a hard copy of PowerPoint slides, you can distribute the slides electronically. Options include sending the slides via email; posting it on cloud storage (such as OneDrive) and sharing the link with others; posting it on social media, a blog, or other website; and sharing a link associated with an online location of the slides. You also can create and share a PDF or XPS image of the slides, so that users can view the file in Acrobat Reader or XPS Viewer instead of in PowerPoint.

To Add a Transition between Slides

A final enhancement you will make in this presentation is to apply the Ripple transition in the Exciting category to all slides and change the transition duration to 3.00. The following steps apply this transition to the presentation.

1. Apply the Ripple transition in the Exciting category (Transitions tab | Transition to This Slide group) to all four slides in the presentation.
2. Change the transition duration from 01.40 to 03.00 for all slides.

To Run a Slide Show with Animations and Video

All changes are complete, so you now can view the Sleep presentation. The following steps start Slide Show view.

1. Click 'Start From Beginning' on the Quick Access Toolbar to display the title slide.
2. Press SPACEBAR to display Slide 2. Watch the WordArt appear. Press SPACEBAR to view the four bulleted paragraphs and watch the video clip.
3. Press SPACEBAR to display Slide 3.

4. Press SPACEBAR to display Slide 4.
5. Press SPACEBAR to end the slide show and then press SPACEBAR again to exit the slide show.

To Save and Print the Presentation

With the presentation completed, you should save the file and print handouts for your audience. The following steps save the file and then print a presentation handout with two slides per page.

1. Save the presentation again in the same storage location with the same file name.
2. Open Backstage view, click the Print tab, click 'Full Page Slides' in the Settings area, click 2 Slides in the Handouts area to display a preview of the handout, and then click Print in the Print gallery to print the presentation.
3. **sam** Because the project now is complete, you can exit PowerPoint.

BTW

Conserving Ink and Toner

If you want to conserve ink or toner, you can instruct PowerPoint to print draft quality documents by clicking File on the ribbon to open Backstage view, clicking Options in Backstage view to display the PowerPoint Options dialog box, clicking Advanced in the left pane (PowerPoint Options dialog box), scrolling to the Print area in the right pane, verifying there is no check mark in the High quality check box, and then clicking OK. Then, use Backstage view to print the document as usual.

Summary

In this module you have learned how to create and format a chart and table, insert a text box, reuse slides from another presentation, move slides in Slide Sorter view, crop a picture and then apply styles, convert text to a WordArt graphic, animate an object and text, and insert a video.

CONSIDER THIS: PLAN AHEAD

What decisions will you need to make when creating your next presentation?

Use these guidelines as you complete the assignments in this module and create your own slide show decks outside of this class.

1. Audiences recall visual concepts more quickly and accurately than text alone, so consider using graphics in your presentation.
   a) Decide the precise message you want to convey to your audience.
   b) Determine if a chart or table is the better method of presenting the information.
2. Choose an appropriate chart or table.
   a) Charts are excellent visuals to show relationships between groups of data, especially numbers.
   b) Tables are effective for organizing information in a grid.
   c) Decide which chart or table type best conveys the points you are attempting to make in your presentation. PowerPoint provides a wide variety of styles within each category, so determine which one is most effective in showing the relationships.
3. Obtain information for the graphic from credible sources.
   a) Text or numbers should be current and correct.
   b) Verify the sources of the information.
   c) Be certain you have typed the data correctly.
   d) Acknowledge the source of the information on the slide or during your presentation.
4. Choose an appropriate WordArt style.
   a) Determine which style best represents the concept you are attempting to present.
5. Test your visual elements.
   a) Show your slides to several friends or colleagues and ask them to interpret what they see.
   b) Have your test audience summarize the information they perceive on the tables and charts and compare their analyses to what you are attempting to convey.

Apply Your Knowledge

Reinforce the skills and apply the concepts you learned in this module.

Creating and Formatting a Chart, Table, and WordArt

Note: To complete this assignment, you will be required to use the Data Files. Please contact your instructor for information about accessing the Data Files.

Instructions: Start PowerPoint. The city council in your town commissioned an analysis of carbon emissions in an attempt to uncover areas of efficiency and cost savings. You have developed slides to accompany a presentation on their findings for next month's council meeting. Open the presentation called SC_PPT_3-1.pptx, which is located in the Data Files. You will create a chart and table, format WordArt and a picture, and insert a video to create the presentation shown in Figure 3–100.

Perform the following tasks:

1. On Slide 1 (Figure 3–100a), convert the title text, Emissions Analysis, to WordArt and then apply the 'Fill: Dark Yellow, Accent color 2; Outline: Dark Yellow, Accent color 2' (third style in first row) style. Change the WordArt outline weight to 3 pt and then apply the Warp Down transform (last effect in fourth Warp row) text effect. Increase the WordArt width to 5.3".
2. Insert a text box below the WordArt title and then type **`Carbon Footprint Survey Results`** as the text box text. Change the font to Georgia and increase the font size to 24 point. Use the smart guides to center the text box below the WordArt.
3. Insert the video with the file name Support_PPT_3_CO2.mp4 in the Slide 1 content placeholder. Start the video Automatically.

   If requested by your instructor, insert a text box on Slide 1 in the lower-right area of the slide and add the name of the first school you attended.
4. On Slide 2 (Figure 3–100b), enter the data shown in Table 3–1. Apply the 'Medium Style 1 – Accent 2' (third style in first Medium row) table style. Change the table height to 4" and the width to 6". Align the table in the center of the slide.

Table 3–1

Method	Time
Bus	45 minutes
Carpool	40 minutes
Drive alone	25 minutes
Walk	15 minutes
Bike	10 minutes

5. Convert the title text, Commute to Work, to WordArt and then apply the 'Fill: Dark Yellow, Accent color 2; Outline: Dark Yellow, Accent color 2' (third style in first row) style. Change the WordArt outline weight to 3 pt and then apply the Deflate (second effect in sixth Warp row) text effect.
6. On Slide 3 (Figure 3–100c), delete the title text placeholder. Insert a Pie chart and change the layout to Doughnut (last layout in gallery). Insert the data shown in Table 3–2.

Table 3–2 Greenhouse Gas Sources

Electricity	45
Natural Gas	35
Travel	11
Waste	9

7. Increase the chart height to 7" and the width to 11.5". Increase the chart title text to 40 point and change the font to Georgia. Increase the legend to 20 point and change the font to Georgia. Use the smart guides to align the chart in the center of the slide.
8. Insert the picture Support_PPT_3_Footprint.jpg. Crop the picture as shown in Figure 3–100c, change the height to 2.4", and then use the smart guides to position it in the center of the slide.
9. Apply the 'Snip Diagonal Corner, White' (first style in third row) picture style to the picture and then change the color tone to 'Temperature: 4700 K' (first thumbnail).
10. Apply the Switch transition in the Exciting category to all slides and then change the duration to 3.00 seconds.

11. View the presentation and then save the file using the file name, `SC_PPT_3_Carbon` and submit the revised presentation in the format specified by your instructor.
12. In this assignment, you formatted WordArt and a picture. You also changed the table chart style. How did these edits enhance the presentation? Does the video clip add interest to the presentation? Why or why not?

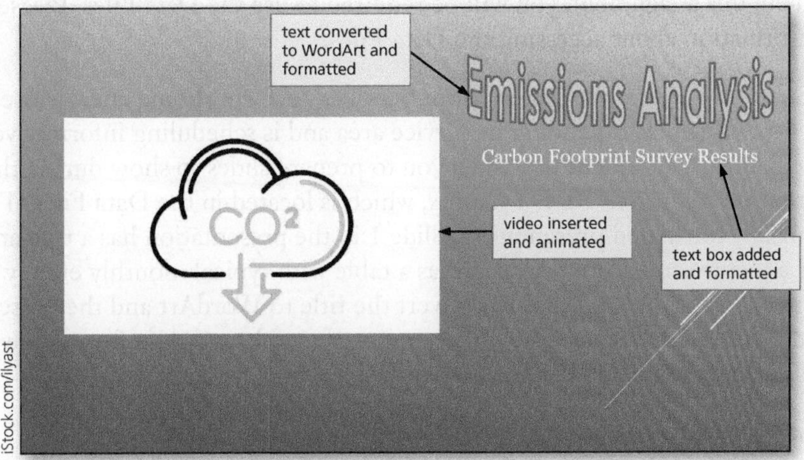

Figure 3–100a – (a) Slide 1

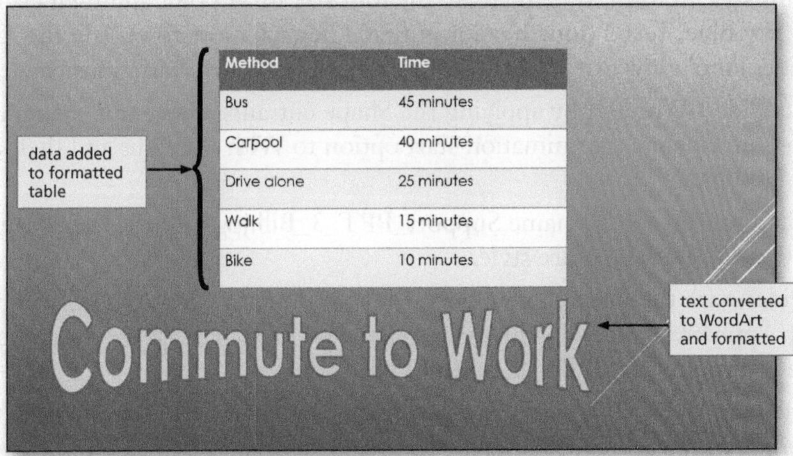

Method	Time
Bus	45 minutes
Carpool	40 minutes
Drive alone	25 minutes
Walk	15 minutes
Bike	10 minutes

Figure 3–100b – (b) Slide 2

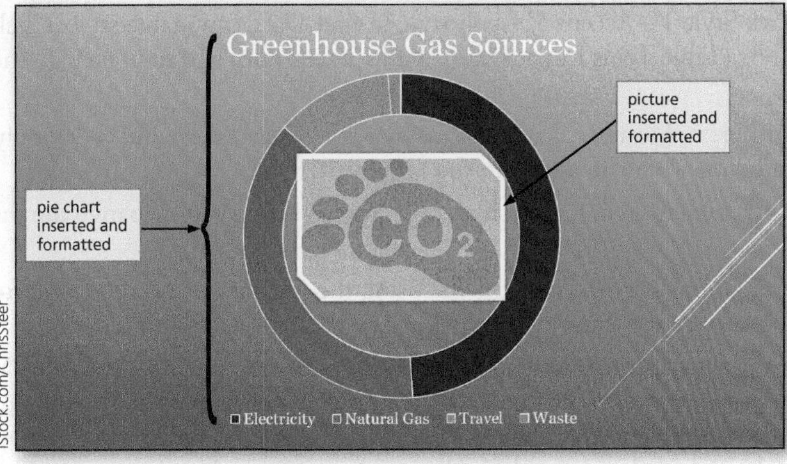

Figure 3–100c – (c) Slide 3

Extend Your Knowledge

Extend the skills you learned in the module and experiment with new skills. You may need to use Help to complete the assignment.

Formatting Graphic Elements and a Table

Note: To complete this assignment, you will be required to use the Data Files. Please contact your instructor for information about accessing the Data Files.

Instructions: Start PowerPoint. Cashman Power Services performs home energy assessments for its customers. The company is expanding its service area and is scheduling informative talks in your home town. The company president has asked you to prepare slides to show during this speech. Open the presentation called SC_PPT_3-2.pptx, which is located in the Data Files. The document you open is a partially formatted presentation. Slide 1 in the presentation has a title and two content placeholders for a picture and a video. Slide 2 has a table with typical monthly energy consumption for several products. On Slide 1, you are to convert the title to WordArt and then insert and format a picture and video. On Slide 2, you are to add a row to the table and then format the table. The slides will look similar to Figure 3–101 before you add the final formatting.

Perform the following tasks:

1. On Slide 1 (Figure 3–101a), convert the title text, Controlling Energy Usage, to WordArt style 'Fill: Blue, Accent color 5; Outline: Black, Background color 1; Hard Shadow: Blue, Accent color 5' (third style in third row). Increase the font size to 54 point and then change the text fill color to Sky Blue, Text 2 (fourth color in first Theme Colors row). Add the 'Glow: 18 point; Teal, Accent color 6' glow text effect (last variation in last Glow Variations row).
2. Animate the Slide 1 WordArt by applying the Shape entrance effect and changing the direction to Out. Change the animation start option to With Previous and then change the duration to 3.00.
3. Insert the picture with the file name Support_PPT_3_Bill.jpg into the left content placeholder. Apply the Rotated, White picture style.
4. Insert the video with the file name Support_PPT_3_Plug.mp4 into the right content placeholder. Apply the Rotated, White video style and then increase the video height to 3.5". Change the start option to 'When Clicked On'.
5. On Slide 2 (Figure 3–101b), insert a row below the Cable modem row and then type `Cell phone charger` in the left cell, `2` in the middle cell, and `$0.11` in the right cell.

   If requested by your instructor, add a row at the bottom of the Slide 2 table and then enter the names of three of your favorite grade school teachers in the cells.
6. Apply the 'Dark Style 1 – Accent 5' (sixth style in first Dark row) table style. Click 'Lock Aspect Ratio' check box (Table Tools Layout tab | Table Size group) and then change the table height to 3".
7. Convert the title text, Monthly Energy Consumption, to WordArt and then apply the same formatting and animation you added to the Slide 1 title text.
8. Apply the Blinds transition in the Exciting category to both slides. Change the duration to 3.00 seconds.
9. View the presentation and then save the file using the file name, `SC_PPT_3_Energy_Usage` and submit the revised presentation in the format specified by your instructor.
10. You applied the same formatting and animation to the title text on both slides. You also applied the same style to the picture and video. Does this consistency help or hinder the presentation? Why? In Step 6 you chose a table style in the Dark category. Was this style effective? How did this style improve the slide and increase the audience's attention to the table content?

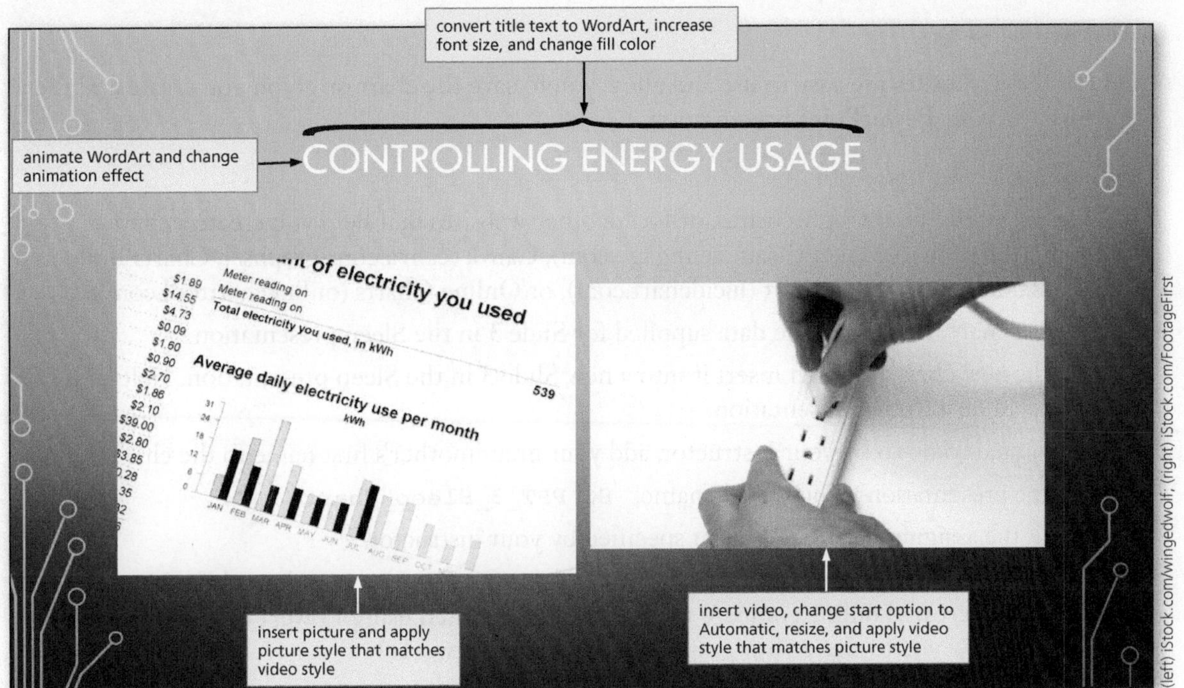

Figure 3–101a – (a) Slide 1

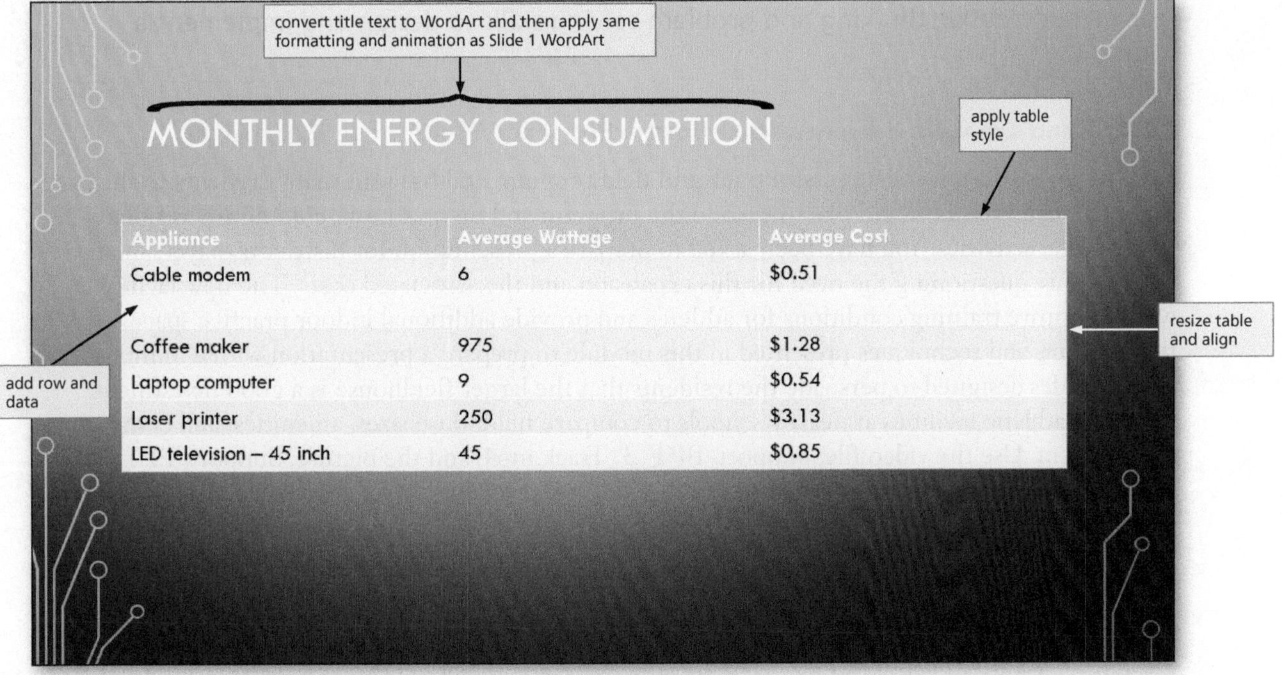

Appliance	Average Wattage	Average Cost
Cable modem	6	$0.51
Coffee maker	975	$1.28
Laptop computer	9	$0.54
Laser printer	250	$3.13
LED television – 45 inch	45	$0.85

Figure 3–101b – (b) Slide 2

Expand Your World

Create a solution that uses cloud or web technologies by learning and investigating on your own from general guidance.

Creating Charts and Graphs Using Websites

Instructions: PowerPoint presents a wide variety of chart and table layouts, and you must decide which one is effective in presenting the relationships between data and indicating important trends. Several websites offer opportunities to create graphics that help explain concepts to your audience.

Continued >

Expand Your World *continued*

Many of these websites are easy to use and allow you to save the chart or graph you create and then import it into your PowerPoint presentation.

Perform the following tasks:

1. Visit one of the following websites, or locate other websites that help you create a chart or graph: Beam Chart Maker (beam.venngage.com), Canva (canva.com/graphs/), Charts Builder (charts.hohli.com), Lucidchart (lucidchart.com), or Online Charts (onlinecharttool.com).
2. Create a chart using the same data supplied for Slide 3 in the Sleep presentation.
3. Save the new chart and then insert it into a new Slide 3 in the Sleep presentation. Delete the original Slide 3 in the presentation.

   If requested to do so by your instructor, add your grandmother's first name to the chart title.
4. Save the presentation using the file name, `SC_PPT_3_Sleep_Chart`.
5. Submit the assignment in the format specified by your instructor.
6. Which features do the websites offer that help you create charts and graphs? How does the graphic you created online compare to the chart you created using PowerPoint? How do the websites allow you to share your graphics using social networks?

In the Lab

Apply your creative thinking and problem-solving skills to design and implement a solution.

Design and Create a Presentation about a Proposed Fieldhouse Expansion

Part 1: Your school has a successful track and field program and has sent many students to the state finals. Administrators would like to expand the program and involve more community residents in recreational activities. You have been asked to prepare a presentation for district taxpayers, many of whom are questioning the need for this expansion and the associated costs. The new facility would improve training conditions for athletes and provide additional indoor practice space. Use the concepts and techniques presented in this module to prepare a presentation with a minimum of four slides designed to persuade the residents that the larger fieldhouse is a good investment. Research athletic facilities at nearby schools to compare fieldhouse sizes, amenities, and community involvement. Use the video file, Support_PPT_3_Track.mp4, and the picture, Support_PPT_3_Fieldhouse.jpg, which are located in the Data Files. Insert a table and chart, format these graphics, format the picture, add animation, and insert WordArt. Review and revise your presentation as needed and then save the file using the file name, `SC_PPT_3_Fieldhouse`. Submit your assignment in the format specified by your instructor.

Part 2: You made several decisions while creating the presentation in this assignment: creating and formatting a table and chart, adding animation, inserting WordArt, and inserting a video and a picture. What was the rationale behind each of these decisions? When you reviewed the document, what further revisions did you make and why? Where would you recommend showing this slide show?

1 Creating a Worksheet and a Chart

Objectives

After completing this module, you will be able to:

- Start an app
- Identify the components of the Microsoft Office ribbon
- Describe the Excel worksheet
- Enter text and numbers
- Use the Sum button to sum a range of cells
- Enter a simple function
- Copy the contents of a cell to a range of cells using the fill handle
- Apply cell styles
- Format cells in a worksheet
- Create a pie chart
- Change a worksheet name and sheet tab color
- Change document properties
- Preview and print a worksheet
- Use the AutoCalculate area to display statistics
- Correct errors on a worksheet
- Use Microsoft Office Help

Introduction

Almost every organization collects vast amounts of data. Often, data is consolidated into a summary so that people in the organization better understand the meaning of the data. An Excel worksheet allows data to be summarized and charted easily. A **chart** is a graphic element that illustrates data. In this module, you will create a worksheet that includes a chart. The data in the worksheet and chart comprise a budget that contains monthly estimates for each income and expense category.

Project: Real Estate Budget Worksheet and Chart

The project in this module follows proper design guidelines and uses Excel to create the worksheet and chart shown in Figure 1–1a and Figure 1–1b. The worksheet contains budget data for Frangold Realty. Mrs. Frangold has compiled a list of her projected expenses and sources of income and wants to use this information to create an easy-to-read worksheet. In addition, she would like a pie chart to show her estimated monthly expenses by category.

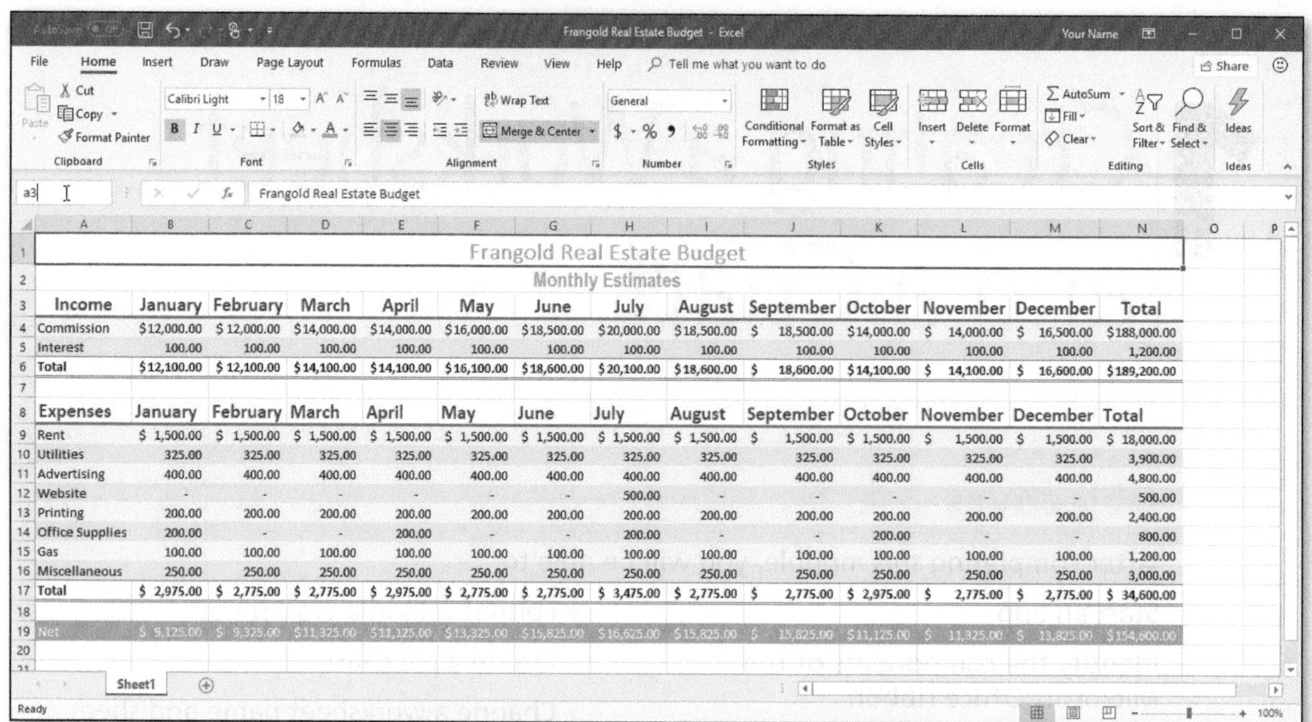

	A	B	C	D	E	F	G	H	I	J	K	L	M	N
1	Frangold Real Estate Budget													
2	Monthly Estimates													
3	Income	January	February	March	April	May	June	July	August	September	October	November	December	Total
4	Commission	$12,000.00	$ 12,000.00	$14,000.00	$14,000.00	$16,000.00	$18,500.00	$20,000.00	$18,500.00	$ 18,500.00	$14,000.00	$ 14,000.00	$ 16,500.00	$188,000.00
5	Interest	100.00	100.00	100.00	100.00	100.00	100.00	100.00	100.00	100.00	100.00	100.00	100.00	1,200.00
6	Total	$12,100.00	$ 12,100.00	$14,100.00	$14,100.00	$16,100.00	$18,600.00	$20,100.00	$18,600.00	$ 18,600.00	$14,100.00	$ 14,100.00	$ 16,600.00	$189,200.00
7														
8	Expenses	January	February	March	April	May	June	July	August	September	October	November	December	Total
9	Rent	$ 1,500.00	$ 1,500.00	$ 1,500.00	$ 1,500.00	$ 1,500.00	$ 1,500.00	$ 1,500.00	$ 1,500.00	$ 1,500.00	$ 1,500.00	$ 1,500.00	$ 1,500.00	$ 18,000.00
10	Utilities	325.00	325.00	325.00	325.00	325.00	325.00	325.00	325.00	325.00	325.00	325.00	325.00	3,900.00
11	Advertising	400.00	400.00	400.00	400.00	400.00	400.00	400.00	400.00	400.00	400.00	400.00	400.00	4,800.00
12	Website	-	-	-	-	-	-	500.00	-	-	-	-	-	500.00
13	Printing	200.00	200.00	200.00	200.00	200.00	200.00	200.00	200.00	200.00	200.00	200.00	200.00	2,400.00
14	Office Supplies	200.00	-	-	200.00	-	-	200.00	-	-	200.00	-	-	800.00
15	Gas	100.00	100.00	100.00	100.00	100.00	100.00	100.00	100.00	100.00	100.00	100.00	100.00	1,200.00
16	Miscellaneous	250.00	250.00	250.00	250.00	250.00	250.00	250.00	250.00	250.00	250.00	250.00	250.00	3,000.00
17	Total	$ 2,975.00	$ 2,775.00	$ 2,775.00	$ 2,975.00	$ 2,775.00	$ 2,775.00	$ 3,475.00	$ 2,775.00	$ 2,775.00	$ 2,975.00	$ 2,775.00	$ 2,775.00	$ 34,600.00
18														
19	Net	$ 9,125.00	$ 9,325.00	$11,325.00	$11,125.00	$13,325.00	$15,825.00	$16,625.00	$15,825.00	$ 15,825.00	$11,125.00	$ 11,325.00	$ 13,825.00	$154,600.00

Figure 1–1(a) Real Estate Budget Worksheet

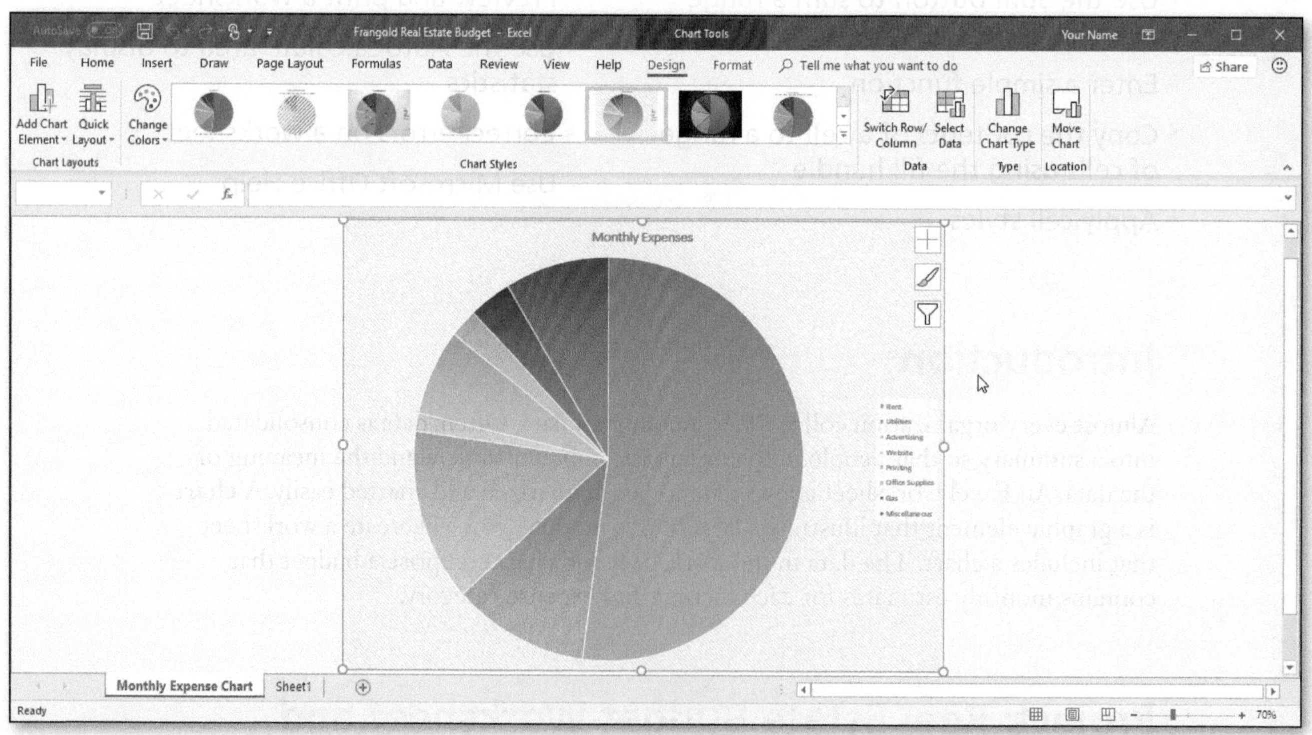

Figure 1–1(b) Pie Chart Showing Monthly Expenses by Category

The first step in creating an effective worksheet is to make sure you understand what is required. The person or persons requesting the worksheet may supply their requirements in a requirements document, or you can create one. A requirements document includes a needs statement, a source of data, a summary of calculations, and any other special requirements for the worksheet, such as charting and web support. Figure 1–2 shows the requirements document for the new workbook to be created in this module.

Worksheet Title	Frangold Real Estate Budget
Need	A yearly projection of Frangold Realty's budget
Source of data	Data supplied by Madelyn Frangold includes monthly estimates for income and expenses
Calculations	The following calculations must be made: 1. For each month, a total for income and expenses 2. For each budget item, a total for the item 3. For the year, total all income and expenses 4. Net income = Total income - Expenses

Figure 1–2

CONSIDER THIS

Why is it important to plan a worksheet?

The key to developing a useful worksheet is careful planning. Careful planning can reduce your effort significantly and result in a worksheet that is accurate, easy to read, flexible, and useful. When analyzing a problem and designing a worksheet solution, what steps should you follow?

1. Define the problem, including need, source of data, calculations, charting, and web or special requirements.
2. Design the worksheet.
3. Enter the data and formulas.
4. Test the worksheet.

After carefully reviewing the requirements document (Figure 1–2) and making the necessary decisions, the next step is to design a solution or draw a sketch of the worksheet based on the requirements, including titles, column and row headings, the location of data values, and the pie chart, as shown in Figure 1–3. The dollar signs and commas that you see in the sketch of the worksheet indicate formatted numeric values.

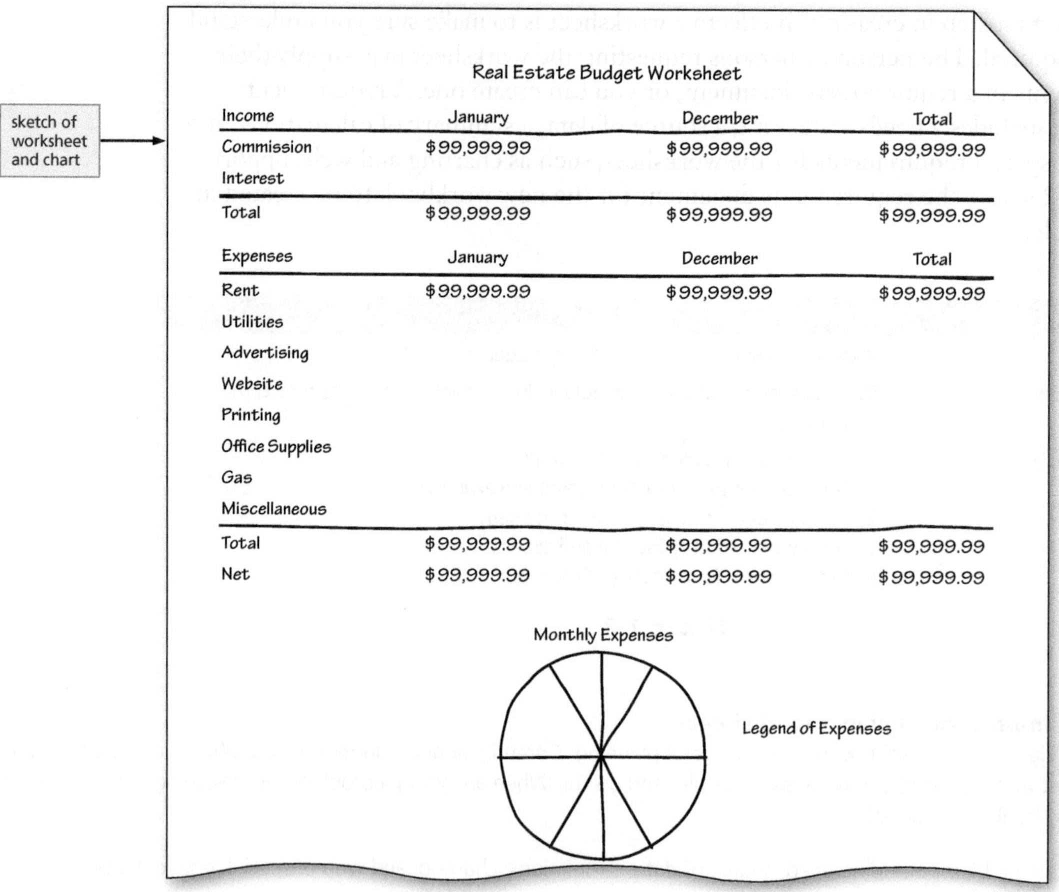

Figure 1–3

With a good understanding of the requirements document, an understanding of the necessary decisions, and a sketch of the worksheet, the next step is to use Excel to create the worksheet and chart.

Starting and Using Excel

What Is Excel?

Excel is a powerful spreadsheet app that allows users to organize data, complete calculations, make decisions, graph data, develop professional-looking reports, publish organized data to the web, and access real-time data from websites. The four major parts of Excel are as follows:

- **Workbooks and Worksheets:** A workbook is like a notebook. Inside the workbook are sheets, each of which is called a worksheet. A **worksheet** is a single sheet in a workbook file that lets you enter and manipulate data, perform calculations with data, and analyze data. Thus, a workbook is a collection of worksheets. Worksheets allow users to enter, calculate, manipulate, and analyze data, such as numbers and text. The terms "worksheet" and "spreadsheet" are interchangeable.
- **Charts:** Excel can draw a variety of charts, such as column charts and pie charts.
- **Tables:** Tables organize and store data within worksheets. For example, once a user enters data into a worksheet, an Excel table can sort the data, search for specific data, and select data that satisfies defined criteria.

- **Web Support:** Web support allows users to save Excel worksheets or parts of a worksheet in a format that a user can view in a browser, so that a user can view and manipulate the worksheet using a browser. Excel web support also provides access to real-time data, such as stock quotes, using web queries.

To Start Excel and Create a Blank Workbook

Across the bottom of the Windows desktop is the taskbar. The taskbar contains the **Start button,** a clickable button at in the lower left corner of the Windows 10 screen that you click to open the Start menu. The **Start menu** provides access to all programs, documents, and settings on the computer. The Start menu may contain one of more folders, and these folders can be used to group related apps together. A **folder** is an electronic container that helps you organize your computer files, like a cardboard folder on your desk; it can contain subfolders for organizing files into smaller groups.

The Start menu allows you to start programs, store and search for documents, customize the computer or mobile device, and sign out of a user account or shut down the computer or mobile device. A **menu** is a list of related items, including folders, programs, and commands. Each **command** on a menu performs a specific action, such as saving a file or obtaining help. ***Why?*** *Commands are one of the principal ways you communicate with an app so you can tell it what you want it to do.*

The following steps, which assume Windows is running, use the Start menu to start Excel and create a blank workbook based on a typical installation. You may need to ask your instructor how to start Excel on your computer.

1

- sam Click the Start button on the Windows taskbar to display the Start menu containing a list of apps installed on the computer or mobile device.
- If necessary, scroll to display Excel (Figure 1–4).

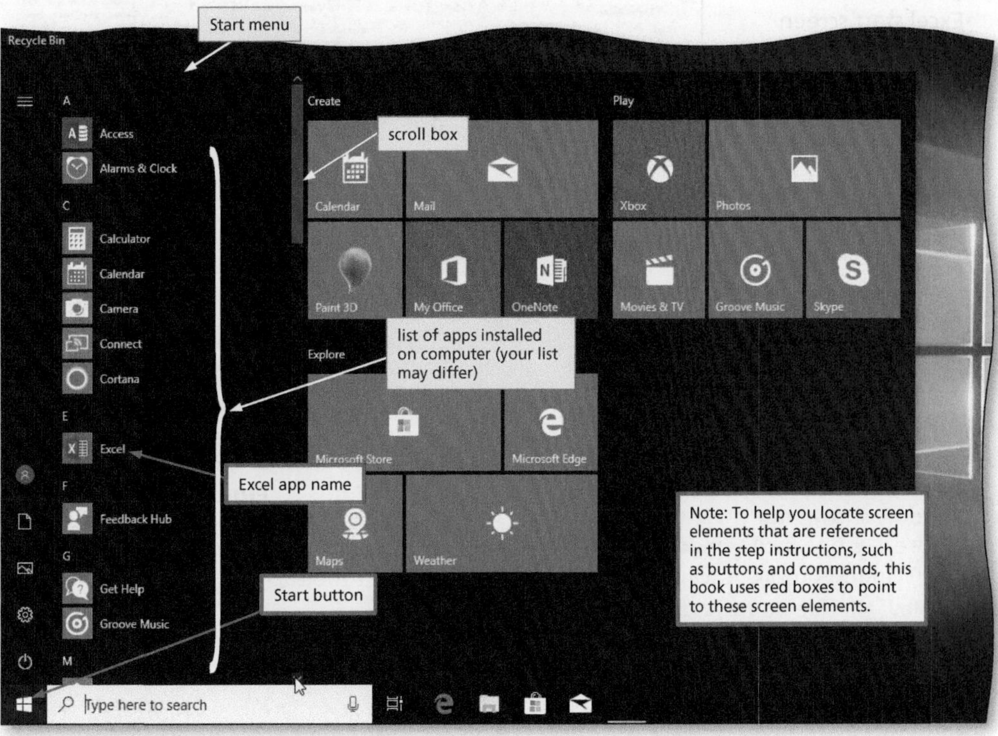

Figure 1–4

- Click Excel to start the app (Figure 1–5).

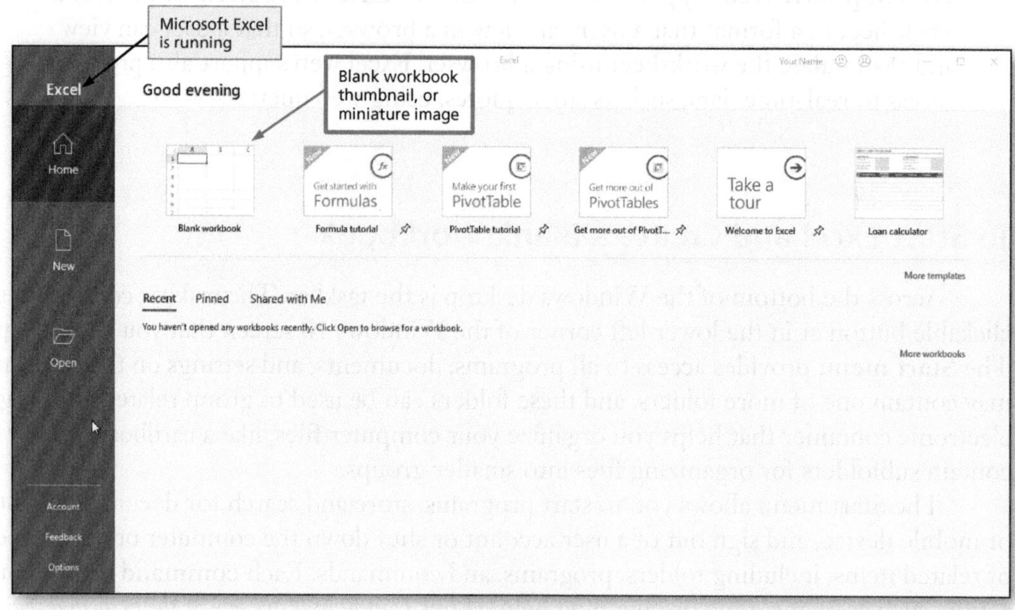

Figure 1–5

- Click the Blank workbook thumbnail on the Excel start screen to create a blank Excel workbook in the Excel window (Figure 1–6).

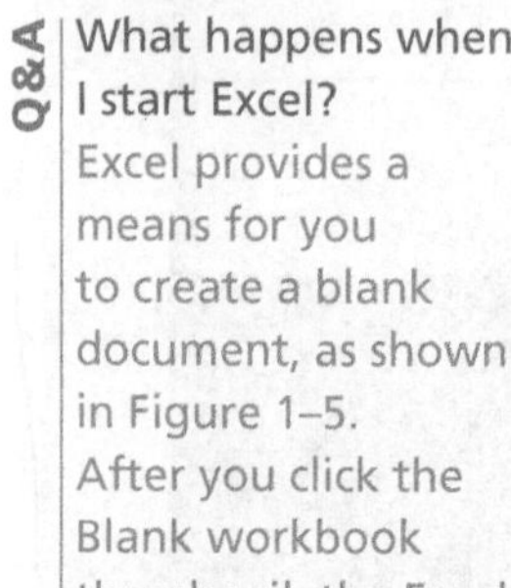

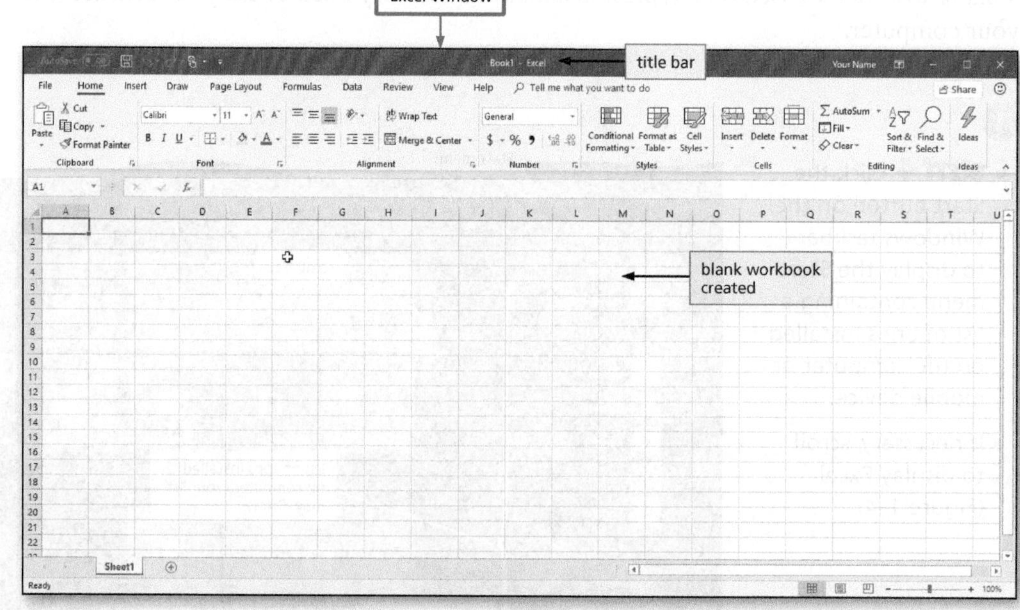

Figure 1–6

Q&A What happens when I start Excel?
Excel provides a means for you to create a blank document, as shown in Figure 1–5. After you click the Blank workbook thumbnail, the Excel window shown in Figure 1–6 opens. A **window** is a rectangular-shaped work area that displays an app or a collection of files, folders, and Windows tools. A window has a **title bar**, an area at the top of a document window or app window that displays the file name and program name.

Other Ways

1. Type app name in search box, click app name in results list
2. Double-click file created in app you want to start

The Excel Window

The Excel window consists of a variety of components to make your work more efficient and worksheets more professional. These include the worksheet window, ribbon, Tell Me box, Quick Access Toolbar, and Microsoft Account area.

Excel opens a new workbook with one worksheet. If necessary, you can add additional worksheets. Each worksheet has a sheet name that appears on a **sheet tab**, an indicator at the bottom of the window that identifies a worksheet. For example, Sheet1 is the name of the active worksheet displayed in the blank workbook shown in Figure 1–7. You can add more sheets to the workbook by clicking the New sheet button.

Worksheet The worksheet is organized into a rectangular grid containing vertical columns and horizontal rows. A column letter in a box above the grid, also called the **column heading**, appears above each worksheet column to identify it. A row number in a box on the left side of a worksheet row, also called the **row heading**, identifies each row.

The intersection of each column and row is a cell. A **cell** is the box, formed by the intersection of a column and a row, where you enter data. Each worksheet in a workbook has 16,384 columns and 1,048,576 rows for a total of 17,179,869,184 cells. Only a small fraction of the active worksheet appears on the screen at one time.

A cell is referred to by its unique address, or **cell reference**, which is the column letter and row number location that identifies a cell within a worksheet, such as A1. To identify a cell, specify the column letter first, followed by the row number. For example, cell reference D5 refers to the cell located at the intersection of column D and row 5 (Figure 1–7).

One cell on the worksheet, designated the **active cell**, is the worksheet cell into which you are entering data. The active cell in Figure 1–7 is A1. The active cell is identified in three ways. First, a heavy border surrounds the cell; second, the active cell reference shows immediately above column A in the Name box; and third, the column heading A and row heading 1 are highlighted so that it is easy to see which cell is active (Figure 1–7).

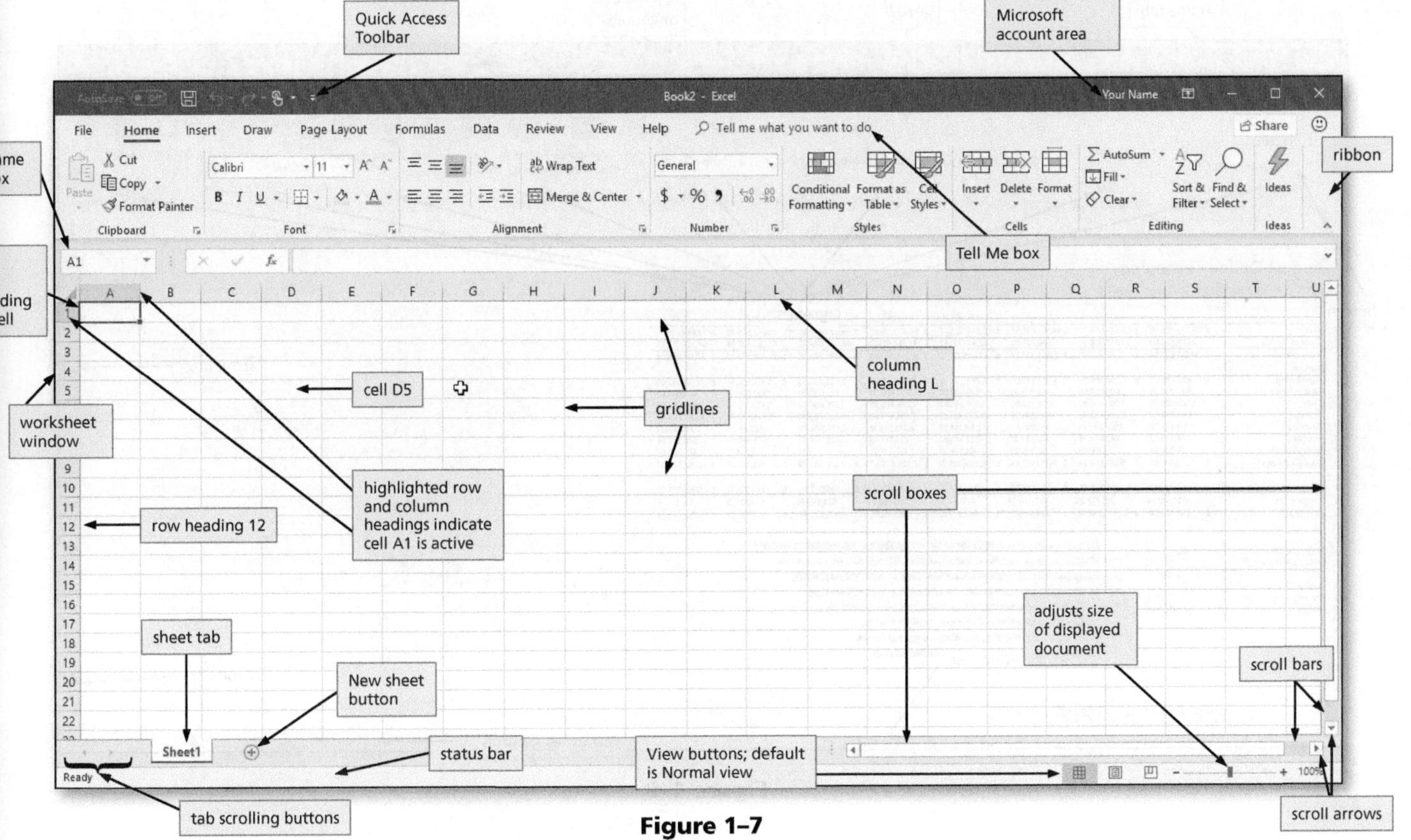

Figure 1–7

The evenly spaced horizontal and/or vertical lines used in a worksheet or chart are called **gridlines**. Gridlines make a worksheet easier to read. If desired, you can turn the gridlines off so that they do not show on the worksheet. While learning Excel, gridlines help you to understand the structure of the worksheet.

The pointer appears as a block plus sign whenever it is located in a cell on the worksheet. Another common shape of the pointer is the block arrow. The pointer turns into the block arrow when you move it outside the worksheet or when you drag cell contents between rows or columns.

Scroll Bars **Scroll bars** on the right edge (vertical scroll bar) and bottom edge (horizontal scroll bar) of a document window let you view a document that is too large to fit on the screen at once. You use a scroll bar to display different portions of a document in the document window. On a scroll bar, the position of the scroll box reflects the location of the portion of the document that is displayed in the document window.

Status Bar The **status bar** is the gray bar at the bottom of the Excel window that shows status information about the currently open worksheet, as well as view buttons and zoom controls. As you type text or perform certain tasks, various indicators and buttons may appear on the status bar. The right side of the status bar includes buttons and controls you can use to change the view of a document and adjust the size of the displayed document.

Ribbon The **ribbon** (shown in Figure 1–8) is a horizontal strip near the top of the window that contains tabs (pages) of grouped command buttons that you click to interact with the app. Each **tab** in the ribbon contains a group of related commands and settings. Each **group** is a tab element on the ribbon that contains related commands. When you start an Office app, such as Excel, it initially displays several main tabs, also called default or top-level tabs. All Office apps have a Home tab, which contains the more frequently used commands. When you start Excel, the ribbon displays ten main tabs: File, Home, Insert, Draw, Page Layout, Formulas, Data, Review, View, and Help. (If you are using a desktop computer, you might not see the Draw tab.)

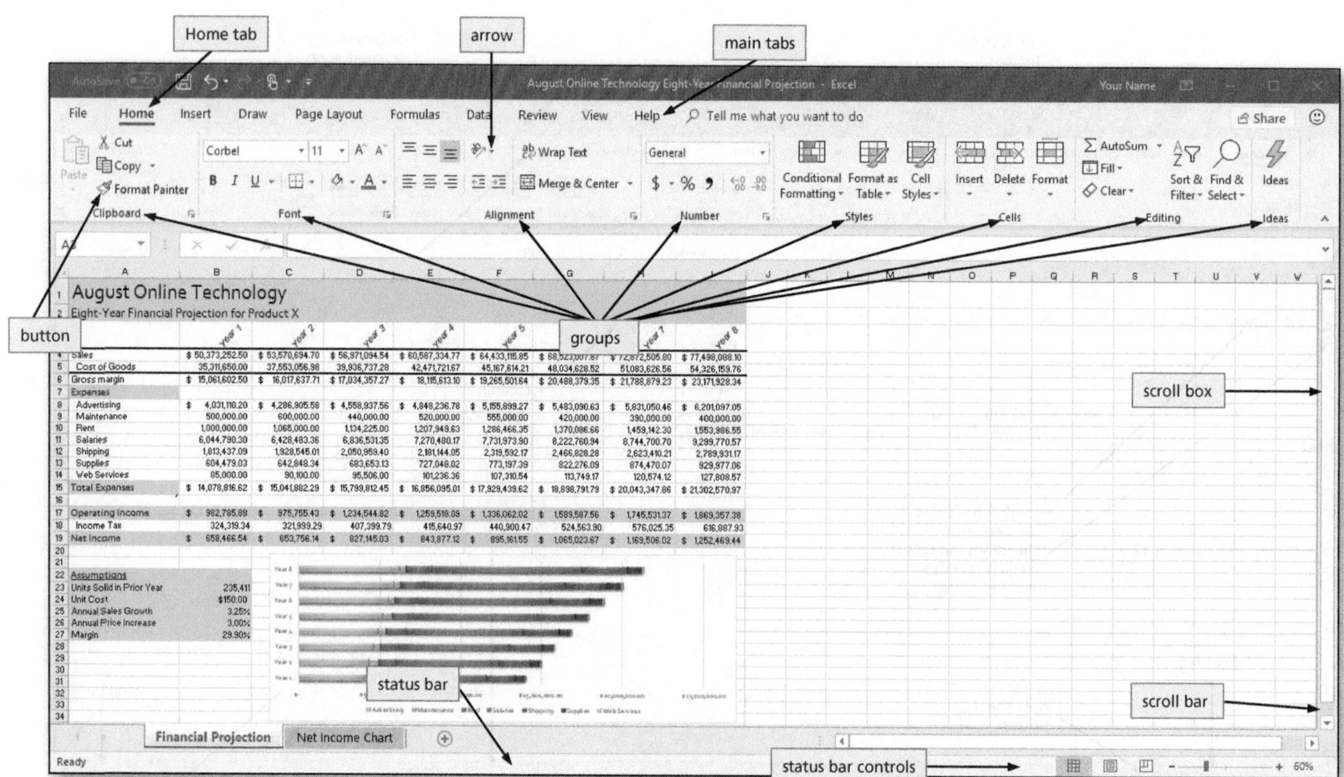

Figure 1–8

In addition to the main tabs, Excel displays **tool tabs**, also called **contextual tabs** (Figure 1–9), tabs that appear in addition to the main tabs on the ribbon when you perform certain tasks or work with objects, such as pictures or tables. If you insert a chart in an Excel workbook, for example, the Chart Tools tab and its related subordinate Design and Format tabs appear, collectively referred to as the Chart Tools Design tab or the Chart Tools Format tab. When you are finished working with the chart, the Chart Tools tabs disappear from the ribbon. Excel determines when tool tabs should appear and disappear based on tasks you perform.

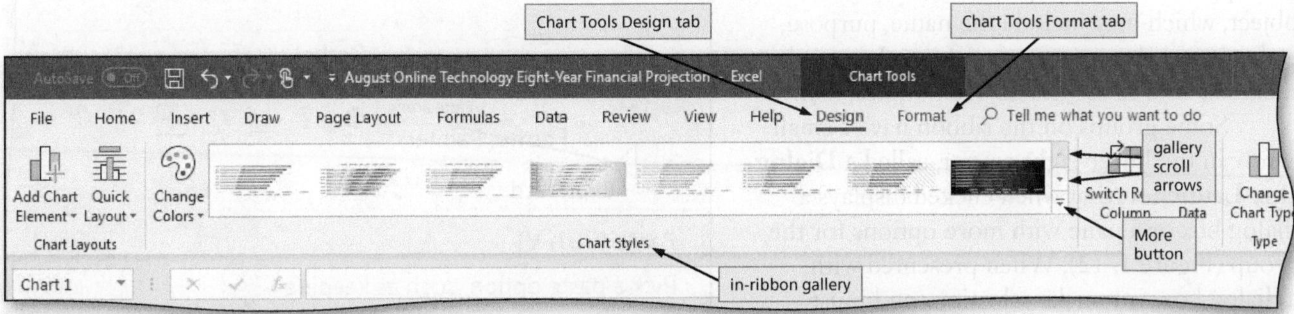

Figure 1–9

Items on the ribbon include buttons and galleries (shown in Figures 1–8 and 1–9). A **gallery** is a collection of choices, arranged in a grid or list, that you can browse through before making a selection of items such as fonts. You can scroll through choices in a gallery by clicking its scroll arrows. Or, you can click a gallery's More button to view more gallery options on the screen at a time.

Some buttons and boxes have arrows that, when clicked, also display a gallery; others always cause a gallery to be displayed when clicked. Most galleries support **live preview**, an Office feature that shows the results that would occur in your file, such as the effects of formatting options on a document's appearance, if you clicked the option you are pointing to (Figure 1–10). Live preview works only if you are using a mouse; if you are using a touch screen, you will not be able to view live previews.

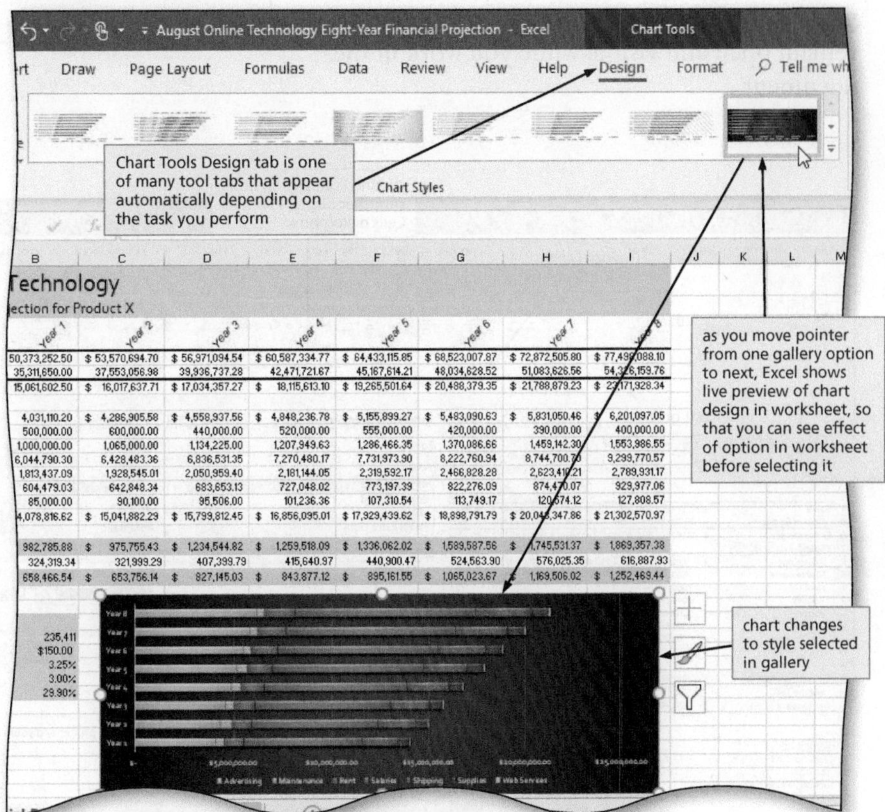

Figure 1–10

Some commands on the ribbon display an image to help you remember their function. When you point to a command on the ribbon, all or part of the command glows in a darker shade of gray, and a ScreenTip appears on the screen. A **ScreenTip** (Figure 1–11) is a label that appears when you point to a button or object, which may include the name, purpose, or keyboard shortcut for the object. It may also include a link to associated Help topics, if any.

Some groups on the ribbon have a small arrow in the lower-right corner, called a **Dialog Box Launcher**, that when clicked displays a dialog box or a pane with more options for the group (Figure 1–12). When presented with a dialog box, you make selections and must close the dialog box before returning to the document. A **pane**, in contrast to a dialog box, is a section of a window, such as the navigation pane in the File Explorer window, that can remain open and visible while you work in the document.

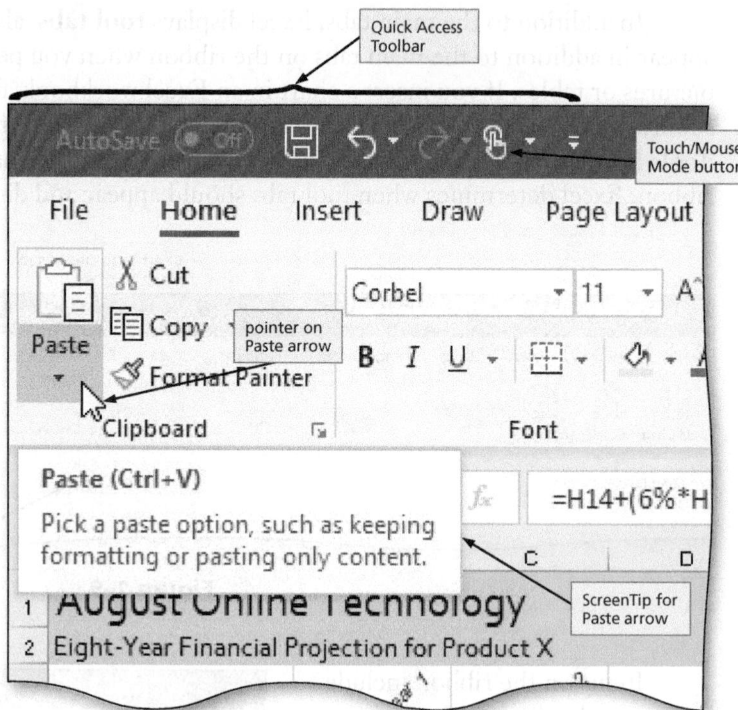

Figure 1–11

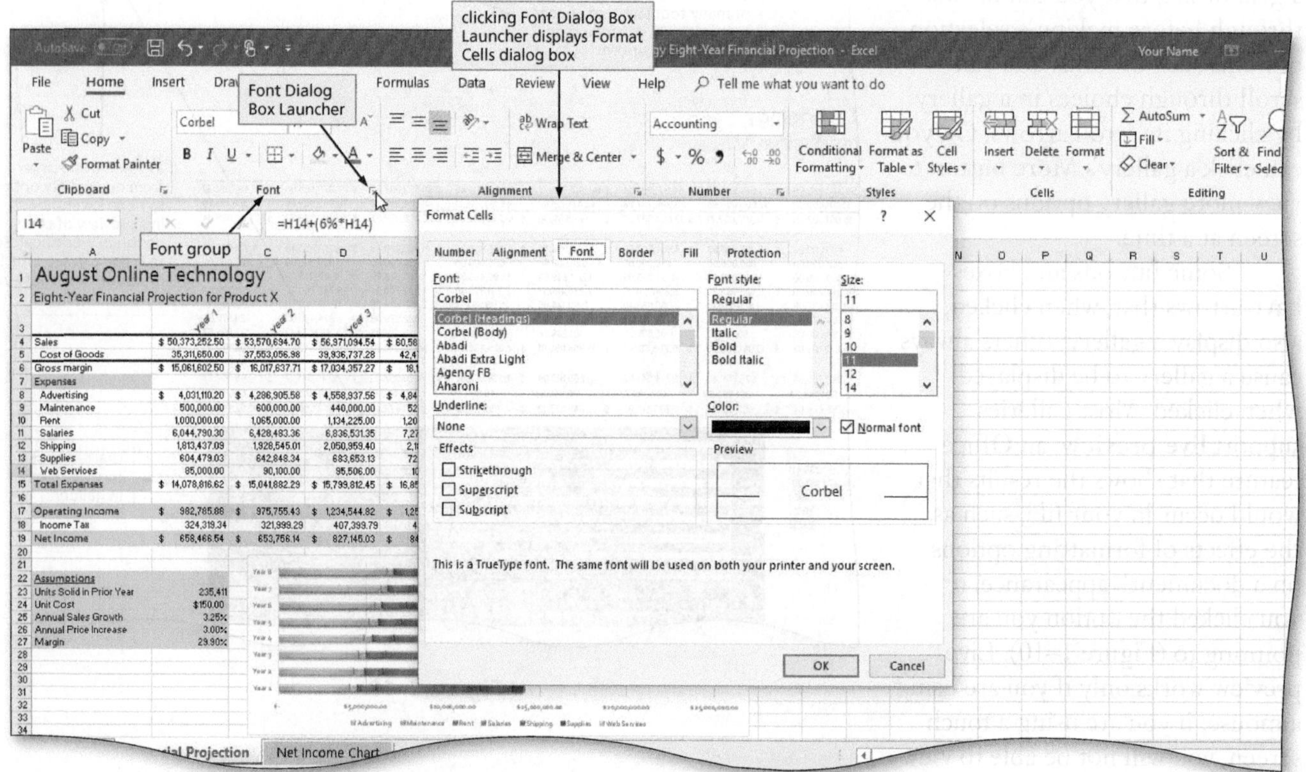

Figure 1–12

Mini Toolbar The **Mini toolbar** is a small toolbar that appears automatically next to selected text and that contains the most frequently used text formatting commands, such as bold, italic, font color, and font size

(Figure 1–13). If you do not use the Mini toolbar, it disappears from the screen. The buttons, arrows, and boxes on the Mini toolbar may vary, depending on whether you are using Touch mode versus Mouse mode. If you right-click an item in the document window, Excel displays both the Mini toolbar and a shortcut menu, which is discussed in a later section in this module.

All commands on the Mini toolbar also exist on the ribbon. The purpose of the Mini toolbar is to minimize hand or mouse movement.

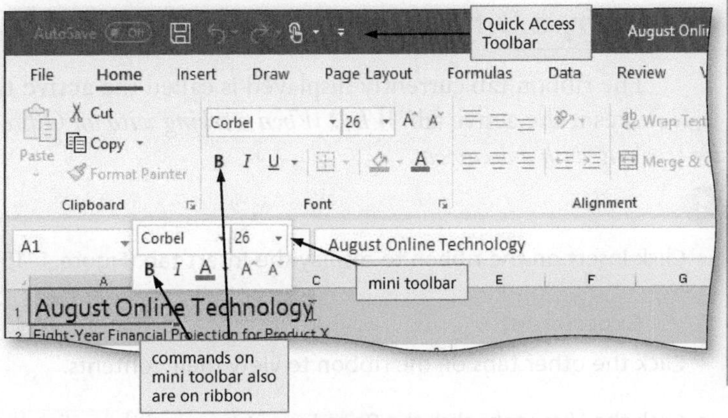

Figure 1–13

Quick Access Toolbar The **Quick Access Toolbar** (shown in Figure 1–13) is a customizable toolbar at the left edge of the title bar that contains buttons you can click to perform frequently used commands. The commands on the Quick Access Toolbar always are available, regardless of the task you are performing. If your computer or mobile device has a touch screen, the Touch/Mouse Mode button will appear on the Quick Access Toolbar and will allow you to switch between Touch mode and Mouse mode. If you are primarily using touch gestures, Touch mode will add more space between commands on menus and on the ribbon so that they are easier to tap. While touch gestures are convenient ways to interact with Office apps, not all features are supported when you are using Touch mode. If you are using a mouse, Mouse mode will not add the extra space between buttons and commands. The Quick Access Toolbar is discussed in more depth later in the module.

KeyTips If you prefer using the keyboard instead of the mouse, you can display KeyTips for certain commands (Figure 1–14). **KeyTips** are labels that appear over each tab and command on the ribbon when the ALT key is pressed. To select a command using the keyboard, press the letter or number displayed in the KeyTip, which may cause additional KeyTips related to the selected command to appear. To remove KeyTips from the screen, press the ALT key or the ESC key until all KeyTips disappear, or click anywhere in the app window.

Formula Bar As you type, Excel displays your entry in the **formula bar**, the area above the worksheet grid where you enter or edit data in the active cell (Figure 1–14). You can make the formula bar larger by dragging the bottom of the formula bar or clicking the expand button to the right of the formula bar. Excel also displays cell information in the **Name box**, a box to the left of the formula bar that shows the cell reference or name of the active cell.

Tell Me Box The **Tell Me box** is a text box to the right of the ribbon tabs that is used to find a command or to access the Office Help system (Figure 1–14). As you type in the Tell Me box, Excel displays search results that are refined as you type. For example, if you want to center text in a document, you can type "center" in the Tell Me box and then select the appropriate command. The Tell Me box also lists related commands and/or the last five commands accessed from the box.

Microsoft Account Area In the **Microsoft Account area**, an area on the right side of the title bar, you can use the Sign in link to sign in to your Microsoft account (Figure 1–14). Once signed in, you will see your account information.

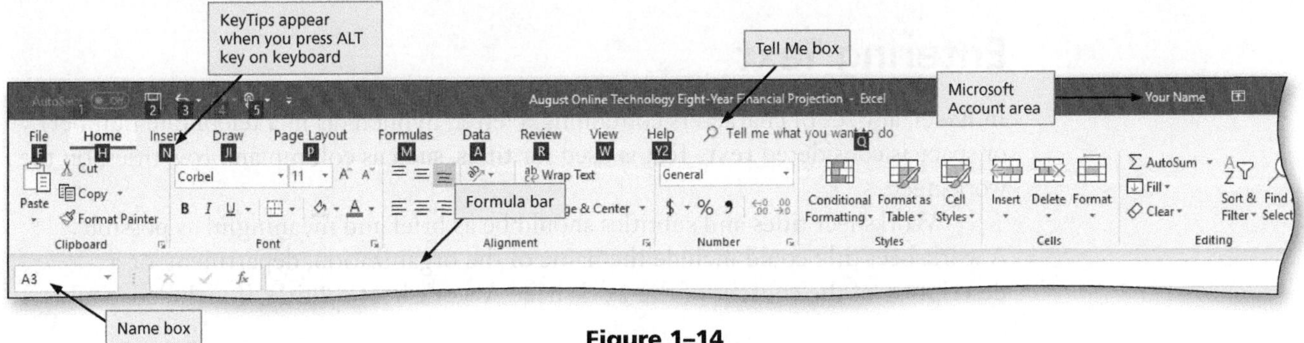

Figure 1–14

To Display a Different Tab on the Ribbon

The ribbon tab currently displayed is called the **active tab**. The following step displays the Insert tab; that is, it makes it the active tab. ***Why?*** *When working with an Office app, you may need to switch tabs to access other options for working with a document.*

- Click Insert on the ribbon to display the Insert tab (Figure 1–15).

Experiment

- Click the other tabs on the ribbon to view their contents.
- Click the View tab, click the Page Layout tab, and then click the Insert tab again.

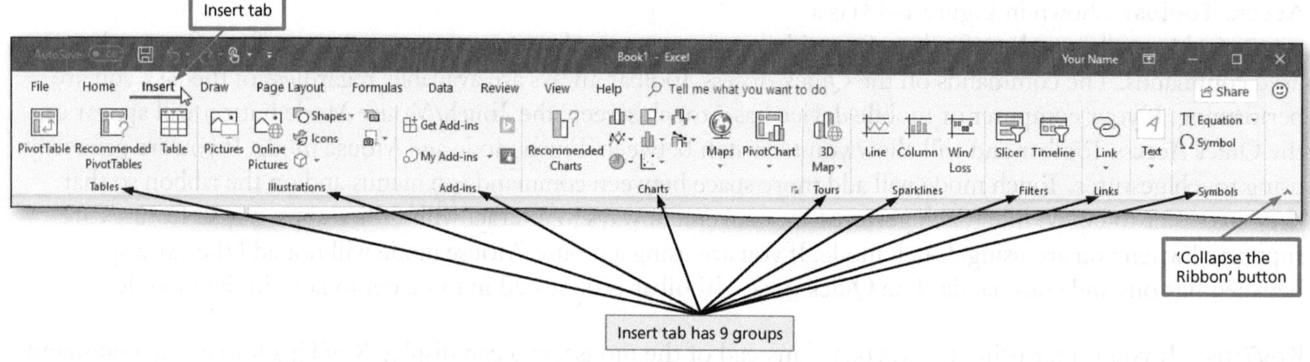

Figure 1–15

Other Ways

1. Press ALT, press letter corresponding to tab to display

Selecting a Cell

BTW
Touch Mode Differences
The Office and Windows interfaces may vary if you are using touch mode. For this reason, you might notice that the function or appearance of your touch screen differs slightly from this module's presentation.

To enter data into a cell, you first must select it. The easiest way to **select** a cell (to make it active) is to use the mouse to move the block plus sign pointer to the cell and then click.

An alternative method is to use the arrow keys that are located on a standard keyboard. An arrow key selects the cell adjacent to the active cell in the direction of the arrow on the key.

You know a cell is selected, or active, when a heavy border surrounds the cell and the active cell reference appears in the Name box on the left side of the formula bar. Excel also changes the color of the active cell's column and row headings to a darker shade.

Entering Text

In Excel, any set of characters containing a letter, hyphen (as in a telephone number), or space is considered **text**. Text is used for titles, such as column and row titles, on the worksheet.

Worksheet titles and subtitles should be as brief and meaningful as possible. A worksheet title could include the name of the organization, department, or a description of the content of the worksheet. A worksheet subtitle, if included, could include a more detailed description of the content of the worksheet. Examples of worksheet titles are January 2021 Payroll and Year 2021 Projected Budget, and examples of subtitles are Finance Department and Monthly Projections, respectively.

As shown in Figure 1–16, data in a worksheet is identified by row and column titles so that the meaning of each entry is clear. Rows typically contain information such as categories of data. Columns typically describe how data is grouped in the worksheet, such as by month or by department.

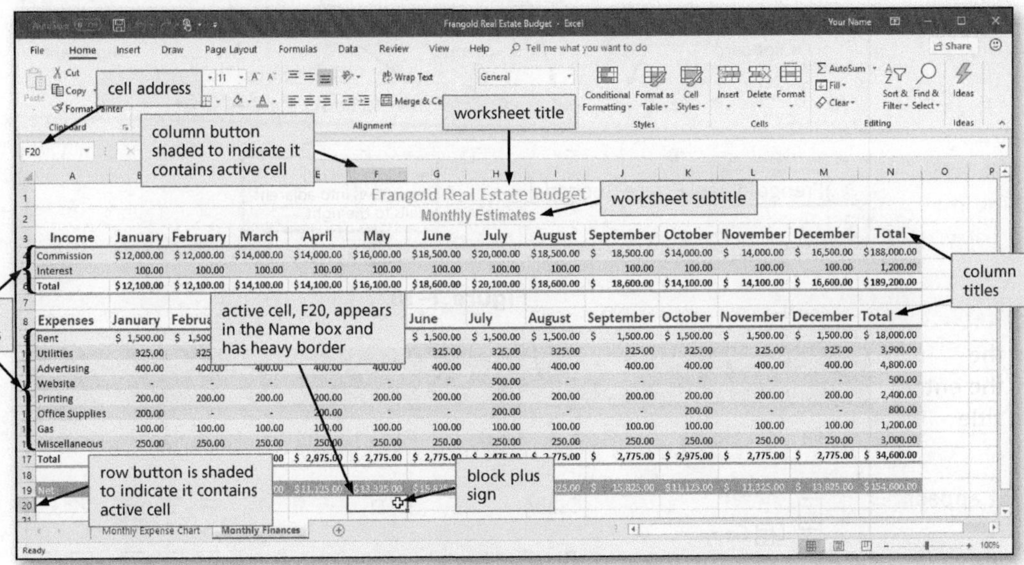

Figure 1–16

BTW

Screen Resolution

If you are using a computer to step through the project in this module and you want your screens to match the figures in this book, you should change your screen's resolution to 1366 × 768.

To Enter the Worksheet Titles

As shown in Figure 1–16, the worksheet title, Frangold Real Estate Budget, identifies the purpose of the worksheet. The worksheet subtitle, Monthly Estimates, identifies the type of data contained in the worksheet. ***Why?*** *A title and subtitle help the reader to understand clearly what the worksheet contains.* The following steps enter the worksheet titles in cells A1 and A2. Later in this module, the worksheet titles will be formatted so that they appear as shown in Figure 1–16.

- Click Home on the ribbon to display the Home tab.
- If necessary, click cell A1 to make cell A1 the active cell (Figure 1–17).

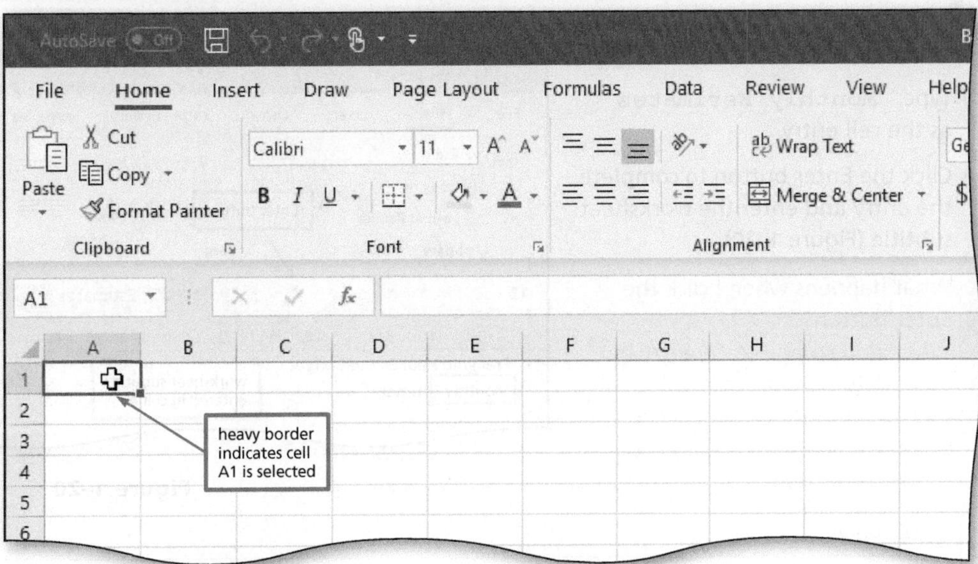

Figure 1–17

2

- Type **`Frangold Real Estate Budget`** in cell A1 (Figure 1–18).

Why did the appearance of the formula bar change?
Excel displays the title in the formula bar and in cell A1. When you begin typing a cell entry, Excel enables two additional boxes in the formula bar: The Cancel button and the Enter button. Clicking the Enter button completes an entry. Clicking the Cancel button cancels an entry.

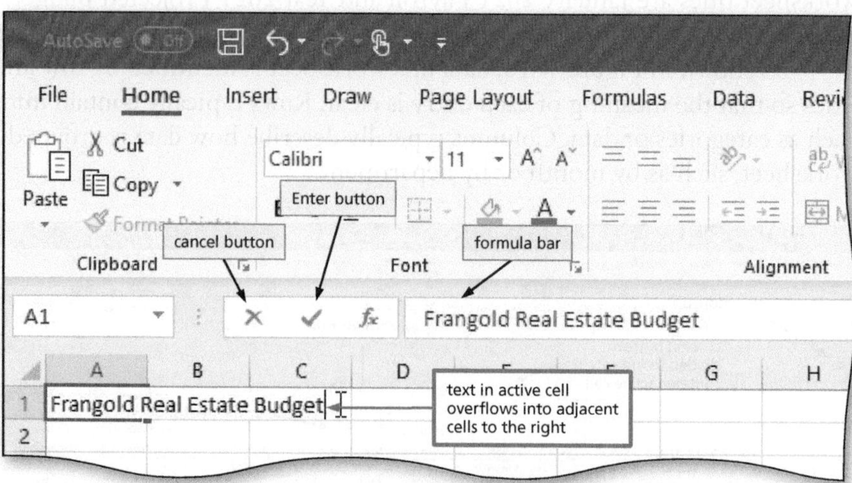

Figure 1–18

3

- Click the Enter button in the formula bar to complete the entry and enter the worksheet title (Figure 1–19).

Why does the entered text appear in three cells?
When the typed text is longer than the width of a cell, Excel displays the overflow characters in adjacent cells to the right as long as those adjacent cells contain no data. If the adjacent cells contain data, Excel hides the overflow characters. The overflow characters are visible in the formula bar whenever that cell is active.

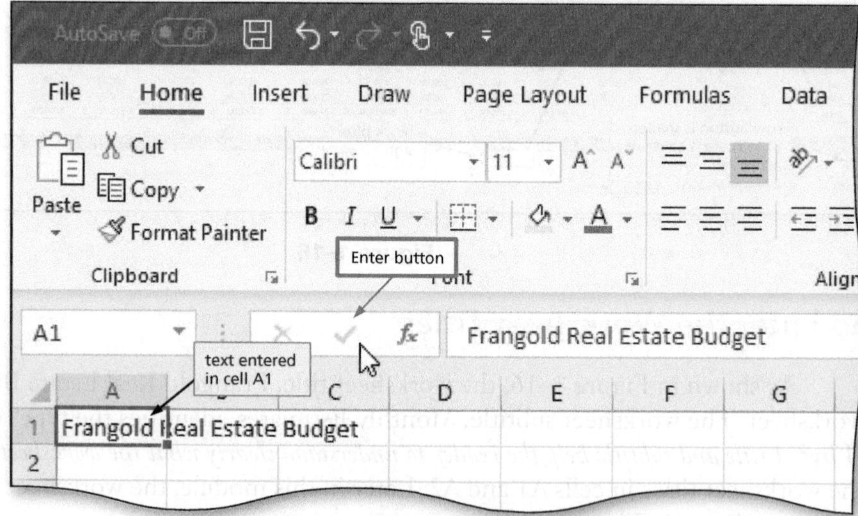

Figure 1–19

4

- Click cell A2 to select it.
- Type **`Monthly Estimates`** as the cell entry.
- Click the Enter button to complete the entry and enter the worksheet subtitle (Figure 1–20).

Q&A
What happens when I click the Enter button?
When you complete an entry by clicking the Enter button, the insertion point disappears and the cell in which the text is entered remains the active cell.

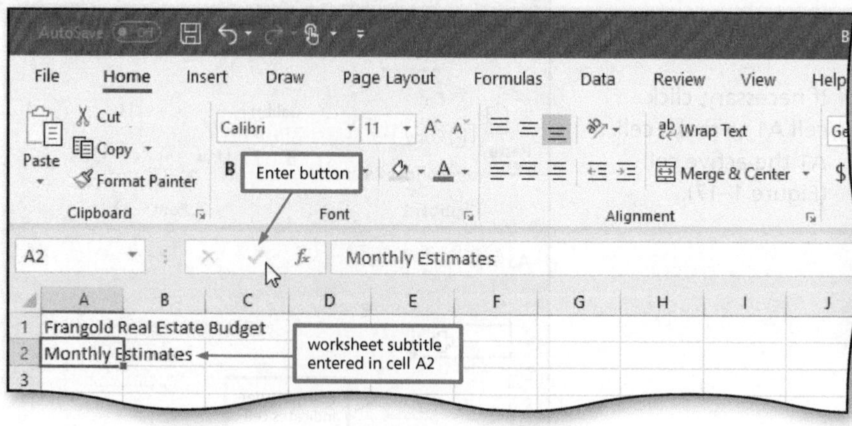

Figure 1–20

Other Ways

1. Click any cell other than active cell
2. Press ENTER
3. Press HOME, PAGE UP, PAGE DOWN, END, UP ARROW, DOWN ARROW, LEFT ARROW, or RIGHT ARROW

CONSIDER THIS

Why is it difficult to read the text on my screen?
If you are having trouble reading the cell values in your spreadsheet, you can zoom in to make the cells larger. When you zoom in, fewer columns and rows display on your screen, and you might have to scroll more often. To zoom in, drag the zoom slider on the right side of the status bar, or click the plus button on the zoom slider, until you reach your desired zoom level. You also can zoom by clicking the Zoom button (View tab | Zoom group), selecting a desired zoom percentage (Zoom dialog box), and then clicking OK (Zoom dialog box).

AutoCorrect

The **AutoCorrect** feature of Excel works behind the scenes, where it automatically detects and corrects typing errors. AutoCorrect makes three types of corrections for you:

1. Corrects two initial uppercase letters by changing the second letter to lowercase.
2. Capitalizes the first letter in the names of days.
3. Replaces commonly misspelled words with their correct spelling. For example, it will change the misspelled word *recieve* to *receive* when you complete the entry. AutoCorrect will correct the spelling of hundreds of commonly misspelled words automatically.

BTW
Ribbon and Screen Resolution
Excel may change how the groups and buttons within the groups appear on the ribbon, depending on the screen resolution of your computer. Thus, your ribbon may look different from the ones in this book if you are using a screen resolution other than 1366 × 768.

To Enter Column Titles

The worksheet is divided into two parts, income and expense, as shown in Figure 1–16. Grouping income and expense data by month is a common method for organizing budget data. The column titles shown in row 3 identify the income section of the worksheet and indicate that the income values will be grouped by month. Likewise, row 8 is clearly identified as the expense section and similarly indicates that the expense values will be estimated on a per-month basis. The following steps enter the column titles in row 3. ***Why?*** *Data entered in columns should be identified using column titles to identify what the column contains.*

- Click cell A3 to make it the active cell.
- Type `Income` to begin entry of a column title in the active cell (Figure 1–21).

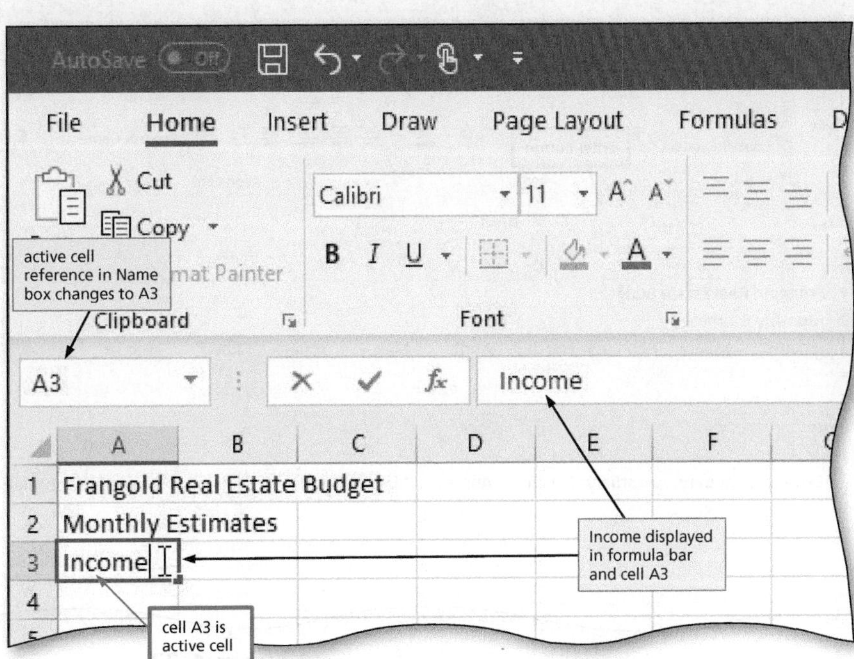

Figure 1–21

2

- Press the RIGHT ARROW key to enter the column title and make the cell to the right the active cell (Figure 1–22).

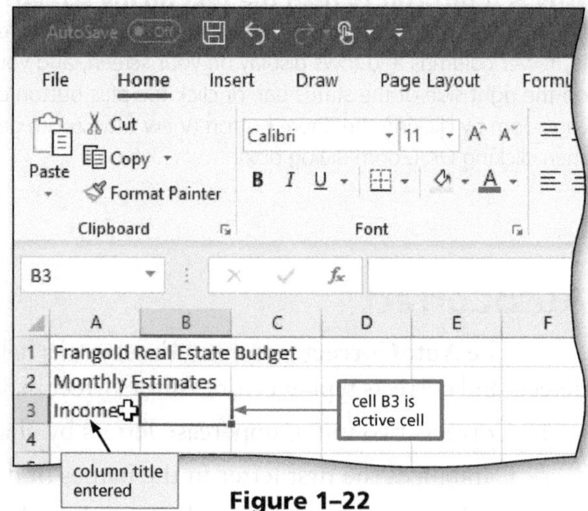

Figure 1–22

Q&A Why is the RIGHT ARROW key used to complete the entry in the cell?

Pressing an arrow key to complete an entry makes the adjacent cell in the direction of the arrow (up, down, left, or right) the next active cell. However, if your next entry is in a nonadjacent cell, you can complete your current entry by clicking the next cell in which you plan to enter data. You also can press ENTER and then click the appropriate cell for the next entry.

3

- Repeat Steps 1 and 2 to enter the remaining column titles; that is, enter `January` in cell B3, `February` in cell C3, `March` in cell D3, `April` in cell E3, `May` in cell F3, `June` in cell G3, `July` in cell H3, `August` in cell I3, `September` in cell J3, `October` in cell K3, `November` in cell L3, `December` in cell M3, and `Total` in cell N3 (complete the last entry in cell N3 by clicking the Enter button in the formula bar).
- Click cell A8 to select it.
- Repeat Steps 1 and 2 to enter the remaining column titles; that is, enter `Expenses` in cell A8, `January` in cell B8, `February` in cell C8, `March` in cell D8, `April` in cell E8, `May` in cell F8, `June` in cell G8, `July` in cell H8, `August` in cell I8, `September` in cell J8, `October` in cell K8, `November` in cell L8, `December` in cell M8, and `Total` in cell N8 (complete the last entry in cell N8 by clicking the Enter button in the formula bar) (Figure 1–23).

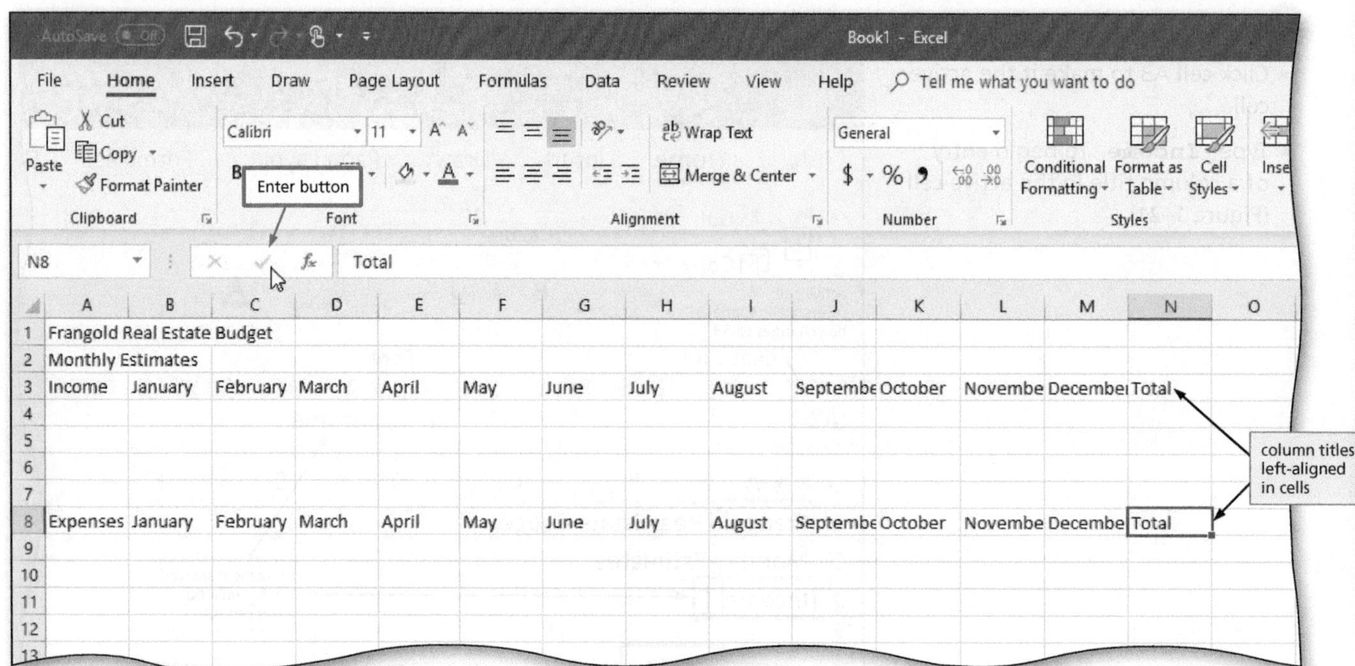

Figure 1–23

To Enter Row Titles

The next step in developing the worksheet for this project is to enter the row titles in column A. For the Frangold Real Estate Budget worksheet data, the row titles contain a list of income types and expense types. Each income or expense item should be placed in its own row. ***Why?*** *Entering one item per row allows for maximum flexibility, in case more income or expense items are added in the future.* The following steps enter the row titles in the worksheet.

- Click cell A4 to select it.
- Type **Commission** and then click cell A5 or press the DOWN ARROW key to enter a row title (Figure 1–24).

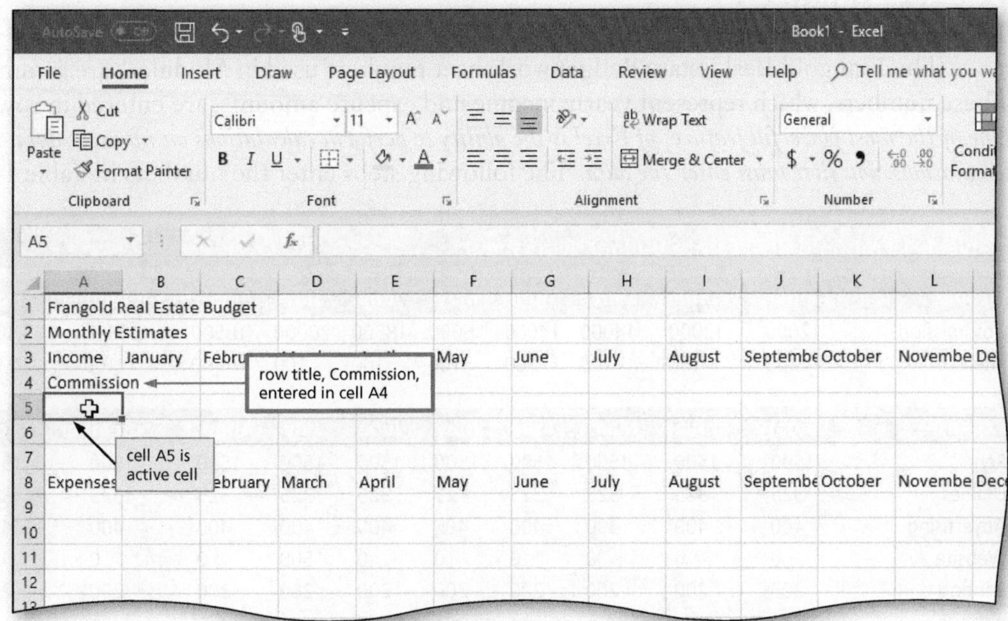

Figure 1–24

2

- Repeat Step 1 to enter the remaining row titles in column A; that is, enter **Interest** in cell A5, **Total** in cell A6, **Rent** in cell A9, **Utilities** in cell A10, **Advertising** in cell A11, **Website** in cell A12, **Printing** in cell A13, **Office Supplies** in cell A14, **Gas** in cell A15, **Miscellaneous** in cell A16, **Total** in cell A17, and **Net** in cell A19 (Figure 1–25).

Q&A Why is the text left-aligned in the cells?
Excel automatically left-aligns the text in the cell. Excel treats any combination of numbers, spaces, and nonnumeric characters as text. For example, Excel would recognize the following entries as text: 401AX21, 921–231, 619 321, 883XTY. How to change the text alignment in a cell is discussed later in this module.

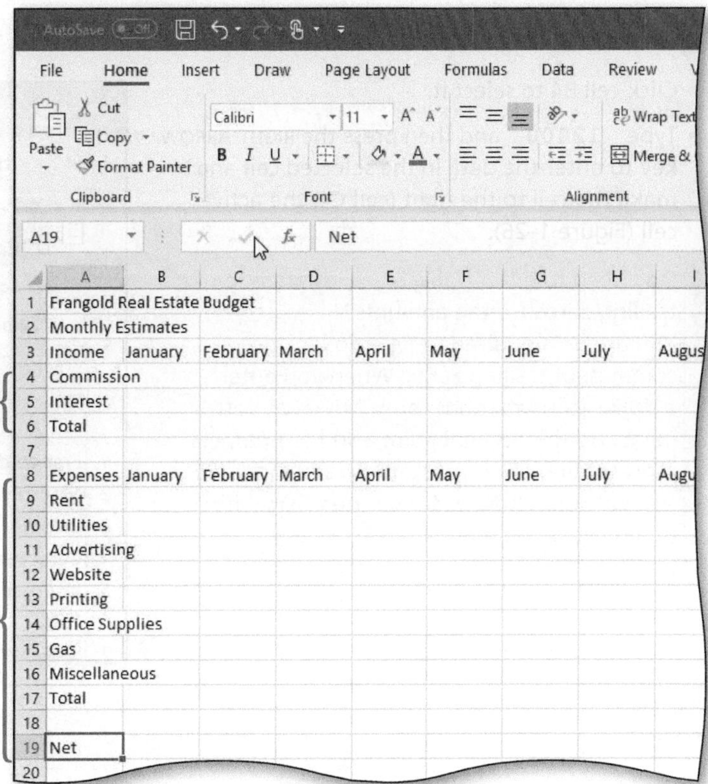

Figure 1–25

Entering Numbers

In Excel, you enter a number into a cell to represent an amount or value. A **number** is an amount or value using any of the following characters: 1 2 3 4 5 6 7 8 9 + - ( ) , / . $ E e. The use of special characters is explained when they are used in this book. If you are entering numbers that will not be used in a calculation, you should format those numbers as text. You can format numeric data as text by typing an apostrophe before the number(s).

To Enter Numbers

The Frangold Real Estate Budget worksheet numbers used in Module 1 are summarized in Table 1–1. These numbers, which represent yearly income and expense amounts, are entered in rows 4–5 and 9–16. ***Why?*** *One of the most powerful features of Excel is the ability to perform calculations on numeric data. Before you can perform calculations, you first must enter the data.* The following steps enter the numbers in Table 1–1 one row at a time.

Table 1–1 Frangold Real Estate Budget Worksheet

Income	January	February	March	April	May	June	July	August	September	October	November	December
Commission	12000	12000	14000	14000	16000	18500	20000	18500	18500	14000	14000	16500
Interest	100	100	100	100	100	100	100	100	100	100	100	100

Expenses	January	February	March	April	May	June	July	August	September	October	November	December
Rent	1500	1500	1500	1500	1500	1500	1500	1500	1500	1500	1500	1500
Utilities	325	325	325	325	325	325	325	325	325	325	325	325
Advertising	400	400	400	400	400	400	400	400	400	400	400	400
Website	0	0	0	0	0	0	500	0	0	0	0	0
Printing	200	200	200	200	200	200	200	200	200	200	200	200
Office Supplies	200	0	0	200	0	0	200	0	0	200	0	0
Gas	100	100	100	100	100	100	100	100	100	100	100	100
Miscellaneous	250	250	250	250	250	250	250	250	250	250	250	250

- Click cell B4 to select it.
- Type `12000` and then press the RIGHT ARROW key to enter the data in the selected cell and make the cell to the right (cell C4) the active cell (Figure 1–26).

Q&A Do I need to enter dollar signs, commas, or trailing zeros for the amounts?

You are not required to type dollar signs, commas, or trailing zeros. When you enter a dollar value that has cents, however, you must add the decimal point and the numbers representing the cents. Later in this module, you will learn how to format numbers with dollar signs, commas, and trailing zeros to improve their appearance and readability.

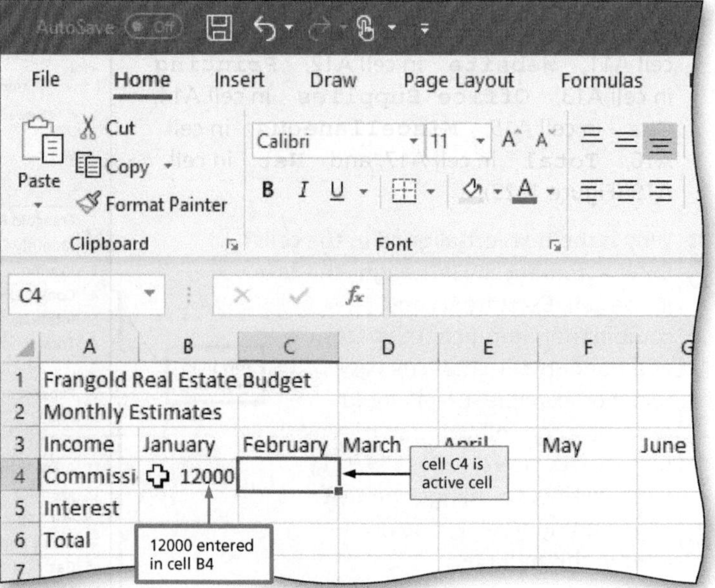

Figure 1–26

2

- Refer to Table 1–1 and enter the appropriate values in cells C4, D4, E4, F4, G4, H4, I4, J4, K4, L4, and M4 to complete the first row of numbers in the worksheet (Figure 1–27).

Q&A Why are the numbers right-aligned?
When you enter numeric data in a cell, Excel recognizes the values as numbers and automatically right-aligns the values in order to vertically align decimal and integer values.

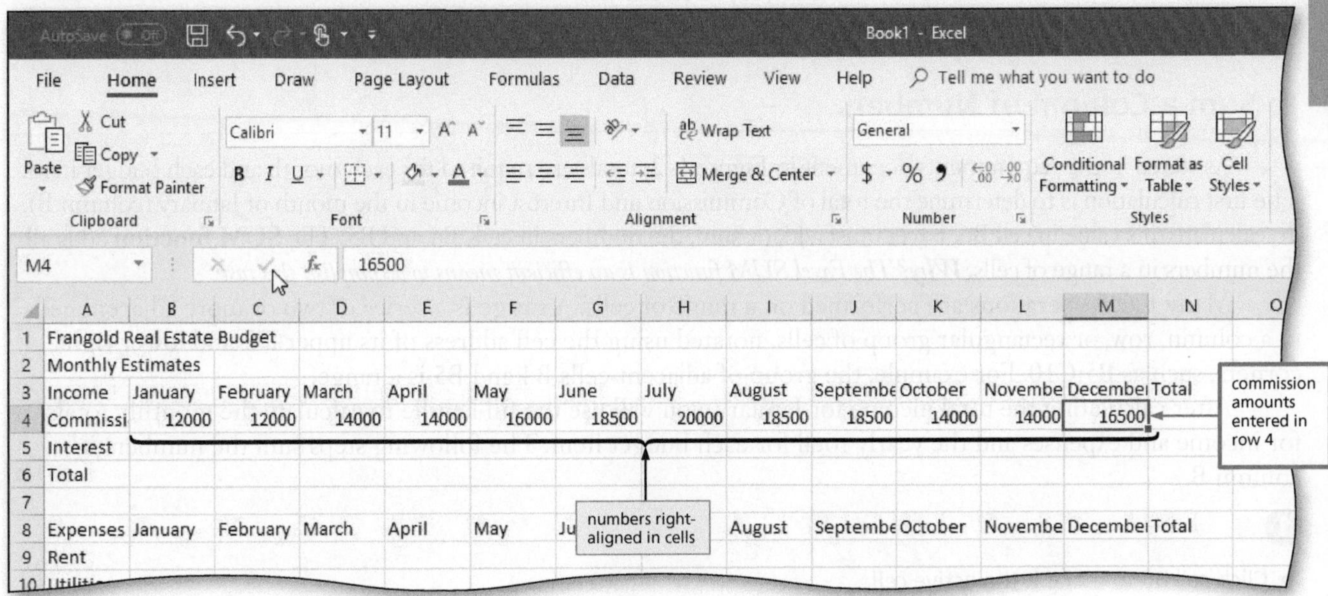

Figure 1–27

- Click cell B5 to select it and complete the entry in the previously selected cell.
- Enter the remaining numbers provided in Table 1–1 for each of the nine remaining budget items in row 5 and rows 9–16 (Figure 1–28).

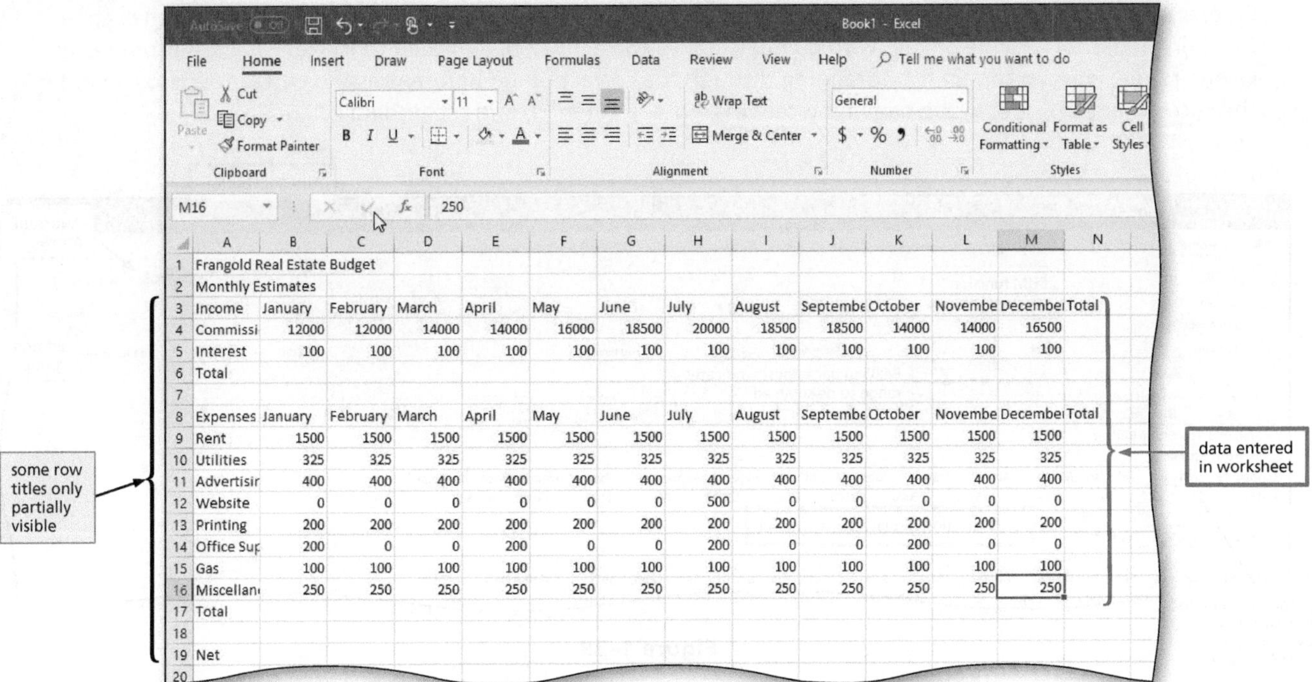

Figure 1–28

Calculating Sums and Using Formulas

The next step in creating the worksheet is to perform any necessary calculations, such as calculating the column and row totals. In Excel, you can easily perform calculations using a function. A **function** is a special, predefined formula that provides a shortcut for a commonly used calculation, for example, SUM or COUNT. When you use functions, Excel performs the calculations for you, which helps to prevent errors and allows you to work more efficiently.

To Sum a Column of Numbers

As stated in the requirements document in Figure 1–2, totals are required for each month and each budget item. The first calculation is to determine the total of Commission and Interest income in the month of January (column B). To calculate this value in cell B6, Excel must add, or sum, the numbers in cells B4 and B5. The **SUM function** adds all the numbers in a range of cells. ***Why?*** *The Excel SUM function is an efficient means to accomplish this task.*

Many Excel operations are performed on a range of cells. A **range** is a series of two or more adjacent cells in a column, row, or rectangular group of cells, notated using the cell address of its upper left and lower right corners, such as B5:C10. For example, the group of adjacent cells B4 and B5 is a range.

After calculating the total income for January, you will use the fill handle to calculate the monthly totals for income and expenses and the yearly total for each budget item. The following steps sum the numbers in column B.

- Click cell B6 to make it the active cell.
- Click the AutoSum button (Home tab | Editing group) to enter a formula in the formula bar and in the active cell (Figure 1–29).

Q&A

What if my screen displays the Sum menu?

If you are using a touch screen, you may not have a separate AutoSum button and AutoSum arrow. In this case, select the desired option (Sum) on the AutoSum menu.

How does Excel know which cells to sum?

Excel automatically selects what it considers to be your choice of the range to sum. When proposing the range, Excel first looks for a range of cells with numbers above the active cell and then to the left. If Excel proposes the wrong range, you can correct it by dragging through the correct range before pressing ENTER. You also can enter the correct range by typing the beginning cell reference, a colon (:), and the ending cell reference.

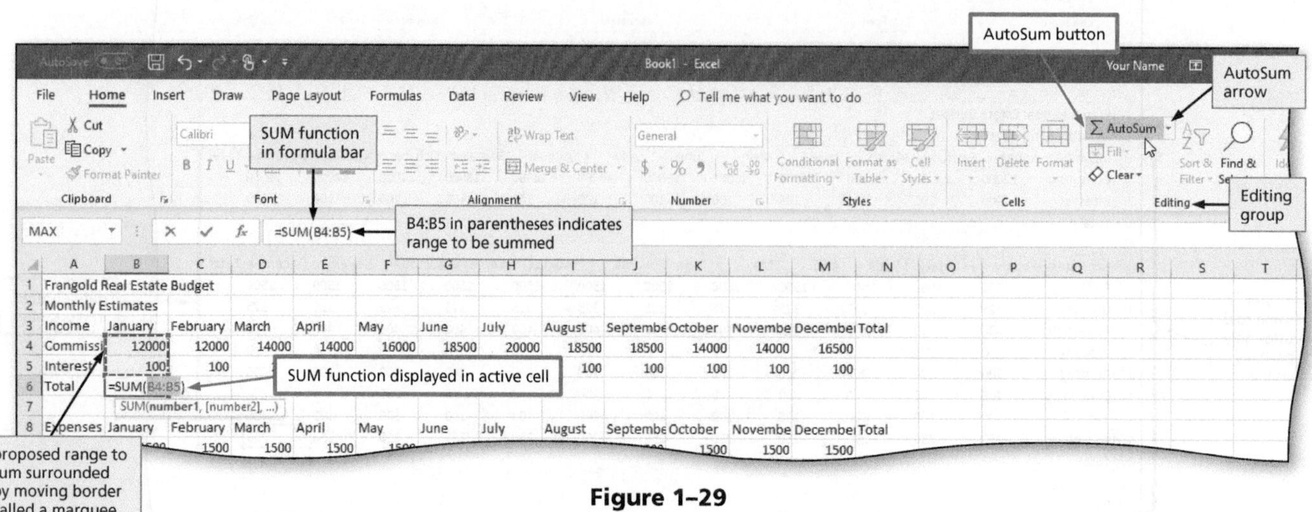

Figure 1–29

2

- Click the Enter button in the formula bar to enter the sum in the active cell.

Q&A What is the purpose of the arrow next to the AutoSum button on the ribbon?
The AutoSum arrow (shown in Figure 1–29) displays a list of functions that allow you to easily determine the average of a range of numbers, the number of items in a selected range, or the maximum or minimum value of a range.

3

- Repeat Steps 1 and 2 to enter the SUM function in cell B17 (Figure 1–30).

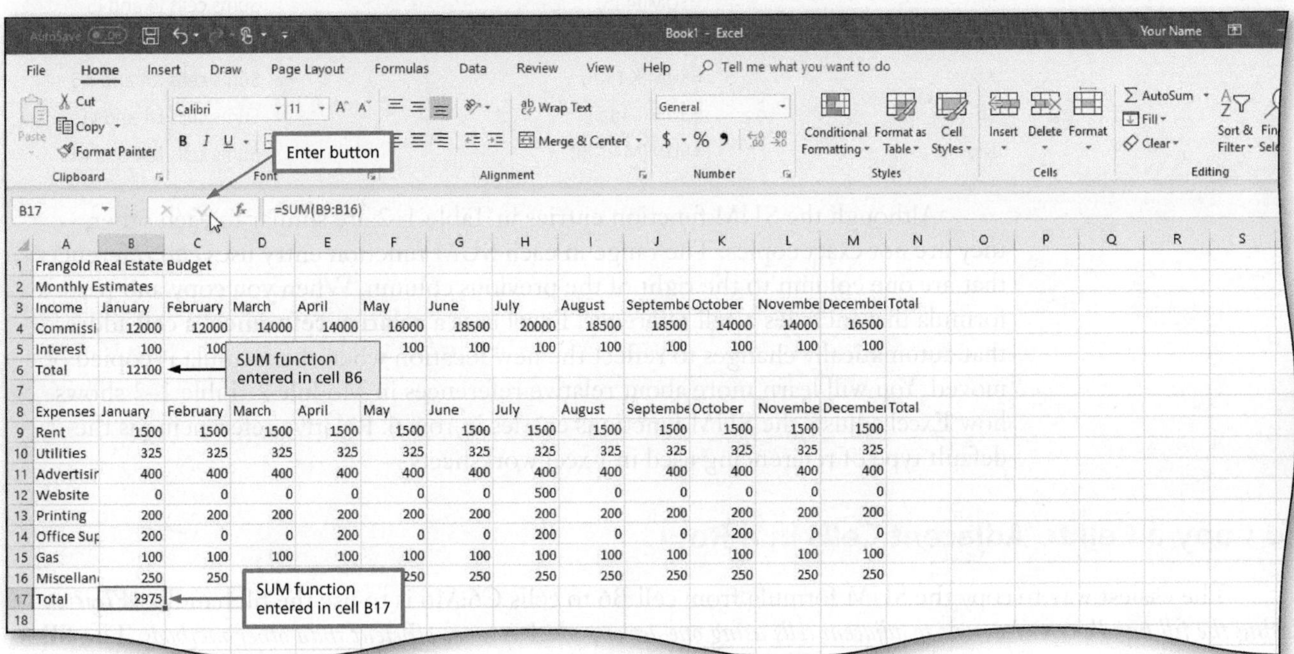

Figure 1–30

Other Ways

1. Click Insert Function button in formula bar, select SUM in Select a function list, click OK (Insert Function dialog box), click OK (Function Arguments dialog box)
2. Click AutoSum arrow (Home tab | Editing group), click More Functions in list, scroll to and then click SUM (Insert Function dialog box), click OK, select range (Function Arguments dialog box), click OK
3. Type **=s** in cell, select SUM in list, select range, click Enter button
4. Press ALT+EQUAL SIGN (=) twice

Using the Fill Handle to Copy a Cell to Adjacent Cells

You want to calculate the income totals for each month in cells C6:M6. Table 1–2 illustrates the similarities between the function and range used in cell B6 and the function and ranges required to sum the totals in cells C6, D6, E6, F6, G6, H6, I6, J6, K6, L6, and M6.

To calculate each total for each range across the worksheet, you could follow the same steps shown previously in Figure 1–29 and Figure 1–30. A more efficient method, however, would be to copy the SUM function from cell B6 to the range C6:M6. A range of cells you are cutting or copying is called the **source area** or **copy area**. The range of cells to which you are pasting is called the **destination area** or **paste area**.

Table 1–2 Sum Function Entries in Row 6

Cell	SUM Function Entries	Result
B6	=SUM(B4:B5)	Sums cells B4 and B5
C6	=SUM(C4:C5)	Sums cells C4 and C5
D6	=SUM(D4:D5)	Sums cells D4 and D5
E6	=SUM(E4:E5)	Sums cells E4 and E5
F6	=SUM(F4:F5)	Sums cells F4 and F5
G6	=SUM(G4:G5)	Sums cells G4 and G5
H6	=SUM(H4:H5)	Sums cells H4 and H5
I6	=SUM(I4:I5)	Sums cells I4 and I5
J6	=SUM(J4:J5)	Sums cells J4 and J5
K6	=SUM(K4:K5)	Sums cells K4 and K5
L6	=SUM(L4:L5)	Sums cells L4 and L5
M6	=SUM(M4:M5)	Sums cells M4 and M5

Although the SUM function entries in Table 1–2 are similar to each other, they are not exact copies. The range in each SUM function entry uses cell references that are one column to the right of the previous column. When you copy and paste a formula that includes a cell reference, Excel uses a **relative reference**, a cell address that automatically changes to reflect the new location when the formula is copied or moved. You will learn more about relative references in Module 2. Table 1–2 shows how Excel adjusts the SUM functions entries in row 6. Relative referencing is the default type of referencing used in Excel worksheets.

To Copy a Cell to Adjacent Cells in a Row

The easiest way to copy the SUM formula from cell B6 to cells C6:M6 is to use the fill handle. ***Why?*** *Using the fill handle copies content to adjacent cells using one action, which is more efficient than other methods.* The **fill handle** is a box that appears in the lower-right corner of a selected cell or range. It is used to fill adjacent cells with duplicate or similar data. The following steps use the fill handle to copy cell B6 to the adjacent cells C6:M6.

- **With cell B6 active, point to the fill handle; your pointer changes to a crosshair (Figure 1–31).**

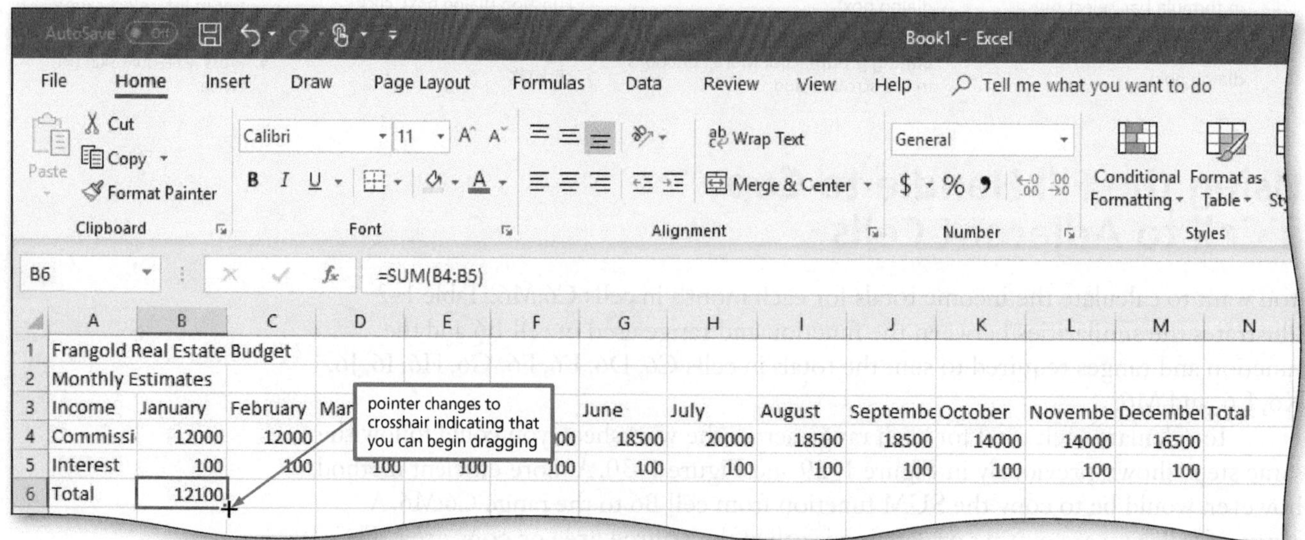

Figure 1–31

2

- Drag the fill handle to select the destination area, the range C6:M6, which will draw a heavy green border around the source area and the destination area (Figure 1–32). Do not release the mouse button.

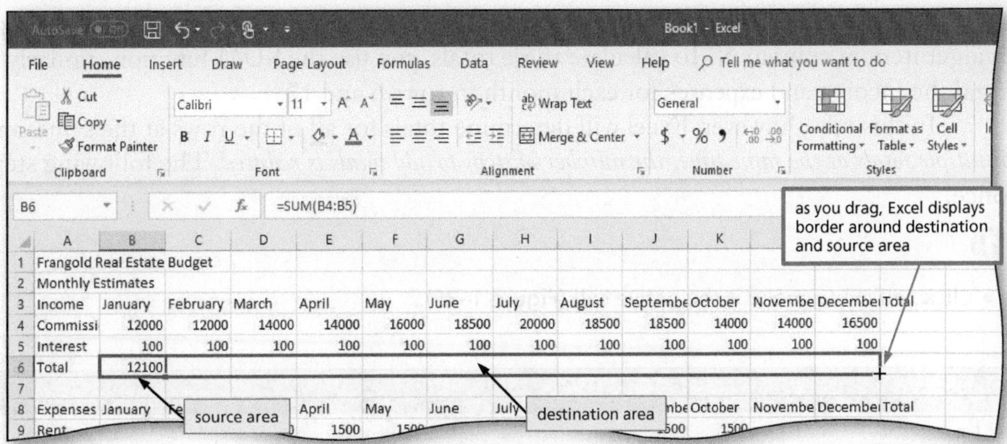

Figure 1–32

3

- Release the mouse button to copy the SUM function from the active cell to the destination area and calculate the sums (Figure 1–33).

Q&A What is the purpose of the Auto Fill Options button?
The Auto Fill Options button allows you to choose whether you want to copy the values from the source area to the destination area with the existing formatting, without the formatting, or with the formatting but without the functions.

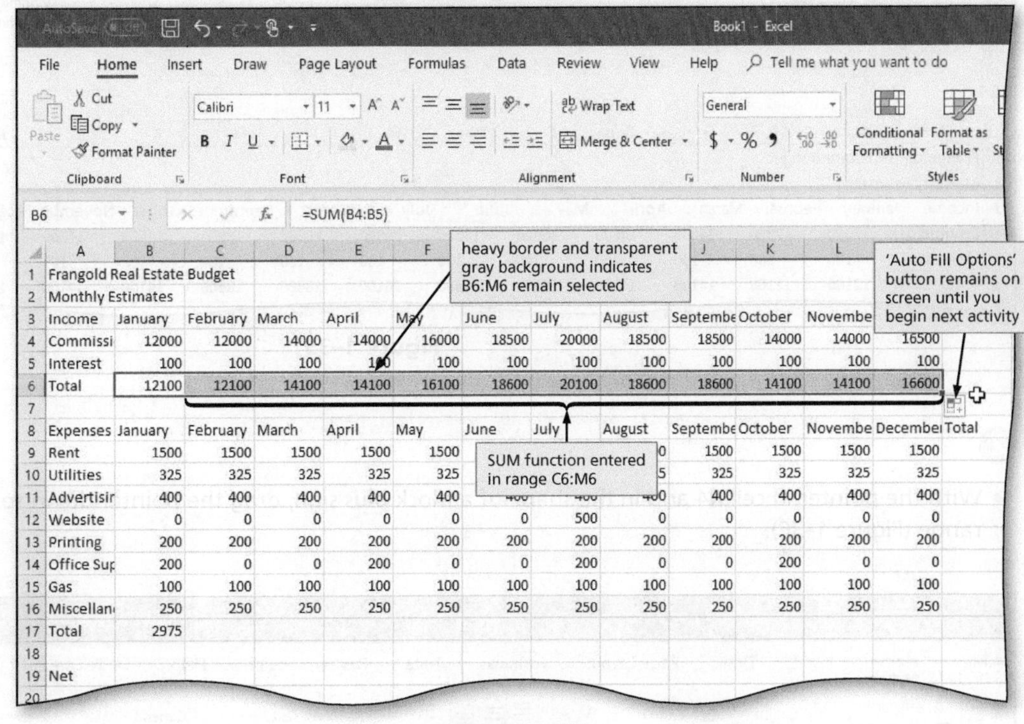

Figure 1–33

4

- Repeat Steps 1–3 to copy the SUM function from cell B17 to the range C17:M17 (Figure 1–34).

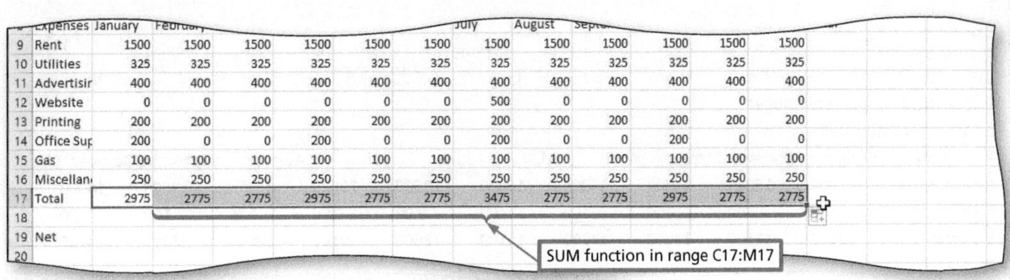

Figure 1–34

Other Ways

1. Select source area, click Copy button (Home tab | Clipboard group), select destination area, click Paste button (Home tab | Clipboard group)
2. Right-click source area, click Copy on shortcut menu, select and right-click destination area, click Paste on shortcut menu
3. Select source and destination areas, click Fill arrow (Home tab | Editing group), click Sum

To Calculate Multiple Totals at the Same Time

The next step in building the worksheet is to determine the total income, total expenses, and total for each budget item in column N. To calculate these totals, you use the SUM function similarly to how you used it to total the income and expenses for each month in rows 6 and 17.

In this case, however, Excel will determine totals for all of the rows at the same time. ***Why?*** *By determining multiple totals at the same time, the number of steps to add totals is reduced.* The following steps sum multiple totals at once.

- Click cell N4 to make it the active cell (Figure 1–35).

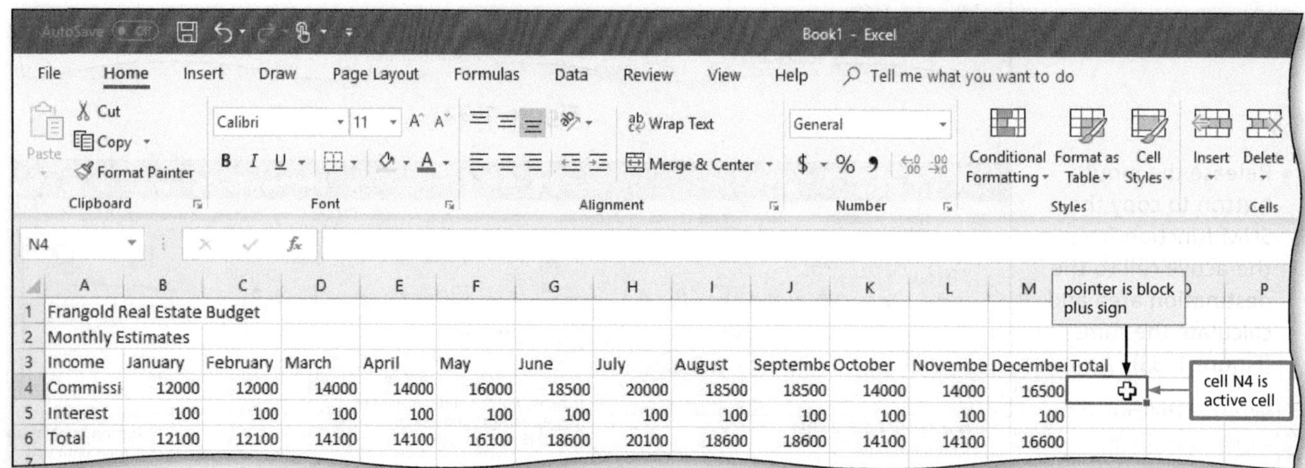

Figure 1–35

2

- With the pointer in cell N4 and in the shape of a block plus sign, drag the pointer down to cell N6 to select the range (Figure 1–36).

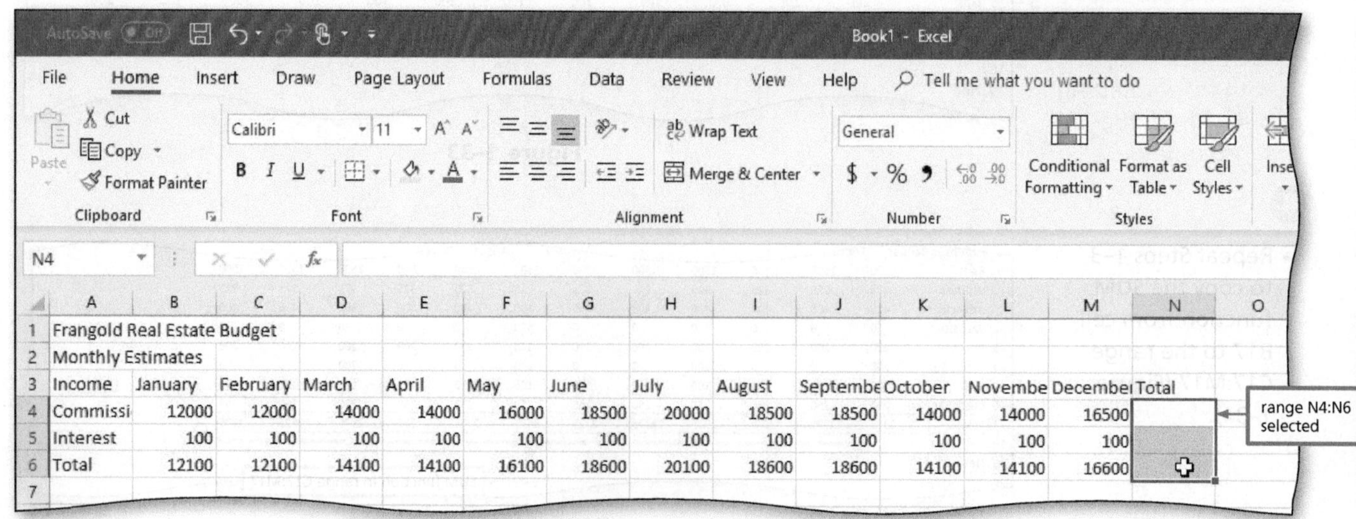

Figure 1–36

3

- Click the AutoSum button (Home tab | Editing group) to calculate the sums of all three rows (Figure 1–37).

Q&A How does Excel create unique totals for each row?
If each cell in a selected range is adjacent to a row of numbers, Excel assigns the SUM function to each cell when you click the Sum button.

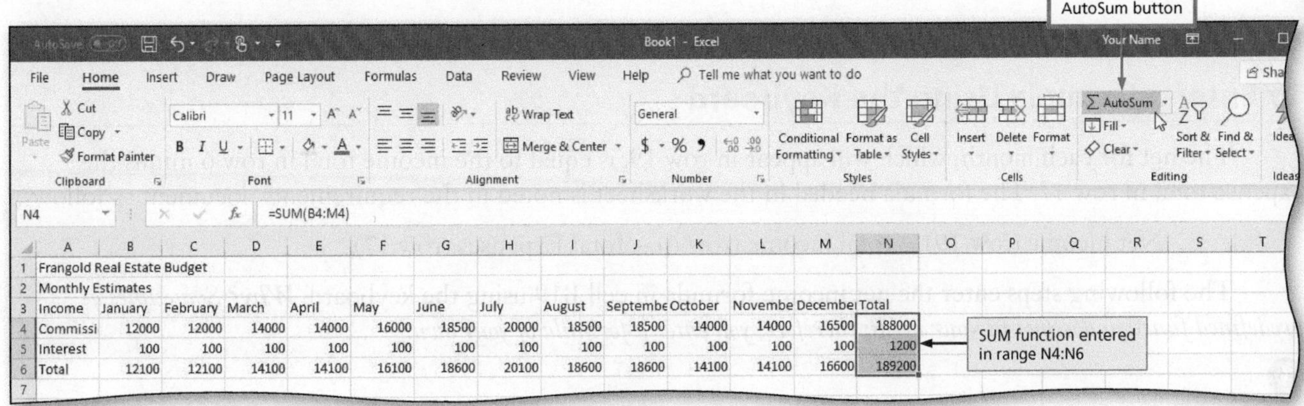

Figure 1–37

4

- Repeat Steps 1–3 to select cells N9 to N17 and calculate the sums of the corresponding rows (Figure 1–38).

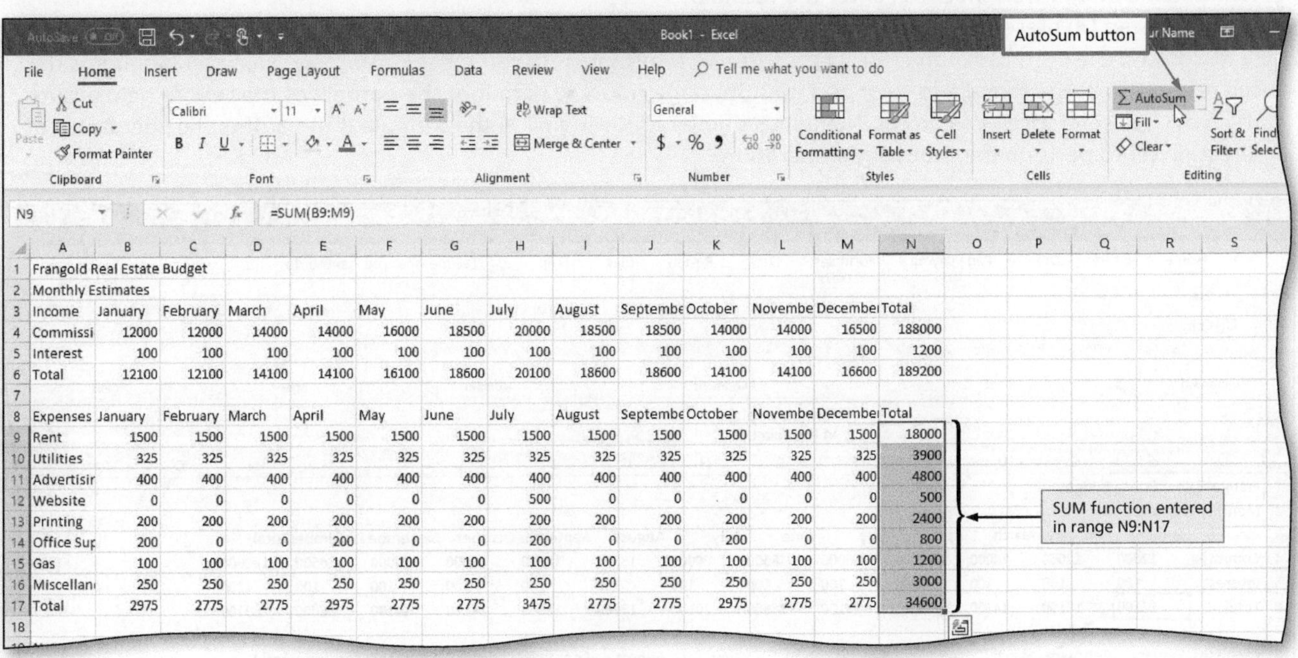

Figure 1–38

Calculating Average, Maximum, and Minimum Values

As you learned earlier in this module, the AutoSum list lets you calculate not only sums but also the average, the number of items, or the maximum or minimum value of a range. You can calculate these using three additional functions: AVERAGE, MAX, and MIN. The AVERAGE function calculates the average value in a range of cells, the MAX function calculates the maximum value in a range of cells, and the MIN function calculates the minimum value in a range of cells. Table 1–3 shows examples of each of these functions.

Table 1–3 AVERAGE, MAX, and MIN Functions	
Function	**Result**
=AVERAGE(H1:H5)	Determines the average of the values in cells H1, H2, H3, H4, and H5
=MAX(H1:H5)	Determines the maximum value entered in cells H1, H2, H3, H4, and H5
=MIN(H1:H5)	Determines the minimum value entered in cells H1, H2, H3, H4, and H5

To Enter a Formula Using the Keyboard

The net for each month, which will appear in row 19, is equal to the income total in row 6 minus the expense total in row 17. The formula needed in the worksheet is noted in the requirements document as follows:

Net income (row 19) = Total income (row 6) – Total Expenses (row 17)

The following steps enter the net income formula in cell B19 using the keyboard. ***Why?*** *Sometimes a predefined function does not fit your needs; therefore, you enter a formula of your own.*

- Select cell B19 to deselect the selected range.
- Type **=b6-b17** in the cell. The formula is displayed in the formula bar and the current cell, and colored borders are drawn around the cells referenced in the formula (Figure 1–39).

Q&A What occurs on the worksheet as I enter the formula?

The equal sign (=) preceding b6–b17 in the formula alerts Excel that you are entering a formula or function and not text. Because the most common error when entering a formula is to reference the wrong cell, Excel highlights the cell references in the formula in color and uses the same colors to highlight the borders of the cells to help ensure that your cell references are correct. The minus sign (–) following b6 in the formula is the arithmetic operator that directs Excel to perform the subtraction operation.

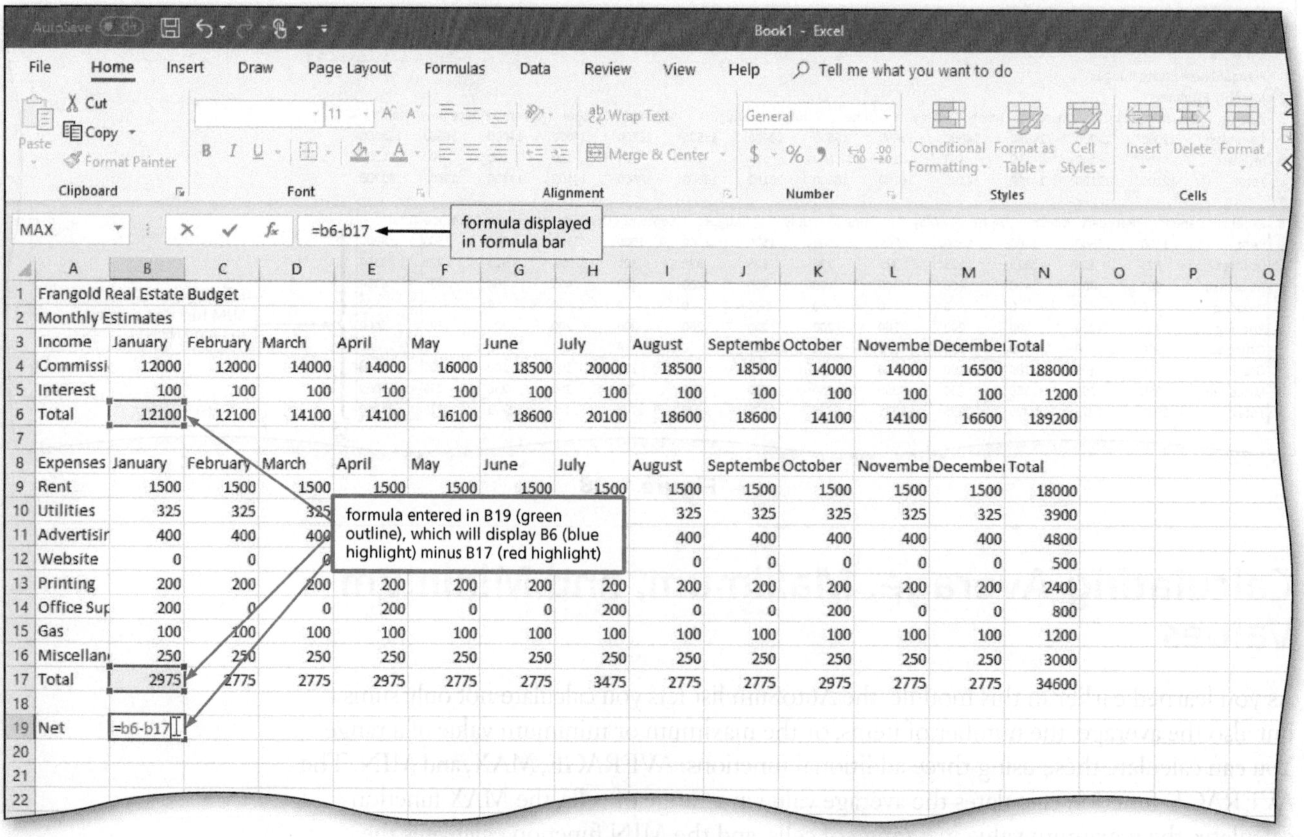

	A	B	C	D	E	F	G	H	I	J	K	L	M	N
1	Frangold Real Estate Budget													
2	Monthly Estimates													
3	Income	January	February	March	April	May	June	July	August	Septembe	October	Novembe	Decembe	Total
4	Commissi	12000	12000	14000	14000	16000	18500	20000	18500	18500	14000	14000	16500	188000
5	Interest	100	100	100	100	100	100	100	100	100	100	100	100	1200
6	Total	12100	12100	14100	14100	16100	18600	20100	18600	18600	14100	14100	16600	189200
7														
8	Expenses	January	February	March	April	May	June	July	August	Septembe	October	Novembe	Decembe	Total
9	Rent	1500	1500	1500	1500	1500	1500	1500	1500	1500	1500	1500	1500	18000
10	Utilities	325	325	325					325	325	325	325	325	3900
11	Advertisir	400	400	400					400	400	400	400	400	4800
12	Website	0	0	0					0	0	0	0	0	500
13	Printing	200	200	200	200	200	200	200	200	200	200	200	200	2400
14	Office Sup	200	0	0	200	0	0	200	0	0	200	0	0	800
15	Gas	100	100	100	100	100	100	100	100	100	100	100	100	1200
16	Miscellan	250	250	250	250	250	250	250	250	250	250	250	250	3000
17	Total	2975	2775	2775	2975	2775	2775	3475	2775	2775	2975	2775	2775	34600
18														
19	Net	=b6-b17												

Figure 1–39

- Click cell C19 to complete the arithmetic operation, display the result in the worksheet, and select the cell to the right (Figure 1–40).

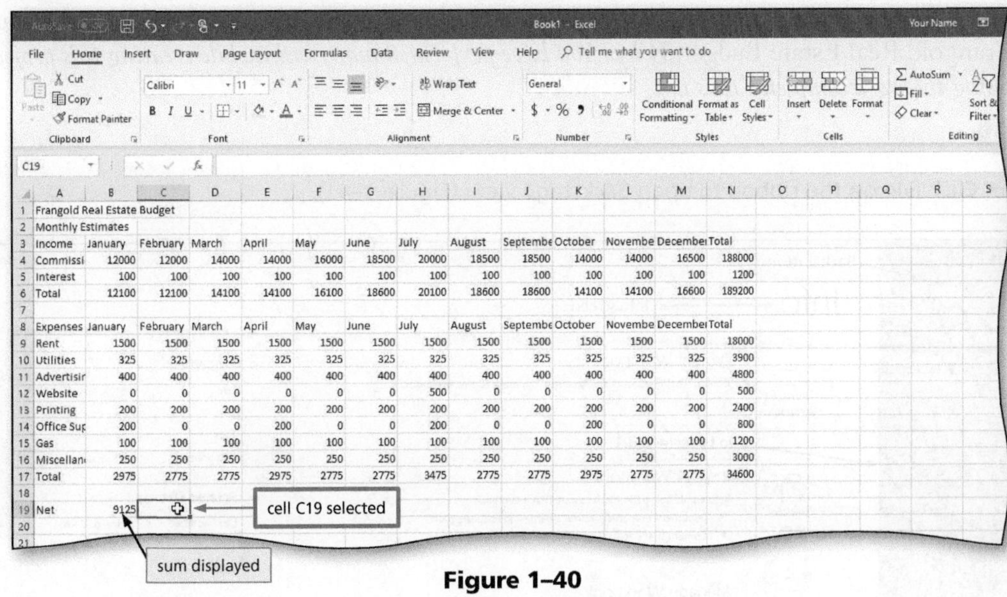

Figure 1–40

To Copy a Cell to Adjacent Cells in a Row Using the Fill Handle

The easiest way to copy the SUM formula from cell B19 to cells C19, D19, E19, F19, G19, H19, I19, J19, K19, L19, M19, and N19 is to use the fill handle. The following steps use the fill handle to copy the formula in cell B19 to the adjacent cells C19:N19.

1. Select cell B19.
2. Drag the fill handle to select the destination area, range C19:N19, which highlights and draws a border around the source area and the destination area. Release the mouse button to copy the function from the active cell to the destination area and calculate the results.

Saving the Project

While you are building a worksheet in a workbook, the computer stores it in memory. When you save a workbook, the computer places it on a storage medium such as a hard drive, USB flash drive, or online using a service such as OneDrive. A saved workbook is called a **file.** A **file name** is the name assigned to a file when you save it. It is important to save the workbook frequently for the following reasons:

- The worksheet in memory will be lost if the computer is turned off or you lose electrical power while Excel is open.
- If you run out of time before completing your workbook, you may finish your worksheet at a future time without starting over.

BTW
Organizing Files and Folders
You should organize and store files in folders so that you can easily find the files later. For example, if you are taking an introductory technology class called CIS 101, a good practice would be to save all Excel files in an Excel folder in a CIS 101 folder.

CONSIDER THIS

Where should you save the workbook?
When saving a workbook, you must decide which storage medium to use:

- If you always work on the same computer and have no need to transport your projects to a different location, then your computer's hard drive will suffice as a storage location. It is a good idea, however, to save a backup copy of your projects on a separate medium, such as an external drive, in case the file becomes corrupted or the computer's hard drive fails. The workbooks used in this book are saved to the computer's hard drive.
- If you plan to work on your workbooks in various locations or on multiple computers or mobile devices, then you should save your workbooks on a portable medium, such as a USB flash drive. Alternatively, you can save your workbooks to an online cloud storage service such as OneDrive.

To Save a Workbook

The following steps save a workbook in the Documents library on the hard drive using the file name, Frangold Real Estate Budget. ***Why?*** *You have performed many tasks while creating this project and do not want to risk losing the work completed thus far.*

- Click File on the ribbon to open Backstage view (Figure 1–41).

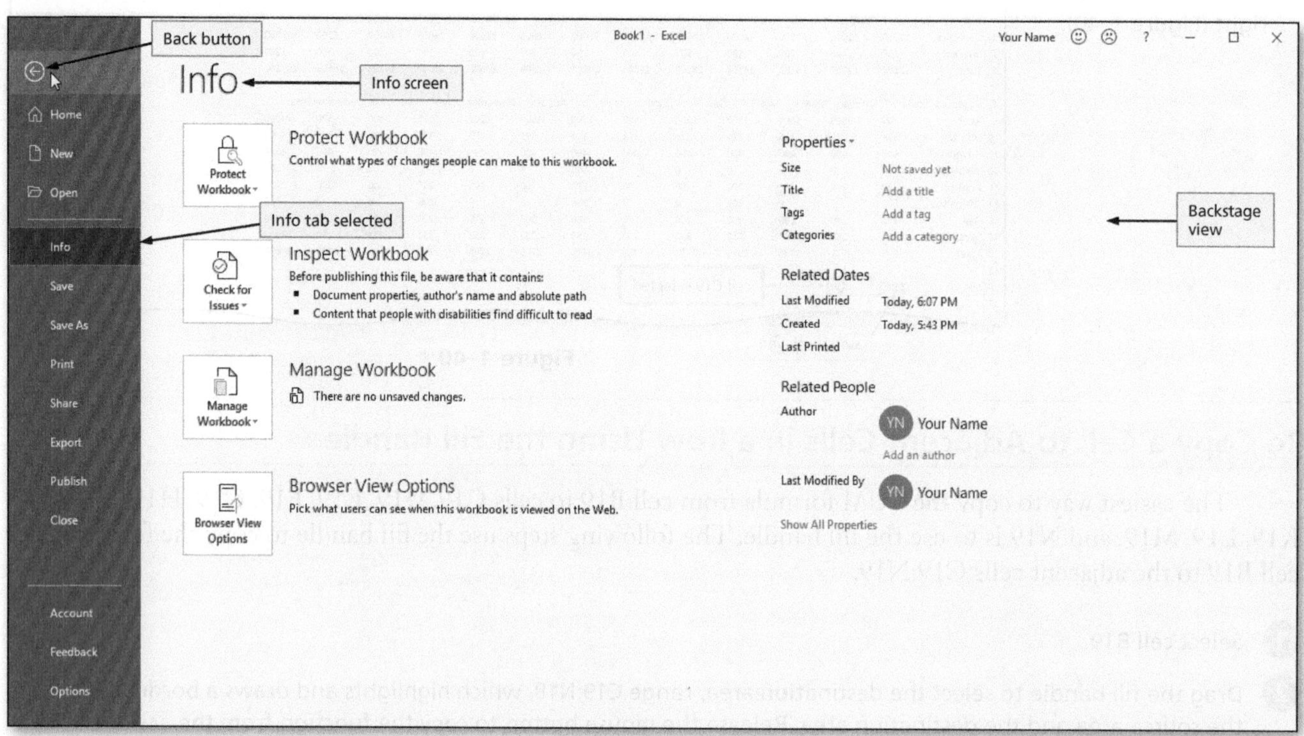

Figure 1–41

- Click Save As in Backstage view to display the Save As screen (Figure 1–42).

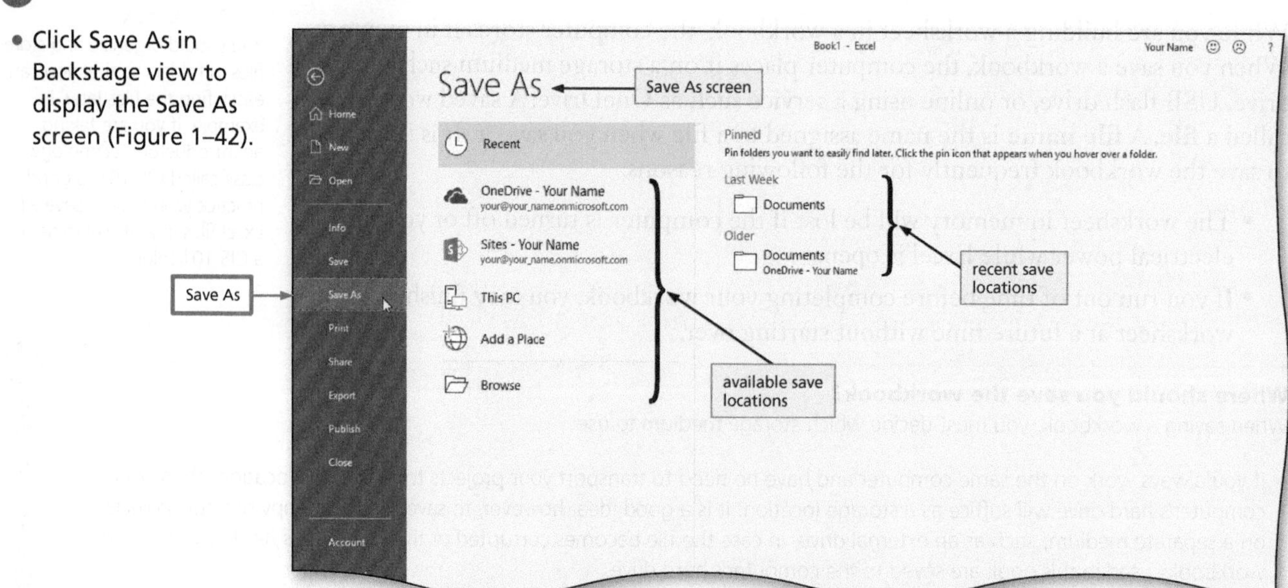

Figure 1–42

3

- Click This PC in the Other locations section to display the default save location on the computer or mobile device (Figure 1–43).

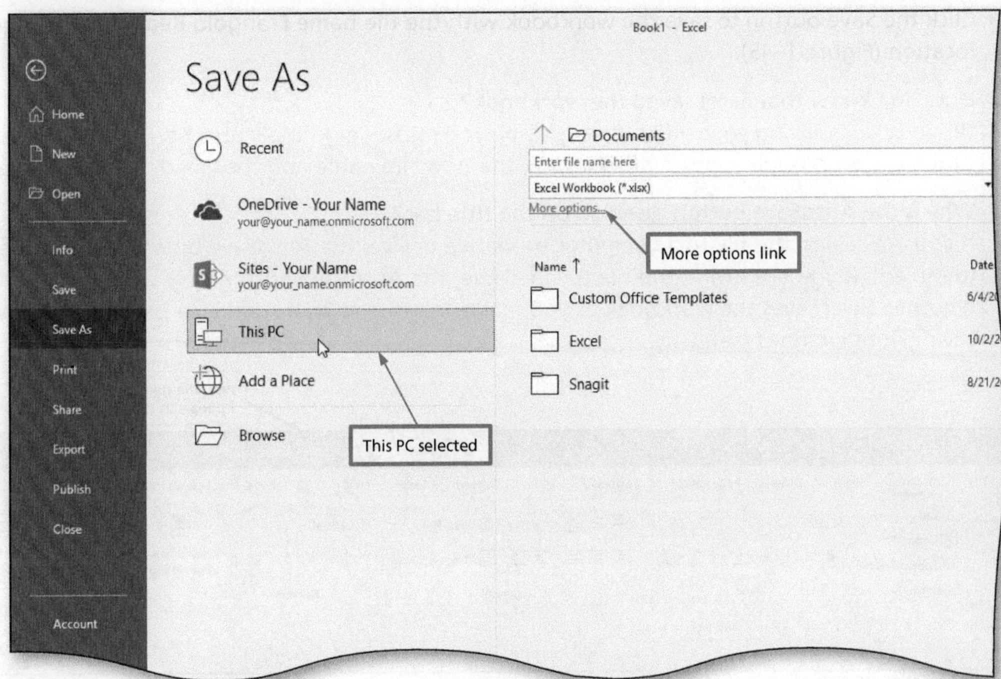

Figure 1–43

4

- Click the More options link to display the Save As dialog box.
- If necessary, click Documents in the Navigation pane to select the Documents library as the save location.
- Type `Frangold Real Estate Budget` in the File name text box to specify the file name for the workbook (Figure 1–44).

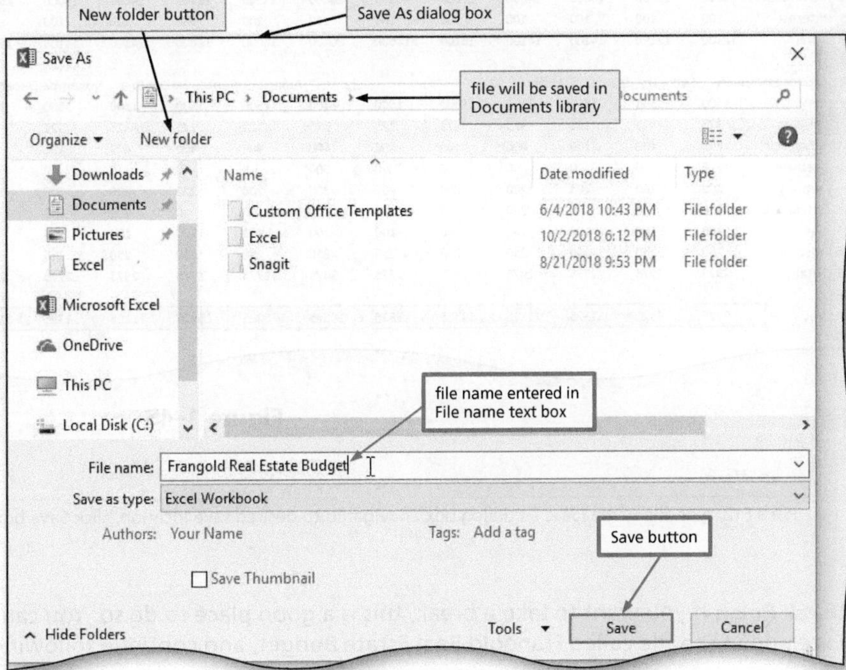

Figure 1–44

Q&A

Do I have to save to the Documents library?

No. You can save to any device or folder. A folder is a specific location on a storage medium. You can save to the default folder or a different folder. You also can create your own folders by clicking the New folder button shown in Figure 1–44. To save to a different location, navigate to that location in the Navigation pane instead of clicking Documents.

What characters can I use in a file name?

The only invalid characters are the backslash (\), slash (/), colon (:), asterisk (*), question mark (?), quotation mark ("), less than symbol (<), greater than symbol (>), and vertical bar (|).

Why is my list of files, folders, and drives arranged and named differently from those shown in the figure?

Your computer or mobile device's configuration determines how the list of files and folders is displayed and how drives are named. You can change the save location by clicking links in the Navigation pane.

- Click the Save button to save the workbook with the file name Frangold Real Estate Budget to the default save location (Figure 1–45).

Q&A

How do I know that Excel saved the workbook?
While Excel is saving your file, it briefly displays a message on the status bar indicating the amount of the file saved. When the workbook appears after saving, the new file name and the word, Saved, appear in the title bar.

Why is the AutoSave button disabled on the title bar?
If you are saving the file to a computer or mobile device, the AutoSave button on the title bar may be disabled (dimmed). If you are saving the file to OneDrive, the AutoSave button may be enabled, allowing you to specify whether Excel saves the workbook as you make changes to it. If AutoSave is turned off, you will need to continue saving your changes manually.

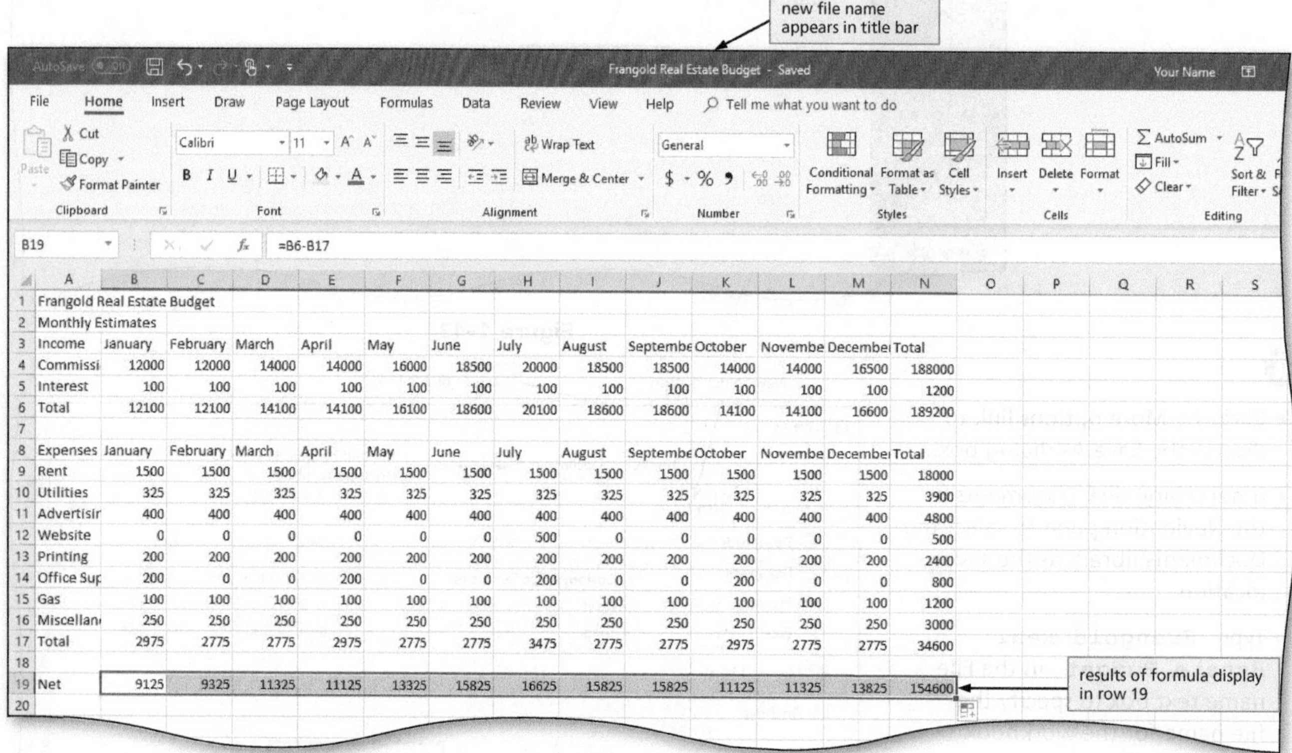

Figure 1–45

Other Ways

1. Press F12, type file name (Save As dialog box), navigated to desired save location, click Save button

Break Point: If you want to take a break, this is a good place to do so. You can exit Excel now. To resume later, start Excel, open the file called Frangold Real Estate Budget, and continue following the steps from this location forward.

Formatting the Worksheet

The text, numeric entries, and functions for the worksheet now are complete. The next step is to format the worksheet. You **format** a worksheet to enhance the appearance of information by changing its font, size, color, or alignment.

Figure 1–46a shows the worksheet before formatting. Figure 1–46b shows the worksheet after formatting. As you can see from the two figures, a worksheet that is formatted not only is easier to read but also looks more professional.

CONSIDER THIS

What steps should you consider when formatting a worksheet?

The key to formatting a worksheet is to consider the ways you can enhance the worksheet so that it appears professional. When formatting a worksheet, consider the following steps:

- Identify in what ways you want to emphasize various elements of the worksheet.
- Increase the font size of cells.
- Change the font color of cells.
- Center the worksheet titles, subtitles, and column headings.
- Modify column widths to best fit text in cells.
- Change the font style of cells.

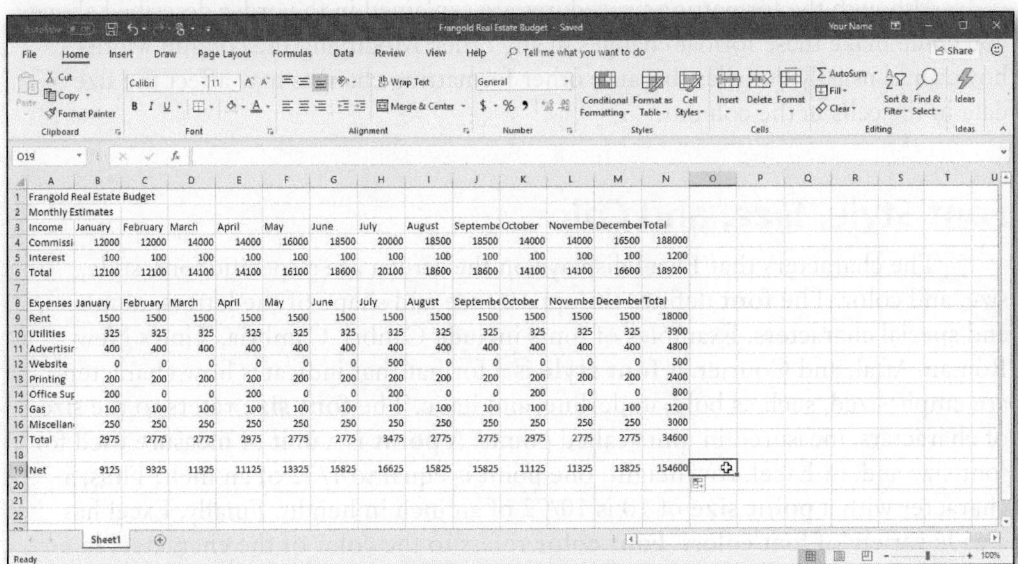

(a) Unformatted Worksheet

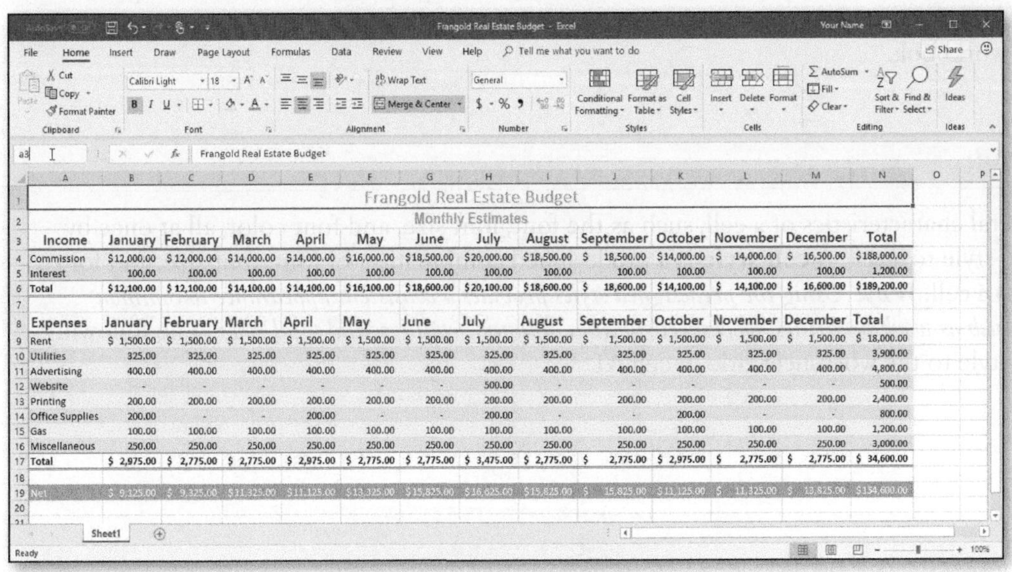

(b) Formatted Worksheet

Figure 1–46

To change the unformatted worksheet in Figure 1–46a so that it looks like the formatted worksheet in Figure 1–46b, the following tasks must be completed:

1. Change the font, change the font style, increase the font size, and change the font color of the worksheet titles in cells A1 and A2.
2. Center the worksheet titles in cells A1 and A2 across columns A through N.
3. Format the body of the worksheet. The body of the worksheet, range A3:N19, includes the column titles, row titles, and numbers. Formatting the body of the worksheet changes the numbers to use a dollars-and-cents format, with dollar signs in rows 4 and 9 and in the total rows (row 6 and 17); changes the styles of some rows; adds underlining that emphasizes portions of the worksheet; and modifies the column widths to fit the text in the columns and make the text and numbers readable.

Although the formatting procedures are explained in the order described above, you could make these format changes in any order. Modifying the column widths, however, is usually done last because other formatting changes may affect the size of data in the cells in the column.

Font Style, Size, and Color

The characters that Excel displays on the screen are a specific font, style, size, and color. The **font** defines the appearance and shape of the letters, numbers, and special characters. Examples of fonts include Calibri, Cambria, Times New Roman, Arial, and Courier. A **font style** is a format that indicates how characters are emphasized, such as bold, underline, and italic. The **font size** refers to the size of characters, measured in units called points. A **point** is a unit of measure used for font size and, in Excel, row height; one point is equal to 1/72 of an inch. Thus, a character with a **point size** of 10 is 10/72 of an inch in height. Finally, Excel has a wide variety of font colors. **Font color** refers to the color of the characters in a spreadsheet.

When Excel first starts, the default font for the entire workbook is Calibri, with a font size, font style, and font color of 11-point regular black. You can change the font characteristics in a single cell, a range of cells, the entire worksheet, or the entire workbook.

To Change a Cell Style

You can change several characteristics of a cell, such as the font, font size, and font color, all at once by assigning a predefined cell style to a cell. A **cell style** is a predesigned combination of font, font size, and font color that you can apply to a cell. ***Why?*** *Using the predesigned styles provides a consistent appearance to common portions of your worksheets, such as worksheet titles, worksheet subtitles, column headings, and total rows.* The following steps assign the Title cell style to the worksheet title in cell A1.

1

- Click cell A1 to make cell A1 the active cell.
- Click the Cell Styles button (Home tab | Styles group) to display the Cell Styles gallery (Figure 1–47).

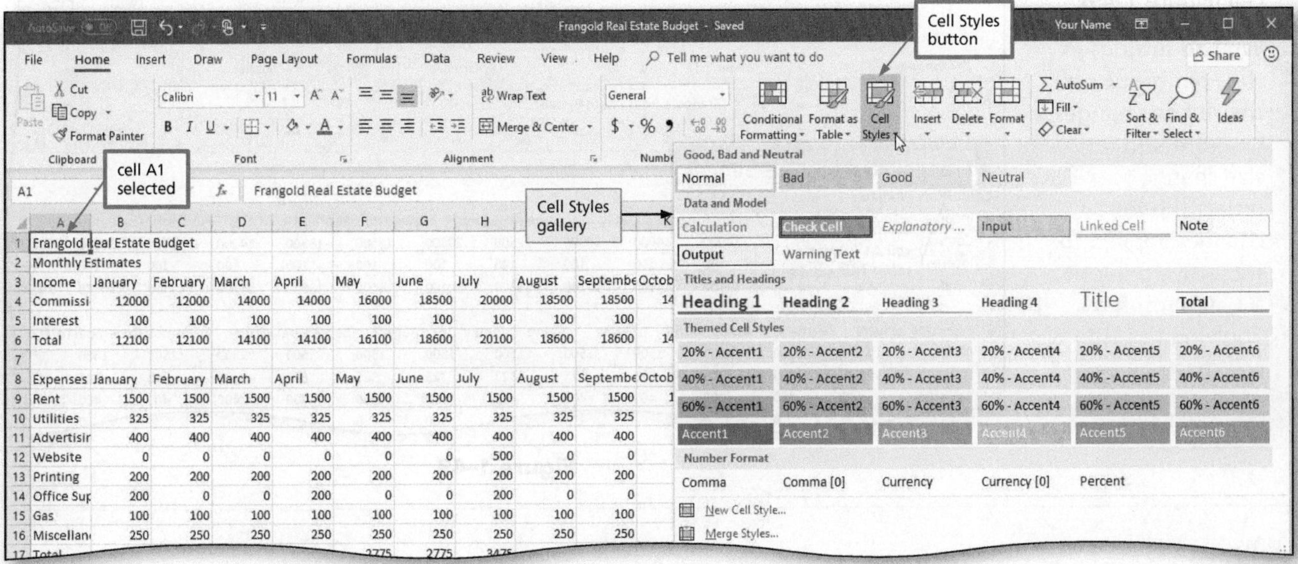

Figure 1–47

2

- Point to the Title cell style in the Titles and Headings area of the Cell Styles gallery to see a live preview of the cell style in the active cell (Figure 1–48).

Experiment

- If you are using a mouse, point to other cell styles in the Cell Styles gallery to see a live preview of those cell styles in cell A1.

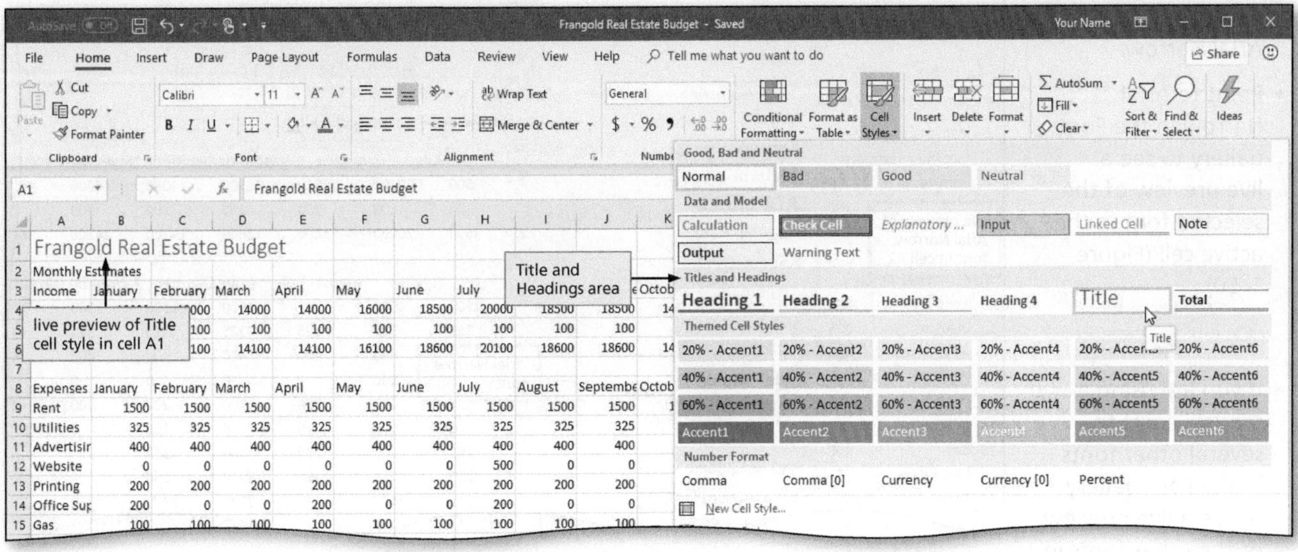

Figure 1–48

- Click the Title cell style to apply the cell style to the active cell (Figure 1–49).

Q&A Why do settings in the Font group on the ribbon change?
The font and font size change to reflect the font changes applied to the active cell, cell A1, as a result of applying the Title cell style.

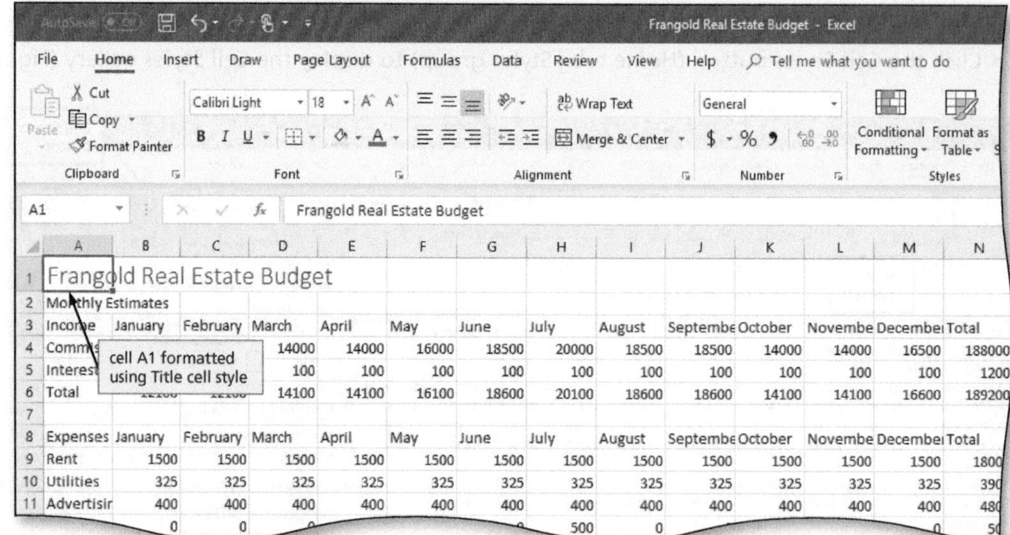

Figure 1–49

To Change the Font

Why? Different fonts are often used in a worksheet to make it more appealing to the reader and to relate or distinguish data in the worksheet. The following steps change the worksheet subtitle's font to Arial Narrow.

- Click cell A2 to make it the active cell.
- Click the Font arrow (Home tab | Font group) to display the Font gallery. If necessary, scroll to Arial Narrow.
- Point to Arial Narrow in the Font gallery to see a live preview of the selected font in the active cell (Figure 1–50).

Experiment

- If you are using a mouse, point to several other fonts in the Font gallery to see a live preview of the other fonts in the selected cell.

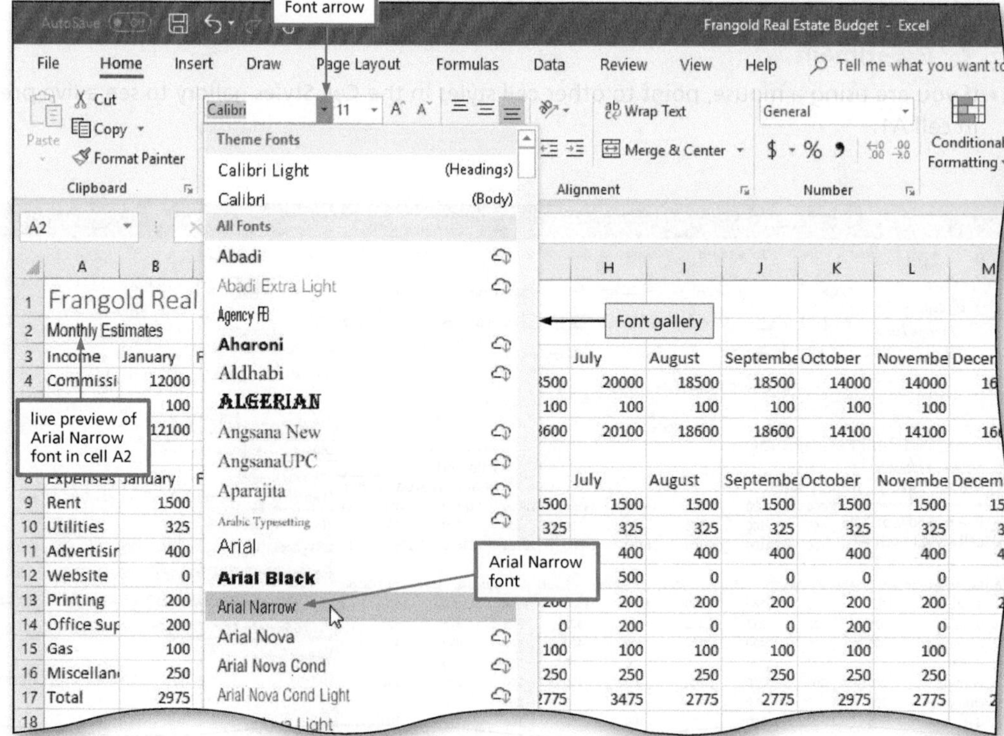

Figure 1–50

- Click Arial Narrow in the Font gallery to change the font of the worksheet subtitle to Arial Narrow (Figure 1–51).

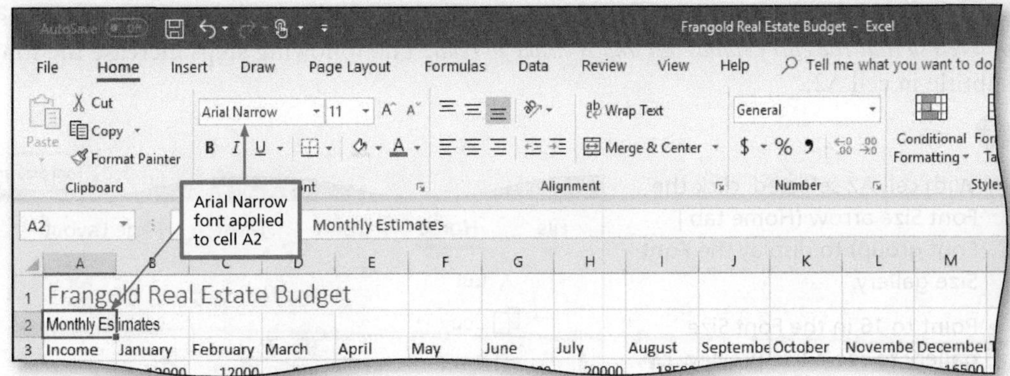

Figure 1–51

Other Ways

1. Click Font Settings Dialog Box Launcher, click Font tab (Format Cells dialog box), click desired color in Color list, click OK
2. Right-click the cell to display Mini toolbar, click Font Color arrow on Mini toolbar, click desired font color in Font Color gallery
3. Right-click selected cell, click Format Cells on shortcut menu, click Font tab (Format Cells dialog box), click desired color in Color list, click OK

To Apply Bold Style to a Cell

Bold, or boldface, text has a darker appearance than normal text. ***Why?*** *You apply bold style to a cell to emphasize it or make it stand out from the rest of the worksheet.* The following steps apply bold style to the worksheet title and subtitle.

- Click cell A1 to make it active and then click the Bold button (Home tab | Font group) to change the font style of the active cell to bold (Figure 1–52).

Q&A What if a cell already has the bold style applied?
If the active cell contains bold text, then Excel displays the Bold button with a darker gray background.

How do I remove the bold style from a cell?
Clicking the Bold button (Home tab | Font group) a second time removes the bold style.

Figure 1–52

- Repeat Step 1 to bold cell A2.

Other Ways

1. Click Font Settings Dialog Box Launcher, click Font tab (Format Cells dialog box), click Bold in Font style list, click OK
2. Right-click selected cell, click Bold button on Mini toolbar
3. Right-click selected cell, click Format Cells on shortcut menu, click Font tab (Format Cells dialog box), click Bold in Font style list, click OK
4. Press CTRL+B

To Increase the Font Size of a Cell Entry

Increasing the font size is the next step in formatting the worksheet subtitle. ***Why?*** *You increase the font size of a cell so that the entry stands out and is easier to read.* The following steps increase the font size of the worksheet subtitle in cell A2.

- With cell A2 selected, click the Font Size arrow (Home tab | Font group) to display the Font Size gallery.
- Point to 16 in the Font Size gallery to see a live preview of the active cell with the selected font size (Figure 1–53).

Experiment

- If you are using a mouse, point to several other font sizes in the Font Size list to see a live preview of those font sizes in the selected cell.

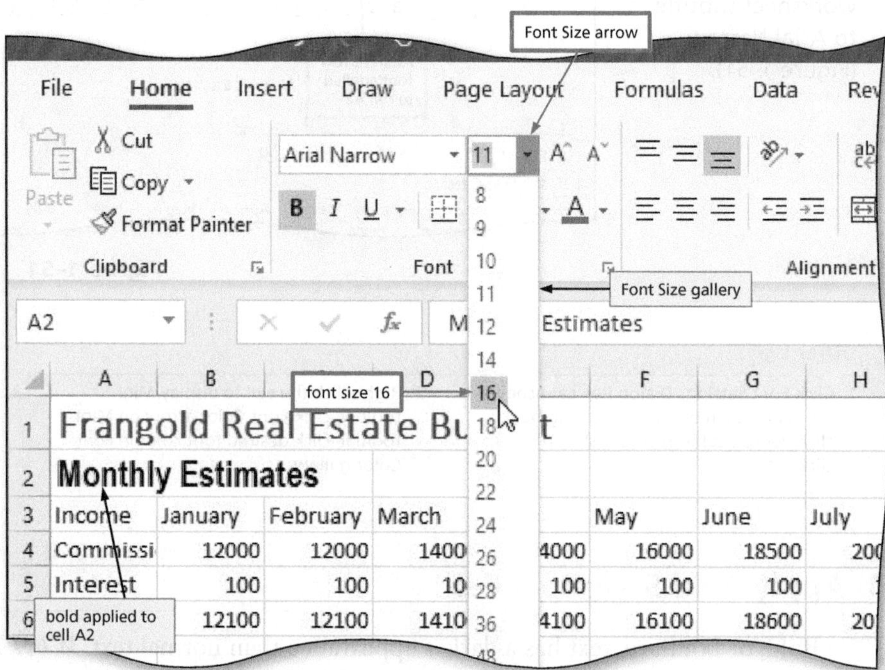

Figure 1–53

2

- Click 16 in the Font Size gallery to change the font size in the active cell (Figure 1–54).

Q&A Can I choose a font size that is not in the Font Size gallery?
Yes. To select a font size not displayed in the Font Size gallery, such as 13, click the Font Size box (Home tab | Font group), type the font size you want, and then press ENTER.

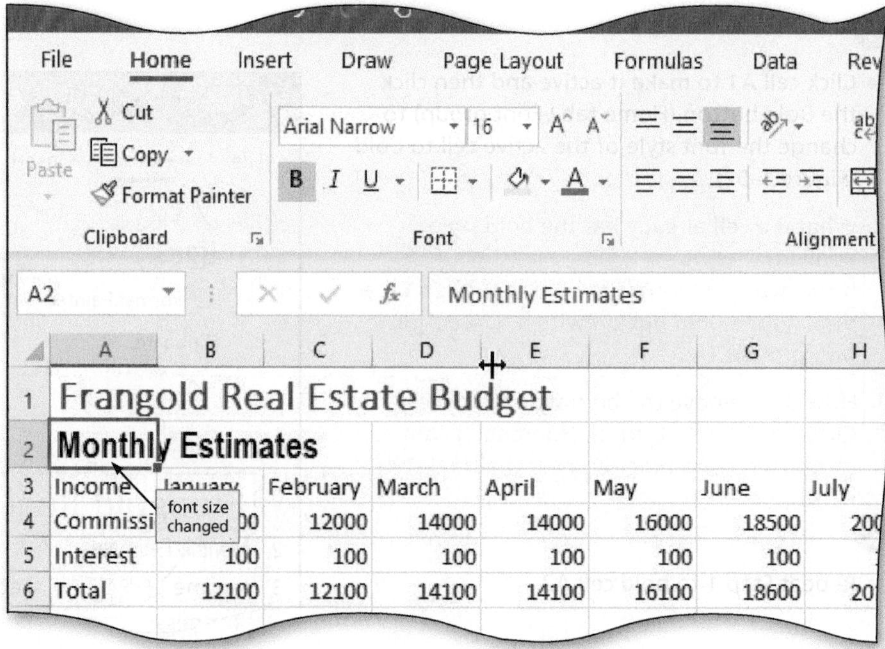

Figure 1–54

Other Ways

1. Click 'Increase Font Size' button (Home tab | Font group) or 'Decrease Font Size' button (Home tab | Font group)
2. Click Font Settings Dialog Box Launcher, click Font tab (Format Cells dialog box), click desired size in Size list, click OK
3. Right-click cell to display Mini toolbar, click Font Size arrow on Mini toolbar, click desired font size in Font Size gallery
4. Right-click selected cell, click Format Cells on shortcut menu, click Font tab (Format Cells dialog box), select font size in Size box, click OK

To Change the Font Color of a Cell Entry

The next step is to change the color of the font in cells A1 and A2 to green. ***Why?*** *Changing the font color of cell entries can help the text stand out more. You also can change the font colors to match a company's or product's brand colors.* The following steps change the font color of a cell entry.

- Click cell A1 and then click the Font Color arrow (Home tab | Font group) to display the Font Color gallery.
- If you are using a mouse, point to Green, Accent 6 (column 10, row 1) in the Theme Colors area of the Font Color gallery to see a live preview of the font color in the active cell (Figure 1–55).

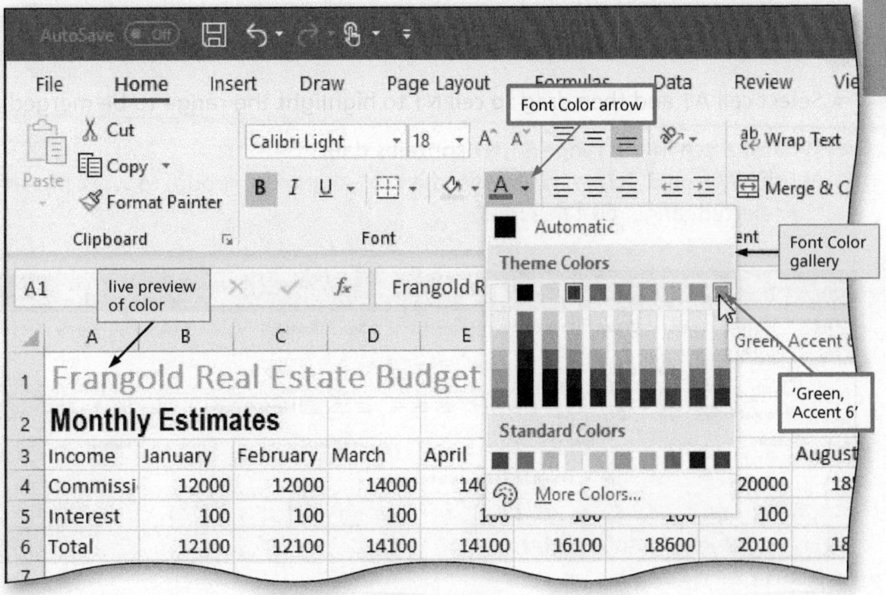

Experiment

- Point to several other colors in the Font Color gallery to see a live preview of other font colors in the active cell.

Figure 1–55

Q&A How many colors are in the Font Color gallery?
You can choose from approximately 70 different font colors in the Font Color gallery. Your Font Color gallery may have more or fewer colors, depending on the color settings of your operating system. The Theme Colors area contains colors that are included in the current workbook's theme.

- Click Green, Accent 6 (column 10, row 1) in the Font Color gallery to change the font color of the worksheet title in the active cell (Figure 1–56).

Q&A Why does the Font Color button change after I select the new font color?
When you choose a color on the Font Color gallery, Excel changes the Font Color button (Home tab | Font group) to your chosen color. Then when you want to change the font color of another cell to the same color, you need only to select the cell and then click the Font Color button (Home tab | Font group).

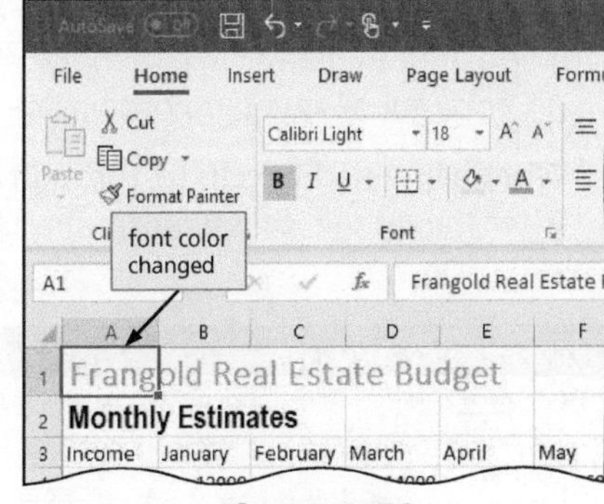

Figure 1–56

3

- Click cell A2.
- Click the Font Color button to apply Green, Accent 6 (column 10, row 1) to cell A2.

Other Ways

1. Click Font Settings Dialog Box Launcher, click Font tab (Format Cells dialog box), click desired font color in Color list, click OK
2. Right-click cell to display Mini toolbar, click Font Color arrow on Mini toolbar, click desired color in Font Color gallery
3. Right-click selected cell, click Format Cells on shortcut menu, click Font tab (Format Cells dialog box), click Color arrow, click desired color, click OK

To Center Cell Entries across Columns by Merging Cells

The final step in formatting the worksheet title and subtitle is to center them across columns A through N. ***Why?*** *Centering a title across the columns used in the body of the worksheet improves the worksheet's appearance.* To do this, the 14 cells in the range A1:N1 are combined, or merged, into a single cell that is the width of the columns in the body of the worksheet. The 14 cells in the range A2:N2 are merged in a similar manner. When you **merge** cells, you combine multiple adjacent cells into one larger cell. To unmerge cells, you **split** them to display the original range of cells. The following steps center the worksheet title and subtitle across columns by merging cells.

- Select cell A1 and then drag to cell N1 to highlight the range to be merged and centered (Figure 1–57).

Q&A What if a cell in the range B1:N1 contains data?
For the 'Merge & Center' button (Home tab | Alignment group) to work properly, all the cells except the leftmost cell in the selected range must be empty.

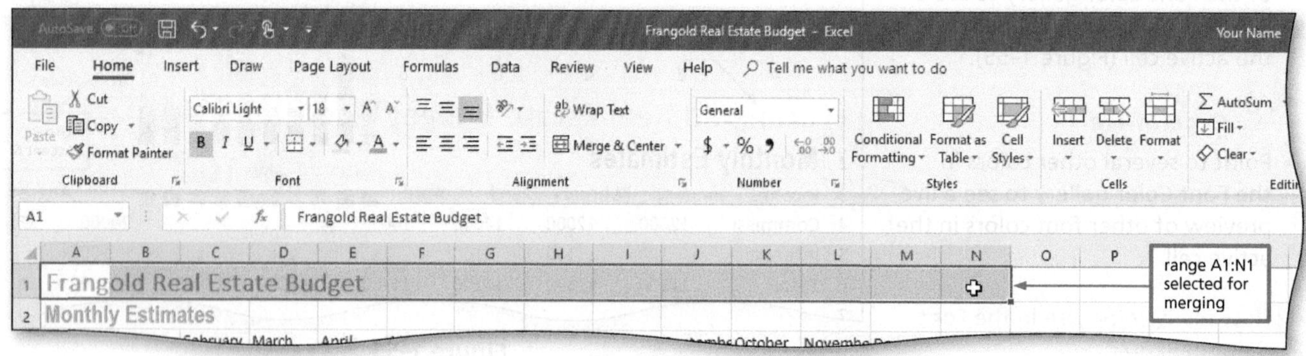

Figure 1–57

- Click the 'Merge & Center' button (Home tab | Alignment group) to merge cells A1 through N1 and center the contents of the leftmost cell across the selected columns (Figure 1–58).

Q&A What if my screen displays a Merge & Center menu?
If you are using a touch screen, Excel might display a Merge & Center menu. Select the desired option on the Merge & Center menu if you do not have a separate 'Merge & Center' button and 'Merge & Center' arrow.

What happened to cells B1 through N1?
After the merge, cells B1 through N1 no longer exist. The new cell A1 now extends across columns A through N.

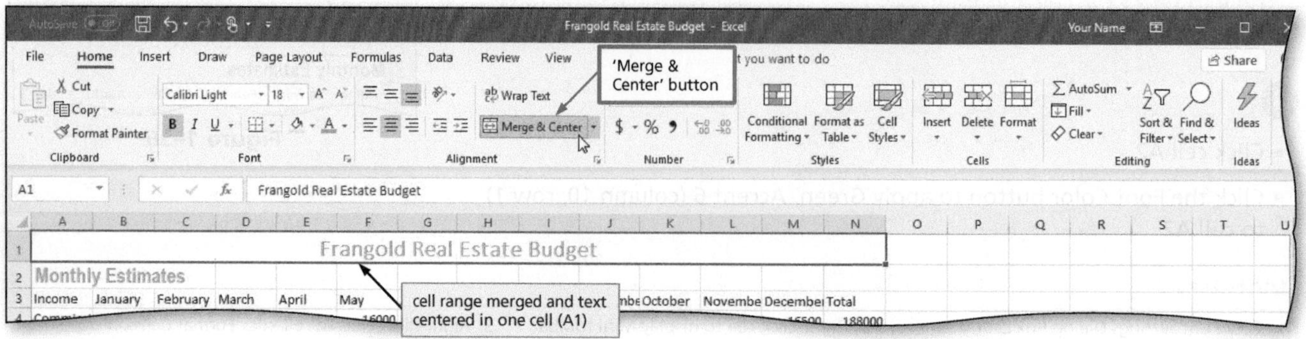

Figure 1–58

- Repeat Steps 1 and 2 to merge and center the worksheet subtitle across cells A2 through N2 (Figure 1–59).

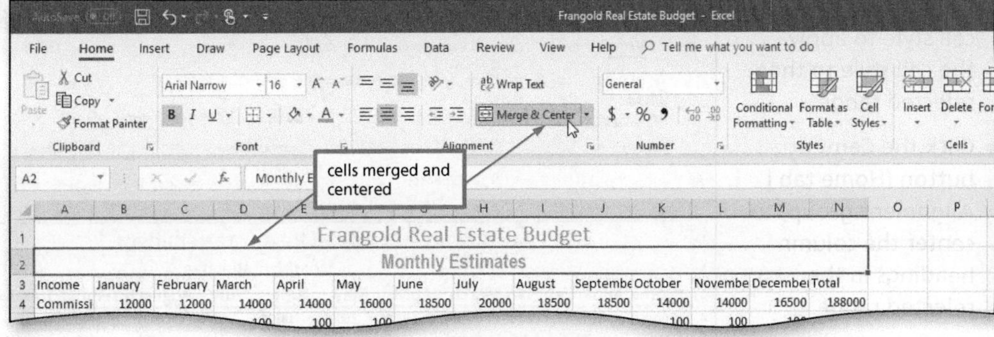

Figure 1–59

Q&A Are cells B1 through N1 and B2 through N2 lost forever? No. You can split a merged cell to redisplay the individual cells. You split a merged cell by selecting it and clicking the 'Merge & Center' button. For example, if you click the 'Merge & Center' button a second time in Step 2, it will split the merged cell A1 into cells A1, B1, C1, D1, E1, F1, G1, H1, I1, J1, K1, L1, M1, and N1, and move the title to its original location in cell A1.

Other Ways

1. Right-click selection, click 'Merge & Center' button on Mini toolbar
2. Right-click selected cell, click Format Cells on shortcut menu, click Alignment tab (Format Cells dialog box), select 'Center Across Selection' in Horizontal list, click OK

To Format Rows Using Cell Styles

The next step to format the worksheet is to format the rows. ***Why?*** *Row titles and the total row should be formatted so that the column titles and total row can be distinguished from the data in the body of the worksheet. Data rows can be formatted to make them easier to read as well.* The following steps format the column titles and total row using cell styles in the default worksheet theme.

- Click cell A3 and then drag to cell N3 to select the range.
- Click the Cell Styles button (Home tab | Styles group) to display the Cell Styles gallery.
- Point to the Heading 1 cell style in the Titles and Headings area of the Cell Styles gallery to see a live preview of the cell style in the selected range (Figure 1–60).

Experiment

- If you are using a mouse, point to other cell styles in the Titles and Headings area of the Cell Styles gallery to see a live preview of other styles.

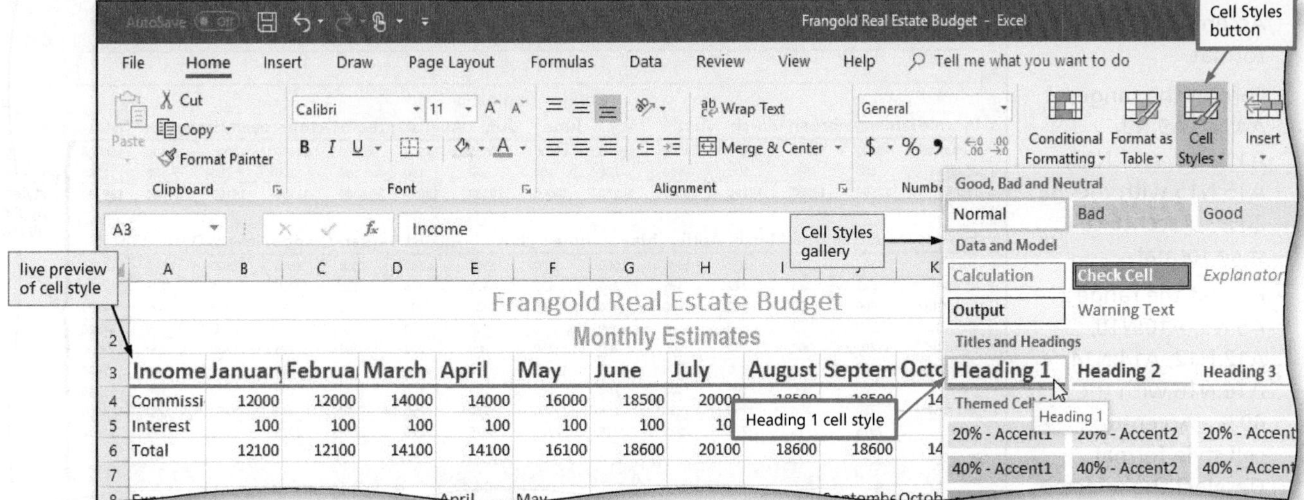

Figure 1–60

2

- Click the Heading 1 cell style to apply the cell style to the selected range.
- Click the Center button (Home tab | Alignment group) to center the column headings in the selected range.
- Select the range A8 to N8 (Figure 1–61).

Center button

Heading 1 style applied and column heading centered

range A8:N8

Figure 1–61

3

- Apply the Heading 1 cell style format and then center the headings (Figure 1–62).

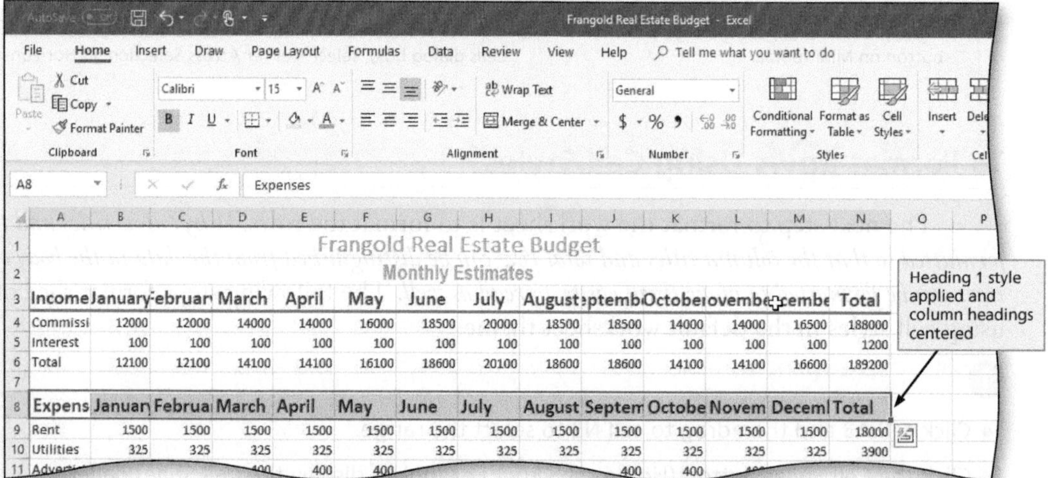

Figure 1–62

4

- Format the ranges A6:N6 and A17:N17 with the Total cell style format.
- Format the range A19:N19 with the Accent6 cell style format.
- Format the ranges A4:N4, A9:N9, A11:N11, A13:N13, A15:N15 with the 20% - Accent6 cell style format.
- Format the range A5:N5, A10:N10, A12:N12, A14:N14, A16:N16 with the 40% - Accent6 cell style format. Deselect the selected ranges (Figure 1–63).

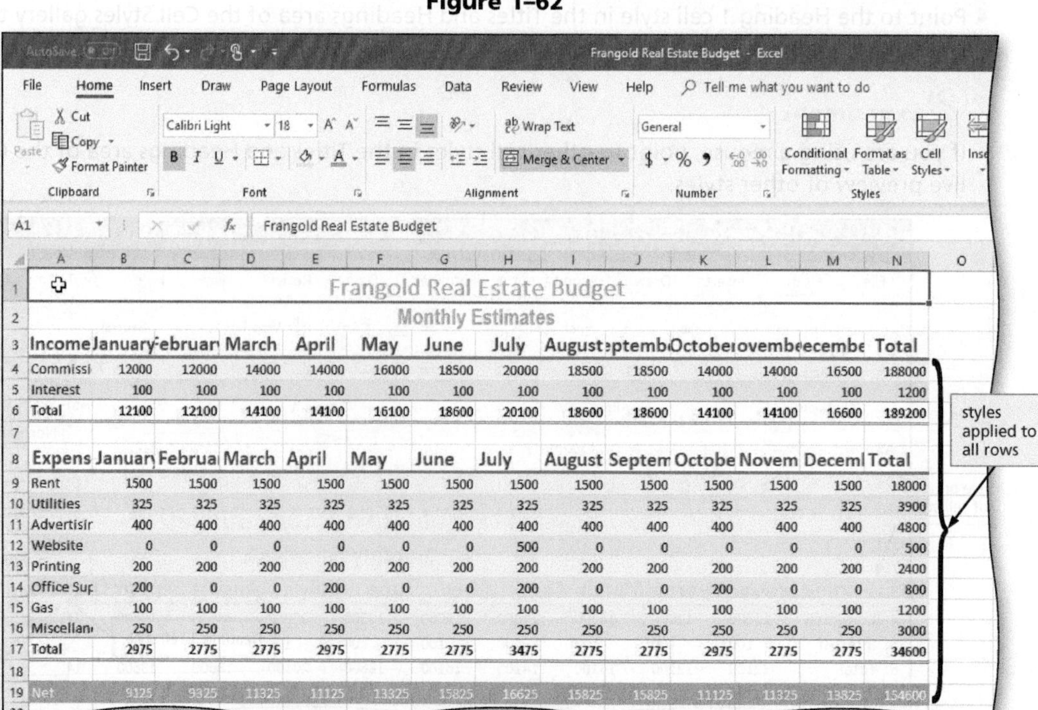

Figure 1–63

To Format Numbers in the Worksheet

The requirements document requested that numbers in the first row and last row of each section should be formatted to use a dollar-and-cents format, while other numbers receive a comma format. ***Why?*** *Using a dollar-and-cents format for selected cells makes it clear to users of the worksheet that the numbers represent dollar values without cluttering the entire worksheet with dollar signs, and applying the comma format makes larger numbers easier to read.* Excel allows you to apply various number formats, many of which are discussed in later modules. The following steps use buttons on the ribbon to format the numbers in the worksheet.

- Select the range B4:N4.
- Click the 'Accounting Number Format' button (Home tab | Number group) to apply the accounting number format to the cells in the selected range.
- Select the range B5:N5 (Figure 1–64).

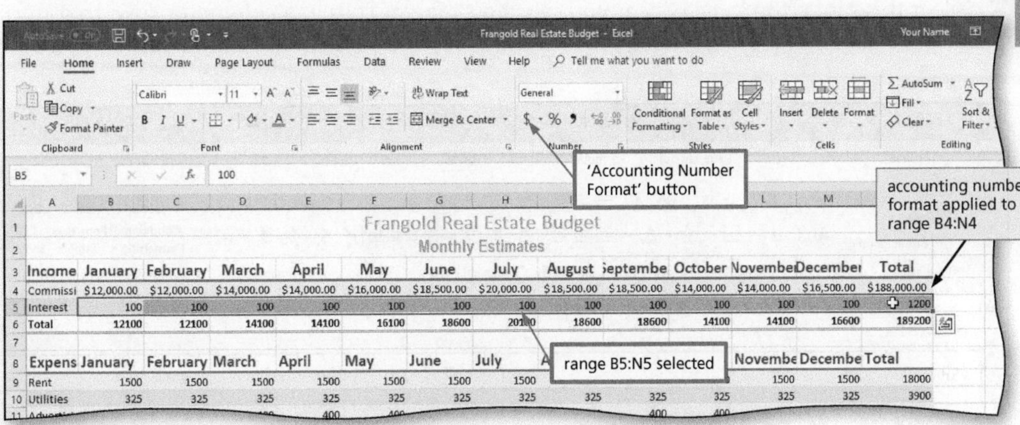

Figure 1–64

Q&A What if my screen displays an Accounting Number Format menu?
If you are using a touch screen, you may not have a separate 'Accounting Number Format' button and 'Accounting Number Format' arrow. In this case, select the desired option on the Accounting Number Format menu.

What effect does the accounting number format have on the selected cells?
The accounting number format causes numbers to be displayed with two decimal places and to align vertically. Cell widths are adjusted automatically to accommodate the new formatting.

2

- Click the Comma Style button (Home tab | Number group) to apply the comma style format to the selected range.

Q&A What effect does the comma style format have on the selected cells?
The comma style format formats numbers to have two decimal places and commas as thousands separators.

- Select the range B6:N6 to make it the active range (Figure 1–65).

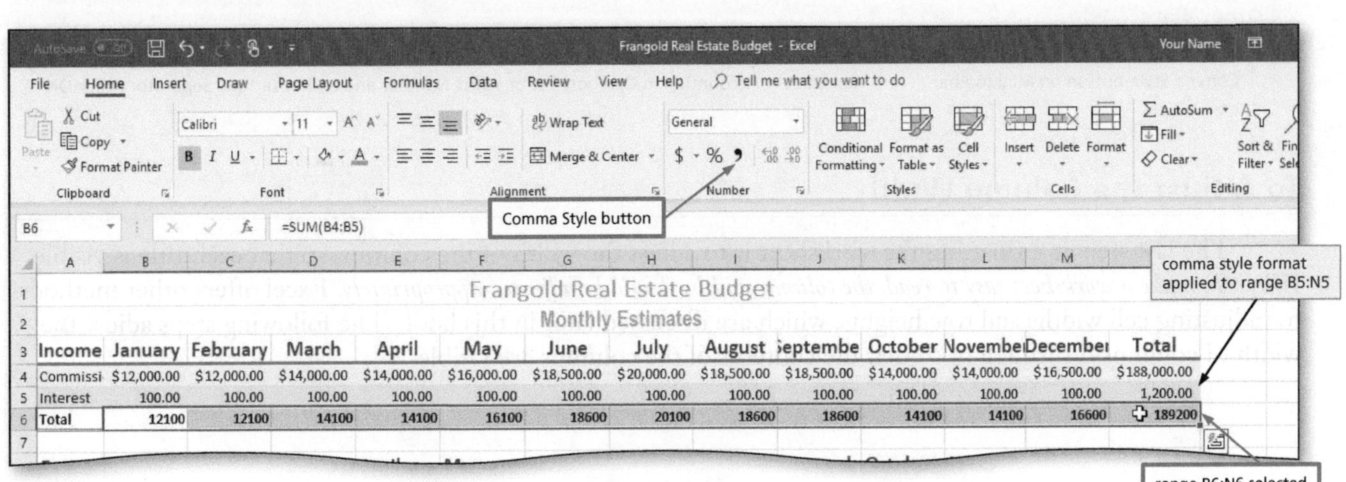

Figure 1–65

- Click the 'Accounting Number Format' button (Home tab | Number group) to apply the accounting number format to the cells in the selected range.

- Format the ranges B9:N9, B17:N17, and B19:N19 with the accounting number format.
- Format the range B10:N16 with the comma style format. Click cell A1 to deselect the selected ranges (Figure 1–66).

Q&A How do I select the range B10:N16?

Select this range the same way as you select a range of cells in a column or row; that is, click the first cell in the range (B10, in this case) and drag to the last cell in the range (N16, in this case).

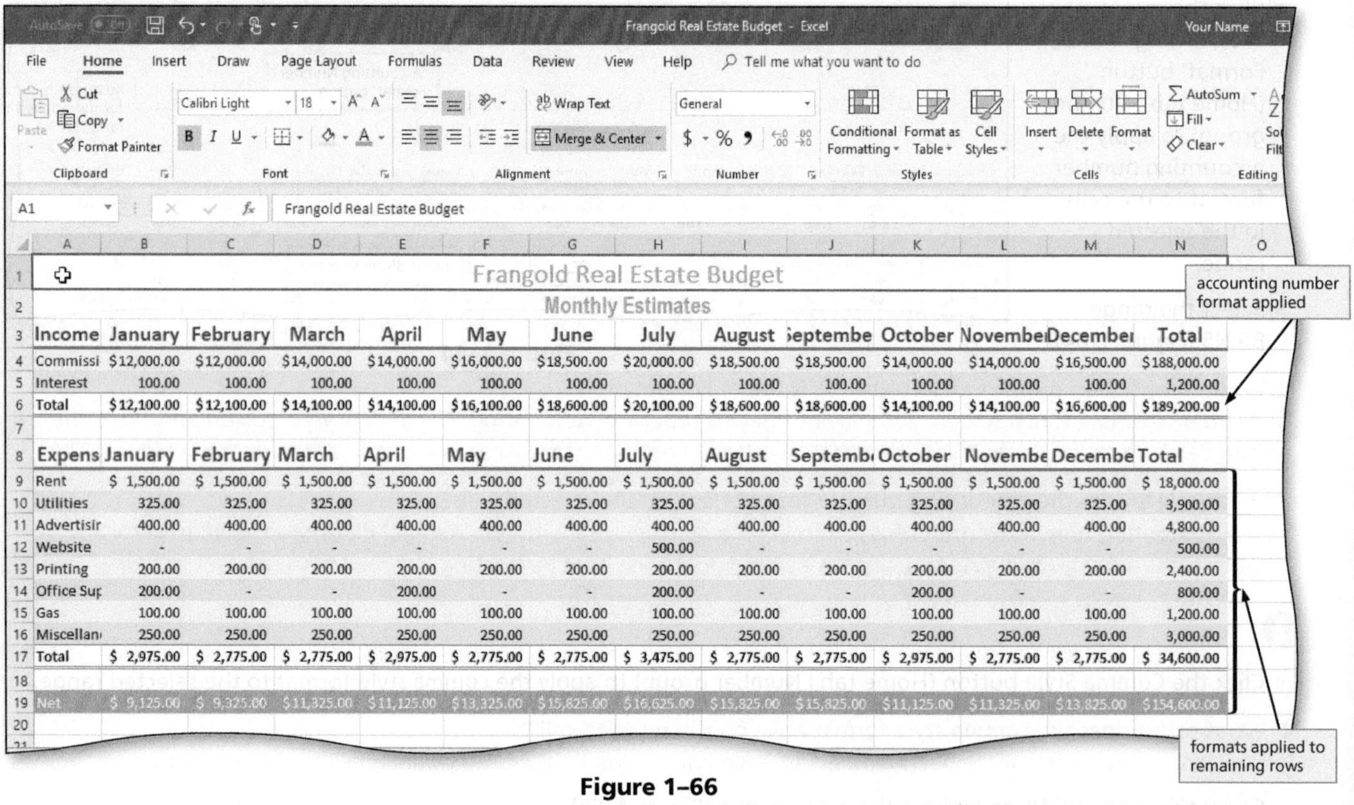

Frangold Real Estate Budget

Monthly Estimates

Income	January	February	March	April	May	June	July	August	Septembe	October	Novembe	Decembe	Total
Commissi	$12,000.00	$12,000.00	$14,000.00	$14,000.00	$16,000.00	$18,500.00	$20,000.00	$18,500.00	$18,500.00	$14,000.00	$14,000.00	$16,500.00	$188,000.00
Interest	100.00	100.00	100.00	100.00	100.00	100.00	100.00	100.00	100.00	100.00	100.00	100.00	1,200.00
Total	$12,100.00	$12,100.00	$14,100.00	$14,100.00	$16,100.00	$18,600.00	$20,100.00	$18,600.00	$18,600.00	$14,100.00	$14,100.00	$16,600.00	$189,200.00

Expens	January	February	March	April	May	June	July	August	Septemb	October	Novembe	Decembe	Total
Rent	$ 1,500.00	$ 1,500.00	$ 1,500.00	$ 1,500.00	$ 1,500.00	$ 1,500.00	$ 1,500.00	$ 1,500.00	$ 1,500.00	$ 1,500.00	$ 1,500.00	$ 1,500.00	$ 18,000.00
Utilities	325.00	325.00	325.00	325.00	325.00	325.00	325.00	325.00	325.00	325.00	325.00	325.00	3,900.00
Advertisir	400.00	400.00	400.00	400.00	400.00	400.00	400.00	400.00	400.00	400.00	400.00	400.00	4,800.00
Website	-	-	-	-	-	-	500.00	-	-	-	-	-	500.00
Printing	200.00	200.00	200.00	200.00	200.00	200.00	200.00	200.00	200.00	200.00	200.00	200.00	2,400.00
Office Sup	200.00	-	-	200.00	-	-	200.00	-	-	200.00	-	-	800.00
Gas	100.00	100.00	100.00	100.00	100.00	100.00	100.00	100.00	100.00	100.00	100.00	100.00	1,200.00
Miscellan	250.00	250.00	250.00	250.00	250.00	250.00	250.00	250.00	250.00	250.00	250.00	250.00	3,000.00
Total	$ 2,975.00	$ 2,775.00	$ 2,775.00	$ 2,975.00	$ 2,775.00	$ 2,775.00	$ 3,475.00	$ 2,775.00	$ 2,775.00	$ 2,975.00	$ 2,775.00	$ 2,775.00	$ 34,600.00
Net	$ 9,125.00	$ 9,325.00	$11,325.00	$11,125.00	$13,325.00	$15,825.00	$16,625.00	$15,825.00	$15,825.00	$11,125.00	$11,325.00	$13,825.00	$154,600.00

accounting number format applied

formats applied to remaining rows

Figure 1–66

Other Ways

1. Click 'Accounting Number Format' or Comma Style button on Mini toolbar
2. Right-click selected cell, click Format Cells on shortcut menu, click Number tab (Format Cells dialog box), select Accounting in Category list or select Number and click 'Use 1000 Separator', click OK

To Adjust the Column Width

The last step in formatting the worksheet is to adjust the width of the columns so that each title is visible. ***Why?*** *To make a worksheet easy to read, the column widths should be adjusted appropriately.* Excel offers other methods for adjusting cell widths and row heights, which are discussed later in this book. The following steps adjust the width of columns A through N so that the contents of the columns are visible.

1

- Point to the boundary on the right side of the column A heading above row 1 to change the pointer to a split double arrow (Figure 1–67).

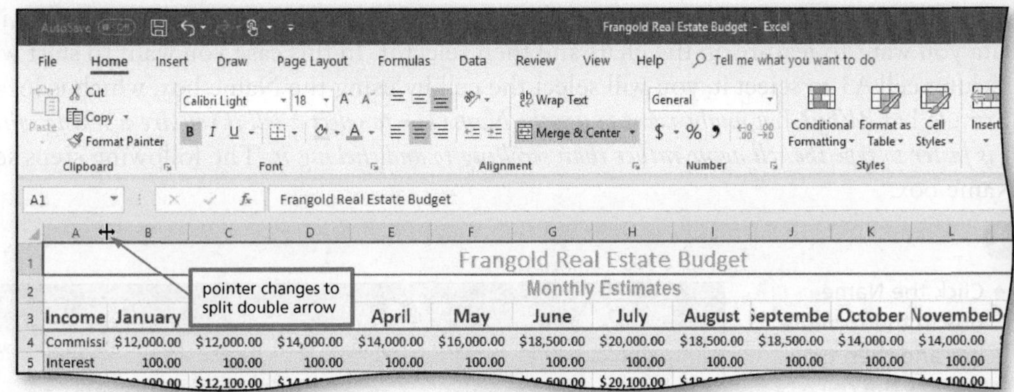

Figure 1–67

2

- Double-click the boundary to adjust the width of the column to accommodate the width of the longest item in the column (Figure 1–68).

Q&A What if all of the items in the column are already visible?
If all of the items are shorter in length than the width of the column and you double-click the column boundary, Excel will reduce the width of the column to the width of the widest entry.

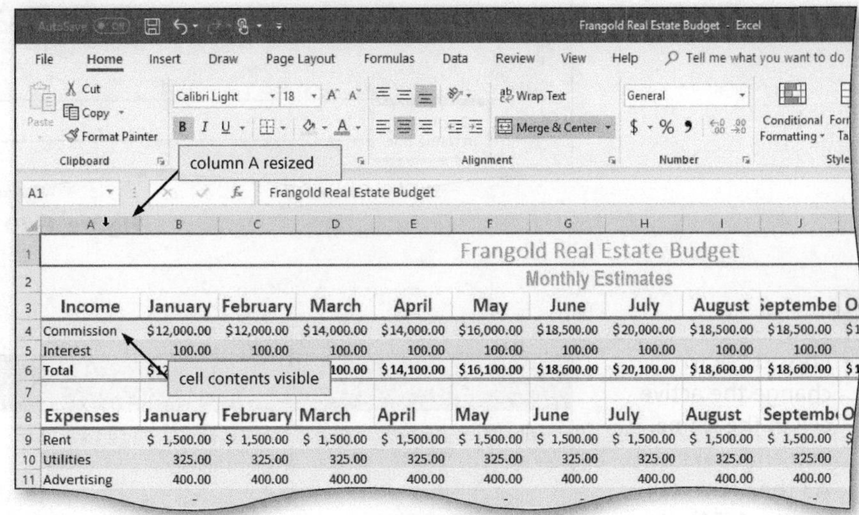

Figure 1–68

3

- Repeat Steps 1 and 2 to adjust the column width of columns B through N (Figure 1–69).

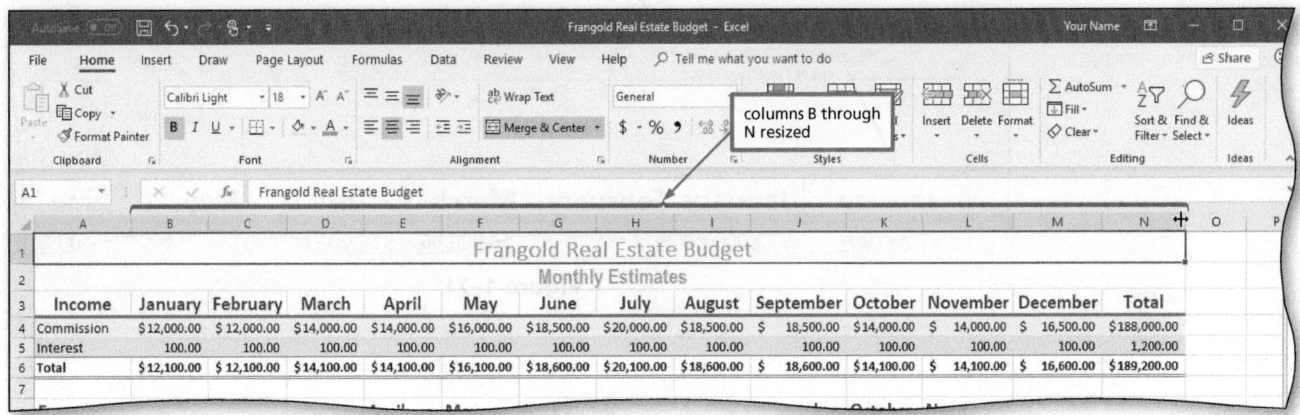

Figure 1–69

Other Ways

1. Select column heading, click Format (Home tab | Cells group), click AutoFit Column Width

To Use the Name Box to Select a Cell

The next step is to chart the monthly expenses. To create the chart, you need to identify the range of the data you want to feature on the chart and then select it. In this case you want to start with cell A3. Rather than clicking cell A3 to select it, you will select the cell by using the Name box, which is located to the left of the formula bar. ***Why?*** *You might want to use the Name box to select a cell if you are working with a large worksheet and it is faster to type the cell name rather than scrolling to and clicking it.* The following steps select cell A3 using the Name box.

- Click the Name box in the formula bar and then type **a3** as the cell you want to select (Figure 1–70).

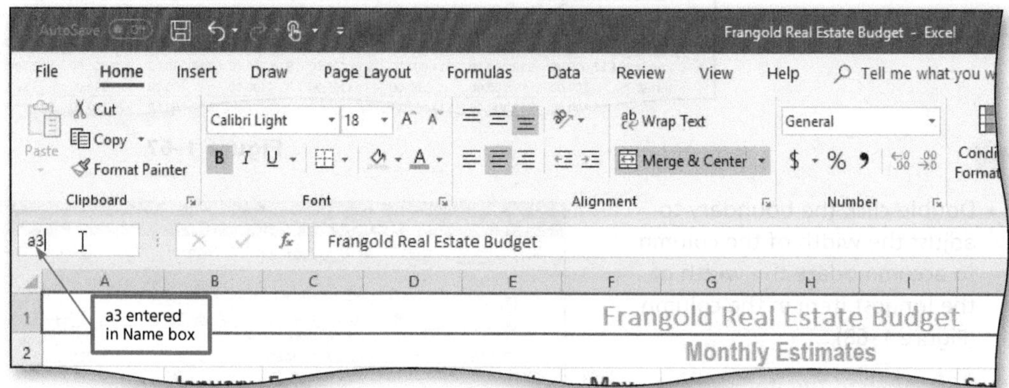

Figure 1–70

- Press ENTER to change the active cell in the Name box and make cell A3 the active cell (Figure 1–71).

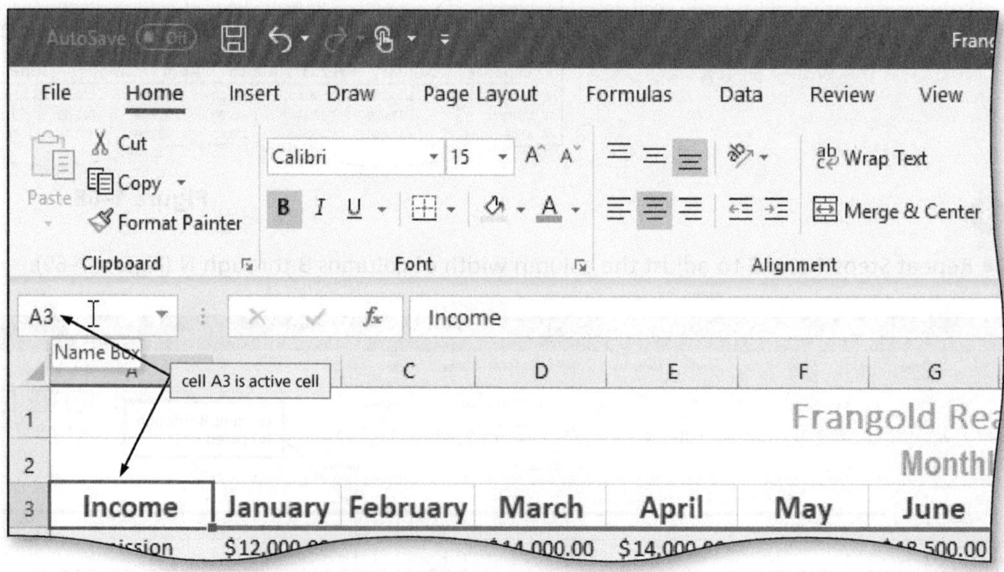

Figure 1–71

Other Ways to Select Cells

As you will see in later modules, in addition to using the Name box to select any cell in a worksheet, you also can use it to assign names to a cell or range of cells. Excel supports several additional ways to select a cell, as summarized in Table 1–4.

Table 1–4 Selecting Cells in Excel

Key, Box, or Command	Function
ALT+PAGE DOWN	Selects the cell one worksheet window to the right and moves the worksheet window accordingly.
ALT+PAGE UP	Selects the cell one worksheet window to the left and moves the worksheet window accordingly.
ARROW	Selects the adjacent cell in the direction of the arrow on the key.
CTRL+ARROW	Selects the border cell of the worksheet in combination with the arrow keys and moves the worksheet window accordingly. For example, to select the rightmost cell in the row that contains the active cell, press CTRL+RIGHT ARROW. You also can press END, release it, and then press the appropriate arrow key to accomplish the same task.
CTRL+HOME	Selects cell A1 or the cell one column and one row below and to the right of frozen titles and moves the worksheet window accordingly.
Find command on Find & Select menu (Home tab | Editing group) or SHIFT+F5	Finds and selects a cell that contains specific contents that you enter in the Find and Replace dialog box. If necessary, Excel moves the worksheet window to display the cell. You also can press CTRL+F to display the Find and Replace dialog box.
Go To command on Find & Select menu (Home tab | Editing group) or F5	Selects the cell that corresponds to the cell reference you enter in the Go To dialog box and moves the worksheet window accordingly. You also can press CTRL+G to display the Go To dialog box and its Special button to go to special worksheet elements, such as formulas.
HOME	Selects the cell at the beginning of the row that contains the active cell and moves the worksheet window accordingly.
Name box	Selects the cell in the workbook that corresponds to the cell reference you enter in the Name box.
PAGE DOWN	Selects the cell down one worksheet window from the active cell and moves the worksheet window accordingly.
PAGE UP	Selects the cell up one worksheet window from the active cell and moves the worksheet window accordingly.

Break Point: If you want to take a break, this is a good place to do so. Be sure to save the Frangold Real Estate Budget file again, and then you can exit Excel. To resume later start Excel, open the file called Frangold Real Estate Budget, and continue following the steps from this location forward.

Adding a Pie Chart to the Worksheet

Excel includes 17 chart types from which you can choose, including column, line, pie, bar, area, X Y (scatter), map, stock, surface, radar, treemap, sunburst, histogram, box & whisker, waterfall, funnel, and combo. The type of chart you choose depends on the type and quantity of data you have and the message or analysis you want to convey.

A column chart is a good way to compare values side by side. A line chart is often used to illustrate changes in data over time. Pie charts show the contribution of each piece of data to the whole, or total, of the data. A pie chart can go even further in comparing values across categories by showing each pie piece in comparison with the others. Area charts, like line charts, illustrate changes over time but are often used to compare more than one set of data, and the area below the lines is filled in with a different color for each set of data. An X Y (scatter) chart is used much like a line chart, but each piece of data is represented by a dot and is not connected with a line. Scatter charts are typically used for viewing scientific, statistical, and engineering data. A map chart depicts data based on geographic location. A stock chart provides a number of methods commonly used in the financial industry to show fluctuations in stock market data. A surface chart compares data from three columns and/or rows in a 3-D manner. A radar chart can compare aggregate values of several sets of data in a manner that resembles a radar screen, with each set of data represented by a different color. A funnel chart illustrates values during various stages. A combo chart allows you to combine multiple types of charts.

As outlined in the requirements document in Figure 1–2, the budget worksheet should include a pie chart to graphically represent the yearly expense totals for each item in Frangold Real Estate's budget. The pie chart shown in Figure 1–72 is on its own sheet in the workbook. The pie chart resides on a separate sheet, called a chart sheet. A **chart sheet** is a separate sheet in a workbook that contains only a chart, which is linked to the workbook data.

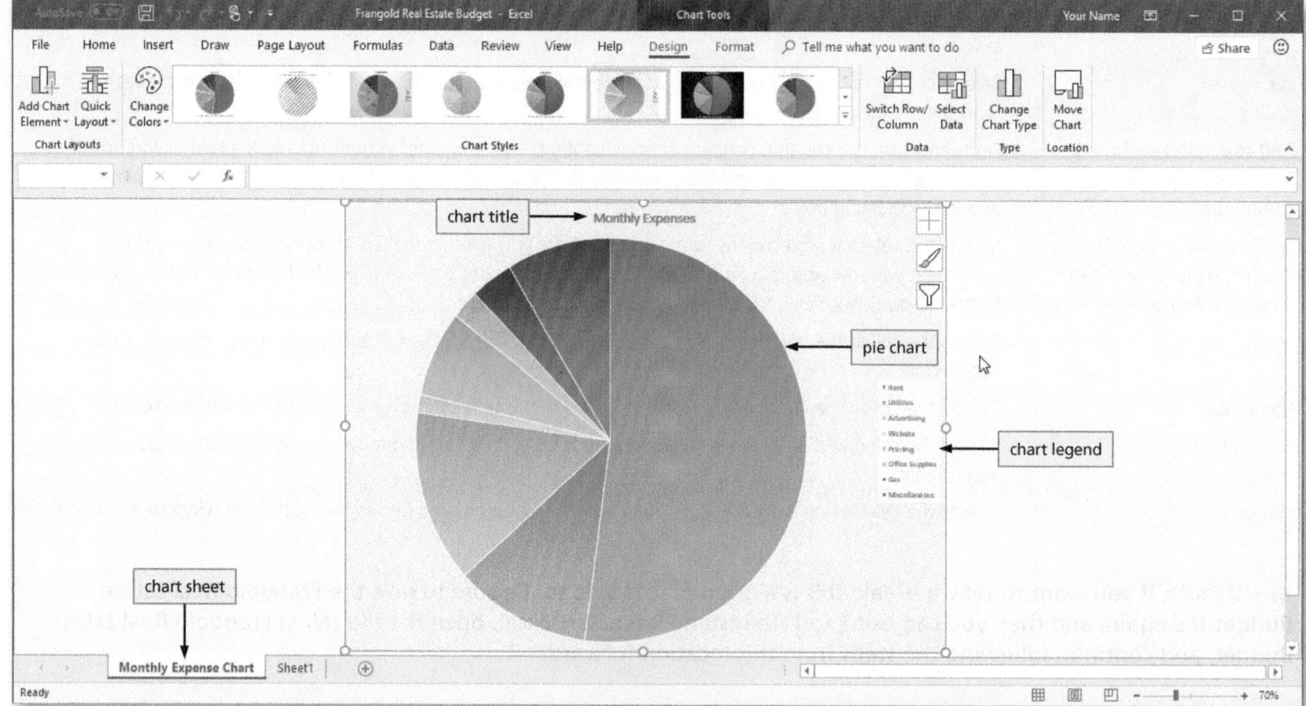

Figure 1–72

In this worksheet, the ranges you want to chart are the nonadjacent ranges A9:A16 (expense titles) and N9:N16 (yearly expense totals). The expense titles in the range A9:A16 will identify the slices of the pie chart; these entries are called category names. The range N9:N16 contains the data that determine the size of the slices in the pie; these entries are called the data series. A **data series** is a column or row in a datasheet and also the set of values represented in a chart. Because eight budget items are being charted, the pie chart contains eight slices.

To Add a Pie Chart

Why? *When you want to see how each part relates to the whole, you use a pie chart.* The following steps draw the pie chart.

1

- Select the range A9:A16 to identify the range of the category names for the pie chart.
- While holding down CTRL, select the nonadjacent range N9:N16.
- Click Insert on the ribbon to display the Insert tab.
- Click the 'Insert Pie or Doughnut Chart' button (Insert tab | Charts group) to display the Insert Pie or Doughnut Chart gallery (Figure 1–73).

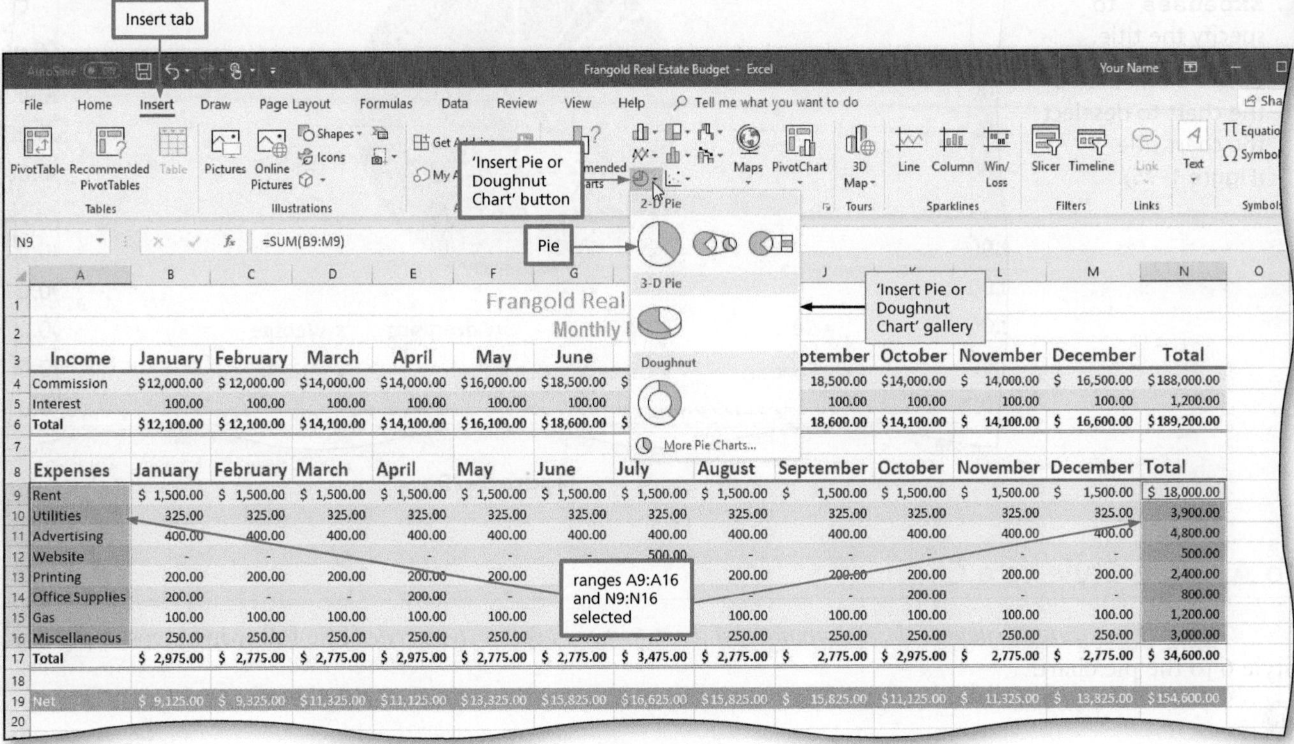

Figure 1–73

2

- Click Pie in the 2-D category of the Insert Pie or Doughnut Chart gallery to insert the chart in the worksheet (Figure 1–74).

Q&A Why have new tabs appeared on the ribbon?

The new tabs provide additional options and functionality when you are working with certain objects, such as charts, and only display when you are working with those objects.

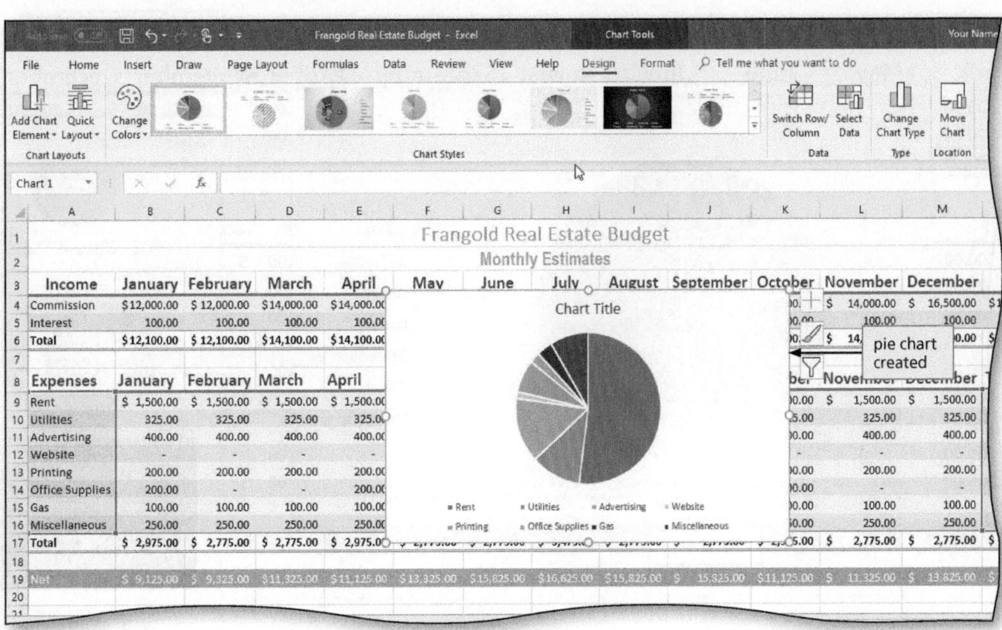

Figure 1–74

- Click the chart title to select it.
- Click and drag to select all the text in the chart title.
- Type **Monthly Expenses** to specify the title.
- Click a blank area of the chart to deselect the chart title (Figure 1–75).

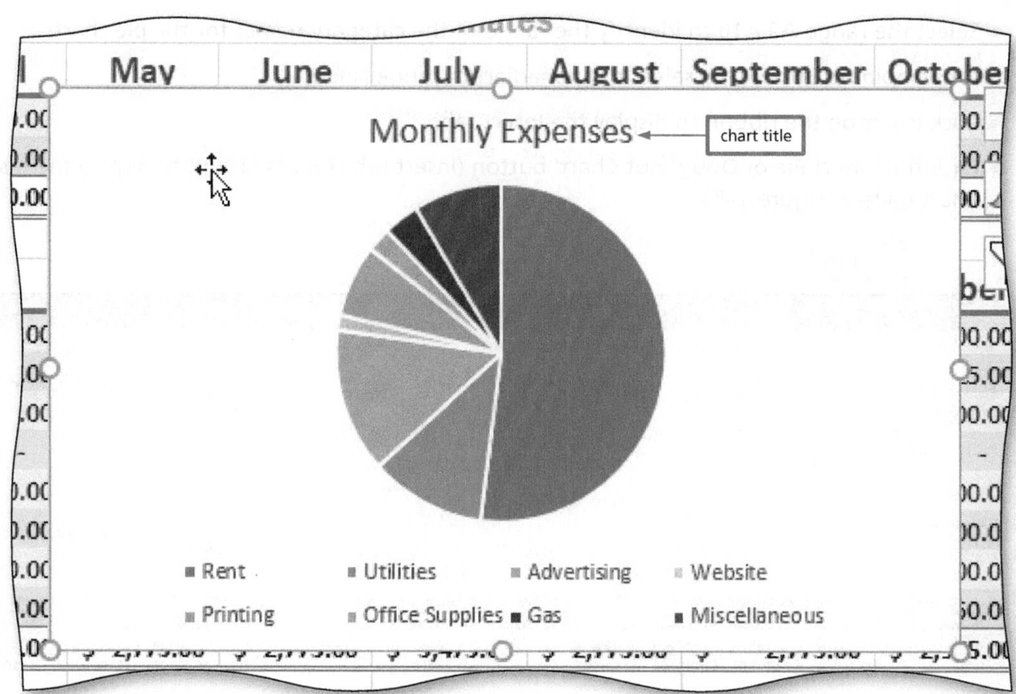

Figure 1–75

To Apply a Style to a Chart

Why? If you want to enhance the appearance of a chart, you can apply a chart style. The following steps apply Style 6 to the pie chart.

- Click the Chart Styles button to the right of the chart to display the Chart Styles gallery.
- Scroll in the Chart Styles gallery to display the Style 6 chart style (Figure 1–76).

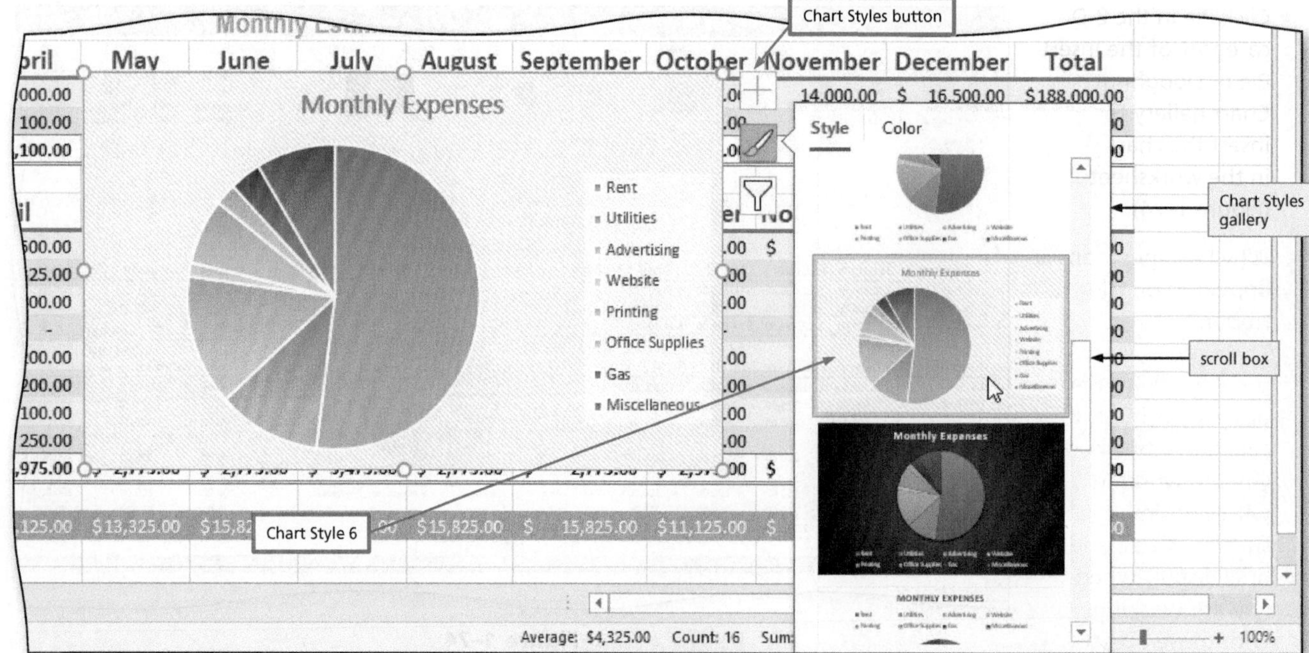

Figure 1–76

2

- Click Style 6 in the Chart Styles gallery to change the chart style to Style 6 (Figure 1–77).

3

- Click the Chart Styles button to close the Chart Styles gallery.

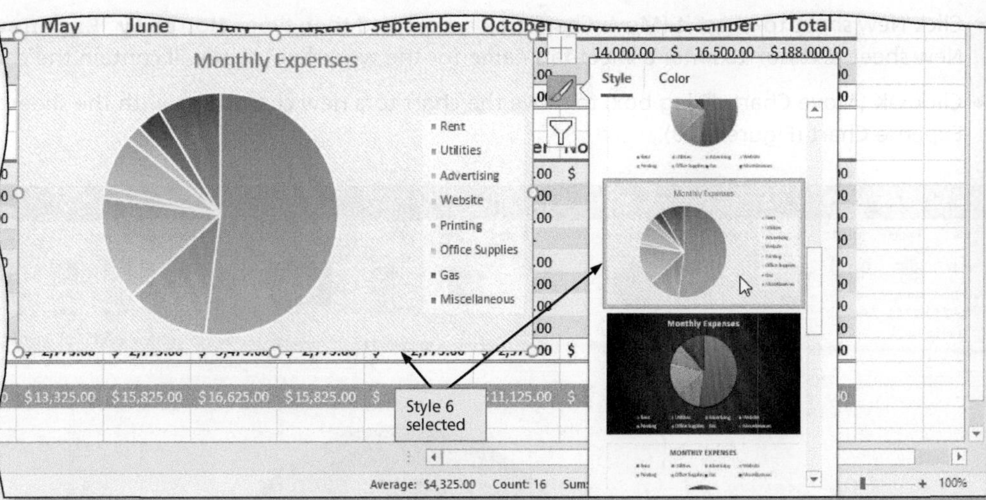

Figure 1–77

Changing the Sheet Tab Names and Colors

The sheet tabs at the bottom of the window allow you to navigate between any worksheet in the workbook. You click the sheet tab of the worksheet you want to view in the Excel window. By default, the worksheets are named Sheet1, Sheet2, and so on. The worksheet names become increasingly important as you move toward more sophisticated workbooks, especially workbooks in which you place objects such as charts on different sheets, which you will do in the next section, or you reference cells between worksheets.

BTW

Exploding a Pie Chart

If you want to draw attention to a particular slice in a pie chart, you can offset the slice so that it stands out from the rest. A pie chart with one or more slices offset is referred to as an exploded pie chart. To offset a slice, click the slice two times to select it (do not double-click) and then drag the slice outward.

To Move a Chart to a New Sheet

Why? By moving a chart to its own sheet, the size of the chart will increase, which can improve readability. The following steps move the pie chart to a chart sheet named Monthly Expenses.

- Click the Move Chart button (Chart Tools Design tab | Location group) to display the Move Chart dialog box (Figure 1–78).

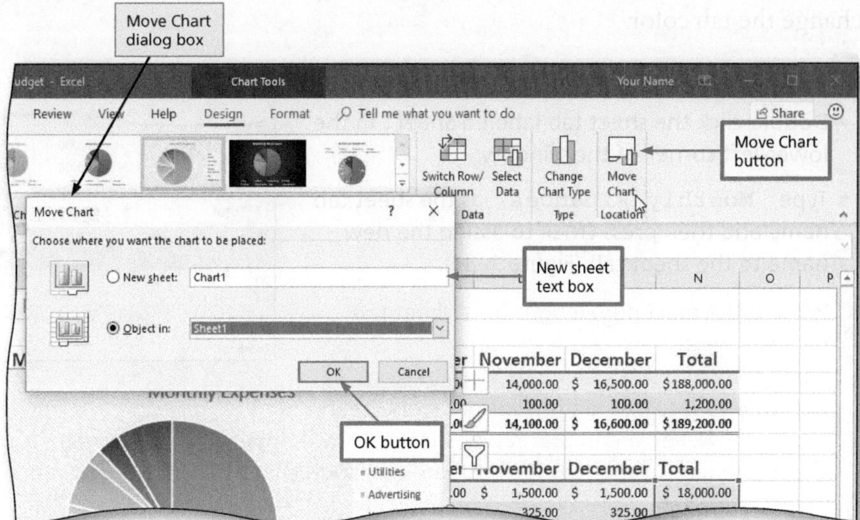

Figure 1–78

- Click New sheet to select it (Move Chart dialog box) and then type `Monthly Expense Chart` in the New sheet text box to enter a sheet tab name for the worksheet that will contain the chart.
- Click OK (Move Chart dialog box) to move the chart to a new chart sheet with the sheet tab name, Monthly Expense Chart (Figure 1–79).

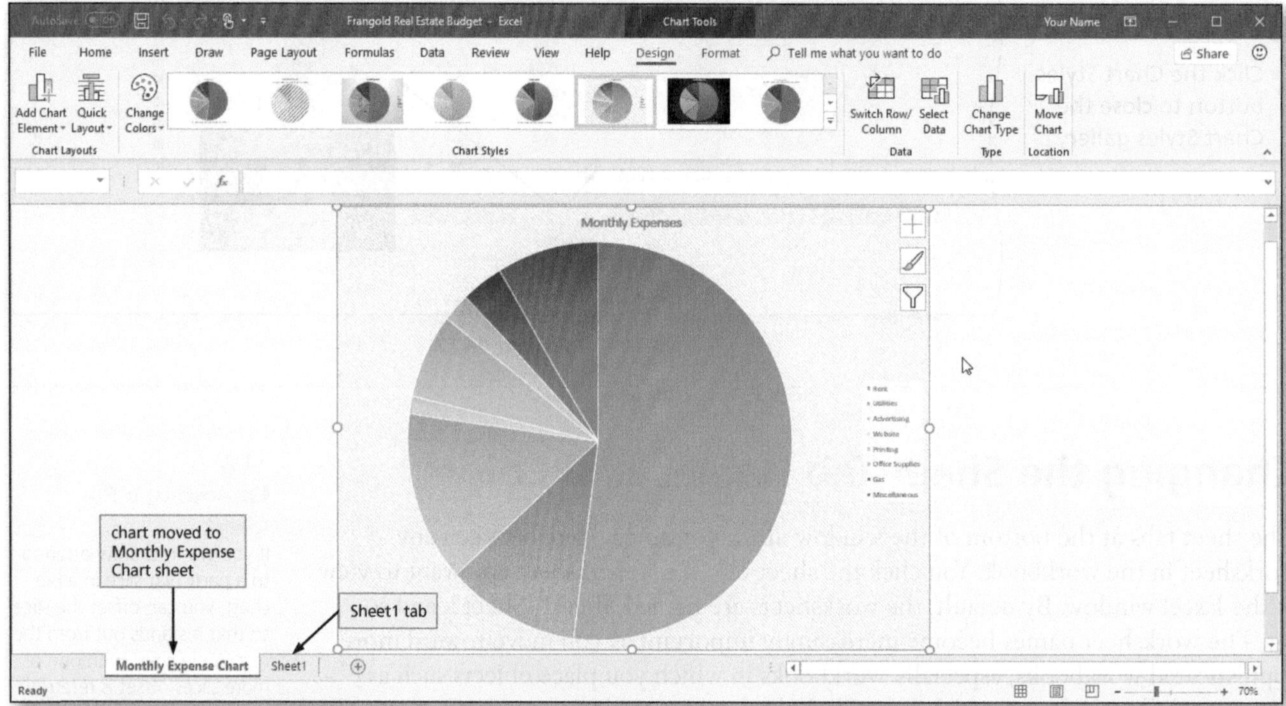

Figure 1–79

To Change the Sheet Tab Name and Color

You decide to change the name and color of the Sheet1 tab to Monthly Finances. ***Why?*** *Use simple, meaningful names for each sheet tab. Sheet tab names often match the worksheet title. If a worksheet includes multiple titles in multiple sections of the worksheet, use a sheet tab name that encompasses the meaning of all of the sections. Changing the tab color also can help uniquely identify a sheet.* The following steps rename the sheet tab and change the tab color.

- Double-click the sheet tab labeled Sheet1 in the lower-left corner of the window.
- Type `Monthly Finances` as the sheet tab name and then press ENTER to assign the new name to the sheet tab (Figure 1–80).

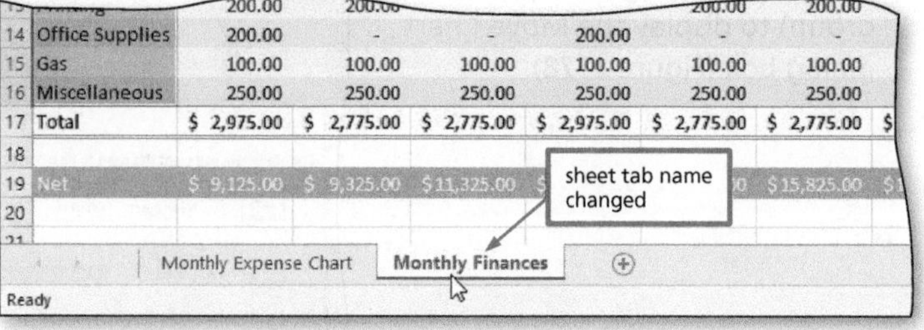

Figure 1–80

Q&A What is the maximum length for a sheet tab name?

Sheet tab names can be up to 31 characters (including spaces) in length. Longer worksheet names, however, mean that fewer sheet tabs will appear on your screen. If you have multiple worksheets with long sheet tab names, you may have to scroll through sheet tabs, making it more difficult to find a particular sheet.

2

- Right-click the sheet tab labeled Monthly Finances, in the lower-left corner of the window, to display a shortcut menu.
- Point to Tab Color on the shortcut menu to display the Tab Color gallery (Figure 1–81).

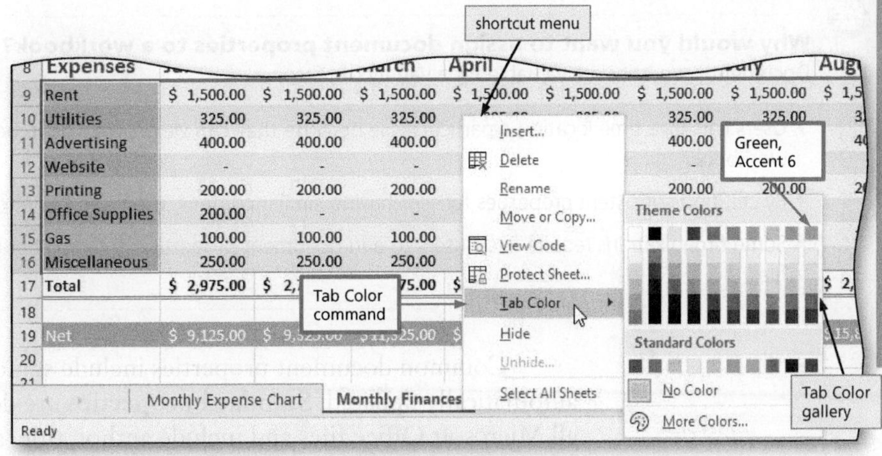

Figure 1–81

3

- Click Green, Accent 6 (column 10, row 1) in the Theme Colors area to change the color of the tab (Figure 1–82).
- If necessary, click Home on the ribbon to display the Home tab.
- Click the Save button on the Quick Access Toolbar to save the workbook again on the same storage location with the same file name.

Q&A

Why should I save the workbook again?
You have made several modifications to the workbook since you last saved it. Thus, you should save it again.

What if I want to change the file name or storage location when I save the workbook?
Click Save As in Backstage view and follow the "To Save a Workbook" steps earlier in this module to specify a different file name and/or storage location.

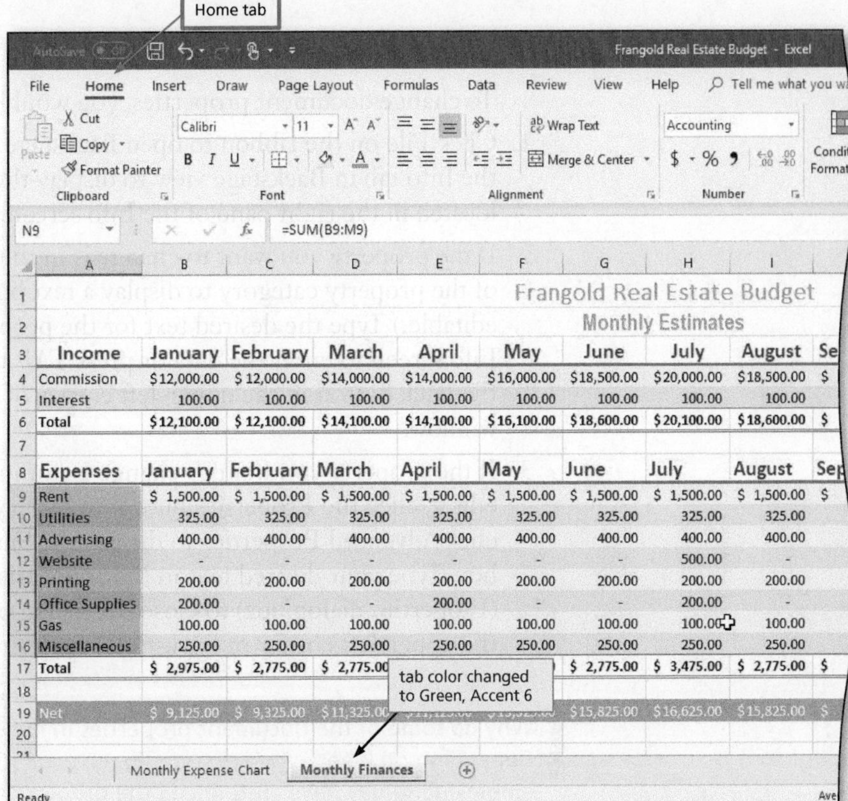

Figure 1–82

Document Properties

Excel helps you organize and identify your files by using **document properties**, which are the details about a file such as the project author, title, and subject. For example, you could use the class name or topic to describe the workbook's purpose or content in the document properties.

CONSIDER THIS

Why would you want to assign document properties to a workbook?
Document properties are valuable for a variety of reasons:

- Users can save time locating a particular file because they can view a file's document properties without opening the workbook.
- By creating consistent properties for files having similar content, users can better organize their workbooks.
- Some organizations require Excel users to add document properties so that other employees can view details about these files.

Common document properties include standard properties and those that are automatically updated. **Standard properties** are document properties associated with all Microsoft Office files and include author, title, and subject. **Automatically updated properties** are file system or document properties, such as the date you create or change a file, and statistics, such as the file size.

To Change Document Properties

To change document properties, you would follow these steps.

1. Click File on the ribbon to open Backstage view and then, if necessary, click the Info tab in Backstage view to display the Info screen. The Properties list is located in the right pane of the Info screen.
2. If the property you want to change is in the Properties list, click to the right of the property category to display a text box. (Note that not all properties are editable.) Type the desired text for the property and then click anywhere in the Info screen to enter the data or press TAB to navigate to the next property. Click the Back button in the upper-left corner of Backstage view to return to the Excel window.
3. If the property you want to change is not in the Properties list or you cannot edit it, click the Properties button to display the Properties menu, and then click Advanced Properties to display the Summary tab in the Properties dialog box. Type your desired text in the appropriate property text boxes. Click OK (Properties dialog box) to close the dialog box and then click the Back button in the upper-left corner of Backstage view to return to the workbook.

Q&A

Why do some of the document properties in my Properties dialog box contain data?
Depending on where you are using Excel, your school, university, or place of employment may have customized the properties.

Printing a Worksheet

After creating a worksheet, you may want to preview and print it. A **preview** is an onscreen view of your document prior to printing, to see exactly how the printed document will look. Printing a worksheet enables you to distribute the worksheet to others in a form that can be read or viewed but not edited. It is a good practice to save a workbook before printing a worksheet, in the event you experience difficulties printing.

CONSIDER THIS

What is the best method for distributing a workbook?

The traditional method of distributing a workbook uses a printer to produce a hard copy. A **hard copy** or **printout** is information that exists on paper. Hard copies can be useful for the following reasons:

- Some people prefer proofreading a hard copy of a workbook rather than viewing it on the screen to check for errors and readability.
- Hard copies can serve as a backup reference if your storage medium is lost or becomes corrupted and you need to recreate the workbook.

Instead of distributing a hard copy of a workbook, users can distribute the workbook as an electronic image that mirrors the original workbook's appearance. An electronic image of a workbook is not an editable file; it simply displays a picture of the workbook. The electronic image of the workbook can be sent as an email attachment, posted on a website, or copied to a portable storage medium such as a USB flash drive. Two popular electronic image formats, sometimes called fixed formats, are PDF by Adobe Systems and XPS by Microsoft. In Excel, you can create electronic image files through the Save As dialog box and the Export, Share, and Print tabs in Backstage view. Electronic images of workbooks, such as PDF and XPS, can be useful for the following reasons:

- Users can view electronic images of workbooks without the software that created the original workbook (e.g., Excel). Specifically, to view a PDF file, you use a program called Adobe Reader, which can be downloaded free from the Adobe website. Similarly, to view an XPS file, you use a program called XPS Viewer, which is included in the latest version of Windows.
- Sending electronic workbooks saves paper and printer supplies. Society encourages users to contribute to **green computing**, which involves reducing the electricity consumed and environmental waste generated when using computers, mobile devices, and related technologies.

To Preview and Print a Worksheet in Landscape Orientation

With the completed workbook saved, you may want to print it. ***Why?*** *A printed copy is sometimes necessary for a report delivered in person.*

An on-screen preview of your worksheet lets you see each page of your worksheet in the current orientation. **Portrait orientation** describes a printed copy with the short (8½") edge at the top of the printout; the printed page is taller than it is wide. **Landscape orientation** describes the page orientation in which the page is wider than it is tall. The print settings allow you to change the orientation as well as the paper size, margins, and scaling. **Scaling** determines how the worksheet fits on the page. You may want to adjust scaling to ensure that your data fits on one sheet of paper. ***Why?*** *A printed worksheet may be difficult to read if it is spread across more than one page.* The following steps print one or more hard copies of the contents of the worksheet.

- **Click File on the ribbon to open Backstage view.**
- **Click Print in Backstage view to display the Print screen (Figure 1–83).**

Q&A

How can I print multiple copies of my worksheet?
Increase the number in the Copies box on the Print screen.

What if I decide not to print the worksheet at this time?
Click the Back button in the upper-left corner of Backstage view to return to the workbook window.

Why does my Print screen look different?
Depending on the type of printer you select, your Print screen may display different options.

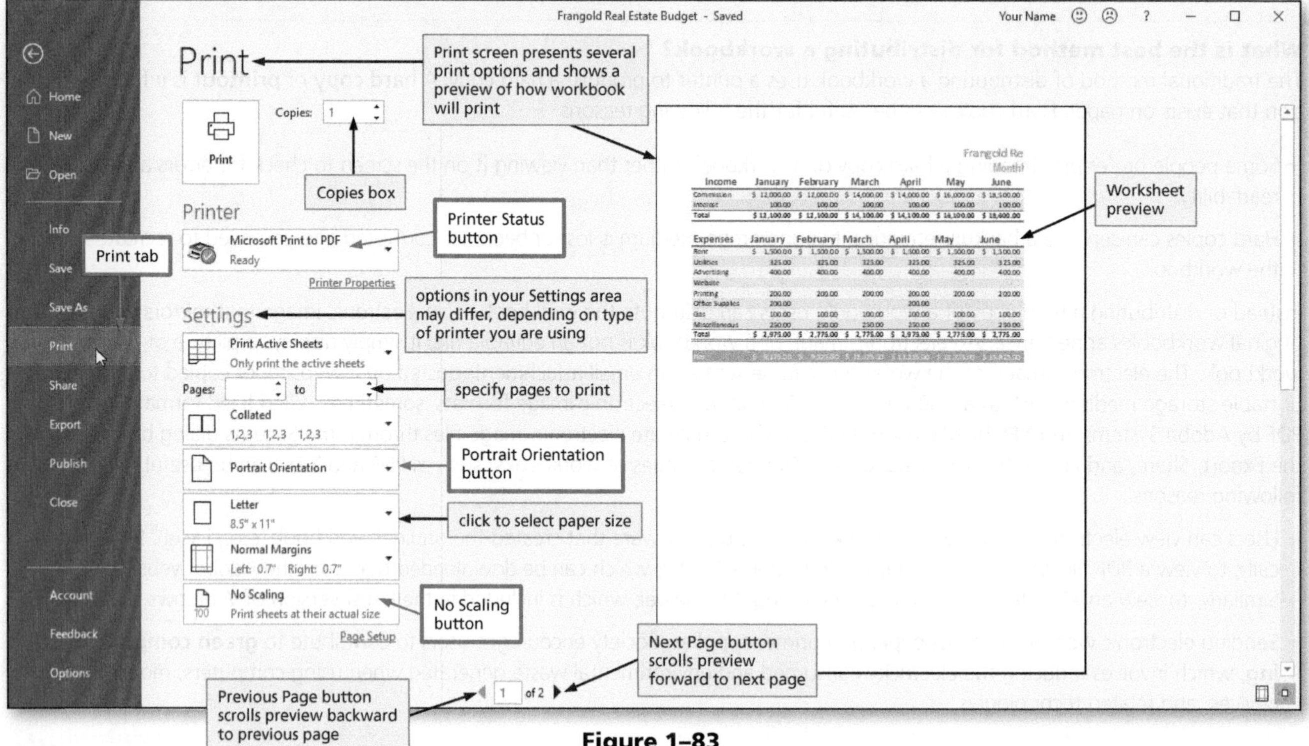

Figure 1–83

2

- Verify that the printer listed on the Printer Status button is the printer you want to use. If necessary, click the Printer Status button to display a list of available printer options and then click the desired printer to change the currently selected printer.
- If you want to print more than one copy, use the Copies up arrow to increase the number.
- If you want to change the paper size, use the paper size arrow (which currently reads Letter 8.5" × 11") to view and select a different one.

3

- Click the Portrait Orientation button in the Settings area and then select Landscape Orientation to change the orientation of the page to landscape.
- Click the No Scaling button and then select 'Fit Sheet on One Page' to print the entire worksheet on one page (Figure 1–84).

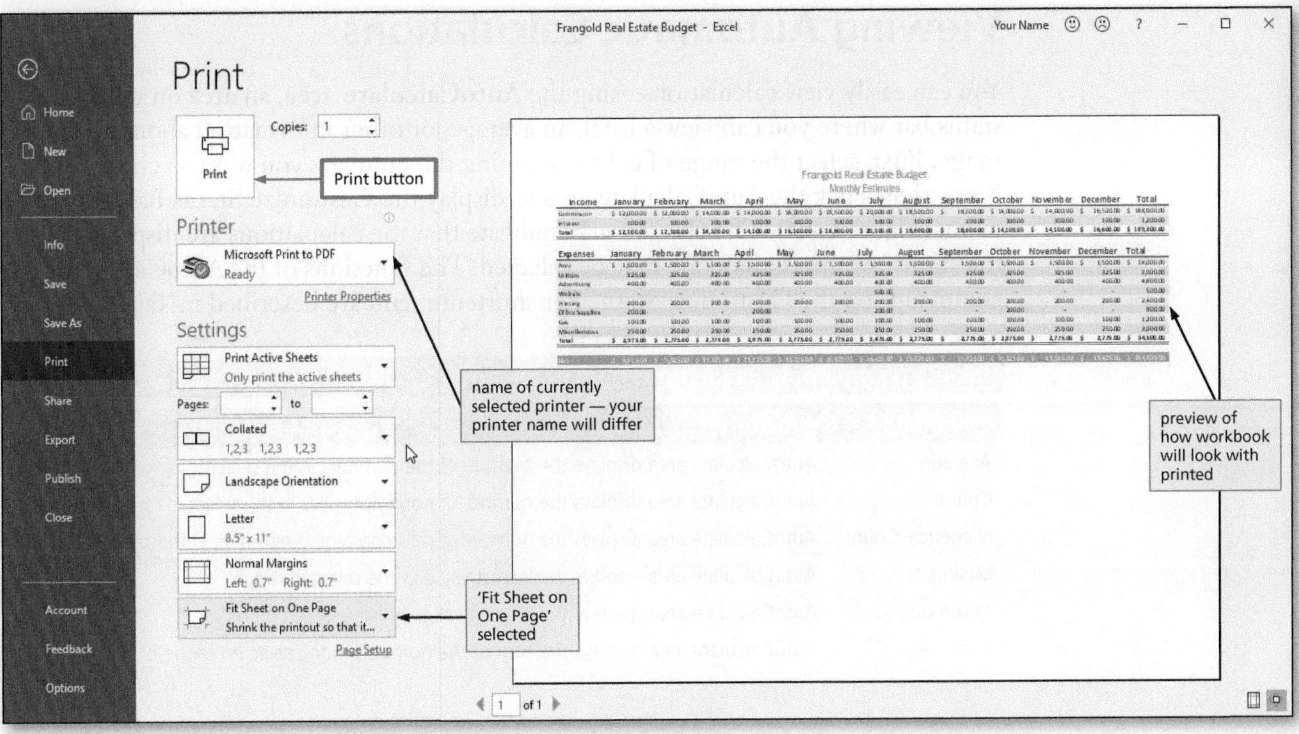

Figure 1–84

4

- **Click the Print button on the Print screen to print the worksheet in landscape orientation on the currently selected printer.**
- **When the printer stops, retrieve the hard copy (Figure 1–85).**

Q&A
Do I have to wait until my worksheet is complete to print it?
No, you can print a document at any time while you are creating it.

Frangold Real Estate Budget

Monthly Estimates

Income	January	February	March	April	May	June	July	August	September	October	November	December	Total
Commission	$ 12,000.00	$ 12,000.00	$ 14,000.00	$ 14,000.00	$ 16,000.00	$ 18,500.00	$ 20,000.00	$ 18,500.00	$ 18,500.00	$ 14,000.00	$ 14,000.00	$ 16,500.00	$ 188,000.00
Interest	100.00	100.00	100.00	100.00	100.00	100.00	100.00	100.00	100.00	100.00	100.00	100.00	1,200.00
Total	**$ 12,100.00**	**$ 12,100.00**	**$ 14,100.00**	**$ 14,100.00**	**$ 16,100.00**	**$ 18,600.00**	**$ 20,100.00**	**$ 18,600.00**	**$ 18,600.00**	**$ 14,100.00**	**$ 14,100.00**	**$ 16,600.00**	**$ 189,200.00**

Expenses	January	February	March	April	May	June	July	August	September	October	November	December	Total
Rent	$ 1,500.00	$ 1,500.00	$ 1,500.00	$ 1,500.00	$ 1,500.00	$ 1,500.00	$ 1,500.00	$ 1,500.00	$ 1,500.00	$ 1,500.00	$ 1,500.00	$ 1,500.00	$ 18,000.00
Utilities	325.00	325.00	325.00	325.00	325.00	325.00	325.00	325.00	325.00	325.00	325.00	325.00	3,900.00
Advertising	400.00	400.00	400.00	400.00	400.00	400.00	400.00	400.00	400.00	400.00	400.00	400.00	4,800.00
Website	-	-	-	-	-	-	500.00	-	-	-	-	-	500.00
Printing	200.00	200.00	200.00	200.00	200.00	200.00	200.00	200.00	200.00	200.00	200.00	200.00	2,400.00
Office Supplies	200.00	-	-	200.00	-	-	200.00	-	-	200.00	-	-	800.00
Gas	100.00	100.00	100.00	100.00	100.00	100.00	100.00	100.00	100.00	100.00	100.00	100.00	1,200.00
Miscellaneous	250.00	250.00	250.00	250.00	250.00	250.00	250.00	250.00	250.00	250.00	250.00	250.00	3,000.00
Total	**$ 2,975.00**	**$ 2,775.00**	**$ 2,775.00**	**$ 2,975.00**	**$ 2,775.00**	**$ 2,775.00**	**$ 3,475.00**	**$ 2,775.00**	**$ 2,775.00**	**$ 2,975.00**	**$ 2,775.00**	**$ 2,775.00**	**$ 34,600.00**
Net	$ 9,125.00	$ 9,325.00	$ 11,325.00	$ 11,125.00	$ 13,325.00	$ 15,825.00	$ 16,625.00	$ 15,825.00	$ 15,825.00	$ 11,125.00	$ 11,325.00	$ 13,825.00	$ 154,600.00

Figure 1–85

Other Ways

1. Press CTRL+P to open the Print screen, press ENTER

Viewing Automatic Calculations

You can easily view calculations using the **AutoCalculate area**, an area on the Excel status bar where you can view a total, an average, or other information about a selected range. First, select the range of cells containing the numbers you want to check. Next, right-click the AutoCalculate area to display the Customize Status Bar shortcut menu (Figure 1–86). The check marks indicate that the calculations are displayed in the status bar; more than one may be selected. The functions of the AutoCalculate commands on the Customize Status Bar shortcut menu are described in Table 1–5.

Table 1–5 Commonly Used Status Bar Commands

Command	Function
Average	AutoCalculate area displays the average of the numbers in the selected range
Count	AutoCalculate area displays the number of nonempty cells in the selected range
Numerical Count	AutoCalculate area displays the number of cells containing numbers in the selected range
Minimum	AutoCalculate area displays the lowest value in the selected range
Maximum	AutoCalculate area displays the highest value in the selected range
Sum	AutoCalculate area displays the sum of the numbers in the selected range

To Use the AutoCalculate Area to Determine a Maximum

The following steps determine the largest monthly total in the budget. ***Why?*** *Sometimes, you want a quick analysis, which can be especially helpful when your worksheet contains a lot of data.*

- Select the range B19:M19. Right-click the status bar to display the Customize Status Bar shortcut menu (Figure 1–86).

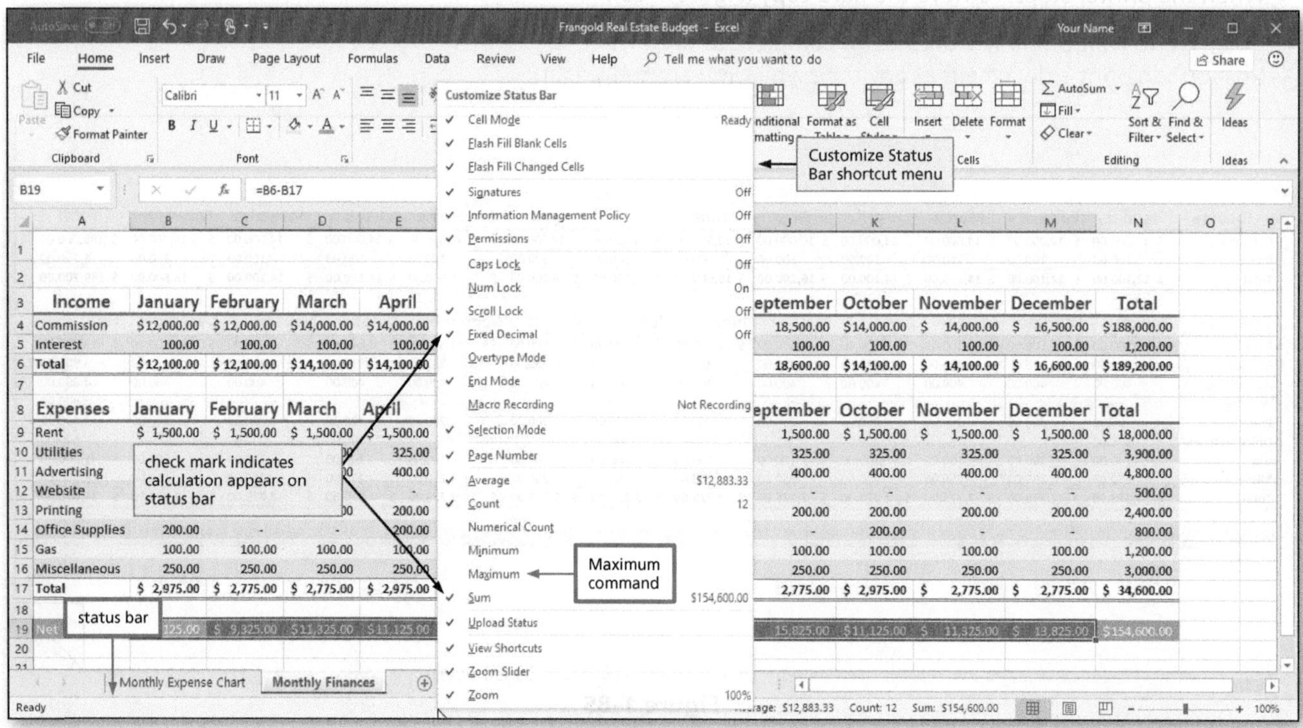

Figure 1–86

2

- Click Maximum on the shortcut menu to display the Maximum value in the range B19:M19 in the AutoCalculate area of the status bar.
- Click anywhere on the worksheet to close the shortcut menu (Figure 1–87).

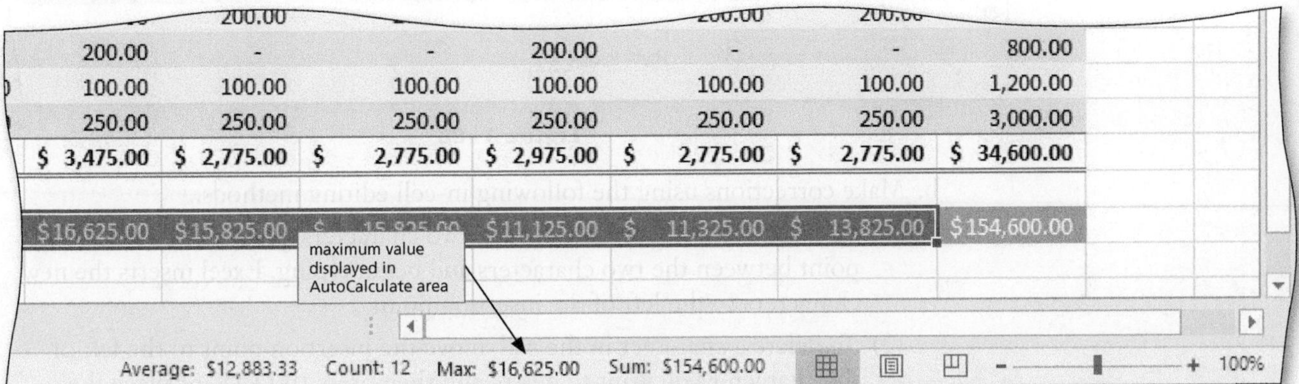

Figure 1–87

3

- Right-click the AutoCalculate area and then click Maximum on the shortcut menu to deselect it. The Maximum value will no longer appear on the status bar.
- Close the shortcut menu.

Correcting Errors

You can correct data entry errors on a worksheet using one of several methods. The method you choose will depend on the extent of the error and whether you notice it while entering the data or after you have entered the incorrect data into the cell.

Correcting Errors while Entering Data into a Cell

If you notice an error while you are entering data into a cell, press BACKSPACE to erase the incorrect character(s) and then enter the correct character(s). If the error is a major one, click the Cancel box in the formula bar or press ESC to erase the entire entry and then reenter the data.

Correcting Errors after Entering Data into a Cell

If you find an error in the worksheet after entering the data, you can correct the error in one of two ways:

1. If the entry is short, select the cell, retype the entry correctly, and then click the Enter button or press ENTER. The new entry will replace the old entry.
2. If the entry in the cell is long and the errors are minor, using Edit mode may be a better choice than retyping the cell entry. In **Edit mode**, a mode that lets you perform in-cell editing, Excel displays the active cell entry in the formula bar and a flashing insertion point in the active cell. There you can edit the contents directly in the cell — a procedure called **in-cell editing.**
   a. Double-click the cell containing the error to switch Excel to Edit mode (Figure 1–88).

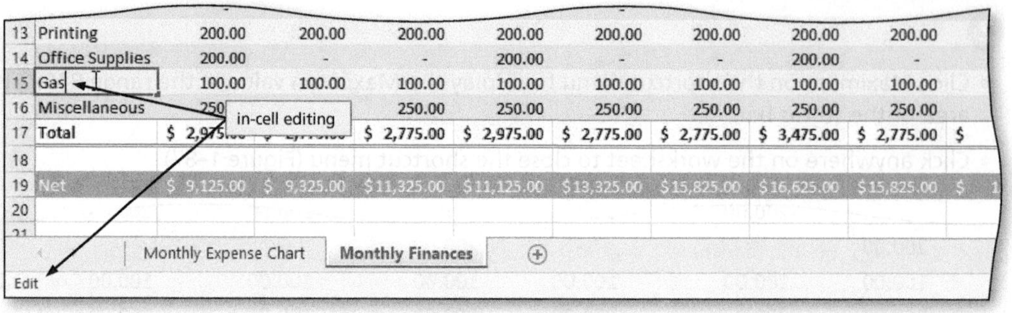

Figure 1–88

b. Make corrections using the following in-cell editing methods.

(1) To insert new characters between two characters, place the insertion point between the two characters and begin typing. Excel inserts the new characters to the left of the insertion point.

(2) To delete a character in the cell, move the insertion point to the left of the character you want to delete and then press DELETE, or place the insertion point to the right of the character you want to delete and then press BACKSPACE. You also can drag to select the character or adjacent characters you want to delete and then press DELETE or CTRL+X OR click the Cut button (Home tab | Clipboard group).

(3) When you are finished editing an entry, click the Enter button or press ENTER.

There are two ways to enter data in Edit mode: Insert mode and Overtype mode. **Insert mode** is the default Excel mode that inserts a character and moves all characters to the right of the typed character one position to the right. You can change to Overtype mode by pressing INSERT. In **Overtype mode**, Excel replaces, or overtypes, the character to the right of the insertion point. The INSERT key toggles the keyboard between Insert mode and Overtype mode.

While in Edit mode, you may want to move the insertion point to various points in the cell, select portions of the data in the cell, or switch from inserting characters to overtyping characters. Table 1–6 summarizes the more common tasks performed during in-cell editing.

Table 1–6 Summary of In-Cell Editing Tasks

	Task	Mouse Operation	Keyboard
1.	Move the insertion point to the beginning of data in a cell.	Point to the left of the first character and click.	Press HOME.
2.	Move the insertion point to the end of data in a cell.	Point to the right of the last character and click.	Press END.
3.	Move the insertion point anywhere in a cell.	Point to the appropriate position and click the character.	Press RIGHT ARROW or LEFT ARROW.
4.	Highlight one or more adjacent characters.	Drag through adjacent characters.	Press SHIFT+RIGHT ARROW or SHIFT+LEFT ARROW.
5.	Select all data in a cell.	Double-click the cell with the insertion point in the cell if the data in the cell contains no spaces.	
6.	Delete selected characters.	Click the Cut button (Home tab | Clipboard group).	Press DELETE.
7.	Delete characters to the left of the insertion point.		Press BACKSPACE.
8.	Delete characters to the right of the insertion point.		Press DELETE.
9.	Toggle between Insert and Overtype modes.		Press INSERT.

Undoing the Last Cell Entry

The Undo button on the Quick Access Toolbar (Figure 1–89) allows you to erase recent cell entries. Thus, if you enter incorrect data in a cell and notice it immediately, click the Undo button and Excel changes the cell entry to what it was prior to the incorrect data entry.

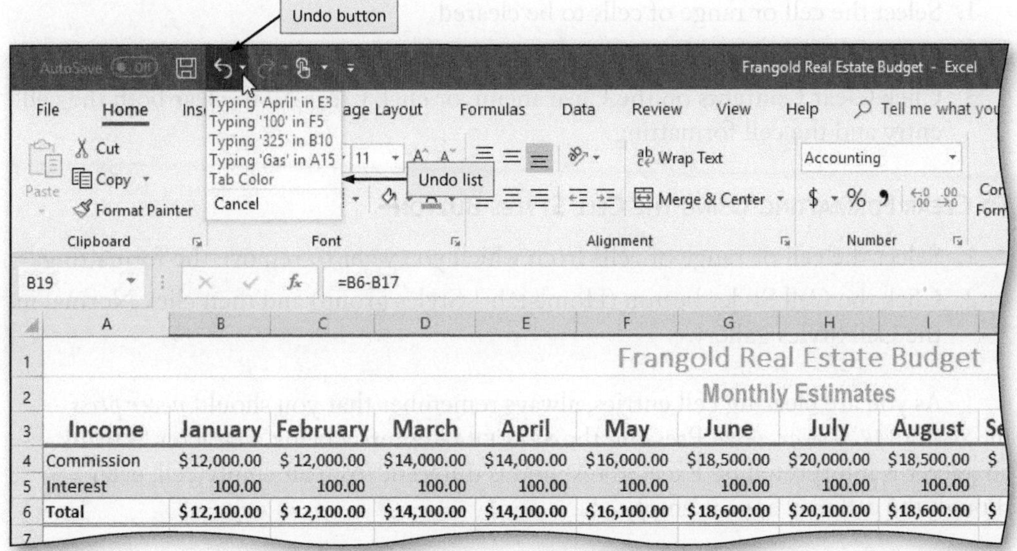

Figure 1–89

Excel remembers the last 100 actions you have completed. Thus, you can undo up to 100 previous actions by clicking the Undo arrow to display the Undo list and then clicking the action to be undone (Figure 1–89). You can drag through several actions in the Undo list to undo all of them at once. If no actions are available for Excel to undo, then the dimmed appearance of the Undo button indicates that it is unavailable.

The Redo button, next to the Undo button on the Quick Access Toolbar, allows you to repeat previous actions; that is, if you accidentally undo an action, you can use the Redo button to perform the action again.

Clearing a Cell or Range of Cells

If you enter data into the wrong cell or range of cells, you can erase, or clear, the data using one of the first four methods listed below. The fifth method clears the formatting from the selected cells. To clear a cell or range of cells, you would perform the following steps:

To Clear Cell Entries Using the Fill Handle

1. Select the cell or range of cells and then point to the fill handle so that the pointer changes to a crosshair.
2. Drag the fill handle back into the selected cell or range until a shadow covers the cell or cells you want to erase.

To Clear Cell Entries Using the Shortcut Menu

1. Select the cell or range of cells to be cleared.
2. Right-click the selection.
3. Click Clear Contents on the shortcut menu.

To Clear Cell Entries Using the Delete Key

1. Select the cell or range of cells to be cleared.
2. Press DELETE.

To Clear Cell Entries and Formatting Using the Clear Button

1. Select the cell or range of cells to be cleared.
2. Click the Clear button (Home tab | Editing group).
3. Click Clear Contents on the Clear menu, or click Clear All to clear both the cell entry and the cell formatting.

To Clear Formatting Using the Cell Styles Button

1. Select the cell or range of cells from which you want to remove the formatting.
2. Click the Cell Styles button (Home tab | Styles group) and then click Normal in the Cell Styles gallery.

As you are clearing cell entries, always remember that you should *never press the SPACEBAR to clear a cell.* Pressing the SPACEBAR enters a blank character. A blank character is interpreted by Excel as text and is different from an empty cell, even though the cell may appear empty.

Clearing the Entire Worksheet

If the required worksheet edits are extensive or if the requirements drastically change, you may want to clear the entire worksheet and start over. To clear the worksheet or delete an embedded chart, you would use the following steps.

To Clear the Entire Worksheet

1. Click the Select All button on the worksheet. The Select All button is located above the row 1 identifier and to the left of the column A heading.
2. Click the Clear button (Home tab | Editing group) and then click Clear All on the menu to delete both the entries and formats.

The Select All button selects the entire worksheet. To clear an unsaved workbook, click the Close Window button on the workbook's title bar or click the Close button in Backstage view. Click the No button if the Microsoft Excel dialog box asks if you want to save changes. To start a new, blank workbook, click the New button in Backstage view.

Using Excel Help

Once an Office app's Help window is open, you can use several methods to navigate Help. You can search for help by using the Help pane or the Tell me box.

To Obtain Help Using the Search Text Box

Assume for the following example that you want to know more about functions. The following steps use the Search text box to obtain useful information about functions by entering the word, functions, as search text. ***Why?*** *You may not know the exact help topic you are looking to find, so using keywords can help narrow your search.*

1

- Click Help on the ribbon to display the Help tab (Figure 1–90).

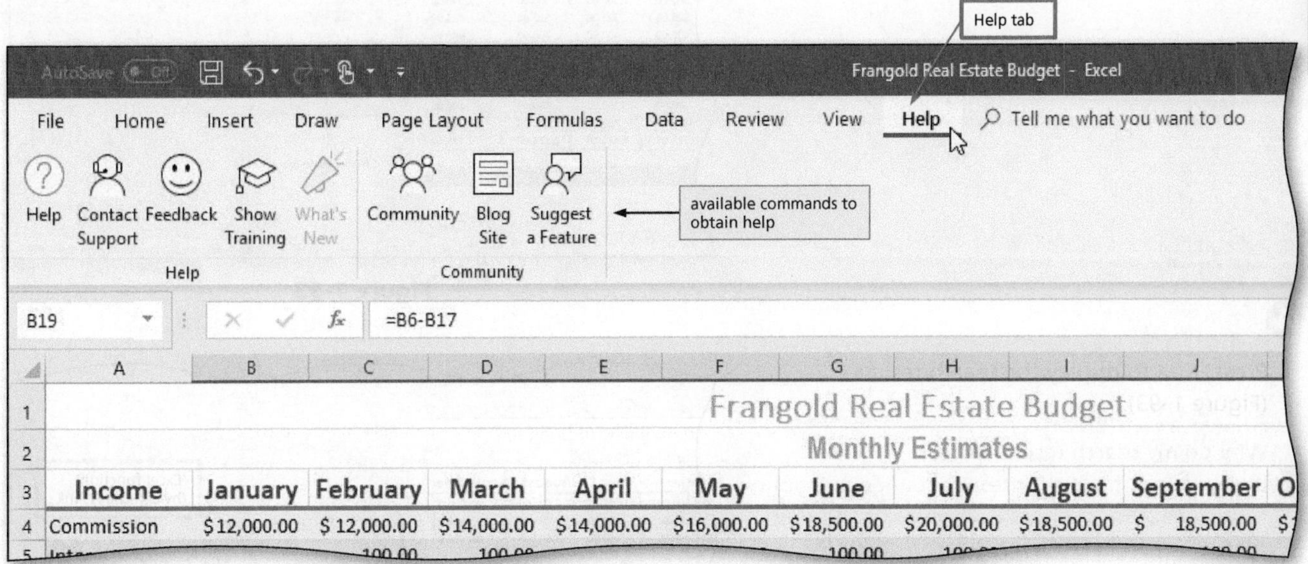

Figure 1–90

2

- Click the Help button (Help group) to display the Help pane (Figure 1–91).

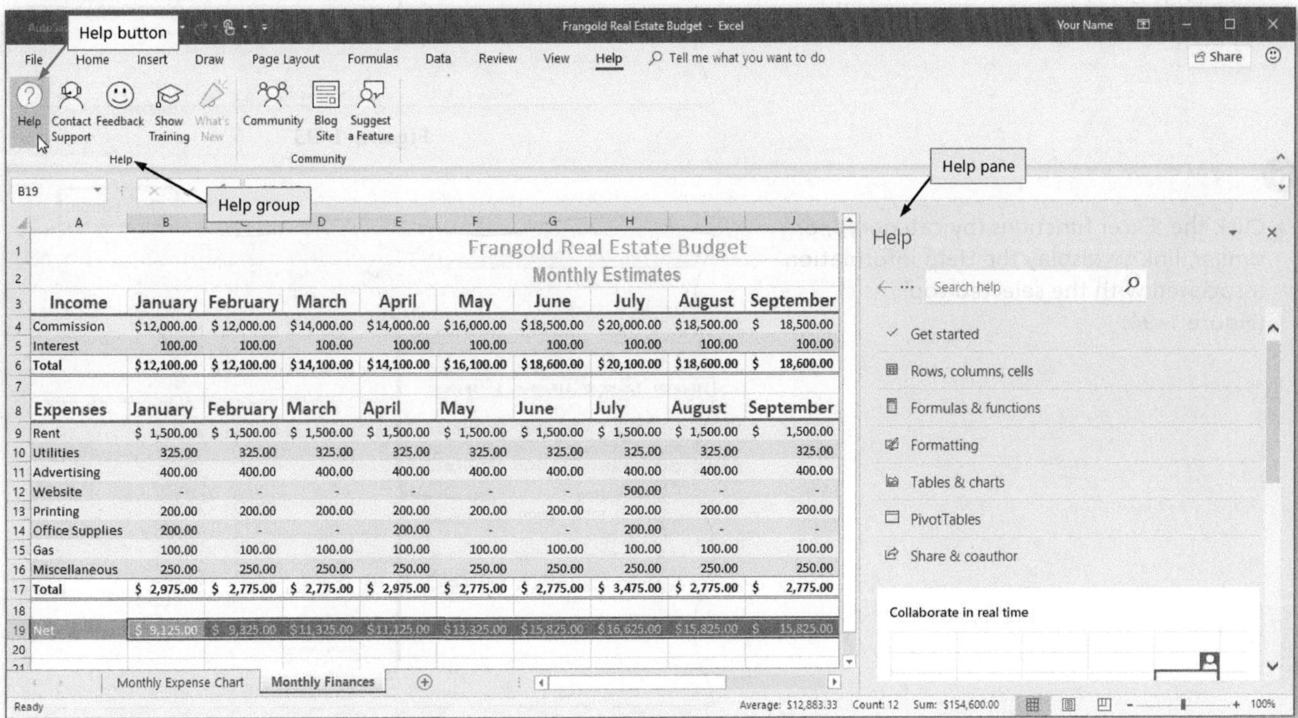

Figure 1–91

- Type **functions** in the Search help box at the top of the Help pane to enter the search text (Figure 1–92).

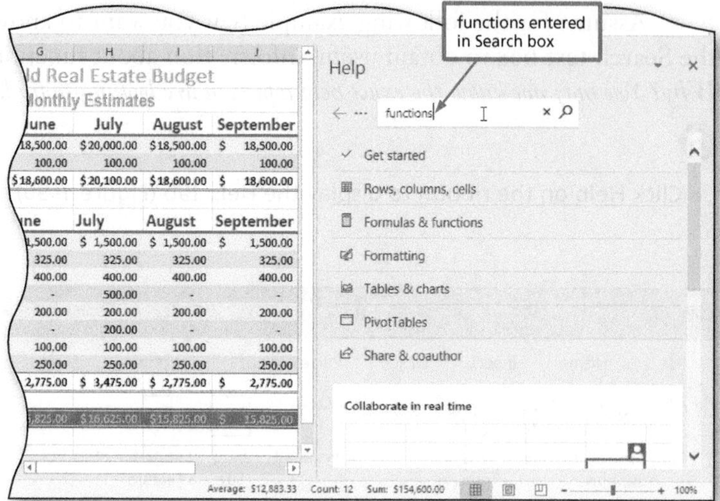

Figure 1–92

- Press ENTER to display the search results (Figure 1–93).

Q&A Why do my search results differ?
If you do not have an Internet connection, your results will reflect only the content of the Help files on your computer. When searching for help online, results also can change as content is added, deleted, and updated on the online Help webpages maintained by Microsoft.

Why were my search results not very helpful?
When initiating a search, be sure to check the spelling of the search text; also, keep your search specific to return the most accurate results.

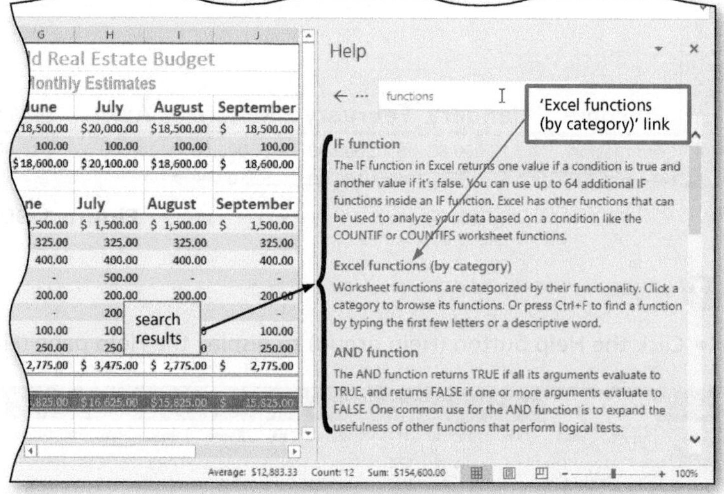

Figure 1–93

5

- Click the 'Excel functions (by category)', or similar, link to display the Help information associated with the selected topic (Figure 1–94).

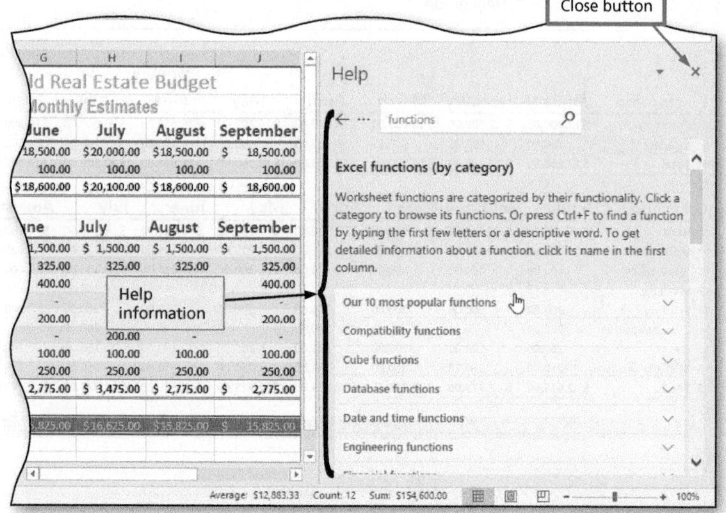

Figure 1–94

- Click the Close button in the Help pane to close the pane.
- Click Home on the ribbon to display the Home tab.

Obtaining Help while Working in an Office App

You also can access the Help functionality without first opening the Help pane and initiating a search. For example, you may be confused about how a particular command works, or you may be presented with a dialog box that you are not sure how to use.

If you want to learn more about a command, point to its button and wait for the ScreenTip to appear, as shown in Figure 1–95. If the Help icon and 'Tell me more' link appear in the ScreenTip, click the 'Tell me more' link (or press F1 while pointing to the button) to open the Help window associated with that command.

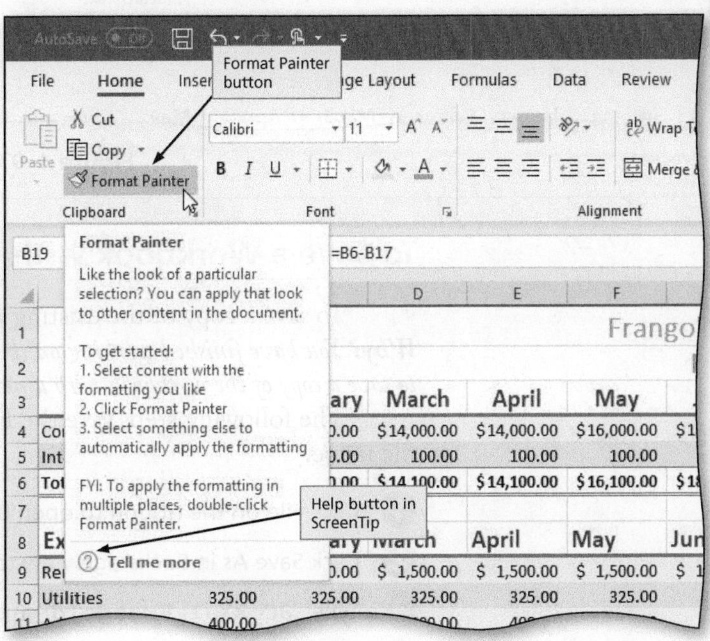

Figure 1–95

Dialog boxes also contain Help buttons, as shown in Figure 1–96. Clicking the Help button (or pressing F1) while the dialog box is displayed opens a Help window, which will display help contents specific to the dialog box, if available. If no help file is available for that particular dialog box, then the window will display the Help home page.

As mentioned previously, the Tell me box is integrated into the ribbon in Excel and most other Office apps and can perform a variety of functions, including providing easy access to commands and help content as you type.

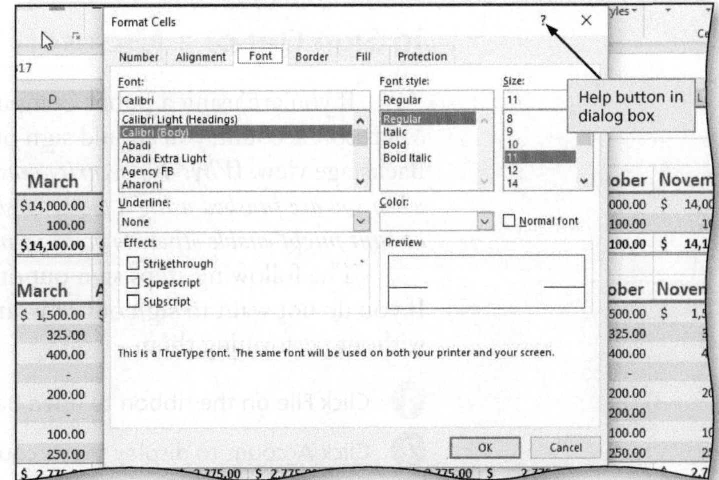

Figure 1–96

To Obtain Help Using the Tell Me Box

If you are having trouble finding a command in Excel, you can use the Tell me box to search for the function you are trying to perform. As you type, the Tell me box will suggest commands that match the search text you are entering. ***Why?*** *You can use the Tell me box to access commands quickly you otherwise may be unable to find on the ribbon.* The following steps find commands related to headers and footers.

- Type **header and footer** in the Tell me box and watch the search results appear (Figure 1–97).

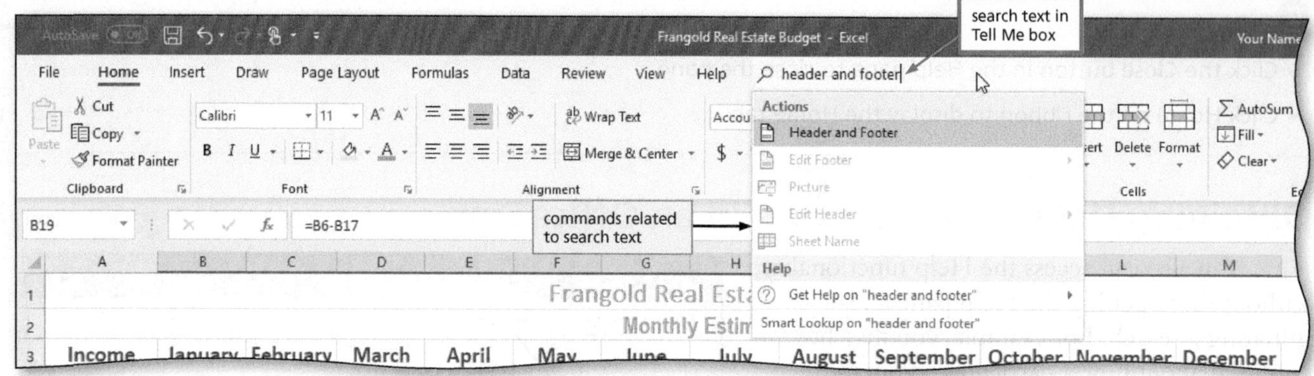

Figure 1–97

To Save a Workbook with a Different File Name

To save a copy of the existing file, you can save the file with a new file name. ***Why?*** *You have finished working on the Frangold Real Estate Budget workbook and would like to save a copy of the workbook with a new file name.*

The following steps save the Frangold Real Estate Budget workbook with a new file name.

1. Click File on the ribbon to open Backstage view.
2. Click Save As in Backstage view to display the Save As screen.
3. Type `SC_EX_1_Frangold` in the File name text box, replacing the existing file name.
4. Click the Save button to save the workbook with the new name.

To Sign Out of a Microsoft Account

If you are using a public computer or otherwise want to sign out of your Microsoft account, you should sign out of the account from the Accounts screen in Backstage view. ***Why?*** *For security reasons, you should sign out of your Microsoft account when you are finished using a public or shared computer. Staying signed in to your Microsoft account might enable others to access your files.*

The following steps sign out of a Microsoft account and exit the Excel program. If you do not want to sign out of your Microsoft account or exit Excel, read these steps without performing them.

1. Click File on the ribbon to open Backstage view.
2. Click Account to display the Account screen (Figure 1–98).
3. Click the Sign out link, which displays the Remove Account dialog box. If a Can't remove Windows accounts dialog box appears instead of the Remove Account dialog box, click OK and skip the remaining steps.

Q&A Why does a Can't remove Windows accounts dialog box appear?
If you signed in to Windows using your Microsoft account, then you also must sign out from Windows rather than signing out from within Excel. When you are finished using Windows, be sure to sign out at that time.

4. Click the Yes button (Remove Account dialog box) to sign out of your Microsoft account on this computer.

Q&A Should I sign out of Windows after removing my Microsoft account?
When you are finished using the computer, you should sign out of Windows for maximum security.

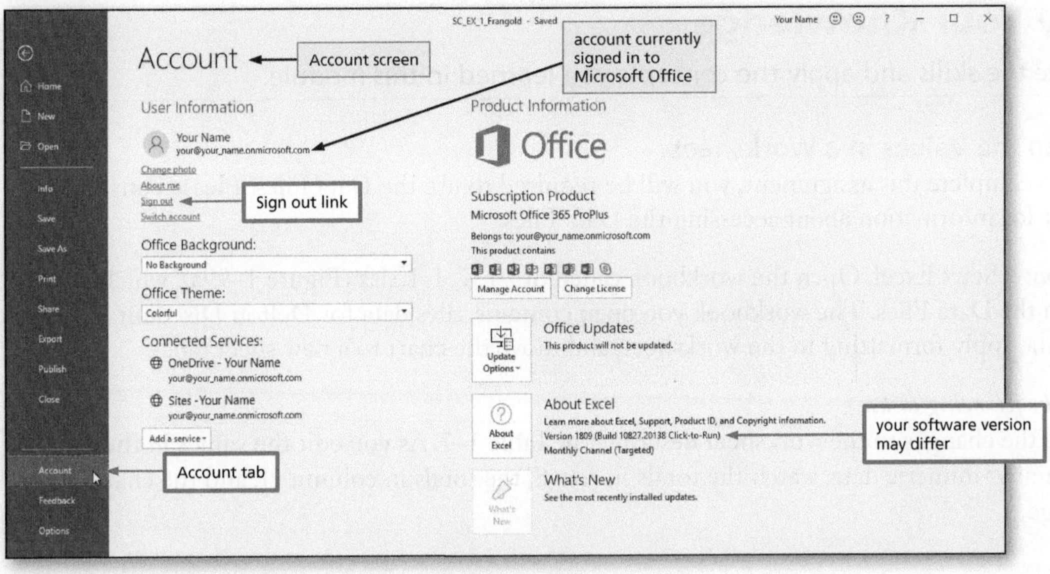

Account screen

account currently signed in to Microsoft Office

Sign out link

Account tab

your software version may differ

Figure 1–98

5 Click the Back button in the upper-left corner of Backstage view to return to the document.

6 **sam** Click the Close button to close the workbook and exit Microsoft Excel. If you are prompted to save changes, click Yes.

Summary

In this module you have learned how to create a real estate budget worksheet and chart. Topics covered included starting Excel and creating a blank workbook, selecting a cell, entering text, entering numbers, calculating a sum, using the fill handle, formatting a worksheet, adding a pie chart, changing sheet tab names and colors, printing a worksheet, using the AutoCalculate area, correcting errors, and obtaining help.

What decisions will you need to make when creating workbooks and charts in the future?

Use these guidelines as you complete the assignments in this module and create your own spreadsheets outside of this class.

1. Determine the workbook structure.
   a) Determine the data you will need for your workbook.
   b) Sketch a layout of your data and your chart.
2. Create the worksheet.
   a) Enter titles, subtitles, and headings.
   b) Enter data, functions, and formulas.
3. Format the worksheet.
   a) Format the titles, subtitles, and headings using styles.
   b) Format the totals.
   c) Format the numbers.
   d) Format the text.
   e) Adjust column widths.
4. Create the chart.
   a) Determine the type of chart to use.
   b) Determine the chart title and data.
   c) Determine the chart location
   d) Format the chart.

Apply Your Knowledge

Reinforce the skills and apply the concepts you learned in this module.

Changing the Values in a Worksheet

Note: To complete this assignment, you will be required to use the Data Files. Please contact your instructor for information about accessing the Data Files.

Instructions: Start Excel. Open the workbook called SC_EX_1-1.xlsx (Figure 1–99a), which is located in the Data Files. The workbook you open contains sales data for Delton Discount. You are to edit data, apply formatting to the worksheet, and move the chart to a new sheet tab.

Perform the following tasks:

1. Make the changes to the worksheet described in Table 1–7. As you edit the values in the cells containing numeric data, watch the totals in row 8, the totals in column H, and the chart change.

Table 1–7 New Worksheet Data

Cell	Change Cell Contents To
A2	Monthly Departmental Sales
B5	13442.36
C7	115528.13
D5	24757.85
E6	39651.54
F7	29667.88
G6	19585.46

2. Change the worksheet title in cell A1 to the Title cell style and then merge and center it across columns A through H.
3. Use buttons in the Font group on the Home tab on the ribbon to change the worksheet subtitle in cell A2 to 14-point font and then merge and center it across columns A through H. Change the font color of cell A2 to Blue, Accent 1, Darker 50%.
4. Name the worksheet, Department Sales, and apply the Blue, Accent 1, Darker 50% color to the sheet tab (Figure 1–99b).
5. Move the chart to a new sheet called Sales Analysis Chart (Figure 1–99c). Change the chart title to MONTHLY SALES TOTALS.

   If requested by your instructor, on the Department Sales worksheet, replace Delton in cell A1 with your last name.
6. Save the workbook with the file name, SC_EX_1_Delton, and submit the revised workbook (shown in Figure 1–99) in the format specified by your instructor and exit Excel.
7. Besides the styles used in the worksheet, what other changes could you make to enhance the worksheet?

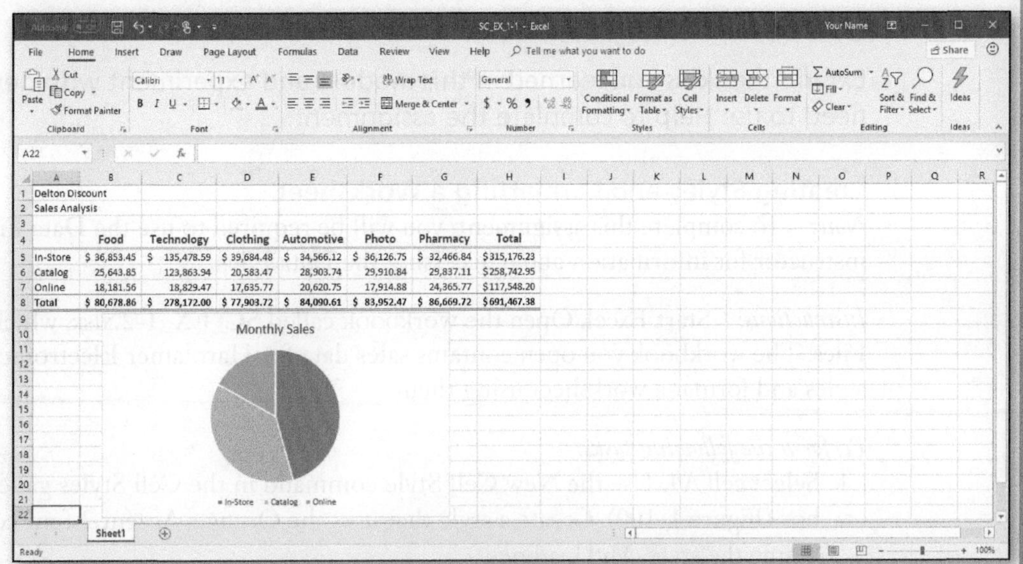

(a) Worksheet before Formatting

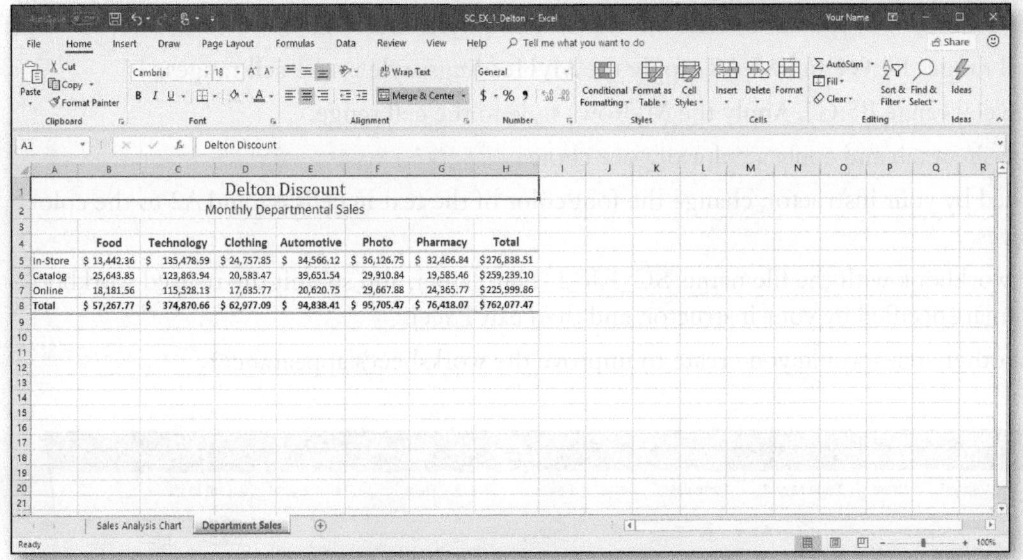

(b) Worksheet after Formatting

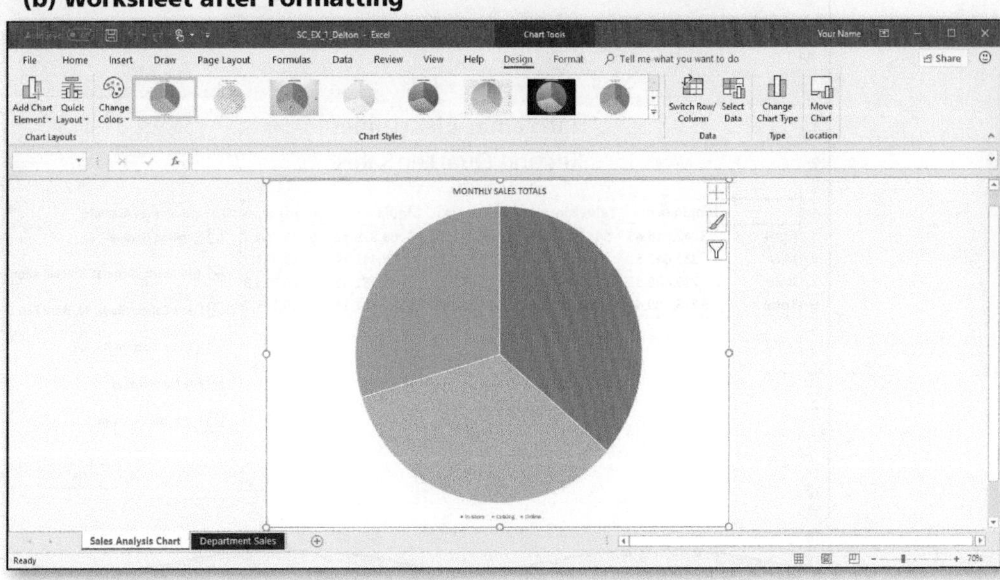

(c) Pie Chart on Separate Sheet

Figure 1–99

Extend Your Knowledge

Extend the skills you learned in this module and experiment with new skills. You may need to use Help to complete the assignment.

Creating Styles and Formatting a Worksheet

Note: To complete this assignment, you will be required to use the Data Files. Please contact your instructor for information about accessing the Data Files.

Instructions: Start Excel. Open the workbook called SC_EX_1-2.xlsx, which is located in the Data Files. The workbook you open contains sales data for Harolamer Electronics. You are to create styles and format a worksheet using them.

Perform the following tasks:

1. Select cell A4. Use the New Cell Style command in the Cell Styles gallery open the Style dialog box (Figure 1-100). Create a style that uses the Orange, Accent 2 font color (row 1, column 6). Name the style, MyHeadings.
2. Select cell A5. Use the New Cell style dialog box to create a style that uses the Orange, Accent 2, Darker 50% (row 6, column 6) font color. Name the style, MyRows.
3. Select cell ranges B4:G4 and A5:A8. Apply the MyHeadings style to the cell ranges.
4. Select the cell range B5:G7. Apply the MyRows style to the cell range.
5. Name the sheet tab and apply a color of your choice.

   If requested by your instructor, change the font color of the text in cells A1 and A2 to the color of your eyes.
6. Save the workbook with the file name, SC_EX_1_Harolamer, and submit the revised workbook in the format specified by your instructor, and then exit Excel.
7. What other styles would you create to improve the worksheet's appearance?

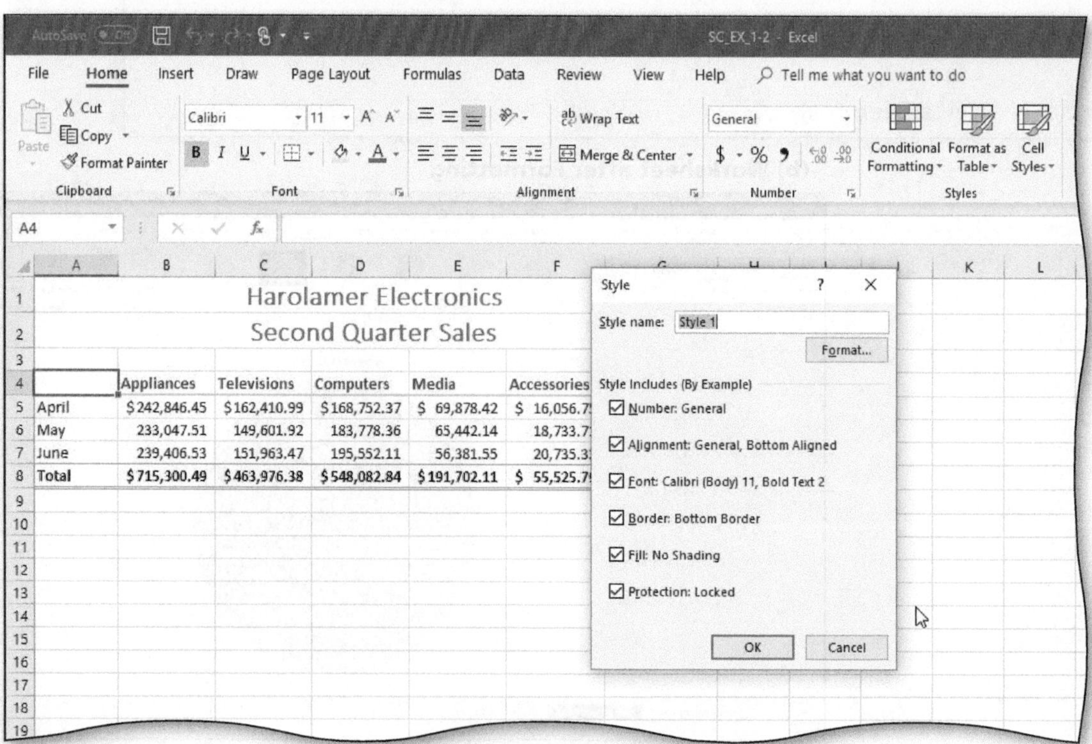

Figure 1-100

Expand Your World

Create a solution that uses cloud or web technologies by learning and investigating on your own from general guidance.

Loan Calculator

Instructions: Start Excel. You are to determine how long it will take you to pay back a loan. You decide to download and use one of the Excel templates to create your worksheet.

Perform the following tasks:

1. Click New in Backstage view and then search for and click a template that can calculate loans for an item you choose, such as a vehicle, mortgage, or general loan.
2. Enter fictitious (but realistic) information for a loan, including loan number, lender, loan amount, annual interest rate, beginning date, and length (in years). If the template you chose does not include a place for this information, add the information in an appropriate location. Search the web to examine current interest rates and typical loan durations.
3. Save the file as SC_EX_1_LoanCalculator, print the worksheet, and submit the assignment in the format specified by your instructor and then exit Excel.
4. Which template would you use if you wanted to plan and keep track of a budget for a wedding?

In the Lab

Design and implement a solution using creative thinking and problem-solving skills.

Create a Worksheet Comparing Laptops

Problem: You are shopping for a new laptop and want to compare the prices of three laptops. You will compare laptops with similar specifications, but where the brands and/or models are different.

Perform the following tasks:

Part 1: Create a worksheet that compares the type, specifications, and the price for each laptop, as well as the costs to add an extended warranty. Use the concepts and techniques presented in this module to calculate the average price of a laptop and average cost of an extended warranty and to format the worksheet. Include a chart to compare the different laptop costs. Submit your assignment in the format specified by your instructor.

Part 2: You made several decisions while creating the worksheet in this assignment: how to organize the data, how to display the text, which calculations to use, and which chart to use. What was your rationale behind each of these decisions?

2 Formulas, Functions, and Formatting

Objectives

After completing this module, you will be able to:

- Use Flash Fill
- Enter formulas using the keyboard
- Enter formulas using Point mode
- Apply the MAX, MIN, and AVERAGE functions
- Verify a formula using Range Finder
- Apply a theme to a workbook
- Apply a date format to a cell or range
- Add conditional formatting to cells
- Change column width and row height
- Check the spelling on a worksheet
- Change margins and headers in Page Layout view
- Preview and print versions and sections of a worksheet

Introduction

In Module 1, you learned how to enter data, sum values, format a worksheet to make it easier to read, and draw a chart. This module continues to illustrate these topics and presents some new ones.

The new topics covered in this module include using formulas and functions to create a worksheet. Recall from Module 1 that a function is a special, predefined formula that provides a shortcut for a commonly used calculation. Other new topics include using option buttons, verifying formulas, applying a theme to a worksheet, adding borders, formatting numbers and text, using conditional formatting, changing the widths of columns and heights of rows, checking spelling, generating alternative worksheet displays and printouts, and adding page headers and footers to a worksheet. One alternative worksheet display and printout shows the formulas in the worksheet instead of the values. When you display the formulas in the worksheet, you see exactly what text, data, formulas, and functions you have entered into it.

Project: Worksheet with Formulas and Functions

The project in this module follows proper design guidelines and uses Excel to create the worksheet shown in Figure 2–1. Every two weeks, the owners of Klapore Engineering create a salary report by hand, where they keep track of employee payroll data. Before paying employees, the owners must summarize the hours worked, pay rate, and tax information for each employee to ensure that the business properly compensates its employees. This report includes the following information for each employee: name, email address, number of dependents, gross pay, deductions, net pay, and hire date. As the complexity of creating the salary report increases, the owners want to use Excel to make the process easier.

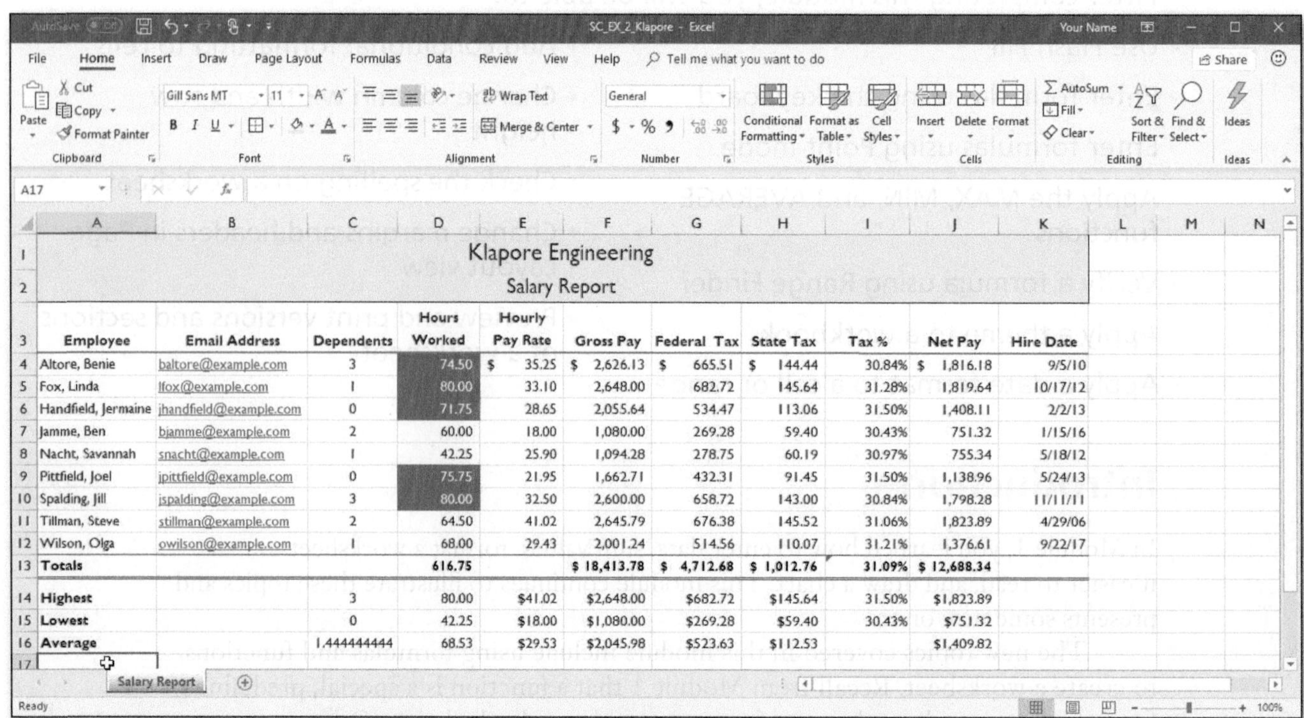

Klapore Engineering
Salary Report

	Employee	Email Address	Dependents	Hours Worked	Hourly Pay Rate	Gross Pay	Federal Tax	State Tax	Tax %	Net Pay	Hire Date
4	Altore, Benie	baltore@example.com	3	74.50	$ 35.25	$ 2,626.13	$ 665.51	$ 144.44	30.84%	$ 1,816.18	9/5/10
5	Fox, Linda	lfox@example.com	1	80.00	33.10	2,648.00	682.72	145.64	31.28%	1,819.64	10/17/12
6	Handfield, Jermaine	jhandfield@example.com	0	71.75	28.65	2,055.64	534.47	113.06	31.50%	1,408.11	2/2/13
7	Jamme, Ben	bjamme@example.com	2	60.00	18.00	1,080.00	269.28	59.40	30.43%	751.32	1/15/16
8	Nacht, Savannah	snacht@example.com	1	42.25	25.90	1,094.28	278.75	60.19	30.97%	755.34	5/18/12
9	Pittfield, Joel	jpittfield@example.com	0	75.75	21.95	1,662.71	432.31	91.45	31.50%	1,138.96	5/24/13
10	Spalding, Jill	jspalding@example.com	3	80.00	32.50	2,600.00	658.72	143.00	30.84%	1,798.28	11/11/11
11	Tillman, Steve	stillman@example.com	2	64.50	41.02	2,645.79	676.38	145.52	31.06%	1,823.89	4/29/06
12	Wilson, Olga	owilson@example.com	1	68.00	29.43	2,001.24	514.56	110.07	31.21%	1,376.61	9/22/17
13	**Totals**			**616.75**		**$ 18,413.78**	**$ 4,712.68**	**$ 1,012.76**	**31.09%**	**$ 12,688.34**	
14	**Highest**		3	80.00	$41.02	$2,648.00	$682.72	$145.64	31.50%	$1,823.89	
15	**Lowest**		0	42.25	$18.00	$1,080.00	$269.28	$59.40	30.43%	$751.32	
16	**Average**		1.444444444	68.53	$29.53	$2,045.98	$523.63	$112.53		$1,409.82	

Figure 2–1

Recall that the first step in creating an effective worksheet is to make sure you understand what is required. The people who request the worksheet usually provide the requirements. The requirements document for the Klapore Engineering Salary Report worksheet includes the following needs: source of data, summary of calculations, and other facts about its development (Figure 2–2).

Worksheet Title	Klapore Engineering Salary Report
Needs	An easy-to-read worksheet that summarizes the company's salary report (Figure 2–3). For each employee, the worksheet is to include the employee's name, email address, number of dependents, hours worked, hourly pay rate, gross pay, federal tax, state tax, total tax percent, net pay, and hire date. The worksheet also should include the total pay for all employees, as well as the highest value, lowest value, and average for each category of data.
Source of Data	Supplied data includes employee names, email addresses, number of dependents, hours worked, hourly pay rate, and hire dates.
Calculations	The following calculations must be made for each of the employees: 1. Gross Pay = Hours Worked * Hourly Pay Rate 2. Federal Tax = 0.26 * (Gross Pay – Number of Dependents * 22.16) 3. State Tax = 0.055 * Gross Pay 4. Tax % = (Federal Tax + State Tax) / Gross Pay 5. Net Pay = Gross Pay – (Federal Tax + State Tax) 6. Compute the totals for hours worked, gross pay, federal tax, state tax, and net pay 7. Compute the total tax percent 8. Use the MAX and MIN functions to determine the highest and lowest values for number of dependents, hours worked, hourly pay rate, gross pay, federal tax, state tax, total tax percent, and net pay 9. Use the AVERAGE function to determine the average for number of dependents, hours worked, hourly pay rate, gross pay, federal tax, state tax, and net pay

Figure 2–2

In addition, using a sketch of the worksheet can help you visualize its design. The sketch for the Klapore Engineering Salary Report worksheet includes a title, a subtitle, column and row headings, and the location of data values (Figure 2–3). It also uses specific characters to define the desired formatting for the worksheet, as follows:

1. The row of Xs below the leftmost column heading defines the cell entries as text, such as employee names.

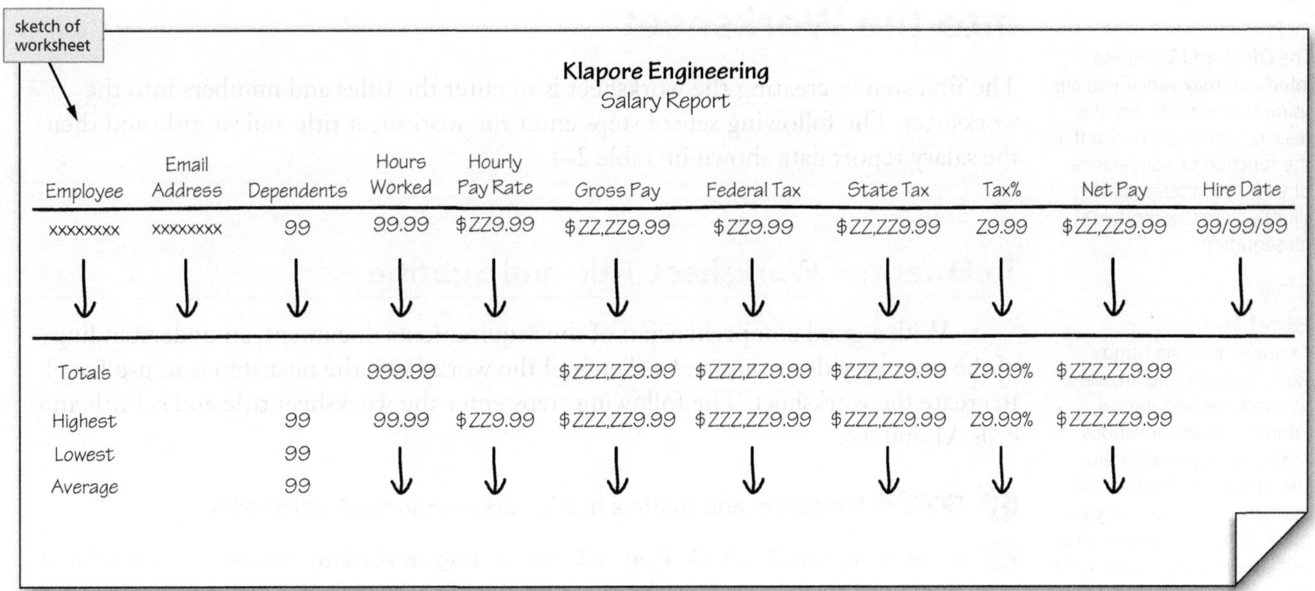

Figure 2–3

2. The rows of Zs and 9s with slashes, dollar signs, decimal points, commas, and percent signs in the remaining columns define the cell entries as numbers. The Zs indicate that the selected format should instruct Excel to suppress leading 0s. The 9s indicate that the selected format should instruct Excel to display any digits, including 0s.
3. The decimal point means that a decimal point should appear in the cell entry and indicates the number of decimal places to use.
4. The slashes in the last column identify the cell entry as a date.
5. The dollar signs that are adjacent to the Zs below the totals row signify a floating dollar sign, or one that appears next to the first significant digit.
6. The commas indicate that the selected format should instruct Excel to display a comma separator only if the number has sufficient digits (values in the thousandths) to the left of the decimal point.
7. The percent sign (%) in the Tax % column indicates a percent sign should appear after the number.

CONSIDER THIS

What is the function of an Excel worksheet?

The function, or purpose, of a worksheet is to provide a user with direct ways to accomplish tasks. In designing a worksheet, functional considerations should supersede visual aesthetics. Consider the following when designing your worksheet:

- Avoid the temptation to use flashy or confusing visual elements within the worksheet.
- Understand the requirements document.
- Choose the proper functions and formulas.

BTW

Touch Mode Differences

The Office and Windows interfaces may vary if you are using touch mode. For this reason, you might notice that the function or appearance of your touch screen differs slightly from this module's presentation.

BTW

Excel Help

At any time while using Excel, you can find answers to questions and display information about various topics through Excel Help. Used properly, this form of assistance can increase your productivity and reduce your frustrations by minimizing the time you spend learning how to use Excel.

Entering the Titles and Numbers into the Worksheet

The first step in creating the worksheet is to enter the titles and numbers into the worksheet. The following sets of steps enter the worksheet title and subtitle and then the salary report data shown in Table 2–1.

To Enter the Worksheet Title and Subtitle

With a good comprehension of the requirements document, an understanding of the necessary decisions, and a sketch of the worksheet, the next step is to use Excel to create the worksheet. The following steps enter the worksheet title and subtitle into cells A1 and A2.

1. sam Start Excel and create a blank workbook in the Excel window.
2. If necessary, select cell A1. Type **Klapore Engineering** in the selected cell and then press the DOWN ARROW key to enter the worksheet title.
3. Type **Salary Report** in cell A2 and then press the DOWN ARROW key to enter the worksheet subtitle.

To Enter the Column Titles

The column titles in row 3 begin in cell A3 and extend through cell K3. The employee names and the row titles begin in cell A4 and continue down to cell A16. The employee data is entered into rows 4 through 12 of the worksheet. The remainder of this section explains the steps required to enter the column titles, payroll data, and row titles, as shown in Figure 2–4, and then to save the workbook. The following steps enter the column titles.

1. With cell A3 selected, type **`Employee`** and then press the RIGHT ARROW key to enter the column heading.
2. Type **`Email Address`** in cell B3 and then press the RIGHT ARROW key.
3. In cell C3, type **`Dependents`** and then press the RIGHT ARROW key.
4. In cell D3, type **`Hours`** and then press ALT+ENTER to enter the first line of the column heading. Type **`Worked`** and then press the RIGHT ARROW key to enter the column heading.

Q&A Why do I use ALT+ENTER?
You press ALT+ENTER in order to start a new line in a cell. The final line can be completed by clicking the Enter button, pressing ENTER, or pressing one of the arrow keys. When you see ALT+ENTER in a step, press ENTER while holding down ALT and then release both keys.

5. Type **`Hourly`** in cell E3, press ALT+ENTER, type **`Pay Rate,`** and then press the RIGHT ARROW key.
6. Type **`Gross Pay`** in cell F3 and then press the RIGHT ARROW key.
7. Type **`Federal Tax`** in cell G3 and then press the RIGHT ARROW key.
8. Type **`State Tax`** in cell H3 and then press the RIGHT ARROW key.
9. Type **`Tax %`** in cell I3 and then press the RIGHT ARROW key.
10. Type **`Net Pay`** in cell J3 and then press the RIGHT ARROW key.
11. Type **`Hire Date`** in cell K3 and then press the RIGHT ARROW key.

BTW
Screen Resolution
If you are using a computer to step through the project in this module and you want your screens to match the figures in this book, you should change your screen's resolution to 1366 x 768.

BTW
Wrapping Text
If you have a long text entry, such as a paragraph, you can instruct Excel to wrap the text in a cell. This method is easier than pressing ALT+ENTER to end each line of text within the paragraph. To wrap text, right-click in the cell, click Format Cells on a shortcut menu, click the Alignment tab, and then click Wrap text. Excel will increase the height of the cell automatically so that the additional lines will fit. If you want to control where each line ends in the cell, rather than letting Excel wrap the text based on the cell width, you must end each line with ALT+ENTER.

To Enter the Salary Data

The salary data in Table 2-1 includes a hire date for each employee. Excel considers a date to be a number, and, therefore, it displays the date right-aligned in the cell. The following steps enter the data for each employee, except their email addresses, which will be entered later in this module.

1. Select cell A4. Type **`Altore, Benie`** and then press the RIGHT ARROW key two times to enter the employee name and make cell C4 the active cell.
2. Type **`3`** in cell C4 and then press the RIGHT ARROW key.
3. Type **`74.50`** in cell D4 and then press the RIGHT ARROW key.

BTW
Two-Digit Years
When you enter a two-digit year value (xx) that is less than 30, Excel changes that value to 20xx; when you enter a value that is 30 or greater (zz), Excel changes the value to 19zz. Use four-digit years, if necessary, to ensure that Excel interprets year values the way you intend.

Q&A **Why did 74.50% change to 74.5% when I pressed the RIGHT ARROW key?**
Depending on the number format applied to the call, Excel might remove trailing zeros from a cell value.

4. Type **35.25** in cell E4.
5. Click cell K4 and then type **9/5/10**.
6. Enter the payroll data in Table 2–1 for the eight remaining employees in rows 5 through 12. Click the Enter button when you have finished entering the value in the last cell.

Q&A **In Step 5, why did the date change from 9/5/10 to 9/5/2010?**
When Excel recognizes a date in mm/dd/yy format, it formats the date as mm/dd/yyyy. Most professionals prefer to view dates in mm/dd/yyyy format as opposed to mm/dd/yy format to avoid confusion regarding the intended year. For example, a date displayed as 3/3/50 could imply a date of 3/3/1950 or 3/3/2050.

Table 2–1 Klapore Engineering Salary Report Data

Employee	Email Address	Dependents	Hours Worked	Hourly Pay Rate	Hire Date
Altore, Benie		3	74.50	35.25	9/5/10
Fox, Linda		1	80.00	33.10	10/17/12
Handfield, Jermaine		0	71.75	28.65	2/2/13
Jamme, Ben		2	60.00	18.00	1/15/16
Nacht, Savannah		1	42.25	25.90	5/18/12
Pittfield, Joel		0	75.75	21.95	5/24/13
Spalding, Jill		3	80.00	32.50	11/11/11
Tillman, Steve		2	64.50	41.02	4/29/06
Wilson, Olga		1	68.00	29.43	9/22/17

BTW
The Ribbon and Screen Resolution
Excel may change how the groups and buttons within the groups appear on the ribbon, depending on the screen resolution of your computer. Thus, your ribbon may look different from the ones in this book if you are using a screen resolution other than 1366 x 768.

Flash Fill

When you are entering data in a spreadsheet, occasionally Excel will recognize a pattern in the data you are entering. **Flash Fill** is an Excel feature that looks for patterns in the data and automatically fills or formats data in remaining cells based on those patterns. For example, if column A contains a list of 10 phone numbers without parentheses around the area code or dashes after the prefix, Flash Fill can help automatically create formatted phone numbers with parentheses and dashes with relative ease. To use Flash Fill, simply start entering formatted phone numbers in cells next to the unformatted numbers. After entering a few formatted phone numbers, Flash Fill will suggest similarly formatted phone numbers for the remaining cells in the column. If you do not want to wait for Excel to offer suggestions, type one or two examples and then click the Flash Fill button (Data tab | Data Tools group). Flash fill will autocomplete the remaining cells. If Flash Fill makes a mistake, simply click the Undo button, enter a few more examples, and try again. In addition to formatting data, Flash Fill can perform tasks such as concatenating data from multiple cells and separating data from one cell into multiple cells.

To Use Flash Fill

In the Klapore Engineering Salary Report worksheet, you can use Flash Fill to generate email addresses using first and last names from another column in the worksheet. ***Why?*** *The Flash Fill feature is a convenient way to avoid entering a lot of data manually.* The following steps use Flash Fill to generate employee email addresses using the names entered in column A.

- Click cell B4 to select it.
- Type **baltore@example.com** and then press the DOWN ARROW key to select cell B5.
- Type **lfox@example.com** and then click the Enter button to enter Linda Fox's email address in cell B5 (Figure 2–4).

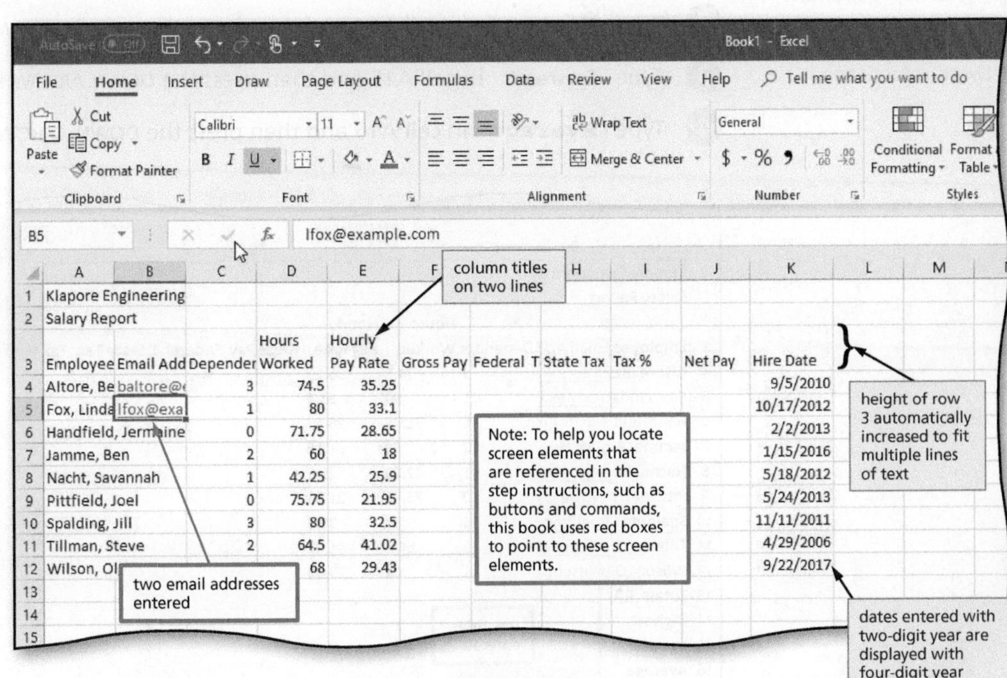

Figure 2–4

- Select the range B4:B12.
- Click Data on the ribbon to select the Data tab.
- Click the Flash Fill button (Data tab | Data Tools group) to enter similarly formatted email addresses in the range B6:B12.
- Remove the entries from cells B1 and B2 (Figure 2–5).

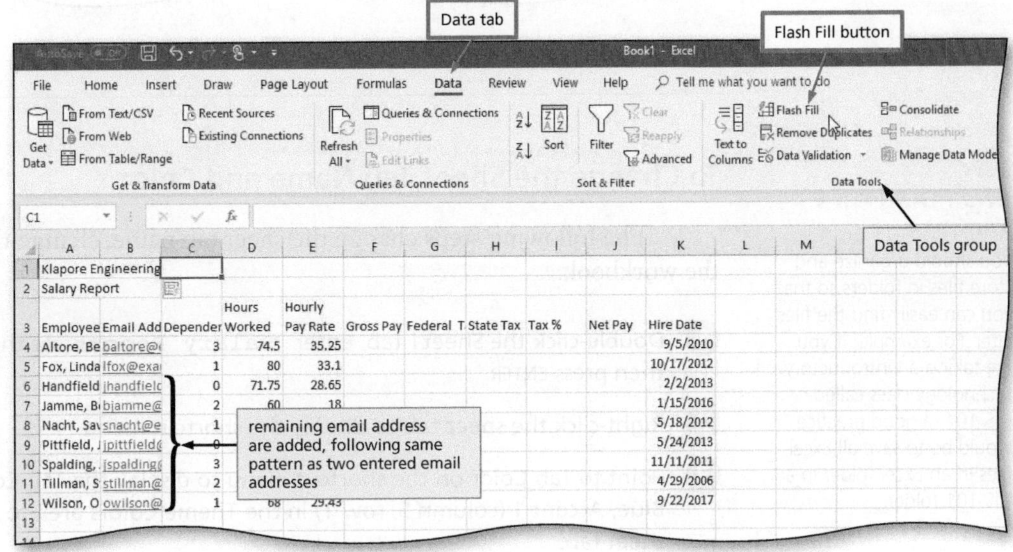

Figure 2–5

Q&A

Why was I unable to click the Flash Fill button after entering the first email address?

One entry might not have been enough for Excel to recognize a pattern. For instance, Flash Fill might have used the letter b before each last name in the email address instead of using the first initial and last name.

What would have happened if I kept typing examples without clicking the Flash Fill button?

As soon as Excel recognized a pattern, it would have displayed suggestions for the remaining cells. Pressing ENTER when the suggestions appear will populate the remaining cells.

BTW
Formatting Worksheets
With early spreadsheet programs, users often skipped rows to improve the appearance of the worksheet. With Excel it is not necessary to skip rows because you can increase row heights to add white space between information.

To Enter the Row Titles

The following steps add row titles for the rows that will contain the totals, highest, lowest, and average amounts.

1. Select cell A13. Type **`Totals`** and then press the DOWN ARROW key to enter a row header.
2. Type **`Highest`** in cell A14 and then press the DOWN ARROW key.
3. Type **`Lowest`** in cell A15 and then press the DOWN ARROW key.
4. Type **`Average`** in cell A16 and then press the DOWN ARROW key (Figure 2–6).

	A	B	C	D	E	F	G	H	I	J	K	L
1	Klapore Engineering											
2	Salary Report											
3	Employee	Email Add	Depender	Hours Worked	Hourly Pay Rate	Gross Pay	Federal T	State Tax	Tax %	Net Pay	Hire Date	
4	Altore, Be	baltore@	3	74.5	35.25						9/5/2010	
5	Fox, Linda	lfox@exa	1	80	33.1						10/17/2012	
6	Handfield	jhandfielc	0	71.75	28.65						2/2/2013	
7	Jamme, B	bjamme@	2	60	18						1/15/2016	
8	Nacht, Sa	snacht@e	1	42.25	25.9						5/18/2012	
9	Pittfield, J	jpittfield@	0	75.75	21.95						5/24/2013	
10	Spalding, .	jspalding@	3	80	32.5						11/11/2011	
11	Tillman, S	stillman@	2	64.5	41.02						4/29/2006	
12	Wilson, O	owilson@	1	68	29.43						9/22/2017	
13	Totals											
14	Highest											
15	Lowest											
16	Average											
17												

row titles entered

Figure 2–6

BTW
Organizing Files and Folders
You should organize and store files in folders so that you can easily find the files later. For example, if you are taking an introductory technology class called CIS 101, a good practice would be to save all Excel files in an Excel folder in a CIS 101 folder.

To Change the Sheet Tab Name and Color

The following steps change the sheet tab name, change the tab color, and save the workbook.

1. Double-click the Sheet1 tab, enter **`Salary Report`** as the sheet tab name and then press ENTER.
2. Right-click the sheet tab to display the shortcut menu.
3. Point to Tab Color on the shortcut menu to display the Tab Color gallery. Click Blue, Accent 1 (column 5, row 1) in the Theme Colors area to apply the color to the sheet tab.
4. Save the workbook using SC_EX_2_Klapore as the file name.

Q&A Why should I save the workbook at this time?
You have performed many tasks while creating this workbook and do not want to risk losing work completed thus far.

Entering Formulas

One of the reasons Excel is such a valuable tool is that you can assign a formula to a cell, and Excel will calculate the result. A **formula** is a mathematical statement in a spreadsheet or table cell that calculates a value using cell references, numbers, and arithmetic operators such as +, –, *, and /. Consider, for example, what would happen if you had to multiply 74.50 by 35.25 and then manually enter the product for Gross Pay, 2,626.13, in cell F4. Every time the values in cells D4 or E4 changed, you would have to recalculate the product and enter the new value in cell F4. By contrast, if you enter a formula in cell F4 to multiply the values in cells D4 and E4, Excel recalculates the product whenever new values are entered into those cells and displays the result in cell F4.

In a spreadsheet, an error that occurs when one of the defining values in a cell is itself is called a **circular reference**. Excel warns you when you create circular references. In almost all cases, circular references are the result of an incorrect formula. A circular reference can be direct or indirect. For example, placing the formula =A1 in cell A1 results in a direct circular reference. A **direct circular reference** occurs when a formula refers to the same cell in which it is entered. An **indirect circular reference** occurs when a formula in a cell refers to another cell or cells that include a formula that refers back to the original cell.

BTW

Entering Numbers in a Range

An efficient way to enter data into a range of cells is to select a range and then enter the first number in the upper-left cell of the range. Excel responds by accepting the value and moving the active cell selection down one cell. When you enter the last value in the first column, Excel moves the active cell selection to the top of the next column.

To Enter a Formula Using the Keyboard

The formulas needed in the worksheet are noted in the requirements document as follows:

1. Gross Pay (column F) = Hours Worked × Hourly Pay Rate
2. Federal Tax (column G) = 0.26 × (Gross Pay – Dependents × 22.16)
3. State Tax (column H) = 0.055 × Gross Pay
4. Tax % (column I) = (Federal Tax + State Tax) / Gross Pay
5. Net Pay (column J) = Gross Pay – (Federal Tax + State Tax)

The gross pay for each employee, which appears in column F, is equal to hours worked in column D times hourly pay rate in column E. Thus, the gross pay for Benie Altore in cell F4 is obtained by multiplying 74.50 (cell D4) by 35.25 (cell E4) or = D4 × E4. The following steps enter the initial gross pay formula in cell F4 using the keyboard. ***Why?** In order for Excel to perform the calculations, you must first enter the formulas.*

1

- With cell F4 selected, type **=d4*e4** in the cell to display the formula in the formula bar and the current cell and to display colored borders around the cells referenced in the formula (Figure 2–7).

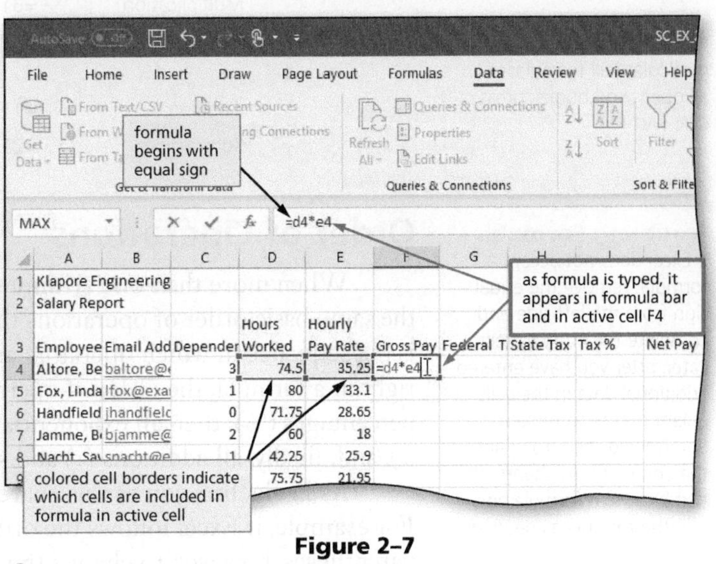

Figure 2–7

Q&A What happens when I enter the formula?

The **equal sign** (=) preceding d4*e4 alerts Excel that you are entering a formula or function — not text. Because the most common error when entering a formula is to reference the wrong cell, Excel colors the cells referenced in the formula. The colored cells help you determine whether the cell references are correct. The asterisk (*) following d4 is the arithmetic operator for multiplication.

Is there a function, similar to the SUM function, that calculates the product of two or more numbers?

Yes. The **PRODUCT function** calculates the product of two or more numbers. For example, the function, =PRODUCT(D4,E4) will calculate the product of cells D4 and E4.

- Press TAB to complete the arithmetic operation indicated by the formula, display the result in the worksheet, and select the cell to the right (Figure 2–8). The number of decimal places on your screen may be different than shown in Figure 2–8, but these values will be adjusted later in this module.

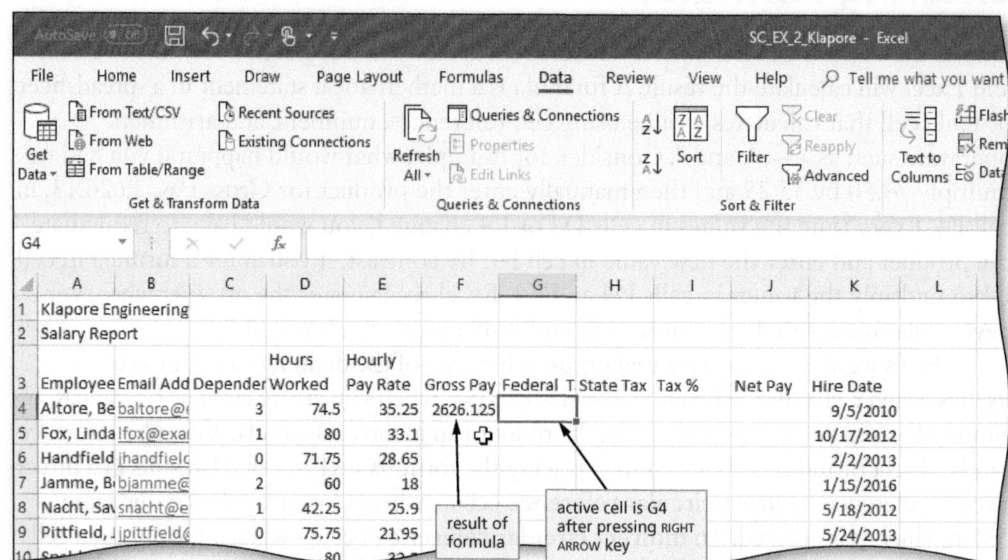

Figure 2–8

BTW

Automatic Recalculation

Every time you enter a value into a cell in the worksheet, Excel automatically recalculates all formulas. You can change to manual recalculation by clicking the Calculation Options button (Formulas tab | Calculation group) and then clicking Manual. In manual calculation mode, pressing F9 instructs Excel to recalculate all formulas on all worksheets. Press SHIFT+F9 to recalculate the active worksheet. To recalculate all formulas in all open workbooks, press CTRL+ALT+F9.

Arithmetic Operations

Excel provides powerful functions and capabilities that allow you to perform arithmetic operations easily and efficiently. Table 2–2 describes multiplication and other valid Excel arithmetic operators, listed in the order in which Excel performs them.

Table 2–2 Arithmetic Operations Listed in Order of Operations

Arithmetic Operator	Meaning	Example of Usage	Result
–	Negation	–78	Negative 78
%	Percentage	=23%	Multiplies 23 by 0.01
^	Exponentiation	=3 ^ 4	Raises 3 to the fourth power
*	Multiplication	=61.5 * C5	Multiplies the contents of cell C5 by 61.5
/	Division	=H3 / H11	Divides the contents of cell H3 by the contents of cell H11
+	Addition	=11 + 9	Adds 11 and 9
–	Subtraction	=22 – F15	Subtracts the contents of cell F15 from 22

BTW

Troubling Formulas

If Excel does not accept a formula, remove the equal sign from the left side and complete the entry as text. Later, after you have entered additional data in the cells reliant on the formula or determined the error, reinsert the equal sign to change the text back to a formula and edit the formula as needed.

Order of Operations

When more than one arithmetic operator is involved in a formula, Excel follows the same basic order of operations that you use in algebra. The **order of operations** is the sequence in which operators are applied in a calculation. Moving from left to right in a formula, the order of operations is as follows: first negation (–), then all percentages (%), then all exponentiations (^), then all multiplications (*) and divisions (/), and, finally, all additions (+) and subtractions (–).

As in algebra, you can use parentheses to override the order of operations. For example, if Excel follows the order of operations, 8 * 3 + 2 equals 26. If you use parentheses, however, to change the formula to 8 * (3 + 2), the result is 40, because the parentheses instruct Excel to add 3 and 2 before multiplying by 8. Table 2–3 illustrates several examples of valid Excel formulas and explains the order of operations.

Table 2–3 Examples of Excel Formulas

Formula	Result
=G15	Assigns the value in cell G15 to the active cell.
=2^4 + 7	Assigns the sum of 16 + 7 (or 23) to the active cell.
=100 + D2 or =D2 +100 or =(100 + D2)	Assigns 100 plus the contents of cell D2 to the active cell.
=25% * 40	Assigns the product of 0.25 times 40 (or 10) to the active cell.
– (K15 * X45)	Assigns the negative value of the product of the values contained in cells K15 and X45 to the active cell. *Tip:* You do not need to type an equal sign before an expression that begins with a minus sign, which indicates a negation.
=(U8 – B8) * 6	Assigns the difference between the values contained in cells U8 and B8 times 6 to the active cell.
=J7 / A5 + G9 * M6 – Z2 ^ L7	Completes the following operations, from left to right: exponentiation (Z2 ^ L7), then division (J7 / A5), then multiplication (G9 * M6), then addition (J7 / A5) + (G9 * M6), and finally subtraction (J7 / A5 + G9 * M6) – (Z2 ^ L7). If cells A5 = 6, G9 = 2, J7 = 6, L7 = 4, M6 = 5, and Z2 = 2, then Excel assigns the active cell the value –5; that is, 6 / 6 + 2 * 5 – 2 ^ 4 = –5.

BTW

Parentheses

Remember that you can use parentheses to override the order of operations. You cannot use brackets or braces in place of parentheses in arithmetic operations.

To Enter Formulas Using Point Mode

The sketch of the worksheet in Figure 2–3 calls for the federal tax, state tax, tax percentage, and net pay for each employee to appear in columns G, H, I, and J, respectively. All four of these values are calculated using formulas in row 4:

Federal Tax (cell G4) = 0.26 × (Gross Pay – Dependents × 22.16) or = 0.26 * (F4 – C4 * 22.16)
State Tax (cell H4) = 0.055 × Gross Pay or = 0.055 * F4
Tax % (cell I4) = (Federal Tax + State Tax) / Gross Pay or = (G4 + H4) / F4
Net Pay (cell J4) = Gross Pay – (Federal Tax + State Tax) or = F4 – (G4 + H4)

An alternative to entering the formulas in cells G4, H4, I4, and J4 using the keyboard is to enter the formulas using the pointer and Point mode. **Point mode** allows you to select cells for use in a formula by using the pointer or a screen tap. The following steps enter formulas using Point mode. ***Why?*** *Using Point mode makes it easier to create formulas without worrying about typographical errors when entering cell references.*

1

- With cell G4 selected, type `=0.26*(` to begin the formula and then click cell F4 to add a cell reference in the formula (Figure 2–9).

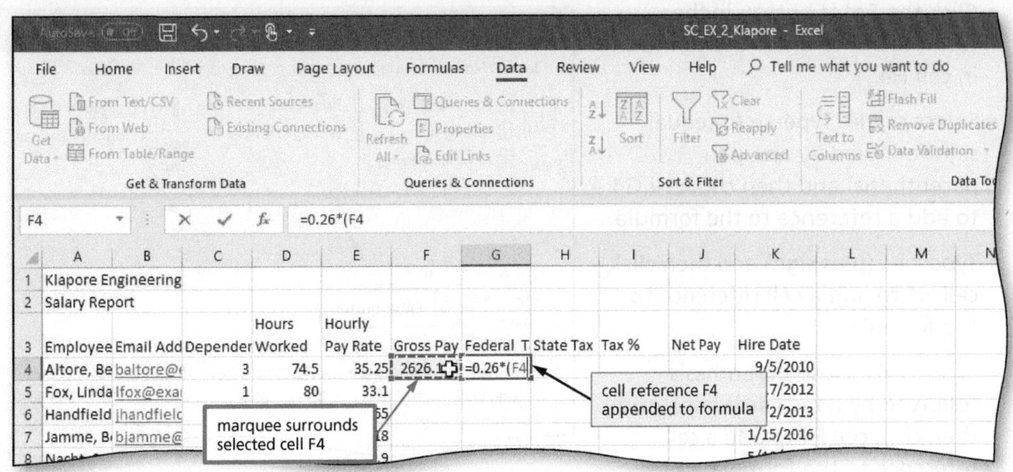

Figure 2–9

- Type – (minus sign) and then click cell C4 to add a subtraction operator and a reference to another cell to the formula.
- Type `*22.16)` to complete the formula (Figure 2–10).

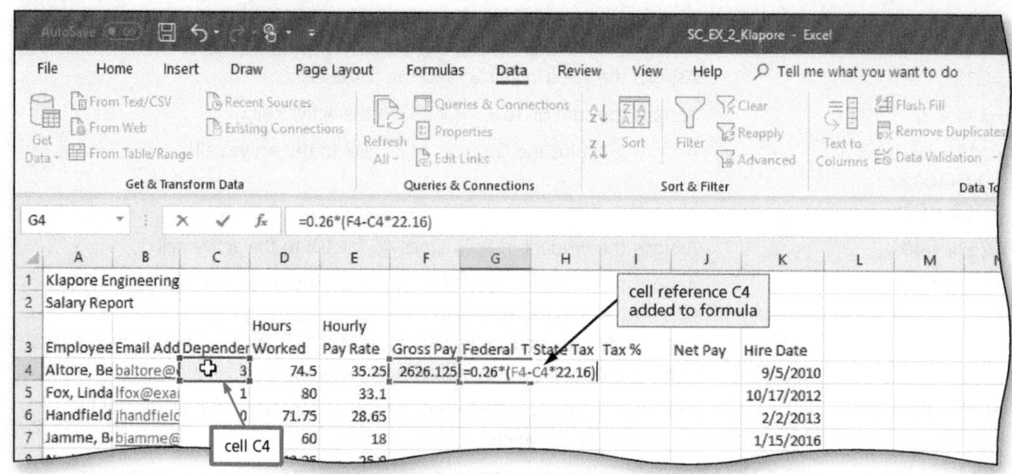

Figure 2–10

- Click the Enter button in the formula bar and then select cell H4 to prepare to enter the next formula.
- Type `=0.055*` and then click cell F4 to add a cell reference to the formula (Figure 2–11).

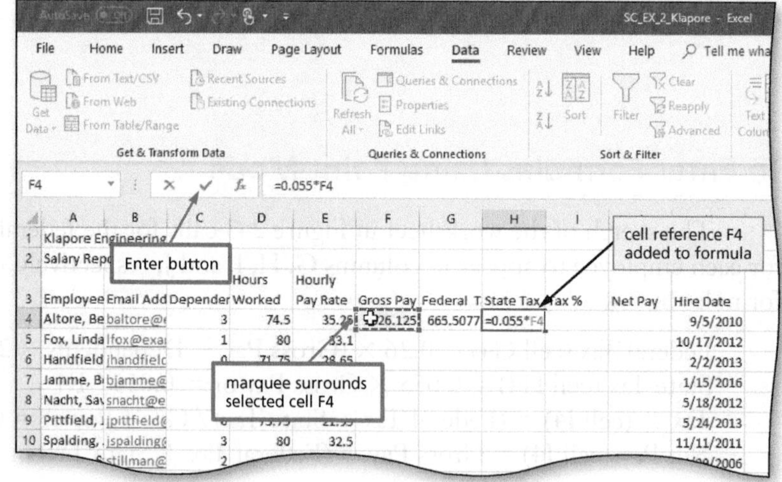

Figure 2–11

Q&A **Why should I use Point mode to enter formulas?**

Using Point mode to enter formulas often is faster and more accurate than using the keyboard, but only when the cell you want to select does not require you to scroll. In many instances, as in these steps, you may want to use both the keyboard and pointer when entering a formula in a cell. You can use the keyboard to begin the formula, for example, and then use the pointer to select a range of cells.

- Click the Enter button in the formula bar to enter the formula in cell H4.
- Select cell I4. Type `=(` (equal sign followed by an open parenthesis) and then click cell G4 to add a reference to the formula.
- Type `+` (plus sign) and then click cell H4 to add a cell reference to the formula.
- Type `)/` (close parenthesis followed by a forward slash), and then click cell F4 to add a cell reference to the formula.
- Click the Enter button in the formula bar to enter the formula in cell I4 (Figure 2–12).

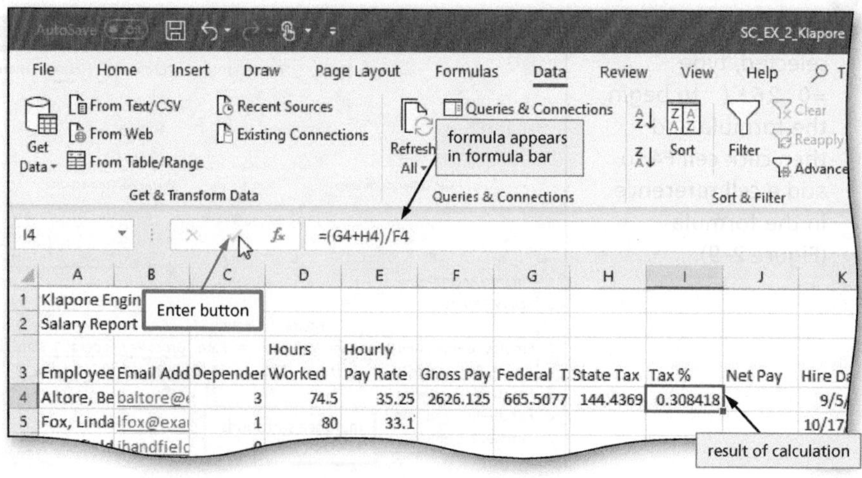

Figure 2–12

5

- Click cell J4, type = (equal sign) and then click cell F4.
- Type -((minus sign followed by an open parenthesis) and then click cell G4.
- Type + (plus sign), click cell H4, and then type) (close parenthesis) to complete the formula (Figure 2–13).
- Click the Enter button.

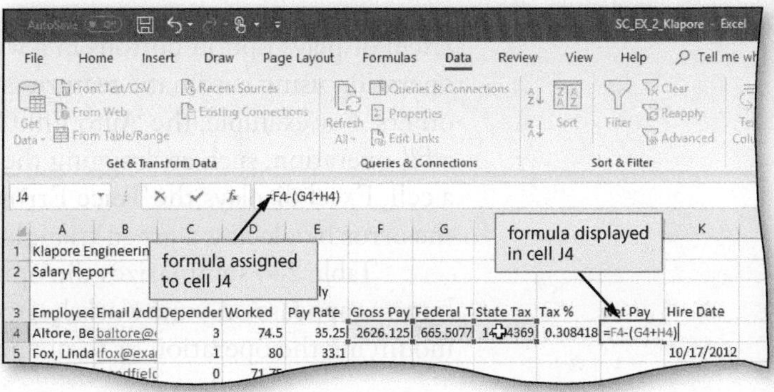

Figure 2–13

To Copy Formulas Using the Fill Handle

The five formulas for Benie Altore in cells F4, G4, H4, I4, and J4 now are complete. The next step is to copy them to the range F5:J12. When copying formulas in Excel, the source area is the cell, or range, from which data or formulas are being copied. When a range is used as a source, it sometimes is called the **source range.** The destination area is the cell, or range, to which data or formulas are being copied. When a range is used as a destination in a data exchange, it sometimes is called the **destination range.** When you copy a formula, Excel adjusts the cell references so that the new formulas contain new cell references corresponding to the new locations and perform calculations using the appropriate values. Thus, if you copy downward, Excel adjusts the row portion of the cell references relative to the source cell. If you copy across, then Excel adjusts the column portion of the cell references to the source of the cell. Cells that automatically change to reflect the new location when the formulas are copied or moved are called **relative references.** Recall from Module 1 that the fill handle is a small square in the lower-right corner of the active cell or active range. The following steps copy the formulas using the fill handle.

1 Select the source range, F4:J4 in this case, point to the fill handle, drag the fill handle down through cell J12, and then continue to hold the mouse button to select the destination range.

2 Release the mouse button to copy the formulas to the destination range (Figure 2–14).

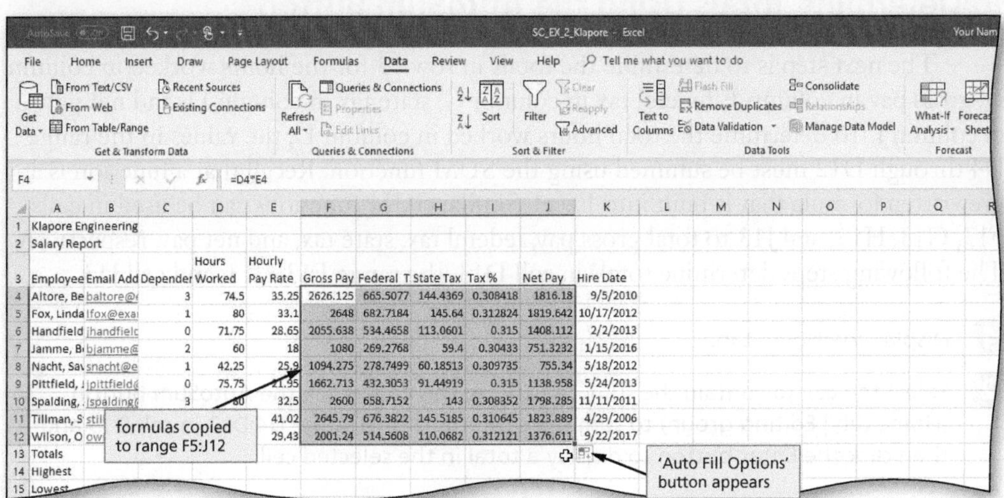

Figure 2–14

Option Buttons

Excel displays option buttons in a worksheet to indicate that you can complete an operation using automatic features such as AutoCorrect, Auto Fill, error checking, and others. For example, the 'Auto Fill Options' button shown in Figure 2–14 appears after a fill operation, such as dragging the fill handle. When an error occurs in a formula in a cell, Excel displays the Trace Error button next to the cell and identifies the cell with the error by placing a green triangle in the upper left of the cell.

Table 2–4 summarizes the option buttons available in Excel. When one of these buttons appears on your worksheet, click its arrow to produce the list of options for modifying the operation or to obtain additional information.

Table 2–4 Option Buttons in Excel

Name	Menu Function
Auto Fill Options	Provides options for how to fill cells following a fill operation, such as dragging the fill handle
AutoCorrect Options	Undoes an automatic correction, stops future automatic corrections of this type, or causes Excel to display the AutoCorrect Options dialog box
Insert Options	Lists formatting options following an insertion of cells, rows, or columns
Paste Options	Specifies how moved or pasted items should appear (for example, with original formatting, without formatting, or with different formatting)
Trace Error	Lists error-checking options following the assignment of an invalid formula to a cell

CONSIDER THIS

Why is the Paste Options button important?

The Paste Options button provides powerful functionality. When performing copy and paste operations, the button allows you great freedom in specifying what it is you want to paste. You can choose from the following options:

- Paste an exact copy of what you copied, including the cell contents and formatting.
- Copy only formulas.
- Copy only formatting.
- Copy only values.
- Copy a combination of these options.
- Copy a picture of what you copied.

BTW

Selecting a Range

You can select a range using the keyboard. Press F8 and then use the arrow keys to select the desired range. After you are finished, make sure to press F8 to turn off the selection process or you will continue to select ranges.

To Determine Totals Using the AutoSum Button

The next step is to determine the totals in row 13 for the hours worked in column D, gross pay in column F, federal tax in column G, state tax in column H, and net pay in column J. To determine the total hours worked in column D, the values in the range D4 through D12 must be summed using the SUM function. Recall that a function is a prewritten formula that is built into Excel. Similar SUM functions can be used in cells F13, G13, H13, and J13 to total gross pay, federal tax, state tax, and net pay, respectively. The following steps determine totals in cell D13, the range F13:H13, and cell J13.

1. Display the Home tab.
2. Select the cell to contain the sum, cell D13 in this case. Click the AutoSum button (Home tab | Editing group) to sum the contents of the range D4:D12 in cell D13 and then click the Enter button to display a total in the selected cell.
3. Select the range to contain the sums, range F13:H13 in this case. Click the AutoSum button (Home tab | Editing group) to display totals in the selected range.

4 Select the cell to contain the sum, cell J13 in this case. Click the AutoSum button (Home tab | Editing group) to sum the contents of the range J4:J12 in cell J13 and then click the Enter button to display a total in the selected cell (Figure 2–15).

Q&A Why did I have to click the Enter button?
When you click the AutoSum button to calculate the sum of a single cell, the formula to calculate the sum appears in that cell. If you want Excel to display the results of the formula, you should click the Enter button.

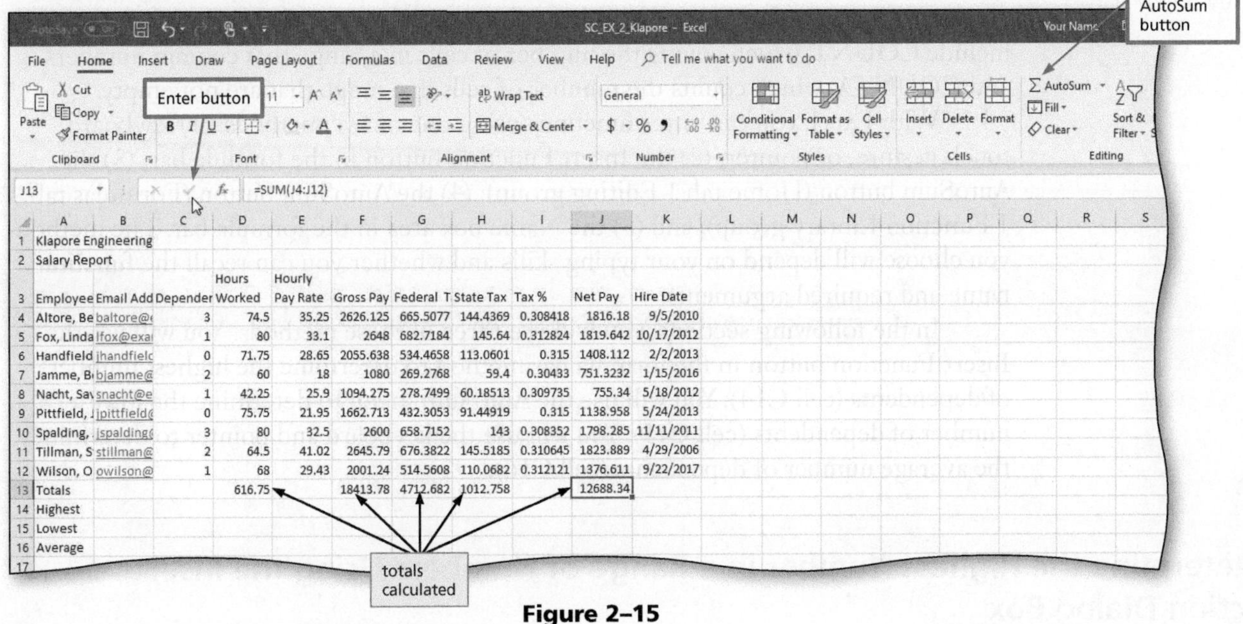

Figure 2–15

To Determine the Total Tax Percentage

With the totals in row 13 determined, the next step is to copy the tax percentage formula in cell I12 to cell I13. The following step copies the tax percentage formula.

1 Select the cell to be copied, I12 in this case, and then drag the fill handle down through cell I13 to copy the formula (Figure 2–16).

Q&A Why was the SUM function not used for tax percentage in I13?
The total tax percentage is calculated using the totals of the Gross Pay, Federal Tax and State Tax columns, not by summing the tax percentage column.

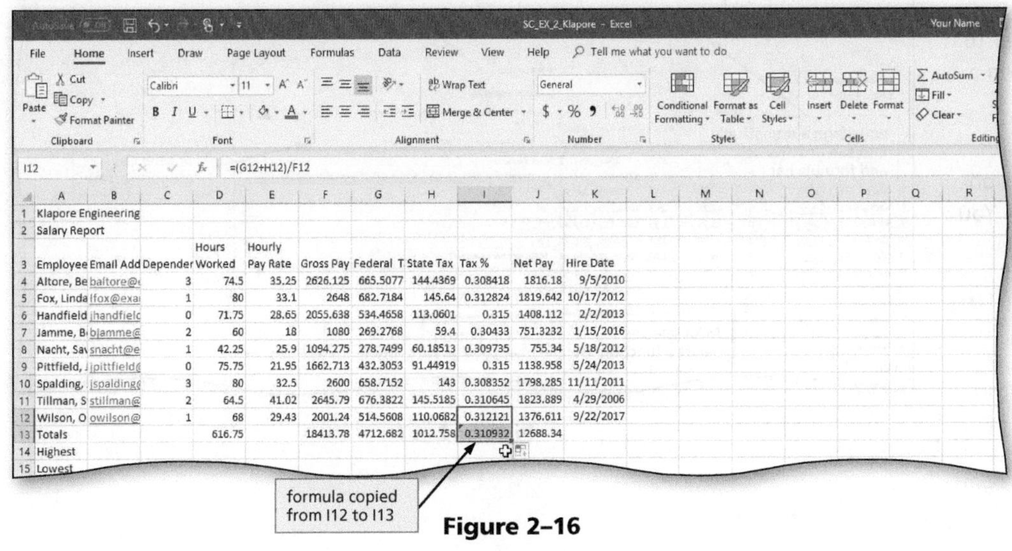

Figure 2–16

BTW
Statistical Functions
Excel usually considers a blank cell to be equal to 0. The statistical functions, however, ignore blank cells. Excel thus calculates the average of three cells with values of 10, blank, and 8 to be 9 [(10 + 8) / 2] and not 6 [(10 + 0 + 8) / 3].

Using the AVERAGE, MAX, MIN, and other Statistical Functions

The next step in creating the Klapore Engineering Salary Report worksheet is to compute the highest value, lowest value, and average value for the number of dependents listed in the range C4:C12 using the MAX, MIN, and AVERAGE functions in the range C14:C16. Once the values are determined for column C, the entries can be copied across to the other columns. Other useful statistical functions include COUNT, which counts the number of cells in a range that contain numbers, and COUNTA, which counts the number of cells in a range that are not empty.

With Excel, you can enter functions using one of five methods: (1) keyboard, touch gesture, or pointer; (2) the Insert Function button in the formula bar; (3) the AutoSum button (Home tab | Editing group); (4) the AutoSum button (Formulas tab | Function Library group); and (5) the Name box area in the formula bar. The method you choose will depend on your typing skills and whether you can recall the function name and required arguments.

In the following sections, you will use three of these methods. You will use the Insert Function button in the formula bar method to determine the highest number of dependents (cell C14). You will use the AutoSum menu to determine the lowest number of dependents (cell C15). You will use the keyboard and pointer to determine the average number of dependents (cell C16).

To Determine the Highest Number in a Range of Numbers Using the Insert Function Dialog Box

The next step is to select cell C14 and determine the highest (maximum) number in the range C4:C12. As discussed in Module 1, Excel includes a function called the **MAX function** that displays the highest value in a range. The following steps use the Insert Function dialog box to enter the MAX function. ***Why?*** *Although you could enter the MAX function using the keyboard and Point mode as described previously, an alternative method to entering the function is to use the Insert Function button in the formula bar to display the Insert Function dialog box. The Insert Function dialog box is helpful if you do not remember the name of a function or need to search for a particular function by what it does.*

- Select the cell to contain the maximum number, cell C14 in this case.
- Click the Insert Function button in the formula bar to display the Insert Function dialog box.
- Click MAX in the Select a function list (Insert Function dialog box; Figure 2–17). You may need to scroll.

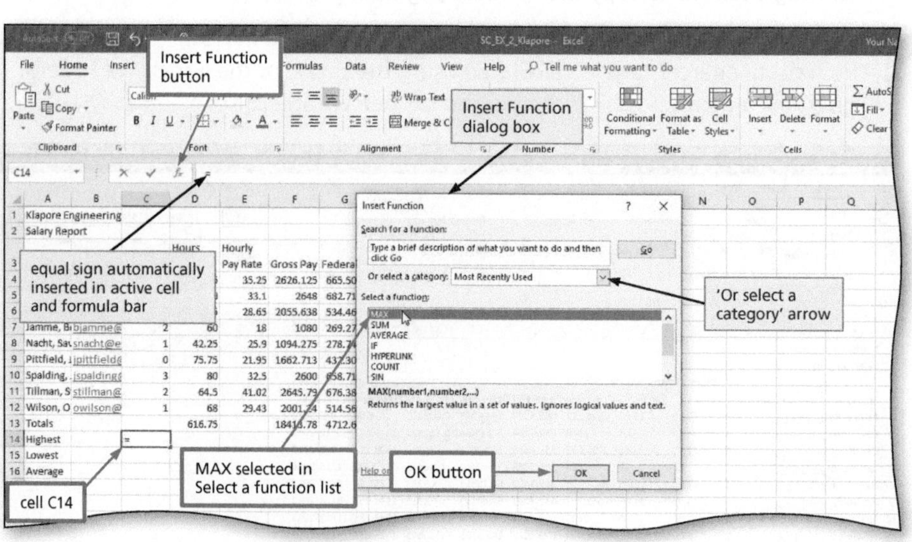

Q&A What if the MAX function is not in the Select a function list?

Click the 'Or select a category' arrow to display the list of function categories, select All, and then scroll down and select the MAX function in the Select a function list.

Figure 2–17

Q&A How can I learn about other functions?
Excel has more than 400 functions that perform nearly every type of calculation you can imagine. These functions are categorized in the Insert Function dialog box shown in Figure 2–17. To view the categories, click the 'Or select a category' arrow. Click the name of a function in the Select a function list to display a description of the function.

2

- Click OK (Insert Function dialog box) to display the Function Arguments dialog box.
- Replace the text in the Number1 box with the text, `c4:c12` (Function Arguments dialog box) to enter the first argument of the function (Figure 2–18).

Q&A What are the numbers that appear to the right of the Number1 box in the Function Arguments dialog box?
The numbers shown to the right of the Number1 box are the values in the selected range (or if the range is large, the first few numbers only). Excel also displays the value the MAX function will return to cell C14 in the Function Arguments dialog box, shown in Figure 2–18.

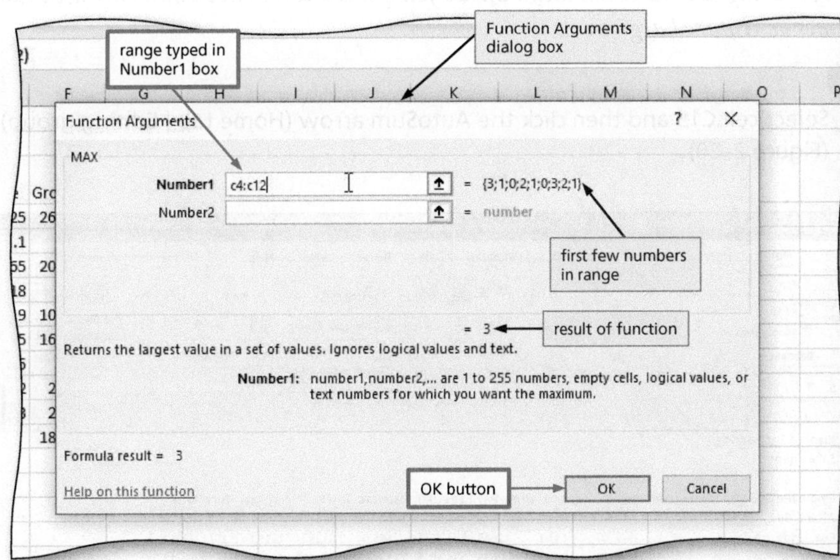

Figure 2–18

3

- Click OK (Function Arguments dialog box) to display the highest value in the chosen range in cell C14 (Figure 2–19).

Q&A Why should I not just enter the highest value that I see in the range C4:C12 in cell C14?
In this example, rather than entering the MAX function, you could examine the range C4:C12, determine that the highest number of dependents is 3, and manually enter the number 3 as a constant in cell C14. Excel would display the number similar to how it appears in Figure 2–19. However, because C14 would then contain a constant, Excel would continue to display 3 in cell C14 even if the values in the range change. If you use the MAX function, Excel will recalculate the highest value in the range each time a new value is entered.

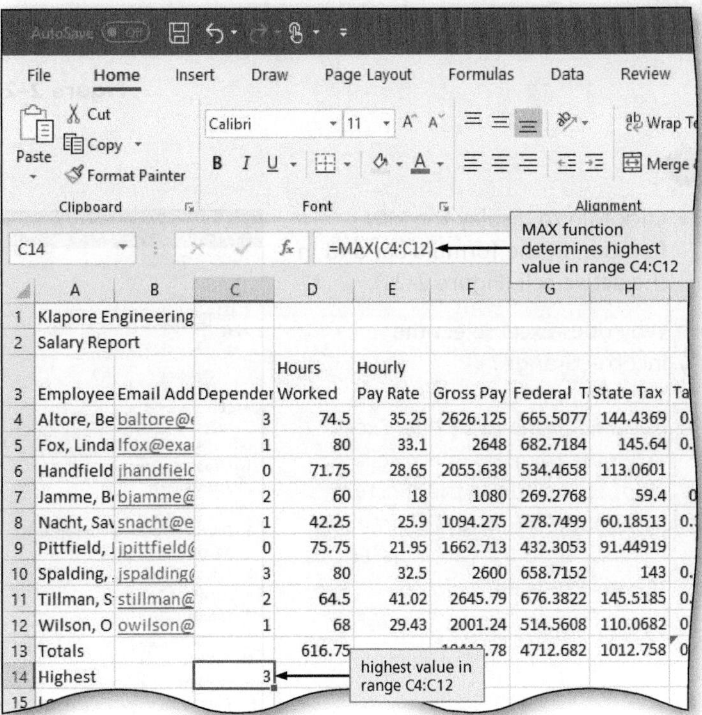

	A	B	C	D	E	F	G	H
1	Klapore Engineering							
2	Salary Report							
3	Employee	Email Add	Depender	Hours Worked	Hourly Pay Rate	Gross Pay	Federal T	State Tax
4	Altore, Be	baltore@	3	74.5	35.25	2626.125	665.5077	144.4369
5	Fox, Linda	lfox@exa	1	80	33.1	2648	682.7184	145.64
6	Handfield	jhandfielc	0	71.75	28.65	2055.638	534.4658	113.0601
7	Jamme, B	bjamme@	2	60	18	1080	269.2768	59.4
8	Nacht, Sa	snacht@e	1	42.25	25.9	1094.275	278.7499	60.18513
9	Pittfield, J	jpittfield@	0	75.75	21.95	1662.713	432.3053	91.44919
10	Spalding, .	jspalding@	3	80	32.5	2600	658.7152	143
11	Tillman, S	stillman@	2	64.5	41.02	2645.79	676.3822	145.5185
12	Wilson, O	owilson@	1	68	29.43	2001.24	514.5608	110.0682
13	Totals			616.75		[illegible].78	4712.682	1012.758
14	Highest		3					

Figure 2–19

Other Ways

1. Click AutoSum arrow (Home tab | Editing group), click Max
2. Click AutoSum arrow (Formulas tab | Function Library group), click Max
3. Type `=MAX(` in cell, specify range, type)

To Determine the Lowest Number in a Range of Numbers Using the Sum Menu

The next step is to enter the **MIN function** in cell C15 to determine the lowest (minimum) number in the range C4:C12. Although you can enter the MIN function using the method used to enter the MAX function, the following steps illustrate an alternative method using the AutoSum button (Home tab | Editing group). ***Why?*** *Using the AutoSum menu allows you quick access to five commonly used functions, without having to memorize their names or required arguments.*

- Select cell C15 and then click the AutoSum arrow (Home tab | Editing group) to display the AutoSum menu (Figure 2–20).

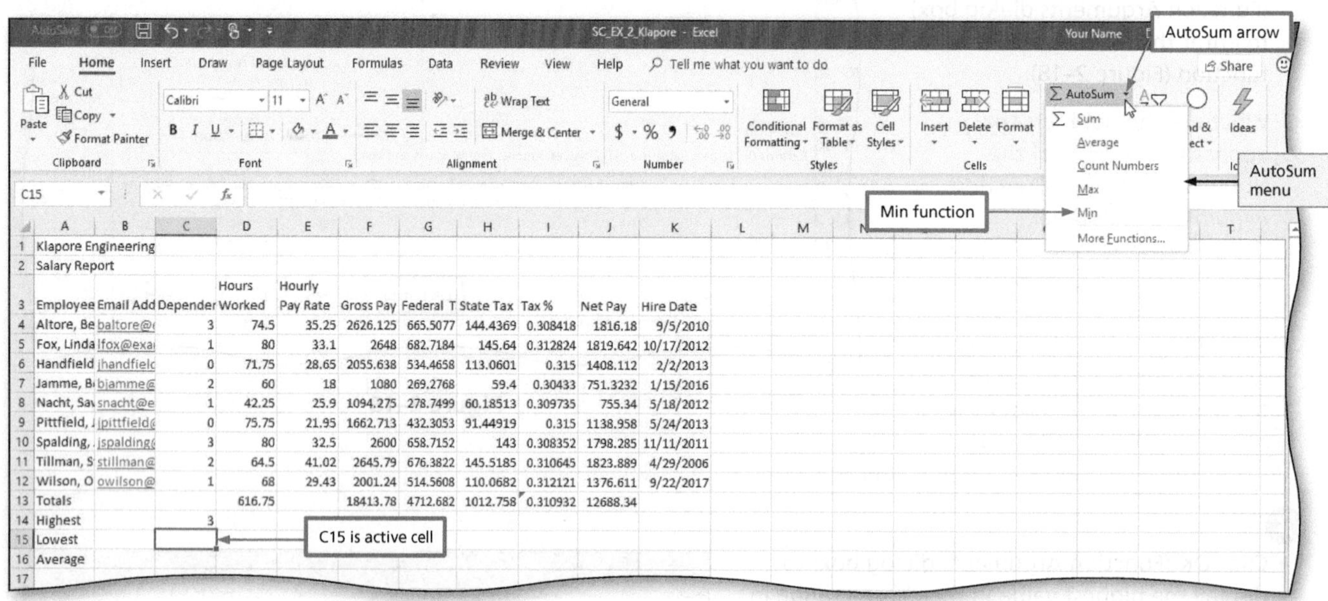

Figure 2–20

- Click Min to display the MIN function in the formula bar and in the active cell (Figure 2–21).

Q&A Why does Excel select the incorrect range?

The range selected by Excel is not always the right one. Excel attempts to guess which cells you want to include in the function by looking for ranges containing numeric data that are adjacent to the selected cell.

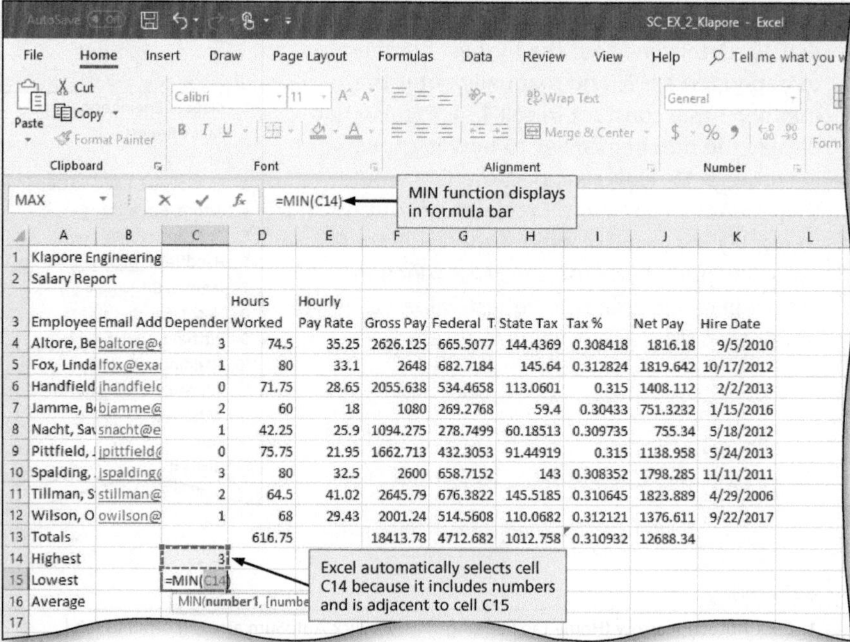

Figure 2–21

3

- Click cell C4 and then drag through cell C12 to update the function with the new range (Figure 2–22).

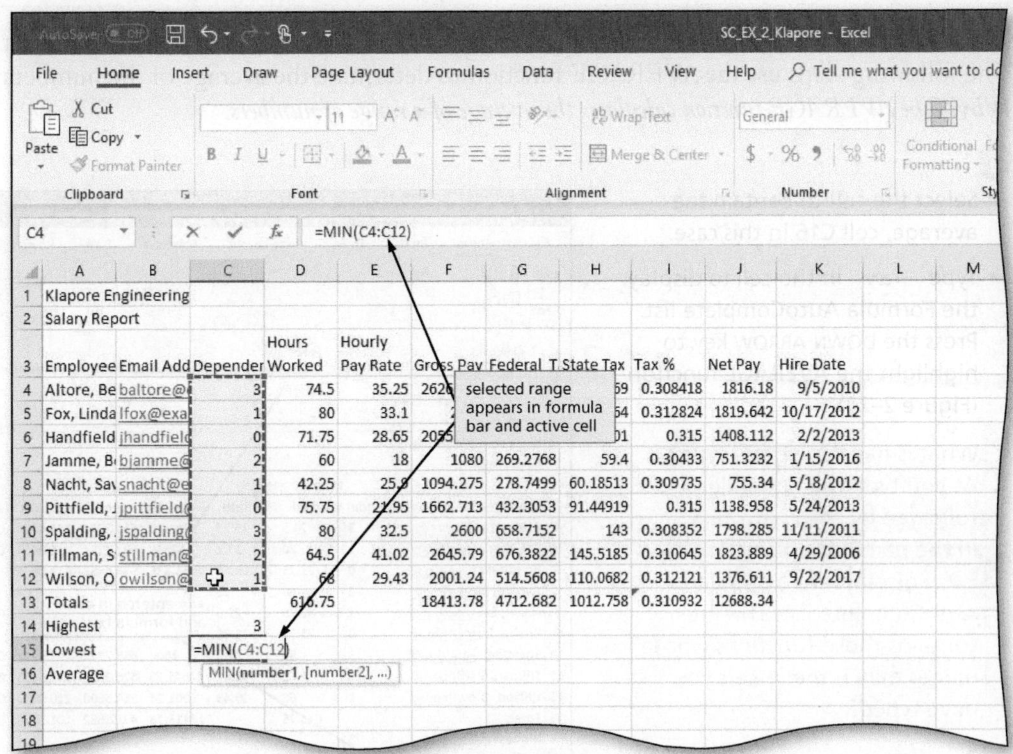

Figure 2–22

4

- Click the Enter button to determine the lowest value in the range C4:C12 and display the result in cell C15 (Figure 2–23).

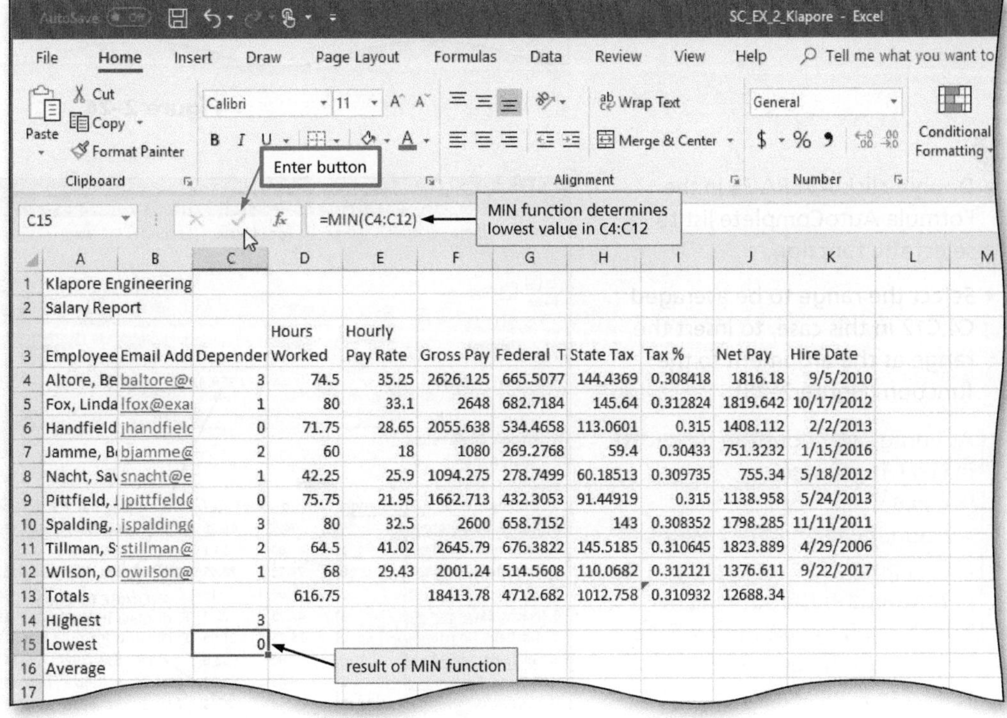

Figure 2–23

Other Ways

1. Click Insert Function button in formula bar, select Statistical category if necessary, click MIN, specify arguments
2. Click AutoSum arrow (Formulas tab | Function Library group), click Min
3. Type `=MIN(` in cell, fill in arguments, type)

To Determine the Average of a Range of Numbers Using the Keyboard

The **AVERAGE function** is an Excel function that calculates the average value of a collection of numbers. The following steps use the AVERAGE function to determine the average of the numbers in the range C4:C12. ***Why?*** *The AVERAGE function calculates the average of a range of numbers.*

- Select the cell to contain the average, cell C16 in this case.
- Type **=av** in the cell to display the Formula AutoComplete list. Press the DOWN ARROW key to highlight the AVERAGE function (Figure 2–24).

Q&A What is happening as I type?
As you type the equal sign followed by the characters in the name of a function, Excel displays the Formula AutoComplete list. This list contains those functions whose names match the letters you have typed.

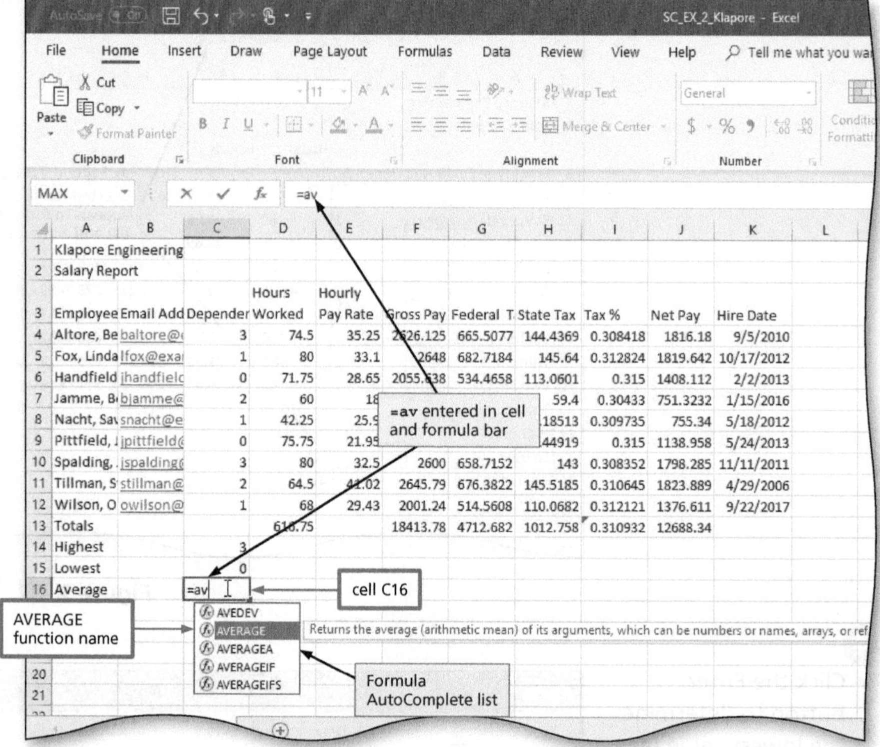

Figure 2–24

- Double-click AVERAGE in the Formula AutoComplete list to select the function.
- Select the range to be averaged, C4:C12 in this case, to insert the range as the argument to the function (Figure 2–25).

Q&A As I drag, why does the function in cell C16 change?
When you click cell C4, Excel surrounds cell C4 with a marquee and appends C4 to the left parenthesis in the formula bar. When you begin dragging, Excel appends to the argument a colon (:) and the cell reference of the cell where the pointer is located.

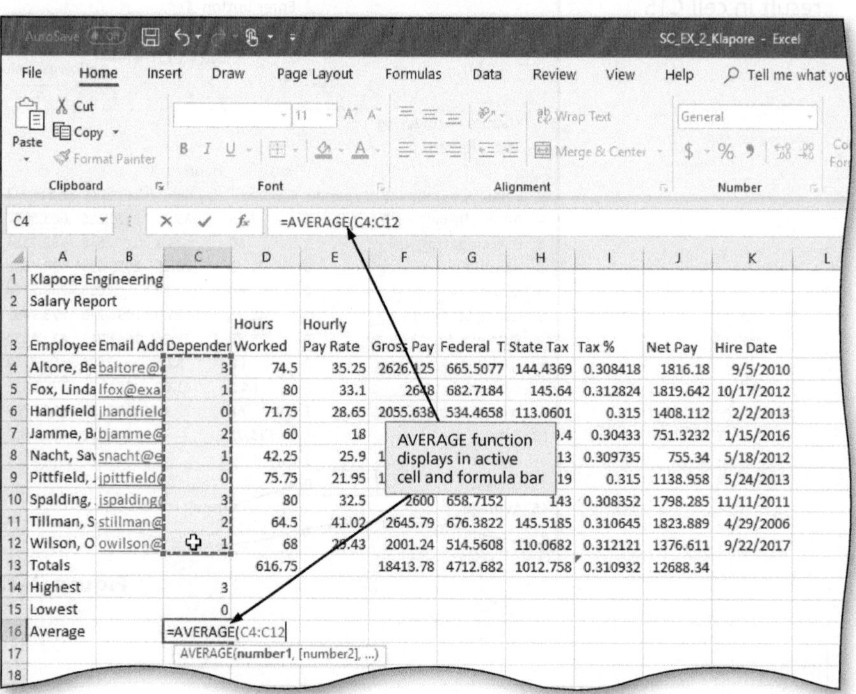

Figure 2–25

3

- Click the Enter button to compute the average of the numbers in the selected range and display the result in the selected cell (Figure 2–26).

Q&A

Can I use the arrow keys to complete the entry instead?
No. While in Point mode, the arrow keys change the selected cell reference in the range you are selecting instead of completing the entry.

What is the purpose of the parentheses in the function?
Most Excel functions require that the argument (in this case, the range C4:C12) be included within parentheses following the function name. In this case, Excel appended the right parenthesis to complete the AVERAGE function when you clicked the Enter button.

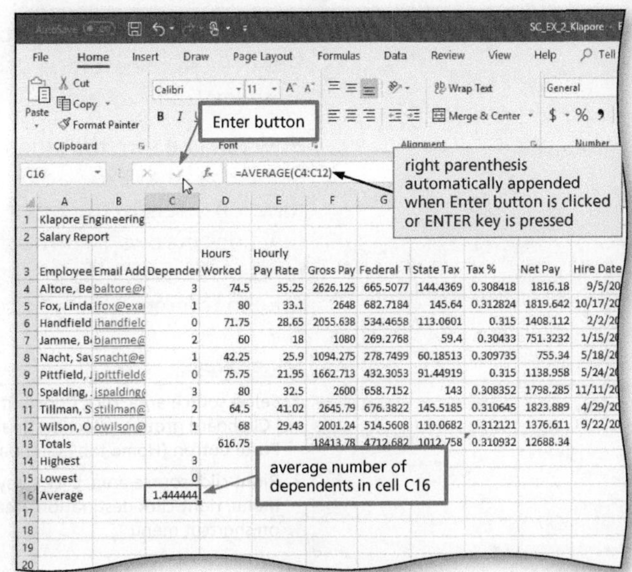

Figure 2–26

To Copy a Range of Cells across Columns to an Adjacent Range Using the Fill Handle

The next step is to copy the AVERAGE, MAX, and MIN functions in the range C14:C16 to the adjacent range D14:J16. The following steps use the fill handle to copy the functions.

1. Select the source range from which to copy the functions, in this case C14:C16.
2. Drag the fill handle in the lower-right corner of the selected range through cell J16 to copy the three functions to the selected range.
3. Select cell I16 and then press DELETE to delete the average of the Tax % (Figure 2–27).

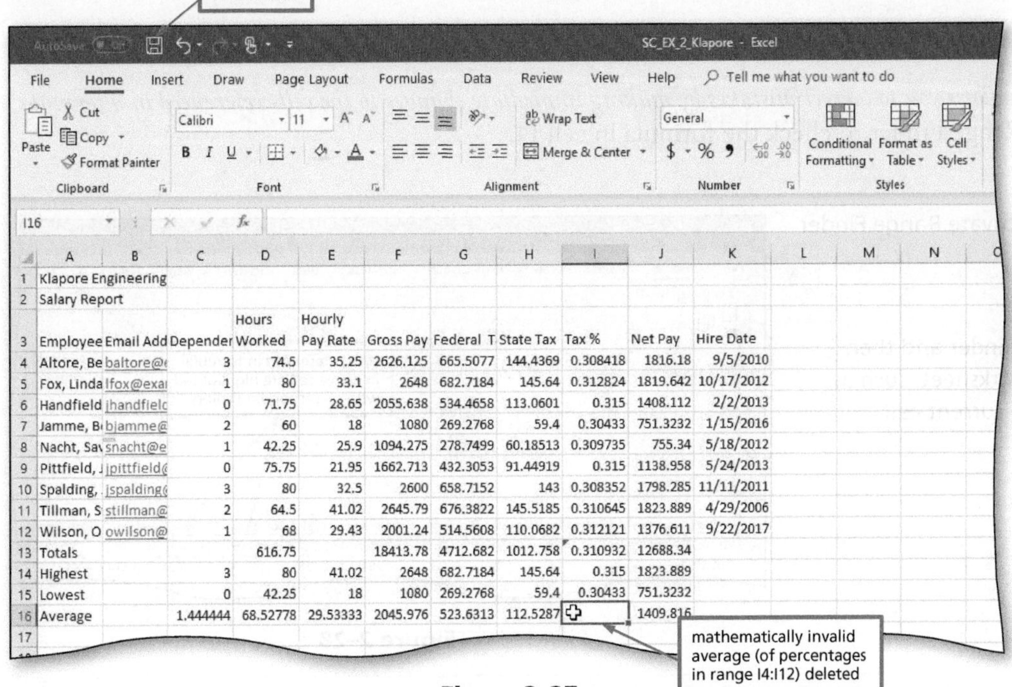

Figure 2–27

4 Save the workbook again with the same file name.

Q&A

Why delete the formula in cell I16?

You deleted the average in cell I16 because averaging this type of percentage is mathematically invalid.

How can I be sure that the function arguments are correct for the cells in range D14:J16?

Remember that Excel adjusts the cell references in the copied functions so that each function refers to the range of numbers above it in the same column. Review the functions in rows 14 through 16 by clicking on individual cells and examining the function as it appears in the formula bar. You should see that the functions in each column reference the appropriate ranges.

Other Ways

1. Select source area, click Copy button (Home tab | Clipboard group), select destination area, click Paste button (Home tab | Clipboard group)
2. Right-click source area, click Copy on shortcut menu; right-click destination area, click Paste icon on shortcut menu
3. Select source area and then point to border of range; while holding down CTRL, drag source area to destination area
4. Select source area, press CTRL+C, select destination area, press CTRL+V

Break Point: If you want to take a break, this is a good place to do so. You can exit Excel now. To resume later, start Excel, open the file called SC_EX_2_Klapore, and continue following the steps from this location forward.

Verifying Formulas Using Range Finder

One of the more common mistakes made with Excel is to include an incorrect cell reference in a formula. An easy way to verify that a formula references the cells you want it to reference is to use Range Finder. **Range Finder** checks which cells are referenced in the formula assigned to the active cell.

To use Range Finder to verify that a formula contains the intended cell references, double-click the cell with the formula you want to check. Excel responds by highlighting the cells referenced in the formula so that you can verify that the cell references are correct.

To Verify a Formula Using Range Finder

Why? Range Finder allows you to correct mistakes by making immediate changes to the cells referenced in a formula. The following steps use Range Finder to check the formula in cell I4.

1

- Double-click cell I4 to activate Range Finder (Figure 2–28).

2

- Press ESC to quit Range Finder and then click anywhere in the worksheet, such as cell A18, to deselect the current cell.

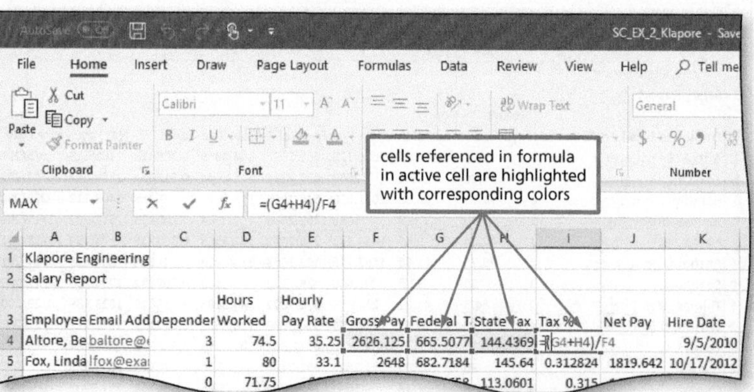

Figure 2–28

Formatting the Worksheet

Although the worksheet contains the appropriate data, formulas, and functions, the text and numbers need to be formatted to improve their appearance and readability.

In Module 1, you used cell styles to format much of the worksheet. This section describes how to change the unformatted worksheet in Figure 2–29a to the formatted worksheet in Figure 2–29b using a theme and other commands on the ribbon. A **theme** formats a worksheet by applying a collection of fonts, font styles, colors, and effects to give it a consistent appearance.

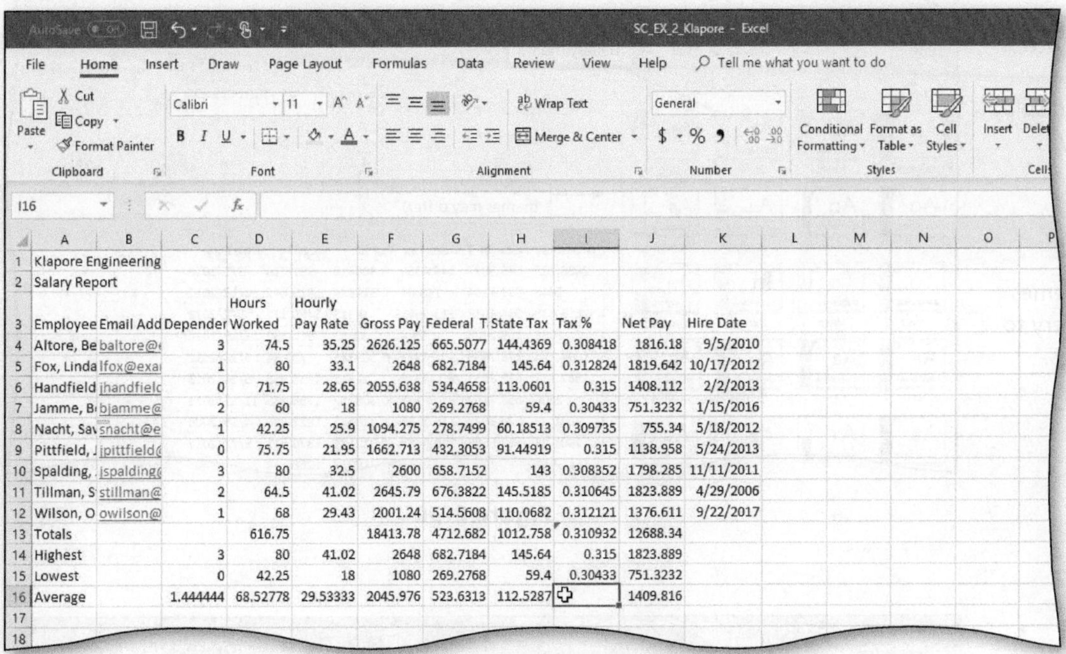

(a) Unformatted Worksheet

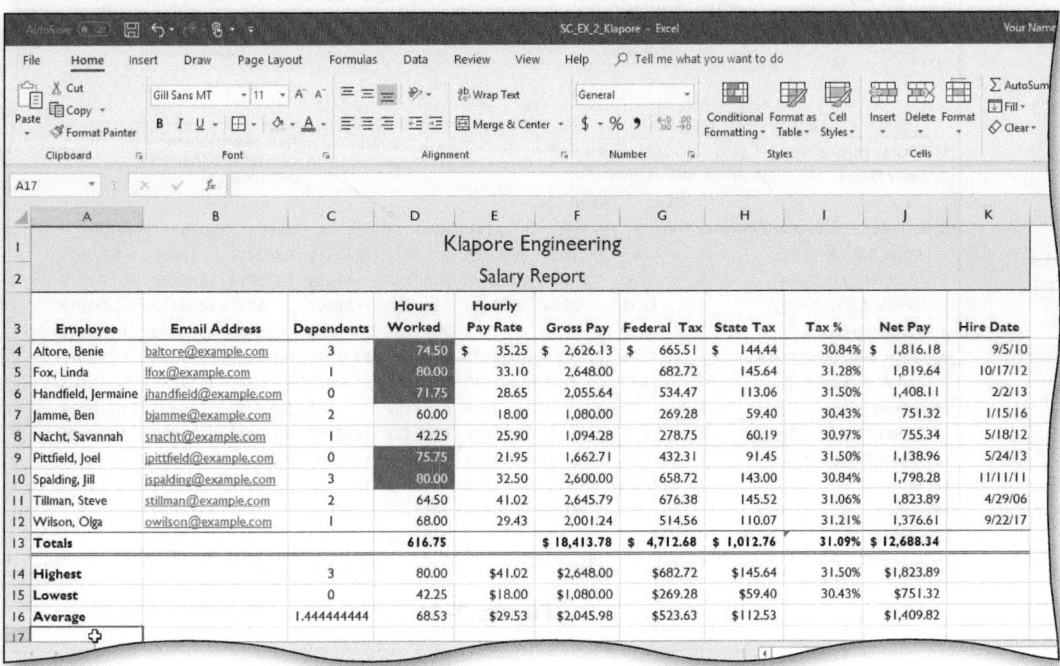

(b) Formatted Worksheet

Figure 2–29

To Change the Workbook Theme

Why? A company or department may choose a specific theme as their standard theme so that all of their documents have a similar appearance. Similarly, you may want to have a theme that sets your work apart from the work of others. Other Office programs, such as Word and PowerPoint, include the same themes so that all of your Microsoft Office documents can share a common look. The following steps change the workbook theme to the Gallery theme.

- Click Page Layout to display the Page Layout tab.
- Click the Themes button (Page Layout tab | Themes group) to display the Themes gallery (Figure 2–30).

Experiment

- Point to several themes in the Themes gallery to preview the themes.

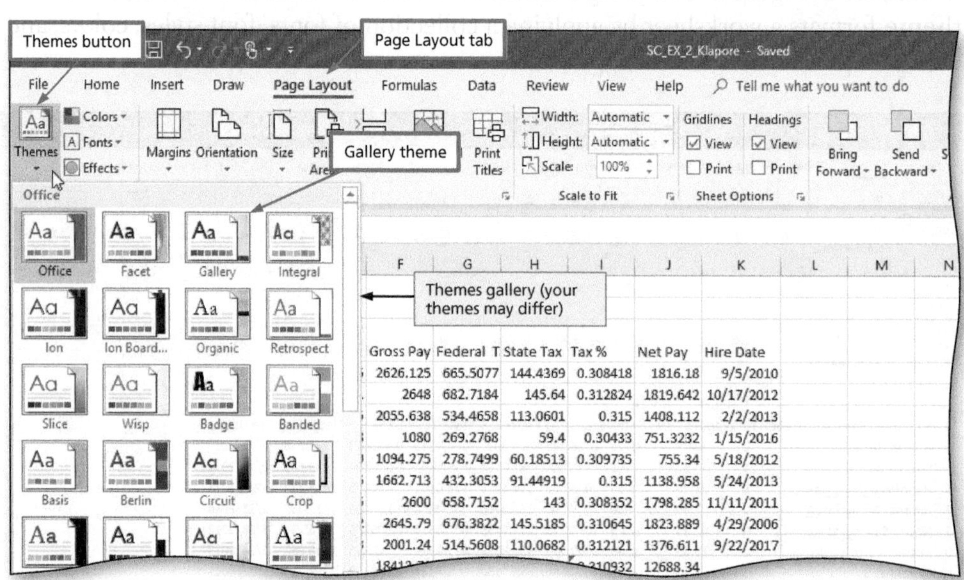

Figure 2–30

- Click Gallery in the Themes gallery to change the workbook theme (Figure 2–31).

Q&A Why did the cells in the worksheet change?
Originally, the cells in the worksheet were formatted with the default font of the default Office theme. The Gallery theme has a different default font than the Office theme, so when you changed the theme, the font changed. If you had modified the font for any cells, those cells would not have changed to the default font of the Gallery theme.

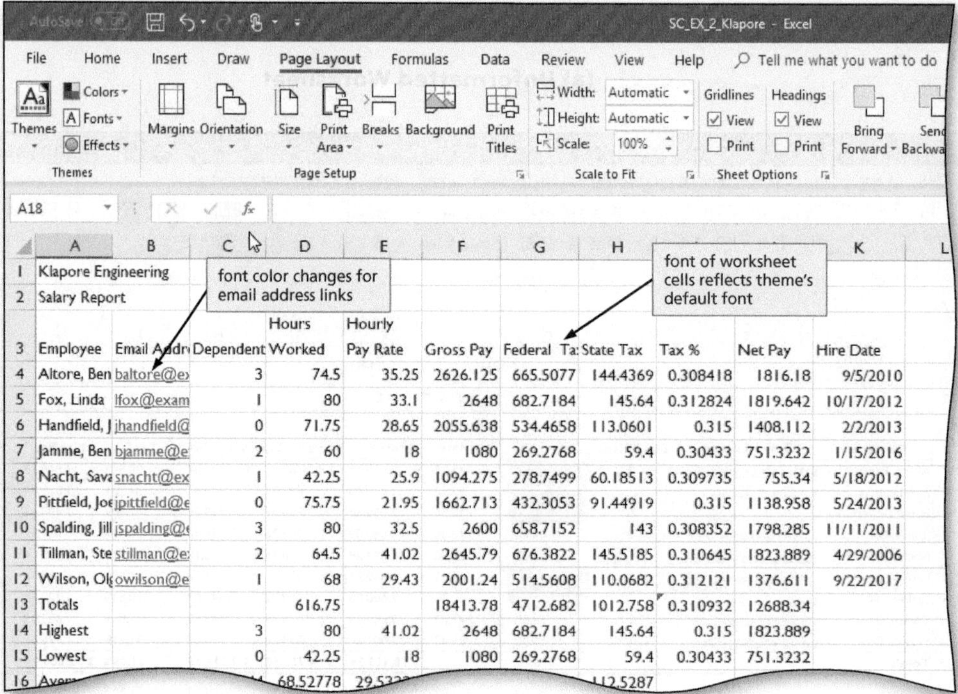

Figure 2–31

To Format the Worksheet Titles

The following steps merge and center the worksheet titles, apply the Title cells style to the worksheet titles, and decrease the font of the worksheet subtitle.

1. Display the Home tab.

2. Select the range to be merged, A1:K1 in this case, and then click the 'Merge & Center' button (Home tab | Alignment group) to merge and center the text in the selected range.

3. Select the range A2:K2 and then click the 'Merge & Center' button (Home tab | Alignment group) to merge and center the text.

4. Select the range to contain the Title cell style, in this case A1:A2, click the Cell Styles button (Home tab | Styles group) to display the Cell Styles gallery, and then click the Title cell style in the Titles and Headings group in the Cell Styles gallery to apply the Title cell style to the selected range.

5. Select cell A2 and then click the 'Decrease Font Size' button (Home tab | Font group) to decrease the font size of the selected cell to the next lower font size (Figure 2–32).

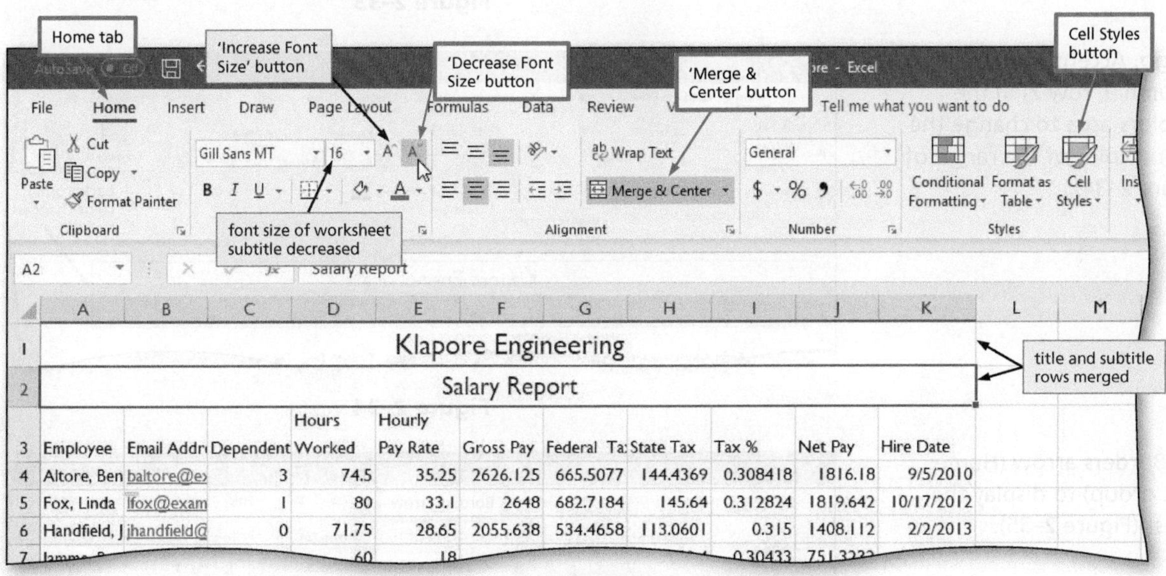

Figure 2–32

Q&A What happens when I click the 'Decrease Font Size' button?
When you click the 'Decrease Font Size' button, Excel assigns the next smaller font size in the Font Size gallery to the selected range. The 'Increase Font Size' button works in a similar manner, assigning the next larger font size in the Font Size gallery to the selected range.

CONSIDER THIS

Which colors work best when formatting your worksheet?
Knowing how people perceive colors can help you focus attention on parts of your worksheet. For example, warmer colors (red and orange) tend to reach toward the reader. Cooler colors (blue, green, and violet) tend to pull away from the reader.

To Change the Background Color and Apply a Box Border to the Worksheet Title and Subtitle

***Why?** A background color and border can draw attention to the title of a worksheet.* The final formats assigned to the worksheet title and subtitle are the blue-gray background color and thick outside border. The following steps complete the formatting of the worksheet titles.

- Select the range A1:A2 and then click the Fill Color arrow (Home tab | Font group) to display the Fill Color gallery (Figure 2–33).

Experiment

- Point to a variety of colors in the Fill Color gallery to preview the selected colors in the range A1:A2.

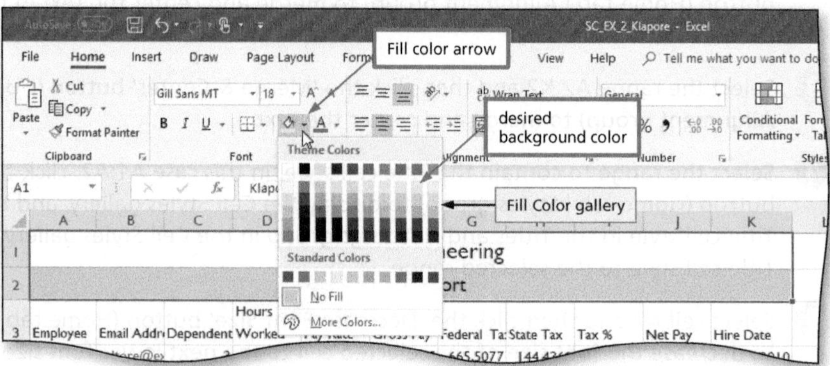

Figure 2–33

2

- Click Indigo, Accent 5, Lighter 80% (column 9, row 2) in the Theme Colors area to change the background color of the range of cells (Figure 2–34).

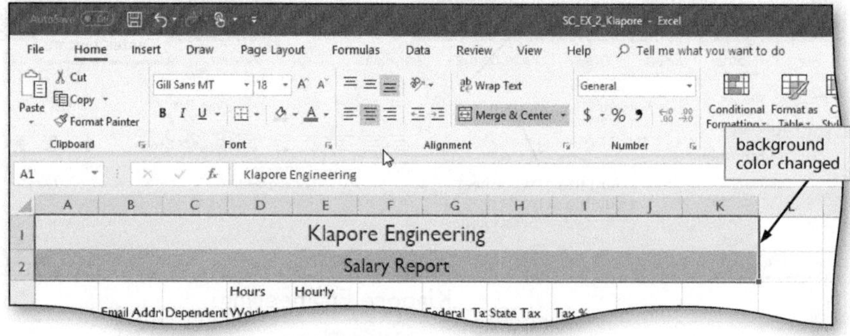

Figure 2–34

3

- Click the Borders arrow (Home tab | Font group) to display the Borders list (Figure 2–35).

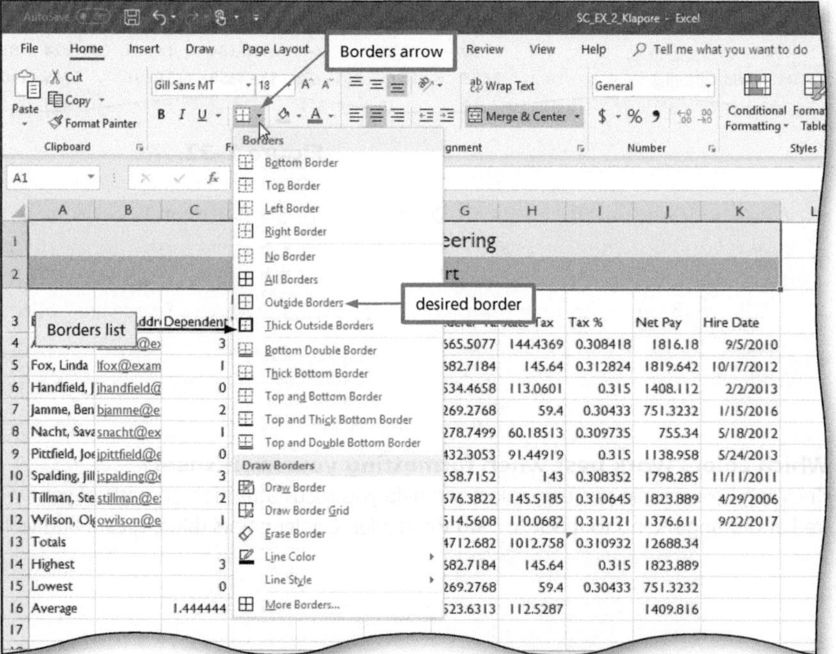

Figure 2–35

4

- Click 'Outside Borders' in the Borders gallery to create an outside border around the selected range.
- Click anywhere in the worksheet, such as cell A17, to deselect the current range (Figure 2–36).

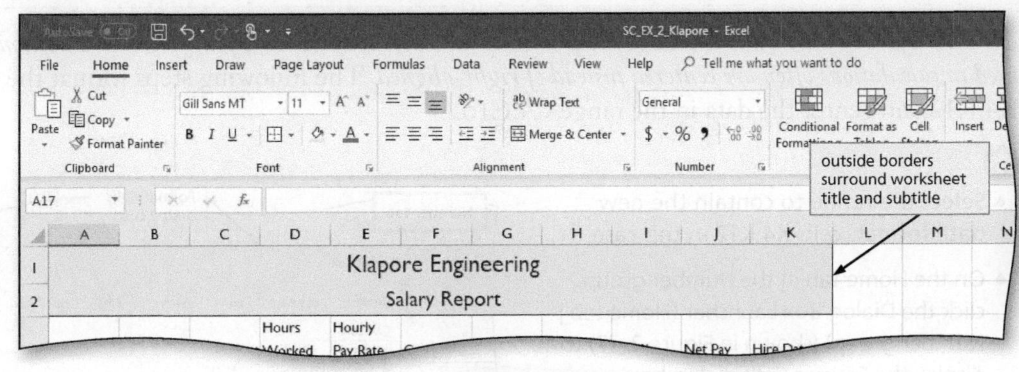

Figure 2–36

Other Ways

1. Click Font Settings Dialog Box Launcher (Home tab | Font group), click Fill tab (Format Cells dialog box), click desired fill, click OK
2. Right-click range, click Format Cells on shortcut menu, click Fill tab (Format Cells dialog box), click desired fill, click OK
3. Press CTRL+1, click Fill tab (Format Cells dialog box), click desired fill, click OK

To Apply a Cell Style to the Column Headings and Format the Total Rows

As shown in Figure 2–29b, the column titles (row 3) should have the Heading 3 cell style and the totals row (row 13) should have the Total cell style. The headings in the range A14:A16 should be bold. The following steps assign these styles and formats to row 3, row 13, and the range A14:A16.

BTW
Color Selection
Bright colors jump out of a dark background and are easiest to see. White or yellow text on a dark blue, green, purple, or black background is ideal for highlighting.

1. Select the range to be formatted, cells A3:K3 in this case.
2. Use the Cell Styles gallery to apply the Heading 3 cell style to the range A3:K3.
3. Click the Center button (Home tab | Alignment group) to center the column headings.
4. Apply the Total cell style to the range A13:K13.
5. Bold the range A14:A16 (Figure 2–37).

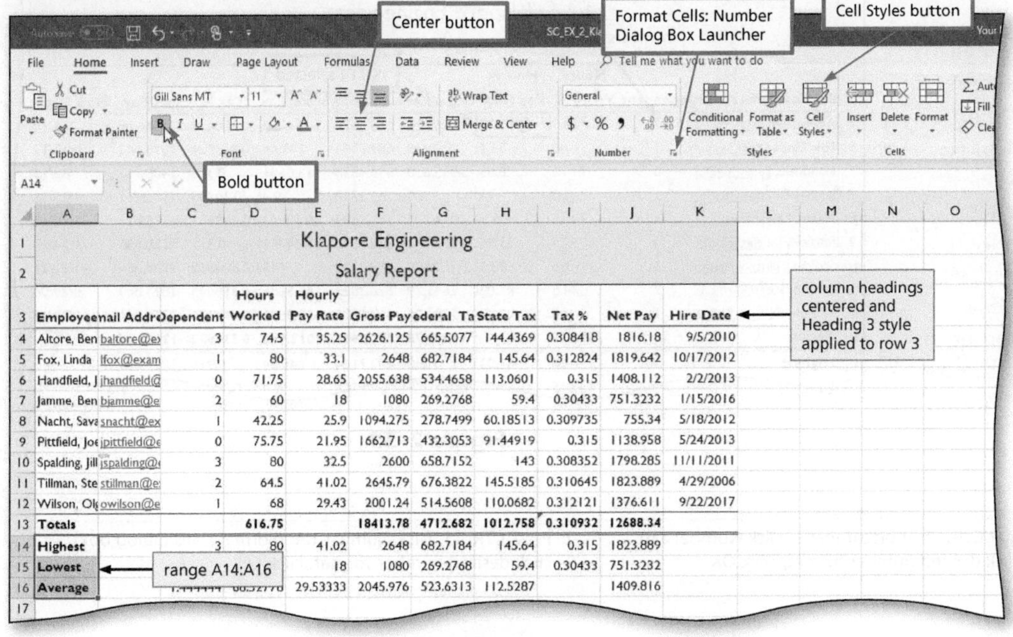

Figure 2–37

BTW
Background Colors
The most popular background color is blue. Research shows that the color blue is used most often because this color connotes serenity, reflection, and proficiency. Use color in spreadsheets to highlight data or to format worksheet elements such as titles. In most cases, colors should not be used for numbers because it may make them less visible.

To Format Dates and Center Data in Cells

***Why?** You may want to change the format of the dates to better suit your needs. In addition, numbers that are not used in calculations often are centered instead of right-aligned.* The following steps format the dates in the range K4:K12 and center the data in the range C4:C16.

- Select the range to contain the new date format, cells K4:K12 in this case.
- On the Home tab in the Number group, click the Dialog Box Launcher (Home tab | Number group) (shown in Figure 2–37) to display the Format Cells dialog box.
- If necessary, click the Number tab (Format Cells dialog box), click Date in the Category list, and then click 3/14/12 in the Type list to choose the format for the selected range (Figure 2–38).

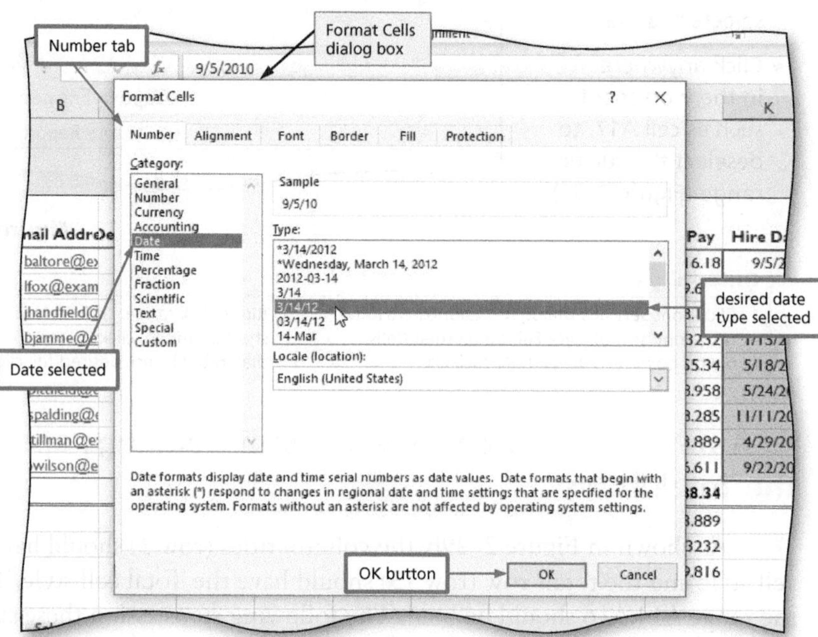

Figure 2–38

- Click OK (Format Cells dialog box) to format the dates in the current column using the selected date format style.

3

- Select the range C4:C16 and then click the Center button (Home tab | Alignment group) to center the data in the selected range.
- Select cell E4 to deselect the selected range (Figure 2–39).

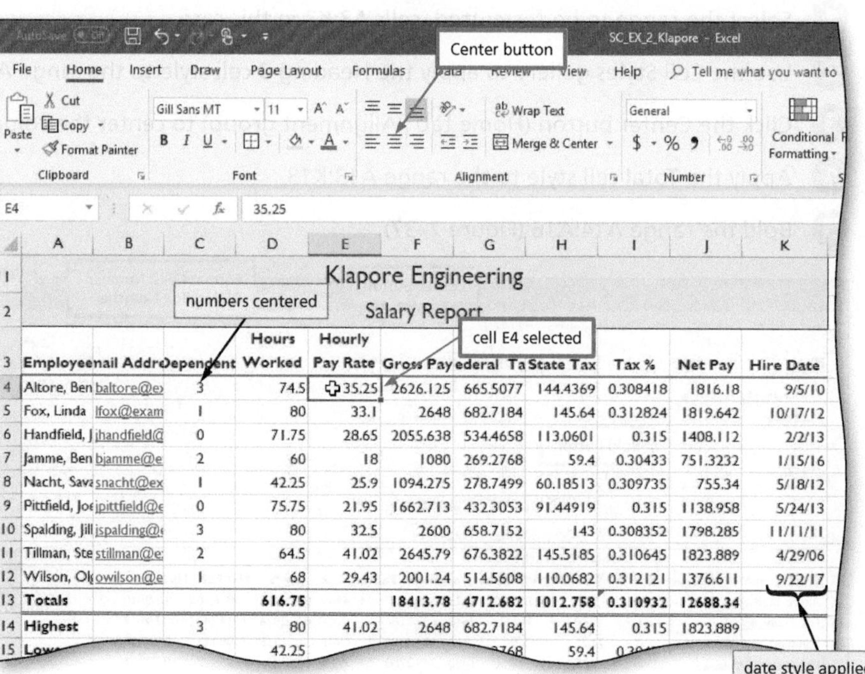

Figure 2–39

Q&A How can I format an entire column at once?

Instead of selecting the range C4:C16 in Step 3, you could have clicked the column C heading immediately above cell C1, and then clicked the Center button (Home tab | Alignment group). In this case, all cells in column C down to the last cell in the worksheet would have been formatted to use center alignment. This same procedure could have been used to format the dates in column K.

Other Ways

1. Right-click range, click Format Cells on shortcut menu, click Number tab (Format Cells dialog box), click desired number format, click OK
2. Press CTRL+1, click Number tab (Format Cells dialog box), click desired number format, click OK

To Apply an Accounting Number Format and Comma Style Format Using the Ribbon

As shown in Figure 2–29b, the worksheet is formatted to resemble an accounting report. In columns E through H and J, the numbers in the first row (row 4), the totals row (row 13), and the rows below the totals (rows 14 through 16) have dollar signs, while the remaining numbers (rows 5 through 12) in columns E through H and column J do not. The following steps assign formats using the 'Accounting Number Format' button and the Comma Style button. ***Why?*** *This gives the worksheet a more professional look.*

1. Select the range to contain the accounting number format, cells E4:H4 in this case.

2. While holding down CTRL, select cell J4, the range F13:H13, and cell J13 to select the nonadjacent ranges and cells.

3. Click the 'Accounting Number Format' button (Home tab | Number group) to apply the accounting number format with fixed dollar signs to the selected nonadjacent ranges.

Q&A What is the effect of applying the accounting number format?
The 'Accounting Number Format' button assigns a fixed dollar sign to the numbers in the ranges and rounds the figure to the nearest 100th. A fixed dollar sign is one that appears to the far left of the cell, with multiple spaces between it and the first digit in the cell.

4. Select the ranges to contain the comma style format, cells E5:H12 and J5:J12 in this case.

5. Click the Comma Style button (Home tab | Number group) to assign the comma style format to the selected ranges.

6. Select the range D4:D16 and then click the Comma Style button (Home tab | Number group) to assign the comma style format to the selected range (Figure 2–40).

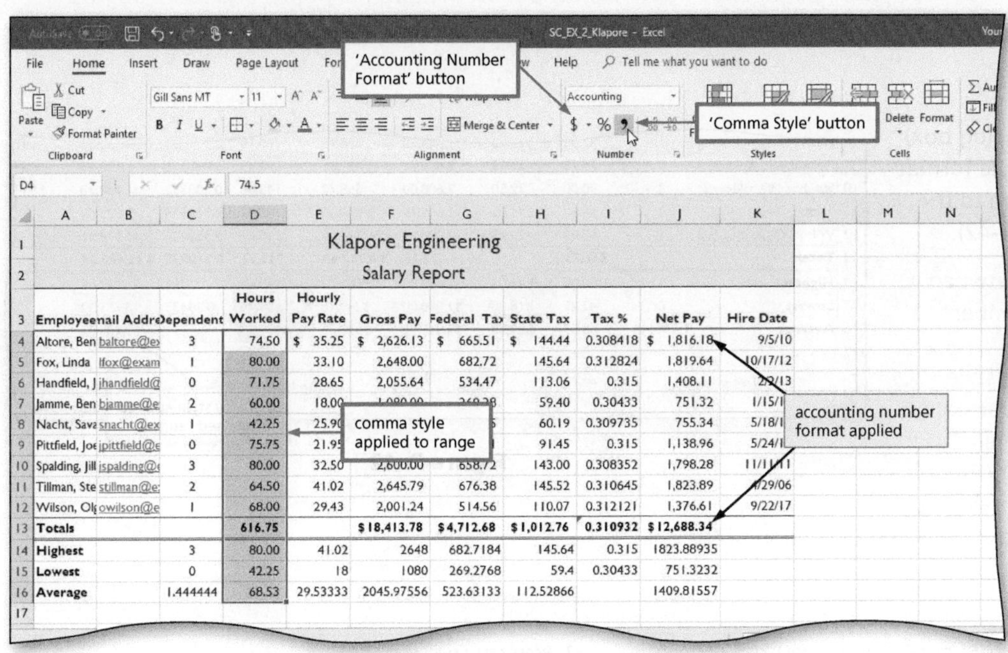

Figure 2–40

To Apply a Currency Style Format with a Floating Dollar Sign Using the Format Cells Dialog Box

Why? *The Currency format places dollar signs immediately to the left of the number (known as floating dollar signs, as they change position depending on the number of digits in the cell) and displays a zero for cells that have a value of zero.* The following steps use the Format Cells dialog box to apply the currency style format with a floating dollar sign to the numbers in the ranges E14:H16 and J14:J16.

- Select the ranges (E14:H16 and J14:J16) and then on the Home tab in the Number group, click the Dialog Box Launcher to display the Format Cells dialog box.
- If necessary, click the Number tab to display the Number sheet (Format Cells dialog box).
- Click Currency in the Category list to select the necessary number format category and then click the third style ($1,234.10) in the Negative numbers list to select the desired currency format for negative numbers (Figure 2–41).

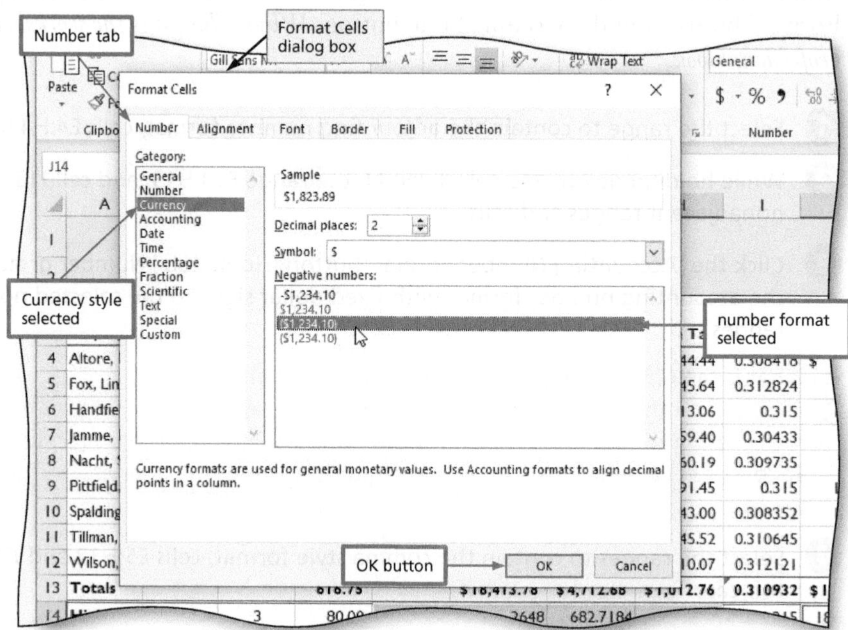

Figure 2–41

Q&A How do I decide which number format to use?

Excel offers many ways to format numbers. Once you select a number category, you can select the number of decimal places, whether to include a dollar sign (or a symbol of another currency), and how negative numbers should appear. Selecting the appropriate negative numbers format is important, because some formats add a space to the right of the number in order to align numbers in the worksheet on the decimal points and some do not.

- Click OK (Format Cells dialog box) to assign the currency style format with a floating dollar sign to the selected ranges (Figure 2–42).

currency style applied to selected ranges

Figure 2–42

Q&A What is the difference between using the accounting number style and currency style?

When using the currency style, recall that a floating dollar sign always appears immediately to the left of the first digit. With the accounting number style, the fixed dollar sign always appears on the left side of the cell.

Other Ways

1. Press CTRL+1, click Number tab (Format Cells dialog box), click Currency in Category list, select format, click OK
2. Press CTRL+SHIFT+DOLLAR SIGN ($)

To Apply a Percent Style Format and Use the Increase Decimal Button

The next step is to format the tax percentage in column I. ***Why?*** *Currently, Excel displays the numbers as decimal fractions when they should appear as percentages.* The following steps format the range I4:I15 to the percent style format with two decimal places.

1

- Select the range to format, cells I4:I15 in this case.
- Click the Percent Style button (Home tab | Number group) to display the numbers in the selected range as a rounded whole percent.

Q&A What is the result of clicking the Percent Style button?
The Percent Style button instructs Excel to display a value as a percentage, which is determined by multiplying the cell entry by 100, rounding the result to the nearest percentage, and adding a percent sign. For example, when cell I4 is formatted using the Percent Style buttons, Excel displays the actual value 0.461282 as 46%.

2

- Click the Increase Decimal button (Home tab | Number group) two times to display the numbers in the selected range with two decimal places (Figure 2–43).

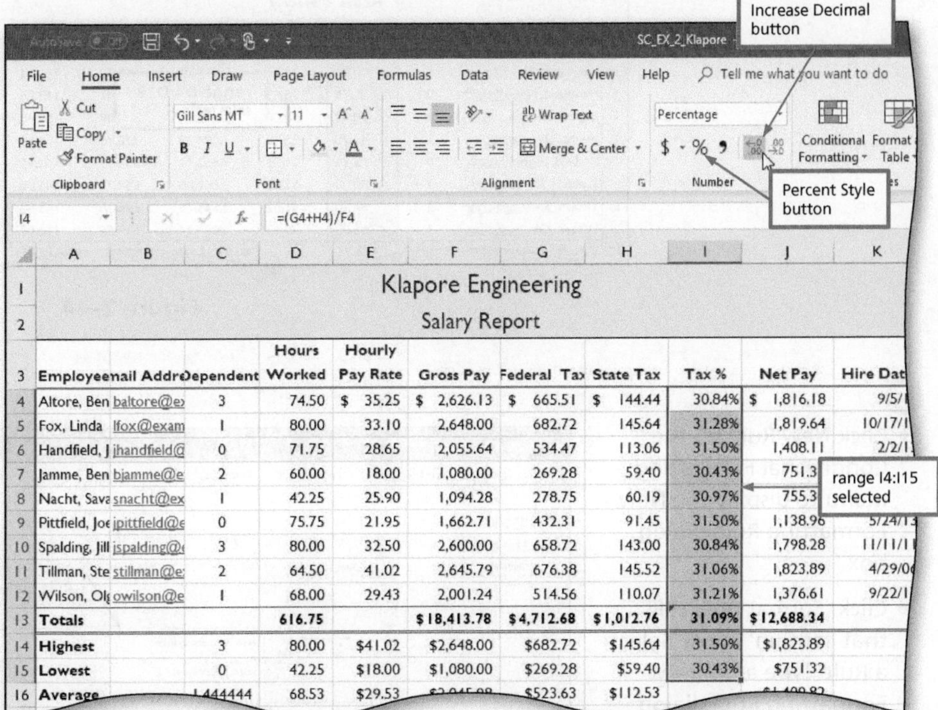

Figure 2–43

Other Ways

1. Right-click selected range, click Format Cells on shortcut menu, click Number tab (Format Cells dialog box), click Percentage in Category list, select format, click OK
2. Press CTRL+1, click Number tab (Format Cells dialog box), click Percentage in Category list, select format, click OK button
3. Press CTRL+SHIFT+PERCENT SIGN (%)

Conditional Formatting

Conditional formatting is special formatting — the font, font color, background fill, and other options — that is applied if cell values meet specified criteria. Excel offers a variety of commonly used conditional formatting rules, along with the ability to create your own custom rules and formatting. The next step is to emphasize the values greater than 70 in column D by formatting them to appear with a purple background and white font color.

BTW
Conditional Formatting
You can assign any format to a cell, a range of cells, a worksheet, or an entire workbook conditionally. If the value of the cell changes and no longer meets the specified condition, Excel suppresses the conditional formatting.

To Apply Conditional Formatting

The following steps assign conditional formatting to the range D4:D12. ***Why?*** *After formatting, any cell with a value greater than 70 in column D will appear with a purple background and a white font.*

- Select the range D4:D12.
- Click the Conditional Formatting button (Home tab | Styles group) to display the Conditional Formatting menu (Figure 2–44).

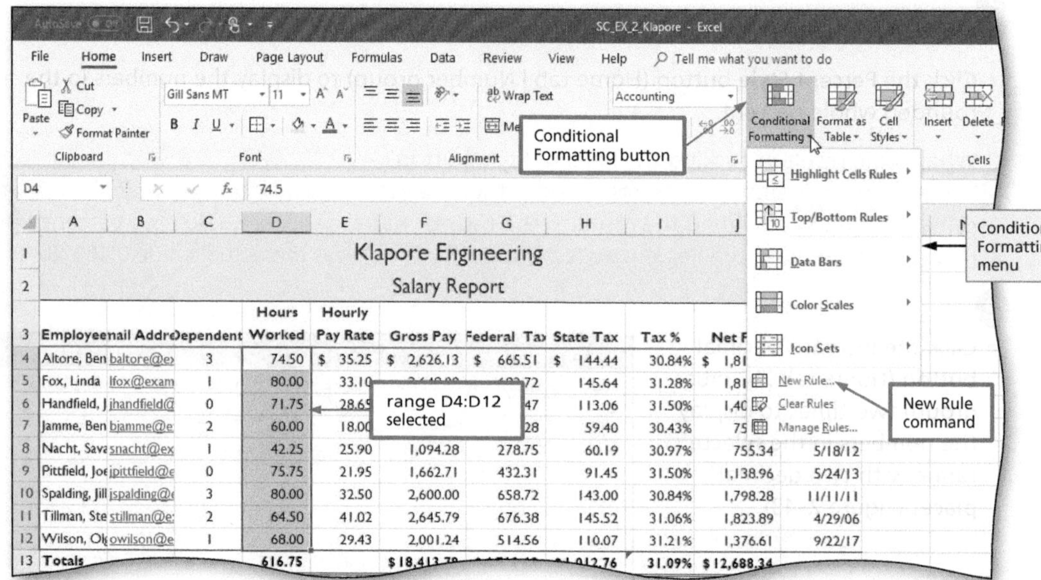

Figure 2–44

- Click New Rule on the Conditional Formatting menu to display the New Formatting Rule dialog box.
- Click 'Format only cells that contain' in the Select a Rule Type area (New Formatting Rule dialog box) to change the Edit the Rule Description area.
- In the Edit the Rule Description area, click the arrow in the relational operator box (second box) to display a list of relational operators, and then select greater than to select the desired operator.

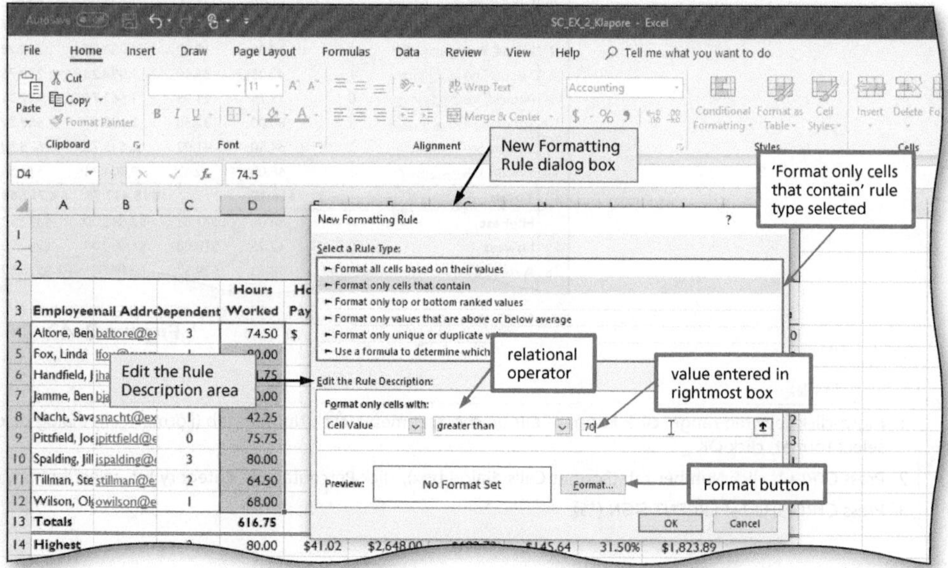

Figure 2–45

- Click in the rightmost box, and then type `70` to enter the value of the rule description (Figure 2–45).

Q&A What do the changes in the Edit the Rule Description area indicate?

The Edit the Rule Description area allows you to view and edit the rules for the conditional format. In this case, the rule indicates that Excel should format only those cells with cell values greater than 70.

3

- Click the Format button (New Formatting Rule dialog box) to display the Format Cells dialog box.
- If necessary, click the Font tab (Format Cells dialog box) to display the Font sheet. Click the Color arrow to display the Color gallery and then click White, Background 1 (column 1, row 1) in the Color gallery to select the font color (Figure 2–46).

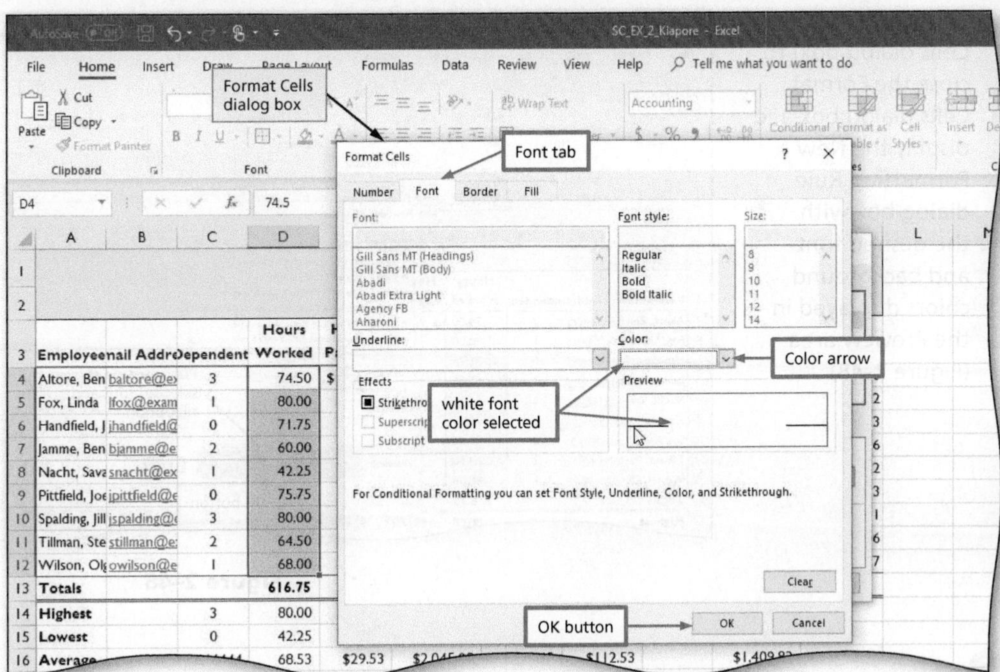

Figure 2–46

4

- Click the Fill tab (Format Cells dialog box) and then click the purple color in column 8, row 1 to select the background color (Figure 2–47).

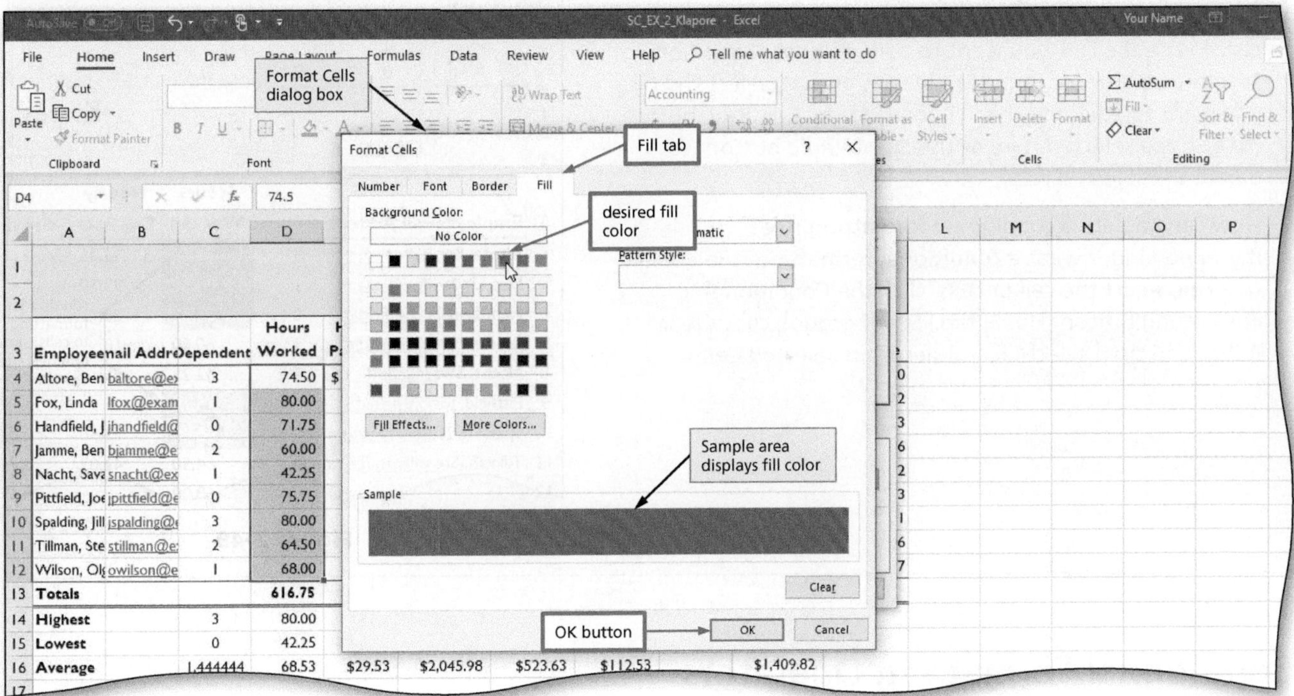

Figure 2–47

- Click OK (Format Cells dialog box) to close the Format Cells dialog box and display the New Formatting Rule dialog box with the desired font and background colors displayed in the Preview area (Figure 2–48).

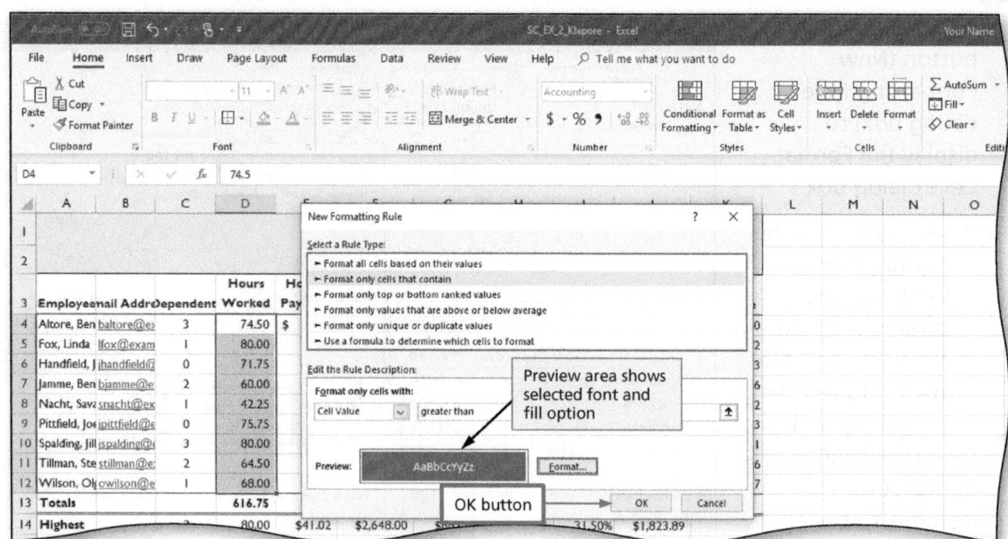

Figure 2–48

- Click OK (New Formatting Rule dialog box) to assign the conditional format to the selected range.
- Click anywhere in the worksheet, such as cell A17, to deselect the current range (Figure 2–49).

Q&A

What should I do if I make a mistake setting up a rule?
If after you have applied the conditional formatting you realize you made a mistake when creating a rule, select the cell(s) with the rule you want to edit, click the Conditional Formatting button (Home tab | Styles group), select the rule you want to edit, and then click either the Edit Rule button (to edit the selected rule) or the Delete Rule button (to delete the selected rule).

How can I delete a conditional formatting rule?
If you no longer want a conditional formatting rule applied to a cell, select the cell or cells, click the Conditional Formatting button (Home tab | Styles group), click Clear Rules, and then select Clear Rules from Selected Cells.

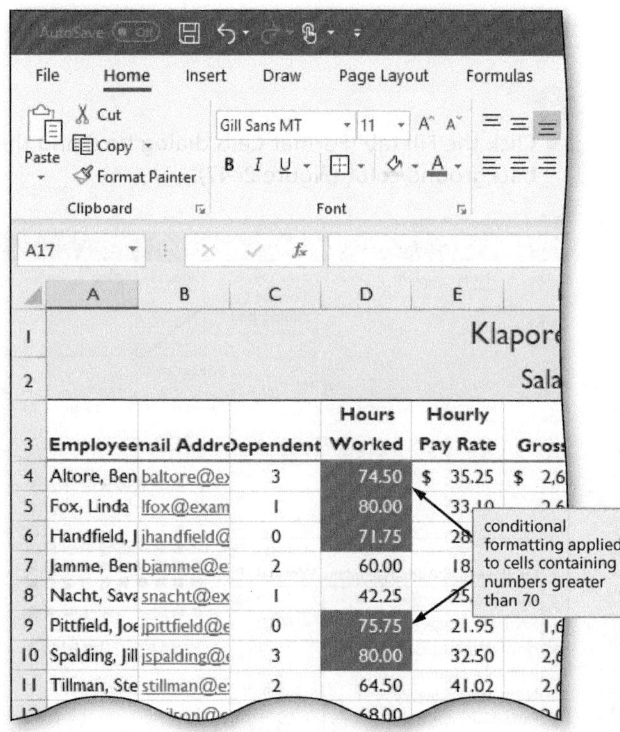

Figure 2–49

Conditional Formatting Operators

As shown in the New Formatting Rule dialog box, when the selected rule type is “Format only the cells that contain,” the second text box in the Edit the Rule Description area allows you to select a relational operator, such as greater than, to use in the condition. The eight different relational operators from which you can choose for conditional formatting are summarized in Table 2–5.

Table 2–5 Summary of Conditional Formatting Relational Operators

Relational Operator	Formatting will be applied if...
between	cell value is between two numbers
not between	cell value is not between two numbers
equal to	cell value is equal to a number
not equal to	cell value is not equal to a number
greater than	cell value is greater than a number
less than	cell value is less than a number
greater than or equal to	cell value is greater than or equal to a number
less than or equal to	cell value is less than or equal to a number

Changing Column Width and Row Height

You can change the width of the columns or height of the rows at any time to make the worksheet easier to read or to ensure that an entry fits properly in a cell. By default, all of the columns in a blank worksheet have a width of 8.43 characters, or 64 pixels. This value may change depending on the theme applied to the workbook. For example, when you applied the Gallery theme to the workbook in this module, the default width of the columns changed to 8.38 characters. A **character** is defined as a letter, number, symbol, or punctuation mark. An average of 8.43 characters in 11-point Calibri font (the default font used by Excel) will fit in a cell.

The default row height in a blank worksheet is 15 points (or 20 pixels), which easily fits the 11-point default font. Recall from Module 1 that a point is equal to 1/72 of an inch. Thus, 15 points is equal to about 1/5 of an inch.

Another measure of the height and width of cells is pixels. A **pixel**, which is short for picture element, is a an individual point of color on a display screen or printout. The size of the dot is based on your screen's resolution. At the resolution of 1366 × 768, for example, 1366 pixels appear across the screen and 768 pixels appear down the screen for a total of 1,049,088 pixels. It is these 1,049,088 pixels that form the font and other items you see on the screen.

In addition to changing column width and row heights, you also can hide columns and rows so that they temporarily do not display. The values in the columns and rows will remain, but they will not display on the screen. To hide a column or row, right-click the column letter or row number and then click hide. To unhide a hidden column or row, select the columns to the left and right of the hidden column, right click the column heading, and then click Unhide. To unhide a hidden row, select the rows above and below the hidden row, right click the row numbers, and then click Unhide.

BTW
Hidden Rows and Columns
For some people, trying to unhide a range of columns using the mouse can be frustrating. An alternative is to use the keyboard: select the columns to the right and left of the hidden columns and then press CTRL+SHIFT+) (RIGHT PARENTHESIS). To use the keyboard to hide a range of columns, press CTRL+0 (zero). You also can use the keyboard to unhide a range of rows by selecting the rows immediately above and below the hidden rows and then pressing CTRL+SHIFT+((LEFT PARENTHESIS). To use the keyboard to hide a range of rows, press CTRL+9.

To Change Column Width

When changing the column width, you can set the width manually or you can instruct Excel to size the column to best fit. **Best fit** is an Excel feature that automatically increases or decreases the width of a column so that the widest entry will fit. ***Why?*** *Sometimes, you may prefer more or less white space in a column than best fit provides. To change the white space, Excel allows you to change column widths manually.*

When the format you assign to a cell causes the entry to exceed the width of a column, Excel changes the column width to best fit. If you do not assign a format to a cell or cells in a column, the column width will remain 8.43 characters. Recall from Module 1 that to set a column width to best fit, double-click the right boundary of the column heading above row 1. The following steps change the column widths.

- Drag through column headings A, B, and C above row 1 to select the columns.
- Point to the boundary on the right side of column heading C to cause the pointer to become a split double arrow (Figure 2–50).

Q&A What if I want to make a large change to the column width?

If you want to increase or decrease column width significantly, you can right-click a column heading and then use the Column Width command on the shortcut menu to change the column's width. To use this command, however, you must select one or more entire columns.

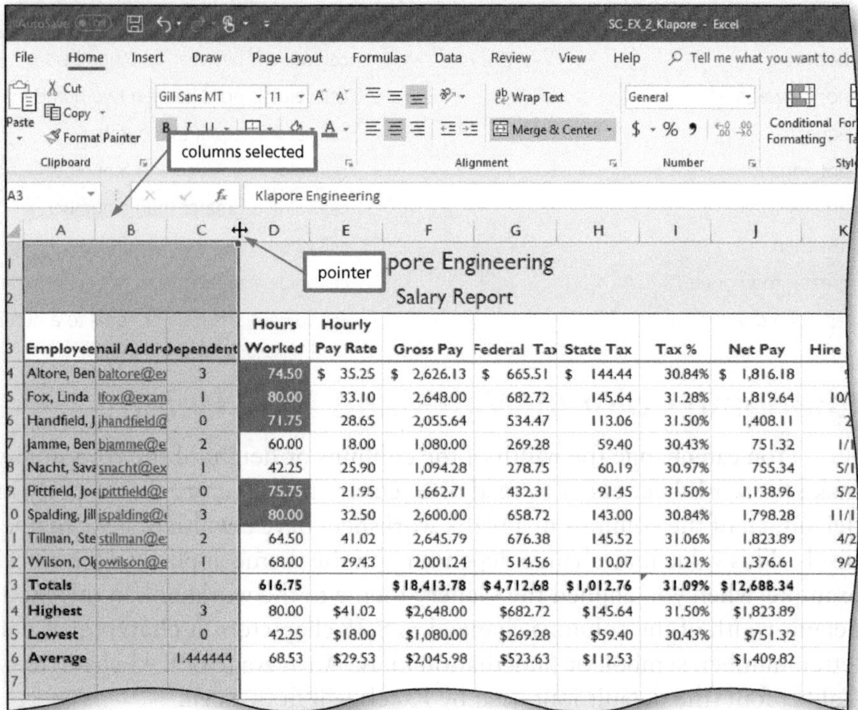

Figure 2–50

2

- Double-click the right boundary of column heading C to change the width of the selected columns to best fit.
- Point to the right boundary of the column H heading above row 1.
- When the pointer changes to a split double arrow, drag until the ScreenTip indicates Width: 10.38 (88 pixels). Do not release the mouse button (Figure 2–51).

Q&A What happens if I change the column width to zero (0)?

If you decrease the column width to 0, the column is hidden. Hiding cells is a technique you can use to hide data that might not be relevant to a particular report. To instruct Excel to display a hidden column, position the mouse pointer to the right of the column heading boundary where the hidden column is located and then drag to the right.

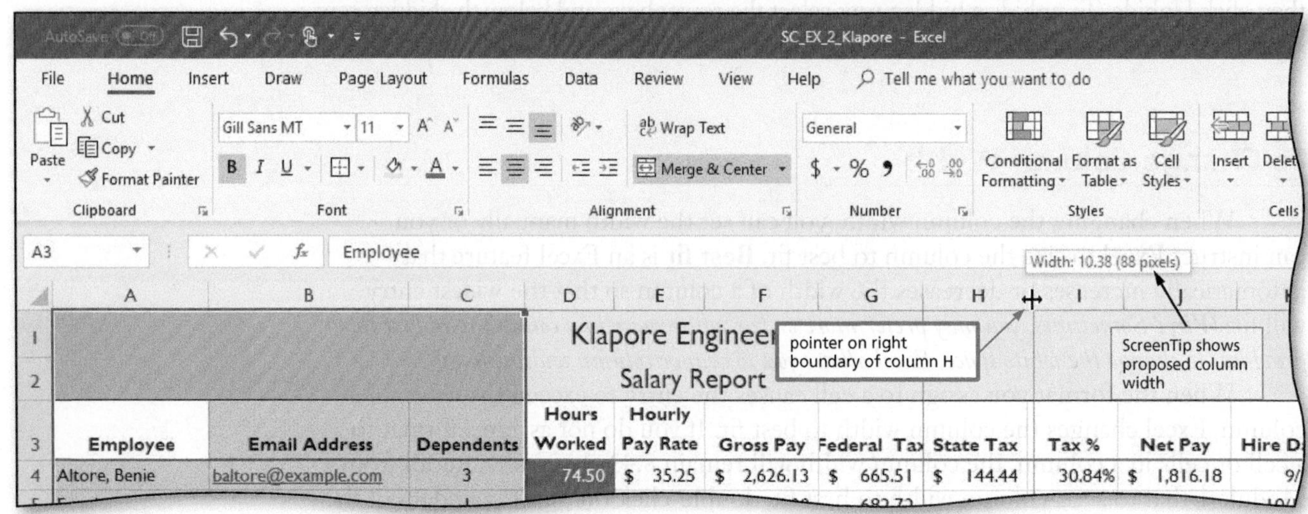

Figure 2–51

3

- Release the mouse button to change the column width.
- Click the column D heading above row 1 to select the column.
- While holding down CTRL, click the column E heading and then the column I heading above row 1 so that nonadjacent columns are selected.
- Point to the boundary on the right side of the column I heading above row 1.
- Drag until the ScreenTip indicates Width: 10.50 (89 pixels). Do not release the mouse button (Figure 2–52).

columns selected

Width: 10.50 (89 pixels)

ScreenTip shows proposed column widths

Figure 2–52

- Release the mouse button to change the column widths.
- Click the column F heading and drag to select the column G heading.
- While holding down CTRL, click the column J heading and drag to select the column K heading above row 1 so that nonadjacent columns are selected.
- Drag the right boundary of column G until the ScreenTip indicates Width: 11.13 (94 pixels). Release the mouse button to change the column widths.
- Click anywhere in the worksheet, such as cell A17, to deselect the columns (Figure 2–53).

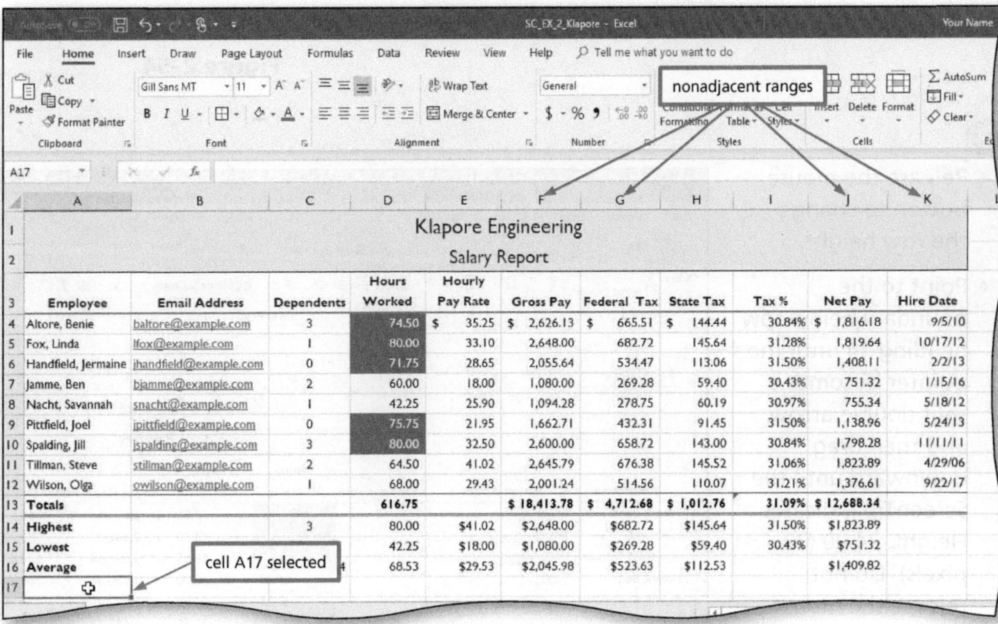

Figure 2–53

Other Ways

1. Click column heading or drag through multiple column headings, right-click selected column, click Column Width on shortcut menu, enter desired column width, click OK

To Change Row Height

Why? You also can increase or decrease the height of a row manually to improve the appearance of the worksheet. When you increase the font size of a cell entry, such as the title in cell A1, Excel increases the row height to best fit so that it can display the characters properly. Recall that Excel did this earlier when you entered multiple lines in a cell in row 3, and when you changed the cell style of the worksheet title and subtitle. The following steps improve the appearance of the worksheet by increasing the height of row 3 to 39.00 points and increasing the height of row 14 to 24.00 points.

- Point to the boundary below row heading 3 until the pointer becomes a split double arrow.
- Drag down until the ScreenTip indicates Height: 39.00 (52 pixels). Do not release the mouse button (Figure 2–54).

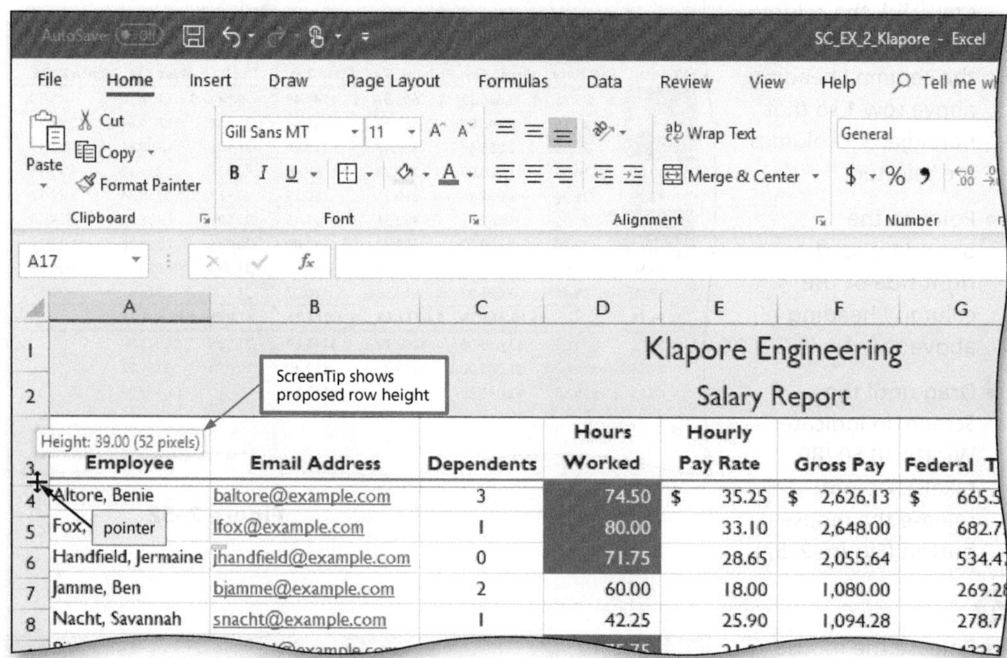

Figure 2–54

- Release the mouse button to change the row height.
- Point to the boundary below row heading 14 until the pointer becomes a split double arrow and then drag downward until the ScreenTip indicates Height: 24.00 (32 pixels). Do not release the mouse button (Figure 2–55).

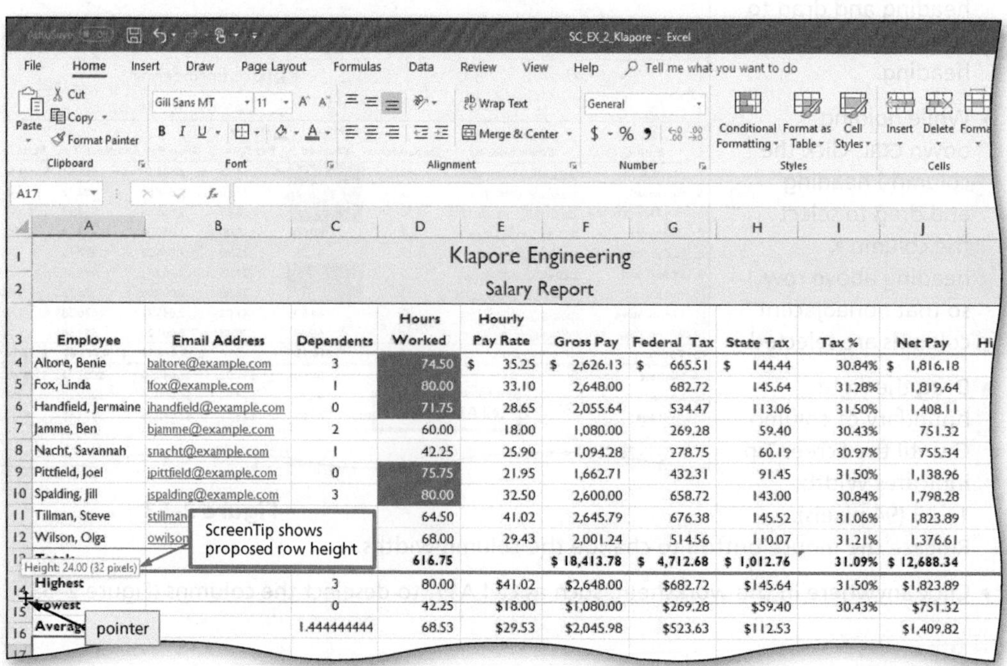

Figure 2–55

3

- **Release the mouse button to change the row height.**
- **Click anywhere in the worksheet, such as cell A17, to deselect the current cell (Figure 2–56).**

Q&A

Can I hide a row?

Yes. As with column widths, when you decrease the row height to 0, the row is hidden. To instruct Excel to display a hidden row, position the pointer just below the row heading boundary where the row is hidden and then drag downward. To set a row height to best fit, double-click the bottom boundary of the row heading. You also can hide and unhide rows by right-clicking the row or column heading and selecting the option to hide or unhide the cells.

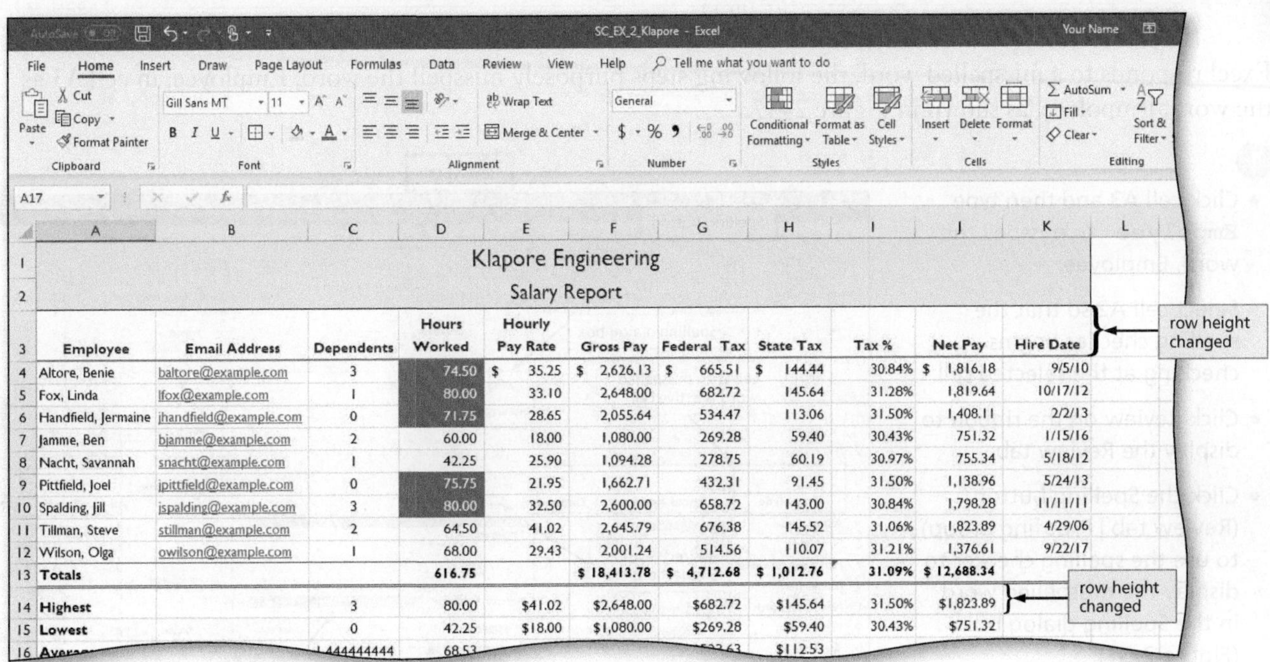

Figure 2–56

Other Ways

1. Right-click row heading or drag through multiple row headings, right-click selected heading, click Row Height on shortcut menu, enter desired row height, click OK

Break Point: If you want to take a break, this is a good place to do so. Be sure to save the SC_EX_2-Klapore file again and then you can exit Excel. To resume later, start Excel, open the file called SC_EX_2_Klapore, and continue following the steps from this location forward.

Checking Spelling

Excel includes a **spelling checker** you can use to check a worksheet for spelling errors. The spelling checker looks for spelling errors by comparing words on the worksheet against words contained in its standard dictionary. If you often use specialized terms that are not in the standard dictionary, you may want to add them to a custom dictionary using the Spelling dialog box. When the spelling checker finds a word that is not in either dictionary, it displays the word in the Spelling dialog box. You then can correct it if it is misspelled.

CONSIDER THIS

Does the spelling checker catch all spelling mistakes?

While Excel's spelling checker is a valuable tool, it is not infallible. You should proofread your workbook carefully by pointing to each word and saying it aloud as you point to it. Be mindful of misused words such as its and it's, through and though, your and you're, and to and too. Nothing undermines a good impression more than a professional report with misspelled words.

To Check Spelling on the Worksheet

Why? Everything in a worksheet should be checked to make sure there are no spelling errors. To illustrate how Excel responds to a misspelled word, the following steps purposely misspell the word, Employee, in cell A3 as the word, Empolyee, as shown in Figure 2–57.

- Click cell A3 and then type **`Empolyee`** to misspell the word, Employee.
- Select cell A2 so that the spelling checker begins checking at the selected cell.
- Click Review on the ribbon to display the Review tab.
- Click the Spelling button (Review tab | Proofing group) to use the spelling checker to display the misspelled word in the Spelling dialog box (Figure 2–57).

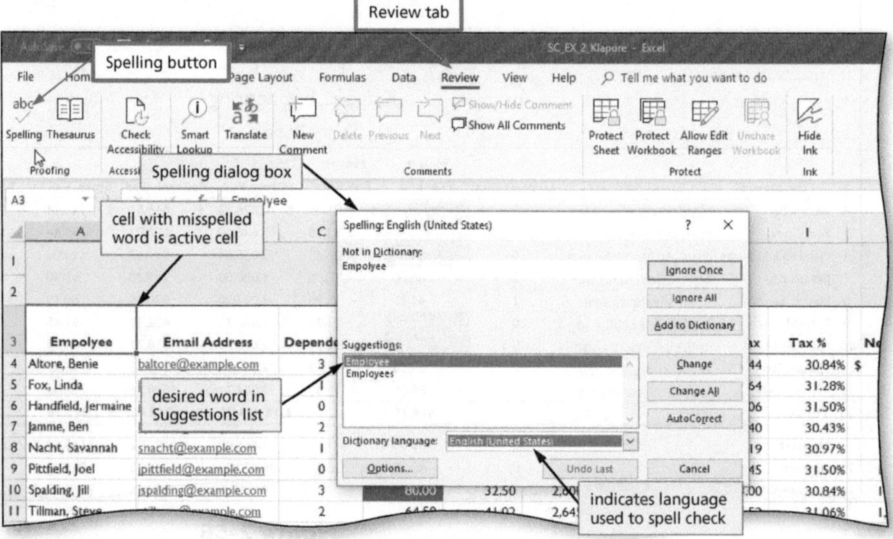

Figure 2–57

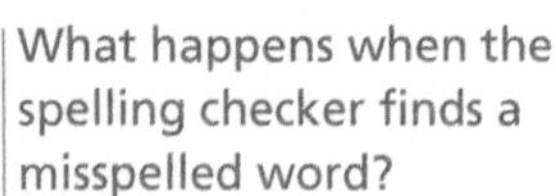

Q&A What happens when the spelling checker finds a misspelled word?

When the spelling checker identifies that a cell contains a word not in its standard or custom dictionary, it selects that cell as the active cell and displays the Spelling dialog box. The Spelling dialog box displays the word that was not found in the dictionary and offers a list of suggested corrections (Figure 2–58).

- Verify that the word highlighted in the Suggestion area is correct.
- Click the Change button (Spelling dialog box) to change the misspelled word to the correct word (Figure 2–58).
- Click the Close button to close the Spelling dialog box.
- If a Microsoft Excel dialog box is displayed, click OK.

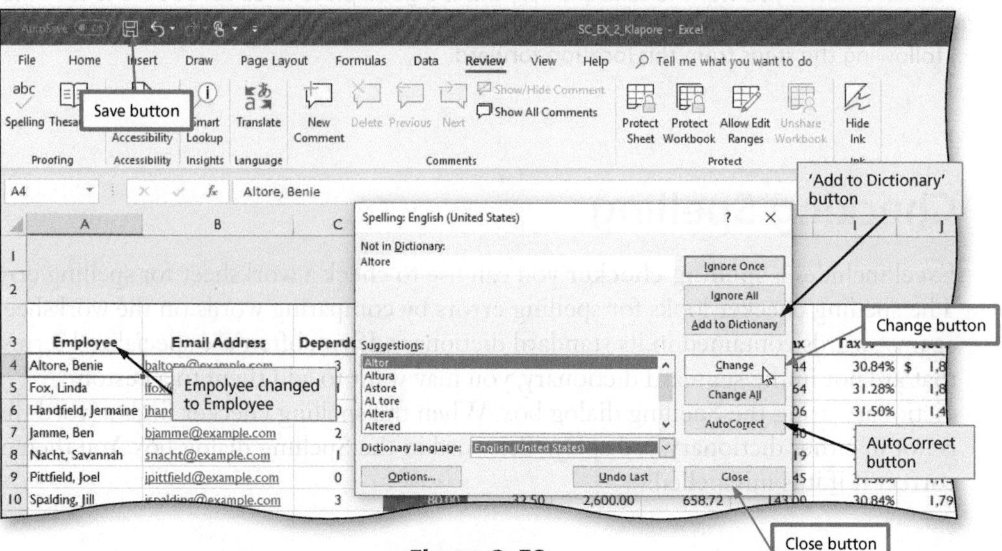

Figure 2–58

3
- Click anywhere in the worksheet, such as cell A17, to deselect the current cell.
- Display the Home tab.
- Save the workbook again on the same storage location with the same file name.

Q&A What other actions can I take in the Spelling dialog box?
If one of the words in the Suggestions list is correct, select it and then click the Change button. If none of the suggested words are correct, type the correct word in the 'Not in Dictionary' text box and then click the Change button. To change the word throughout the worksheet, click the Change All button instead of the Change button. To skip correcting the word, click the Ignore Once button. To have Excel ignore the word for the remainder of the worksheet, click the Ignore All button.

Other Ways

1. Press F7

Additional Spelling Checker Considerations

Consider these additional guidelines when using the spelling checker:

- To check the spelling of the text in a single cell, double-click the cell to make the formula bar active and then click the Spelling button (Review tab | Proofing group).
- If you select a single cell so that the formula bar is not active and then start the spelling checker, Excel checks the remainder of the worksheet, including notes and embedded charts.
- If you select a cell other than cell A1 before you start the spelling checker, Excel displays a dialog box when the spelling checker reaches the end of the worksheet, asking if you want to continue checking at the beginning.
- If you select a range of cells before starting the spelling checker, Excel checks the spelling of the words only in the selected range.
- To check the spelling of all the sheets in a workbook, right-click any sheet tab, click 'Select All Sheets' on the sheet tab shortcut menu, and then start the spelling checker.
- To add words to the dictionary, such as your last name, click the 'Add to Dictionary' button in the Spelling dialog box (shown in Figure 2–58) when Excel flags the word as not being in the dictionary.
- Click the AutoCorrect button (shown in Figure 2–58) to add the misspelled word and the correct version of the word to the AutoCorrect list. For example, suppose that you misspell the word, do, as the word, dox. When the spelling checker displays the Spelling dialog box with the correct word, do, in the Suggestions list, click the AutoCorrect button. Then, any time in the future that you type the word, dox, Excel will change it to the word, do.

BTW
Error Checking
Always take the time to check the formulas of a worksheet before submitting it to your supervisor. You can check formulas by clicking the Error Checking button (Formulas tab | Formula Auditing group). You also should test the formulas by employing data that tests the limits of formulas. Experienced spreadsheet specialists spend as much time testing a workbook as they do creating it, and they do so before placing the workbook into production.

BTW
Distributing a Workbook
Instead of printing and distributing a hard copy of a workbook, you can distribute the workbook electronically. Options include sending the workbook via email; posting it on cloud storage (such as OneDrive) and sharing the file with others; posting it on social media, a blog, or other website; and sharing a link associated with an online location of the workbook. You also can create and share a PDF or XPS image of the workbook, so that users can view the file in Acrobat Reader or XPS Viewer instead of in Excel.

Printing the Worksheet

Excel allows for a great deal of customization in how a worksheet appears when printed. For example, the margins on the page can be adjusted. A header or footer can be added to each printed page as well. A **header** is text and graphics that print at the top of each page. Similarly, a **footer** is text and graphics that print at the bottom of each page. When you insert a header or footer in a workbook, they can display the same on all pages, you can have a different header and footer on the first page of the workbook, or you can have different headers and footers on odd and even pages. With the header or footer area selected on the Header & Footer Tools Design tab, click the desired check box in the Options group. Excel also has the capability to alter the worksheet in Page Layout view. **Page Layout view** provides an accurate view of how a worksheet will look when printed, including headers and footers. The default view that you have worked in up until this point in the book is called Normal view.

To Change the Worksheet's Margins, Header, and Orientation in Page Layout View

The following steps change to Page Layout view, narrow the margins of the worksheet, change the header of the worksheet, and set the orientation of the worksheet to landscape. ***Why?*** *You may want the printed worksheet to fit on one page. You can do that by reducing the page margins and changing the page orientation to fit wider printouts across a sheet of paper. You can use the header to identify the content on each page.* **Margins** are the space between the page content and the edges of the page. The current worksheet is too wide for a single page and requires landscape orientation to fit on one page in a readable manner.

- Click the Page Layout button on the status bar to view the worksheet in Page Layout view (Figure 2–59).

Q&A What are the features of Page Layout view?

Page Layout view shows the worksheet divided into pages. A gray background separates each page. The white areas surrounding each page indicate the print margins. The top of each page includes a Header area, and the bottom of each page includes a Footer area. Page Layout view also includes rulers at the top and left margin of the page that assists you in placing objects on the page, such as charts and pictures.

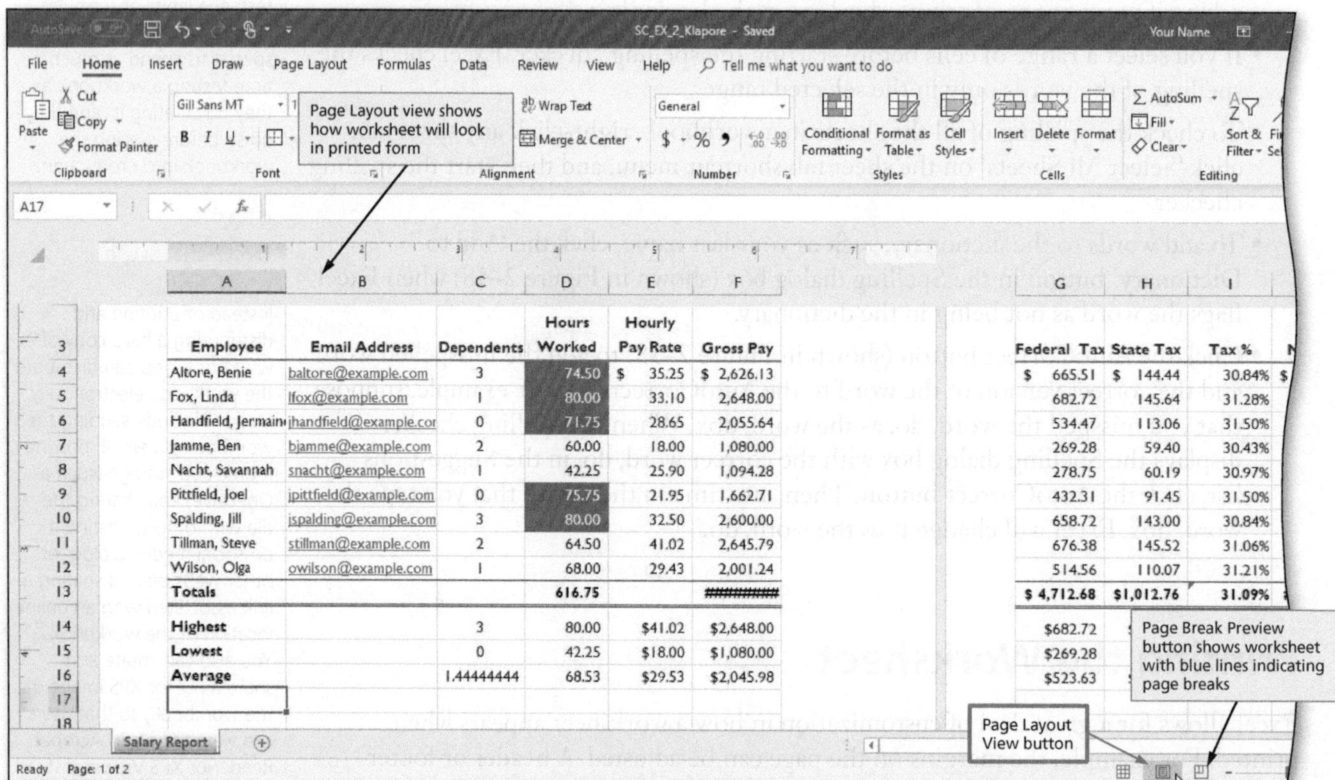

Figure 2–59

2

- Display the Page Layout tab.
- Click the Margins button (Page Layout tab | Page Setup group) to display the Margins gallery (Figure 2–60).

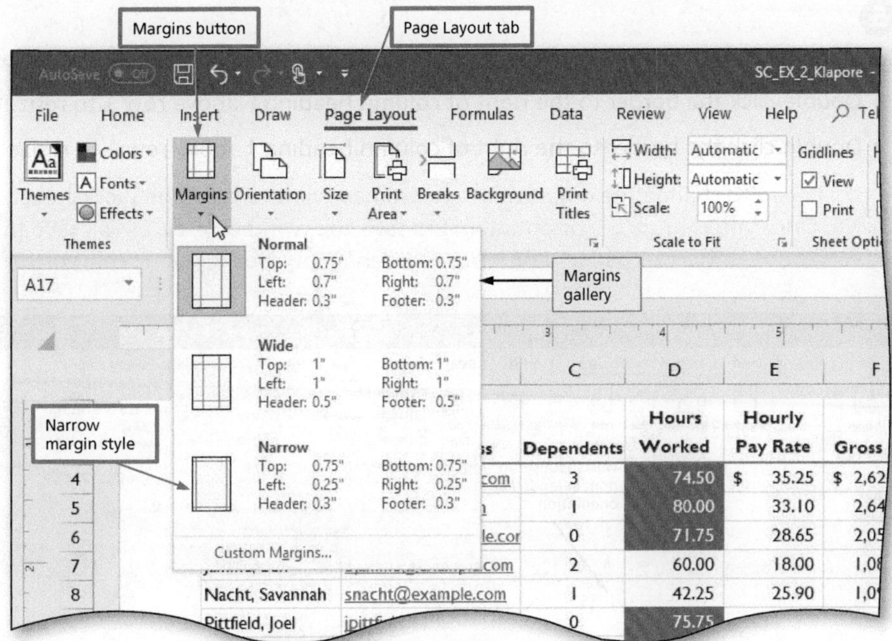

Figure 2–60

3

- Click Narrow in the Margins gallery to change the worksheet margins to the Narrow margin style.
- If necessary, scroll up to display the Header area.
- Click the center of the Header area above the worksheet title.
- Type **`Madelyn Samuels`** and then press ENTER. Type **`Chief Financial Officer`** to complete the worksheet header (Figure 2–61).

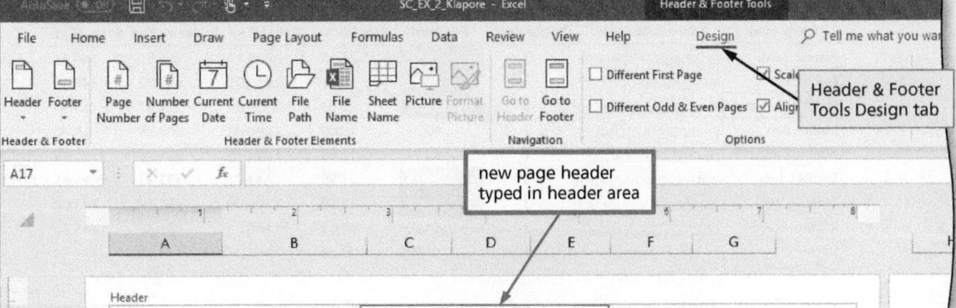

Figure 2–61

- If requested by your instructor, type your name instead of Madelyn Samuels.
- Select cell A6 to deselect the header.

Q&A What else can I place in a header?

You can add additional text, page number information, date and time information, the file path of the workbook, the file name of the workbook, the sheet name of the workbook, and pictures to a header.

4

- Display the Page Layout tab.
- Click the Orientation button (Page Layout tab | Page Setup group) to display the Orientation gallery (Figure 2–62).

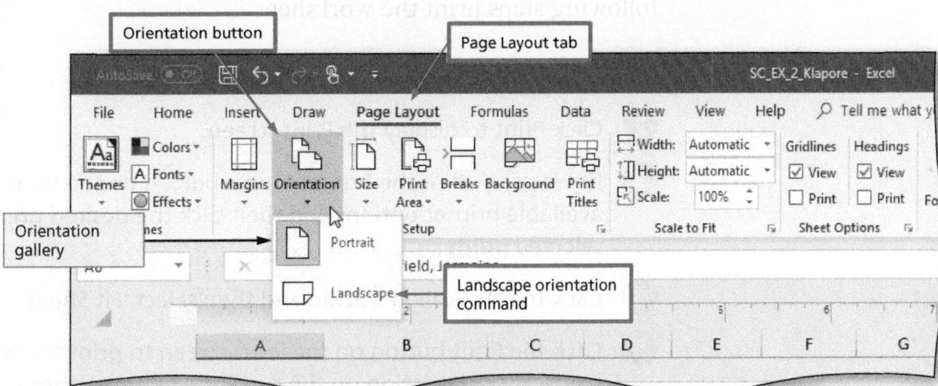

Figure 2–62

- Click Landscape in the Orientation gallery to change the worksheet's orientation to landscape.
- Double-click the border to the right of column heading F above row 1 to resize the column to best fit.
- Double-click the border to the right of column heading J above row 1 to resize the column to best fit (Figure 2–63).

Q&A | Do I need to change the orientation every time I want to print the worksheet?
No. Once you change the orientation and save the workbook, Excel will save the orientation setting for that workbook until you change it. When you open a new workbook, Excel sets the orientation to portrait.

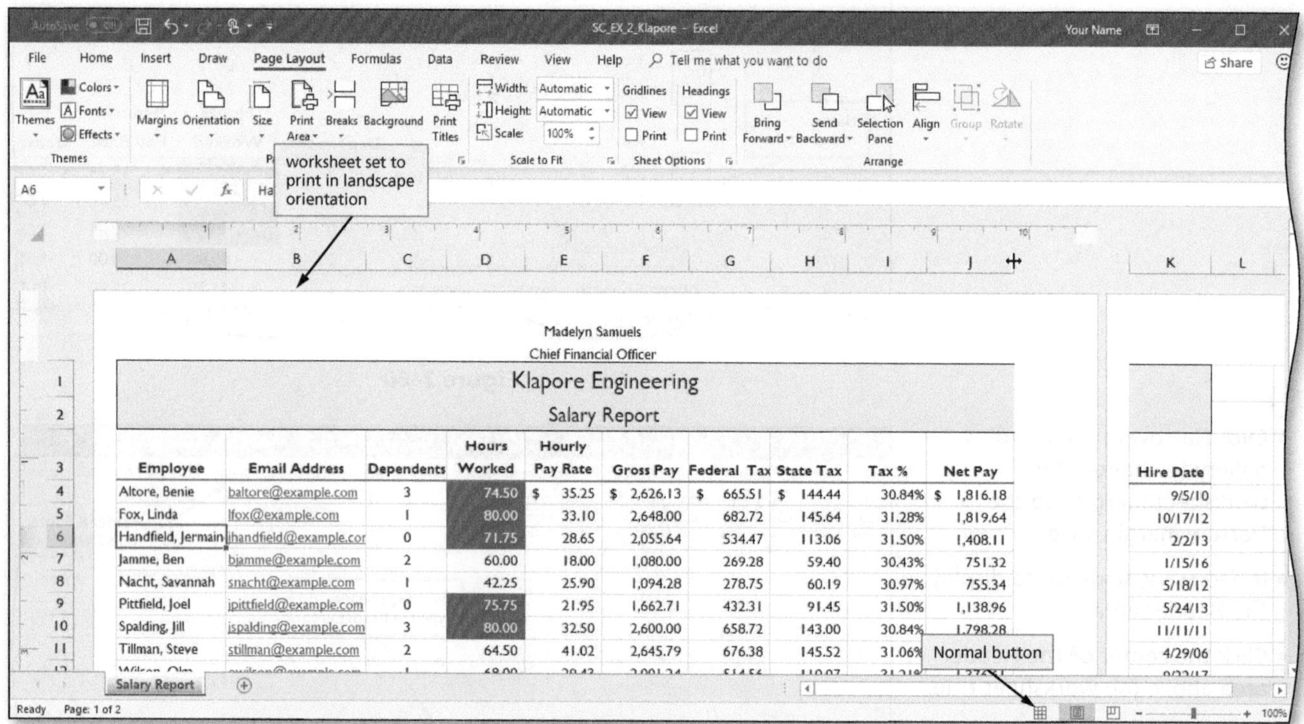

Figure 2–63

Other Ways

1. Click Page Setup Dialog Box Launcher (Page Layout tab | Page Setup group), click Page tab (Page Setup dialog box), click Portrait or Landscape, click OK

To Print a Worksheet

Excel provides multiple options for printing a worksheet. In the following sections, you first print the worksheet and then print a section of the worksheet. The following steps print the worksheet.

1. Click File on the ribbon to open Backstage view.
2. Click Print to display the Print screen.
3. If necessary, click the Printer Status button on the Print screen to display a list of available printer options and then click the desired printer to change the currently selected printer.
4. Click the No Scaling button and then select 'Fit Sheet on One Page' to select it.
5. Click the Print button on the Print screen to print the worksheet on one page in landscape orientation on the currently selected printer.

6 When the printer stops, retrieve the hard copy (Figure 2–64).

Madelyn Samuels
Chief Financial Officer

Klapore Engineering
Salary Report

Employee	Email Address	Dependents	Hours Worked	Hourly Pay Rate	Gross Pay	Federal Tax	State Tax	Tax %	Net Pay	Hire Date
Altore, Benie	baltore@example.com	3	74.50	$ 35.25	$ 2,626.13	$ 665.51	$ 144.44	30.84%	$ 1,816.18	9/5/10
Fox, Linda	lfox@example.com	1	80.00	33.10	2,648.00	682.72	145.64	31.28%	1,819.64	10/17/12
Handfield, Jermain	jhandfield@example.con	0	71.75	28.65	2,055.64	534.47	113.06	31.50%	1,408.11	2/2/13
Jamme, Ben	bjamme@example.com	2	60.00	18.00	1,080.00	269.28	59.40	30.43%	751.32	1/15/16
Nacht, Savannah	snacht@example.com	1	42.25	25.90	1,094.28	278.75	60.19	30.97%	755.34	5/18/12
Pittfield, Joel	jpittfield@example.com	0	75.75	21.95	1,662.71	432.31	91.45	31.50%	1,138.96	5/24/13
Spalding, Jill	jspalding@example.com	3	80.00	32.50	2,600.00	658.72	143.00	30.84%	1,798.28	11/11/11
Tillman, Steve	stillman@example.com	2	64.50	41.02	2,645.79	676.38	145.52	31.06%	1,823.89	4/29/06
Wilson, Olga	owilson@example.com	1	68.00	29.43	2,001.24	514.56	110.07	31.21%	1,376.61	9/22/17
Totals			**616.75**		**$18,413.78**	**$ 4,712.68**	**$1,012.76**	**31.09%**	**$12,688.34**	
Highest		3	80.00	$41.02	$2,648.00	$682.72	$145.64	31.50%	$1,823.89	
Lowest		0	42.25	$18.00	$1,080.00	$269.28	$59.40	30.43%	$751.32	
Average		1.444444444	68.53	$29.53	$2,045.98	$523.63	$112.53		$1,409.82	

Figure 2–64

To Print a Section of the Worksheet

You can print portions of the worksheet by selecting the range of cells to print and then clicking the Selection option button in the Print what area in the Print dialog box. ***Why?*** *To save paper, you only want to print the portion of the worksheet you need, instead of printing the entire worksheet.* The following steps print the range A3:F16.

- Select the range to print, cells A3:F16 in this case.
- Click File on the ribbon to open Backstage view.
- Click Print to display the Print screen.
- Click 'Print Active Sheets' in the Settings area (Print screen | Print list) to display a list of options that determine what Excel should print (Figure 2–65).

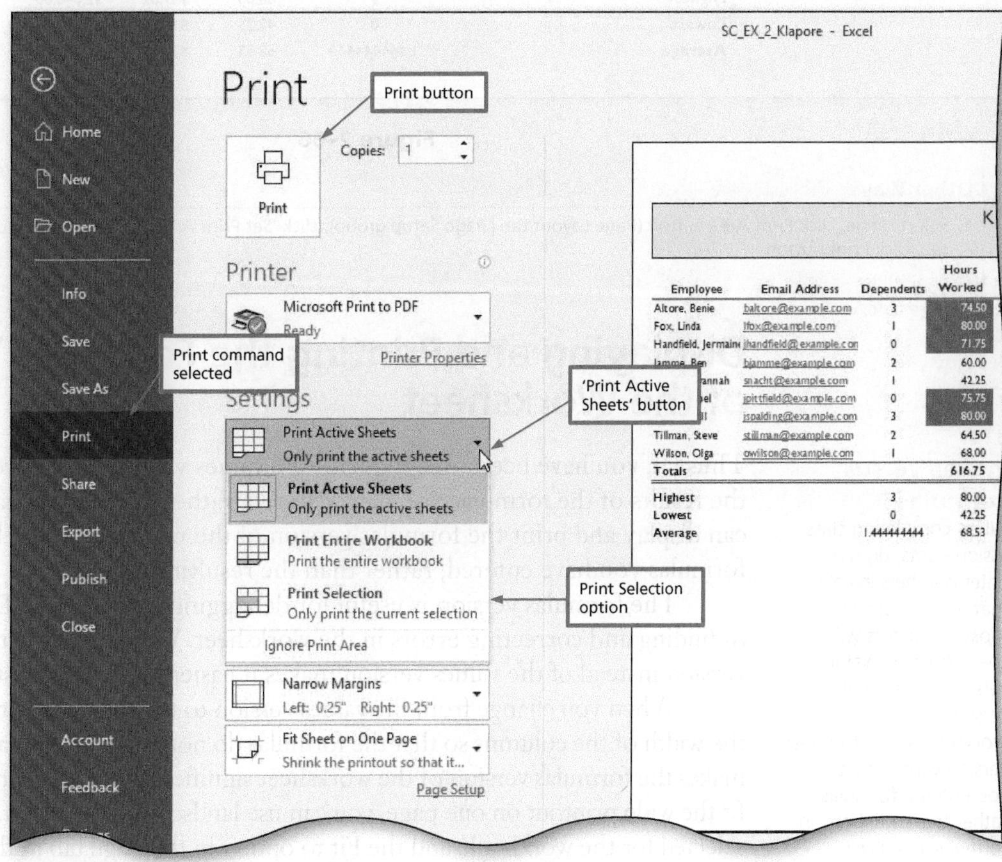

Figure 2–65

- Click Print Selection to instruct Excel to print only the selected range and display only the selected range in the preview area.
- Click the Print button in the Print screen to print the selected range of the worksheet on the currently selected printer (Figure 2–66).
- Click the Normal button on the status bar to return to Normal view.
- Click anywhere in the worksheet, such as cell A17, to deselect the range A3:F16.

Q&A What can I print?
Excel includes three options for selecting what to print (Figure 2–65). As shown in the previous steps, the Print Selection option instructs Excel to print the selected range. The 'Print Active Sheets' option instructs Excel to print the active worksheet (the worksheet currently on the screen) or selected worksheets. Finally, the 'Print Entire Workbook' option instructs Excel to print all of the worksheets in the workbook.

Madelyn Samuels
Chief Financial Officer

Employee	Email Address	Dependents	Hours Worked	Hourly Pay Rate	Gross Pay
Altore, Benie	baltore@example.com	3	74.50	$ 35.25	$ 2,626.13
Fox, Linda	lfox@example.com	1	80.00	33.10	2,648.00
Handfield, Jermain	jhandfield@example.con	0	71.75	28.65	2,055.64
Jamme, Ben	bjamme@example.com	2	60.00	18.00	1,080.00
Nacht, Savannah	snacht@example.com	1	42.25	25.90	1,094.28
Pittfield, Joel	jpittfield@example.com	0	75.75	21.95	1,662.71
Spalding, Jill	jspalding@example.com	3	80.00	32.50	2,600.00
Tillman, Steve	stillman@example.com	2	64.50	41.02	2,645.79
Wilson, Olga	owilson@example.com	1	68.00	29.43	2,001.24
Totals			**616.75**		**$18,413.78**
Highest		3	80.00	$41.02	$2,648.00
Lowest		0	42.25	$18.00	$1,080.00
Average		1.444444444	68.53	$29.53	$2,045.98

Figure 2–66

Other Ways

1. Select range, click Print Area button (Page Layout tab | Page Setup group), click 'Set Print Area', click File tab to open Backstage view, click Print tab, click Print button

Displaying and Printing the Formulas Version of the Worksheet

BTW
Values versus Formulas
When completing class assignments, do not enter numbers in cells that require formulas. Most instructors will check both the values version and formulas version of your worksheets. The formulas version verifies that you entered formulas, rather than numbers, in formula-based cells.

Thus far, you have been working with the values version of the worksheet, which shows the results of the formulas you have entered, rather than the actual formulas. Excel also can display and print the formulas version of the worksheet, which shows the actual formulas you have entered, rather than the resulting values.

The formulas version is useful for debugging a worksheet. **Debugging** is the process of finding and correcting errors in the worksheet. Viewing and printing the formulas version instead of the values version makes it easier to see any mistakes in the formulas.

When you change from the values version to the formulas version, Excel increases the width of the columns so that the formulas do not overflow into adjacent cells, which makes the formulas version of the worksheet significantly wider than the values version. To fit the wide printout on one page, you can use landscape orientation, which already has been selected for the workbook, and the Fit to option in the Page tab in the Page Setup dialog box.

To Display the Formulas in the Worksheet and Fit the Printout on One Page

The following steps change the view of the worksheet from the values version to the formulas version of the worksheet and then print the formulas version on one page. ***Why?*** *Printing the formulas in the worksheet can help you verify that your formulas are correct and that the worksheet displays the correct calculations.*

1

- Press CTRL+ACCENT MARK (`) to display the worksheet with formulas.
- Click the right horizontal scroll arrow until column K appears (Figure 2–67).

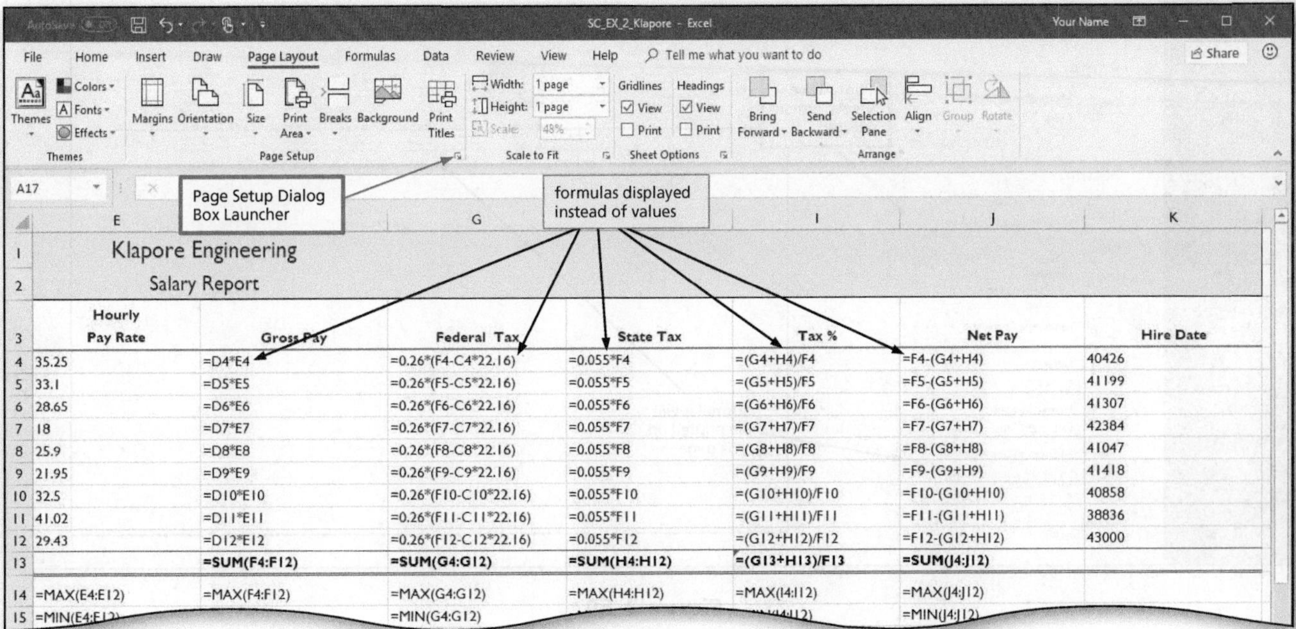

Figure 2–67

2

- Click the Page Setup Dialog Box Launcher (Page Layout tab | Page Setup group) to display the Page Setup dialog box (Figure 2–68).
- If necessary, click Landscape in the Orientation area in the Page tab to select it.
- If necessary, click the Fit to option button in the Scaling area to select it.

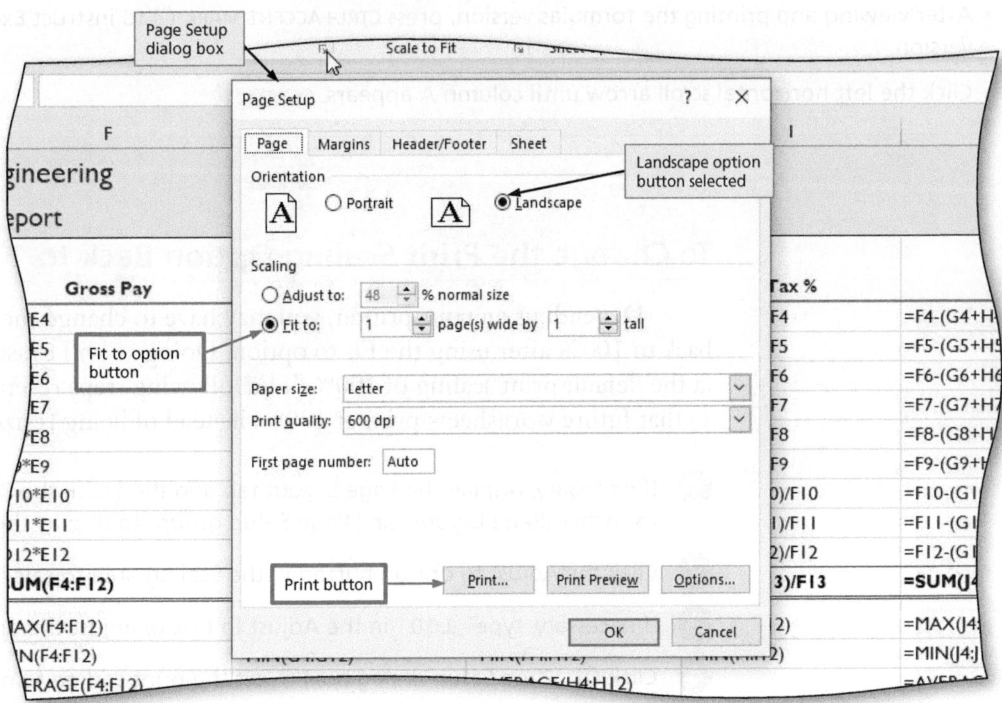

Figure 2–68

- Click the Print button (Page Setup dialog box) to open the Print screen in Backstage view. In Backstage view, select the Print Selection button in the Settings area of the Print gallery and then click Print Active Sheets (Figure 2–69).
- Click the Print button to print the worksheet.

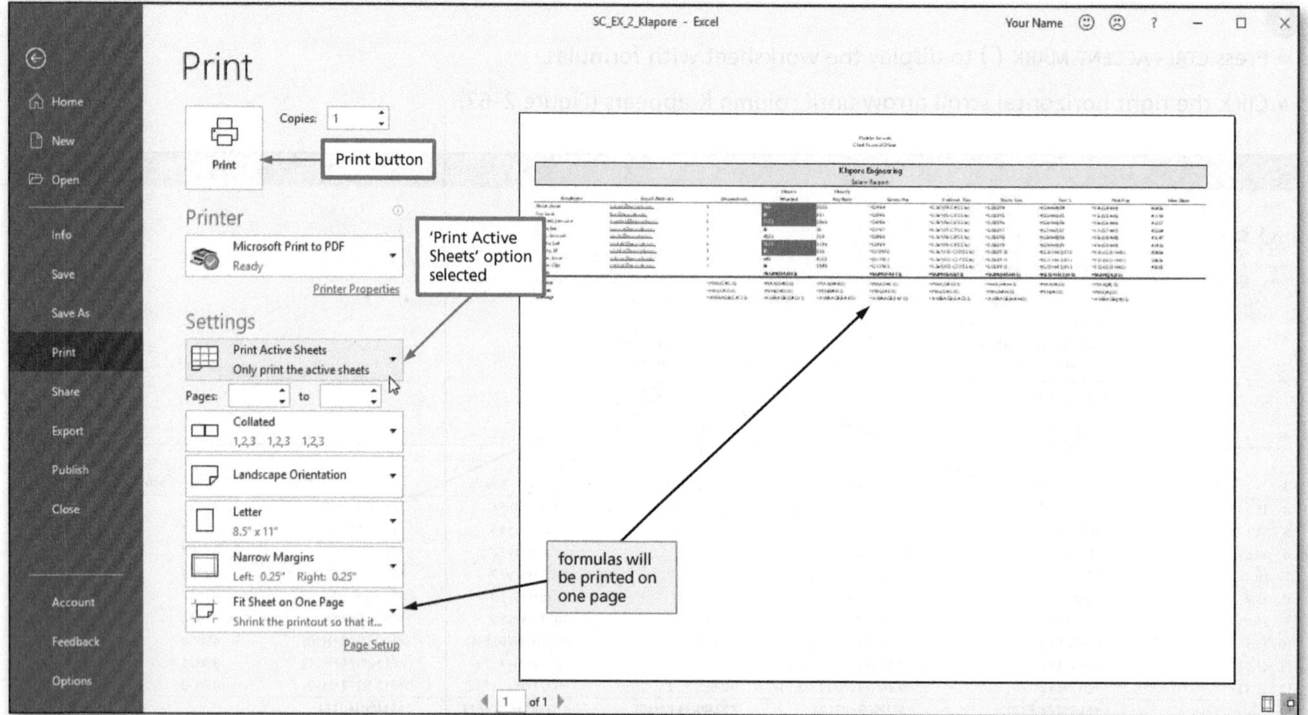

Figure 2–69

- After viewing and printing the formulas version, press CTRL+ACCENT MARK (`) to instruct Excel to display the values version.
- Click the left horizontal scroll arrow until column A appears.

To Change the Print Scaling Option Back to 100%

Depending on your printer, you may have to change the Print Scaling option back to 100% after using the Fit to option. Doing so will cause the worksheet to print at the default print scaling of 100%. The following steps reset the Print Scaling option so that future worksheets print at 100%, instead of being resized to print on one page.

1. If necessary, display the Page Layout tab and then click the Page Setup Dialog Box Launcher (Page Layout tab | Page Setup group) to display the Page Setup dialog box.
2. Click the Adjust to option button in the Scaling area to select the Adjust to setting.
3. If necessary, type `100` in the Adjust to box to adjust the print scaling to 100%.
4. Click OK (Page Setup dialog box) to set the print scaling to normal.

5 Display the Home tab.

6 Save the workbook again on the same storage location with the same file name.

7 If desired, sign out of your Microsoft account.

8 sam Exit Excel.

Q&A What is the purpose of the Adjust to box in the Page Setup dialog box?
The Adjust to box allows you to specify the percentage of reduction or enlargement in the printout of a worksheet. The default percentage is 100%. When you click the Fit to option button, this percentage changes to the percentage required to fit the printout on one page.

Summary

In this module you have learned how to enter formulas, calculate an average, find the highest and lowest numbers in a range, verify formulas using Range Finder, add borders, align text, format numbers, change column widths and row heights, and add conditional formatting to a range of numbers. In addition, you learned how to use the spelling checker to identify misspelled words in a worksheet, print a section of a worksheet, and display and print the formulas version of the worksheet using the Fit to option.

CONSIDER THIS: PLAN AHEAD

What decisions will you need to make when creating workbooks in the future?

1. Determine the workbook structure.
   a) Determine the formulas and functions you will need for your workbook.
   b) Sketch a layout of your data and functions.
2. Create the worksheet.
   a) Enter the titles, subtitles, and headings.
   b) Enter the data, desired functions, and formulas.
3. Format the worksheet.
   a) Determine the theme for the worksheet.
   b) Format the titles, subtitles, and headings using styles.
   c) Format the totals, minimums, maximums, and averages.
   d) Format the numbers and text.
   e) Resize columns and rows.

Apply Your Knowledge

Reinforce the skills and apply the concepts you learned in this module.

Cost Analysis Worksheet

Note: To complete this assignment, you will be required to use the Data Files. Please contact your instructor for information about accessing the Data Files.

Instructions: Start Excel. Open the workbook called SC_EX_2-1.xlsx, which is located in the Data Files. The workbook you open contains information about vehicles driven for Prontix Courier Services. You are to enter and copy formulas and functions and apply formatting to the worksheet in order to analyze the costs associated with a bus company's fleet of vehicles, as shown in Figure 2–70.

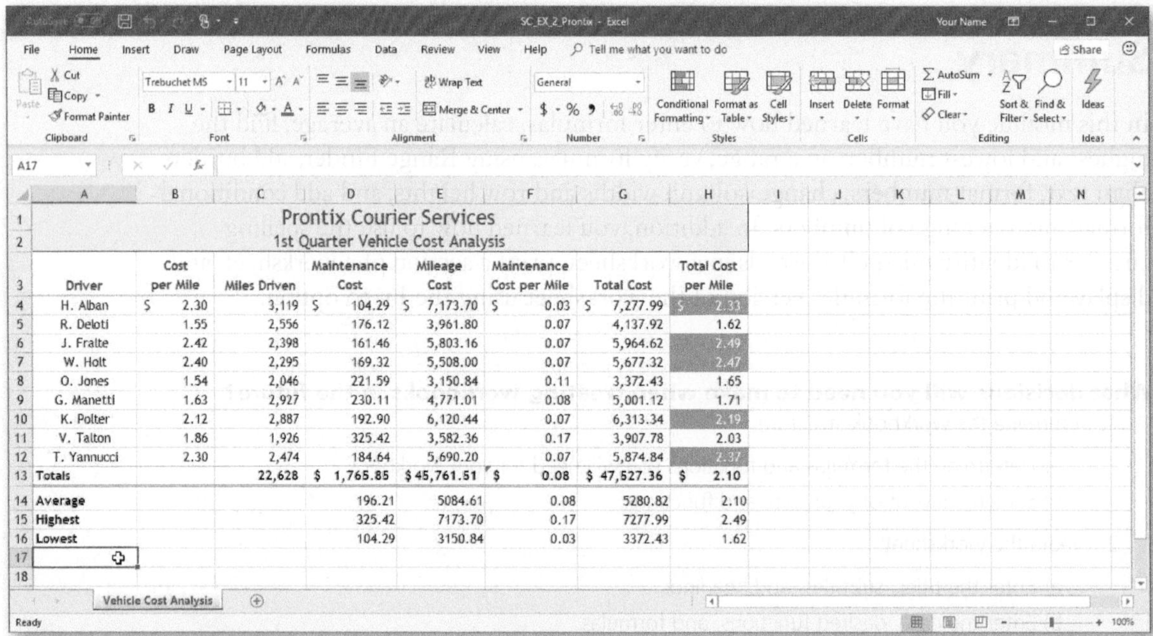

Prontix Courier Services							
1st Quarter Vehicle Cost Analysis							
Driver	Cost per Mile	Miles Driven	Maintenance Cost	Mileage Cost	Maintenance Cost per Mile	Total Cost	Total Cost per Mile
H. Alban	$ 2.30	3,119	$ 104.29	$ 7,173.70	$ 0.03	$ 7,277.99	$ 2.33
R. Deloti	1.55	2,556	176.12	3,961.80	0.07	4,137.92	1.62
J. Fralte	2.42	2,398	161.46	5,803.16	0.07	5,964.62	2.49
W. Holt	2.40	2,295	169.32	5,508.00	0.07	5,677.32	2.47
O. Jones	1.54	2,046	221.59	3,150.84	0.11	3,372.43	1.65
G. Manetti	1.63	2,927	230.11	4,771.01	0.08	5,001.12	1.71
K. Polter	2.12	2,887	192.90	6,120.44	0.07	6,313.34	2.19
V. Talton	1.86	1,926	325.42	3,582.36	0.17	3,907.78	2.03
T. Yannucci	2.30	2,474	184.64	5,690.20	0.07	5,874.84	2.37
Totals		22,628	$ 1,765.85	$ 45,761.51	$ 0.08	$ 47,527.36	$ 2.10
Average			196.21	5084.61	0.08	5280.82	2.10
Highest			325.42	7173.70	0.17	7277.99	2.49
Lowest			104.29	3150.84	0.03	3372.43	1.62

Figure 2–70

Perform the following tasks:

1. Use the following formulas in cells E4, F4, G4, and H4:
   Mileage Cost (cell E4) = Cost per Mile * Miles Driven or = B4 * C4
   Maintenance Cost per Mile (cell F4) = Maintenance Cost/Miles Driven or = D4/C4
   Total Cost (cell G4) = Maintenance Cost + Mileage Cost or = D4 + E4
   Total Cost per Mile (cell H4) = Total Cost / Miles Driven or = G4 / C4
   Use the fill handle to copy the three formulas in the range E4:H4 to the range E5:H12.
2. Determine totals for the miles driven, maintenance cost, mileage cost, and total cost in row 13. Copy the formula in cell F12 to F13 to assign the formula in cell F12 to F13 in the total line. Copy the formula in cell H12 to H13 to assign the formula in cell H12 to H13 in the total line. Reapply the Total cell style to cells F13 and H13.
3. In the range D14:D16, determine the average value, highest value, and lowest value, respectively, for the values in the range D4:D12. Use the fill handle to copy the three functions to the range E14:H16.
4. Format the worksheet as follows:
   a. Change the workbook theme to Berlin by using the Themes button (Page Layout tab | Themes group)
   b. Cell A1 — change to Title cell style
   c. Cell A2 — change to Title cell style and a font size of 14

d. Cells A1:A2 — Rose, Accent 6, Lighter 80% fill color and add outside borders
e. Cells B4, D4:H4, and D13:H13 — accounting number format with two decimal places and fixed dollar signs by using the 'Accounting Number Format' button (Home tab | Number group)
f. Cells B5:B12, and D5:H12 — comma style format with two decimal places by using the Comma Style button (Home tab | Number group)
g. Cells C4:C13 — comma style format with no decimal places.
h. Cells H4:H12 — apply conditional formatting so that cells with a value greater than 2.15 appear with an orange background color and white font

5. If necessary increase the size of any columns that do not properly display data.
6. Switch to Page Layout view. Enter your name, course, and any other information, as specified by your instructor, in the header area.
7. Preview and print the worksheet in landscape orientation so that it appears on one page. Save the workbook using the file name, SC_EX_2_Prontix.
8. Use Range Finder to verify the formula in cell H13.
9. Print the range A3:D16. Press CTRL+ACCENT MARK (`) to change the display from the values version of the worksheet to the formulas version. Print the formulas version in landscape orientation on one page by using the Fit to option in the Page tab in the Page Setup dialog box. Press CTRL+ACCENT MARK (`) to change the display of the worksheet back to the values version. Close the workbook without saving it.
10. Submit the workbook in the format specified by your instructor and exit Excel.
11. Besides adding a header to your document, can you think of anything else that could be added when printing the worksheet?

Extend Your Knowledge

Extend the skills you learned in this module and experiment with new skills. You may need to use Help to complete the assignment.

Creating a Customer Tracking Worksheet for Kalto Security Outlet

Note: To complete this assignment, you will be required to use the Data Files. Please contact your instructor for information about accessing the Data Files.

Instructions: Start Excel. Open the workbook SC_EX_2-2.xlsx, which is located in the Data Files. The workbook you open contains vendor information for Kalto Security Outlet. You are to apply Flash Fill and four types of conditional formatting to cells in a worksheet.

Perform the following tasks:

1. Add the account identifiers to the cells in the range E4:E16. The account identifier is determined by taking the first initial of the vendor's first name, the first initial of the vendor's last name, followed by the entire vendor number. For example, the account identifier for John Abrahms is JA28689. Continue entering two or three account identifiers, then use Flash Fill to complete the remaining cells. Add the thick bottom border back to cell E16 (Figure 2–71).
2. Select the range F4:F16. Click the Conditional Formatting button (Home tab | Styles group) and then click New Rule on the Conditional Formatting menu. Select 'Format only top or bottom ranked values' in the Select a Rule Type area (New Formatting Rule dialog box).
3. If requested by your instructor, enter 35 in the Edit the Rule Description (New Formatting Rule dialog box) area, and then click the '% of the selected range' check box to select it.
4. Click the Format button, and choose a light orange background on the Fill tab to assign this conditional format. Click OK in each dialog box and view the worksheet.

Continued >

Extend Your Knowledge *continued*

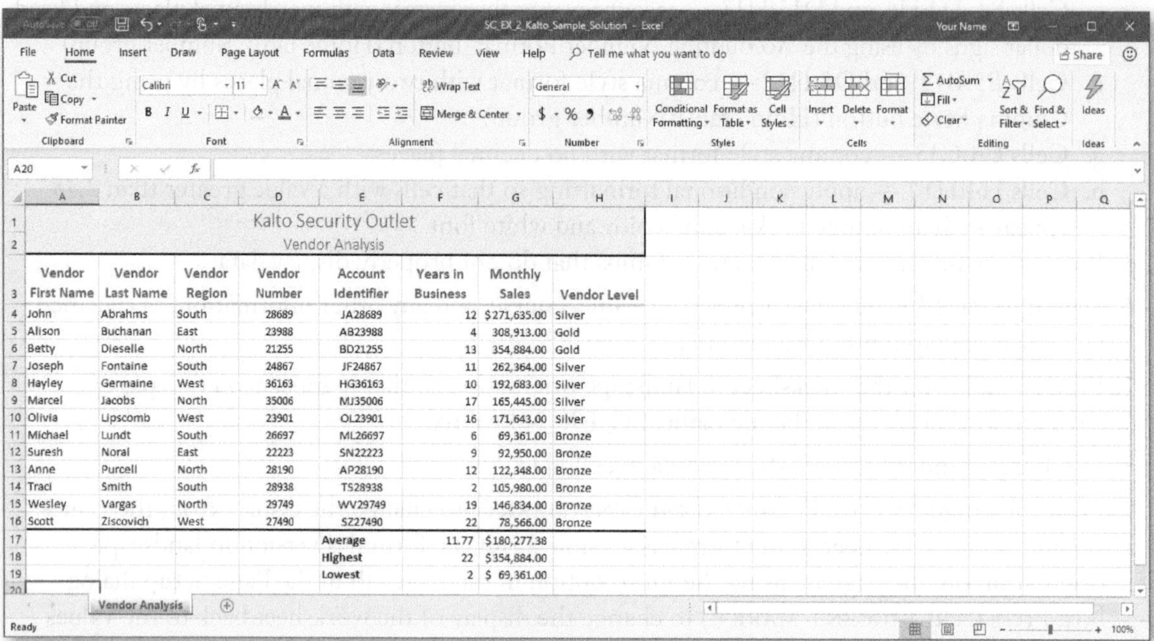

Vendor First Name	Vendor Last Name	Vendor Region	Vendor Number	Account Identifier	Years in Business	Monthly Sales	Vendor Level
John	Abrahms	South	28689	JA28689	12	$271,635.00	Silver
Alison	Buchanan	East	23988	AB23988	4	308,913.00	Gold
Betty	Dieselle	North	21255	BD21255	13	354,884.00	Gold
Joseph	Fontaine	South	24867	JF24867	11	262,364.00	Silver
Hayley	Germaine	West	36163	HG36163	10	192,683.00	Silver
Marcel	Jacobs	North	35006	MJ35006	17	165,445.00	Silver
Olivia	Lipscomb	West	23901	OL23901	16	171,643.00	Silver
Michael	Lundt	South	26697	ML26697	6	69,361.00	Bronze
Suresh	Noral	East	22223	SN22223	9	92,950.00	Bronze
Anne	Purcell	North	28190	AP28190	12	122,348.00	Bronze
Traci	Smith	South	28938	TS28938	2	105,980.00	Bronze
Wesley	Vargas	North	29749	WV29749	19	146,834.00	Bronze
Scott	Ziscovich	West	27490	SZ27490	22	78,566.00	Bronze
				Average	11.77	$180,277.38	
				Highest	22	$354,884.00	
				Lowest	2	$ 69,361.00	

Figure 2–71

5. With range F4:F16 selected, apply a conditional format to the range that uses a light red fill with dark red text to highlight cells with scores that are below average. *Hint:* Explore some of the preset conditional rules to assist with formatting this range of cells.
6. With range G4:G16 selected, apply a conditional format to the range that uses a light blue background to highlight cells that contain a value between 150,000 and 299,999.
7. With range H4:H16 selected, apply a conditional format to the range that uses a background color of your choice to highlight cells that contain Silver and another background color of your choice for cells that contain Gold. Silver, and a yellow background color to highlight the cells that contain Gold. (*Hint:* You need to apply two separate formats, one for Silver and one for Gold.)
8. Save the file with the file name, SC_EX_2_Kalto, and submit the revised workbook in the format specified by your instructor.
9. Why did you choose the background colors for the Silver and Gold loyalty levels in Step 7?

Expand Your World

Create a solution that uses cloud or web technologies by learning and investigating on your own from general guidance.

Four-Year College Cost Calculator

Instructions: You are to create an estimate of the cost for attending your college for four years. You decide to create the worksheet using Excel Online so that you can share it with your friends online.

Perform the following tasks:

1. If necessary, sign in to your Microsoft account on the web and start Excel Online.
2. Create a blank workbook. In the first worksheet, use column headings for each year of college (Freshman, Sophomore, Junior, and Senior). For the row headings, use your current expenses (such as car payment, rent, utilities, tuition, and food).

3. Enter expenses for each year based upon estimates you find by searching the web.
4. Calculate the total for each column. Also determine highest, lowest, and average values for each column.
5. Using the techniques taught in this module, create appropriate titles and format the worksheet accordingly.
6. Save the file with the file name, SC_EX_2_CollegeExpenses, and submit the workbook in the format specified by your instructor.
7. When might you want to use Excel Online instead of the Excel app installed on your computer?

In the Lab

Design and implement a solution using creative thinking and problem-solving skills.

Create a Cell Phone Service Summary

Problem: You and your friends have decided to sign up for new cell phone service. You would like to maximize services while keeping costs low.

Perform the following tasks:

Part 1: Research and find three cell phone providers in your area. If you cannot find three providers in your area, you can research three providers in another area of your choosing. For each company, find the best service package as well as the basic service package. Using the cost figures you find, calculate the cost per month for each service for a year. Include totals, minimum, maximum, and average values. Use the concepts and techniques presented in this module to create and format the worksheet.

Part 2: You made several decisions while creating the worksheet in this assignment: how to display the data, how to format the worksheet, and which formulas to use. What was the rationale behind each of these decisions?

3 Working with Large Worksheets, Charting, and What-If Analysis

Objectives

After completing this module, you will be able to:

- Rotate text in a cell
- Create a series of month names
- Copy, paste, insert, and delete cells
- Format numbers using format symbols
- Enter and format the system date
- Use absolute and mixed cell references in a formula
- Use the IF function to perform a logical test
- Create and format sparkline charts
- Change sparkline chart types and styles
- Use the Format Painter button to format cells
- Create a clustered column chart on a separate chart sheet
- Use chart filters to display a subset of data in a chart
- Change the chart type and style
- Reorder sheet tabs
- Change the worksheet view
- Freeze and unfreeze rows and columns
- Answer what-if questions
- Goal seek to answer what-if questions
- Use Smart Lookup
- Understand accessibility features

Introduction

This module introduces you to techniques that will enhance your ability to create worksheets and draw charts. This module also covers other methods for entering values in cells, such as allowing Excel to automatically enter and format values based on a perceived pattern in the existing values. In addition, you will learn how to use absolute cell references and how to use the IF function to assign a value to a cell based on a logical test.

When you set up a worksheet, you should use cell references in formulas whenever possible, rather than constant values. The use of a cell reference allows you to change a value in multiple formulas by changing the value in a single cell. The cell references in a formula are called assumptions. **Assumptions** are cell values that you can change to determine new values for formulas. This module emphasizes the use of assumptions and shows how to use assumptions to answer what-if questions, such as what happens to the six-month operating income if you decrease the Marketing expenses assumption by 5%. Being able to analyze the effect of changing values in a worksheet is an important skill in making business decisions.

Worksheets are normally much larger than those you created in the previous modules, often extending beyond the size of the Excel window. When you cannot view the entire worksheet on the screen at once, working with a large worksheet can be frustrating. This module introduces several Excel commands that allow you to control what is displayed on the screen so that you can focus on critical parts of a large worksheet. One command allows you to freeze rows and columns so that they remain visible, even when you scroll. Another command splits the worksheet into separate panes so that you can view different parts of a worksheet on the screen at once. Another changes the magnification to allow you to see more content, albeit at a smaller size. This is useful for reviewing the general layout of content on the worksheet.

From your work in Module 1, you know how easily you can create charts in Excel. This module covers additional charting techniques that allow you to convey meaning visually, such as by using sparkline charts or clustered column charts. This module also introduces the Accessibility checker.

Project: Financial Projection Worksheet with What-If Analysis and Chart

The project in this module uses Excel to create the worksheet and clustered column chart shown in Figures 3–1a and 3–1b. Manola Department Stores, Incorporated, operates a store in Manchester, New Hampshire. The store has multiple departments such as electronics, clothing, appliances, and toys. Each December and June, the chief executive officer projects monthly sales revenues, costs of goods sold, gross margin, expenses, and operating income for the upcoming six-month period, based on figures from the previous six months. The CEO requires an easy-to-read worksheet that shows financial projections for the upcoming six months to use for procuring partial financing and for determining staffing needs. The worksheet should allow for quick analysis when projected numbers change, such as the percentage of expenses allocated

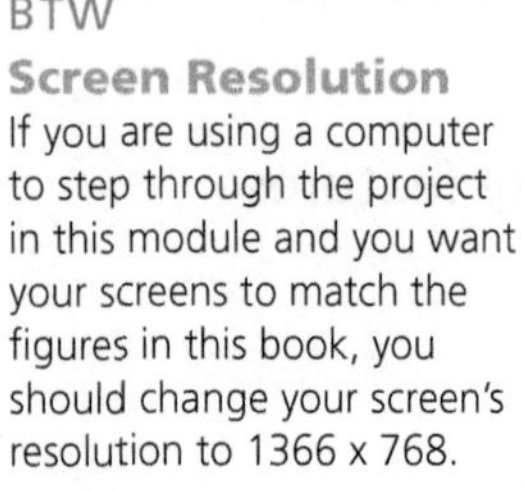

BTW
Screen Resolution
If you are using a computer to step through the project in this module and you want your screens to match the figures in this book, you should change your screen's resolution to 1366 x 768.

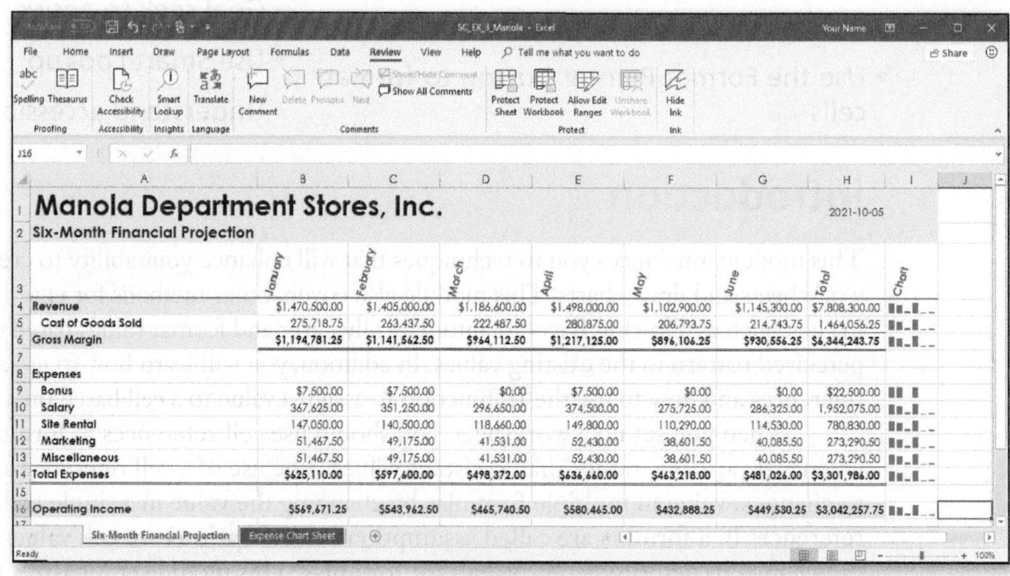

Manola Department Stores, Inc.							2021-10-05
Six-Month Financial Projection							
	January	February	March	April	May	June	Total
Revenue	$1,470,500.00	$1,405,000.00	$1,186,600.00	$1,498,000.00	$1,102,900.00	$1,145,300.00	$7,808,300.00
Cost of Goods Sold	275,718.75	263,437.50	222,487.50	280,875.00	206,793.75	214,743.75	1,464,056.25
Gross Margin	$1,194,781.25	$1,141,562.50	$964,112.50	$1,217,125.00	$896,106.25	$930,556.25	$6,344,243.75
Expenses							
Bonus	$7,500.00	$7,500.00	$0.00	$7,500.00	$0.00	$0.00	$22,500.00
Salary	367,625.00	351,250.00	296,650.00	374,500.00	275,725.00	286,325.00	1,952,075.00
Site Rental	147,050.00	140,500.00	118,660.00	149,800.00	110,290.00	114,530.00	780,830.00
Marketing	51,467.50	49,175.00	41,531.00	52,430.00	38,601.50	40,085.50	273,290.50
Miscellaneous	51,467.50	49,175.00	41,531.00	52,430.00	38,601.50	40,085.50	273,290.50
Total Expenses	$625,110.00	$597,600.00	$498,372.00	$636,660.00	$463,218.00	$481,026.00	$3,301,986.00
Operating Income	$569,671.25	$543,962.50	$465,740.50	$580,465.00	$432,888.25	$449,530.25	$3,042,257.75

(a) Worksheet

Figure 3–1

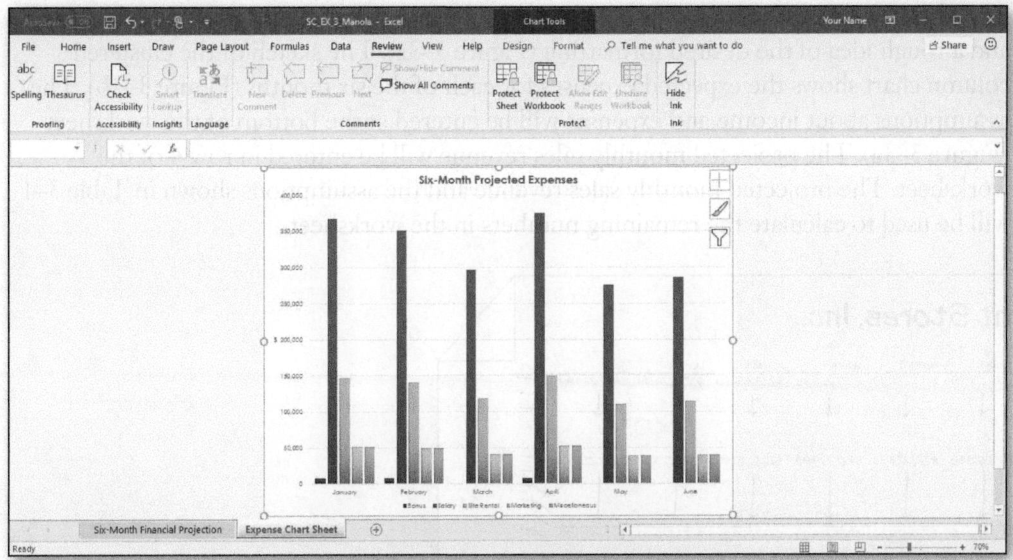

(b) Clustered Column Chart

Figure 3–1 (Continued)

to commission or the cost of miscellaneous expenses. In addition, you need to create a column chart that shows the breakdown of expenses for each month in the period.

The requirements document for the Manola Department Stores, Inc. Six-Month Financial Projection worksheet is shown in Figure 3–2. It includes the needs, source of data, summary of calculations, and chart requirements.

BTW
Touch Mode Differences
The Office and Windows interfaces may vary if you are using Touch mode. For this reason, you might notice that the function or appearance of your touch screen differs slightly from this module's presentation.

Worksheet Title	Manola Department Stores, Inc. Six-Month Financial Projection
Needs	• A worksheet that shows Manola Department Stores, Inc.'s projected monthly sales revenue, cost of goods sold, gross margin, expenses, and operating income for a six-month period. • A clustered column chart that shows the expected contribution of each expense category to total expenses.
Source of Data	Data supplied by the business owner includes projections of the monthly sales and expenses based on prior year figures (see Table 3–1). Remaining numbers in the worksheet are based on formulas.
Calculations	The following calculations are needed for each month: • Cost of Goods Sold = Revenue * (1 – Margin) • Gross Margin = Revenue – Cost of Goods Sold • Bonus expense = Predetermined bonus amount if Revenue exceeds the Revenue for Bonus, otherwise Bonus = 0 • Salary expense = Revenue × Salary percentage • Site Rental expense = Revenue × Site Rental percentage • Marketing expense = Revenue × Marketing percentage • Miscellaneous expense = Revenue × Miscellaneous expense percentage • Total expenses = Sum of all expenses • Operating Income = Gross Margin – Total expenses
Chart Requirements	• Show sparkline charts for revenue and each of the items noted in the calculations area above. • Show a clustered column chart that shows the contributions of each month's expense categories to the total monthly expense figure.

Figure 3–2

Using a sketch of the worksheet can help you visualize its design. The sketch of the worksheet consists of titles, column and row headings, location of data values, calculations, and a rough idea of the desired formatting (Figure 3–3a). The sketch of the clustered column chart shows the expected expenses for each of the six months (Figure 3–3b). The assumptions about income and expenses will be entered at the bottom of the worksheet (Figure 3–3a). The projected monthly sales revenue will be entered in row 4 of the worksheet. The projected monthly sales revenue and the assumptions shown in Table 3–1 will be used to calculate the remaining numbers in the worksheet.

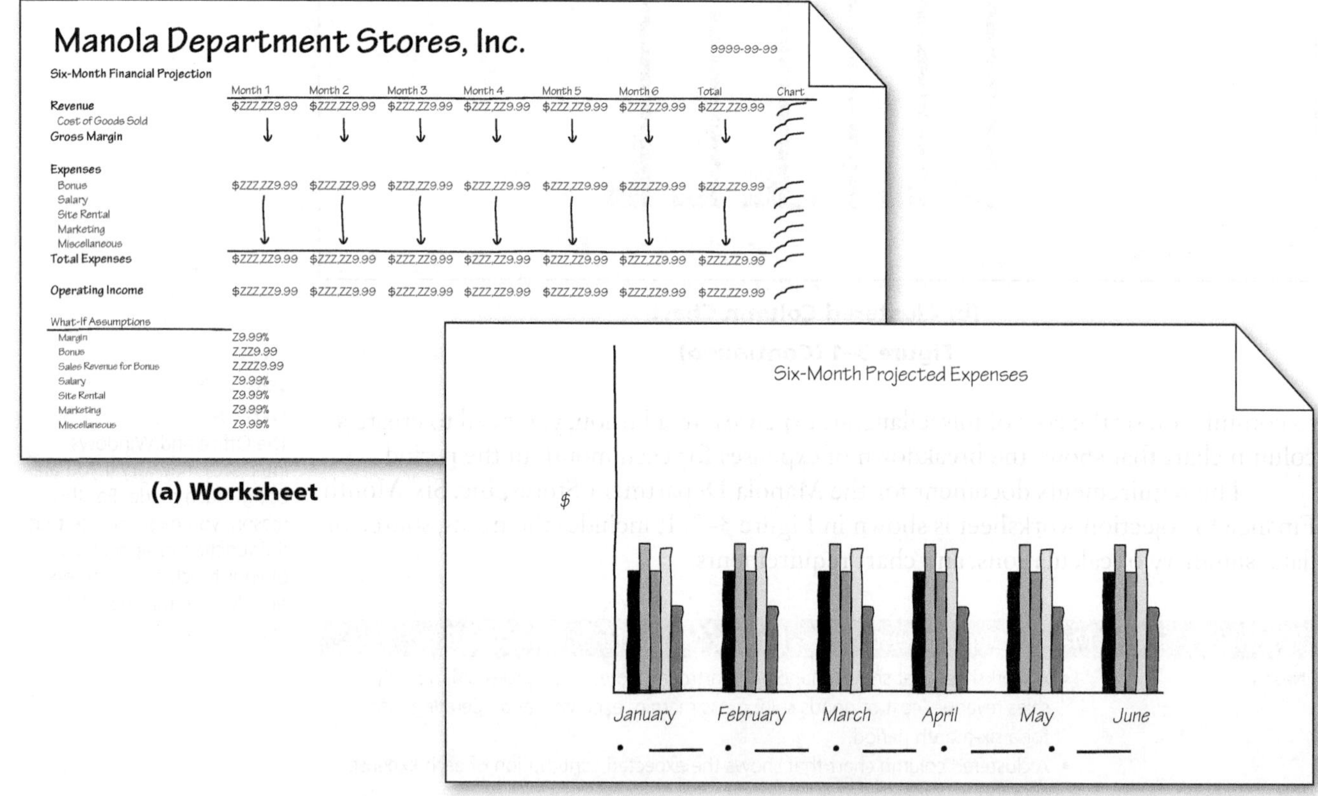

(a) Worksheet

(b) Clustered Column Chart

Figure 3–3

Table 3–1 Manola Department Stores, Inc. Six-Month Financial Projections Data and What-If Assumptions	
Projected Monthly Total Sales Revenues	
January	1,470,500.00
February	1,405,000.00
March	1,186,600.00
April	1,498,000.00
May	1,102,900.00
June	1,145,300.00
What-If Assumptions	
Margin	81.25%
Bonus	$5,000.00
Sales Revenue for Bonus	1,250,000.00
Salary	20.00%
Site Rental	10.00%
Marketing	3.50%
Miscellaneous	5.00%

With a solid understanding of the requirements document, an understanding of the necessary decisions, and a sketch of the worksheet, the next step is to use Excel to create the worksheet.

BTW

Excel Help

At any time while using Excel, you can find answers to questions and display information about various topics through Excel Help. Used properly, this form of assistance can increase your productivity and reduce your frustrations by minimizing the time you spend learning how to use Excel.

To Enter the Worksheet Titles and Apply a Theme

The worksheet contains two titles in cells A1 and A2. In the previous modules, titles were centered across the worksheet. With large worksheets that extend beyond the size of a window, it is best to leave titles left-aligned, as shown in the sketch of the worksheet in Figure 3–3a, so that the worksheet will print the title on the first page if the worksheet requires multiple pages. This allows the user to easily find the worksheet title when necessary. The following steps enter the worksheet titles and change the workbook theme to Slice.

BTW

Ribbon and Screen Resolution

Excel may change how the groups and buttons within the groups appear on the ribbon, depending on the screen resolution of your computer. Thus, your ribbon may look different from the ones in this book if you are using a screen resolution other than 1366 x 768

1. **sam** Start Excel and create a blank workbook in the Excel window.
2. Select cell A1 and then type `Manola Department Stores, Inc.` as the worksheet title.
3. Select cell A2, type `Six-Month Financial Projection` as the worksheet subtitle, and then press ENTER to enter the worksheet subtitle.
4. Apply the Slice theme to the workbook.

Rotating Text and Using the Fill Handle to Create a Series

The data on the worksheet, including month names and the What-If Assumptions section, now can be added to the worksheet.

BTW

Rotating Text in a Cell

In Excel, you use the Alignment sheet in the Format Cells dialog box (shown in Figure 3–5) to position data in a cell by centering, left-aligning, or right-aligning; indenting; aligning at the top, bottom, or center; and rotating.

CONSIDER THIS

What should you take into account when planning a worksheet layout?

Using Excel, you can change text and number formatting in many ways, which affects the visual impact of the worksheet. Rotated text often provides a strong visual appeal. Rotated text also allows you to fit more text into a smaller column width. When laying out a worksheet, keep in mind the content you want to emphasize and the length of the cell titles relative to the numbers.

To Rotate Text in a Cell

The design of the worksheet calls specifically for data for the six months of the selling season. Because there always will be only six months of data in the worksheet, place the months across the top of the worksheet as column headings rather than as row headings. Place the income and expense categories in rows, as they are more numerous than the number of months. This layout allows you to easily navigate the worksheet. Ideally, a proper layout will create a worksheet that is longer than it is wide.

When you first enter text, its angle is zero degrees (0°), and it reads from left to right in a cell. Excel allows you to rotate text in a cell counterclockwise by entering a number between 1° and 90°. If you specify an exact value by entering 90 in the Degrees box in the Orientation area, the text will appear vertically and read from bottom to top in the cell. ***Why?*** *Rotating text is one method of making column headings visually distinct.* The following steps enter the month name, January, in cell B3 and format cell B3 by rotating the text.

- If necessary, click the Home tab and then select cell B3 because this cell will include the first month name in the series of month names.
- Type `January` as the cell entry and then click the Enter button.
- On the Home tab in the Alignment group, click the Dialog Box Launcher to display the Format Cells dialog box (Figure 3–4).

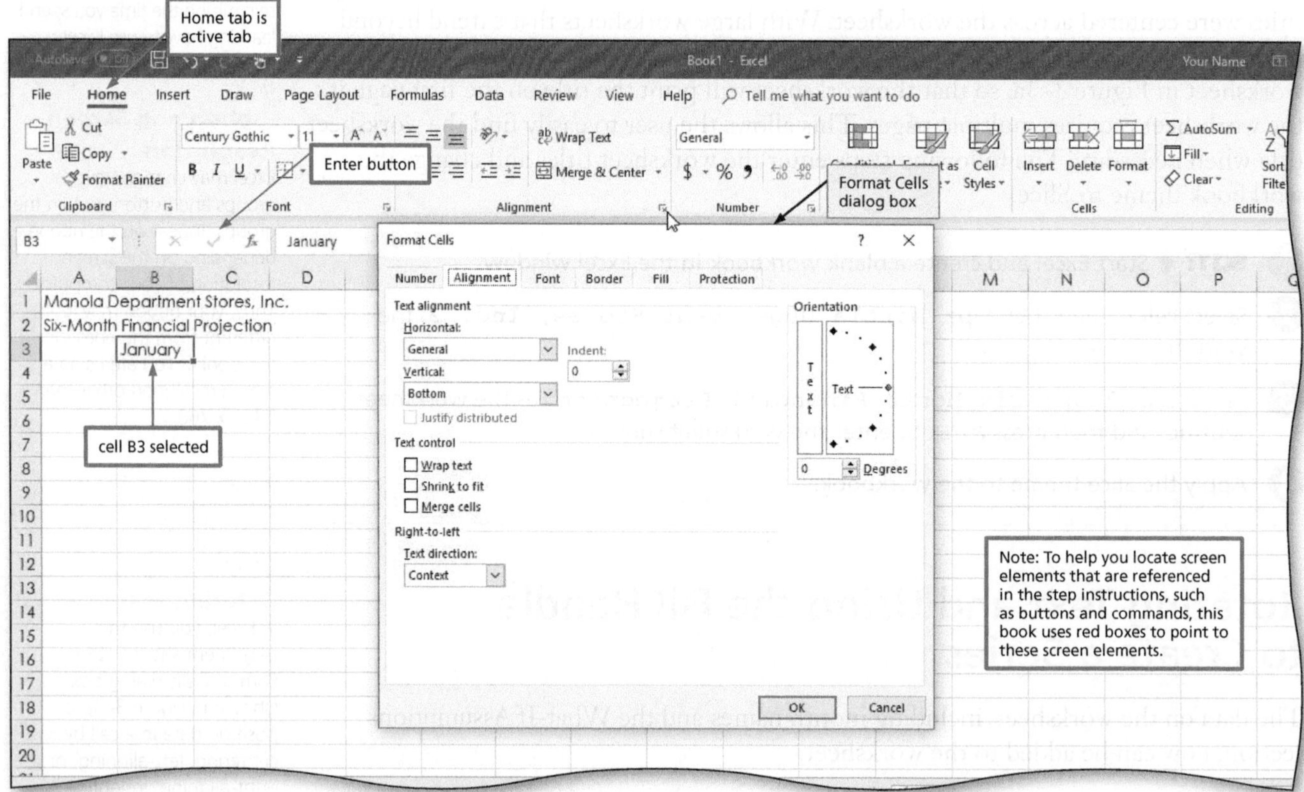

Figure 3–4

2

- Click the 75° point in the Orientation area (Format Cells dialog box) to move the indicator in the Orientation area to the 75° point and display a new orientation in the Degrees box (Figure 3–5).

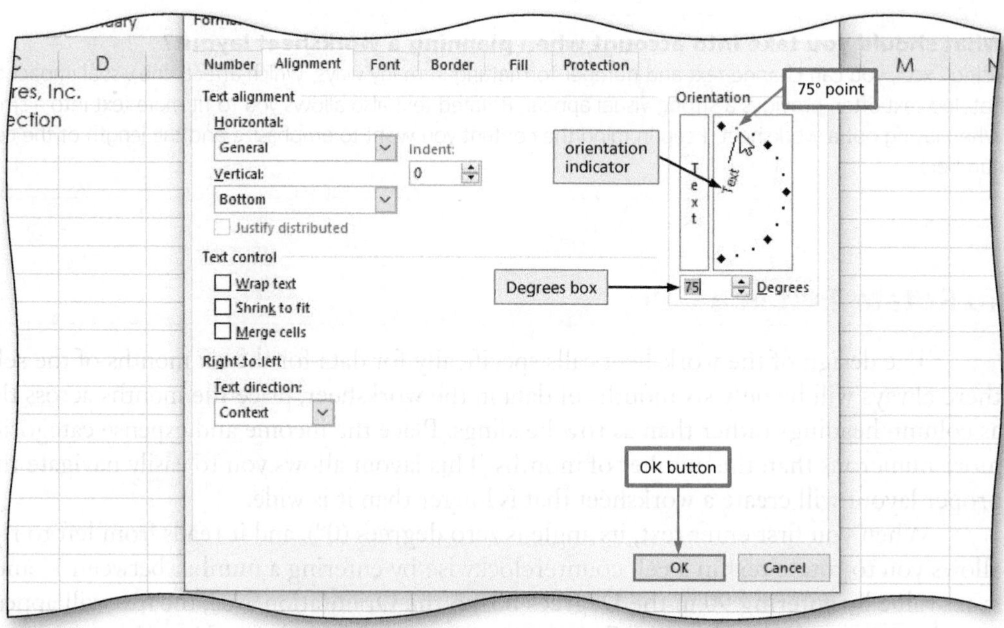

Figure 3–5

- Click OK (Format Cells dialog box) to rotate the text to the preset angle in the active cell and increase the height of the current row to best fit the rotated text (Figure 3–6).

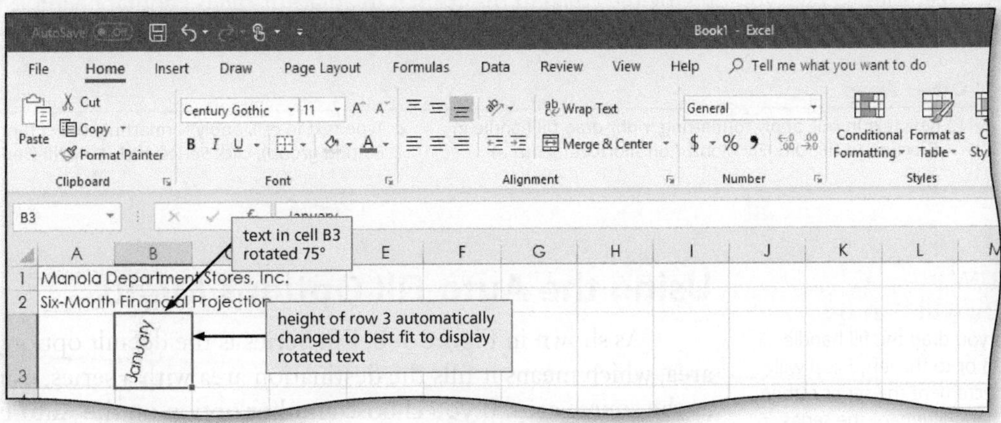

Figure 3–6

Other Ways

1. Right-click selected cell, click Format Cells on shortcut menu, click Alignment tab (Format Cells dialog box), click 75° point, click OK

To Use the Fill Handle to Create a Series of Month Names

Why? *Once the first month in the series has been entered and formatted, you can complete the data series using the fill handle rather than typing and formatting all the entries.* The following steps use the fill handle and the entry in cell B3 to create a series of month names in cells C3:G3.

- Drag the fill handle on the lower-right corner of cell B3 to the right to select the range to fill, C3:G3 in this case. Do not release the mouse button (Figure 3–7).

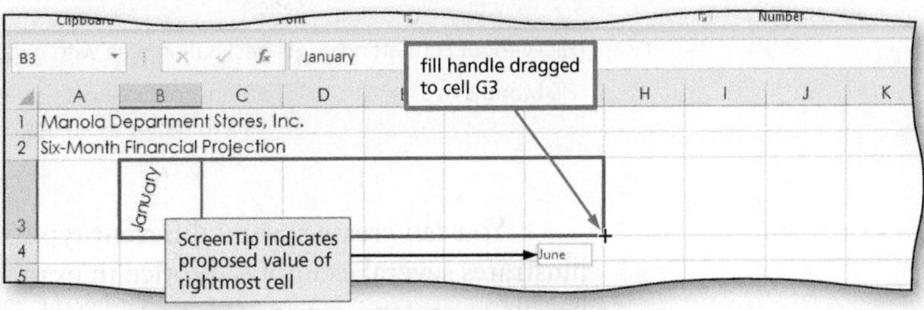

Figure 3–7

2

- Release the mouse button to create a month name series in the selected range and copy the format of the selected cell to the selected range.
- Click the 'Auto Fill Options' button below the lower-right corner of the fill area to display the Auto Fill Options menu (Figure 3–8).

Q&A What if I do not want to copy the format of cell B3 during the auto fill operation?

In addition to creating a series of values, dragging the fill handle instructs Excel to copy the format of cell B3 to the range C3:G3. With some fill operations, you may not want to copy the formats of the source cell or range to the destination cell or range. If this is the case, click the 'Auto Fill Options' button after the range fills and then select the desired option on the Auto Fill Options menu (Figure 3–8).

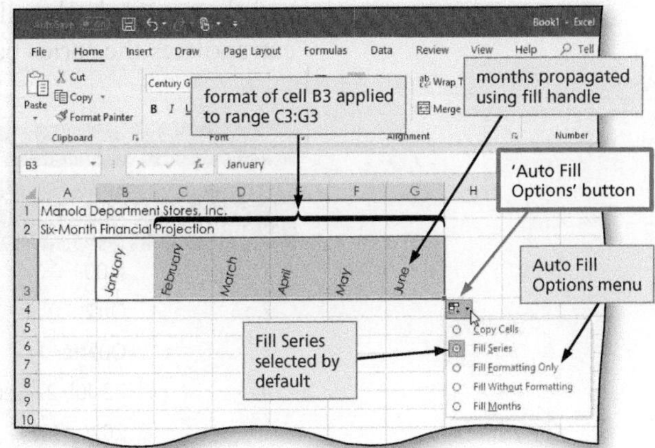

Figure 3–8

- Click the 'Auto Fill Options' button to hide the Auto Fill Options menu.
- Select cell H3, type `Total`, and then press the RIGHT ARROW key to enter a column heading.
- Type `Chart` in cell I3 and then press the RIGHT ARROW key.

Q&A Why is the word, Total, formatted with a 75° rotation?
Excel tries to save you time by recognizing the format in adjacent cell G3 and applying it to cell H3. Such behavior also occurs when typing the column heading in cell I3.

Other Ways

1. Type text in cell, apply formatting, right-drag fill handle in direction to fill, click Fill Months on shortcut menu
2. Type text in cell, apply formatting, select range, click Fill button (Home tab | Editing group), click Series, click AutoFill (Series dialog box), click OK

BTW
The Fill Handle
If you drag the fill handle up or to the left, Excel will decrement the series rather than increment the series. To copy a word, such as January or Monday, which Excel might interpret as the start of a series, hold down CTRL while you drag the fill handle to a destination area. If you drag the fill handle back into the middle of a cell, Excel erases the contents of the cell.

Using the Auto Fill Options Menu

As shown in Figure 3–8, Fill Series is the default option that Excel uses to fill an area, which means it fills the destination area with a series, using the same formatting as the source area. If you choose another option on the Auto Fill Options menu, Excel changes the contents of the destination range. Following the use of the fill handle, the 'Auto Fill Options' button remains active until you begin the next Excel operation. Table 3–2 summarizes the options on the Auto Fill Options menu.

Table 3–2 Options Available on the Auto Fill Options Menu

Auto Fill Option	Description
Copy Cells	Fill destination area with contents using format of source area. Do not create a series.
Fill Series	Fill destination area with series using format of source area. This option is the default.
Fill Formatting Only	Fill destination area using format of source area. No content is copied unless fill is series.
Fill Without Formatting	Fill destination area with contents, without applying the formatting of source area.
Fill Months	Fill destination area with series of months using format of source area. Same as Fill Series and shows as an option only if source area contains the name of a month.

You can create several different types of series using the fill handle. Table 3–3 illustrates several examples. Notice in examples 4, 7, 9, and 11 that, if you use the fill handle to create a series of nonsequential numbers or months, you must enter the first item in the series in one cell and the second item in the series in an adjacent cell, and then select both cells and drag the fill handle through the destination area. Excel extrapolates the series based on the previous input.

Table 3–3 Examples of Series Using the Fill Handle

Example	Contents of Cell(s) Copied Using the Fill Handle	Next Three Values of Extended Series
1	4:00	5:00, 6:00, 7:00
2	Qtr2	Qtr3, Qtr4, Qtr1
3	Quarter 1	Quarter 2, Quarter 3, Quarter 4
4	22-Jul, 22-Sep	22-Nov, 22-Jan, 22-Mar
5	2020, 2021	2022, 2023, 2024
6	1, 2	3, 4, 5
7	625, 575	525, 475, 425
8	Mon	Tue, Wed, Thu
9	Sunday, Tuesday	Thursday, Saturday, Monday
10	4th Section	5th Section, 6th Section, 7th Section
11	2205, 2208	2211, 2214, 2217

You can create your own custom fill sequences for use with the fill handle. For example, if you often type the same list of products or names in Excel, you can create a custom fill sequence. You then can type the first product or name and then use the fill handle to automatically fill in the remaining products or names. To create a custom fill sequence, display the Excel Options dialog box by clicking Options in Backstage view. Click the Advanced tab (Excel Options dialog box) and then click the 'Edit Custom Lists' button in the General section (Excel Options dialog box).

To Increase Column Widths

Why? In Module 2, you increased column widths after the values were entered into the worksheet. Sometimes, you may want to increase the column widths before you enter values and, if necessary, adjust them later. You can resize columns to exact widths using dragging, as described below. You can also resize columns to an approximate value by dragging until the cell contents are displayed in a visually pleasing way, without regard for the numbers displayed. The following steps increase the column widths to specific values.

1

- Move the pointer to the boundary between column heading A and column heading B so that the pointer changes to a split double arrow in preparation for adjusting the column widths.
- Drag the pointer to the right until the ScreenTip displays the desired column width, Width: 38.50 (313 pixels) in this case. Do not release the mouse button (Figure 3–9).

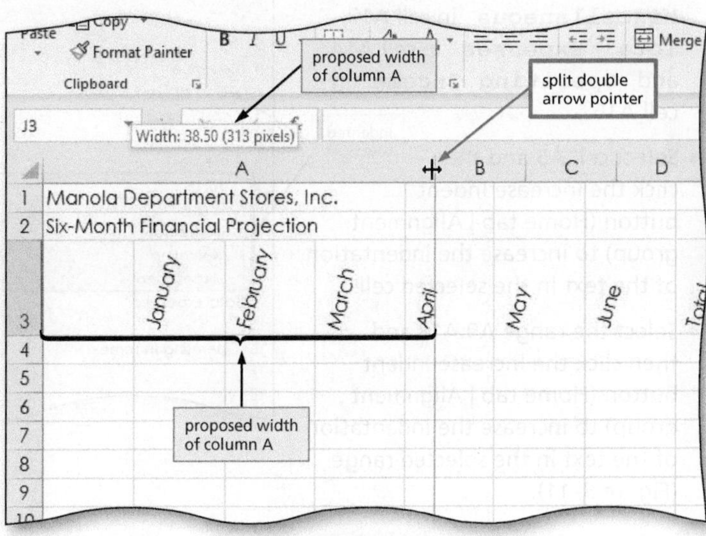

Figure 3–9

2

- Release the mouse button to change the width of the column.
- Click column heading B to select the column and then drag through column heading G to select the range in which to change the widths.
- Move the pointer to the boundary between column headings B and C in preparation for resizing column B and then drag the pointer to the right until the ScreenTip displays the desired width, Width: 15.00 (125 pixels) in this case. Do not lift your finger or release the mouse button (Figure 3–10).

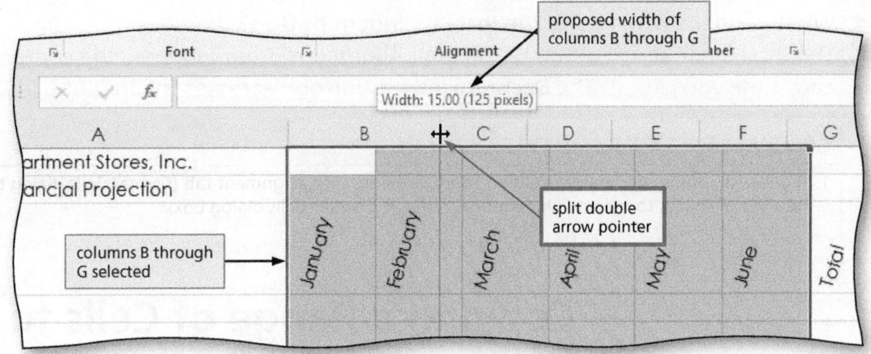

Figure 3–10

- Release the mouse button to change the width of the selected columns.
- If necessary, scroll the worksheet so that column H is visible and then use the technique described in Step 1 to increase the width of column H to 18.00 (149 pixels).

To Enter and Indent Row Titles

Excel allows you to indent text in cells. The following steps enter the row titles in column A and indent several of the row titles. ***Why?*** *Indenting rows helps you create a visual hierarchy by indenting some of the row titles, like in an outline or table of contents.*

- If necessary, scroll the worksheet so that column A and row 4 are visible and then enter **Revenue** in cell A4, **Cost of Goods Sold** in cell A5, **Gross Margin** in cell A6, **Expenses** in cell A8, **Bonus** in cell A9, **Salary** in cell A10, **Site Rental** in cell A11, **Marketing** in cell A12, **Miscellaneous** in cell A13, **Total Expenses** in cell A14, and **Operating Income** in cell A16.
- Select cell A5 and then click the Increase Indent button (Home tab | Alignment group) to increase the indentation of the text in the selected cell.
- Select the range A9:A13 and then click the Increase Indent button (Home tab | Alignment group) to increase the indentation of the text in the selected range (Figure 3–11).

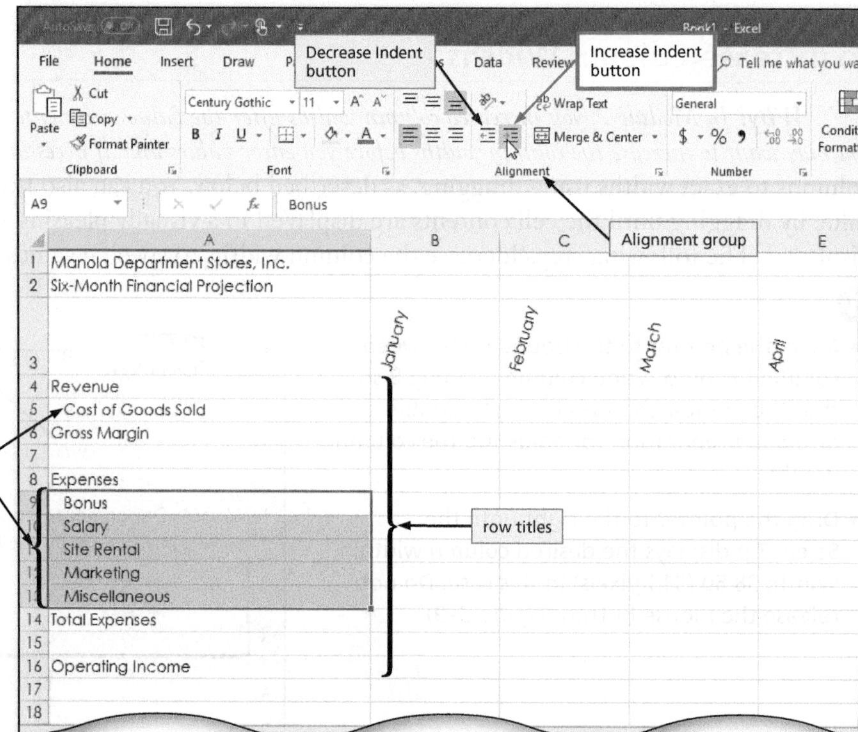

Figure 3–11

- Select cell A18 to finish entering the row titles and deselect the current cell.

Q&A What happens when I click the Increase Indent button?
The Increase Indent button (Home tab | Alignment group) indents the contents of a cell two spaces to the right each time you click it. The Decrease Indent button decreases the indent by two spaces each time you click it.

Other Ways

1. Right-click range, click Format Cells on shortcut menu, click Alignment tab (Format Cells dialog box), click Left (Indent) in Horizontal list, type number of spaces to indent in Indent box, click OK (Format Cells dialog box)

Copying a Range of Cells to a Nonadjacent Destination Area

The What-If Assumptions section should be placed in an area of the worksheet that is accessible yet does not impair the view of the main section of the worksheet. As shown in Figure 3–3a, the What-If Assumptions will be placed below the calculations in the worksheet. This will allow the reader to see the main section of the worksheet when first opening the workbook. Additionally, the row titles in the Expenses area are the same as the row titles in the What-If Assumptions table, with the exception of the two additional entries in cells A19 (Margin) and A21 (Sales Revenue for Bonus). Hence, the row titles in the What-If Assumptions table can be created by copying the range A9:A13 to the range A19:A23 and then inserting two rows for the additional entries in cells A19 and A21. You cannot use the fill handle to copy the range because the source area (range A9:A13) is not adjacent to the destination area (range A19:A23).

A more versatile method of copying a source area is to use the Copy button and Paste button (Home tab | Clipboard group). You can use these two buttons to copy a source area to an adjacent or nonadjacent destination area.

BTW

Fitting Entries in a Cell

An alternative to increasing column widths or row heights is to shrink the characters in a cell to fit the current width of the column. To shrink to fit, on the Home tab in the Alignment group, click the Dialog Box Launcher and then place a check mark in the 'Shrink to fit' check box in the Text control area (Format Cells dialog box).

To Copy a Range of Cells to a Nonadjacent Destination Area

The Copy button copies the contents and format of the source area to the **Office Clipboard**, a temporary storage area in the computer's memory that allows you to collect text and graphics from any Office document and then paste them into almost any other type of document; the Office Clipboard can hold a maximum of 24 items. The Paste button pastes a copy of the contents of the Office Clipboard in the destination area. ***Why?*** *Copying the range of cells rather than reentering the content ensures consistency within the worksheet.* The following steps enter the What-If Assumptions row heading and then use the Copy and Paste buttons to copy the range A9:A13 to the nonadjacent range A19:A23.

- With cell A18 selected, type **`What-If Assumptions`** as the new row title and then click the Enter button.
- Select the range A9:A13 and then click the Copy button (Home tab | Clipboard group) to copy the values and formats of the selected range, A9:A13 in this case, to the Office Clipboard.
- If necessary, click the down scroll arrow to display cell A19, and then select cell A19, the top cell in the destination area (Figure 3–12).

Q&A

Why do I not select the entire destination area?

You are not required to select the entire destination area (A19:A23) because Excel only needs to know the upper-left cell of the destination area. In the case of a single column range, such as A19:A23, the top cell of the destination area (cell A19) also is the upper-left cell of the destination area.

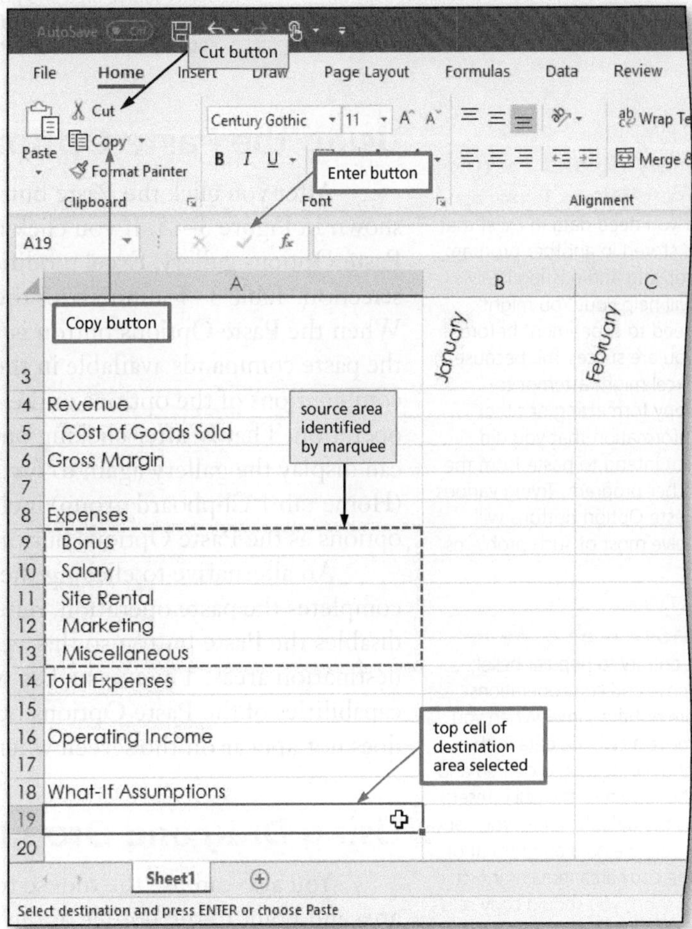

Figure 3–12

- Click the Paste button (Home tab | Clipboard group) to copy the values and formats of the last item placed on the Office Clipboard, range A9:A13, to the destination area, A19:A23. If necessary, scroll down to see the complete destination area (Figure 3–13).

Q&A What if there was data in the destination area before I clicked the Paste button?

Any data contained in the destination area prior to the copy and paste would be lost. When you complete a copy, the values and formats in the destination area are replaced with the values and formats of the source area. If you accidentally delete valuable data, click the Undo button on the Quick Access Toolbar or press CTRL+Z.

3

- Press ESC to remove the marquee from the source area and deactivate the Paste button (Home tab | Clipboard group).

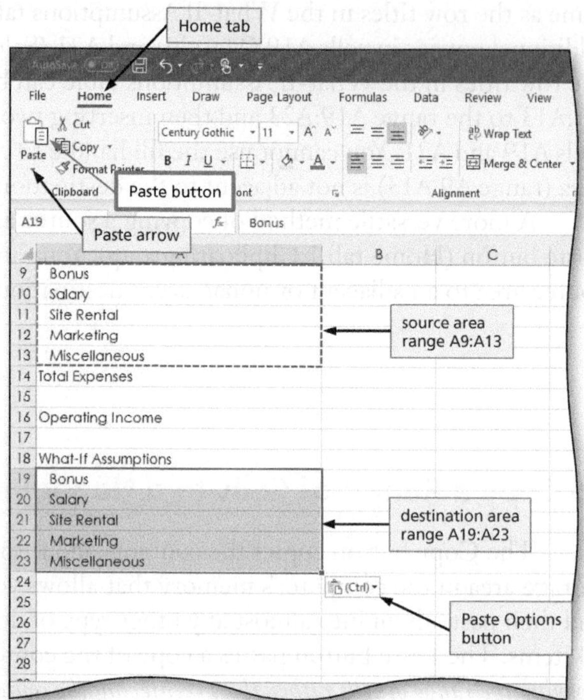

Figure 3–13

Other Ways

1. Right-click source area, click Copy on shortcut menu, right-click destination area, click Paste icon on shortcut menu
2. Select source area and point to border of range; while holding down CTRL, drag source area to destination area
3. Select source area, press CTRL+C, select destination area, press CTRL+V

BTW

Copying and Pasting from Other Programs

If you need data in Excel that is stored in another program, copying and pasting likely will help you. You might need to experiment before you are successful, because Excel might attempt to copy formatting or other information that you did not intend to paste from the other program. Trying various Paste Option buttons will solve most of such problems.

BTW

Move It or Copy It

Contrary to popular belief, move and copy operations are not the same. When you move a cell, the data in the original location is cleared and the format of the cell is reset to the default. When you copy a cell, the data and format of the copy area remains intact. In short, you should copy cells to duplicate entries and move cells to rearrange entries.

Using the Paste Options Menu

After you click the Paste button, Excel displays the Paste Options button, as shown in Figure 3–13. If you click the Paste Options arrow and select an option in the Paste Options gallery, Excel modifies the most recent paste operation based on your selection. Table 3–4 summarizes the options available in the Paste Options gallery. When the Paste Options button is visible, you can use keyboard shortcuts to access the paste commands available in the Paste Options gallery. Additionally, you can use combinations of the options in the Paste Options gallery to customize your paste operation. That is, after clicking one of the icons in the Paste Options gallery, you can display the gallery again to further adjust your paste operation. The Paste button (Home tab | Clipboard group) includes an arrow that, when clicked, displays the same options as the Paste Options button.

An alternative to clicking the Paste button is to press ENTER. Pressing ENTER completes the paste operation, removes the marquee from the source area, and disables the Paste button so that you cannot paste the copied source area to other destination areas. The ENTER key was not used in the previous set of steps so that the capabilities of the Paste Options button could be discussed. The Paste Options button does not appear on the screen when you use ENTER to complete the paste operation.

Using Drag and Drop to Move or Copy Cells

You also can use the mouse to move or copy cells. First, you select the source area and point to the border of the cell or range. You know you are pointing to the border of the cell or range when the pointer changes to a four-headed arrow. To move the selected cell or cells, drag the selection to the destination area. To copy a selection,

Table 3–4 Paste Gallery Commands

Paste Option Icon	Paste Option	Description
	Paste	Copy contents and format of source area. This option is the default.
	Formulas	Copy formulas from the source area, but not the contents and format.
	Formulas & Number Formatting	Copy formulas and format for numbers and formulas of source area, but not the contents.
	Keep Source Formatting	Copy contents, format, and styles of source area.
	No Borders	Copy contents and format of source area, but not any borders.
	Keep Source Column Widths	Copy contents and format of source area. Change destination column widths to source column widths.
	Transpose	Copy the contents and format of the source area, but transpose, or swap, the rows and columns.
	Values	Copy contents of source area but not the formatting for formulas.
	Values & Number Formatting	Copy contents and format of source area for numbers or formulas, but use format of destination area for text.
	Values & Source Formatting	Copy contents and formatting of source area but not the formula.
	Formatting	Copy format of source area but not the contents.
	Paste Link	Copy contents and format and link cells so that a change to the cells in source area updates the corresponding cells in destination area.
	Picture	Copy an image of the source area as a picture.
	Linked Picture	Copy an image of the source area as a picture so that a change to the cells in source area updates the picture in destination area.

hold down CTRL while dragging the selection to the destination area. You know Excel is in Copy mode when a small plus sign appears next to the pointer. Be sure to release the mouse button before you release CTRL. Using the mouse to move or copy cells is called **drag and drop**.

Using Cut and Paste to Move Cells

Another way to move cells is to select them, click the Cut button (Home tab | Clipboard group) (Figure 3–12) to remove the cells from the worksheet and copy them to the Office Clipboard, select the destination area, and then click the Paste button (Home tab | Clipboard group) or press ENTER. The cell(s) you move using the Cut command either can contain a static value or a formula. You also can use the Cut command on the shortcut menu instead of the Cut button on the ribbon.

BTW

Cutting

When you cut a cell or range of cells using the Cut command on a shortcut menu or Cut button (Home tab | Clipboard group), Excel copies the cells to the Office Clipboard; it does not remove the cells from the source area until you paste the cells in the destination area by either clicking the Paste button (Home tab | Clipboard group) or pressing ENTER. When you complete the paste, Excel clears the cell's or range of cell's entries and their formats from the source area.

Inserting and Deleting Cells in a Worksheet

At any time while the worksheet is on the screen, you can insert cells to enter new data or delete cells to remove unwanted data. You can insert or delete individual cells; a range of cells, rows, or columns; or entire worksheets. As you insert cells into your worksheet, making the worksheet larger, it may print on multiple pages. If you want to indicate where one page should stop and the next page should start, you can insert a page break. To insert a page break, first select the cell immediately below where you want to insert the page break. Next, click the Breaks button (Page Layout tab | Page Setup group) and then click Insert Page Break. If you want to remove a page break, you should instead click the 'Remove Page Break' command. To remove all page breaks from a worksheet, click the 'Reset All Page Breaks' command.

To Insert a Row

Why? *According to the sketch of the worksheet in Figure 3–3a, two rows must be inserted in the What-If Assumptions table, one above Bonus for the Margin assumption and another between Bonus and Salary for the Sales Revenue for Bonus assumption.* The following steps insert the new rows into the worksheet.

- Right-click row heading 20, the row below where you want to insert a row, to display the shortcut menu and the mini toolbar (Figure 3–14).

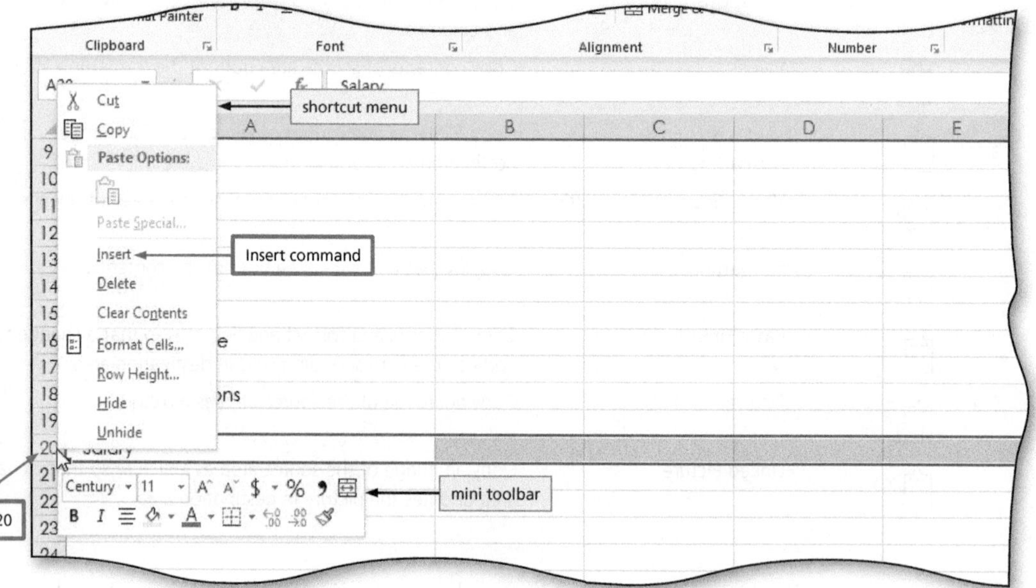

Figure 3–14

- Click Insert on the shortcut menu to insert a new row in the worksheet by shifting the selected row and all rows below it down one row.
- Select cell A20 in the new row and then type `Sales Revenue for Bonus` to enter a new row title (Figure 3–15).

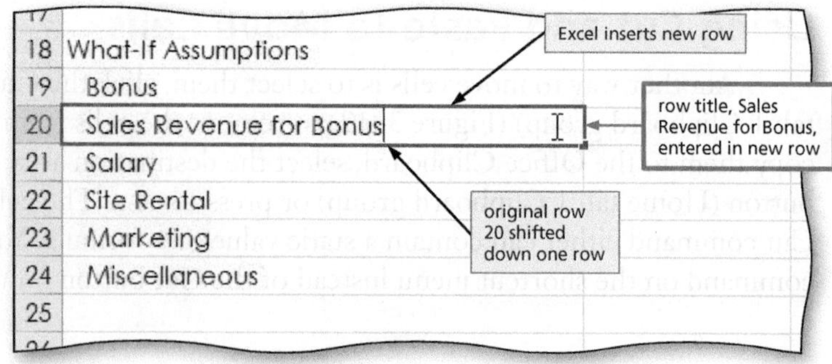

Figure 3–15

Q&A What is the resulting format of the new row?
The cells in the new row inherit the formats of the cells in the row above them. You can change this behavior by clicking the Insert Options button that appears below the inserted row. Following the insertion of a row, the Insert Options button allows you to select from the following options: (1) 'Format Same As Above', (2) 'Format Same As Below', and (3) Clear Formatting. The 'Format Same as Above' option is the default. The Insert Options button remains active until you begin the next Excel operation. Excel does not display the Insert Options button if the initial row does not contain any formatted data.

3

- Right-click row heading 19, the row below where you want to insert a row, to display the shortcut menu and the mini toolbar.
- Click Insert on the shortcut menu to insert a new row in the worksheet.
- Click the Insert Options button below row 19 (Figure 3–16).
- Click 'Format Same As Below' on the menu.
- Select cell A19 in the new row and then enter `Margin` as a new row title.

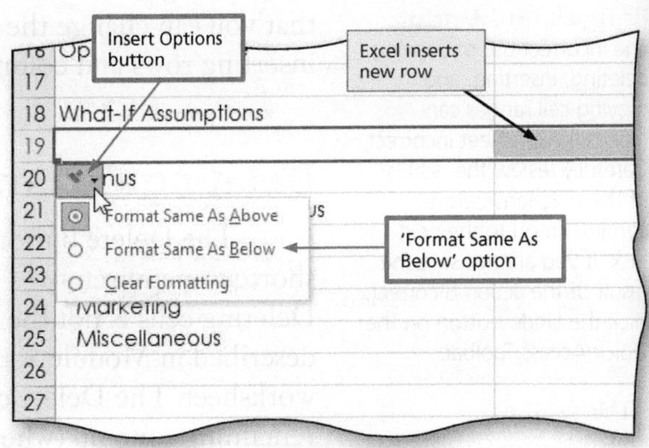

Figure 3–16

Q&A What would happen if cells in the shifted rows were included in formulas?

If the rows that shift down included cell references in formulas located in the worksheet, Excel would automatically adjust the cell references in the formulas to their new locations. Thus, in Step 2, if a formula in the worksheet referenced a cell in row 19 before the insert, then Excel would adjust the cell reference in the formula to row 20 after the insert.

4

- Save the workbook using `SC_EX_3_Manola` as the file name.

Other Ways

1. Click Insert Cells arrow (Home tab | Cells group), click 'Insert Sheet Rows'
2. Press CTRL+SHIFT+PLUS SIGN, click Entire row (Insert dialog box), OK

BTW

Inserting Multiple Rows

If you want to insert multiple rows, you have two choices. You can insert a single row by using the Insert command on the shortcut menu and then repeatedly press F4 to continue inserting rows. Alternatively, you can select a number of existing rows equal to the number of rows that you want to insert. For instance, if you want to insert five rows, select five existing rows in the worksheet, right-click the selected rows, and then click Insert on the shortcut menu.

Inserting Columns

You insert columns into a worksheet in the same way you insert rows. To insert columns, select one or more columns immediately to the right of where you want Excel to insert the new column or columns. Select the number of columns you want to insert, click the Insert arrow (Home tab | Cells group), and then click 'Insert Sheet Columns' in the Insert list; or right-click the selected column(s) and then click Insert on the shortcut menu. The Insert command on the shortcut menu requires that you select an entire column (or columns) to insert a column (or columns). Following the insertion of a column, Excel displays the Insert Options button, which allows you to modify the insertion in a fashion similar to that discussed earlier when inserting rows.

BTW

Dragging Ranges

You can move and insert a selected cell or range between existing cells by holding down SHIFT while you drag the selection to the gridline where you want to insert the selected cell or range. You also can copy and insert by holding down CTRL+SHIFT while you drag the selection to the desired gridline.

Inserting Single Cells or a Range of Cells

You can use the Insert command on the shortcut menu or the Insert Cells command on the Insert menu—produced by clicking the Insert button (Home tab | Cells group)—to insert a single cell or a range of cells. You should be aware that if you shift a single cell or a range of cells, however, it no longer lines up with its associated cells. To ensure that the values in the worksheet do not get out of order, spreadsheet experts recommend that you insert only entire rows or entire columns. When you insert a single cell or a range of cells, Excel displays the Insert Options button so that you can change the format of the inserted cell, using options similar to those for inserting rows and columns.

BTW

Ranges and Undo

The incorrect use of copying, deleting, inserting, and moving cell ranges can makes a worksheet incorrect. Carefully review the results of these actions before continuing on to the next task. If you are not sure the result of the action is correct, click the Undo button on the Quick Access Toolbar.

BTW

Organizing Files and Folders

You should organize and store files in folders so that you easily can find the files later. For example, if you are taking an introductory technology class called CIS 101, a good practice would be to save all Excel files in an Excel folder in a CIS 101 folder.

Deleting Columns and Rows

The Delete button (Home tab | Cells group) or the Delete command on the shortcut menu removes cells (including the data and format) from the worksheet. Deleting cells is not the same as clearing cells. The Clear Contents command, described in Module 1, clears the data from the cells, but the cells remain in the worksheet. The Delete command removes the cells from the worksheet and shifts the remaining rows up (when you delete rows) or shifts the remaining columns to the left (when you delete columns). If formulas located in other cells reference cells in the deleted row or column, Excel does not adjust these cell specifically references. Excel displays the error message **#REF!** in those cells to indicate a cell reference error. For example, if cell A7 contains the formula =A4+A5 and you delete row 5, Excel assigns the formula =A4+#REF! to cell A6 (originally cell A7) and displays the error message, #REF!, in cell A6. Excel also displays an Error Options button when you select the cell containing the error message, #REF!, which allows you to select options to determine the nature of the problem.

To Enter Numbers with Format Symbols

The next step in creating the Financial Projection worksheet is to enter the what-if assumptions values in the range B19:B25. The numbers in the table can be entered and then formatted using techniques from Modules 1 and 2, or each number can be entered with **format symbols**, which assign a format to numbers as they are entered. When a number is entered with a format symbol, Excel displays it with the assigned format. Valid format symbols include the dollar sign ($), comma (,), and percent sign (%).

If you enter a whole number, it appears without any decimal places. If you enter a number with one or more decimal places and a format symbol, Excel displays the number with two decimal places. Table 3–5 illustrates several examples of numbers entered with format symbols. The number in parentheses in column 4 indicates the number of decimal places.

Table 3–5 Numbers Entered with Format Symbols

Format Symbol	Typed in Formula Bar	Displays in Cell	Comparable Format
,	374,149	374,149	Comma(0)
	5,833.6	5,833.60	Comma(2)
$	$58917	$58,917	Currency(0)
	$842.51	$842.51	Currency(2)
	$63,574.9	$63,574.90	Currency(2)
%	85%	85%	Percent(0)
	12.80%	12.80%	Percent(2)
	68.2242%	68.2242%	Percent(4)

Why? *In some cases, using a format symbol is the most efficient method for entering and formatting data.*
The following step enters the numbers in the What-If Assumptions table with format symbols.

1

- Enter the following values, using format symbols to apply number formatting: `81.25%` in cell B19, `5,000.00` in cell B20, `1,250,000.00` in cell B21, `20.00%` in cell B22, `10.00%` in cell B23, `3.50%` in cell B24, and `5.00%` in cell B25 (Figure 3–17).

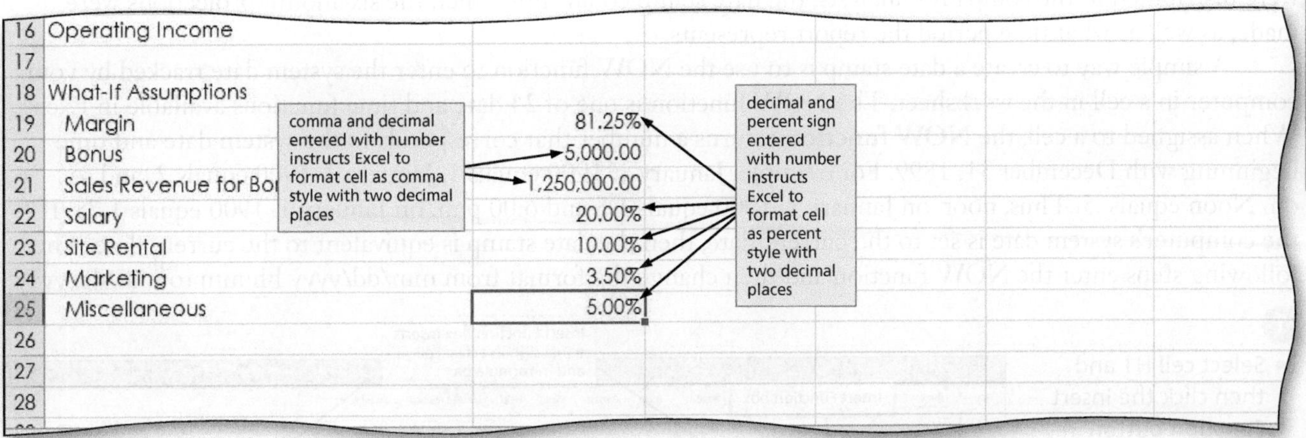

Figure 3–17

Other Ways

1. Right-click range, click Format Cells on shortcut menu, click Number tab (Format Cells dialog box), click category in Category list, select desired format, click OK
2. Press CTRL+1, click Number tab (Format Cells dialog box), click category in Category list, select desired format, click OK

To Enter the Projected Monthly Sales

The following steps enter the projected revenue, listed previously in Table 3–1, in row 4 and compute the projected six-month revenue in cell H4.

1. If necessary, display the Home tab.
2. Enter `1,470,500.00` in cell B4, `1,405,000.00` in cell C4, `1,186,600.00` in cell D4, `1,498,000.00` in cell E4, `1,102,900.00` in cell F4, and `1,145,300.00` in cell G4.
3. Select cell H4 and then click the Auto Sum button (Home tab | Editing group) twice to create a sum (7,808,300.00) in the selected cell (Figure 3–18).

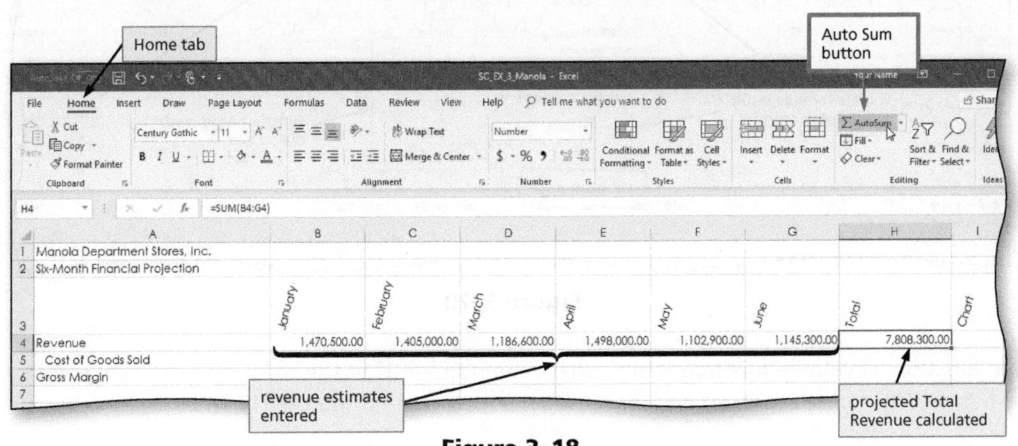

Figure 3–18

To Enter and Format the System Date

Why? The sketch of the worksheet in Figure 3–3a includes a date stamp on the right side of the heading section. A date stamp shows the date a workbook, report, or other document was created or the time period it represents. In business, a report is often meaningless without a date stamp. For example, if a printout of the worksheet in this module were distributed to the company's analysts, the date stamp could show when the six-month projections were made, as well as what time period the report represents.

A simple way to create a date stamp is to use the NOW function to enter the system date tracked by your computer in a cell in the worksheet. The NOW function is one of 24 date and time functions available in Excel. When assigned to a cell, the **NOW function** returns a number that corresponds to the system date and time beginning with December 31, 1899. For example, January 1, 1900 equals 1, January 2, 1900 equals 2, and so on. Noon equals .5. Thus, noon on January 1, 1900 equals 1.5 and 6:00 p.m. on January 1, 1900 equals 1.75. If the computer's system date is set to the current date, then the date stamp is equivalent to the current date. The following steps enter the NOW function and then change the format from mm/dd/yyyy hh:mm to mm/dd/yyyy.

1

- Select cell H1 and then click the Insert Function button in the formula bar to display the Insert Function dialog box.
- Click the 'Or select a category' arrow (Insert Function dialog box) and then select 'Date & Time' to populate the 'Select a function' list with date and time functions.
- Scroll down in the 'Select a function' list and then click NOW to select the required function (Figure 3–19).

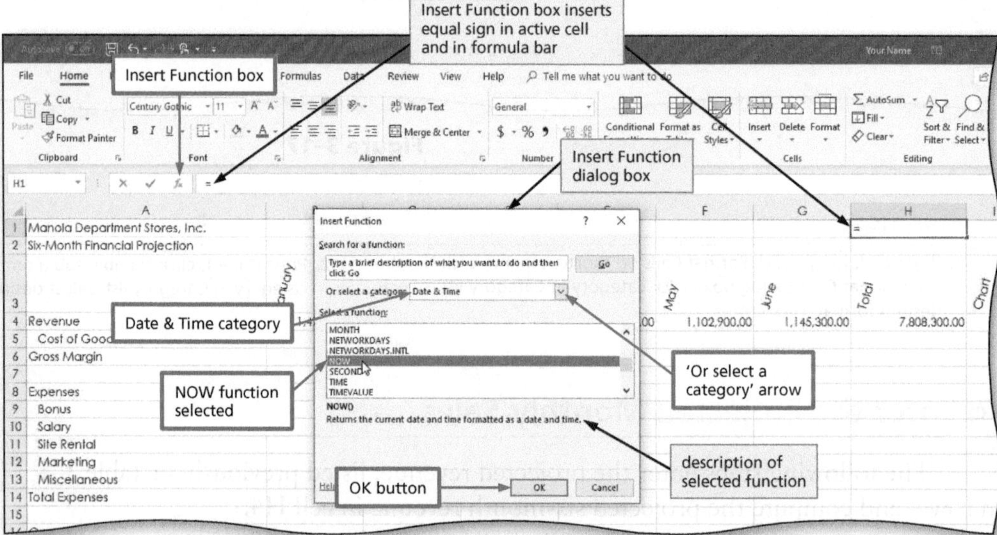

Figure 3–19

2

- Click OK (Insert Function dialog box) to close the Insert Function dialog box and display the Function Arguments dialog box (Figure 3–20).

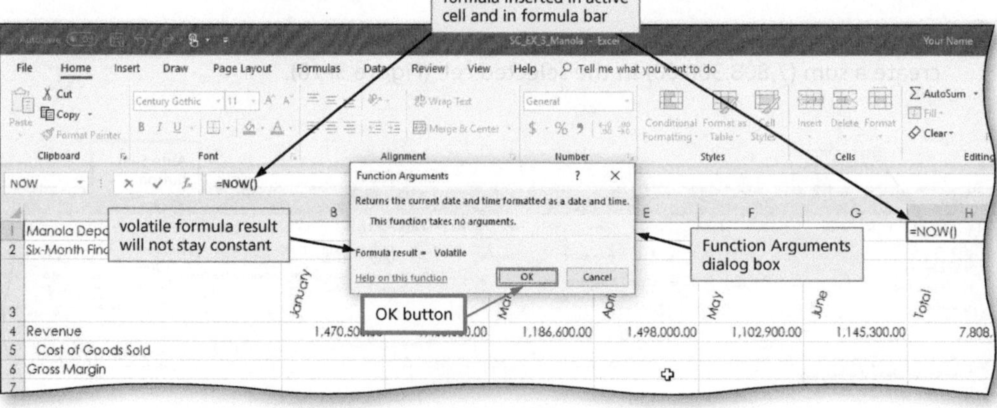

Figure 3–20

Q&A What is meant by 'Formula result = Volatile' in the Function Arguments dialog box?
The NOW function is an example of a volatile function. A **volatile function** is one where the number that the function returns is not constant but changes each time the worksheet is opened. As a result, any formula using the NOW function will have a variable result.

3

- Click OK (Function Arguments dialog box) to display the system date and time in the selected cell, using the default date and time format, which is mm/dd/yyyy hh:mm.

Q&A What does the mm/dd/yyyy hh:mm format represent?
The mm/dd/yyyy hh:mm format can be explained as follows: the first mm is the two-digit month, dd is the two-digit day of the month, yyyy is the four-digit year, hh is the two-digit hour of the day, and the second mm is the two-digit minutes past the hour. Excel applies this date and time format to the result of the NOW function.

- Right-click cell H1 to display a shortcut menu and mini toolbar.
- Click Format Cells on the shortcut menu to display the Format Cells dialog box.
- If necessary, click the Number tab (Format Cells dialog box) to display the Number sheet.
- Click Date in the Category list (Format Cells dialog box) to display the date format options in the Type list. Click 2012-03-14 to display a sample of the data in the Sample area in the dialog box (Figure 3–21).

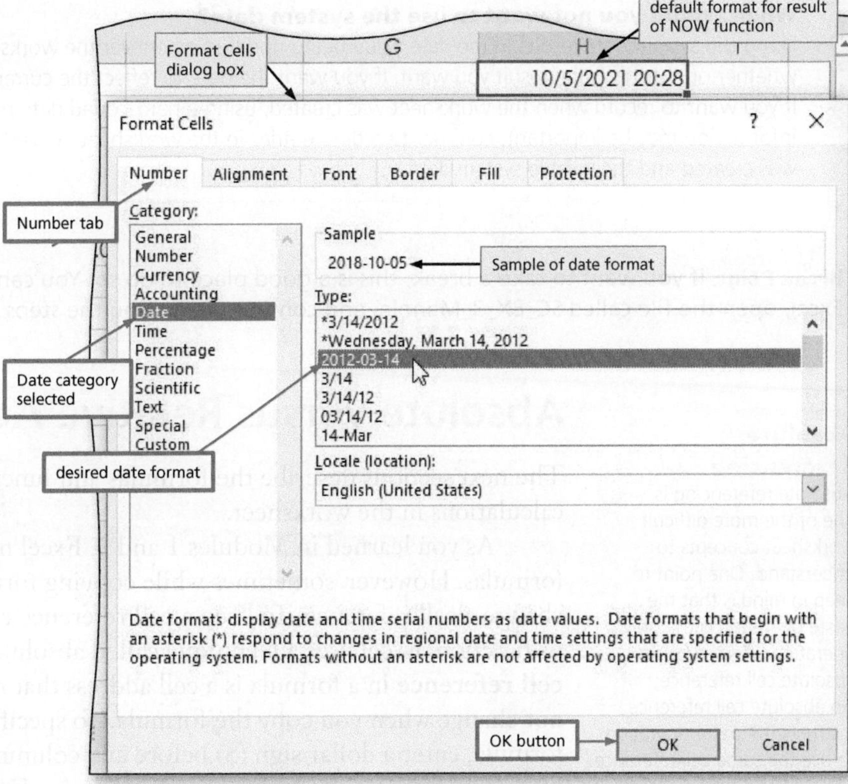

Figure 3–21

Q&A Why do the dates in the Type box show March 14, 2012, instead of the current date?
March 14, 2012, is just used as a sample date in this version of Office.

4

- Click OK (Format Cells dialog box) to display the system date (the result of the NOW function).
- Double-click the border between columns H and I to change the width of the column to best fit (Figure 3–22).
- Save the workbook again on the same storage location with the same file name.

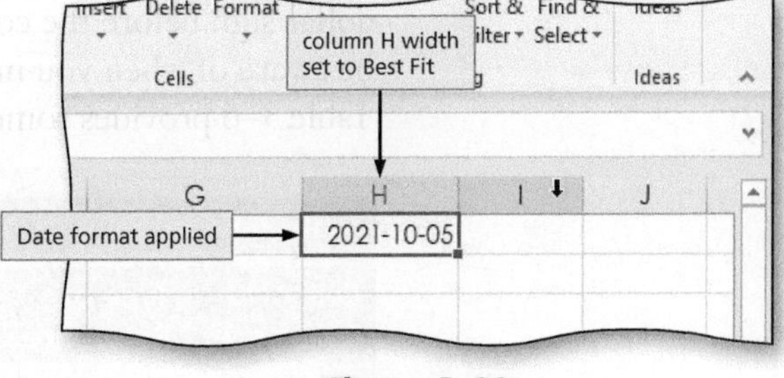

Figure 3–22

Q&A Why should I save the workbook again?
You have made several modifications to the workbook since you last saved it. Thus, you should save it again to make sure all your changes become part of the saved file.

Other Ways

1. Click 'Date & Time' button (Formulas tab | Function Library group), click NOW
2. Press CTRL+SEMICOLON (this enters the date as a static value, meaning the date will not change when the workbook is opened at a later date)
3. Press CTRL+SHIFT+# to format date as day-month-year

CONSIDER THIS

When would you not want to use the system date?

Using the system date results in the date value being updated whenever the worksheet is opened. Think carefully about whether or not this is the result you want. If you want the date to reflect the current date, using the system date is appropriate. If you want to record when the worksheet was created, using a hard-coded date makes more sense. If both pieces of information may be important, consider two date entries in the worksheet: a fixed entry identifying the date the worksheet was created and the volatile system date.

Break Point: If you want to take a break, this is a good place to do so. You can exit Excel now. To resume later, start Excel, open the file called SC_EX_3_Manola, and continue following the steps from this location forward.

BTW
Absolute Referencing
Absolute referencing is one of the more difficult worksheet concepts to understand. One point to keep in mind is that the paste operation is the only operation affected by an absolute cell reference. An absolute cell reference instructs the paste operation to use the same cell reference as it copies a formula from one cell to another.

Absolute versus Relative Addressing

The next sections describe the formulas and functions needed to complete the calculations in the worksheet.

As you learned in Modules 1 and 2, Excel modifies cell references when copying formulas. However, sometimes while copying formulas you do not want Excel to change a cell reference. To keep a cell reference constant when copying a formula or function, Excel uses a technique called absolute cell referencing. An **absolute cell reference** in a formula is a cell address that refers to a specific cell and does not change when you copy the formula. To specify an absolute cell reference in a formula, enter a dollar sign ($) before any column letters or row numbers you want to keep constant in formulas you plan to copy. For example, B4 is an absolute cell reference, whereas B4 is a relative cell reference. Both reference the same cell. The difference becomes apparent when they are copied to a destination area. A formula using the absolute cell reference B4 instructs Excel to keep the cell reference B4 constant (absolute) in the formula as it is copied to the destination area. A formula using the relative cell reference B4 instructs Excel to adjust the cell reference as it is copied to the destination area. A **relative cell reference** is a cell address in a formula that automatically changes to reflect the new location when the formula is copied or moved. This is the default type of referencing used in Excel worksheets and is also called a relative reference. When a cell reference combines both absolute and relative cell addressing, it is called a **mixed cell reference.** A mixed cell reference includes a dollar sign before the column or the row, not before both. When planning formulas, be aware of when you might need to use absolute, relative, and mixed cell references. Table 3–6 provides some additional examples of each of these types of cell references.

Table 3–6 Examples of Absolute, Relative, and Mixed Cell References

Cell Reference	Type of Reference	Meaning
B4	Absolute cell reference	Both column and row references remain the same when you copy this cell, because the cell references are absolute.
B4	Relative cell reference	Both column and row references are relative. When copied to another cell, both the column and row in the cell reference are adjusted to reflect the new location.
B$4	Mixed reference	This cell reference is mixed. The column reference changes when you copy this cell to another column because it is relative. The row reference does not change because it is absolute.
$B4	Mixed reference	This cell reference is mixed. The column reference does not change because it is absolute. The row reference changes when you copy this cell reference to another row because it is relative.

Figure 3–23 illustrates how the type of cell reference used affects the results of copying a formula to a new place in a worksheet. In Figure 3–23a, cells D6:D9 contain formulas. Each formula multiplies the content of cell A2 by 2; the difference between formulas lies in how cell A2 is referenced. Cells C6:C9 identify the type of reference: absolute, relative, or mixed.

Figure 3–23b shows the values that result from copying the formulas in cells D6:D9 to ranges E6:E9, F7:F10, and G11:G14. Figure 3–23c shows the formulas that result from copying the formulas. While all formulas initially multiplied the content of cell A2 by 2, the values and formulas in the destination ranges illustrate how Excel adjusts cell references according to how you reference those cells in original formulas.

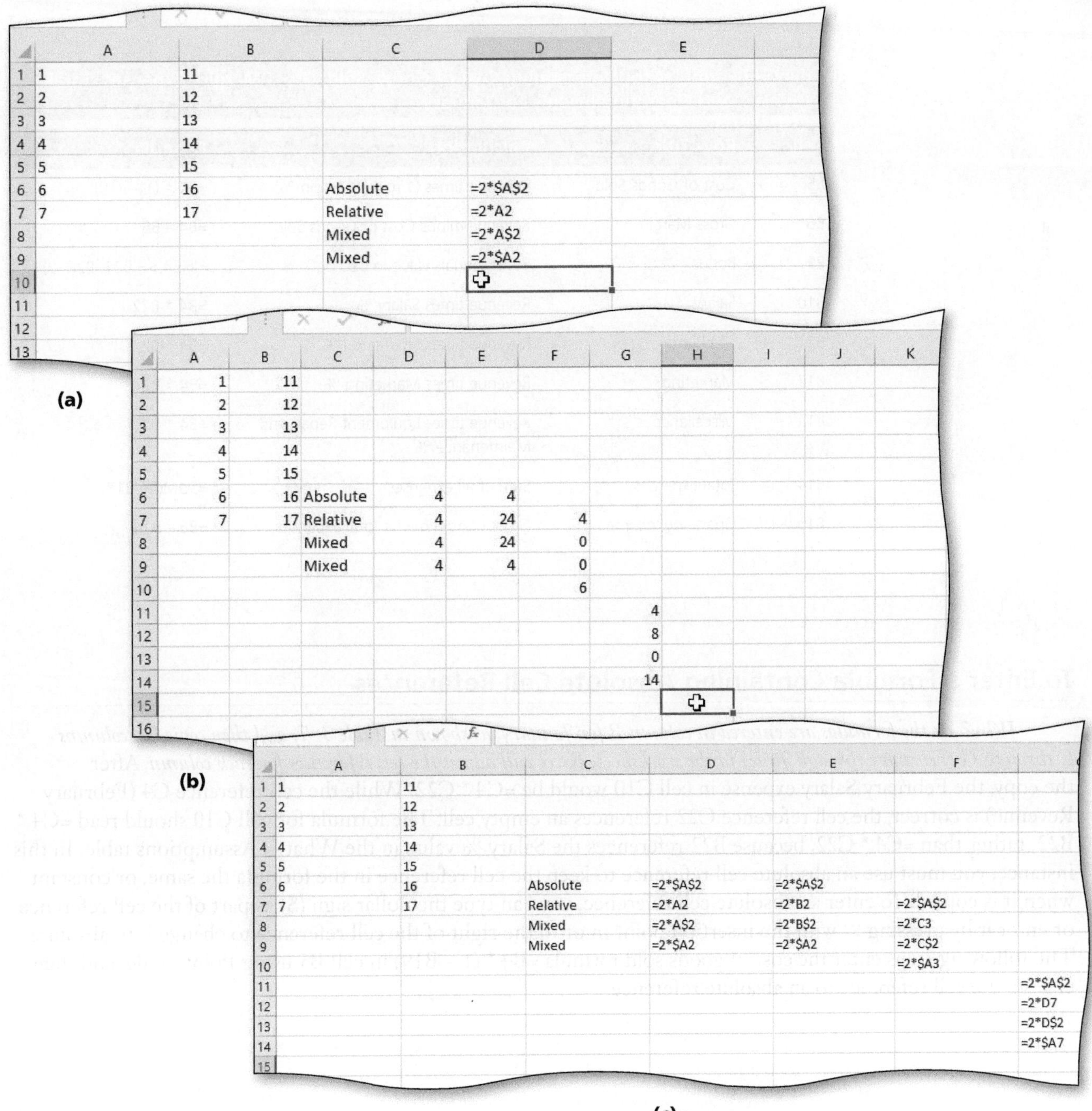

(a)

(b)

(c)

Figure 3–23

In the SC_EX_3_Manola worksheet, you need to enter formulas that calculate the following values for January: cost of goods sold (cell B5), gross margin (cell B6), expenses (range B9:B13), total expenses (cell B14), and operating income (cell B16). The formulas are based on the projected monthly revenue in cell B4 and the assumptions in the range B19:B25.

The calculations for each column (month) are the same, except for the reference to the projected monthly revenue in row 4, which varies according to the month (B4 for January, C4 for February, and so on). Thus, the formulas for January can be entered in column B and then copied to columns C through G. Table 3–7 shows the formulas for determining the January cost of goods sold, gross margin, expenses, total expenses, and operating income in column B.

Table 3–7 Formulas for Determining Cost of Goods Sold, Gross Margin, Expenses, Total Expenses, and Operating Income for January

Cell	Row Title	Calculation	Formula
B5	Cost of Goods Sold	Revenue times (1 minus Margin %)	=B4 * (1 – B19)
B6	Gross Margin	Revenue minus Cost of Goods Sold	=B4 – B5
B9	Bonus	Bonus equals value in B20 or 0	=IF(B4 >= B21, B20, 0)
B10	Salary	Revenue times Salary %	=B4 * B22
B11	Site Rental	Revenue times Site Rental %	=B4 * B23
B12	Marketing	Revenue times Marketing %	=B4 * B24
B13	Miscellaneous	Revenue times Equipment Repair and Maintenance %	=B4 * B25
B14	Total Expenses	Sum of all expenses	=SUM(B9:B13)
B16	Operating Income	Gross Margin minus Total Expenses	=B6 – B14

To Enter a Formula Containing Absolute Cell References

Why? *As the formulas are entered in column B for January, as shown in Table 3–7, and then copied to columns C through G (February through June) in the worksheet, Excel will adjust the cell references for each column.* After the copy, the February Salary expense in cell C10 would be =C4 * C22. While the cell reference C4 (February Revenue) is correct, the cell reference C22 references an empty cell. The formula for cell C10 should read =C4 * B22, rather than =C4 * C22, because B22 references the Salary % value in the What-If Assumptions table. In this instance, you must use an absolute cell reference to keep the cell reference in the formula the same, or constant, when it is copied. To enter an absolute cell reference, you can type the dollar sign ($) as part of the cell reference or enter it by pressing F4 with the insertion point in or to the right of the cell reference to change it to absolute. The following steps enter the cost of goods sold formula =B4 * (1 – B19) in cell B5 using Point mode, and then change the cell reference to an absolute reference.

1

- Click cell B5 to select the cell in which to enter the first formula.
- Type = (equal sign), select cell B4, type `*(1-B19` to continue entering the formula, and then press F4 to change the cell reference from a relative cell reference to an absolute cell reference. Type) (closing parenthesis) to complete the formula (Figure 3–24).

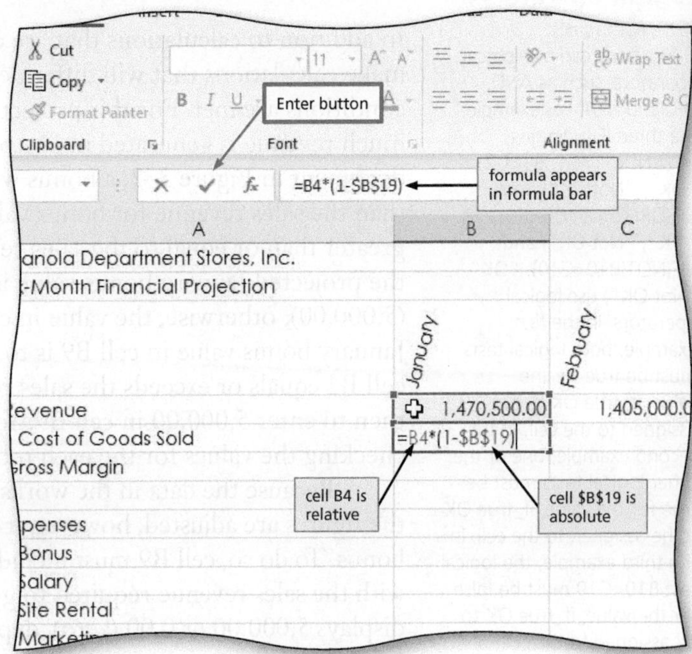

Figure 3–24

Q&A Is an absolute reference required in this formula?

No, a mixed cell reference also could have been used. The formula in cell B5 will be copied across columns, rather than down rows. So, the formula entered in cell B5 in Step 1 could have been entered as =B4*(1–$B19) using a mixed cell reference, rather than =B4*(1–B19), because when you copy a formula across columns, the row does not change. The key is to ensure that column B remains constant as you copy the formula across columns. To change the absolute cell reference to a mixed cell reference, continue to press F4 until you achieve the desired cell reference.

2

- Click the Enter button in the formula bar to display the result, 275718.75, instead of the formula in cell B5 (Figure 3–25).

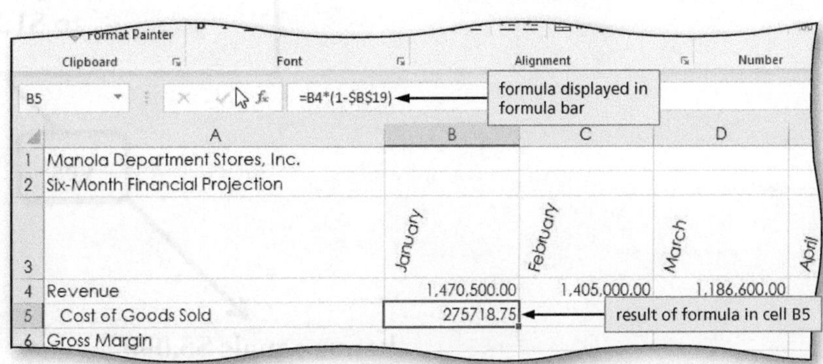

Figure 3–25

3

- Click cell B6 to select the cell in which to enter the next formula, type = (equal sign), click cell B4, type – (minus sign), and then click cell B5 to add a reference to the cell to the formula.
- Click the Enter button in the formula bar to display the result in the selected cell, in this case gross margin for January, 1,194,781.25, in cell B6 (Figure 3–26).

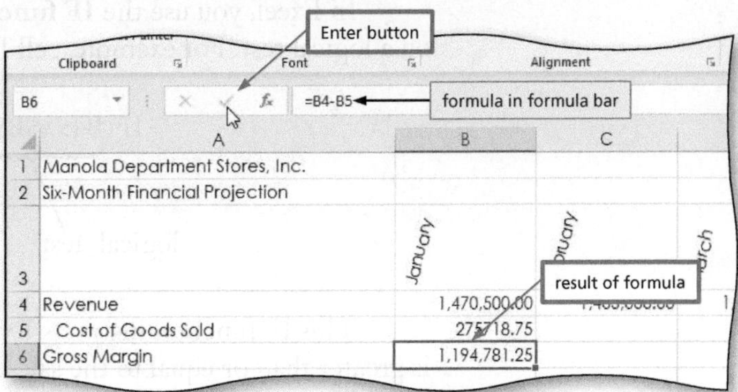

Figure 3–26

BTW
Logical Operators in IF Functions
IF functions can use logical operators, such as AND, OR, and NOT. For example, the three IF functions =IF(AND(A1>C1, B1<C2), "OK", "Not OK") and =IF(OR(K5>J5, C3<K6), "OK", "Not OK") and =IF(NOT(B10<C10), "OK", "Not OK") use logical operators. In the first example, both logical tests must be true for the value_if_true OK to be assigned to the cell. In the second example, one or the other logical tests must be true for the value_if_true OK to be assigned to the cell. In the third example, the logical test B10<C10 must be false for the value_if_true OK to be assigned to the cell.

Making Decisions—The IF Function

In addition to calculations that are constant across all categories, you may need to make calculations that will differ depending on whether a particular condition or set of conditions are met. For this project, you need to vary compensation according to how much revenue is generated in any particular month. According to the requirements document in Figure 3–2, a bonus will be paid in any month where revenue is greater than the sales revenue for bonus value. If the projected January revenue in cell B4 is greater than or equal to the sales revenue for bonus in cell B21 (1,250,000.00), then the projected January bonus value in cell B9 is equal to the bonus value in cell B20 (5,000.00); otherwise, the value in cell B9 is equal to 0. One way to assign the projected January bonus value in cell B9 is to manually check to see if the projected revenue in cell B4 equals or exceeds the sales revenue for the bonus amount in cell B21 and, if so, then to enter 5,000.00 in cell B9. You can use this manual process for all six months by checking the values for the each month.

Because the data in the worksheet changes each time a report is prepared or the figures are adjusted, however, it is preferable to have Excel calculate the monthly bonus. To do so, cell B9 must include a function that compares the projected revenue with the sales revenue required to generate a bonus (Sales Revenue for Bonus), and displays 5,000.00 or 0.00 (zero), depending on whether the projected January revenue in cell B4 is greater than, equal to, or less than the sales revenue for bonus value in cell B21. This decision-making process is a **logical test**. It can be represented in diagram form, as shown in Figure 3–27.

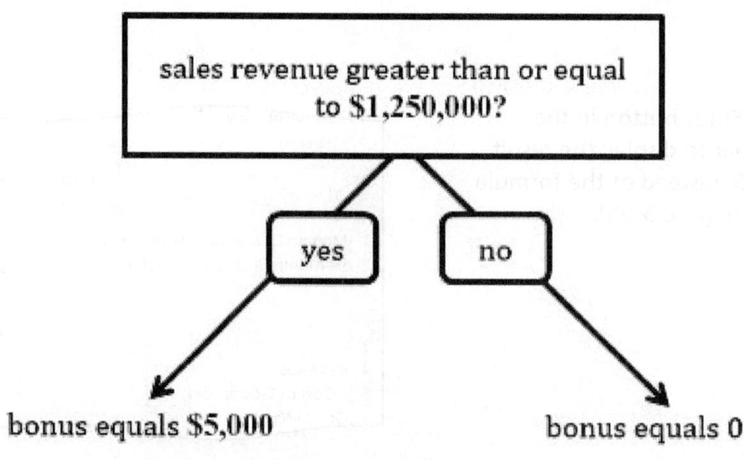

Figure 3–27

In Excel, you use the **IF function** when you want to assign a value to a cell based on a logical test. For example, cell B9 can be assigned the following IF function:

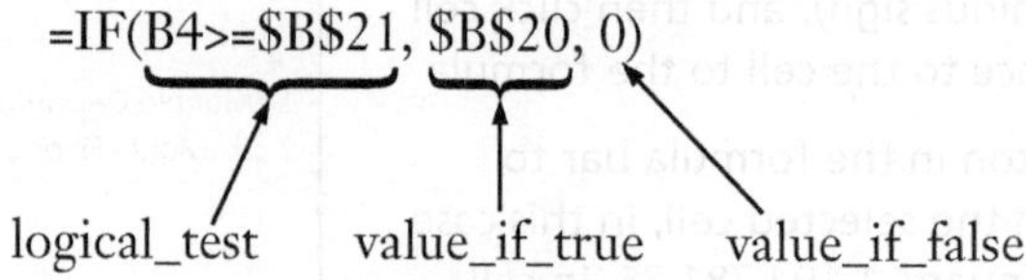

This IF function instructs Excel that if the projected January revenue in cell B4 is greater than or equal to the sales revenue for bonus value in cell B21, then Excel should display the bonus value found in cell B20 in cell B9. If the projected January revenue in cell B4 is not greater than or equal to the sales revenue for bonus value in cell B21, then Excel should display a 0 (zero) in cell B9.

The general form of the IF function is:

=IF(logical_test, value_if_true, value_if_false)

The argument, logical_test, is made up of two expressions and a comparison operator. Each expression can be a cell reference, a number, text, a function, or a formula. In this example, the logical test compares the projected revenue with the Sales Revenue for Bonus amount, using the comparison operator greater than or equal to. Valid comparison operators, their meanings, and examples of their use in IF functions are shown in Table 3–8. The argument, value_if_true, is the value you want Excel to display in the cell when the logical test is true. The argument, value_if_false, is the value you want Excel to display in the cell when the logical test is false.

Table 3–8 Comparison Operators

Comparison Operator	Meaning	Example
=	Equal to	=IF(A1=A2, "True", "False")
<	Less than	=IF(A1<A2, "True", "False")
>	Greater than	=IF(A1>A2, "True", "False")
>=	Greater than or equal to	=IF(A1>=A2, "True", "False")
<=	Less than or equal to	=IF(A1<=A2, "True", "False")
<>	Not equal to	=IF(A1<>A2, "True", "False")

To Enter an IF Function

Why? Use an IF function to determine the value for a cell based on a logical test. The following steps assign the IF function =IF(B4>=B21,B20,0) to cell B9. This IF function determines whether or not the worksheet assigns a bonus for January.

- Click cell B9 to select the cell for the next formula.
- Click the Insert Function button in the formula bar to display the Insert Function dialog box.
- Click the 'Or select a category' arrow (Insert Function dialog box) and then select Logical in the list to populate the 'Select a function' list with logic functions.
- Click IF in the 'Select a function' list to select the required function (Figure 3–28).

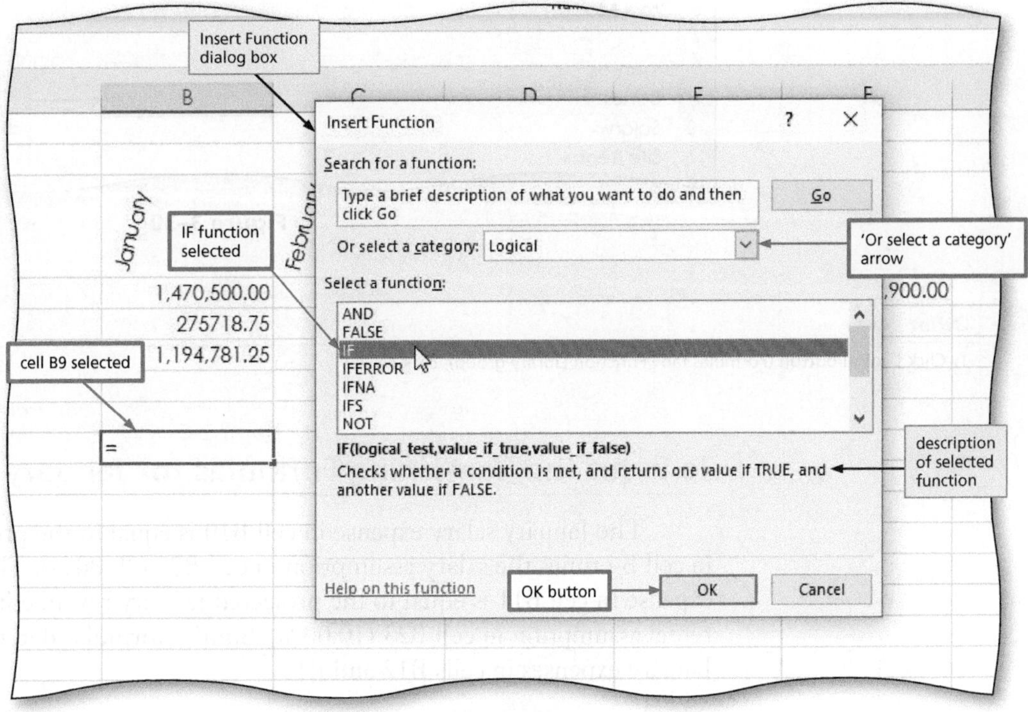

Figure 3–28

- Click OK (Insert Function dialog box) to display the Function Arguments dialog box.
- Type **b4>=b21** in the Logical_test box to enter a logical test for the IF function.
- Type **b20** in the Value_if_true box to enter the result of the IF function if the logical test is true.
- Type **0** (zero) in the Value_if_false box to enter the result of the IF function if the logical test is false (Figure 3–29).

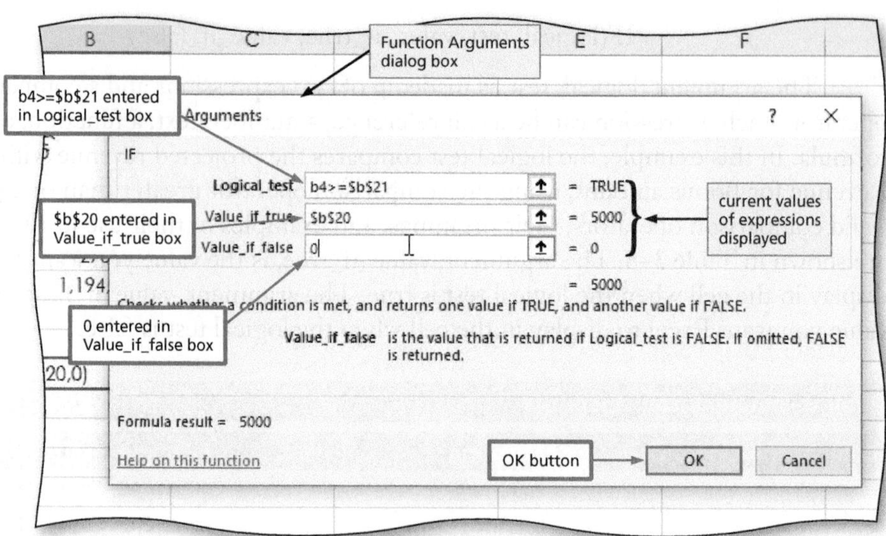

Figure 3–29

- Click OK (Function Arguments dialog box) to insert the IF function in the selected cell (Figure 3–30).

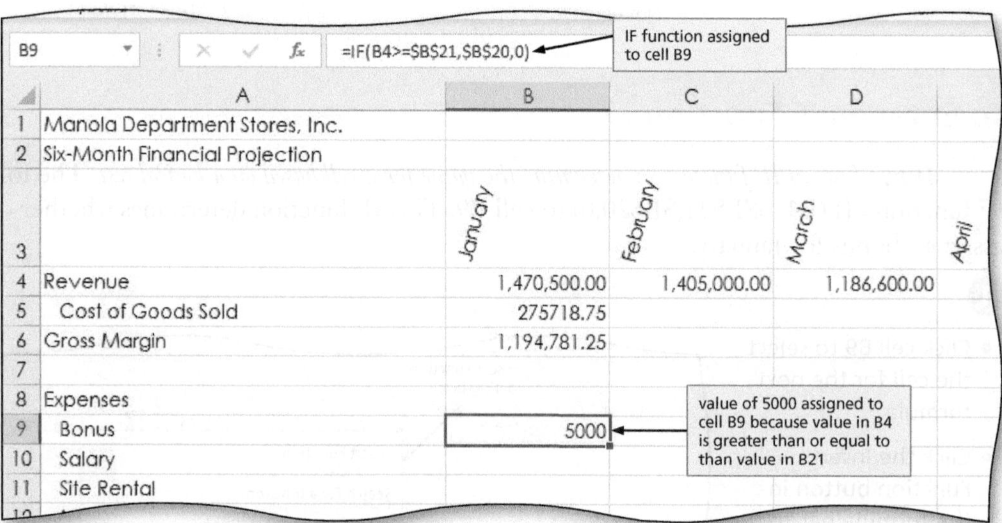

Figure 3–30

Other Ways

1. Click Logical button (Formulas tab | Function Library group), click IF

To Enter the Remaining Formulas for January

The January salary expense in cell B10 is equal to the projected January revenue in cell B4 times the salary assumption in cell B22 (20.00%). The January site rental expense in cell B11 is equal to the projected January revenue in cell B4 times the site rental assumption in cell B23 (10.00%). Similar formulas determine the remaining January expenses in cells B12 and B13.

The total expenses value in cell B14 is equal to the sum of the expenses in the range B9:B13. The operating income in cell B16 is equal to the gross margin in cell B6 minus the total expenses in cell B14. Because the formulas are short, you will type them in the following steps, rather than using Point mode.

1. Select cell B10. Type **=b4*b22** and then press the DOWN ARROW key to enter the formula in the selected cell. Type **=b4*b23** and then press the DOWN ARROW key to enter the formula in cell B11. Type **=b4*b24,** press the DOWN ARROW key, type **=b4*b25,** and then press the DOWN ARROW key again.

2. With cell B14 selected, click the Auto Sum button (Home tab | Editing group) twice to insert a SUM function in the selected cell. Select cell B16 to prepare to enter the next formula. Type **=b6-b14** and then press ENTER to enter the formula in the selected cell.

3. Press CTRL+ACCENT MARK (`) to display the formulas version of the worksheet (Figure 3–31).

4. When you are finished viewing the formulas version, press CTRL+ACCENT MARK (`) again to return to the values version of the worksheet.

Q&A

Why should I view the formulas version of the worksheet?
Viewing the formulas version (Figure 3–31) of the worksheet allows you to check the formulas you entered in the range B5:B16. Recall that formulas were entered in lowercase. You can see that Excel converts all the formulas from lowercase to uppercase.

BTW

Replacing a Formula with a Constant

Using the following steps, you can replace a formula with its result so that the cell value remains constant: (1) click the cell with the formula; (2) press F2 or click in the formula bar; (3) press F9 to display the value in the formula bar; and (4) press ENTER.

BTW

Error Messages

When Excel cannot calculate a formula, it displays an error message in a cell. These error messages always begin with a number sign (#). The more commonly occurring error messages are as follows: #DIV/0! (tries to divide by zero); #NAME? (uses a name Excel does not recognize); #N/A (refers to a value not available); #NULL! (specifies an invalid intersection of two areas); #NUM! (uses a number incorrectly); #REF (refers to a cell that is not valid); #VALUE! (uses an incorrect argument or operand); and ##### (refers to cells not wide enough to display entire entry).

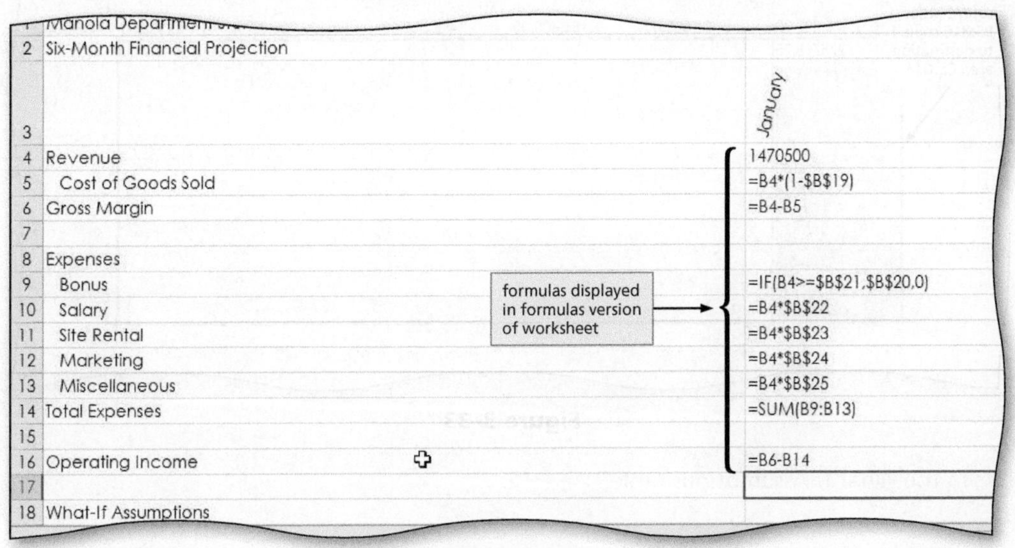

Figure 3–31

To Copy Formulas with Absolute Cell References Using the Fill Handle

Why? *Using the fill handle ensures a quick, accurate copy of the formulas.* The following steps use the fill handle to copy the January formulas in column B to the other five months in columns C through G.

- Select the range B5:B16 and then point to the fill handle in the lower-right corner of the selected cell, B16 in this case, to display the crosshair pointer (Figure 3–32).

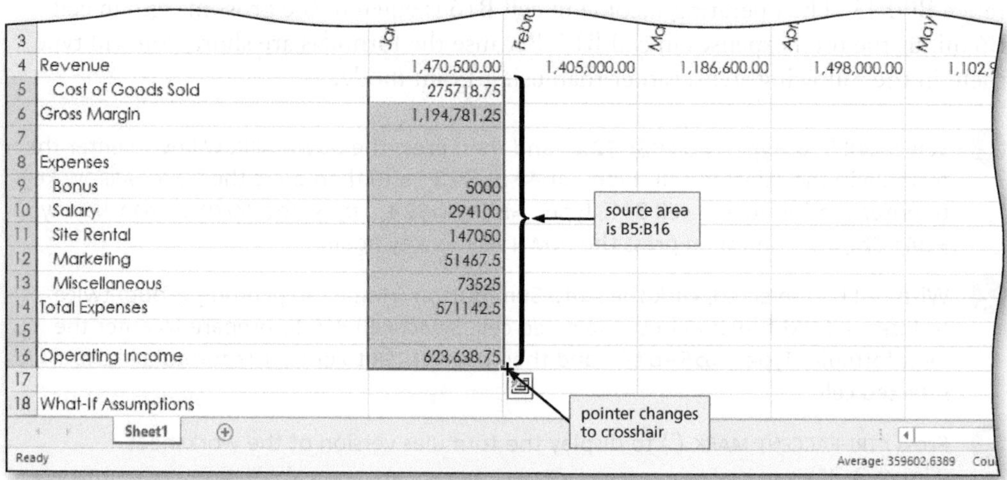

Figure 3–32

2

- Drag the fill handle to the right to copy the formulas from the source area, B5:B16 in this case, to the destination area, C5:G16 in this case, and display the calculated amounts (Figure 3–33).

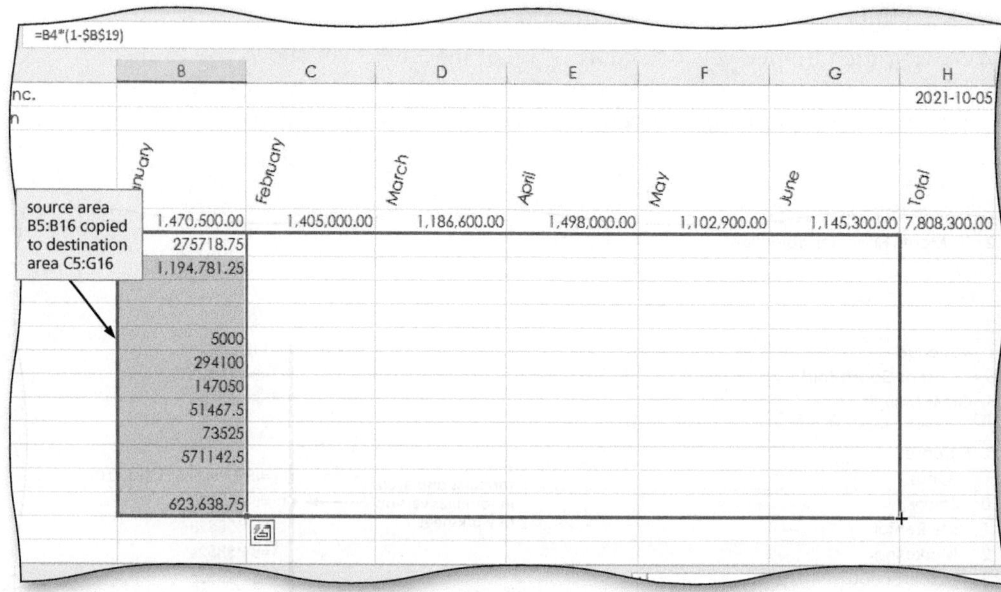

Figure 3–33

Q&A What happens to the formulas after performing the copy operation?
Because the formulas in the range B5:B16 use absolute cell references, when they are copied to the range C5:G16, they still refer to the values in the What-If Assumptions table.

To Determine Row Totals in Nonadjacent Cells

The following steps determine the row totals in column H. To determine the row totals using the Sum button, select only the cells in column H containing numbers in adjacent cells to the left. If, for example, you select the range H5:H16, Excel will display 0s as the sum of empty rows in cells H7, H8, and H15.

1. Select the range H5:H6. While holding down CTRL, select the range H9:H14 and cell H16, as shown in Figure 3–34.

2. Click the Auto Sum button (Home tab | Editing group) to display the row totals in the selected ranges (Figure 3–34).

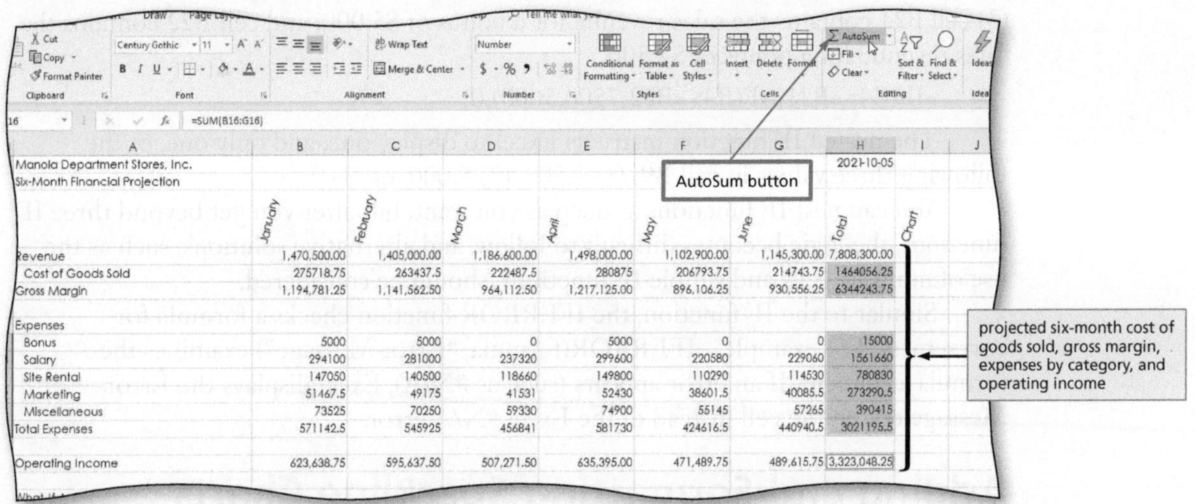

Figure 3–34

3. Save the workbook again in the same storage location with the same file name.

Nested Forms of the IF Function

A **nested IF function** is one in which the action to be taken for the true or false case includes another IF function. The second IF function is considered to be nested, or layered, within the first. You can use a nested IF function to add another condition to the decision-making process. Study the nested IF function below, which would add another level of bonus to the compensation at Manola Department Stores. In this case, Manola's assigns a bonus for sales of $1,250,000 and above. For months where sales make that level, additional bonus money is available for sales of $1,450,000 and above. In this case, three outcomes are possible, two of which involve paying a bonus. Figure 3–35 depicts a decision tree for this logical test.

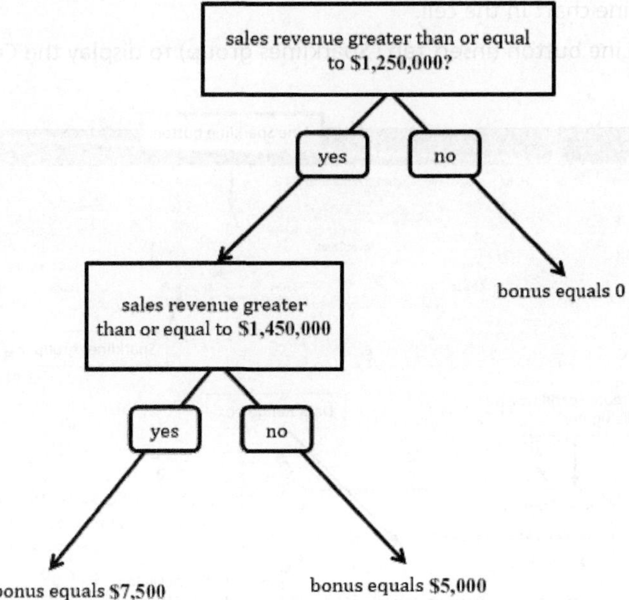

Figure 3–35

Assume the following in this example: (1) the nested IF function is assigned to cell B9, which will display one of three values; (2) cell B4 contains the sales revenue;

(3) cell B21 contains the sales revenue for a bonus of $5,000; and cell B22 contains the sales revenue for a bonus of $7,500.

=IF(B4>=B21, IF(B4>=B22,7500,5000),0)

The nested IF function instructs Excel to display one, and only one, of the following three values in cell B9: (1) 7,500, (2) 5,000, or (3) 0.

You can nest IF functions as deep as you want, but after you get beyond three IF functions, the logic becomes difficult to follow, and alternative solutions, such as the use of multiple cells and simple IF functions, should be considered.

Similar to the IF function, the IFERROR function checks a formula for correctness. For example, =IFERROR(formula, "Error Message") examines the formula argument. If an error appears (such as #N/A), Excel displays the Error Message text in the cell instead of the Excel #N/A error.

Adding and Formatting Sparkline Charts

Sometimes you may want to condense a range of data into a small chart in order to show a trend or variation in the range, and Excel's standard charts may be too large or extensive for your needs. A sparkline chart provides a simple way to show trends and variations in a range of data within a single cell. Excel includes three types of sparkline charts: line, column, and win/loss. Because sparkline charts appear in a single cell, you can use them to convey succinct, eye-catching summaries of the data they represent.

To Add a Sparkline Chart to the Worksheet

Each row of monthly data, including those containing formulas, provides useful information that can be summarized by a line sparkline chart. ***Why?*** *A line sparkline chart is a good choice because it shows trends over the six-month period for each row of data.* The following steps add a line sparkline chart to cell I4 and then use the fill handle to create line sparkline charts in the range I5:I16 to represent the monthly data shown in rows 4 through 16.

- If necessary, scroll the worksheet so that both columns B and I and row 3 are visible on the screen.
- Select cell I4 to prepare to insert a sparkline chart in the cell.
- Display the Insert tab and then click the Line button (Insert tab | Sparklines group) to display the Create Sparklines dialog box (Figure 3–36).

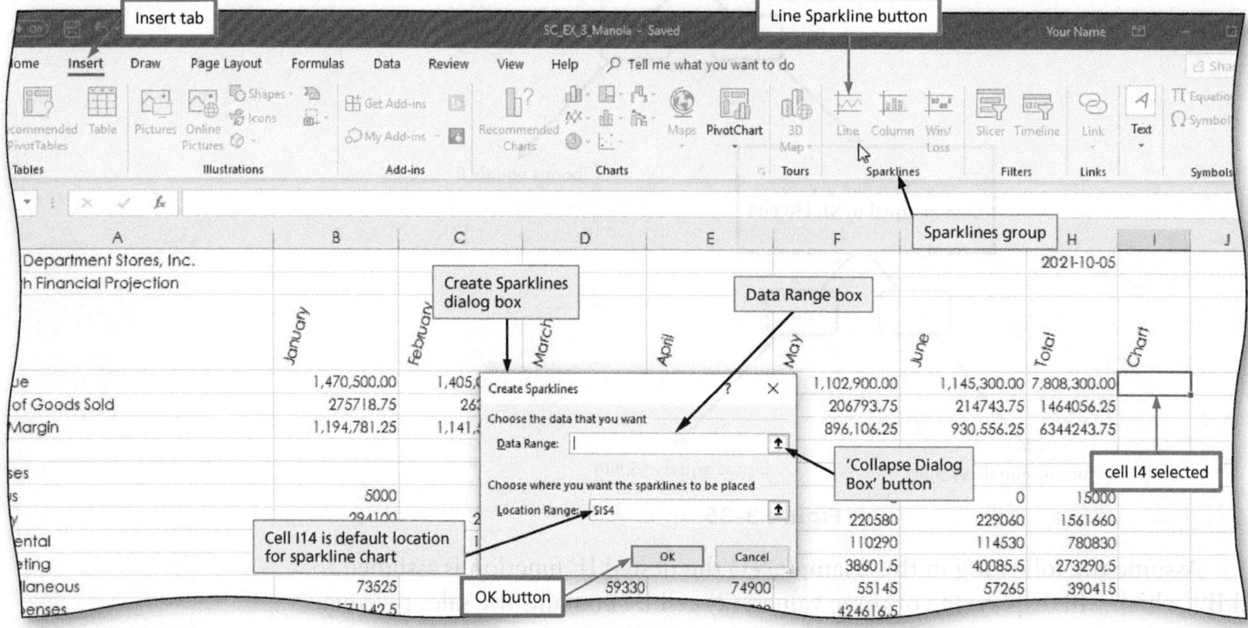

Figure 3–36

2

- Drag through the range B4:G4 to select the range. Do not release the mouse button (Figure 3–37).

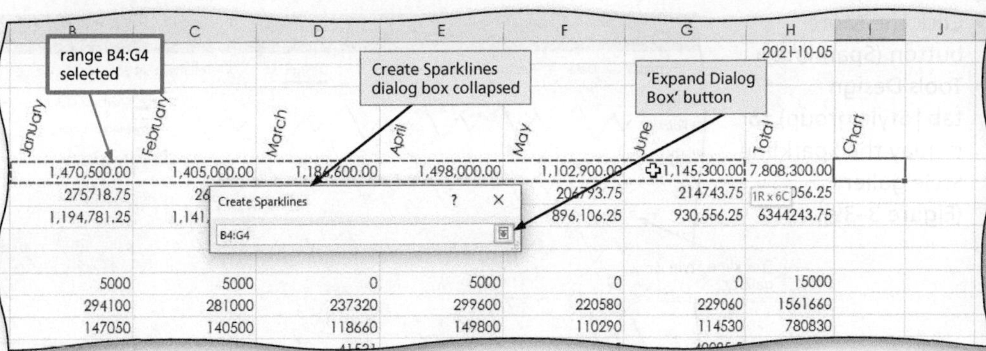

Figure 3–37

Q&A What happened to the Create Sparklines dialog box?
When a dialog box includes a 'Collapse Dialog Box' button (Figure 3–36), selecting cells or a range collapses the dialog box so that only the current text box is visible. This allows you to select your desired range without the dialog box getting in the way. Once the selection is made, the dialog box expands back to its original size. You also can click the 'Collapse Dialog Box' button to make your selection and then click the 'Expand Dialog Box' button (Figure 3–37) to expand the dialog box.

3

- **Release the mouse button to insert the selected range, B4:G4 in this case, in the Data Range box.**
- **Click OK as shown in Figure 3–36 (Create Sparklines dialog box) to insert a line sparkline chart in the selected cell and display the Sparkline Tools Design tab (Figure 3–38).**

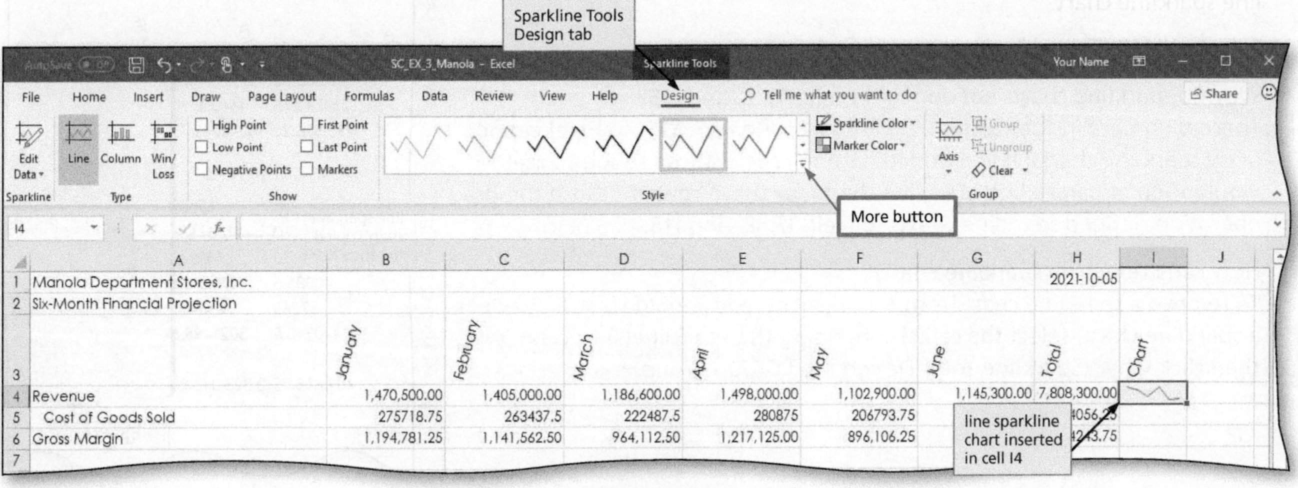

Figure 3–38

To Change the Sparkline Style and Copy the Sparkline Chart

***Why?** The default style option may not provide the visual impact you seek. Changing the sparkline style allows you to alter how the sparkline chart appears.* The following steps change the sparkline chart style.

- Click the More button (Sparkline Tools Design tab | Style group) to display the Sparkline Style gallery (Figure 3–39).

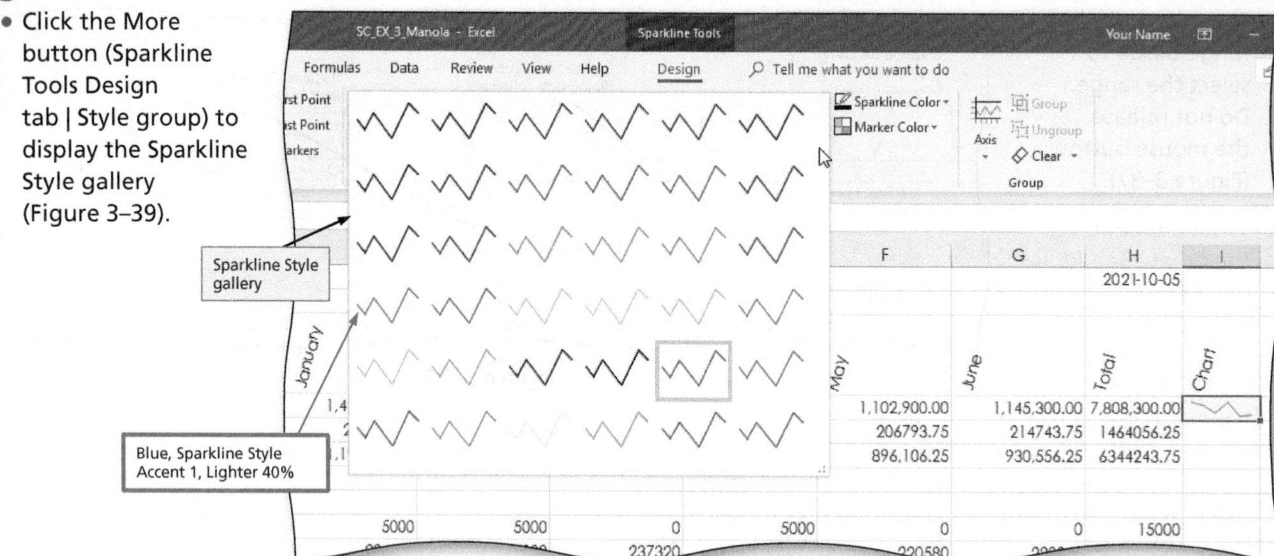

Figure 3–39

- Click 'Blue, Sparkline Style Accent 1, Lighter 40%' in the Sparkline Style gallery to apply the style to the sparkline chart in the selected cell, I4 in this case.
- Point to the fill handle in cell I4 and then drag through cell I16 to copy the line sparkline chart.
- Select cell I18 (Figure 3–40).

Q&A Why do sparkline charts not appear in cells I7, I8, and I15?
There is no data in the ranges B7:G7, B8:G8, and B15:G15, so Excel cannot draw sparkline charts. If you added data to cells in those ranges, Excel would then generate line sparkline charts for those rows, because the drag operation defined sparkline charts for cells I7, I8, and I15.

How can I remove a sparkline chart?
To remove a sparkline chart from a worksheet, you should clear it. To clear a sparkline chart, select the cell(s) containing the sparkline(s) to clear, and then click Clear (Sparkline Tools Design tab | Group group).

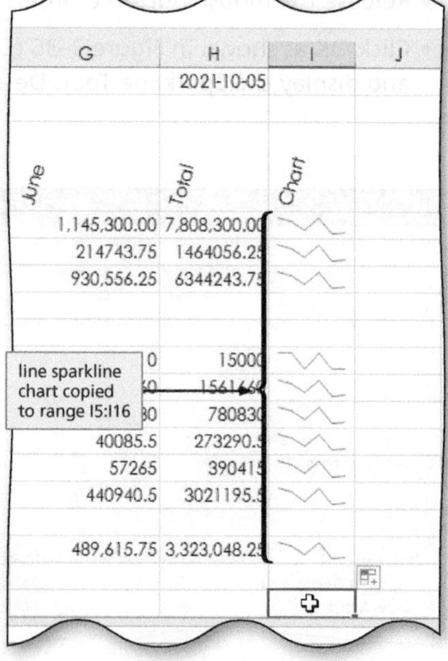

Figure 3–40

To Change the Sparkline Type

In addition to changing the sparkline chart style, you also can change the sparkline chart type. ***Why?*** *You may decide that a different chart type will better illustrate the characteristics of your data.* As shown in Figure 3–40, most of the sparkline charts look similar. Changing the sparkline chart type allows you to decide if a different chart type will better present your data to the reader. The following steps change the line sparkline charts to column sparkline charts.

- Select the range I4:I16 to select the sparkline charts.
- Click the Sparkline Tools Design tab to make it the active tab.

- Click the Column button (Sparkline Tools Design tab | Type group) to change the sparkline charts in the selected range to the column type (Figure 3–41).

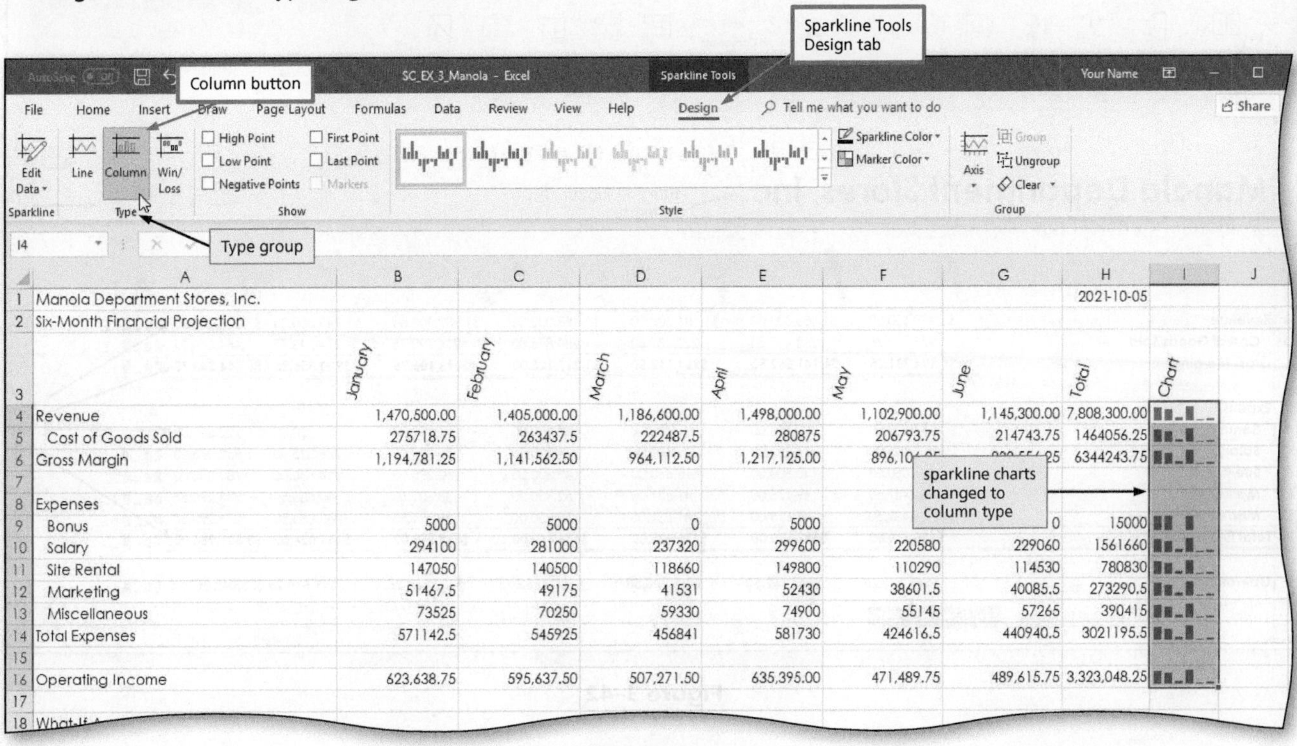

Figure 3–41

2

- Select cell I18.
- Save the workbook again in the same storage location with the same file name.

Customizing Sparkline Charts

You can customize sparkline charts using commands on the Sparkline Tools Design tab. To show markers on specific values on the sparkline chart, such as the highest value, lowest value, any negative numbers, the first point, or the last point, use the corresponding check boxes in the Show group. To show markers on all line sparkline points, select the Markers check box in the Show group. You can change the color of sparklines or markers by using the Sparkline Color and Marker Color buttons in the Style group. You can group sparklines so changes apply to all sparklines in the group by using the Group command in the Group group.

Formatting the Worksheet

The worksheet created thus far shows the financial projections for the six-month period from January to June. Its appearance is uninteresting, however, even though you have performed some minimal formatting earlier (formatting assumptions numbers, changing the column widths, formatting the date, and formatting the sparkline chart). This section completes the formatting of the worksheet by making the numbers easier to read and emphasizing the titles, assumptions, categories, and totals, as shown in Figure 3–42.

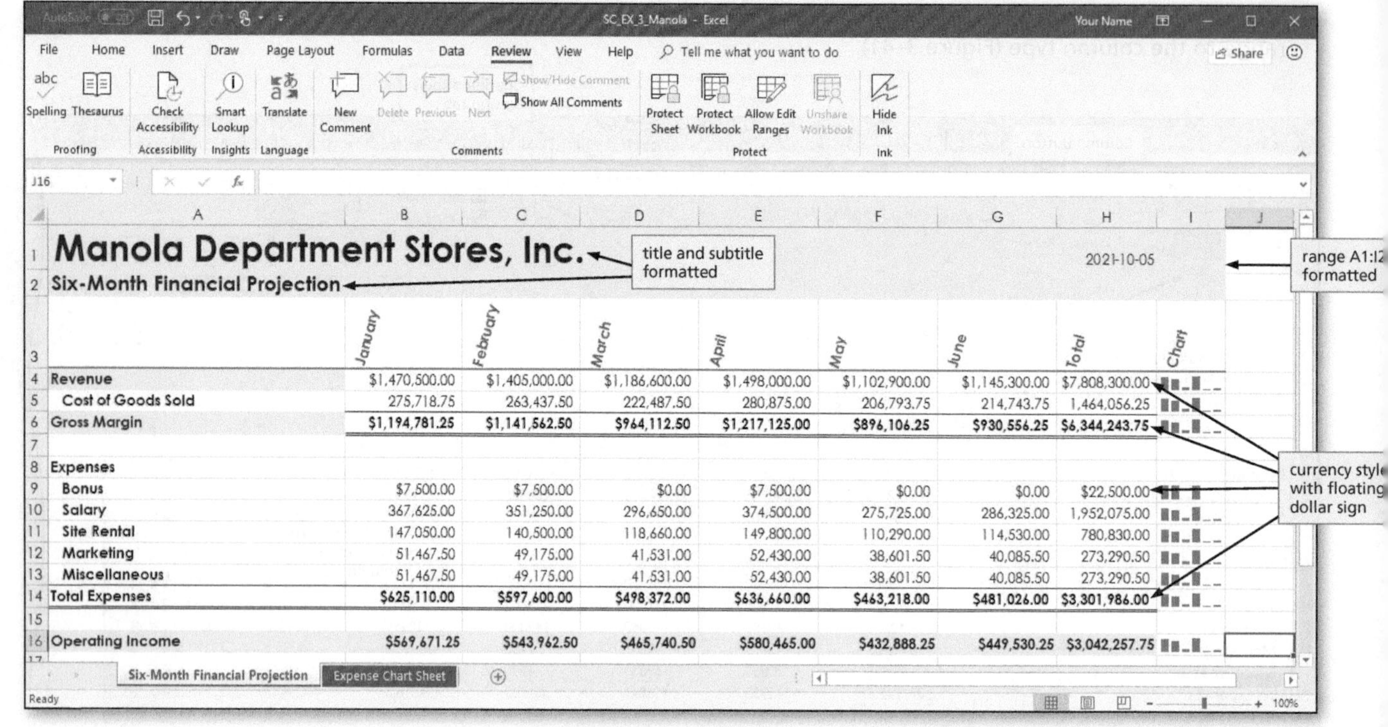

Figure 3–42

CONSIDER THIS

How should you format various elements of the worksheet?

A worksheet, such as the one presented in this module, should be formatted in the following manner: (1) format the numbers; (2) format the worksheet title, column titles, row titles, and total rows; and (3) format the assumptions table. Numbers in heading rows and total rows should be formatted with a currency symbol. Other dollar amounts should be formatted with a comma style. The assumptions table should be diminished in its formatting so that it does not distract from the main data and calculations in the worksheet. Assigning a smaller font size to the data in the assumptions table would visually illustrate that it is supplementary information and set it apart from other data formatted with a larger font size.

To Assign Formats to Nonadjacent Ranges

The following steps assign formats to the numbers in rows 4 through 16. ***Why?*** *These formats increase the readability of the data.*

1

- Select the range B4:H4 as the first range to format.
- While holding down CTRL, select the nonadjacent ranges B6:H6, B9:H9, B14:H14, and B16:H16, and then release CTRL to select nonadjacent ranges.
- On the Home tab in the Number group, click the Dialog Box Launcher to display the Format Cells dialog box.
- Click Currency in the Category list (Format Cells dialog box), if necessary select 2 in the Decimal places box and then select $ in the Symbol list to ensure a dollar sign shows in the cells to be formatted, and select the red font color ($1,234.10) in the Negative numbers list to specify the desired currency style for the selected ranges (Figure 3–43).

Q&A

Why was this particular style chosen for the negative numbers?

In accounting, negative numbers often are shown with parentheses surrounding the value rather than with a negative sign preceding the value. Although the data being used in this module contains no negative numbers, you still must select a negative number format. It is important to be consistent when selecting negative number formats if you are applying different formats in a column; otherwise, the decimal points may not line up.

Q&A Why is the Format Cells dialog box used to create the format for the ranges in this step?
The requirements for this worksheet call for a floating dollar sign. You can use the Format Cells dialog box to assign a currency style with a floating dollar sign, instead of using the 'Accounting Number Format' button (Home tab | Number group), which assigns a fixed dollar sign.

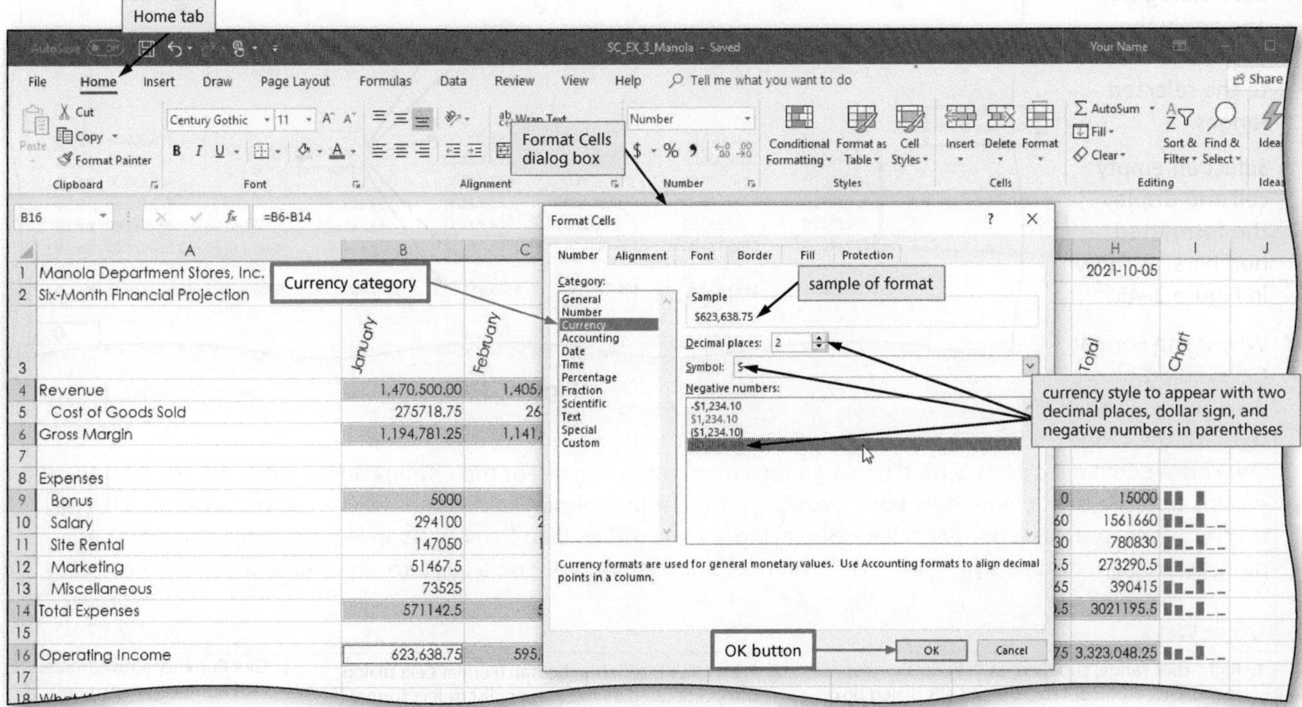

Figure 3–43

2

- Click OK (Format Cells dialog box) to close the Format Cells dialog box and apply the desired format to the selected ranges.
- Select the range B5:H5 as the next range to format.
- While holding down CTRL, select the range B10:H13, and then release CTRL to select nonadjacent ranges.
- On the Home tab in the Number group, click the Dialog Box Launcher to display the Format Cells dialog box.
- Click Currency in the Category list (Format Cells dialog box), if necessary select 2 in the Decimal places box, select None in the Symbol list so that a dollar sign does not show in the cells to be formatted, and select the red font color (1,234.10) in the Negative numbers list (Figure 3–44).

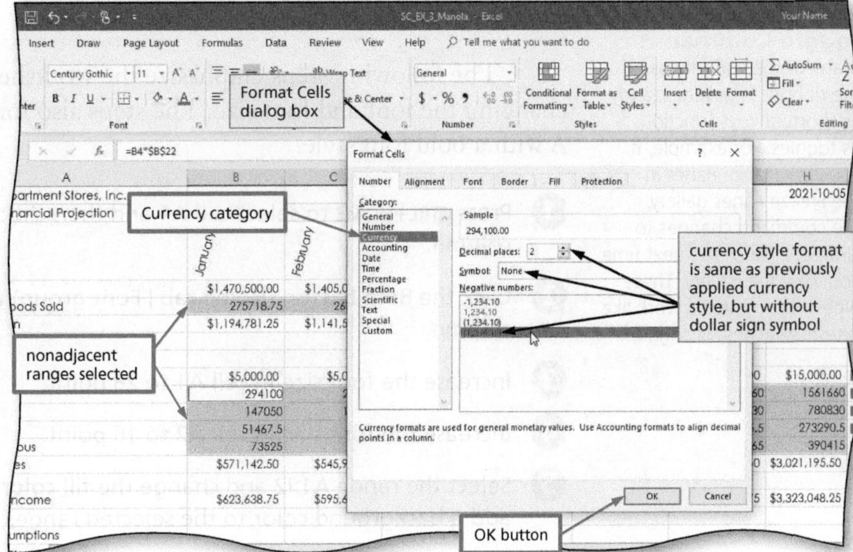

Figure 3–44

3

- Click OK (Format Cells dialog box) to close the Format Cells dialog box and apply the desired format to the selected ranges.
- Select an empty cell and display the formatted numbers, as shown in Figure 3–45.

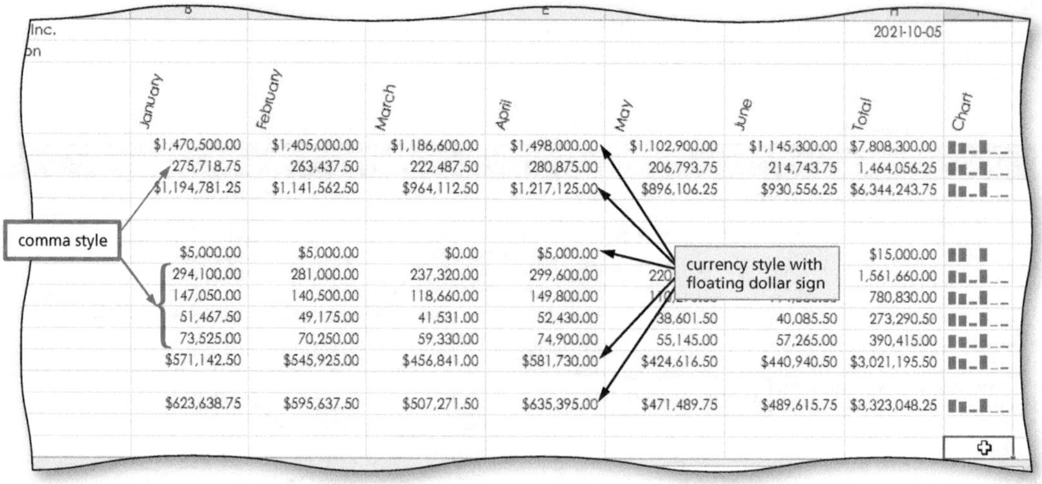

January	February	March	April	May	June	Total	Chart
$1,470,500.00	$1,405,000.00	$1,186,600.00	$1,498,000.00	$1,102,900.00	$1,145,300.00	$7,808,300.00	
275,718.75	263,437.50	222,487.50	280,875.00	206,793.75	214,743.75	1,464,056.25	
$1,194,781.25	$1,141,562.50	$964,112.50	$1,217,125.00	$896,106.25	$930,556.25	$6,344,243.75	
$5,000.00	$5,000.00	$0.00	$5,000.00			$15,000.00	
294,100.00	281,000.00	237,320.00	299,600.00	220		1,561,660.00	
147,050.00	140,500.00	118,660.00	149,800.00			780,830.00	
51,467.50	49,175.00	41,531.00	52,430.00	38,601.50	40,085.50	273,290.50	
73,525.00	70,250.00	59,330.00	74,900.00	55,145.00	57,265.00	390,415.00	
$571,142.50	$545,925.00	$456,841.00	$581,730.00	$424,616.50	$440,940.50	$3,021,195.50	
$623,638.75	$595,637.50	$507,271.50	$635,395.00	$471,489.75	$489,615.75	$3,323,048.25	

Figure 3–45

Q&A Why is the Format Cells dialog box used to create the style for the ranges in Steps 2 and 3?

The Format Cells dialog box is used to assign the comma style instead of the Comma Style button (Home tab | Number group), because the Comma Style button assigns a format that displays a dash (–) when a cell has a value of 0. The specifications for this worksheet call for displaying a value of 0 as 0.00 (see cell D9 in Figure 3–45) rather than as a dash. To create a comma style using the Format Cells dialog box, you use a currency style with no dollar sign.

Other Ways

1. Right-click range, click Format Cells on shortcut menu, click Number tab (Format Cells dialog box), click category in Category list, select format, click OK (Format Cells dialog box)
2. Press CTRL+1, click Number tab (Format Cells dialog box), click category in Category list, select format, click OK (Format Cells dialog box)
3. Click Currency arrow (Home tab | Number group), select desired format

BTW

Toggle Commands

Many of the commands on the ribbon, in galleries, and as shortcut keys function as toggles. For example, if you click Freeze Panes in the Freeze Panes gallery, the command changes to Unfreeze Panes the next time you view the gallery. These types of commands work like on-off switches, or toggles.

To Format the Worksheet Titles

The following steps emphasize the worksheet titles in cells A1 and A2 by changing the font and font size. The steps also format all of the row headers in column A with a bold font style.

1. Press CTRL+HOME to select cell A1 and then click the column A heading to select the column.
2. Click the Bold button (Home tab | Font group) to bold all of the data in the selected column.
3. Increase the font size in cell A1 to 28 point.
4. Increase the font size in cell A2 to 16 point.
5. Select the range A1:I2 and change the fill color to Dark Blue, Text 2, Lighter 80% to add a background color to the selected range.
6. With A1:I2 selected, change the font color to Dark Blue, Accent 1.
7. Click an empty cell to deselect the range (Figure 3–46).

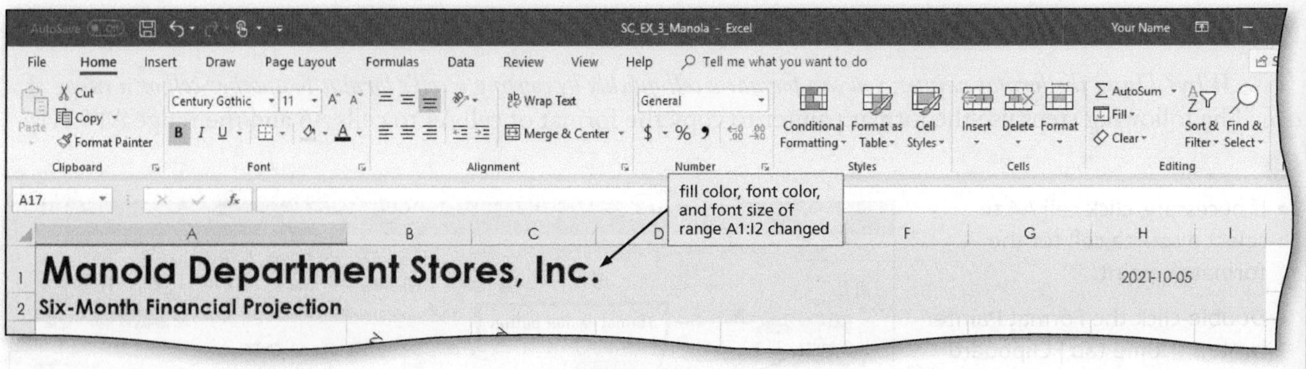

Figure 3–46

Other Ways

1. Right-click range, click Format Cells on shortcut menu, click Fill tab (Format Cells dialog box) to color background (or click Font tab to color font), click OK
2. Press CTRL+1, click Fill tab (Format Cells dialog box) to color background (or click Font tab to color font), click OK

To Assign Cell Styles to Nonadjacent Rows and Colors to a Cell

The following steps improve the appearance of the worksheet by formatting the headings in row 3 and the totals in rows 6, 14, and 16. Cell A4 also is formatted with a background color and font color.

1. Select the range A3:I3 and apply the Heading 3 cell style.
2. Select the range A6:H6 and while holding down CTRL, select the ranges A14:H14 and A16:H16.
3. Apply the Total cell style to the selected nonadjacent ranges.
4. Select cell A4 and click the Fill Color button (Home tab | Font group) to apply the last fill color used (Dark Blue, Text 2, Lighter 80%) to the cell contents.
5. Click the Font Color button (Home tab | Font group) to apply the last font color used (Dark Blue, Accent 1) to the cell contents (Figure 3–47).

BTW

The Fill and Font Color Buttons

You may have noticed that the color bar at the bottom of the Fill Color and Font Color buttons (Home tab | Font group) (Figure 3–46) changes to the most recently selected color. To apply this same color to a cell background or text, select a cell and then click the Fill Color button to use the color as a background or click the Font Color button to use the color as a font color.

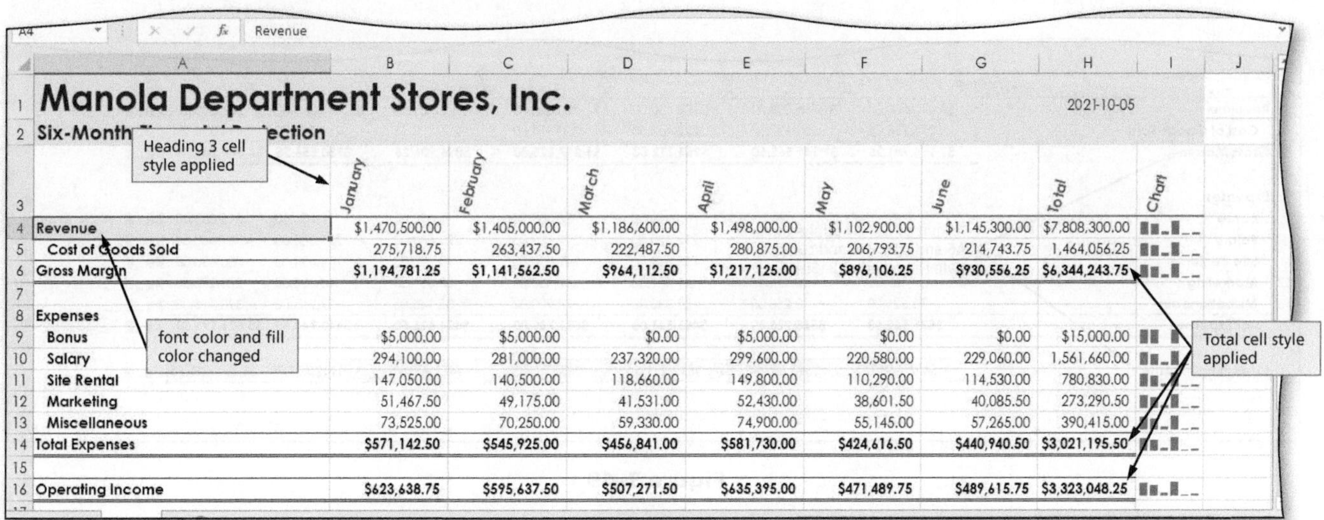

Figure 3–47

To Copy a Cell's Format Using the Format Painter Button

Why? *Using the format painter, you can format a cell quickly by copying a cell's format to another cell or a range of cells.* The following steps use the format painter to copy the format of cell A4 to cells A6 and the range A16:H16.

- If necessary, click cell A4 to select a source cell for the format to paint.
- Double-click the Format Painter button (Home tab | Clipboard group) and then move the pointer onto the worksheet to cause the pointer to change to a block plus sign with a paintbrush (Figure 3–48).

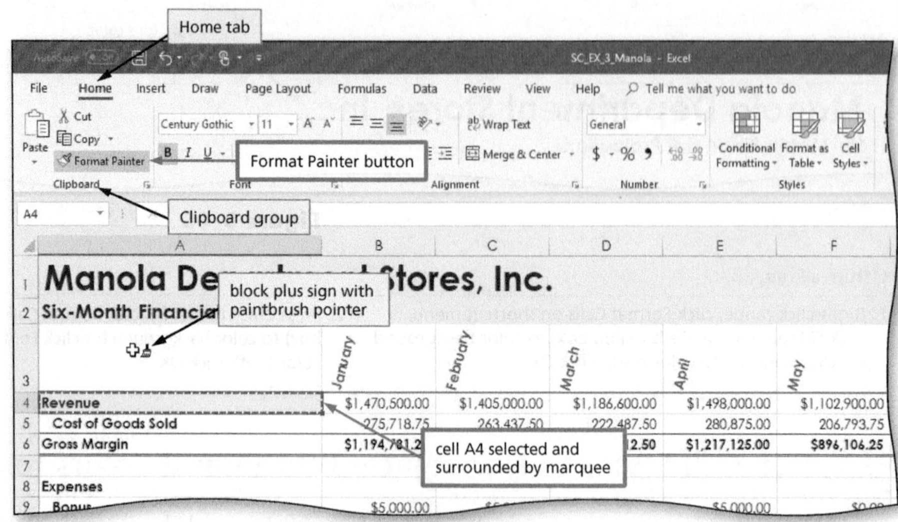

Figure 3–48

2

- Click cell A6 to assign the format of the source cell, A4 in this case, to the destination cell, A6 in this case.
- With the pointer still a block plus sign with a paintbrush, drag through the range A16:H16 to assign the format of the source cell, A4 in this case, to the destination range, A16:H16 in this case.
- Click the Format Painter button or press ESC to turn off the format painter.
- Apply the currency style to the range B16:H16 to cause the cells in the range to appear with a floating dollar sign and two decimal places (Figure 3–49).

Q&A Why does the currency style need to be reapplied to the range B16:H16?
Sometimes, the use of the format painter results in unintended outcomes. In this case, changing the background fill color and font color for the range B16:H16 resulted in the loss of the currency style because the format being copied did not include the currency style. Reapplying the currency style to the range results in the proper number style, fill color, and font color.

		January	Febru	Marc	April	May	June	Total	Chart
3									
4	Revenue	$1,470,500.00	$1,405,000.00	$1,186,600.00	$1,498,000.00	$1,102,900.00	$1,145,300.00	$7,808,300.00	
5	Cost of Goods Sold	275,718.75	263,437.50	222,487.50	280,875.00	206,793.75	214,743.75	1,464,056.25	
6	Gross Margin	$1,194,781.25	$1,141,562.50	$964,112.50	$1,217,125.00	$896,106.25	$930,556.25	$6,344,243.75	
7									
8	Expenses								
9	Bonus			$0.00	$5,000.00	$0.00	$0.00	$15,000.00	
10	Salary			237,320.00	299,600.00	220,580.00	229,060.00	1,561,660.00	
11	Site Rental			118,660.00	149,800.00	110,290.00	114,530.00	780,830.00	
12	Marketing			41,531.00	52,430.00	38,601.50	40,085.50	273,290.50	
13	Miscellaneous	73,525.00	70,250.00	59,330.00	74,900.00	55,145.00	57,265.00	390,415.00	
14	Total Expenses	$571,142.50	$545,925.00	$456,841.00	$581,730.00	$424,616.50	$440,940.50	$3,021,195.50	
15									
16	Operating Income	$623,638.75	$595,637.50	$507,271.50	$635,395.00	$471,489.75	$489,615.75	$3,323,048.25	

format of cell A4 applied to cells A6 and A16:H16 and currency style reapplied to B16:H16

Sheet1

Ready Average: $949,442.36 Count: 7 Sum: $6,646,096.50 100%

Figure 3–49

Other Ways

1. Click Copy button (Home tab | Clipboard group), select cell, click Paste arrow (Home tab | Clipboard group), click Formatting button in Paste gallery
2. Right-click cell, click Copy on shortcut menu, right-click cell, click Formatting icon on shortcut menu

To Format the What-If Assumptions Table

The following steps format the What-If Assumptions table, the final step in improving the appearance of the worksheet.

1. Select cell A18.
2. Change the font size to 9 pt.
3. Italicize and underline the text in cell A18.
4. Select the range A19:B25, and change the font size to 9 pt.
5. Select the range A18:B25 and then click the Fill Color button (Home tab | Font group) to apply the most recently used background color to the selected range.
6. Click the Font Color button (Home tab | Font group) to apply the most recently used font color to the selected range.
7. Deselect the range A18:B25 and display the What-If Assumptions table, as shown in Figure 3–50.
8. Save the workbook on the same storage location with the same file name.

Q&A What happens when I click the Italic and Underline buttons?
When you assign the italic font style to a cell, Excel slants the characters slightly to the right, as shown in cell A18 in Figure 3–50. The underline format underlines only the characters in the cell, rather than the entire cell, as is the case when you assign a cell a bottom border.

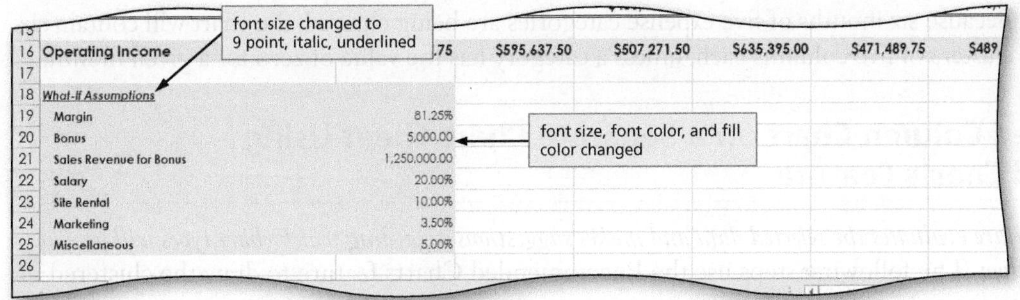

Figure 3–50

BTW
Painting a Format to Nonadjacent Ranges
Double-click the Format Painter button (Home tab | Clipboard group) and then drag through the nonadjacent ranges to paint the formats to the ranges. Click the Format Painter button again to deactivate it.

BTW
Selecting Nonadjacent Ranges
One of the more difficult tasks to learn is selecting nonadjacent ranges. To complete this task, do not hold down CTRL when you select the first range because Excel will consider the current active cell to be the first selection, and you may not want the current active cell in the selection. Once the first range is selected, hold down CTRL and drag through the nonadjacent ranges. If a desired range is not visible in the window, use the scroll arrows to view the range. You need not hold down CTRL while you scroll.

Break Point: If you want to take a break, this is a good place to do so. You can exit Excel now. To resume later, start Excel, open the file called SC_EX_3_Manola, and continue following the steps from this location forward.

Adding a Clustered Column Chart to the Workbook

The next step in the module is to create a clustered column chart on a separate sheet in the workbook, as shown in Figure 3–51. Use a clustered column chart to compare values side by side, broken down by category. Each column shows the value for a particular category, by month in this case.

The clustered column chart in Figure 3–51 shows the projected expense amounts, by category, for each of the six months. The clustered column chart allows the user to see how the various expense categories compare with each other each month, and across months.

The clustered column is a two-dimensional chart. Excel also lets you create three-dimensional charts, but some experts feel that three-dimensional charts are more difficult to read and may not represent certain types of data accurately.

Recall that charts can either be embedded in a worksheet or placed on a separate chart sheet. The clustered column chart will reside on its own sheet, because if placed on the worksheet, it would not be visible when the worksheet first opens and could be missed.

BTW
Charts
When you change a value on which a chart is dependent, Excel immediately redraws the chart based on the new value.

BTW
Chart Items
When you rest the pointer over a chart item, such as a legend, bar, or axis, Excel displays a chart tip containing the name of the item.

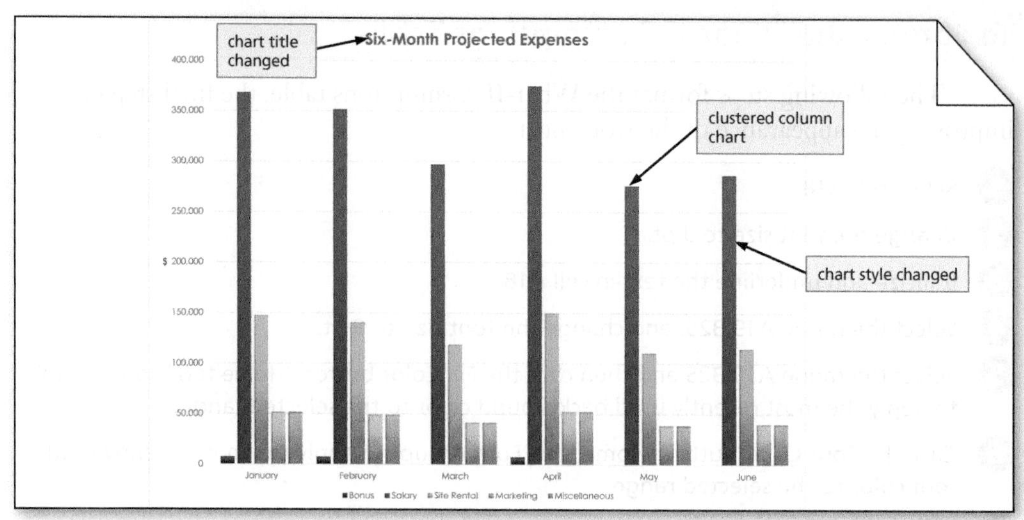

Figure 3–51

In this worksheet, the ranges to chart are the nonadjacent ranges B3:G3 (month names) and A9:G13 (monthly projected expenses, by category). The month names in the range B3:G3 will identify the major groups for the chart; these entries are called **category names**. The range A9:G13 contains the data that determines the individual columns in each month cluster, along with the names that identify each column; these entries are called the **data series**, which is the set of values represented in a chart. Because six months of five expense categories are being charted, the chart will contain six clusters of five columns each, unless a category has the value of zero for a given month.

To Draw a Clustered Column Chart on a Separate Chart Sheet Using the Recommended Charts Feature

Why? This Excel feature evaluates the selected data and makes suggestions regarding which chart types will provide the most suitable representation. The following steps use the Recommended Charts feature to draw the clustered column chart on a separate chart sheet.

1

- Select the range A3:G3 to identify the range of the categories.
- Hold down CTRL and select the data range A9:G13.
- Display the Insert tab.
- Click the Recommended Charts button (Insert tab | Charts group) to display the Insert Chart dialog box with the Recommended Charts tab active (Figure 3–52).

 **Experiment**

- Click the various recommended chart types, reading the description for each of its best use and examining the chart preview.

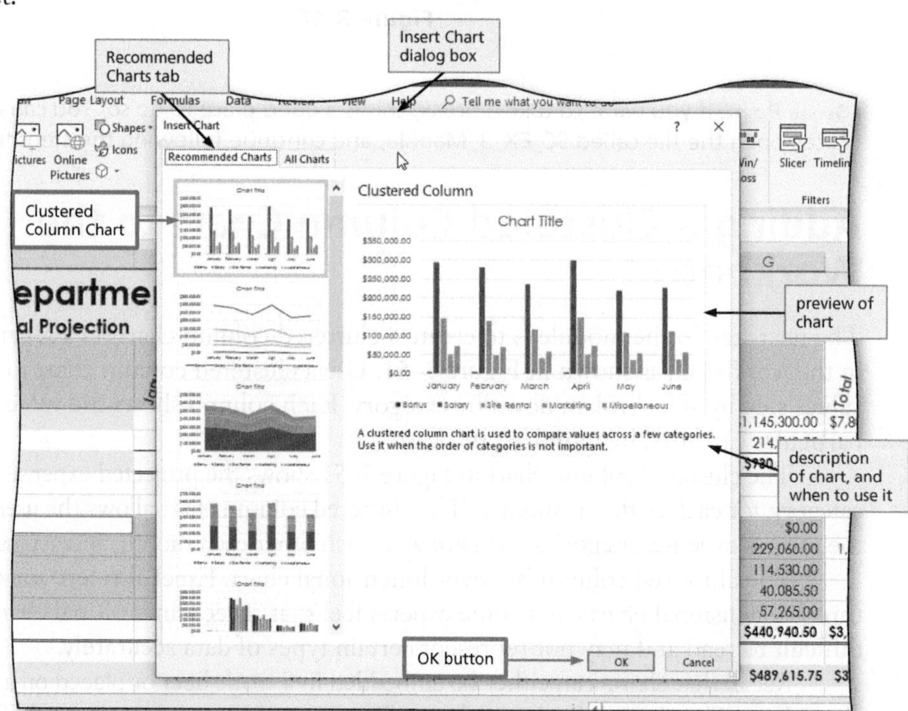

Figure 3–52

2

- Click the first Clustered Column recommended chart to select it and then click OK (Insert Chart dialog box).
- After Excel draws the chart, click the Move Chart button (Chart Tools Design tab | Location group) to display the Move Chart dialog box.
- Click the New sheet option button (Move Chart dialog box) and then type `Expense Chart Sheet` in the New sheet text box to enter a sheet tab name for the chart sheet (Figure 3–53).

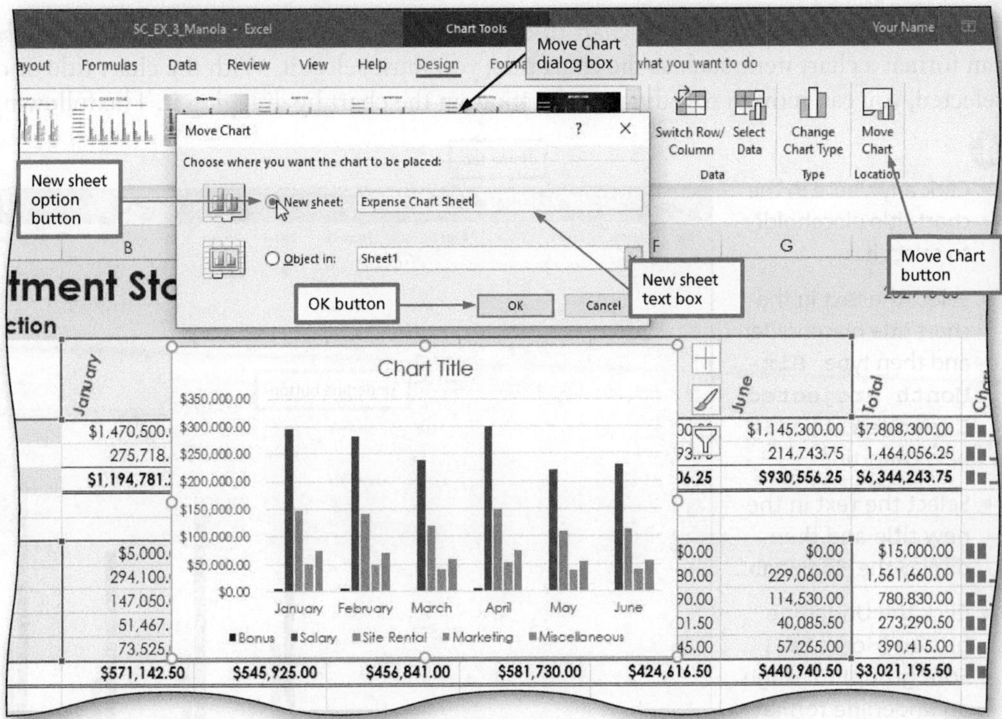

Figure 3–53

3

- Click OK (Move Chart dialog box) to move the chart to a new chart sheet with a new sheet tab name, Expense Chart (Figure 3–54).

Q&A Why do March, May, and June have only four columns charted?

March, May, and June have a value of $0 for the Bonus category. Values of zero are not charted in a column chart, so these three months have one fewer column than the other months.

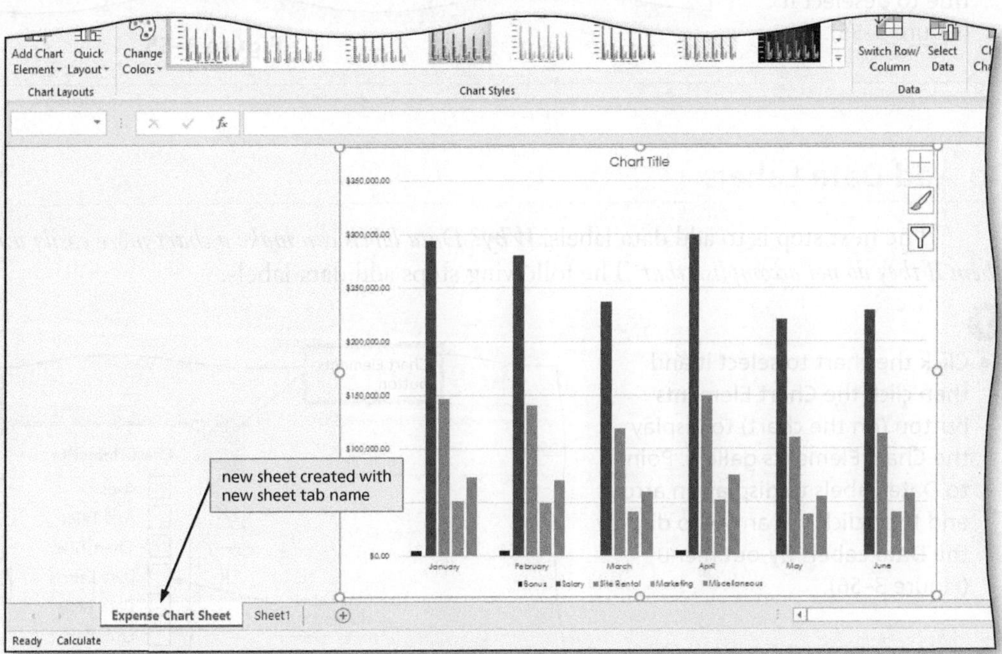

Figure 3–54

Other Ways

1. Select range to chart, press F11

To Insert a Chart Title

The next step is to insert a chart title. ***Why?*** *A chart title identifies the chart content for the viewer.* Before you can format a chart item, such as the chart title, you must select it. With the chart title or other chart element selected, you can move it to a different location on the chart by dragging it. The following step inserts a chart title.

- Click anywhere in the chart title placeholder to select it.
- Select the text in the chart title placeholder and then type **`Six-Month Projected Expenses`** to add a new chart title.
- Select the text in the new title and then display the Home tab.
- Click the Underline button (Home tab | Font group) to assign an underline format to the chart title.
- Click anywhere outside of the chart title to deselect it (Figure 3–55).

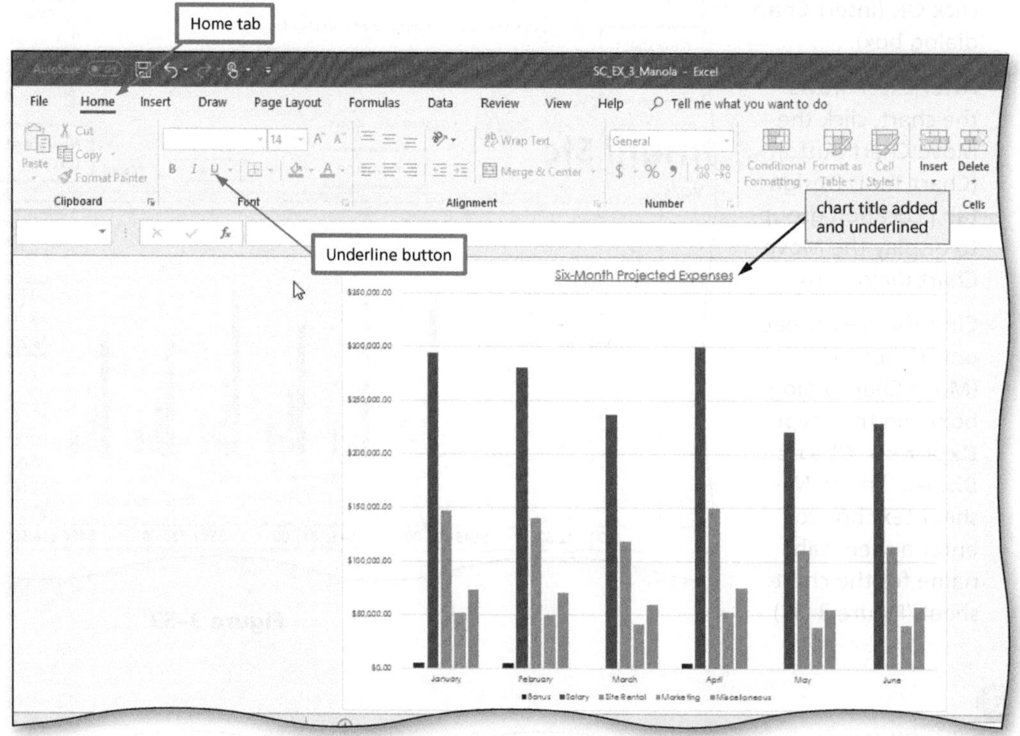

Figure 3–55

To Add Data Labels

The next step is to add data labels. ***Why?*** *Data labels can make a chart more easily understood. You can remove them if they do not accomplish that.* The following steps add data labels.

- Click the chart to select it and then click the Chart Elements button (on the chart) to display the Chart Elements gallery. Point to Data Labels to display an arrow and then click the arrow to display the Data Labels fly-out menu (Figure 3–56).

Experiment

- If you are using a mouse, point to each option on the Data Labels fly-out menu to see a live preview of the data labels.

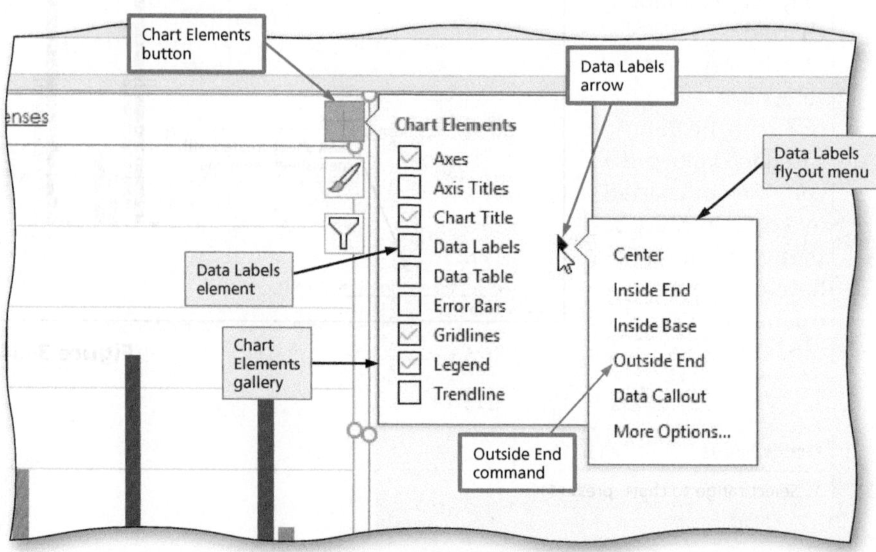

Figure 3–56

2

- Click Outside End on the Data Labels fly-out menu so that data labels are displayed outside the chart at the end of each column.
- Click the Chart Elements button to close the gallery (Figure 3–57).

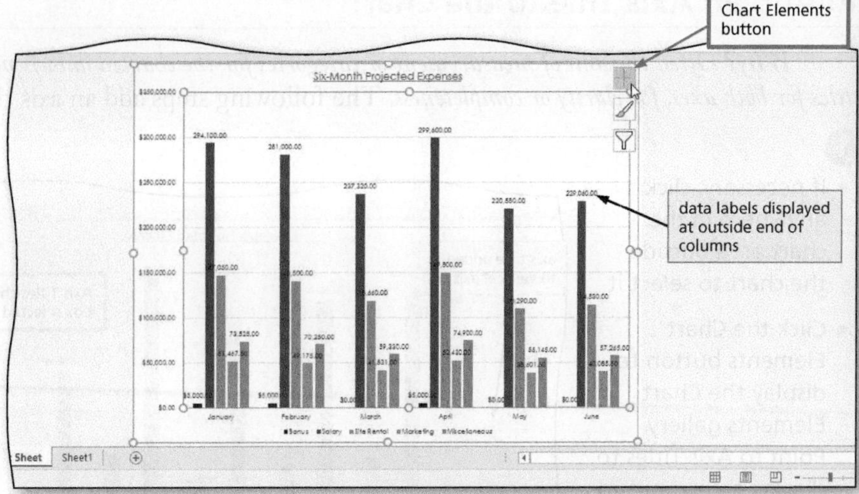

Figure 3–57

To Apply Chart Filters

***Why?** With some data, you may find that certain data series or categories make it difficult to examine differences and patterns between other series or categories. Excel allows you to easily filter data series and categories to allow more in-depth examinations of subsets of data.* In this case, filters can be used to temporarily remove the compensation categories Bonus and Salary from the chart, to allow a comparison across the noncompensation expenses. The following steps apply filters to the clustered column chart.

1

- Click the Chart Filters button (on the chart) to display the Chart Filters gallery.
- In the Series section, click the Bonus and Salary check boxes to remove their check marks and then click the Apply button to filter these series from the chart (Figure 3–58).

Q&A What happens when I remove the check marks from Bonus and Salary?
When you remove the check marks from Bonus and Salary, Excel filters the Bonus and Salary series out and redraws the chart without them.

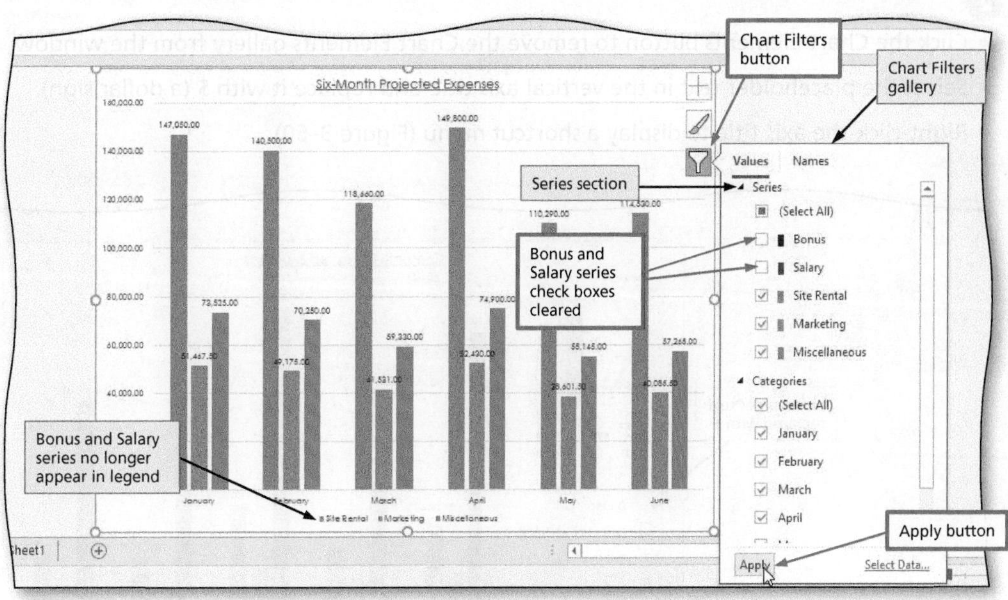

Figure 3–58

2

- Click the Chart Filters button to close the gallery.

To Add an Axis Title to the Chart

Why? Often the unit of measurement or categories for the charted data is not obvious. You can add an axis title, or titles for both axes, for clarity or completeness. The following steps add an axis title for the vertical axis.

- If necessary, click anywhere in the chart area outside the chart to select it.
- Click the Chart Elements button to display the Chart Elements gallery. Point to Axis Titles to display an arrow and then click the arrow to display the Axis Titles fly-out menu.

Experiment

- Point to each option on the fly-out menu to see a live preview of the axes' titles.

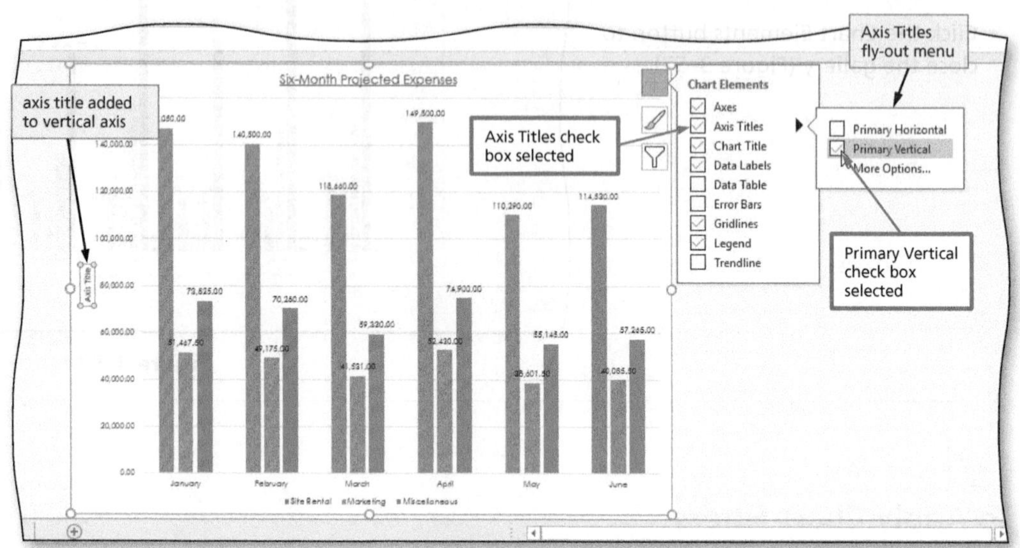

Figure 3–59

- Click Primary Vertical on the Axis Titles fly-out menu to add an axis title to the vertical axis (Figure 3–59).

2

- Click the Chart Elements button to remove the Chart Elements gallery from the window.
- Select the placeholder text in the vertical axis title and replace it with $ (a dollar sign).
- Right-click the axis title to display a shortcut menu (Figure 3–60).

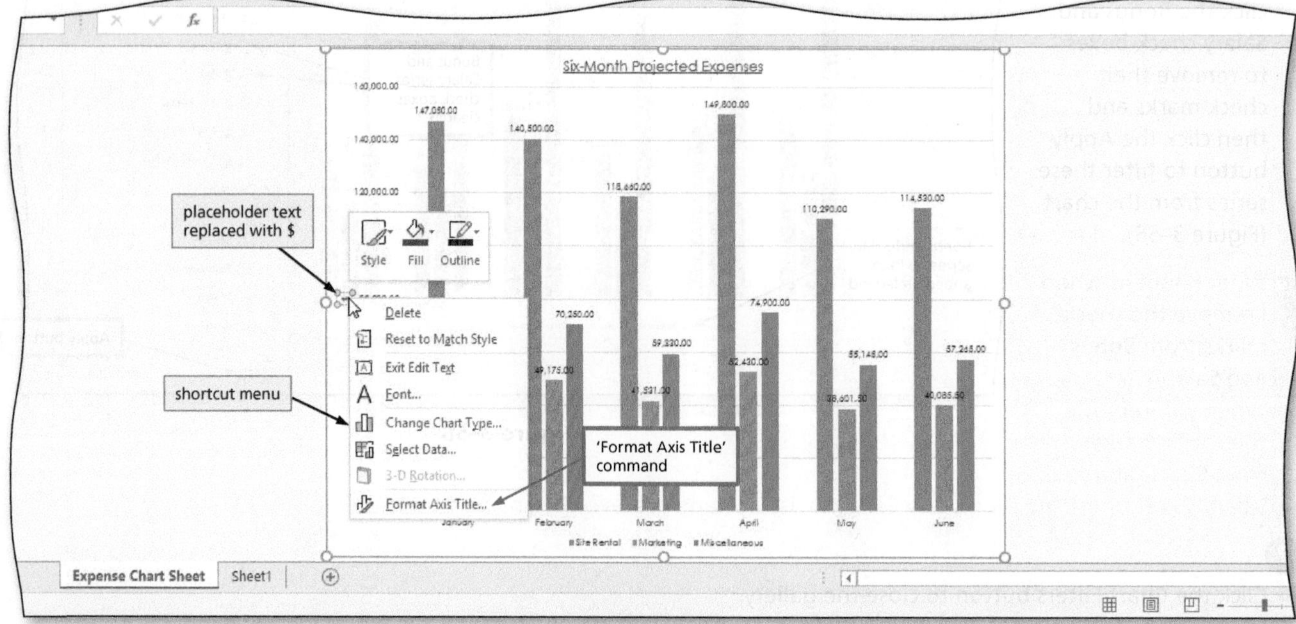

Figure 3–60

3

- Click 'Format Axis Title' on the shortcut menu to open the Format Axis Title pane.
- If necessary, click the Title Options tab, click the 'Size & Properties' button, and then, if necessary, click the Alignment arrow to expand the Alignment section.
- Click the Text direction arrow to display the Text direction list (Figure 3–61).
- Click Horizontal in the Text direction list to change the orientation of the vertical axis title.
- Click the Close button (shown in Figure 3–61) on the task pane to close the Format Axis Title task pane.

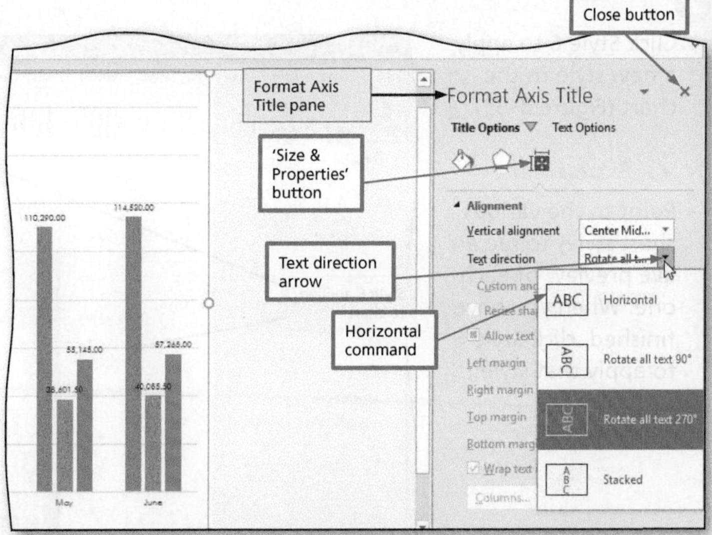

Figure 3–61

To Change the Chart Style

Why? You decide that a chart with a different look would better convey meaning to viewers. The following steps change the chart style.

1

- Display the Chart Tools Design tab and then click the More button (Chart Tools Design tab | Chart Styles group) to display the Chart Styles gallery (Figure 3–62).

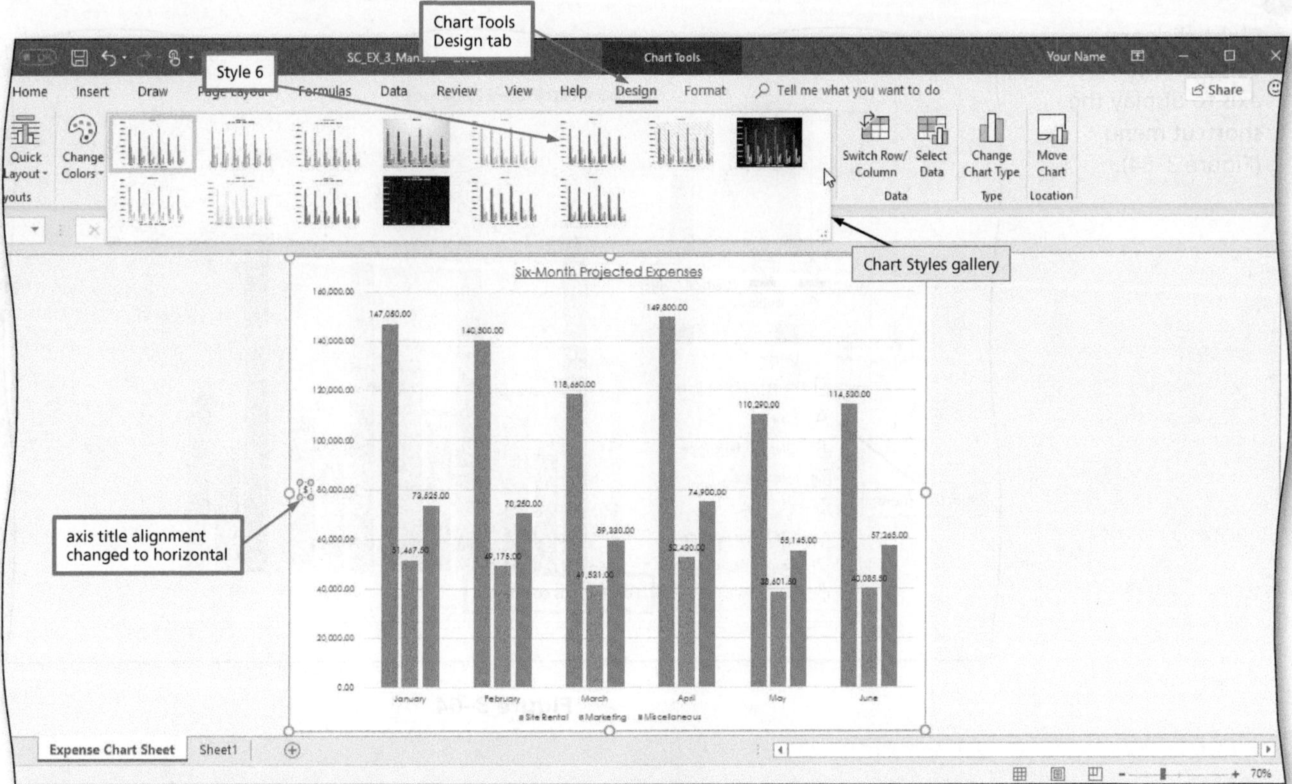

Figure 3–62

2

- Click Style 6 to apply a new style to the chart (Figure 3–63).

Experiment

- Point to the various chart styles to see a live preview of each one. When you have finished, click Style 6 to apply that style.

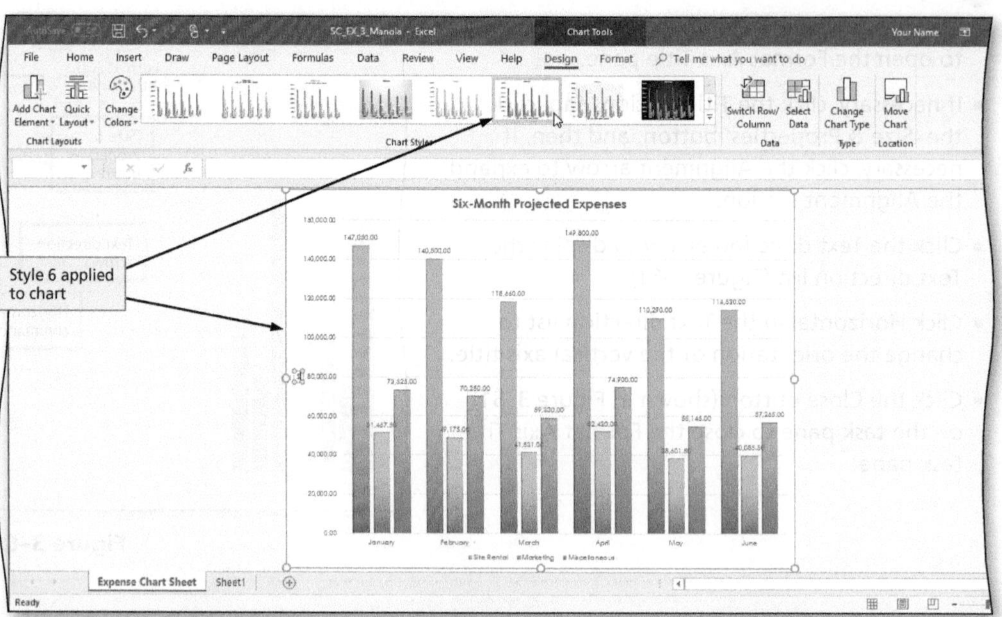

Figure 3–63

To Modify the Chart Axis Number Format

Why? *The two decimal places in the vertical chart axis numbers are not necessary and make the axis appear cluttered.* The following steps format the numbers in the chart axis to contain no decimal places.

1

- Right-click any value on the vertical axis to display the shortcut menu (Figure 3–64).

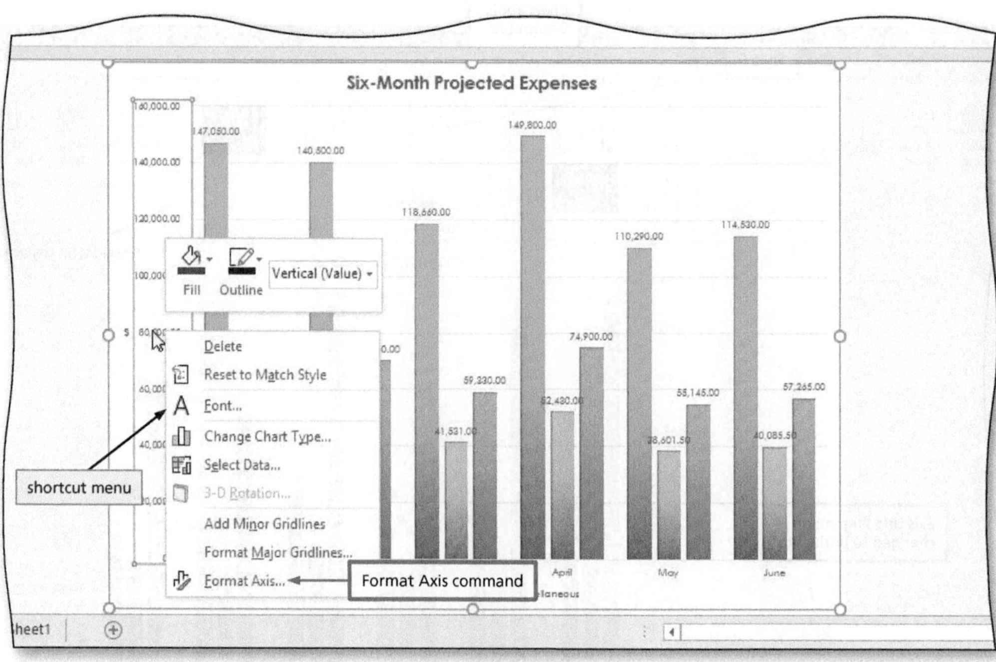

Figure 3–64

2

- Click Format Axis on the shortcut menu to open the Format Axis pane.
- If necessary, click the Axis Options tab in the Format Axis task pane and then scroll until Number is visible. Click the Number arrow to expand the Number section and then scroll to review options related to formatting numbers.
- Change the number in the Decimal places text box to 0 (Figure 3–65).

Can I change the minimum and maximum bounds displayed on the axis?

Yes. In the Format Axis pane, expand the Axis Options area and then enter the desired values in the Minimum and Maximum text boxes.

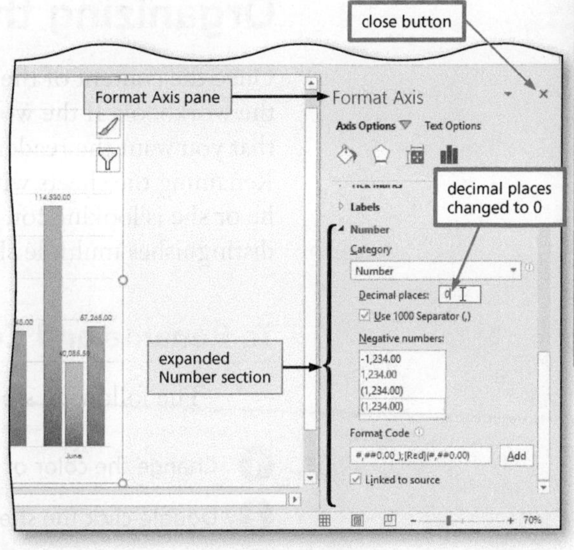

Figure 3–65

3

- Close the Format Axis pane.

To Remove Filters and Data Labels

You decide that the data labels on the bars are distracting and add no value to the chart. You decide to remove the data labels and filters so that all expense data is once again visible. You also can experiment with various chart layouts that specify which chart elements display and where they display. To change the layout of a chart, click the Quick Layout button (Chart Tools Design tab | Chart Layouts group) and then select the desired layout. You also can change the chart type by selecting the chart, clicking the 'Change Chart Type' button (Chart Tools Design tab | Type group), and then selecting the desired chart in the Change Chart Type dialog box. The following steps remove the data labels and the filters.

BTW

Chart Templates

Once you create and format a chart to your liking, consider saving the chart as a template so that you can use it to format additional charts. Save your chart as a chart template by right-clicking the chart to display the shortcut menu and then selecting 'Save as Template' from that shortcut menu. The chart template will appear in the Templates folder for Charts. When you want to use the template, click the Templates folder in the All Charts sheet (Insert Chart dialog box) and then select your template.

1. Click the Chart Elements button to display the Chart Elements gallery.
2. Click the Data Labels check box to remove the check mark for the data labels.
3. Click the Chart Elements button again to close the gallery.
4. Click the Chart Filters button to display the Chart Filters fly-out menu.
5. In the Series section, click Bonus and then Salary, click the Apply button to add the compensation data back into the chart, and then click the Chart Filters button again to close the menu (Figure 3–66).

Figure 3–66

Organizing the Workbook

Once the content of the workbook is complete, you can address the organization of the workbook. If the workbook has multiple worksheets, place the worksheet on top that you want the reader to see first. Default sheet names in Excel are not descriptive. Renaming the sheets with descriptive names helps the reader find information that he or she is looking for. Modifying the sheet tabs through the use of color further distinguishes multiple sheets from each other.

To Rename and Color Sheet Tabs

The following steps rename the sheets and color the sheet tabs.

1. Change the color of the Expense Chart Sheet tab to Dark Blue, Text 2 (column 4, row 1).
2. Double-click the sheet tab labeled Sheet1 at the bottom of the screen.
3. Type **`Six-Month Financial Projection`** as the new sheet tab name and then press ENTER.
4. Change the sheet tab color of the Six-Month Financial Projection sheet to Light Turquoise, Background 2 (column 3, row 1) and then select an empty cell (Figure 3–67).

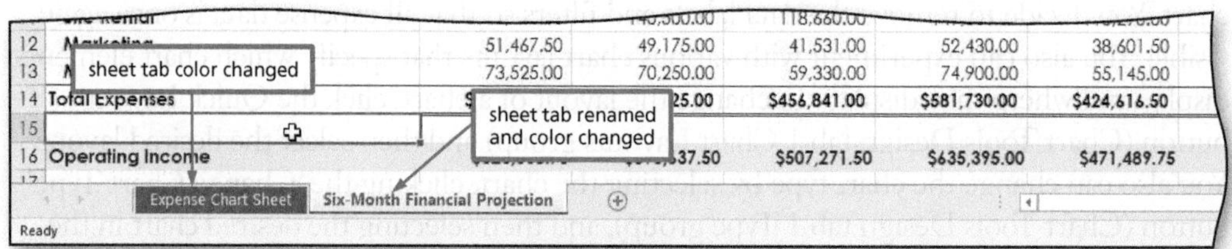

Figure 3–67

To Reorder the Sheet Tabs

Why? *You want the most important worksheets to appear first in a workbook, so you need to change the order of sheets.* The following step reorders the sheets so that the worksheet precedes the chart sheet in the workbook.

- Drag the Six-Month Financial Projection tab to the left so that it precedes the Expense Chart sheet tab to rearrange the sequence of the sheets (Figure 3–68).

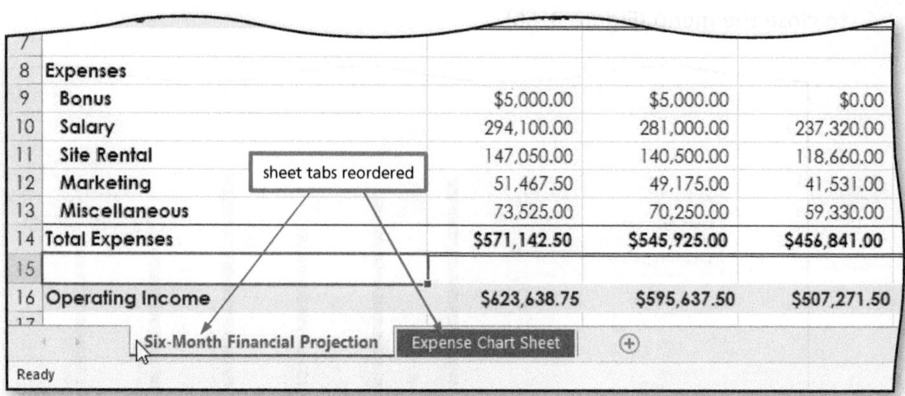

Figure 3–68

Other Ways

1. To move sheet, right-click sheet tab, click Move or Copy on shortcut menu, click OK

To Check Spelling in Multiple Sheets

By default, the spelling checker reviews spelling only in the selected sheets. It will check all the cells in the selected sheets unless you select a range of two or more cells. Before checking the spelling, the following steps select both worksheets in the workbook so that both are checked for any spelling errors.

1. With the Six-Month Financial Projection sheet active, press CTRL+HOME to select cell A1. Hold down CTRL and then click the Expense Chart Sheet tab to select both sheets.
2. Display the Review tab and then click the Spelling button (Review tab | Proofing group) to check spelling in the selected sheets.
3. Correct any errors and then click OK (Spelling dialog box or Microsoft Excel dialog box) when the spelling checker is finished.

BTW

Checking Spelling

Unless you first select a range of cells or an object before starting the spelling checker, Excel checks the entire selected worksheet, including all cell values, cell comments, embedded charts, text boxes, buttons, and headers and footers.

To Preview and Print the Worksheet

After checking the spelling, the next step is to preview and print the worksheets. As with spelling, Excel previews and prints only the selected sheets. In addition, because the worksheet is too wide to print in portrait orientation, the orientation must be changed to landscape. The following steps adjust the orientation and scale, preview the worksheets, and then print the worksheets.

1. If both sheets are not selected, hold down CTRL and then click the tab of the inactive sheet.
2. Click File on the ribbon to open Backstage view.
3. Click Print in Backstage view to display the Print screen.
4. Click the Portrait Orientation button in the Settings area and then select Landscape Orientation to select the desired orientation.
5. Click the No Scaling button in the Settings area and then select 'Fit Sheet on One Page' to cause the worksheets to print on one page.
6. Verify that the desired printer is selected. If necessary, click the printer button to display a list of available printer options and then click the desired printer to change the currently selected printer.
7. Click the Print button in the Print gallery to print the worksheet in landscape orientation on the currently selected printer.
8. When the printer stops, retrieve the printed worksheets (shown in Figure 3–69a and Figure 3–69b).
9. Right-click the Six-Month Financial Projection tab, and then click Ungroup Sheets on the shortcut menu to deselect the Expense Chart tab.
10. Save the workbook again in the same storage location with the same file name.

BTW

Distributing a Workbook

Instead of printing and distributing a hard copy of a workbook, you can distribute the workbook electronically. Options include sending the workbook via email; posting it on cloud storage (such as OneDrive) and sharing the file with others; posting it on social media, a blog, or other website; and sharing a link associated with an online location of the workbook. You also can create and share a PDF or XPS image of the workbook, so that users can view the file in Acrobat Reader or XPS Viewer instead of in Excel.

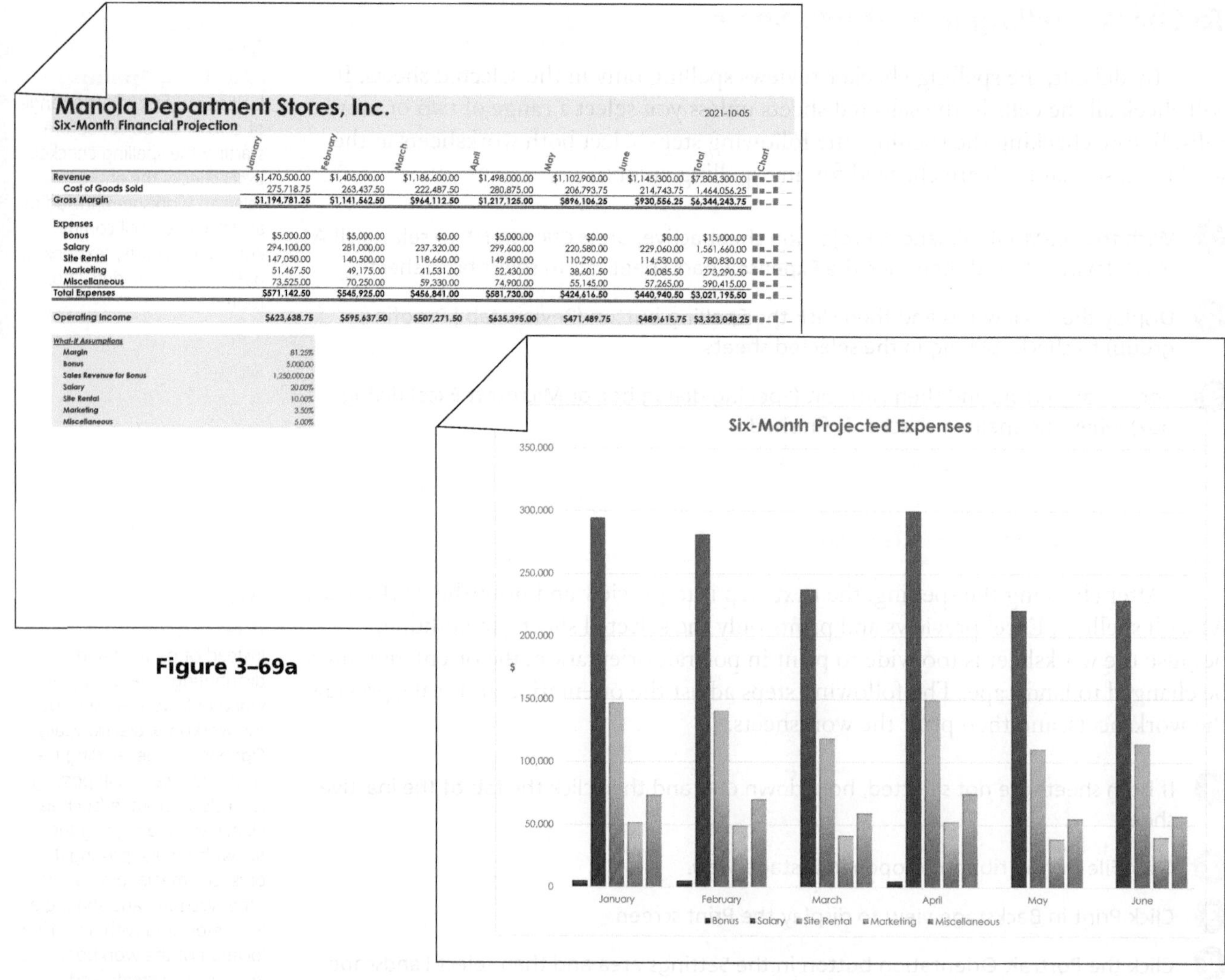

Manola Department Stores, Inc.
Six-Month Financial Projection
2021-10-05

	January	February	March	April	May	June	Total	Chart
Revenue	$1,470,500.00	$1,405,000.00	$1,186,600.00	$1,498,000.00	$1,102,900.00	$1,145,300.00	$7,808,300.00	
Cost of Goods Sold	275,718.75	263,437.50	222,487.50	280,875.00	206,793.75	214,743.75	1,464,056.25	
Gross Margin	$1,194,781.25	$1,141,562.50	$964,112.50	$1,217,125.00	$896,106.25	$930,556.25	$6,344,243.75	
Expenses								
Bonus	$5,000.00	$5,000.00	$0.00	$5,000.00	$0.00	$0.00	$15,000.00	
Salary	294,100.00	281,000.00	237,320.00	299,600.00	220,580.00	229,060.00	1,561,660.00	
Site Rental	147,050.00	140,500.00	118,660.00	149,800.00	110,290.00	114,530.00	780,830.00	
Marketing	51,467.50	49,175.00	41,531.00	52,430.00	38,601.50	40,085.50	273,290.50	
Miscellaneous	73,525.00	70,250.00	59,330.00	74,900.00	55,145.00	57,265.00	390,415.00	
Total Expenses	$571,142.50	$545,925.00	$456,841.00	$581,730.00	$424,616.50	$440,940.50	$3,021,195.50	
Operating Income	$623,638.75	$595,637.50	$507,271.50	$635,395.00	$471,489.75	$489,615.75	$3,323,048.25	

What-If Assumptions	
Margin	81.25%
Bonus	5,000.00
Sales Revenue for Bonus	1,250,000.00
Salary	20.00%
Site Rental	10.00%
Marketing	3.50%
Miscellaneous	5.00%

Figure 3–69a

Figure 3–69b

Changing the View of the Worksheet

With Excel, you easily can change the view of the worksheet. For example, you can magnify or shrink the worksheet on the screen. You also can view different parts of the worksheet at the same time by using panes.

To Shrink and Magnify the View of a Worksheet or Chart

You can magnify (zoom in) or shrink (zoom out) the appearance of a worksheet or chart by using the Zoom button (View tab | Zoom group). ***Why?*** *When you magnify a worksheet, Excel enlarges the view of the characters on the screen but shows fewer columns and rows. Alternatively, when you shrink a worksheet, Excel is able to display more columns and rows.* Magnifying or shrinking a worksheet affects only the view; it does not change the window size or the size of the text on the worksheet or chart. If you have a range of cells selected, you can click the 'Zoom to Selection' button (View tab | Zoom group) to zoom the worksheet so that the selected range fills the entire window. The following steps shrink and magnify the view of the worksheet.

1

- If cell A1 is not active, press CTRL+HOME.
- Display the View tab and then click the Zoom button (View tab | Zoom group) to display a list of magnifications in the Zoom dialog box (Figure 3–70).

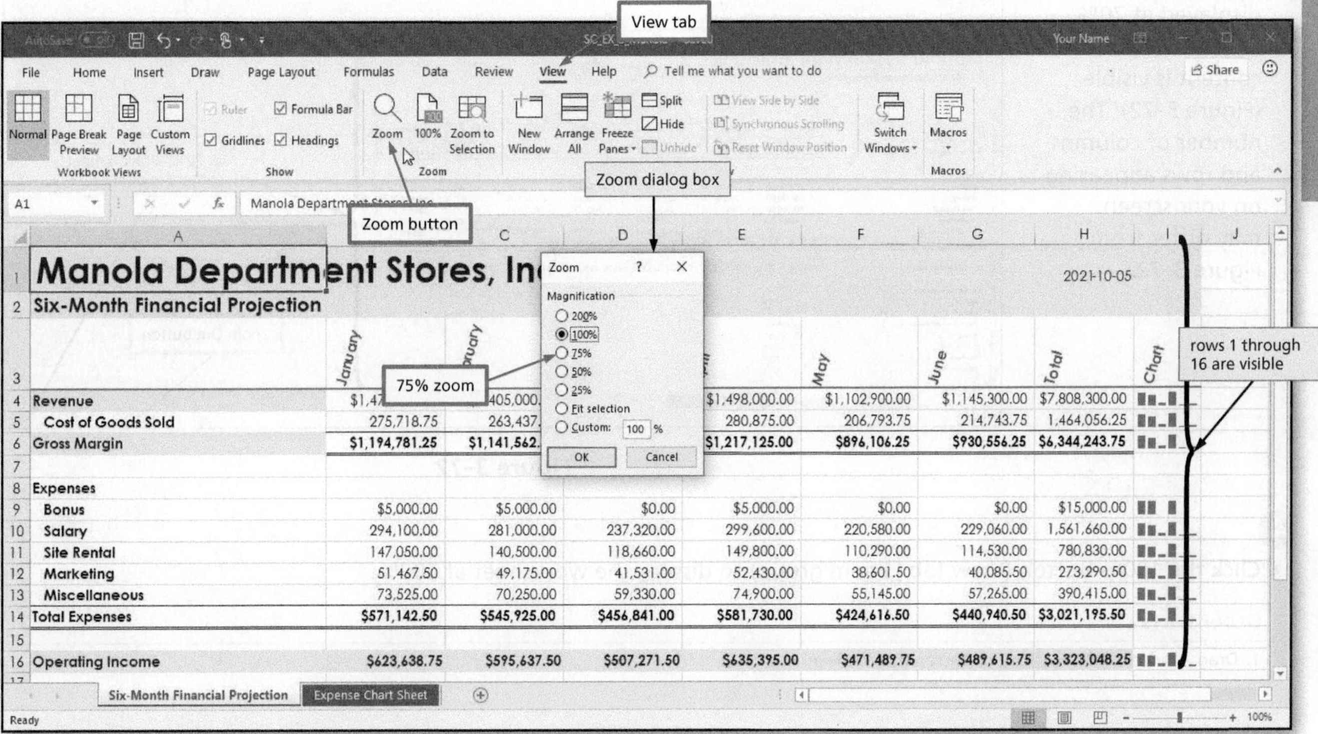

Figure 3–70

2

- Click 75% and then click OK (Zoom dialog box) to shrink the display of the worksheet (Figure 3–71). The number of columns and rows appearing on your screen may differ from Figure 3–71.

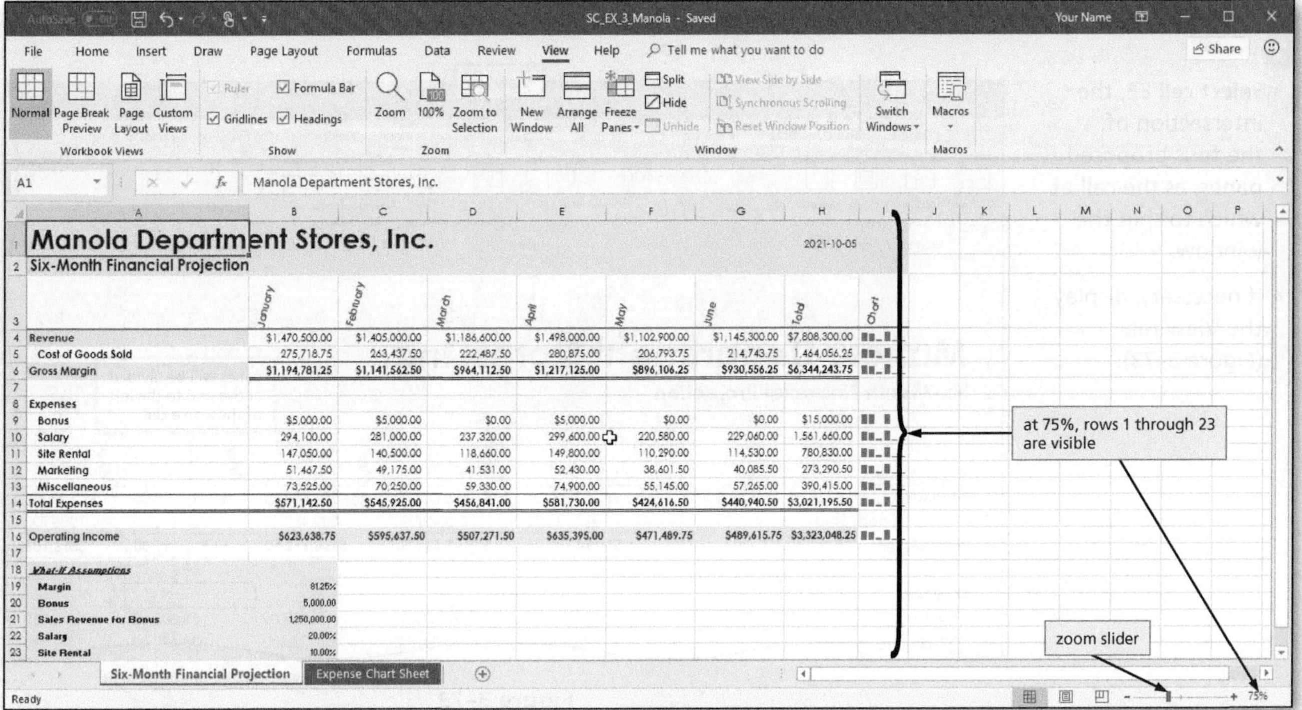

Figure 3–71

- Click the Zoom Out button on the status bar until the worksheet is displayed at 70% and all worksheet content is visible (Figure 3–72). The number of columns and rows appearing on your screen may differ from Figure 3–72.

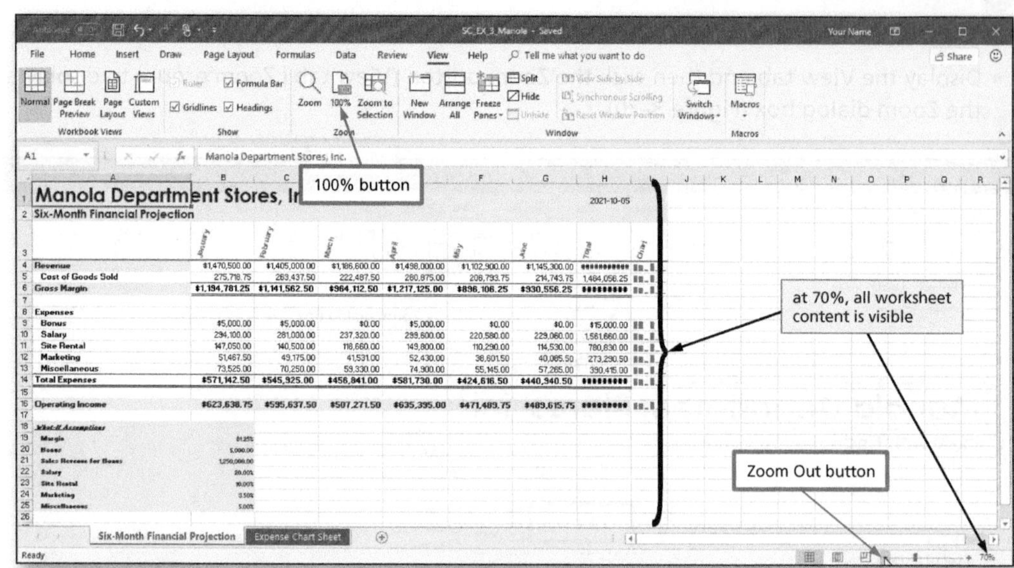

Figure 3–72

- Click the 100% button (View tab | Zoom group) to display the worksheet at 100%.

Other Ways

1. Drag zoom slider to increase or decrease zoom level

To Split a Window into Panes

When working with a large worksheet, you can split the window into two or four panes to view different parts of the worksheet at the same time. ***Why?*** *Splitting the Excel window into four panes at cell E8 allows you to view all four corners of the worksheet simultaneously.* The following steps split the Excel window into four panes.

- Select cell E8, the intersection of the four proposed panes, as the cell at which to split the window.
- If necessary, display the View tab (Figure 3–73).

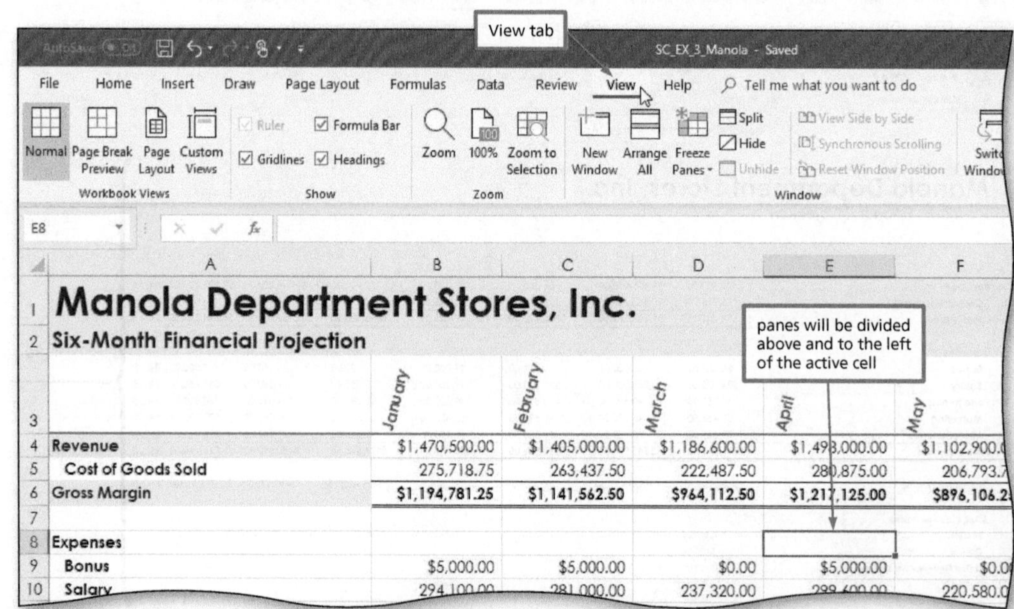

Figure 3–73

2

- Click the Split button (View tab | Window group) to divide the window into four panes.
- Use the scroll arrows to show the four corners of the worksheet at the same time (Figure 3–74).

Q&A What is shown in the four panes?
The four panes in Figure 3–74 show the following: (1) range A1:D7 in the upper-left pane; (2) range E1:J7 in the upper-right pane; (3) range A17:D25 in the lower-left pane; and (4) range E17:J25 in the lower-right pane. The vertical split bar is the vertical bar running up and down the middle of the window. The horizontal split bar is the horizontal bar running across the middle of the window. If you use the scroll bars below the window, you will see that the panes split by the horizontal split bar scroll together horizontally. The panes split by the vertical split bar scroll together vertically when using the scroll bars to the right of the window. To resize the panes, drag either split bar to the desired location.

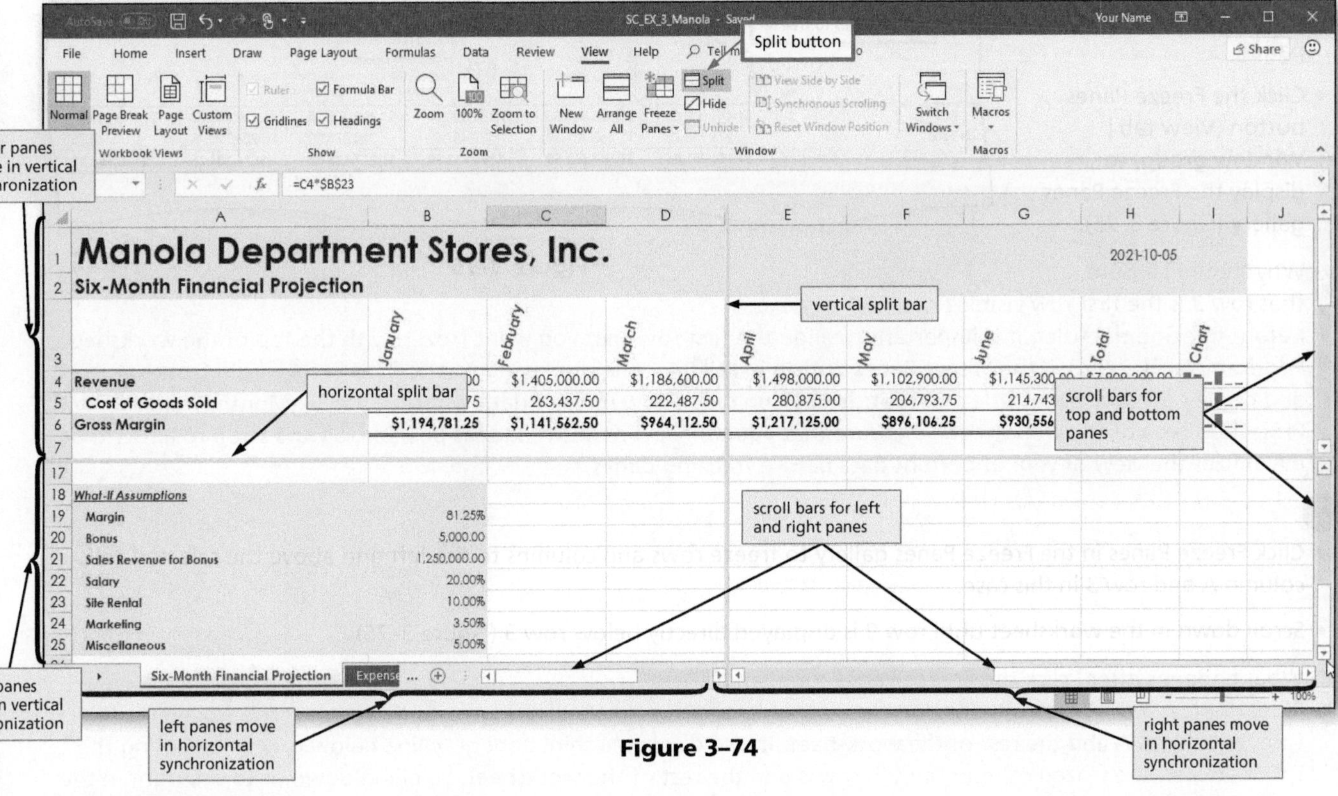

Figure 3–74

To Remove the Panes from the Window

The following step removes the panes from the window.

1 Click the Split button (View tab | Window group) to remove the four panes from the window.

Other Ways

1. Double-click intersection of horizontal and vertical split bars

To Freeze Worksheet Columns and Rows

***Why?** Freezing worksheet columns and rows is a useful technique for viewing large worksheets that extend beyond the window.* Normally, when you scroll down or to the right, the column content in the top rows and the row content in the leftmost columns no longer appear on the screen. When the content of these rows and/or columns helps to identify or define other content still visible on the worksheet, it can make it difficult to remember what the numbers in the visible cells represent. To alleviate this problem, Excel allows you to freeze columns and rows, so that their content, typically column or row titles, remains on the screen, no matter how far down or to the right you scroll. You also may wish to keep numbers visible that you need to see when making changes to content in another part of the worksheet, such as the revenue, cost of goods sold, and gross margin information in rows 4 through 6. The following steps use the Freeze Panes button (View tab | Window group) to freeze the worksheet title and column titles in row 3, and the row titles in column A.

- Scroll the worksheet until Excel displays row 3 as the first row and column A as the first column on the screen.
- Select cell B4 as the cell on which to freeze panes.
- Click the Freeze Panes button (View tab | Window group) to display the Freeze Panes gallery (Figure 3–75).

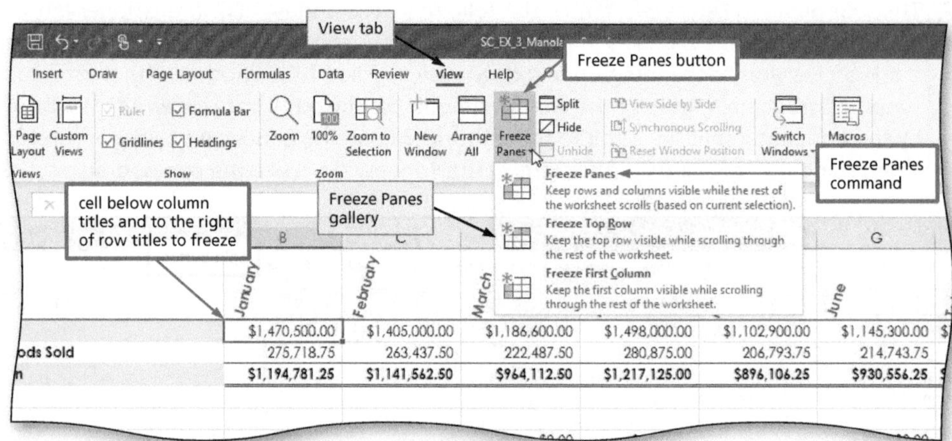

Figure 3–75

Q&A Why should I ensure that row 3 is the first row visible?
Before freezing the titles, it is important to align the first row that you want frozen with the top of the worksheet. For example, if you used the Freeze Panes button in cell B4 while displaying row 1, then Excel would freeze and display the worksheet title and subtitle, leaving only a few rows of data visible in the Six-Month Financial Projection area of the worksheet. To ensure that you can view as much data as possible, always scroll to a row that maximizes the view of your important data before freezing panes.

- Click Freeze Panes in the Freeze Panes gallery to freeze rows and columns to the left and above the selected cell, column A and row 3 in this case.
- Scroll down in the worksheet until row 9 is displayed directly below row 3 (Figure 3–76).

Q&A What happens after I click the Freeze Panes command?
Excel displays a thin, dark gray line on the right side of column A, indicating the split between the frozen row titles in column A and the rest of the worksheet. It also displays a thin, dark gray line below row 3, indicating the split between the frozen column titles in row 3 and the rest of the worksheet. Scrolling down or to the right in the worksheet will not scroll the content of row 3 or column A off the screen (Figure 3–76).

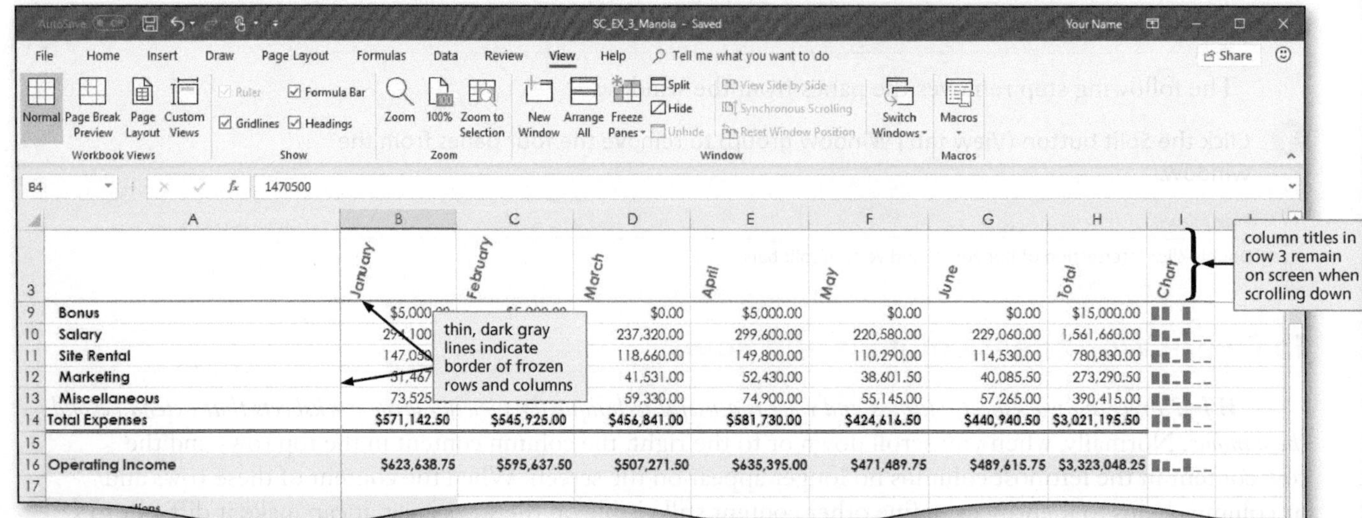

Figure 3–76

To Unfreeze the Worksheet Columns and Rows

Why? When you no longer need to view frozen columns and rows at all times, you should unfreeze them so that all columns and rows are displayed. The following steps unfreeze the titles in column A and row 3 to allow you to work with the worksheet without frozen rows and columns, or to freeze the worksheet at a different location.

1. Press CTRL+HOME to select cell B4 and view the upper-left corner of the screen.
2. Click the Freeze Panes button (View tab | Window group) to display the Freeze Panes gallery.
3. Click Unfreeze Panes in the Freeze Panes gallery to unfreeze the frozen columns and rows.
4. Save the workbook again in the same storage location with the same file name.

Q&A Why does pressing CTRL+HOME select cell B4?
When the titles are frozen and you press CTRL+HOME, Excel selects the upper-leftmost cell of the unfrozen section of the worksheet. For example, in Step 1 of the previous steps, Excel selected cell B4. When the titles are unfrozen, pressing CTRL+HOME selects cell A1.

BTW
Freezing Titles
If you want to freeze only column headings, select the appropriate cell in column A before you click the Freeze Panes button (View tab | Window group). If you want to freeze only row titles, select the appropriate cell in row 1 before you click the Freeze Panes button. To freeze both column headings and row titles, select the cell that is the intersection of the column and row titles before you click the Freeze Panes button.

What-If Analysis

The automatic recalculation feature of Excel is a powerful tool that can be used to analyze worksheet data. **What-if analysis** is a decision-making tool in which changing input values recalculate formulas, in order to predict various possible outcomes. When new data is entered, Excel not only recalculates all formulas in a worksheet but also redraws any associated charts.

In the workbook created in this module, many of the formulas are dependent on the assumptions in the range B19:B25. Thus, if you change any of the assumption values, Excel recalculates all formulas. Excel redraws the clustered column chart as well, because it is based on these numbers.

To Analyze Data in a Worksheet by Changing Values

Why? The effect of changing one or more values in the What-If Assumptions table—essentially posing what-if questions—allows you to review the results of different scenarios. In this case, you are going to examine what would happen to the six-month operating income (cell H16) if the following changes were made in the What-If Assumptions table: Bonus $5,000.00 to $7,500.00; Salary 20.00% to 25.00%; Miscellaneous 5.00% to 3.50%. To answer a question like this, you need to change only the second, fourth, and seventh values in the What-If Assumptions table. The following step splits the screen, which allows you to view income and expense figures simultaneously, and then changes values in the worksheet to answer a what-if question. When a new value is entered, Excel recalculates the formulas in the worksheet and redraws the clustered column chart to reflect the new data.

- Scroll the worksheet so that row 4 is the first row visible on the worksheet.
- Click in cell A7 to select the row above which to split the window.
- Click the Split button (View tab | Window group) to split the window after row 6.
- Use the scroll arrows in the lower-right pane to scroll the window content until row 9 is the first row visible in the lower part of the screen, as shown in Figure 3–77.

- Enter **7,500** in cell B20, **25.00%** in cell B22, and **3.50%** in cell B25 (Figure 3–77), which causes the six-month operating income in cell H16 to decrease from $3,323,048.25 to $3,042,257.75.
- Save the workbook again on the same storage location with the same file name.

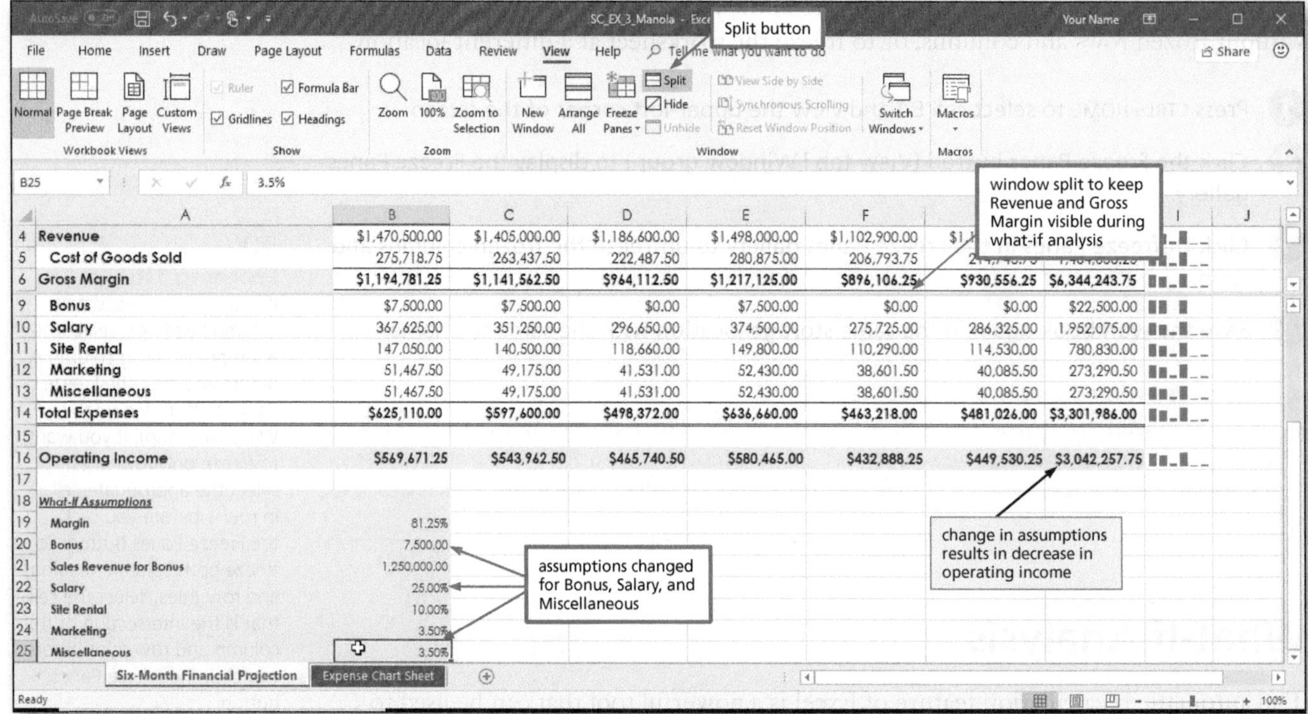

Figure 3–77

Goal Seeking

Goal seek is a problem-solving method in which you specify a solution and then find the input value that produces the answer you want. In this example, to change the six-month operating income in cell H16 to $3,500,000.00, the Site Rental percentage in cell B23 must decrease by 5.86% from 10.00% to 4.14%.

You can see from this goal seeking example that the cell to change (cell B23) does not have to be referenced directly in the formula or function. For example, the six-month operating income in cell H16 is calculated by the function =SUM(B16:G16). Cell B23 is not referenced in this function. Instead, cell B23 is referenced in the formulas in row 11, on which the monthly operating incomes in row 16 are based. By tracing the formulas and functions, Excel can obtain the desired six-month operating income by varying the value for the Site Rental assumption.

To Goal Seek

Why? *If you know the result you want a formula to produce, you can use goal seeking to determine the value of a cell on which the formula depends.* The previous step, which made changes to the What-If Assumptions table, resulted in an operating income that approaches but does not reach $3,500,000.00. The following steps use the Goal Seek command (Data tab | Forecast group) to determine what Site Rental percentage (cell B23), in conjunction with the earlier changes in assumptions, will yield a six-month operating income of $3,500,000.00 in cell H16, rather than the $3,042,257.75 calculated in the previous set of steps.

1

- If necessary, use the scroll arrows in the lower pane to ensure that you can view all of the What-If Assumptions table and the Operating Income figures.
- Select cell H16, the cell that contains the six-month operating income.
- Display the Data tab and then click the 'What-If Analysis' button (Data tab | Forecast group) to display the What-If Analysis menu (Figure 3–78).

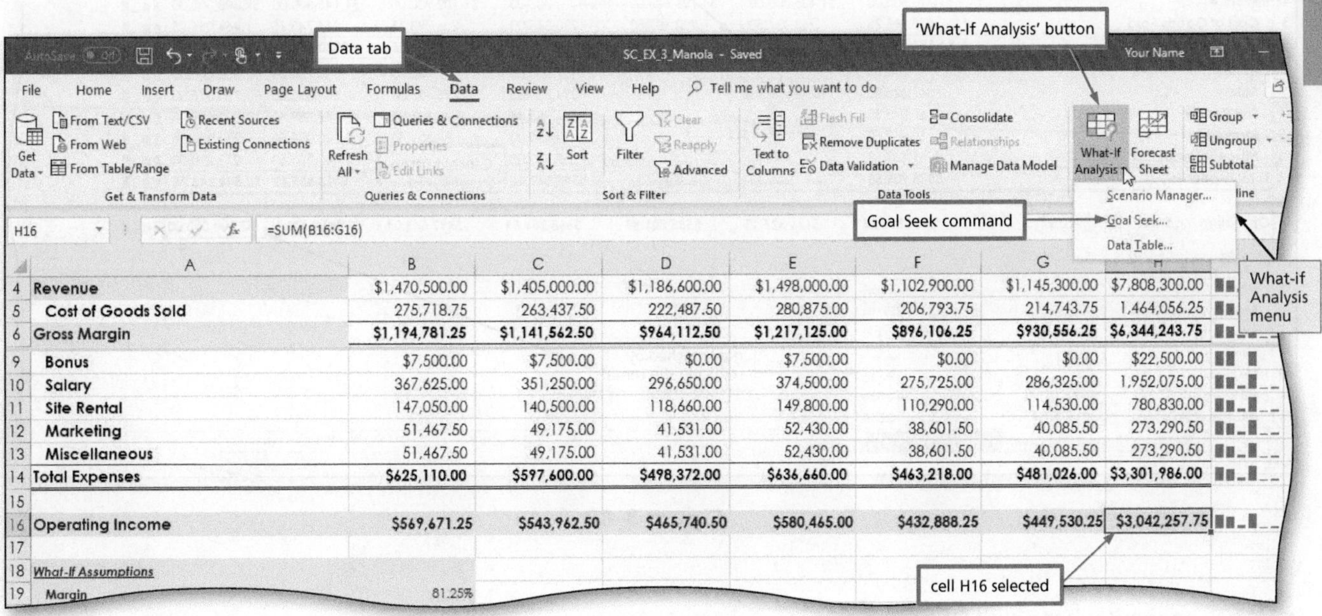

Figure 3–78

2

- Click Goal Seek to display the Goal Seek dialog box with the Set cell box set to the selected cell, H16 in this case.
- Click the To value text box, type 3,500,000 and then click the 'By changing cell' box to select the 'By changing cell' box.
- Click cell B23 on the worksheet to assign the current cell, B23 in this case, to the 'By changing cell' box (Figure 3–79).

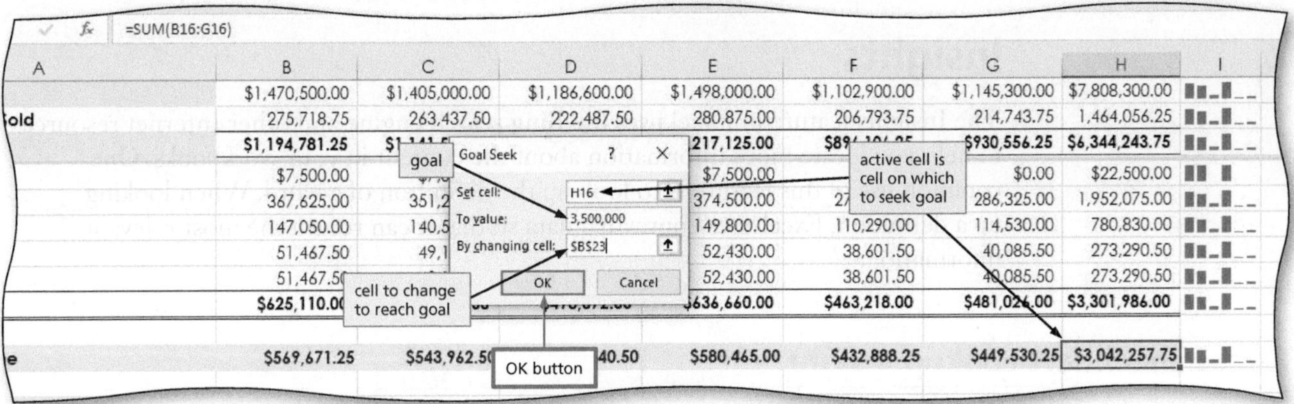

Figure 3–79

- Click OK (Goal Seek dialog box) to goal seek for the sought-after value in the To value text box, $3,500,000.00 in cell H16 in this case (Figure 3–80).

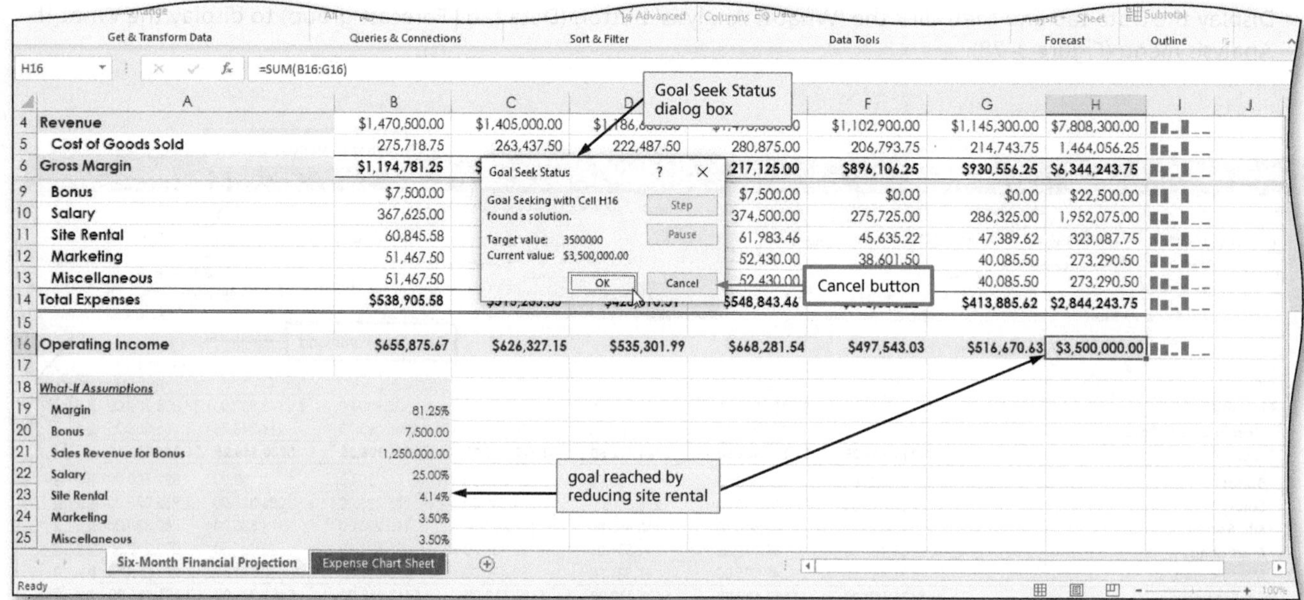

Figure 3–80

Q&A

What happens when I click OK?

Excel changes cell H16 to the desired value of $3,500,000.00. More importantly, Excel changes the Site Rental assumption in cell B23 to 4.14% (Figure 3–80). Excel also displays the Goal Seek Status dialog box. If you click OK, Excel keeps the new values in the worksheet. If you click the Cancel button, Excel redisplays the original values.

- Click the Cancel button in the Goal Seek Status dialog box to redisplay the original values in the worksheet.

- Click the Split button (View tab | Window group) to remove the two panes from the window.

Insights

The Insights feature in Excel uses the Bing search engine and other Internet resources to help you locate more information about the content in your workbooks. One common use of this feature is to look up the definition of a word. When looking up a definition, Excel uses contextual data so that it can return the most relevant information.

To Use the Smart Lookup Insight

Smart Lookup locates useful information about text in your spreadsheet and then displays that information in the Insights task pane. ***Why?*** *You want to locate additional information about the contents of your worksheet.* The following steps use Smart Lookup to look up information about the text in cell A6.

1

- Select cell A6.
- Display the Review tab and then click Smart Lookup (Review tab | Insights group) to display the Smart Lookup pane containing information about the text in the selected cell. If necessary, click the Turn on button to turn on intelligent services (Figure 3–81).

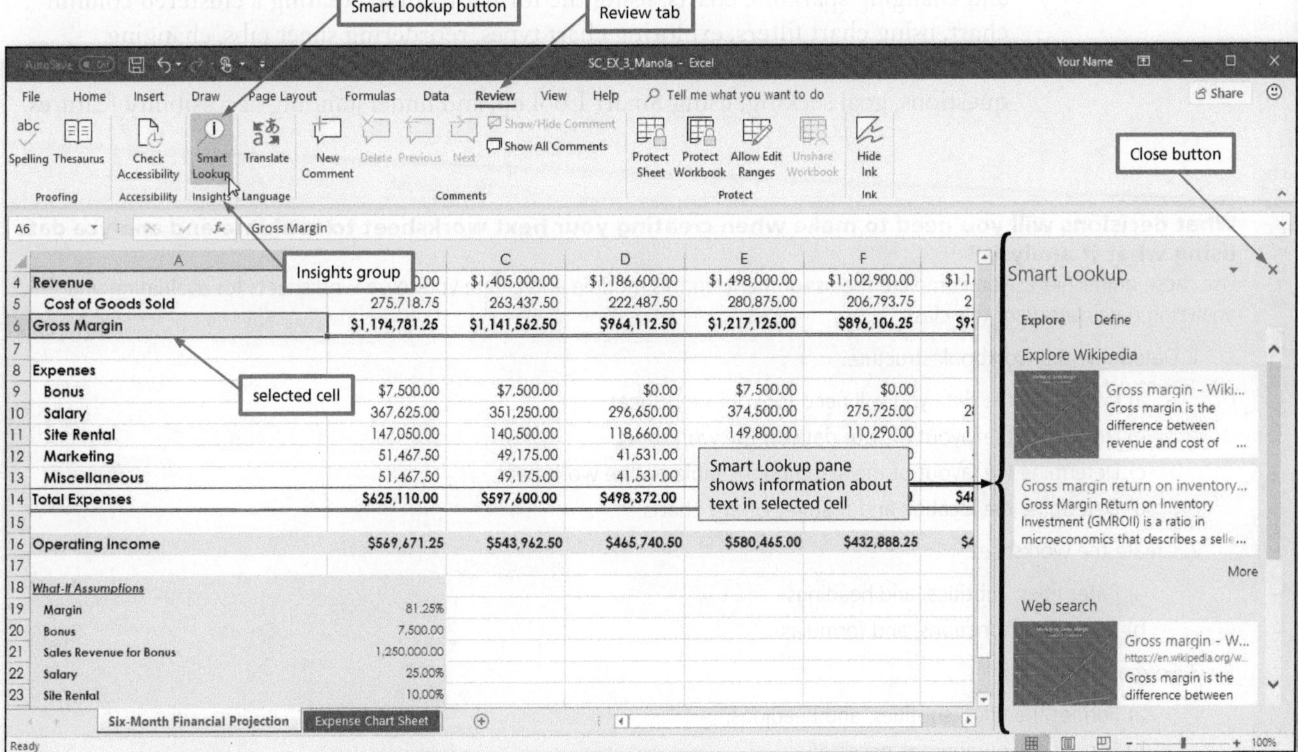

Figure 3–81

2

- sam Click the Close button on the Smart Lookup pane to close the task pane.
- If desired, sign out of your Microsoft account.
- Exit Excel.

Accessibility Features

Excel provides a utility that can be used to check a workbook for potential issues related to accessibility. **Accessibility** refers to the practice of removing barriers that may prevent individuals with disabilities from interacting with data or an app. To use the Check Accessibility command, click File on the ribbon to open Backstage view, click Info, click the 'Check for Issues' button, and then click Check Accessibility. Excel will check your workbook for content that could prove difficult for people with disabilities to read, either alone or with adaptive tools. The resulting report (Figure 3–82 shows an example) will identify issues and offer suggestions for addressing the reported issues.

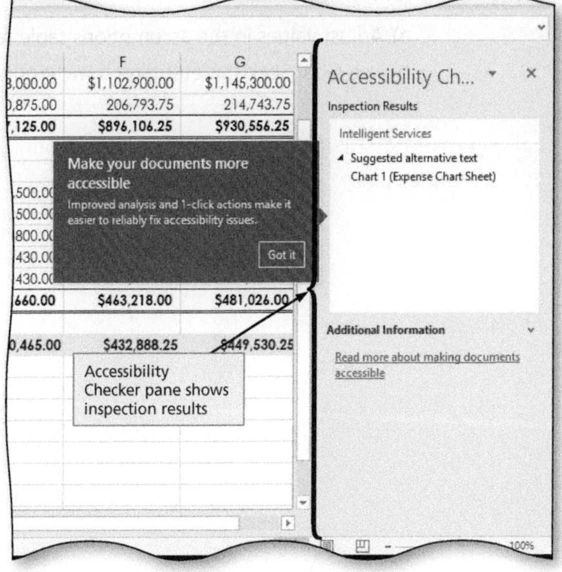

Figure 3–82

Summary

In this module, you learned how to use Excel to create a six-month financial projection workbook. Topics covered included rotating text in a cell, creating a series of month names, copying, pasting, inserting, and deleting cells, entering and formatting the system date, using absolute and mixed cell references, using the IF function, creating and changing sparkline charts, using the format painter, creating a clustered column chart, using chart filters, exploring chart types, reordering sheet tabs, changing the worksheet view, freezing and unfreezing rows and columns, answering what-if questions, goal seeking, using Smart Lookup, and understanding accessibility features.

CONSIDER THIS: PLAN AHEAD

What decisions will you need to make when creating your next worksheet to evaluate and analyze data using what-if analysis?

Use these guidelines as you complete the assignments in this module and create your own worksheets for evaluating and analyzing data outside of this class.

1. Determine the workbook structure.
   a) Determine the data you will need for your worksheet.
   b) Determine the layout of your data on the worksheet.
   c) Determine the layout of the assumptions table on the worksheet.
   d) Determine the location and features of any charts.
2. Create the worksheet.
   a) Enter titles, subtitles, and headings.
   b) Enter data, functions, and formulas.
3. Format the worksheet.
   a) Format the titles, subtitles, and headings.
   b) Format the numbers as necessary.
   c) Format the text.
4. Create and use charts.
   a) Select data to chart.
   b) Select a chart type for selected data.
   c) Format the chart elements.
   d) Filter charts if necessary to view subsets of data.
5. Perform what-if analyses.
   a) Adjust values in the assumptions table to review scenarios of interest.
   b) Use Goal Seek to determine how to adjust a variable value to reach a particular goal or outcome.

Apply Your Knowledge

Reinforce the skills and apply the concepts you learned in this module.

Understanding Logical Tests and Absolute Cell Referencing

Note: To complete this assignment, you will be required to use the Data Files. Please contact your instructor for information about accessing the Data Files.

Instructions Part 1: For each of the following logical tests, indicate whether an IF function in Excel would return a value of True or False; given the following cell values: C2 = 41; H12 = 13; L3 = 32; M14 = 125; and G4 = 2.

1. C2 < H12 Returned value: ____________
2. L3 = G4 Returned value: ____________
3. M14 + 15 * H12 / 10 <= L3 Returned value: ____________
4. M14 + G4 < H12 / C2 Returned value: ____________
5. (C2 + H12) * 2 >= L3 – (L3 / 4) * 2 Returned value: ____________
6. L3 + 300 > H12 * G4 + 10 Returned value: ____________
7. G4 * M14 >= 2 * (M14 – 25) Returned value: ____________
8. H12 = 10 * (C2 + 8) Returned value: ____________

Instructions Part 2: Write cell L23 as a relative reference, absolute reference, mixed reference with the column varying, and mixed reference with the row varying.

____________ ____________ ____________ ____________

Instructions Part 3: Start Excel. Open the workbook called SC_EX_3-1.xlsx. The workbook you open contains sample data that you will reference to create formulas. You are to re-create the numerical grid pictured in Figure 3–83.

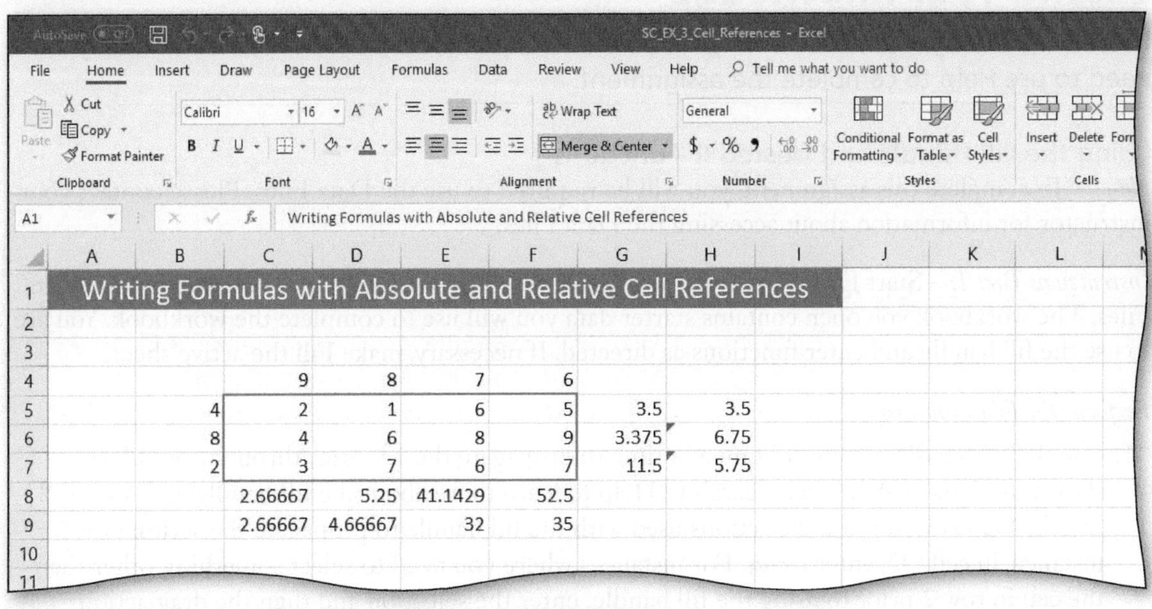

Figure 3–83

Continued >

Apply Your Knowledge *continued*

Perform the following tasks:

1. Enter a formula in cell G5 that divides the sum of cells C5 through F5 by cell B5. Write the formula so that when you copy it to cells G6:G7, Excel adjusts all the cell references according to the destination cells. Verify your formula by checking it against the values found in cells G5, G6, and G7 in Figure 3–83.
2. Enter a formula in cell C8 that divides the product of cells C5 through C7 by cell C4. Write the formula so that when you copy the formula to cells D8:F8, Excel adjusts all the cell references according to the destination cells. Verify your formula by checking it against the values found in cells C8, D8, E8, and F8 in Figure 3–83.
3. Enter a formula in cell C9 that divides the product of cells C5 through C7 by cell C4. Write the formula using an absolute cell reference so that when you copy the formula to cells D9:F9, cell C4 remains absolute. Verify your formula by checking it against the values found in cells C9, D9, E9, and F9 in Figure 3–83.
4. Enter a formula in cell H5 that divides the sum of cells C5:F5 by cell B5. Write the formula using an absolute cell reference so that when you copy the formula to cells H6 and H7, cell B5 remains absolute. Verify your formula by checking it with the values found in cells H5, H6, and H7 in Figure 3–83.
5. Apply the worksheet name, Cell References, to the sheet tab and apply the Blue, Accent 1, Darker 25% Theme color to the sheet tab.

   If requested by your instructor, add a dash followed by your name to the worksheet title in cell A1.
6. Save the revised workbook (shown in Figure 3–83) using the file name, SC_EX_3_Cell_References. Submit the revised workbook as specified by your instructor and exit Excel.
7. Exit Excel.
8. How would you rewrite the formula in cell H5 using relative and mixed cell references only, to come up with the same result as showing in Figure 3–83, and to produce the results currently showing in cells G6 and G7 in cells H6 and H7 when the formula in cell H5 is copied to those cells?

Extend Your Knowledge

Extend the skills you learned in this module and experiment with new skills. You may need to use Help to complete the assignment.

Using the Fill Handle and Nested IF Functions

Note: To complete this assignment, you will be required to use the Data Files. Please contact your instructor for information about accessing the Data Files.

Instructions Part 1: Start Excel. Open the workbook SC_EX_3-2.xlsx, which is located in the Data Files. The workbook you open contains starter data you will use to complete the workbook. You are to use the fill handle and enter functions as directed. If necessary, make Fill the active sheet.

Perform the following tasks:

1. Use the fill handle on one column at a time to propagate the 12 series through row 14, as shown in Figure 3–84. (*Hint:* Search in Help to learn more about the fill handle and Auto Fill.) In cells O2:O13, indicate the actions used with the fill handle to propagate the series. For instance, in cell O2, enter `Drag`. For instances where you need to select something other than the cell in row 2 prior to using the fill handle, enter the selection and then the drag action, `A2:A3 Drag` for example.

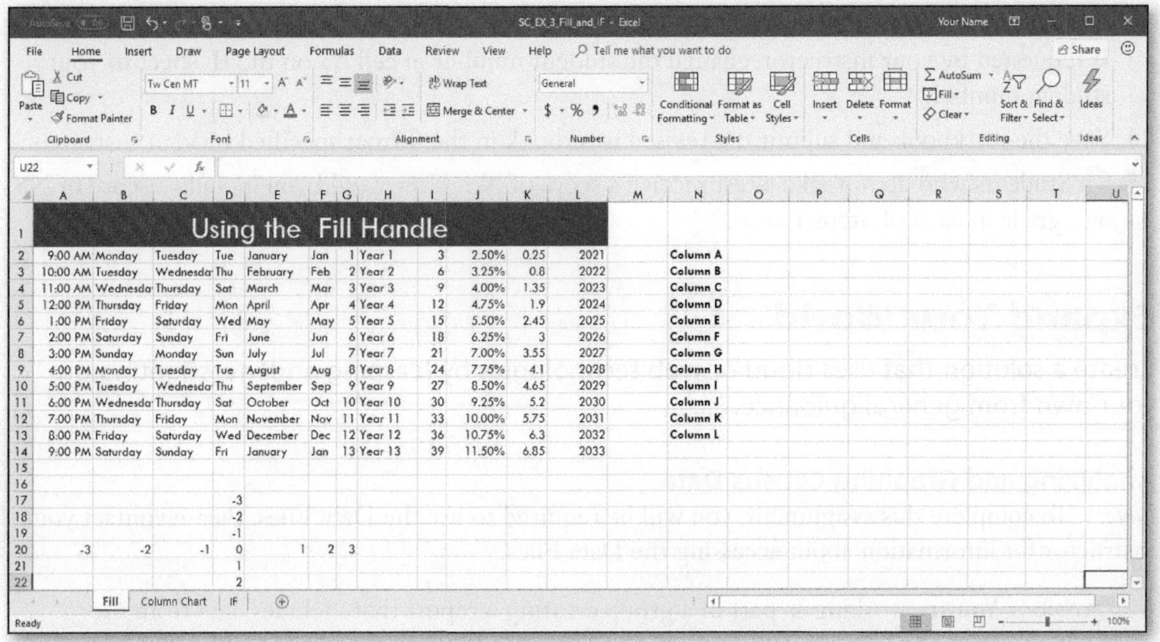

Figure 3–84

2. Select cell D20. While holding down CTRL, one at a time drag the fill handle three cells to the right, to the left, up, and down to generate four series of numbers beginning with zero and incremented by one.
3. Select cell H20. Point to the cell border so that the pointer changes to a plus sign with four arrows. Drag the pointer down to cell H22 to move the contents of cell H20 to cell H22.
4. If necessary, select cell H22. Point to the cell border so that the pointer changes to a plus sign with four arrows. While holding down CTRL, drag the pointer to cell K22 to copy the contents of cell H22 to cell K22.
5. Select cell K20. Drag the fill handle in to the center of cell K20 until that the cell is shaded and the cell contents are deleted.
6. Select cell range H2:I14, and insert a 3-D clustered column chart on a new sheet.
7. Change the chart title to Annual Breakdown.
8. Add a data table with legend keys to the chart. Change the chart colors to Colorful Palette 4.
9. Name the chart sheet, Column Chart, and move the sheet to follow the Fill sheet.
10. Save the workbook using the file name, SC_EX_3_Fill_and_IF.

Instructions Part 2: Switch to the IF sheet in the SC_EX_3_Fill_and_IF workbook.

1. Write an IF function in cell C3 that assigns a grade of "Pass" if the score in cell B3 is 70 or above, and a grade of "Fail" if the score in cell B3 is below 70. Copy this function to cells C4:C19.
2. Write a nested IF function in cell D3 that assigns a grade of A for scores between 90 and 100, a grade of B for scores between 80 and 89, a grade of C for scores between 70 and 79, and a grade of F for scores below 70. (*Hint*: Search in Help for nested IF when constructing your function.) Copy this function to cells D4:D19.
3. Calculate the average grade in cell B21. In cells C21 and D21, use a formula to determine whether the average grade is a passing grade, and the overall grade achieved by the class.

Continued >

Extend Your Knowledge *continued*

If requested by your instructor, change the student number in cell A3 on the IF sheet to your student number.

4. Save the workbook and submit the revised workbook in the format specified by your instructor.
5. Students who do not take a test receive a score of NS. How would you include a score of NS as a grade in each of Steps 1 and 2?

Expand Your World

Create a solution that uses cloud or web technologies by learning and investigating on your own from general guidance.

Analyzing and Graphing Census Data

Note: To complete this assignment, you will be required to use the Data Files. Please contact your instructor for information about accessing the Data Files.

Instructions: You are working as part of a group creating a report that includes data from the most recent census. Your task is to complete and format the worksheet using information from the census.gov website, chart the data, and make the chart available to your group using OneDrive. Start Excel. Open the workbook called SC_EX_3-3.xlsx, which is located in the Data Files. This workbook contains a basic structure to represent data from the last census.

Perform the following tasks:

1. Save the workbook using the file name, SC_EX_3_Census.
2. Identify three U.S. cities of your choice and enter the city and state names in cells A4, A5, and A6.
3. Open a web browser and navigate to the factfinder.census.gov website. Use the most recent census data to locate the population, median age, number of housing units, and median income for each city. Enter the information into the respective cells in the worksheet, as shown in Figure 3–85 but using cities of your own choosing. If you are unable to locate the necessary data, either choose a different city or perform a search for another website containing the necessary data.

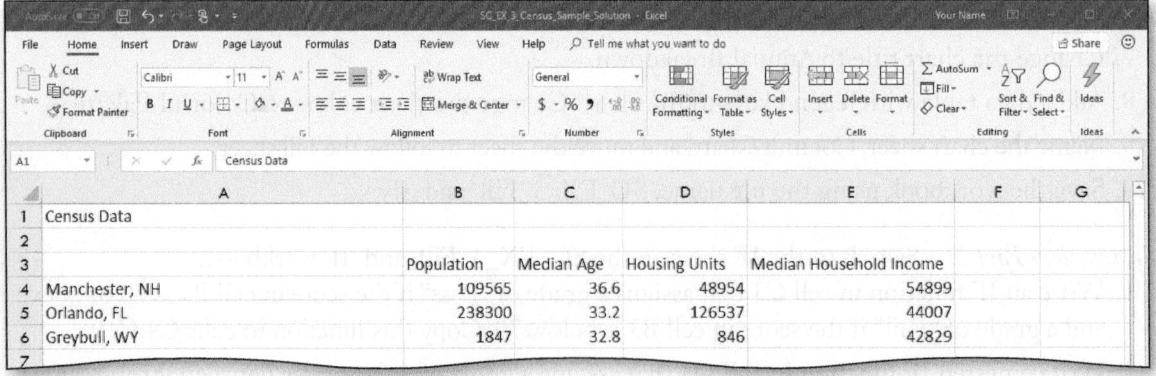

	A	B	C	D	E
1	Census Data				
2					
3		Population	Median Age	Housing Units	Median Household Income
4	Manchester, NH	109565	36.6	48954	54899
5	Orlando, FL	238300	33.2	126537	44007
6	Greybull, WY	1847	32.8	846	42829

Figure 3–85

4. Format the worksheet using techniques you have learned to present the data in a visually appealing form.
5. Create charts that present the data for each of the four categories of data. Decide which chart types will best present the data. (*Hint:* If you are not sure which types to use, consider selecting

the data and using the Recommended Chart button to narrow down and preview suitable choices.) Place each chart on a separate sheet and format the charts to best present the data in a clear, attractive format.

6. Give each worksheet a descriptive name and color the tabs using theme colors. Reorder the sheets so that the data table appears first, followed by the charts.
7. If requested by your instructor, export the file to OneDrive.
8. Submit the revised workbook as specified by your instructor.
9. Justify your choice of chart types in Step 5. Explain why you selected these types over other suitable choices.

In the Lab

Design and implement a solution using creative thinking and problem-solving skills.

Comparing Transportation Costs

Problem: You are thinking about buying a new vehicle, and you want to make sure that you buy one that offers the highest fuel savings. You decide to research hybrid cars as well as gas-only cars. Your friends are also interested in your results. Together, you decide to research the fuel costs associated with various types of vehicles.

Perform the following tasks:

Part 1: Research the gas mileage for eight vehicles: four should run only on gas, and the others should be hybrid vehicles, combining gas and battery power. After you find the gas mileage for each vehicle, you will use formulas to calculate the fuel cost for one month, six months, and two years. Assume that in a typical month, you will drive 1,250 miles. Develop a worksheet following the general layout in Table 3–9 that shows the fuel cost analysis. Use the formulas listed in Table 3–10 and the concepts and techniques presented in this module to create the worksheet. You will need to find the average price of gas for your market. Add a chart showing the cost comparisons as an embedded chart.

Table 3–9 Fuel Cost Analysis

Vehicle	Miles Per Gallon	Fuel Cost 1 Month	Fuel Cost 6 Months	Fuel Cost 2 Years
Gas 1		Formula A	Formula B	Formula C
Gas 2		—	—	—
Gas 3		—	—	—
Gas 4		—	—	—
Hybrid 1		—	—	—
Hybrid 2		—	—	—
Hybrid 3		—	—	—
Hybrid 4		—	—	—
Assumptions				
Distance per Month	1,250			
Price of Gas				

Continued >

In the Lab *continued*

Table 3–10 Fuel Cost Analysis Formulas
Formula A = (Distance per Month / Miles per Gallon)*Price of Gas
Formula B = ((Distance per Month / Miles per Gallon)*Price of Gas)*6
Formula C = ((Distance Per Month / Miles per Gallon)*Price of Gas)*24

Part 2: You made several decisions while creating the workbook for this assignment: how to lay out the data in the worksheet and which chart types to use. What was the rationale behind each of these decisions? What other costs might you want to consider when making your purchase decision?

1 Databases and Database Objects: An Introduction

Objectives

You will have mastered the material in this module when you can:

- Describe the features of the Access window
- Create a database
- Create tables in Datasheet and Design views
- Add records to a table
- Close a database
- Open a database
- Create and use a query
- Create and use a form
- Create a report
- Perform special database operations

Introduction

The term **database** describes a collection of data organized in a manner that allows access, retrieval, and use of that data. Microsoft Access 2019, usually referred to as simply Access, is a database management system. A **database management system** is software that allows you to use a computer to create a database; add, change, and delete data in the database; ask and answer questions concerning the data; and create forms and reports using the data.

Project—Database Creation

CanisMajorFelis Veterinary, or CMF Vets as its commonly known, is a veterinary practice that takes care of all cat and dog pet needs. Up until now, the appointment system has been paper-based. The staff records appointments in a large book with each page containing a specific date and time. Each page has slots for appointments, which are made in pencil to allow for changes. CMF Vets wants to computerize the appointment system with an Access database. The practice owns multiple veterinary clinics in the southwest. The practice wants to make the appointment system easier to use and more efficient. To accomplish that goal, the practice needs better record keeping.

CMF Vets needs to record all information about the pet owners. Name and full mailing address are essential pieces of information. In addition, the practice must be able to contact pet owners quickly. The staff needs to record home phone numbers, mobile phone numbers, and email addresses for appointment reminders, test results, and emergency calls.

Patient information is paramount. The patient's breed, animal type, name, and owner should be always recorded so that information can be easily retrieved. The database should also contain each patient's appointments with specific date, time, and procedure. For example, the staffing requirements of a surgical procedure will differ from those of a check-up.

Each treatment has a specific cost, which needs to be recorded and applied as patients undergo these treatments. The database system must also track the veterinarians who perform these treatments.

By recording all of its practice information, CMF Vets keeps its data current and accurate and can analyze it for trends. Using a database also allows CMF Vets to create a variety of useful reports; for example, tracking the frequency of certain procedures. These reports are vital for planning purposes.

In a **relational database,** such as those maintained by Access, a database consists of a collection of tables, each of which contains information on a specific subject. Figure 1–1 shows the database for CMF Vets. It consists of five tables: the Owners table (Figure 1–1a) contains information about the pet owners, the Patients table (Figure 1–1b) contains contact information for each pet's owner, the Appointments table (Figure 1–1c) contains information about the scheduling of appointments, the Treatment Cost table (Figure 1–1d) contains information about the cost of each treatment, and the Veterinarians table (Figure 1–1e) contains a listing of the veterinarians in the practice.

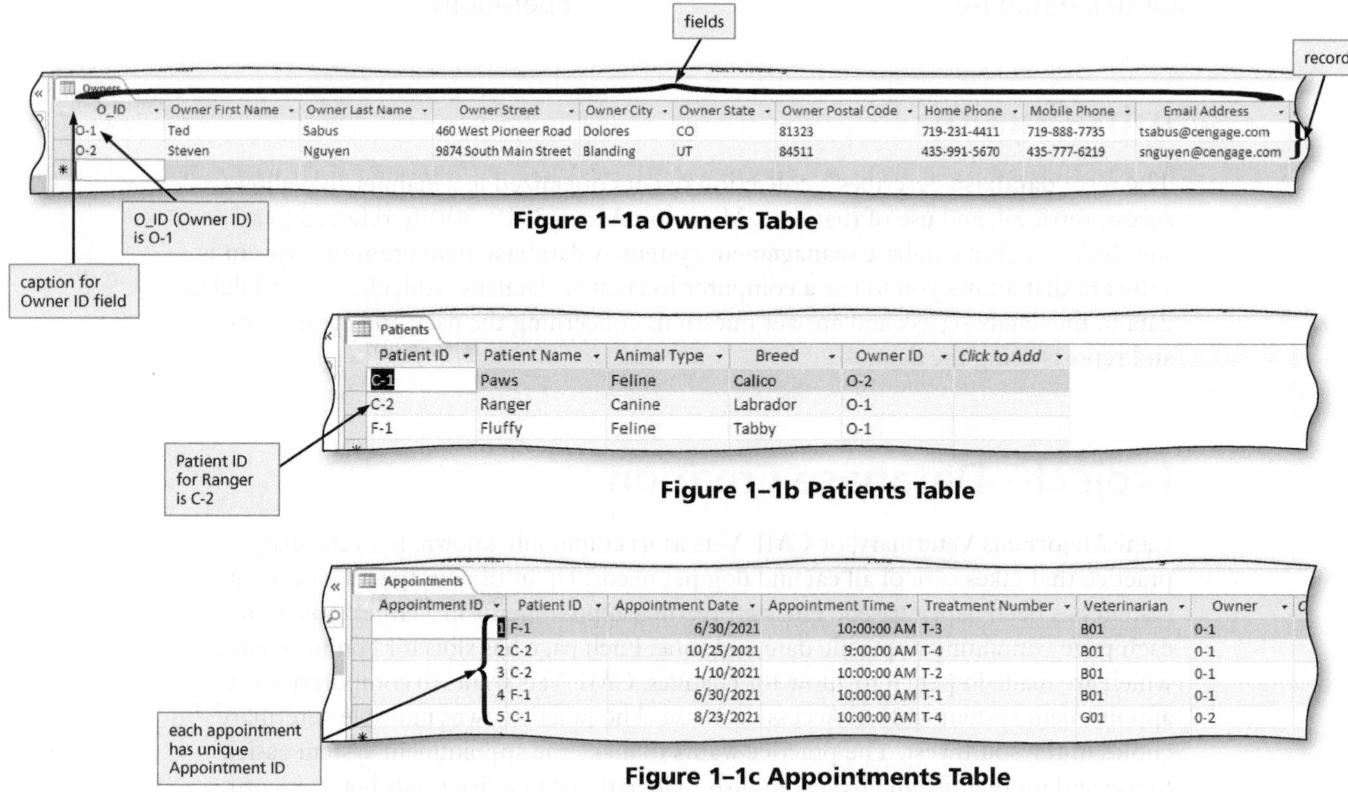

Owners

O_ID	Owner First Name	Owner Last Name	Owner Street	Owner City	Owner State	Owner Postal Code	Home Phone	Mobile Phone	Email Address
O-1	Ted	Sabus	460 West Pioneer Road	Dolores	CO	81323	719-231-4411	719-888-7735	tsabus@cengage.com
O-2	Steven	Nguyen	9874 South Main Street	Blanding	UT	84511	435-991-5670	435-777-6219	snguyen@cengage.com

Figure 1–1a Owners Table

Patients

Patient ID	Patient Name	Animal Type	Breed	Owner ID	Click to Add
C-1	Paws	Feline	Calico	O-2	
C-2	Ranger	Canine	Labrador	O-1	
F-1	Fluffy	Feline	Tabby	O-1	

Figure 1–1b Patients Table

Appointments

Appointment ID	Patient ID	Appointment Date	Appointment Time	Treatment Number	Veterinarian	Owner
1	F-1	6/30/2021	10:00:00 AM	T-3	B01	0-1
2	C-2	10/25/2021	9:00:00 AM	T-4	B01	0-1
3	C-2	1/10/2021	10:00:00 AM	T-2	B01	0-1
4	F-1	6/30/2021	10:00:00 AM	T-1	B01	0-1
5	C-1	8/23/2021	10:00:00 AM	T-4	G01	0-2

Figure 1–1c Appointments Table

Table Tools Database13 : D

File Home Create External Data Database Tools Help Fields Table Tell me what you war

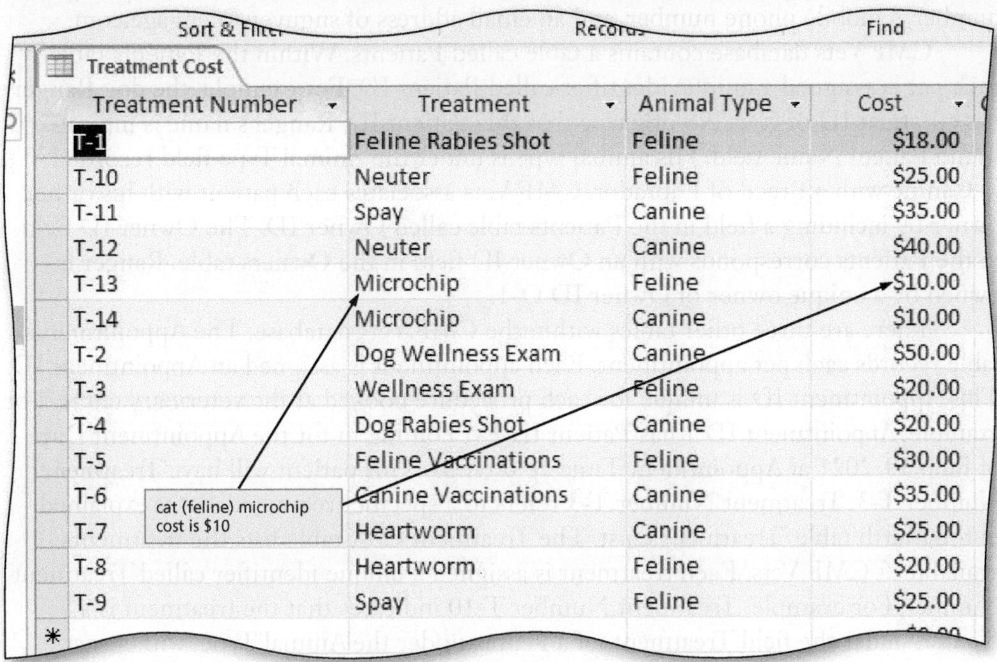

Treatment Number	Treatment	Animal Type	Cost
T-1	Feline Rabies Shot	Feline	$18.00
T-10	Neuter	Feline	$25.00
T-11	Spay	Canine	$35.00
T-12	Neuter	Canine	$40.00
T-13	Microchip	Feline	$10.00
T-14	Microchip	Canine	$10.00
T-2	Dog Wellness Exam	Canine	$50.00
T-3	Wellness Exam	Feline	$20.00
T-4	Dog Rabies Shot	Canine	$20.00
T-5	Feline Vaccinations	Feline	$30.00
T-6	Canine Vaccinations	Canine	$35.00
T-7	Heartworm	Canine	$25.00
T-8	Heartworm	Feline	$20.00
T-9	Spay	Feline	$25.00

Figure 1–1d Treatment Cost Table

Veterinarians

Veterinarian ID	First Name	Last Name	Office Phone	Cell Phone	Email Address	Street Address	City	State	ZIP Code
B01	William	Black	719-238-6682	719-334-9856	wblack@newmail.com	9887 Dover	Dolores	CO	81323
G01	Teresa	Gomez	435-222-4545	435-229-5612	tgomez@newmail.com	6214 Lansing	Blanding	UT	84511

each veterinarian has a Veterinarian ID

Figure 1–1e Veterinarians Table

The rows in the tables are called **records**. A record contains information about a given person (or in this case, pet), product, or event. A row in the Owners table, for example, contains information about a specific owner, such as the owner's name, address, and other data.

The columns in the tables are called fields. A **field** contains a specific piece of information within a record. In the Owners table, for example, the fifth field, Owner City, contains the name of the city where the owner is located.

The first field in the Owners table is Owner ID, which is an abbreviation for Owner Identification Number. CMF Vets assigns each owner an identifying number; the Owner ID consists of one uppercase letter followed by a number.

The Owner IDs are unique; that is, no two owners have the same number. Such a field is a **unique identifier**. A unique identifier, as its name suggests, is a way of uniquely identifying each record in the database. A given owner number will appear only in a single record in the table. Only one record exists, for example, in which the Owner ID is O-2. A unique identifier is also called a **primary key**. Thus, the Owner ID field is the primary key for the Owners table. This means the Owner ID field can be used to uniquely identify a record in the table. No two records can have the same value in the Owner ID field.

The next nine fields in the Owners table are Owner First Name, Owner Last Name, Owner Street, Owner City, Owner State, Owner Postal Code, Home Phone, Mobile Phone, and Email Address. For example, Owner ID O-2 is Steven Nguyen,

BTW

Captions

You can change a field's caption, or the wording that appears as the field's name, to language that is more descriptive, shorter, or meets some other requirement.

BTW

Naming Fields

Access 2019 has a number of reserved words, words that have a special meaning to Access. You cannot use these reserved words as field names. For example, Name is a reserved word and could not be used in the Owners table to describe a pet owner's name. For a complete list of reserved words in Access 2019, consult Access Help.

who lives at 9874 South Main Street in Blanding UT, 84511. Steven has a home phone number, a mobile phone number, and an email address of snguyen@cengage.com.

CMF Vets database contains a table called Patients. Within the Patients table, each pet is assigned a unique identifier called Patient ID. For example, the dog Ranger has a Patient ID of C-2. No other pet has this Patient ID. Ranger's name is indicated in the Patient Name field. His animal type is under the Animal Type field recorded as Canine with a Breed of Labrador. CMF Vets associates each patient with his or her owner by including a field in the Patients table called Owner ID. The Owner ID field in the Patients corresponds with an Owner ID field in the Owners table. Ranger is owned by a unique owner of Owner ID O-1.

There are three other tables within the CMF Vets database. The Appointments table records each pet appointment. Each appointment is assigned an Appointment ID. This Appointment ID is unique for each procedure booked at the veterinary clinic. For example, Appointment ID 1 has Patient ID F-1 coming in for the Appointment Date of June 30, 2021 at Appointment Time 10:00 A.M. This patient will have Treatment Number T-3. Treatment Number T-3 refers to a specific treatment that is explained in the fourth table, Treatment Cost. The Treatment Cost table lists the treatments available at CMF Vets. Each treatment is assigned a unique identifier called Treatment Number. For example, Treatment Number T-10 indicates that the treatment is a Neuter, under the field Treatment, of a Feline, under the Animal Type, with a cost of $25, under the field Cost. Finally, there is a table called Veterinarians that lists the veterinarians in the practice. Each doctor has a unique Veterinarian ID that is associated with the veterinarian's contact details. For example, Veterinarian ID G01 is Teresa Gomez, in Blanding, Utah, with a cell phone number of 435-229-5612.

How would you find the owner of a specific patient?

If CMF Vets had a test result of a specific patient, Ranger, Patient ID C-2, and the veterinarian wanted to telephone the owner with the test results, the vet could easily find that telephone number by looking in the Patients table and then in Owners table. In the Patients table, locate the Patient C-2 and read across until you come to the Owner ID field, which is O-1. Then, in the Owner table, locate the record which has the Owner ID O-1, and read across to find the owners name, Ted Sabus, and his phone numbers, home and mobile.

CONSIDER THIS

How would you find appointment information for a specific patient?

First, look in the Patients table to identify the specific pet and its Patient ID. Assume that the Patient's Owner is O-1 and the Patient's name is Fluffy. Fluffy's Patient ID is F-1. Next, look in the appointments table for Patient F-1 and find that Fluffy is scheduled to come into the clinic on June 30, 2021 at 10:00 A.M.

Creating a Database

In Access, all the tables, reports, forms, and queries that you create are stored in a single file called a database. A database is a structure that can store information about multiple types of objects, the properties of those objects, and the relationships among the objects. The first step is to create the database that will hold your tables, reports, forms, and queries. You can use either the Blank desktop database option or a template to create a new database. If you already know the tables and fields you want in your database, you would use the Blank desktop database option. If not, you can use a template. Templates can guide you by suggesting some commonly used databases.

To Create a Database

Because you already know the tables and fields you want in the CMF Vets database, you will use the Blank desktop database option rather than a template to create the database. ***Why?*** *The Blank desktop database is the most efficient way to create a database for which you already know the intended data needs.* The following steps create the database.

1

- Click the Windows Start button to display the Windows menu.
- Click the Access button to start Access (Figure 1–2a).

Figure 1–2a

2

- Click the Blank database button to specify the type of database to create.
- **sam** Type `CMF Vets` in the File Name text box, and then click the Create button to create the database (Figure 1–2).

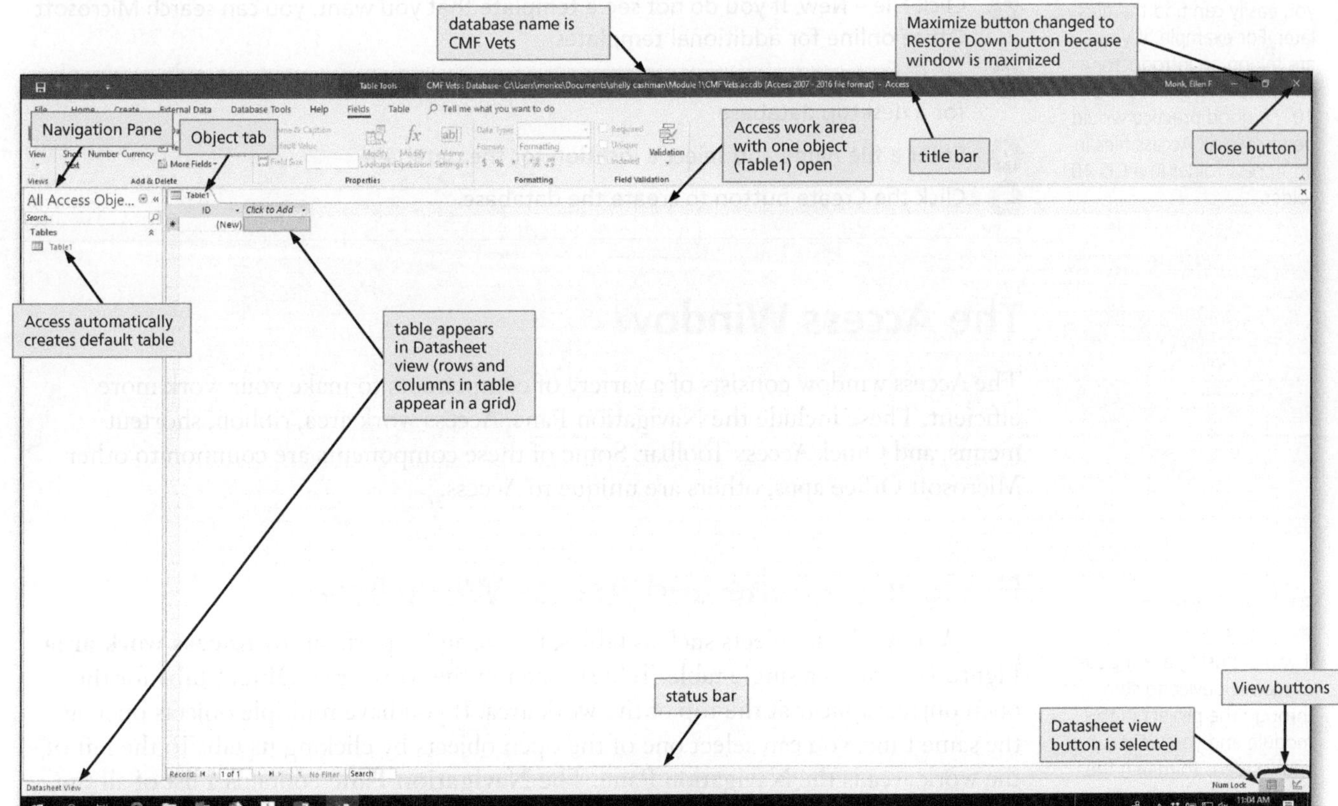

Figure 1–2

CONSIDER THIS

Saving a Microsoft Access Database File
Unlike other Microsoft Office applications, the Access app allocates storage space when the database is created, even before any tables have been designed and data has been entered. In other Microsoft Office applications, you can enter data before saving. In Access, as you are working and saving each object, such as a table, the entire database is being saved in the app's designated storage space.

BTW
Available Templates
The templates gallery includes both desktop and web-based templates. If you are creating an Access database for your own use, select a desktop template. Web-based templates allow you to create databases that you can publish to a SharePoint server.

Q&A
The title bar for my Navigation Pane contains All Tables rather than All Access Objects, as in the figure. Is that a problem?
It is not a problem. The title bar indicates how the Navigation Pane is organized. You can carry out the steps in the text with either organization. To make your screens match the ones in the text, click the Navigation Pane arrow and then click Object Type.

I do not have the Search bar that appears in the figure. Is that a problem?
It is not a problem. If your Navigation Pane does not display a Search bar and you want your screens to match the ones in the text, right-click the Navigation Pane title bar arrow to display a shortcut menu, and then click Search Bar.

To Create a Database Using a Template

Ideally, you will design your own database, create a blank database, and then create the tables you have determined that your database should contain. If you are not sure what database design you will need, you can use a template. Templates can guide you by suggesting some commonly used databases. To create a database using a template, you would use the following steps.

BTW
Organizing Files and Folders
You should organize and store files in folders so that you easily can find the files later. For example, if you are taking an introductory computer class called CIS 101, a good practice would be to save all Access files in an Access folder in a CIS 101 folder.

1. If you have another database open, close it without exiting Access by clicking File on the ribbon to open the Backstage view and then clicking Close.
2. Click File – New. If you do not see a template that you want, you can search Microsoft Office online for additional templates.
3. Click the template you want to use. Be sure you have selected one that indicates it is for a desktop database.
4. Enter a file name and select a location for the database.
5. Click the Create button to create the database.

The Access Window

The Access window consists of a variety of components to make your work more efficient. These include the Navigation Pane, Access work area, ribbon, shortcut menus, and Quick Access Toolbar. Some of these components are common to other Microsoft Office apps; others are unique to Access.

BTW
Access Screen Resolution
If you are using a computer or mobile device to step through the project in this module and you want your screens to match the figures in this book, you should change your screen's resolution to 1366 x 768.

Navigation Pane and Access Work Area

You work on objects such as tables, forms, and reports in the **Access work area**. Figure 1–2 shows a single table, Table1, open in the work area. **Object tabs** for the open objects appear at the top of the work area. If you have multiple objects open at the same time, you can select one of the open objects by clicking its tab. To the left of the work area is the Navigation Pane. The **Navigation Pane** contains a list of all the objects in the database. You use this pane to open an object. You can also customize the way objects are displayed in the Navigation Pane.

The **status bar**, located at the bottom of the Access window, presents information about the database object, the progress of current tasks, and the status of certain commands and keys; it also provides controls for viewing the object. As you type text or perform certain commands, various indicators might appear on the status bar. The left edge of the status bar in Figure 1–2 shows that the table object is open in **Datasheet view**. In Datasheet view, the table is represented as a collection of rows and columns called a **datasheet**. Toward the right edge are View buttons, which you can use to change the view that currently appears.

BTW
Naming Tables
Database users typically have their own guidelines for naming tables. Some use the singular version of the object being described while others use the prefix tbl with a table name. This book uses the singular and plural version of the object (Owners, Patients, Appointments, Treatment Cost).

Determining Tables and Fields

Once you have created the database, you need to create the tables and fields that your database will contain. Before doing so, however, you need to make some decisions regarding the tables and fields.

Naming Tables and Fields

In creating your database, you must name tables, fields, and other objects. Before beginning the design process, you must understand the rules Access applies to table and field names. These rules are:

1. Names can be up to 64 characters in length.
2. Names can contain letters, digits, and spaces, as well as most of the punctuation symbols.
3. Names cannot contain periods (.), exclamation points (!), accent graves (`), or square brackets ([ ]).
4. Each field in a table must have a unique name.

BTW
Multiple-Word Names
There are several ways to handle multiple-word names. You can leave in the space (Patient ID), omit the space (PatientID) or use an underscore in place of the space (Patient_ID). Another option is to use an underscore in place of a space, but use the same case for all letters (PATIENT_ID or patient_id).

The approach to naming tables and fields used in this text is to begin all names with an uppercase letter. In multiple-word names, each word begins with an uppercase letter, and there is a space between words (for example, Owner Street).

Determining the Primary Key

For each table, you need to determine the primary key, the unique identifier. In many cases, you will have obvious choices, such as Patient ID or Owner ID. If you do not have an obvious choice, you can use the primary key that Access creates automatically. It is a field called ID. It is an **autonumber field**, which means that Access will assign the value 1 to the first record, 2 to the second record, and so on.

Determining Data Types for the Fields

For each field in your database, you must determine the field's **data type**, that is, the type of data that can be stored in the field. Four of the most commonly used data types in Access are:

1. **Short Text —** The field can contain any characters. A maximum number of 255 characters is allowed in a field whose data type is Short Text.
2. **Number —** The field can contain only numbers. The numbers can be either positive or negative. Fields assigned this type can be used in arithmetic

BTW
Data Types
Different database management systems have different available data types. Even data types that are essentially the same can have different names. The Currency data type in Access, for example, is referred to as Money in SQL Server.

BTW
AutoNumber Fields
AutoNumber fields also are called AutoIncrement fields. In Design view, the New Values field property allows you to increment the field sequentially (Increment) or randomly (Random). The default is sequential.

operations. You usually assign fields that contain numbers but will not be used for arithmetic operations (such as postal codes) a data type of Short Text.

3. **Currency** — The field can contain only monetary data. The values will appear with currency symbols, such as dollar signs, commas, and decimal points, and with two digits following the decimal point. Like numeric fields, you can use currency fields in arithmetic operations. Access assigns a size to currency fields automatically.
4. **Date & Time** — The field can contain dates and/or times.

Table 1–1 shows the other data types that are available in Access.

Table 1–1 Additional Data Types

Data Type	Description
Long Text	Field can store up to a gigabyte of text.
AutoNumber	Field can store a unique sequential number that Access assigns to a record. Access will increment the number by 1 as each new record is added.
Yes/No	Field can store only one of two values. The choices are Yes/No, True/False, or On/Off.
OLE Object	Field can store an OLE object, which is an object linked to or embedded in the table.
Hyperlink	Field can store text that can be used as a hyperlink address.
Attachment	Field can contain an attached file. Images, spreadsheets, documents, charts, and other elements can be attached to this field in a record in the database. You can view and edit the attached file.
Calculated	Field specified as a calculation based on other fields. The value is not actually stored.

BTW
Currency Symbols
To show the symbol for the Euro (€) instead of the dollar sign, change the Format property for the field whose data type is currency. To change the default symbols for currency, change the settings in Windows.

In the Owners table, because the Owner ID, Owner First Name, Owner Last Name, Owner Street, Owner City, Owner State, Owner Postal Code, Home Phone, Mobile Phone, and Email Address can all contain letters or symbols, their data types should be Short Text. The data type for Owner Postal Code is Short Text instead of Number because you typically do not use postal codes in arithmetic operations; you do not add postal codes or find an average postal code, for example. The Owner ID field contains numbers, but you will not use these numbers in arithmetic operations, so its data type should be Short Text.

Similarly, in the Appointments table, the data type for the Account Manager Appointment ID, Patient ID and Treatment Number fields should all be Short Text. The Appointment Date and Appointment Time fields should have a data type of Date & Time. In the Treatment Cost table, the Cost contains monetary amounts, so its data type should be Currency.

For fields whose data type is Short Text, you can change the field size, that is, the maximum number of characters that can be entered in the field. If you set the field size for the State field to 2, for example, Access will not allow the user to enter more than two characters in the field. On the other hand, fields whose data type is Number often require you to change the field size, which is the storage space assigned to the field by Access. Table 1–2 shows the possible field sizes for Number fields.

Table 1–2 Field Sizes for Number Fields

Field Size	Description
Byte	Integer value in the range of 0 to 255
Integer	Integer value in the range of -32,768 to 32,767
Long Integer	Integer value in the range of -2,147,483,648 to 2,147,483,647
Single	Numeric values with decimal places to seven significant digits—requires 4 bytes of storage
Double	Numeric values with decimal places to more accuracy than Single—requires 8 bytes of storage
Replication ID	Special identifier required for replication
Decimal	Numeric values with decimal places to more accuracy than Single or Double—requires 12 bytes of storage

CONSIDER THIS

What is the appropriate size for the Owner Postal Code field?

A Short Text field created will allocate 255 spaces for data. However, a postal code normally would only take up 9 spaces. It is more accurate to change the Short Text field size to limit to 9 spaces to account for the postal code plus 4 (5 numbers, a dash, followed by 4 numbers).

Creating a Table in Datasheet View

BTW

Naming Files

The following characters cannot be used in a file name: question mark (?), quotation mark ("), slash (/), backslash (\ ), colon (:), asterisk (*), vertical bar (|), greater than symbol (>), and less than symbol (<).

To create a table in Access, you must define its structure. That is, you must define all the fields that make up the table and their characteristics. You must also indicate the primary key.

In Access, you can use two different views to create a table: Datasheet view and Design view. Although the main reason to use Datasheet view is to add or update records in a table, you can also use it to create a table or to later modify its structure. The other view, **Design view**, is only used to create a table or to modify the structure of a table.

As you might expect, Design view has more functionality for creating a table than Datasheet view. That is, there are certain actions that can only be performed in Design view. One such action is assigning Short Text as the field size for the Owner ID. In this module, you will create the first table, the Owners table, in Datasheet view. Once you have created the table in Datasheet view, you will use Design view to change the field size.

Whichever view you choose to use, before creating the table, you need to know the names and data types of the fields that will make up the table. You can also decide to enter a description for a particular field to explain important details about the field. When you select this field, this description will appear on the status bar. You might also choose to assign a **caption** to a particular field. If you assign a caption, Access will display the value you assign, rather than the field name, in datasheets and in forms. If you do not assign a caption, Access will display the field name.

CONSIDER THIS

When would you want to use a caption?

You would use a caption whenever you wanted something other than the field name displayed. One common example is when the field name is relatively long and the data in the field is relatively short. In the Owners table, the name of the first field is Owner ID, but the field contains data that is only at most five characters long. You will change the caption for this field to O_ID, which is much shorter than Owner ID, yet still describes the field. Doing so will enable you to greatly reduce the width of the column.

The results of these decisions for the fields in the Owners table are shown in Table 1–3. The table also shows the data types and field sizes of the fields as well as any special properties that need to be changed. The Owner ID short text field has a caption of O_ID, enabling the width of the Owner ID column to be reduced in the datasheet.

Table 1–3 Structure of Owners Table

Field Name	Data Type	Field Size	Description
Owner ID	Short Text	5	Primary Key **Description:** Unique identifier of pet owner **Caption:** O_ID
Owner First Name	Short Text	50	
Owner Last Name	Short Text	50	
Owner Street	Short Text	255	
Owner City	Short Text	50	
Owner State	Short Text	2	
Owner Postal Code	Short Text	9	
Home Phone	Short Text	25	
Mobile Phone	Short Text	25	
Email Address	Short Text	50	

CONSIDER THIS

How do you determine the field size?

You need to determine the maximum number of characters that can be entered in the field. In some cases, it is obvious. Field sizes of 2 for the State field and 9 for the Postal Code field are certainly the appropriate choices. In other cases, you need to determine how many characters you want to allow. In the list shown in Table 1–3, CMF Vets decided allowing 50 characters was sufficient for last names. You can change this field size later if it proves to be insufficient.

To Modify the Primary Key

When you first create a database, Access automatically creates a table for you. You can immediately begin defining the fields. If, for any reason, you do not have this table or inadvertently delete it, you can create the table by clicking Create on the ribbon and then clicking the Table button (Create tab | Tables group). In either case, you are ready to define the fields.

The following steps change the name, data type, and other properties of the first field to match the Owner ID field in Table 1–3, which is the primary key. ***Why?*** *Access has already created the first field as the primary key field, which it has named ID. Owner ID is a more appropriate name.*

- Right-click the column heading for the ID field to display a shortcut menu (Figure 1–3).

Q&A

Why does my shortcut menu look different?

You displayed a shortcut menu for the column instead of the column heading. Be sure you right-click the column heading.

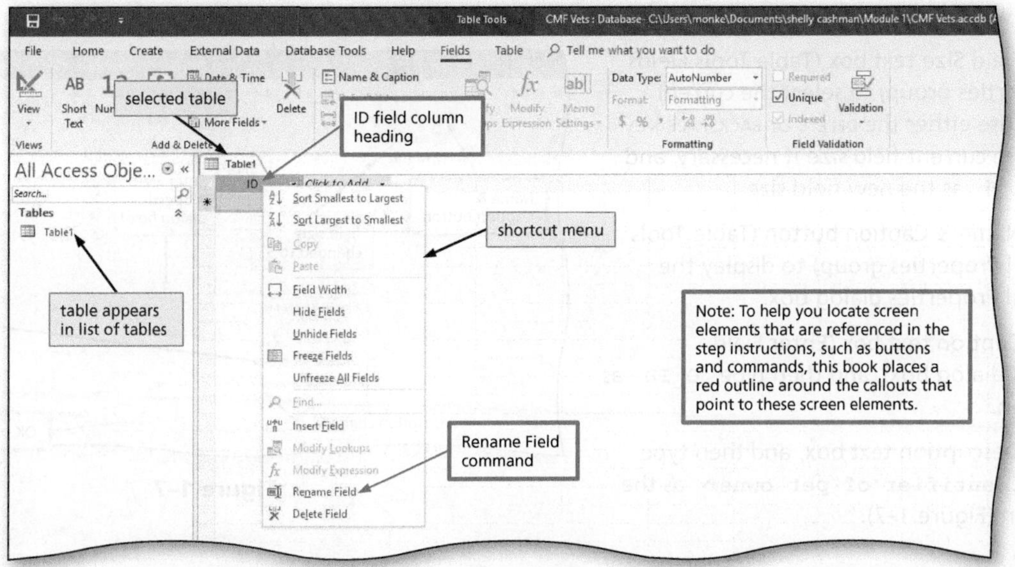

Figure 1–3

2

- Click Rename Field on the shortcut menu to highlight the current name.
- Type `Owner ID` to assign a name to the new field.
- Click the white space immediately below the field name to complete the addition of the field (Figure 1–4).

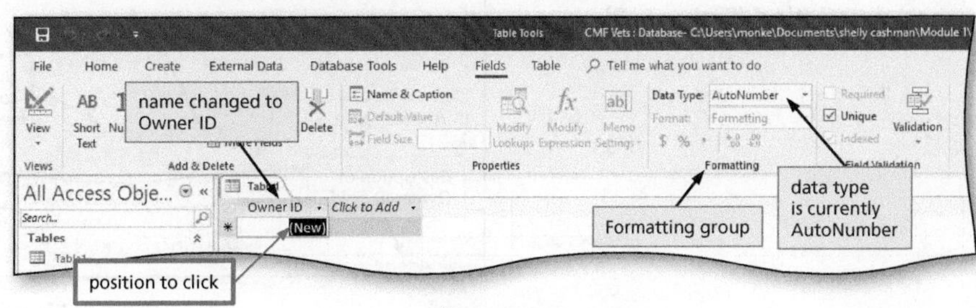

Figure 1–4

Q&A Why does the full name of the field not appear?
The default column size might not be large enough for Owner ID, or a later field such as Owner Last Name, to be displayed in its entirety. If necessary, you will address this issue in later steps.

3

- Because the data type needs to be changed from AutoNumber to Short Text, click the Data Type arrow (Table Tools Fields tab | Formatting group) to display a menu of available data types (Figure 1–5).

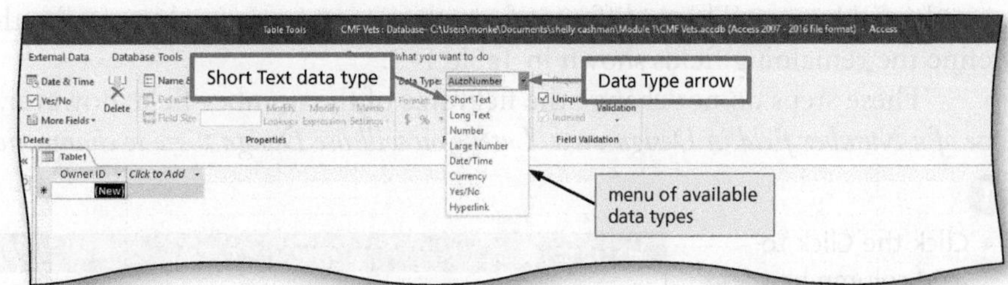

Figure 1–5

4 Click Short Text to select the data type for the field (Figure 1–6).

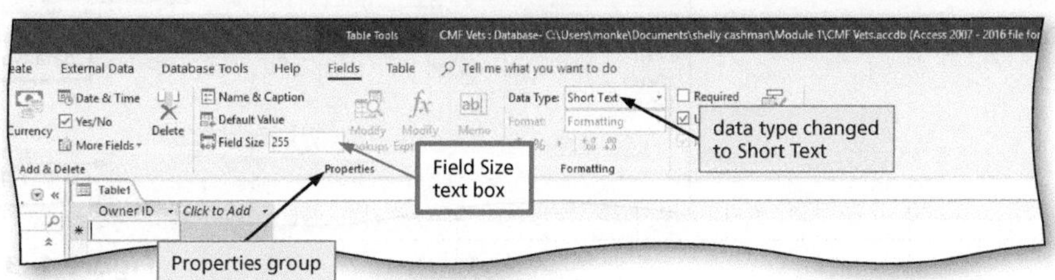

Figure 1–6

- Click the Field Size text box (Table Tools Fields tab | Properties group) to select the current field size, use either the DELETE or BACKSPACE key to erase the current field size if necessary, and then type `5` as the new field size.
- Click the Name & Caption button (Table Tools Fields tab | Properties group) to display the Enter Field Properties dialog box.
- Click the Caption text box (Enter Field Properties dialog box), and then type `O_ID` as the caption.
- Click the Description text box, and then type **`Unique identifier of pet owner`** as the description (Figure 1–7).

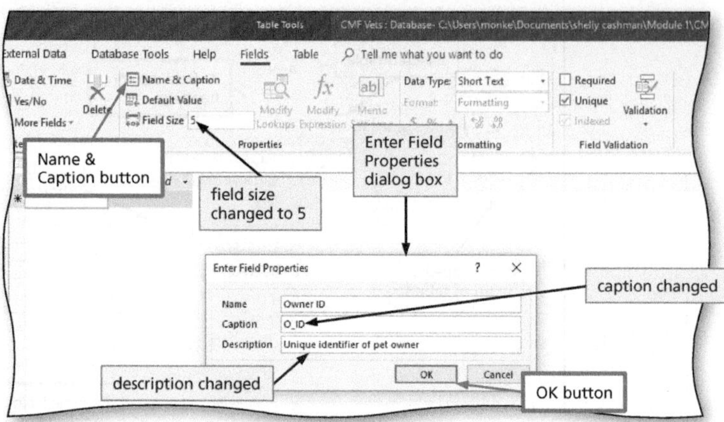

Figure 1–7

- Click OK (Enter Field Properties dialog box) to change the caption and description (Figure 1–8).

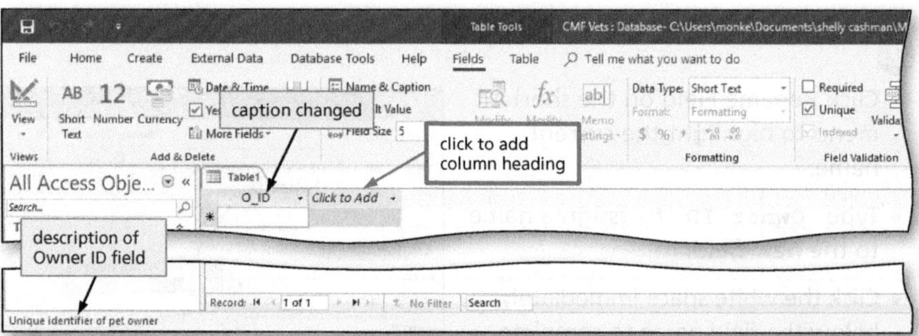

Figure 1–8

To Define the Remaining Fields in a Table

To define an additional field, you click the Click to Add column heading, select the data type, and then type the field name. This is different from the process you used to modify the ID field. The following steps define the remaining fields shown in Table 1–3.

These steps do not change the field size of the number field, however. ***Why?*** *You can only change the field size of a Number field in Design view. Later, you will use Design view to change field size and change the format.*

- Click the Click to Add column heading to display a menu of available data types (Figure 1–9).

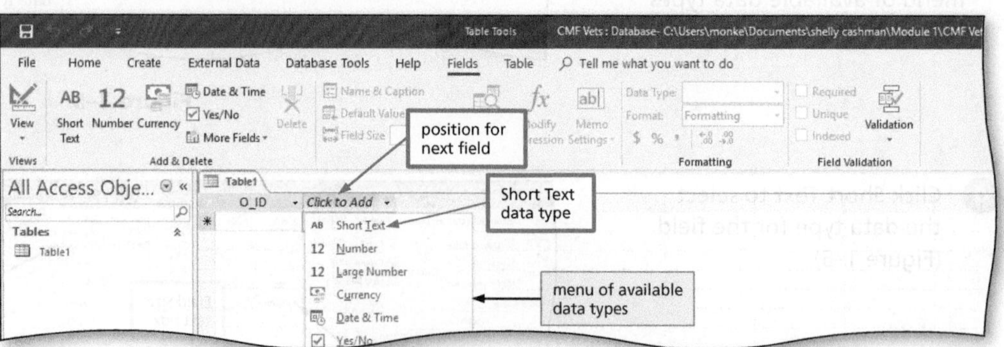

Figure 1–9

2

- Click Short Text in the menu of available data types to select the Short Text data type.
- Type **`Owner First Name`** to enter a field name.
- Click the blank space below the field name to complete the change of the name. Click the blank space a second time to select the field (Figure 1–10).
- If necessary, enlarge the field name box to display the entire name by clicking between Owner First Name and the Click to Add box. Drag the pointer, which is now a double-tipped arrow, to the right so that the entire field name of Owner First Name is visible.

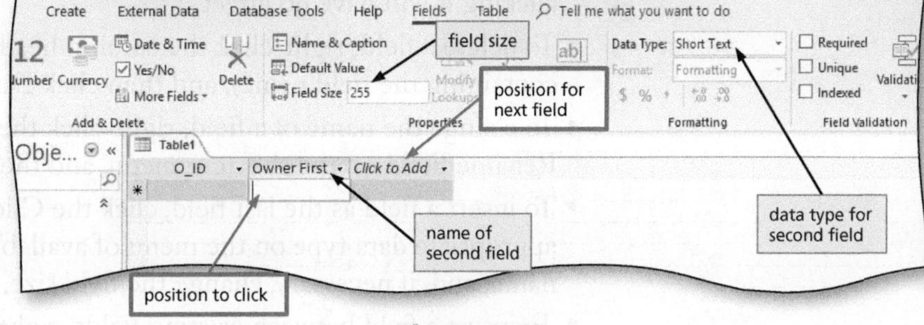

Figure 1–10

Q&A After entering the field name, I realized that I selected the wrong data type. How can I correct it?
Click the Data Type arrow, and then select the correct type.

I inadvertently clicked the blank space before entering the field name. How can I correct the name?
Right-click the field name, click Rename Field on the shortcut menu, and then type the new name.

3

- Change the field size to 50 just as you changed the field size of the Owner ID field.
- Using the same technique, add the remaining fields in the Owners table. For the Owner Last Name, Owner Street, Owner City, Owner State, Owner Postal Code, Home Phone, Mobile Phone, and Email Address fields, use the Short Text data type, but change the field sizes to match Table 1–3. Your Owners table should look like Figure 1–11.

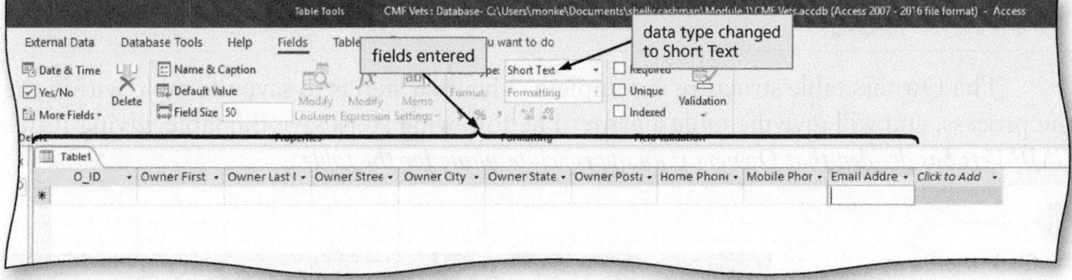

Figure 1–11

Q&A I have an extra row between the row containing the field names and the row that begins with the asterisk. What happened? Is this a problem? If so, how do I fix it?
You inadvertently added a record to the table by pressing a key. Even pressing the SPACEBAR adds a record. You now have an unwanted record. To fix it, press the ESC key or click the Undo button to undo the action. You may need to do this more than once.

When I try to move on to specify another field, I get an error message indicating that the primary key cannot contain a null value. How do I correct this?
First, click the OK button to remove the error message. Next, press the ESC key or click the Undo button to undo the action. You may need to do this more than once.

Making Changes to the Structure

When creating a table, check the entries carefully to ensure they are correct. If you discover a mistake while still typing the entry, you can correct the error by repeatedly pressing the BACKSPACE key until the incorrect characters are removed. Then, type the correct characters. If you do not discover a mistake until later, you can use the following techniques to make the necessary changes to the structure:

BTW
Touch Screen Differences
The Office and Windows interfaces may vary if you are using a touch screen. For this reason, you might notice that the function or appearance of your touch screen differs slightly from this module's presentation.

- To undo your most recent change, click the Undo button on the Quick Access Toolbar. If there is nothing that Access can undo, this button will be dim, and clicking it will have no effect.
- To delete a field, right-click the column heading for the field (the position containing the field name), and then click Delete Field on the shortcut menu.
- To change the name of a field, right-click the column heading for the field, click Rename Field on the shortcut menu, and then type the desired field name.
- To insert a field as the last field, click the Click to Add column heading, click the appropriate data type on the menu of available data types, type the desired field name, and, if necessary, change the field size.
- To insert a field between existing fields, right-click the column heading for the field that will follow the new field, and then click Insert Field on the shortcut menu. Right-click the column heading for the field, click Rename Field on the shortcut menu, and then type the desired field name.
- To move a field, click the column heading for the field to be moved to select the field, and then drag the field to the desired position.

As an alternative to these steps, you might want to start over. To do so, click the Close button for the table, and then click the No button in the Microsoft Access dialog box. Click Create on the ribbon, and then click the Table button to create a table. You then can repeat the process you used earlier to define the fields in the table.

To Save a Table

The Owners table structure is complete. The final step is to save the table within the database. As part of the process, you will give the table a name. The following steps save the table, giving it the name Owners. ***Why?*** *CMF Vets has decided that Owners is an appropriate name for the table.*

- Click the Save button on the Quick Access Toolbar to display the Save As dialog box (Figure 1–12).

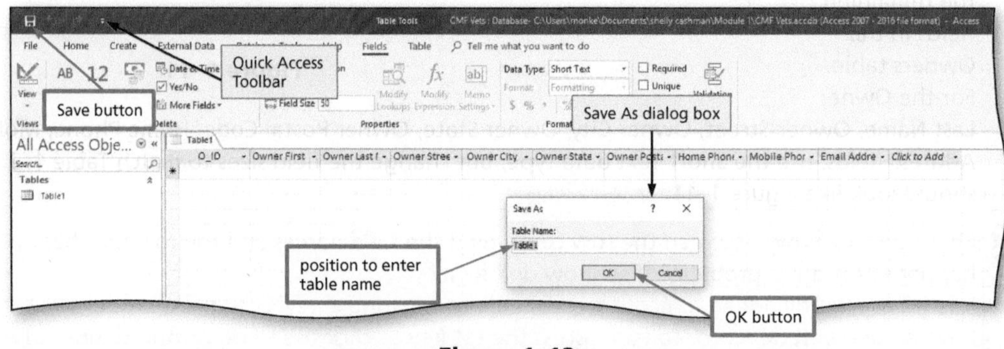

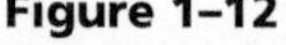
Figure 1–12

- Type `Owners` to change the name assigned to the table.
- Click OK (Save As dialog box) to save the table (Figure 1–13).

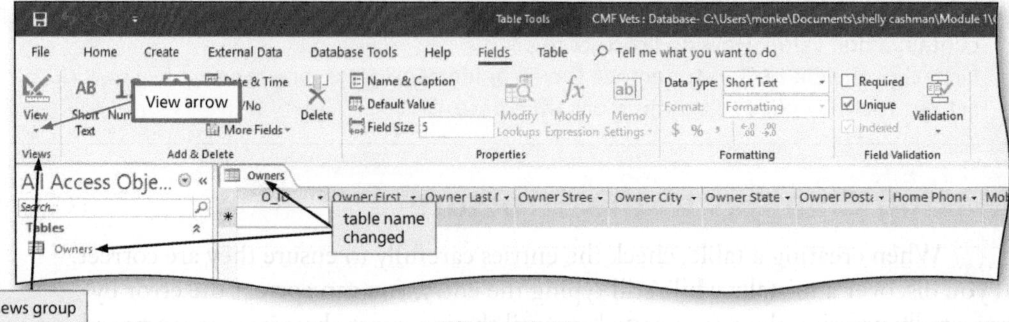

Figure 1–13

Other Ways

1. Click File on the ribbon, click Save in the Backstage view
2. Right-click tab for table, click Save on shortcut menu
3. Press CTRL+S

To View the Table in Design View

Even when creating a table in Datasheet view, Design view can be helpful. ***Why?*** *You easily can view the fields, data types, and properties to ensure you have entered them correctly. It is also easier to determine the primary key in Design view.* The following steps display the structure of the Owner table in Design view so that you can verify the design is correct.

1

- Click the View arrow (Table Tools Fields tab | Views group) to display the View menu (Figure 1–14).

Q&A Could I just click the View button rather than the arrow?
Yes. Clicking the button is equivalent to clicking the command represented by the icon that currently appears on the button. Because the icon on the button in Figure 1–14 is for Design view, clicking the button would display the table in Design view. If you are uncertain, you can always click the arrow and select Design View from the menu.

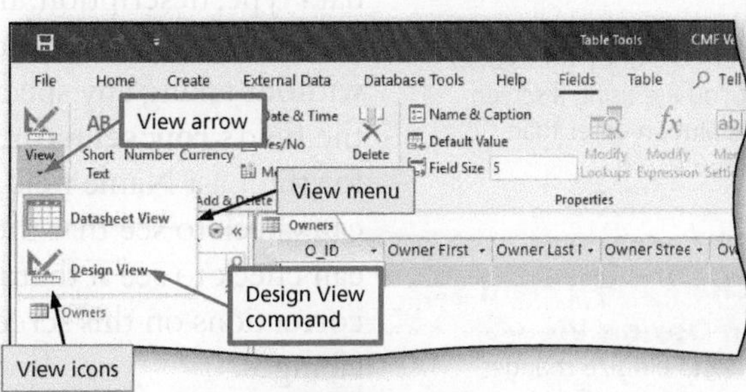

Figure 1–14

2

- Click Design View on the View menu to view the table in Design view (Figure 1–15).

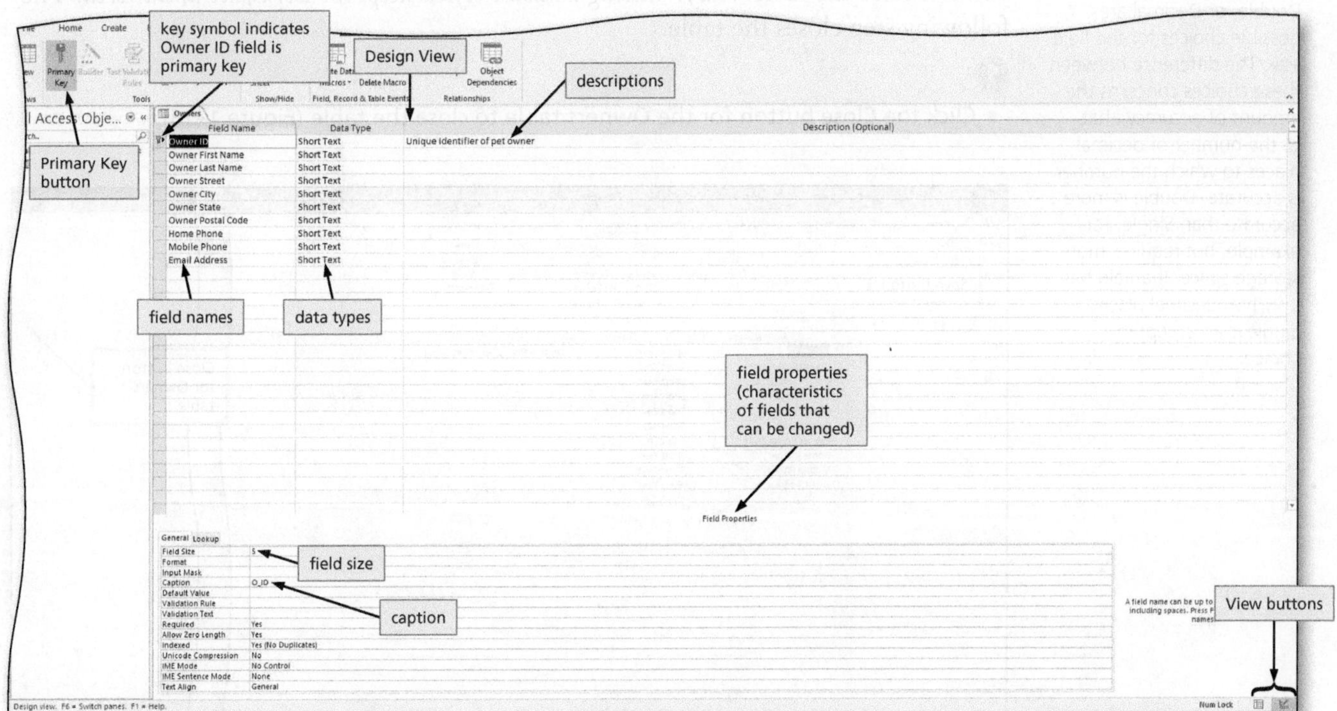

Figure 1–15

Other Ways

1. Click Design View button on status bar

BTW
The Ribbon and Screen Resolution
Access may change how the groups and buttons within the groups appear on the ribbon, depending on the computer or mobile device's screen resolution. Thus, your ribbon may look different from the ones in this book if you are using a screen resolution other than 1366 × 768.

BTW
Changing a Field Size in Design View
Most field size changes can be made in either Datasheet view or Design view. However, changing the field size for Number fields can only be done in Design view. If field values have decimal places, only Single, Double, or Decimal are possible choices for the field size. The difference between these choices concerns the amount of accuracy, that is, the number of decimal places to which the number is accurate. Double is more accurate than Single, for example, but requires more storage space. If a field has only two decimal places, Single is an acceptable choice.

Checking the Structure in Design View

You should use Design view to carefully check the entries you have made. In Figure 1–15, for example, the key symbol in front of the Owner ID field name indicates that the Owner ID field is the primary key of the Owners table. If your table does not have a key symbol, you can click the Primary Key button (Table Tools Design tab | Tools group) to designate a field as the primary key. You can also check that the data type, description, field size, and caption are all correct.

For the other fields, you can see the field name, data type, and description without taking any special action. To see the field size and/or caption for a field, click the field's **row selector**, the small box to the left of the field. Clicking the row selector for the Last Name field, for example, displays the properties for that field. You then can check to see that the field size is correct. In addition, if the field has a caption, you can check to see if that is correct. If you find any mistakes, you can make the necessary corrections on this screen. When you have finished, click the Save button to save your changes.

To Close the Table

Once you are sure that your entries are correct and you have saved your changes, you can close the table. ***Why?*** *Closing database objects keeps the workspace uncluttered.* The following step closes the table.

- Click the Close button for the Owners table to close the table (Figure 1–16).

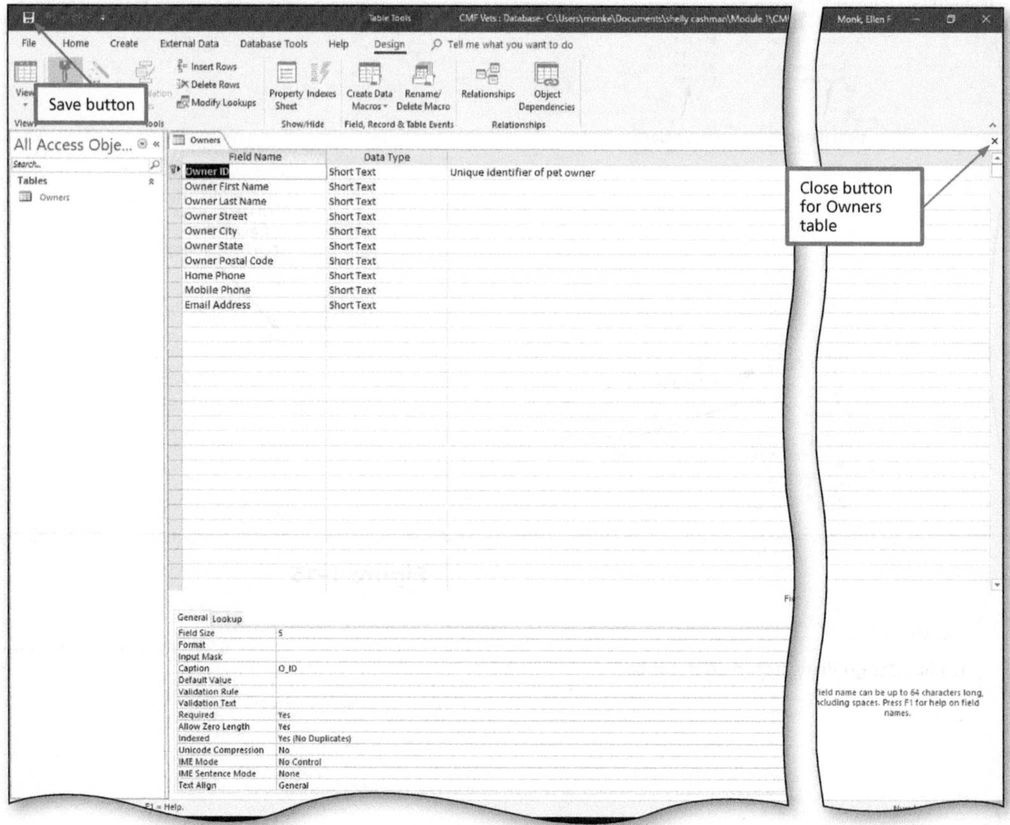

Figure 1–16

- If necessary, click Yes to save changes to the design of the table and then close the table. The dialog box will not appear if you did not make any changes.

Other Ways

1. Right-click tab for table, click Close on shortcut menu

To Add Records to a Table

Creating a table by building the structure and saving the table is the first step in the two-step process of using a table in a database. The second step is to add records to the table. To add records to a table, the table must be open. When making changes to records, you work in Datasheet view.

You often add records in phases. ***Why?*** *You might not have enough time to add all the records in one session, or you might not have all the records currently available.* The following steps open the Owners table in Datasheet view and then add the two records in the Owners table (Figure 1–17).

O_ID	Owner First Name	Owner Last Name	Owner Street	Owner City	Owner State	Owner Postal Code	Home Phone	Mobile Phone	Email Address
O-1	Ted	Sabus	460 West Pioneer Road	Dolores	CO	81323	719-231-4411	719-888-7735	tsabus@cengage.com
O-2	Steven	Nguyen	9874 South Main Street	Blanding	UT	84511	435-991-5670	435-777-6219	snguyen@cengage.com

Figure 1–17

- Right-click the Owners table in the Navigation Pane to display the shortcut menu (Figure 1–18).

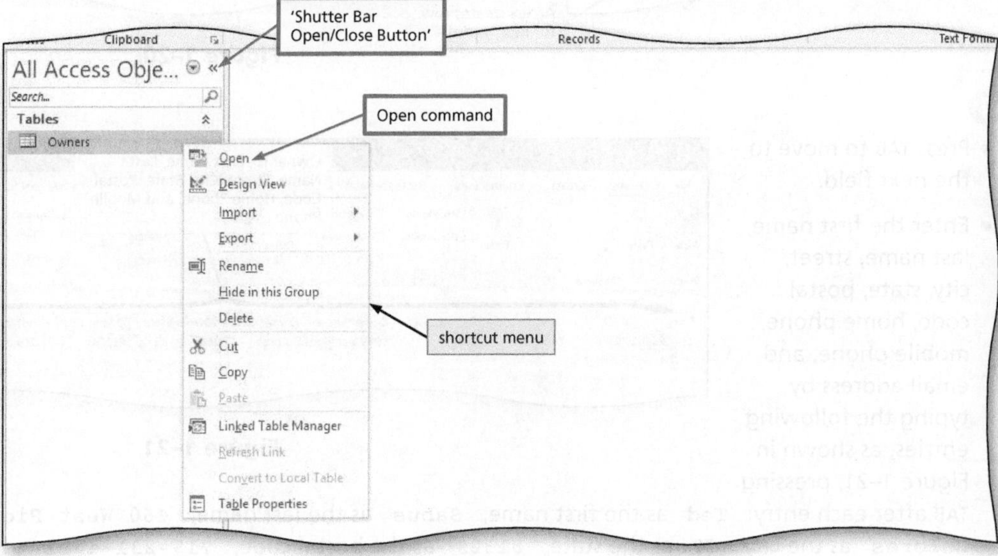

Figure 1–18

- Click Open on the shortcut menu to open the table in Datasheet view.
- Click the 'Shutter Bar Open/Close Button' to close the Navigation Pane (Figure 1–19).

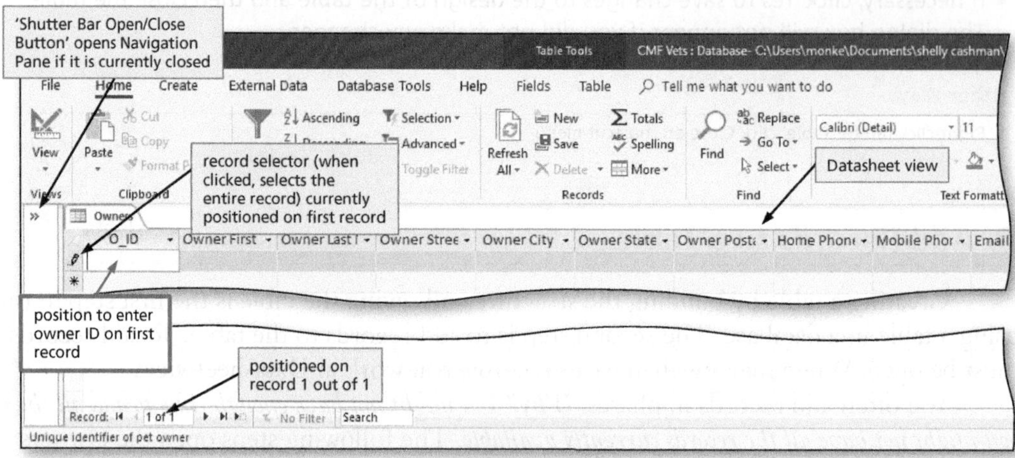

Figure 1–19

- Click the first row in the O_ID field if necessary to display an insertion point, and type `O-1` (the letter "O" followed by a hyphen and the number 1) to enter the first owner ID (Figure 1–20).

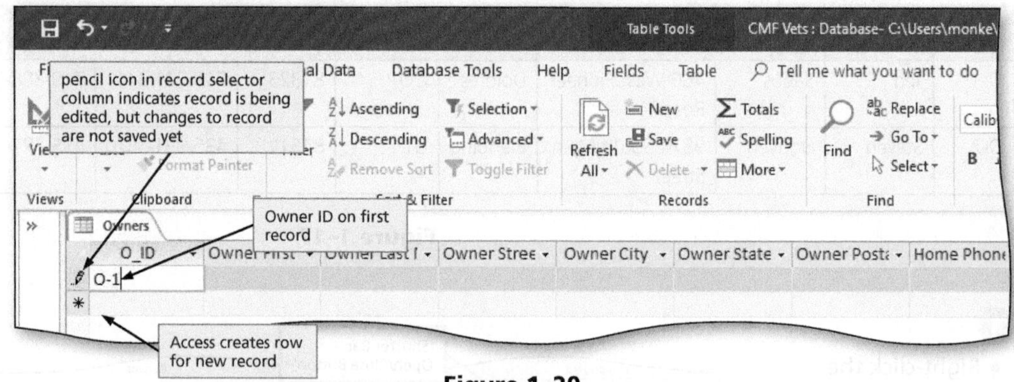

Figure 1–20

- Press TAB to move to the next field.
- Enter the first name, last name, street, city, state, postal code, home phone, mobile phone, and email address by typing the following entries, as shown in Figure 1–21, pressing TAB after each entry: `Ted` as the first name, `Sabus` as the last name, `460 West Pioneer Road` as the street, `Dolores` as the city, `CO` as the state, `81323` as the postal code, `719-231-4411` as the home phone, and `719-888-7735` as the mobile phone.

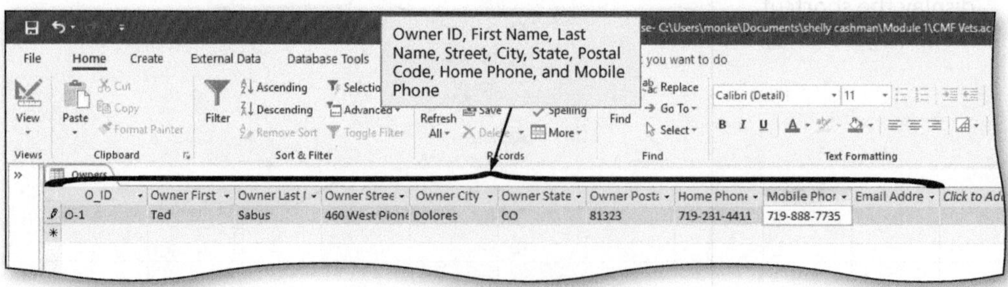

Figure 1–21

- If requested by your instructor, enter your address instead of 460 West Pioneer Road as the street. If your address is longer than 50 characters, enter the first 50 characters.

- Press TAB to complete the entry for the Email Address field.
- If requested by your instructor, enter your email address instead of tsabus@cengage.com in the Email Address field. If your email address is longer than 50 characters, shorten the part of the Email Address field so that it ends before the @ symbol.
- Press the TAB key to complete the entry of the first record (Figure 1–22).

Q&A How and when do I save the record?
As soon as you have entered or modified a record and moved to another record, Access saves the original record. This is different from other applications. The rows entered in an Excel worksheet, for example, are not saved until the entire worksheet is saved.

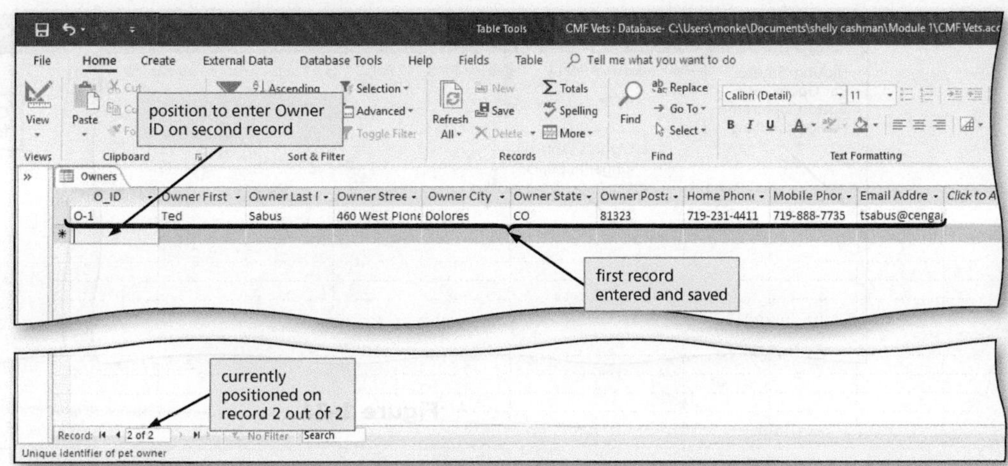

Figure 1–22

- Use the techniques in Steps 3 through 5 to enter the owner data (found in Figure 1–17) to complete the second record (Figure 1–23).

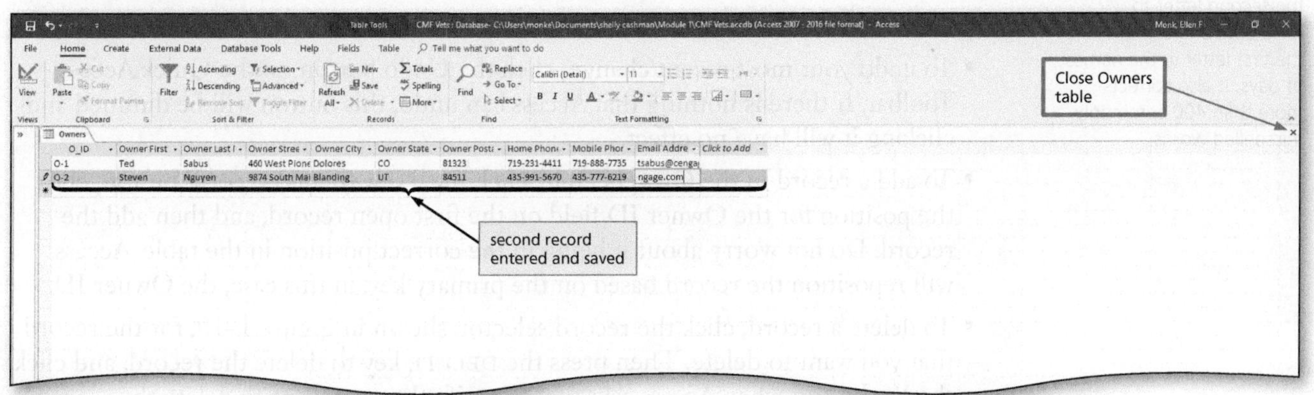

Figure 1–23

Q&A Does it matter that I entered Owner ID O-1 after I entered Owner ID O-2? Should the Owner IDs be in order?
The order in which you enter the records is not important. When you close and later reopen the table, the records will be in Owner ID order, because the Owner ID field is the primary key.

I made a mistake in entering the data. When should I fix it?
It is a good idea to fix it now, although you can fix it later as well. In any case, the following section gives you the techniques you can use to make any necessary corrections. If you want to fix it now, read that section and make your corrections before proceeding to the next step.

- Click the Close button for the Owners table, shown in Figure 1–23, to close the table (Figure 1–24).
- Exit Access.

Q&A Is it necessary for me to exit Access at this point?
No. The step is here for two reasons. First, you will often not be able to add all the records you need to add in one sitting. In such a case, you will add some records, and then exit Access. When you are ready to resume adding the records, you will run Access, open the table, and then continue the addition process. Second, there is a break point coming up in the module. If you want to take advantage of that break, you need to first exit Access.

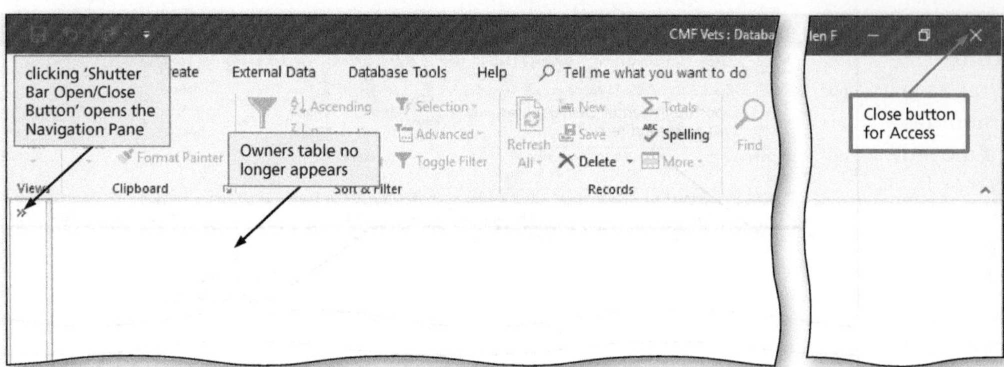

Figure 1–24

BTW
AutoCorrect Feature
The AutoCorrect feature of Access corrects common data entry errors. For example, AutoCorrect corrects two capital letters by changing the second letter to lowercase and capitalizes the first letter in the names of days. It also corrects more than 400 commonly misspelled words.

Making Changes to the Data

As you enter data in the datasheet view, check your entries carefully to ensure they are correct. If you make a mistake and discover it before you press the TAB key, correct it by pressing the BACKSPACE key until the incorrect characters are removed, and then type the correct characters. If you do not discover a mistake until later, you can use the following techniques to make the necessary corrections to the data:

- To undo your most recent change, click the Undo button on the Quick Access Toolbar. If there is nothing that Access can undo, this button will be dimmed and clicking it will have no effect.
- To add a record in the Owners table, click the 'New (blank) record' button, click the position for the Owner ID field on the first open record, and then add the record. Do not worry about it being in the correct position in the table. Access will reposition the record based on the primary key, in this case, the Owner ID.
- To delete a record, click the record selector, shown in Figure 1–19, for the record that you want to delete. Then press the DELETE key to delete the record, and click the Yes button when Access asks you to verify that you want to delete the record.
- To change the contents of one or more fields in a record, the record must be on the screen. If it is not, use any appropriate technique, such as the UP ARROW and DOWN ARROW keys or the vertical scroll bar, to move to the record. If the field you want to correct is not visible on the screen, use the horizontal scroll bar along the bottom of the screen to shift all the fields until the one you want appears. If the value in the field is currently highlighted, you can simply type the new value. If you would rather edit the existing value, you must have an insertion point in the field. You can place the insertion point by clicking in the field or by pressing the F2 key. You then can use the arrow keys, the DELETE key, and the BACKSPACE key for making the correction. You can also use the INSERT key to switch between Insert and Overtype mode. When you have made the change, press the TAB key to move to the next field.

BTW
Spell Checking
To check the spelling in a table, Select the Home tab, Records group, Spelling.

CONSIDER THIS

Duplicate Key Fields

When typing in new records, if you inadvertently type in the same key field as another record, Access will display a dialog box saying that the changes were not successful because they would create duplicate values in the index, primary key, or relationship. To correct this problem, change the primary key to a different field that has already been entered. You can then delete the record if you no longer need this.

If you cannot determine how to correct the data, you may find that you are "stuck" on the record, in which case Access neither allows you to move to another record nor allows you to close the table until you have made the correction. If you encounter this situation, simply press the ESC key. Pressing the ESC key will remove from the screen the record you are trying to add. You then can move to any other record, close the table, or take any other action you desire.

BTW
Other AutoCorrect Options
Using the Office AutoCorrect feature, you can create entries that will replace abbreviations with spelled-out names and phrases automatically. To specify AutoCorrect rules, click File on the ribbon to open the Backstage view, click Options, and then click Proofing in the Access Options dialog box.

Break Point: If you wish to take a break, this is a good place to do so. You can exit Access now. To resume at a later time, run Access, open the database called CMF Vets, and continue following the steps from this location forward.

BTW
Enabling Content
If the database is one that you created, or if it comes from a trusted source, you can enable the content. You should disable the content of a database if you suspect that your database might contain harmful content or damaging macros.

Navigation Buttons

You will often need to update tables with new records. You can open a table that already contains data and add records using a process similar to that used to add records to an empty table. The only difference is that you place the insertion point after the last record before you enter the additional data. To position the insertion point after the last record, you can use the **Navigation buttons**, which are buttons used to move within a table, found near the lower-left corner of the screen when a table is open. It is a good habit to use the 'New (blank) record' button. Once a table contains more records than will fit on the screen, it is easier to click the 'New (blank) record' button. The purpose of each Navigation button is described in Table 1–4.

Table 1–4 Navigation Buttons in Datasheet View

Button	Purpose
First record	Moves to the first record in the table
Previous record	Moves to the previous record
Next record	Moves to the next record
Last record	Moves to the last record in the table
New (blank) record	Moves to the end of the table to a position for entering a new record

To Resize Columns in a Datasheet

Access assigns default column sizes, which do not always provide space to display all the data in the field. In some cases, the data might appear but the entire field name is not visible. You can correct this problem by resizing the column (changing its size) in the datasheet. In some instances, you might want to reduce the size of a column. ***Why?*** *Some fields, such as the Owner State field, are short enough that they do not require all the space on the screen that is allotted to them.* Changing a column width changes the layout, or design, of a table. The following steps resize the columns in the Owners table and save the changes to the layout.

- Run Access, unless it is already running.
- Open the CMF Vets database from your hard drive, OneDrive, or other storage location (Figure 1–25).
- If a Security Warning appears, click the Enable Content button.

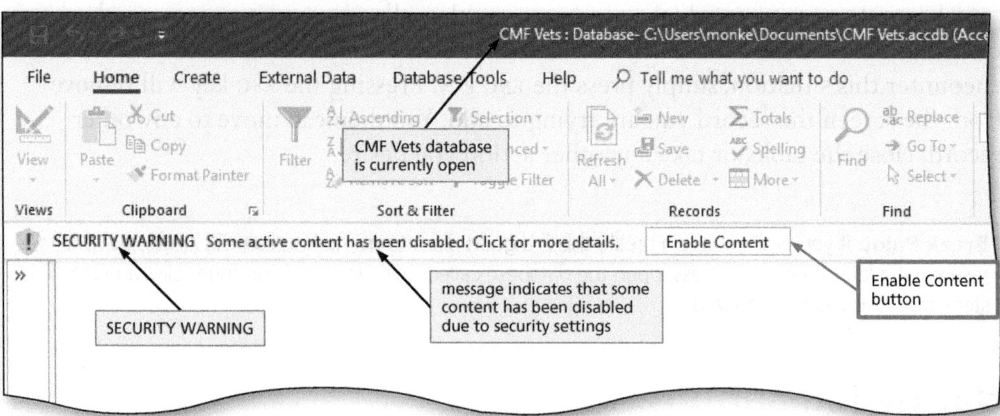

Figure 1–25

- If the Navigation Pane is closed, click the 'Shutter Bar Open/Close Button,' shown in Figure 1–24, to open the Navigation Pane (Figure 1–26).

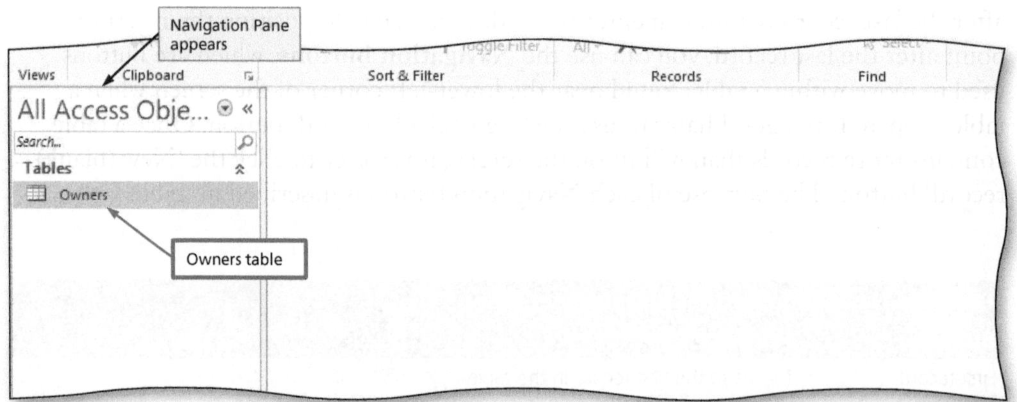

Figure 1–26

- Right-click the Owners table in the Navigation Pane to display a shortcut menu.
- Click Open on the shortcut menu to open the table in Datasheet view.

Q&A Why do the records appear in a different order from how I entered them?
When you open the table, they are sorted in the order of the primary key. In this case, that means they will appear in Owner ID order.

4

- Point to the right boundary of the field selector for the Owner First Name field (Figure 1–27) so that the pointer becomes a two-headed arrow.

Q&A I am using touch and I cannot see the pointer. Is this a problem?
It is not a problem. Remember that if you are using your finger on a touch screen, you will not see the pointer.

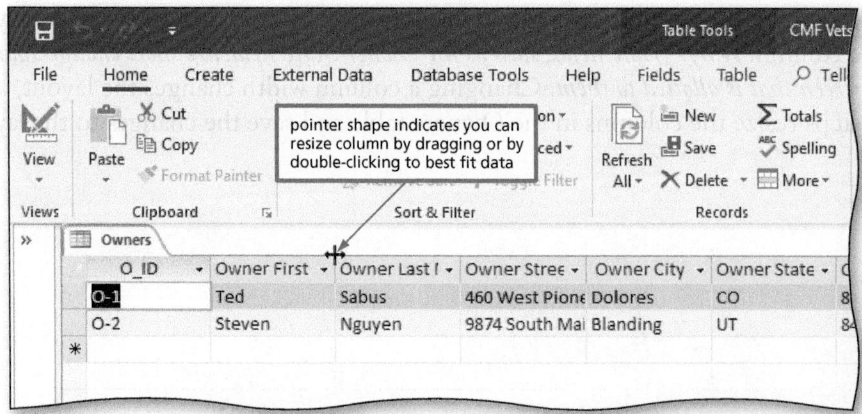

Figure 1–27

5

- **Double-click the right boundary of the field selector to resize the field so that it best fits the data.**
- **Use the same technique to resize all the other fields to best fit the data.**
- **Save the changes to the layout by clicking the Save button on the Quick Access Toolbar (Figure 1–28).**

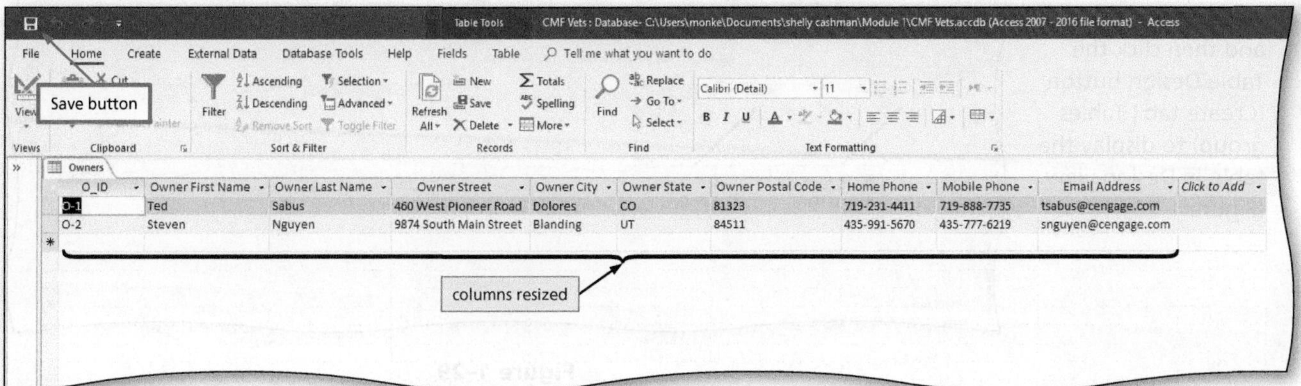

Figure 1–28

- **Click the table's Close button (shown in Figure 1–23) to close the table.**

Q&A What if I closed the table without saving the layout changes?
You would be asked if you want to save the changes.

Other Ways

1. Right-click field name, click Field Width

CONSIDER THIS

What is the best method for distributing database objects?

The traditional method of distributing database objects such as tables, reports, and forms uses a printer to produce a hard copy. A hard copy or printout is information that exists on a physical medium such as paper. Hard copies can be useful for the following reasons:

- Some people prefer proofreading a hard copy of a document rather than viewing it on the screen to check for errors and readability.
- Hard copies can serve as a backup reference if your storage medium is lost or becomes corrupted and you need to recreate the document. Instead of distributing a hard copy, users can distribute the document as an electronic image that mirrors the original document's appearance. The electronic image of the document can be emailed, posted on a website, or copied to a portable storage medium such as a USB flash drive. Two popular electronic image formats, sometimes called fixed formats, are PDF by Adobe Systems and XPS by Microsoft.

In Access, you can create electronic image files through the External Data tab on the ribbon. Electronic images of documents, such as PDF and XPS, can be useful for the following reasons:

- Users can view electronic images of documents without the software that created the original document (e.g., Access). Specifically, to view a PDF file, you use a program called Adobe Reader, which can be downloaded free from Adobe's website. Similarly, to view an XPS file, you use a program called XPS Viewer, which is included in the latest versions of Windows and Edge.
- Sending electronic documents saves paper and printer supplies. Society encourages users to contribute to **green computing**, which involves reducing the electricity consumed and environmental waste generated when using computers, mobile devices, and related technologies.

To Create a Table in Design View

The following steps use Design view to create a table. ***Why?*** *Instead of using Datasheet view, Design view is the most efficient way to create a table because you specify field name, data type, and size all in one view.*

1

- To create a table in Design view, display the Create tab, and then click the Table Design button (Create tab | Tables group) to display the table in Design view (Figure 1–29).

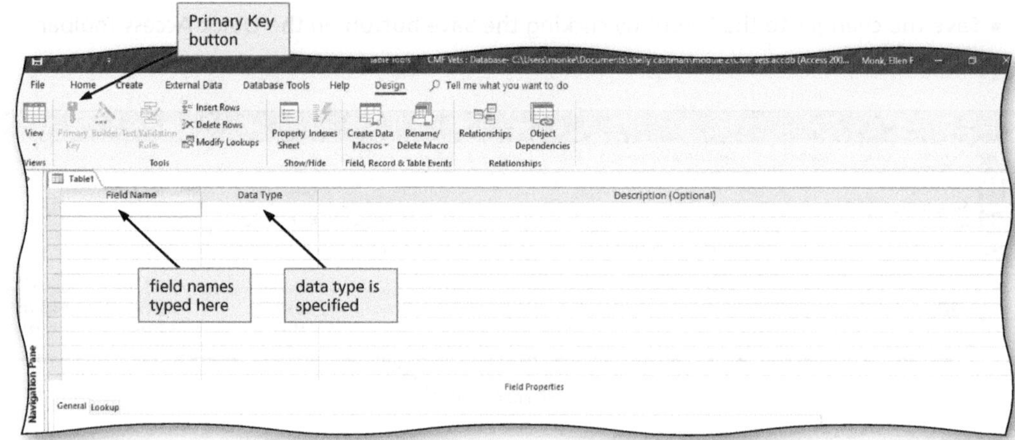

Figure 1–29

2

- Click in the empty field below Field Name, and then type **`Patient ID`** to enter the data for the first field. Continue entering the data for the Patients table, as shown in Figure 1–30.

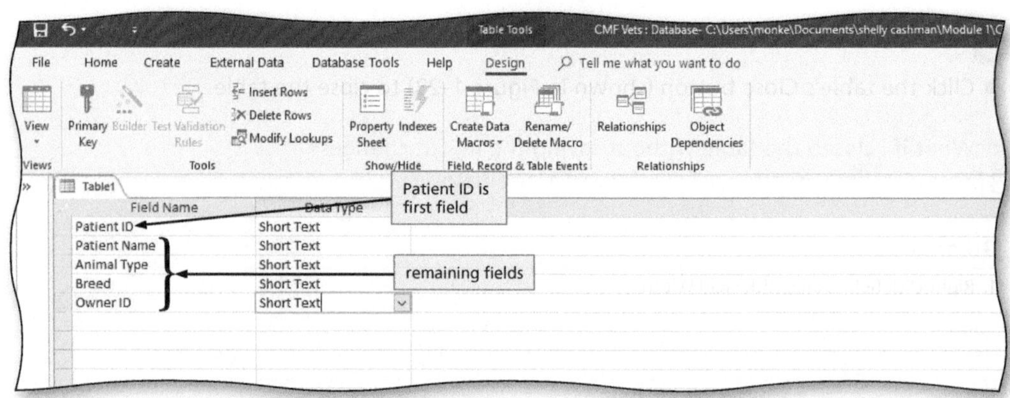

Figure 1–30

- Click the Patient ID row selector, if necessary, and then click the Primary Key button to assign Patient ID as the primary key field (Figure 1–31).
- Click the Save button on the Quick Access toolbar and enter **`Patients`** in the text box to save the table with the name, Patients.

Q&A How do I rename a field in Design view?

In Design view, place your pointer on the end of the field you want to rename and press the BACKSPACE key until the name is removed. Enter the correct name.

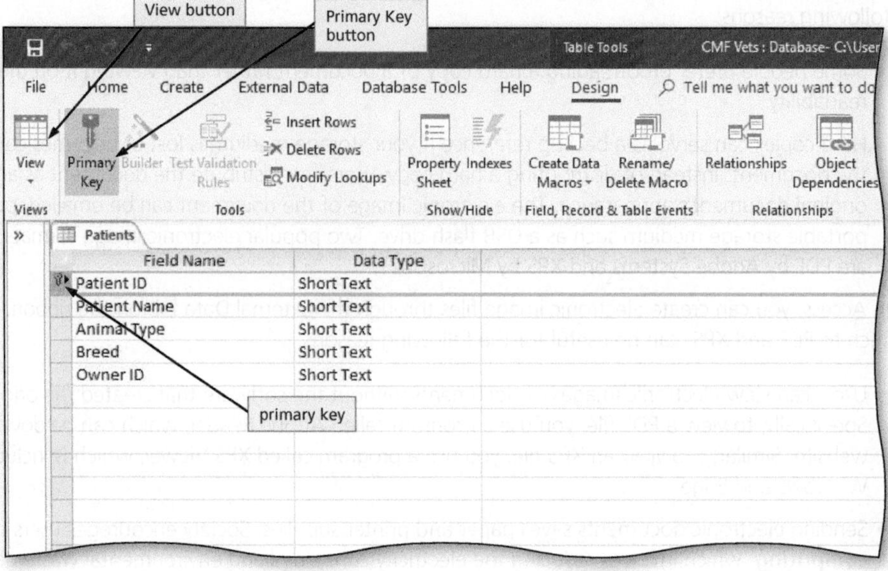

Figure 1–31

Correcting Errors in the Structure

Whenever you create or modify a table in Design view, you should check the entries carefully to ensure they are correct. If you make a mistake and discover it before you press the TAB key, you can correct the error by repeatedly pressing the BACKSPACE key until the incorrect characters are removed. Then, type the correct characters. If you do not discover a mistake until later, you can click the entry, type the correct value, and then press the ENTER key. You can use the following techniques to make changes to the structure:

- If you accidentally add an extra field to the structure, select the field by clicking the row selector (the leftmost column on the row that contains the field to be deleted). Once you have selected the field, press the DELETE key. This will remove the field from the structure.
- If you forget to include a field, select the field that will follow the one you want to add by clicking the row selector, and then press the INSERT key. The remaining fields move down one row, making room for the missing field. Make the entries for the new field in the usual manner.
- If you made the wrong field a primary key field, click the correct primary key entry for the field and then click the Primary Key button (Table Tools Design tab | Tools group).
- To move a field, click the row selector for the field to be moved to select the field, and then drag the field to the desired position.

As an alternative to these steps, you might want to start over. To do so, click the Close button for the window containing the table, and then click the No button in the Microsoft Access dialog box. You then can repeat the process you used earlier to define the fields in the table.

Populating the Patients Table

Now that you have created the Patients table, you can populate the table by entering the data in Datasheet view. Populating the table means entering data into the tables.

1. Click the View button (Table Tools Design tab | Views group) to change to Datasheet view.
2. If necessary, click the View button (Table Tools Fields tab | Views group) to confirm that you are in Datasheet view (see Figure 1–31).
3. Enter the patient data, as shown in Figure 1–32.

Patients				
Patient ID	**Patient Name**	**Animal Type**	**Breed**	**Owner ID**
C-1	Paws	Feline	Calico	O-2
C-2	Ranger	Canine	Labrador	O-1
F-1	Fluffy	Feline	Tabby	O-1

Figure 1–32

To Close the Table

Now that you have completed and saved the Patients table, you can close it. The following step closes the table.

1 Click the Close button for the Patients table (Figure 1–33) to close the table.

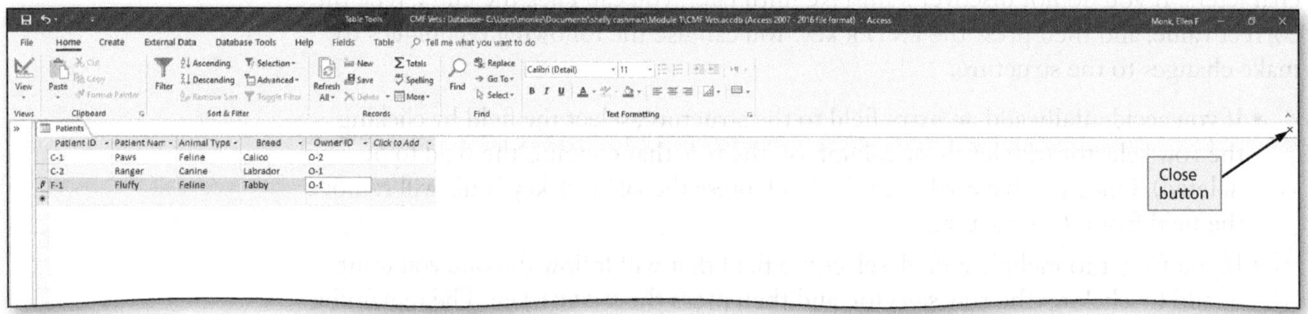

Figure 1–33

To Resize Columns in a Datasheet

You can resize the columns in the datasheet for the Patients table just as you resized the columns in the datasheet for the Owners table. The following steps resize the columns in the Patients table to best fit the data.

1 Open the Patients table in Datasheet view.

2 Double-click the right boundary of the field selectors of each of the fields to resize the columns so that they best fit the data.

3 Save the changes to the layout by clicking the Save button on the Quick Access Toolbar.

4 Close the table.

BTW
Resizing Columns
To resize all columns in a datasheet to best fit simultaneously, select the column heading for the first column, hold down SHIFT and select the last column in the datasheet. Then, double-click the right boundary of any field selector.

Importing Additional Access Database Tables into an Existing Database

Access users frequently need to import tables that contain data into an existing database. ***Why?*** *Organizations have data in tables that needs to be used in other databases. Importing tables ensures efficiency and accuracy.* In addition to owners and patients, CMF Vets must also keep track of its procedures and appointments, and the veterinarians assigned to those appointments. This information exists in another database. The following steps import three tables into the CMF Vets database.

- Open the database file Support_AC_CMF Vets Extra Tables from the Data Files and save it to the storage location specified by your instructor.
- Open the CMF Vets database.
- Click External Data on the ribbon to display the External Data tab (Figure 1–34).

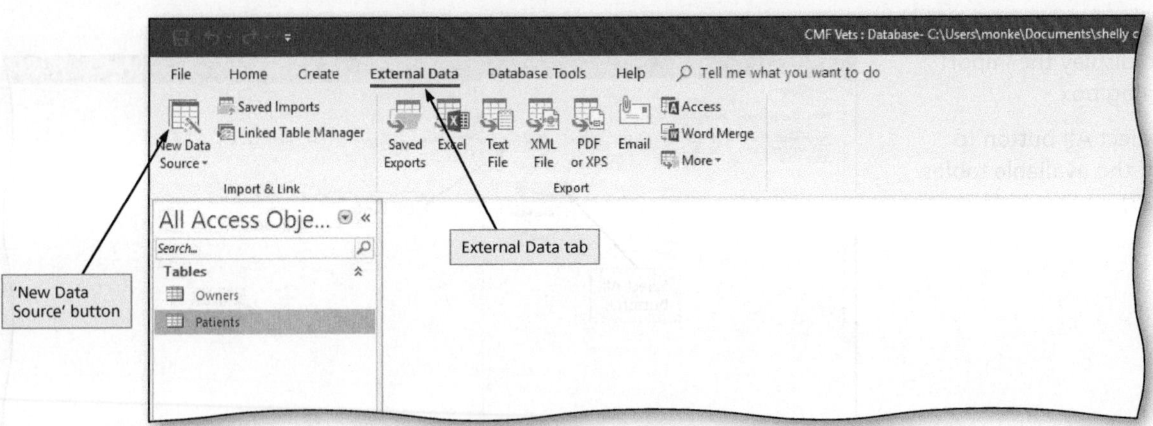

Figure 1–34

2

- Click the 'New Data Source' button (External Data tab | Import & Link group) to open a menu.
- Point to From Database to display a menu (Figure 1–35) and then click Access to display the Get External Data, Access Database dialog box.

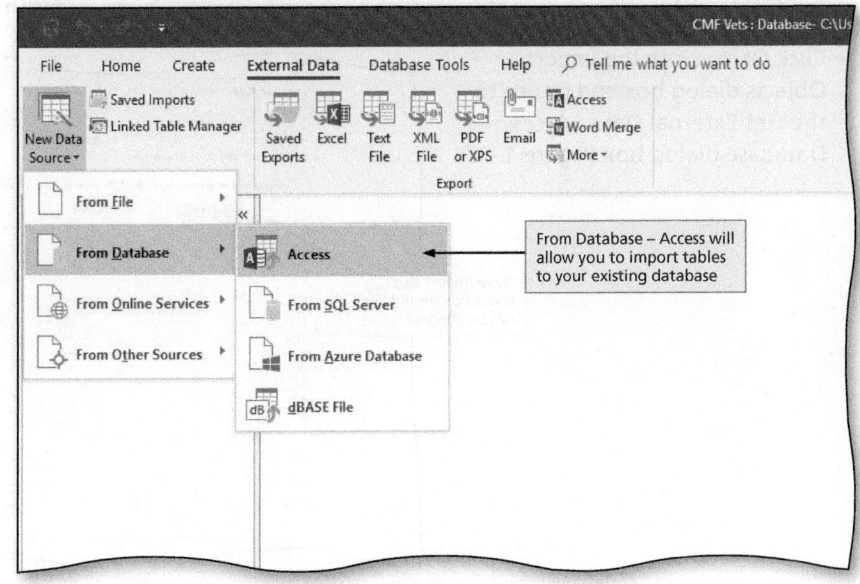

Figure 1–35

3

- Click the Browse button, and then navigate to the storage location for the CMF Vets Extra Tables file to specify the source of the data you are importing.
- Click the 'Import tables, queries, forms, reports, macros, and modules into the current database' option box to specify how and where you want to store the data. (Figure 1–36).

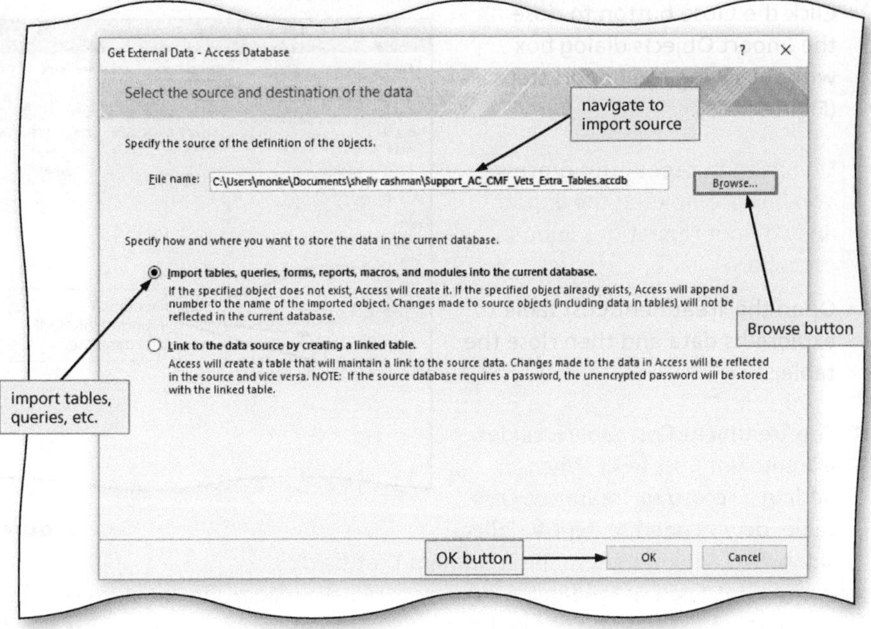

Figure 1–36

- Click OK to display the Import Objects dialog box.
- Click the Select All button to select all of the available tables (Figure 1–37).

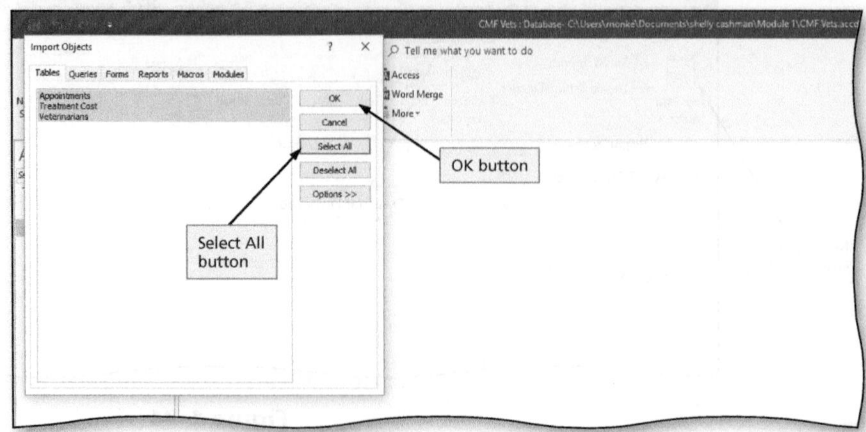

Figure 1–37

- Click OK to close the Import Objects dialog box and return to the Get External Data - Access Database dialog box (Figure 1–38)

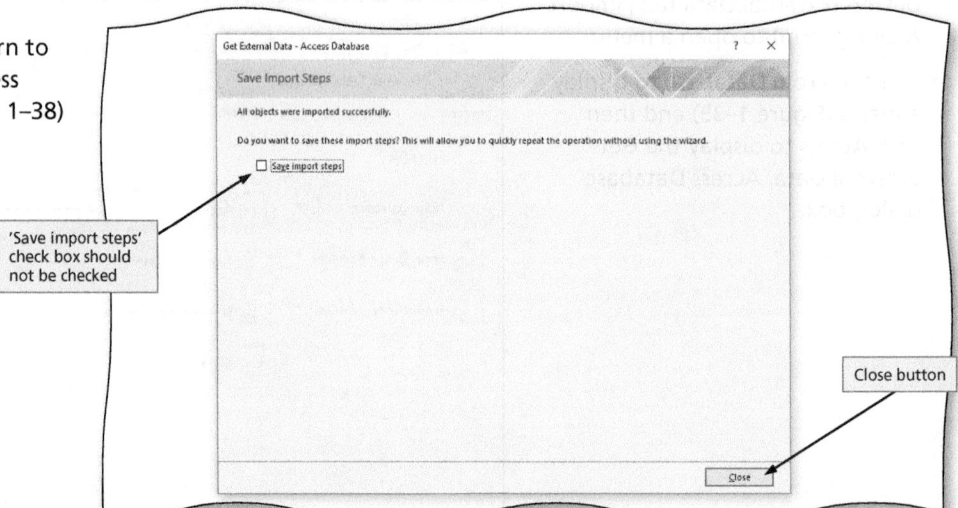

Figure 1–38

- Click the Close button to close the Import Objects dialog box without saving the Import steps (Figure 1–39).

Q&A Do I need to repeat this process?
You have completed the import and will not repeat this import procedure.

- Open the Treatment Cost table to explore its data and then close the table.

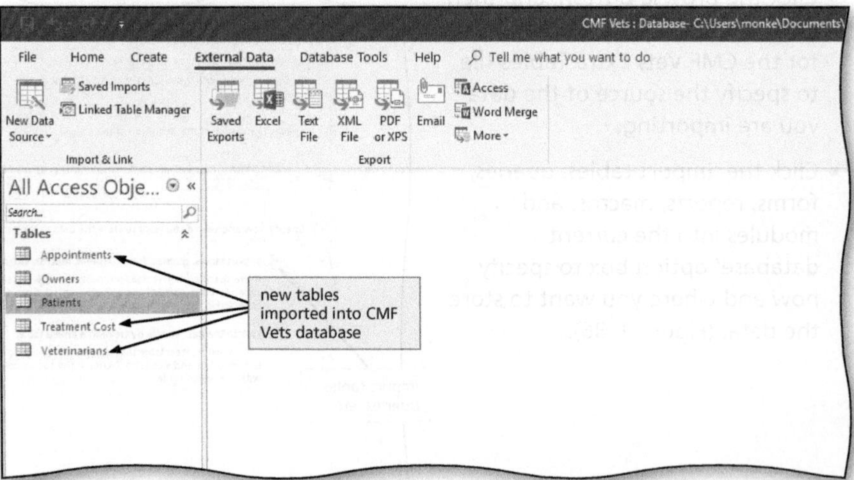

Figure 1–39

Q&A The Treatment Cost table includes a Treatment Cost field. When adding a record to Treatment Cost table, do you need to type a dollar sign when adding data to the Treatment Cost field?
You do not need to type dollar signs or commas. In addition, because the digits to the right of the decimal point are both zeros, you do not need to type either the decimal point or the zeros.

Break Point: If you wish to take a break, this is a good place to do so. You can exit Access now. To resume at a later time, start Access, open the database called CMF Vets, and continue following the steps from this location forward.

Additional Database Objects

A database contains many types of objects. Tables are the objects you use to store and manipulate data. Access supports other important types of objects as well; each object has a specific purpose that helps maximize the benefits of a database. Through queries (questions), Access makes it possible to ask complex questions concerning the data in the database and then receive instant answers. Access also allows the user to produce attractive and useful forms for viewing and updating data. Additionally, Access includes report creation tools that make it easy to produce sophisticated reports for presenting data.

BTW
Creating Queries
The Simple Query Wizard is a convenient way to create straightforward queries. It is a good method to learn about queries, although you will find that many of the queries you create require more control than the wizard provides.

Creating Queries

Queries are simply questions, the answers to which are in the database. Access contains a powerful query feature that helps you find the answers to a wide variety of questions. Once you have examined the question you want to ask to determine the fields involved in the question, you can begin creating the query. If the query involves no special sort order, restrictions, or calculations, you can use the Simple Query Wizard.

To Use the Simple Query Wizard to Create a Query

The following steps use the Simple Query Wizard to create a query that CMF Vets can use to obtain a list of their owners to send out a mailing. *Why? The Simple Query Wizard is the quickest and easiest way to create a query.* This query displays the Owner's first and last name, the street address, city, state, and postal code.

1

- If the Navigation Pane is closed, click the 'Shutter Bar Open/Close Button' to open the Navigation Pane.
- If necessary, click the Owners table to select it.
- Click Create on the ribbon to display the Create tab.
- Click the Query Wizard button (Create tab | Queries group) to display the New Query dialog box (Figure 1–40).

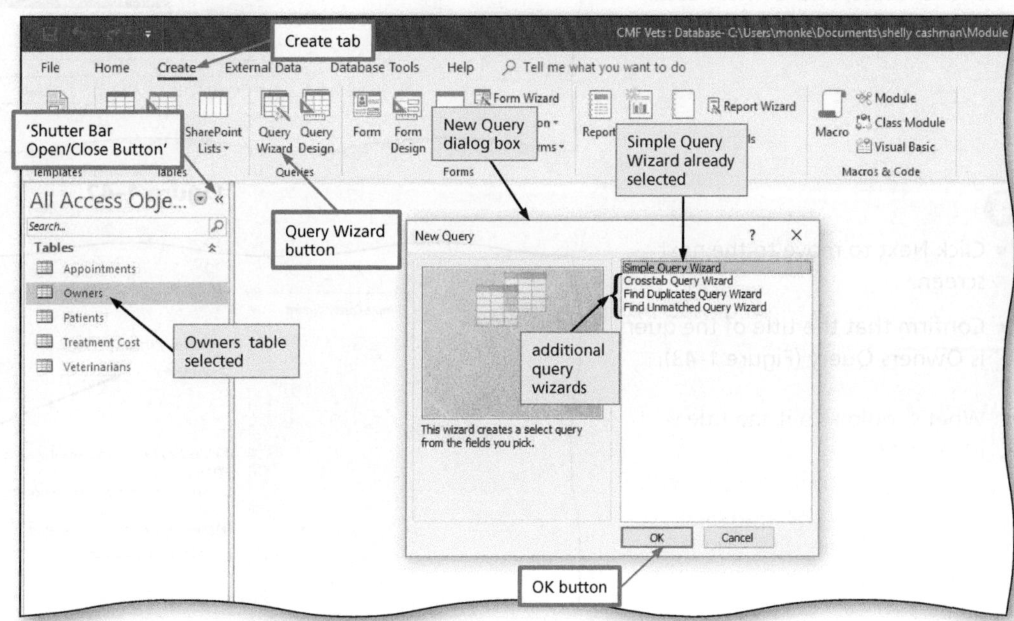

Figure 1–40

2

- Be sure Simple Query Wizard is selected, and then click OK (New Query dialog box) to display the Simple Query Wizard dialog box (Figure 1–41).

Q&A What would happen if the Patients table were selected instead of the Owners table?
The list of available fields would contain fields from the Patients table rather than the Owners table.

If the list contained Patients table fields, how could I make it contain Owners table fields?
Click the arrow in the Tables/Queries box, and then click the Owners table in the list that appears.

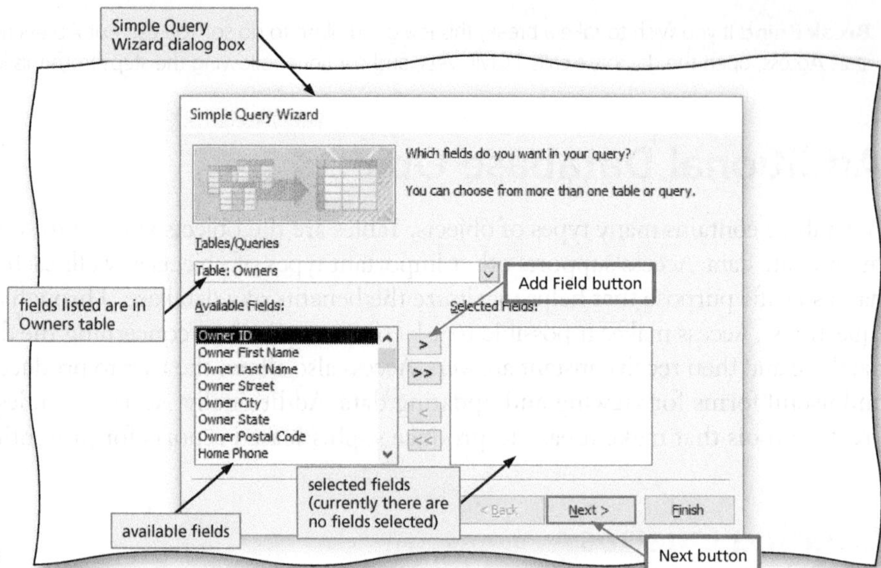

Figure 1–41

3

- If necessary, select the Owner First Name field, and then click the Add Field button to add the field to the query.
- With the Owner Last Name field selected, click the Add Field button a second time to add the field.
- Using the same technique, add the Owner Street, Owner City, Owner State, and Owner Postal Code fields (Figure 1–42).

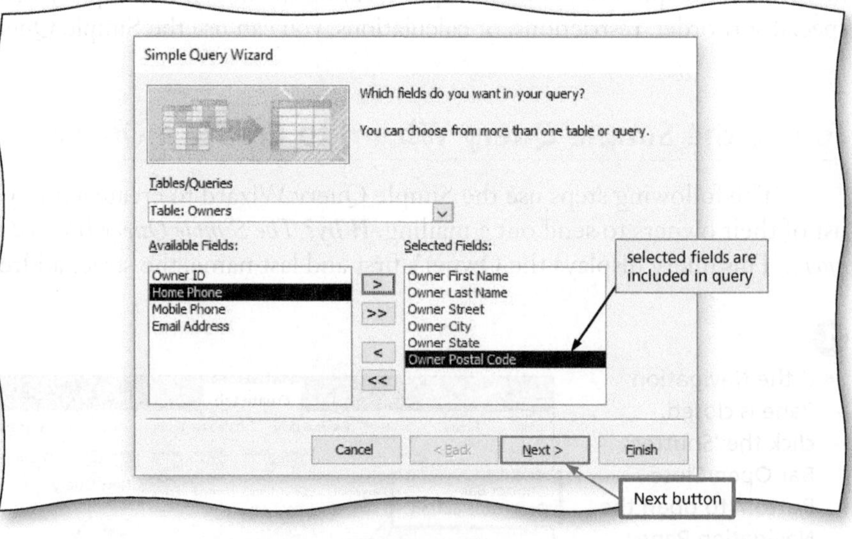

Figure 1–42

4

- Click Next to move to the next screen.
- Confirm that the title of the query is Owners Query (Figure 1–43).

Q&A What should I do if the title is incorrect?
Click the box containing the title to produce an insertion point. Erase the current title and then type Owners Query.

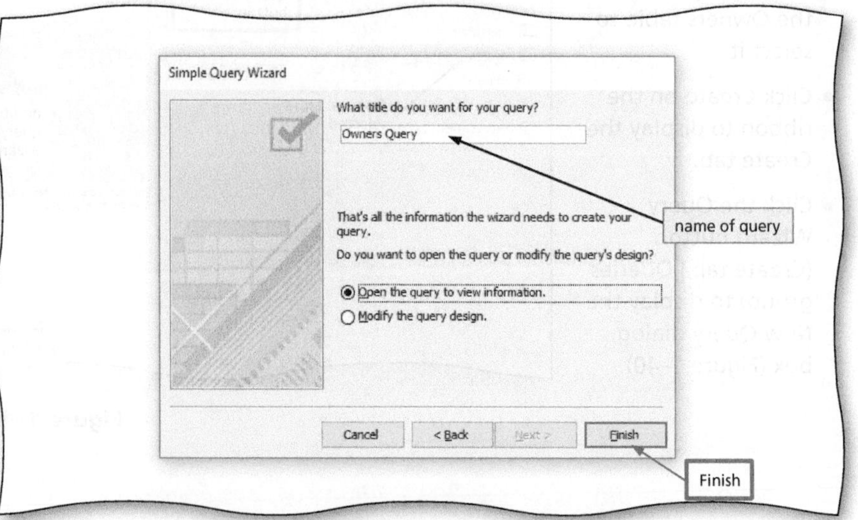

Figure 1–43

- Click the Finish button to create the query (Figure 1–44).
- Click the Close button for the Owners Query to remove the query results from the screen.

Q&A If I want to use this query in the future, do I need to save the query?
Normally you would. The one exception is a query created by the wizard. The wizard automatically saves the query it creates.

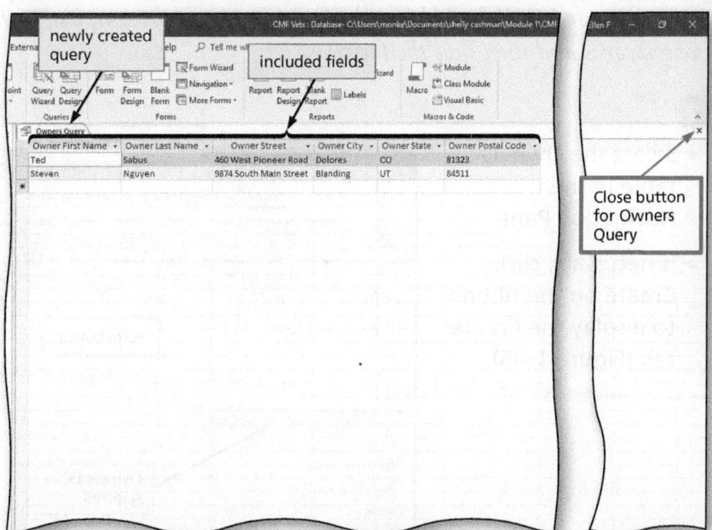

Figure 1–44

Using Queries

After you have created and saved a query, Access stores it as a database object and makes it available for use in a variety of ways:

- If you want to change the design of the query, right-click the query in the Navigation Pane and then click Design View on the shortcut menu to open the query in Design view.
- To view the results of the query from Design view, click the Run button to instruct Access to **run** the query, that is, to perform the necessary actions to produce and display the results in Datasheet view.
- To view the results of the query from the Navigation Pane, open it by right-clicking the query and clicking Open on the shortcut menu. Access automatically runs the query and displays the results in Datasheet view.

You can switch between views of a query using the View button (Home tab | Views group). Clicking the arrow in the bottom of the button produces the View button menu. You then click the desired view in the menu. The two query views you will use in this module are Datasheet view (which displays the query results) and Design view (for changing the query design). You can also click the top part of the View button, in which case you will switch to the view identified by the icon on the button. For the most part, the icon on the button represents the view you want, so you can usually simply click the button.

Creating Forms

In Datasheet view, you can view many records at once. If there are many fields, however, only some of the fields in each record might be visible at a time. In **Form view**, where data is displayed in a form on the screen, you can usually see all the fields, but only for one record.

To Create a Form

Like a paper form, a **form** in a database is a formatted document with fields that contain data. Forms allow you to view and maintain data. Forms can also be used to print data, but reports are more commonly used for that purpose. The simplest type of form in Access is one that includes all the fields in a table stacked one above the other, which can be achieved by simply clicking the Form button. The following steps use the Form button to create a form. ***Why?*** *Using the Form button is the simplest way to create this type of form. The steps use the form to view records and then save the form.*

- Select the Owners table in the Navigation Pane.
- If necessary, click Create on the ribbon to display the Create tab (Figure 1–45).

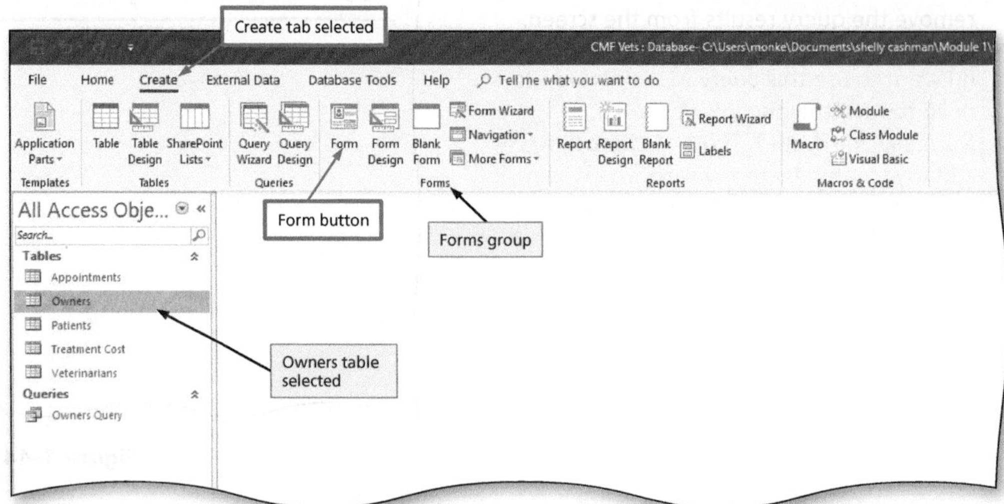

Figure 1–45

- Click the Form button (Create tab | Forms group) to create a simple form (Figure 1–46).

Q&A A Field list appeared on my screen. What should I do?
Click the 'Add Existing Fields' button (Form Layout Tools Design tab | Tools group) to remove the Field list from the screen.

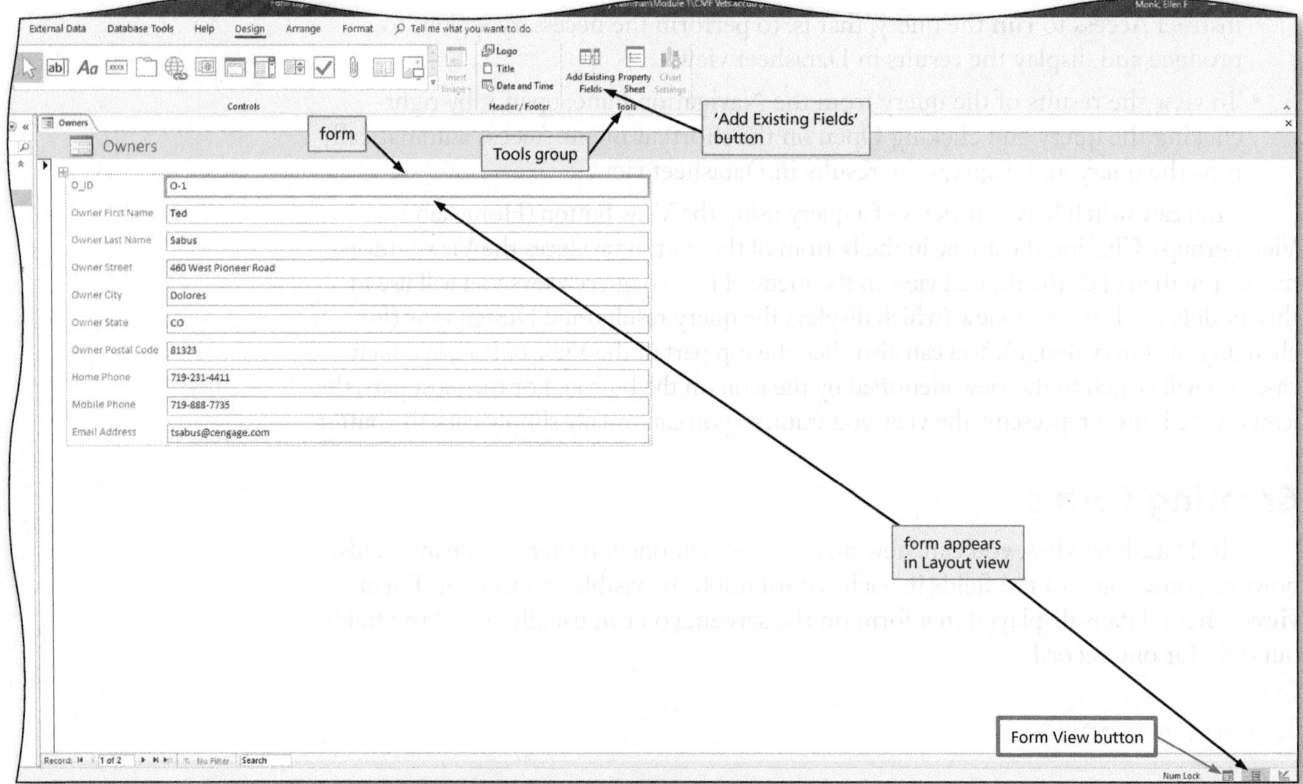

Figure 1–46

3

- Click the Form View button on the Access status bar to display the form in Form view rather than Layout view.

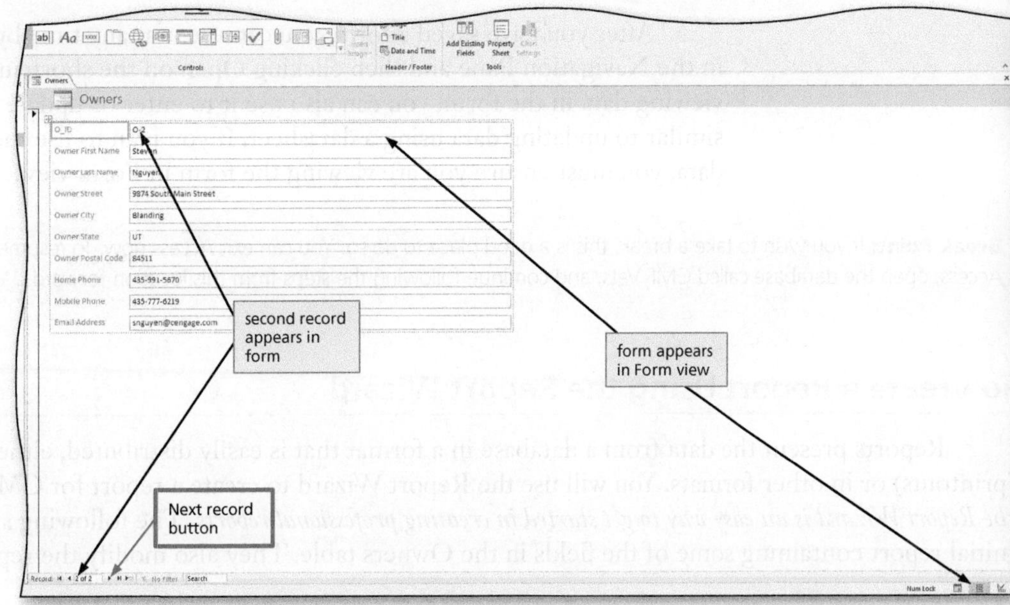

Figure 1–47

What is the difference between Layout view and Form view?
Layout view allows you to make changes to the look of the form. Form view is the view you use to examine or make changes to the data.

How can I tell when I am in Layout view?
Access identifies Layout view in three ways. The left side of the status bar will contain the words Layout View, shading will appear around the outside of the selected field in the form, and the Layout View button will be selected on the right side of the status bar.

- Click the Next record button once to advance through the records (Figure 1–47).

4

- Click the Save button on the Quick Access Toolbar to display the Save As dialog box (Figure 1–48).

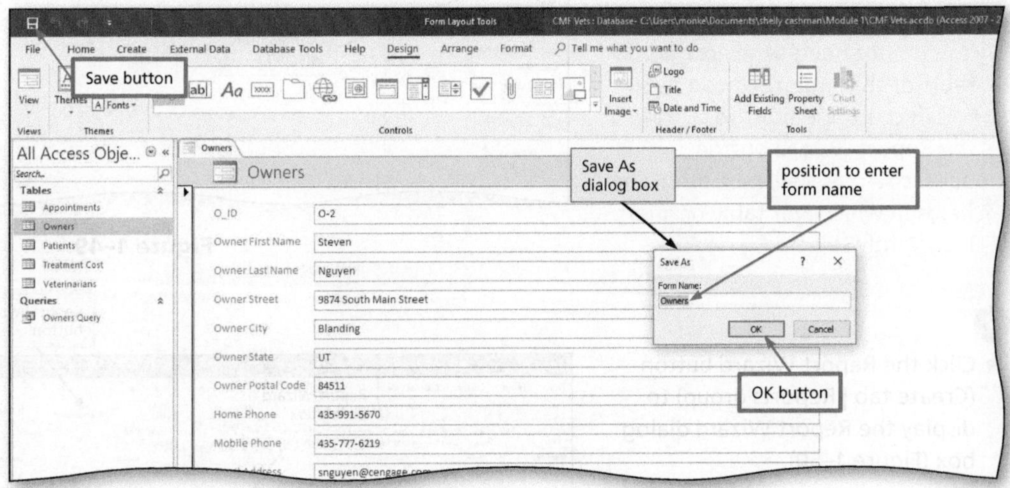

Figure 1–48

Do I have to click the Next record button before saving?
No. The only reason you were asked to click the button was so that you could experience navigation within the form.

5

- Type `Owners Form` as the form name, and then click OK to save the form.
- Click Close for the form to close the form.

Other Ways

1. Click View button (Form Layout Tools Design tab | Views group)

Using a Form

After you have saved a form, you can use it at any time by right-clicking the form in the Navigation Pane and then clicking Open on the shortcut menu. In addition to viewing data in the form, you can also use it to enter or update data, a process that is similar to updating data using a datasheet. If you plan to use the form to enter or revise data, you must ensure you are viewing the form in Form view.

Break Point: If you wish to take a break, this is a good place to do so. You can exit Access now. To resume at a later time, start Access, open the database called CMF Vets, and continue following the steps from this location forward.

To Create a Report Using the Report Wizard

Reports present the data from a database in a format that is easily distributed, either as hard copy (printouts) or in other formats. You will use the Report Wizard to create a report for CMF Vets. ***Why?*** *Using the Report Wizard is an easy way to get started in creating professional reports.* The following steps create and save an initial report containing some of the fields in the Owners table. They also modify the report title.

- Be sure the Owners table is selected in the Navigation Pane.
- Click Create on the ribbon to display the Create tab (Figure 1–49).

Q&A Do I need to select the Owners table prior to clicking Create on the ribbon?
You do not need to select the table at that point. You do need to select a table prior to clicking the Report Wizard button, because Access will include all the fields in whichever table or query is currently selected.

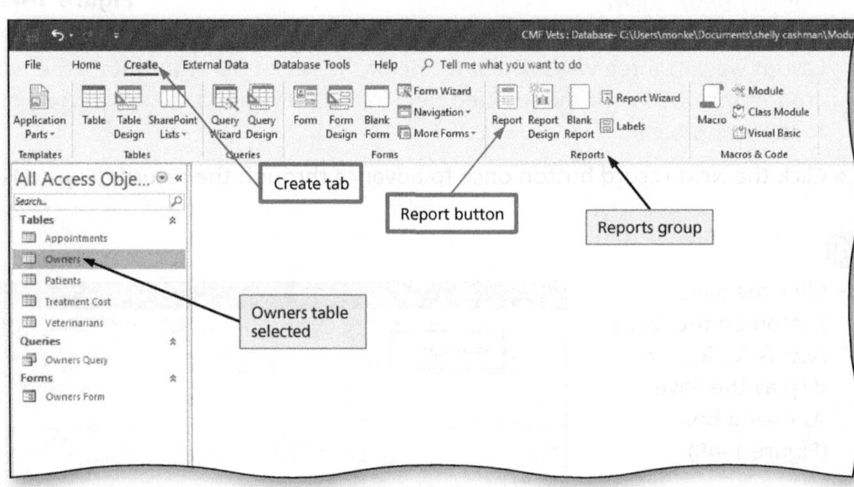

Figure 1–49

- Click the Report Wizard button (Create tab | Reports group) to display the Report Wizard dialog box (Figure 1–50).

Q&A Why is the report title Owners?
Access automatically assigns the name of the table or query as the title of the report. It also automatically includes the date and time. You can change either of these later.

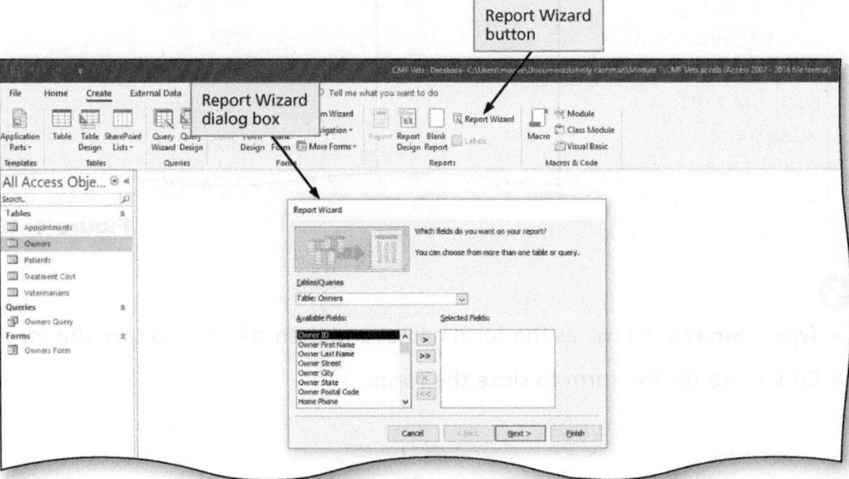

Figure 1–50

3

- In Available Fields area, select Owner First Name and then click the Add Field button to add the field to the Selected Fields area.
- Click the arrow button a second time to move the Owner Last Name field to the Selected Fields area.
- Move the Owner Street, Owner City, and Owner State to the Selected Fields box. (Figure 1–51)

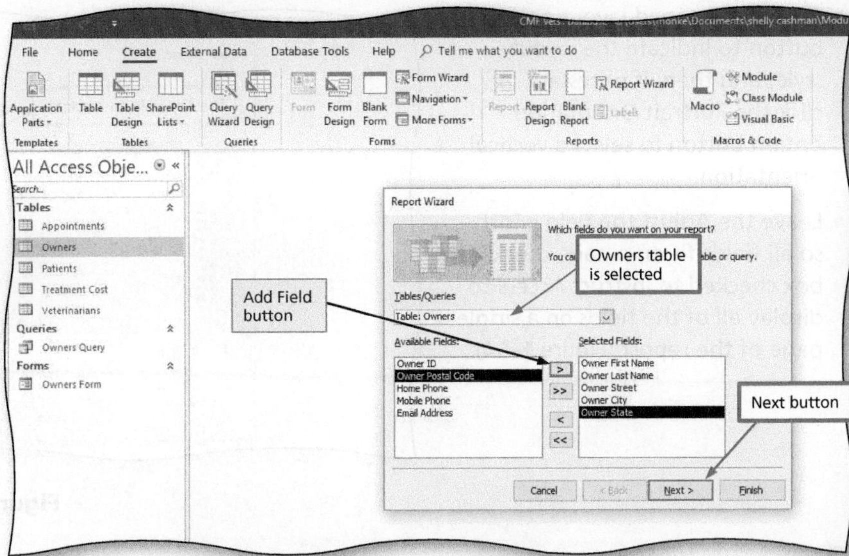

Figure 1–51

- Click Next, and select Owner State, and then click the Add Field button In the Do you want to add any grouping levels area to indicate that the report will be grouped by Owner State. (Figure 1–52).

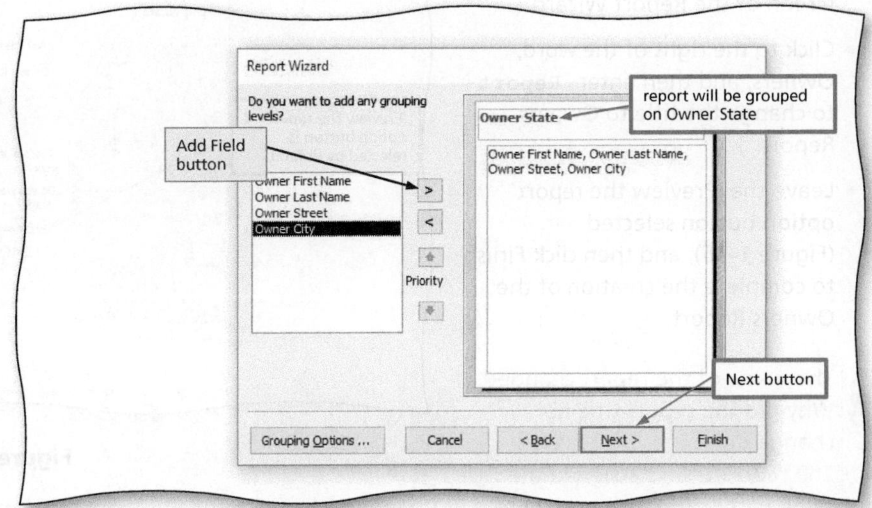

Figure 1–52

- Click Next to move to the next screen in the Report Wizard.

Q&A How do I correct a mistake I made in the Report Wizard?
The Report Wizard lets you click the Back button at any time to undo an action.

- Click Next again to move to the next screen without indicating a sort order for detail records. (Figure 1–53).

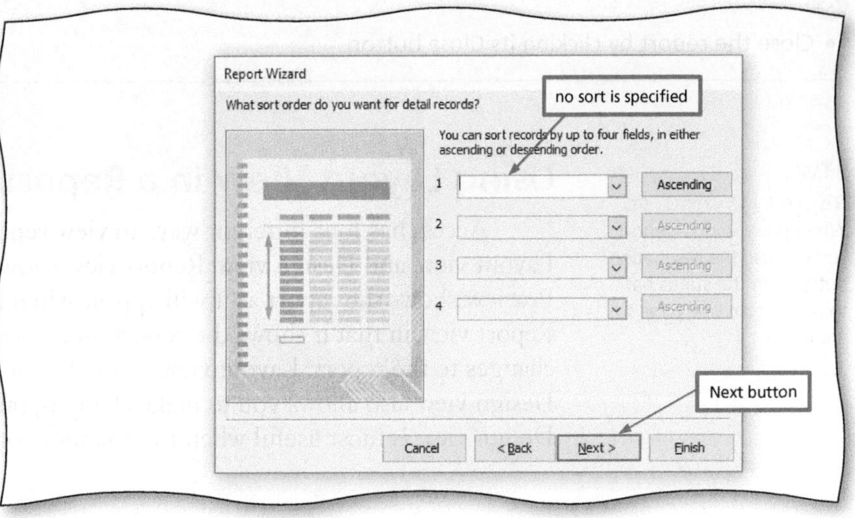

Figure 1–53

- Click the Stepped layout option button to indicate the layout style, and then, if necessary, click the Portrait Orientation option button to select a vertical orientation.
- Leave the Adjust the field width so all fields fit on a page check box checked to instruct Access to display all of the fields on a single page of the report (Figure 1–54).

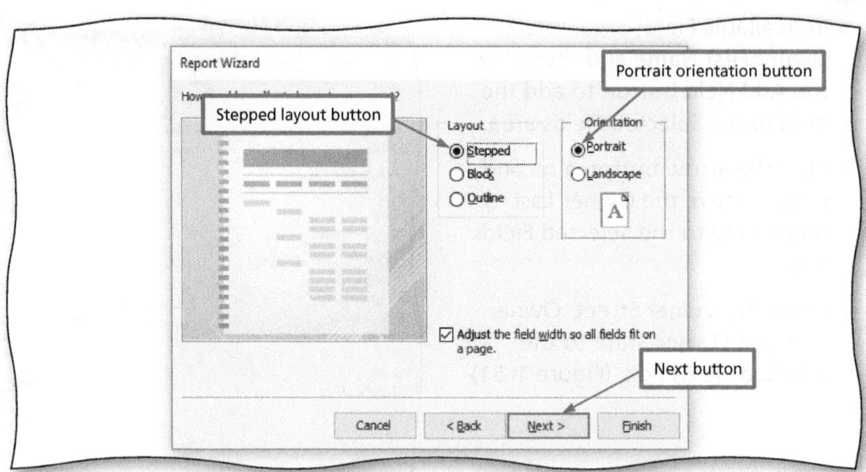

Figure 1–54

- Click Next to move to the next screen of the Report Wizard.
- Click to the right of the word, Owners, and then enter **Report** to change the title to Owners Report.
- Leave the 'Preview the report' option button selected (Figure 1–55), and then click Finish to complete the creation of the Owners Report.

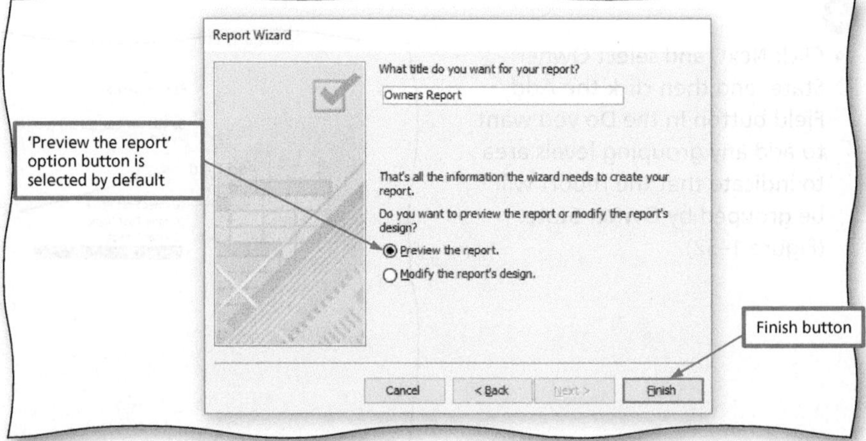

Figure 1–55

Q&A The name of the report changed. Why did the report title not change?

The report title is assigned the same name as the report by default. Changing the name of the report does not change the report title. You can change the title at any time to anything you like.

- Close the report by clicking its Close button.

BTW

Report Navigation

When previewing a report, you can use the Navigation buttons on the status bar to move from one page to another.

Using Layout View in a Report

Access has four different ways to view reports: Report view, Print Preview, Layout view, and Design view. Report view shows the report on the screen. Print Preview shows the report as it will appear when printed. Layout view is similar to Report view in that it shows the report on the screen, but it also allows you to make changes to the report. Layout view is usually the easiest way to make such changes. Design view also allows you to make changes, but does not show you the actual report. Design view is most useful when the changes you need to make are especially complex.

Database Properties

Access helps you organize and identify your databases by using **database properties,** which are the details about a file. Database properties, also known as **metadata**, can include such information as the project author, title, or subject. **Keywords** are words or phrases that further describe the database. For example, a class name or database topic can describe the file's purpose or content.

Five different types of database properties exist, but the more common ones used in this book are standard and automatically updated properties. **Standard properties** are associated with all Microsoft Office documents and include author, title, and subject. **Automatically updated properties** include file system properties, such as the date you create or change a file, and statistics, such as the file size.

CONSIDER THIS

Why would you want to assign database properties to a database?
Database properties are valuable for a variety of reasons:

- Users can save time locating a particular file because they can view a file's database properties without opening the database.
- By creating consistent properties for files having similar content, users can better organize their databases.
- Some organizations require Access users to add database properties so that other employees can view details about these files.

To Change Database Properties

To change database properties, you would follow these steps.

1. Click File on the ribbon to open the Backstage view and then, if necessary, click the Info tab in the Backstage view to display the Info gallery.
2. Click the 'View and edit database properties' link in the right pane of the Info gallery to display the CMF Vets Properties dialog box.

Q&A Why are some of the database properties already filled in?
The person who installed Office 2019 on your computer or network might have set or customized the properties.

3. If the property you want to change is displayed in the Properties dialog box, click the text box for the property and make the desired change. Skip the remaining steps.
4. If the property you want to change is not displayed in the Properties dialog box, click the appropriate tab so the property is displayed and then make the desired change.
5. Click the OK button in the Properties dialog box to save your changes and remove the dialog box from the screen.

Special Database Operations

Additional operations involved in maintaining a database are backup, recovery, compacting, and repairing.

Backup and Recovery

It is possible to damage or destroy a database. Users can enter data that is incorrect, programs that are updating the database can end abnormally during an update, a hardware problem can occur, and so on. After any such event has occurred, the database might contain invalid data or it might be totally destroyed.

BTW
Tabbed Documents Versus Overlapping Windows
By default, Access 2019 displays database objects in tabbed documents instead of in overlapping windows. If your database is in overlapping windows mode, click File on the ribbon, click Options in the Backstage view, click Current Database in the Access Options dialog box, and select the 'Display Document Tabs' check box and the Tabbed Documents option button.

Obviously, you cannot allow a situation in which data has been damaged or destroyed to go uncorrected. You must somehow return the database to a correct state. This process is called recovery; that is, you **recover** the database.

The simplest approach to recovery involves periodically making a copy of the database (called a **backup copy** or a **save copy**). This is referred to as **backing up** the database. If a problem occurs, you correct the problem by overwriting the actual database—often referred to as the **live database**—with the backup copy.

To back up the database that is currently open, you use the Back Up Database command on the Save As tab in the Backstage view. In the process, Access suggests a name that is a combination of the database name and the current date. For example, if you back up the CMF Vets database on October 20, 2021, Access will suggest the name, CMF Vets_2021-10-20. You can change this name if you desire, although it is a good idea to use this name. By doing so, it will be easy to distinguish between all the backup copies you have made to determine which is the most recent. In addition, if you discover that a critical problem occurred on October 18, 2021, you might want to go back to the most recent backup before October 18. If, for example, the database was not backed up on October 17 but was backed up on October 16, you would use CMF Vets_2021-10-16.

To Back Up a Database

You would use the following steps to back up a database to a file on a hard drive, high-capacity removable disk, or other storage location.

1. Open the database to be backed up.
2. Click File on the ribbon to open the Backstage view, and then click the Save As tab.
3. With Save Database As selected in the File Types area, click 'Back Up Database' in the Save Database As area, and then click the Save As button.
4. Navigate to the desired location in the Save As box. If you do not want the name Access has suggested, enter the desired name in the File name text box.
5. Click the Save button to back up the database.

Access creates a backup copy with the desired name in the desired location. Should you ever need to recover the database using this backup copy, you can simply copy it over the live version.

Compacting and Repairing a Database

As you add more data to a database, it naturally grows larger. When you delete an object (records, tables, forms, or queries), the space previously occupied by the object does not become available for additional objects. Instead, the additional objects are given new space; that is, space that was not already allocated. To remove this empty space from the database, you must **compact** the database. The same option that compacts the database also repairs problems that might have occurred in the database.

To Compact and Repair a Database

You would use the following steps to compact and repair a database.

1. Open the database to be compacted.
2. Click File on the ribbon to open the Backstage view, and then, if necessary, select the Info tab.
3. Click the 'Compact & Repair Database' button in the Info gallery to compact and repair the database.

The database now is the compacted form of the original.

Additional Operations

Additional special operations include opening another database, closing a database without exiting Access, and saving a database with another name. They also include deleting a table (or another object) as well as renaming an object.

When you are working in a database and you open another database, Access will automatically close the database that was previously open. Before deleting or renaming an object, you should ensure that the object has no dependent objects; that is, other objects that depend on the object you want to delete.

To Close a Database without Exiting Access

You would use the following steps to close a database without exiting Access.

1. Click File on the ribbon to open the Backstage view.
2. Click Close.

To Save a Database with Another Name

To save a database with another name, you would use the following steps.

1. Click File on the ribbon to open the Backstage view, and then select the Save As tab.
2. With Save Database As selected in the File Types area and Access Database selected in the Save Database As area, click the Save As button.
3. Enter a name and select a location for the new version.
4. Click the Save button.

CONSIDER THIS

If you want to make a backup, could you just save the database with another name?
You could certainly do that. Using the backup procedure discussed earlier is useful because doing so automatically includes the current database name and the date in the name of the file it creates.

To Delete a Table or Other Object in the Database

You would use the following steps to delete a database object.

1. Right-click the object in the Navigation Pane.
2. Click Delete on the shortcut menu.
3. Click the Yes button in the Microsoft Access dialog box.

To Rename an Object in the Database

You would use the following steps to rename a database object.

1. Right-click the object in the Navigation Pane.
2. Click Rename on the shortcut menu.
3. Type the new name and press the ENTER key.

BTW
Access Help
At any time while using Access, you can find answers to questions and display information about various topics through Access Help. Used properly, this form of assistance can increase your productivity and reduce your frustration by minimizing the time you spend learning how to use Access. For instructions about Access Help and exercises that will help you gain confidence in using it, read the Office and Windows module at the beginning of this book.

To Exit Access

All the steps in this module are now complete.

1. If desired, sign out of your Microsoft account.
2. sam Exit Access.

Summary

In this module you have learned to create an Access database, create tables and add records to a database, import tables, create queries, create forms, create reports, and change database properties.

CONSIDER THIS

What decisions will you need to make when creating your next database?

Use these guidelines as you complete the assignments in this module and create your own databases outside of this class.

1. Identify the information you want to record in the tables.
2. Determine the fields within those tables.
3. Determine the primary key for each table.
4. Determine the data types for the fields in the table.
5. Determine additional properties for fields.
    a. Determine if a caption if warranted.
    b. Determine if a description of the field is warranted.
    c. Determine field sizes.
    d. Determine formats.
6. Determine a storage location for the database.
7. Determine any simple queries, forms, or reports needed.

Apply Your Knowledge

Reinforce the skills and apply the concepts you learned in this module.

Adding a Caption, Changing a Data Type, and Creating a Query, Form, and Report

Note: To complete this assignment, you will be required to use the Data Files. Please contact your instructor for information about accessing the Data Files.

Instructions: Financial Services provides financial planning advice to the community. The company employs a number of trained and certified financial advisors to help their clients navigate the complex world of financial investing. Financial Services has a database that keeps track of its advisors and its clients. Each client is assigned to a single advisor; each advisor may be assigned many clients. The database has two tables. The Client table contains data on the clients who use Financial Services. The Advisor table contains data on the advisors. You will add a caption, change a data type, and create a query, a form, and a report, as shown in Figure 1–56.

Perform the following tasks:

1. Start Access, open the Support_AC_Financial Services database from the Data Files, and enable the content.
2. Open the Advisor table in Datasheet view, add AU # as the caption for the Advisor Number field, and resize all columns to best fit the data. Save the changes to the layout of the table and close the table.
3. Open the Client table in Design view and change the data type for the Advisor Number field to Short Text. Change the field size for the field to 4 and add AU # as the caption for the Advisor Number field. Save the changes to the table and close the table.
4. Use the Simple Query Wizard to create a query for the Client table that contains the Client Number, Client Name, and Advisor Number. Use the name Client Query for the query and close the query.
5. Create a simple form for the Advisor table. Save the form and use the name Advisor for the form. Close the form.
6. Create the report shown in Figure 1–56 for the Client table. Move the page number so that it is within the margins. Save the report as Client Advisor Report.
7. If requested by your instructor, add your last name to the title of the report, that is, change the title to Client Advisor Report LastName where LastName is your actual last name.
8. Compact and repair the database.
9. Submit the revised database in the format specified by your instructor.
10. How would you change the field name of the Street field in the Client table to Address?

Continued >

Apply Your Knowledge *continued*

Client Advisor Report

Advisor Number	Client Name	Street	City
103			
	Kirk D'Elia	378 Stout Ave.	Carlton
	Heidi Croft	245 Beard St.	Kady
	Cindy Platt	178 Fletcher Rd.	Conradt
	Alton Repart	220 Beard St.	Kady
	Patricia Singer	234 Hartwell Dr.	Carlton
	Moss Manni	109 Fletcher Dr.	Carlton
	Carly Cohen	87 Fletcher Rd.	Conradt
120			
	Timothy Edwards	876 Redfern Rd.	Kady
	Katy Cline	255 Main St.	Kady
	Bob Schwartz	443 Cheddar St.	Kady

Figure 1–56

Extend Your Knowledge

Extend the skills you learned in this module and experiment with new skills. You may need to use Help to complete the assignment.

Using a Database Template to Create a Student Database

Instructions: Access includes both desktop database templates and web-based templates. You can use a template to create a beginning database that can be modified to meet your specific needs. You will use a template to create a Students database. The database template includes sample tables, queries, forms, and reports. You will modify the database and create the Guardians Relationship Query shown in Figure 1–57.

Perform the following tasks:

1. Run Access.
2. Select the Students template in the template gallery and create a new database with the file name Students.
3. Close the welcome dialog box, and then close the Student List form.
4. Open the Navigation Pane and change the organization to Object Type.
5. Open the Guardians table in Datasheet view and delete the Attachments field in the table. The Attachments field has a paperclip as the column heading.
6. Add the Guardian Relationship field to the end of the table. Assign the Short Text data type with a field size of 15.
7. Save the changes to the Guardians table and close the table.
8. Use the Simple Query Wizard to create the Guardian Relationship Query shown in Figure 1–57. Close the query.

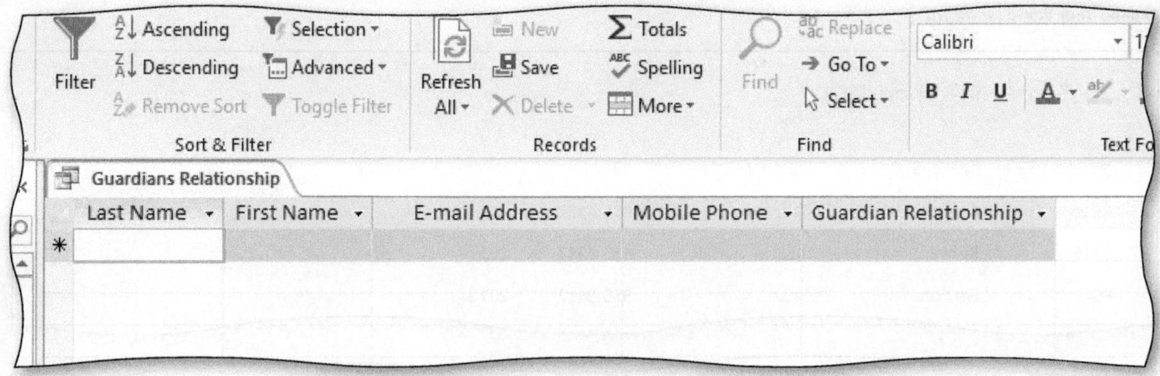

Figure 1–57

9. Open the Emergency Contact Information report in Layout view. Delete the controls containing the current date and current time in the upper-left corner of the report. Change the title of the report to Student Emergency Contact List.
10. Save the changes to the report.
11. If requested to do so by your instructor, add your first and last names to the end of the title and save the changes to the report.
12. Submit the revised database in the format specified by your instructor.
13. a. Why would you use a template instead of creating a database from scratch with just the fields you need?
    b. The Attachment data type allows you to attach files to a database record. If you were using this database to keep track of students, what specific documents might you attach to a Guardian record?

Expand Your World

Create a solution, which uses cloud and web technologies, by learning and investigating on your own from general guidance.

Problem: As a volunteer project, you and a few friends are creating a database for a local physical therapy clinic that provides therapy to the elderly in their homes. You want to be able to share query results and reports, so you have decided to store the items in the cloud. You are still learning Access, so you are going to create a sample query and the report shown in Figure 1–58, export the results, and save them to a cloud storage location, such as Microsoft OneDrive, Dropbox, or Google Drive.

Note: To complete this assignment, you will be required to use the Data Files. Please contact your instructor for information about accessing the Data Files.

Instructions:

1. Open the Support_AC_Physical Therapy database from the Data Files and enable the content. If your instructor wants you to submit your work as a SAM Project for automatic grading, you must download the Data Files from the assignment launch page.
2. Use the Simple Query Wizard to create a query that includes the Client Number, First Name, Last Name, and Therapist Number. Save the query as Client Query.
3. Export the Client Query as an XPS document to a cloud-based storage location of your choice.
4. Create the report shown in Figure 1–58. Save the report as Client Therapist Report.

Continued >

Expand Your World *continued*

Client Therapist Report

Client Number	Last Name	First Name	Phone	Therapist Number
AB10	Autley	Francis	555-4321	203
BR16	Behrens	Alexa	555-6987	205
FE45	Ferdon	Jean	555-3412	207
KL12	Klingman	Cynthia	555-4576	203
MA34	Marston	Libby	555-8787	207
PR80	Priestly	Martin	555-4454	205
SA23	Sanders	Marya	555-9780	207
TR35	Teeter	Rich	555-2222	205

Figure 1–58

5. Export the Client Status Report as a PDF document to a cloud-based storage location of your choice. You do not need to change any optimization or export settings. Do not save the export steps.
6. If requested to do so by your instructor, open the Therapist table and change the last name and first name for Therapist 203 to your last name and your first name.
7. Submit the assignment in the format specified by your instructor.
8. Which cloud-based storage location did you use for this assignment? Why?

In the Lab

Design, create, modify, and/or use a database following the guidelines, concepts, and skills presented in this module. This Lab requires you to create solutions based on what you learned in the module.

Lab: Creating Objects for the Lancaster College Intramural Sports Database

Problem: Lancaster College runs an intramural sports program. One of the students attending Lancaster College is familiar with Microsoft Access and created a database to use to keep track of the program. This database keeps track of all aspects of the intramural program such as the equipment, the fields, the maintenance personnel, the coaches, the teams, the students and their participation. The database and the Coach table have been created, but the Sport field needs to be added to the table. The records shown in Figure 1–59 must be added to the Coach table. The Lancaster College Intramural Sports department would like to finish storing this data in a database and has asked you to help.

Note: To complete this assignment, you will be required to use the Data Files. Please contact your instructor for information about accessing the Data Files.

Part 1: Open the Support_AC_1_Lab Lancaster College database from the Data Files, and enable the content. If your instructor wants you to submit your work as a SAM Project for automatic grading, you must download the Data Files from the assignment launch page. Add a field SportName to the Coach table. Assign the correct data type and a caption to the field.

Add the records shown in Figure 1–59.

Coach ID	FirstName	LastName	Office	Phone	Cell	SportName
17893	Lakisha	Black	WM-18	7178798787	7172451245	Track
18797	Bill	Brinkly	SM-1	7178798797	7175643751	Tennis
18798	Tom	Smith	SM-0	7178795467	7175432495	Wrestling
18990	William	Gutierez	WM-10	7178798789	7174597655	Football
18999	Sharon	Stone	WM-10	7178794681	7174231021	Softball
78978	Frank	Terranova	SM-10	7178798798	7172031543	Pool
78979	Gail	French	SM-12	7178792543	7172468713	Ping Pong
79798	Daniel	Costner	SM-15	7178798793	7172403120	Swimming
79879	Gary	Faulkner	SM-18	7178795432	7178965532	Soccer
82374	Jean	Epperson	JK-18	7178795402	7179845411	Basketball

Figure 1–59

Change the Student table's fields to be the correct data type and length. Add an appropriate caption to the Student ID field. Save your changes. Create a query that displays the StudentID, FirstName, LastName and Waiver, and save the query. Create the report shown in Figure 1–60 for the Coach table. Save the report.

Coach Sport Specialty Report

FirstName	LastName	Office	SN
Lakisha	Black	WM-18	Track
Bill	Brinkly	SM-1	Tennis
Tom	Smith	SM-0	Wrestling
Sharon	Stone	WM-15	Softball
Frank	Terranova	SM-10	Pool
Gail	French	SM-12	Ping Pong
Daniel	Costner	SM-15	Swimming
Gary	Faulkner	SM-18	Soccer
Jean	Epperson	JK-18	Basketball

Figure 1–60

Continued >

In the Lab *continued*

If requested to do so by your instructor, change any data in the database to reflect your own personal information. Submit the revised database in the format specified by your instructor.

Part 2: The Waiver and the Academic fields in the Student table are Yes/No Data Types. Why is this appropriate?

File Home Create External Data Database Tools Help Fields Table Tell me what you war

2 Querying a Database

Objectives

You will have mastered the material in this module when you can:

- Create queries using Design view
- Include fields in the design grid
- Use text and numeric data in criteria
- Save a query and use the saved query
- Create and use parameter queries
- Use compound criteria in queries
- Sort data in queries
- Join tables in queries
- Create a report and a form from a query
- Export data from a query to another application
- Perform calculations and calculate statistics in queries
- Create crosstab queries
- Customize the Navigation Pane

Introduction

One of the primary benefits of using a database management system such as Access is having the ability to find answers to questions related to data stored in the database. When you pose a question to Access, or any other database management system, the question is called a query. A query is simply a question presented in a way that Access can process.

To find the answer to a question, you first create a corresponding query using the techniques illustrated in this module. After you have created the query, you instruct Access to run the query, that is, to perform the steps necessary to obtain the answer. Access then displays the answer in Datasheet view.

Project — Querying a Database

Examples of questions related to the data in the CMF Vets database are shown in Figure 2–1. In addition to these questions, CMF Vets managers need to find information about a patient like the animal type, such as canine or feline. The managers can use a parameter query to accomplish this task. A **parameter query** prompts you to enter a search term and then displays the results based on the search term you entered. CMF Vets managers also want to summarize data in a specific way, such as by animal type or treatment cost, which might involve performing calculations, and they can use a crosstab query to present the data in the desired form.

In this module, you will learn how to create and use the queries shown in Figure 2–1.

File Home Create External Data Database Tools Help Fields Table Tell me what you war

O_ID	Owner First Name	Owner Last Name	Owner Street Address	Owner City	Owner State	Owner Postal Code	Home Phone	Mobile Phone	Email Address
O-1	Ted	Sabus	460 West Pioneer Road	Dolores	CO	81323	719-231-4411	719-888-7735	tsabus@cengage.com
O-2	Steven	Nguyen	9874 South Main Street	Blanding	UT	84511	435-991-5670	435-777-6219	snguyen@cengage.com

Figure 2–1a Pet Owner Addresses

Appointment ID	Patient ID	Appointment Date	Appointment Time	Treatment Number	Veterinarian	Owner
1	F-1	6/30/2021	10:00:00 AM	T-3	B01	O-1
2	C-2	10/25/2021	9:00:00 AM	T-4	B01	O-1
3	C-2	1/10/2021	10:00:00 AM	T-2	B01	O-1
4	F-1	6/30/2021	10:00:00 AM	T-1	B01	O-1
5	C-1	8/23/2021	10:00:00 AM	T-4	G01	O-2
6						

Figure 2–1b Appointment Dates and Times

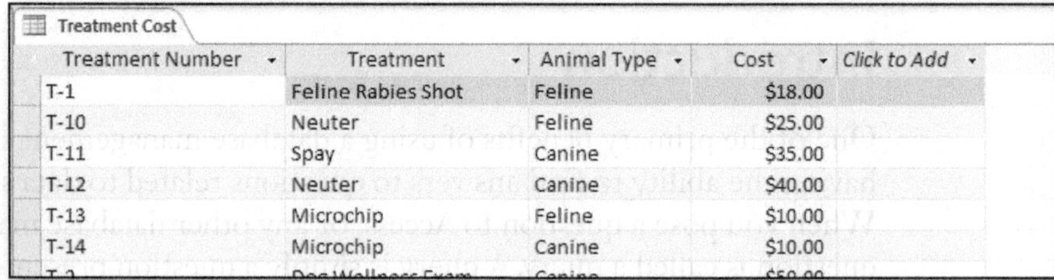

Treatment Number	Treatment	Animal Type	Cost
T-1	Feline Rabies Shot	Feline	$18.00
T-10	Neuter	Feline	$25.00
T-11	Spay	Canine	$35.00
T-12	Neuter	Canine	$40.00
T-13	Microchip	Feline	$10.00
T-14	Microchip	Canine	$10.00

Figure 2–1c Treatments and their Costs

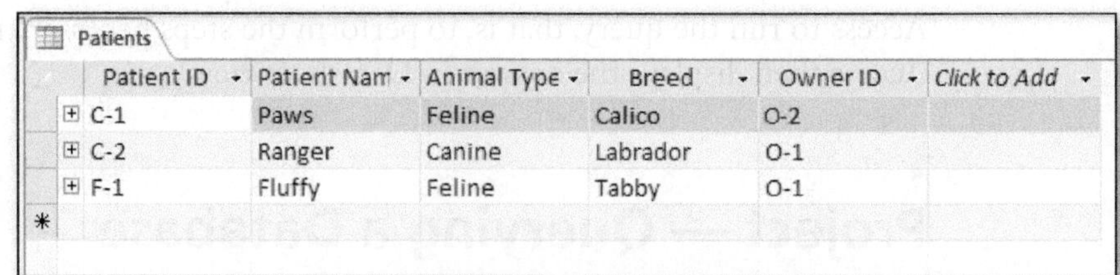

Patient ID	Patient Name	Animal Type	Breed	Owner ID
C-1	Paws	Feline	Calico	O-2
C-2	Ranger	Canine	Labrador	O-1
F-1	Fluffy	Feline	Tabby	O-1

Figure 2–1d Patient Names, Types, and Breeds

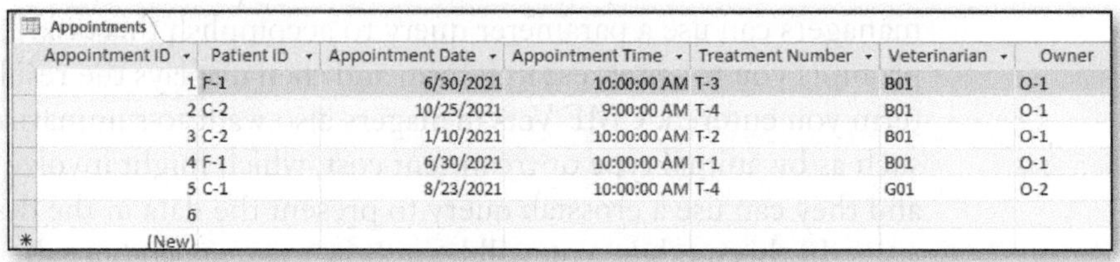

Appointment ID	Patient ID	Appointment Date	Appointment Time	Treatment Number	Veterinarian	Owner
1	F-1	6/30/2021	10:00:00 AM	T-3	B01	O-1
2	C-2	10/25/2021	9:00:00 AM	T-4	B01	O-1
3	C-2	1/10/2021	10:00:00 AM	T-2	B01	O-1
4	F-1	6/30/2021	10:00:00 AM	T-1	B01	O-1
5	C-1	8/23/2021	10:00:00 AM	T-4	G01	O-2
6						
(New)						

Figure 2–1e Owners and Pet Treatments

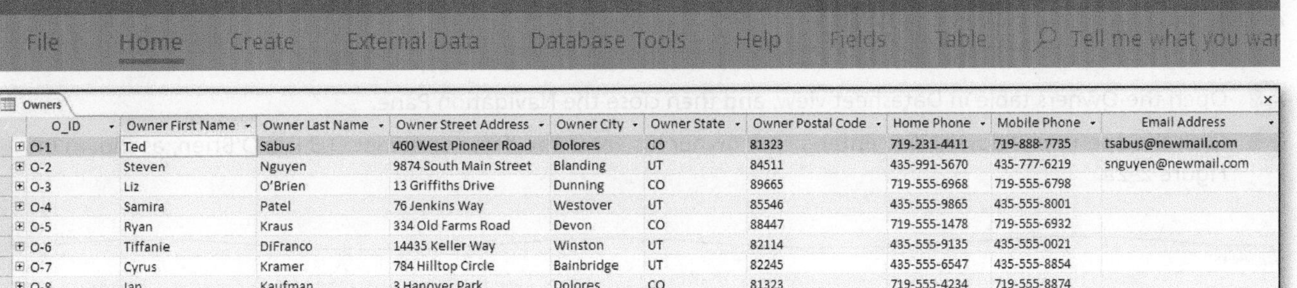

O_ID	Owner First Name	Owner Last Name	Owner Street Address	Owner City	Owner State	Owner Postal Code	Home Phone	Mobile Phone	Email Address
O-1	Ted	Sabus	460 West Pioneer Road	Dolores	CO	81323	719-231-4411	719-888-7735	tsabus@newmail.com
O-2	Steven	Nguyen	9874 South Main Street	Blanding	UT	84511	435-991-5670	435-777-6219	snguyen@newmail.com
O-3	Liz	O'Brien	13 Griffiths Drive	Dunning	CO	89665	719-555-6968	719-555-6798	
O-4	Samira	Patel	76 Jenkins Way	Westover	UT	85546	435-555-9865	435-555-8001	
O-5	Ryan	Kraus	334 Old Farms Road	Devon	CO	88447	719-555-1478	719-555-6932	
O-6	Tiffanie	DiFranco	14435 Keller Way	Winston	UT	82114	435-555-9135	435-555-0021	
O-7	Cyrus	Kramer	784 Hilltop Circle	Bainbridge	UT	82245	435-555-6547	435-555-8854	
O-8	Ian	Kaufman	3 Hanover Park	Dolores	CO	81323	719-555-4234	719-555-8874	

Figure 2–1f Pet Owners and Their Contact Information

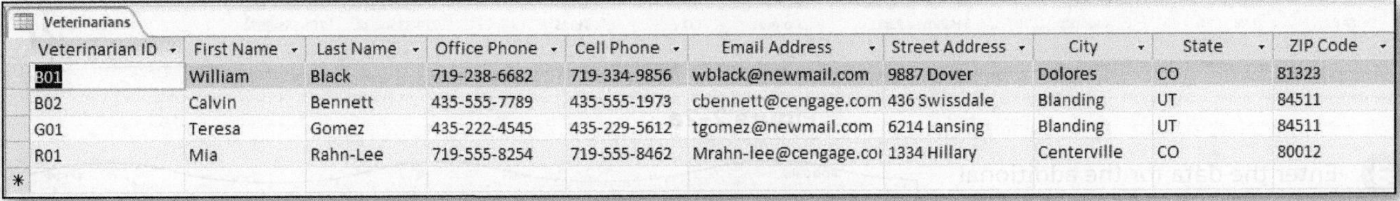

Veterinarian ID	First Name	Last Name	Office Phone	Cell Phone	Email Address	Street Address	City	State	ZIP Code
B01	William	Black	719-238-6682	719-334-9856	wblack@newmail.com	9887 Dover	Dolores	CO	81323
B02	Calvin	Bennett	435-555-7789	435-555-1973	cbennett@cengage.com	436 Swissdale	Blanding	UT	84511
G01	Teresa	Gomez	435-222-4545	435-229-5612	tgomez@newmail.com	6214 Lansing	Blanding	UT	84511
R01	Mia	Rahn-Lee	719-555-8254	719-555-8462	Mrahn-lee@cengage.coı	1334 Hillary	Centerville	CO	80012

Figure 2–1g Veterinarians

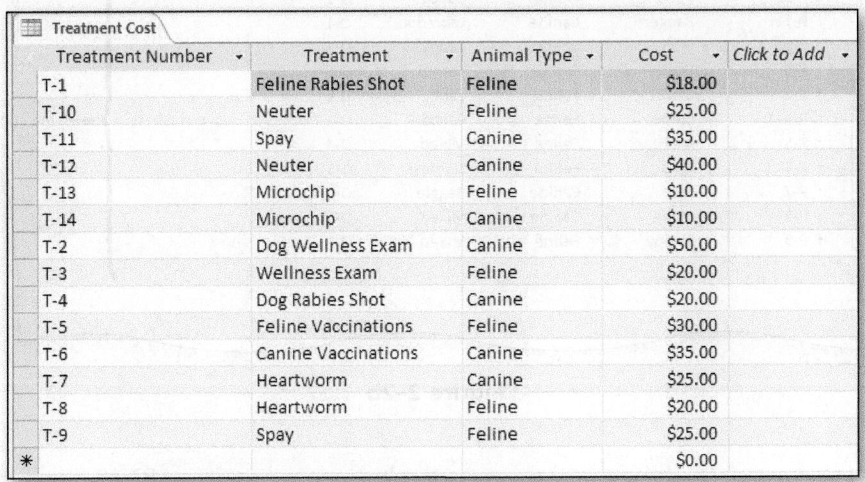

Treatment Number	Treatment	Animal Type	Cost	Click to Add
T-1	Feline Rabies Shot	Feline	$18.00	
T-10	Neuter	Feline	$25.00	
T-11	Spay	Canine	$35.00	
T-12	Neuter	Canine	$40.00	
T-13	Microchip	Feline	$10.00	
T-14	Microchip	Canine	$10.00	
T-2	Dog Wellness Exam	Canine	$50.00	
T-3	Wellness Exam	Feline	$20.00	
T-4	Dog Rabies Shot	Canine	$20.00	
T-5	Feline Vaccinations	Feline	$30.00	
T-6	Canine Vaccinations	Canine	$35.00	
T-7	Heartworm	Canine	$25.00	
T-8	Heartworm	Feline	$20.00	
T-9	Spay	Feline	$25.00	
			$0.00	

Figure 2–1h Treatments for Pets

Creating Queries

As you learned previously, you can use queries in Access to find answers to questions about the data contained in the database. *Note:* In this module, you will save each query example. When you use a query for another task, such as to create a form or report, you will assign a specific name to a query, for example, Manager-Appointments Query. In situations in which you will not use the query again, you will assign a name using a convention that includes the module number and a query number, for example, m02q01. Queries are numbered consecutively.

BTW
Select Queries
The queries you create in this module are select queries. In a select query, you retrieve data from one or more tables using criteria that you specify and display the data in a datasheet.

To Add Records to the Database

Because the practice continues to grow, with new patients and their owners coming to CMF Vets for care, the managers need to add records to reflect the growth of the business. The following steps open the Owners, Patients, and Veterinarians tables and add data.

1. Open the Owners table in Datasheet view, and then close the Navigation Pane.
2. Click the open cell below O-2 to enter a new owner ID. Enter the data for owner O-3, Liz O'Brien, as shown in Figure 2–2a.

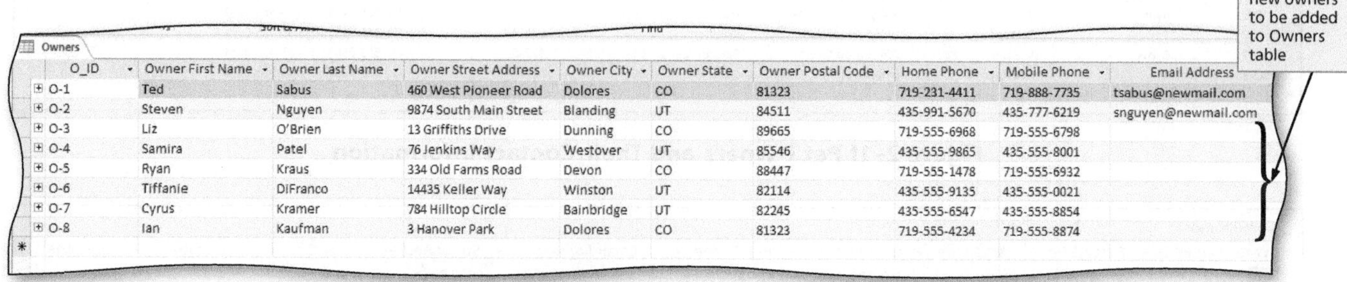

O_ID	Owner First Name	Owner Last Name	Owner Street Address	Owner City	Owner State	Owner Postal Code	Home Phone	Mobile Phone	Email Address
O-1	Ted	Sabus	460 West Pioneer Road	Dolores	CO	81323	719-231-4411	719-888-7735	tsabus@newmail.com
O-2	Steven	Nguyen	9874 South Main Street	Blanding	UT	84511	435-991-5670	435-777-6219	snguyen@newmail.com
O-3	Liz	O'Brien	13 Griffiths Drive	Dunning	CO	89665	719-555-6968	719-555-6798	
O-4	Samira	Patel	76 Jenkins Way	Westover	UT	85546	435-555-9865	435-555-8001	
O-5	Ryan	Kraus	334 Old Farms Road	Devon	CO	88447	719-555-1478	719-555-6932	
O-6	Tiffanie	DiFranco	14435 Keller Way	Winston	UT	82114	435-555-9135	435-555-0021	
O-7	Cyrus	Kramer	784 Hilltop Circle	Bainbridge	UT	82245	435-555-6547	435-555-8854	
O-8	Ian	Kaufman	3 Hanover Park	Dolores	CO	81323	719-555-4234	719-555-8874	

Figure 2–2a

3. Enter the data for the additional owners shown in Figure 2-2a.
4. Close the Owners table.
5. Open the Patients table in Datasheet view, and then close the Navigation Pane.
6. Click the open cell below Patient ID to enter an ID for Patient P-1, Pepper. Enter Pepper's information as shown in Figure 2–2b.
7. Change the Patient ID numbers for the existing patients so that they are consistent with Figure 2–2b.
8. Enter the data for the remaining patients as shown in the figure.

Patient ID	Patient Nam	Animal Type	Breed	Owner ID	Click to Add
P-1	Pepper	Canine	Weimaraner	O-2	
P-10	Paws	Feline	Calico	O-2	
P-11	Ranger	Canine	Labrador	O-1	
P-12	Fluffy	Feline	Tabby	O-1	
P-2	Hooper	Canine	Terrier	O-6	
P-3	Oliver	Feline	Tabby	O-6	
P-4	Chloe	Feline	Calico	O-1	
P-5	Max	Feline	Mixed	O-4	
P-6	Elvis	Feline	Siamese	O-3	
P-7	Milo	Canine	Beagle	O-8	
P-8	Millie	Canine	Mixed	O-5	
P-9	Skippy	Feline	Mixed	O-1	

patients in Patients table

Figure 2–2b

9. Close the Patients table.
10. Open the Veterinarians table in Datasheet view, and then close the Navigation Pane.
11. Click the open cell below Gomez to enter a new veterinarian last name. Enter the data for Calvin Bennett as shown in Figure 2–2c, and then enter the data for Mia Rahn-Lee.
12. Close the Veterinarians table.

BTW
Row Order
Your row order will not match Figure 2-2b until you save, close, and reopen the file. Doing so will automatically sort all rows to match the figure.

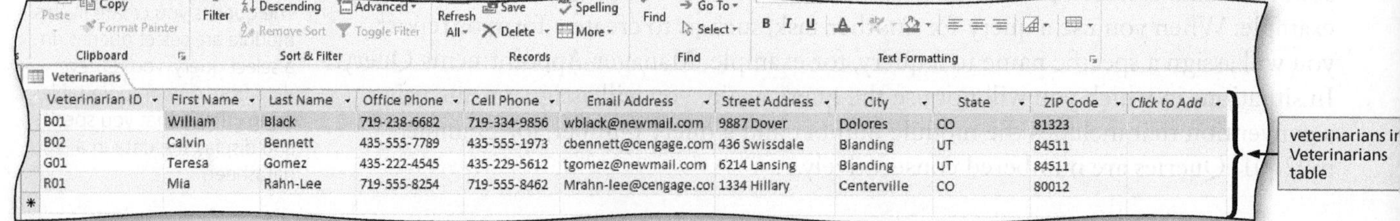

Veterinarian ID	First Name	Last Name	Office Phone	Cell Phone	Email Address	Street Address	City	State	ZIP Code	Click to Add
B01	William	Black	719-238-6682	719-334-9856	wblack@newmail.com	9887 Dover	Dolores	CO	81323	
B02	Calvin	Bennett	435-555-7789	435-555-1973	cbennett@cengage.com	436 Swissdale	Blanding	UT	84511	
G01	Teresa	Gomez	435-222-4545	435-229-5612	tgomez@newmail.com	6214 Lansing	Blanding	UT	84511	
R01	Mia	Rahn-Lee	719-555-8254	719-555-8462	Mrahn-lee@cengage.coı	1334 Hillary	Centerville	CO	80012	

Figure 2–2c

To Create a Query in Design View

You have already used the Simple Query Wizard to create a query. Most of the time, however, you will use Design view, which is the primary option for creating queries. ***Why?** Once you have created a new query in Design view, you have more options than with the wizard and can specify fields, criteria, sorting, calculations, and so on.* The following steps create a new query in Design view.

1

- **sam** Start Access and open the database named CMF Vets from your hard drive, OneDrive, or other storage location.
- Click the 'Shutter Bar Open/Close Button' to close the Navigation Pane.
- Click Create on the ribbon to display the Create tab (Figure 2–3).

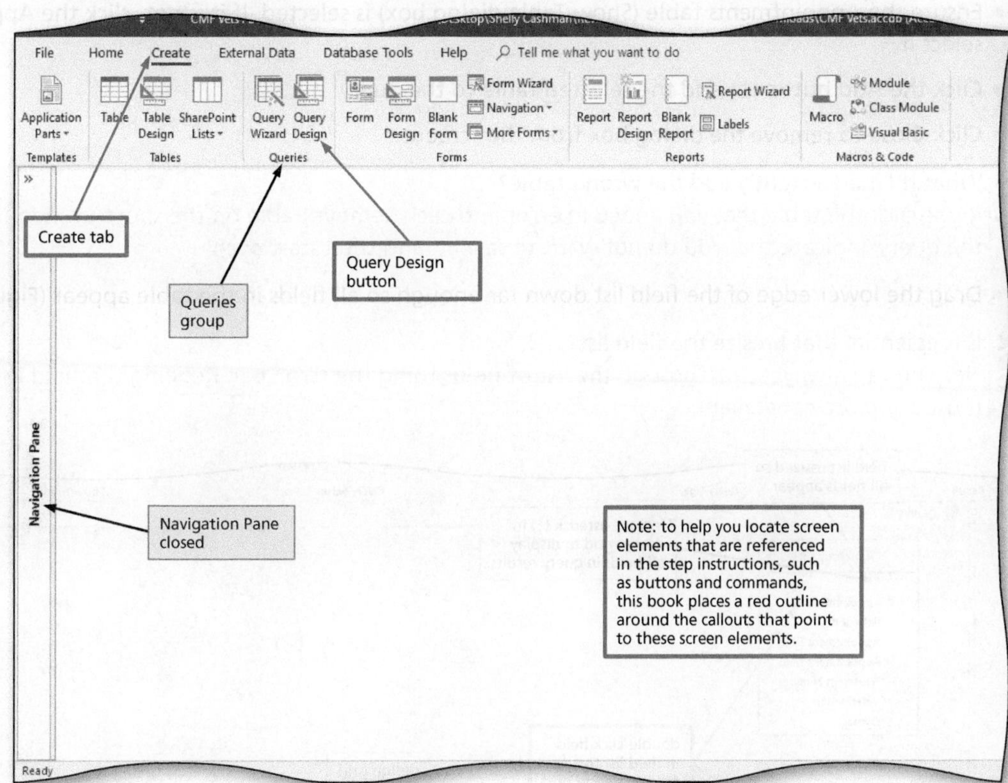

Figure 2–3

2

- Click the Query Design button (Create tab | Queries group) to create a new query (Figure 2–4).

Q&A Is it necessary to close the Navigation Pane?
No. Closing the pane gives you more room for the query, however, so it is usually a good practice.

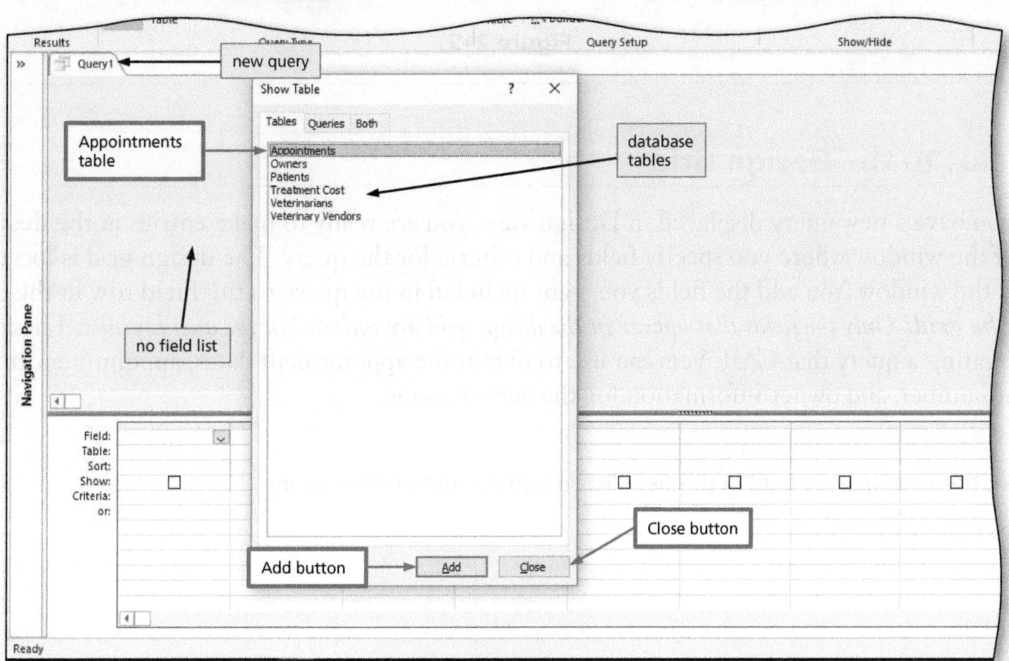

Figure 2–4

3

- Ensure the Appointments table (Show Table dialog box) is selected. If it is not, click the Appointments table to select it.
- Click the Add button to add the selected table to the query.
- Click Close to remove the dialog box from the screen.

Q&A What if I inadvertently add the wrong table?
Right-click the table that you added in error and click Remove Table on the shortcut menu. You also can just close the query, indicate that you do not want to save it, and then start over.

- Drag the lower edge of the field list down far enough so all fields in the table appear (Figure 2–5).

Q&A Is it essential that I resize the field list?
No. You can always scroll through the list of fields using the scroll bar. Resizing the field list so that all fields appear is usually more convenient.

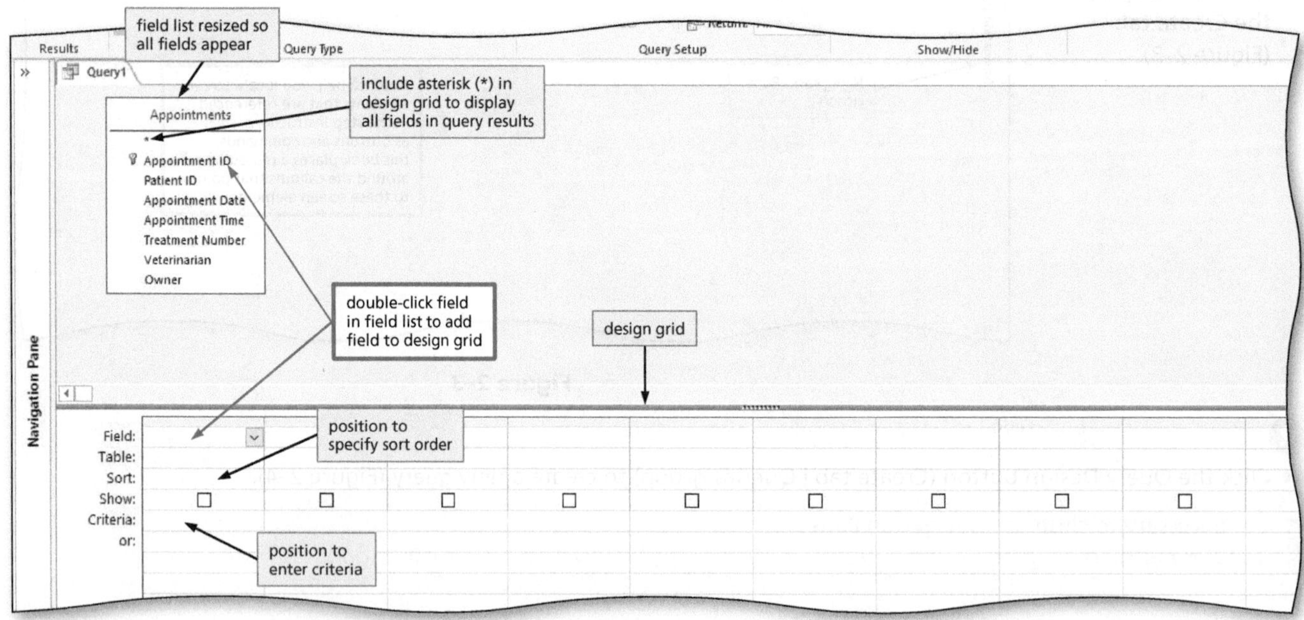

Figure 2–5

To Add Fields to the Design Grid

Once you have a new query displayed in Design view, you are ready to make entries in the **design grid**, the portion of the window where you specify fields and criteria for the query. The design grid is located in the lower pane of the window. You add the fields you want included in the query to the Field row in the grid. ***Why add fields to the grid?*** *Only the fields that appear in the design grid are included in the query results.* The following step begins creating a query that CMF Vets can use to obtain the appointment dates, appointment times, patient ID, treatment number, and owner information for the veterinarians.

1

- Double-click the Veterinarian field in the field list to add the field to the query.

Q&A What if I add the wrong field?
Click just above the field name in the design grid to select the column, and then press DELETE to remove the field.

- Double-click the Appointment Date field in the field list to add the field to the query.
- Add the Appointment Time, Patient ID, Treatment Number, and Owner fields to the query (Figure 2–6).

Q&A What if I want to include all fields? Do I have to add each field individually?

No. Instead of adding individual fields, you can double-click the asterisk (*) to add the asterisk to the design grid. The asterisk is a shortcut indicating all fields are to be included.

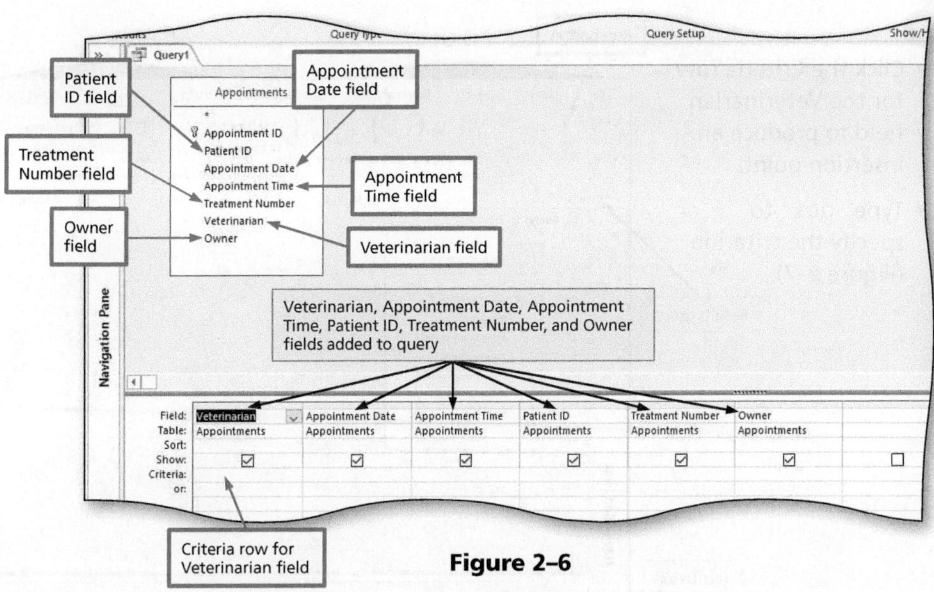

Figure 2–6

Determining Criteria

When you use queries, usually you are looking for those records that satisfy some criterion. For example, you might want to see appointment dates, appointment times, patient ID, types of treatments, and owner information for one of the veterinarians. You enter criteria in the Criteria row in the design grid below the field name to which the criterion applies. For example, to find appointments for Dr. Gomez, you first must add the Veterinarian field to the design grid. For ease of typing, the veterinarians were given ID numbers, for example, Dr. Teresa Gomez's ID is G01, and Dr. William Black's ID is B01. Therefore, when you enter the Veterinarian ID, you will only need to type G01 or B01 in the Criteria row. For example, you only need to type G01 for Gomez in the Criteria row below the Veterinarian field.

BTW

Touch Screen Differences

The Office and Windows interfaces may vary if you are using a touch screen. For this reason, you might notice that the function or appearance of your touch screen differs slightly from this module's presentation.

BTW

Access Screen Resolution

If you are using a computer or mobile device to step through the project in this module and you want your screens to match the figures in this book, you should change your screen's resolution to 1366 × 768.

Running the Query

After adding the appropriate fields and defining the query's criteria, you must run the query to get the results. To view the results of the query from Design view, click the Run button to instruct Access to run the query, that is, to perform the necessary actions to produce and display the results in Datasheet view.

To Use Text Data in a Criterion

To use **text data** (data in a field whose data type is Short Text) in criteria, simply type the text in the Criteria row below the corresponding field name, just as you did previously. In Access, you typically do not need to enclose text data in quotation marks as you do in many other database management systems. ***Why?*** *Access will enter the quotation marks automatically, so you can simply type the desired text.* The following steps finish creating a query that CMF Vets managers might use to obtain Dr. Gomez's appointment dates, appointment times, patient IDs, types of treatments, and pet owner information. These steps also save the query.

1

- Click the Criteria row for the Veterinarian field to produce an insertion point.
- Type `G01` to specify the criterion (Figure 2–7).

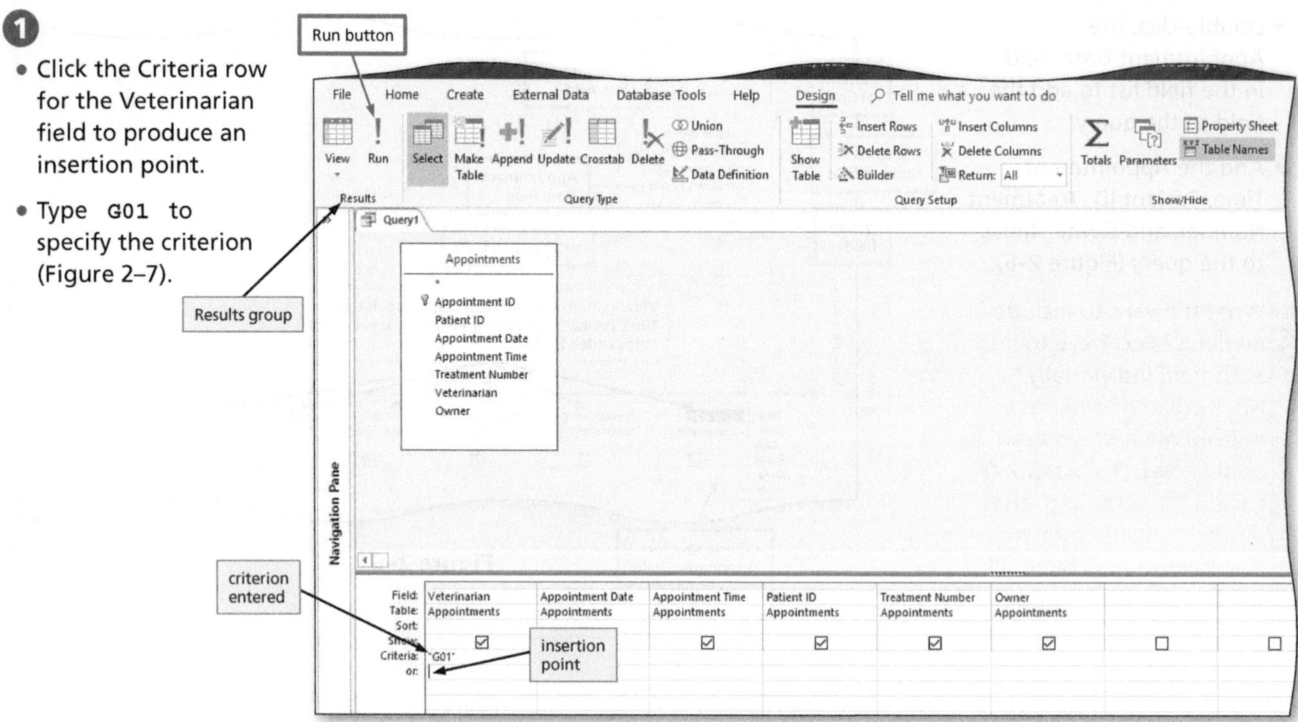

Figure 2–7

2

- Click the Run button (Query Tools Design tab | Results group) to run the query (Figure 2–8) and display Dr. Gomez's appointments.

Q&A Can I also use the View button in the Results group to run the query?
Yes. You can click the View button to view the query results in Datasheet view.

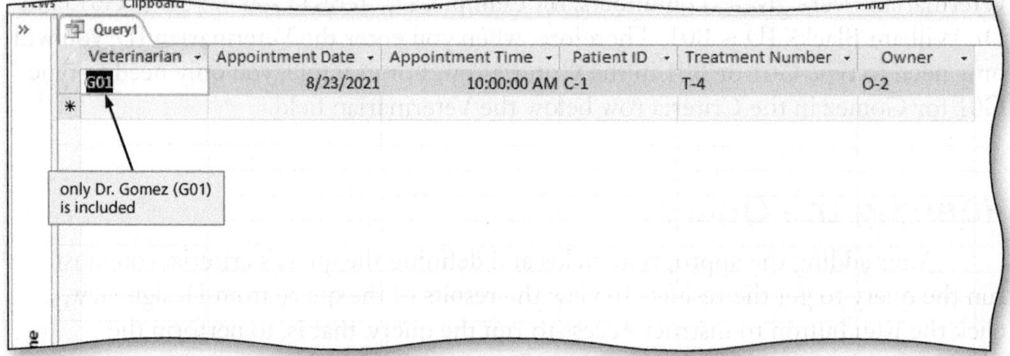

Figure 2–8

3

- Click the Save button on the Quick Access Toolbar to display the Save As dialog box.
- Type `m02q01` as the name of the query (Figure 2–9).

Q&A Can I also save from Design view?
Yes. You can save the query when you view it in Design view just as you can save it when you view query results in Datasheet view.

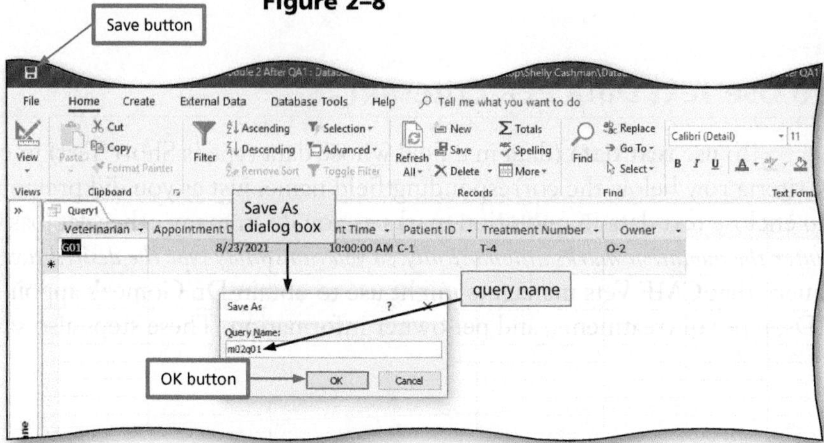

Figure 2–9

4

- Click OK (Save As dialog box) to save the query (Figure 2–10), and then click Close for the m02q01 query to close the query.

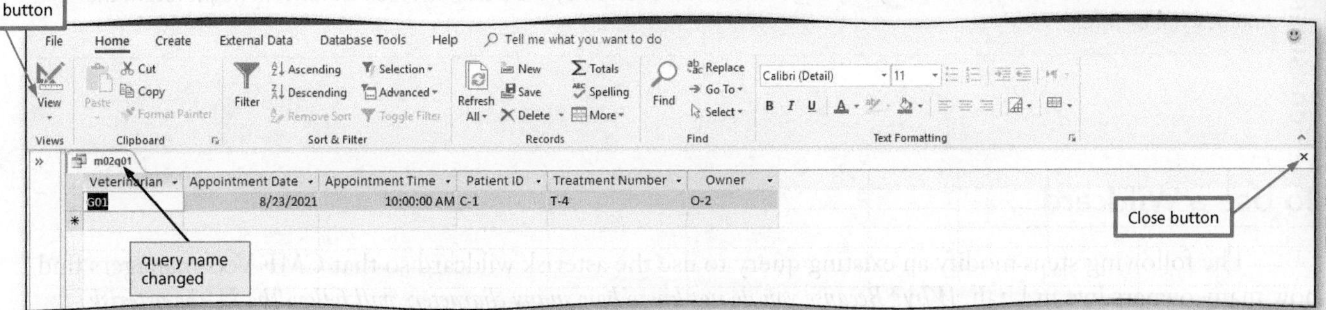

Figure 2–10

Other Ways

1. Right-click query tab, click Save on shortcut menu or Press CTRL+S.

Using Saved Queries

After you have created and saved a query, you can use it in a variety of ways:

- To view the results of a query that is not currently open, open it by right-clicking the query in the Navigation Pane and clicking Open on the shortcut menu.
- If you want to change the design of a query that is already open, return to Design view and make the changes.
- If you want to change the design of a query that is not currently open, right-click the query in the Navigation Pane and then click Design View on the shortcut menu to open the query in Design view.
- To print the results with a query open, click File on the ribbon, click the Print tab in the Backstage view, and then click Quick Print.
- To print a query without first opening it, be sure the query is selected in the Navigation Pane and click File on the ribbon, click the Print tab in the Backstage view, and then click Quick Print.
- You can switch between views of a query using the View button (Home tab | Views group). Clicking the arrow at the bottom of the button produces the View button menu. You then click the desired view in the menu. The two query views you use in this module are Datasheet view (to see the results) and Design view (to change the design). You can also click the top part of the View button, in which case you will switch to the view identified by the icon on the button. In Figure 2–10, the View button displays the icon for Design view, so clicking the button would change to Design view. For the most part, the icon on the button represents the view you want, so you can usually simply click the button.

BTW
The Ribbon and Screen Resolution
Access may change how the groups and buttons within the groups appear on the ribbon, depending on the computer or mobile device's screen resolution. Thus, your ribbon may look different from the ones in this book if you are using a screen resolution other than 1366 × 768.

Wildcards

Microsoft Access supports wildcards. **Wildcards** are symbols that represent any character or combination of characters. One common wildcard, the **asterisk** (*), represents any collection of characters. Another wildcard symbol is the **question mark (?)**, which represents any individual character.

BTW
Organizing Files and Folders
You should organize and store files in folders so that you easily can find the files later. For example, if you are taking an introductory computer class called CIS 101, a good practice would be to save all Access files in an Access folder in a CIS 101 folder.

CONSIDER THIS

What does S* represent? What does T?m represent?

S* represents the letter, S, followed by any collection of characters. A search for S* might return System, So, or Superlative. T?m represents the letter, T, followed by any single character, followed by the letter, m. A search for T?m might return the names Tim or Tom.

To Use a Wildcard

The following steps modify an existing query to use the asterisk wildcard so that CMF Vets managers find how many owners live in Utah. ***Why?*** *Because you do not know how many characters will follow the U, the asterisk wildcard symbol is appropriate.* The steps also save the query with a new name using Save As.

- Open the Owners Query in Design View.
- Click the Criteria row below the Owner State field to produce an insertion point.
- If there were any existing data in the Criteria row, you would use the DELETE or BACKSPACE key. But, since there is no existing criteria, you can simply type the criteria.
- Type `U*` as the criterion (Figure 2–11).

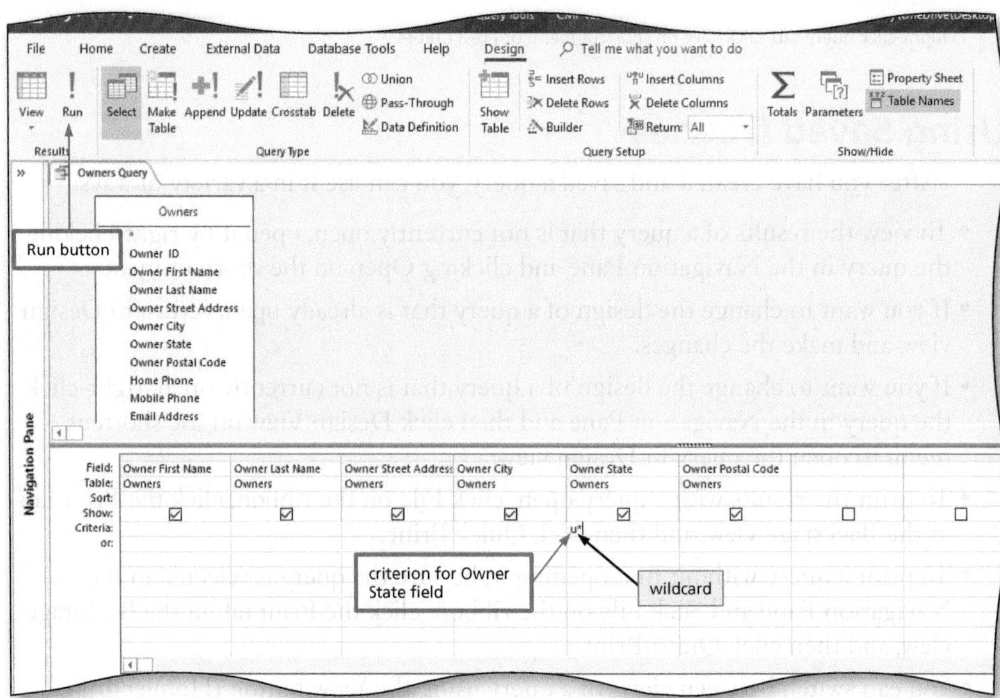

Figure 2–11

- Run the query by clicking the Run button (Query Tools Design tab | Results group) (Figure 2–12).

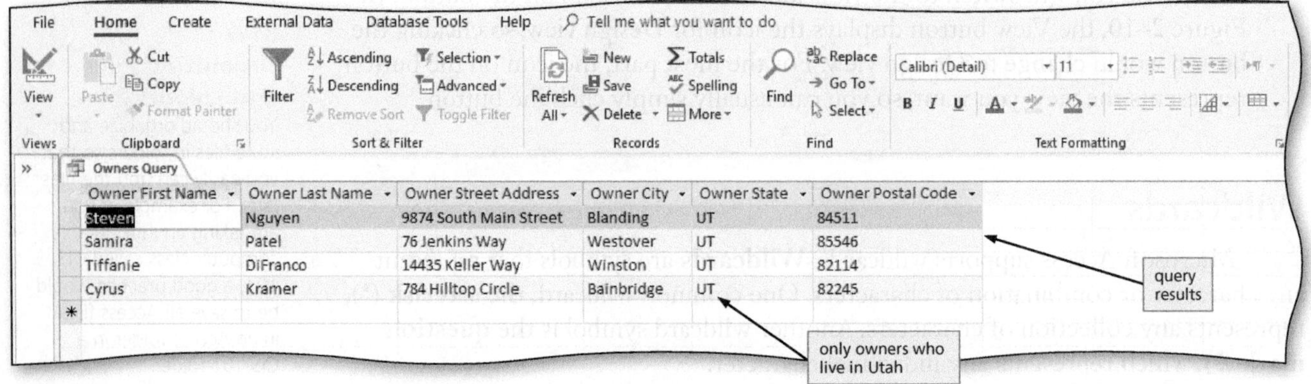

Owner First Name	Owner Last Name	Owner Street Address	Owner City	Owner State	Owner Postal Code
Steven	Nguyen	9874 South Main Street	Blanding	UT	84511
Samira	Patel	76 Jenkins Way	Westover	UT	85546
Tiffanie	DiFranco	14435 Keller Way	Winston	UT	82114
Cyrus	Kramer	784 Hilltop Circle	Bainbridge	UT	82245

Figure 2–12

Experiment

- Change the letter U to lowercase in the criterion and run the query to determine whether case makes a difference when entering a wildcard.

3

- Click File on the ribbon to open the Backstage view.
- Click the Save As tab in the Backstage view to display the Save As gallery.
- Click 'Save Object As' in the File Types area (Figure 2–13).

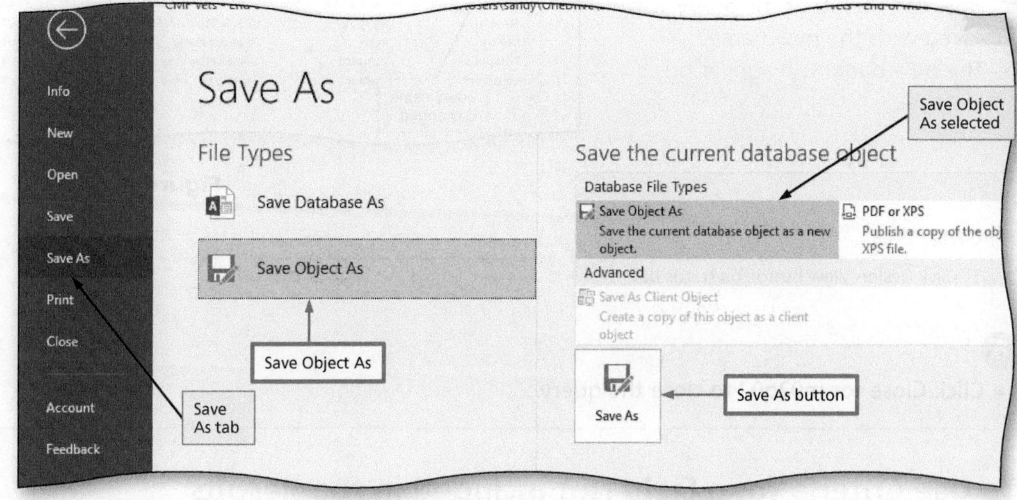

Figure 2–13

Q&A The text I entered is now preceded by the word, Like. What happened?
Criteria that include wildcards need to be preceded by the word, Like. However, you do not have to type it; Access adds the word automatically to any criterion involving a wildcard.

Can I just click the Save button on the Quick Access Toolbar as I did when saving the previous query?
If you clicked the Save button, you would replace the previous query with the version you just created. Because you want to save both the previous query and the new one, you need to save the new version with a different name. To do so, you must use Save Object As, which is available through the Backstage view.

4

- With Save Object As selected in the File Types gallery, click the Save As button to display the Save As dialog box.
- Erase the name of the current query and type `m02q02` as the name for the saved query (Figure 2–14).

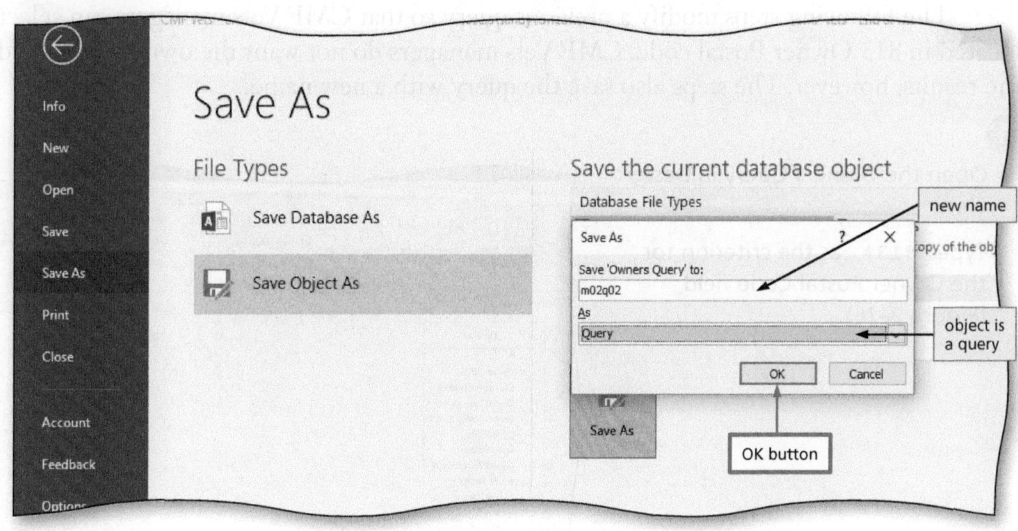

Figure 2–14

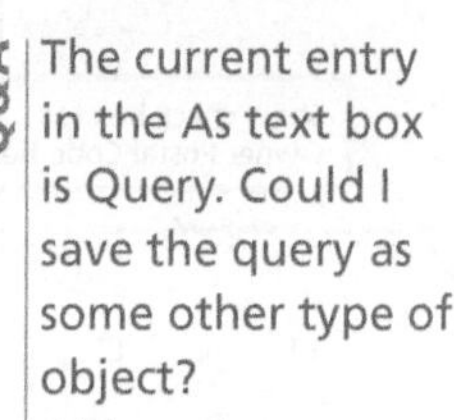

Q&A The current entry in the As text box is Query. Could I save the query as some other type of object?
Although you usually would want to save the query as another query, you can also save it as a form or report by changing the entry in the As text box. If you do, Access would create either a simple form or a simple report for the query.

- Click OK (Save As dialog box) to save the query with the new name and close the Backstage view (Figure 2–15).

Q&A How can I tell that the query was saved with the new name?

The new name will appear on the tab.

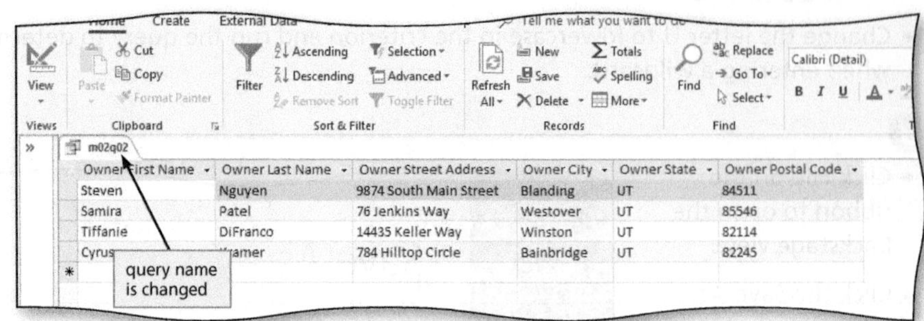

Figure 2–15

Other Ways

1. Click Design View button on status bar

- Click Close for m02q02 to close the query.

To Use Criteria for a Field Not Included in the Results

In some cases, you might require criteria for a particular field that should not appear in the results of the query. For example, you may want to see the Mobile Phone number for all Owners located in the 813 Owners Postal code in an Owners Query. The criteria involve the Owners Postal field, but you do not want to include the Owners Postal Code field in the results since this information is sensitive and you do not want everyone viewing the query to see this information.

To enter a criterion for the Owner Postal Code field, it must be included in the design grid. Normally, it would then appear in the results. To prevent this from happening, remove the check mark from its check box in the Show row of the grid. ***Why?*** *A check mark in the Show check box instructs Access to show the field in the result. If you remove the check mark, you can use the field in the query without displaying it in the query results.*

The following steps modify a previous query so that CMF Vets managers can select only those customers located in 813 Owner Postal code. CMF Vets managers do not want the owner postal code field to appear in the results, however. The steps also save the query with a new name.

- Open the Owners Query in Design view.
- Type `813*` as the criterion for the Owner Postal Code field (Figure 2–16).

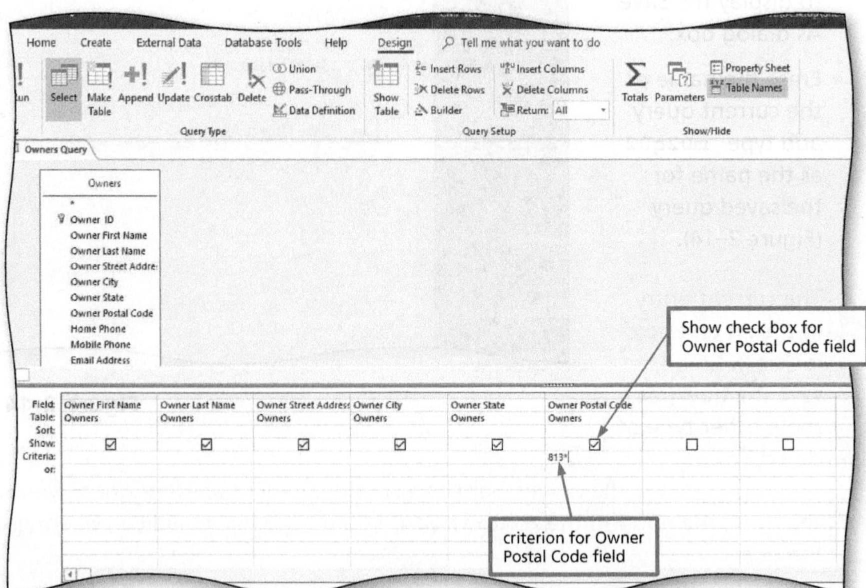

Figure 2–16

2

- Click the Show check box for the Owner Postal Code field to remove the check mark (Figure 2–17).

Q&A Could I have removed the check mark before entering the criterion?

Yes. The order in which you perform the two operations does not matter.

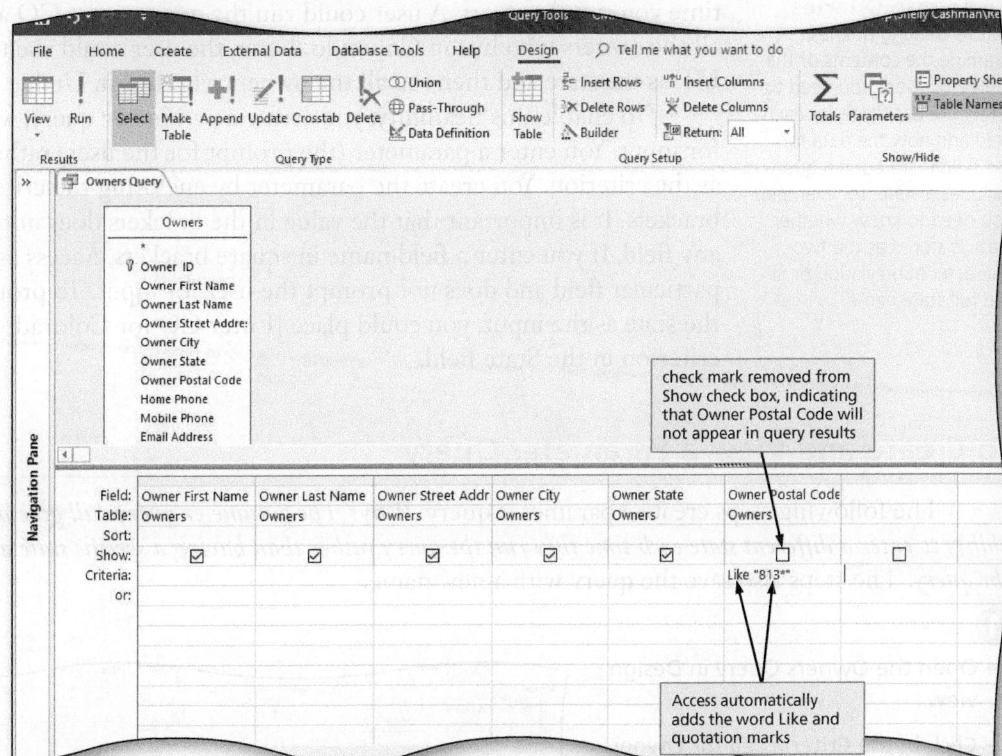

Figure 2–17

3

- Run the query (Figure 2–18).

Experiment

- Click the View button to return to Design view, enter a different Postal Code, such as 821*, as the criterion, and run the query. Repeat this process with additional Postal Codes, including at least one Postal Code that is not in the database. When finished, remove the Owner Postal Code Criteria field and then close the query without saving the changes.

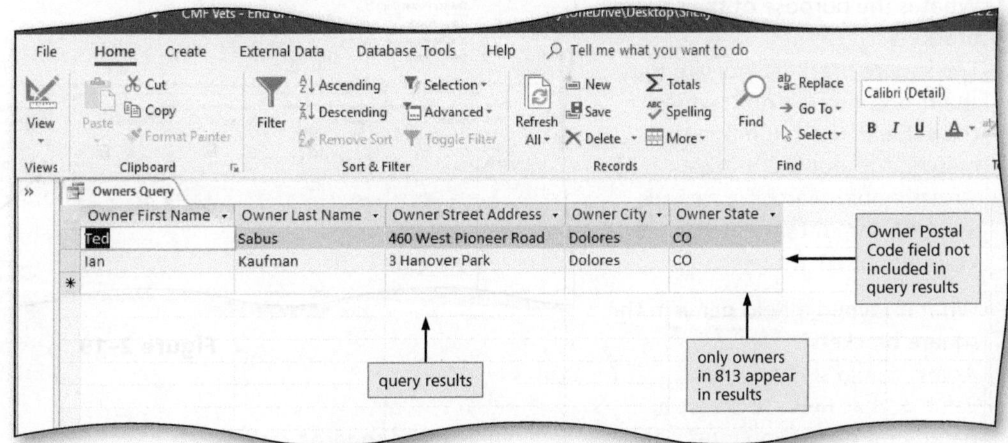

Figure 2–18

Creating a Parameter Query

If you wanted to find owners that lived in Colorado or Utah, you would either have to create a new query or modify the existing query by replacing CO with UT as the criterion. Rather than giving a specific criterion when you first create the query, occasionally you may want to be able to enter part of the criterion when you run the query and then have the appropriate results appear. For example, you might want a

BTW
Designing Queries
Before creating queries, examine the contents of the tables involved. You need to know the data type for each field and how the data for the field is stored. If a query includes a state, for example, you need to know whether state is stored as the two-character abbreviation or as the full state name.

query to return the owners and their associated states, specifying a different state each time you run the query. A user could run the query, enter CO as the state, and then see all the owners who live in Colorado. Later, the user could use the same query but enter UT as the state and then see all the owners who live in Utah.

To enable this flexibility, you create a parameter query, which prompts the user for input. You enter a parameter (the prompt for the user) rather than a specific value as the criterion. You create the parameter by enclosing the criterion value in square brackets. It is important that the value in the brackets does not match the name of any field. If you enter a field name in square brackets, Access assumes you want that particular field and does not prompt the user for input. To prompt the user to enter the state as the input, you could place [Enter CO for Colorado or UT for Utah] as the criterion in the State field.

To Create and View a Parameter Query

The following steps create a parameter query. ***Why?*** *The parameter query will give managers at CMF Vets the ability to enter a different state each time they run the query rather than having a specific state as part of the criterion in the query.* The steps also save the query with a new name.

- Open the Owners Query in Design view.
- Click in the Criteria cell for Owner State and enter [Enter CO for Colorado or UT for Utah] as the new criterion (Figure 2–19).

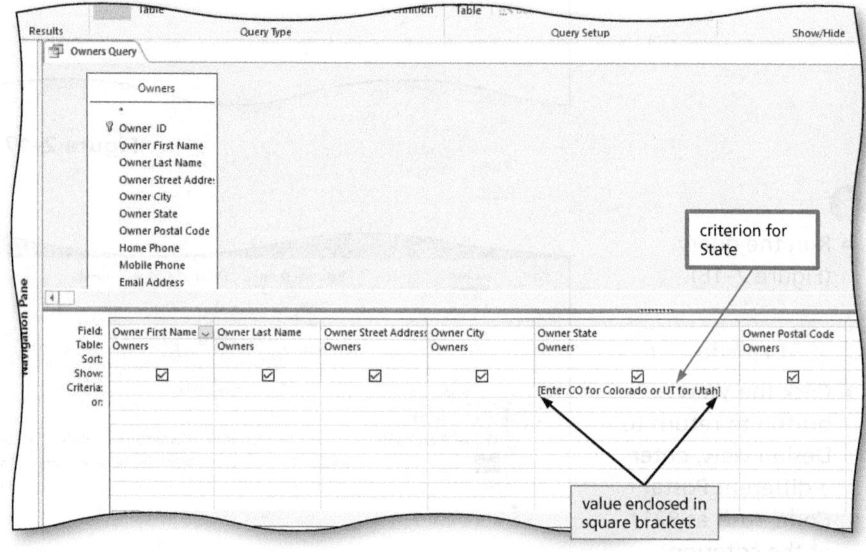

Figure 2–19

Q&A

What is the purpose of the square brackets?
The square brackets indicate that the text entered is not text that the value in the column must match. Without the brackets, Access would search for records in which the state is Enter CO for Colorado or UT for Utah.

What if I typed a field name in the square brackets?
Access would simply use the value in that field. To create a parameter query, you must not use a field name in the square brackets.

- Click the Run button (Query Tools Design tab | Results group) to display the Enter Parameter Value dialog box (Figure 2–20).

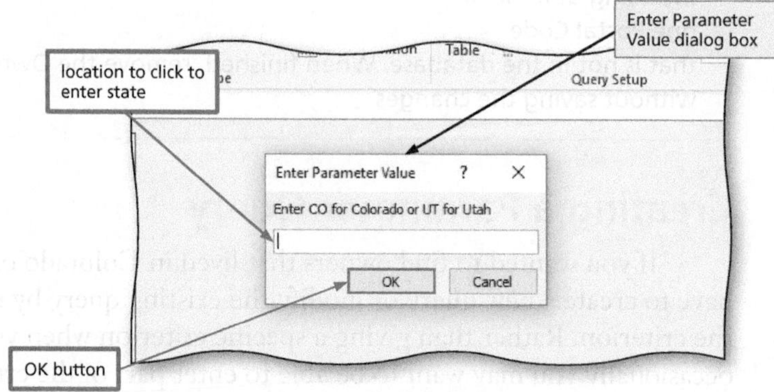

Figure 2–20

3

- Type `CO` as the parameter value in the Enter Parameter Value text box, and then click OK (Enter Parameter Value dialog box) to close the dialog box and view the query (Figure 2–20).

Experiment

- Try using other characters between the square brackets. In each case, run the query. When finished, change the characters between the square brackets back to Enter CO for Colorado or UT for Utah.

4

- Click File on the ribbon to open the Backstage view.
- Click the Save As tab in the Backstage view to display the Save As gallery.
- Click 'Save Object As' in the File Types area.
- With Save Object As selected in the File Types area, click the Save As button to display the Save As dialog box.
- Type `Owner-State Query` as the name for the saved query.
- Click OK (Save As dialog box) to save the query with the new name and close the Backstage view (Figure 2–21).

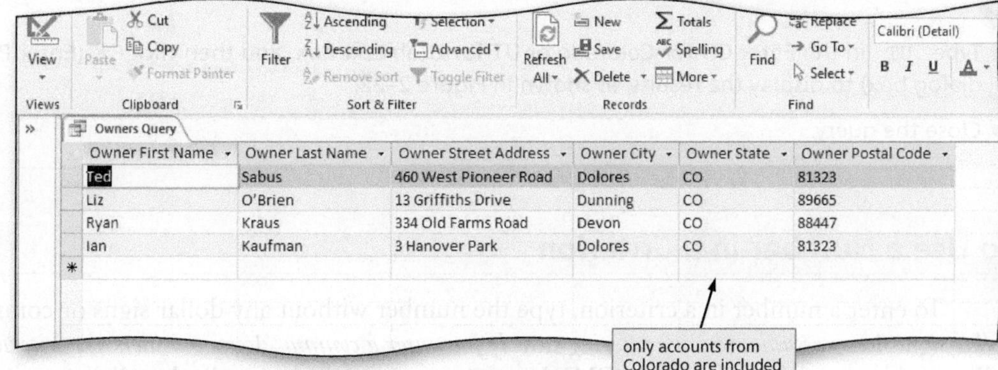

Figure 2–21

5

- Click Close for the Owner-State Query to close the query.

Break Point: If you wish to take a break, this is a good place to do so. You can exit Access now. To resume later, start Access, open the database called CMF Vets, and continue following the steps from this location forward.

To Use a Parameter Query

You use a parameter query like any other saved query. You can open it or you can print the query results. In either case, Access prompts you to supply a value for the parameter each time you use the query. If changes have been made to the data since the last time you ran the query, the results of the query may be different, even if you enter the same value for the parameter. ***Why?*** *In addition to the ability to enter different field values each time the parameter query is run, the query always uses the data that is currently in the table.* The following steps use the parameter query named Owner-State Query.

1

- Open the Navigation Pane.
- Right-click the Owner-State Query to produce a shortcut menu.
- Click Open on the shortcut menu to open the query and display the Enter Parameter Value dialog box (Figure 2–22).

Q&A

The title bar for my Navigation Pane contains Tables and Related Views rather than All Access Objects as it did previously. What should I do?

Click the Navigation Pane arrow and then click 'All Access Objects'.

I do not have the Search bar at the top of the Navigation Pane that I had previously. What should I do?

Right-click the Navigation Pane title bar arrow to display a shortcut menu, and then click Search Bar.

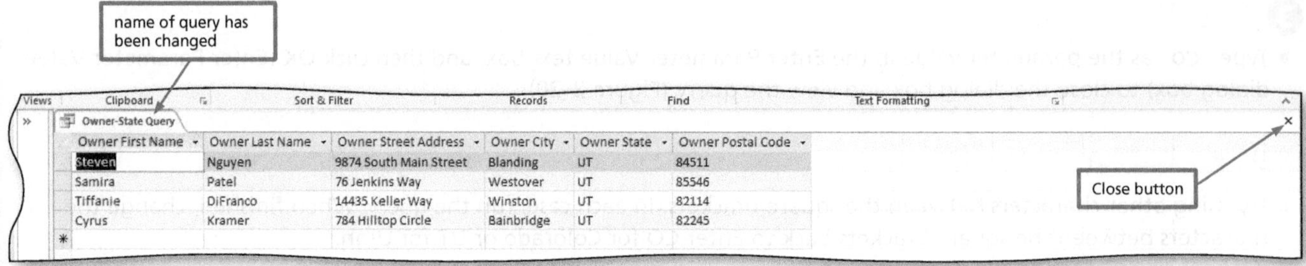

Figure 2–22

- Type UT in the Enter CO for Colorado or UT for Utah text box, and then click OK (Enter Parameter Value dialog box) to display the results, as shown in Figure 2–22.
- Close the query.

To Use a Number in a Criterion

To enter a number in a criterion, type the number without any dollar signs or commas. ***Why?** If you enter a dollar sign, Access assumes you are entering text. If you enter a comma, Access considers the criterion invalid.* The following steps create a query that CMF Vets managers might use to display all treatments whose current price is $25. The steps also save the query with a new name.

- Close the Navigation Pane.
- Click Create on the ribbon to display the Create tab.
- Click the Query Design button (Create tab | Queries group) to create a new query.
- If necessary, click the Treatment Cost table (Show Table dialog box) to select the table.
- Click the Add button to add the selected table to the query.
- Click Close to remove the dialog box from the screen.
- Drag the lower edge of the field list down far enough so all fields in the list are displayed.

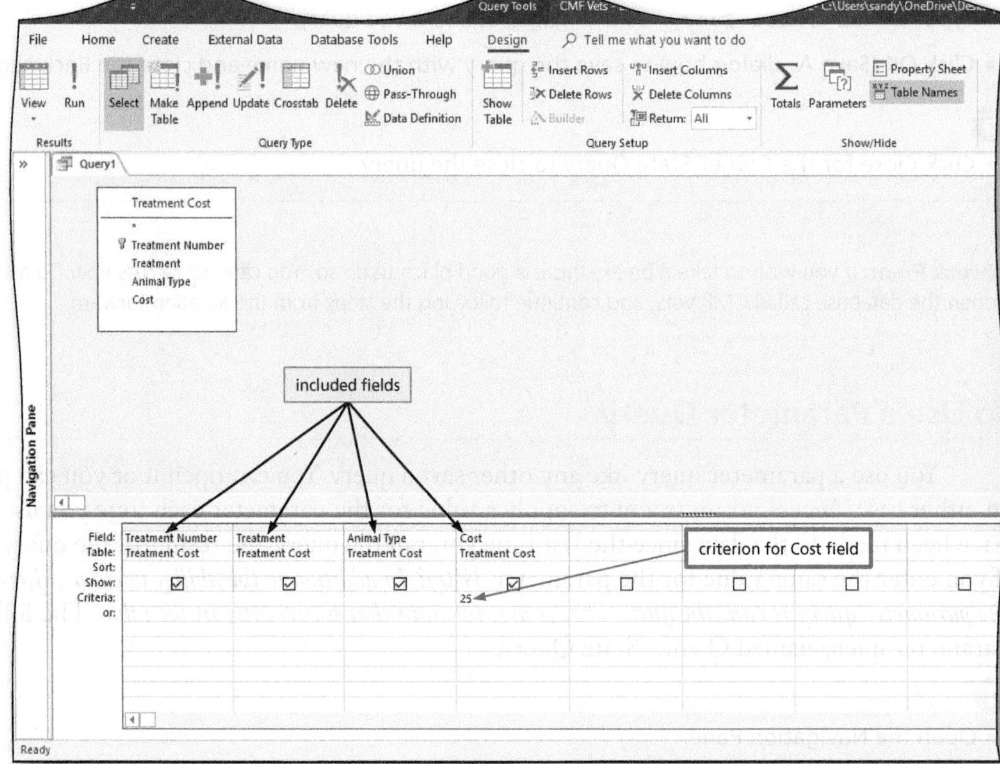

Figure 2–23

- Include the Treatment Number, Treatment, Animal Type, and Cost fields in the query.
- Type 25 as the criterion for the Cost field (Figure 2–23).

Q&A Do I need to enter a dollar sign and decimal point?
No. Access will interpret 25 as $25 because the data type for the Cost field is currency.

2

- Run the query (Figure 2–24).

Q&A Why did Access display the results as $25.00 when I only entered 25?
Access uses the format for the field to determine how to display the result. In this case, the format indicated that Access should include the dollar sign, decimal point, and two decimal places.

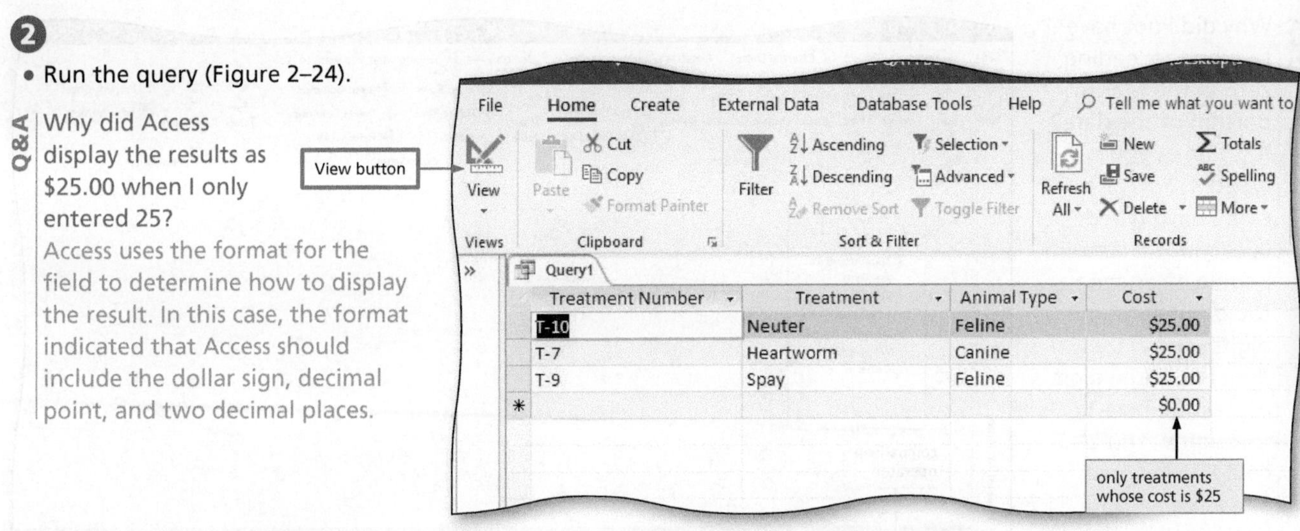

Figure 2–24

3

- Save the query as m02q03.

Q&A How do I know when to use the Save button to save a query or use the Backstage view to perform a Save As?
If you are saving a new query, the simplest way is to use the Save button on the Quick Access Toolbar. If you are saving changes to a previously saved query but do not want to change the name, use the Save button. If you want to save a previously saved query with a new name, you must use the Backstage view and perform a Save Object As.

- Close the query.

Comparison Operators

Unless you specify otherwise, Access assumes that the criteria you enter involves equality (exact matches). In the last query, for example, you were requesting those treatments that cost $25. In other situations, you might want to find a range of results; for example, you could request appointments whose appointment date is greater than 06/30/2021. If you want a query to return something other than an exact match, you must enter the appropriate **comparison operator**. The comparison operators are > (greater than), < (less than), >= (greater than or equal to), <= (less than or equal to), and NOT (not equal to).

To Use a Comparison Operator in a Criterion

The following steps use the > operator to create a query that CMF Vets managers might use to find all appointments whose appointment date is after 6/30/2021. ***Why?*** *A date greater than 6/30/2021 means the date comes after 7/1/2021 when both veterinarians are scheduled for vacations.* The steps also save the query with a new name.

1

- Start a new query using the Appointments table.
- Include the Appointment Date, Appointment Time, Treatment Number, Veterinarian, and Patient ID fields.
- Type `>6/30/2021` as the criterion for the Appointment Date field (Figure 2–25).

Q&A **Why did I not have to type the leading zero in the Month portion of the date?**
It is fine as you typed it. You also could have typed 06/30/2021. Some people often type the day using two digits even if the date is a single digit as the numbers 1 through 9. You also could have typed a leading zero for both the month and the day: 06/30/2021.

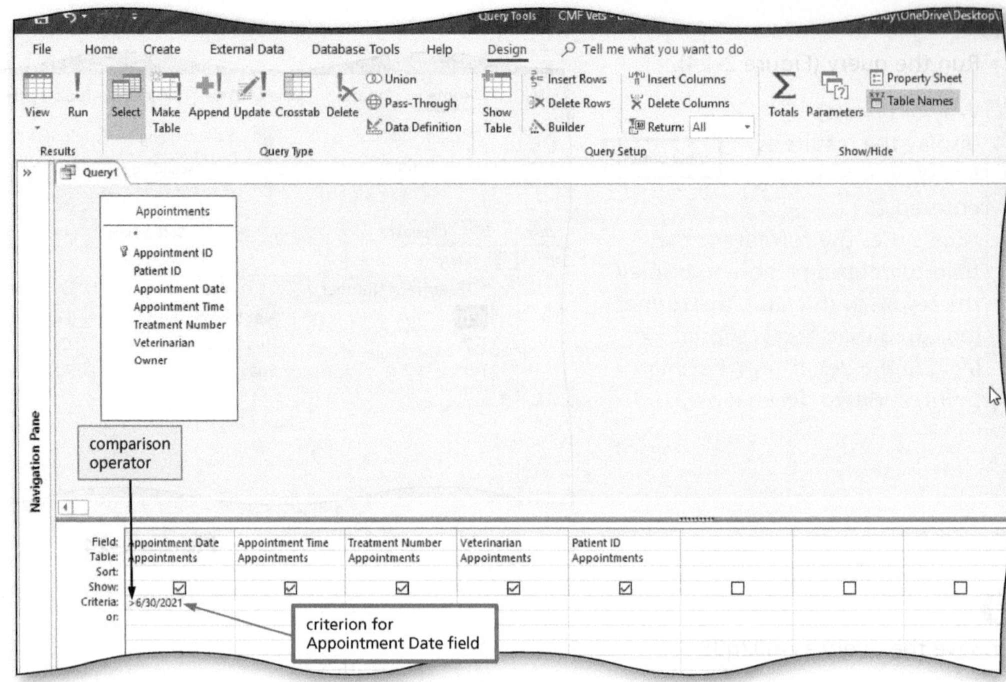

Figure 2–25

2

- Run the query (Figure 2–26).

Experiment

- Return to Design view. Try a different criterion involving a comparison operator in the Appointment Date field and run the query. When finished, return to Design view, enter the original criterion (>6/30/2021) in the Start Date field, and run the query.

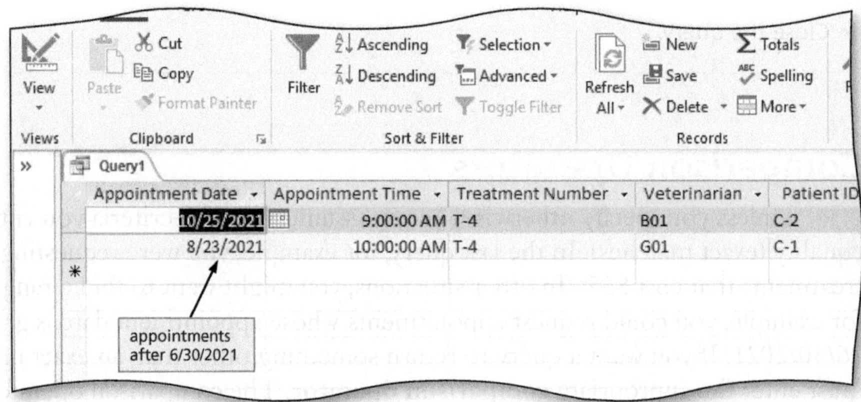

Figure 2–26

Q&A I returned to Design view and noticed that Access changed >6/30/2021 to >#6/30/2021#. Why does the date now have number signs around it?
This is the date format in Access. You usually do not have to enter the number signs because in most cases Access will insert them automatically.

My records are in a different order. Is this a problem?
No. The important thing is which records are included in the results. You will see later in this module how you can specify the specific order you want for cases when the order is important.

Can I use the same comparison operators with text data?
Yes. Comparison operators function the same whether you use them with number fields, currency fields, date fields, or text fields. With a text field, comparison operators use alphabetical order in making the determination.

- Save the query as m02q04.
- Close the query.

Using Compound Criteria

Often your search data must satisfy more than one criterion. This type of criterion is called a **compound criterion** and is created using the words AND or OR.

In an **AND criterion**, each individual criterion must be true in order for the compound criterion to be true. For example, an AND criterion would allow you to find appointments after 6/30/2021 that are treated by Veterinarian B01.

An **OR criterion** is true if either individual criterion is true. An OR criterion would allow you to find appointments after 6/30/2021 or appointments that have Veterinarian B0l . In this case, any appointment after 6/30/2021 or whose Veterinarian is B01 will both be displayed.

BTW
Queries: Query-by-Example
Query-By-Example, often referred to as QBE, was a query language first proposed in the mid-1970s. In this approach, users asked questions by filling in a table on the screen. The Access approach to queries is based on Query-by-Example.

To Use a Compound Criterion Involving AND

To combine criteria with AND, place the criteria on the same row of the design grid. ***Why?*** *Placing the criteria in the same row indicates that both criteria must be true in Access.* It is important to note that sometimes when you view the results of a query, there are no records that meet the criterion entered. At this point, you might want to check to be certain the criterion was entered correctly. And, if the criterion is entered correctly, it becomes easier to trust the results even though you might have expected another result. The following steps use an AND criterion to enable CMF Vets managers to find those appointments with an appointment date after 06/30/2021 and the Veterinarian B01. The steps also save the query.

- Start a new query using the Appointments table.
- Include the Appointment Date, Appointment Time, Treatment Number, Veterinarian, and Owner fields.
- Type `>06/30/2021` as the criterion for the Appointment Date field.
- Type `B01` as the criterion for the Veterinarian field (Figure 2–27).

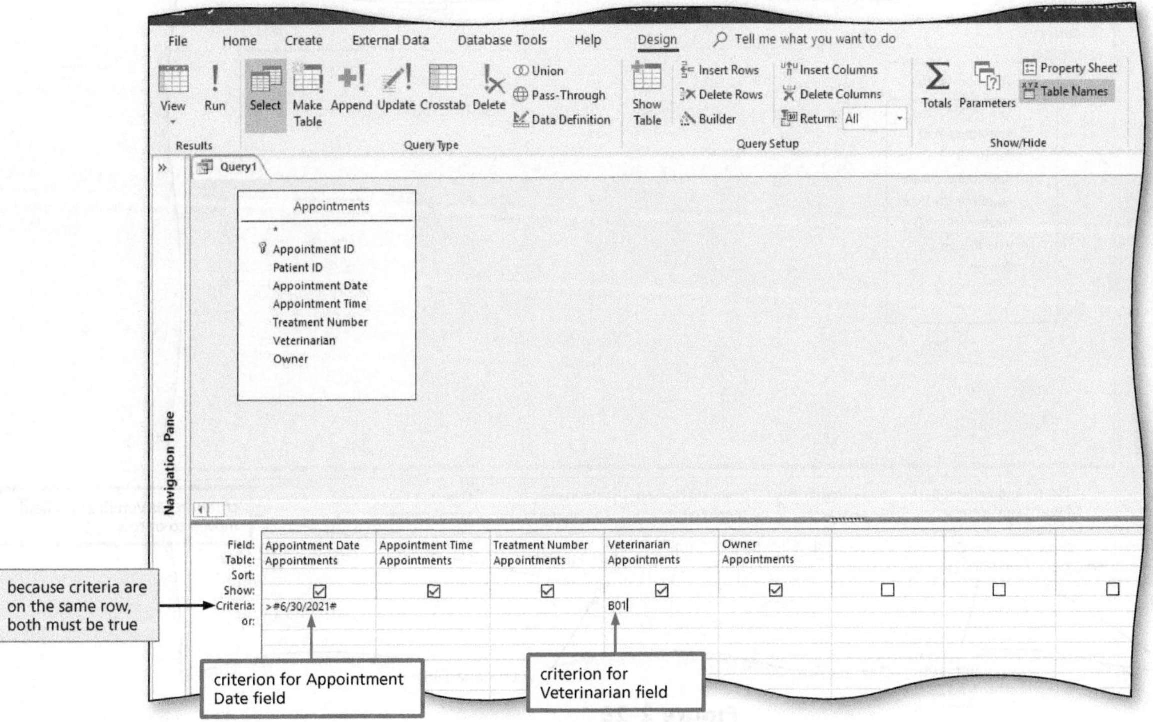

Figure 2–27

- Run the query (Figure 2–28) and Notice that Veterinarian B01 does have an appointment after 6/30/2021.

- Save the query as m02q05.

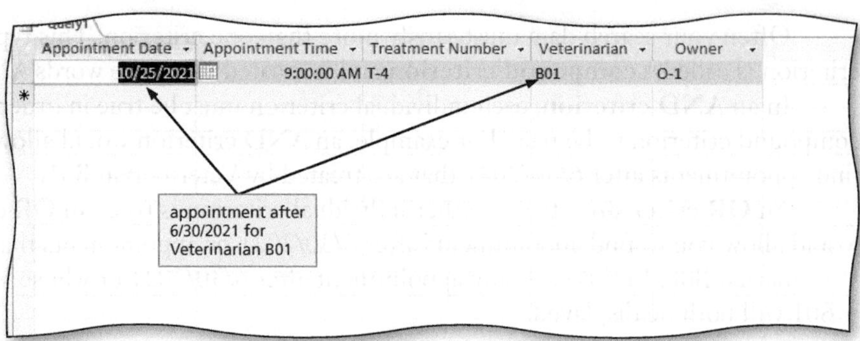

Figure 2–28

To Use a Compound Criterion Involving OR

To combine criteria with OR, each criterion must go on separate rows in the Criteria area of the grid. ***Why?*** *Placing criteria on separate rows indicates at least one criterion must be true in Access and also shows true if both criterion are true.* The following steps use an OR criterion to enable CMF Vets managers to find those Appointments who have an Appointment Date greater than 6/30/2021 or Appointments for B01. The steps also save the query with a new name.

- Return to Design view.
- If necessary, click the Criteria entry for the Veterinarian field and delete any existing text.
- Click the or row (the row below the Criteria row) for the Veterinarian field, delete any existing text if necessary, and then enter `B01` as the entry (Figure 2–29).

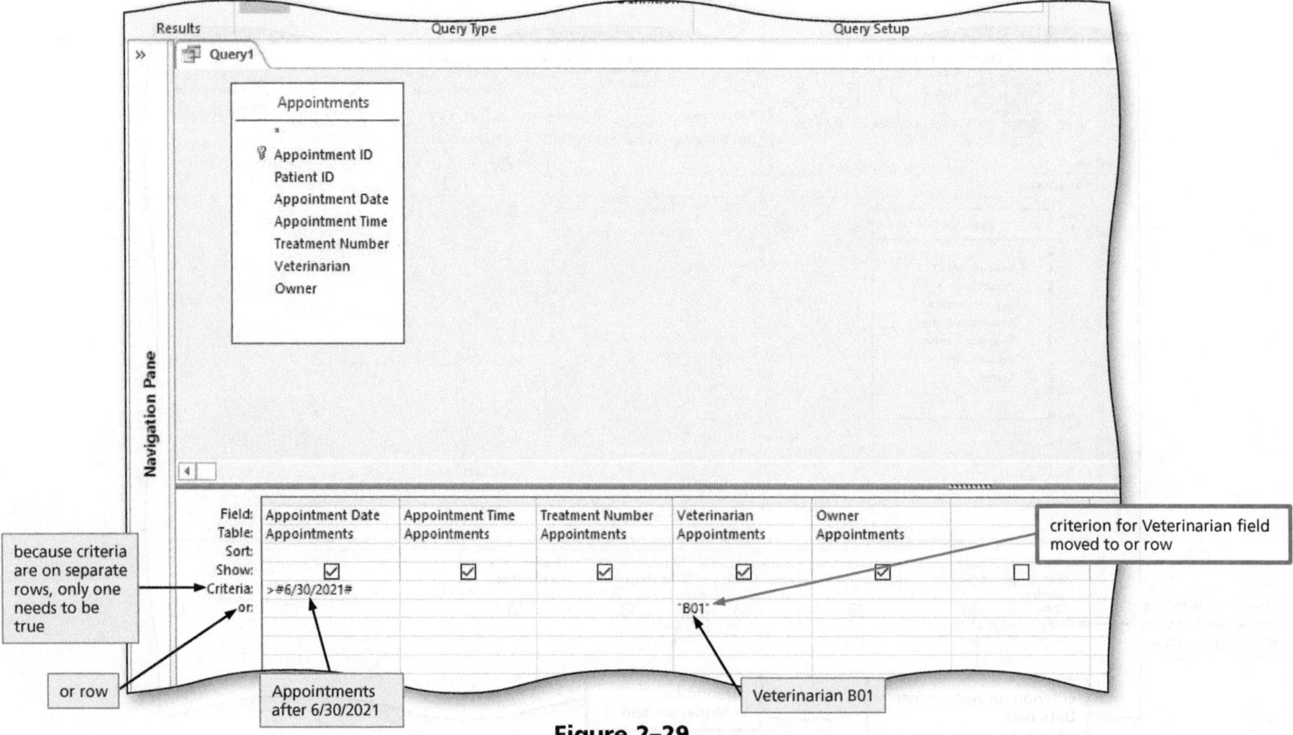

Figure 2–29

2

- Run the query (Figure 2–30).

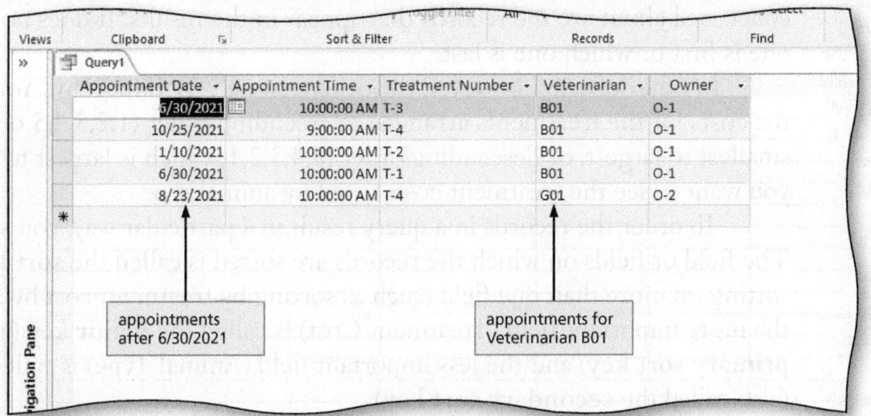

Figure 2–30

- Use Save As to save the query as m02q06.

Special Criteria

You can use three special criteria in queries:

1. If you want to create a criterion involving a range of values in a single field, you can use the **AND operator**. You place the word AND between the individual conditions. For example, if you wanted to find all Treatments whose cost is greater than or equal to $20 and less than or equal to $35, you would enter >= 20 AND <= 35 as the criterion in the Treatment Cost column.
2. You can select values in a given range by using the **BETWEEN operator**. This is often an alternative to the AND operator. For example, to find all appointments between 1/10/2021 and 10/25/2021, inclusive, you would enter BETWEEN 1/10/2021 AND 10/25/2021 as the criterion in the Appointment Date column. This is equivalent to entering >=1/10/2021 and <=10/25/2021.
3. You can select a list of values by using the **IN operator**. You follow the word IN with the list of values in parentheses. For example, to find the owners that live in Colorado (CO) **or** Utah (UT) you would enter IN ('CO', 'UT'). Unlike when you enter a simple criterion, you must enclose text values in quotation marks. The IN operator is like the OR operator, but it returns multiple values.

BTW

Rearranging Fields in a Query

To move a field in the design grid, click the column selector for the field to select the field and drag it to the appropriate location.

CONSIDER THIS

How would you find owners who live in Colorado or Utah without using the IN operator?

Place the text CO in the Criteria row of the State column. Place the text UT in the or row of the State column.

BTW
Sorting Data in a Query
When sorting data in a query, the records in the underlying tables (the tables on which the query is based) are not actually rearranged. Instead, the DBMS determines the most efficient method of simply displaying the records in the requested order. The records in the underlying tables remain in their original order.

BTW
Clearing the Design Grid
You can also clear the design grid using the ribbon. To do so, click the Home tab, click the Advanced button to display the Advanced menu, and then click Clear Grid on the Advanced menu.

Sorting

In some queries, the order in which the records appear is irrelevant. All you need to be concerned about are the records that appear in the results. It does not matter which one is first or which one is last.

In other queries, however, the order can be very important. You may want to see the costs for the treatments arranged in ascending order (1,2,3,4,5,on so on), which is smallest to largest, or descending order (5,4,3,2,1, which is largest to smallest. Perhaps you want to see the treatment costs listed by animal type.

To order the records in a query result in a particular way, you **sort** the records. The field or fields on which the records are sorted is called the **sort key**. If you are sorting on more than one field (such as sorting by treatment cost by animal type), the more important field (Treatment Cost) is called the **major key** (also called the **primary sort key**) and the less important field (Animal Type) is called the **minor key** (also called the **secondary sort key**).

To sort in Microsoft Access, specify the sort order in the Sort row of the design grid below the field that is the sort key. If you specify more than one sort key, the sort key on the left will be the major sort key, and the one on the right will be the minor key.

To Clear the Design Grid

Why? *If the fields you want to include in the next query are different from those in the previous query, it is usually simpler to start with a clear grid, that is, one with no fields already in the design grid.* You always can clear the entries in the design grid by closing the query and then starting over. A simpler approach to clearing the entries is to select all the entries and then press the DELETE key. The following steps return to Design view and clear the design grid.

- If necessary, click the Design View button to display m02q06 in Design view.
- Click just above the Appointment Date column heading in the grid to select the column.

Q&A I clicked above the column heading, but the column is not selected. What should I do?
You did not point to the correct location. Be sure the pointer changes into a down-pointing arrow, and then click again.

- Press and hold SHIFT and click just above the Owner column heading to select all the columns (Figure 2–31).

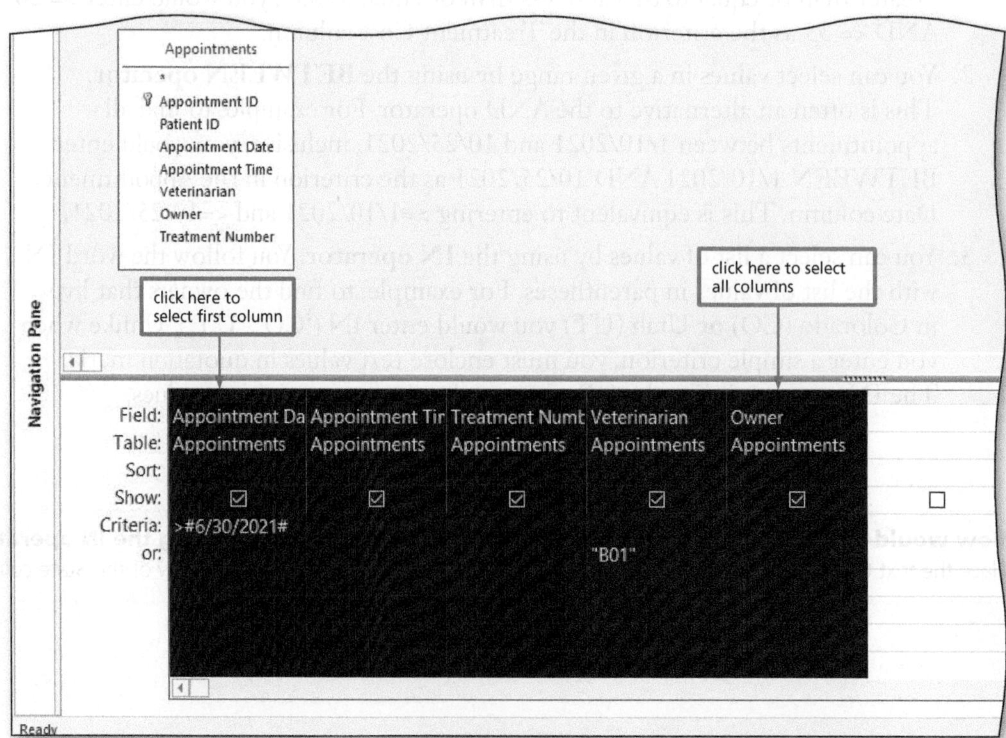

Figure 2–31

2

- Press DELETE to clear the design grid.

3

- Close the query without saving these changes.

To Import a Table

CMF Vets requires additional data to be able to run some of its required queries. As you learned previously, you can import data from external sources. The following steps import the Veterinary Vendors table from the CMF Vets Extra Tables database.

1. Open the Support_AC_CMF_Vets Extra Tables database from the Data Files on your hard drive, OneDrive, or other storage location, and then click the External Data tab. You should now have both databases open in Access.
2. With the CMF Vets database already open, click the 'New Data Source button' (External Data tab | Import & Link group).
3. Click From Database in the New Data Source menu, and then click Access to display the Get External Data - Access Database dialog box.
4. Click the Browse button and navigate to your storage location for the file, Support_AC_CMF_Vets Extra Tables.
5. Select Support_AC_CMF_Vets Extra Tables, and then click the Open button to select it as the data source.
6. If necessary, click the 'Import tables, queries, forms, reports, macros, and modules Into the current database' option button to indicate how and where to store the data in the current database
7. Click OK to display the Import Objects dialog box.
8. Select the Veterinary Vendors table to indicate the file to import, and then click OK to import the table.
9. Close the Get External Data – Access Database dialog box without saving the import steps.
10. Click Close and confirm that the Veterinary Vendors table is listed as a table object in the Navigation Pane.

To Sort Data in a Query

If you determine that the query results should be sorted, you will need to specify the sort key. The following steps sort the costs in the Treatment Cost table by indicating that the Cost field is to be sorted. The steps specify Ascending sort order. ***Why?*** *When sorting numerical data, Ascending sort order arranges the results in ascending order.*

- Create a new query based on the Treatment Cost table.
- Include the Treatment and Cost fields in the design grid.
- Click the Sort row in the Cost field column, and then click the Sort arrow to display a menu of possible sort orders (Figure 2–32).

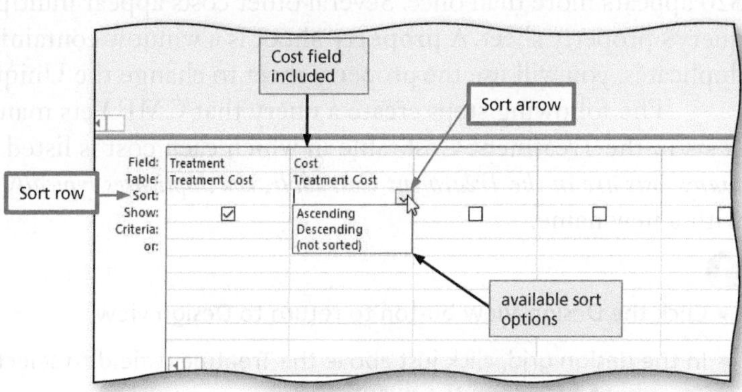

Figure 2–32

- Click Ascending to select the sort order (Figure 2–33).

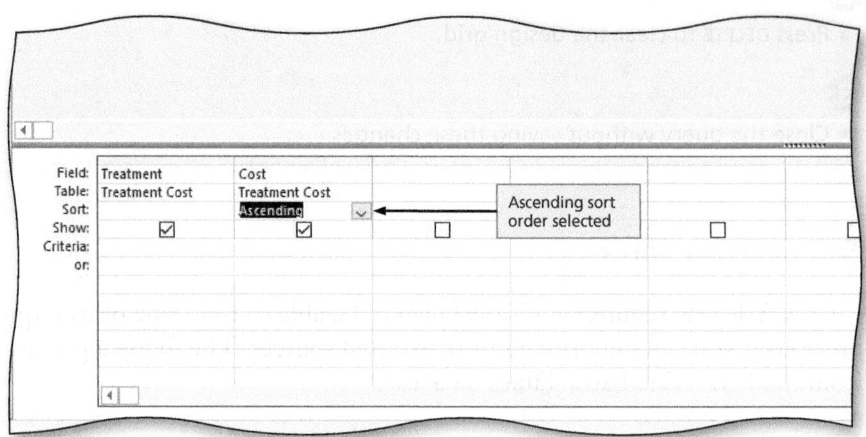

Figure 2–33

- Run the query (Figure 2–34) to display the treatment costs sorted in ascending order (lowest to highest).
- Save the query as m02q07.

Experiment

- Return to Design view and change the sort order to Descending. Run the query. Return to Design view and change the sort order back to Ascending. Run the query.

Q&A Why do some costs appear more than once?
The same cost is associated with various treatments for felines and canines.

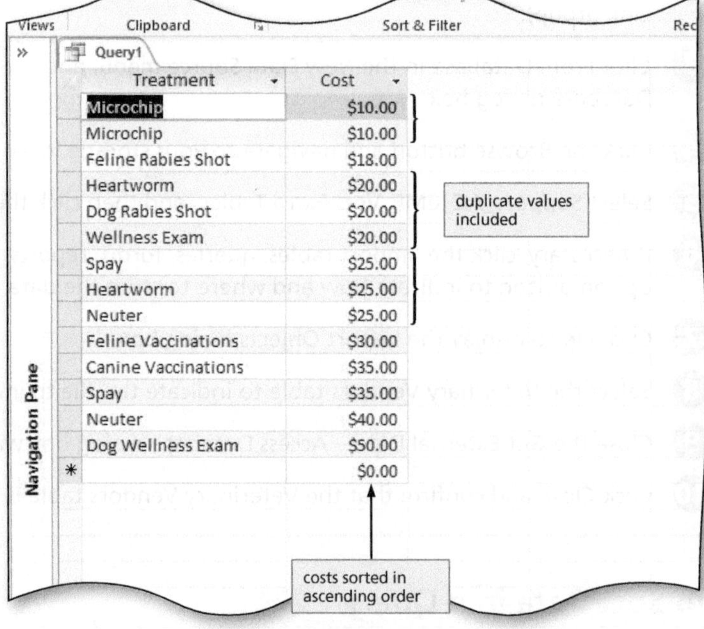

Treatment	Cost
Microchip	$10.00
Microchip	$10.00
Feline Rabies Shot	$18.00
Heartworm	$20.00
Dog Rabies Shot	$20.00
Wellness Exam	$20.00
Spay	$25.00
Heartworm	$25.00
Neuter	$25.00
Feline Vaccinations	$30.00
Canine Vaccinations	$35.00
Spay	$35.00
Neuter	$40.00
Dog Wellness Exam	$50.00
*	$0.00

Figure 2–34

To Omit Duplicates

When you sort data, duplicates normally are included. In the query shown in Figure 2–34, for example, $20 appears more than once. Several other costs appear multiple times as well. You eliminate duplicates using the query's property sheet. A **property sheet** is a window containing the various properties of the object. To omit duplicates, you will use the property sheet to change the Unique Values property from No to Yes.

The following steps create a query that CMF Vets managers might use to obtain a sorted list of the costs in the Treatment Cost table in which each cost is listed only once. ***Why?*** *Unless you wanted to know how many costs are in the Treatment Cost table, the duplicates typically do not add any value.* The steps also save the query with a new name.

- Click the Design View button to return to Design view.
- In the design grid, click just above the Treatment field to select the field and then click DELETE to remove the Treatment field from the query.

- Click the second field (the empty field to the right of Cost) in the design grid to produce an insertion point.
- If necessary, click Design on the ribbon to display the Design tab.
- Click the Property Sheet button (Query Tools Design tab | Show/Hide group) to display the property sheet (Figure 2–35).

Q&A My property sheet looks different. What should I do?
If your sheet looks different, close the property sheet and repeat this step.

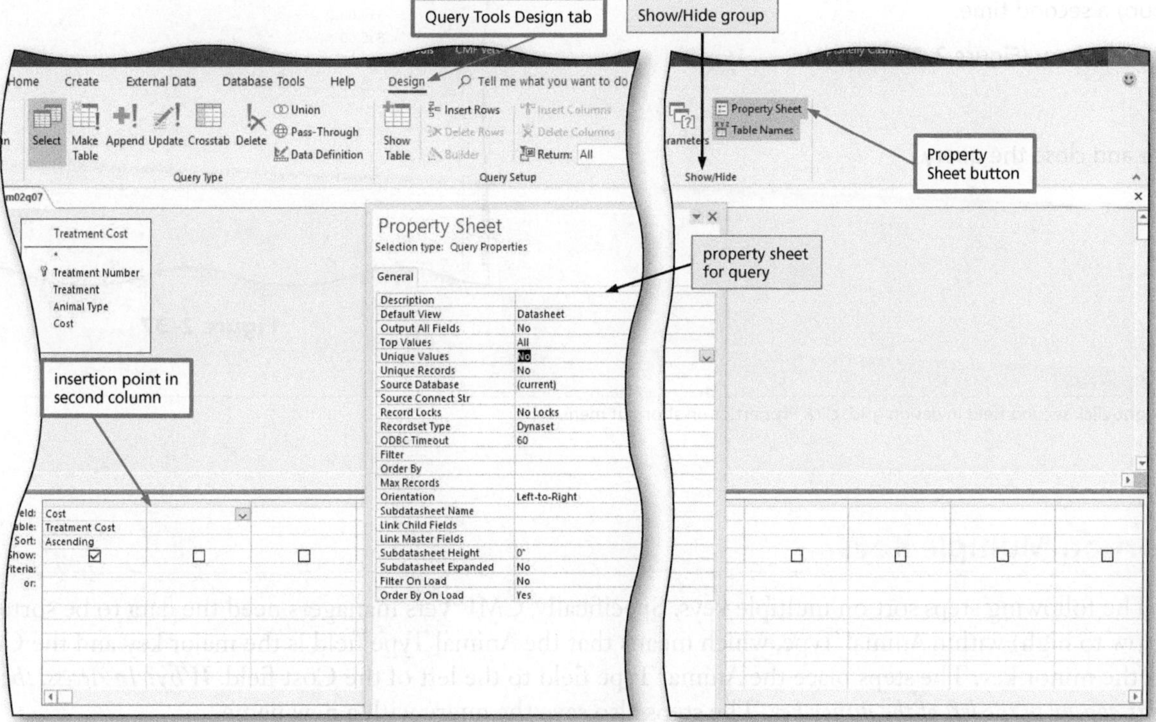

Figure 2–35

2

- Click the Unique Values property box, and then click the Unique Values arrow to display a list of available choices (Figure 2–36).

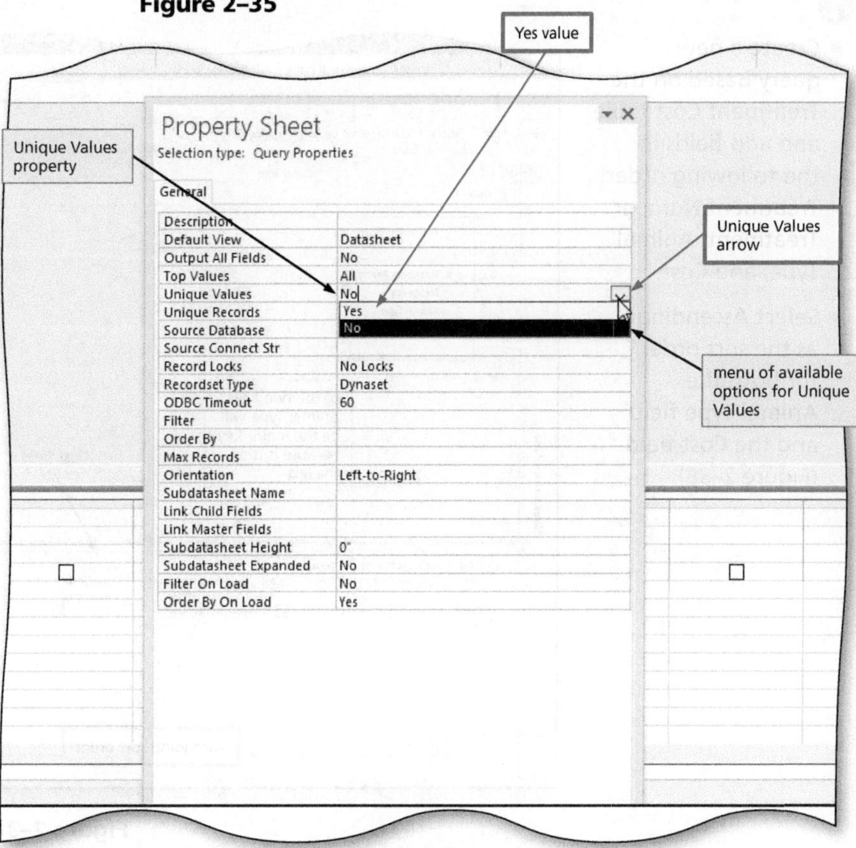

Figure 2–36

- Click Yes to indicate that the query will return unique values, which means that each value will appear only once in the query results.
- Close the Query Properties property sheet by clicking the Property Sheet button (Query Tools Design tab | Show/Hide group) a second time.
- Run the query (Figure 2–37).

- Save and close the query.

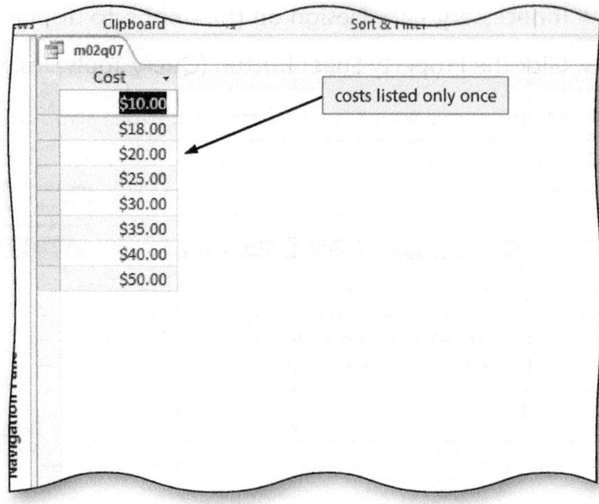

Figure 2–37

Other Ways

1. Right-click second field in design grid, click Properties on shortcut menu

To Sort on Multiple Keys

The following steps sort on multiple keys. Specifically, CMF Vets managers need the data to be sorted by Cost (low to high) within Animal Type, which means that the Animal Type field is the major key and the Cost field is the minor key. The steps place the Animal Type field to the left of the Cost field. ***Why?** In Access, the major key must appear to the left of the minor key.* The steps also save the query with a new name.

- Create a new query based on the Treatment Cost table and add fields in the following order: Treatment Number, Treatment, Animal Type, and Cost.
- Select Ascending as the sort order for both the Animal Type field and the Cost field (Figure 2–38).

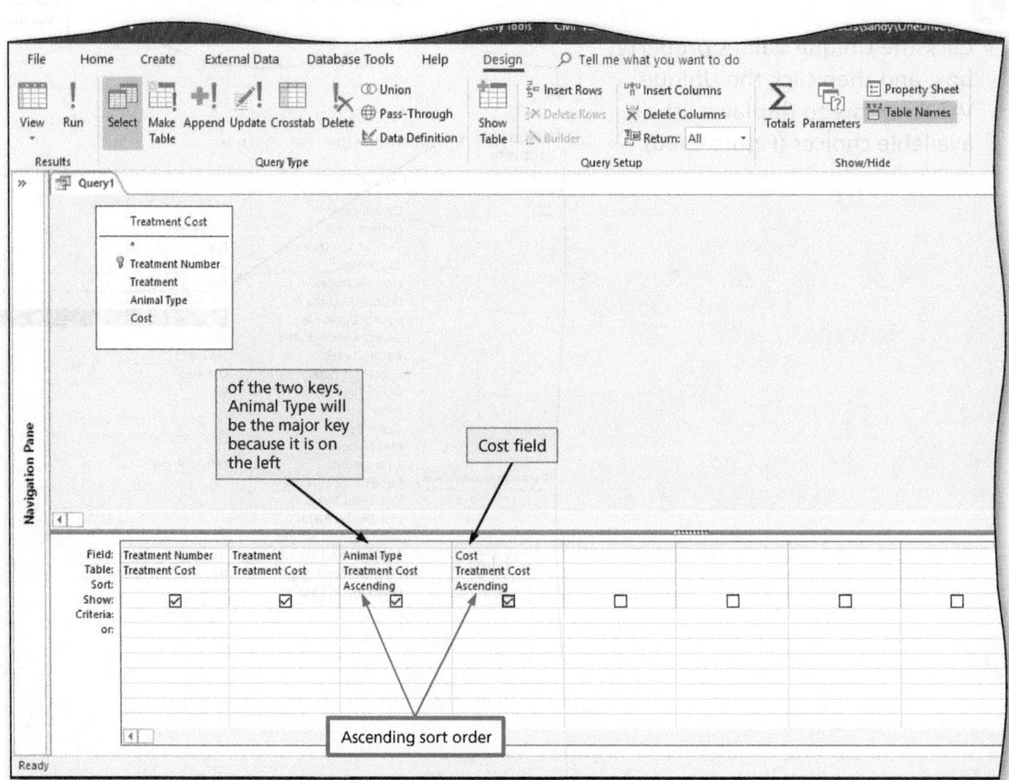

Figure 2–38

2

- Run the query (Figure 2–39) to display the treatment costs sorted first by animal type and then by cost.

Experiment

- Return to Design view and try other sort combinations for the Animal Type and Cost fields, such as Descending for Animal Type and Ascending for Cost. In each case, run the query to see the effect of the changes. When finished, select Ascending as the sort order for both fields.

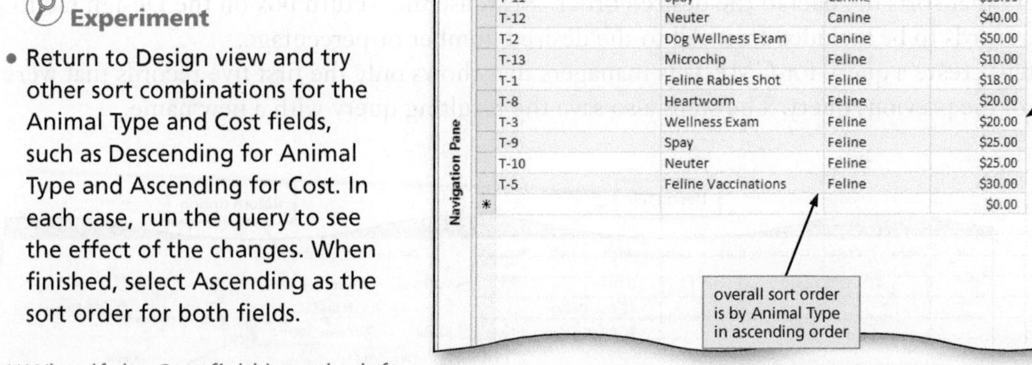

Treatment Number	Treatment	Animal Type	Cost
T-14	Microchip	Canine	$10.00
T-4	Dog Rabies Shot	Canine	$20.00
T-7	Heartworm	Canine	$25.00
T-6	Canine Vaccinations	Canine	$35.00
T-11	Spay	Canine	$35.00
T-12	Neuter	Canine	$40.00
T-2	Dog Wellness Exam	Canine	$50.00
T-13	Microchip	Feline	$10.00
T-1	Feline Rabies Shot	Feline	$18.00
T-8	Heartworm	Feline	$20.00
T-3	Wellness Exam	Feline	$20.00
T-9	Spay	Feline	$25.00
T-10	Neuter	Feline	$25.00
T-5	Feline Vaccinations	Feline	$30.00
*			$0.00

Figure 2–39

Q&A What if the Cost field is to the left of the Animal Type field?

It is important to remember that the major sort key must appear to the left of the minor sort key in the design grid. If you attempted to sort by Cost within Animal Type but placed the Cost field to the left of the Animal Type field, your results would not accurately represent the intended sort.

- Save the query as m02q08.

CONSIDER THIS

Is there any way to sort the records in this same order, but have the Cost field appear to the left of the Animal Type field in the query results?

Yes. Remove the check mark from the Animal Type field, and then add an additional Animal Type field at the end of the query. The first Animal Type field will be used for sorting but will not appear in the results. The second will appear in the results but will not be involved in the sorting process.

CONSIDER THIS

How do you approach the creation of a query that might involve sorting?

Examine the query or request to see if it contains words such as *order* or *sort*. Such words imply that the order of the query results is important. If so, you need to sort the query.

- If sorting is required, identify the field or fields on which the results are to be sorted. In the request, look for language such as *ordered by* or *sort the results by*, both of which would indicate that the specified field is a sort key.
- If using multiple sort keys, determine the major and minor keys. If you are using two sort keys, determine which one is the more important, or the major key. Look for language such as *view treatment costs within each animal type*, which implies that the overall order is by animal type. In this case, the Animal Type field would be the major sort key and the Cost field would be the minor sort key.
- Determine sort order. Words such as *increasing*, *ascending*, or *low-to-high* imply Ascending order. Words such as *decreasing*, *descending*, or *high-to-low* imply Descending order. Sorting in *alphabetical order* implies Ascending order. If there were no words to imply a particular order, you would typically use Ascending.
- Examine the query or request to see if there are any special restrictions. One common restriction is to exclude duplicates. Another common restriction is to list only a certain number of records, such as the first five records.

To Create a Top-Values Query

Rather than show all the results of a query, you may want to show only a specified number of records or a percentage of records. ***Why?*** *You might not need to see all the records, just enough to get a general idea of the results.* Creating a **top-values query** allows you to restrict the number of records that appear. When you sort records, you can limit results to those records having the highest (descending sort) or lowest (ascending sort) values. To do so, first create a query that sorts the data in the desired order. Next, use the Return box on the Design tab to change the number of records to be included from All to the desired number or percentage.

The following steps create a query for CMF Vets managers that shows only the first five records that were included in the results of the previous query. The steps also save the resulting query with a new name.

1

- Return to Design view.
- If necessary, click Design on the ribbon to display the Design tab.
- Click the Return arrow (Query Tools Design tab | Query Setup group) to display the Return menu (Figure 2–40).

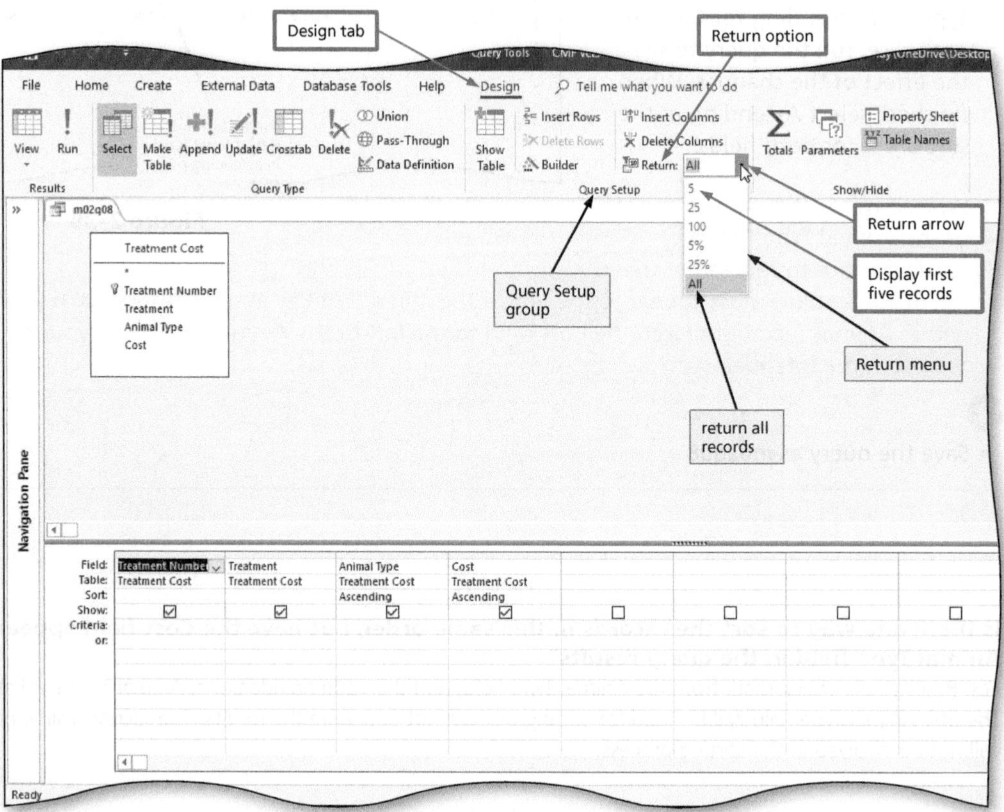

Figure 2–40

2

- Click 5 in the Return menu to specify that the query results should contain the first five rows.

Q&A Could I have typed the 5? What about other numbers that do not appear in the list?

Yes, you could have typed the 5. For numbers not appearing in the list, you must type the number.

- Run the query (Figure 2–41) to display only the first five records.

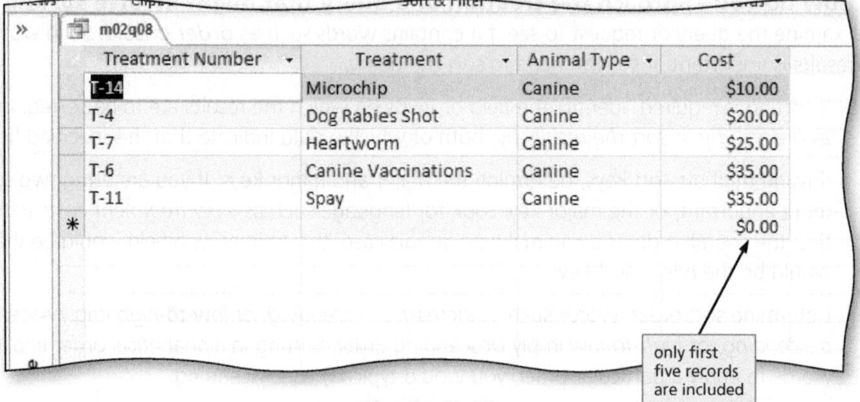

Treatment Number	Treatment	Animal Type	Cost
T-14	Microchip	Canine	$10.00
T-4	Dog Rabies Shot	Canine	$20.00
T-7	Heartworm	Canine	$25.00
T-6	Canine Vaccinations	Canine	$35.00
T-11	Spay	Canine	$35.00
*			$0.00

Figure 2–41

3

- Save the query as m02q09.
- Close the query.

Q&A Do I need to close the query before creating my next query?
Not necessarily. When you use a top-values query, however, it is important to change the value in the Return box back to All. If you do not change the Return value back to All, the previous value will remain in effect. Consequently, you might not get all the records you should in the next query. A good practice whenever you use a top-values query is to close the query as soon as you are done. That way, you will begin your next query from scratch, which ensures that the value is reset to All.

Joining Tables

In designing a query, you need to determine whether more than one table is required. For example, if the question being asked involves data from both the Appointments and Treatment Cost tables, then both tables are required for the query. For example, you might want a query that shows the appointment dates (from the Appointments table) along with the cost of the treatment and animal type (from the Treatment Cost table). Both the Appointments and Treatment Cost tables are required for this query. You need to **join** the tables to find records in the two tables that have identical values in matching fields (Figure 2–42). In this example, you need to find records in the Appointments table that have the same value in the Treatment Cost fields.

BTW
Ad Hoc Relationships
When you join tables in a query, you are creating an ad hoc relationship, that is, a relationship between tables created for a specific purpose and not a permanent change. To create general-purpose relationships, you use the Relationships window.

BTW
Join Types
The type of join that finds records from both tables that have identical values in matching fields is called an inner join. An inner join is the default join in Access. Outer joins are used to show all the records in one table as well as the common records; that is, the records that share the same value in the join field. In a left outer join, all rows from the table on the left are included. In a right outer join, all rows from the table on the right are included.

Appointments Table

Appointment ID	Patient ID	Appointment Date	Appointment Time	Treatment Number	Veterinarian	Owner
1	F-1	6/30/2021	10:00 AM	T-3	B01	0-1
2	C-2	10/25/2021	9:00 AM	T-4	B01	0-1
3	C-2	1/10/2021	10:00 AM	T-2	B01	0-1
4	F-1	6/30/2021	10:00 AM	T-1	B01	0-1
5	C-1	8/23/2021	10:00 AM	T-4	G01	0-2

Treatment Cost Table

Treatment Number	Treatment	Animal Type	Cost
T-1	Feline Rabies Shot	Feline	$18
T-10	Neuter	Feline	$25
T-11	Spay	Canine	$35
T-12	Neuter	Canine	$40
T-13	Microchip	Feline	$10
T-14	Microchip	Canine	$10
T-2	Dog Wellness Exam	Canine	$50
T-3	Wellness	Feline	$20
T-4	Dog Rabies Shot	Canine	$20
T-5	Feline Vaccinations	Feline	$30
T-6	Canine Vaccinations	Canine	$35
T-7	Heartworm	Canine	$25
T-8	Heartworm	Feline	$20
T-9	Spay	Feline	$25

for each appointment date, give the Treatment, Animal Type, and Cost

Figure 2–42

To Join Tables

If you have determined that you need to join tables, you first will bring field lists for both tables to the upper pane of the query window while working in Design view. Access will draw a line, called a **join line**, between matching fields in the two tables, indicating that the tables are related. You then can select fields from either table. Access joins the tables automatically.

The first step is to create a new query and add the Appointments table to the query. Then, add the Treatment Cost table to the query. A join line should appear, connecting the Treatment Number fields in the two field lists. ***Why might the join line not appear?*** *If the names of the matching fields differ from one table to the other, Access will not insert the line. You can insert it manually, however, by clicking one of the two matching fields and dragging the pointer to the other matching field.*

The following steps create a query to display information from both the Appointments table and the Treatment Cost table.

- Click the Query Design button (Create tab | Queries group) to create a new query.
- If necessary, click the Appointments table (Show Table dialog box) to select the table.
- Click the Add button (Show Table dialog box) to add a field list for the Appointments Table to the query (Figure 2–43).

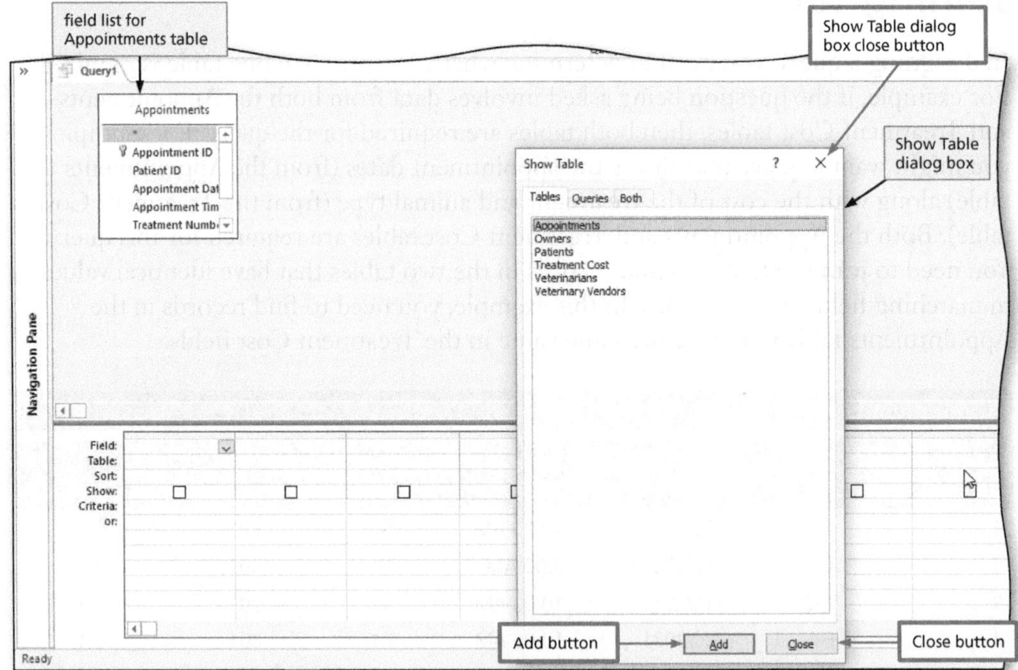

Figure 2–43

- Click the Treatment Cost table (Show Table dialog box).
- Click the Add button (Show Table dialog box) to add a field list for the Treatment Cost table.
- Close the Show Table dialog box by clicking its Close button.
- Expand the size of the two field lists so all the fields in the Appointments and Treatment Cost tables appear (Figure 2–44).

Q&A I did not get a join line. What should I do?
Ensure that the names of the matching fields are the same, the data types are the same, and the matching field is the primary key in one of the two tables. If all of these factors are true and you still do not have a join line, you can produce one by pointing to a matching field and dragging to the other matching field.

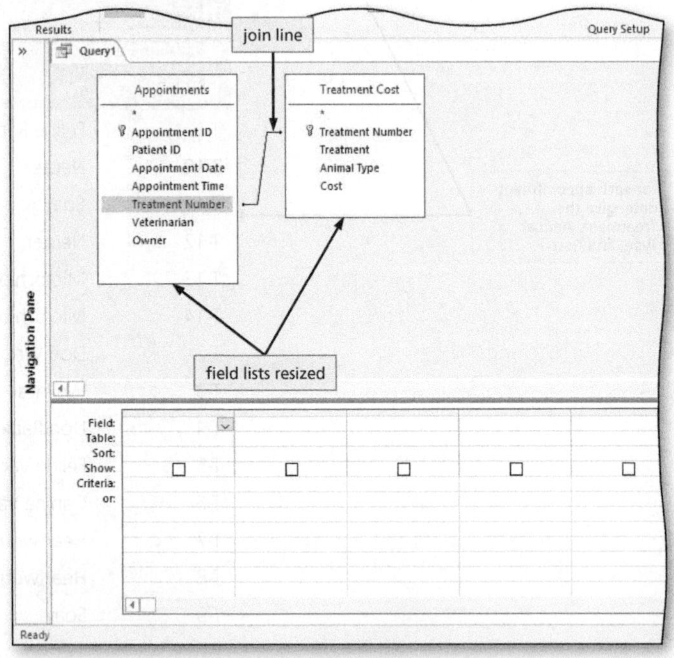

Figure 2–44

3

- In the design grid, include the Appointment Date field from the Appointments Table as well as the Treatment, Animal Type, and Cost fields from the Treatment Cost Table.
- Select Ascending as the sort order for both the Appointment Date field and the Treatment field (Figure 2–45).

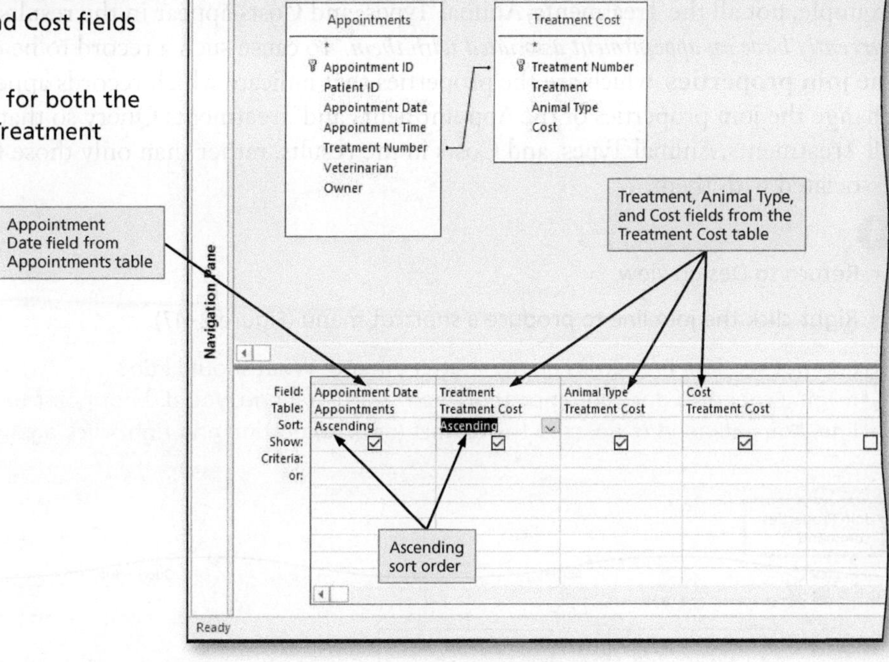

Figure 2–45

4

- Run the query (Figure 2–46).

5

- Click the Save button on the Quick Access Toolbar to display the Save As dialog box.
- Enter `Appointments and Treatments` as the query name.
- Click OK (Save As dialog box) to save the query.

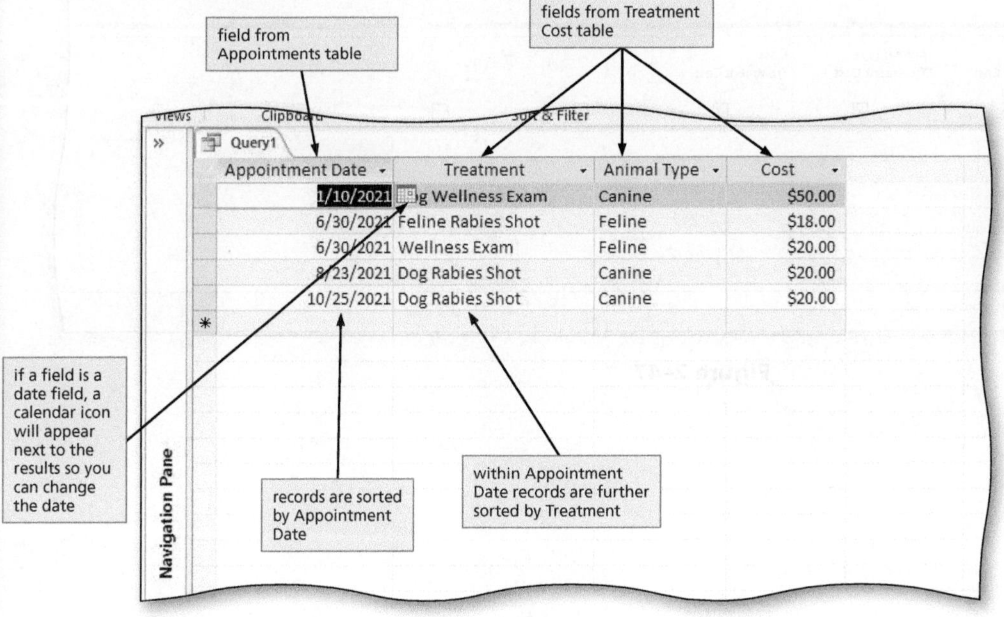

Figure 2–46

BTW

Join Line

If you do not get a join line automatically, there might be a problem with one of your table designs. Open each table in Design view and make sure that the data types are the same for the matching field in both tables and that one of the matching fields is the primary key in a table. If not, correct these errors and create the query again.

To Change Join Properties

Normally, records that do not match the query conditions do not appear in the results of a join query. For example, not all the Treatments, Animal Types, and Costs appear in the results. ***Why?*** *Not all of the treatments currently have an appointment associated with them.* To cause such a record to be displayed, you need to change the **join properties**, which are the properties that indicate which records appear in a join. The following steps change the join properties of the Appointments and Treatments Query so that CMF Vets managers can include all Treatments, Animal Types, and Costs in the results, rather than only those fields that have Appointments associated with them.

- Return to Design view.
- Right-click the join line to produce a shortcut menu (Figure 2–47).

Q&A I do not see Join Properties on my shortcut menu. What should I do?
If Join Properties does not appear on your shortcut menu, you did not point to the appropriate portion of the join line. You will need to point to the correct (middle) portion and right-click again.

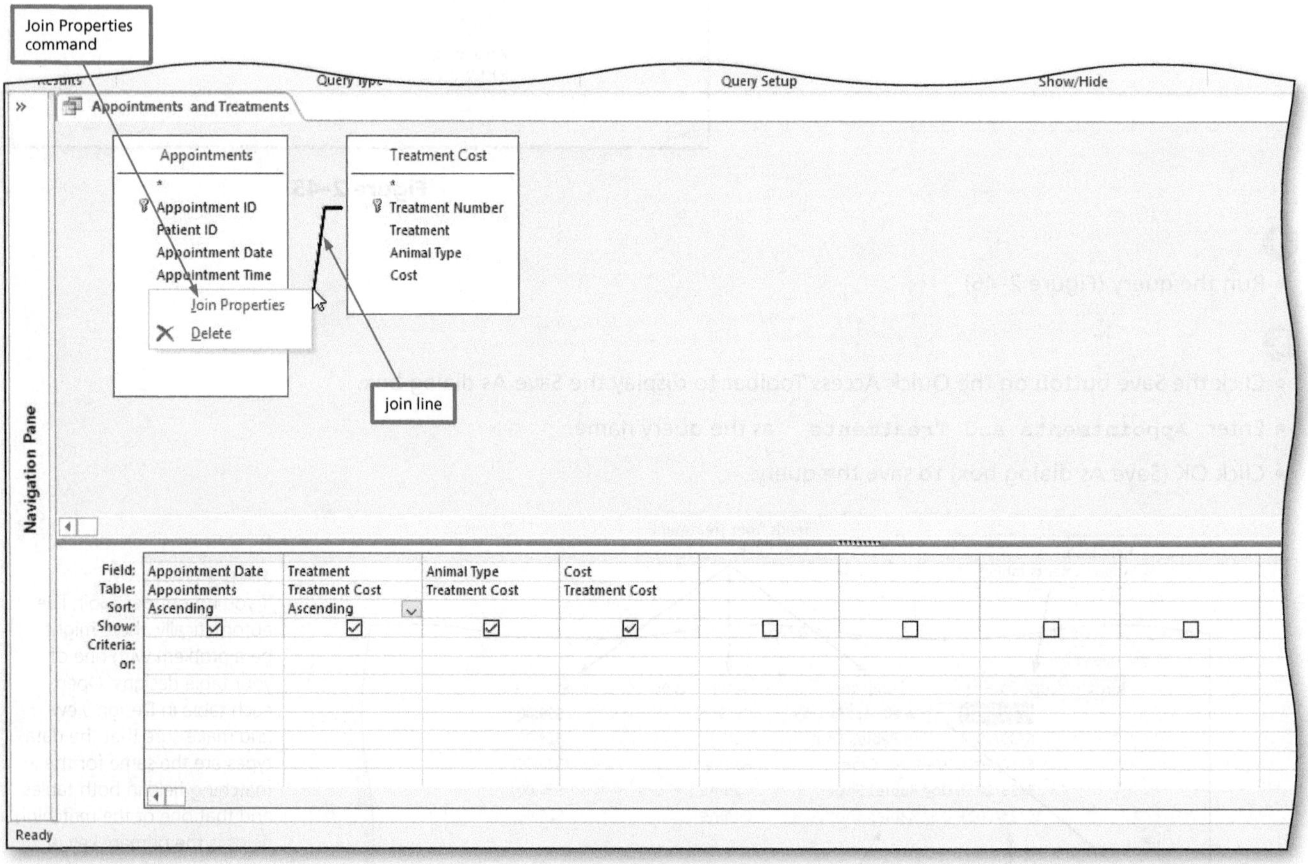

Figure 2–47

2

- Click Join Properties on the shortcut menu to display the Join Properties dialog box (Figure 2–48).

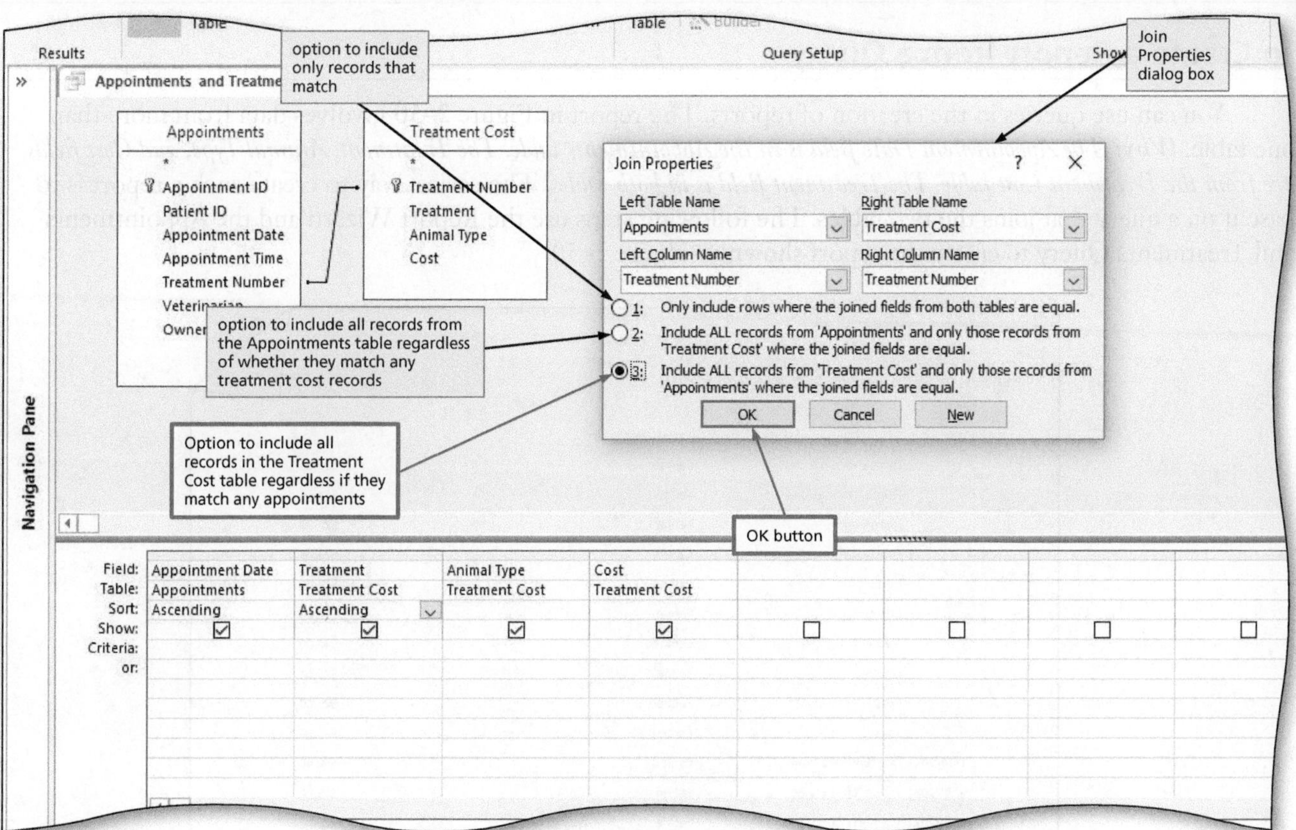

Figure 2–48

3

- Click option button 3 (Join Properties dialog box) to include all records from the Treatment Cost Table regardless of whether they match any appointments.
- Click OK (Join Properties dialog box) to modify the join properties and close the Join Properties dialog box.
- Run the query (Figure 2–49).

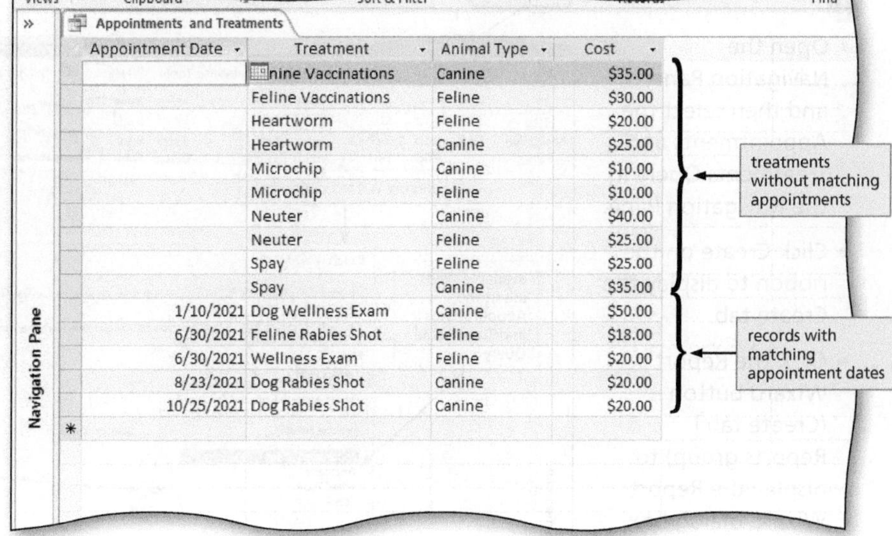

Appointment Date	Treatment	Animal Type	Cost
	Canine Vaccinations	Canine	$35.00
	Feline Vaccinations	Feline	$30.00
	Heartworm	Feline	$20.00
	Heartworm	Canine	$25.00
	Microchip	Canine	$10.00
	Microchip	Feline	$10.00
	Neuter	Canine	$40.00
	Neuter	Feline	$25.00
	Spay	Feline	$25.00
	Spay	Canine	$35.00
1/10/2021	Dog Wellness Exam	Canine	$50.00
6/30/2021	Feline Rabies Shot	Feline	$18.00
6/30/2021	Wellness Exam	Feline	$20.00
8/23/2021	Dog Rabies Shot	Canine	$20.00
10/25/2021	Dog Rabies Shot	Canine	$20.00

Figure 2–49

Experiment

- Return to Design view, change the Join properties, and select option button 2. Run the query to see the effect of this option. When done, return to Design view, change the join properties, and once again select option button 3.

4

- Click the Save button on the Quick Access Toolbar to save the changes to the query.
- Close the Appointments and Treatments Query.

Q&A I see a dialog box that asks if I want to save the query. What should I do?
Click OK to save the query.

To Create a Report from a Query

You can use queries in the creation of reports. The report in Figure 2–50 involves data from more than one table. ***Why?*** *The Appointment Date field is in the Appointments table. The Treatment, Animal Type, and Cost fields are from the Treatment Cost table. The Treatment field is in both tables.* The easiest way to create such a report is to base it on a query that joins the two tables. The following steps use the Report Wizard and the Appointments and Treatments Query to create the report shown in Figure 2–50.

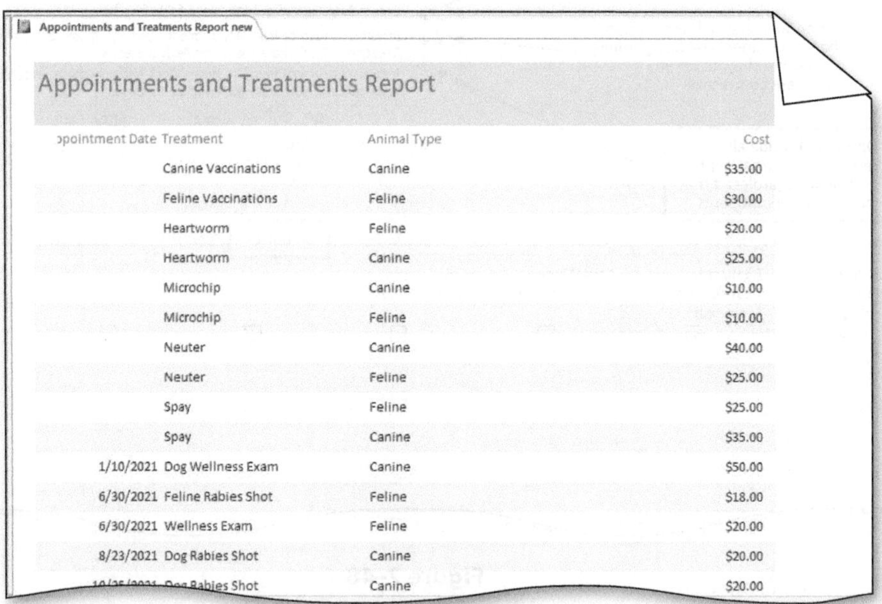

Figure 2–50

- Open the Navigation Pane, and then select the Appointments and Treatments Query in the Navigation Pane.
- Click Create on the ribbon to display the Create tab.
- Click the Report Wizard button (Create tab | Reports group) to display the Report Wizard dialog box (Figure 2–51).

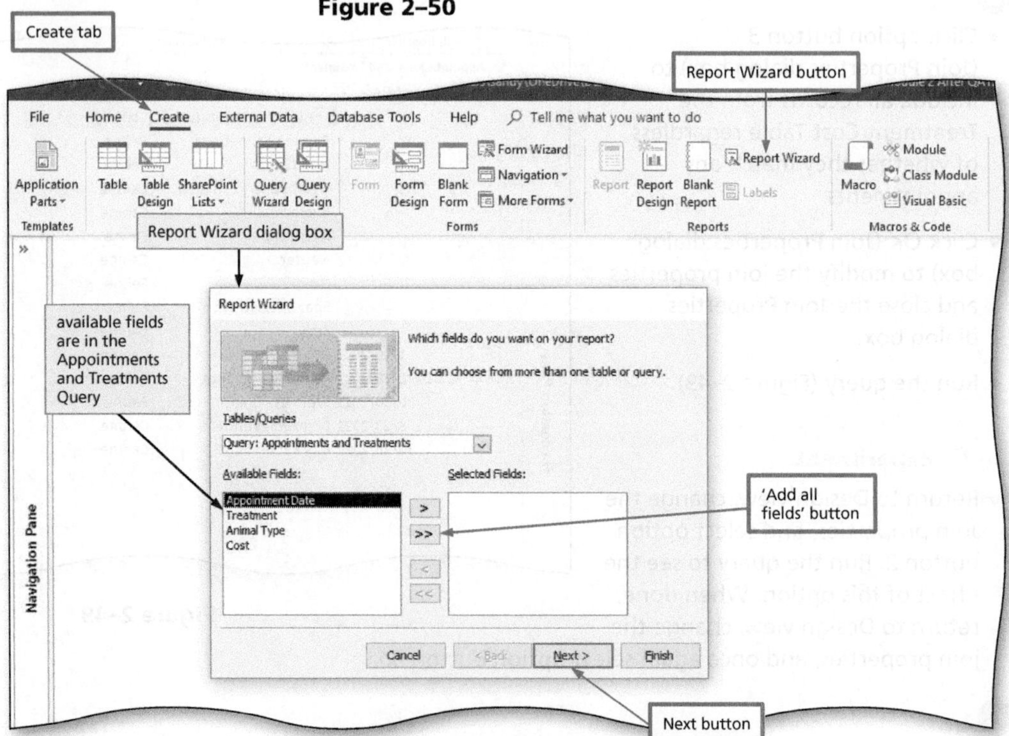

Figure 2–51

2

- Click the 'Add All Fields' button (Report Wizard dialog box) to add all the fields in the Appointments and Treatments Query.
- Click Next to display the next Report Wizard screen (Figure 2–52).

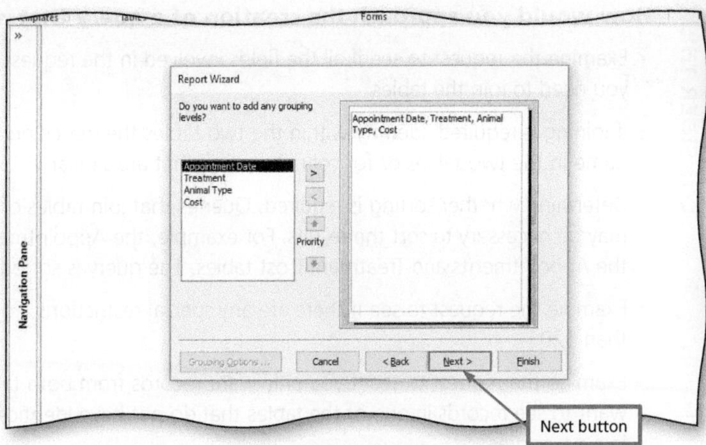

Figure 2–52

- Because you will not specify any grouping, click Next again to display the next Report Wizard screen.
- Because you already specified the sort order in the query, click Next again to display the next Report Wizard screen.
- Make sure that Tabular is selected as the Layout and Portrait is selected as the Orientation.
- Click Next to display the next Report Wizard screen.
- If necessary, erase the current title, and then type **`Appointments and Treatments Report`** as the new title.
- Click the Finish button to produce the report (Figure 2–53).

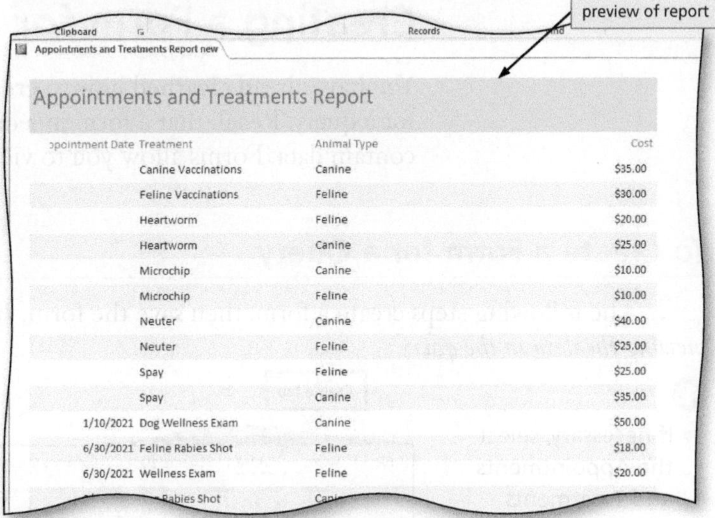

Figure 2–53

Q&A My report is very small and does not look like the one in the figure. What should I do?
Click the pointer, which should look like a magnifying glass, anywhere in the report to magnify the report.

- Close the Appointments and Treatments Report.

To Print a Report

Often, users will need to distribute database information in a printed format. CMF Vets would like to share the Appointments and Treatments reports with stakeholders who prefer a hard copy. The following steps print a hard copy of the report.

1 With the Appointments and Treatments Report selected in the Navigation Pane, click File on the ribbon to open the Backstage view.

2 Click the Print tab in the Backstage view to display the Print gallery.

3 Click the Quick Print button to print the report.

CONSIDER THIS

How would you approach the creation of a query that might involve multiple tables?

- Examine the request to see if all the fields involved in the request are in one table. If the fields are in two (or more) tables, you need to join the tables.
- If joining is required, identify within the two tables the matching fields that have identical values. Look for the same column name in the two tables or for column names that are similar.
- Determine whether sorting is required. Queries that join tables often are used as the basis for a report. If this is the case, it may be necessary to sort the results. For example, the Appointments and Treatments Report is based on a query that joins the Appointments and Treatment Cost tables. The query is sorted by Appointment Date and Treatment.
- Examine the request to see if there are any special restrictions. For example, the user may only want treatment costs higher than $20.
- Examine the request to see if you only want records from both tables that have identical values in matching fields. If you want to see records in one of the tables that do not have identical values in the other table, then you need to change the join properties.

Creating a Form for a Query

You have already learned how to create a form for a table. You can also create a form for a query. Recall that a form in a database is a formatted document with fields that contain data. Forms allow you to view and maintain data.

To Create a Form for a Query

The following steps create a form, then save the form. ***Why?*** *The form will be available for future use in viewing the data in the query.*

- If necessary, select the Appointments and Treatments Query in the Navigation Pane.
- Click Create on the ribbon to display the Create tab (Figure 2–54).

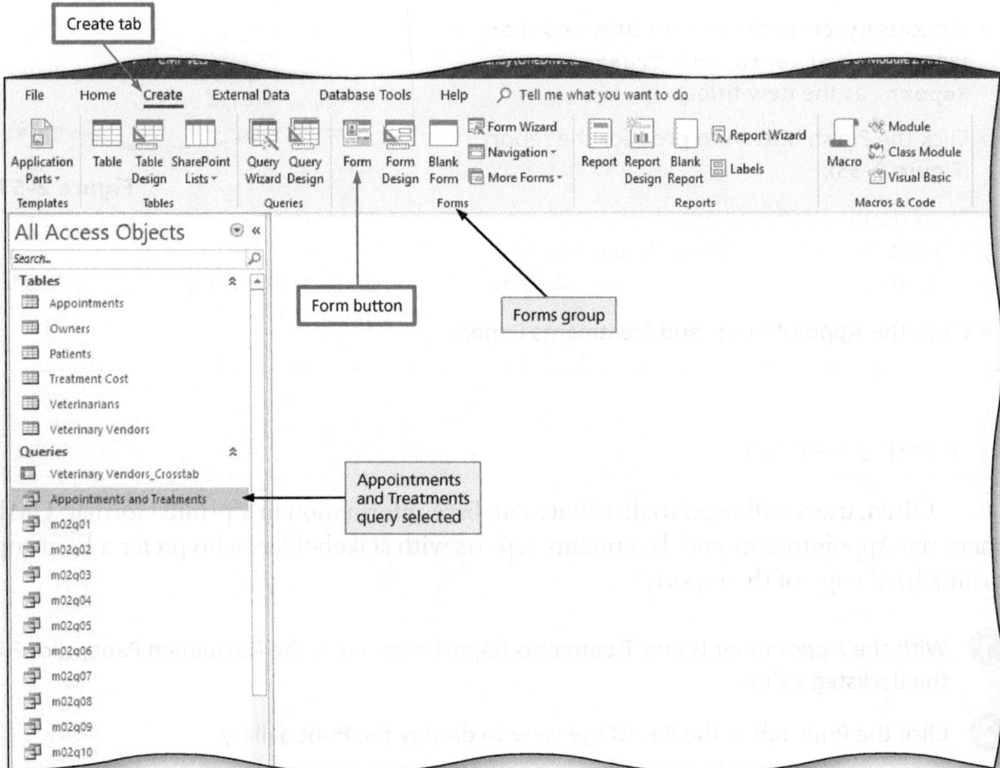

Figure 2–54

2

- Click the Form button (Create tab | Forms group) to create a simple form (Figure 2–55).

Q&A I see a field list also. What should I do?
Click Close for the Field List.

3

- Click the Save button on the Quick Access Toolbar to display the Save As dialog box.

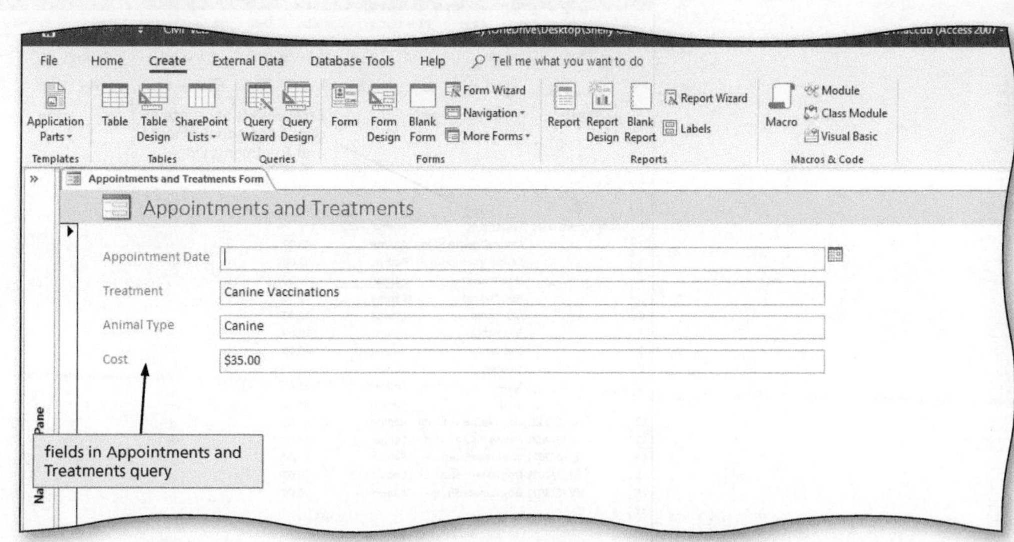

Figure 2–55

- Enter `Form` at the end of the Appointments and Treatments name so that Appointments and Treatments Form appears as the complete name.

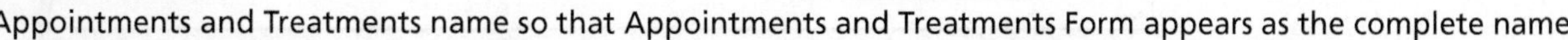

- Click OK to save the form.
- Click Close for the form to close the form.

Using a Form

After you have saved a form, you can use it at any time by right-clicking the form in the Navigation Pane and then clicking Open on the shortcut menu. If you plan to use the form to enter data, you must ensure you are viewing the form in Form view.

Break Point: If you wish to take a break, this is a good place to do so. You can exit Access now. To resume later, start Access, open the database called CMF Vets, and continue following the steps from this location forward.

Exporting Data from Access to Other Applications

You can **export**, or copy, tables or queries from an Access database so that another application (for example, Excel or Word) can use the data. The application that will receive the data determines the export process to be used. You can export to text files in a variety of formats. For applications to which you cannot directly export data, you often can export an appropriately formatted text file that the other application can import. Figure 2–56 shows the workbook produced by exporting the Appointments and Treatments Query to Excel. The columns in the workbook have been resized to best fit the data.

BTW
Exporting Data
You frequently need to export data so that it can be used in other applications and by other users in an organization. For example, the Accounting department might require financial data in an Excel format to perform certain financial functions. Marketing might require a list of owner names and addresses in Word or RTF format for marketing campaigns.

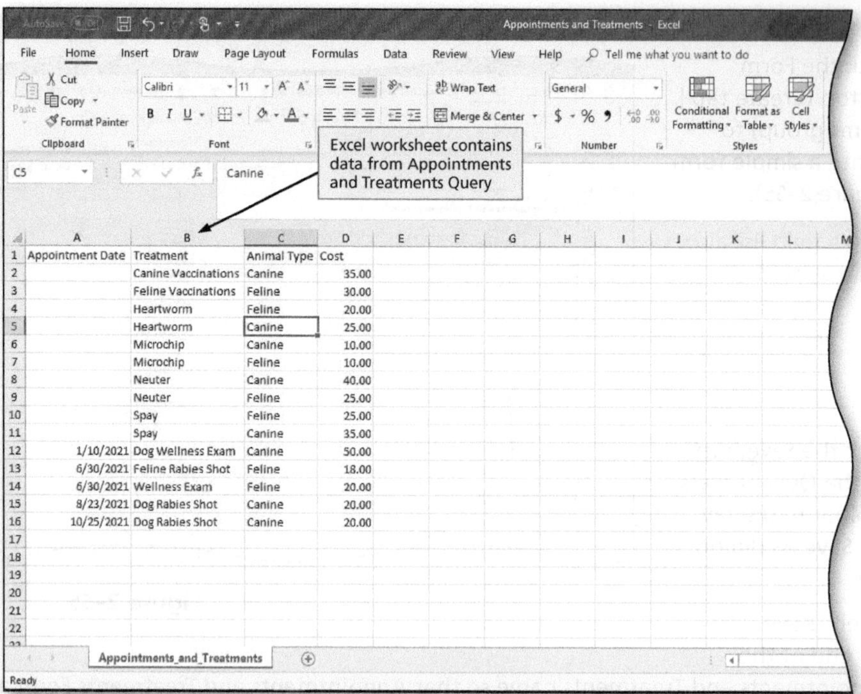

Appointment Date	Treatment	Animal Type	Cost
	Canine Vaccinations	Canine	35.00
	Feline Vaccinations	Feline	30.00
	Heartworm	Feline	20.00
	Heartworm	Canine	25.00
	Microchip	Canine	10.00
	Microchip	Feline	10.00
	Neuter	Canine	40.00
	Neuter	Feline	25.00
	Spay	Feline	25.00
	Spay	Canine	35.00
1/10/2021	Dog Wellness Exam	Canine	50.00
6/30/2021	Feline Rabies Shot	Feline	18.00
6/30/2021	Wellness Exam	Feline	20.00
8/23/2021	Dog Rabies Shot	Canine	20.00
10/25/2021	Dog Rabies Shot	Canine	20.00

Figure 2–56

To Export Data to Excel

For CMF Vets managers to make the Appointments and Treatments Query available to Excel users, they need to export the data. To export data to Excel, select the table or query to be exported and then click the Excel button in the Export group on the External Data tab. The following steps export the Appointments and Treatments Query to Excel and save the export steps. ***Why save the export steps?*** *By saving the export steps, you could easily repeat the export process whenever you like without going through all the steps.* You would use the saved steps to export data in the future by clicking the Saved Exports button (External Data tab | Export group) and then selecting the steps you saved.

- If necessary, click the Appointments and Treatments Query in the Navigation Pane to select it.
- Click External Data on the ribbon to display the External Data tab (Figure 2–57).

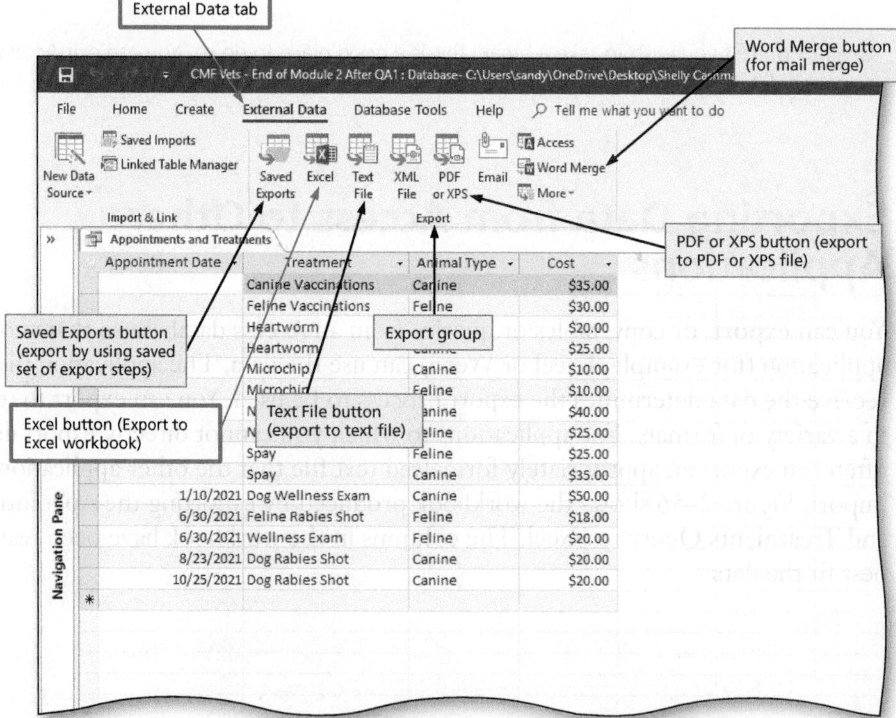

Appointment Date	Treatment	Animal Type	Cost
	Canine Vaccinations	Canine	$35.00
	Feline Vaccinations	Feline	$30.00
	Heartworm	Feline	$20.00
	Heartworm	Canine	$25.00
	Microchip	Canine	$10.00
	Microchip	Feline	$10.00
	Neuter	Canine	$40.00
	Neuter	Feline	$25.00
	Spay	Feline	$25.00
	Spay	Canine	$35.00
1/10/2021	Dog Wellness Exam	Canine	$50.00
6/30/2021	Feline Rabies Shot	Feline	$18.00
6/30/2021	Wellness Exam	Feline	$20.00
8/23/2021	Dog Rabies Shot	Canine	$20.00
10/25/2021	Dog Rabies Shot	Canine	$20.00

Figure 2–57

2

- Click the Excel button (External Data tab | Export group) to display the Export-Excel Spreadsheet dialog box.
- Click the Browse button (Export-Excel Spreadsheet dialog box), and then navigate to the location where you want to export the query (your hard drive, OneDrive, or other storage location).
- Confirm that the file format is Excel Workbook (*.xlsx), and the file name is Appointments and Treatments as the query name and then click the Save button (File Save dialog box) to select the file name and location (Figure 2–58).

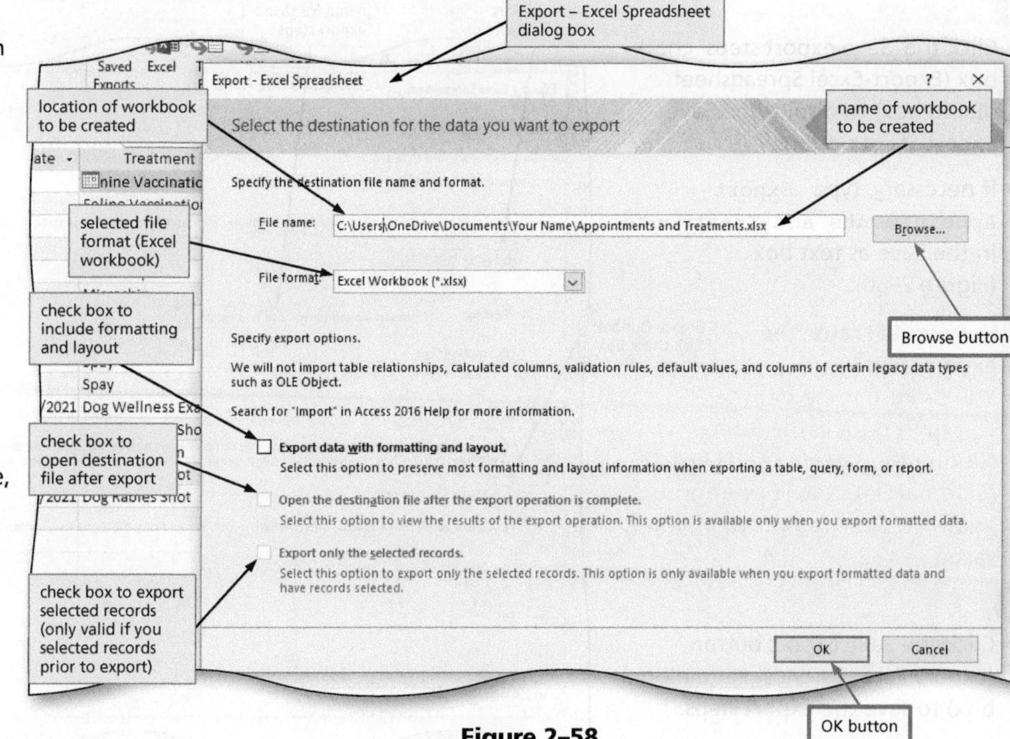

Figure 2–58

Q&A

Did I need to browse?
No. You could type the appropriate file location.

Could I change the name of the file?
You could change it. Simply replace the current file name with the one you want.

What if the file I want to export already exists?
Access will indicate that the file already exists and ask if you want to replace it. If you click Yes, the file you export will replace the old file. If you click No, you must either change the name of the export file or cancel the process.

3

- Click OK (Export-Excel Spreadsheet dialog box) to export the data (Figure 2–59).

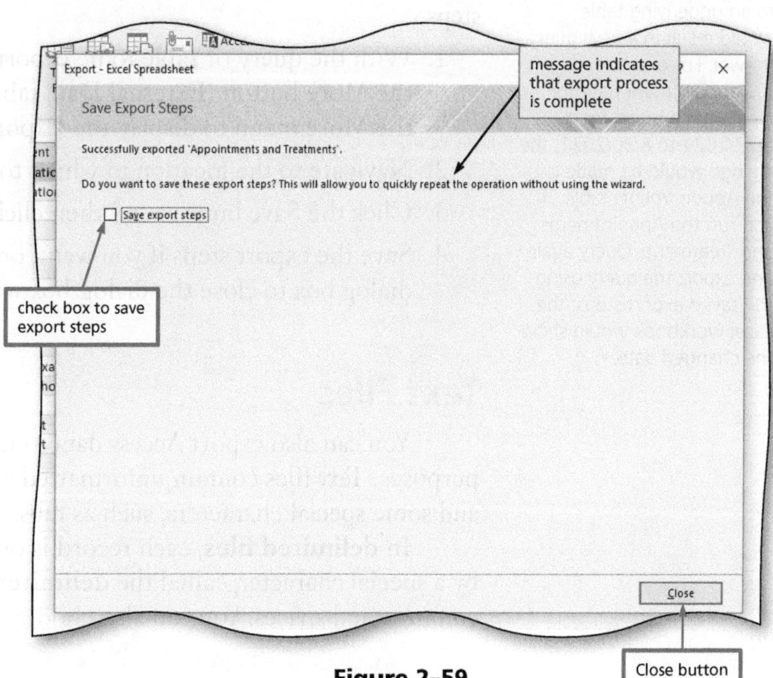

Figure 2–59

4

- Click the 'Save export steps' check box (Export-Excel Spreadsheet dialog box) to display the Save Export Steps options.
- If necessary, type **`Export-Appointments and Treatments`** in the Save as text box (Figure 2–60).

Q&A How could I reuse the export steps?
You can use these steps to export data in the future by clicking the Saved Exports button (External Data tab | Export group) and then selecting the steps you saved.

5

- Click the Save Export button (Export-Excel Spreadsheet dialog box) to save the export steps.

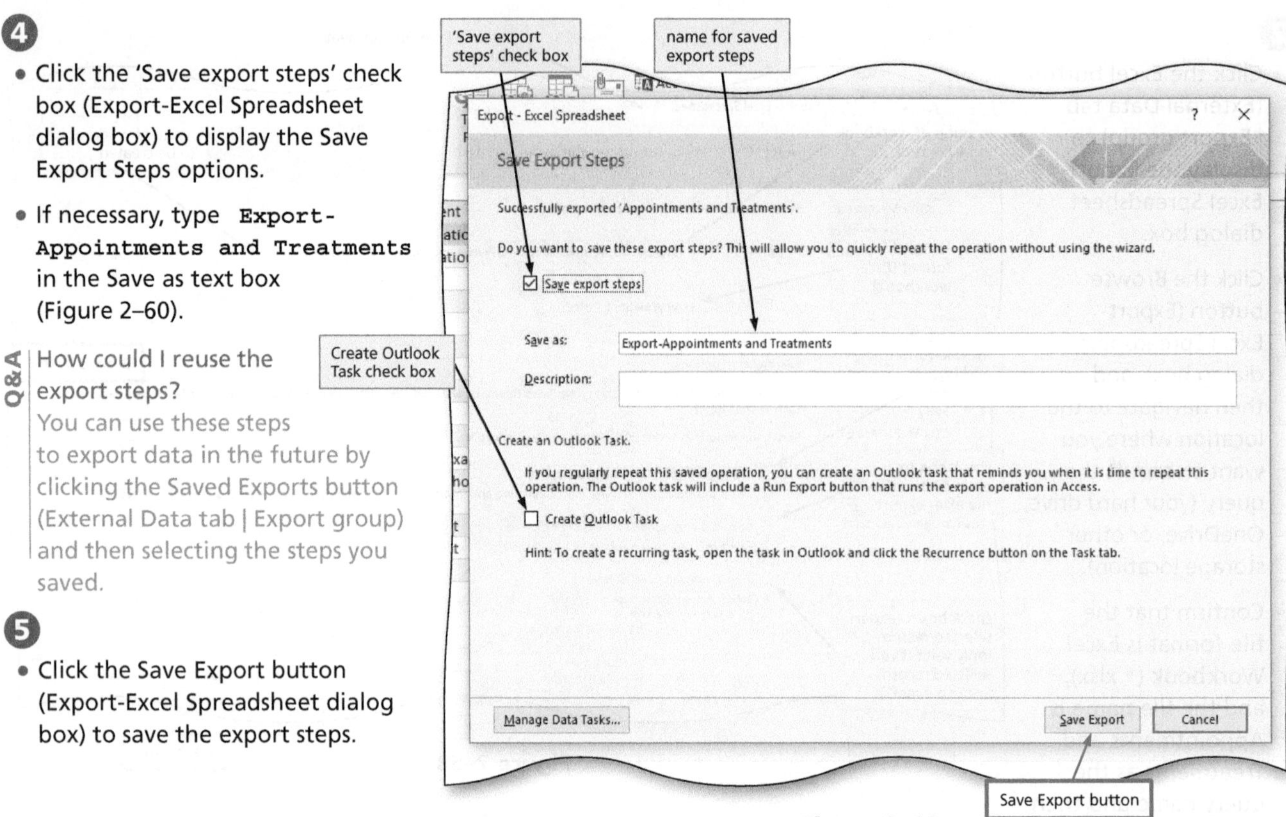

Figure 2–60

Other Ways

1. Right-click database object in Navigation Pane, click Export

BTW

Saving Export Steps
Because query results are based on the data in the underlying tables, a change to an underlying table would result in a new query answer. For example, if the appointment date for a patient changed from 8/23/2021 to 8/30/2021, the change would be made in the Appointments table. If you run the Appointments and Treatments Query again and export the query using the saved export steps, the Excel workbook would show the changed date.

To Export Data to Word

It is not possible to export data from Access to the standard Word format. It is possible, however, to export the data as a rich text format (RTF) file, which Word can use. To export data from a query or table to an RTF file, you would use the following steps.

1. With the query or table to be exported selected in the Navigation Pane, click the More button (External Data tab | Export group) and then click Word on the More menu to display the Export-RTF File dialog box.
2. Navigate to the location in which to save the file and assign a file name.
3. Click the Save button, and then click OK to export the data.
4. Save the export steps if you want, or simply click Close in the Export-RTF File dialog box to close the dialog box without saving the export steps.

Text Files

You can also export Access data to text files, which can be used for a variety of purposes. Text files contain unformatted characters, including alphanumeric characters, and some special characters, such as tabs, carriage returns, and line feeds.

In **delimited files**, each record is on a separate line and the fields are separated by a special character, called the **delimiter**. Common delimiters are tabs, semicolons, commas, and spaces. You can also choose any other value that does not appear within the field contents as the delimiter. The comma-separated values (CSV) file often used in Excel is an example of a delimited file.

In **fixed-width files**, the width of any field is the same on every record. For example, if the width of the first field on the first record is 12 characters, the width of the first field on every other record must also be 12 characters.

TO EXPORT DATA TO A TEXT FILE

When exporting data to a text file, you can choose to export the data with formatting and layout. This option preserves much of the formatting and layout in tables, queries, forms, and reports. For forms and reports, this is the only option for exporting to a text file.

If you do not need to preserve the formatting, you can choose either delimited or fixed-width as the format for the exported file. The most common option, especially if formatting is not an issue, is delimited. You can choose the delimiter. You can also choose whether to include field names on the first row. In many cases, delimiting with a comma and including the field names is a good choice.

To export data from a table or query to a comma-delimited file in which the first row contains the column headings, you would use the following steps.

1. With the query or table to be exported selected in the Navigation Pane, click the Text File button (External Data tab | Export group) to display the Export-Text File dialog box.
2. Select the name and location for the file to be created.
3. If you need to preserve formatting and layout, be sure the 'Export data with formatting and layout' check box is checked. If you do not need to preserve formatting and layout, make sure the check box is not checked. Once you have made your selection, click OK in the Export-Text File dialog box.
4. To create a delimited file, be sure the Delimited option button is selected in the Export Text Wizard dialog box. To create a fixed-width file, be sure the Fixed Width option button is selected. Once you have made your selection, click the Next button.
5. a. If you are exporting to a delimited file, choose the delimiter that you want to separate your fields, such as a comma. Decide whether to include field names on the first row and, if so, click the 'Include Field Names on First Row' check box. If you want to select a text qualifier, select it in the Text Qualifier list. When you have made your selections, click the Next button.
   b. If you are exporting to a fixed-width file, review the position of the vertical lines that separate your fields. If any lines are not positioned correctly, follow the directions on the screen to reposition them. When you have finished, click the Next button.
6. Click the Finish button to export the data.
7. Save the export steps if you want, or simply click Close in the Export-Text File dialog box to close the dialog box without saving the export steps.

BTW
Distributing a Document
Instead of printing and distributing a hard copy of a document, you can distribute the document electronically. Options include sending the document via email; posting it on cloud storage (such as OneDrive) and sharing the file with others; posting it on social media, a blog, or other website; and sharing a link associated with an online location of the document. You also can create and share a PDF or XPS image of the document, so that users can view the file in Acrobat Reader or XPS Viewer instead of in Access.

Adding Criteria to a Join Query

Sometimes you will want to join tables, but you will not want to include all possible records. For example, you would like to create a report showing only those treatments whose cost is greater than $10.00. In this case, you would relate the tables and include fields just as you did before. You will also include criteria. To include only those treatments whose amount cost is more than $10.00, you will include >10 as a criterion for the Cost field.

To Restrict the Records in a Join

The following steps modify the Appointments and Treatments Query so that the results for CMF Vets managers include a criterion. ***Why?** CMF Vets managers want to include only those treatments whose cost is more than $10.*

- Open the Navigation Pane, if necessary, and then right-click the Appointments and Treatments Query to produce a shortcut menu.
- Click Design View on the shortcut menu to open the Appointments and Treatments Query in Design view.
- Close the Navigation Pane.
- Type `>10` as the criterion for the Cost field (Figure 2–61).

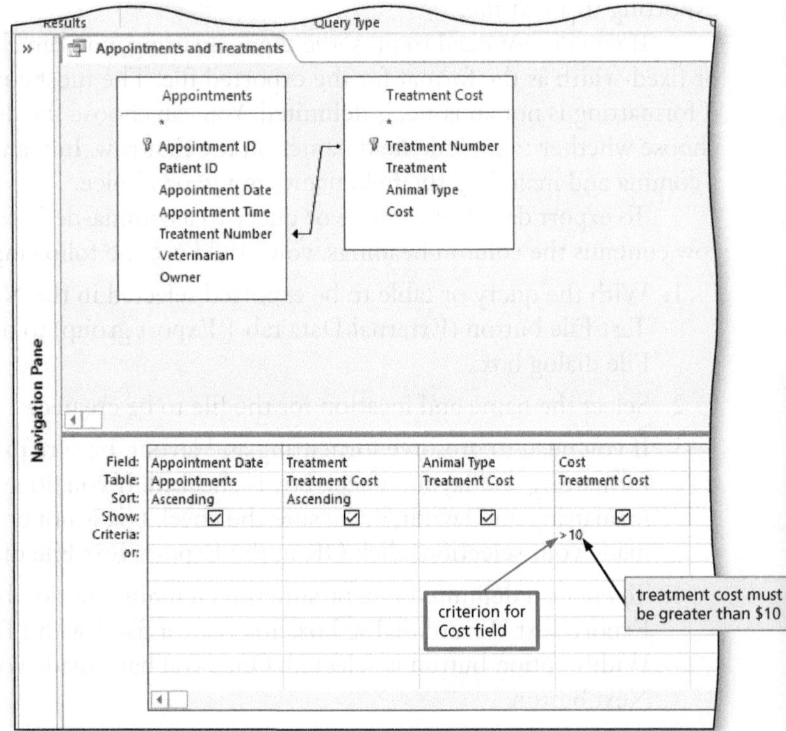

Figure 2–61

2

- Run the query (Figure 2–62).

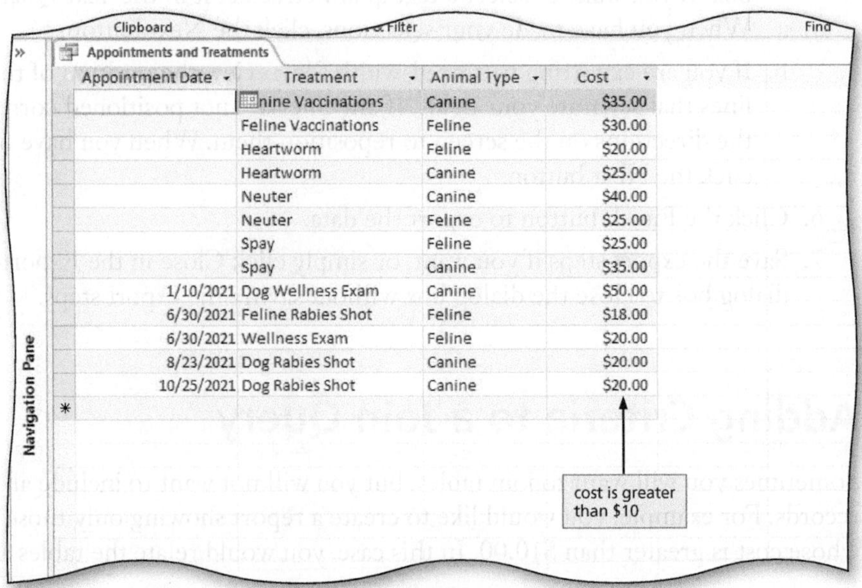

Appointment Date	Treatment	Animal Type	Cost
	[Ca]nine Vaccinations	Canine	$35.00
	Feline Vaccinations	Feline	$30.00
	Heartworm	Feline	$20.00
	Heartworm	Canine	$25.00
	Neuter	Canine	$40.00
	Neuter	Feline	$25.00
	Spay	Feline	$25.00
	Spay	Canine	$35.00
1/10/2021	Dog Wellness Exam	Canine	$50.00
6/30/2021	Feline Rabies Shot	Feline	$18.00
6/30/2021	Wellness Exam	Feline	$20.00
8/23/2021	Dog Rabies Shot	Canine	$20.00
10/25/2021	Dog Rabies Shot	Canine	$20.00

Figure 2–62

3

- Close the query.
- When asked if you want to save your changes, click No.

Q&A What would happen if I saved the changes?
The next time you used this query, you would only see treatments whose cost is more than $10.

Calculations

BTW
Expression Builder
Access includes a tool to help you create complex expressions. If you click Build on the shortcut menu (see Figure 2–63), Access displays the Expression Builder dialog box, which includes an expression box, operator buttons, and expression elements. You can type parts of the expression directly and paste operator buttons and expression elements into the box. You also can use functions in expressions.

If a special calculation is required for a query, you need to determine whether the calculation is an **individual record calculation** (for example, adding the values in two fields for one record) or a **group calculation** (for example, finding the total of the values in a particular field on all the records).

CMF Vets managers might want to know the total cost of their inventory in the Veterinary Vendors table (quantity and cost) for each veterinary supply. This would seem to pose a problem because the table does not include a field for total cost. You can calculate it, however, because the total amount is equal to the quantity times the cost. A field that can be computed from other fields is called a **calculated field** or a **computed field** and is not usually included in the table. Including it introduces the possibility for errors in the table. If the value in the field does not happen to match the results of the calculation, the data is inconsistent. A calculated field is an individual record calculation because each calculation only involves fields in a single record.

CMF Vets managers might also want to calculate the average amount paid for the veterinary supplies of each vendor. That is, they may want the average paid for supplies from Duncan Veterinary Supplies, the average paid for supplies of Gaines Vet Supplies, and so on. This type of calculation is called a **group calculation** because each calculation involves groups of records. In this example, the supplies of Duncan Veterinary Supplies would form one group, the supplies of Gaines Vet Supplies would be a second group, and the supplies of Mayes Supplies Corporation would form a third group.

To Use a Calculated Field in a Query

If you need a calculated field in a query, you enter a name, or alias, for the calculated field, a colon, and then the calculation in one of the columns in the Field row of the design grid for the query. Any fields included in the expression must be enclosed in square brackets ([ ]). For example, for the total amount, you will type Total Cost:[Quantity]*[Cost] as the expression.

You can type the expression directly into the Field row in Design view. The preferred method, however, is to select the column in the Field row and then use the Zoom command on its shortcut menu. When Access displays the Zoom dialog box, you can enter the expression. ***Why use the Zoom command?*** *You will not be able to see the entire entry in the Field row, because the space available is not large enough.*

You can use addition (+), subtraction (-), multiplication (*), or division (/) in calculations. If you have multiple calculations in an expression, you can include parentheses to indicate which calculations should be done first.

The following steps create a query that CMF Vets managers might use to obtain financial information on its inventory, including the total cost (quantity * cost), which is a calculated field.

- Create a query with a field list for the Veterinary Vendors table.
- Add the Vendor Name, State, Veterinary Supply, Quantity, and Cost fields to the query.

- Right-click the Field row in the first open column in the design grid to display a shortcut menu (Figure 2–63).

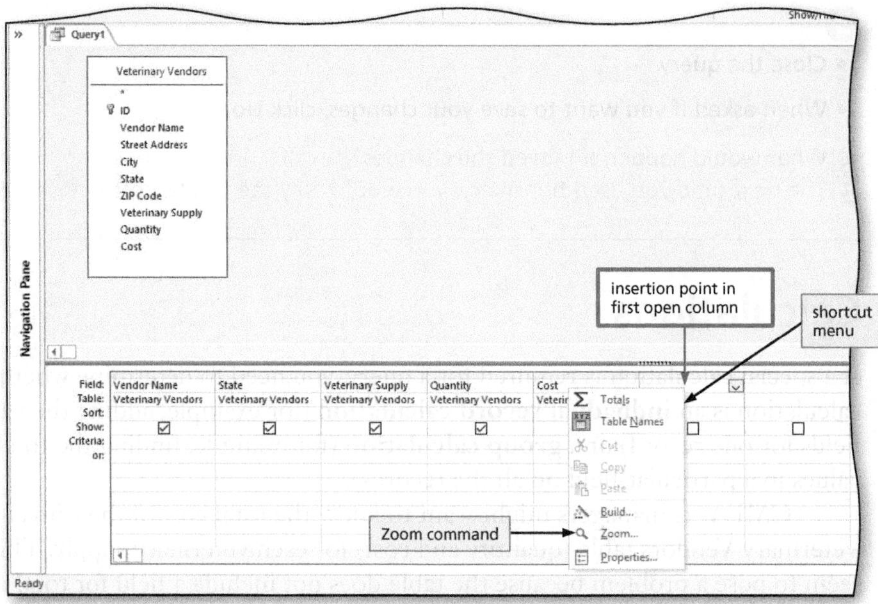

Figure 2–63

2

- Click Zoom on the shortcut menu to display the Zoom dialog box.
- Type `Total Cost:[Quantity]*[Cost]` in the Zoom dialog box (Figure 2–64) to enter the expression.

Q&A Do I always need to put square brackets around field names?
If the field name does not contain spaces, square brackets are technically not required. It is a good practice, however, to get in the habit of using the brackets in field calculations.

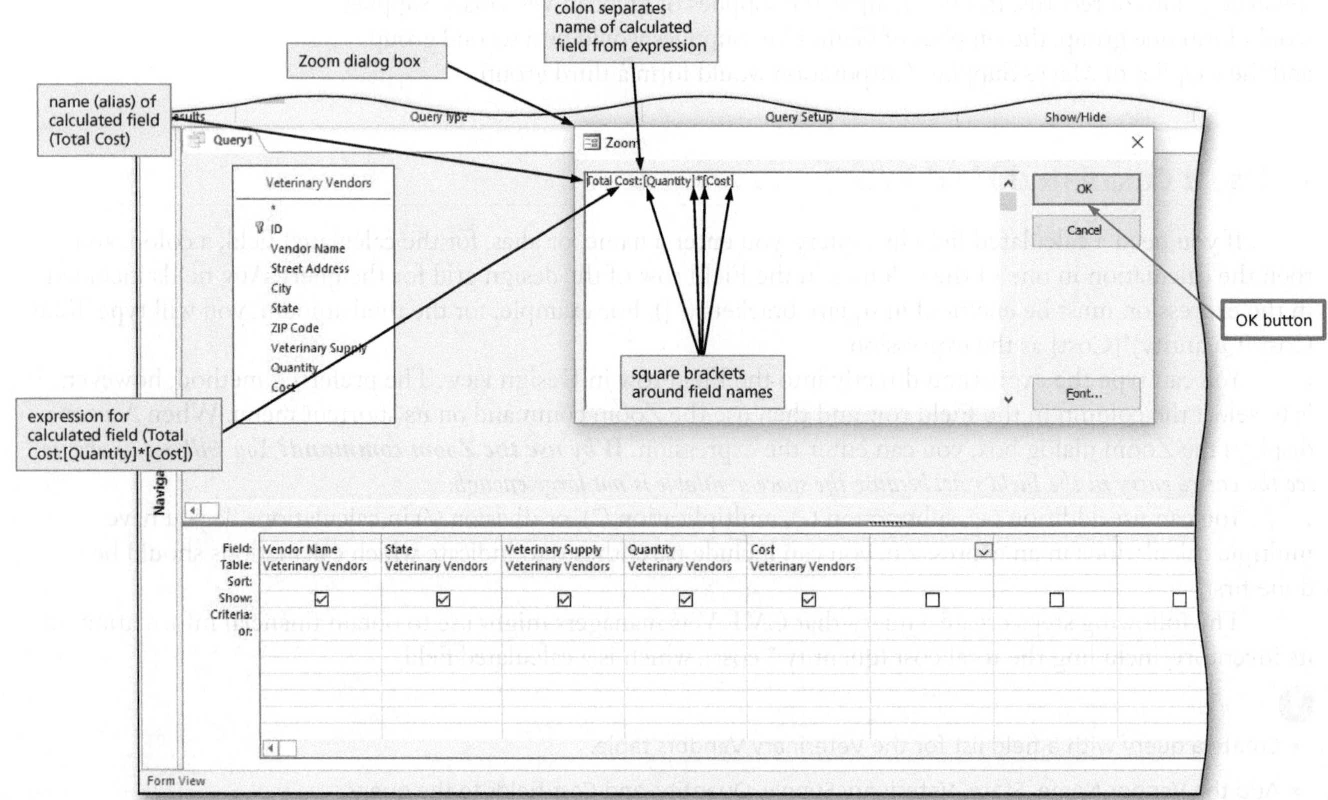

Figure 2–64

3

- Click OK (Zoom dialog box) to complete the expression (Figure 2–65) and close the dialog box.
- Widen the column if necessary to view the entire expression.

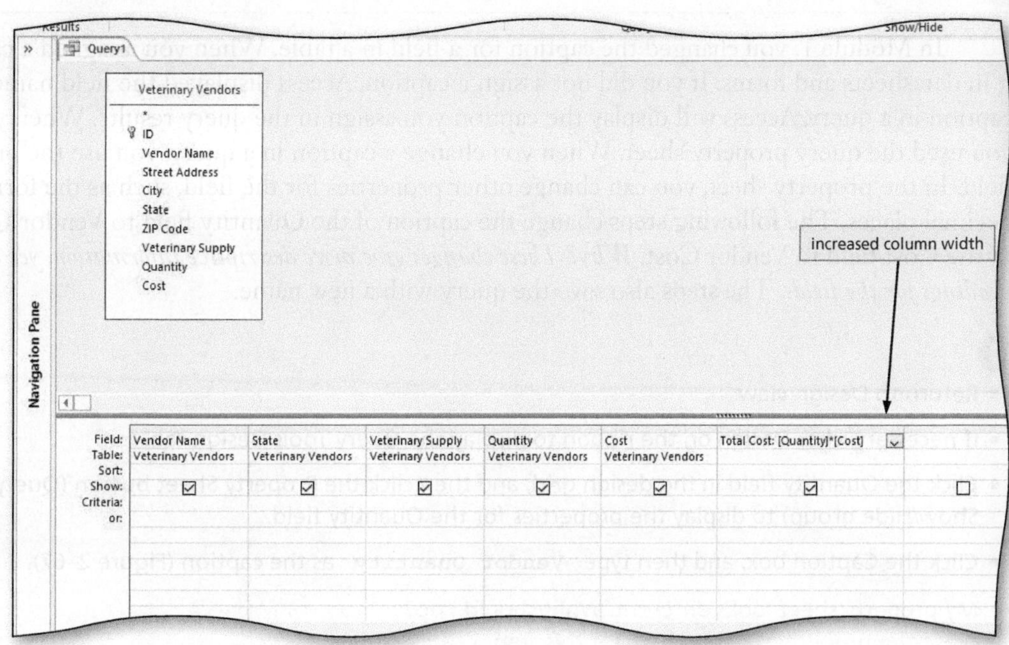

Figure 2–65

4

- Run the query (Figure 2–66) to see the calculated results for the new Total Cost field.

 **Experiment**

- Return to Design view and try other expressions. In at least one case, omit the Total Cost and the colon. In at least one case, intentionally misspell a field name. In each case, run the query to see the effect of your changes. When finished, re-enter the original expression.

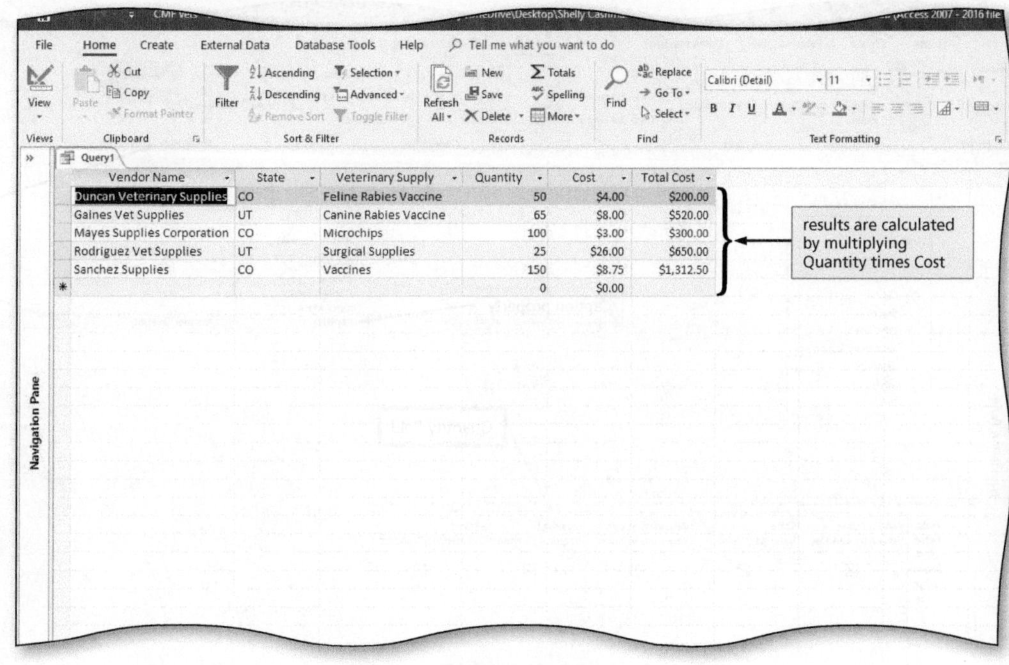

Vendor Name	State	Veterinary Supply	Quantity	Cost	Total Cost
Duncan Veterinary Supplies	CO	Feline Rabies Vaccine	50	$4.00	$200.00
Gaines Vet Supplies	UT	Canine Rabies Vaccine	65	$8.00	$520.00
Mayes Supplies Corporation	CO	Microchips	100	$3.00	$300.00
Rodriguez Vet Supplies	UT	Surgical Supplies	25	$26.00	$650.00
Sanchez Supplies	CO	Vaccines	150	$8.75	$1,312.50
*			0	$0.00	

Figure 2–66

Q&A Does the Total Cost field now exist as a field in the Vendors table?

When a field is created in Table Design View as a new calculated field in the table, it will appear as a field in the table.

Other Ways

1. Press SHIFT+F2

To Change a Caption

In Module 1, you changed the caption for a field in a table. When you assigned a caption, Access displayed it in datasheets and forms. If you did not assign a caption, Access displayed the field name. You can also change a caption in a query. Access will display the caption you assign in the query results. When you omitted duplicates, you used the query property sheet. When you change a caption in a query, you use the property sheet for the field. In the property sheet, you can change other properties for the field, such as the format and number of decimal places. The following steps change the caption of the Quantity field to Vendor Quantity and the caption of the Cost field to Vendor Cost. ***Why?*** *These changes give more descriptive information, yet very readable, column headings for the fields.* The steps also save the query with a new name.

- Return to Design view.
- If necessary, click Design on the ribbon to display the Query Tools Design tab.
- Click the Quantity field in the design grid, and then click the Property Sheet button (Query Tools Design tab | Show/Hide group) to display the properties for the Quantity field.
- Click the Caption box, and then type `Vendor Quantity` as the caption (Figure 2–67).

Q&A | My property sheet looks different. What should I do?
Close the property sheet and repeat this step.

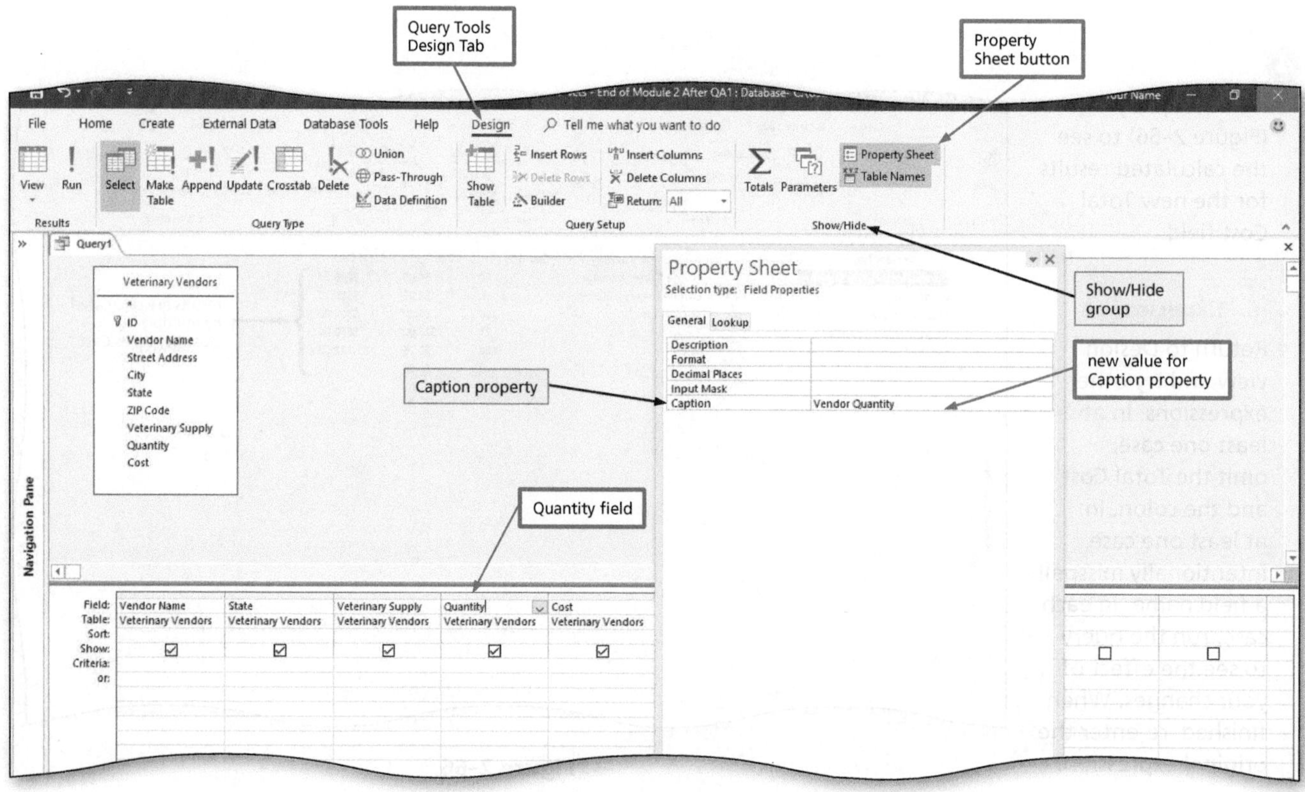

Figure 2–67

2

- Click the Cost field in the design grid to view its properties in the Property Sheet.
- Click the Caption box, and then type `Vendor Cost` as the caption.
- Close the Property Sheet by clicking the Property Sheet button a second time.
- Run the query (Figure 2–68).

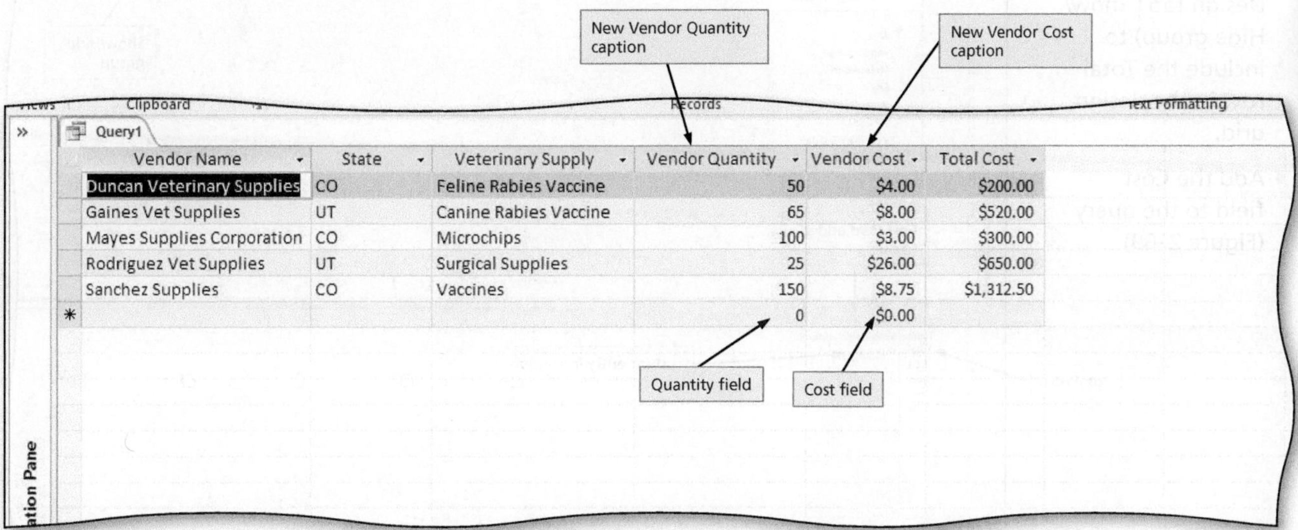

Figure 2–68

3

- Save the query as m02q10.
- Close the query.

Other Ways

1. Right-click field in design grid, click Properties on shortcut menu

To Calculate Statistics

For group calculations, Microsoft Access supports several built-in statistics: COUNT (count of the number of records), SUM (total), AVG (average), MAX (largest value), MIN (smallest value), STDEV (standard deviation), VAR (variance), FIRST (first value), and LAST (last value). These statistics are called aggregate functions. An **aggregate function** is a function that performs some mathematical function against a group of records. To use an aggregate function in a query, you include it in the Total row in the design grid. In order to do so, you must first include the Total row by clicking the Totals button on the Design tab. ***Why?*** *The Total row usually does not appear in the grid. Statistical calculations are performed regularly in Access queries by some, but not all learners. So, the process for these calculations requires extra steps.*

The following steps create a new query for the Veterinary Vendors table. The steps include the Total row in the design grid, and then calculate the average cost for all veterinary supplies.

- Create a new query with a field list for the Veterinary Vendors table.
- Click the Totals button (Query Tools Design tab | Show/Hide group) to include the Total row in the design grid.
- Add the Cost field to the query (Figure 2–69).

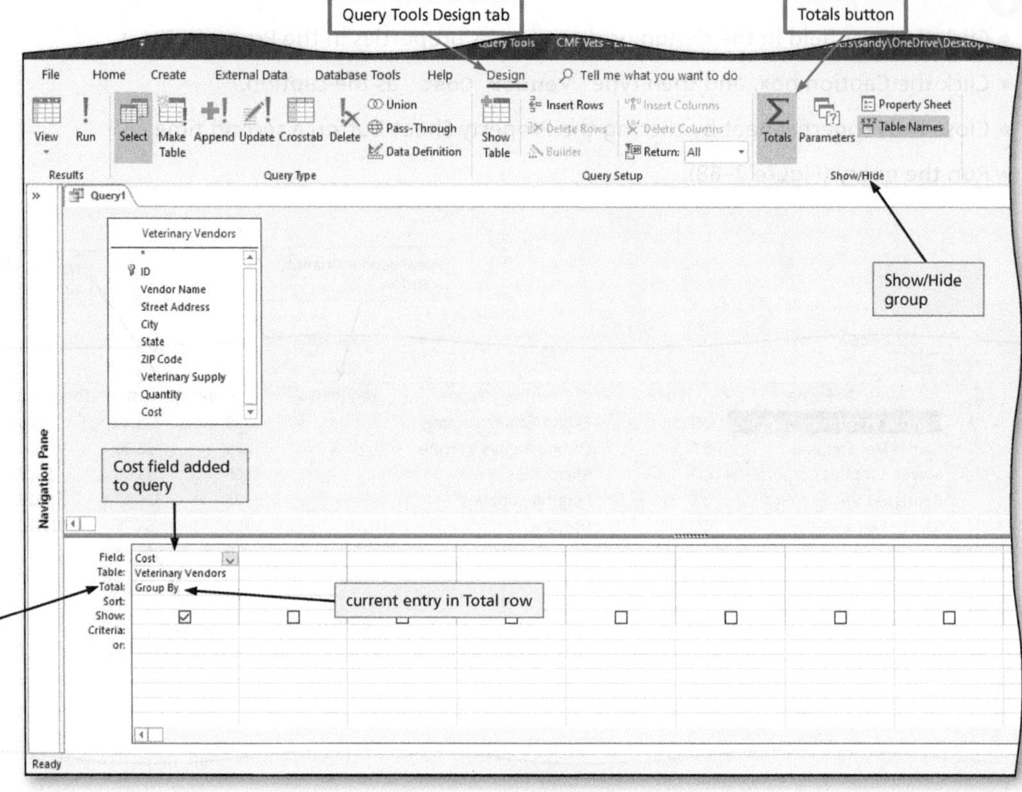

Figure 2–69

- Click the Total row in the Cost column to display the Total arrow.
- Click the Total arrow to display the Total list (Figure 2–70).

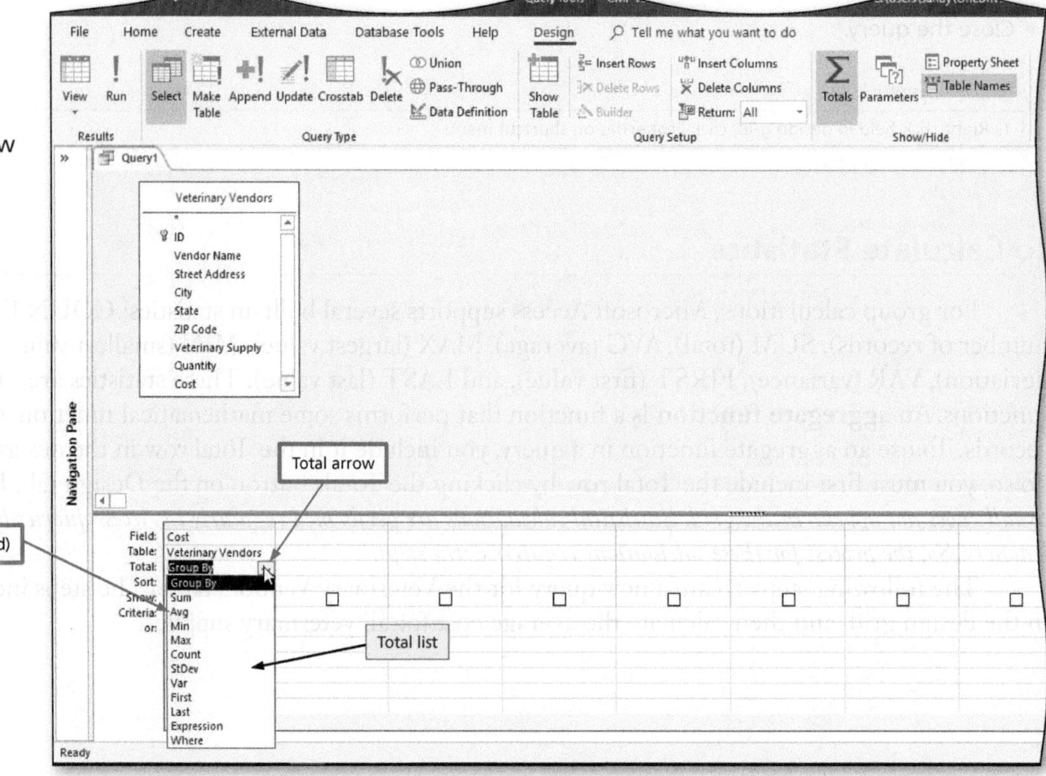

Figure 2–70

3

- Click Avg to select the calculation that Access is to perform (Figure 2–71).

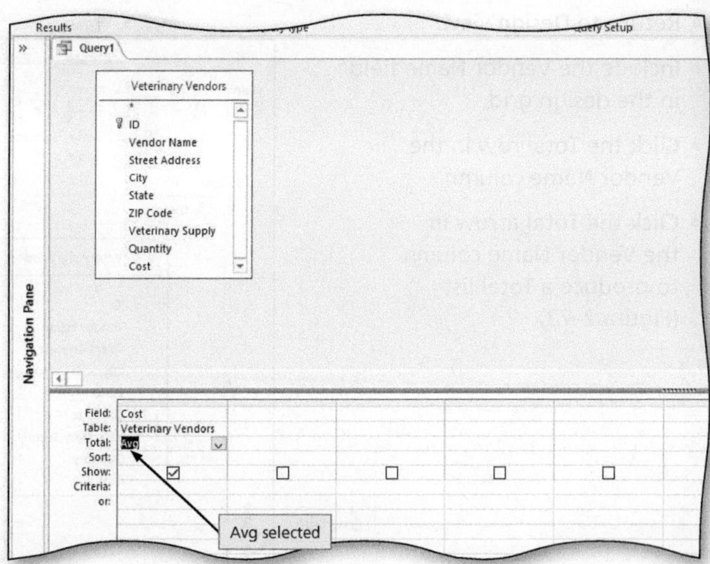

Figure 2–71

4

- Run the query (Figure 2–72).

Experiment

- Return to Design view and try other aggregate functions. In each case, run the query to see the effect of your selection. When finished, select Avg once again.

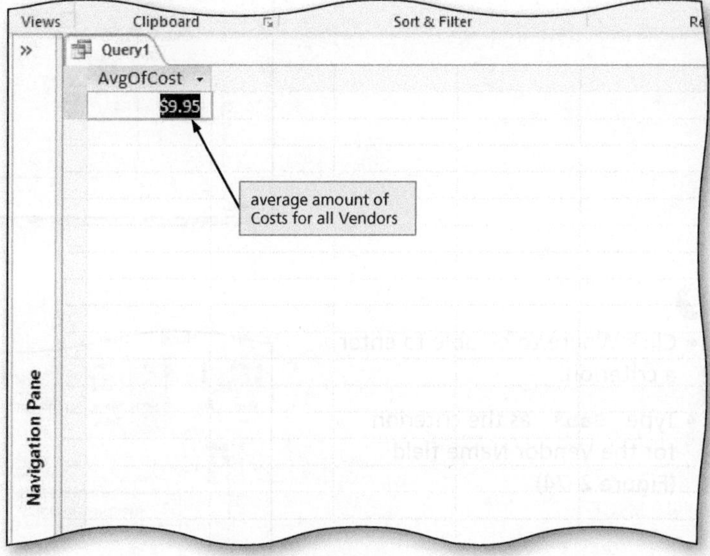

Figure 2–72

To Use Criteria in Calculating Statistics

Why? *Sometimes calculating statistics for all the records in the table is appropriate. In other cases, however, you will need to calculate the statistics for only those records that satisfy certain criteria.* To enter a criterion in a field, first you select Where as the entry in the Total row for the field, and then enter the criterion in the Criteria row. Access uses the word, Where, to indicate that you will enter a criterion. The following steps use this technique to calculate the average costs for purchases from Sanchez Supplies. The steps also save the query with a new name.

1

- Return to Design view.
- Include the Vendor Name field in the design grid.
- Click the Total row in the Vendor Name column.
- Click the Total arrow in the Vendor Name column to produce a Total list (Figure 2–73).

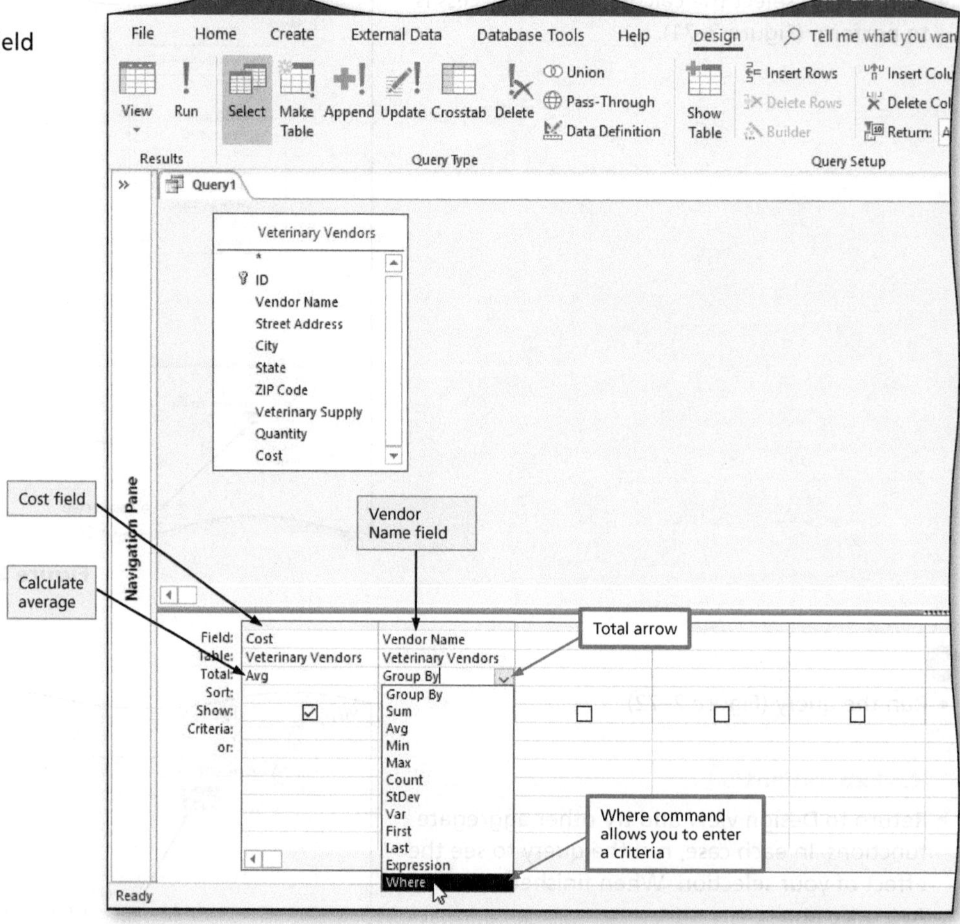

Figure 2–73

- Click Where to be able to enter a criterion.
- Type **San*** as the criterion for the Vendor Name field (Figure 2–74).

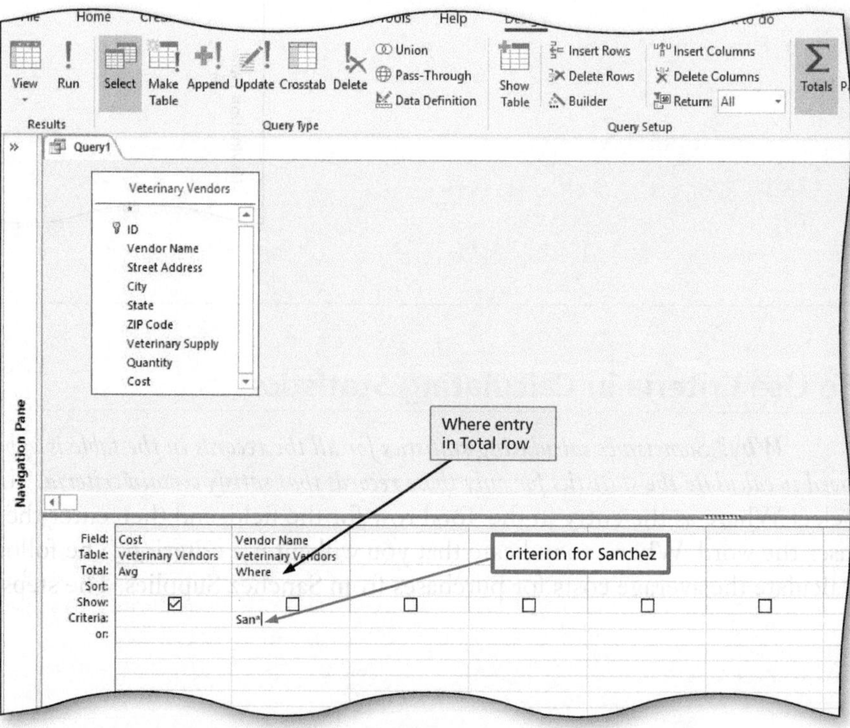

Figure 2–74

3

- Run the query (Figure 2–75) and display the average cost of supplies for Sanchez Supplies.

4

- Save the query as m02q11.

BTW

Criterion for Where

Access treats the criterion for the Where object just as it would for any criterion in a field. Therefore, if you want to use a wildcard rather than spelling out the entire criterion, such as Rod* for the Rod Supplies, Access recognizes and utilizes the wildcard to find the desired result.

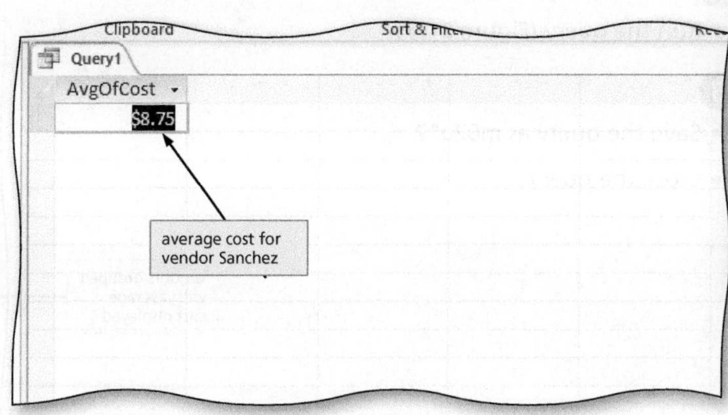

Figure 2–75

To Use Grouping

Why? *Statistics are often used in combination with grouping; that is, statistics are calculated for groups of records. For example, CMF Vets managers could calculate the average amount paid for each veterinary supplier, which would require the average for the vendor specified in the criteria.* **Grouping** means creating groups of records that share some common characteristic. In grouping by Veterinary Vendor, for example, the costs of Duncan Veterinary Supplies would form one group, the costs of Gaines Vet Supplies would form a second, and the costs of Mayes Supplies Corporation would form a third group. The calculations are then made for each group. To indicate grouping in Access, select Group By as the entry in the Total row for the field to be used for grouping. Even though the entry indicates Group By, the vendors will appear individually. Access needs to know the field that you want to review the averages on, and it indicates this by the text Group By. Group By does not mean that it will group together all the vendors, just refers to looking at that particular group.

The following steps create a query that calculates the average amount paid for each vendor supplier account at CMF Vets. The steps also save the query with a new name.

1

- Return to Design view and clear the design grid.
- Include the Vendor Name field in the query.
- Include the Cost field in the query.
- Select Avg as the calculation in the Total row for the Cost field (Figure 2–76).

Q&A Why was it not necessary to change the entry in the Total row for the Vendor Name field?

Group By, which is the initial entry in the Total row when you add a field, is correct. Thus, you did not need to change the entry.

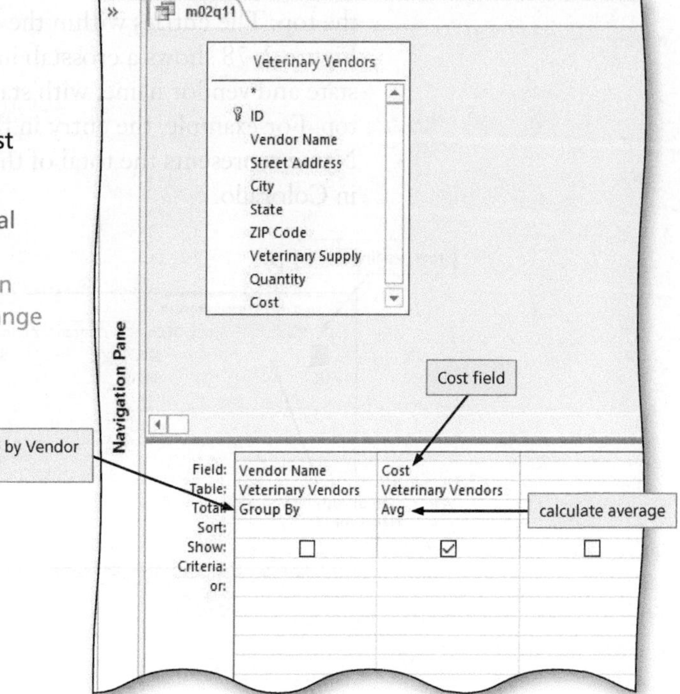

Figure 2–76

2

- Run the query (Figure 2–77).

3

- Save the query as m02q12.
- Close the query.

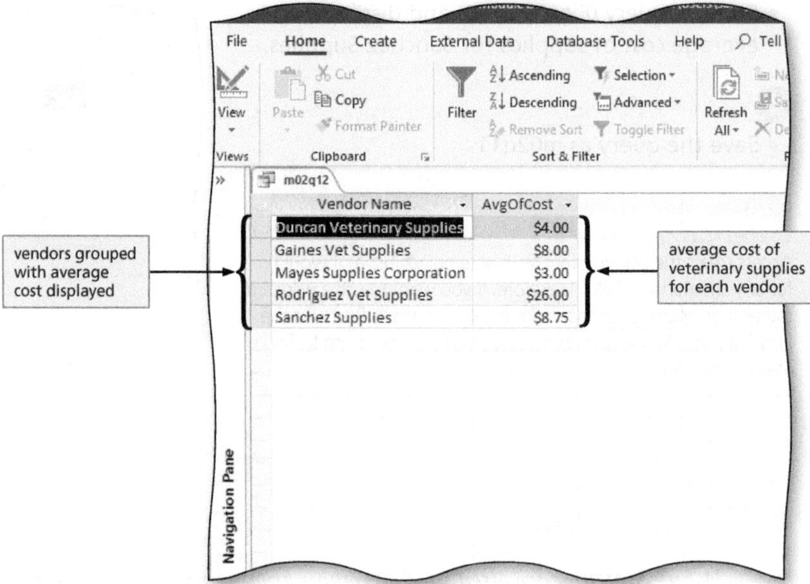

Figure 2–77

Crosstab Queries

A **crosstab query**, or simply, crosstab, calculates a statistic (for example, sum, average, or count) for data that is grouped by two different types of information. One of the types will appear down the side of the resulting datasheet, and the other will appear across the top. Crosstab queries are useful for summarizing data by category or group.

For example, if a query must summarize the sum of the current costs grouped by both state and vendor name, you could have states as the row headings, that is, down the side. You could have vendor names as the column headings, that is, across the top. The entries within the datasheet represent the total of the cost amounts. Figure 2–78 shows a crosstab in which the total of cost amounts is grouped by both state and vendor name, with states down the left side and vendor name across the top. For example, the entry in the row labeled CO and in the column labelled Vendor Name represents the total of the current cost amounts by all vendors who are located in Colorado.

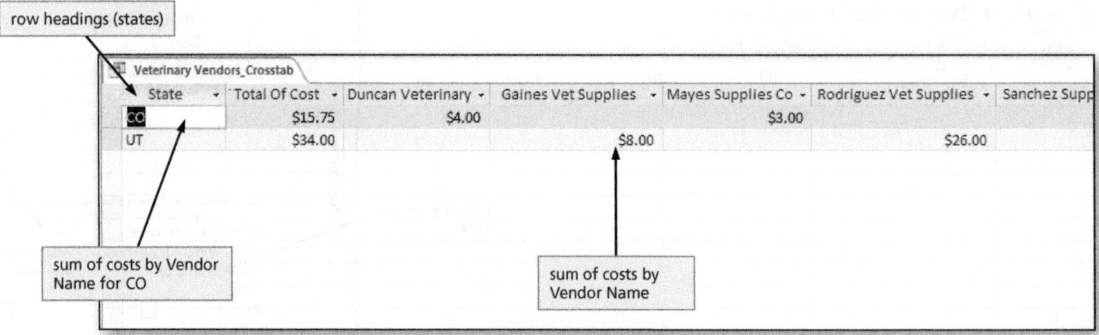

Figure 2–78

CONSIDER THIS

How do you know when to use a crosstab query?

If data is to be grouped by two different types of information, you can use a crosstab query. You will need to identify the two types of information. One of the types will form the row headings and the other will form the column headings in the query results.

To Create a Crosstab Query

The following steps use the Crosstab Query Wizard to create a crosstab query. ***Why?*** *CMF Vets managers want to group data on cost by two types of information: state and vendor name.*

1

- Click Create on the ribbon to display the Create tab.
- Click the Query Wizard button (Create tab | Queries group) to display the New Query dialog box (Figure 2–79).

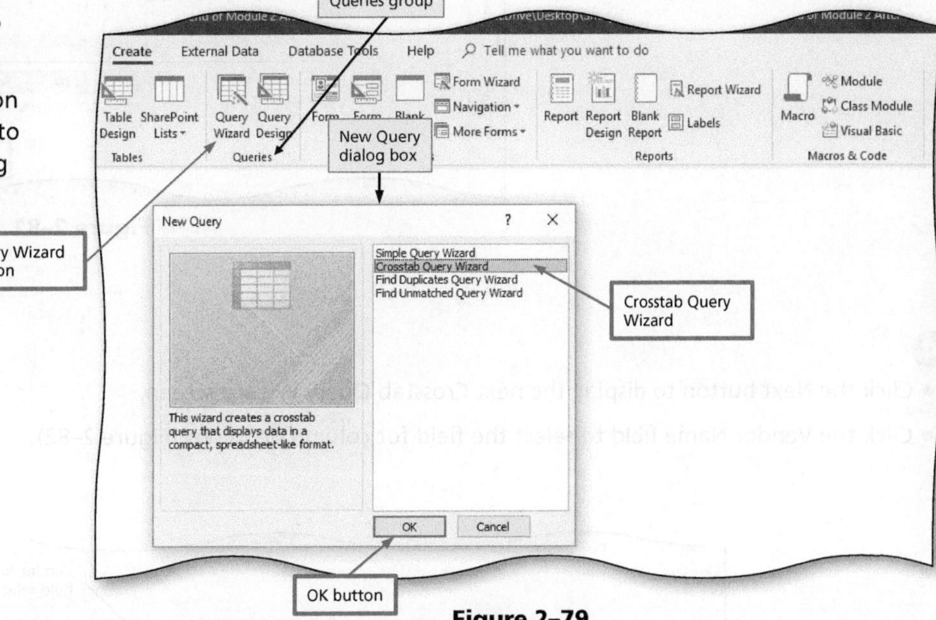

Figure 2–79

2

- Click Crosstab Query Wizard (New Query dialog box).
- Click OK to display the Crosstab Query Wizard dialog box (Figure 2–80).

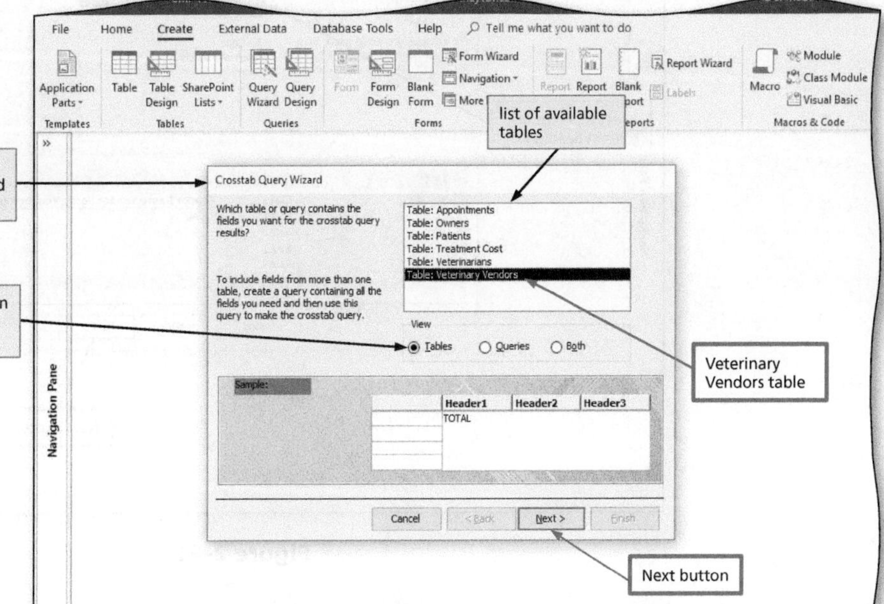

Figure 2–80

3

- With the Tables option button selected, click Table: Veterinary Vendors to select the Veterinary Vendors table, and then click the Next button to display the next Crosstab Query Wizard screen.
- Click the State field, and then click the Add Field button to select the State field for row headings (Figure 2–81).

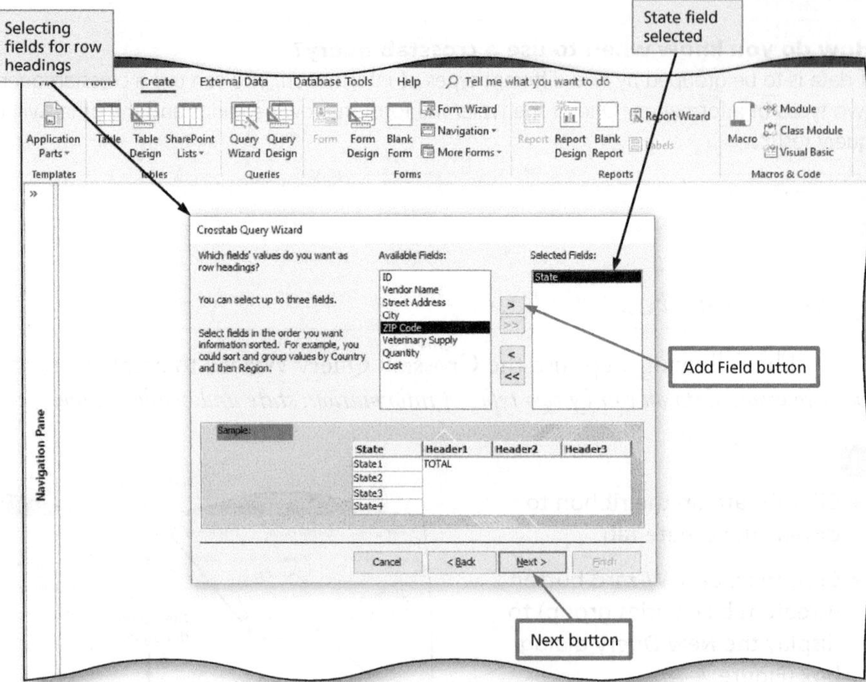

Figure 2–81

4

- Click the Next button to display the next Crosstab Query Wizard screen.
- Click the Vendor Name field to select the field for column headings (Figure 2–82).

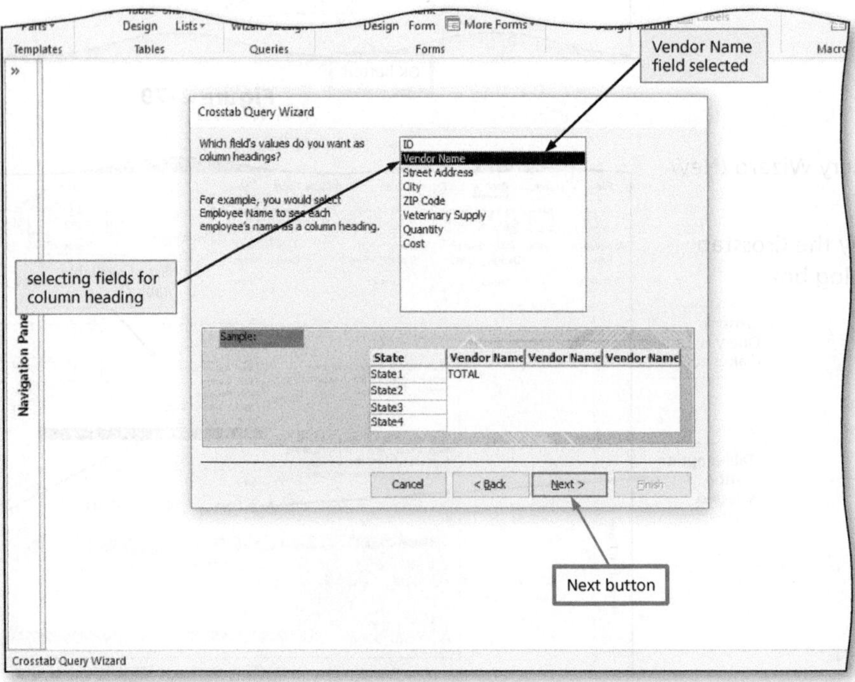

Figure 2–82

- Click Next to display the next Crosstab Query Wizard screen.
- Click the Cost field to select the field for calculations.

Experiment

- Click other fields. For each field, examine the list of calculations that are available. When finished, click the Cost field again.
- Click Sum to select the calculation to be performed (Figure 2–83).

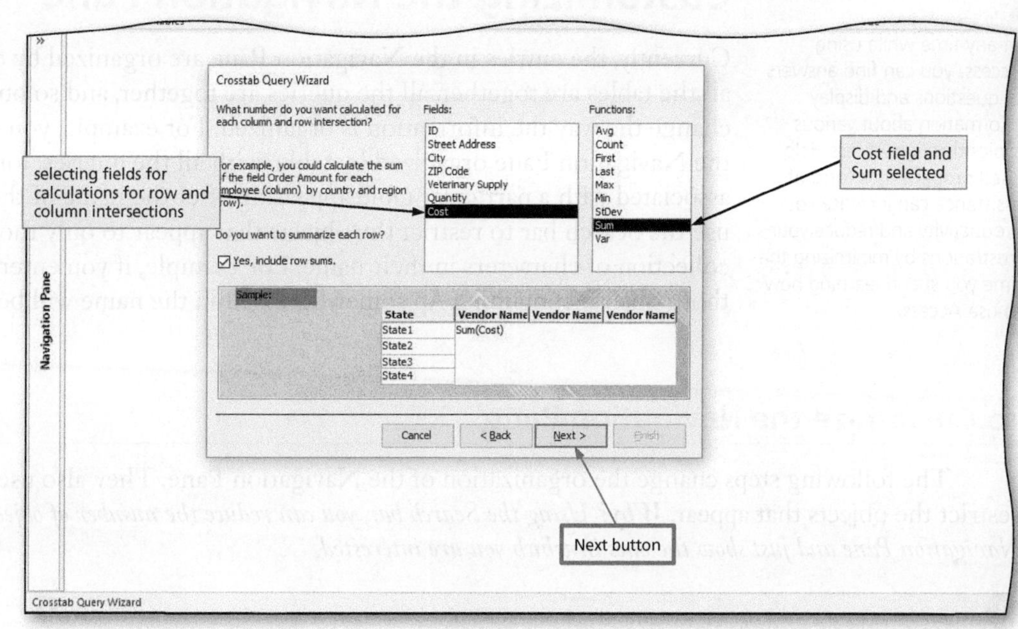

Figure 2–83

Q&A My list of functions is different. What did I do wrong?
Either you clicked the wrong field, or the Cost field has the wrong data type. For example, if you mistakenly assigned it the Short Text data type, you would not see Sum in the list of available calculations.

- Click Next to display the next Crosstab Query Wizard screen.
- If necessary, erase the text in the name text box and type `Veterinary Vendors_Crosstab` as the name of the query (Figure 2–84).

- If requested to do so by your instructor, name the crosstab query as FirstName LastName Crosstab where FirstName and LastName are your first and last names.
- Click the Finish button to produce the crosstab shown in Figure 2–78.
- Close the query.

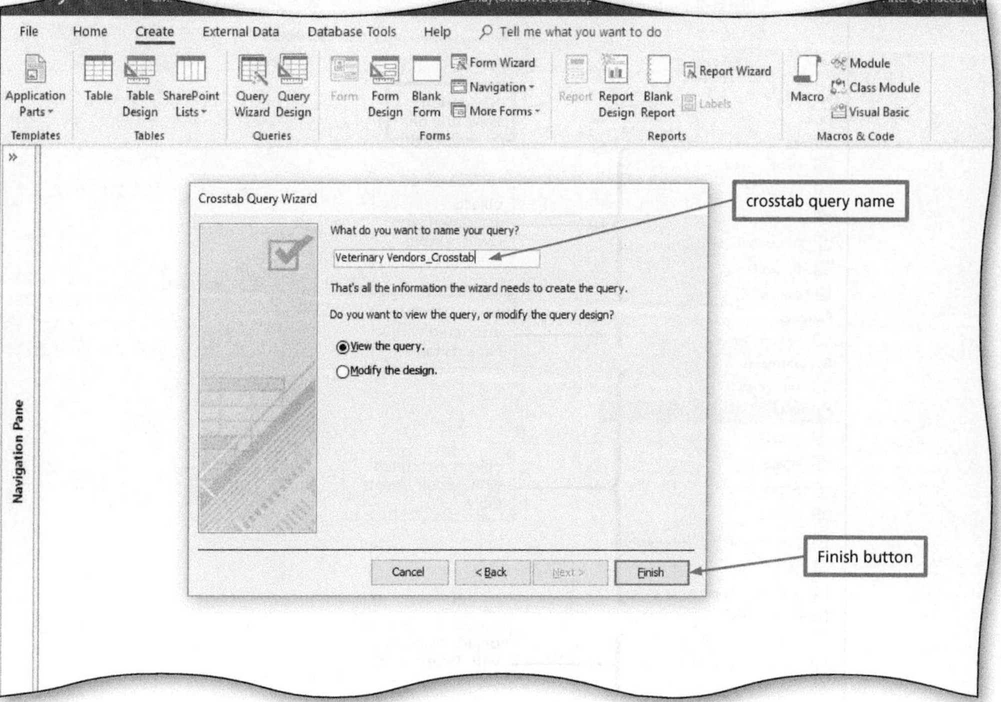

Figure 2–84

BTW
Access Help
At any time while using Access, you can find answers to questions and display information about various topics through Access Help. Used properly, this form of assistance can increase your productivity and reduce your frustrations by minimizing the time you spend learning how to use Access.

Customizing the Navigation Pane

Currently, the entries in the Navigation Pane are organized by object type. That is, all the tables are together, all the queries are together, and so on. You might want to change the way the information is organized. For example, you might want to have the Navigation Pane organized by table, with all the queries, forms, and reports associated with a particular table appearing after the name of the table. You can also use the Search bar to restrict the objects that appear to only those that have a certain collection of characters in their name. For example, if you entered the letters, Ap, only those objects containing Ap somewhere within the name will be included.

To Customize the Navigation Pane

The following steps change the organization of the Navigation Pane. They also use the Search bar to restrict the objects that appear. ***Why?*** *Using the Search bar, you can reduce the number of objects that appear in the Navigation Pane and just show the ones in which you are interested.*

- If necessary, click the 'Shutter Bar Open/Close Button' to open the Navigation Pane.
- Click the Navigation Pane arrow to produce the Navigation Pane menu and then click 'Tables and Related Views' to organize the Navigation Pane by table rather than by the type of object (Figure 2–85).

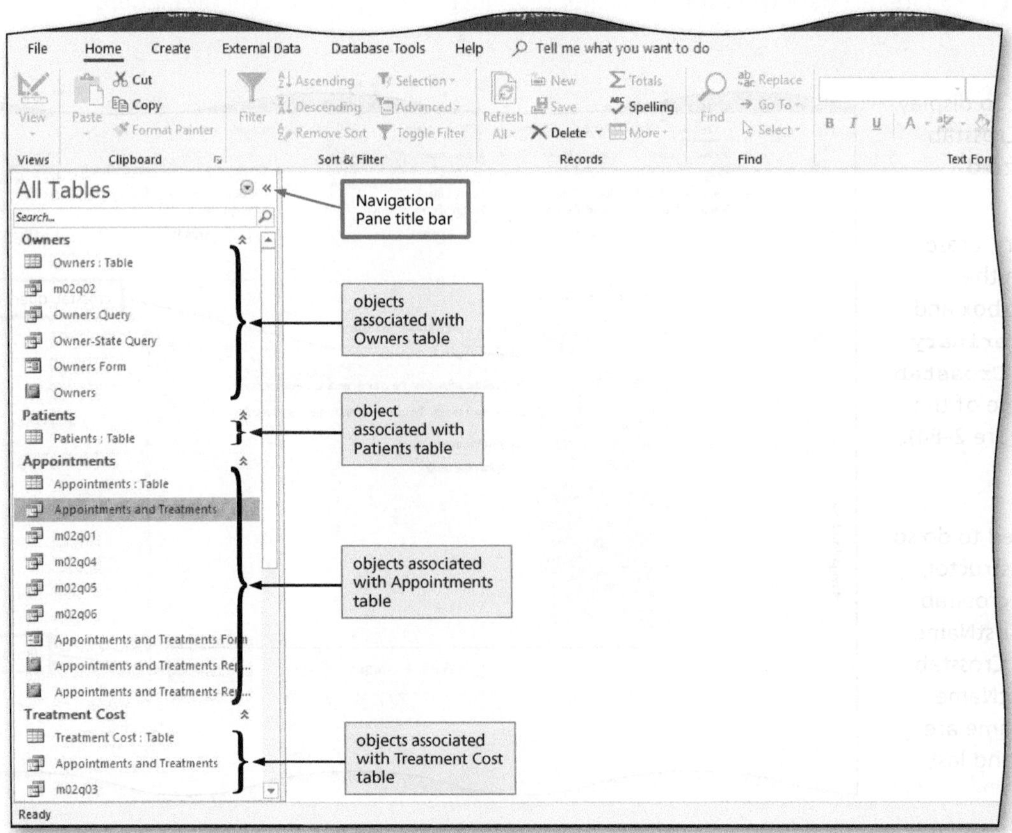

Figure 2–85

- Click the Navigation Pane arrow to produce the Navigation Pane menu.
- Click Object Type to once again organize the Navigation Pane by object type.

Experiment

- Select different Navigate To Category options to see the effect of the option. With each option you select, select different Filter By Group options to see the effect of the filtering. When you have finished experimenting, select the 'Object Type Navigate To Category' option and the 'All Access Objects Filter By Group' option.

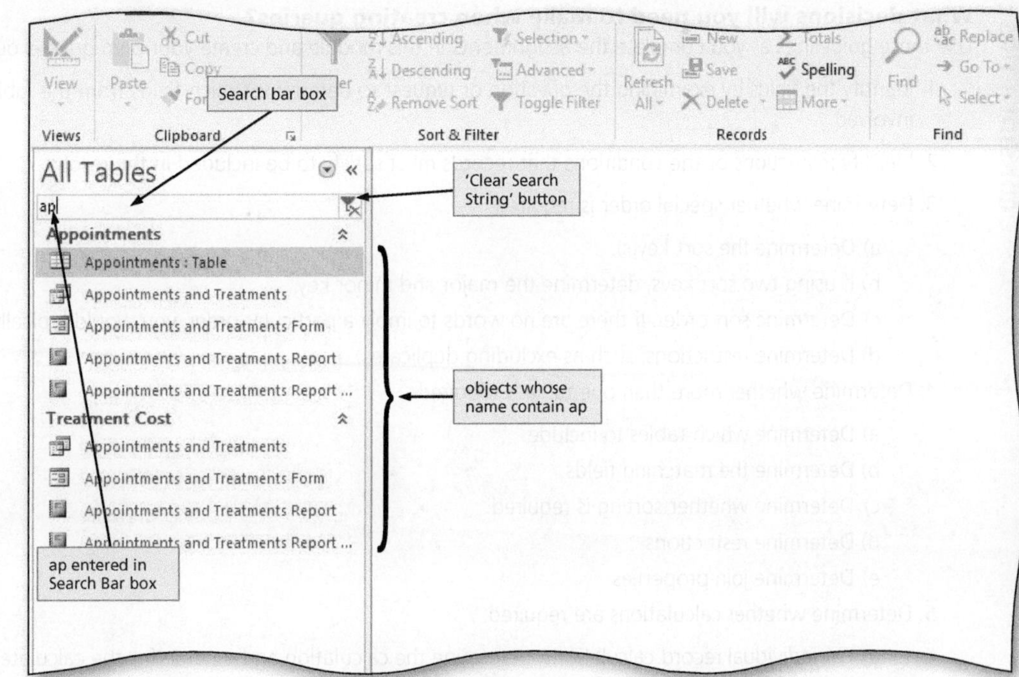

Figure 2–86

- If the Search bar does not appear, right-click the Navigation Pane and click Search Bar on the shortcut menu.
- Click in the Search box to produce an insertion point.
- Type ap as the search string to restrict the objects displayed to only those containing the desired string (Figure 2–86).

- Click the 'Clear Search String' button to remove the search string and redisplay all objects.

Q&A Did I have to click the button to redisplay all objects? Could I simply have erased the current string to achieve the same result?
You did not have to click the button. You could have used the DELETE or BACKSPACE keys to erase the current search string.

- If desired, sign out of your Microsoft account.
- **sam** Exit Access.

Summary

In this module you have learned to create queries, enter fields, enter criteria, use text and numeric data in queries, use wildcards, use compound criteria, create parameter queries, sort data in queries, join tables in queries, perform calculations in queries, and create crosstab queries. You also learned to create a report and a form that used a query, to export a query, and to customize the Navigation Pane.

CONSIDER THIS

What decisions will you need to make when creating queries?

Use these guidelines as you complete the assignments in this module and create your own queries outside of this class.

1. Identify the fields by examining the question or request to determine which fields from the tables in the database are involved.
2. Identify restrictions or the conditions that records must satisfy to be included in the results.
3. Determine whether special order is required.
   a) Determine the sort key(s).
   b) If using two sort keys, determine the major and minor key.
   c) Determine sort order. If there are no words to imply a particular order, you would typically use Ascending sort order.
   d) Determine restrictions, such as excluding duplicates.
4. Determine whether more than one table is required.
   a) Determine which tables to include.
   b) Determine the matching fields.
   c) Determine whether sorting is required.
   d) Determine restrictions.
   e) Determine join properties.
5. Determine whether calculations are required.
   a) For individual record calculations, determine the calculation and a name for the calculated field.
   b) For group calculations, determine the calculation as well as the field to be used for grouping.
6. If data is to be summarized and the data is to be grouped by two different types of information, create a crosstab query.

CONSIDER THIS

How should you submit solutions to questions in the assignments identified with a symbol?

Every assignment in this book contains one or more questions identified with a symbol. These questions require you to think beyond the assigned database. Present your solutions to the questions in the format required by your instructor. Possible formats may include one or more of these options: write the answer; create a document that contains the answer; present your answer to the class; discuss your answer in a group; record the answer as audio or video using a webcam, smartphone, or portable media player; or post answers on a blog, wiki, or website.

Apply Your Knowledge

Reinforce the skills and apply the concepts you learned in this module.

Using Wildcards in a Query, Creating a Parameter Query, Joining Tables, and Creating a Report

Instructions: Start Access. Open the Support_AC_Financial Services database from the Data Files. (If you did not previously complete the exercise, see your instructor for a copy of the modified database.)

Perform the following tasks:

1. Import the Accounting table from the Support_AC Financial Services – Extra Tables database.
2. Create a query for the Accounting table and add the CL #, Client Name, Amount Paid, and AU# fields to the design grid. Sort the records in descending order by Amount Paid. Add a criterion for the AU# field that allows the user to enter a different advisor each time the query is run. Run the query and enter 114 as the advisor to test the query. Save the query as Apply 2 Step 2 Query.
3. Create a query for the Accounting table and add the CL #, Client Name, and Current Due fields to the design grid. Add a criterion to find all clients whose current due amount is less than $500. Run the query and then save it as Apply 2 Step 3 Query.
4. Create a query that joins the Advisor and Client tables. Add the Advisor Number, Last Name, and First Name fields from the Advisor table and the Client Number and Client Name fields from the Client table to the design grid. Sort the records in ascending order by Client Number within Advisor. Run the query and save it as Advisor-Client Query. Note: if any error messages appear, check the field types of the fields in the query tables and make changes as necessary.
5. Create the report shown in Figure 2–87. The report uses the Advisor-Client Query.

Advisor-Client

AU#	Last Name	First Name	CL #	Client Name
103	Estevez	Enrique	AT13	Alton Repart
110	Hillsdale	Rachel	AZ01	Amanda Zito
110	Hillsdale	Rachel	BB35	Barbara Black
120	Short	Chris	BS24	Bob Schwartz
114	Liu	Chou	CC25	Carly Cohen
110	Hillsdale	Rachel	CJ45	Carl Jones
103	Estevez	Enrique	CP03	Cindy Platt
103	Estevez	Enrique	HC17	Heidi Croft
110	Hillsdale	Rachel	HN23	Henry Niemer
120	Short	Chris	KC12	Katy Cline
103	Estevez	Enrique	KD15	Kirk D'Elia
114	Liu	Chou	MM01	Moss Manni
110	Hillsdale	Rachel	PL03	Paul Loon
114	Liu	Chou	PS67	Patricia Singer

Figure 2–87

Continued >

Apply Your Knowledge *continued*

6. If requested to do so by your instructor, rename the Advisor-Client Report in the Navigation Pane as LastName-Client Report where LastName is your last name.
7. Submit the revised database in the format specified by your instructor.
8. What criteria would you enter in the Street field if you wanted to find all clients whose businesses were on Beard?

Extend Your Knowledge

Extend the skills you learned in this module and experiment with new skills. You may need to use Help to complete the assignment.

Creating Queries Using Criteria and Exporting a Query

Note: To complete this assignment, you will be required to use the Data Files. Please contact your instructor for information about accessing the Data Files.

Instructions: Start Access. Open the Students database, which you created from a template. The Students database provides a database structure for students and their guardians. The data will be entered next semester as new students register for classes.

1. Enter the student information shown in Figure 2–88 into the Student List that appears as the database is opened.

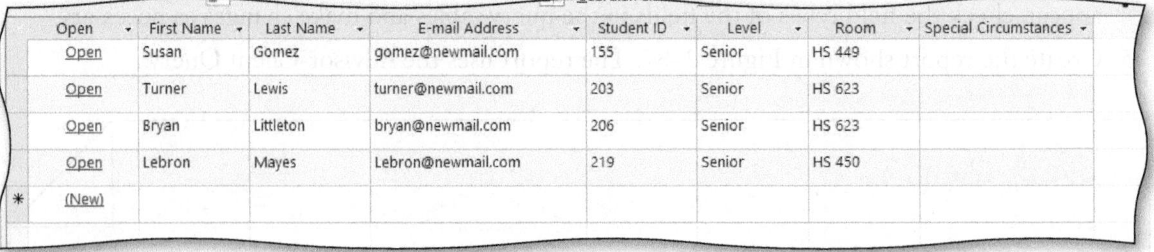

	Open	First Name	Last Name	E-mail Address	Student ID	Level	Room	Special Circumstances
	Open	Susan	Gomez	gomez@newmail.com	155	Senior	HS 449	
	Open	Turner	Lewis	turner@newmail.com	203	Senior	HS 623	
	Open	Bryan	Littleton	bryan@newmail.com	206	Senior	HS 623	
	Open	Lebron	Mayes	Lebron@newmail.com	219	Senior	HS 450	
*	(New)							

Figure 2–88

2. Create a query to find all Students located in room HS 623. Save the query as Extend 2-1 Step 2 Query.
3. Enter information for Tyron Black into the Guardian Details form, as shown in Figure 2–89.
4. Open the All Students Report and delete the date from the upper-left corner of the report.
5. Export the report as a Word file with the name All Students List.rtf and save the export steps.
6. Save the database and the exported RTF file in the format specified by your instructor.
7. How would you create the query in Step 1 that shows students who are not in room HS 623?

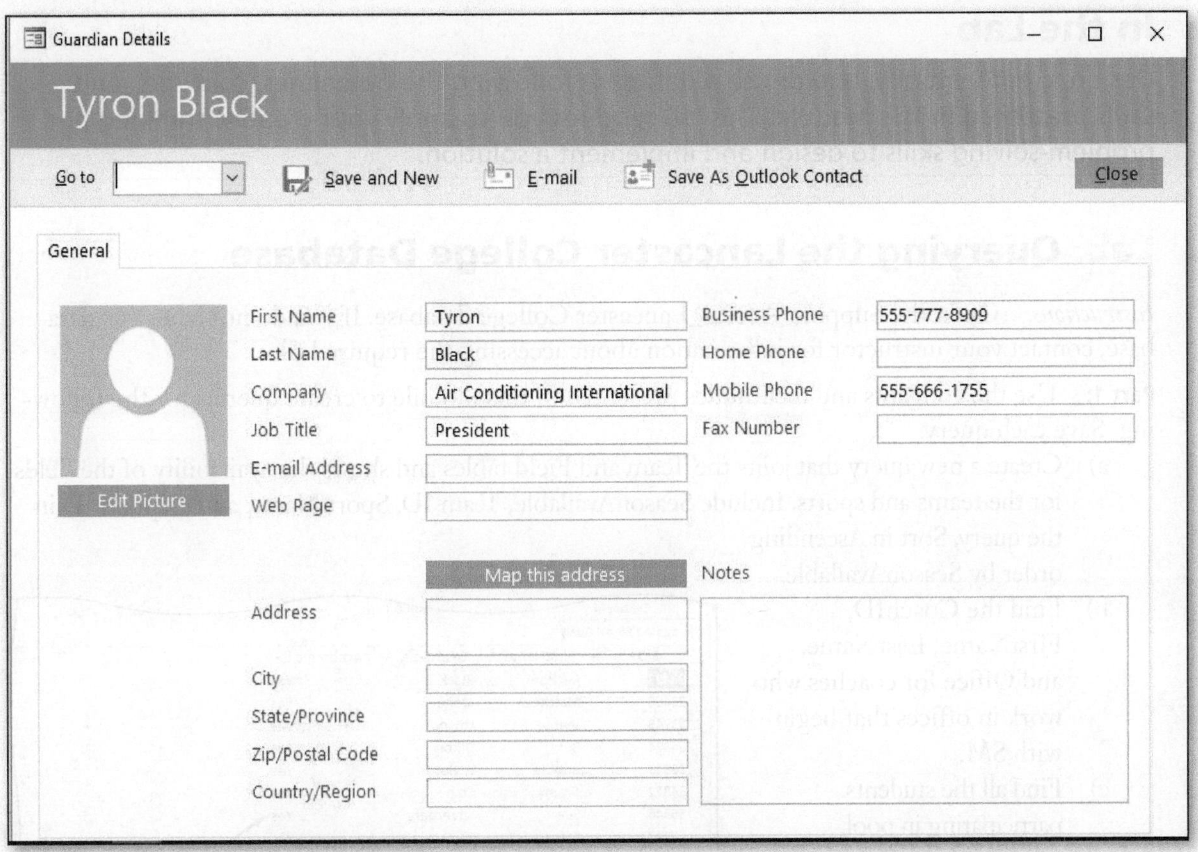

Figure 2–89

Expand Your World

Create a solution, which uses cloud and web technologies, by learning and investigating on your own from general guidance.

Problem: You are taking a general science course and the instructor would like you to gather some statistics and query the statistics on the dietary intake from community gardens.

Instructions:

1. Examine a website that contains research data on how individuals and families participate in growing their own food. Select data from both small and large cities near your current location.
2. Create a database containing one table that contains the following fields: Five-year increase in percentage of households gardening, percentage increase in low-income family gardening participants, and percentage increase in home gardens.
3. Create queries that do the following:
   a. return the largest quantity of increases in gardening.
   b. Calculate the difference between the largest gardening percentage increase and the lowest gardening percentage increase.
4. Submit the database in the format specified by your instructor.
5. Use an Internet search engine to find the most successful community garden near your location.
6. Which websites did you use to gather data and search for statistical information? How did the query result in Step 3 differ from historical averages? Do you think these statistics are significant? Why or why not?

In the Lab

Design, create, modify, and/or use a database following the guidelines, concepts, and skills presented in this module. This lab requires you to apply your creative thinking and problem-solving skills to design and implement a solution.

Lab: Querying the Lancaster College Database

Instructions: Open the Support_Access_Lancaster College database. If you do not have this database, contact your instructor for information about accessing the required files.

Part 1: Use the concepts and techniques presented in this module to create queries for the following. Save each query.

a) Create a new query that joins the Team and Field tables and shows the availability of the fields for the teams and sports. Include SeasonAvailable, Team ID, Sport Name, and Captain ID in the query. Sort in Ascending order by SeasonAvailable.

b) Find the CoachID, FirstName, LastName, and Office for coaches who work in offices that begin with SM.

c) Find all the students participating in pool activities. Include the StudentID and SportName fields.

d) Find all the students who are academically qualified to participate in sports. Include their ID, first and last names, and academic status. The result should appear as shown in Figure 2–90.

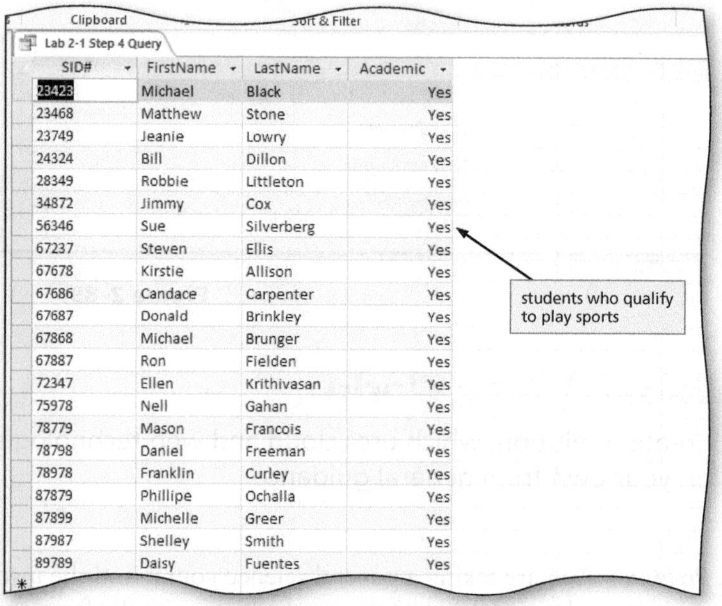

Clipboard | Sort & Filter

Lab 2-1 Step 4 Query

SID#	FirstName	LastName	Academic
23423	Michael	Black	Yes
23468	Matthew	Stone	Yes
23749	Jeanie	Lowry	Yes
24324	Bill	Dillon	Yes
28349	Robbie	Littleton	Yes
34872	Jimmy	Cox	Yes
56346	Sue	Silverberg	Yes
67237	Steven	Ellis	Yes
67678	Kirstie	Allison	Yes
67686	Candace	Carpenter	Yes
67687	Donald	Brinkley	Yes
67868	Michael	Brunger	Yes
67887	Ron	Fielden	Yes
72347	Ellen	Krithivasan	Yes
75978	Nell	Gahan	Yes
78779	Mason	Francois	Yes
78798	Daniel	Freeman	Yes
78978	Franklin	Curley	Yes
87879	Phillipe	Ochalla	Yes
87899	Michelle	Greer	Yes
87987	Shelley	Smith	Yes
89789	Daisy	Fuentes	Yes

students who qualify to play sports

Figure 2–90

Submit your assignment in the format specified by your instructor.

Part 2: You made several decisions while creating the queries in this assignment. What was the rationale behind your decisions? How would you modify the query in Step d to include students who already have waivers? How would you further modify the query to show the percentage of students that have waivers?

File Home Create External Data Database Tools Help Fields Table Tell me what you war

Table Tools Database13 : D

3 Maintaining a Database

Objectives

You will have mastered the material in this module when you can:

- Add, change, and delete records
- Search for records
- Filter records
- Update a table design
- Use action queries to update records
- Use delete queries to delete records
- Specify validation rules, default values, and formats
- Create and use single-value lookup fields
- Create and use multivalued lookup fields
- Format a datasheet
- Specify referential integrity
- Use a subdatasheet
- Sort records

Introduction

Once you have created a database and loaded it with data, you must maintain it. **Maintaining the database** means modifying the data to keep it up to date by adding new records, changing the data for existing records, and deleting records. Updating can include mass updates or mass deletions (i.e., updates to, or deletions of, many records at the same time).

Maintenance of a database can also involve the need to **restructure the database** periodically. Restructuring can include adding new fields to a table, changing the characteristics of existing fields, and removing existing fields. Restructuring also includes the creation of validation rules and referential integrity. Validation rules ensure the validity of the data in the database, whereas referential integrity ensures the validity of the relationships between entities. Maintaining a database can also include filtering records, a process that ensures that only the records that satisfy some criterion appear when viewing and updating the data in a table. Changing the appearance of a datasheet is also a maintenance activity.

BTW
Organizing Files and Folders
You should organize and store files in folders so that you easily can find the files later. For example, if you are taking an introductory computer class called CIS 101, a good practice would be to save all Access files in an Access folder in a CIS 101 folder.

Project — Maintaining a Database

The CMF Veterinarian practice faces the task of keeping its database up to date. As the practice takes on new vendors, it will need to add new records, make changes to existing records, and delete records. CMF believes that it can serve its vendors better by changing the structure of the database to categorize the vendors by type of product they supply. The company will do this by adding a Product Type field to the Veterinary Vendors table. Additionally, the practice manager has realized that pet appointments need to be streamlined. Because appointments might involve more than one treatment, the appointment field will be a multivalued field, which is a field that can store multiple values or entries. Along with these changes, CMF wants to change the appearance of a datasheet when displaying data.

CMF would like the ability to make mass updates, that is, to update or delete many records in a single operation. It wants rules that limit users to entering only valid, or appropriate, data into the database. CMF also wants to ensure that the database cannot contain the name of a patient that is not associated with a specific owner.

Figure 3–1 summarizes some of the various types of activities involved in maintaining the CMF database.

Figure 3–1

BTW
The Ribbon and Screen Resolution
Access may change how the groups and buttons within the groups appear on the ribbon, depending on the computer or mobile device's screen resolution. Thus, your ribbon may look different from the ones in this book if you are using a screen resolution other than 1366 x 768.

Updating Records

Keeping the data in a database current requires updating records in three ways: adding new records, changing the data in existing records, and deleting existing records. You can add records to a database using Datasheet view and as you add records, the records appear on the screen in a datasheet. The data looks like a table. When you need to add additional records, you can use the same techniques.

You can use a simple form to view records. You can also use a **split form**, a form that allows you to simultaneously view both simple form and Datasheet views of the data. You can use either portion of a split form to add or update records. To add new records, change existing records, or delete records, you use the same techniques you used in Datasheet view.

To Create a Split Form

The following steps create a split form. ***Why?*** *With a split form, you have the advantage of seeing a single record in a form while simultaneously viewing several records in a datasheet.*

- **sam** Start Access and open the database named CMF Vets from your hard disk, OneDrive, or other storage location.
- Open the Navigation Pane if it is currently closed.
- If necessary, click the Veterinary Vendors table in the Navigation Pane to select it.
- Click Create on the ribbon to display the Create tab.
- Click the More Forms button (Create tab | Forms group) to display the More Forms menu (Figure 3–2).

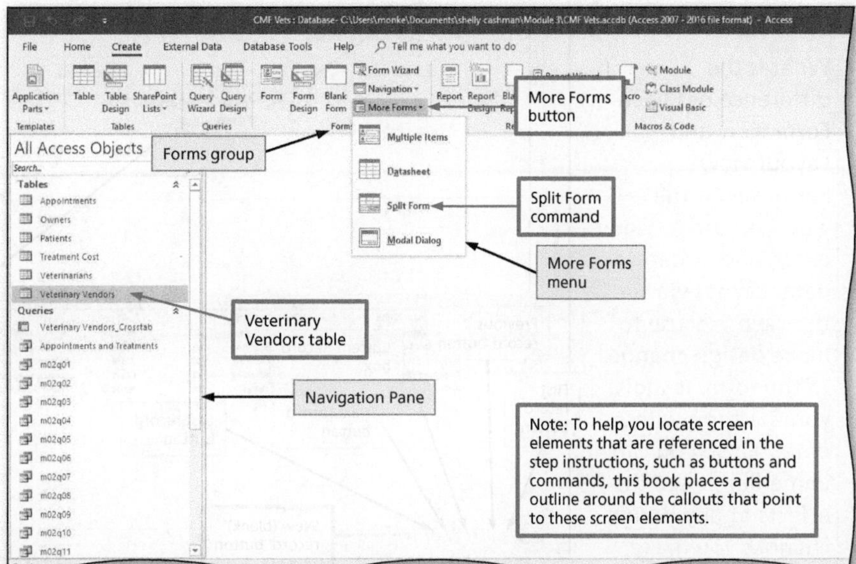

Figure 3–2

- Click Split Form to create a split form based on the Veterinary Vendors table.
- Close the Navigation Pane (Figure 3–3).

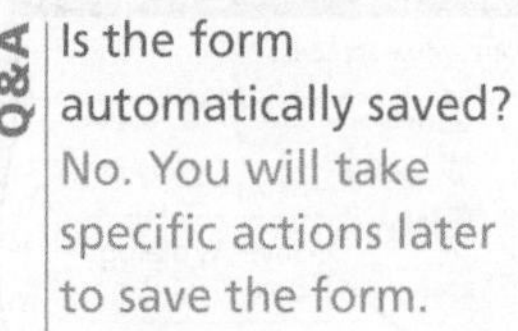

Q&A Is the form automatically saved?
No. You will take specific actions later to save the form.

A field list appeared when I created the form. What should I do?
Click the 'Add Existing Fields' button (Design tab | Tools group) to remove the field list.

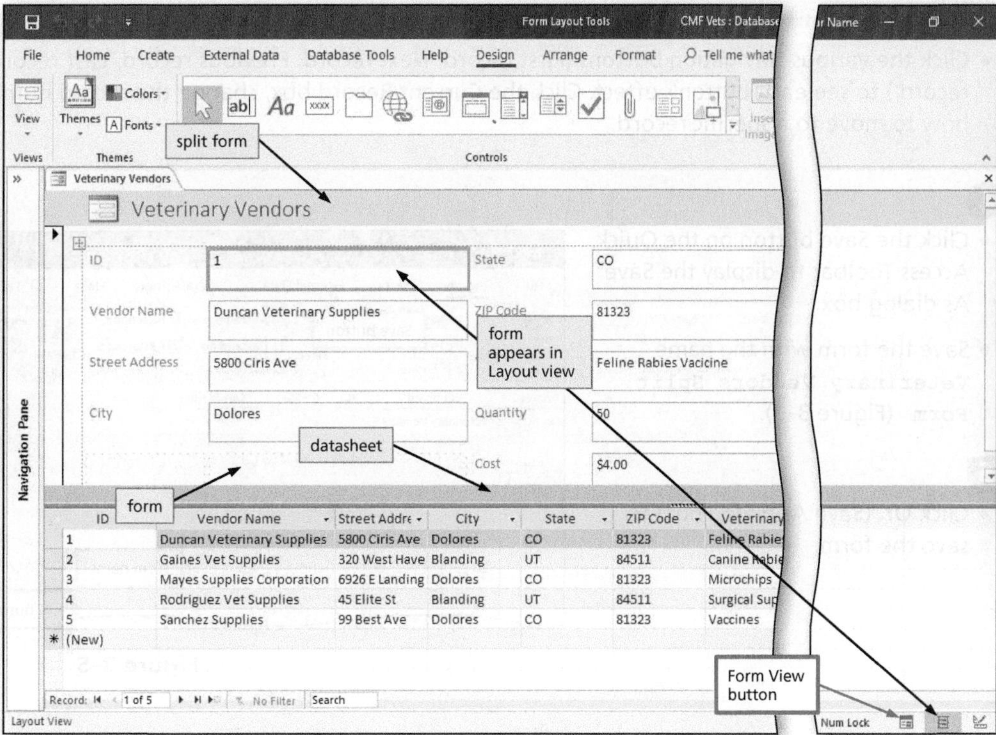

Figure 3–3

- Click the Form View button on the Access status bar to display the form in Form view rather than Layout view (Figure 3–4).

Q&A What is the difference between Form view and Layout view?
Form view is the view you use to view, enter, and update data. Layout view is the view you use to make design changes to the form. It shows you the form with data in it so you can immediately see the effects of any design changes you make, but it is not intended to be used to enter and update data.

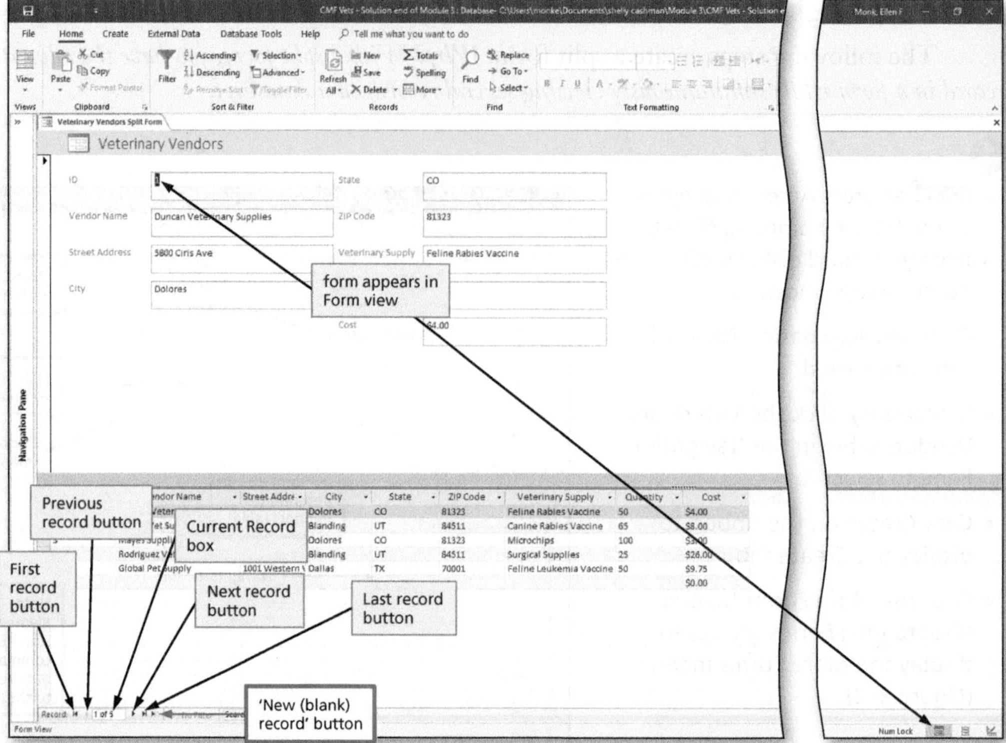

Figure 3–4

Experiment

- Click the various Navigation buttons (First record, Next record, Previous record, Last record, and 'New (blank) record') to see each button's effect. Click the Current Record box, change the record number, and press ENTER to see how to move to a specific record.

- Click the Save button on the Quick Access Toolbar to display the Save As dialog box.
- Save the form with the name `Veterinary Vendors Split Form` (Figure 3–5).

- Click OK (Save As dialog box) to save the form.

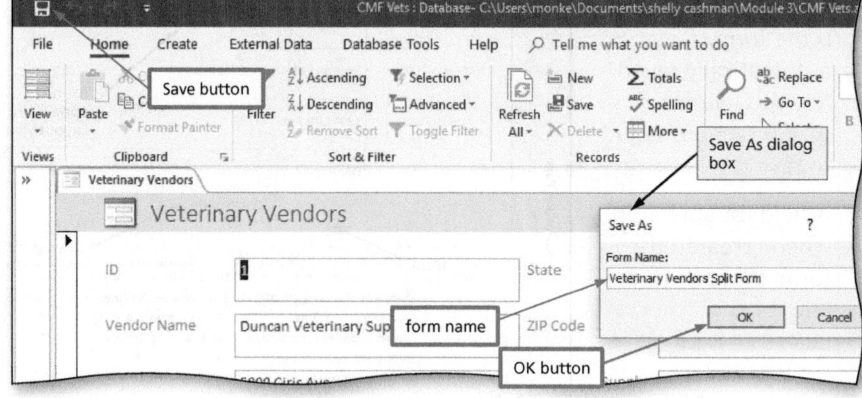

Figure 3–5

Other Ways

1. Right-click tab for form, click Form View on shortcut menu

To Use a Form to Add Records

Once a form or split form is open in Form view, you can add records using the same techniques you used to add records in Datasheet view. In a split form, the changes you make on the form are automatically made on the datasheet. You do not need to take any special action. The following steps use the split form that you just created to add records. ***Why?*** *With a split form, as you add a record, you can immediately see the effect of the addition on the datasheet.*

- Click the 'New (blank) record' button on the Navigation bar to enter a new record, and then type the data for the new record, as shown in Figure 3–6, keeping in mind that the ID field is an autonumber and will appear automatically when typing in a new record. Press TAB after typing the data in each field, except after typing the data for the final field (Cost).
- Press TAB to complete the entry of the record.
- Close the form.

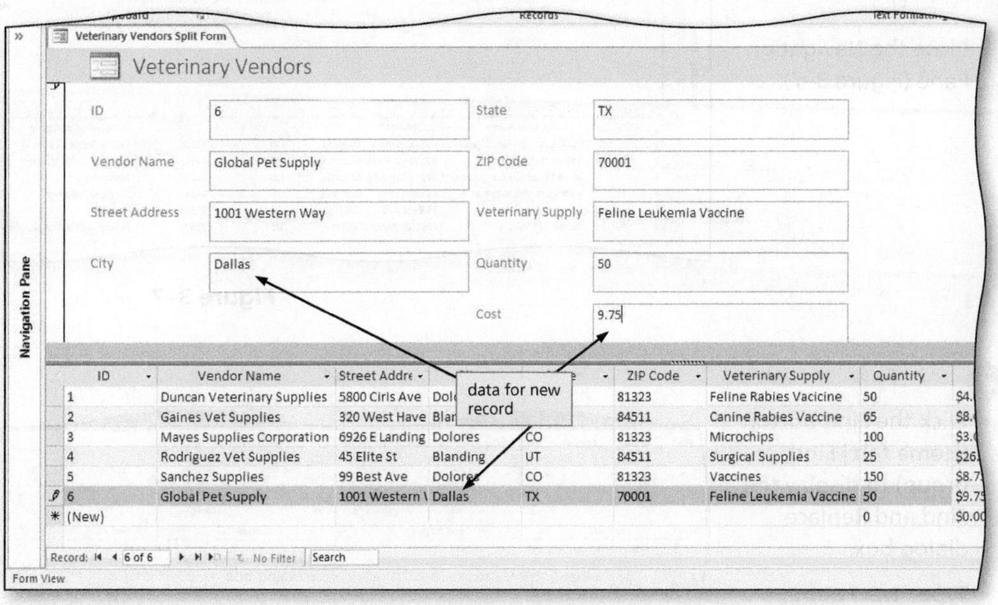

Figure 3–6

Other Ways

1. Click New button (Home tab | Records group)
2. Press CTRL+PLUS SIGN (+)

To Search for a Record

In the database environment, **searching** means looking for records that satisfy some criterion. Looking for the veterinary vendor that sells microchips is an example of searching. Running a query is another way of searching. In a query, Access has to locate those records that satisfied the criteria.

You can perform a search in Form view or Datasheet view without creating a query. The following steps search for the vendor that sells microchips. ***Why?*** *You want to locate the record quickly so you can update this vendor's record.*

- Open the Navigation Pane.
- Scroll down in the Navigation Pane, if necessary, so that Veterinary Vendors Split Form appears on your screen, right-click Veterinary Vendors Split Form to display a shortcut menu, and then click Open on the shortcut menu to open the form in Form view.
- Click the Veterinary Supply field.

Q&A Which command on the shortcut menu gives me Form view? I see both Layout view and Design view, but no option for Form view.
The Open command opens the form in Form view.

- Close the Navigation Pane (Figure 3–7).

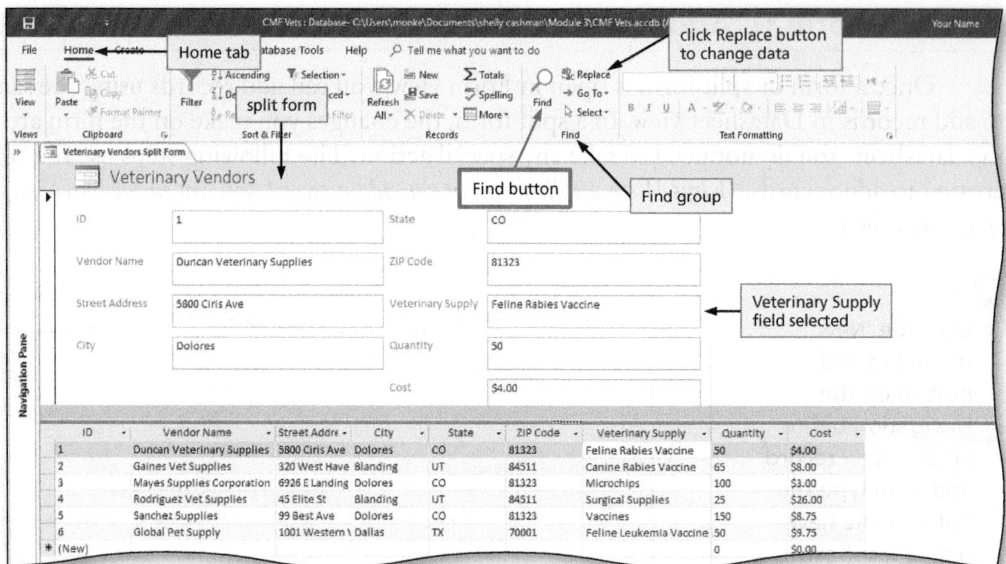

Figure 3–7

2

- Click the Find button (Home tab | Find group) to display the Find and Replace dialog box.
- Type **Microchips** in the Find What text box (Find and Replace dialog box), and then click the Find Next button to find veterinary supply microchips and display the record in the form (Figure 3–8).

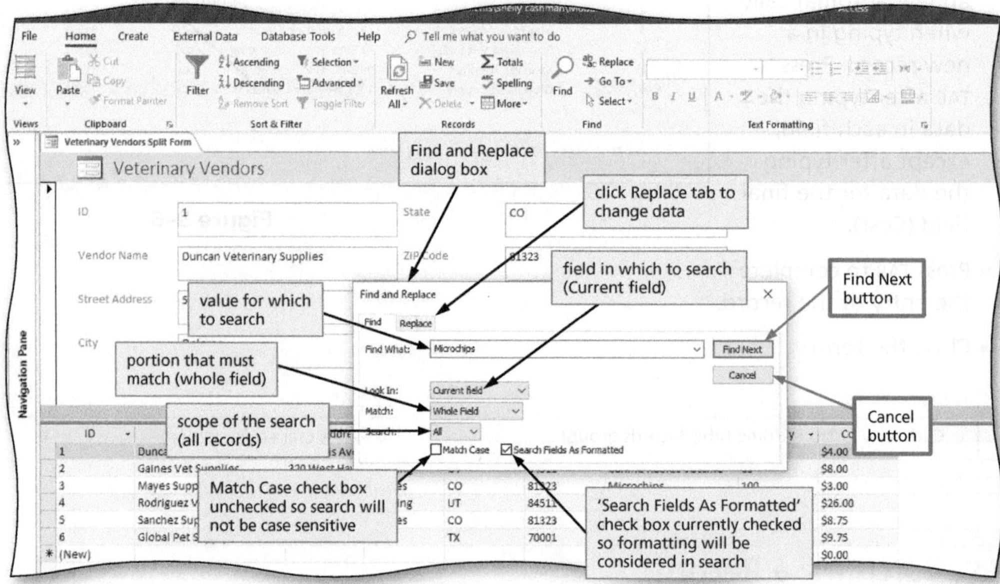

Figure 3–8

Q&A Can I find records using this method in both Datasheet view and Form view?
Yes. You use the same process to find (and replace) records whether you are viewing the data with a split form, in Datasheet view, or in Form view.

3

- Click Cancel (Find and Replace dialog box) to remove the dialog box from the screen.

Q&A Why does the button in the dialog box read Find Next, rather than simply Find?
In some cases, after locating a record that satisfies a criterion, you might need to find the next record that satisfies the same criterion. For example, if you just found the first supplier of microchips, you might then want to find the second supplier, then the third, and so on. To do so, click the Find Next button. You will not need to retype the value each time.

Other Ways

1. Press CTRL+F

Can you replace one value with another using the Find and Replace dialog box?
Yes. Either click the Replace button (Home tab | Find group) or click the Replace tab in the Find and Replace dialog box. You can then enter both the value to find and the new value.

To Update the Contents of a Record

The following step uses Form view to change the name of Veterinary Vendor ID 3 from Mayes Supplies Corporation to Mayes Supplies LLC. ***Why?*** *CMF determined that this supplier's name was incorrect and must be changed.* After locating the record to be changed, select the field to be changed by clicking the field. You can also press TAB repeatedly until the desired field is selected. Then make the appropriate changes. (Clicking the field automatically produces an insertion point. If you use TAB, you will need to press F2 to produce an insertion point.)

1

- Click in the Vendor Name field in the form for ID 3 immediately to the right of the "n" in Corporation.
- Backspace and replace the word Corporation with **LLC**.
- Press TAB to complete the change and move to the next field (Figure 3–9).

Could I have changed the contents of the field in the datasheet portion of the split form?
Yes. You first need to ensure the record to be changed appears in the datasheet. You then can change the value just as in the form.

Do I need to save my change?
No. Once you move to another record or close this form, the change to the name becomes permanent.

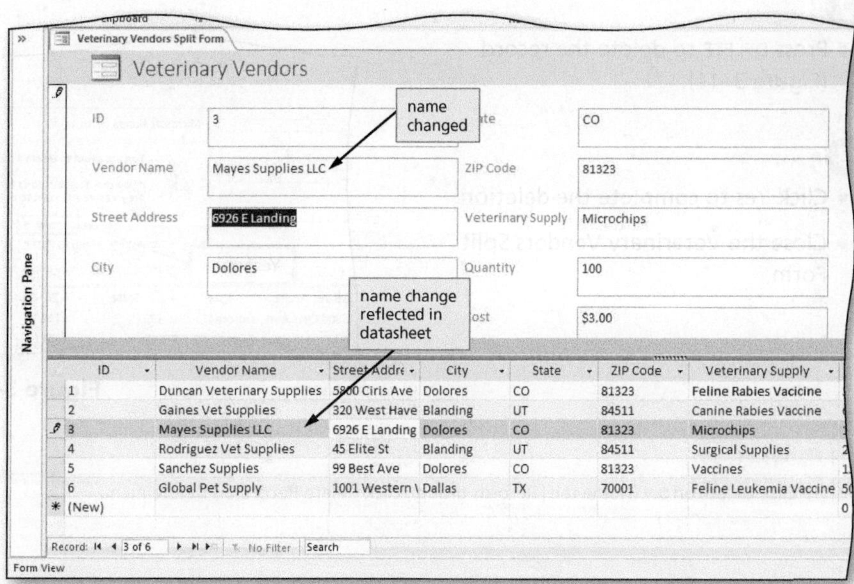

Figure 3–9

To Delete a Record

When records are no longer needed, you should delete them (remove them) from the table. The following steps delete ID 5, Sanchez Supplies. ***Why?*** *Sanchez has been providing an inferior product and CMF no longer wants to use them as a supplier, so the record can be deleted.*

1

- With the Veterinary Vendors Split Form open, click the record selector in the datasheet for ID 5, Vendor Name Sanchez Supplies, to select the record (Figure 3–10).

That technique works in the datasheet portion. How do I select the record in the form portion?
With the desired record appearing in the form, click the record selector (the triangle in front of the record) to select the entire record.

What do I do if the record I want to delete does not appear on the screen?
First search for the record you want to delete using the Find and Replace dialog box.

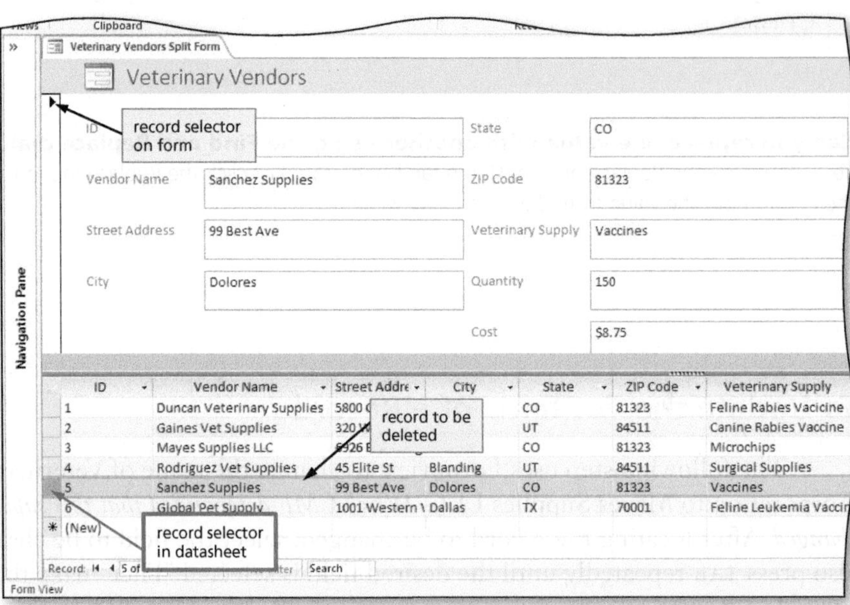

Figure 3–10

2

- Press DELETE to delete the record (Figure 3–11).

3

- Click Yes to complete the deletion.
- Close the Veterinary Vendors Split Form.

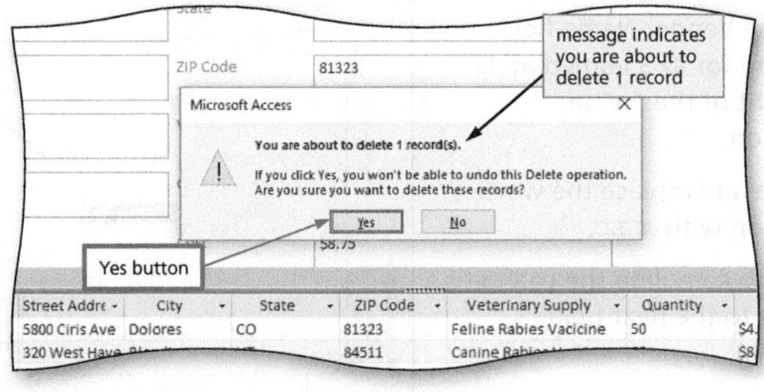

Figure 3–11

Other Ways

1. Click Delete arrow (Home tab | Records group), click Delete Record on Delete menu

BTW
Touch Screen Differences
The Office and Windows interfaces may vary if you are using a touch screen. For this reason, you might notice that the function or appearance of your touch screen differs slightly from this module's presentation.

Filtering Records

You can use the Find button in either Datasheet view or Form view to locate a record quickly that satisfies some criterion (for example, the ID 2). However, using these approaches returns all records, not just the record or records that satisfy the criterion. To have only the record or records that satisfy the criterion appear, use a **filter**. Four types of filters are available: Filter By Selection, Common Filters, Filter By Form, and Advanced Filter/Sort. You can use a filter in either Datasheet view or Form view.

To Use Filter By Selection

To use Filter By Selection, you give Access an example of the data you want by selecting the data within the table. You then choose the option you want on the Selection menu. The following steps use Filter By Selection in Datasheet view to display only the records for vendors in Blanding. ***Why?*** *Filter By Selection is appropriate for displaying these records and is the simplest type of filter.*

- Open the Navigation Pane.
- Open the Veterinary Vendors table, and then close the Navigation Pane.
- Click the City field on the second record to specify Blanding as the city (Figure 3–12).

Q&A Could I have selected the City field on another record where the city is also Blanding to select the same city?

Yes. It does not matter which record you select, as long as the city is Blanding.

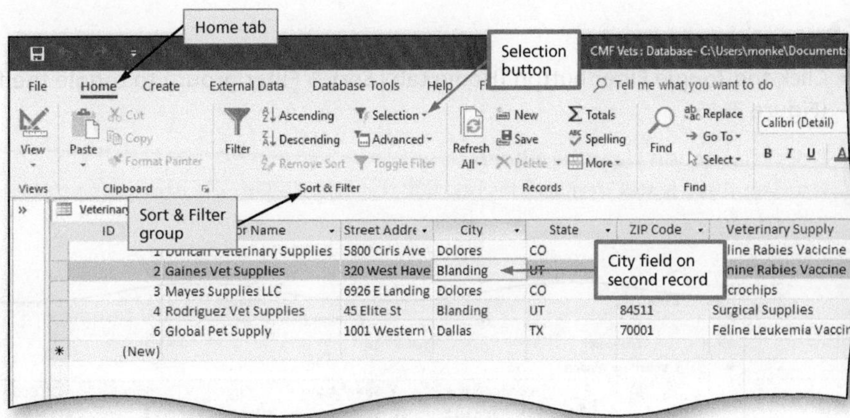

Figure 3–12

- Click the Selection button (Home tab | Sort & Filter group) to display the Selection menu (Figure 3–13).

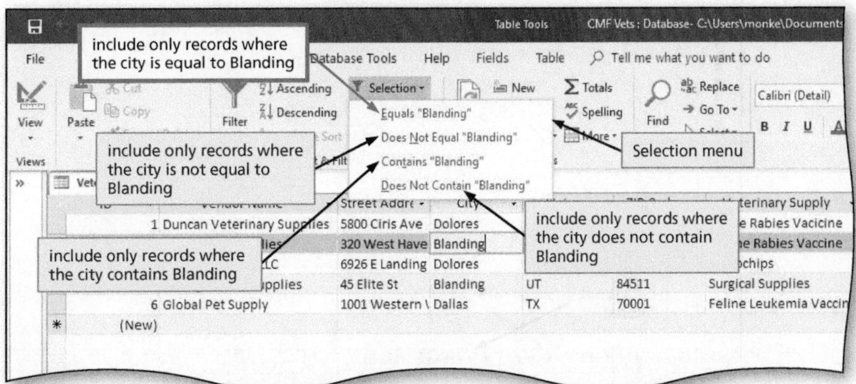

Figure 3–13

3

- Click Equals "Blanding" to select only those accounts whose city is Blanding (Figure 3–14).

Q&A Can I also filter in Form view?

Yes. Filtering works the same whether you are viewing the data with a split form, in Datasheet view, or in Form view.

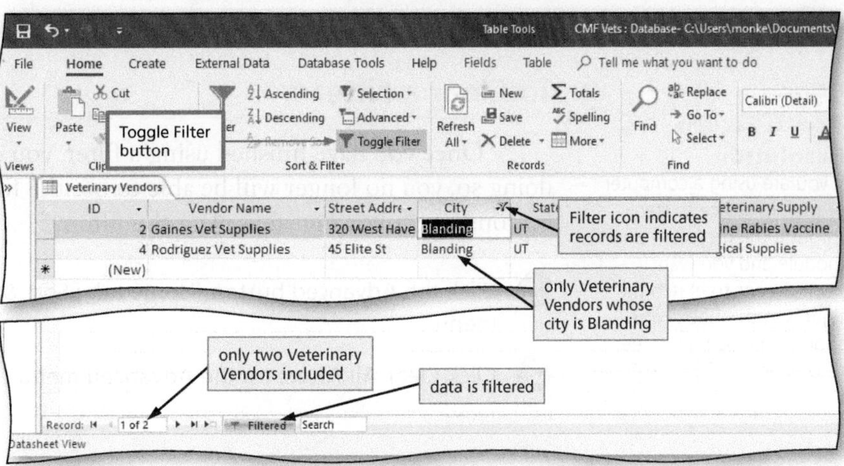

Figure 3–14

To Toggle a Filter

The Toggle Filter button switches between filtered and unfiltered displays of the records in the table. That is, if only filtered records currently appear, clicking the Toggle Filter button will redisplay all records. If all records are currently displayed and there is a filter that is in effect, clicking the Toggle Filter button will display only the filtered records. If no filter is active, the Toggle Filter button will be dimmed, so clicking it would have no effect.

The following step toggles the filter. ***Why?*** *CMF wants to once again view all the records.*

- Click the Toggle Filter button (Home tab | Sort & Filter group) to toggle the filter and redisplay all records (Figure 3–15).

Q&A

Does that action clear the filter?

No. The filter is still in place. If you click the Toggle Filter button a second time, you will again see only the filtered records.

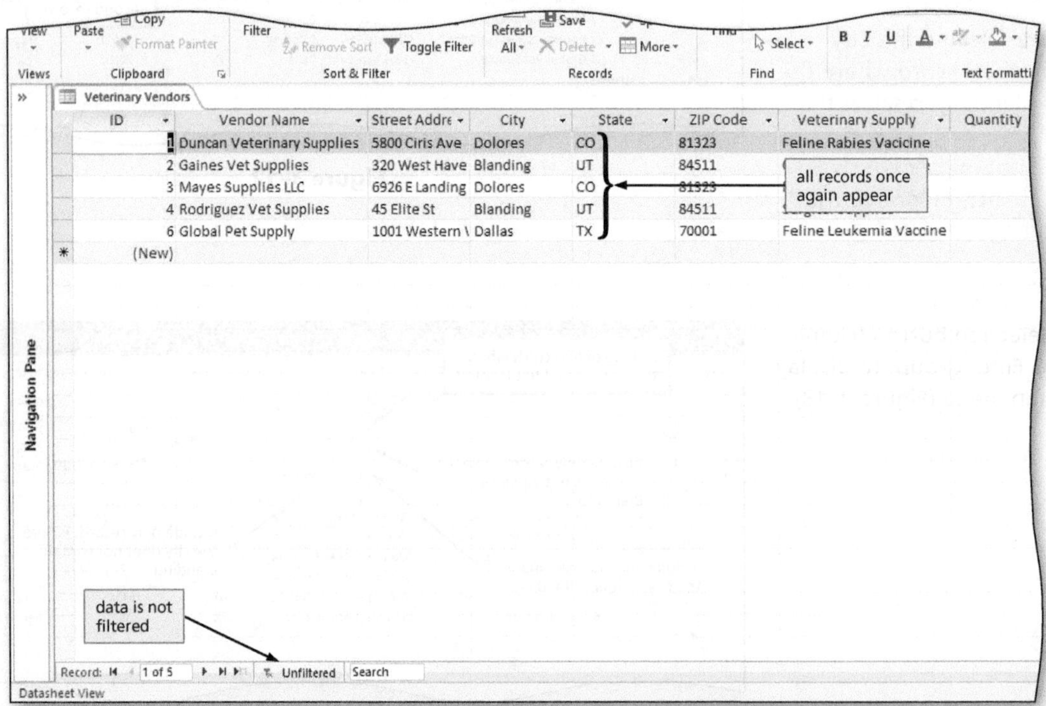

Figure 3–15

BTW

Access Screen Resolution

If you are using a computer or mobile device to step through the project in this module and you want your screens to match the figures in this book, you should change your screen's resolution to 1366 x 768.

To Clear a Filter

Once you have finished using a filter, you can clear (remove) the filter. After doing so, you no longer will be able to use the filter by clicking the Toggle Filter button. The following steps clear the filter.

1. Click the Advanced button (Home tab | Sort & Filter group) to display the Advanced menu.
2. Click Clear All Filters on the Advanced menu.

To Use a Common Filter

If you have determined you want to include those accounts whose city begins with B, Filter By Selection would not be appropriate. ***Why?*** *None of the options within Filter By Selection would support this type of criterion.* You can filter individual fields by clicking the arrow to the right of the field name and using one of the **common filters** that are available for the field. Access includes a collection of filters that perform common filtering tasks; you can modify a common filter by customizing it for the specific field. The following steps customize a common filter to include only those accounts whose city begins with B.

1

- Click the City arrow to display the common filter menu.
- Point to the Text Filters command to display the custom text filters (Figure 3–16).

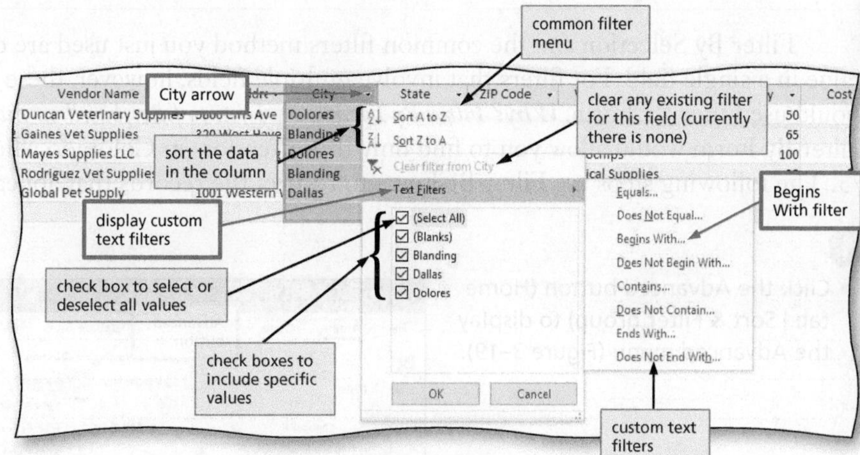

Figure 3–16

Q&A I selected the City field and then clicked the Filter button on the Home tab | Sort & Filter group. My screen looks the same. Is this right?

Yes. That is another way to display the common filter menu.

If I wanted certain cities included, could I use the check boxes?

Yes. Be sure the cities you want are the only ones checked.

2

- Click Begins With to display the Custom Filter dialog box.
- Type `B` as the City begins with value (Figure 3–17).

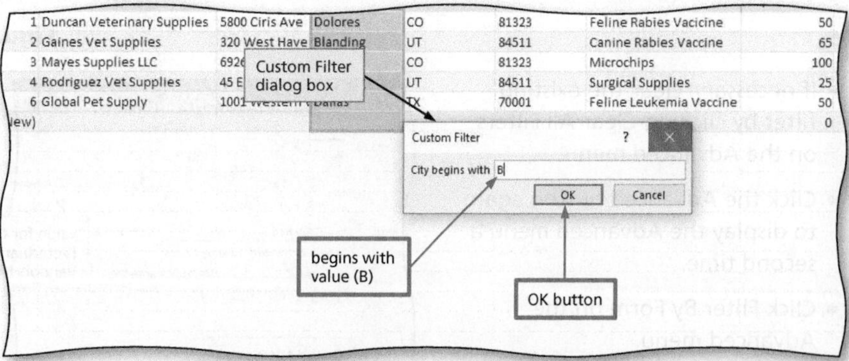

Figure 3–17

Experiment

- Try other options in the common filter menu to see their effects. When done, once again select those accounts whose city begins with B.

3

- Click the OK button to filter the records (Figure 3–18).

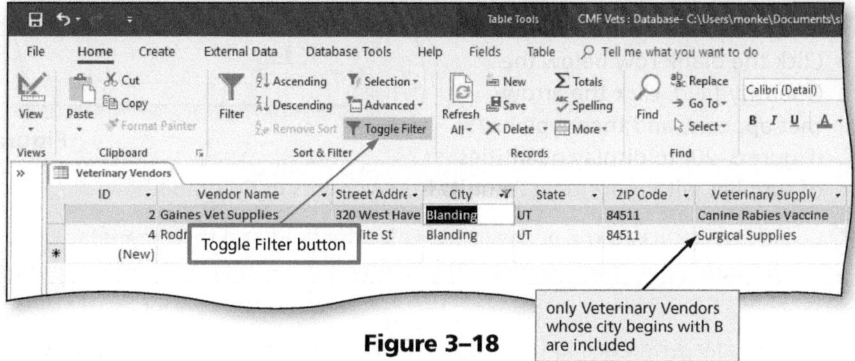

Figure 3–18

Q&A Can I use the same technique in Form view?

In Form view, you would need to click the field and then click the Filter button to display the Common Filter menu. The rest of the process is the same.

- Click the Toggle Filter button (Home tab | Sort & Filter group) to toggle the filter and redisplay all records.

Other Ways

1. Right-click field, click Text Filters on shortcut menu

To Use Filter By Form

Filter By Selection and the common filters method you just used are quick and easy ways to filter by the value in a single field. For filters that involve multiple fields, however, these methods are not appropriate, so you would use Filter By Form. ***Why?*** *Filter By Form allows you to filter based on multiple fields and criteria.* For example, Filter By Form would allow you to find only those vendors in Colorado whose quantity ordered is greater than 75. The following steps use Filter By Form to restrict the records that appear.

- Click the Advanced button (Home tab | Sort & Filter group) to display the Advanced menu (Figure 3–19).

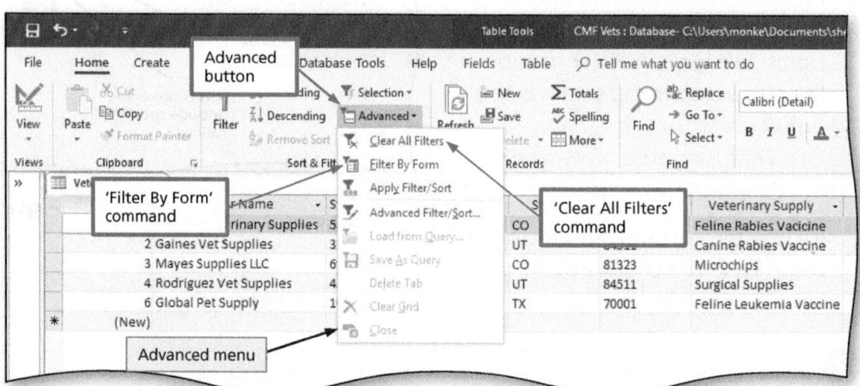

Figure 3–19

2

- If necessary, clear the existing filter by clicking Clear All Filters on the Advanced menu.
- Click the Advanced button again to display the Advanced menu a second time.
- Click Filter By Form on the Advanced menu.
- Click the blank row in the State field, and then choose CO from the menu to enter a criterion for the State field.
- Click the blank row below the Quantity field, click the arrow that appears, and then type `>75` (Figure 3–20) to display quantities of supplies with more than 75 units from vendors in Colorado.

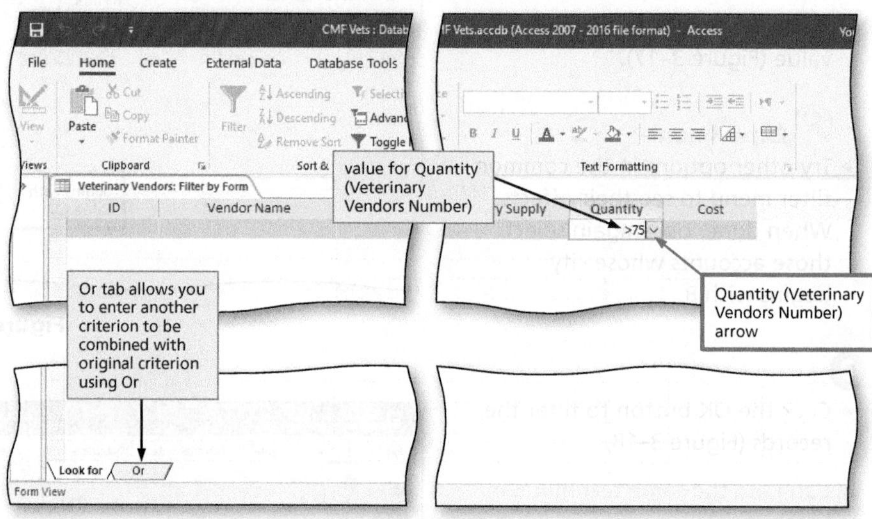

Figure 3–20

Q&A Could I have clicked the arrow in the Quantity field and then made a selection, rather than typing a criterion?
No. Because your criterion involves something other than equality, you need to type the criterion rather than selecting from a list.

Is there any difference in the process if I am viewing a table in Form view rather than in Datasheet view?
In Form view, you will make your entries in a form rather than a datasheet. Otherwise, the process is the same.

3

- Click the Toggle Filter button (Home tab | Sort & Filter group) to apply the filter (Figure 3–21).

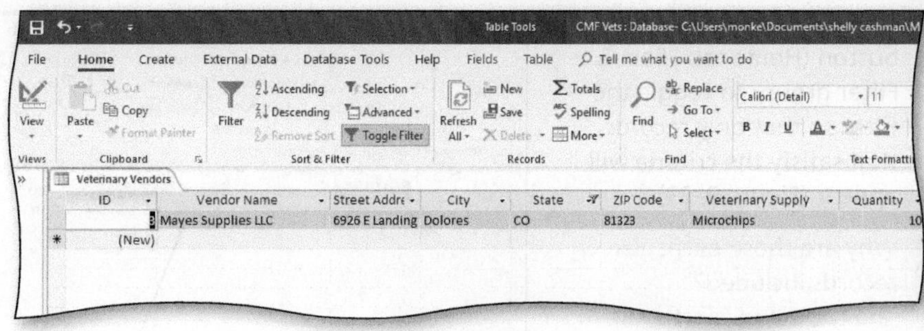

Figure 3–21

Experiment

- Select Filter By Form again and enter different criteria. In each case, toggle the filter to see the effect of your selection. When done, once again select those vendors whose State is CO and whose Quantity is >75.

Other Ways

1. Click the Advanced button (Home tab | Sort & Filter group), click Apply Filter/Sort on Advanced menu

To Use Advanced Filter/Sort

In some cases, your criteria will be too complex even for Filter By Form. You might decide you want to include any vendor in Colorado whose Quantity is greater than 75. Additionally, you might want to include any account whose quantity is lower than 40, no matter which state the account is in. Further, you might want to have the results sorted by account name. The following steps use Advanced Filter/Sort to accomplish this task. ***Why?*** *Advanced Filter/Sort supports complex criteria as well as the ability to sort the results.*

1

- Click the Advanced button (Home tab | Sort & Filter group) to display the Advanced menu, and then click Clear All Filters on the Advanced menu to clear the existing filter.
- Click the Advanced button to display the Advanced menu a second time.
- Click Advanced Filter/Sort on the Advanced menu.
- Expand the size of the field list so all the fields in the Veterinary Vendors table appear.
- Add the Vendor Name field and select Ascending as the sort order to specify the order in which the filtered records will appear.
- Include the State field and enter `CO` as the criterion to limit the search to vendors in Colorado.
- Include the Quantity field and enter `>75` as the criterion in the Criteria row and `<40` as the criterion in the or row (Figure 3–22) to limit the search to vendors whose quantities are less than 40 or greater than 75.

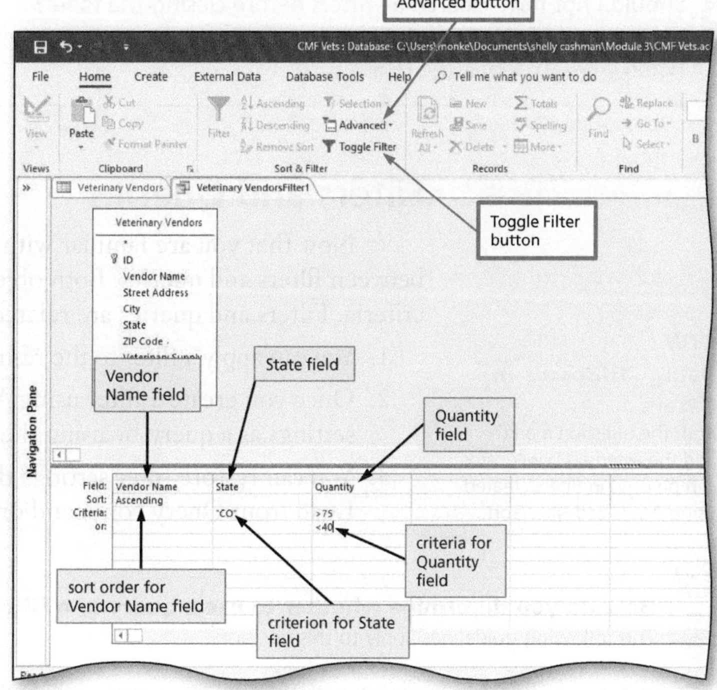

Figure 3–22

2

- Click the Toggle Filter button (Home tab | Sort & Filter group) to toggle the filter so that only records that satisfy the criteria will appear (Figure 3–23).

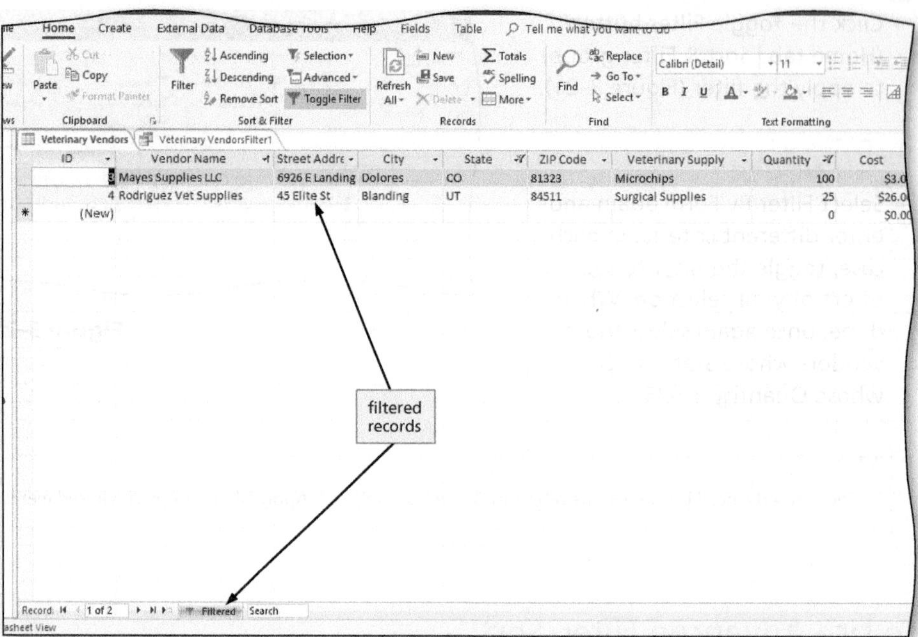

Figure 3–23

Q&A Why are those particular records included?
The third and fourth records are included because the State is Colorado and the quantity is greater than 75. The other record is included because the quantity is less than 40.

Experiment

- Select Advanced Filter/Sort again, and enter different sorting options and criteria. In each case, toggle the filter to see the effect of your selection. When done, change back to the sorting options and criteria you entered in Step 1.

3

- Close the Veterinary Vendors table. When asked if you want to save your changes, click the No button.

Q&A Should I not have cleared all filters before closing the table?
If you are closing a table and not saving the changes, it is not necessary to clear the filter. No filter will be active when you next open the table.

Filters and Queries

Now that you are familiar with how filters work, you might notice similarities between filters and queries. Both objects are used to locate data that meets specific criteria. Filters and queries are related in three ways.

1. You can apply a filter to the results of a query just as you can apply a filter to a table.
2. Once you create a filter using Advanced Filter/Sort, you can save the filter settings as a query by using the Save as Query command on the Advanced menu.
3. You can restore filter settings that you previously saved in a query by using the Load from Query command on the Advanced menu.

BTW

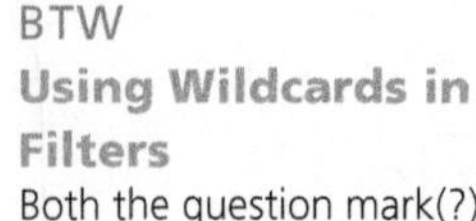

Using Wildcards in Filters
Both the question mark(?) and the asterisk (*) wildcards can be used in filters created using Advanced Filter/Sort.

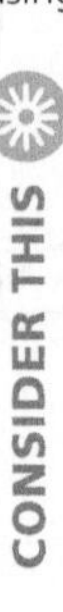

CONSIDER THIS

How do you determine whether to use a query or a filter?
The following guidelines apply to this decision.

- If you think that you will frequently want to display records that satisfy this exact criterion, you should consider creating a query whose results only contain the records that satisfy the criterion. To display those records in the future, simply open the query.
- If you are viewing data in a datasheet or form and decide you want to restrict the records to be included, it is easier to create a filter than a query. You can create and use the filter while you are viewing the data.
- If you have created a filter that you would like to be able to use again, you can save the filter as a query.

CONSIDER THIS

Once you have decided to use a filter, how do you determine which type of filter to use?

- If your criterion for filtering is that the value in a particular field matches or does not match a certain specific value, you can use Filter By Selection.
- If your criterion only involves a single field but is more complex (for example, the criterion specifies that the value in the field begins with a certain collection of letters), you can use a common filter.
- If your criterion involves more than one field, use Filter By Form.
- If your criterion involves more than a single And or Or, or if it involves sorting, you will probably find it simpler to use Advanced Filter/Sort.

Break Point: If you wish to take a break, this is a good place to do so. You can quit Access now. To resume at a later time, run Access, open the database called CMF Vets, and continue following the steps from this location forward.

Changing the Database Structure

When you initially create a database, you define its **structure**; that is, you assign names and types to all the fields. In many cases, the structure you first define will not continue to be appropriate as you use the database.

Perhaps a field currently in the table is no longer necessary. If no one ever uses a particular field, it is not needed in the table. Because it is occupying space and serving no useful purpose, you should remove it from the table. You would also need to delete the field from any forms, reports, or queries that include it.

More commonly, an organization will find that it needs to add data that was not anticipated at the time the database was first designed. The organization's own requirements may have changed. In addition, outside regulations that the organization must satisfy may change as well. Either case requires the addition of fields to an existing table.

Although you can make some changes to the database structure in Datasheet view, it is usually easier and better to make these changes in Design view.

BTW

Using the Find Button

You can use the Find button (Home tab | Find group) to search for records in datasheets, forms, query results, and reports.

To Change a Field's Data Type, Properties, and Primary Key

A field in one of your tables might need a change of its data type and properties; for example, the data type might have been set that prevents the users from making calculations with the field. To make a change to the data type and properties of a field, you would use the following steps.

1. Open the table in Design view.
2. Next to the field name, click the box under Data Type.
3. Choose the correct data type from the menu.
4. A description of the field may be added under the column Description.
5. If necessary, change the field size in the Field Properties General tab below.
6. To change the key field, select the new key field by clicking in the grey box to the left of the field name. Choose Design tab | Tools Group click Primary Key.
7. When you close the table, you will be prompted to save the changes. Select Yes.

BTW

Changing Data Types

It is possible to change the data type for a field that already contains data. Before doing so, you should consider the effect on other database objects, such as forms, queries, and reports. For example, you could convert a Short Text field to a Long Text field if you find that you do not have enough space to store the data that you need. You also could convert a Number field to a Currency field or vice versa.

To Change a Field's Properties in Datasheet View

Alternatively, some of these changes may be done in Datasheet view. To use Datasheet view to change a field's name, caption, or data type, you would use the following steps.

1. Open the table in Datasheet view.
2. Select the desired field and Click the Fields tab | Properties Group.
3. Click Name and Caption, set a caption and description for the field.
4. In the Formatting group, you can set a data type.

To Delete a Field in Design View

If a field in one of your tables is no longer needed, you should delete the field; for example, it might not serve a useful purpose, or it might have been included by mistake. To delete a field, you would use the following steps.

1. Open the table in Design view.
2. Click the row selector for the field to be deleted.
3. Press DELETE.
4. When Access displays the dialog box requesting confirmation that you want to delete the field, click Yes.

To Delete a Field in Datasheet View

1. In Datasheet view, right-click the field and then click Delete Field.

To Move a Field in Design View

If you decide you would rather have a field in one of your tables in a different position in the table, you can move it. To move a field, you would use the following steps.

1. Open the table in Design view.
2. Click the row selector for the field to be deleted.
3. Drag the field to the desired position.
4. Release the mouse button to place the field in the new position.

To Move a Field in Datasheet View

If you are working in Datasheet view and want to move a field, you would use the following steps.

1. In Datasheet view, select the field and then hold down the mouse button. A dark line will appear on the left side of the column.
2. Drag the field to the desired position.
3. Release the mouse button to place the field in the new position.

To Change a Number Field Size in Design View

Most field size changes can be made in either Datasheet view or Design view. However, changing the field size for Number fields, such as the Quantity field, can only be done in Design view. Because the values in the Quantity field could have decimal places, such as a vendor product sold in bulk such as pounds or ounces, only Single, Double, or Decimal are possible choices for the field size. The difference between these choices concerns the amount of accuracy, that is, the number of decimal places to which the number is accurate. Double is more accurate than Single, for example, but requires more storage space. Because the quantity could only be two decimal places, Single is an acceptable choice.

The following steps change the field size of the Quantity field to Single, the format to Fixed, and the number of decimal places to 2, along with extending those changes to any form or report that uses this field. ***Why change the format and number of decimal places?*** *Changing the format and number ensures that each value will appear with precisely two decimal places.*

1

- Open the Navigation Pane, open the Veterinary Vendors table in Design view, and then close the Navigation Pane.
- If necessary, click the vertical scroll bar to display the Quantity field, and then click the row selector for the Quantity field to select the field (Figure 3–24).

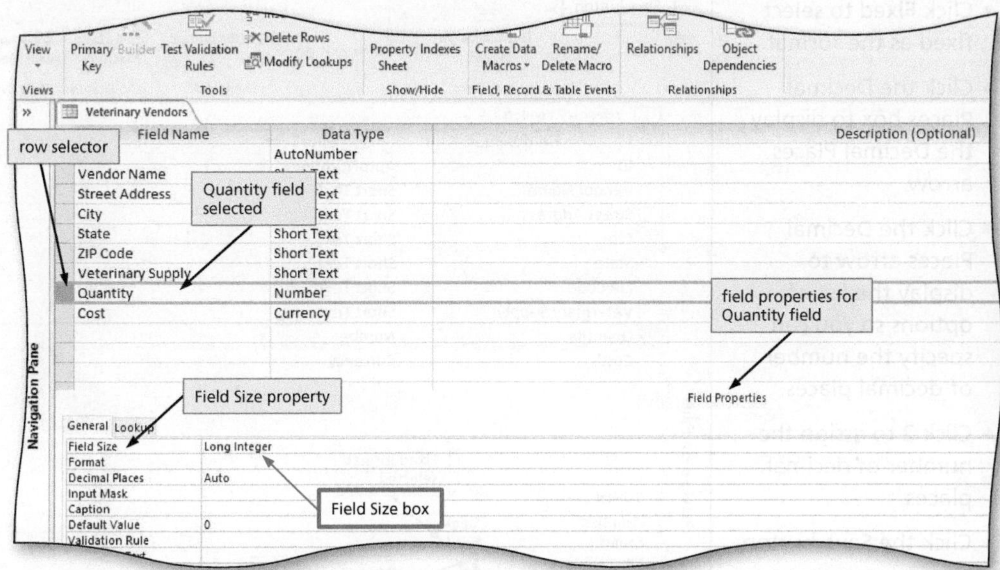

Figure 3–24

2

- Click the Field Size box to display the Field Size arrow.
- Click the Field Size arrow to display the Field Size menu (Figure 3–25).

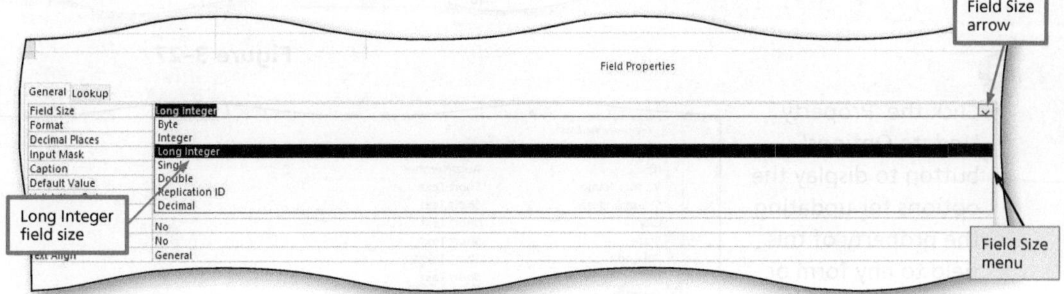

Figure 3–25

Q&A What would happen if I left the field size set to Long Integer?
If the field size is Long Integer, Integer, or Byte, no decimal places can be stored. For example, a value of .10 would be stored as 0. If you enter rates and the values all appear as 0, chances are you did not change the field size property.

3

- Click Single to select single precision as the field size.
- Click the Format box to display the Format arrow (Figure 3–26).

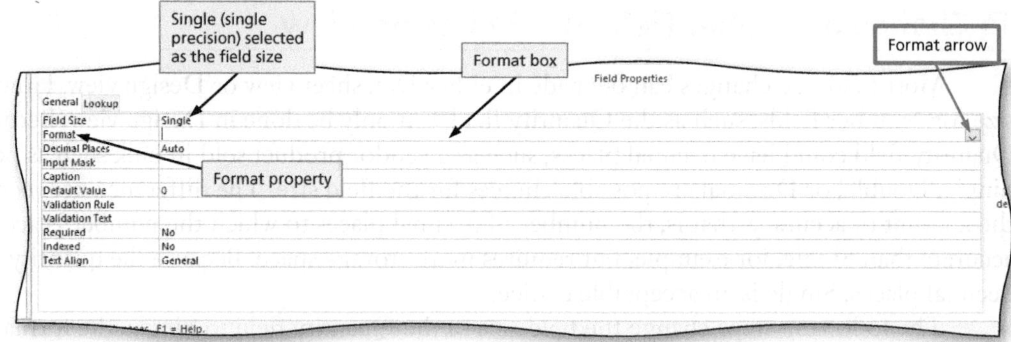

Figure 3–26

4

- Click the Format arrow to display the Format menu.
- Click Fixed to select fixed as the format.
- Click the Decimal Places box to display the Decimal Places arrow.
- Click the Decimal Places arrow to display the list of options so you can specify the number of decimal places.
- Click 2 to assign the number of decimal places.
- Click the Save button to save your changes (Figure 3–27).

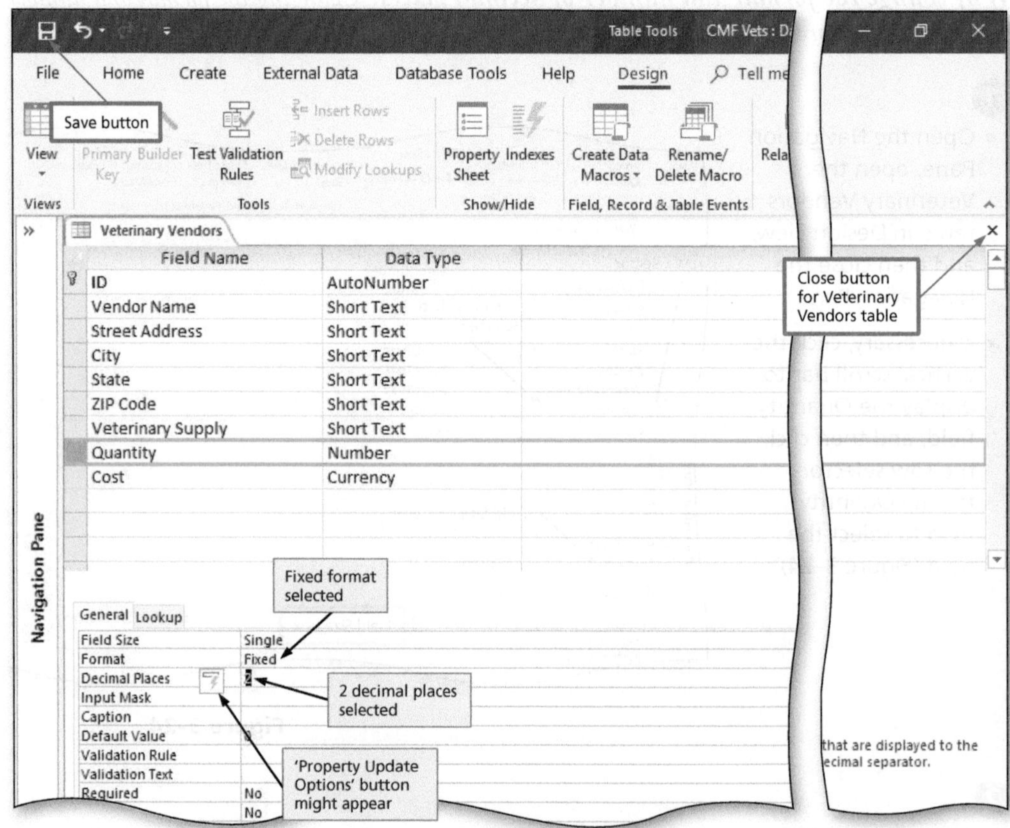

Figure 3–27

5

- Click the 'Property Update Options' button to display the options for updating the property of this field to any form or report that uses this field (Figure 3–28).
- Click Update Decimal Places everywhere Quantity is used to display the Update Properties dialog box (Figure 3–28).

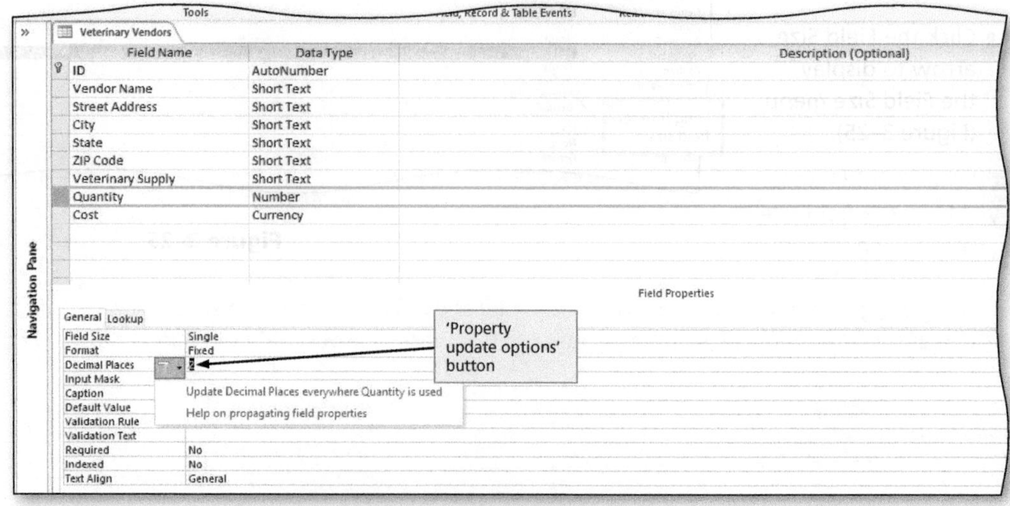

Figure 3–28

6

- In the Update Properties dialog box, ensure that Form: Veterinary Vendors Split Form is selected, and then click Yes to update that form to include the new decimal places for the Quantity field. (Figure 3–29).

Q&A Why did the 'Property Update Options' button appear?
You changed the number of decimal places. The 'Property Update Options' button offers a quick way of making the same change everywhere Quantity appears

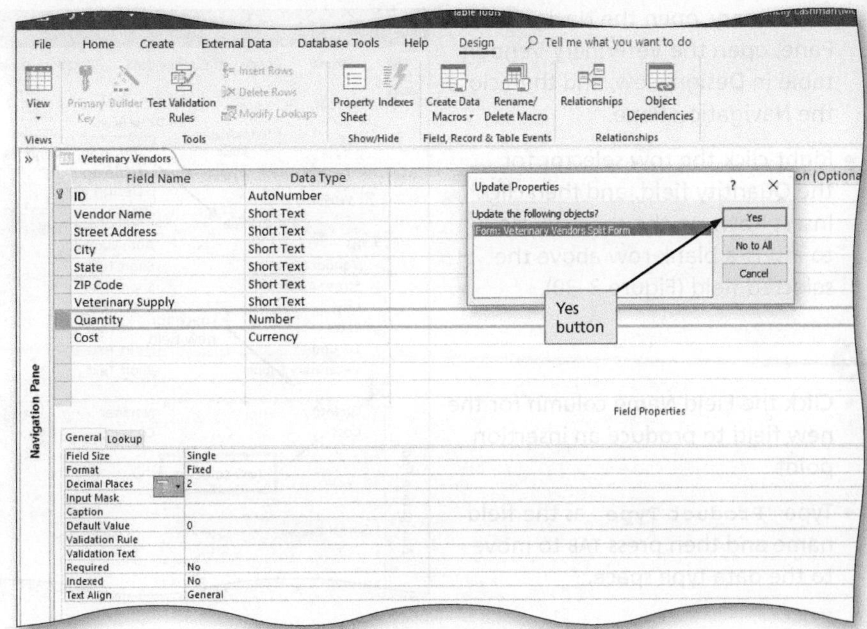

Figure 3–29

To Change the Format of a Number Field in Datasheet

Although the field size of number formatted fields cannot be changed in Datasheet view, the format of a number field can be changed in the datasheet. The number format can be General Number, Currency, Euro, Fixed, Standard, Percent, or Scientific. To change the format of a number field in the datasheet, you would use the following steps.

1. Open the table in Datasheet view.
2. Select the field that you want to change.
3. Click the Data Type arrow (Fields tab | Formatting Group) to display the Data Type menu, and then select the desired number format.

To Add a New Field

You can add fields to a table in a database. The following steps add the Product Type field to the Veterinary Vendors table immediately after the Veterinary Supply field. ***Why?*** *CMF has decided that it needs to categorize its suppliers by adding an additional field, Product Type. The possible values for Product Type are VAC (which indicates the vendor supplies vaccines), MC (which indicates the vendor supplies microchips), or SUP (which indicates the vendor sells surgical supplies).*

- If necessary, open the Navigation Pane, open the Veterinary Vendors table in Design view, and then close the Navigation Pane.
- Right-click the row selector for the Quantity field, and then click Insert Rows on the shortcut menu to insert a blank row above the selected field (Figure 3–30).

- Click the Field Name column for the new field to produce an insertion point.
- Type **`Product Type`** as the field name and then press TAB to move to the data type space.

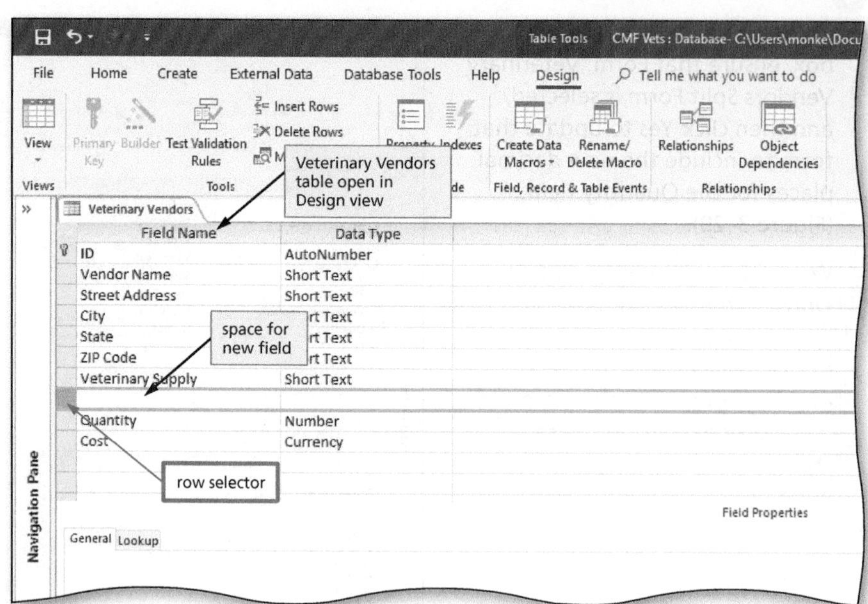

Figure 3–30

Other Ways

1. Click Insert Rows button (Table Tools Design tab | Tools group)

To Create a Lookup Field

A **lookup field** allows the user to select from a list of values when updating the contents of the field. The following steps make the Product Type field a lookup field. ***Why?*** *The Product Type field has only three possible values, making it an appropriate lookup field.*

- If necessary, click the Data Type column for the Product Type field, and then click the Data Type arrow to display the menu of available data types (Figure 3–31).

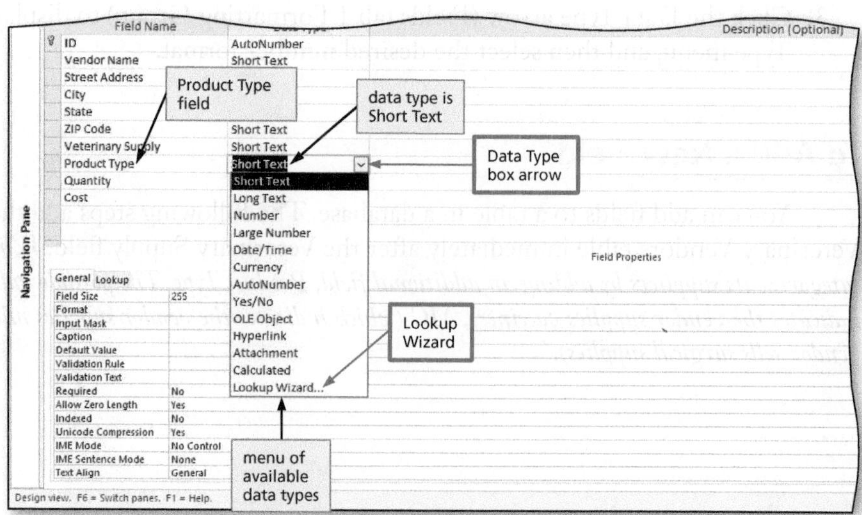

Figure 3–31

2

- Click Lookup Wizard, and then click the 'I will type in the values that I want.' option button (Lookup Wizard dialog box) to indicate that you will type in the values (Figure 3–32).

Q&A When would I use the other option button?
You would use the other option button if the data to be entered in this field were found in another table or query.

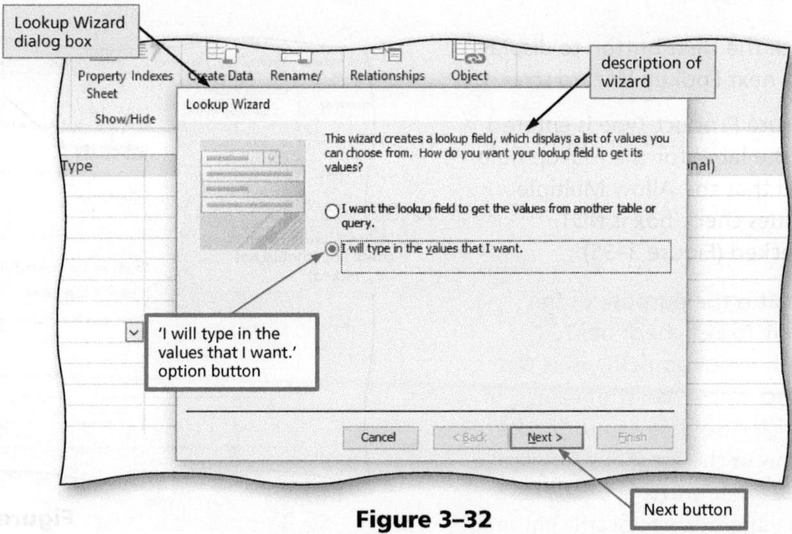

Figure 3–32

3

- Click the Next button to display the next Lookup Wizard screen (Figure 3–33).

Q&A Why did I not change the field size for the Product Type field?
You could have changed the field size to 3, but it is not necessary. When you create a lookup field and indicate specific values for the field, you automatically restrict the field size.

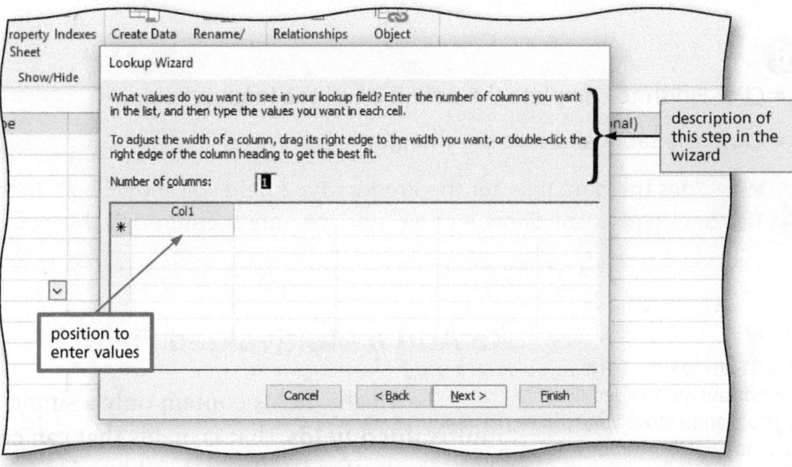

Figure 3–33

4

- Click the first row of the table (below Col1), and then type `VAC` as the value in the first row.
- Press the DOWN ARROW key, and then type `MC` as the value in the second row.
- Press the DOWN ARROW key, and then type `SUP` as the value in the third row (Figure 3–34).

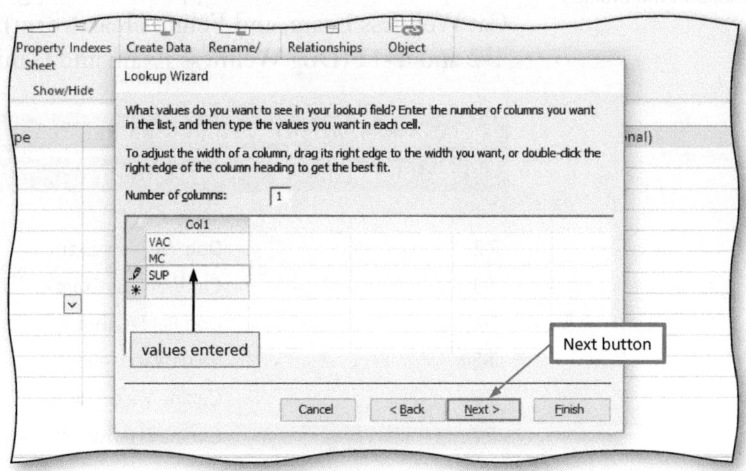

Figure 3–34

- Click the Next button to display the next Lookup Wizard screen.
- Ensure Product Type is entered as the label for the lookup field and that the Allow Multiple Values check box is NOT checked (Figure 3–35).

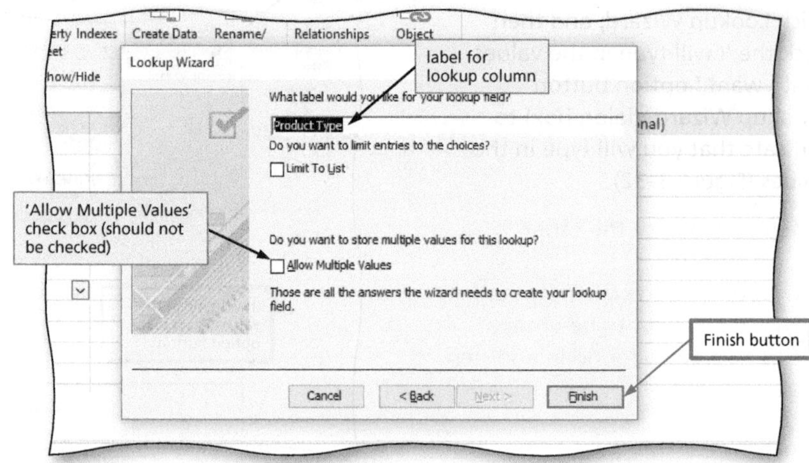

Figure 3–35

Q&A What is the purpose of the Limit To List check box?

With a lookup field, users can select from the list of values, in which case they can only select items in the list. They can also type their entry, in which case they are not necessarily limited to items in the list. If you check the Limit To List check box, users would be limited to items in the list, even if they type their entry. You will accomplish this same restriction later in this module with a validation rule, so you do not need to check this box.

- Click Finish to complete the definition of the lookup field.
- Close the table and save the changes.

Q&A Why does the data type for the Product Type field still show Short Text?

The data type is still Short Text because the values entered in the wizard were entered as text.

BTW

Multivalued Fields

Do not use multivalued fields if you plan to move your data to another relational database management system, such as SQL Server, at a later date. SQL Server and other relational DBMSs do not support multivalued fields.

To Add a Multivalued Field

Normally, fields contain only a single value. In Access, it is possible to have **multivalued fields**, that is, fields that can contain more than one value. CMF wants to use such a field to store the abbreviations of the various treatments done during appointments (see Table 3–1 for the treatment abbreviations and descriptions). Unlike the Product Type, where each product had only one type, appointments can require multiple treatments. One appointment might need T-1, T-3, and T-8 (Feline Rabies, Cat Wellness Exam, and Feline Heartworm). Another appointment might only need T-2 and T-12 (Dog Wellness Exam and Canine Neuter).

Table 3–1 Service Abbreviations and Descriptions

Service Abbreviation	Description	Service Abbreviation	Description
T-1	Feline Rabies	T-8	Feline Heartworm
T-2	Dog Wellness Exam	T-9	Feline Spay
T-3	Cat Wellness Exam	T-10	Feline Neuter
T-4	Dog Rabies Shot	T-11	Canine Spay
T-5	Feline Vaccinations	T-12	Canine Neuter
T-6	Canine Vaccinations	T-13	Feline Microchip
T-7	Canine Heartworm	T-14	Canine Microchip

Creating a multivalued field uses the same process as creating a lookup field, with the exception that you check the Allow Multiple Values check box. The following steps create a multivalued field.

1. Open the Appointments table in Design view.
2. Click the row selector for the Treatment Number.
3. Click the Data Type arrow to display the menu of available data types for the Treatment Number field, and then click Lookup Wizard in the menu of available data types to start the Lookup Wizard.
4. Click the 'I will type in the values that I want.' option button to indicate that you will type in the values.
5. Click the Next button to display the next Lookup Wizard screen.
6. Click the first row of the table (below Col1), and then type `T-1` as the value in the first row.
7. Enter the remaining values from the first column in Table 3–1. Before typing each value, press the DOWN ARROW to move to a new row.
8. Click the Next button to display the next Lookup Wizard screen.
9. Ensure that Treatment Number is entered as the label for the lookup field.
10. Click the Allow Multiple Values check box to allow the user to enter multiple values.
11. Click the Finish button to complete the definition of the Lookup Wizard field.
12. You will see a warning that says, You have changed the Treatment Number lookup column to store multiple values. You will not be able to undo this change once you save the table. Do you want to change Treatment Number to store multiple values? Click the Yes button.
13. Close the table and save the changes.

BTW

Modifying Table Properties

You can change the properties of a table by opening the table in Design view and then clicking the Property Sheet button. To display the records in a table in an order other than primary key (the default sort order), use the Order By property. For example, to display the Appointments table automatically in Patient ID order, change the Order By property setting to Appointments.Patient ID in the property box, close the property sheet, and save the change to the table design. When you open the Appointments table in Datasheet view, the records will be sorted in Patient ID order.

To Modify Single Valued or Multivalued Lookup Fields

At some point you might want to change the list of choices in a lookup field. If you needed to modify a single value or multivalued lookup field, you would use the following steps.

1. Open the table in Design view and select the field to be modified.
2. Click the Lookup tab in the Field Properties pane.
3. Change the list in the Row Source property to the desired list of values.

To Add a Calculated Field

A field that can be computed from other fields is called a **calculated field** or a **computed field**. You can create a calculated field in a query. In Access 2019 it is also possible to include a calculated field in a table. Users will not be able to update this field. ***Why?*** *Access will automatically perform the necessary calculation and display the correct value whenever you display or use this field in any way.* The following steps add to the Veterinary Vendors table a field that calculates the product of the Quantity and Cost fields.

1

- Open the Veterinary Vendors table in Design view.
- Click in the blank row under Cost field.
- Type `Total Amount` as the field name, and then press the TAB key.
- Click the Data Type arrow to display the menu of available data types (Figure 3–36).

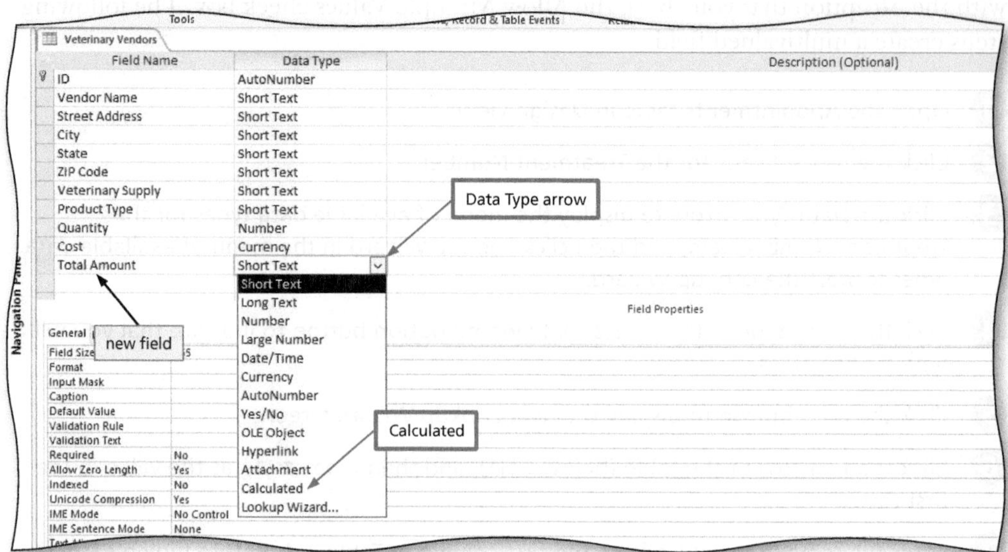

Figure 3–36

2

- Click Calculated to select the Calculated data type and display the Expression Builder dialog box (Figure 3–37).

Q&A I do not have the list of fields in the Expression Categories area. What should I do?
Click Veterinary Vendors in the Expression Elements area.

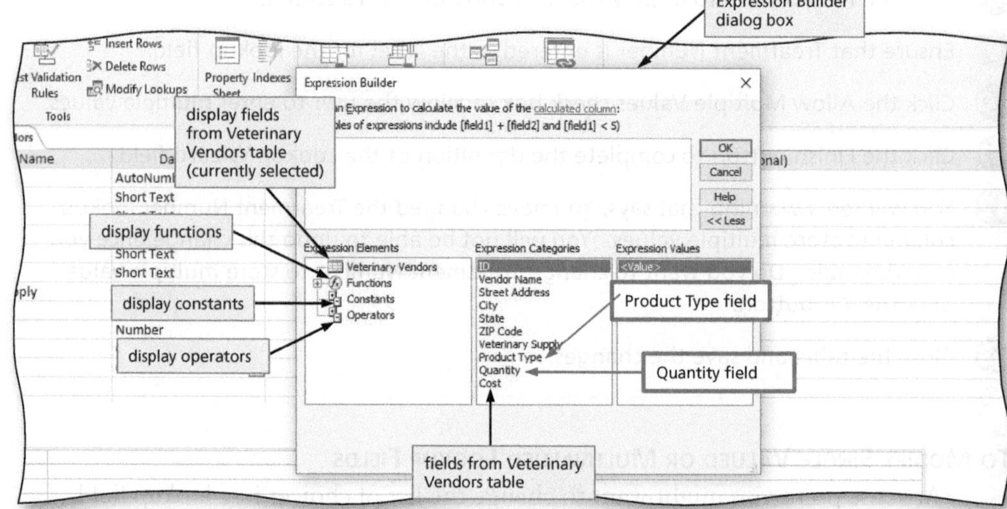

Figure 3–37

3

- Double-click the Quantity field in the Expression Categories area (Expression Builder dialog box) to add the field to the expression.
- Type a multiplication sign (*).

Q&A Could I select the multiplication sign from a list rather than typing it?
Yes. Click Operators in the Expression Elements area to display available operators, and then double-click the multiplication sign.

- Double-click the Cost field in the Expression Categories area (Expression Builder dialog box) to add the field to the expression (Figure 3–38).

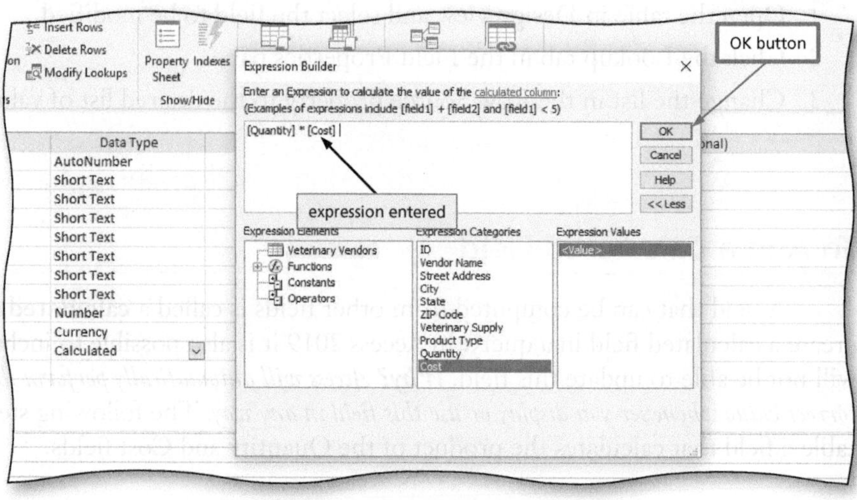

Figure 3–38

4

- Click OK (Expression Builder dialog box) to enter the expression in the Expression property of the Total Amount (Figure 3–39).

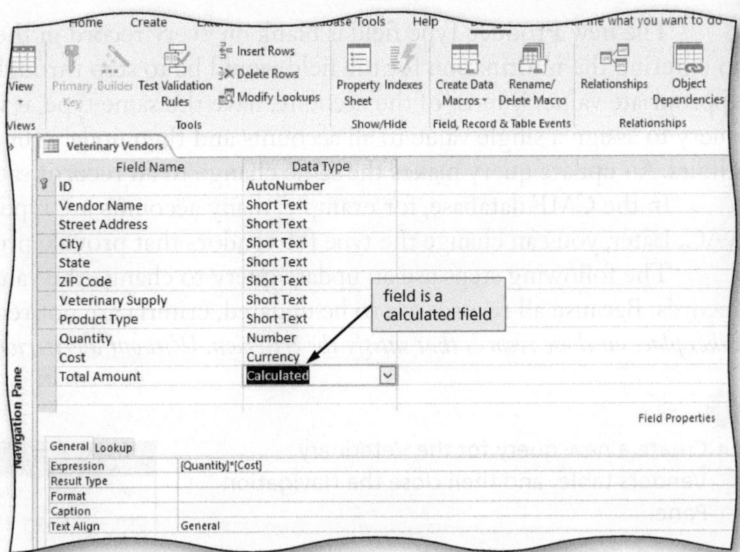

Figure 3–39

Q&A

Could I have typed the expression in the Expression Builder dialog box rather than selecting the fields from a list?
Yes. You can use whichever technique you find more convenient.

When I entered a calculated field in a query, I typed the expression in the Zoom dialog box. Could I have used the Expression Builder instead?
Yes. To do so, you would click Build rather than Zoom on the shortcut menu.

Could I make a calculated field in Datasheet view of a table?
Yes, to do so, open the table in Datasheet view, click the Click to Add arrow in rightmost blank field space, select Calculated Field, and then indicate the type of data you want in that calculated field. Access displays the Expression Builder, where you can complete the calculated field.

Can I modify the calculated field in Design view?
Yes, in Design view, select the calculated field. In the property sheet for the selected field, click the General tab, if necessary, and click to the right of the Expression property. Click the small box with three dots the Expression Builder dialog box.

To Save the Changes and Close the Table

The following steps save the changes; that is, they save the addition of the new field and close the table.

1 Click the Save button on the Quick Access Toolbar to save the changes.

2 Close the Veterinary Vendors table.

Mass Changes

BTW
Database Backup
If you are doing mass changes to a database, be sure to back up the database prior to doing the updates.

In some cases, rather than making individual changes to records, you will want to make mass changes. That is, you will want to add, change, or delete many records in a single operation. You can do this with action queries. Unlike select queries, which simply present data in specific ways, an **action query** adds, deletes, or changes data in a table. An **update query** allows you to make the same change to all records satisfying some criterion. If you omit the criterion, you will make the same changes to all records in the table. A **delete query** allows you to delete all the records satisfying some criterion. You can add the results of a query to an existing table by using an **append query**. You also can add the query results to a new table by using a **make-table query**.

To Use an Update Query

The new Product Type field is blank on every record in the Veterinary Vendors table. One approach to entering the information for the field would be to step through the entire table, assigning each record its appropriate value. If most of the accounts have the same type, it would be more convenient to use an update query to assign a single value to all accounts and then update the Product Type for those accounts whose type differs. An update query makes the same change to all records satisfying a criterion.

In the CMF database, for example, many accounts are type VAC. Initially, you can set all the values to VAC. Later, you can change the type for vendors that provide products other than vaccines.

The following steps use an update query to change the value in the Product Type field to VAC for all the records. Because all records are to be updated, criteria are not required. ***Why?*** *If there is a criterion, the update only takes place on those records that satisfy the criterion. Without a criterion, the update applies to all records.*

- Create a new query for the Veterinary Vendors table, and then close the Navigation Pane.
- Click the Update button (Query Tools Design tab | Query Type group) to specify an update query, double-click the Product Type field to select the field, click the Update To row in the first column of the design grid, and then type **VAC** as the new value (Figure 3–40).

Q&A If I change my mind and do not want an update query, how can I change the query back to a select query?

Click the Select button (Query Tools Design tab | Query Type group).

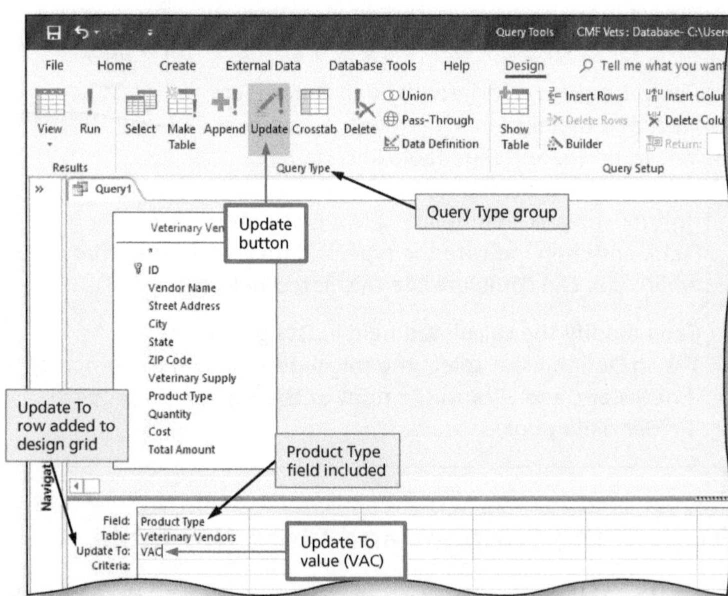

Figure 3–40

- Click the Run button (Query Tools Design tab | Results group) to run the query and update the records (Figure 3–41).

Q&A The dialog box did not appear on my screen when I ran the query. What happened?

If the dialog box did not appear, it means that you did not click the Enable Content button when you first opened the database. Close the database, open it again, and enable the content. Then, create and run the query again.

- Click the Yes button to make the changes.

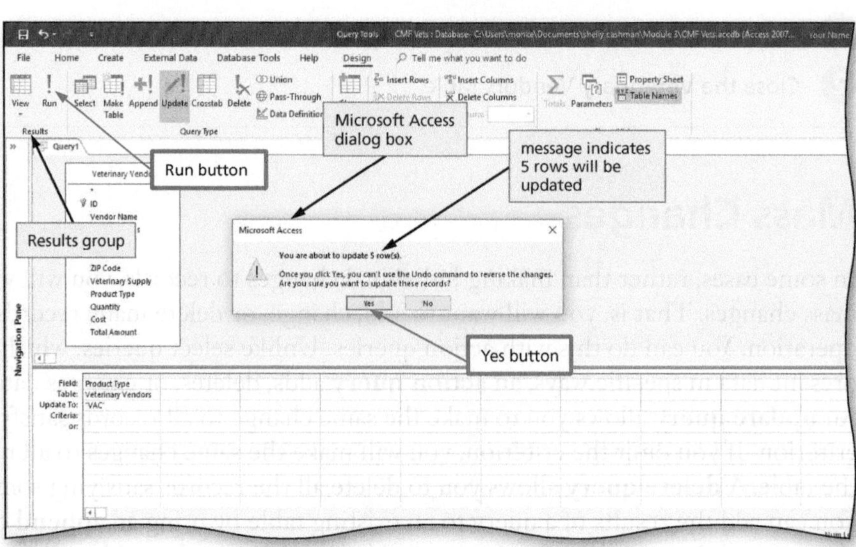

Figure 3–41

Experiment

- Create an update query to change the account type to MC. Enter a criterion to restrict the records to be updated, and then run the query. Open the table to view your changes. When finished, create and run an update query to change the account type to VAC on all records.
- Close the query. Because you do not need to use this update query again, do not save the query.

Other Ways

1. Right-click any open area in upper pane, point to Query Type on shortcut menu, click Update Query on Query Type submenu

BTW

Viewing Records before Updating

You can view records affected by an update query before running the query. To do so, use the Select button to convert the query to a select query, add any additional fields that would help you identify the records, and then view the results. Make any necessary corrections to the query in Design view. When you are satisfied, use the Update button to once again convert the query to an update query.

To Use a Delete Query

In some cases, you might need to delete several records at a time. If, for example, CMF no longer dealt with any vendors in Texas (TX), the vendors with this value in the State field can be deleted from the CMF database. Instead of deleting these accounts individually, which could be very time-consuming in a large database, you can delete them in one operation by using a delete query, which is a query that deletes all the records satisfying the criteria entered in the query. To create a delete query, you would use the following steps.

1. Create a query for the table containing the records to be deleted.
2. In Design view, indicate the fields and criteria that will specify the records to delete.
3. Click the Delete button (Query Tools Design tab | Query Type group).
4. Run the query by clicking the Run button (Query Tools Design tab | Results group).
5. When Access indicates the number of records to be deleted, click the Yes button.

To Use an Append Query

An append query adds a group of records from one table, called the Source table, to the end of another table, called the Destination table. For example, suppose that CMF acquires some new vendors; these new vendors are accompanied by a related database. To avoid entering all this information manually, you can append it to the Veterinary Vendors table in the CMF database using the append query. To create an append query, you would use the following steps.

1. Create a query for the Source table.
2. In Design view, indicate the fields to include, and then enter any necessary criteria.
3. View the query results to be sure you have specified the correct data, and then return to Design view.
4. Click the Append button (Query Tools Design tab | Query Type group).
5. When Access displays the Append dialog box, specify the name of the Destination table and its location. Run the query by clicking the Run button (Query Tools Design tab | Results group).
6. When Access indicates the number of records to be appended, click the OK button.

BTW

Delete Queries

If you do not specify any criteria in a delete query, Access will delete all the records in the table.

BTW
Archive Tables
You can use a make table query to create an archive table. An archive table is a table that contains data that is no longer used in operations but that might still be needed by the organization.

To Use a Make-Table Query

In some cases, you might want to create a new table that contains only records from an existing table. If so, use a make-table query to add the records to a new table. To create a make-table query, you would use the following steps.

1. Create a query for the Source table.
2. In Design view, indicate the fields to include, and then enter any necessary criteria.
3. View the query results to be sure you have specified the correct data, and then return to Design view.
4. Click the Make Table button (Query Tools Design tab | Query Type group).
5. When Access displays the Make Table dialog box, specify the name of the Destination table and its location. Run the query by clicking the Run button (Query Tools Design tab | Results group).
6. When Access indicates the number of records to be inserted, click the OK button.

Break Point: If you wish to take a break, this is a good place to do so. You can quit Access now. To resume at a later time, start Access, open the database called CMF, and continue following the steps from this location forward.

BTW
Using Wildcards in Validation Rules
You can include wildcards in validation rules. For example, if you enter the expression, like T?, in the validation rule for the State field, the only valid entries for the field will be TN or TX. However, erroneous data could be entered, such as TE or TA.

Validation Rules

You now have created, loaded, queried, and updated a database. Nothing you have done so far, however, restricts users to entering only valid data, that is, data that follows the rules established for data in the database. An example of such a rule would be that product types can only be VAC, MC, or SUP. To ensure the entry of valid data, you create **validation rules**, or rules that a user must follow when entering the data. When the database contains validation rules, Access prevents users from entering data that does not follow the rules. You can also specify **validation text**, which is the message that appears if a user attempts to violate the validation rule.

Validation rules can indicate a **required field**, a field in which the user *must* enter data; failing to enter data into a required field generates an error. Validation rules can also restrict a user's entry to a certain **range of values**; for example, the values in the Quantity field must be between 0 and 1,000. Alternatively, rules can specify a **default value**, that is, a value that Access will display on the screen in a particular field before the user begins adding a record. To make data entry of account numbers more convenient for the user, you can also have lowercase letters appear automatically as uppercase letters. Finally, validation rules can specify a collection of acceptable values.

BTW
Using the BETWEEN Operator in Validation Rules
You can use the BETWEEN operator to specify a range of values. For example, to specify that entries in the Quantity field must be between 0 and 1,000, type BETWEEN 0 and 1000 as the rule.

To Change a Field Size

The Field Size property for text fields represents the maximum number of characters a user can enter in the field. Because the field size for the ZIP Code field in the Veterinary Vendors table is the default 255, but a user would never enter a ZIP code that long. Conversely, if the field had been set to be only 5 spaces, then the ZIP code plus four would not fit into that field. Occasionally, you will find that the field size that seemed appropriate when you first created a table is no longer appropriate. In the Veterinary Vendors table, the ZIP code needs to be adjusted to fit 20 characters, in the case that there is a foreign postal code that is longer than the ZIP code plus four. To allow this longer postal code in the table, you need to change the field size for the

ZIP Code field to a Short Text that is smaller so it doesn't take up excess storage. The following step changes the field size for the ZIP code field from 255 to 20.

1 Open the Veterinary Vendors table in Design view and close the Navigation Pane.

2 Select the ZIP Code field by clicking its row selector.

3 Click the Field Size property to select it, delete the current entry (255), and then type 20 as the new field size.

To Specify a Required Field

To specify that a field is to be required, change the value for the Required property from No to Yes. The following step specifies that the Vendor Name field is a required field. ***Why?*** *Users will not be able to leave the Vendor Name field blank when entering or editing records.*

- Select the Vendor Name field by clicking its row selector.
- Click the Required property box in the Field Properties pane, and then click the arrow that appears.
- Click Yes in the list to make Vendor Name a required field (Figure 3–42).

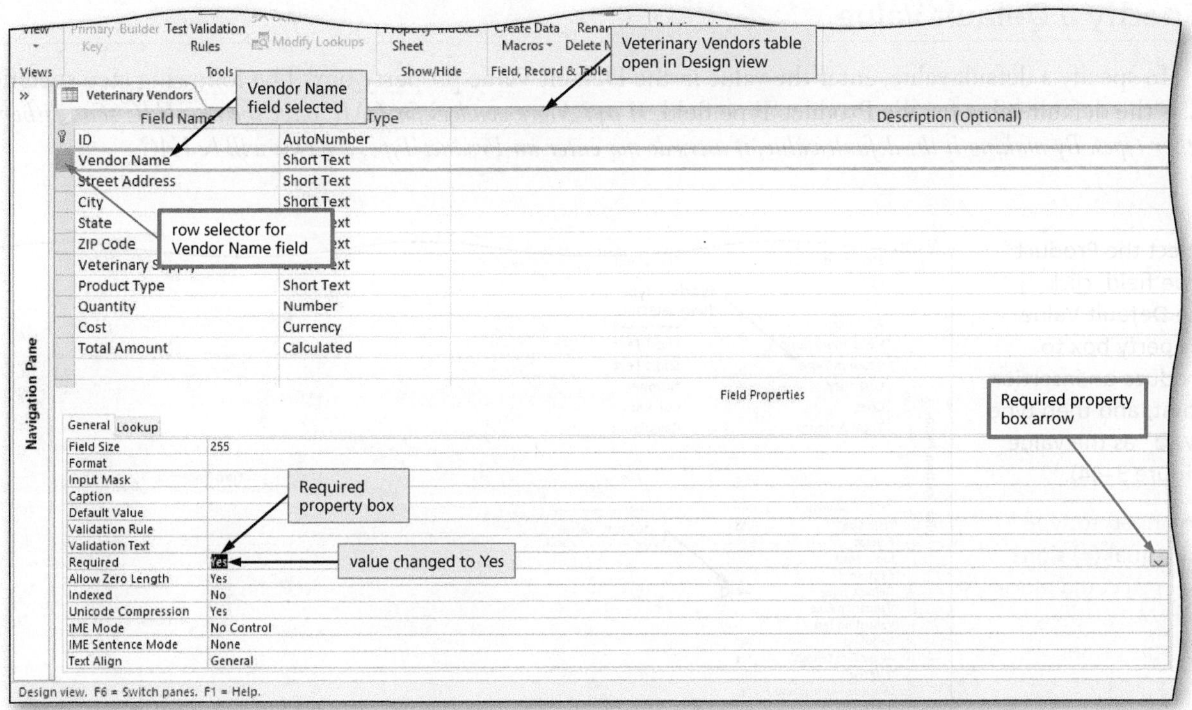

Figure 3–42

To Specify a Range

The following step specifies that entries in the Quantity field must greater than 0 and less than or equal to 1,000. To indicate this range, the criterion specifies that the Quantity amount must be both > 0 (greater than) and <= 1000 (less than or equal to 1,000). ***Why?*** *Combining these two criteria with the word, and, is logically equivalent to being between 0.00 and 1,001.00.*

- Select the Quantity field by clicking its row selector, click the Validation Rule property box to produce an insertion point, and then type `>0 and <=1000` as the rule.
- Click the Validation Text property box to produce an insertion point, and then type `Must be greater than 0.00 and at most 1,000.00` as the text (Figure 3–43).

Q&A What is the effect of this change?
Users will now be prohibited from entering a Quantity amount that is either less than or equal to 0.00 or greater than 1,000.00 when they add records or change the value in the Quantity field.

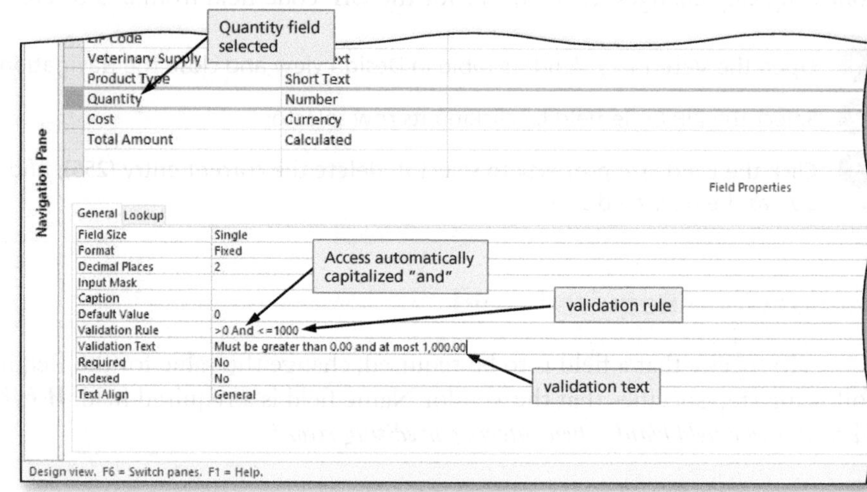

Figure 3–43

To Specify a Default Value

To specify a default value, enter the value in the Default Value property box. The following step specifies VAC as the default value for the Product Type field. ***Why?*** *More vendors for CMF have the type VAC than either of the other types. By making it the default value, if users do not enter an Product Type, the type will be VAC.*

- Select the Product Type field, click the Default Value property box to produce an insertion point, and then type `=VAC` as the value (Figure 3–44).

Q&A Do I need to type the equal (=) sign?
No. You could enter just VAC as the default value.

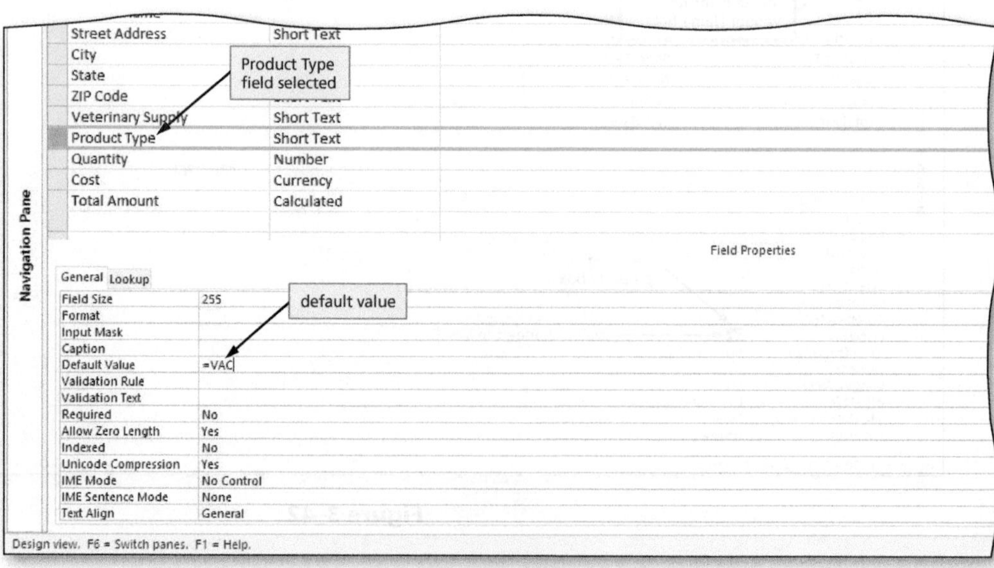

Figure 3–44

To Specify a Collection of Legal Values

The only **legal values**, or **allowable values**, for the Product Type field are VAC, MC, and SUP. The following step creates a validation rule to specify these as the only legal values for the Account Type field. ***Why?*** *The validation rule prohibits users from entering any other value in the Product Type field.*

1

- **With the Product Type field selected, click the Validation Rule property box to produce an insertion point and then type `=VAC or =MC or =SUP` as the validation rule.**
- **Click the Validation Text property box, and then type `Must be VAC, MC, or SUP` as the validation text (Figure 3–45).**

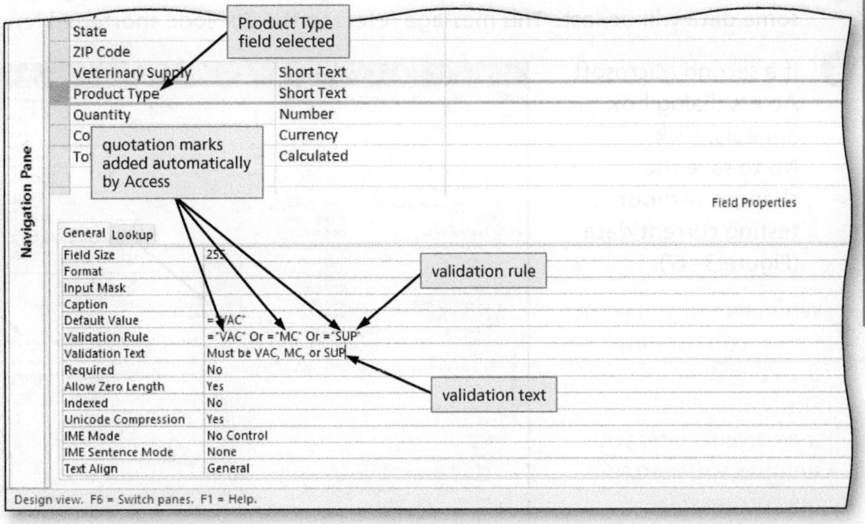

Q&A What is the effect of this change?

Users will now only be allowed to enter VAC, MC, or SUP in the Product Type field when they add records or make changes to this field.

Do I have to put quotation marks around VAC, MC and SUP?

No, you can just type in =VAC or =MC or =SUP. Access automatically will put quotation marks around the product types.

Figure 3–45

To Save the Validation Rules, Default Values, and Formats

The following steps save the validation rules, default values, and formats.

1 **Click the Save button on the Quick Access Toolbar to save the changes (Figure 3–46).**

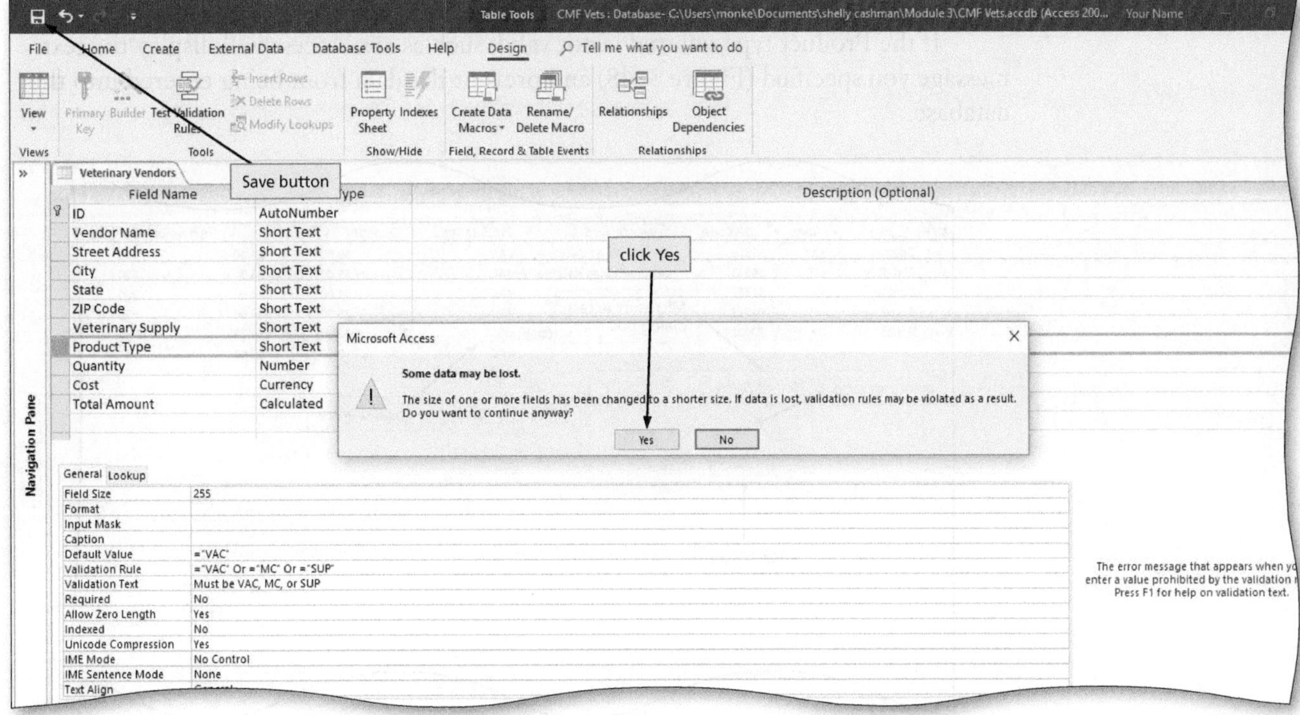

Figure 3–46

2. Click the Yes button (Microsoft Access dialog box) to save the changes, even though the message warns that some data will be lost. This message refers to the ZIP code shortened length.

3. If a second Microsoft Access dialog box appears, click No to save the changes without testing current data (Figure 3–47).

Q&A When would you want to test current data?
If you have any doubts about the validity of the current data, you should be sure to test the current data.

4. Close the Veterinary Vendors table.

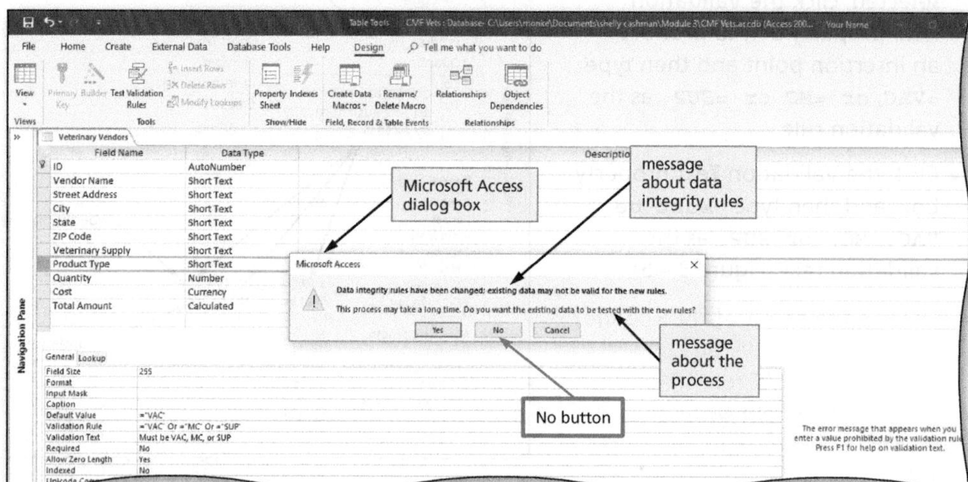

Figure 3–47

Q&A Can I set validation rules, validation text, and properties in Datasheet view?
Yes, in Datasheet view, select the field and display the Fields. In the Properties group, you can also modify lookups. In the Field Validation group, you can set validation.

Updating a Table That Contains Validation Rules

Now that the CMF database contains validation rules, Access restricts the user to entering data that is valid and is formatted correctly. If a user enters a number that is out of the required range, for example, or enters a value that is not one of the permitted choices, Access displays an error message in the form of a dialog box. The user cannot update the database until the error is corrected.

If the Product type entered is not valid, such as xxx, Access will display the text message you specified (Figure 3–48) and prevent the data from being entered into the database.

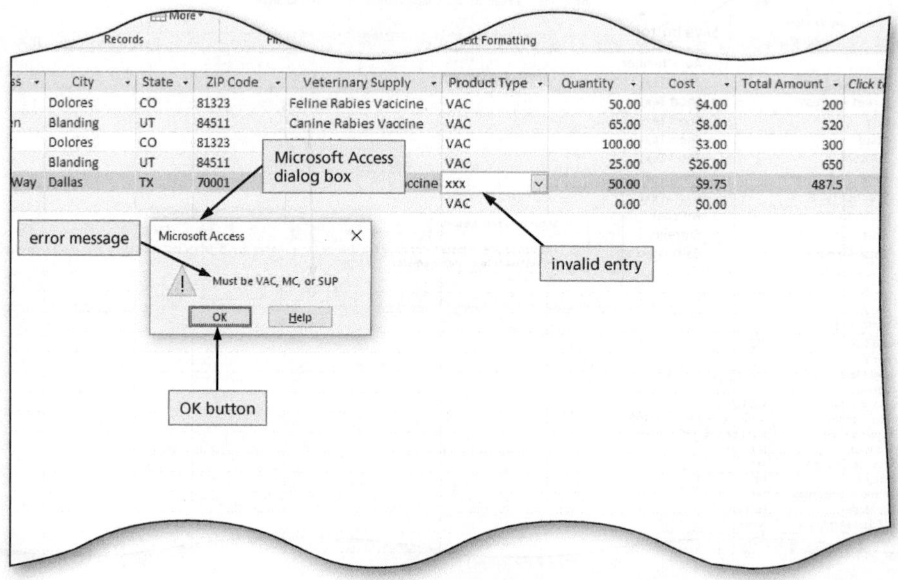

Figure 3–48

If the Current Due amount entered is not valid, such as 5000, which is too large, Access also displays the appropriate message (Figure 3–49) and refuses to accept the data.

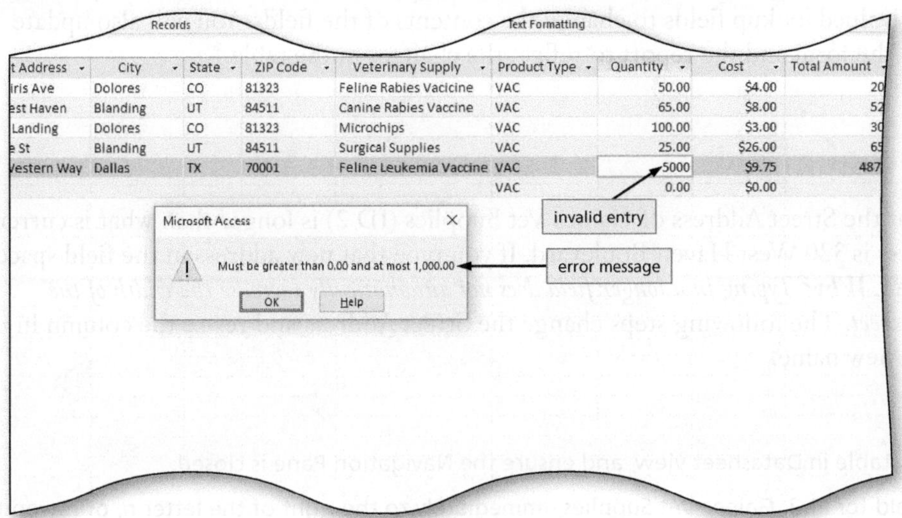

Figure 3–49

If a required field contains no data, Access indicates this by displaying an error message as soon as you attempt to leave the record (Figure 3–50). The field must contain a valid entry before Access will move to a different record, even if you did not specify validation text.

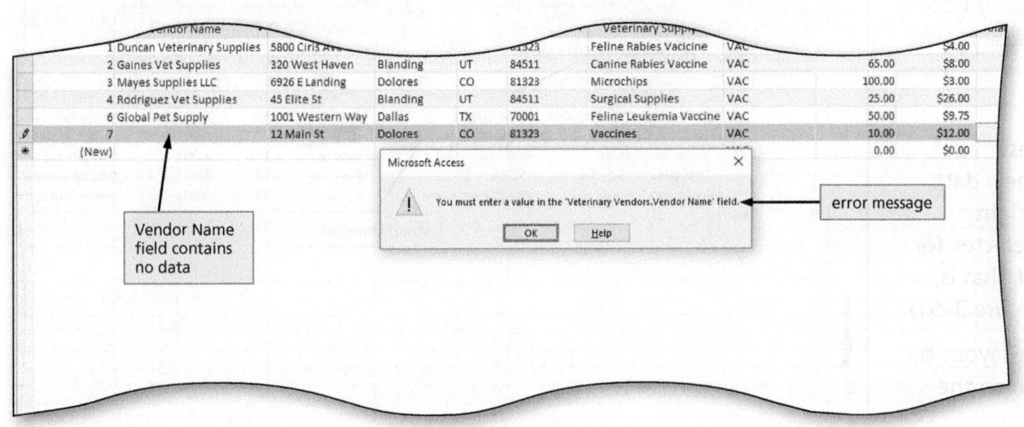

Figure 3–50

CONSIDER THIS

When entering invalid data into a field with a validation rule, is it possible that you could not enter the data correctly? What would cause this? If it happens, what should you do?

If you cannot remember the validation rule you created or if you created the rule incorrectly, you might not be able to enter the data. In such a case, you will be unable to leave the field or close the table because you have entered data into a field that violates the validation rule.

If this happens, first try again to type an acceptable entry. If this does not work, repeatedly press BACKSPACE to erase the contents of the field, and then try to leave the field. If you are unsuccessful using this procedure, press ESC until the record is removed from the screen. The record will not be added to the database.

Should the need arise to take this drastic action, you probably have a faulty validation rule. Use the techniques of the previous sections to correct the existing validation rules for the field.

Making Additional Changes to the Database

Now that you have changed the structure and created validation rules, there are additional changes to be made to the database. You will use both the lookup and multivalued lookup fields to change the contents of the fields. You will also update both the form and the report to reflect the changes in the table.

To Change the Contents of a Field

Perhaps you realized that the Street Address of Gaines Vet Supplies (ID 2) is longer than what is currently in the table. The correct address is 320 West Haven Boulevard. If you type that new address in the field space, the full address will be obscured. ***Why?*** *Typing in a longer field does not automatically increase the width of the corresponding column in the datasheet.* The following steps change the Street Address and resize the column in the datasheet to accommodate the new name.

- Open the Veterinary Vendors table in Datasheet view, and ensure the Navigation Pane is closed.
- Click in the Street Address field for ID 2, Gaines Vet Supplies, immediately to the right of the letter n, of Haven to produce an insertion point.
- Press SPACEBAR to enter a space.
- Enter the word `Boulevard`, and then press TAB to update the address.

Q&A I cannot add the extra characters. Whatever I type replaces what is currently in the cell. What happened and what should I do?
You are typing in Overtype mode, not Insert mode. Press INSERT and correct the entry.

- Resize the Street Address column to best fit the new data by double-clicking the right boundary of the field selector for the Street Address field, that is, the column heading (Figure 3–51).
- Save the changes to the layout by clicking the Save button on the Quick Access Toolbar.
- Close the Veterinary Vendors table.

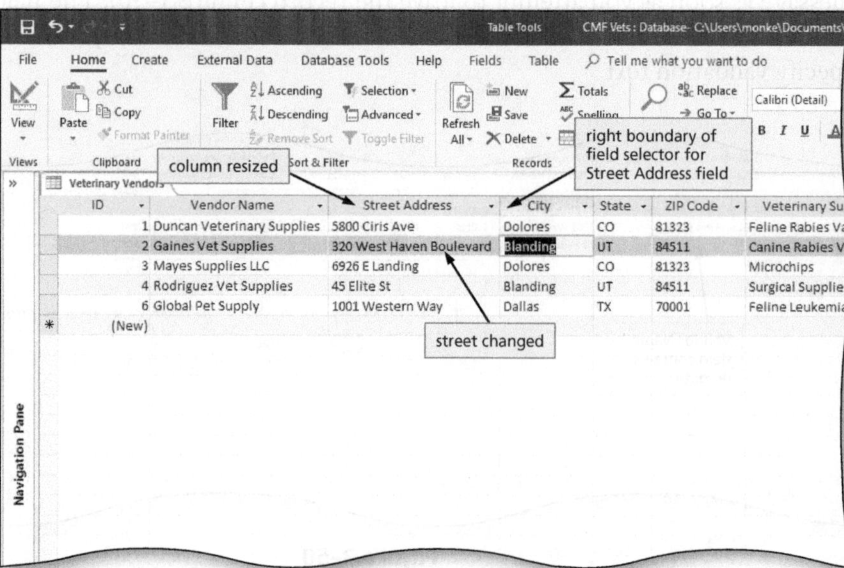

Figure 3–51

To Use a Lookup Field

Earlier, you changed all the entries in the Product Type field to VAC. You have created a rule that will ensure that only legitimate values (VAC, MC, or SUP) can be entered in the field. You also made Product Type a lookup field. ***Why?*** *You can make changes to a lookup field for individual records by simply clicking the field to be changed, clicking the arrow that appears in the field, and then selecting the desired value from the list.* The following steps change the incorrect Product Type values to the correct values.

1

- Open the Veterinary Vendors table in Datasheet view and ensure the Navigation Pane is closed.
- Click in the Product Type field on the third record (ID 3) to display an arrow.
- Click the arrow to display the drop-down list of available choices for the Product Type field (Figure 3–52).

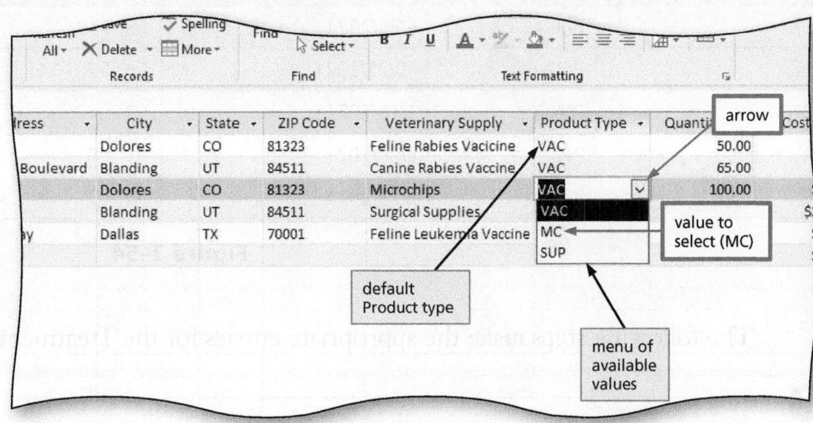

Figure 3–52

Q&A I got the drop-down list as soon as I clicked. I did not need to click the arrow. What happened?
If you click in the position where the arrow would appear, you will get the drop-down list. If you click anywhere else, you would need to click the arrow.

Could I type the value instead of selecting it from the list?
Yes. Once you have either deleted the previous value or selected the entire previous value, you can begin typing. You do not have to type the full entry. When you begin with the letter, M, for example, Access will automatically add the C.

2

- Click MC to change the value.
- In a similar fashion, change the values on the other record to match that shown in Figure 3–53.
- Close the table.

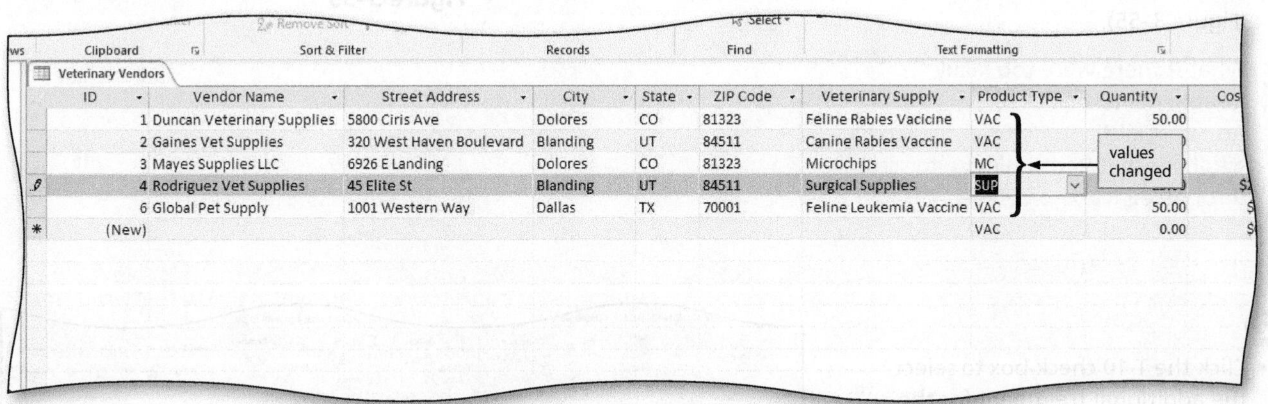

Figure 3–53

To Use a Multivalued Lookup Field

Using a multivalued lookup field is similar to using a regular lookup field. The difference is that when you display the list, the entries are all preceded by check boxes. ***Why?** Having the check boxes allows you to make multiple selections. You check all the entries that you want.* The appropriate entries are shown for the Appointments table in Figure 3–54. As indicated in the figure, most animals come into the CMF Veterinary office for more than one treatment.

Appointment ID	Patient ID	Appointment Date	Treatment Number	Veterinarian	Owner
1	P-3	6/30/2021	T-3, T-10	B01	O-6
2	P-7	10/25/2021	T-4, T-7, T-14	B01	O-8
3	P-2	1/10/2021	T-2	B01	O-5
4	P-4	6/30/2021	T-1, T-8	B01	O-1
5	P-5	8/23/2021	T-4, T-7	G01	O-4

Figure 3–54

The following steps make the appropriate entries for the Treatment Number field in the Appointments table.

- Open the Appointments table.
- Since the Patient IDs were changed in the Patients table in an earlier module, there need to be some corrections to the Appointments table. Before entering the Treatment Numbers in this section, change the data in the Appointments table's Patient ID and Owner ID fields to match those in Figure 3–54.
- Click the Treatment Number field on the first record to display the arrow.
- Click the arrow to display the list of Treatment Numbers available (Figure 3–55).

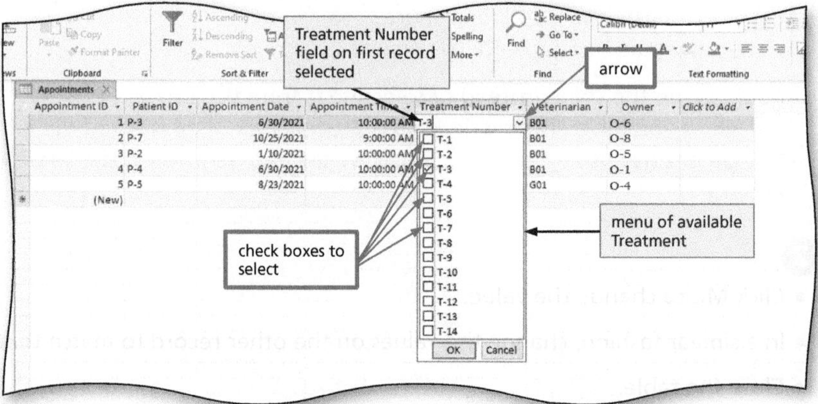

Figure 3–55

Q&A What if there were too many treatments to fit?

Access would automatically include a scroll bar that you could use to scroll through all the choices.

- Click the T-10 check box to select the additional treatment for the first appointment; T-3 treatment has already been selected (Figure 3–56).

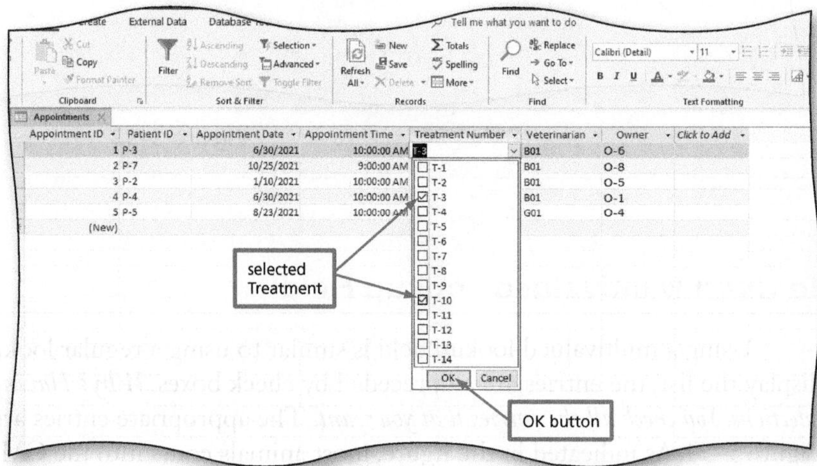

Figure 3–56

- Click the OK button to complete the selection.
- Using the same technique, enter the services given in Figure 3–54 for the remaining accounts.
- Double-click the right boundary of the field selector for the Treatment Number field to resize the field so that it best fits the data (Figure 3–57).

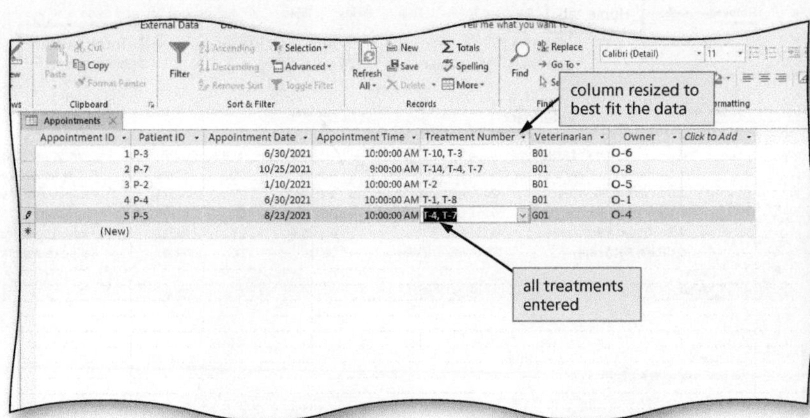

Figure 3–57

- Save the changes to the layout by clicking the Save button on the Quick Access Toolbar.
- Close the Appointments table.

Q&A What if I closed the table without saving the layout changes?
You would be asked if you want to save the changes.

Changing the Appearance of a Datasheet

You can change the appearance of a datasheet in a variety of ways. You can include totals in the datasheet. You can also change the appearance of gridlines or the text colors and font.

To Include Totals in a Datasheet

The following steps first include an extra row, called the Total row, in the datasheet for the Veterinary Vendors table. Note that this is not a calculated field. ***Why?*** *It is possible to include totals and other statistics at the bottom of a datasheet in the Total row.* The steps then display the total amount of money spent on all vendors.

- Open the Veterinary Vendors table in Datasheet view and close the Navigation Pane.
- Click the Totals button (Home tab | Records group) to include the Total row in the datasheet. Note that a blank row will appear above the Totals row.
- Click the Total row in the Total Amount column to display an arrow.
- Click the arrow to display a menu of available calculations (Figure 3–58).

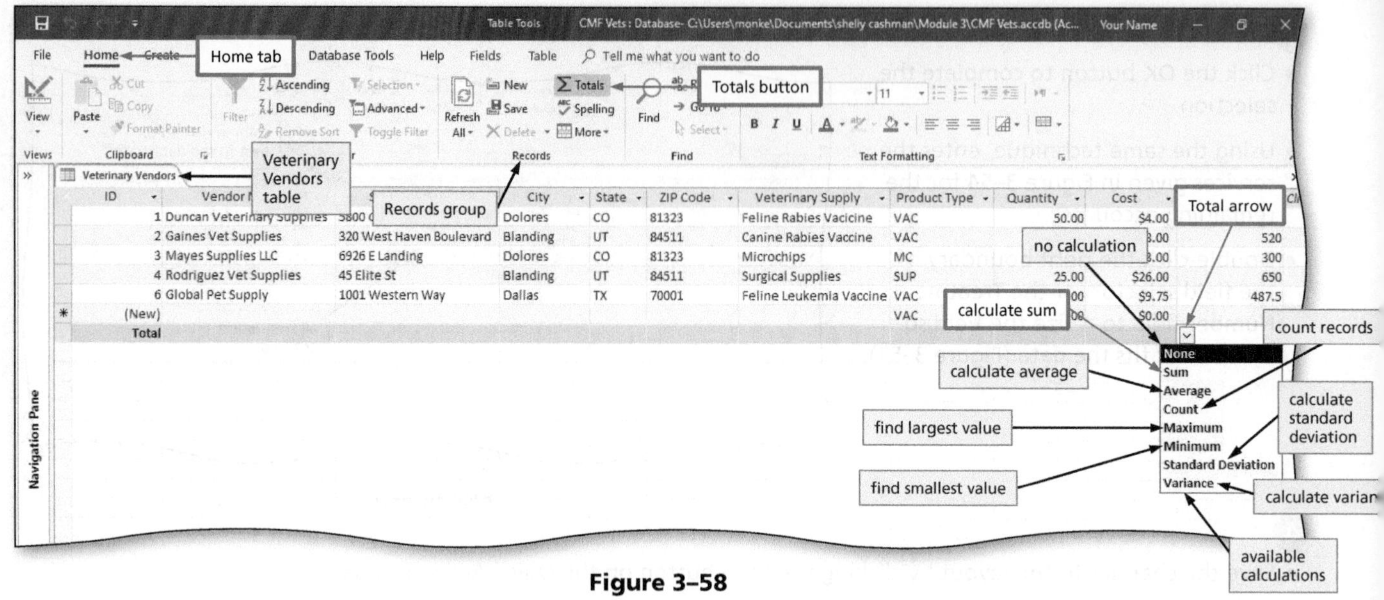

Figure 3–58

Q&A

Can I also create a totals row in a query?
Yes, you can create a totals row in the Datasheet view of a query just like you did in the Datasheet view of the table.

Will I always get the same list?
No. You will only get the items that are applicable to the type of data in the column. You cannot calculate the sum of text data, for example.

2

- Click Sum to calculate the total of the total amounts.
- Resize the Total Amount column to best fit the total amount (Figure 3–59), if necessary.

Experiment

- Experiment with other statistics. When finished, once again select the sum.

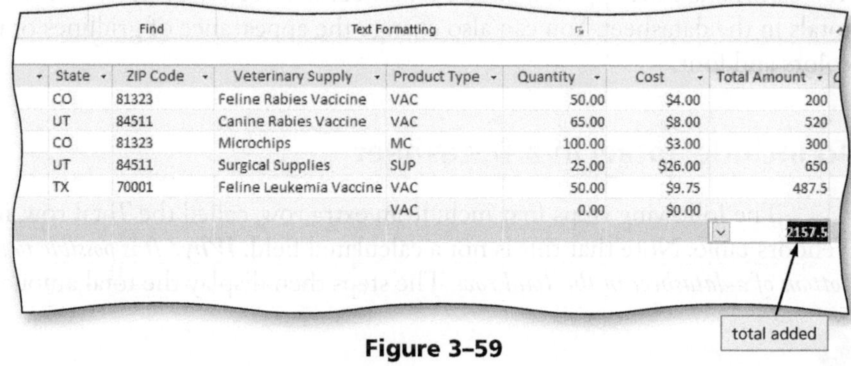

Figure 3–59

To Remove Totals from a Datasheet

If you no longer want the totals to appear as part of the datasheet, you can remove the Total row. The following step removes the Total row.

1 Click the Totals button (Home tab | Records group), which is shown in Figure 3–58, to remove the Total row from the datasheet.

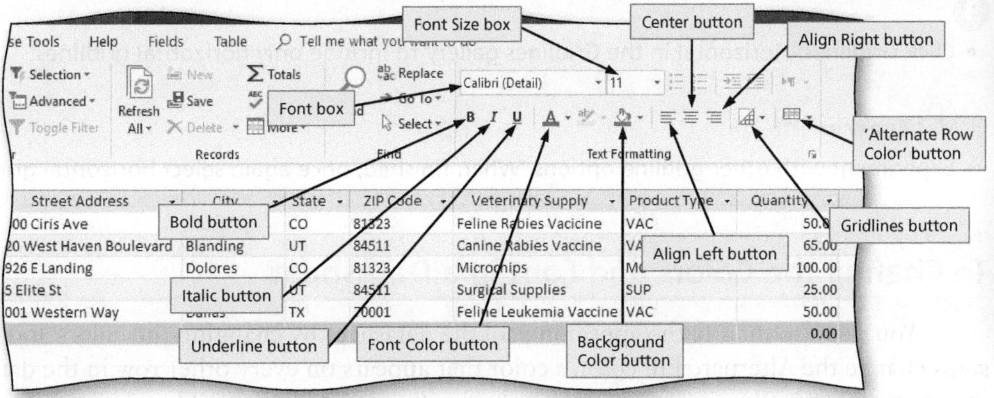

Figure 3–60

Figure 3–60 shows the various buttons, located in the Text Formatting group on the Home tab, that are available to change the datasheet appearance. The changes to the datasheet will be reflected not only on the screen, but also when you print or preview the datasheet.

To Change Gridlines in a Datasheet

The following steps change the datasheet so that only horizontal gridlines are included. ***Why?** You might prefer the appearance of the datasheet with only horizontal gridlines.*

1

- Open the Veterinary Vendors table in Datasheet view, if it is not already open.
- If necessary, close the Navigation Pane.
- Click the datasheet selector, the box in the upper-left corner of the datasheet, to select the entire datasheet (Figure 3–61).

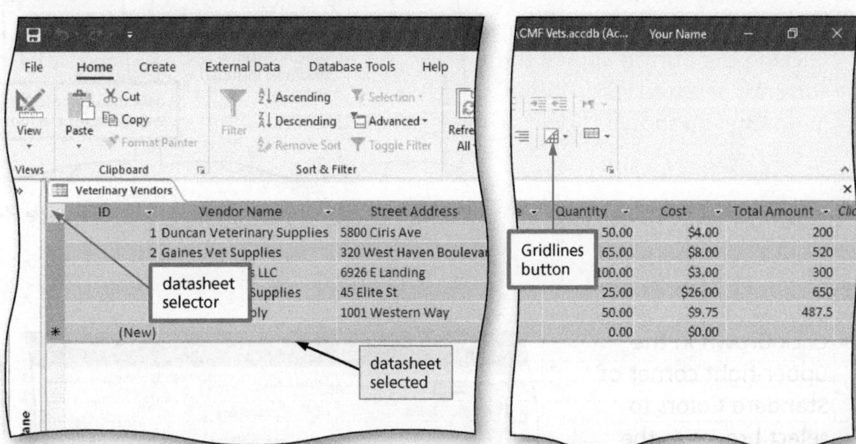

Figure 3–61

2

- Click the Gridlines button (Home tab | Text Formatting group) to display the Gridlines gallery (Figure 3–62).

Q&A Does it matter whether I click the button or the arrow?

In this case, it does not matter. Either action will display the gallery.

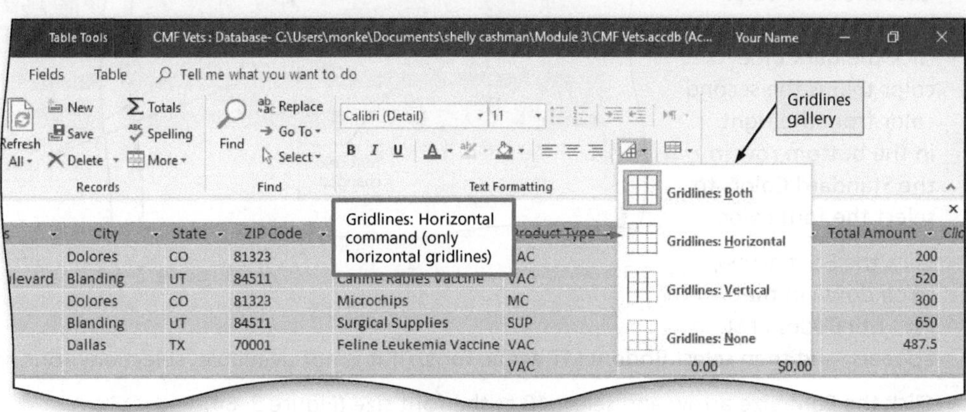

Figure 3–62

- Click Gridlines: Horizontal in the Gridlines gallery to include only horizontal gridlines.

- Experiment with other gridline options. When finished, once again select horizontal gridlines.

To Change the Colors and Font in a Datasheet

You can also modify the appearance of the datasheet by changing the colors and the font. The following steps change the Alternate Fill color, a color that appears on every other row in the datasheet. ***Why?*** *Having rows appear in alternate colors is an attractive way to visually separate the rows.* The steps also change the font color, the font, and the font size.

- With the datasheet for the Veterinary Vendors table selected, click the Alternate Row Color button arrow (Home tab | Text Formatting group) to display the color palette (Figure 3–63).

Q&A Does it matter whether I click the button or the arrow?
Yes. Clicking the arrow produces a color palette. Clicking the button applies the currently selected color. When in doubt, you should click the arrow.

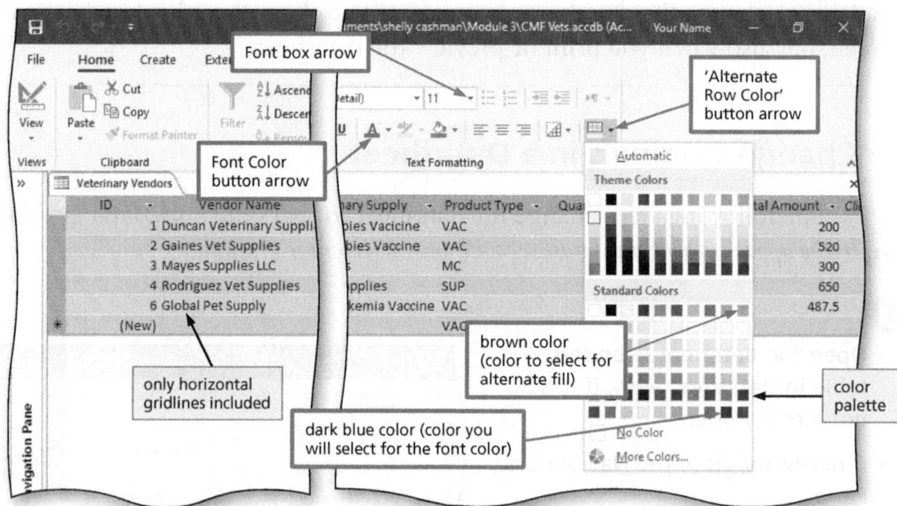

Figure 3–63

- Click Brown in the upper-right corner of Standard Colors to select brown as the alternate color.
- Click the Font Color button arrow, and then click the dark blue color that is the second color from the right in the bottom row in the Standard Colors to select the font color.
- Click the Font arrow, scroll down in the list until Bodoni MT appears, and then select Bodoni MT as the font. (If it is not available, select any font of your choice.)
- Click the Font Size arrow and select 10 as the font size (Figure 3–64).

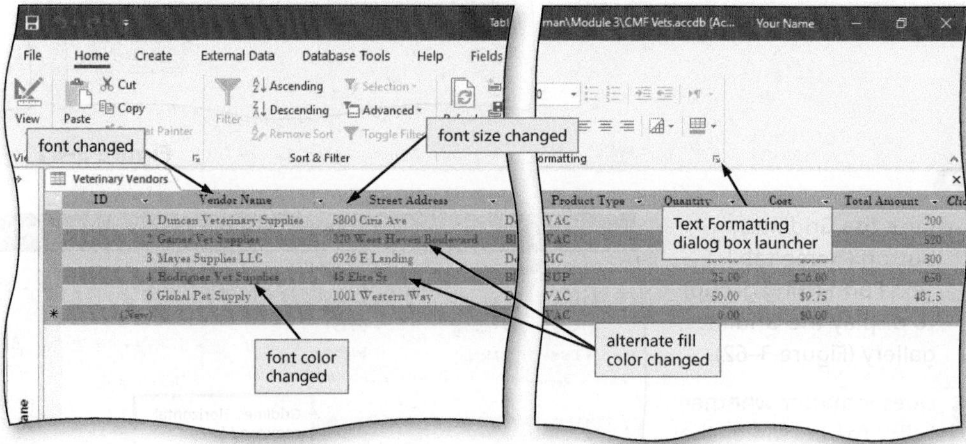

Figure 3–64

Q&A Does the order in which I make these selections make a difference?
No. You could have made these selections in any order.

Experiment

- **Experiment with other colors, fonts, and font sizes. When finished, return to the options selected in these steps.**

Using the Datasheet Formatting Dialog Box

As an alternative to using the individual buttons, you can click the Datasheet Formatting dialog box launcher, which is the arrow at the lower-right of the Text Formatting group, to display the Datasheet Formatting dialog box (Figure 3–65). You can use the various options within the dialog box to make changes to the datasheet format. Once you are finished, click the OK button to apply your changes.

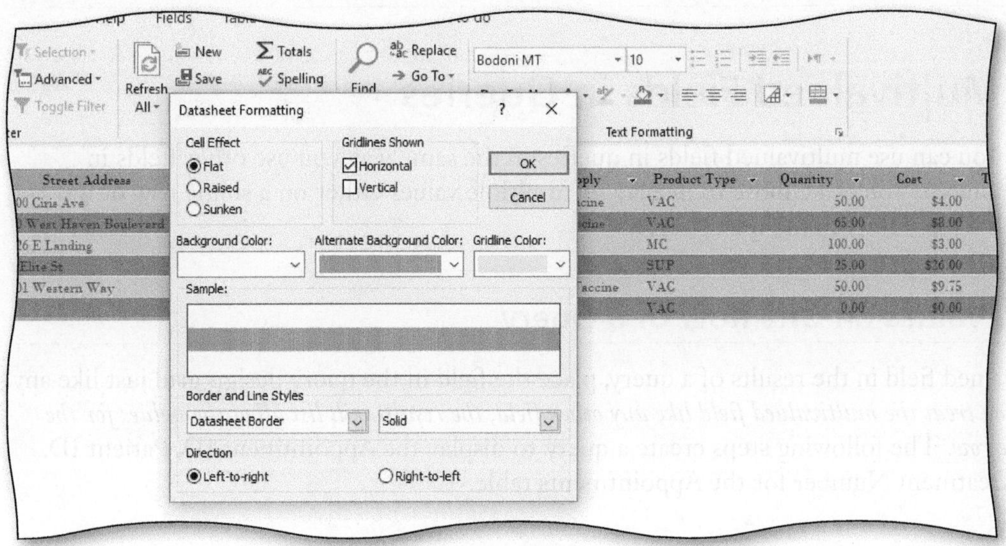

Figure 3–65

Q&A Can I also format my datasheet in other ways?
There are many other formatting options for your table in Datasheet view. You can select all the records as shown in Figure 3–61 by clicking the datasheet selector. Then you can bold, underline, or italicize your font in the Home tab | Text formatting group. Additionally, you can set the background color and align the data.

To Close the Datasheet without Saving the Format Changes

The following steps close the datasheet without saving the changes to the format. Because the changes are not saved, the next time you open the Account Manager table in Datasheet view it will appear in the original format. If you had saved the changes, the changes would be reflected in its appearance.

1. Close the Veterinary Vendors table.
2. Click the No button in the Microsoft Access dialog box when asked if you want to save your changes.

CONSIDER THIS

What kind of decisions should I make in determining whether to change the format of a datasheet?

- Would totals or other calculations be useful in the datasheet? If so, include the Total row and select the appropriate computations.
- Would another gridline style make the datasheet more useful? If so, change to the desired gridlines.
- Would alternating colors in the rows make them easier to read? If so, change the alternate fill color.
- Would a different font and/or font color make the text stand out better? If so, change the font color and/or the font.
- Is the font size appropriate? Can you see enough data at one time on the screen and yet have the data be readable? If not, change the font size to an appropriate value.
- Is the column spacing appropriate? Are some columns wider than they need to be? Do some columns not display all the data? Change the column sizes as necessary.

As a general guideline, once you have decided on a particular look for a datasheet, all datasheets in the database should have the same look, unless there is a compelling reason for a datasheet to differ.

Multivalued Fields in Queries

You can use multivalued fields in queries in the same way you use other fields in queries. You can choose to display the multiple values either on a single row or on multiple rows in the query results.

To Include Multiple Values on One Row of a Query

To include a multivalued field in the results of a query, place the field in the query design grid just like any other field. ***Why?*** *When you treat the multivalued field like any other field, the results will list all of the values for the multivalued field on a single row.* The following steps create a query to display the Appointment ID, Patient ID, Appointment Date, and Treatment Number for the Appointments table.

- Create a query for the Appointments table and close the Navigation Pane.
- Include the Appointment ID, Patient ID, Appointment Date, and Treatment Number fields in the query (Figure 3–66).

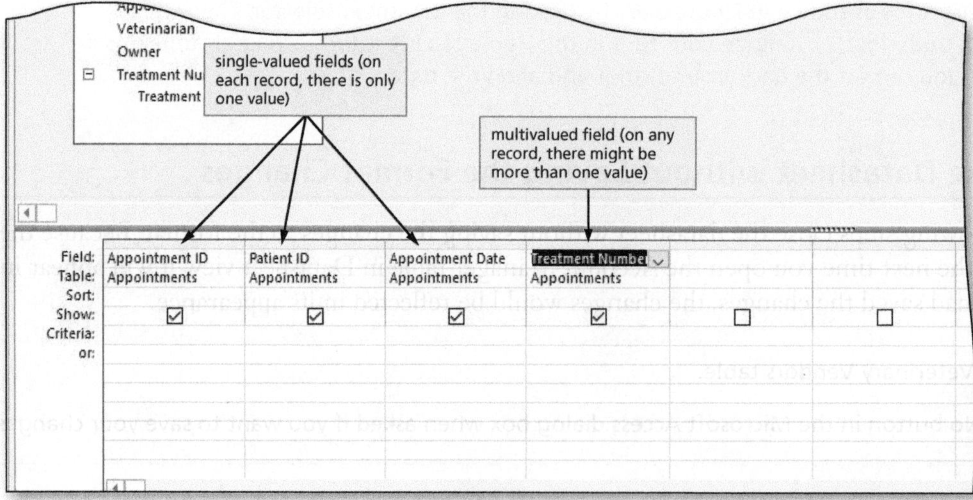

Figure 3–66

2

- Run the query and view the results (Figure 3–67).

Q&A Can I include criteria for the multivalued field?
Yes. You can include criteria for the multivalued field.

- Save the query as m03q01.

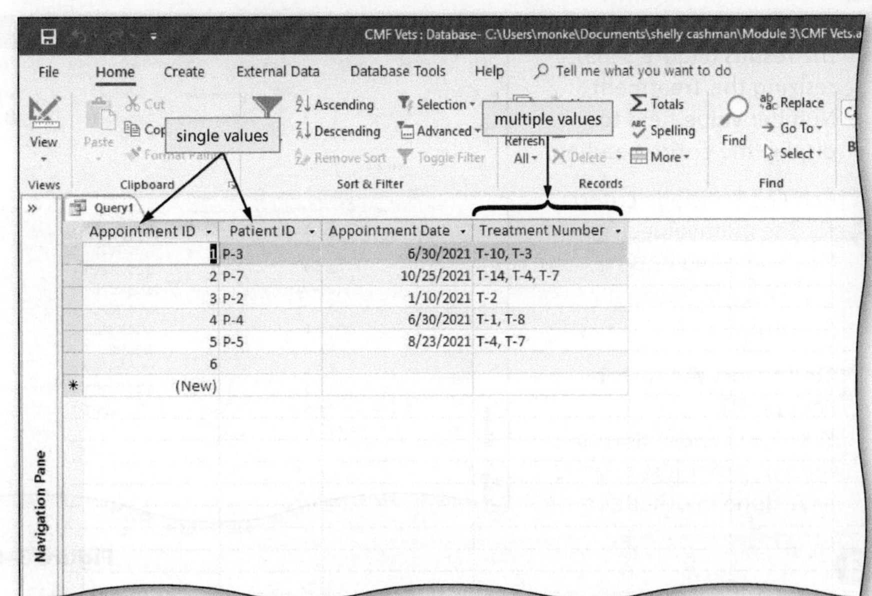

Figure 3–67

To Include Multiple Values on Multiple Rows of a Query

You might want to see the multiple treatment numbers needed for an appointment on separate rows rather than a single row. ***Why?*** *Each row in the results will focus on one specific treatment that is needed.* To do so, you need to use the Value property of the Treatment ID field by following the name of the field with a period and then the word, Value. The following steps use the Value property to display each service on a separate row.

1

- Switch to Design view and ensure that the Appointment ID, Patient ID, Appointment Date, and Treatment Number fields are included in the design grid.
- Click the Treatment Number field to produce an insertion point, press the RIGHT ARROW as necessary to move the insertion point to the end of the field name, and then type a period.

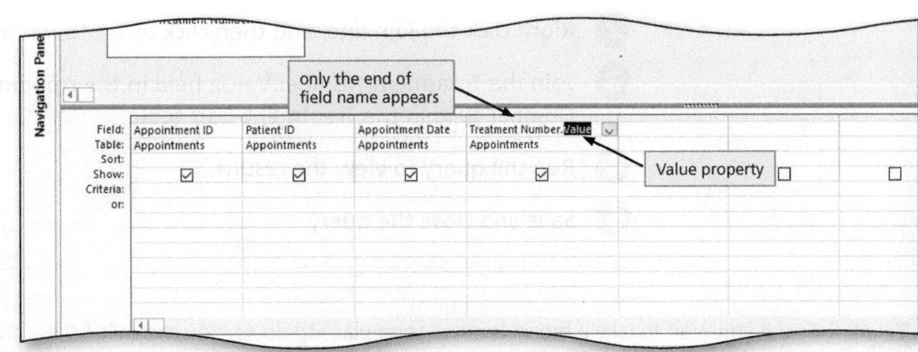

Figure 3–68

- If the word, Value, does not automatically appear after the period, type the word `Value` after the period following the word, Number, to use the Value property (Figure 3–68).

Q&A I do not see the word, Value. Did I do something wrong?
No. There is not enough room to display the entire name. If you wanted to see it, you could point to the right boundary of the column selector and then either drag or double-click.

I see Treatment Number.Value as a field in the field list. Could I have deleted the Treatment Number field and added the Treatment Number.Value field?
Yes. Either approach is fine.

2

- Run the query and view the results (Figure 3–69), resizing the Treatment Number.Value field to display the entire heading.

Q&A Can I now include criteria for the multivalued field?
Yes. You could enter a criterion just like in any other query.

Could I sort the rows by Patient ID?
Yes. Select Ascending as the sort order just as you have done in other queries.

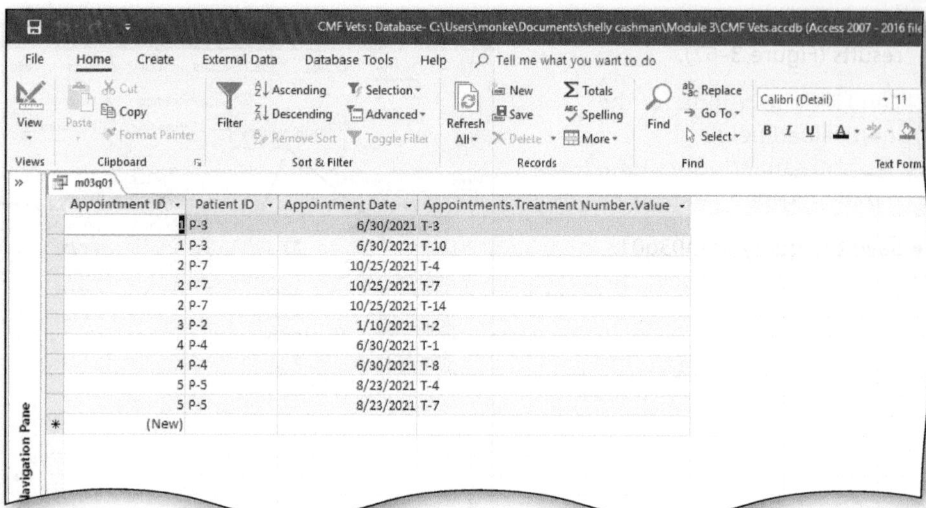

Figure 3–69

3

- Save the query as a new object in the database named m03q02.
- Close the query.

To Test an Existing Query with a Multivalued Field

Because the current join does not connect the common individual fields since it was changed to multivalued, you need to modify the join. The following steps change the join on an existing query that uses a multivalued field.

1. Open the Appointments and Treatments query in Design view.
2. Right click the join line, and then click DELETE to remove the join.
3. Join the Treatment Number.Value field in the Appointments table to the Treatment Number field in the Treatment Cost table.
4. Run the query to view the results.
5. Save and close the query.

Break Point: If you wish to take a break, this is a good place to do so. You can quit Access now. To resume at a later time, start Access, open the database called CMF Vets, and continue following the steps from this location forward.

BTW
Using Criteria with Multivalued Fields
To enter criteria in a multivalued field, simply enter the criteria in the Criteria row. For example, to find all patients who need feline rabies shots in the Appointments table, enter T-1 in the Criteria row under Treatment Number.

Referential Integrity

When you have two related tables in a database, it is essential that the data in the common fields match. There should not be a patient in the Patients table whose owner ID is O-2, for example, unless there is a record in the Owners table whose Owner ID is O-2. This restriction is enforced through **referential integrity**, which is the property that ensures that the value in a foreign key must match that of another table's primary key.

A **foreign key** is a field in one table whose values are required to match the *primary key* of another table. In the Patients table, the Owner ID field is a foreign key that must match the primary key of the Owners table; that is, the Owner ID for any patient must exist as an Owner ID currently in the Owners table. A patient whose Owner ID is O-9, for example, should not be stored in the Patients table because no such owner exists in the Owners table.

In Access, to specify referential integrity, you must explicitly define a relationship between the tables by using the Relationships button. As part of the process of defining a relationship, you indicate that Access is to enforce referential integrity. Access then prohibits any updates to the database that would violate the referential integrity.

The type of relationship between two tables specified by the Relationships command is referred to as a **one-to-many relationship**. This means that *one* record in the first table is related to, or matches, *many* records in the second table, but each record in the second table is related to only *one* record in the first. In the CMF Vets database, for example, a one-to-many relationship exists between the Owners table and the Patients table. *One* owner is associated with *many* patients, but each patient is associated with only a single owner. In general, the table containing the foreign key will be the *many* part of the relationship.

CONSIDER THIS

When specifying referential integrity, what special issues do you need to address?

You need to decide how to handle deletions of fields. In the relationship between owners and patients, for example, deletion of an owner for whom patients exist, such as Patient ID C-2, would violate referential integrity. The owner for Patient ID C-2 would no longer relate to any owner in the Owners table in the database. You can handle this in two ways. For each relationship, you need to decide which of the approaches is appropriate.

The normal way to avoid this problem is to prohibit such a deletion. The other option is to **cascade the delete**. This means that Access would allow the deletion but then delete all related records. For example, it would allow the deletion of the patient from the Patients table but then automatically delete any owners related to the deleted patient. In this example, cascading the delete would obviously not be appropriate.

You also need to decide how to handle the update of the primary key. In the relationship between owners and patients, for example, changing the Owner ID in the Owners table from C-2 to C-9 would cause a problem because some accounts in the Patients table have Owner ID C-2. These patients no longer would relate to any owner. You can handle this in two ways. For each relationship, you need to decide which of the approaches is appropriate.

The normal way to avoid this problem is to prohibit this type of update. The other option is to **cascade the update**. This means to allow the change, but make the corresponding change in the foreign key on all related records. In the relationship between owners and patients, for example, Access would allow the update but then automatically make the corresponding change for any account whose Owner ID is C-2. It will now be C-9.

To Specify Referential Integrity

The following steps use the Relationships button on the Database Tools tab to specify referential integrity by explicitly indicating a relationship between the Owners and Patients tables. The steps also ensure that updates will cascade, but that deletes will not. ***Why?*** *By indicating a relationship between tables, and specifying that updates will cascade, it will be possible to change the Owner ID for an owner, and the same change will automatically be made for all pets of that owner. By not specifying that deletes will cascade, it will not be possible to delete and owner who has patients (pets).*

- Click Database Tools on the ribbon to display the Database Tools tab. (Figure 3–70).

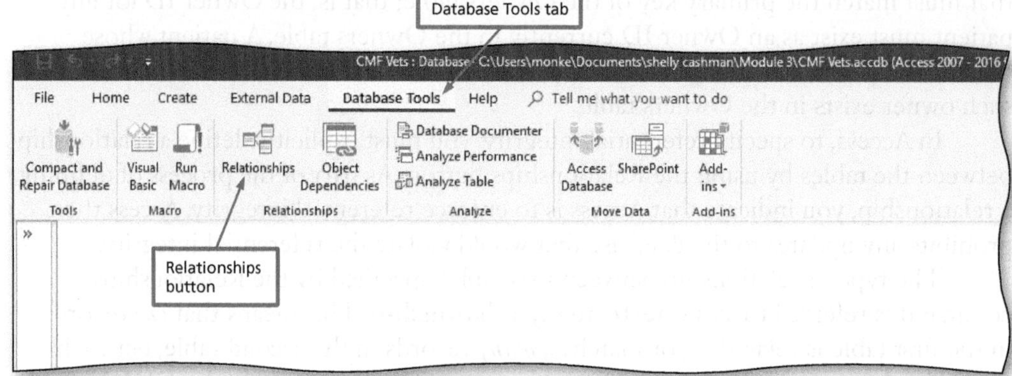

Figure 3–70

- Click the Relationships button (Database Tools tab | Relationships group) to open the Relationships window and display the Show Table dialog box (Figure 3–71).

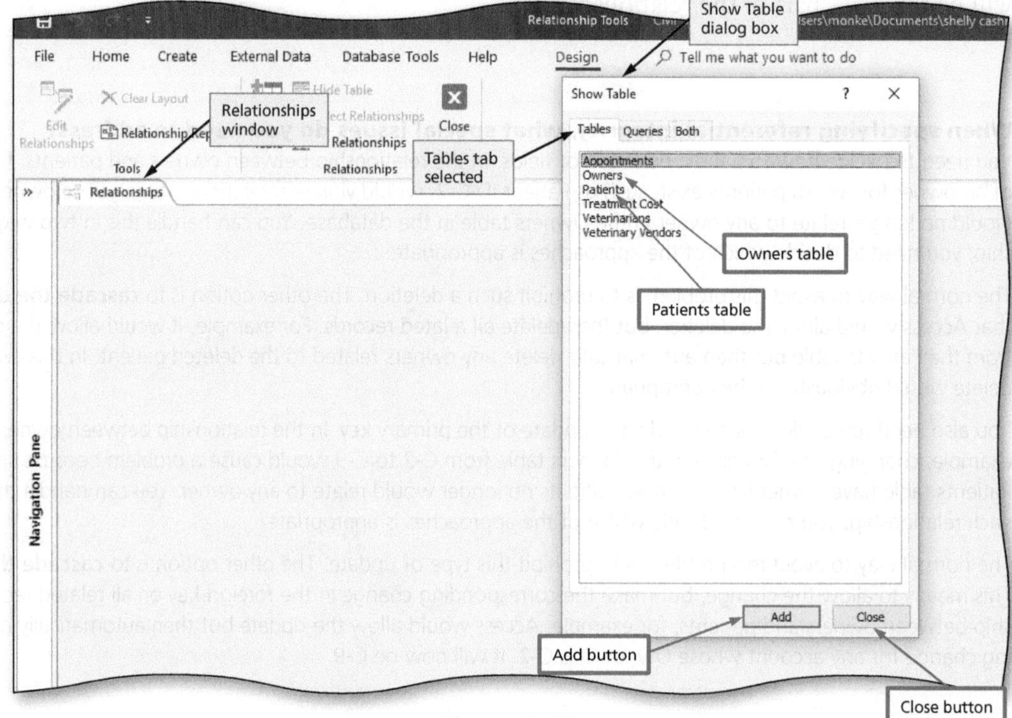

Figure 3–71

- Click the Owners table (Show Table dialog box), and then click the Add button to add a field list for the Owners table to the Relationships window.
- Click the Patients table (Show Table dialog box), and then click the Add button to add a field list for the Patients table to the Relationships window.
- Click the Close button (Show Table dialog box) to close the dialog box.

- Resize the field lists that appear so all fields are visible (Figure 3–72).

Q&A Do I need to resize the field lists?
No. You can use the scroll bars to view the fields. Before completing the next step, however, you would need to make sure the Owner ID fields in both tables appear on the screen.

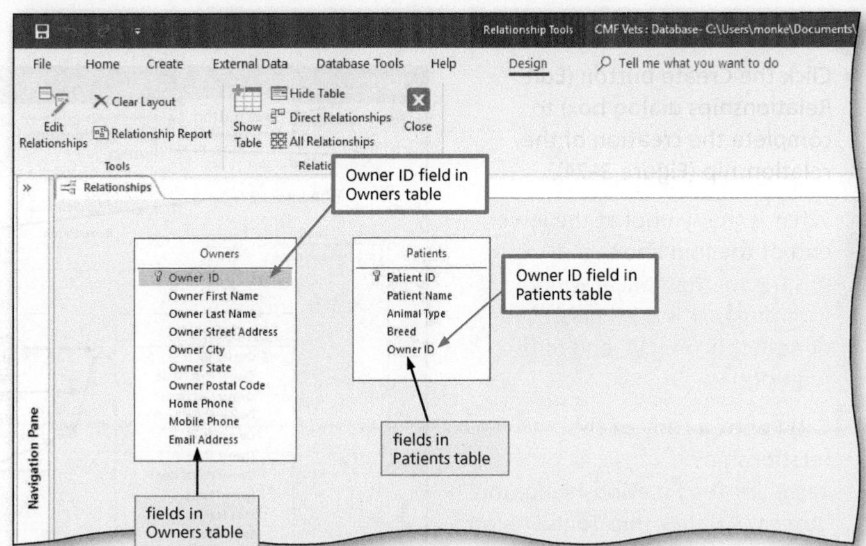

Figure 3–72

4

- Drag the Owner ID field in the Owners table field list to the Owner ID field in the Patients table field list to display the Edit Relationships dialog box and create a relationship.

Q&A Do I actually move the field from the Owners table to the Patients table?
No. The pointer will change shape to indicate you are in the process of dragging, but the field does not move.

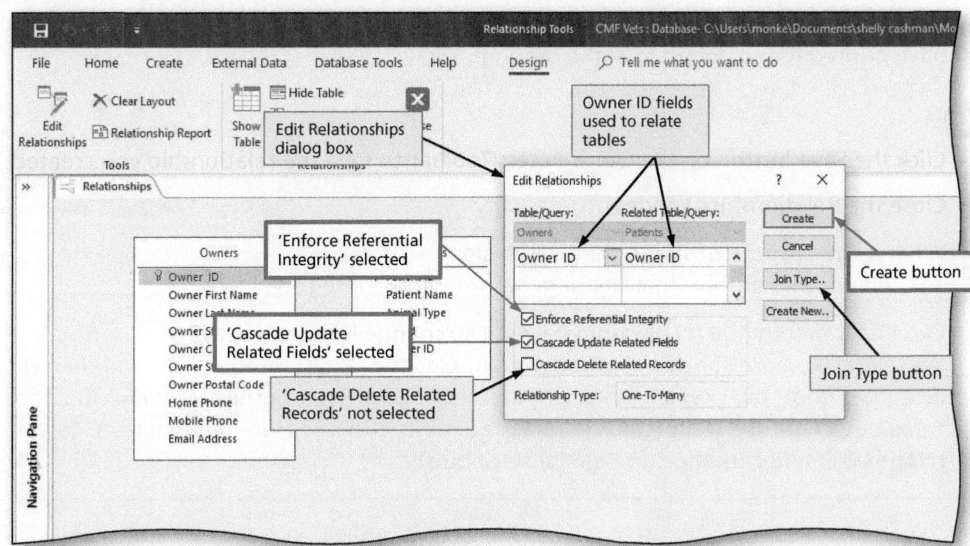

Figure 3–73

- Click the 'Enforce Referential Integrity' check box (Edit Relationships dialog box).
- Click the Cascade Update Related Fields check box (Figure 3–73).

Q&A The Cascade check boxes were dim until I clicked the Enforce Referential Integrity check box. Is that correct?
Yes. Until you have chosen to enforce referential integrity, the cascade options are not applicable.

- Click the Create button (Edit Relationships dialog box) to complete the creation of the relationship (Figure 3–74).

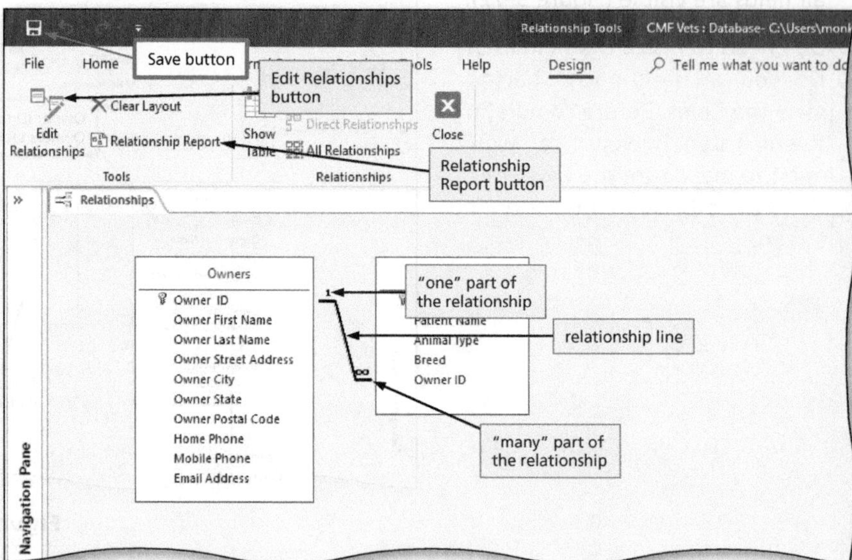

Figure 3–74

Q&A What is the symbol at the lower end of the join line?

It is the mathematical symbol for infinity. It is used here to denote the "many" end of the relationship.

Can I print a copy of the relationship?

Yes. Click the Relationship Report button (Relationship Tools Design tab | Tools group) to produce a report of the relationship. You can print the report. You can also save it as a report in the database for future use. If you do not want to save it, close the report after you have printed it and do not save the changes.

- Click the Save button on the Quick Access Toolbar to save the relationship you created.
- Close the Relationships window.

Q&A What is the purpose of saving the relationship?

The relationship ensures that the data has referential integrity.

Can I later modify the relationship if I want to change it in some way?

Yes. Click Database Tools on the ribbon to display the Database Tools tab, and then click the Relationships button (Database Tools tab | Relationships group) to open the Relationships window. To add another table, click the Show Table button on the Design tab. To remove a table, click the Hide Table button. To edit a relationship, select the relationship and click the Edit Relationships button.

CONSIDER THIS

Can I change the join type as I can in queries?

Yes. Click the Join Type button in the Edit Relationships dialog box. Click option button 1 to create an INNER join, that is, a join in which only records with matching values in the join fields appear in the result. Click option button 2 to create a LEFT join, that is, a join that includes all records from the left-hand table, but only records from the right-hand table that have matching values in the join fields. Click option button 3 to create a RIGHT join, that is, a join that includes all records from the right-hand table, but only records from the left-hand table that have matching values in the join fields.

Effect of Referential Integrity

Referential integrity now exists between the Owners and the Patients tables. Access now will reject any number in the Owner ID field in the Patients table that does not match an Owner ID in the Owners table. Attempting to change the Owner ID for a patient to one that does not match any Owner ID in the Owner table would result in the error message shown in Figure 3–75. Similarly, attempting to add a patient whose Owner ID does not match would produce the same error message.

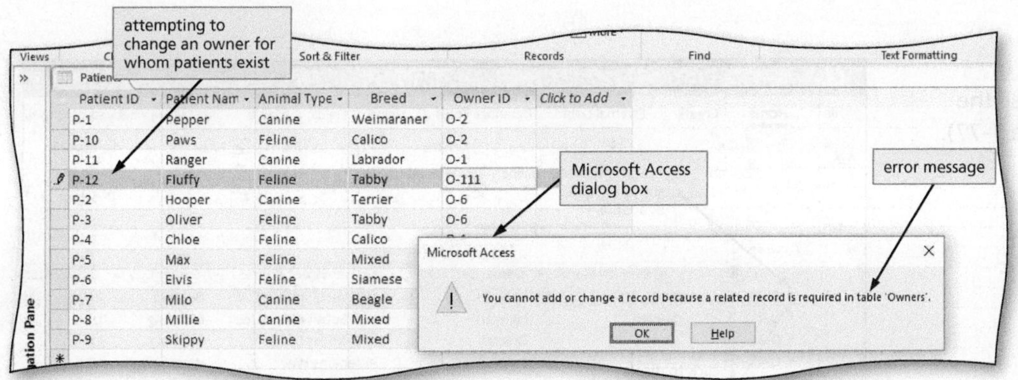

Figure 3–75

Access also will reject the deletion of an Owner ID for whom related accounts exist. Attempting to delete Owner ID O-2 from the Owners table, for example, would result in the message shown in Figure 3–76.

Access would, however, allow the change of an Owner ID in the Owners table. It would then automatically make the corresponding change to the Owner ID for all the patients that belong to that owner. For example, if you changed the Owner ID in the Owner table from O-2 to O-3, the Owner ID O-3 would appear in the Owner ID field for patients whose Owner ID had been O-2.

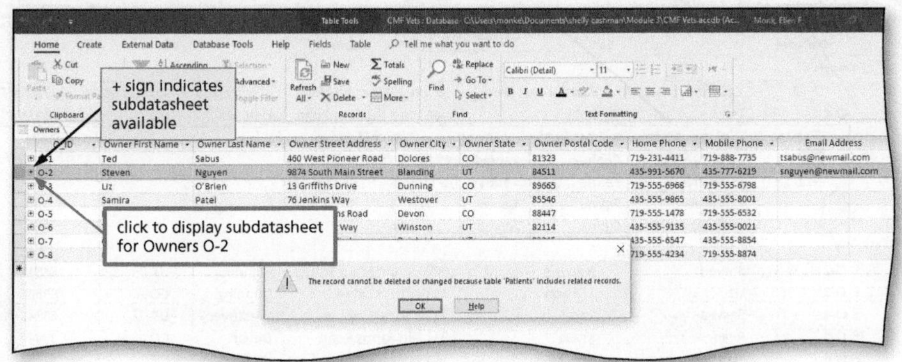

Figure 3–76

BTW

Relationships

You also can use the Relationships window to specify a one-to-one relationship. In a one-to-one relationship, the matching fields are both primary keys. If CMF maintained a mobile veterinary pet van for each veterinarian, the data concerning the van might be kept in a Van table, in which the primary key is Veterinarian ID — the same primary key as the Veterinarians table. Thus, there would be a one-to-one relationship between veterinarians and vans.

BTW

Exporting a Relationship Report

You also can export a relationship report. To export a report as a PDF or XPS file, right-click the report in the Navigation Pane, click Export on the shortcut menu, and then click PDF or XPS as the file type.

To Use a Subdatasheet

One consequence of the tables being explicitly related is that the patients for an owner can appear below the Owner ID in a **subdatasheet**. Because the two tables are joined by a common field, the data for the patient belonging to the owner can be embedded within that particular owner. ***Why is a subdatasheet useful?*** *A subdatasheet is useful when you want to review or edit data in joined or related tables.* The availability of such a subdatasheet is indicated by a plus sign that appears in front of the rows in the Owners table. The following steps display the subdatasheet for Owner O-1.

- Open the Owners table in Datasheet view and close the Navigation Pane (Figure 3–77).

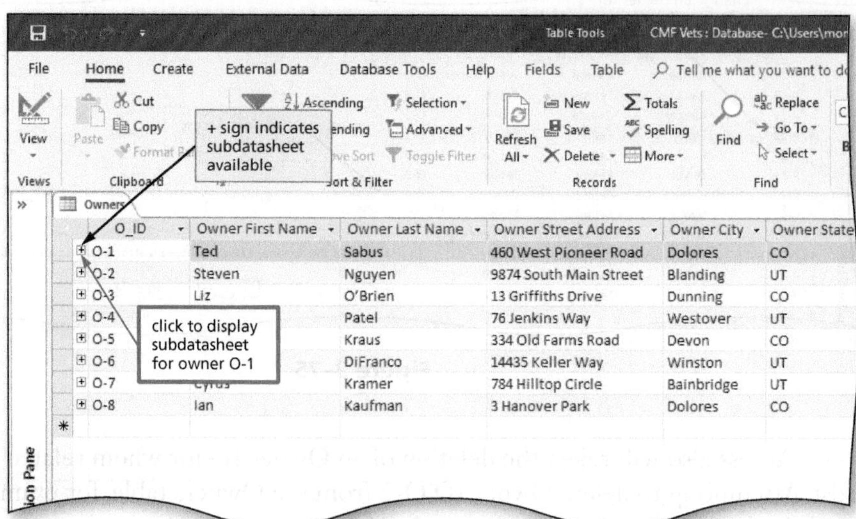

Figure 3–77

- Click the plus sign in front of the row for Owner ID O-1 to display the subdatasheet (Figure 3–78).

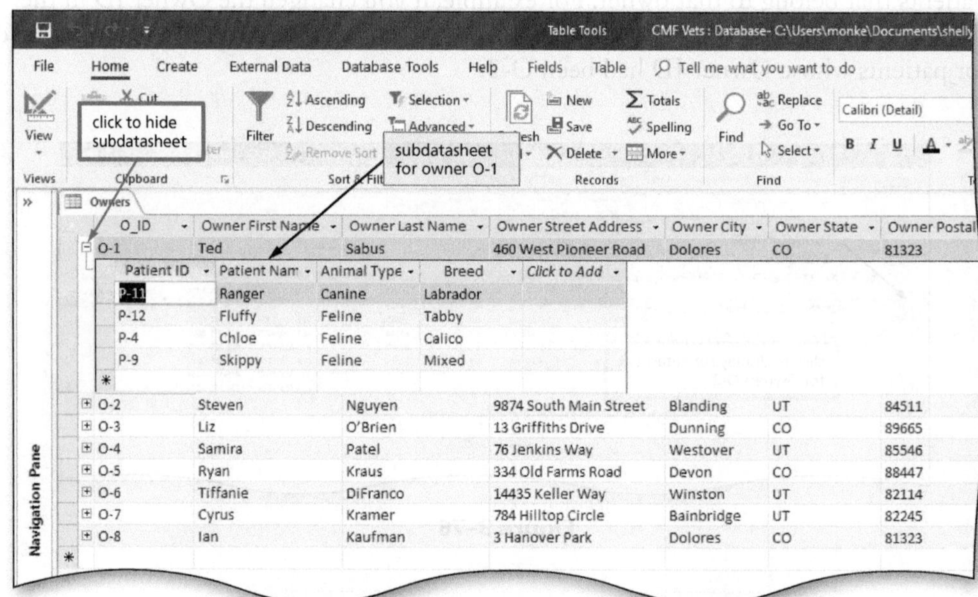

Figure 3–78

Q&A How do I hide the subdatasheet when I no longer want it to appear?

When you clicked the plus sign, it changed to a minus sign. Click the minus sign.

How do I remove a subdatasheet?

Open the table with the subdatasheet closed and click the More button (Home tab | Records Group) to display a menu. Select Subdatasheet, Remove.

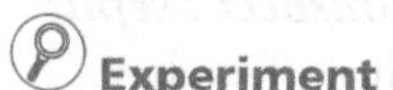

Experiment

- Display subdatasheets for other owners. Display more than one subdatasheet at a time. Remove the subdatasheets from the screen.

- If requested by your instructor, replace the city and state for Owner ID O-1 with your city and state.
- Close the Owners table.

Handling Data Inconsistency

In many organizations, databases evolve and change over time. One department might create a database for its own internal use. Employees in another department may decide they need their own database containing much of the same information. For example, the Purchasing department of an organization might create a database of products that it buys and the Receiving department may create a database of products that it receives. Each department is keeping track of the same products. When the organization eventually merges the databases, they might discover inconsistencies and duplication. The Find Duplicates Query Wizard and the Find Unmatched Query Wizard can assist in clearing the resulting database of duplication and errors.

BTW
Database Design: Validation
In most organizations, decisions about what is valid and what is invalid data are made during the requirements gathering process and the database design process.

To Find Duplicate Records

One reason to include a primary key for a table is to eliminate duplicate records. A possibility still exists, however, that duplicate records can get into your database. You would use the following steps to find duplicate records using the Find Duplicates Query Wizard.

1. Click Create on the ribbon, and then click the Query Wizard button (Create tab | Queries group).
2. When Access displays the New Query dialog box, click Find Duplicates Query Wizard and then click the OK button.
3. Identify the table and field or fields that might contain duplicate information.
4. Indicate any other fields you want displayed.
5. Finish the wizard to see any duplicate records.

To Find Unmatched Records

Occasionally, you might need to find records in one table that have no matching records in another table. For example, you might want to determine which owners currently have no patients. You would use the following steps to find unmatched records using the Find Unmatched Query Wizard.

1. Click Create on the ribbon, and then click the Query Wizard button (Create tab | Queries group).
2. When Access displays the New Query dialog box, click Find Unmatched Query Wizard and then click the OK button.
3. Identify the table that might contain unmatched records, and then identify the related table.
4. Indicate the fields you want displayed.
5. Finish the wizard to see any unmatched records.

Ordering Records

Normally, Access sequences the records in the Owners table by Owner ID whenever listing them because the Owner ID field is the primary key. You can change this order, if desired.

To Use the Ascending Button to Order Records

To change the order in which records appear, use the Ascending or Descending buttons. Either button reorders the records based on the field in which the insertion point is located. The following steps order the records by city using the Ascending button. ***Why?*** *Using the Ascending button is the quickest and easiest way to order records.*

- Open the Owners table in Datasheet view.
- Click the Owner City field on the first record to select the field (Figure 3–79).

Q&A Did I have to click the field on the first record?

No. Any other record would have worked as well.

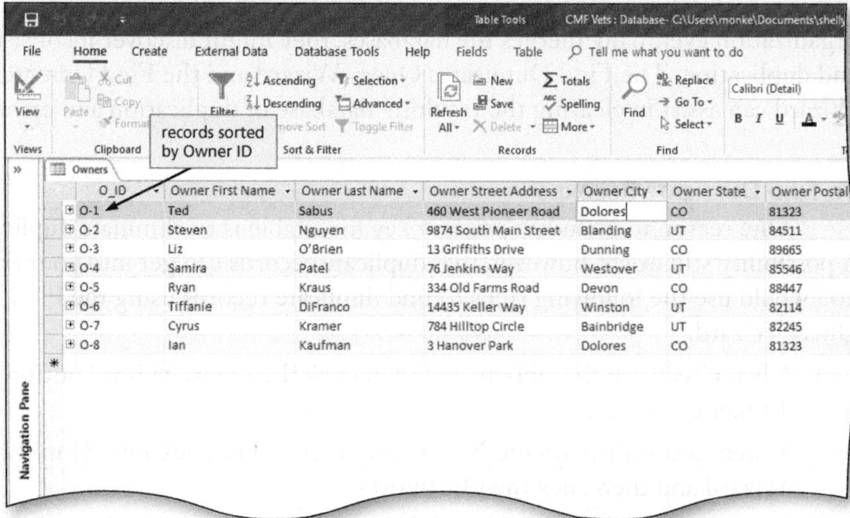

Figure 3–79

- Click the Ascending button (Home tab | Sort & Filter group) to sort the records by City (Figure 3–80).

- Close the Owners table.
- Click the No button (Microsoft Access dialog box) when asked if you want to save your changes.

Q&A What if I saved the changes?

The next time you open the table the records will be sorted by city.

- If desired, sign out of your Microsoft account.
- **sam** Exit Access.

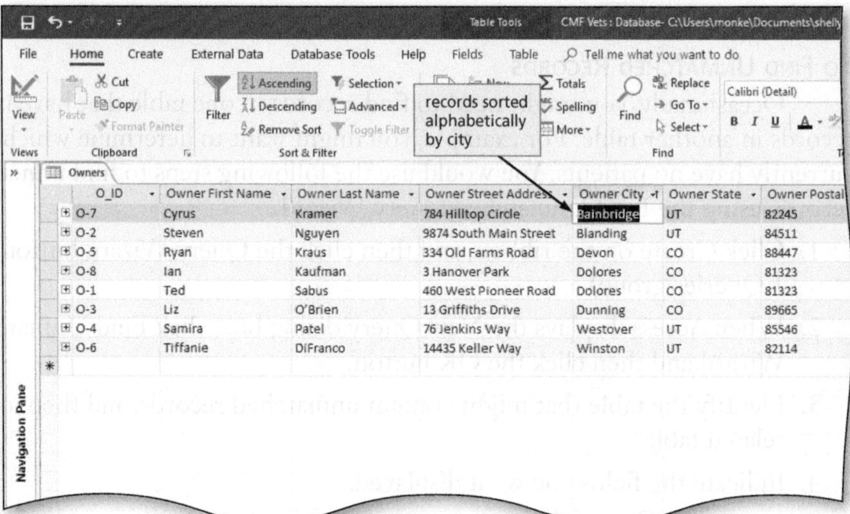

Figure 3–80

Other Ways

1. Right-click field name, click Sort A to Z (for ascending) or Sort Z to A (for descending)
2. Click field selector arrow, click Sort A to Z or Sort Z to A

To Use the Ascending Button to Order Records on Multiple Fields

Just as you are able to sort the answer to a query on multiple fields, you can also sort the data that appears in a datasheet on multiple fields. To do so, the major and minor keys must be next to each other in the datasheet with the major key on the left. If this is not the case, you can drag the columns into the correct position. Instead of dragging, however, usually it will be easier to use a query that has the data sorted in the desired order.

To sort on a combination of fields where the major key is just to the left of the minor key, you would use the following steps.

1. Click the field selector at the top of the major key column to select the entire column.
2. Hold down SHIFT and then click the field selector for the minor key column to select both columns.
3. Click the Ascending button to sort the records.

BTW

Access Help

At any time while using Access, you can find answers to questions and display information about various topics through Access Help. Used properly, this form of assistance can increase your productivity and reduce your frustrations by minimizing the time you spend learning how to use Access.

Summary

In this module you have learned how to use a form to add records to a table, search for records, delete records, filter records, change the database structure, create and use lookup fields, create calculated fields, create and use multivalued fields, make mass changes, create validation rules, change the appearance of a datasheet, specify referential integrity, and use subdatasheets.

CONSIDER THIS

What decisions will you need to make when maintaining your own databases?

Use these guidelines as you complete the assignments in this module and maintain your own databases outside of this class.

1. Determine when it is necessary to add, change, or delete records in a database.
2. Determine whether you should filter records.
   a) If your criterion for filtering is that the value in a particular field matches or does not match a certain specific value, use Filter By Selection.
   b) If your criterion only involves a single field but is more complex, use a common filter.
   c) If your criterion involves more than one field, use Filter By Form.
   d) If your criterion involves more than a single And or Or, or if it involves sorting, use Advanced Filter/Sort.
3. Determine whether additional fields are necessary or whether existing fields should be deleted.
4. Determine whether validation rules, default values, and formats are necessary.
   a) Can you improve the accuracy of the data entry process by enforcing data validation?
   b) What values are allowed for a particular field?
   c) Are there some fields in which one particular value is used more than another?
   d) Should some fields be required for each record?
   e) Are there some fields for which special formats would be appropriate?
5. Determine whether changes to the format of a datasheet are desirable.
   a) Would totals or other calculations be useful in the datasheet?
   b) Would different gridlines make the datasheet easier to read?
   c) Would alternating colors in the rows make them easier to read?
   d) Would a different font and/or font color make the text stand out better?
   e) Is the font size appropriate?
   f) Is the column spacing appropriate?
6. Identify related tables in order to implement relationships between the tables.
   a) Is there a one-to-many relationship between the tables?
   b) If so, which table is the one table?
   c) Which table is the many table?
7. When specifying referential integrity, address deletion and update policies.
   a) Decide how to handle deletions. Should deletion be prohibited or should the delete cascade?
   b) Decide how to handle the update of the primary key. Should the update be prohibited or should the update cascade?

CONSIDER THIS

How should you submit solutions to questions in the assignments identified with a symbol?
Every assignment in this book contains one or more questions identified with a symbol. These questions require you to think beyond the assigned database. Present your solutions to the questions in the format required by your instructor. Possible formats may include one or more of these options: write the answer; create a document that contains the answer; present your answer to the class; discuss your answer in a group; record the answer as audio or video using a webcam, smartphone, or portable media player; or post answers on a blog, wiki, or website.

Apply Your Knowledge

Reinforce the skills and apply the concepts you learned in this module.

Adding Lookup Fields, Specifying Validation Rules, Updating Records, Updating Reports, and Creating Relationships

Instructions: Run Access. Open the Support_AC_Financial Services database (If you do not have the database, see your instructor for a copy of the modified database.)

Perform the following tasks:

1. Open the Client table in Design view.
2. Add a Lookup field called Client Type to the Client table. The field should be inserted after the Advisor Number field. The field will contain data on the type of client. The client types are TRT (trust), INV (invest), and RET (retirement). Save the changes to the Client table.
3. Create the following validation rules for the Client table.
   a. Specify the legal values TRT, INV, and RET for the Client Type field. Enter `Must be TRT, INV, or RET` as the validation text.
   b. Make the Client Name field a required field.
4. Save the changes and close the table. You do not need to test the current data.
5. Create an update query for the Client table. Change all the entries in the Client Type field to INV. Run the query and save it as Client Type Update Query.
6. Open the Client table in Datasheet view, update the following records, and then close the table:
   a. Change the client type for clients BB35, CC25, CJ45, and CP03 to RET.
   b. Change the client type for clients MM01 and PS67 to TRT.
7. Create a split form for the Client table. Save the form as Client Split Form.
8. Open the Client Split Form in Form view, find client HN23, and change the client name from Henry Niemer to Henry Neimer. Close the form.
9. Establish referential integrity between the Advisor table (the one table) and the Client table (the many table). Cascade the update but not the delete. Save the relationship.
10. If requested to do so by your instructor, rename the Client Split Form as Split Form for First Name Last Name where First Name Last Name is your name.
11. Submit the revised database in the format specified by your instructor.
12. The values in the Client Type field are currently in the order TRT, INV, and RET. How would you reorder the values to INV, RET, and TRT in the Client Type list?

Extend Your Knowledge

Extend the skills you learned in this module and experiment with new skills. You may need to use Help to complete the assignment.

Creating Action Queries, Changing Table Properties, and Adding Totals to a Datasheet

Note: To complete this assignment, you will be required to use the Data Files. Please contact your instructor for information about accessing the Data Files.

Instructions: Healthy Pets is a small veterinary practice in Lebanon, Colorado that is run by a veterinarian that would like to retire. CMF Vets has been approached about buying the Healthy Pets practice. Healthy Pets needs to do some database maintenance by finding duplicate records and finding unmatched records.

Perform the following tasks:

1. Run Access and open the Support_AC Healthy Vets database. Create a make-table query to create the Potential Clients table in the Healthy Vets database shown in Figure 3–81. Run the query and save it as Make Table Query.

Potential Clients

Client Number	Client Name	Street	City	State	Postal Code	Amount Paid	Balance Due	Technician Number
A54	Magnus Afton	612 Walnut St	Cortez	CO	81321	$575.00	$315.00	22
A62	Deadre Alinger	227 Chestnut St	Cortez	CO	81321	$250.00	$175.00	24
B26	Sammy Brown	557 Spring St	Cortez	CO	81321	$875.00	$250.00	24
C29	Jenna Carlisle	123 Federal St	Cortez	CO	81321	$0.00	$250.00	34
D76	Gregory D'Amico	446 Federal St	Cortez	CO	81321	$1,015.00	$325.00	22
G56	Carl Giomaco	337 E. High St	Cortez	CO	81321	$485.00	$165.00	24
H21	Carol Sue Hill	247 Cumberland St	Cortez	CO	81321	$0.00	$285.00	34
J77	Peter Jones	75 South 1st Ave	Cortez	CO	81321	$685.00	$0.00	22
M26	Art Moravia	665 Pershing Ave	Cortez	CO	81321	$125.00	$185.00	24
S56	Ira Singer	31 Walnut St	Cortez	CO	81321	$1,200.00	$645.00	22
T45	Rita Tate	824 Spring St	Cortez	CO	81321	$345.00	$200.00	34
W24	Saul Woodruff	578 Walnut St	Cortez	CO	81321	$975.00	$0.00	34

Figure 3–81

2. Open the Potential Clients table and change the font to Arial with a font size of 10. Resize the columns to best fit the data. Save the changes to the table and close the table.
3. Open the Technician table and add the Totals row to the table. Calculate the average hourly rate and the total Earnings YTD. Save the changes to the table layout and close the table.
4. Use the Find Duplicates Query Wizard to find duplicate information in the City field of the Client table. Include the Client Name in the query. Save the query as City Duplicates Query and close the query.
5. Use the Find Unmatched Query Wizard to find all records in the Technician table that do not match records in the Client table. Technician Number is the common field in both tables. Include the Technician Number, Last Name, and First Name in the query. Save the query as Technician Unmatched Query and close the query.
6. If requested to do so by your instructor, change the client name in the Client table for client number S56 to First Name Last Name where First Name Last Name is your name. If your name is longer than the space allowed, simply enter as much as you can.
7. Submit the revised database in the format specified by your instructor.
8. What differences, if any, are there between the Client table and the Potential Clients table you created with the make-table query?

Expand Your World

Create a solution, which uses cloud and web technologies, by learning and investigating on your own from general guidance.

Problem: The Physical Therapy clinic wants to ensure that all Clients are matched with Therapists. The database needs a relationship created to ensure this matching. Your boss wants a copy of the report of this relationship.

Perform the following tasks:
Run Access and open the Support_AC_Physical Therapy database. (If you do not have the database, see your instructor for a copy of the modified database.)

1. Create a relationship between the Client table and the Therapist table on the Therapist Number field. Enforce referential integrity and Cascade Update Related Fields.
2. Create a relationship report for the relationship and save the report as First Name Last Name Relationship Report where First Name Last Name is your name.
3. Export the relationship as an RTF/Word document to a cloud-based storage location of your choice. Do not save the export steps.
4. Research the web to find a graphic that depicts a one-to-many relationship for a relational database. (*Hint:* Use your favorite search engine and enter keywords such as ERD diagram, entity-relationship diagram, or one to many relationship.)
5. Insert the graphic into the relationship report using an app of your choice, such as Word Online, and save the modified report.
6. Share the modified report with your instructor.
7. Submit the revised database in the format specified by your instructor.
8. Which cloud-based storage location did you use? How did you locate your graphic? Which app did you use to modify the report?

In the Labs

Design, create, modify, and/or use a database following the guidelines, concepts, and skills presented in this module.

Lab: Maintaining the Lancaster College Database

Instructions: Open the Support_AC_Lancaster College database (If you do not have the database, see your instructor for a copy of the modified database.)

Part 1: Use the concepts and techniques presented in this module to modify the database according to the following requirements:

1. Import the table Students Payments Extra table from your data files.
2. The coaches are concerned that there is no backup activity if they are ill. They would like an additional multivalued lookup field, Alternative SportsName, added to the Coach table. Table 3–2 lists the SportsName abbreviations that coaches would like.

Table 3–2 Alternative SportsName Abbreviations and Descriptions

SportsName Abbreviations	SportsName
TRK	Track
TEN	Tennis
WRS	Wrestling
FTB	Football
STB	Softball
POL	Pool
PING	PingPong
SWIM	Swimming
SOC	Soccer
BKB	Basketball

3. The accountant in charge of the student payments has asked for a calculated field that will figure the addition of the amount that the students have paid already plus their balance due. Add that calculated field to the appropriate table.
4. Create the following rule for the Coach table and save the changes: Make Coach First Name and Last Name required fields.
5. Using Filter By Form, delete all the records in the Student Payments table where any student's amount paid is zero and the balance due is greater than zero.
6. Add the data shown in Figure 3–82 to the Coach table for the Alternative SportsName field. Resize the field to best fit.

Coach ID	First Name	Last Name	SN	Alternative SportsName
17893	Lakisha	Black	Track	SOC
18797	Bill	Brinkly	Tennis	
18798	Tom	Smith	Wrestling	
18990	William	Gutierez	Football	STB, WRS
18999	Sharon	Stone	Softball	
78978	Frank	Terranova	Pool	
78979	Gail	French	Ping Pong	
79798	Daniel	Costner	Swimming	POL
79879	Gary	Faulkner	Soccer	
82374	Jean	Epperson	Basketball	SOC, TEN, TRK

Figure 3–82

7. Change the field size for the Alternative SportsName to 50.
8. In the Team table, find the record for CaptainID 78978, and change the CaptainID to 78797.
9. If requested to do so by your instructor, in the Student table, change the last name for Student ID 34872 to your last name. If your last name is longer than 15 characters, simply enter as much as you can.

Continued >

In the Labs *continued*

10. In the Participation table change the Student ID field to Short Text 20.
11. Establish referential integrity between the Student table (the one table) and the Participation table (the many table). Cascade the update but not the delete.

Submit the revised database in the format specified by your instructor.

Part 2: The Alternative SportsName field currently has 10 values. If Lancaster College picked up another sport, such as fencing, how would you add FEN to the Alternative SportsName field list? You added a calculated field in the Student Payments table. Does the calculated field actually exist in the database? Are there any issues that you need to consider when you create a calculated field?

Index

F

Q

R

U

X

Y

Z

ISBN-13: 978-0357119204
ISBN-10: 0357119207
90000
9 780357 119204

3 Creating a Business Letter

Objectives

After completing this module, you will be able to:

- Insert and format a shape
- Change text wrapping
- Insert an online picture and format it
- Insert a symbol
- Add a border to a paragraph
- Clear formatting
- Apply a style
- Set and use tab stops
- Insert the current date
- Insert a Word table, enter data in the table, and format the table
- Format a paragraph border
- Use the format painter
- Insert and format a SmartArt graphic
- Address and print an envelope

Introduction

In a business environment, people use documents to communicate with others. Business documents can include letters, memos, newsletters, proposals, and resumes. An effective business document clearly and concisely conveys its message and has a professional, organized appearance. You can use your own creative skills to design and compose business documents. Using Word, for example, you can develop the content and decide on the location of each item in a business document.

Project: Business Letter

At some time, you more than likely will prepare a business letter. Contents of business letters include requests, inquiries, confirmations, acceptances, applications, acknowledgements, recommendations, notifications, responses, thank you letters, invitations, offers, referrals, references, complaints, and more.

The project in this module follows generally accepted guidelines for writing letters and uses Word to create the business letter shown in Figure 3–1. This letter, written by the services coordinator for the director of admissions at Sunset State College, is an acceptance

page 1 of business letter

Sunset State College

Office of Admissions, 1001 Canton Street, MC 3300, Novato, CA 94945 • 415-555-0199• sunset.edu

letterhead

April 19, 2021 ← date line

inside address →

Mr. Caleb Thomas
982 Bartlett Street
Live Oak, CA 95953

salutation → Dear Caleb,

Congratulations on your admission to the School of Liberal Arts and Sciences at Sunset State for the fall semester of 2021! On behalf of our students, faculty, and staff, I welcome you to our academic community. Our decision to admit you to our college is an acknowledgement of your potential and our confidence in you as a valuable addition to our student body.

We would like to inform you of important upcoming dates:

table →

Date	Event	*Notes*
July 12-16 and July 19-23	Orientation and registration	*See brief schedule on next page*
August 16-17	Move-in days	*Assigned by Housing Services*
August 16-20	Welcome week	*Get schedule during orientation*
August 23	Fall term begins	*First day of classes*

body, or message

Before orientation, you must do the following through our campus website:

bulleted list →

- Complete a housing contract or housing exemption form
- Schedule your math placement exam
- Reserve your orientation dates

I am confident you will pursue your passions and accomplish your goals as a Sunset State Flying Eagle!

Sincerely, ← complimentary close

Lucy R. Song
Director of Admissions ← signature block

page 2 of business letter

Orientation and Registration Student Schedule

We look forward to meeting you! Below you will find a general schedule for the two days you will be on campus for orientation and registration.

During orientation, we will walk around campus so please dress accordingly.

Day 1

- Check-in (9:00-10:00)
- Welcome and general info session (10:15-11:45)
- Lunch (12:00-12:45)
- Student accounts and services session (1:00-1:45)
- Meetings with advisors (2:00-2:45)
- Department meetings (3:00-3:45)
- Expo (4:00-5:15)
- Dinner (5:30-6:45)
- Evening activities (7:00-10:00)

Day 2

- Breakfast (7:00-7:45)
- Housing services session (8:00-8:30)
- Dining services session (8:35-9:05)
- Health services session (9:10-9:40)
- Campus tour (10:00-11:45)
- Lunch (12:00-12:45)
- General education session (1:00-1:45)
- Register for classes (2:00-3:15)
- Welcome week overview (3:30-4:00)

SmartArt graphic

Figure 3–1

letter that welcomes the student to the campus and presents important information related to upcoming deadlines and events. The letter includes a custom letterhead, as well as all essential business letter components: date line, inside address, salutation, body, complimentary close, and signature block. To easily present the important upcoming dates for the student, the letter shows this information in a table. The immediate requirements appear in a bulleted list. The second page contains a visual of the schedule for orientation and registration.

In this module, you will learn how to create the letter shown in Figure 3–1. You will perform the following general tasks as you progress through this module:

1. Create and format a letterhead with graphics.
2. Specify the letter formats according to business letter guidelines.
3. Insert a table in the letter.
4. Format the table in the letter.
5. Insert a bulleted list in the letter.
6. On a second page, insert and format a SmartArt graphic.
7. Address an envelope for the letter.

To Start Word and Change Word Settings

If you are using a computer to step through the project in this module and you want your screens to match the figures in this book, you should change your screen's resolution to 1366 × 768.

The following steps start Word, display formatting marks, and change the zoom to page width.

1. **sam** Start Word and create a blank document in the Word window. If necessary, maximize the Word window.
2. If the Print Layout button on the status bar is not selected (shown in Figure 3–2), click it so that your screen is in Print Layout view.
3. If the 'Show/Hide ¶' button (Home tab | Paragraph group) is not selected already, click it to display formatting marks on the screen.
4. To display the page the same width as the document window, if necessary, click the Page Width button (View tab | Zoom group).
5. If you are using a mouse and you want your screens to match the figures in the book, verify that you are using Mouse mode by clicking the Touch/Mouse Mode button on the Quick Access Toolbar and then, if necessary, clicking Mouse on the menu. (If your Quick Access Toolbar does not display the Touch/Mouse Mode button, click the 'Customize Quick Access Toolbar' button on the Quick Access Toolbar and then click Touch/Mouse Mode on the menu to add the button to the Quick Access Toolbar.)

BTW

Touch Mode Differences

The Office and Windows interfaces may vary if you are using Touch mode. For this reason, you might notice that the function or appearance of your touch screen differs slightly from this module's presentation.

Creating a Letterhead

The cost of preprinted letterhead can be high; thus, some organizations and individuals create their own letterhead and save it in a file. Then, when you want to create a letter at a later time, you can start by using the letterhead file. The following sections create a letterhead and then save it in a file for future use.

CONSIDER THIS

What is a letterhead?

A **letterhead**, which often appears at the top of a letter, is the section of a letter that identifies an organization or individual. Although you can design and print a letterhead yourself, many businesses pay an outside firm to design and print their letterhead, usually on higher-quality paper. They then use the professionally preprinted paper for external business communications.

If you do not have preprinted letterhead paper, you can design a creative letterhead. It is important the letterhead appropriately represent the essence of the organization or individual (i.e., formal, technical, creative, etc.). That is, it should use text, graphics, formats, and colors that reflect the organization or individual. The letterhead should leave ample room for the contents of the letter.

When designing a letterhead, consider its contents, placement, and appearance.

- **Contents of letterhead.** A letterhead should contain these elements:
  - Complete legal name of the individual, group, or company
  - Complete mailing address: street address including building, room, suite number, or post office box, along with city, state, and postal code
  - Phone number(s) and fax number, if applicable
  - Email address, if applicable
  - Web address, if applicable
  - Many letterheads also include a logo or other image; if an image is used, it should express the organization or individual's personality or goals
- **Placement of elements in the letterhead.** Many letterheads center their elements across the top of the page. Others align some or all of the elements with the left or right margins. Sometimes, the elements are split between the top and bottom of the page. For example, a name and logo may be at the top of the page with the address at the bottom of the page.
- **Appearance of letterhead elements.** Use fonts that are easy to read. Give the organization or individual name impact by making its font size larger than the rest of the text in the letterhead. For additional emphasis, consider formatting the name in bold, italic, or a different color. Choose colors that complement each other and convey the goals of the organization or individual.

When finished designing the letterhead, determine if a divider line would help to visually separate the letterhead from the remainder of the letter.

The letterhead for the letter in this module consists of the school name, postal address, phone number, web address, and images of an eagle (the school's mascot). The name and images are enclosed in a rectangular shape (shown in Figure 3–1), and the contact information is below the shape. You will follow these general steps to create the letterhead in this module:

1. Insert and format a shape.
2. Enter and format the school name in the shape.
3. Insert, format, and position the images in the shape.
4. Enter the contact information below the shape.
5. Add a border below the contact information.

To Insert a Shape

Word has a variety of predefined shapes, which are a type of drawing object, that you can insert in documents. A **drawing object** is a graphic that you create using Word. Examples of shape drawing objects include rectangles, circles, triangles, arrows, flowcharting symbols, stars, banners, and callouts. The following steps insert a rectangle shape in the letterhead. ***Why?*** *The school name is placed in a rectangle for emphasis and visual appeal.*

- Display the Insert tab.
- Click the Shapes button (Insert tab | Illustrations group) to display the Shapes gallery (Figure 3–2).

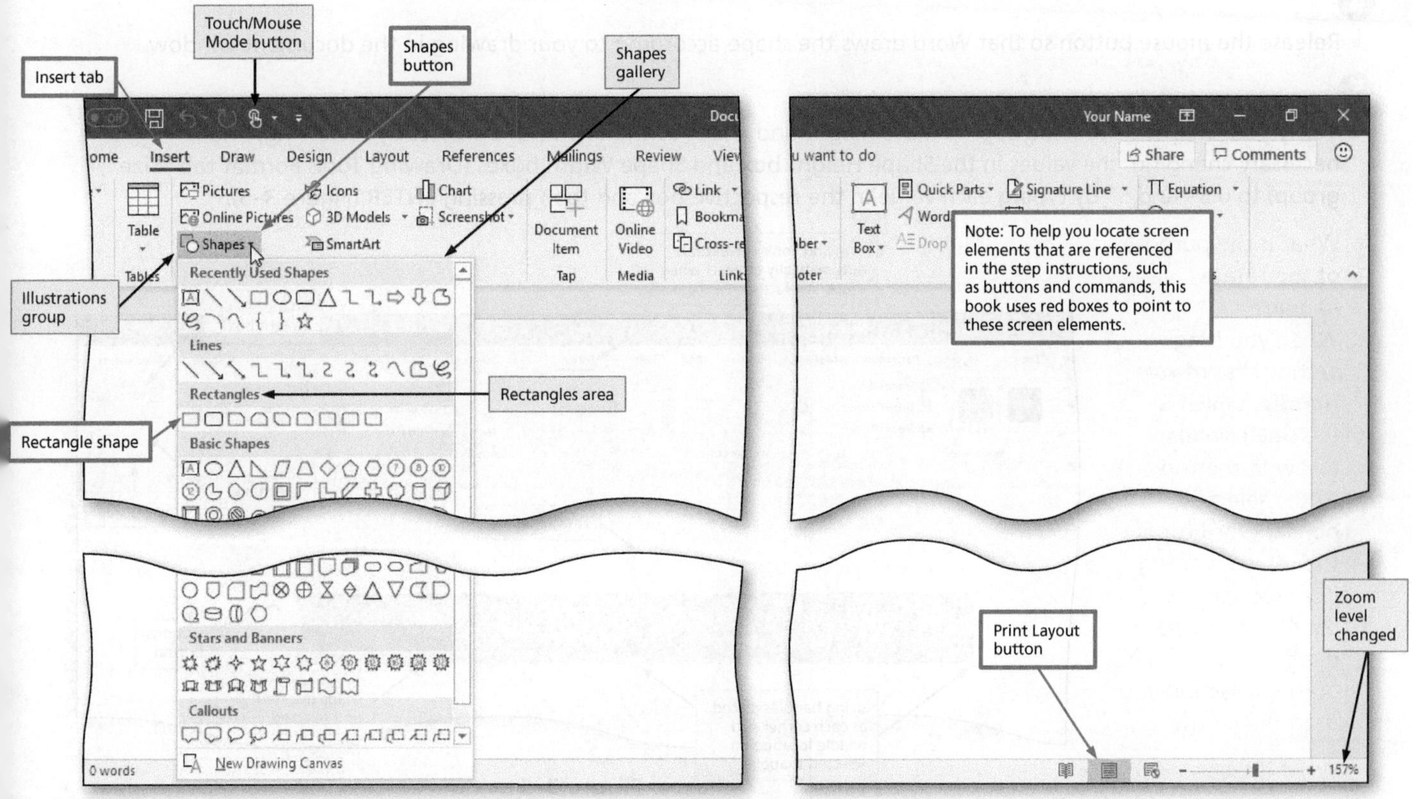

Figure 3–2

- Click the Rectangle shape in the Rectangles area in the Shapes gallery, which removes the gallery.

Q&A What if I am using a touch screen?
The shape is inserted in the document window. Skip Steps 3 and 4, and proceed to Step 5.

- Position the pointer (a crosshair) in the approximate location for the upper-left corner of the desired shape (Figure 3–3).

Q&A What is the purpose of the crosshair pointer?
You drag the crosshair pointer from the upper-left corner to the lower-right corner to form the desired location and size of the shape.

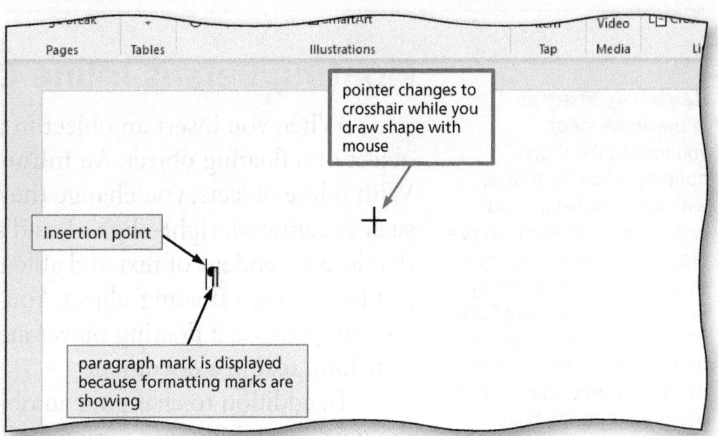

Figure 3–3

- Drag the mouse to the right and downward to form the boundaries of the shape, as shown in Figure 3–4. Do not release the mouse button.

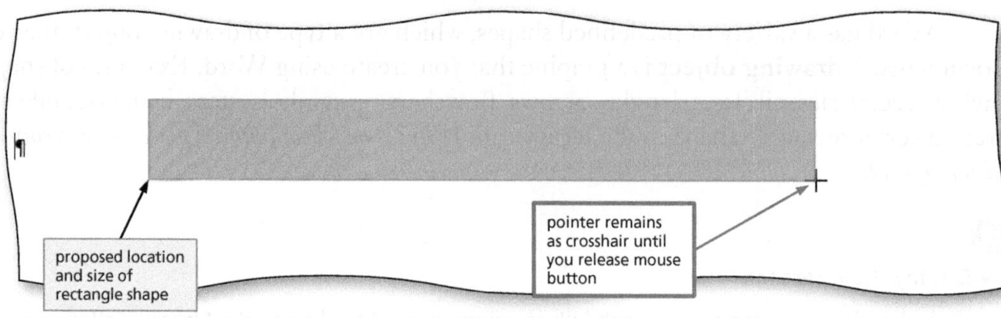

Figure 3–4

- Release the mouse button so that Word draws the shape according to your drawing in the document window.

- Verify your shape is the same approximate height and width as the one in this project by reviewing, and if necessary changing, the values in the Shape Height box and Shape Width boxes (Drawing Tools Format tab | Size group) to 0.5" and 5" by typing each value in the respective box and then pressing ENTER (Figure 3–5).

Q&A

What is the purpose of the rotate handle?
When you drag an object's **rotate handle**, which is the small circular arrow at the top of the selected object, Word turns the selected object in a clockwise or counterclockwise direction, depending on the direction you drag the mouse.

What if I wanted to delete a shape and start over?
With the shape selected, you would press DELETE.

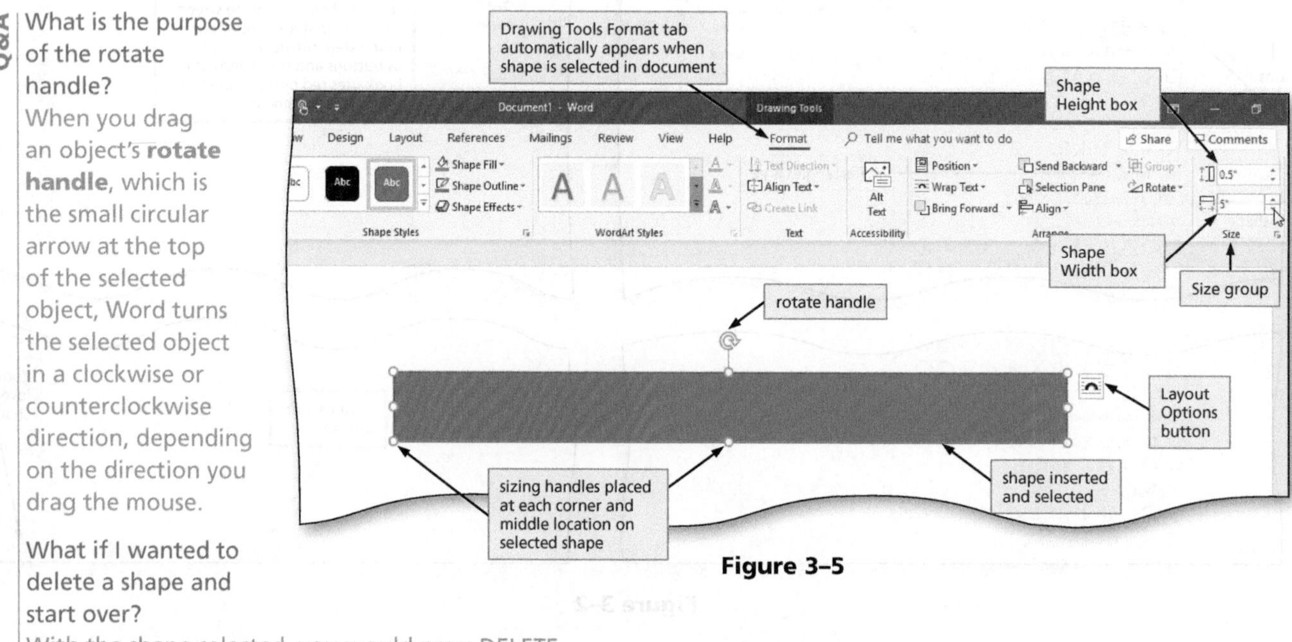

Figure 3–5

BTW
Resizing Shapes
In the above steps, you resized the shape nonproportionally, that is, with different height and width values. To maintain size proportions when resizing a shape, click the Size Dialog Box Launcher (Drawing Tools Format tab | Size group) and then place a check mark in the 'Lock aspect ratio' check box (Layout dialog box).

Floating versus Inline Objects

When you insert an object in a document, Word inserts it as either an inline object or a floating object. An **inline object** is an object that is part of a paragraph. With inline objects, you change the location of the object by setting paragraph options, such as centered, right-aligned, and so on. A **floating object**, by contrast, is an object that is independent of text and able to be moved anywhere on a page. The shape you just inserted is a floating object. You have more flexibility with floating objects because you can position a floating object at a specific location in a document or in a layer over or behind text in a document.

In addition to changing an object from inline to floating and vice versa, Word provides several floating options, which (along with inline) are called text wrapping options because they affect how text wraps with or around the object. Table 3–1 presents the various text wrapping options.

Table 3–1 Text Wrapping Options

Text Wrapping Option	Object Type	How It Works
In Line with Text	Inline	Object positioned according to paragraph formatting; for example, if the paragraph is centered, the object will be centered with any text in the paragraph.
Square	Floating	Text wraps around the object, with the text forming a box around the object.
Tight	Floating	Text wraps around the object, with the text forming to the shape of the object.
Through	Floating	Object appears at the beginning, middle, or end of text. Moving the object changes location of the text.
Top and Bottom	Floating	Object appears above or below text. Moving the object changes location of the text.
Behind Text	Floating	Object appears behind the text.
In Front of Text	Floating	Object appears in front of the text and may cover the text.

To Change an Object's Position

You can specify an object's vertical position within the margins on a page (top, middle, bottom) and its horizontal position (left, center, right). The following steps change the position of an object, specifically, the rectangle shape. ***Why?*** *You want the shape to be centered at the top of the page in the letterhead.*

1

- With the shape still selected, click the Position button (Drawing Tools Format tab | Arrange group) to display the Position gallery (Figure 3–6).

Q&A What if the shape is not still selected?
Click the shape to select it.

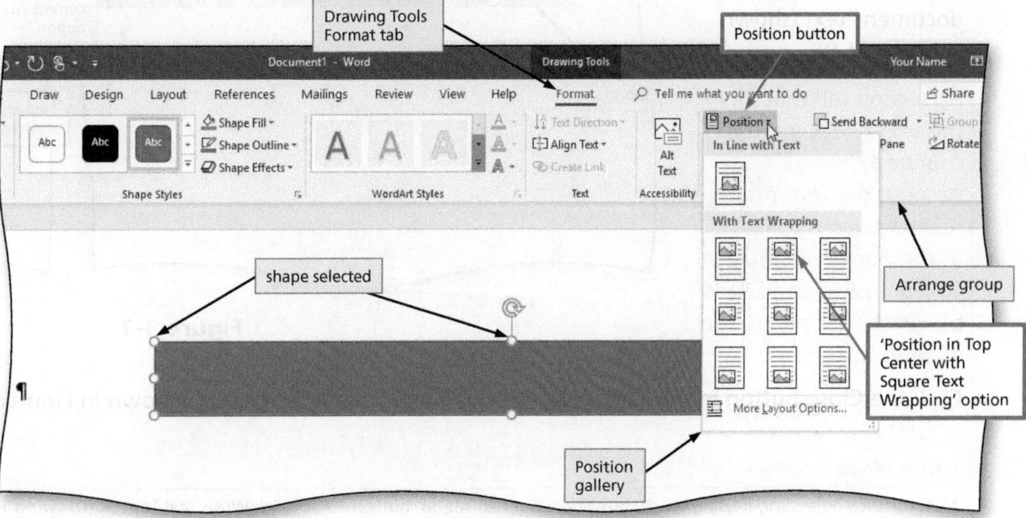

Figure 3–6

 **Experiment**

- Point to various options in the Position gallery and watch the shape move to the selected position option.

2

- Click 'Position in Top Center with Square Text Wrapping' in the Position gallery so that the object does not cover the document and is centered at the top margin of the document.

Q&A What if I wanted to center the object in its current vertical location (and not at the top, center, or bottom of the page)?
You would click the Align button (Drawing Tools Format tab | Arrange group) (shown in Figure 3–7) and then click the desired alignment in the list.

Other Ways

1. Click Layout Options button attached to object (shown in Figure 3–5), click See more link in Layout Options gallery, click Horizontal Alignment arrow and select alignment (Layout dialog box), click Vertical Alignment arrow and select alignment, click OK
2. Click a Size Dialog Box Launcher (Drawing Tools Format tab | Size group), click Position tab (Layout dialog box), click Horizontal Alignment arrow and select alignment, click Vertical Alignment arrow and select alignment, click OK

To Change an Object's Text Wrapping

When you insert a shape in a Word document, the default text wrapping is In Front of Text, which means the object will cover any text behind it. The previous steps, which changed the shape's position, changed the text wrapping to Square. In the letterhead, you want the shape's text wrapping to be Top and Bottom. ***Why?*** *You want the letterhead above the contents of the letter when you type it, instead of covering the contents of the letter.* The following steps change an object's text wrapping, specifically, the shape.

1

- With the shape still selected, click the Layout Options button attached to the object to display the Layout Options gallery (Figure 3–7).

2

- Click 'Top and Bottom' in the Layout Options gallery so that the object does not cover the document text (shown in Figure 3–9).

Q&A How can I tell that the text wrapping has changed?
Because the letter has no text, you need to look at the paragraph mark, which now is positioned below the shape instead of to its left.

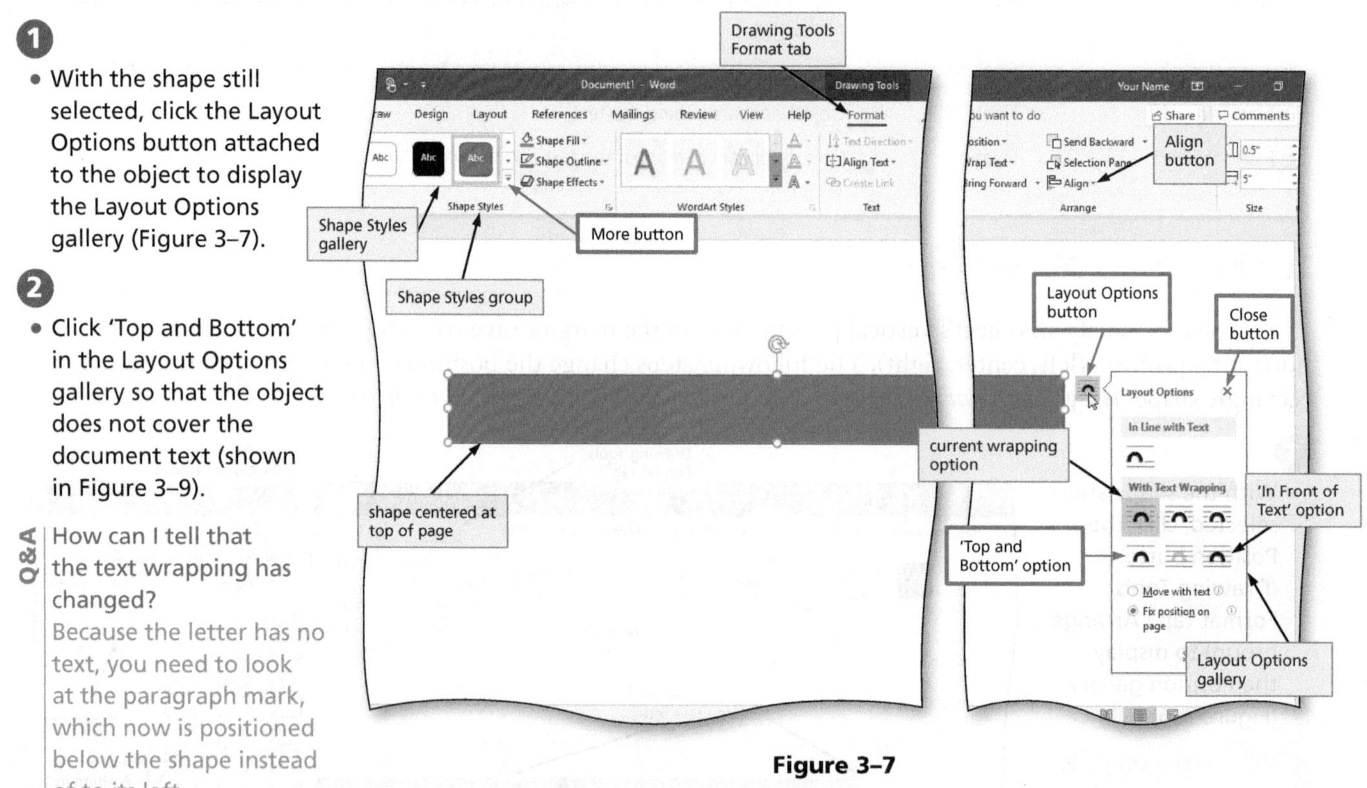

Figure 3–7

- Click the Close button in the Layout Options gallery to close the gallery (shown in Figure 3–9).

Other Ways

1. Right-click object (or, if using touch, tap 'Show Context Menu' button on Mini toolbar), point to Wrap Text on shortcut menu, click desired wrapping option
2. Click Wrap Text button (Drawing Tools Format tab | Arrange group), select desired wrapping option

To Apply a Shape Style

Why apply a shape style? *Word provides a Shape Styles gallery so that you easily can change the appearance of the shape.* The following steps apply a shape style to the rectangle shape.

1

- With the shape still selected, click the More button (shown in Figure 3–7) in the Shape Styles gallery (Drawing Tools Format tab | Shape Styles group) to expand the gallery.

What if the shape no longer is selected?
Click the shape to select it.

- Point to 'Moderate Effect - Orange, Accent 2' (third style in fifth row) in the Shape Styles gallery to display a Live Preview of that style applied to the shape in the document (Figure 3–8).

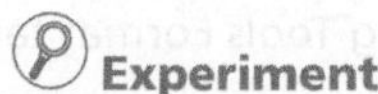

- Point to various styles in the Shape Styles gallery and watch the style of the shape change in the document.

- Click 'Moderate Effect - Orange, Accent 2' in the Shape Styles gallery to apply the selected style to the shape.

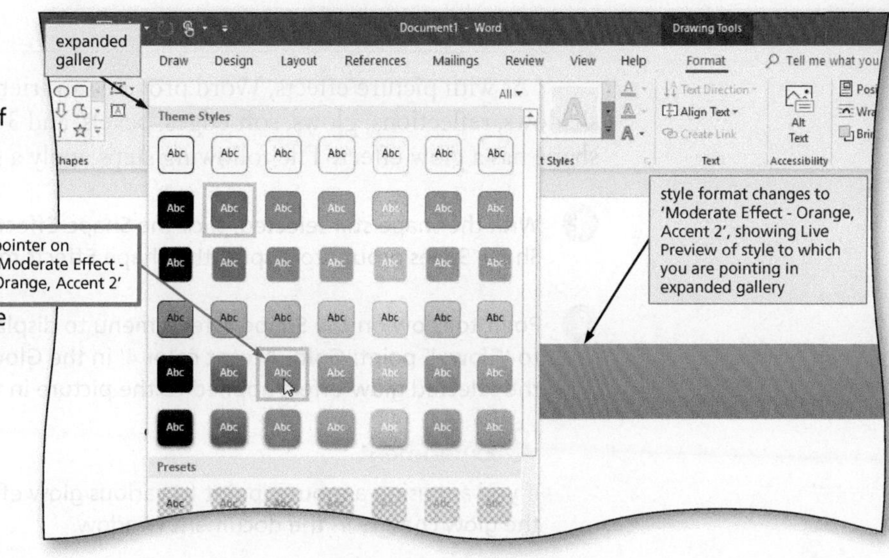

Figure 3–8

Other Ways

1. Right-click shape, click Style button on Mini toolbar, select desired style
2. Click Shape Styles Dialog Box Launcher (Drawing Tools Format tab | Shape Styles group), click 'Fill & Line' button (Format Shape pane), expand Fill section, select desired colors, click Close button

To Change the Shape Outline

The rectangle shape currently has an orange outline that matches the fill color inside the shape. The following steps change the outline color on the shape. ***Why?*** *You would like to differentiate the outline from the fill color on the shape.*

- Click the Shape Outline arrow (Drawing Tools Format tab | Shape Styles group) to display the Shape Outline gallery.
- Point to 'Gold, Accent 4' (eighth color in first row) in the Shape Outline gallery to display a Live Preview of that outline color around the shape (Figure 3–9).

Experiment

- Point to various colors in the Shape Outline gallery and watch the outline color on the shape change in the document window.

- Click 'Gold, Accent 4' in the Shape Outline gallery to change the shape outline color.

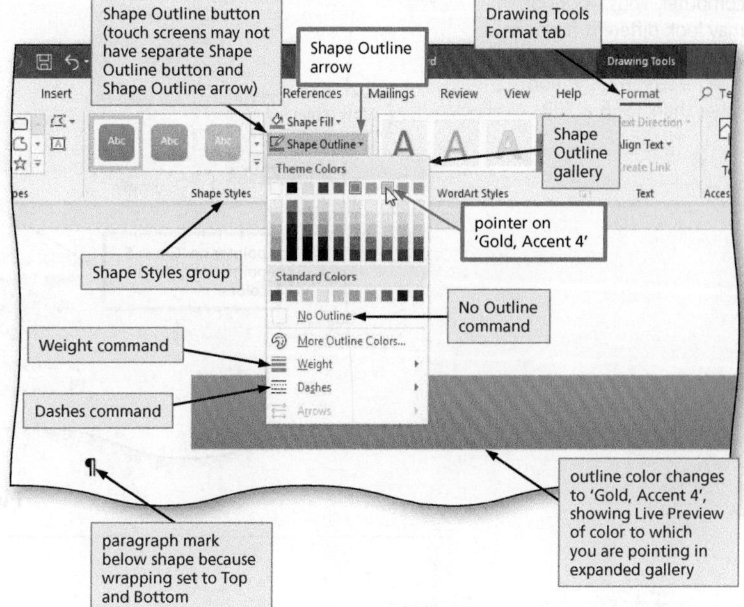

Figure 3–9

Q&A

How would I remove an outline color from a shape?
With the graphic selected, you would click No Outline in the Shape Outline gallery.

When would I use the Weight and Dashes commands in the Shape Outline gallery?
The Weight command enables you to change the thickness of the outline, and the Dashes command provides a variety of dashed outline options.

To Apply a Shape Effect

As with picture effects, Word provides a variety of shape effects, including shadows, reflections, glows, soft edges, bevels, and 3-D rotations. In this letterhead, the shape has a glow effect. The following steps apply a shape effect to the selected shape.

1. With the shape still selected, click the Shape Effects button (Drawing Tools Format tab | Shape Styles group) to display the Shape Effects menu.

2. Point to Glow on the Shape Effects menu to display the Glow gallery and then point to 'Glow: 5 point; Gold, Accent color 4' in the Glow gallery to display a Live Preview of the selected glow effect applied to the picture in the document window (Figure 3–10).

   Experiment

   If you are using a mouse, point to various glow effects in the Glow gallery and watch the glow change in the document window.

3. Click 'Glow: 5 point; Gold, Accent color 4' in the Glow gallery to apply the selected glow effect.

BTW

The Ribbon and Screen Resolution

Word may change how the groups and buttons within the groups appear on the ribbon, depending on the screen resolution of your computer. Thus, your ribbon may look different from the ones in this book if you are using a screen resolution other than 1366 × 768.

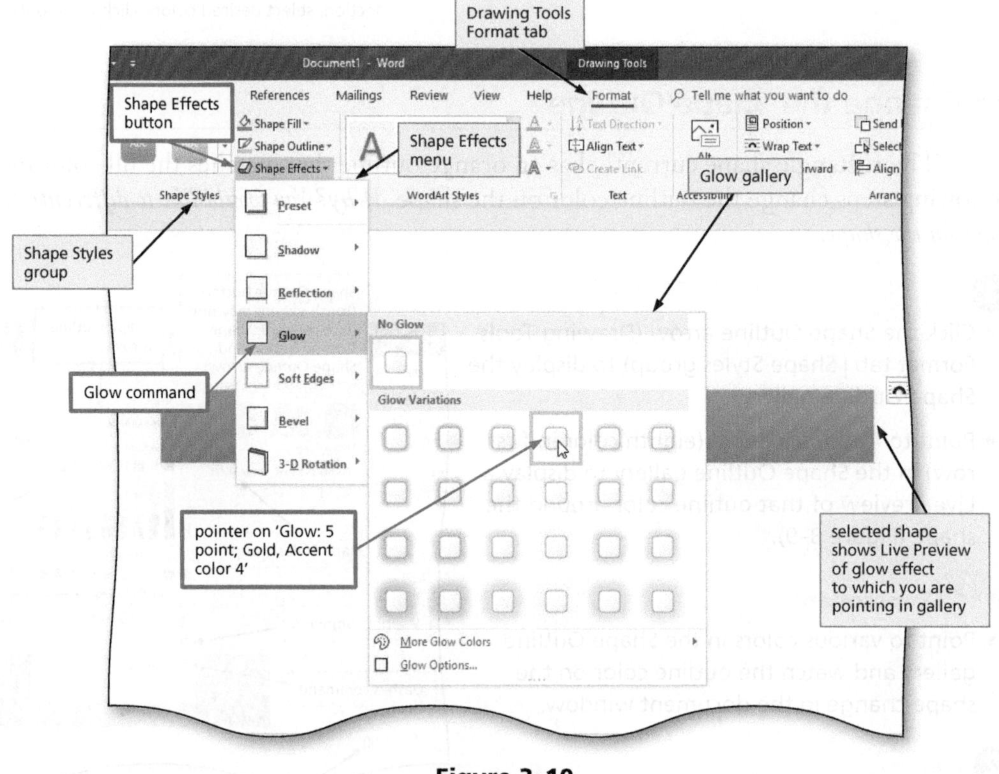

Figure 3–10

To Add Text to a Shape

The following steps add text (the school name) to a shape. ***Why?*** *In the letterhead for this module, the name is in the shape. Similarly, an individual could put his or her name in a shape on a letterhead in order to create personalized letterhead.*

1

- Right-click the shape to display a Mini toolbar and/or shortcut menu (Figure 3–11).

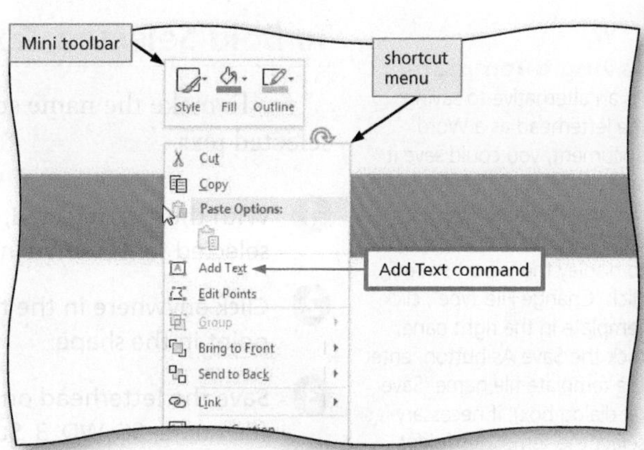

Figure 3–11

2

- Click Add Text on the shortcut menu to place an insertion point in the shape.

Q&A What if I am using a touch screen?
Tap the Edit Text button on the Mini toolbar.

Why do the buttons on my Mini toolbar differ?
If you are using a mouse in Mouse mode, the buttons on your Mini toolbar will differ from those that appear when you use a touch screen in Touch mode.

- If the insertion point and paragraph mark are not centered in the shape, click the Center button (Home tab | Paragraph group) to center them.
- Type `Sunset State College` as the name in the shape (Figure 3–12).

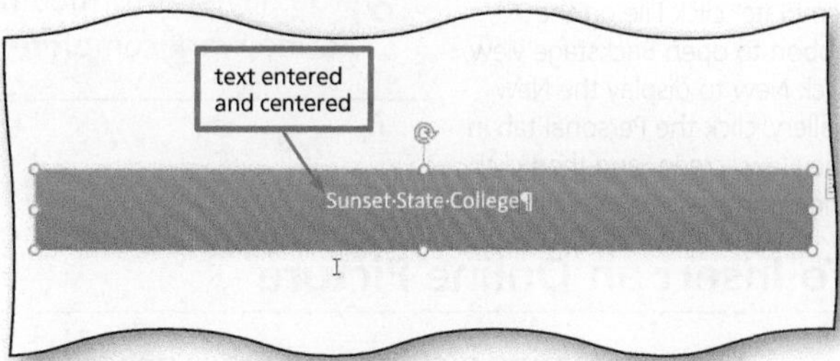

Figure 3–12

To Use the 'Increase Font Size' Button

While you can use the Font Size arrow (Home tab | Font group) to change the font size of text, Word also provides an 'Increase Font Size' button (Home tab | Font group) that increases the font size of selected text each time you click the button. The following steps use the 'Increase Font Size' button to increase the font size of the name in the shape to 24 point. ***Why?*** *You want the name to be larger in the shape.*

- Drag through the text to be formatted (in this case, the name in the shape).

- If necessary, display the Home tab.
- Repeatedly click the 'Increase Font Size' button (Home tab | Font group) until the Font Size box displays 24 to increase the font size of the selected text (Figure 3–13).

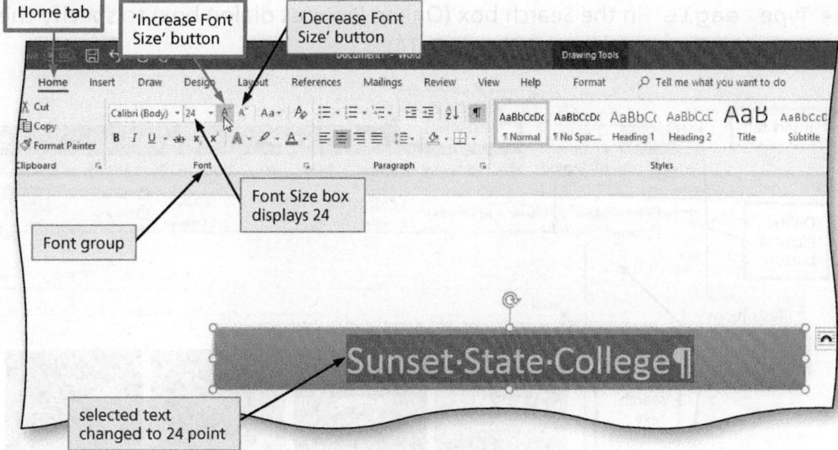

Figure 3–13

Q&A What if I click the 'Increase Font Size' button (Home tab | Font group) too many times, causing the font size to be too big?
Click the 'Decrease Font Size' button (Home tab | Font group) until the desired font size is displayed.

Experiment

- Repeatedly click the 'Increase Font Size' and 'Decrease Font Size' buttons (Home tab | Font group) and watch the font size of the selected text change in the document window. When you are finished experimenting with these two buttons, set the font size to 24.

Other Ways

1. Press CTRL+SHIFT+>

BTW

Saving a Template
As an alternative to saving the letterhead as a Word document, you could save it as a template. To do so, click File on the ribbon to open Backstage view, click Export to display the Export screen, click 'Change File Type', click Template in the right pane, click the Save As button, enter the template file name (Save As dialog box), if necessary select the Templates folder, and then click the Save button in the dialog box. To use the template, click File on the ribbon to open Backstage view, click New to display the New gallery, click the Personal tab in the New screen, and then click the template icon or file name.

To Bold Selected Text and Save the Letterhead Document

To make the name stand out even more, bold it. The following steps bold the selected text.

1. With the text selected, click the Bold button (Home tab | Font group) to bold the selected text (shown in Figure 3–16).
2. Click anywhere in the text in the shape to remove the selection and place the insertion point in the shape.
3. Save the letterhead on your hard drive, OneDrive, or other storage location using the file name, SC_WD_3_SunsetStateLetterhead.

Q&A

Why should I save the letterhead at this time?

You have performed many tasks while creating this letterhead and do not want to risk losing work completed thus far.

To Insert an Online Picture

Files containing pictures and other images are available from a variety of sources. In this project, you insert a picture from the web. Microsoft Office applications can access a collection of royalty-free photos and animations.

The letterhead in this project contains a picture of a flying eagle (shown in Figure 3–1). ***Why?*** *The school mascot is a flying eagle.* The following steps insert an online picture in the document.

- If necessary, click the paragraph mark below the shape to position the insertion point where you want to insert the picture.
- Display the Insert tab.
- Click the Online Pictures button (Insert tab | Illustrations group) to display the Online Pictures dialog box.
- Type `eagle` in the Search box (Online Pictures dialog box) to specify the search text, which indicates the type of image you want to locate (Figure 3–14).

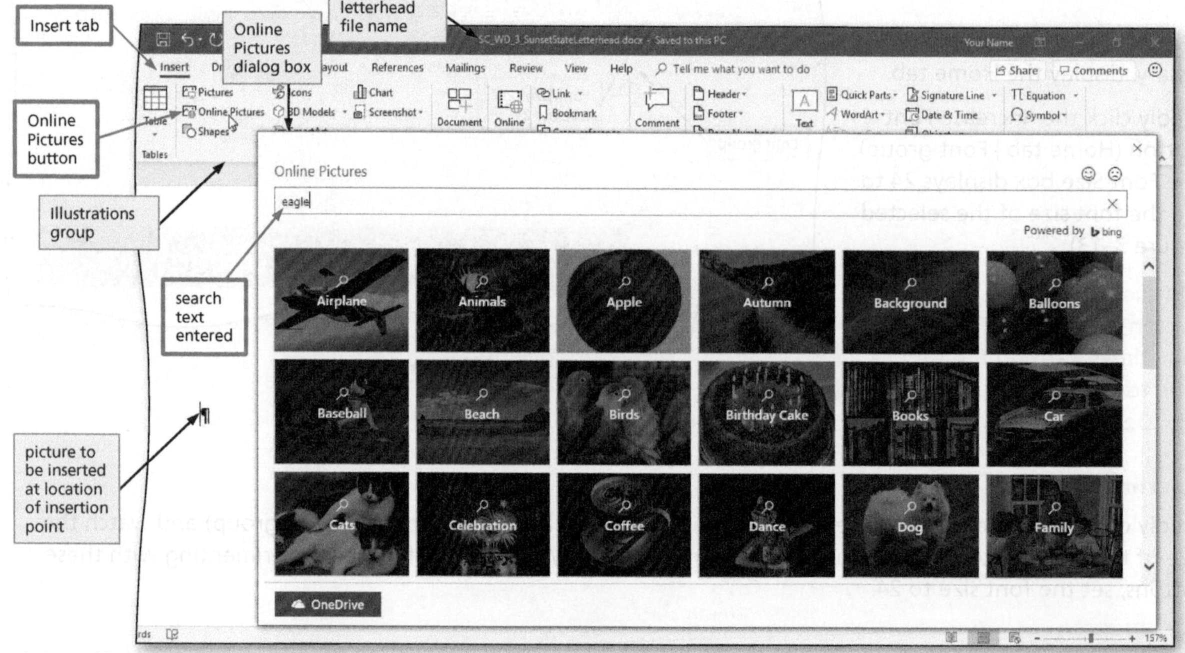

Figure 3–14

- Press ENTER to display a list of online pictures that matches the entered search text.
- Scroll through the list of pictures to locate the one shown in Figure 3–15, or a similar image.

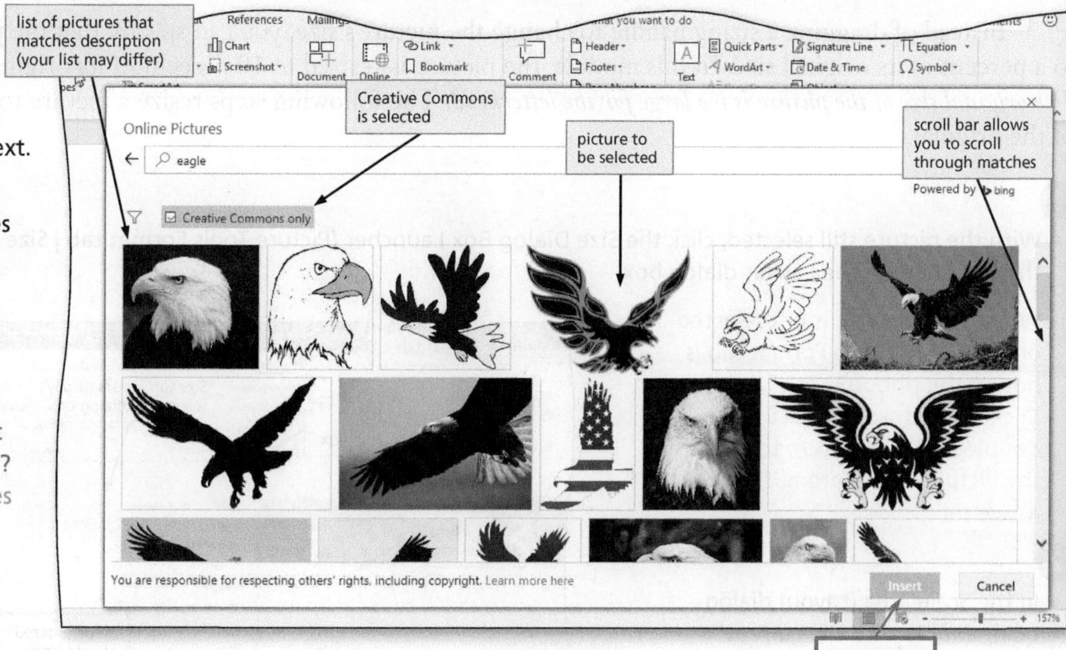

Figure 3–15

Q&A Why is my list of pictures different from Figure 3–15?
The online images are continually updated.

What is Creative Commons?
Creative Commons is a nonprofit organization that makes it easy for content creators to license and share their work by supplying easy-to-understand copyright licenses; the creator chooses the conditions under which the work can be used. Be sure to follow an image's guidelines when using it in a document.

What if I cannot locate the image in Figure 3–15, and I would like to use that exact image?
The image is located in the Data Files. You can click the Cancel button (Online Pictures dialog box) and then click the Pictures button (Insert tab | Illustrations group), navigate to the file called Support_WD_3_FlamingEagle.png in the Data Files, and then click the Insert button (Insert Picture dialog box).

- Click the desired picture to select it.
- Click the Insert button to insert the selected image in the document at the location of the insertion point. If necessary, scroll to display the image (picture) in the document window (Figure 3–16).

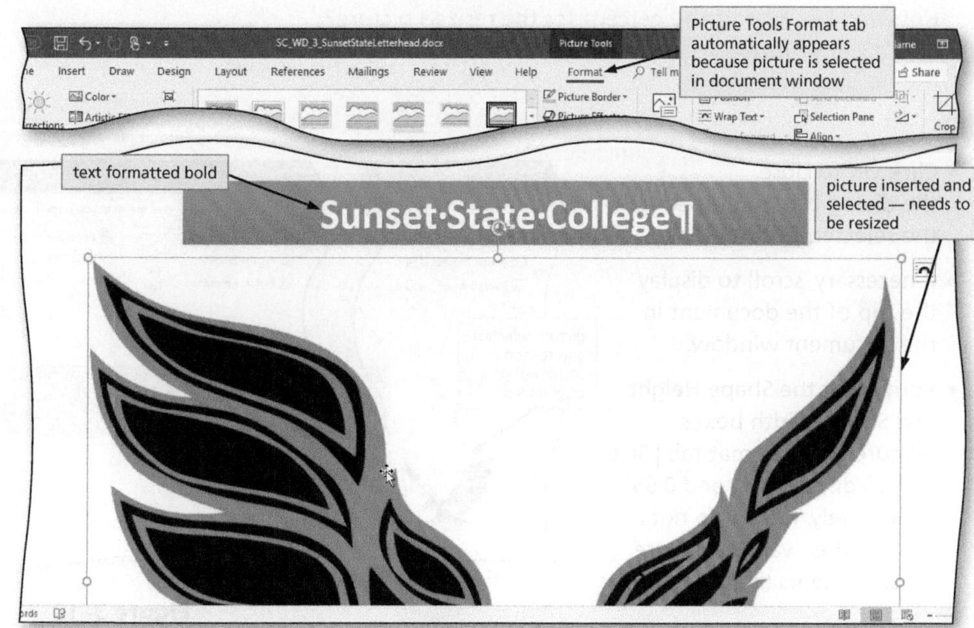

Figure 3–16

To Resize a Picture to a Percent of the Original Size

Instead of dragging a sizing handle to change the picture's size, you can specify that the picture be resized to a percent of its original size. In this module, the picture is resized to 10 percent of its original size. ***Why?*** *The original size of the picture is too large for the letterhead.* The following steps resize a picture to a percent of the original.

- With the picture still selected, click the Size Dialog Box Launcher (Picture Tools Format tab | Size group) to display the Size sheet in the Layout dialog box.

Q&A What if the picture is not selected or the Picture Tools Format tab is not on the ribbon?
Click the picture to select it or double-click the picture to make the Picture Tools Format tab the active tab.

- In the Scale area (Layout dialog box), double-click the current value in the Height box to select it.
- Type `10` in the Height box and then press TAB to display the same percent value in the Width box (Figure 3–17).

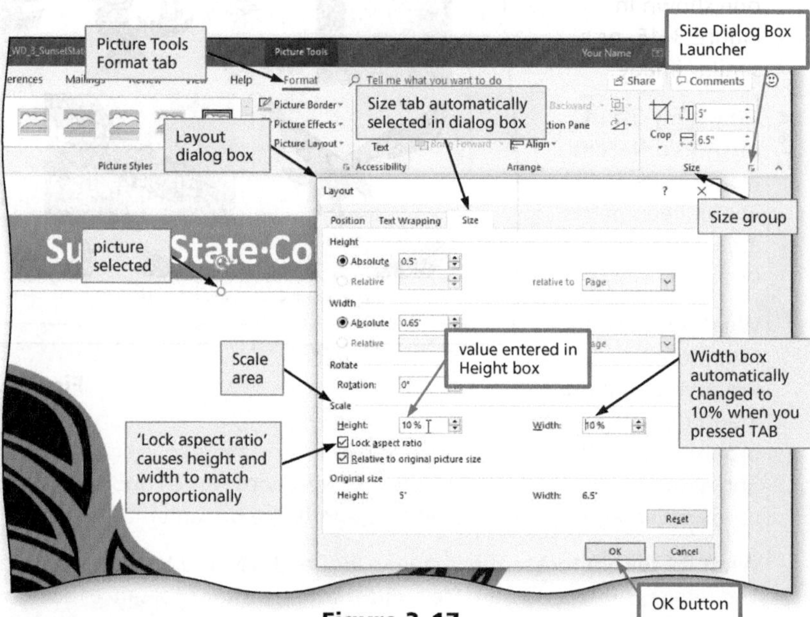

Figure 3–17

Q&A Why did Word automatically fill in the value in the Width box?
When the 'Lock aspect ratio' check box (Layout dialog box) is selected, Word automatically maintains the size proportions of the selected picture. If you wanted to resize the picture nonproportionally, you would remove the check mark from this check box.

How do I know to use 10 percent for the resized picture?
The larger picture consumed too much room on the page. Try various percentages to determine the size that works best in the letterhead design.

- Click OK to close the dialog box and resize the selected picture.
- If necessary, scroll to display the top of the document in the document window.
- Verify that the Shape Height and Shape Width boxes (Picture Tools Format tab | Size group) display 0.5" and 0.65", respectively. If they do not, change their values to these measurements (Figure 3–18).

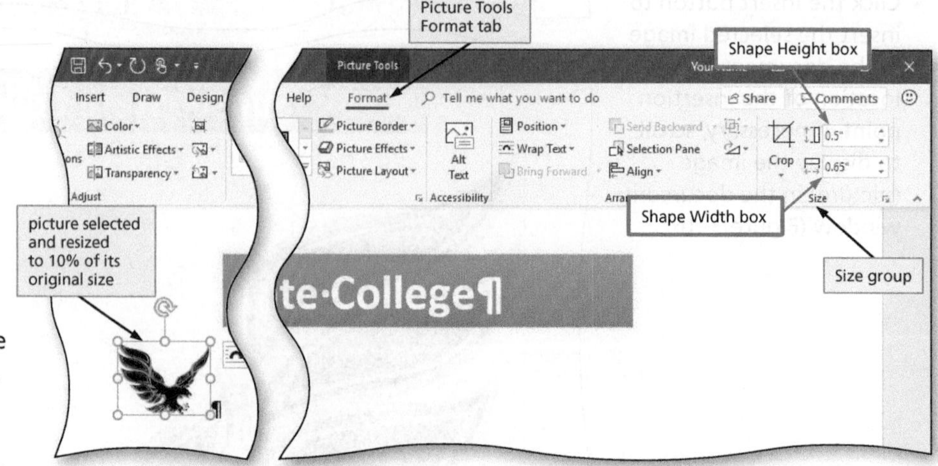

Figure 3–18

Other Ways

1. Click Layout Options button attached to picture, click See more link in the Layout Options gallery, click Size tab (Layout dialog box), enter height and width values, click OK
2. Right-click picture, click 'Size and Position' on shortcut menu, enter height and width values (Layout dialog box), click OK

To Change the Color of a Picture

In Word, you can change the color of a picture. The flying eagle picture currently is bright orange and black colors. The following steps change the color of the picture. ***Why?*** *Because the image in this project will be placed beside the rectangle shape, you prefer to use lighter colors.*

- With the picture still selected (shown in Figure 3–18), click the Color button (Picture Tools Format tab | Adjust group) to display the Color gallery.
- Point to 'Gold, Accent color 4 Dark' in the Recolor area in the Color gallery (fifth color in second row), which would display a Live Preview of that color applied to the selected picture in the document if the picture was not hidden by the Color gallery (Figure 3–19).

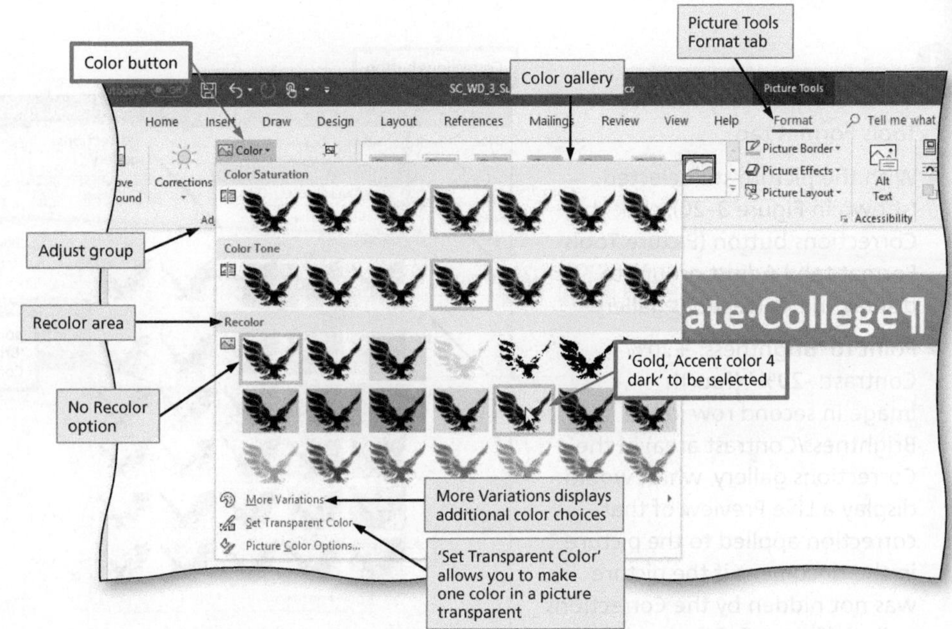

Figure 3–19

- Click 'Gold, Accent color 4 Dark' in the Color gallery to change the color of the selected picture (Figure 3–20).

Q&A How would I change a picture back to its original colors?
With the picture selected, you would click No Recolor, which is the upper-left color in the Color gallery.

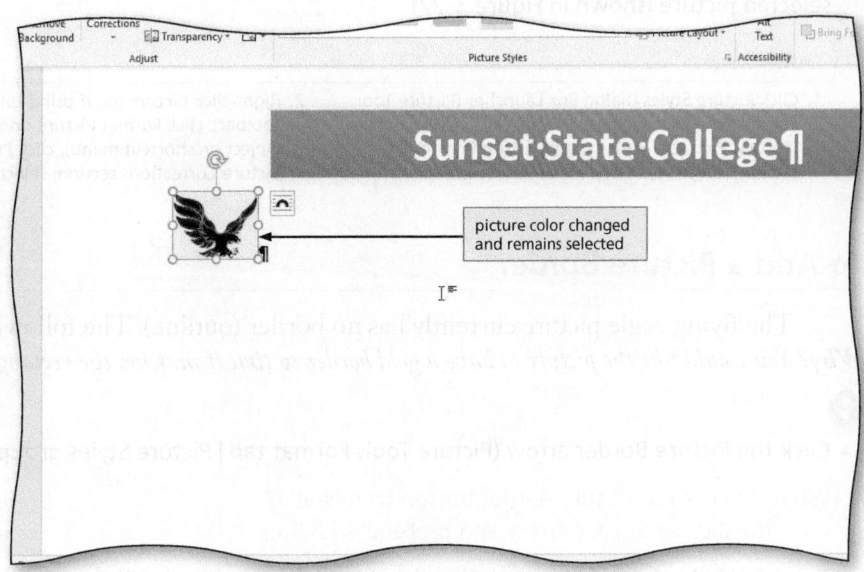

Figure 3–20

Other Ways

1. Click Picture Styles Dialog Box Launcher (Picture Tools Format tab | Picture Styles group), click Picture button (Format Picture pane), expand Picture Color section, select desired options
2. Right-click picture (or, if using touch, tap 'Show Context Menu' button on Mini toolbar), click Format Picture on shortcut menu (or, if using touch, tap Format Object), click Picture button (Format Picture pane), expand Picture Color section, select desired options

To Adjust the Brightness and Contrast of a Picture

In Word, you can adjust the brightness, or lightness, of a picture and also the **contrast**, or the difference between the lightest and darkest areas of the picture. The following steps increase the brightness of the flying eagle picture by 20% and decrease contrast by 20%. ***Why?*** *You want to lighten the picture slightly and, at the same time, decrease the difference between the light and dark areas of the picture.*

- If necessary, display the Picture Tools Format tab.
- With the picture still selected (shown in Figure 3–20), click the Corrections button (Picture Tools Format tab | Adjust group) to display the Corrections gallery.
- Point to 'Brightness: +20% Contrast: -20%' (fourth image in second row in the Brightness/Contrast area) in the Corrections gallery, which would display a Live Preview of that correction applied to the picture in the document if the picture was not hidden by the Corrections gallery (Figure 3–21).

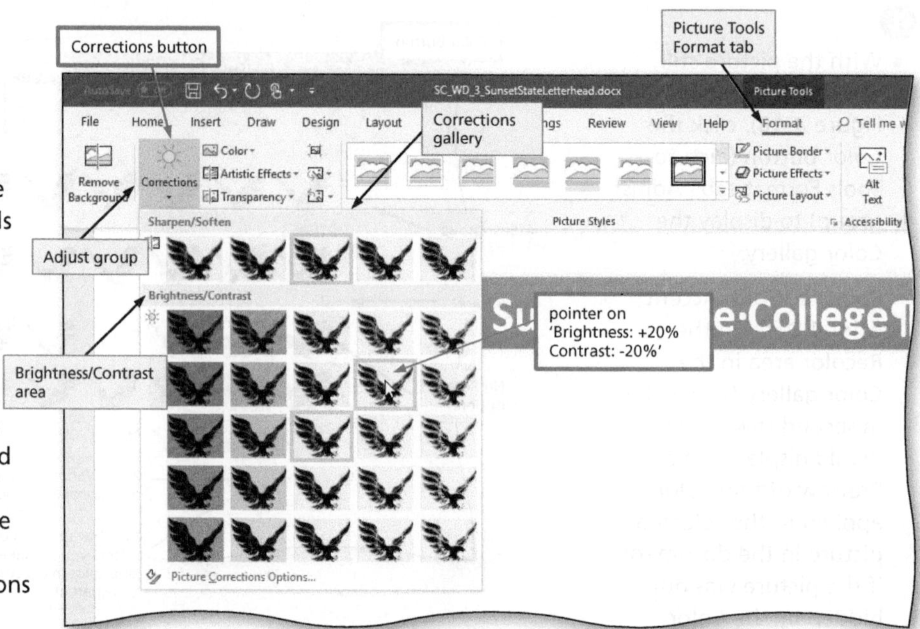

Figure 3–21

- Click 'Brightness: +20% Contrast: -20%' in the Corrections gallery to change the brightness and contrast of the selected picture (shown in Figure 3–22).

Other Ways

1. Click Picture Styles Dialog Box Launcher (Picture Tools Format tab | Picture Styles group), click Picture button (Format Picture pane), expand Picture Corrections section, select desired options
2. Right-click picture (or, if using touch, tap 'Show Context Menu' button on Mini toolbar), click Format Picture on shortcut menu (or, if using touch, tap Format Object on shortcut menu), click Picture button (Format Picture pane), expand Picture Corrections section, select desired options

To Add a Picture Border

The flying eagle picture currently has no border (outline). The following steps add a border to the picture. ***Why?*** *You would like the picture to have a gold border so that it matches the rectangle shape outline.*

- Click the Picture Border arrow (Picture Tools Format tab | Picture Styles group) to display the Picture Border gallery.

Q&A What if I click the Picture Border button by mistake?
Click the Picture Border arrow and proceed with Step 2.

- Point to 'Gold, Accent 4' (eighth theme color in first row) in the Picture Border gallery to display a Live Preview of that border color around the picture (Figure 3–22).

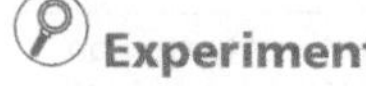

Experiment

- Point to various colors in the Picture Border gallery and watch the border color on the picture change in the document window.

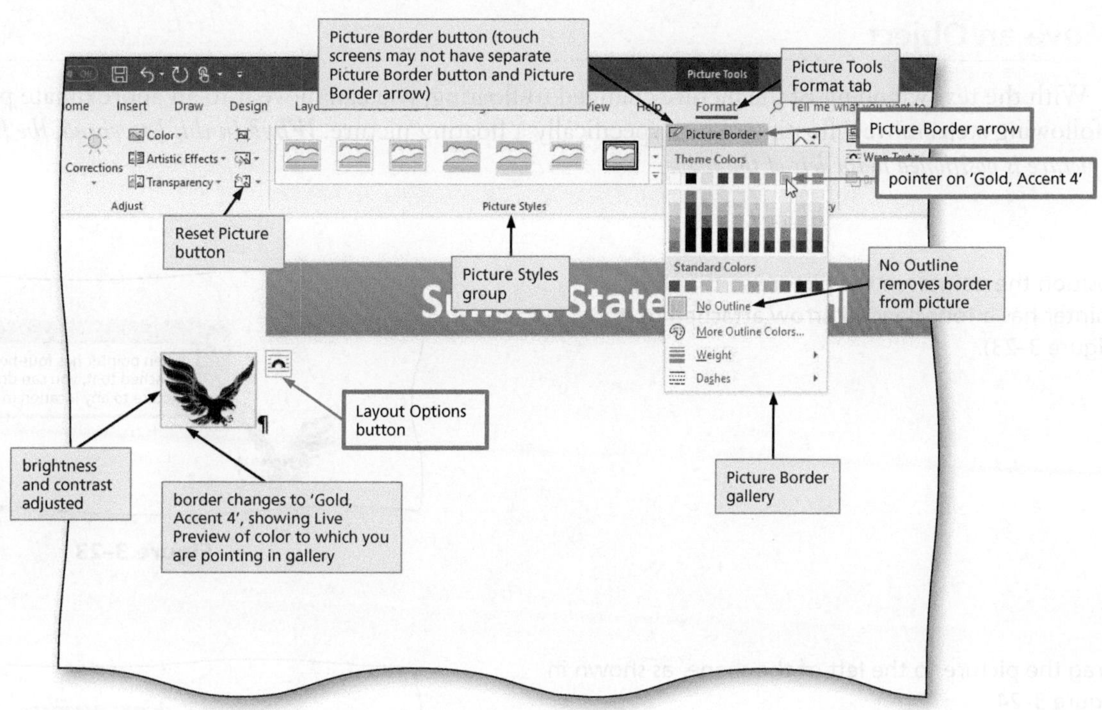

Figure 3–22

2

- Click 'Gold, Accent 4' in the Picture Border gallery to change the picture border color.

Q&A

How would I remove a border from a picture?
With the picture selected, you would click No Outline in the Picture Border gallery.

Can I remove all formatting applied to a picture and start over?
Yes. With the picture selected, you would click the Reset Picture button (Picture Tools Format tab | Adjust group).

To Change an Object's Text Wrapping

The flying eagle picture is to be positioned to the left of the shape. By default, when you insert a picture, it is formatted as an inline graphic. Inline graphics cannot be moved to a precise location on a page. Recall that inline graphics are part of a paragraph and, thus, can be positioned according to paragraph formatting, such as centered or left-aligned. To move the picture to the left of the shape, you format it as a floating object with In Front of Text wrapping. The following steps change a picture's text wrapping.

1. If necessary, click the picture to select it.
2. Click the Layout Options button attached to the picture (shown in Figure 3–22) to display the Layout Options gallery.
3. Click 'In Front of Text' in the Layout Options gallery (shown in Figure 3–7) so that you can position the object on top of any item in the document, in this case, on top of the rectangular shape.
4. Click the Close button to close the Layout Options gallery.

To Move an Object

With the text wrapping of the picture changed to floating, you can move it to an approximate position. The following steps move a floating object, specifically a floating picture. ***Why?*** *In this letterhead, the first flying eagle picture is positioned to the left of the shape.*

- Position the pointer in the picture so that the pointer has a four-headed arrow attached to it (Figure 3–23).

Figure 3–23

- Drag the picture to the left of the shape, as shown in Figure 3–24.

Q&A

What if I moved the picture to the wrong location?
Repeat these steps. You can drag a floating picture to any location in a document.

Why do green lines appear on my screen as I drag a picture?
You have alignment guides set, which help you line up objects. To set alignment guides, click the Align button (Picture Tools Format tab | Arrange group) and then click 'Use Alignment Guides'.

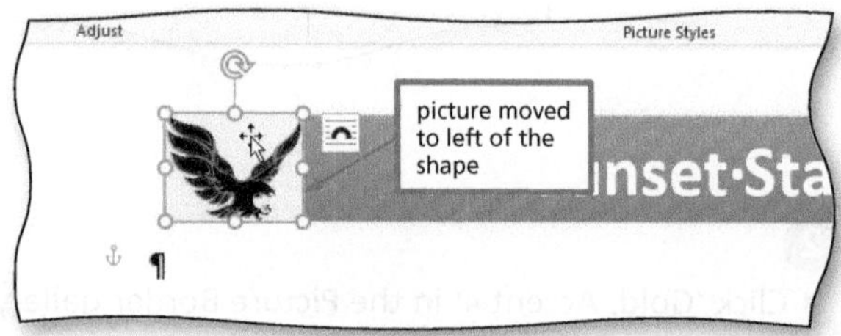

Figure 3–24

To Copy an Object

In this project, the same flying eagle picture is to be placed to the right of the shape. Instead of performing the same steps to insert and format a second identical flying eagle picture, you can copy the picture to the Office Clipboard, paste it from the Office Clipboard, and then move it to the desired location.

You use the same steps to copy a picture as to copy text. The following steps copy a picture.

1. If necessary, click the picture to select it.
2. Display the Home tab and then click the Copy button, shown in Figure 3–25 (Home tab | Clipboard group), or press CTRL+C to copy the selected item to the Office Clipboard.

To Use Paste Options to Paste an Object

The following steps paste a picture using the Paste Options gallery. ***Why?*** *You can specify the format of a pasted item using Paste Options.*

- If necessary, display the Home tab.
- Click the Paste arrow (Home tab | Clipboard group) to display the Paste gallery.

Q&A What if I accidentally click the Paste button?
Click the Paste Options button below the picture pasted in the document to display a Paste Options gallery.

- Point to the 'Keep Source Formatting' button in the Paste gallery to display a Live Preview of that paste option (Figure 3–25).

Experiment

- Point to the two buttons in the Paste gallery and watch the appearance of the pasted picture change.

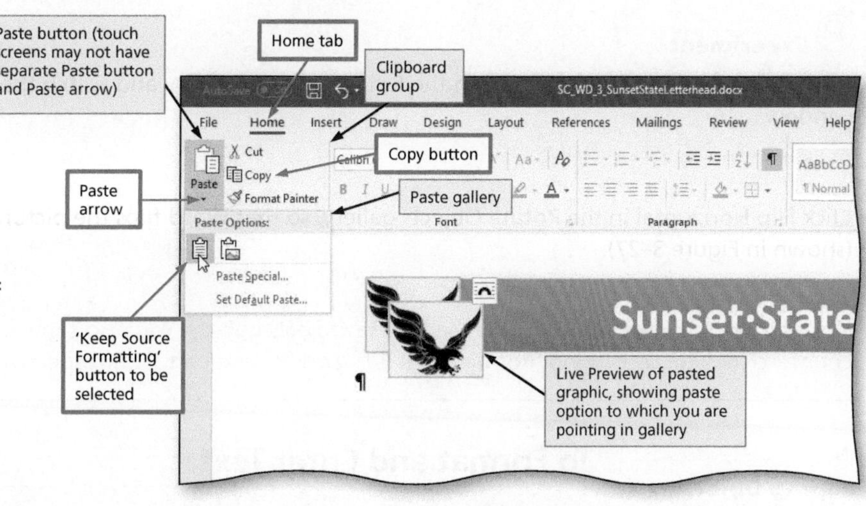

Figure 3–25

Q&A What do the buttons in the Paste gallery mean?
The 'Keep Source Formatting' button indicates the pasted object should have the same formats as it did in its original location. The Picture button removes some formatting from the object.

Why are these paste buttons different from when you paste text?
The buttons that appear in the Paste gallery differ depending on the item you are pasting. Use Live Preview to see how the pasted object will look in the document.

2

- Click the 'Keep Source Formatting' button in the Paste gallery to paste the picture using the same formatting as the original.

To Move an Object

The next step is to move the second flying eagle picture so that it is positioned to the right of the rectangle shape. The following steps move an object.

1. If you are using a mouse, position the pointer in the picture so that the pointer has a four-headed arrow attached to it.
2. Drag the picture to the location shown in Figure 3–26.

To Flip an Object

The following steps flip a selected object horizontally. ***Why?** In this letterhead, you want the flying eagle pictures to face each other.*

1

- If necessary, display the Picture Tools Format tab.
- With the picture still selected, click the Rotate Objects button (Picture Tools Format tab | Arrange group) to display the Rotate Objects gallery (Figure 3–26).

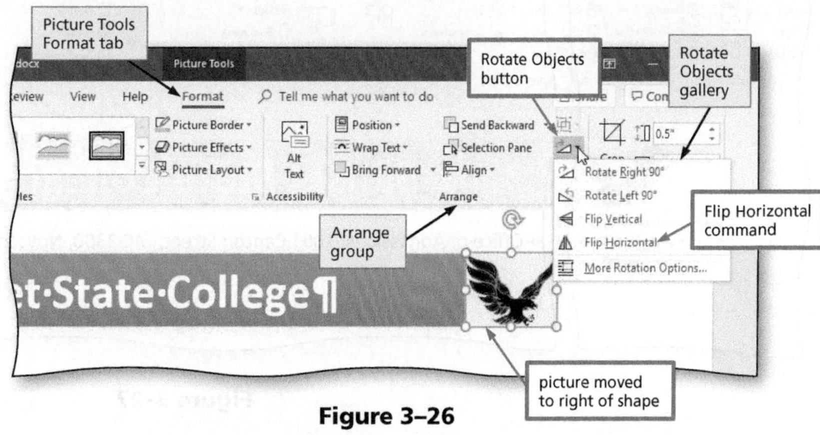

Figure 3–26

Experiment

- Point to the various rotate options in the Rotate Objects gallery and watch the picture rotate in the document window.

2

- Click Flip Horizontal in the Rotate Objects gallery, so that Word flips the picture to display its mirror image (shown in Figure 3–27).

Q&A Can I flip a object vertically?
Yes, you would click Flip Vertical in the Rotate Objects gallery. You also can rotate an object clockwise or counterclockwise by clicking 'Rotate Right 90°' and 'Rotate Left 90°', respectively, in the Rotate Objects gallery.

BTW
Grouping Objects
You can group objects together if you want to move or format them together as a group. To group multiple objects, you select the first object and then CTRL+click each additional object until all objects are selected. Then click the Group button (Drawing Tools Format tab | Arrange group) and click Group on the Group menu to group the selected objects into a single selected object.

To Format and Enter Text

The contact information for the letterhead in this project is located on the line below the shape containing the name. The following steps enter the mailing address in the letterhead.

1. Position the insertion point on the line below the shape containing the name.
2. If necessary, display the Home tab. Click the Center button (Home tab | Paragraph group) or press CTRL+E to center the paragraph.
3. Type `Office of Admissions, 1001 Canton Street, MC 3300, Novato, CA 94945` and then press SPACEBAR (shown in Figure 3–27).

To Insert a Symbol from the Symbol Gallery

Word provides a method of inserting dots and other symbols, such as letters in the Greek alphabet and mathematical characters, that are not on the keyboard. In the letterhead, a dot symbol separates the phone number from the email address. The following steps use the Symbol gallery to insert a dot symbol in the letterhead. ***Why?*** *You want a visual separator between the mailing address and the phone number.*

- Display the Insert tab.

- Click the Symbol button (Insert tab | Symbols group) to display the Symbol gallery (Figure 3–27).

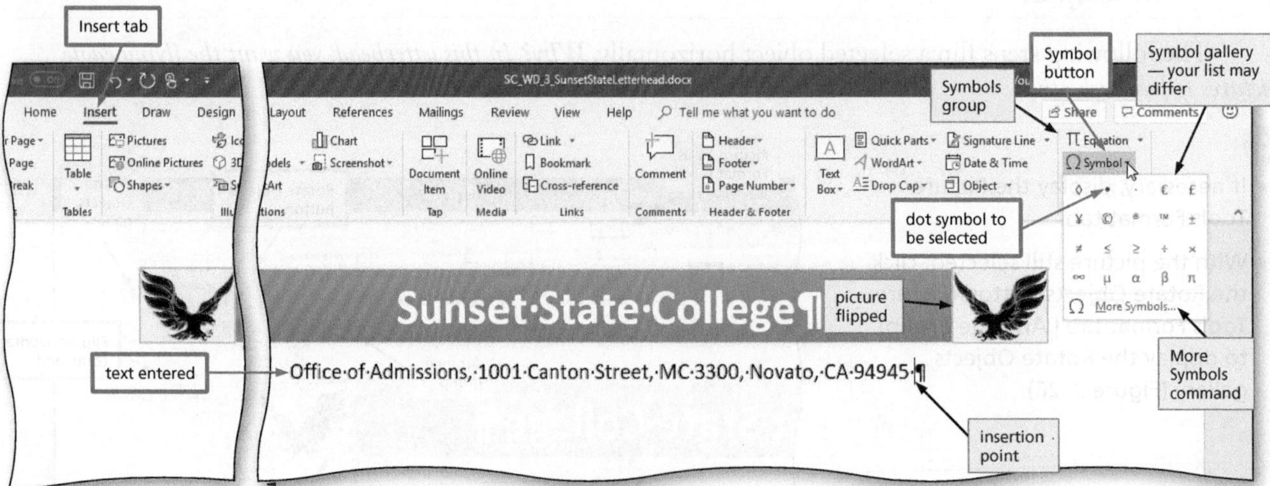

Figure 3–27

3

- Click the dot symbol in the Symbol gallery to insert the symbol at the location of the insertion point (shown in Figure 3–28).

Q&A What if the dot symbol is not in the Symbol gallery?
Click the More Symbols command in the Symbol gallery to display the Symbol dialog box, scroll through the symbols in the dialog box to locate the desired symbol, click the desired symbol to select it, and then click the Insert button in the dialog box to insert the symbol in the document.

To Enter Text

The following steps finish the text in the letterhead.

1. Press SPACEBAR. Type **`415-555-0199`** and then press SPACEBAR.
2. Click the Symbol button (Insert tab | Symbols group) to display the Symbol gallery and then click the dot symbol to insert another dot symbol in the letterhead at the location of the insertion point.
3. Press SPACEBAR and then type **`sunset.edu`** to finish the text in the letterhead (Figure 3–28).

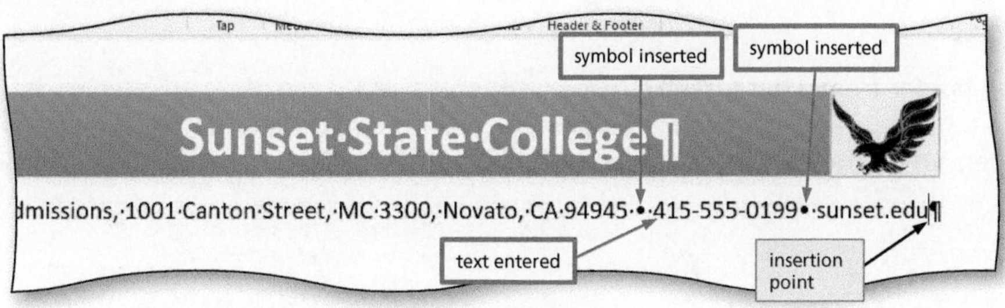

Figure 3–28

BTW
Inserting Special Characters
In addition to symbols, you can insert a variety of special characters, including dashes, hyphens, spaces, apostrophes, and quotation marks. Click More Symbols in the Symbol gallery (shown in Figure 3–27), click the Special Characters tab in the Symbol dialog box, click the desired character in the Character list, click the Insert button, and then click the Close button (Symbol dialog box).

To Add a Paragraph Border

In Word, you can draw a solid line, called a **border**, at any edge of a paragraph. That is, borders may be added above or below a paragraph, to the left or right of a paragraph, or in any combination of these sides.

The letterhead in this project has a border that extends from the left margin to the right margin immediately below the mailing address, phone, and web address information. ***Why?** The horizontal line separates the letterhead from the rest of the letter.* The following steps add a border to the bottom of a paragraph.

- Display the Home tab.
- With the insertion point in the paragraph to border, click the Borders arrow (Home tab | Paragraph group) to display the Borders gallery (Figure 3–29).

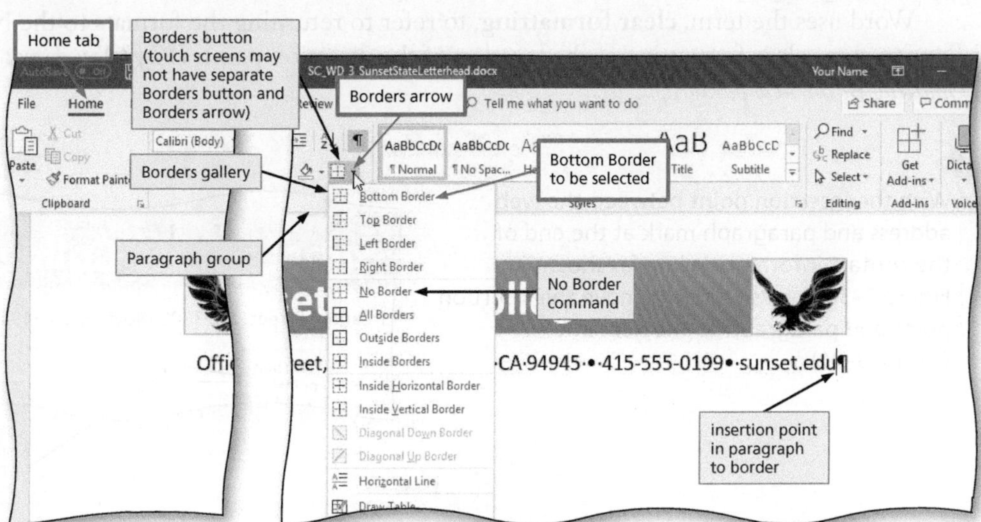

Figure 3–29

- Click Bottom Border in the Borders gallery to place a border below the paragraph containing the insertion point (Figure 3–30).

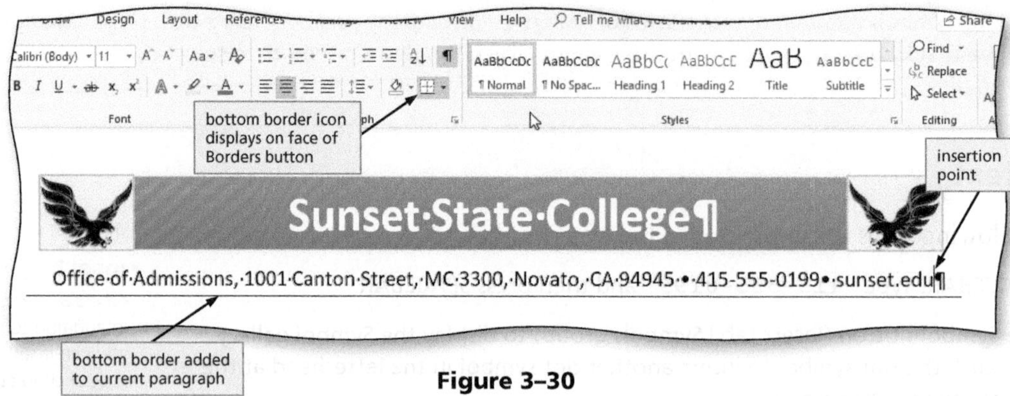

Figure 3–30

Q&A

If the face of the Borders button displays the border icon I want to use, can I click the Borders button instead of using the Borders arrow?

Yes.

How would I remove an existing border from a paragraph?

If, for some reason, you wanted to remove a border from a paragraph, you would position the insertion point in the paragraph, click the Borders arrow (Home tab | Paragraph group), and then click No Border in the Borders gallery.

Other Ways

1. Click Page Borders button (Design tab | Page Background group), click Borders tab (Borders and Shading dialog box), select desired border options, click OK

To Clear Formatting

The next step is to position the insertion point below the letterhead, so that you can type the contents of the letter. When you press ENTER at the end of a paragraph containing a border, Word moves the border forward to the next paragraph. The paragraph also retains all current settings, such as the center format. Instead, you want the paragraph and characters on the new line to use the Normal style: black font with no border.

Word uses the term, **clear formatting**, to refer to returning the formats to the Normal style. The following steps clear formatting at the location of the insertion point. ***Why?*** *You do not want to retain the current formatting in the new paragraph.*

- With the insertion point between the web address and paragraph mark at the end of the contact information line (as shown in Figure 3–30), press ENTER to move the insertion point and paragraph to the next line (Figure 3–31).

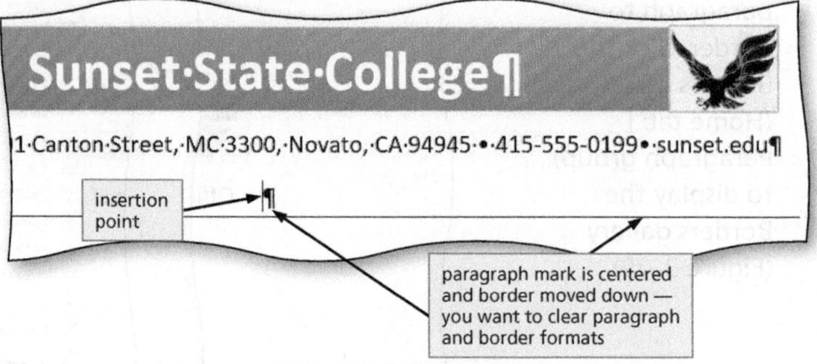

Figure 3–31

2

- Click the 'Clear All Formatting' button (Home tab | Font group) to apply the Normal style to the location of the insertion point (Figure 3–32).

3

- Save the letterhead again on the same storage location with the same file name.

Q&A Why should I save the letterhead at this time?
You are finished editing the letterhead.

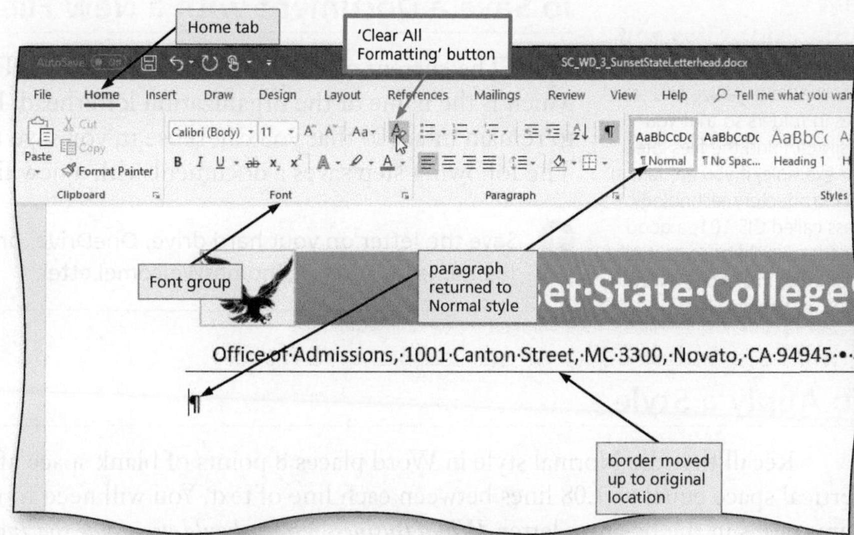

Figure 3–32

Other Ways

1. Click More button in Styles gallery (Home tab | Styles group), click Clear Formatting
2. Click Styles Dialog Box Launcher (Home tab | Styles group), click Clear All in Styles pane
3. Select text, press CTRL+SPACEBAR, press CTRL+Q

Break Point: If you want to take a break, this is a good place to do so. You can exit Word now. To resume later, start Word, open the file called SC_WD_3_SunsetStateLetterhead.docx, and continue following the steps from this location forward.

Creating a Business Letter

With the letterhead for the business letter complete, the next task is to create the remainder of the content in the letter. The following sections use Word to create a business letter that contains a table and a bulleted list.

CONSIDER THIS

What should you consider when writing a business letter?

A finished business letter should look like a symmetrically framed picture with evenly spaced margins, all balanced below an attractive letterhead. The letter should be well written, properly formatted, logically organized, and use visuals where appropriate. The content of a letter should contain proper grammar, correct spelling, logically constructed sentences, flowing paragraphs, and sound ideas.

Be sure to include all essential elements, use proper spacing and formats, and determine which letter style to use.

- **Include all essential letter elements.** All business letters contain the same basic elements, including the date line, inside address, message, and signature block (shown in Figure 3–1 at the beginning of this module). If a business letter does not use a letterhead, then the top of the letter should include return address information in a heading.
- **Use proper spacing and formats for the contents of the letter below the letterhead.** Use a font that is easy to read, in a size between 8 and 12 point. Add emphasis with bold, italic, and lists where appropriate, and use tables to present numeric information. Paragraphs should be single-spaced, with double-spacing between paragraphs.
- **Determine which letter style to use.** You can follow many different styles when creating business letters. A letter style specifies guidelines for the alignment and spacing of elements in the business letter.

If possible, keep the length of a business letter to one page. Be sure to proofread the finished letter carefully.

BTW
Organizing Files and Folders
You should organize and store files in folders so that you easily can find the files later. For example, if you are taking an introductory technology class called CIS 101, a good practice would be to save all Word files in a Word folder in a CIS 101 folder.

To Save a Document with a New File Name

The current open file has the name SC_WD_3_SunsetStateLetterhead.docx, which is the name of the organization letterhead. Because you want the letterhead file to remain intact so that you can reuse it, you save the document with a new file name. The following step saves a document with a new file name.

Save the letter on your hard drive, OneDrive, or other storage location using a new file name, SC_WD_3_ThomasWelcomeLetter.

To Apply a Style

Recall that the Normal style in Word places 8 points of blank space after each paragraph and inserts a vertical space equal to 1.08 lines between each line of text. You will need to modify the spacing used for the paragraphs in the business letter. ***Why?*** *Business letters should use single spacing for paragraphs and double spacing between paragraphs.*

Word has many built-in, or predefined, styles that you can use to format text. The No Spacing style, for example, defines line spacing as single and does not insert any additional blank space between lines when you press ENTER. To apply a style to a paragraph, you first position the insertion point in the paragraph. The following step applies the No Spacing style to a paragraph.

- With the insertion point positioned in the paragraph to be formatted, click No Spacing in the Styles gallery (Home tab | Styles group) to apply the selected style to the current paragraph (Figure 3–33).

Q&A Will this style be used in the rest of the document?
Yes. The paragraph formatting, which includes the style, will carry forward to subsequent paragraphs each time you press ENTER.

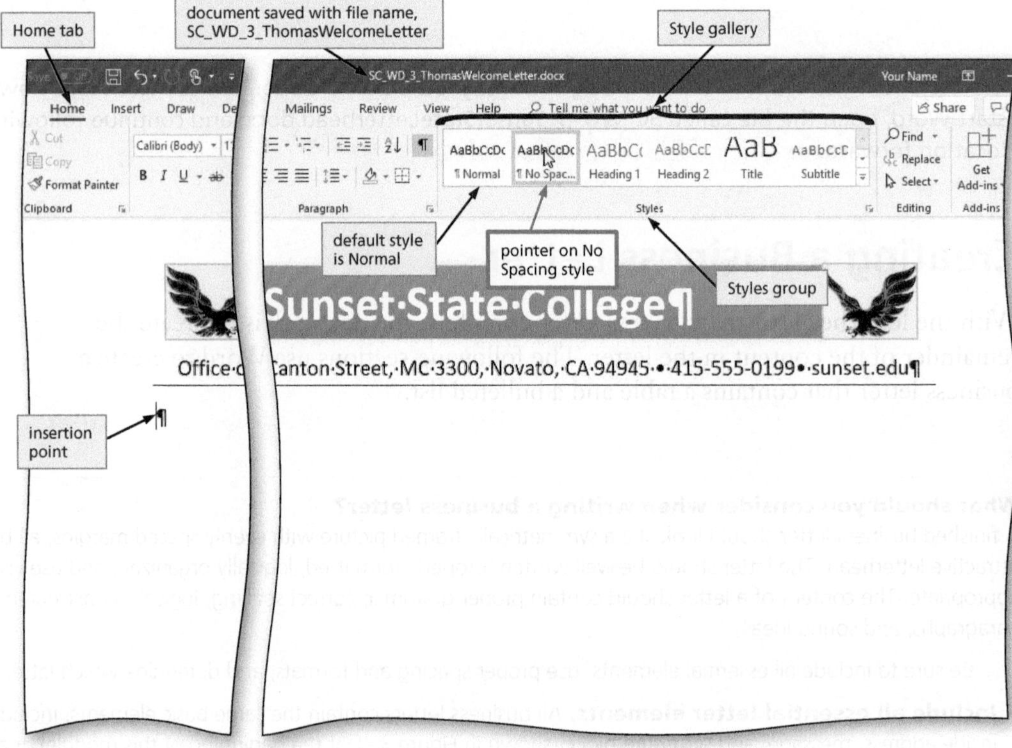

Figure 3–33

Other Ways

1. Click Styles Dialog Box Launcher (Home tab | Styles group), click desired style in Styles pane
2. Press CTRL+SHIFT+S, click Style Name arrow in Apply Styles pane, click desired style in list

CONSIDER THIS

What elements should a business letter contain?

Be sure to include all essential business letter elements, properly spaced, in your letter:

- The **date line**, which consists of the month, day, and year, is positioned two to six lines below the letterhead.
- The **inside address**, placed three to eight lines below the date line, usually contains the addressee's courtesy title plus full name, job title, business affiliation, and full geographical address.
- The **salutation**, if present, is the greeting in the letter that begins two lines below the last line of the inside address. If you do not know the recipient's name, avoid using the salutation "To whom it may concern" — it is impersonal. Instead, use the recipient's title in the salutation, e.g., Dear Personnel Director. In a formal business letter, use a colon (:) at the end of the salutation; in a casual business letter or personal letter, use a comma.
- The body of the letter, the **message**, begins two lines below the salutation. Within the message, paragraphs are single-spaced with one blank line between paragraphs.
- Two lines below the last line of the message, the closing line or **complimentary close** is displayed. Capitalize only the first word in a complimentary close.
- Type the **signature block** at least four blank lines below the complimentary close, allowing room for the author to sign his or her name.

CONSIDER THIS

What are the common styles of business letters?

Three common business letter styles are the block, the modified block, and the modified semi-block. Each style specifies different alignments and indentations.

- In the block letter style, all components of the letter begin flush with the left margin.
- In the modified block letter style, the date, complimentary close, and signature block are positioned approximately one-half inch to the right of center or at the right margin. All other components of the letter begin flush with the left margin.
- In the modified semi-block letter style, the date, complimentary close, and signature block are centered, positioned approximately one-half inch to the right of center or at the right margin. The first line of each paragraph in the body of the letter is indented one-half to one inch from the left margin. All other components of the letter begin flush with the left margin.

The business letter in this project follows the modified block style.

Using Tab Stops to Align Text

A **tab stop** is a location on the horizontal ruler that tells Word where to position the insertion point when you press TAB on the keyboard. Word, by default, places a tab stop at every one-half inch mark on the ruler. You also can set your own custom tab stops. Tab settings are a paragraph format. Thus, each time you press ENTER, any custom tab stops are carried forward to the next paragraph.

To move the insertion point from one tab stop to another, press TAB on the keyboard. When you press TAB, a **tab character** formatting mark appears in the empty space between the tab stops.

When you set a custom tab stop, you specify how the text will align at a tab stop. The tab marker on the ruler reflects the alignment of the characters at the location of the tab stop. Table 3–2 shows types of tab stop alignments in Word and their corresponding tab markers.

BTW

Tabs Dialog Box

You can use the Tabs dialog box to set, change the alignment of, and remove custom tab stops. To display the Tabs dialog box, click the Paragraph Dialog Box Launcher (Home tab or Layout tab | Paragraph group) and then click the Tabs button (Paragraph dialog box). To set a custom tab stop, enter the desired tab position (Tabs dialog box) and then click the Set button. To change the alignment of a custom tab stop, click the tab stop position to be changed, click the new alignment, and then click the Set button. To remove an existing tab stop, click the tab stop position to be removed and then click the Clear button. To remove all tab stops, click the Clear All button in the Tabs dialog box.

Table 3–2 Types of Tab Stop Alignments

Tab Stop Alignment	Tab Marker	Result of Pressing TAB	Example
Left Tab	⌊	Left-aligns text at the location of the tab stop	toolbar ruler
Center Tab	⊥	Centers text at the location of the tab stop	toolbar ruler
Right Tab	⌋	Right-aligns text at the location of the tab stop	toolbar ruler
Decimal Tab	⊥.	Aligns text on decimal point at the location of the tab stop	45.72 223.75
Bar Tab	|	Aligns text at a bar character at the location of the tab stop	| toolbar | ruler

To Display the Ruler

One way to set custom tab stops is by using the horizontal ruler. Thus, the following steps display the ruler in the document window.

1. If the rulers are not showing, display the View tab.
2. Click the Ruler check box (View tab | Show group) to place a check mark in the check box and display the horizontal and vertical rulers on the screen (shown in Figure 3–34).

To Set Custom Tab Stops

The first required element of the business letter is the date line, which in this letter is positioned two lines below the letterhead. The date line contains the month, day, and year, and begins 3½ inches from the left margin. ***Why?*** *Business letter guidelines specify to begin the date line approximately one-half inch to the right of center. Thus, you should set a custom tab stop at the 3.5" mark on the ruler.* The following steps set a left-aligned tab stop.

1

- With the insertion point on the paragraph mark below the border (shown in Figure 3–33), press ENTER so that a blank line appears above the insertion point.
- If necessary, click the tab selector at the left edge of the horizontal ruler until it displays the type of tab you wish to use, which is the Left Tab icon in this case.
- Position the pointer on the 3.5" mark on the ruler, which is the location of the desired custom tab stop (Figure 3–34).

Q&A What is the purpose of the tab selector?
Before using the ruler to set a tab stop, ensure the correct tab stop icon appears in the tab selector. Each time you click the tab selector, its icon changes. The Left Tab icon is the default. For a list of the types of tab stops, see Table 3–2.

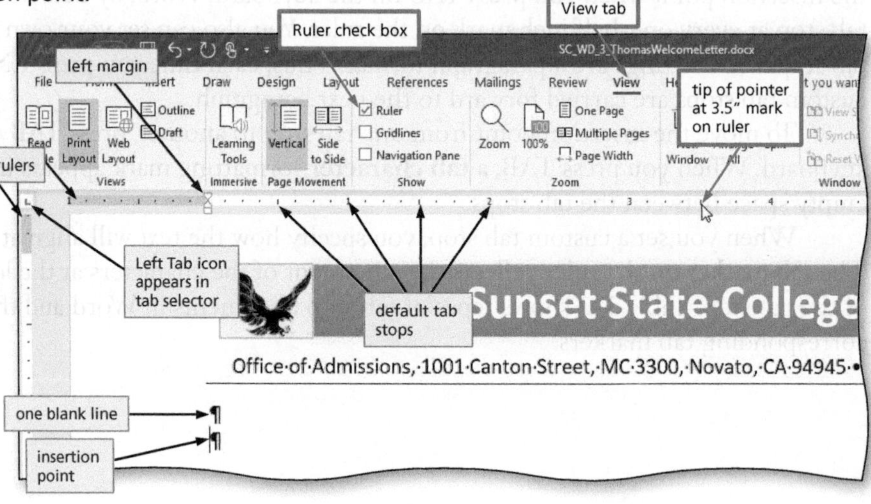

Figure 3–34

2

- Click the 3.5" mark on the ruler to place a tab marker at that location (Figure 3–35).

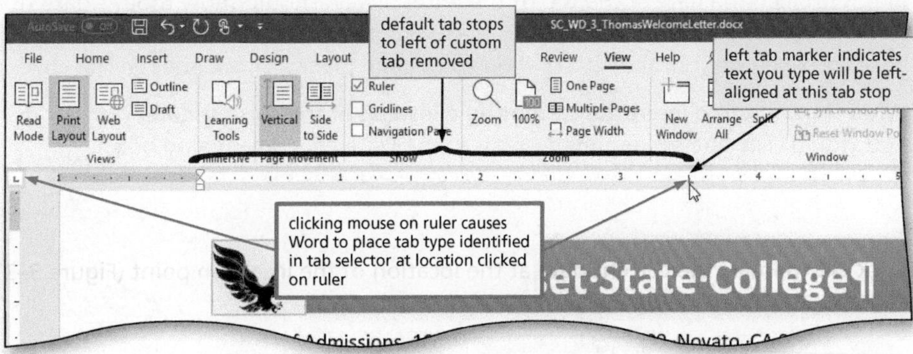

Figure 3–35

Q&A What if I click the wrong location on the ruler?
You can move a custom tab stop by dragging the tab marker to the desired location on the ruler. Or, you can remove an existing custom tab stop by pointing to the tab marker on the ruler and then dragging the tab marker down and out of the ruler.

What if I am using a touch screen?
Display the Home tab, tap the Paragraph Dialog Box Launcher (Home tab | Paragraph group), tap the Tabs button (Paragraph dialog box), type `3.5` in the Tab stop position box (Tabs dialog box), tap the Set button, and then tap OK to set a custom tab stop and place a corresponding tab marker on the ruler.

Other Ways

1. Click Paragraph Dialog Box Launcher (Home tab or Layout tab | Paragraph group), click Tabs button (Paragraph dialog box), type tab stop position (Tabs dialog box), click Set button, click OK

To Insert the Current Date in a Document

The next step is to enter the current date at the 3.5" tab stop in the document. ***Why?*** *The date in this letter will be positioned according to the guidelines for a modified block style letter.* In Word, you can insert a computer's system date in a document. The following steps insert the current date in the letter.

1

- Press TAB to position the insertion point at the location of the tab stop in the current paragraph.
- Display the Insert tab.
- Click the 'Date and Time' button (Insert tab | Text group) to display the Date and Time dialog box.
- Select the desired format (Date and Time dialog box), in this case April 19, 2021.
- If the Update automatically check box is selected, click the check box to remove the check mark (Figure 3–36).

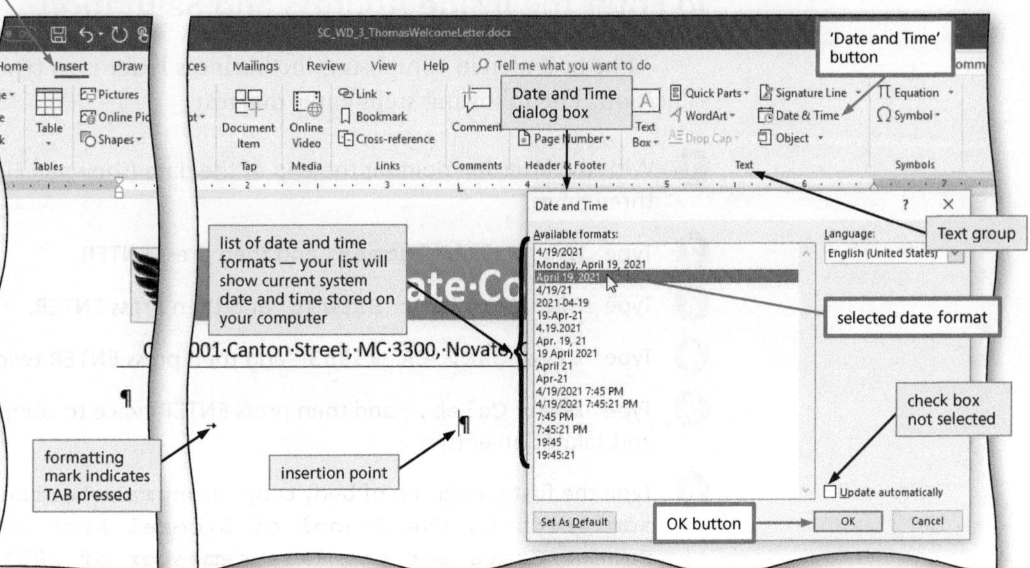

Figure 3–36

Why should the Update automatically check box not be selected?
In this project, the date at the top of the letter always should show today's date (for example, April 19, 2021). If, however, you wanted the date always to change to reflect the current computer date (for example, showing the date you open or print the letter), then you would place a check mark in this check box.

What if I wanted to insert the current time instead of the current date?
You would click one of the time formats in the Date and Time dialog box.

2

- Click OK to insert the current date at the location of the insertion point (Figure 3–37).

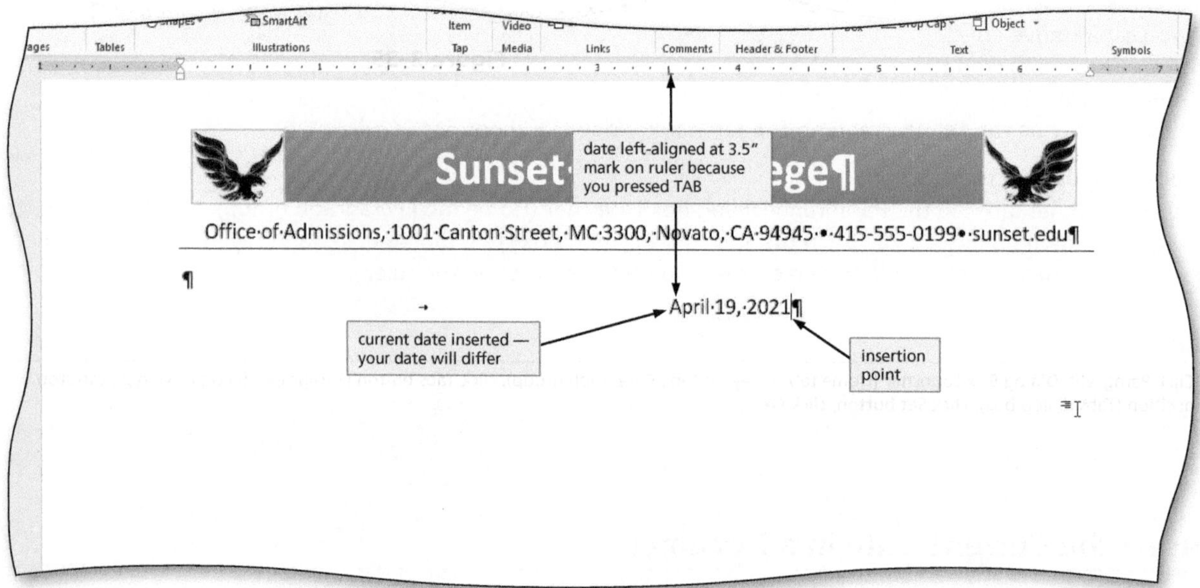

Figure 3–37

To Enter the Inside Address and Salutation

The next step in composing the business letter is to type the inside address and salutation. The following steps enter this text.

1. With the insertion point at the end of the date (shown in Figure 3–37), press ENTER three times.
2. Type `Mr. Caleb Thomas` and then press ENTER.
3. Type `982 Bartlett Street` and then press ENTER.
4. Type `Live Oak, CA 95953` and then press ENTER twice.
5. Type `Dear Caleb,` and then press ENTER twice to complete the inside address and salutation entries.
6. Type the first paragraph of body copy: **Congratulations on your admission to the School of Liberal Arts and Sciences at Sunset State for the fall semester of 2021! On behalf of our students, faculty, and staff, I welcome you to our academic**

community. Our decision to admit you to our college is an acknowledgement of your potential and our confidence in you as a valuable addition to our student body.

7 Press ENTER twice.

8 Type **We would like to inform you of important upcoming dates:** and then press ENTER twice (Figure 3–38).

Q&A Why does my document wrap on different words?
Differences in wordwrap may relate to the printer connected to your computer. Thus, it is possible that the same document could wordwrap differently if associated with a different printer.

9 Save the letter again on the same storage location with the same file name.

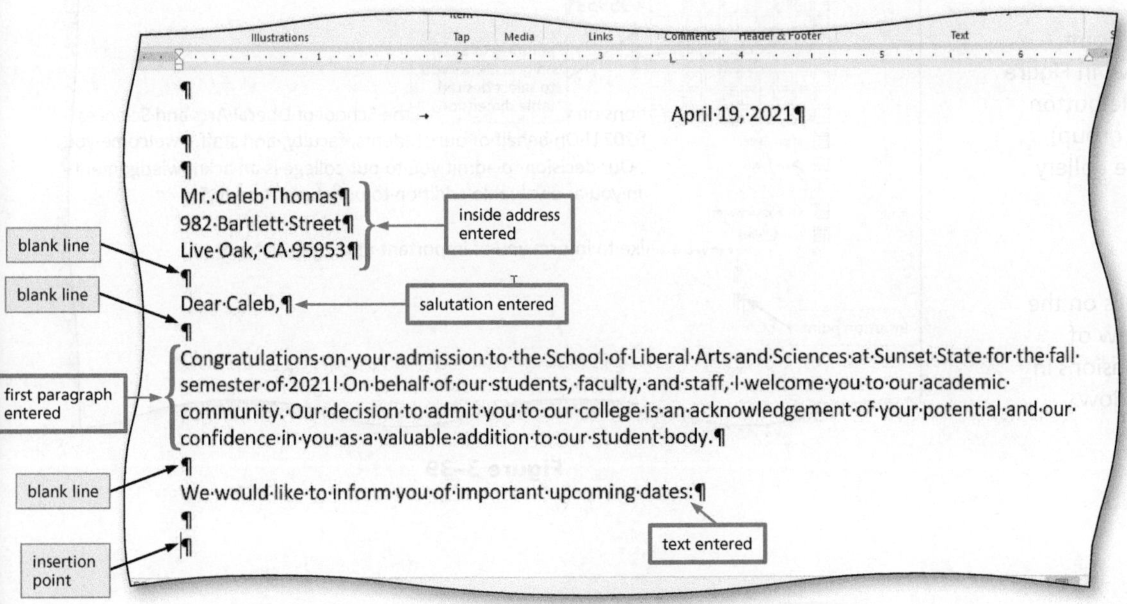

Figure 3–38

Tables

The next step in composing the business letter is to place a table listing the important upcoming dates (shown in Figure 3–1). A Word **table** is a grid of rows and columns that can contain text and graphics. The intersection of a row and a column is called a **cell** (which looks like a box), and cells are filled with data.

The first step in creating a table is to insert an empty table in the document. When inserting a table, you must specify the total number of rows and columns required, which is called the **dimension** of the table. The table in this project has three columns. You often do not know the total number of rows in a table. Thus, many Word users create one row initially and then add more rows as needed. In Word, the first number in a dimension is the number of columns, and the second is the number of rows. For example, in Word, a 3 × 1 (pronounced "three by one") table consists of three columns and one row.

BTW

Word Help

At any time while using Word, you can find answers to questions and display information about various topics through Word Help. Used properly, this form of assistance can increase your productivity and reduce your frustrations by minimizing the time you spend learning how to use Word.

To Insert an Empty Table

The next step is to insert an empty table in the letter. The following steps insert a table with three columns and one row at the location of the insertion point. ***Why?*** *The first column will identify the date(s), the second will identify the event, and the third will identify notes. You will start with one row and add more rows as needed.*

- Scroll the document so that you will be able to see the table in the document window.
- If necessary, display the Insert tab.
- With the insertion point positioned as shown in Figure 3–39, click the Table button (Insert tab | Tables group) to display the Table gallery (Figure 3–39).

Experiment

- Point to various cells on the grid to see a preview of various table dimensions in the document window.

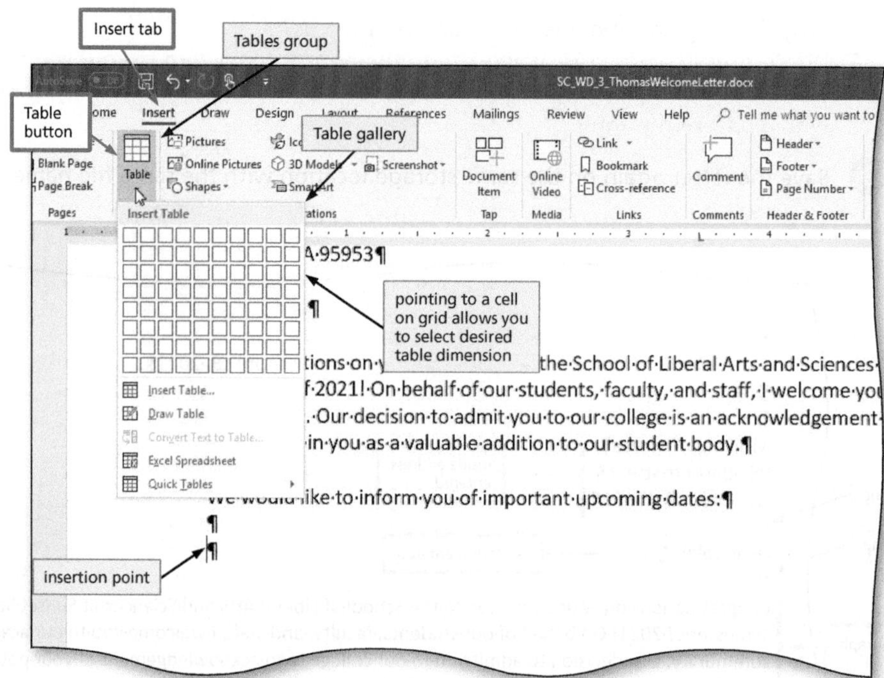

Figure 3–39

- Position the pointer on the cell in the first row and third column of the grid to preview the desired table dimension in the document (Figure 3–40).

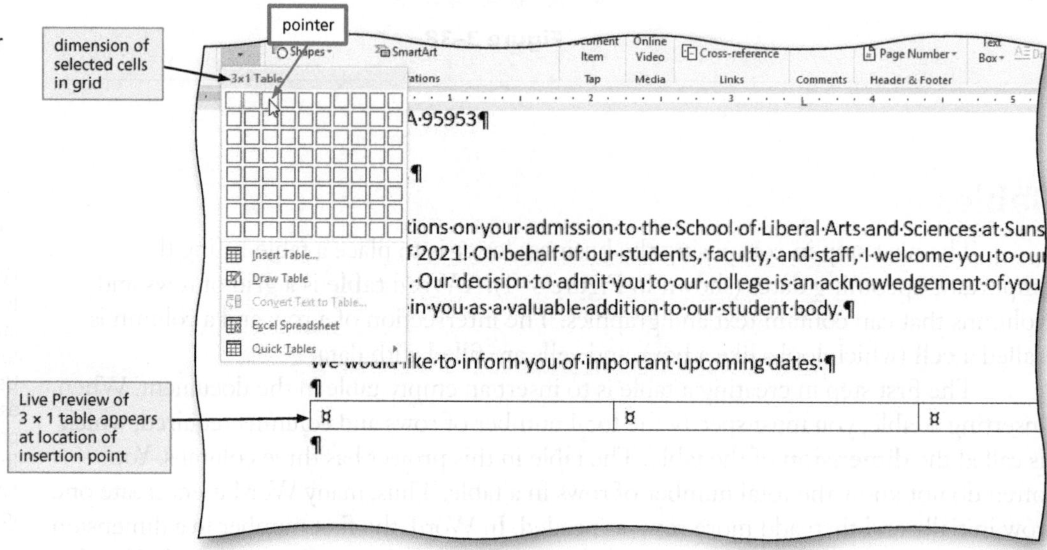

Figure 3–40

3

- Click the cell in the first row and third column of the grid to insert an empty table with one row and three columns in the document.
- If necessary, scroll the document so that the table is visible (Figure 3–41).

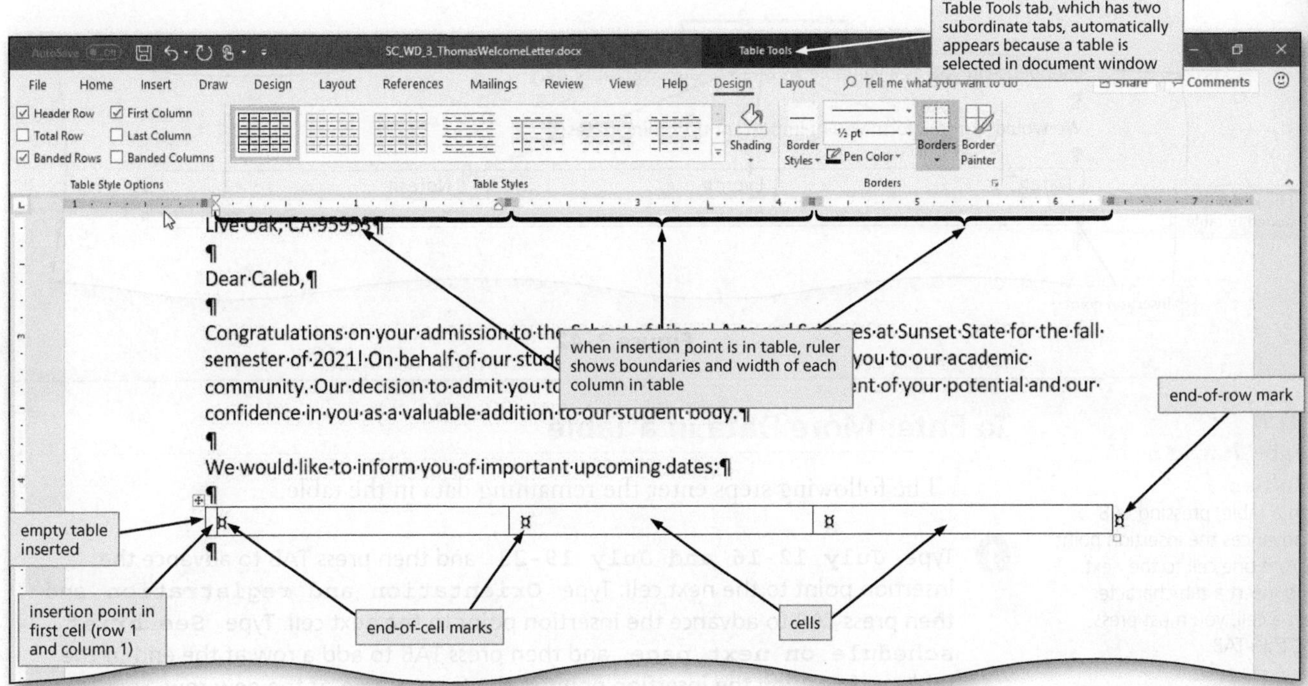

Figure 3–41

Q&A

What are the small circles in the table cells?

Each table cell has an **end-of-cell mark**, which is a formatting mark that assists you with selecting and formatting cells. Similarly, each row has an **end-of-row mark**, which is a formatting mark that you can use to add columns to the right of a table. Recall that formatting marks do not print on a hard copy. The end-of-cell marks currently are left-aligned, that is, positioned at the left edge of each cell.

Other Ways

1. Click Table button (Insert tab | Tables group), click Insert Table in Table gallery, enter number of columns and rows (Insert Table dialog box), click OK

To Enter Data in a Table

The next step is to enter data in the cells of the empty table. The data you enter in a cell wordwraps just as text wordwraps between the margins of a document. To place data in a cell, you click the cell and then type.

To advance rightward from one cell to the next, press TAB. When you are at the rightmost cell in a row, press TAB to move to the first cell in the next row; do not press ENTER. ***Why?** You press ENTER when you want to begin a new paragraph within a cell.* One way to add new rows to a table is to press TAB when the insertion point is positioned in the bottom-right corner cell of the table. The following step enters data in the first row of the table and then inserts a blank second row.

- With the insertion point in the left cell of the table, type `Date` and then press TAB to advance the insertion point to the next cell.

- Type **Event** and then press TAB to advance the insertion point to the next cell.
- Type **Notes** and then press TAB to add a second row at the end of the table and position the insertion point in the first column of the new row (Figure 3–42).

Q&A How do I edit cell contents if I make a mistake?
Click in the cell and then correct the entry.

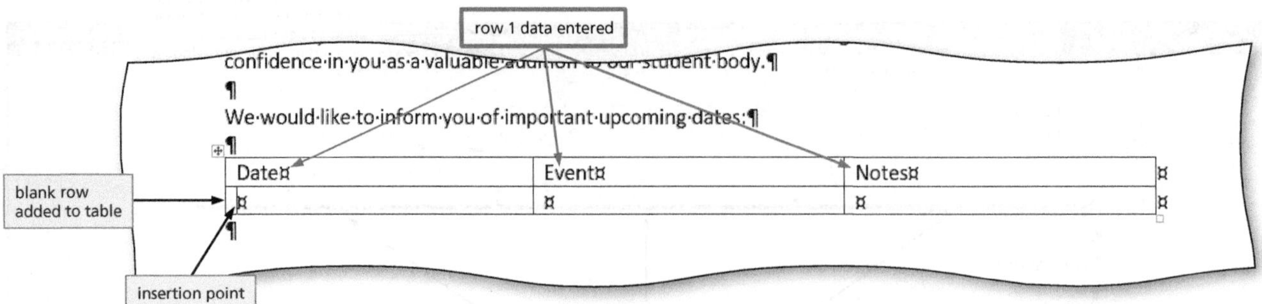

Figure 3–42

BTW
Tab Character in Tables
In a table, pressing TAB advances the insertion point from one cell to the next. To insert a tab character in a cell, you must press CTRL+TAB.

To Enter More Data in a Table

The following steps enter the remaining data in the table.

1. Type **July 12-16 and July 19-23** and then press TAB to advance the insertion point to the next cell. Type **Orientation and registration** and then press TAB to advance the insertion point to the next cell. Type **See brief schedule on next page** and then press TAB to add a row at the end of the table and position the insertion point in the first column of the new row.

2. In the third row, type **August 16-17** in the first column, **Move-in days** in the second column, and **Assigned by Housing Services** in the third column. Press TAB to position the insertion point in the first column of a new row.

3. In the fourth row, type **August 23** in the first column, **Fall term begins** in the second column, and **First day of classes** in the third column (Figure 3–43).

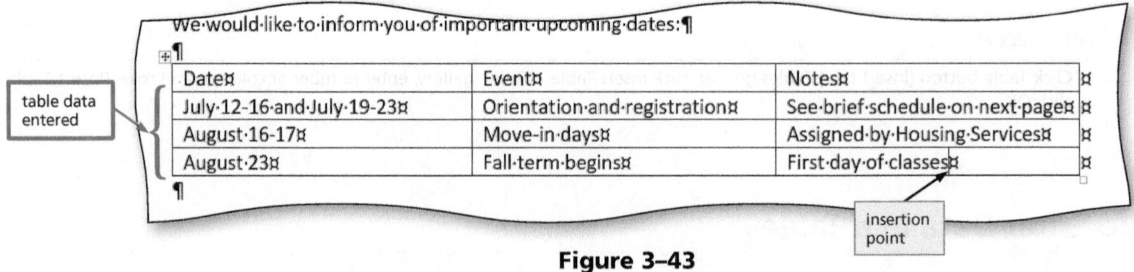

Figure 3–43

To Apply a Table Style

Word provides a gallery of more than 90 table styles, which include a variety of colors and shading. ***Why?*** *Table styles allow you to change the basic table format to a more visually appealing style.* The following steps apply a table style to the table in the letter.

- If the First Column check box in the Table Style Options group (Table Tools Design tab) contains a check mark, click the check box to remove the check mark because you do not want the first column in the table formatted differently from the rest of the table. Be sure the remaining check marks match those in the Table Style Options group (Table Tools Design tab) (Figure 3–44).

What if the Table Tools Design tab no longer is the active tab?
Click in the table and then display the Table Tools Design tab.

What do the options in the Table Style Options group mean?
When you apply table styles, if you want the top row of the table (header row), a row containing totals (total row), first column, or last column to be formatted differently, select those check boxes. If you want the rows or columns to alternate with colors, select Banded Rows or Banded Columns, respectively.

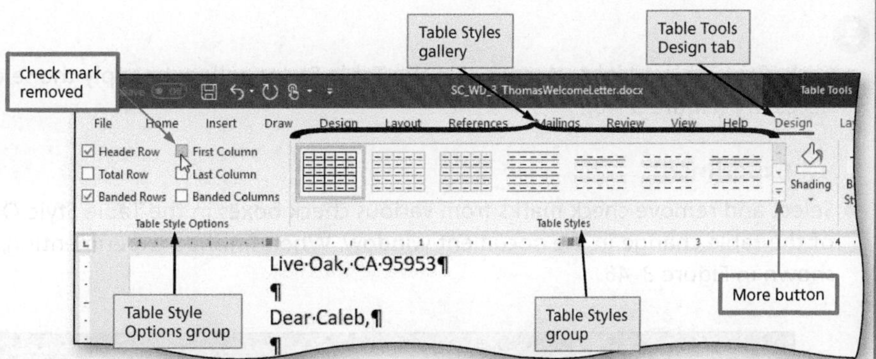

Figure 3–44

2

- **With the insertion point in the table, click the More button in the Table Styles gallery (Table Tools Design tab | Table Styles group), shown in Figure 3–44, to expand the gallery.**
- **Scroll and then point to 'Grid Table 1 Light - Accent 2' in the Table Styles gallery to display a Live Preview of that style applied to the table in the document (Figure 3–45).**

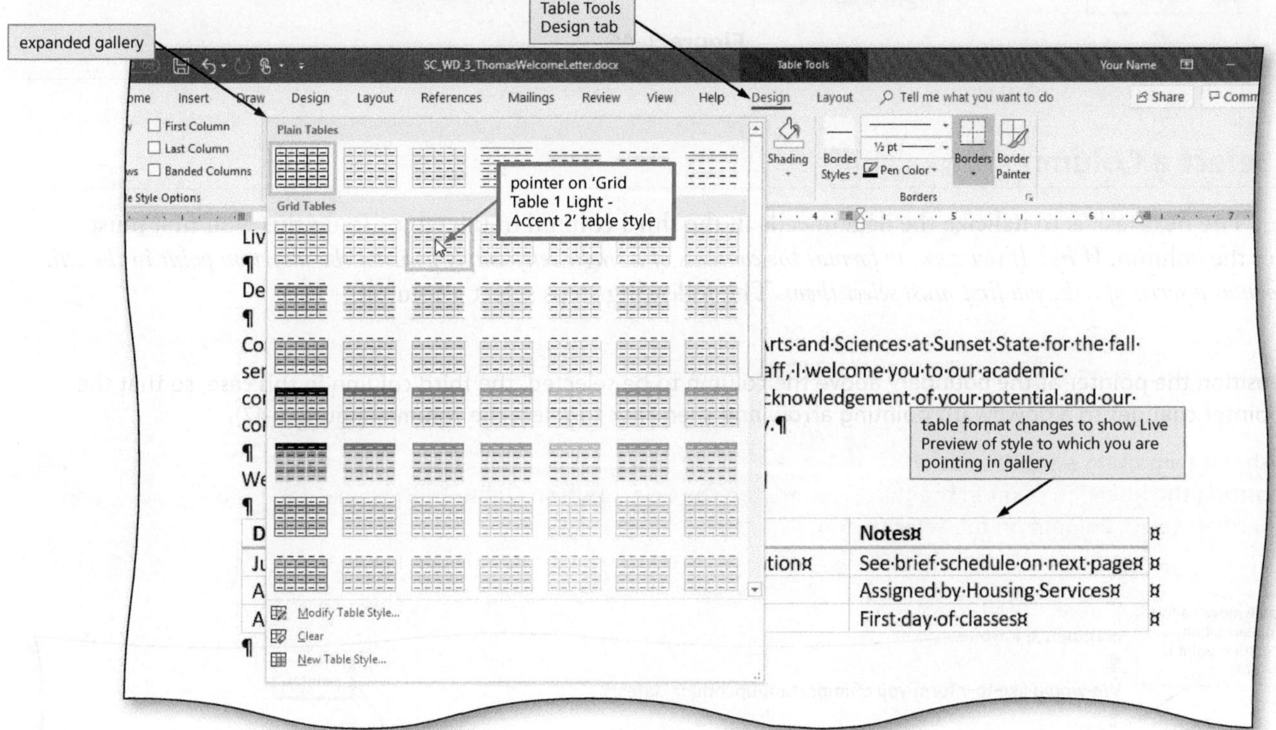

Figure 3–45

Experiment

- Point to various styles in the Table Styles gallery and watch the format of the table change in the document window.

- Click 'Grid Table 1 Light - Accent 2' in the Table Styles gallery to apply the selected style to the table. Scroll up, if necessary (Figure 3–46).

Experiment

- Select and remove check marks from various check boxes in the Table Style Options group and watch the format of the table change in the document window. When finished experimenting, be sure the check marks match those shown in Figure 3–46.

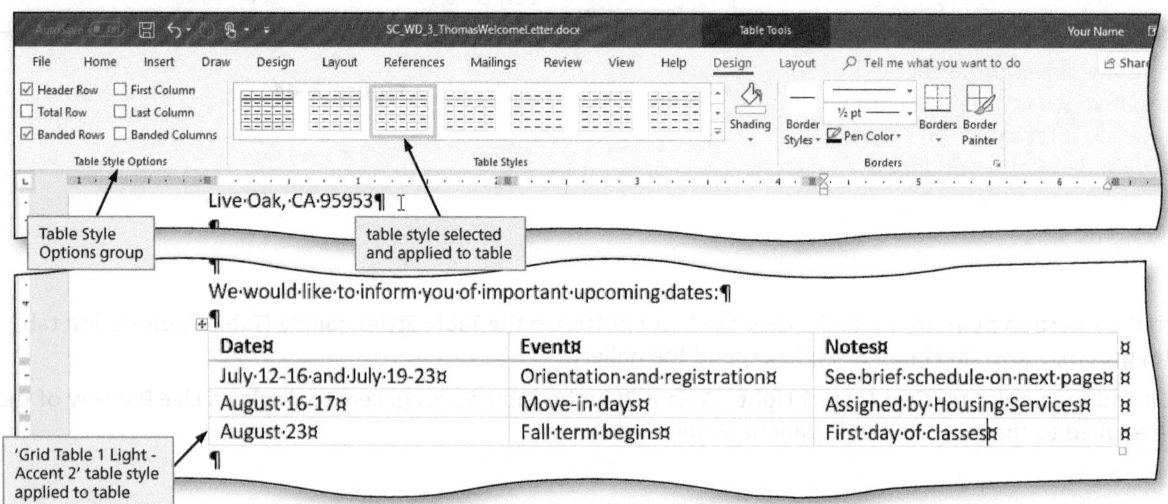

Figure 3–46

To Select a Column

The next task is to italicize the data in cells in the third column of the table. To do this, you first must select the column. ***Why?*** *If you want to format the contents of a single cell, simply position the insertion point in the cell. To format a series of cells, you first must select them.* The following steps select a column.

- Position the pointer at the boundary above the column to be selected, the third column in this case, so that the pointer changes to a downward pointing arrow and then click to select the column (Figure 3–47).

Q&A

What if I am using a touch screen?

Position the insertion point in the third column, tap the Select button (Table Tools Layout tab | Table group), and then tap Select Column on the Select menu.

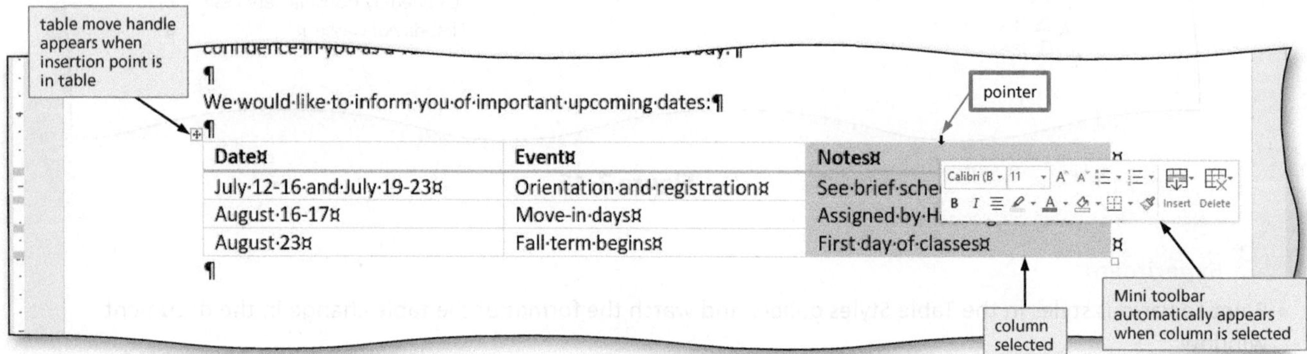

Figure 3–47

- Press CTRL+I to italicize the selected text.
- Click anywhere to remove the selection from the table.

Other Ways

1. Click Select button (Table Tools Layout tab | Table group), click Select Column on Select menu

Selecting Table Contents

When working with tables, you may need to select the contents of cells, rows, columns, or the entire table. Table 3–3 identifies ways to select various items in a table.

BTW
Moving Tables
If you wanted to move a table to a new location, you would point to the upper-left corner of the table until the table move handle appears (shown in Figure 3–47), point to the table move handle, and then drag it to move the entire table to a new location.

Table 3–3 Selecting Items in a Table

Item to Select	Action
Cell	Point to left edge of cell and then click when the pointer changes to a small solid upward angled pointing arrow. Or Position insertion point in cell, click Select button (Table Tools Layout tab | Table group), and then click Select Cell on the Select menu.
Column	Point to border at top of column and then click when the pointer changes to a small solid downward-pointing arrow. Or Position insertion point in column, click Select button (Table Tools Layout tab | Table group), and then click Select Column on the Select menu.
Row	Point to the left of the row and then click when pointer changes to a right-pointing block arrow. Or Position insertion point in row, click Select button (Table Tools Layout tab | Table group), and then click Select Row on the Select menu.
Multiple cells, rows, or columns adjacent to one another	Drag through cells, rows, or columns.
Multiple cells, rows, or columns not adjacent to one another	Select first cell, row, or column (as described above) and then hold down CTRL while selecting next cell, row, or column.
Next cell	Press TAB.
Previous cell	Press SHIFT+TAB
Table	Point somewhere in table and then click table move handle that appears in upper-left corner of table (shown in Figure 3–47). Or Position insertion point in table, click Select button (Table Tools Layout tab | Table group), and then click Select Table on the Select menu.

BTW
Tables
For simple tables, such as the one just created, Word users often select the table dimension in the Table gallery to create the table. For a more complex table, such as one with a varying number of columns per row, Word has a Draw Table feature that allows users to draw a table in the document using a pencil pointer. To use this feature, click the Table button (Insert tab | Tables group) and then click Draw Table on the Table menu.

To Insert a Row in a Table

The next step is to insert a row in the table. ***Why?*** *You want to add a row about welcome week.* As discussed earlier, you can insert a row at the end of a table by positioning the insertion point in the bottom-right corner cell and then pressing TAB. You cannot use TAB to insert a row at the beginning or middle of a table. Instead, you use Insert Above or Insert Below command (Table Tools Layout tab | Rows & Columns group) or the Insert Control. The **Insert Control**, which allows you to insert rows or columns in a table, is a circle containing a plus sign that appears when you use a mouse to point immediately above or to the left of columns or rows in a table. The following steps insert a row in the middle of a table.

- Position the pointer to the left of the table between the rows where you want the row to be inserted to display the Insert Control (Figure 3–48).

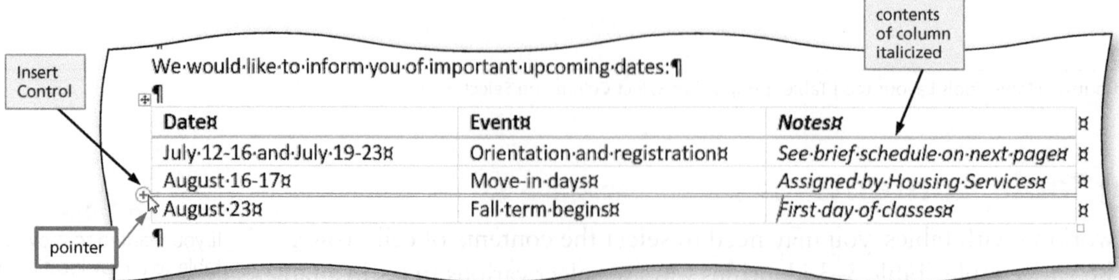

Figure 3–48

2

- Click the Insert Control to insert a row at the location of the pointer and then select the newly inserted row (Figure 3–49).

Experiment

- Click the Table Tools Layout tab to see the options available on this tab (shown in Figure 3–49).

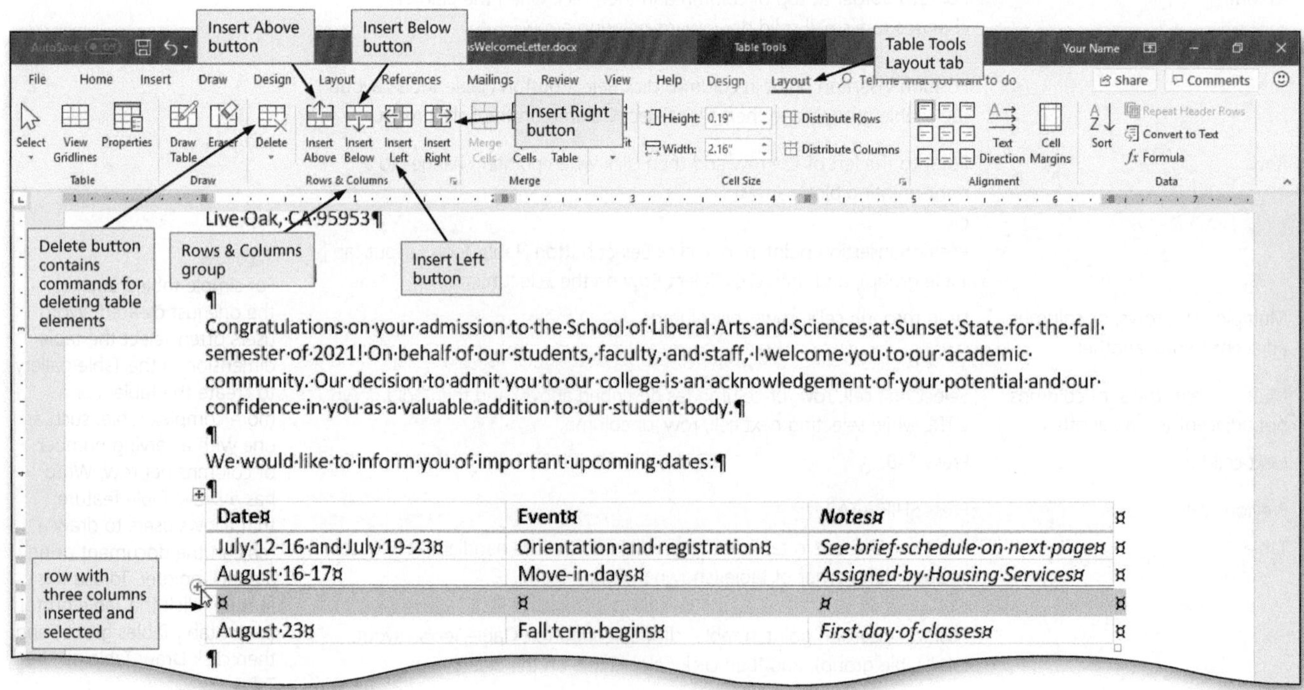

Figure 3–49

- Type **`August 16-20`** and then press TAB.
- Type **`Welcome week`** and then press TAB.
- Type **`Get schedule during orientation`** (Figure 3–50).

we·would·like·to·inform·you·of·important·upcoming·dates:¶

¶

Date¤	Event¤	Notes¤
July·12-16·and·July·19-23¤	Orientation·and·registration¤	*See·brief·schedule·on·next·page¤*
August·16-17¤	Move-in·days¤	*Assigned·by·Housing·Services¤*
August·16-20¤	Welcome·week¤	*Get·schedule·during·orientation¤*
August·23¤	Fall·term·begins¤	*First·day·of·classes¤*

¶

row inserted and data entered

Figure 3–50

Other Ways

1. Click Insert Above or Insert Below button (Table Tools Layout tab | Rows & Columns group)
2. Right-click row, point to Insert on shortcut menu (or, if using touch, tap Insert button on Mini toolbar), click desired option on Insert submenu

To Insert a Column in a Table

If you wanted to insert a column in a table, instead of inserting rows, you would perform the following steps.

1. Point above the table and then click the desired Insert Control.

or

1. Position the insertion point in the column to the left or right of where you want to insert the column.
2. Click the Insert Left button (Table Tools Layout tab | Rows & Columns group) to insert a column to the left of the current column, or click the Insert Right button (Table Tools Layout tab | Rows & Columns group) to insert a column to the right of the current column.

or

1. Right-click the table, point to Insert on the shortcut menu (or, if using touch, tap Insert button on the Mini toolbar), and then click Insert Left or Insert Right on the Insert submenu (or, if using touch, tap Insert Left or Insert Right).

BTW
Resizing Table Columns and Rows
To change the width of a column or height of a row to an exact measurement, hold down ALT while dragging markers on the ruler. Or, enter values in the Width or Height boxes (Table Tools Layout tab | Cell Size group).

Deleting Table Data

If you want to delete row(s) or delete column(s) from a table, position the insertion point in the row(s) or column(s) to delete, click the Delete button (Table Tools Layout tab | Rows & Columns group) (shown in Figure 3–49), and then click Delete Rows or Delete Columns on the Delete menu. Or, select the row or column to delete, right-click the selection, and then click Delete Rows or Delete Columns on the Mini toolbar or shortcut menu.

To delete the contents of a cell, select the cell contents and then press DELETE or BACKSPACE. You also can drag and drop or cut and paste the contents of cells. To delete an entire table, select the table, click the Delete button (Table Tools Layout tab | Rows & Columns group), and then click Delete Table on the Delete menu. To delete the contents of a table and leave an empty table, you would select the table and then press DELETE.

BTW
Aligning Tables
To align an entire table, such as centering it between the margins on the page, select the table and then press CTRL+E or click the Center button (Home tab | Paragraph group). To align contents of cells, select the cells and then click the desired alignment button in the Alignment group on the Table Tools Layout tab.

To Add More Text

The table now is complete. The next step is to enter text below the table. The following steps enter text.

1. Scroll up, if necessary, to see the space below the table on the letter.
2. Position the insertion point on the paragraph mark below the table and then press ENTER.
3. Type `Before orientation, you must do the following through our campus website:` and then press ENTER (shown in Figure 3–51).

To Bullet a List as You Type

If you know before you type that a list should be bulleted, you can use Word's AutoFormat As You Type feature to bullet the paragraphs as you type them instead of formatting the paragraphs with bullets after you enter them. ***Why?*** *The AutoFormat As You Type feature saves you time because it applies formats automatically.* The following steps add bullets to a list as you type.

1

- Press the ASTERISK key (*) as the first character on the line (Figure 3–51).

2

- Press SPACEBAR to convert the asterisk to a bullet character.

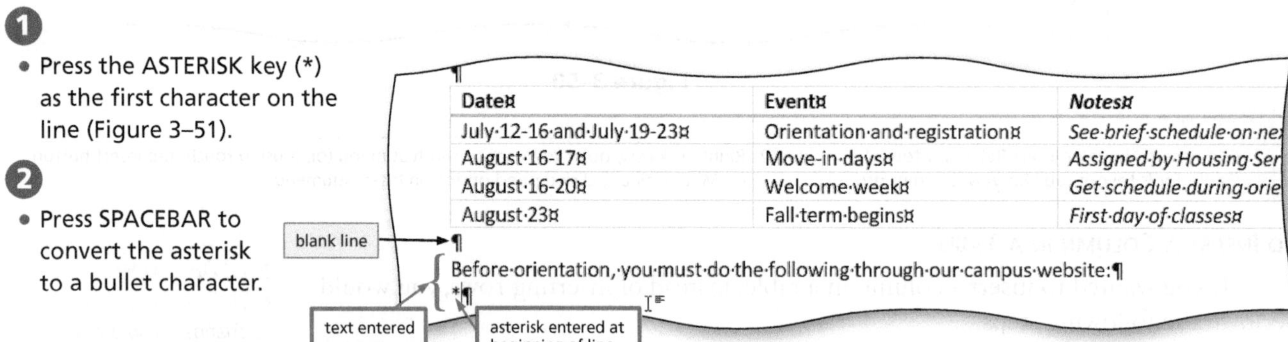

Date	Event	Notes
July·12-16·and·July·19-23	Orientation·and·registration	See·brief·schedule·on·ne
August·16-17	Move-in·days	Assigned·by·Housing·Ser
August·16-20	Welcome·week	Get·schedule·during·orie
August·23	Fall·term·begins	First·day·of·classes

Before·orientation,·you·must·do·the·following·through·our·campus·website:¶
*¶

Figure 3–51

Q&A What if I did not want the asterisk converted to a bullet character?
You could undo the AutoFormat by clicking the Undo button; pressing CTRL+Z; clicking the AutoCorrect Options button that appears to the left of the bullet character as soon as you press SPACEBAR and then clicking 'Undo Automatic Bullets' on the AutoCorrect Options menu; or clicking the Bullets button (Home tab | Paragraph group).

3

- Type `Complete a housing contract or housing exemption form` as the first bulleted item.
- Press ENTER to place another bullet character at the beginning of the next line (Figure 3–52).

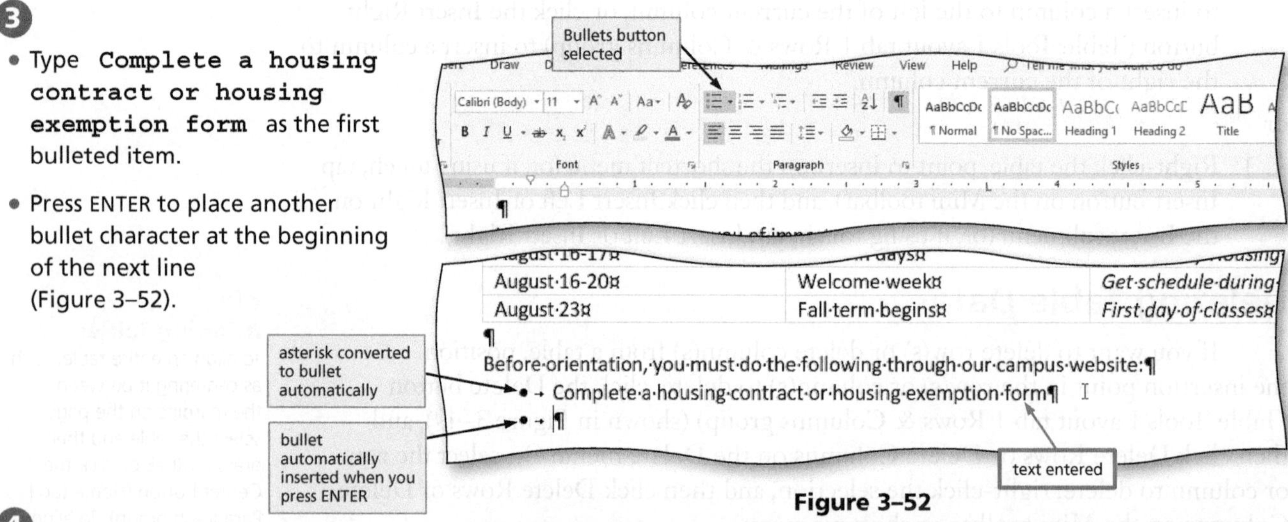

Figure 3–52

4

- Type `Schedule your math placement exam` and then press ENTER.
- Type `Reserve your orientation dates` and then press ENTER.
- Press ENTER again to turn off automatic bullets as you type (Figure 3–53).

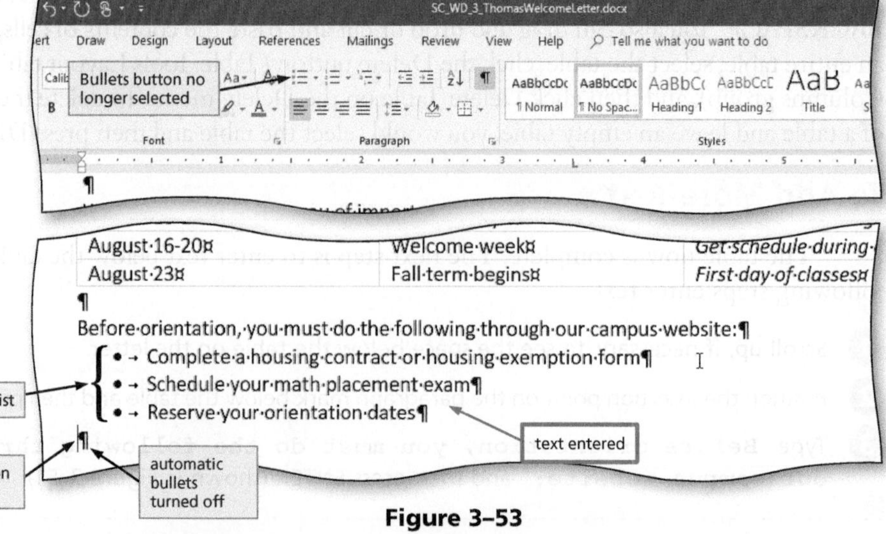

Figure 3–53

Q&A Why did automatic bullets stop?
When you press ENTER without entering any text after the automatic bullet character, Word turns off the automatic bullets feature.

Other Ways

1. Click Bullets arrow (Home tab | Paragraph group), click desired bullet style
2. Right-click paragraph to be bulleted, click Bullets button on Mini toolbar, click desired bullet style, if necessary

To Enter More Text and then Save the Letter

The following steps enter the remainder of text in the letter.

1. With the insertion point positioned on the paragraph below the bulleted list, press ENTER and then type the sentence: **I am confident you will pursue your passions and accomplish your goals as a Sunset State Flying Eagle!**
2. Press ENTER twice. Press TAB to position the insertion point at the tab stop set at the 3.5" mark on the ruler. Type **Sincerely,** and then press ENTER four times.
3. Press TAB to position the insertion point at the tab stop set at the 3.5" mark on the ruler. Type **Lucy R. Song** and then press ENTER.
4. Press TAB to position the insertion point at the tab stop set at the 3.5" mark on the ruler. Type **Director of Admissions** to finish the letter. Scroll up, if necessary (Figure 3–54).
5. Save the letter again on the same storage location with the same file name.

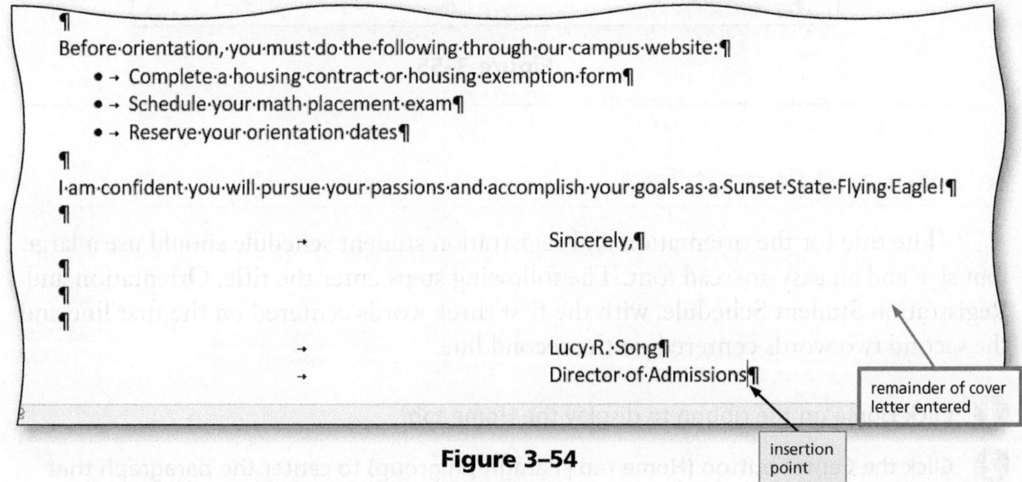

Figure 3–54

BTW
Nonbreaking Spaces and Hyphens
If you do not want a compound word, such as a proper noun, date, unit of time and measure, abbreviations, and geographic destinations, to be split, where part of the compound word appears at the end of one line and the other part appears at the beginning of the next line, you can insert a nonbreaking space or a nonbreaking hyphen. To insert a nonbreaking space, you would press CTRL+SHIFT+SPACEBAR instead of SPACEBAR in the middle of the compound word. To insert a nonbreaking hyphen, you would press CTRL+SHIFT+HYPHEN instead of a hyphen in the middle of the compound word.

Working with SmartArt Graphics

The acceptance letter to the student referenced a brief schedule for the orientation and registration. This schedule is to appear on a separate page after the content of the letter. The following sections insert a page break and then create the content for the orientation and registration student schedule.

To Insert a Page Break

The first step in creating the page that will contain the student schedule for orientation and registration is to insert a page break at the end of the acceptance letter. The following steps insert a page break.

BTW
Sections and Section Breaks
Every document has at least one section. You can create multiple sections if you need to change page formatting in a portion of a document. A section break divides one section from another. To insert a next page section break, click the Breaks button (Layout tab | Page Setup group) and then click Next Page in the Section Breaks area of the Breaks gallery. Other section break options are in the Breaks gallery, as well.

1. Verify that the insertion point is positioned at the end of text in the letter, as shown in Figure 3–54.
2. Click Insert on the ribbon to display the Insert tab.
3. Click the Page Break button (Insert tab | Pages group) to insert a page break immediately to the left of the insertion point and position the insertion point at the beginning of a new blank page (Figure 3–55).

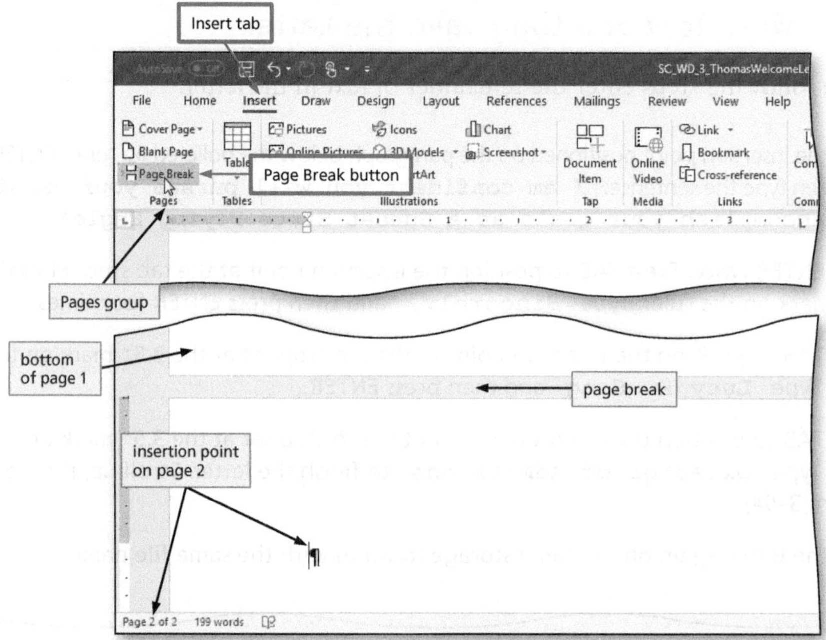

Figure 3–55

To Enter and Format Text

The title for the orientation and registration student schedule should use a large font size and an easy-to-read font. The following steps enter the title, Orientation and Registration Student Schedule, with the first three words centered on the first line and the second two words centered on the second line.

1. Click Home on the ribbon to display the Home tab.
2. Click the Center button (Home tab | Paragraph group) to center the paragraph that will contain the title.
3. Click the Bold button (Home tab | Font group), so that the text you type will be formatted with bold characters.
4. Click the Font Size arrow (Home tab | Font group) and then click 36 in the Font Size gallery, so that the text you type will use the selected font size.
5. Click the Font Color arrow (Home tab | Font group) and then click 'Orange, Accent 2, Darker 25%' (sixth color, fifth row) in the Font Color gallery, so that the text you type will use the selected font color.
6. Scroll, if necessary, to see the insertion point and paragraph mark. Type `Orientation and Registration` and then press ENTER to enter the first line of the title.
7. Type `Student Schedule` as the second line of the title (Figure 3–56).

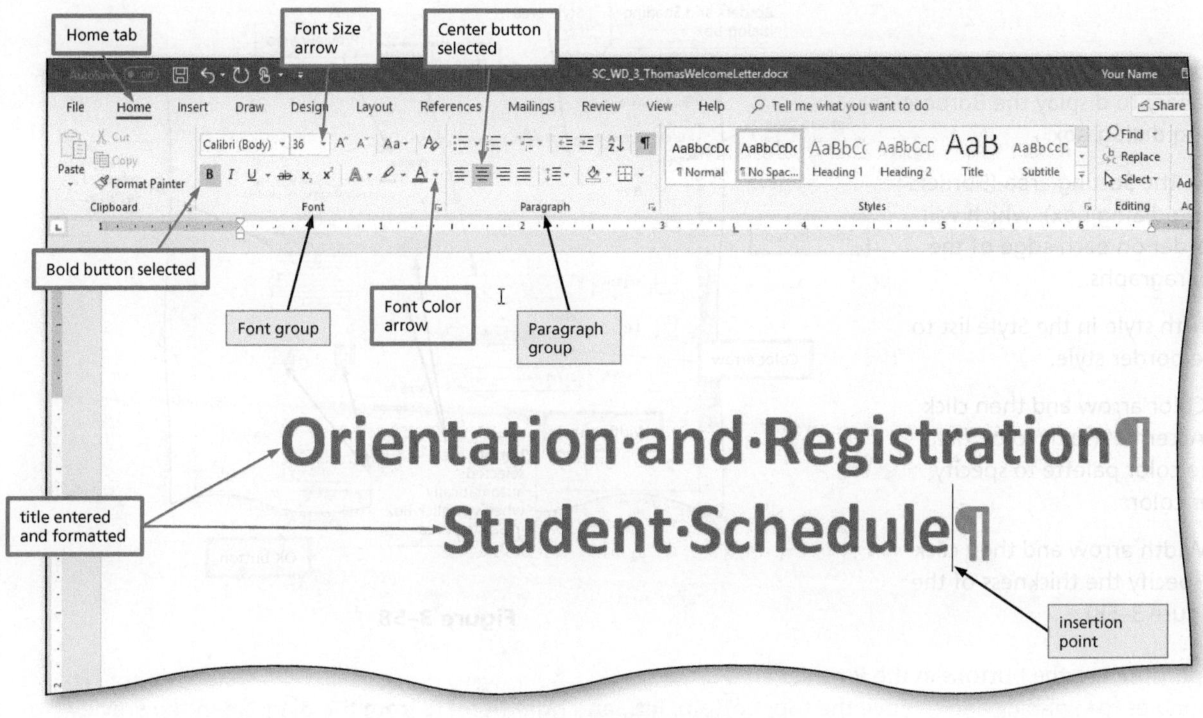

Figure 3–56

To Add and Format a Paragraph Border

If you click the Borders button (Home tab | Paragraph group), Word applies the most recently defined border, or, if one has not been defined, it applies the default border to the current paragraph. To specify a border different from the most recently defined border, you click the Borders arrow (Home tab | Paragraph group).

In this project, the title in the orientation schedule has a 2¼-point orange border around it. ***Why?*** *You want the title to stand out on the page.* The following steps add a border to all edges of the selected paragraphs.

1

- Select the paragraphs to border, in this case, the first two lines of the page.
- Click the Borders arrow (Home tab | Paragraph group) to display the Borders gallery (Figure 3–57).

Q&A What if I wanted to border just a single paragraph?
You would position the insertion point in the paragraph before clicking the Borders arrow.

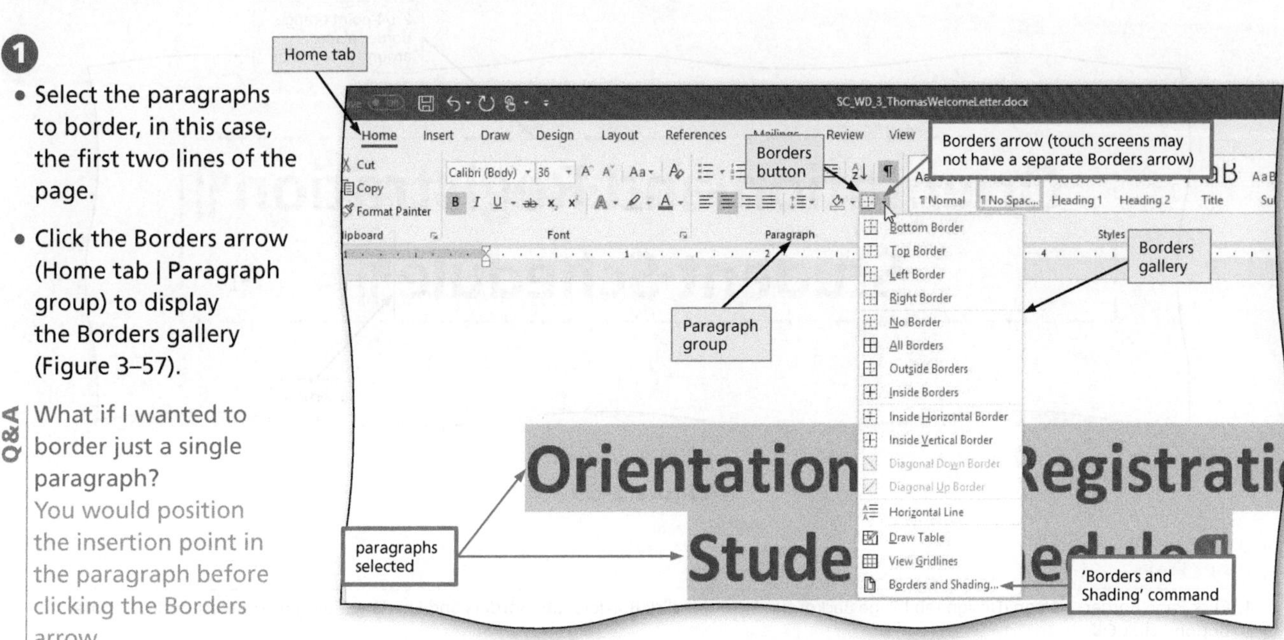

Figure 3–57

- Click 'Borders and Shading' in the Borders gallery to display the Borders and Shading dialog box.
- Click Box in the Setting area (Borders and Shading dialog box), which will place a border on each edge of the selected paragraphs.
- Click the fifth style in the Style list to specify the border style.
- Click the Color arrow and then click 'Orange, Accent 2' (sixth color, first row) in the color palette to specify the border color.
- Click the Width arrow and then click 2 ¼ pt to specify the thickness of the border (Figure 3–58).

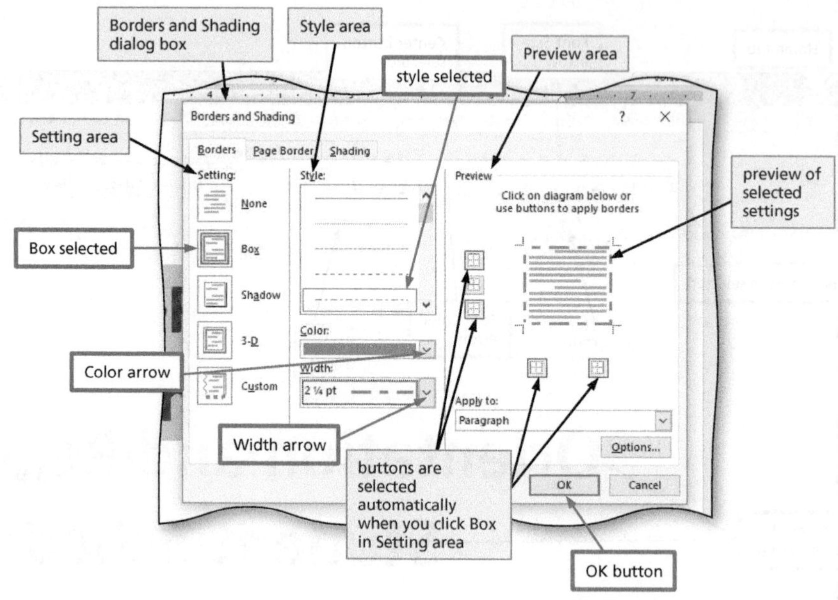

Figure 3–58

Q&A For what purpose are the buttons in the Preview area used?
They are toggles that display and remove the top, bottom, left, and right borders from the diagram in the Preview area.

- Click OK (Borders and Shading dialog box) to place the border shown in the preview area of the dialog box around the selected paragraphs in the document.
- Click anywhere in the title to remove the selection (Figure 3–59).

Q&A How would I remove an existing border from a paragraph?
Click the Borders arrow (Home tab | Paragraph group) and then click the border in the Borders gallery that identifies the border you wish to remove, or click No Border to remove all borders.

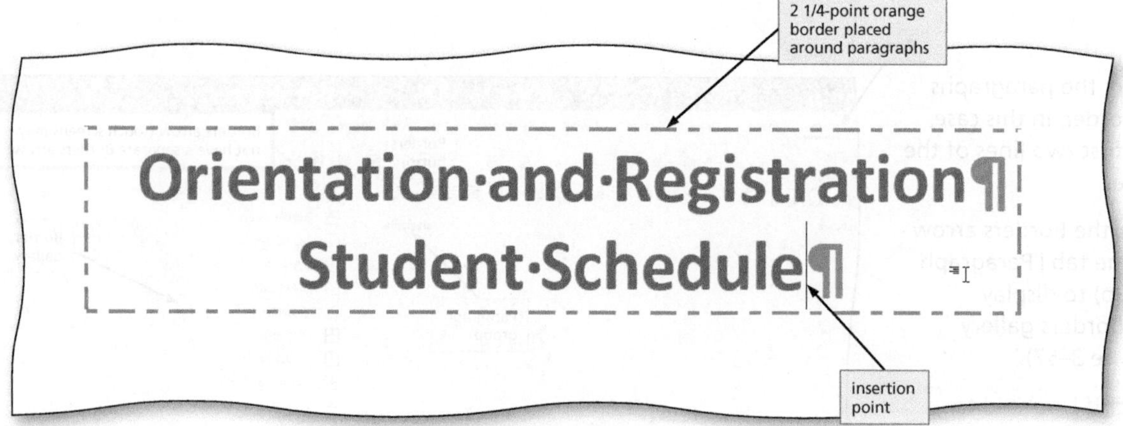

Figure 3–59

Other Ways

1. Click Page Borders button (Design tab | Page Background group), click Borders tab (Borders and Shading dialog box), select desired border options, click OK

To Clear Formatting

When you press ENTER, Word carries forward any formatting at the location of the insertion point to the next line. You want the text you type below the title to be returned to the Normal style. Thus, the following steps clear formatting.

1. Position the insertion point at the end of the second line of the title, as shown in Figure 3–59, and then press ENTER.
2. Click the 'Clear All Formatting' button (Home tab | Font group) to apply the Normal style to the location of the insertion point (Figure 3–60).

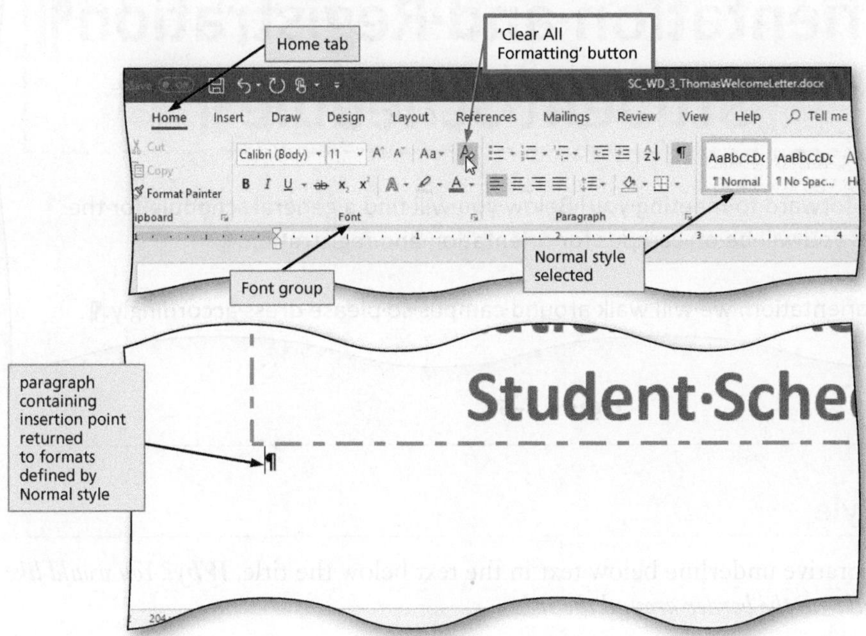

Figure 3–60

To Apply a Style and Enter More Text

The text below the title should use single spacing with double spacing between paragraphs. Thus, the following steps apply the No Spacing style and then enter two paragraphs of text.

1. With the insertion point positioned below the title, click No Spacing in the Styles gallery (Home tab | Styles group) to apply the selected style to the current paragraph.
2. Click the Font Size arrow (Home tab | Font group) and then click 14 in the Font Size gallery, so that the text you type will use the selected font size.
3. Press ENTER and then type `We look forward to meeting you! Below you will find a general schedule for the two days you will be on campus for orientation and registration.`
4. Press ENTER twice and then type `During orientation, we will walk around campus so please dress accordingly.` (Figure 3–61)

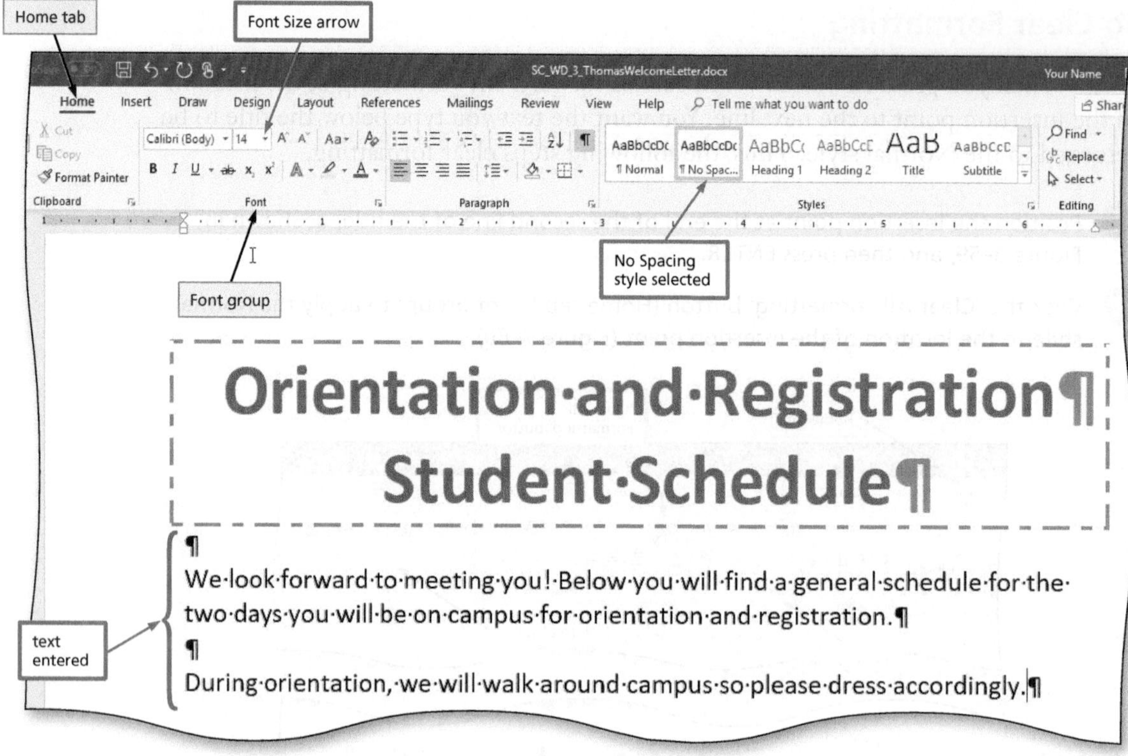

Figure 3–61

To Change the Underline Style

The following steps place a decorative underline below text in the text below the title. ***Why?*** *You would like to emphasize text and use a line style similar to the border around the title.*

- Select the text to format (the words, two days, in this case).
- Click the Underline arrow (Home tab | Font group) to display the Underline gallery (Figure 3–62).

Experiment

- Point to various underline styles in the Underline gallery and watch the underline style on the selected text change in the document window.

- Click the sixth underline style in the Underline gallery to apply the selected underline style to the selected text.

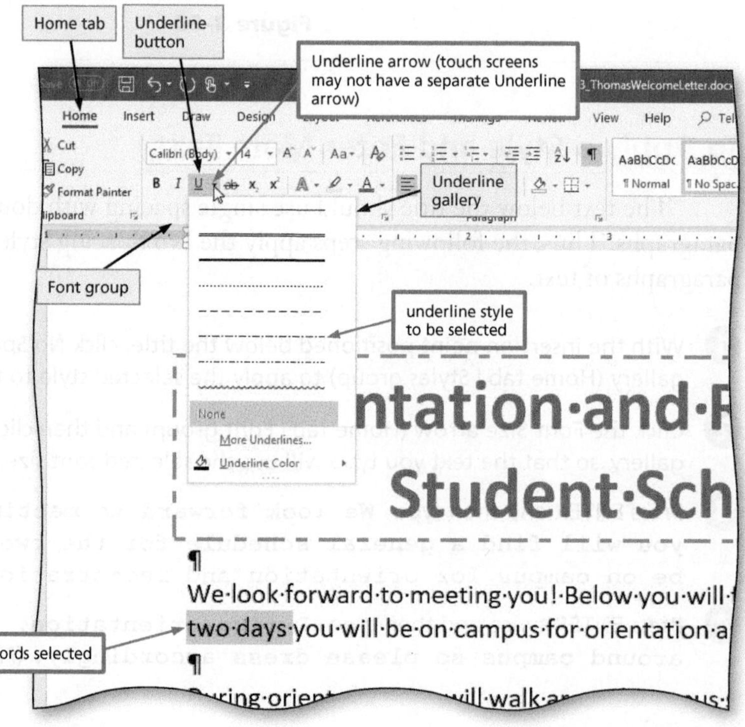

Figure 3–62

- Click the Underline arrow (Home tab | Font group) to display the Underline gallery again.
- Point to Underline Color in the Underline gallery to display a color palette.
- Point to 'Orange, Accent 2' (sixth color in first row) in the color palette to display a Live Preview of that underline color on the selected text (Figure 3–63).

Experiment

- Point to various underline colors in the color palette and watch the underline color on the selected text change in the document window.

Q&A How would I remove underline from text?
With the text selected, you would click the Underline button (Home tab | Font group).

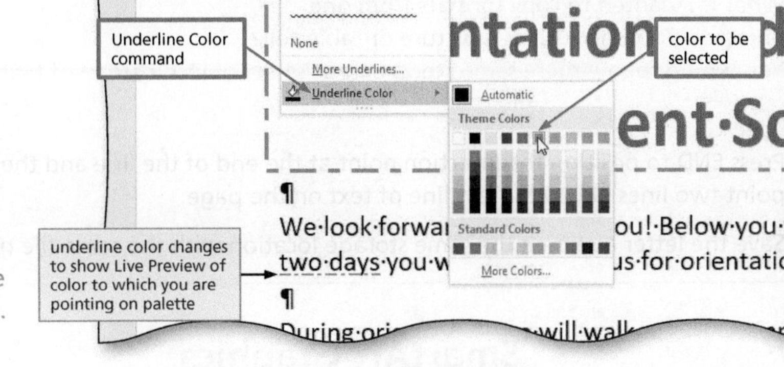

Figure 3–63

- Click 'Orange, Accent 2' in the color palette to apply the selected color to the underline.

Other Ways

1. Click Font Dialog Box Launcher (Home tab | Font group), click Underline style arrow (Font dialog box), select desired underline style, click Underline color arrow, select desired underline color, click OK

To Use the Format Painter Button

The last two words in the next sentence, dress accordingly, are to use the same decorative underline as the words, two days, that you just formatted. ***Why?*** *You would like the underline format to be consistent.* Instead of selecting the words, dress accordingly, and following the steps to apply the same underline format, you will copy the format from the currently selected text. The following steps copy formatting using the Format Painter button.

1

- With the text selected that contains the formatting you wish to copy (the text, two days, in this case), click the Format Painter button (Home tab | Clipboard group) to turn on the format painter.

Q&A What if I wanted to copy a format to multiple locations?
To copy formats to only one other location, click the Format Painter button (Home tab | Clipboard group) once. If you want to copy formatting to multiple locations, double-click the Format Painter button so that the format painter remains active until you turn it off, or click it again.

- Move the pointer to where you want to copy the formatting (the text, dress accordingly, in this case) and notice that the format painter is active (Figure 3–64).

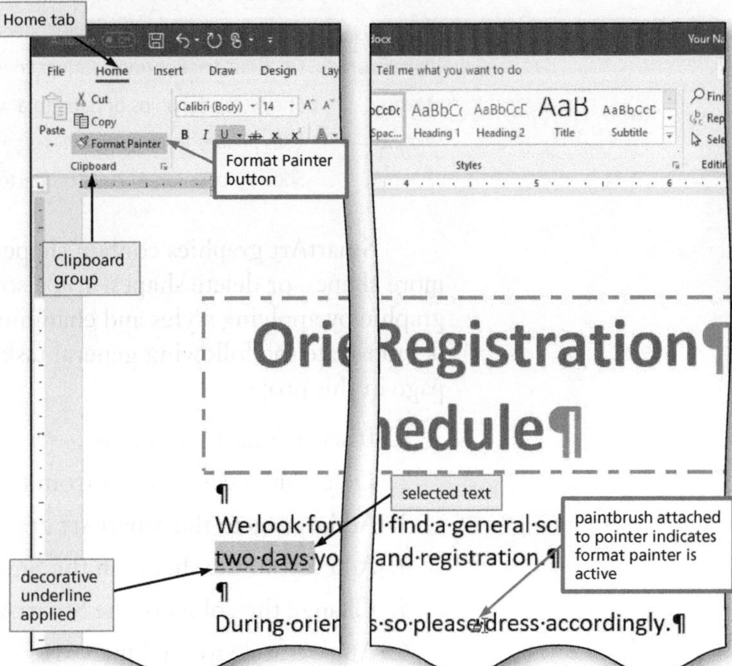

Figure 3–64

How can I tell if the format painter is active?
The pointer has a paintbrush attached to it when the format painter is active.

- Select the text that should have the same underline format (the text, dress accordingly, in this case) to paste the copied format to the selected text (Figure 3–65).

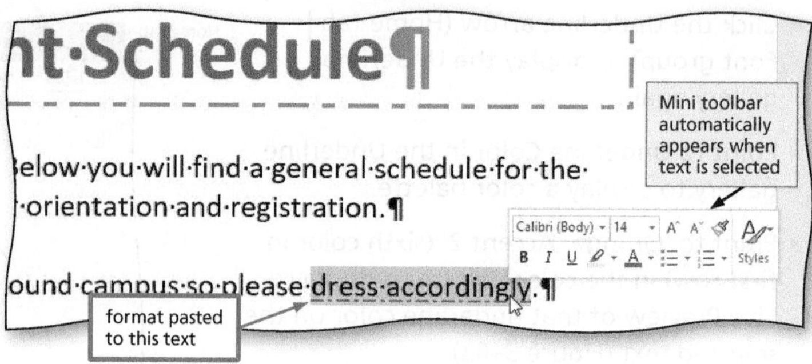

Figure 3–65

Q&A What if I wanted to copy formats from one object to another, such as a picture or table cell?
You would follow these same steps, except select object instead of text.

3

- Press END to position the insertion point at the end of the line and then press ENTER twice to position the insertion point two lines below the last line of text on the page.
- Save the letter again on the same storage location with the same file name.

BTW
Format Painter
If you also want to copy paragraph formatting, such as alignment and line spacing, select the paragraph mark at the end of the paragraph prior to clicking the Format Painter button (Home tab | Clipboard group). If you want to copy only character formatting, such as fonts and font sizes, do not include the paragraph mark in your selected text.

SmartArt Graphics

Microsoft Office 2019 includes **SmartArt graphics**, which are customizable diagrams that you use to pictorially present lists, processes, and relationships. Many different types of SmartArt graphics are available, allowing you to choose one that illustrates your message best. Table 3–4 identifies the purpose of some of the more popular types of SmartArt graphics. Within each type, Office provides numerous layouts. For example, you can select from 40 different layouts of the list type.

Table 3–4 SmartArt Graphic Types

Type	Purpose
List	Shows nonsequential or grouped blocks of information.
Process	Shows progression, timeline, or sequential steps in a process or workflow.
Cycle	Shows a continuous sequence of steps or events.
Hierarchy	Illustrates organization charts, decision trees, and hierarchical relationships.
Relationship	Compares or contrasts connections between concepts.
Matrix	Shows relationships of parts to a whole.
Picture	Uses images to present a message.
Pyramid	Shows proportional or interconnected relationships with the largest component at the top or bottom.

SmartArt graphics contain shapes. You can add text or pictures to shapes, add more shapes, or delete shapes. You also can modify the appearance of a SmartArt graphic by applying styles and changing its colors. The next several sections demonstrate the following general tasks to create the SmartArt graphic on the title page in this project:

1. Insert a SmartArt graphic.
2. Delete unneeded shapes from the SmartArt graphic.
3. Add shapes to the SmartArt graphic.
4. Add text to the shapes in the SmartArt graphic.
5. Change the colors of the SmartArt graphic.
6. Apply a style to the SmartArt graphic.

To Insert a SmartArt Graphic

Below the paragraphs of text you wish to add a Grouped List SmartArt graphic. ***Why?*** *The Grouped List SmartArt graphic allows you to place multiple lists side by side on the document, which works well for the student schedule for the two days of orientation and registration.* The following steps insert a SmartArt graphic centered at the location of the insertion point.

- With the insertion point on the blank paragraph, click the Center button (Home tab | Paragraph group) so that the inserted SmartArt graphic will be centered at the location of the insertion point.
- Display the Insert tab.
- Click the SmartArt button (Insert tab | Illustrations group) to display the Choose a SmartArt Graphic dialog box (Figure 3–66).

Experiment

- Click various SmartArt graphic types in the left pane of the dialog box and watch the related layout choices appear in the middle pane.
- Click various layouts in the list of layouts in the middle pane to see the preview and description of the layout appear in the right pane of the dialog box.

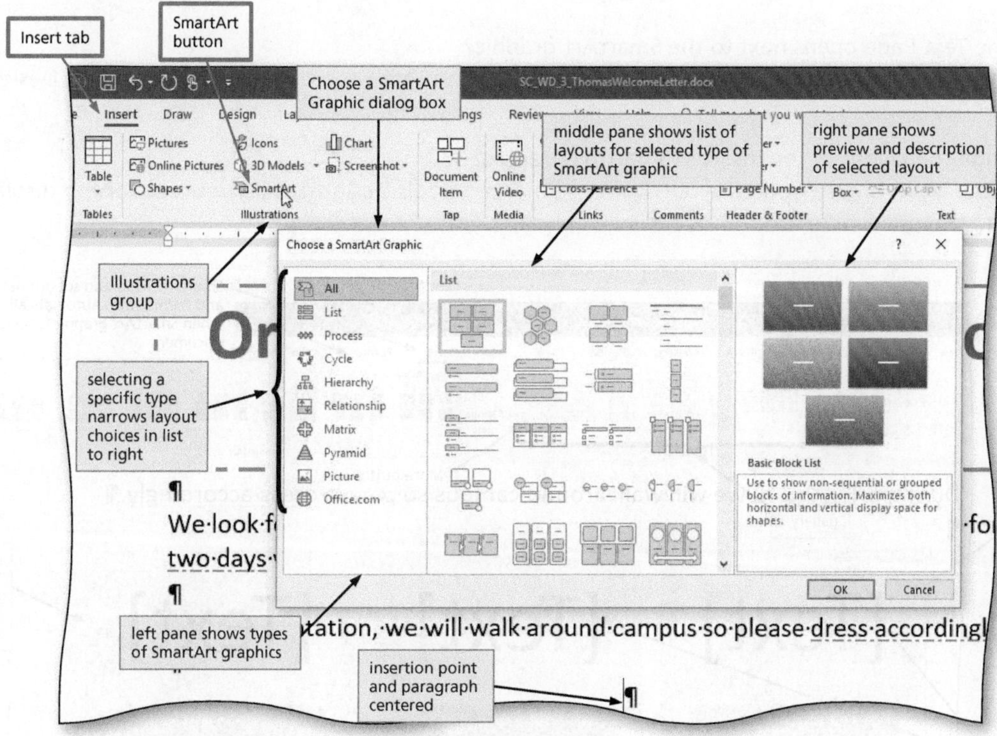

Figure 3–66

- Click List in the left pane (Choose a SmartArt Graphic dialog box) to display the layout choices related to the selected SmartArt graphic type.
- Click Grouped List in the middle pane, which displays a preview and description of the selected layout in the right pane (Figure 3–67).

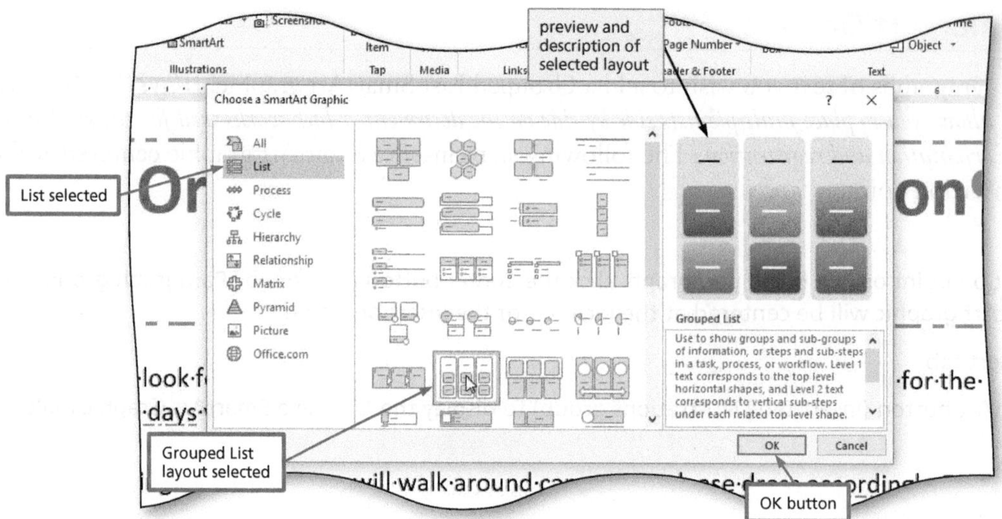

Figure 3–67

3

- Click OK to insert the selected SmartArt graphic in the document at the location of the insertion point (Figure 3–68). Scroll up, if necessary, to see the SmartArt graphic.

Q&A

What if the Text Pane opens next to the SmartArt graphic?

Close the Text Pane by clicking its Close button or clicking the Text Pane button (SmartArt Tools Design tab | Create Graphic group).

Can I change the layout of the inserted SmartArt graphic?

Yes. Click the More button in the Layouts gallery (SmartArt Tools Design tab | Layouts group) to display the list of layouts and then select the desired layout.

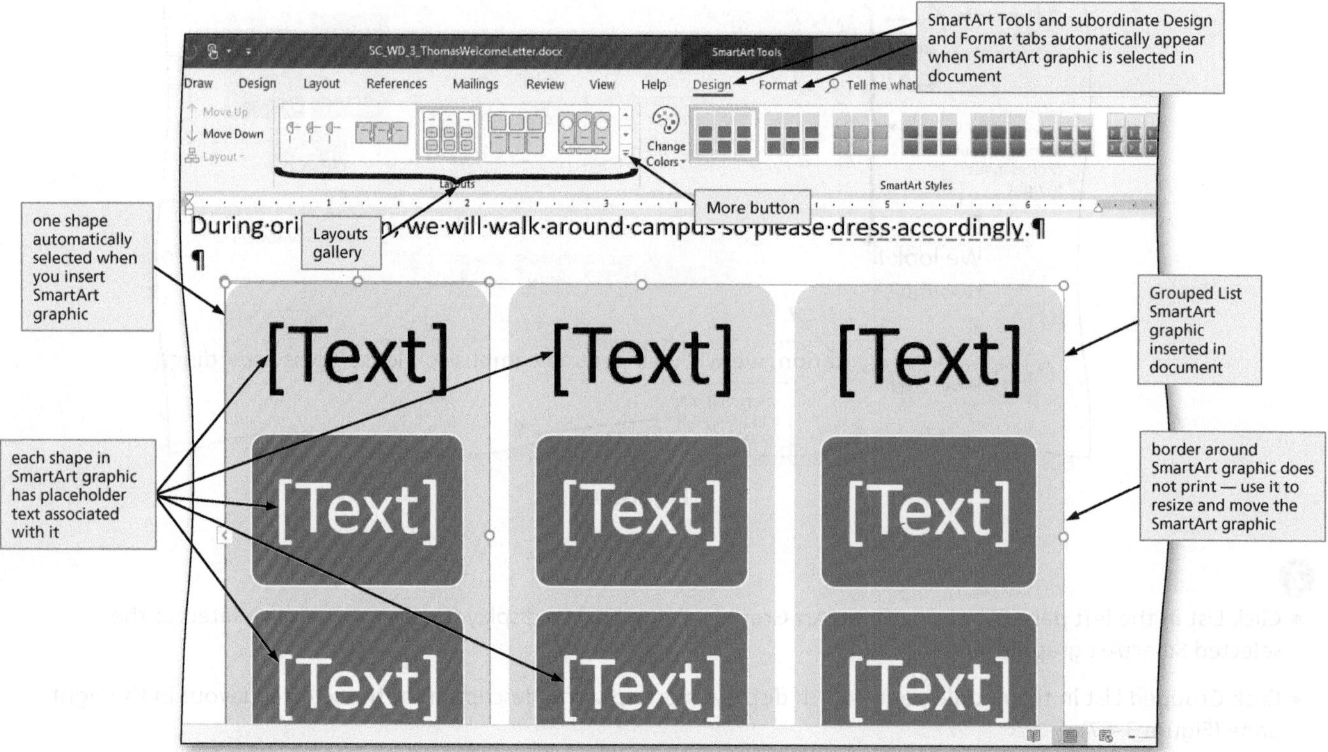

Figure 3–68

To Delete Shapes from a SmartArt Graphic

The Grouped List SmartArt graphic initially has three outer groups that consist of nine different shapes (shown in Figure 3–68). Notice that each shape in the SmartArt graphic initially shows **placeholder text**, which indicates where text can be typed. The next step in this project is to delete one entire group. ***Why?*** *The SmartArt graphic in this project consists of only two major groups (Day 1 and Day 2).* The following steps delete one entire group, or three shapes, in the SmartArt graphic.

- Click one of the edges of the shapes that says the word, [Text], in the rightmost group in the SmartArt graphic to select it (Figure 3–69).

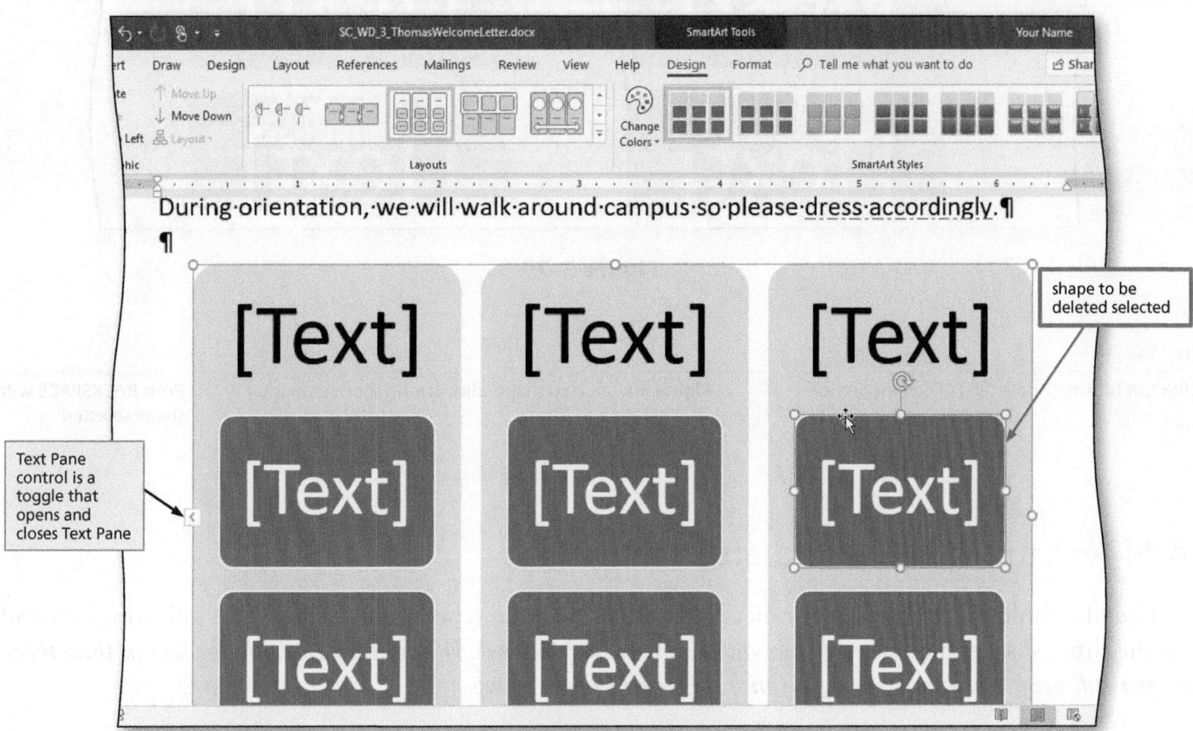

Figure 3–69

- Press DELETE to delete the selected shape from the SmartArt graphic (or, if using touch, tap the Cut button (Home tab | Clipboard group)).

Q&A What if the text inside the shape is selected instead the shape itself?
Click the shape again, ensuring you click the edge of the shape.

- Repeat Steps 1 and 2 to delete the next shape in the rightmost group.

- Repeat Steps 1 and 2 to delete the rightmost group and notice the other shapes resize and relocate in the graphic (Figure 3–70).

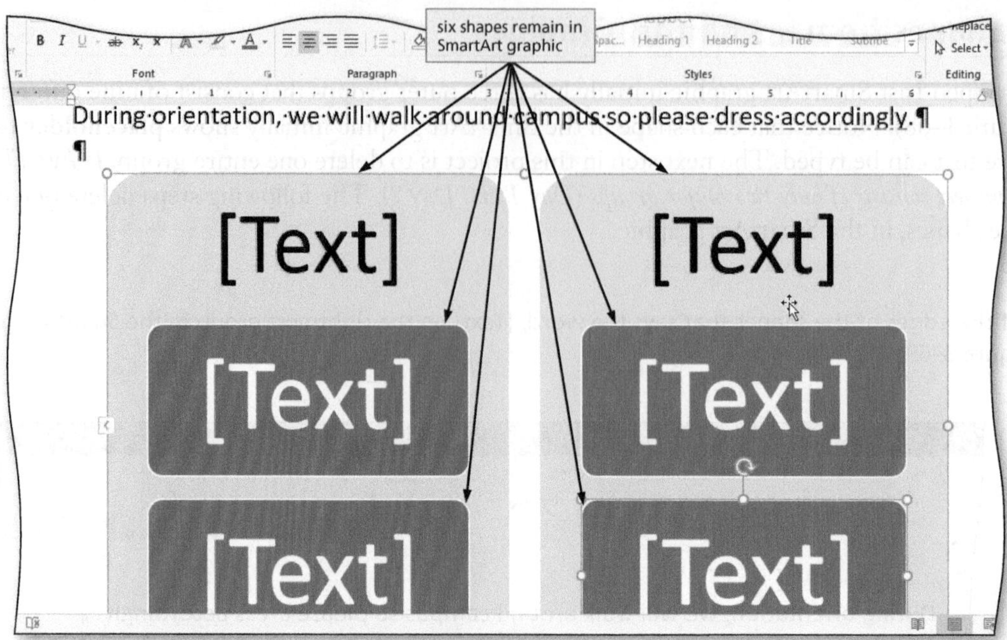

Figure 3–70

Other Ways

1. Click Cut button (Home tab | Clipboard group)
2. Right-click selected shape, click Cut on shortcut menu
3. Press BACKSPACE with shape selected

To Add Text to Shapes in a SmartArt Graphic

The placeholder text in a shape indicates where text can be typed in the shape. The following steps add text to the three shapes in the first group via their placeholder text. ***Why?*** *After entering the text in these three shapes, you will need to add more shapes to finish the content in the group.*

1

- Click the top-left shape to select it and then type `Day 1` to replace the placeholder text, [Text], with the entered text (Figure 3–71).

Q&A

How do I edit placeholder text if I make a mistake?

Click the placeholder text to select it and then correct the entry.

What if my typed text is longer than the shape?

The font size of the text in the shape may be adjusted or the text may wordwrap within the shape.

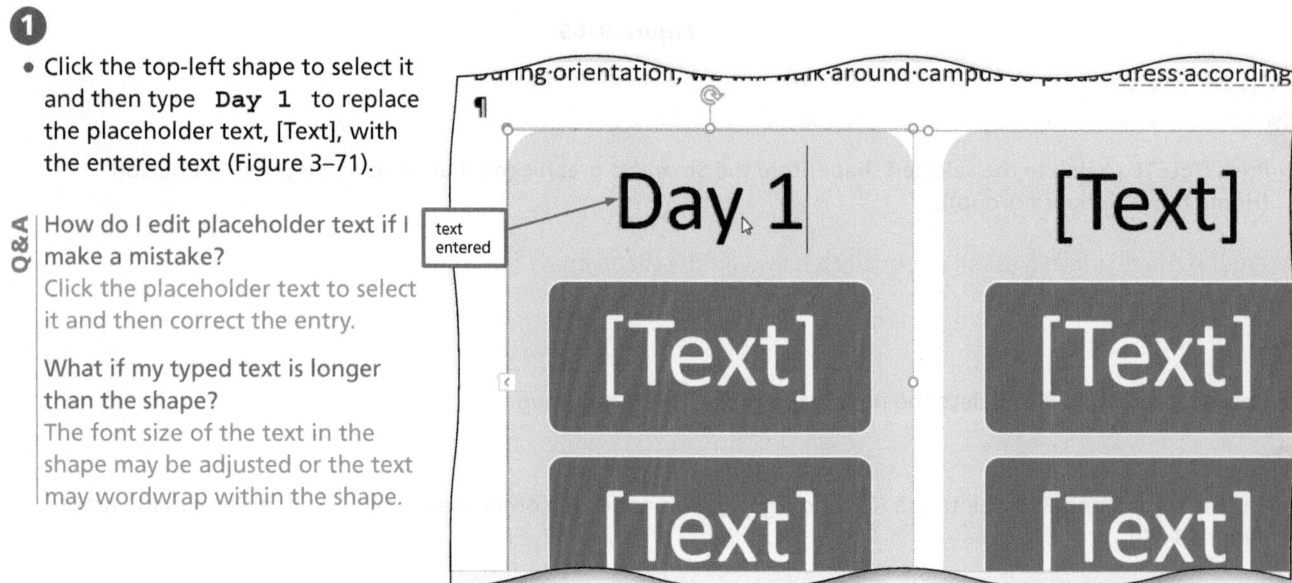

Figure 3–71

2

- Click the middle-left shape to select it and then type `Check-in (9:00-10:00)` as the new text.
- Click the lower-left shape to select it and then type `Welcome and general info session (10:15-11:45)` as the new text (Figure 3–72). Scroll up, if necessary, to see the entered text.

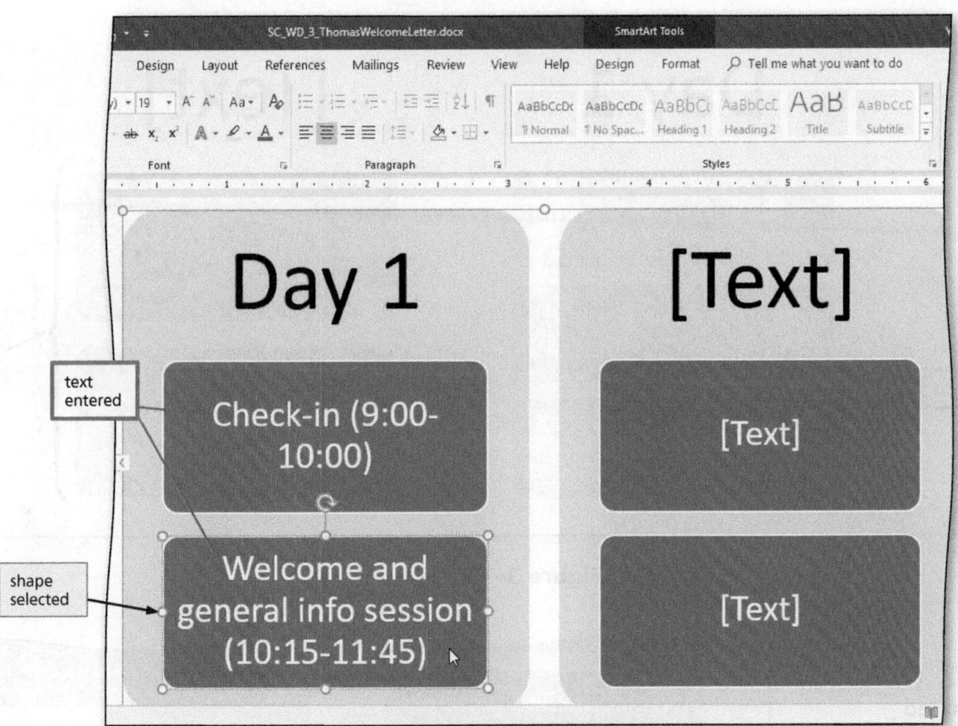

Figure 3–72

Other Ways

1. Click Text Pane control, enter text in Text Pane, close Text Pane
2. Click Text Pane button (SmartArt Tools Design tab | Create Graphic group), enter text in Text Pane, click Text Pane button again
3. Right-click shape (or, if using touch, tap Edit Text button on Mini toolbar), click 'Exit Edit Text' on shortcut menu, enter text

To Add a Shape to a SmartArt Graphic

The following steps add shapes to the SmartArt graphic. ***Why?*** *Each group in this project has nine subordinate items, which means seven shapes need to be added to each group.*

- Click SmartArt Tools Design on the ribbon to display the SmartArt Tools Design tab.
- With a shape in the left group selected (as shown in Figure 3–72), click the Add Shape button (SmartArt Tools Design tab | Create Graphic group) to add a shape to the SmartArt graphic (or, if using touch, tap the Add Shape button (SmartArt Tools Design tab | Create Graphic group) and then tap 'Add Shape After') (Figure 3–73).

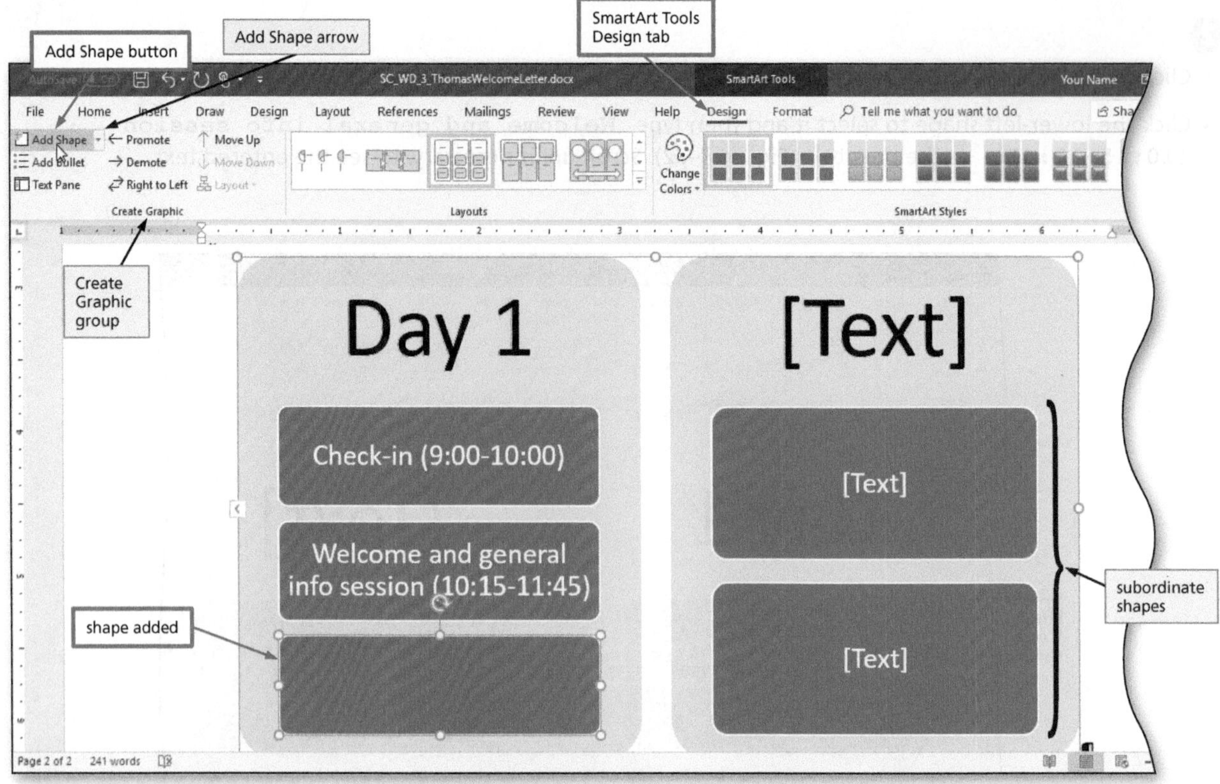

Figure 3–73

2

- Type **Lunch (12:00-12:45)** as the text for the added shape (Figure 3–74).

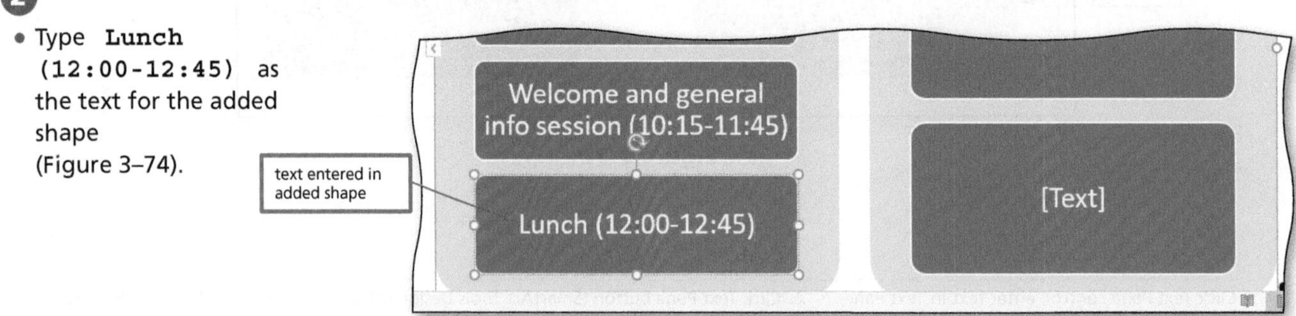

Figure 3–74

Other Ways

1. Click Add Shape arrow (SmartArt Tools Design tab), click desired shape position
2. Right-click paragraph (or, if using touch, tap 'Show Context Menu' button on Mini toolbar), point to Add Shape on shortcut menu, click desired shape position

To Add More Shapes and Text to a SmartArt Graphic

The following steps add the remaining shapes and text in the SmartArt graphic.

1 With a shape in the left group selected, click the Add Shape button (SmartArt Tools Design tab | Create Graphic group) to add a shape to the SmartArt graphic (or, if using touch, tap the Add Shape button (SmartArt Tools Design tab | Create Graphic group) and then tap 'Add Shape After') and then type **Student accounts and services session (1:00-1:45)** as the text for the shape.

2 Add another shape to the left group and then type **Meetings with advisors (2:00-2:45)** as the text for the shape.

3 Add another shape to the left group and then type **Department meetings (3:00-3:45)** as the text for the shape.

4. Add another shape to the left group and then type `Expo (4:00-5:15)` as the text for the shape.
5. Add another shape to the left group and then type `Dinner (5:30-6:45)` as the text for the shape.
6. Add another shape to the left group and then type `Evening activities (7:00-10:00)` as the text for the shape.
7. In the top of the right group, type `Day 2` in the placeholder text.
8. In the first shape below Day 2 in the right group, type `Breakfast (7:00-7:45)` as the text.
9. In the second shape below Day 2 in the right group, type `Housing services session (8:00-8:30)` as the text.
10. With a shape in the right group selected, click the Add Shape button (SmartArt Tools Design tab | Create Graphic group) to add a shape to the SmartArt graphic (or, if using touch, tap the Add Shape button (SmartArt Tools Design tab | Create Graphic group) and then tap 'Add Shape After') and then type `Dining services session (8:35-9:05)` as the text for the shape.
11. Add another shape to the right group and then type `Health services session (9:10-9:40)` as the text for the shape.
12. Add another shape to the right group and then type `Campus tour (10:00-11:45)` as the text for the shape.
13. Add another shape to the right group and then type `Lunch (12:00-12:45)` as the text for the shape.
14. Add another shape to the right group and then type `General education session (1:00-1:45)` as the text for the shape.
15. Add another shape to the right group and then type `Register for classes (2:00-3:15)` as the text for the shape.
16. Add another shape to the right group and then type `Welcome week overview (3:30-4:00)` as the text for the shape (Figure 3–75).

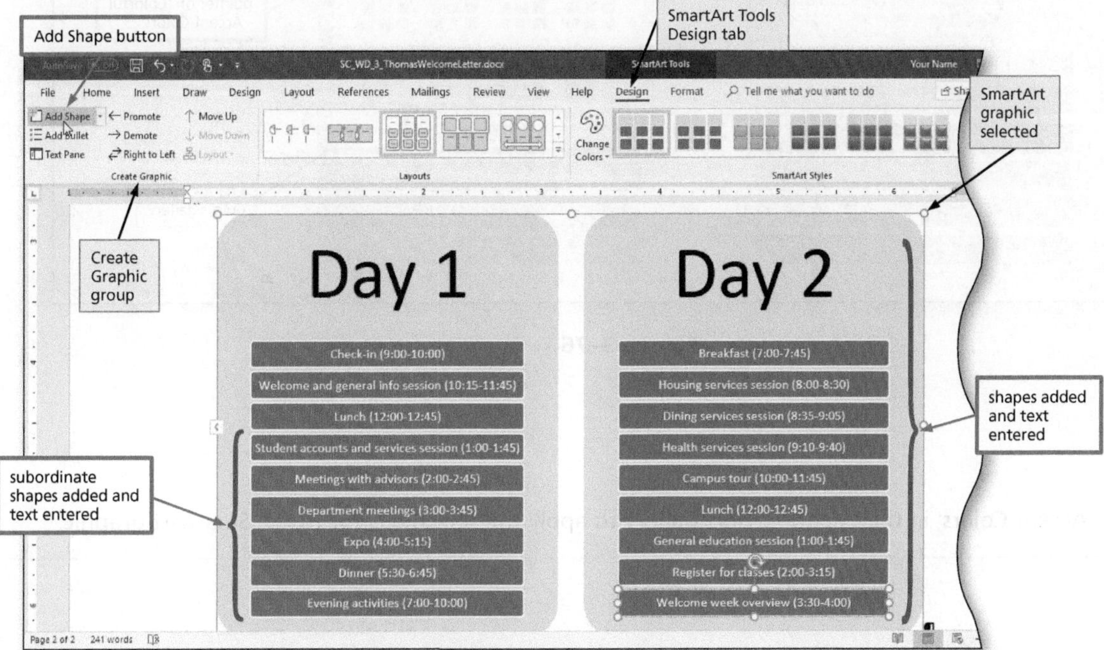

Figure 3–75

To Change Colors of a SmartArt Graphic

Word provides a variety of colors for a SmartArt graphic and the shapes in the graphic. In this project, the inside shapes are multicolor, instead of blue. ***Why?*** *You want more vibrant colors for the shapes.* The following steps change the colors of a SmartArt graphic.

- With the SmartArt graphic selected (shown in Figure 3–75), click the Change Colors button (SmartArt Tools Design tab | SmartArt Styles group) to display the Change Colors gallery.

Q&A What if the SmartArt graphic is not selected?
Click the SmartArt graphic to select it.

- Point to 'Colorful - Accent Colors' in the Change Colors gallery to display a Live Preview of the selected color applied to the SmartArt graphic in the document (Figure 3–76).

Experiment

- Point to various colors in the Change Colors gallery and watch the colors of the graphic change in the document window.

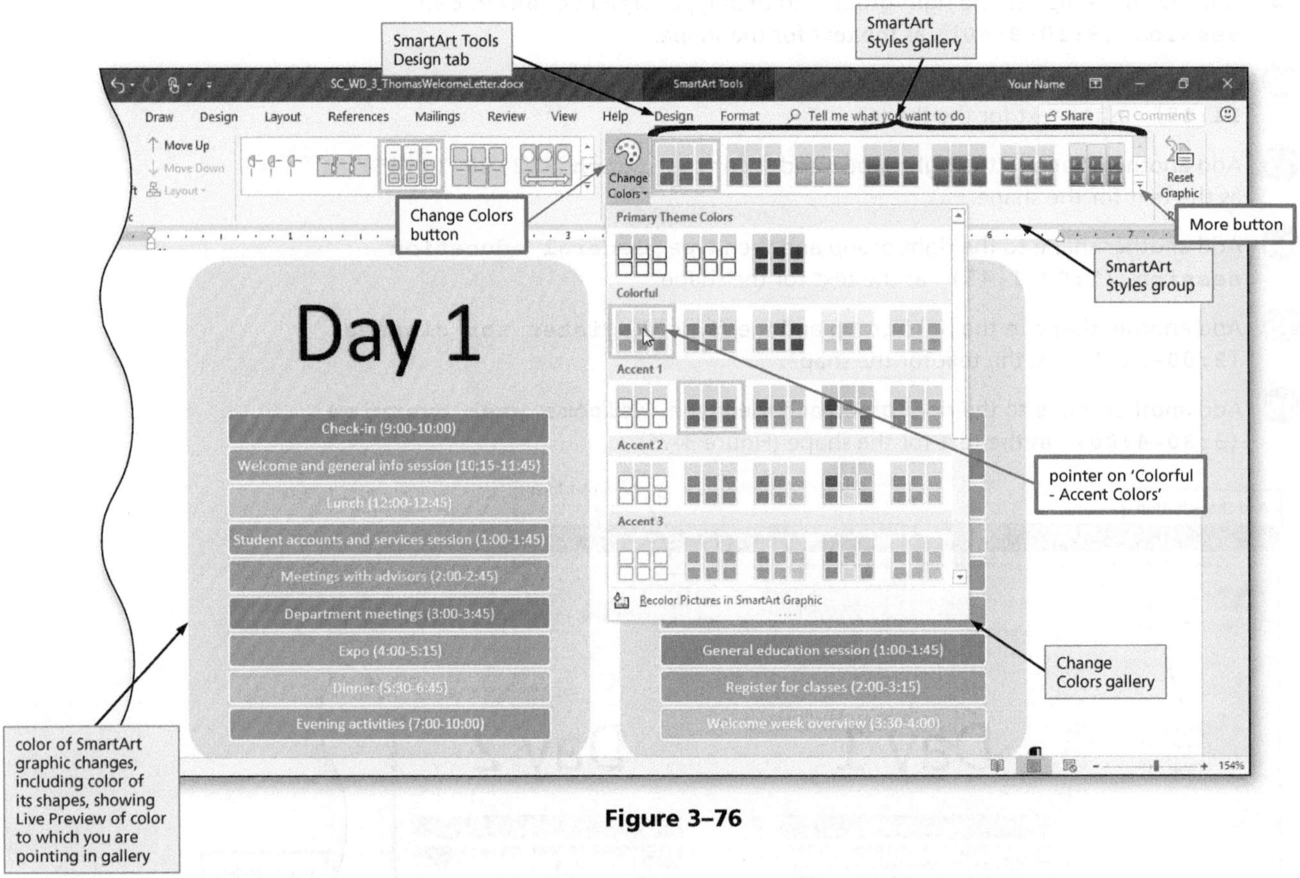

Figure 3–76

- Click 'Colorful - Accent Colors' in the Change Colors gallery to apply the selected color to the SmartArt graphic.

To Apply a SmartArt Style

The next step is to apply a SmartArt style to the SmartArt graphic. ***Why?*** *Word provides a SmartArt Styles gallery, allowing you to change the SmartArt graphic's format to a more visually appealing style.* The following steps apply a SmartArt style to a SmartArt graphic.

- With the SmartArt graphic still selected, click the More button in the SmartArt Styles gallery (shown in Figure 3–76) to expand the SmartArt Styles gallery.
- Point to Subtle Effect in the SmartArt Styles gallery to display a Live Preview of that style applied to the graphic in the document (Figure 3–77).

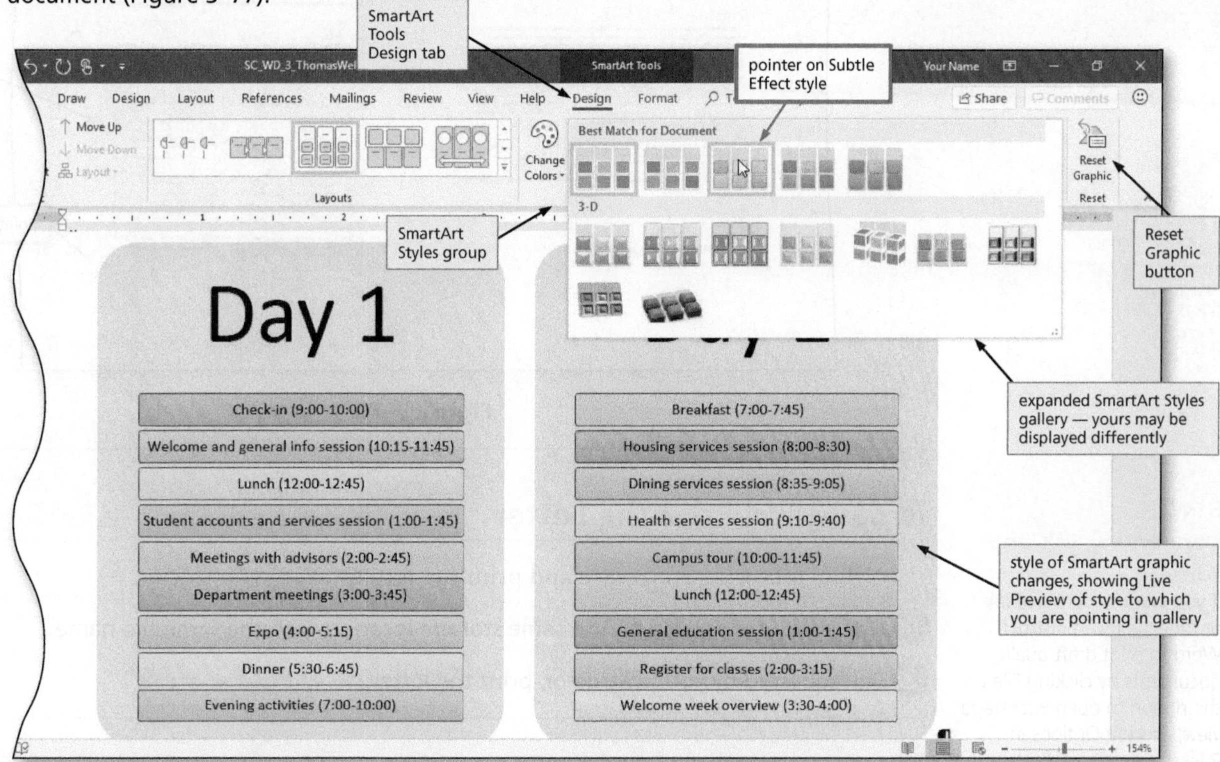

Figure 3–77

Experiment

- Point to various SmartArt styles in the SmartArt Styles gallery and watch the style of the graphic change in the document window.

2

- Click Subtle Effect in the SmartArt Styles gallery to apply the selected style to the SmartArt graphic.

To Resize the SmartArt Graphic

The following steps resize the SmartArt graphic.

1. Display both pages on the screen at once by displaying the View tab and then clicking the Multiple Pages button (View tab | Zoom group).
2. Click the outer edge of the SmartArt graphic to select the entire graphic.
3. Drag the lower-right sizing handle on the SmartArt graphic until it is the same approximate size as in Figure 3–78.
4. Change the zoom to page width by clicking the Page Width button (View tab | Zoom group).

BTW

Resetting Graphics

If you want to remove all formats from a SmartArt graphic and start over, you would click the Reset Graphic button (SmartArt Tools Design tab | Reset group), which is shown in Figure 3–77.

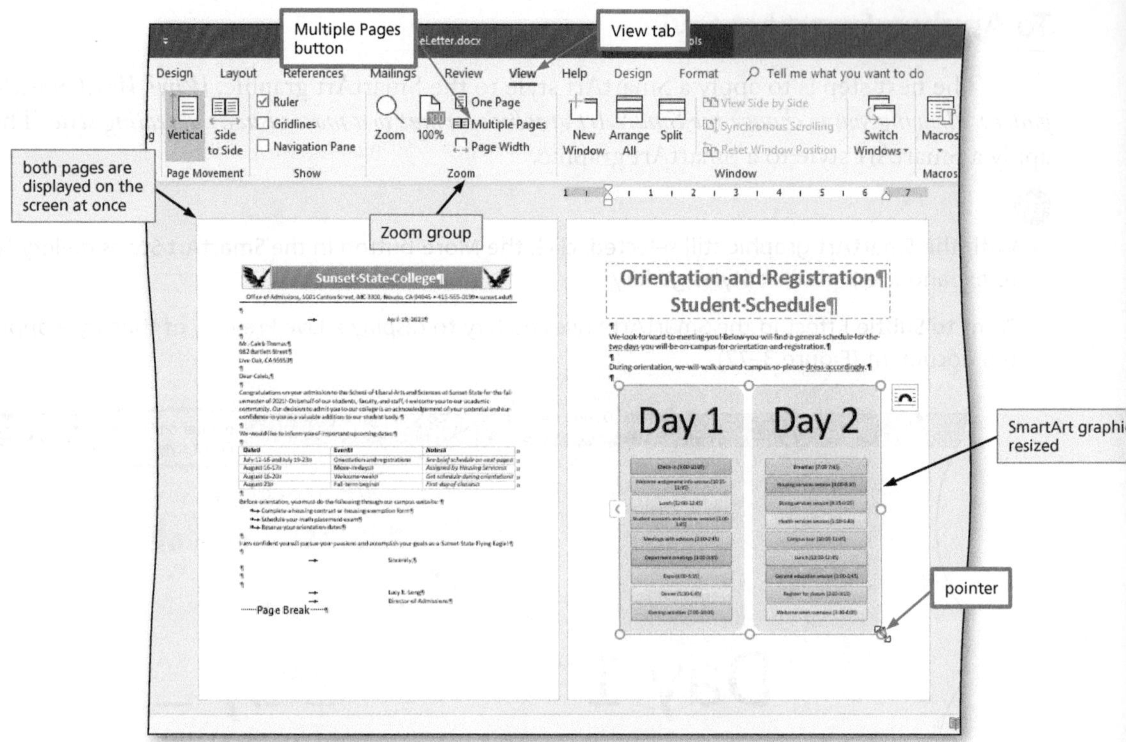

Figure 3–78

BTW

Conserving Ink and Toner

If you want to conserve ink or toner, you can instruct Word to print draft quality documents by clicking File on the ribbon to open Backstage view, clicking Options in Backstage view to display the Word Options dialog box, clicking Advanced in the left pane (Word Options dialog box), scrolling to the Print area in the right pane, placing a check mark in the 'Use draft quality' check box, and then clicking OK. Then, use Backstage view to print the document as usual.

To Save and Print the Letter

The following steps save and print the letter.

1. Save the letter again on the same storage location with the same file name.
2. If requested by your instructor, print the letter.

Enhancing a Document's Accessibility

Word provides several options for enhancing the accessibility of documents for individuals who have difficulty reading. Some tasks you can perform to assist users include increasing zoom and font size, ensuring tab/reading order in tables is logical, and using Read mode. You also can use the accessibility checker to locate and address problematic issues, and you can add alternative text to graphics and tables.

To Use the Accessibility Checker

The accessibility checker scans a document and identifies issues that could affect a person's ability to read the content. Once identified, you can address each individual issue in the document. If you wanted to check accessibility of a document, you would perform the following steps.

1. Open Backstage view and then, if necessary, display the Info gallery.
2. Click the 'Check for Issues' button to display the Check for Issues menu.
3. Click Check Accessibility on the Check for Issues menu, which scans the document and then displays accessibility issues in the Accessibility Checker task pane.
4. Address the errors and warnings in the Accessibility Checker pane and then close the pane.

To Add Alternative Text to Graphics

For users who have difficulty seeing images on the screen, you can include **alternative text**, also called **alt text**, to your graphics so that these users can see or hear the alternative text when working with your document. Graphics you can add alt text to include pictures, shapes, text boxes, SmartArt graphics, and charts. If you wanted to add alternative text to graphics, you would perform the following steps.

1. Click the Alt Text button (Picture Tools Format tab or Drawing Tools Format tab | Accessibility group), or right-click the object and then click Edit Alt Text on the shortcut menu to display the Alt Text pane.
2. Type a narrative description of the graphic in the text box.
3. Close the pane.

To Add Alternative Text to Tables

For users who have difficulty seeing tables on the screen, you can include alternative text to your tables so that these users can see or hear the alternative text when working with your document. If you wanted to add alternative text to a table, sometimes called a table title, you would perform the following steps.

1. Click the Properties button (Table Tools Layout tab | Table group), or right-click the table and then click Table Properties on the shortcut menu to display the Table Properties dialog box.
2. Click the Alt Text tab (Table Properties dialog box) to display the Alt Text sheet.
3. Type a brief title and then type a narrative description of the table in the respective text boxes.
4. Click OK to close the dialog box.

Addressing and Printing Envelopes and Mailing Labels

With Word, you can print mailing address information on an envelope or on a mailing label. Computer-printed addresses look more professional than handwritten ones.

To Address and Print an Envelope

The following steps address and print an envelope. If you are in a lab environment, check with your instructor before performing these steps. ***Why?** Some printers may not accommodate printing envelopes; others may stop printing until an envelope is inserted.*

- Scroll through the letter to display the inside address in the document window.
- Drag through the inside address to select it (Figure 3–79).

- Display the Mailings tab.
- Click the Envelopes button (Mailings tab | Create group) to display the Envelopes and Labels dialog box.

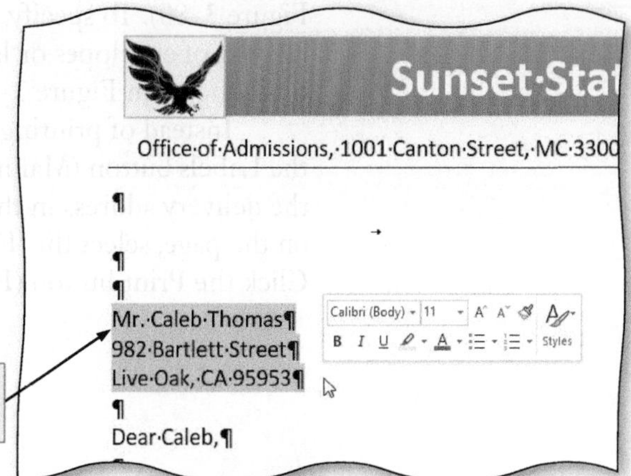

Figure 3–79

- If necessary, click the Envelopes tab (Envelopes and Labels dialog box), which automatically displays the selected delivery address in the dialog box.
- Type the return address as shown in Figure 3–80.

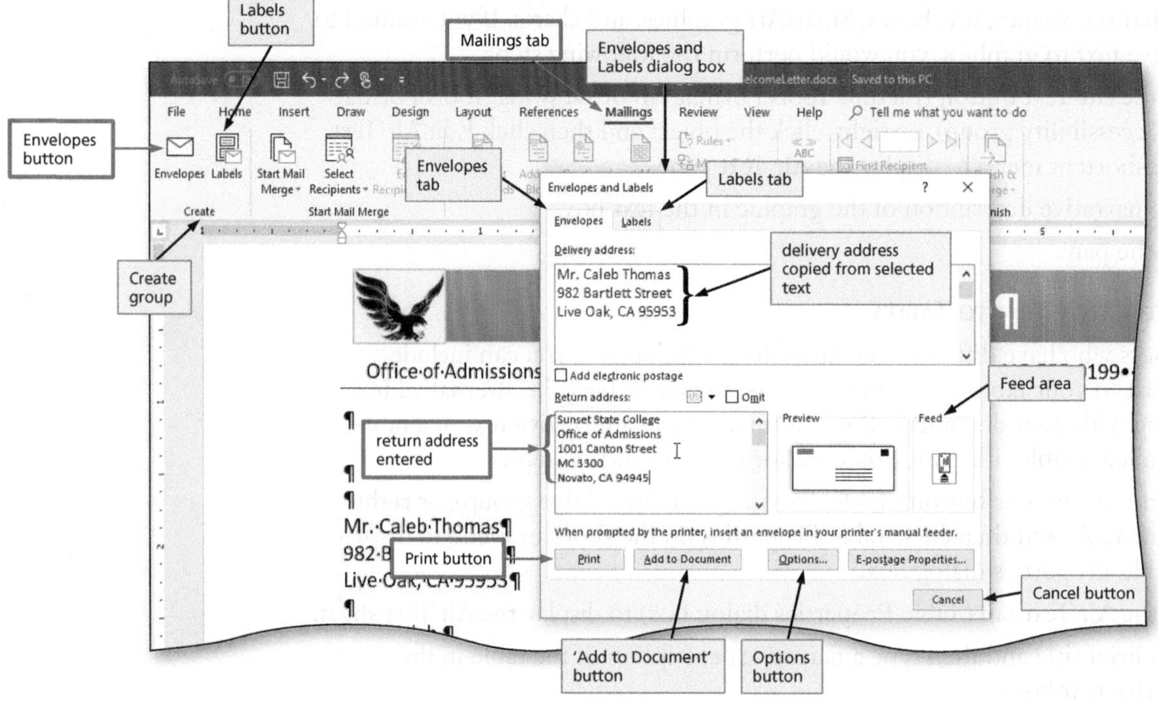

Figure 3–80

- Insert an envelope in your printer, as shown in the Feed area of the dialog box (your Feed area may be different depending on your printer).
- If your printer can print envelopes, click Print (Envelopes and Labels dialog box) to print the envelope; otherwise, click Cancel to close the dialog box.
- **sam** Because the project now is complete, you can exit Word.

Envelopes and Labels

Instead of printing the envelope immediately, you can add it to the document by clicking the 'Add to Document' button (Envelopes and Labels dialog box) (shown in Figure 3–80). To specify a different envelope or label type (identified by a number on the box of envelopes or labels), click the Options button (Envelopes and Labels dialog box) (shown in Figure 3–80).

Instead of printing an envelope, you can print a mailing label. To do this, click the Labels button (Mailings tab | Create group) (shown in Figure 3–80) and then type the delivery address in the Delivery address box. To print the same address on all labels on the page, select the 'Full page of the same label' option button in the Print area. Click the Print button (Envelopes and Labels dialog box) to print the label(s).

Summary

In this module, you have learned how to use Word to insert and format a shape, change text wrapping, insert and format a picture, move and copy objects, insert symbols, add a border, clear formatting, set and use tab stops, insert the current date, insert and format tables, use the format painter, insert and format a SmartArt graphic, and address and print envelopes and mailing labels.

CONSIDER THIS: PLAN AHEAD

What decisions will you need to make when creating your next business letter?

Use these guidelines as you complete the assignments in this module and create your own business letters outside of this class.

1. Create a letterhead.
   a) Ensure that the letterhead contains a complete legal name, mailing address, phone number, and if applicable, fax number, email address, web address, logo, or other image.
   b) Place elements in the letterhead in a visually appealing location.
   c) Format the letterhead with appropriate fonts, font sizes, font styles, and color.
2. Compose an effective business letter.
   a) Include a date line, inside address, message, and signature block.
   b) Use proper spacing and formats for letter contents.
   c) Follow the alignment and spacing guidelines based on the letter style used (i.e., block, modified block, or modified semi-block).
   d) Ensure the message is well written, properly formatted, and logically organized.

BTW

Distributing a Document

Instead of printing and distributing a hard copy of a document, you can distribute the document electronically. Options include sending the document via email; posting it on cloud storage (such as OneDrive) and sharing the file with others; posting it on social media, a blog, or other website; and sharing a link associated with an online location of the document. You also can create and share a PDF or XPS image of the document, so that users can view the file in Acrobat Reader or XPS Viewer instead of in Word.

Apply Your Knowledge

Reinforce the skills and apply the concepts you learned in this module.

Working with Tabs, Tables, and SmartArt Graphics

Note: To complete this assignment, you will be required to use the Data Files. Please contact your instructor for information about accessing the Data Files.

Instructions: Start Word. Open the document called SC_WD_3-1.docx, which is located in the Data Files. The document you open contains a Word table. As relationship coordinator for Pine River Wildlife Refuge, you reach out to previous donors each year and ask if they would consider donating again. Although letters will not go out for several weeks, you want to create some of the letter components at this time. You began composing a Word table of donor categories that you need to edit and format. You also want to create a SmartArt graphic for the letter that identifies how donations are used at the refuge. The revised table, along with the SmartArt graphic you create, is shown in Figure 3–81.

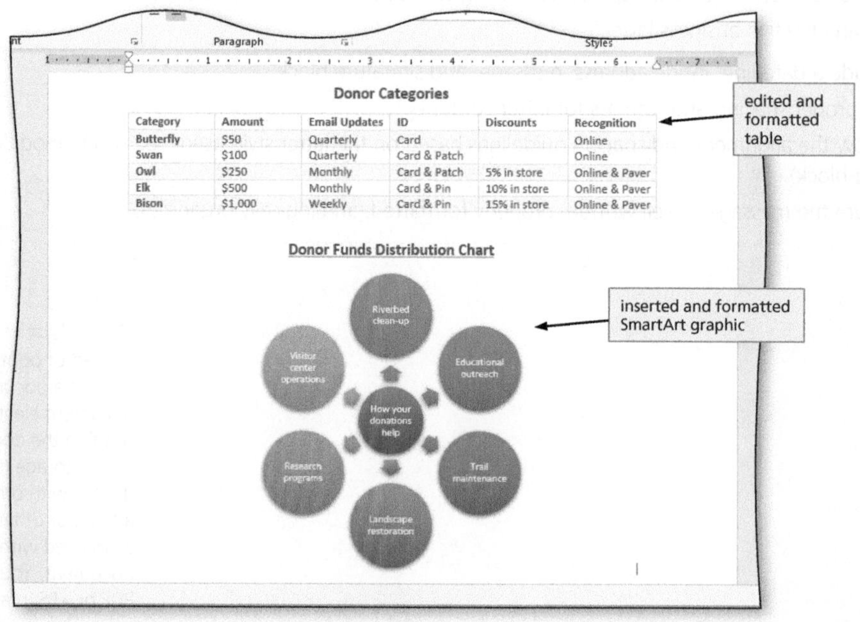

Donor Categories

Category	Amount	Email Updates	ID	Discounts	Recognition
Butterfly	$50	Quarterly	Card		Online
Swan	$100	Quarterly	Card & Patch		Online
Owl	$250	Monthly	Card & Patch	5% in store	Online & Paver
Elk	$500	Monthly	Card & Pin	10% in store	Online & Paver
Bison	$1,000	Weekly	Card & Pin	15% in store	Online & Paver

Figure 3–81

Perform the following tasks:

1. Click File on the ribbon, click Save As, and then save the document using the new file name, SC_WD_3_DonorTableAndSmartArt.
2. In the line containing the table title, Donor Categories, remove the tab stop at the 1" mark on the ruler.
3. Set a centered tab at the 3" mark on the ruler. Move the centered tab stop to the 3.25" mark on the ruler.
4. In the line containing the SmartArt graphic title, Donor Funds Distribution Chart, remove (clear) all tab stops.
5. Bold the characters in the Donor Categories title. Use the 'Increase Font Size' button to increase their font size to 16. Use the 'Decrease Font Size' button to decrease their font size to 14. Change their color to Blue, Accent 1, Darker 25%.

6. Use the format painter to copy the formatting from the table title paragraph to the SmartArt graphic title paragraph (so that the SmartArt graphic title has a centered tab stop at the 3.25" mark on the ruler and has the same text formats).
7. Apply the underline style called Thick underline below the characters in the Donor Funds Distribution Chart title. Change the underline color to Orange, Accent 2, Lighter 40%.
8. In the table, select one of the duplicate rows containing the Butterfly category and delete the row.
9. In the table, select one of the duplicate columns containing the Recognitions and delete the column.
10. Insert a column between the Amount and ID columns. Fill in the column as follows:

    Column Title – Email Updates

    Butterfly – Quarterly

    Swan – Quarterly

    Owl – Monthly

    Bison – Weekly
11. Insert a new row above the bison row. In the first cell of the new row, enter the word, Elk, in the cell. Fill in the cells in the remainder of the row as follows:

    Amount – $500

    Email Updates – Monthly

    ID – Card & Pin

    Discounts – 10% in store

    Recognition – Online & Paver
12. In the Table Style Options group (Table Tools Design tab), ensure that these check boxes have check marks: Header Row, Banded Rows, and First Column. The Total Row, Last Column, and Banded Columns check boxes should not have check marks.
13. Apply the Grid Table 6 Colorful - Accent 4 style to the table.
14. Select the entire table. Change the font color of all text in the selected table to Blue, Accent 1, Darker 25%.
15. Position the insertion point at the end of the Donor Funds Distribution Chart title and then press ENTER. Clear formatting on this new line and then center the insertion point on the line.
16. On the blank line below the title Donor Funds Distribution Chart, insert a Diverging Radial SmartArt graphic (in the Cycle category). Add two shapes to the inserted SmartArt graphic.
17. In the SmartArt graphic, enter the text, How your donations help, in the center shape. In the exterior shapes, starting with the top and moving clockwise, enter this text: Riverbed clean-up, Educational outreach, Trail maintenance, Landscape restoration, Research programs, and Visitor center operations. (Note: if the placeholder text does not appear, open the Text Pane to add the text.)
18. Change the SmartArt colors to Colorful Range - Accent Colors 2 to 3, and apply the SmartArt Style called Intense Effect.
19. If requested by your instructor, enter your name on the line below the table.
20. Save the document again with the same file name.
21. Submit the modified document, shown in Figure 3–81, in the format specified by your instructor.
22. Exit Word.
23. If you wanted to add a row to the end of the table, how would you add the row?

Extend Your Knowledge

Extend the skills you learned in this module and experiment with new skills. You may need to use Help to complete the assignment.

Working with Shapes and Pictures

Note: To complete this assignment, you will be required to use the Data Files. Please contact your instructor for information about accessing the Data Files.

Instructions: Start Word. Open the document, SC_WD_3-2.docx, which is located in the Data Files. The document is a draft of a letter you began earlier this week. As community education coordinator for Midland Medical Center, you are responsible for sending confirmation letters to those who have signed up for education workshops offered by the center. You will work with shapes and pictures to design the letterhead in the letter and will complete the table so that the letter is ready to send.

Perform the following tasks:

1. Use Help to learn about grouping objects and the formatting pictures and shapes.
2. Click File on the ribbon, click Save As, and then save the document using the new file name, SC_WD_3_ConfirmationLetter.
3. Select the arrow shape at the top of the letter. Drag the rotate handle on top of the selected shape clockwise and watch the shape rotate. Delete the selected shape.
4. Insert a Rectangle: Rounded Corners shape at the top of the letter, sizing it across the top of the page. Drag the edges to form a rectangle. After drawing the shape, specify the exact dimensions of a height of 0.7" and a width of 6.5".
5. Position the shape in the 'Position in Top Center with Square Text Wrapping' using the Position button (Drawing Tools Format tab | Arrange group). Then, change the text wrapping to 'Top and Bottom'.
6. Apply a shape style of your choosing to the shape. Enter the text, Midland Medical Center, in the shape. Format the text as you deem appropriate. Apply an appropriate shape outline to the shape. Apply a shape effect of your choosing to the shape.
7. Resize the caduceus picture to 50 percent of its original size. With the picture inline, click the paragraph mark to the right of the picture and then click the Center button (Home tab | Paragraph group). Then, click the Align Right button (Home tab | Paragraph group). How do you move inline pictures?
8. Resize the picture so its height is exactly 0.6" and its width is 0.48". Change the text wrapping of the picture to 'In Front of Text'. Click the Position button (Picture Tools Format tab | Arrange group) and select different options. Click the Align button (Picture Tools Format tab | Arrange group) and select different alignments. Drag the picture into the shape (Figure 3–82). How do you move floating pictures?
9. Change the brightness and contrast of the picture as you deem appropriate. Copy the picture. Use Paste Options arrow to paste as a Picture. Is the pasted picture an inline or floating object? Delete the pasted picture. Use the Paste Options arrow to paste with source formatting. Why did it paste the picture as a floating object this time? Drag the picture into the shape.
10. Rotate one of the pictures 90 degrees to the right. Rotate the same picture 90 degrees to the right again. Flip the same picture vertically. Flip the same picture horizontally.
11. Recolor one of the pictures to a color of your choice. Add a border color of your choice to the same picture. Use the Reset Picture button (Picture Tools Format tab | Adjust group) to clear the formatting of this picture. How would you reset the formatting and the size of the picture?

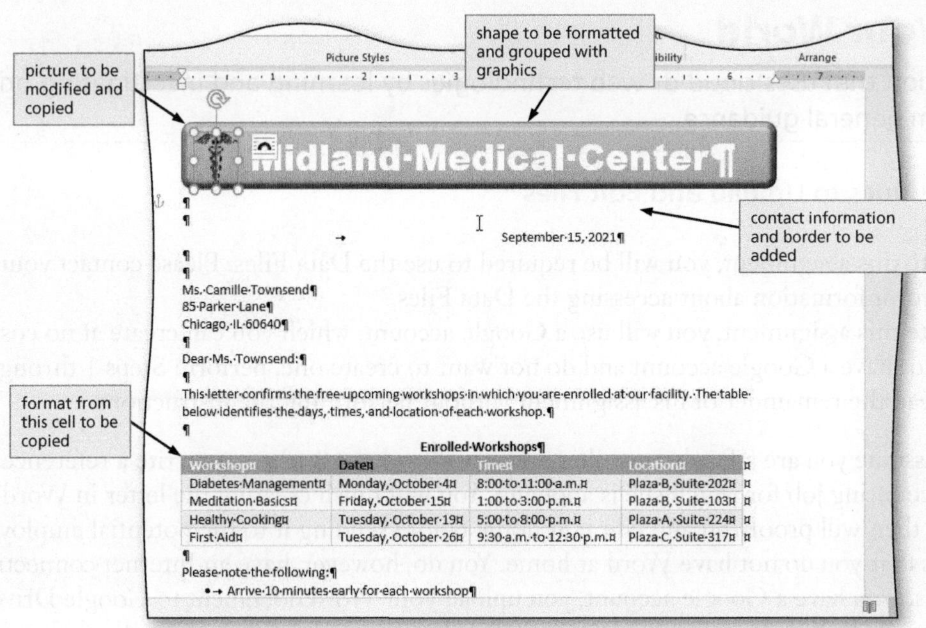

Figure 3–82

12. Select the shape around the Midland Medical Center title and then use the Edit Shape button (Drawing Tools Format tab | Insert Shapes group) to change the shape to a shape of your preference.
13. Group the two caduceus pictures with the shape. Change the text wrapping of the grouped shape to Top and Bottom.
14. Add the contact information below the shape, using a symbol of your choice from the Symbol gallery between the mailing address (101 Carrington Road, Chicago, IL 60640), phone number (312-555-0198), web address (midlandmc.net), and email address (info@midlandmc.net).
15. Add a bottom border to the paragraph containing the contact information.
16. Select the table in the letter and center it between the margins.
17. Select the upper-left cell in the table that contains the text, Workshop. Use the format painter to copy the formats of the selected cell to the cell immediately to the right with the text, Date.
18. Position the insertion point in the table and one at a time, select and deselect each check box in the Table Style Options group. What are the functions of each check box: Header Row, Total Row, Banded Rows, First Column, Last Column, and Banded Columns? Select the check boxes you prefer for the table.
19. If requested by your instructor, change the name in the signature block to your name.
20. Save the document again with the same file name.
21. Submit the modified document in the format specified by your instructor.
22. If requested by your instructor, create an envelope for the letter.
23. If requested by your instructor, print a single mailing label for the letter and then a full page of mailing labels, each containing the address shown in Figure 3–82.
24. Answer the questions posed in #7, #8, #9, #11, and #18. Why would you group objects? (If requested by your instructor, insert a next page section break at the end of the letter and write your responses on the inserted blank page and insert the current time.)

Expand Your World

Create a solution that uses cloud or web technologies by learning and investigating on your own from general guidance.

Using Google Docs to Upload and Edit Files

Notes:

- To complete this assignment, you will be required to use the Data Files. Please contact your instructor for information about accessing the Data Files.
- To complete this assignment, you will use a Google account, which you can create at no cost. If you do not have a Google account and do not want to create one, perform Steps 1 through 3 and then read the remainder of his assignment without performing the instructions.

Instructions: Assume you are a faculty member and a student has asked you to write a reference letter for an accounting job for which she is applying. You will finish creating the letter in Word at your office and then will proofread and edit it at home before sending it to the potential employer. The problem is that you do not have Word at home. You do, however, have an Internet connection at home. Because you have a Google account, you upload your Word document to Google Drive so that you can view and edit it later from a computer that does not have Word installed.

Perform the following tasks:

1. In Word, open the document, SC_WD_3-3.docx, from the Data Files. Click File on the ribbon, click Save As, and then save the document using the new file name, SC_WD_3_ReferenceLetter.
2. Add a box border around the two paragraphs containing the name, Prof. Kim Chung, and the contact information in the letterhead. Select style, width, and color for the box border other than the default. Apply a shading color to the paragraph containing the name.
3. Look through the letter so that you are familiar with its contents and formats. If desired, print the letter so that you easily can compare it to the Google Docs converted file. Close the document.
4. Start a browser. Search for the text, google docs, using a search engine. Visit several websites to learn about Google Docs and Google Drive. Navigate to the Google website. Read about how to create files in Google Docs and upload files to Google Drive. If you do not have a Google account and you want to create one, follow the instructions to create an account. If you do not have a Google account and you do not want to create one, read the remaining instructions without performing them. If you have a Google account, sign in to your account.
5. If necessary, display Google Drive. Upload the file, SC_WD_3_ReferenceLetter.docx, to Google Drive.
6. Rename the file on Google Drive to SC_WD_3_ReferenceLetter_inGoogle. Open the file in Google Docs (Figure 3–83). What differences do you see between the Word document and the Google Docs converted document?
7. Modify the document in Google Docs as follows: change the font and font size of the name in the letterhead, bold the name in the letterhead, change the font color of the name in the letterhead, change the background color for the paragraph containing the name, change the border color around the letterhead, change the name of the insurance company to Wide Country Insurance, and then display the document at various zoom levels.
8. If requested by your instructor, change the name in the letterhead and signature block to your name.

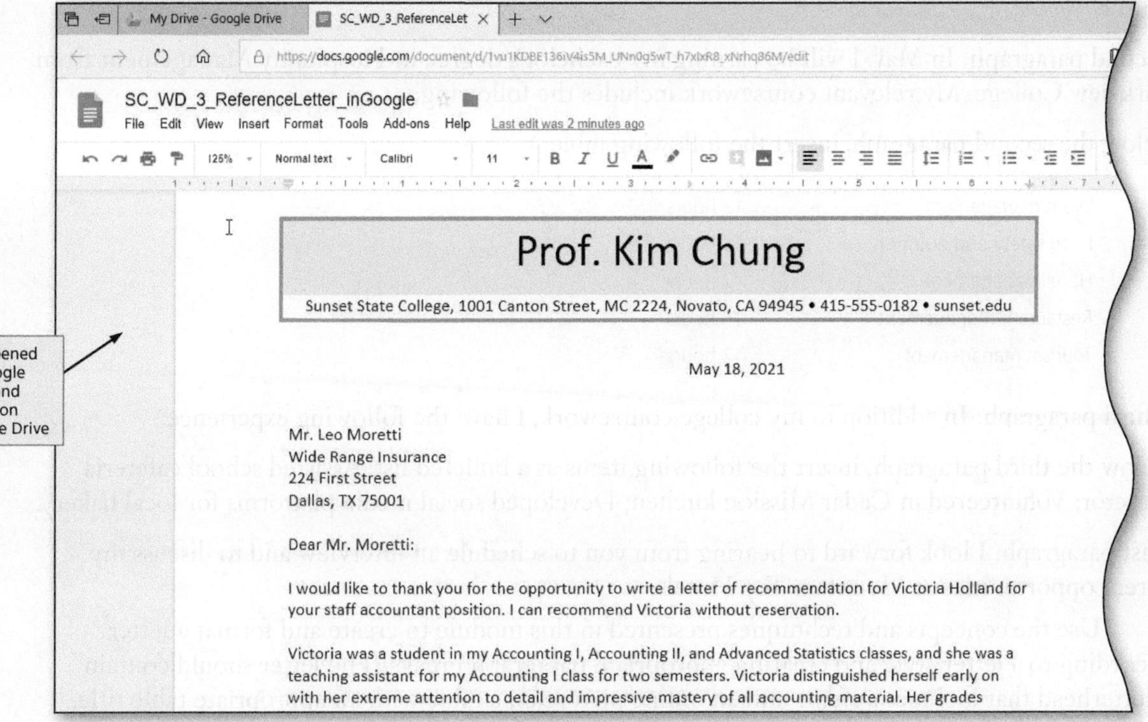

Figure 3–83

9. Download the revised document to your local storage media, changing its format to Microsoft Word. Submit the document in the format requested by your instructor.
10. What is Google Drive? What is Google Docs? Answer the question posed in #6. Do you prefer using Google Docs or Word? Why?

In the Lab

Design and implement a solution using creative thinking and problem-solving skills.

Create a Letter to a Potential Employer

Problem: As an extern in the career development office at your school, your boss has asked you to prepare a sample letter to a potential employer in the hospitality industry. Students on campus seeking employment will use this letter as a reference document when creating their own letters.

Perform the following tasks:

Part 1: Using your name, mailing address, phone number, and email address, create a letterhead for the letter. Be sure to include an image in the letterhead and appropriate separator lines and marks. Once the letterhead is designed, write the letter to this potential employer: Ms. Lynette Galens, Human Resources Director, Mountain Top Hotels, 125 Cedar Road, P.O. Box 1250, Denver, CO 80230.

The draft wording for the letter is as follows:

First paragraph: I am responding to your online advertisement for the assistant manager position. I have the credentials you are seeking and believe I can be a valuable asset to Mountain Top Hotels.

Continued >

In the Lab *continued*

Second paragraph: In May, I will be earning my bachelor's degree in Hospitality Management from Parkview College. My relevant coursework includes the following:

Below the second paragraph, insert the following table:

Event management	12 hours
Food safety and nutrition	15 hours
Hotel management	12 hours
Restaurant management	18 hours
Tourism management	12 hours

Third paragraph: In addition to my college coursework, I have the following experience:

Below the third paragraph, insert the following items as a bulleted list: Assisted school cafeteria director; Volunteered in Cedar Mission kitchen; Developed social media platforms for local bakery.

Last paragraph: I look forward to hearing from you to schedule an interview and to discuss my career opportunities at Mountain Top Hotels.

Use the concepts and techniques presented in this module to create and format a letter according to a letter style and creating appropriate paragraph breaks. The letter should contain a letterhead that includes a shape and an online picture(s); a table with an appropriate table title, column headings, and table style applied (unformatted table contents listed above); and a bulleted list (unformatted experience list items above). If requested by your instructor, insert nonbreaking spaces in the company name, Mountain Top Hotels. If requested by your instructor, set a transparent color in the picture.

While creating the letter, be sure to do the following:

1. Create a letterhead: insert and format a shape, insert and format at least one online picture, insert symbols from the Symbol gallery in the contact line, and add a paragraph border.
2. Create the letter contents: apply the No Spacing style, set left-aligned tab stops where appropriate, insert the current date, insert the table and format it, center the table, bullet the list as you type it, and use your name in the signature line in the letter.
3. Be sure to check the spelling and grammar of the finished letter.
4. Add alt text to the table and to the picture(s) in the document. Check the document accessibility of the finished letter.

When you are finished with the letter, save it with the file name, SC_WD_3_LetterToEmployer. Submit your assignment and answers to the Part 2 critical thinking questions in the format specified by your instructor.

Part 2: You made several decisions while creating the letter in this assignment: where to position elements in the letterhead, how to format elements in the letterhead, which shape and picture(s) to use in the letterhead, which font size to use for the letter text, which table style to use, and which letter style to use. What was the rationale behind each of these decisions?

File Home Insert Draw Design Transitions Animations Slide Show Review View Hel

1 Creating and Editing Presentations with Pictures

Objectives

After completing his module, you will be able to:

- Create a blank presentation
- Select and change a document theme
- Create a title slide and a text slide with a multilevel bulleted list
- Add new slides and change slide layouts
- Change font size and color
- Bold, italicize, and underline text
- Insert pictures into slides with and without content placeholders
- Move and resize pictures
- Arrange slides
- Change theme colors
- Check spelling
- Review a presentation in different views
- Enter slide notes
- Save a presentation
- Print a presentation

What Is PowerPoint?

BTW
Office Suite
PowerPoint is part of the Microsoft Office 365 suite; other apps in the suite include Microsoft Word, Microsoft Excel, Microsoft Outlook, Microsoft OneNote, and Microsoft OneDrive, and on your PC, Microsoft Access and Microsoft Publisher. Apps in a suite, such as Microsoft Office, typically use a similar interface and share features.

Microsoft PowerPoint, or PowerPoint, is a full-featured presentation app that allows you to produce compelling presentations to deliver and share with an audience. A PowerPoint **presentation** also is called a **slide show**. The collection of slides in a presentation is called a **deck**, resembling a deck of cards that are stacked on top of each other. A common use of slide decks is to enhance an oral presentation. A speaker might desire to convey information, such as urging students to volunteer at a fund-raising event, explaining changes in employee compensation packages, or describing a new laboratory procedure. The PowerPoint slides should reinforce the speaker's message and help the audience retain the information presented. PowerPoint contains many features to plan, develop, and organize slides, including providing design ideas, formatting text, adding and editing video and audio clips, creating tables and charts, applying artistic effects to pictures, animating graphics, and collaborating with friends and colleagues. An accompanying handout gives audience members reference notes and review material for your presentation.

BTW

The PowerPoint Window

The modules in this book begin with the PowerPoint window appearing as it did at the initial installation of the software. Your PowerPoint window may look different depending on your screen resolution and other PowerPoint settings.

A PowerPoint presentation can help you deliver a dynamic, professional-looking message to an audience. PowerPoint allows you to produce slides to use in academic, business, or other environments. Custom slides can fit your specific needs and contain diagrams, charts, tables, pictures, shapes, video, sound, and animation effects to make your presentation more effective. You then can print a handout, turn your presentation into a video, broadcast your slide show on the web, or create a photo album.

To illustrate the features of PowerPoint, this book presents a series of projects that use PowerPoint to create presentations like those you will encounter in business environments.

Project: Presentation with a Bulleted List and Pictures

In this module's project, you will follow proper design guidelines and learn to use PowerPoint to create, save, and view the slides shown in Figures 1–1a through 1–1d. The objective is to produce a presentation, titled Pet Hospital, to promote the care provided at the Shelly Pet Hospital & Wellness Center. This slide show has a variety of pictures and visual elements to add interest and give facts about the Center. Some of the text has formatting and color enhancements, and the slides have a variety of layouts.

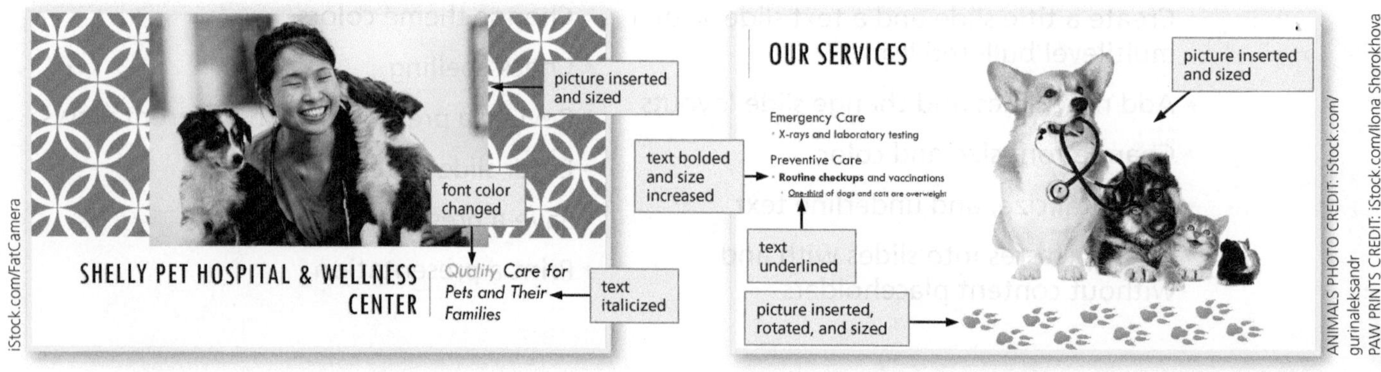

iStock.com/FatCamera

ANIMALS PHOTO CREDIT: iStock.com/gurinaleksandr
PAW PRINTS CREDIT: iStock.com/Ilona Shorokhova

(a) Slide 1 (Title Slide with Picture)

(b) Slide 2 (Multilevel Bulleted List with Picture)

iStock.com/M_a_y_a

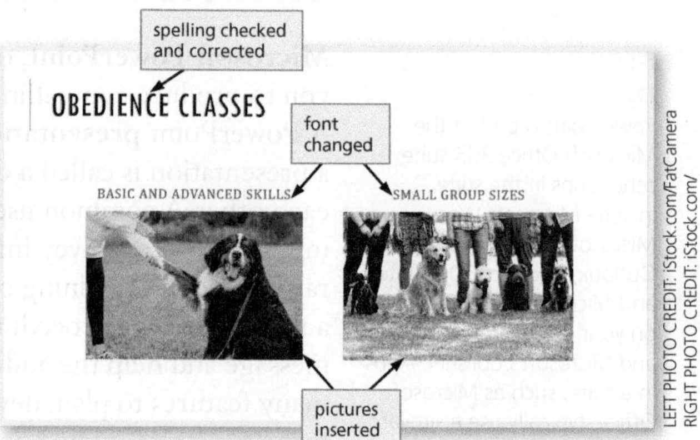

LEFT PHOTO CREDIT: iStock.com/FatCamera
RIGHT PHOTO CREDIT: iStock.com/Highwaystarz-Photography

(c) Slide 3 (Title and Picture)

(d) Slide 4 (Comparison Layout and Pictures)

Figure 1–1

In this module, you will learn how to perform basic tasks using PowerPoint. You will perform the following general tasks as you progress through this module:

1. Start and use PowerPoint.
2. Insert four presentation slides, using various layouts.
3. Enter and format the text on each slide.
4. Insert, size, and position pictures.
5. Display the slides.
6. Correct errors and print the slides.

BTW
Ribbon and Screen Resolution
PowerPoint may change how the groups and buttons within the groups appear on the ribbon, depending on the screen resolution of your computer. Thus, your ribbon may look different from the ones in this book if you are using a screen resolution other than 1366 × 768.

Starting and Using PowerPoint

To use PowerPoint, you must instruct the operating system (such as Windows) to start the app. The following sections start PowerPoint and discuss some elements of PowerPoint.

If you are using a computer or device to step through the project in this module and you want your screen to match the figures in this book, you should change your screen's resolution to 1366 × 768.

BTW
Resolution
For information about how to change a computer's resolution, search for 'change resolution' in your operating system's help files.

To Start PowerPoint and Create a Blank Presentation

The following steps, which assume Windows is running, start PowerPoint and create a blank presentation based on a typical installation. You may need to ask your instructor how to start PowerPoint on your computer or device.

1 sam

- Click Start on the Windows taskbar to display the Start menu.

Q&A What is a menu?
A **menu** contains a list of related items, including commands, apps, and folders. Each **command** on a menu performs a specific action, such as saving a file or obtaining help. A **folder** is a named location on a storage medium that usually contains related documents.

- If necessary, scroll through the list of apps on the Start menu until the PowerPoint app name appears (Figure 1–2).

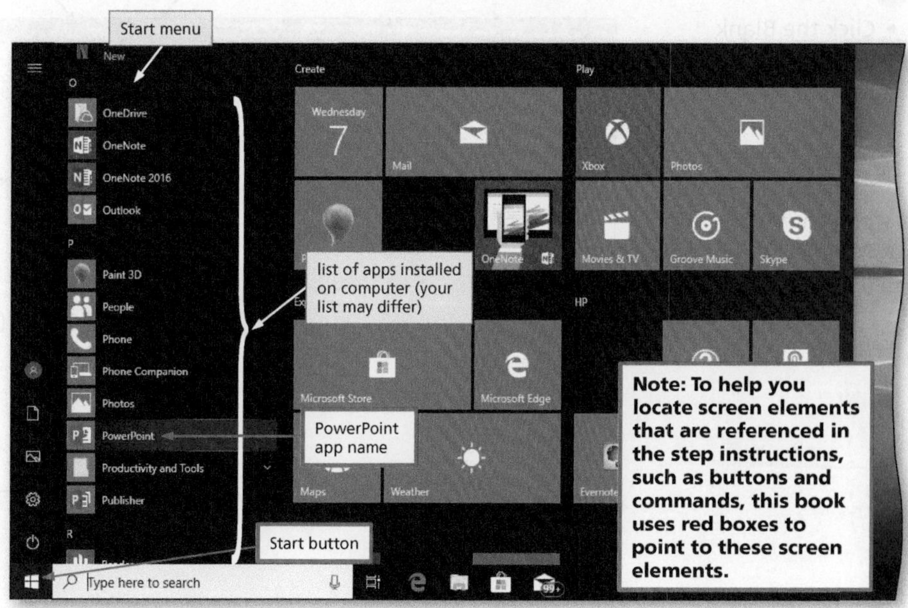

Figure 1–2

Q&A What if my PowerPoint app is in a folder?
Click the appropriate folder name to display the contents of the folder and then click the PowerPoint app name.

2

- Click PowerPoint on the Start menu to start PowerPoint (Figure 1–3).

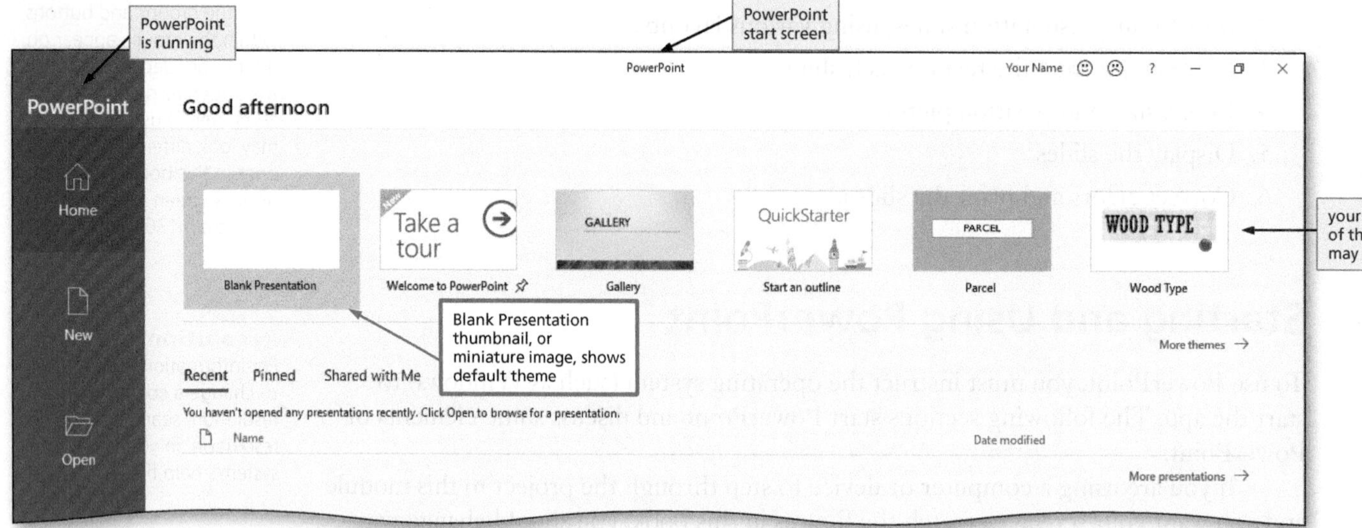

Figure 1–3

Other Ways

1. Type app name in Windows search box, click app name in results list
2. Double-click PowerPoint icon on desktop, if one is present

3

- Click the Blank Presentation thumbnail on the PowerPoint start screen to create a blank PowerPoint presentation in the PowerPoint window (Figure 1–4).

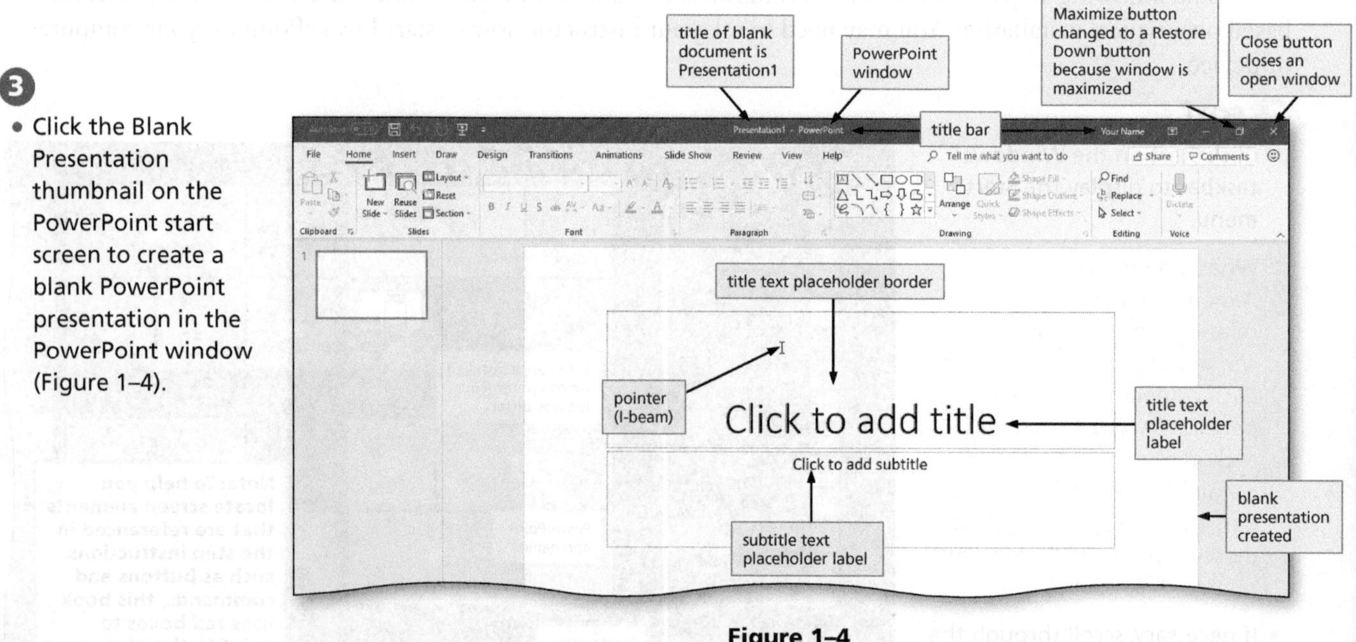

Figure 1–4

4

- If the PowerPoint window is not maximized, click the Maximize button next to the Close button on the title bar to maximize the window.

Q&A

How do I know whether a window is maximized?

A window is maximized if it fills the entire display area and the Restore Down button is displayed on the title bar.

The PowerPoint Window

The PowerPoint window consists of a variety of components to make your work more efficient and presentations more professional: the window, ribbon, Tell Me box, Mini toolbar, shortcut menus, Quick Access Toolbar, and Microsoft Account area. Most of these elements are common to other Microsoft Office apps; others are unique to PowerPoint.

The basic unit of a PowerPoint presentation is a **slide**. A slide may contain text and objects, such as graphics, tables, charts, and drawings. When you create a new presentation, the default **Title Slide** layout appears (shown in Figure 1–4). PowerPoint includes several other built-in standard layouts. All layouts except the Blank slide layout contain placeholders for text or other content such as pictures, charts, or videos. The title slide in Figure 1–4 has two text placeholders for the main heading, or title, and the subtitle.

In the slide, the **insertion point** is a blinking vertical line that indicates where text, pictures, and other objects will be inserted. When you type, the insertion point moves to the right, and when you reach the end of a placeholder, it moves down to the beginning of the next line. The **pointer** is a small screen icon that moves as you move a mouse or pointing device on a surface and becomes different shapes depending on the task you are performing in PowerPoint. You move the pointer with a pointing device, such as a mouse or touchpad. The pointer in Figure 1–4 is the shape of an I-beam.

Scroll Bar You use a **scroll bar** to display different portions of a presentation in the window. At the right edge of the window is a vertical scroll bar. If a slide is too wide to fit in the window, a horizontal scroll bar also appears at the bottom of the window. On a scroll bar, the position of the **scroll box** reflects the location of the portion of the slide that is displayed in the window. A small triangular **scroll arrow** is located at each end of a scroll bar. To scroll through or display different portions of the slide in the window, you can click a scroll arrow or drag the scroll box.

Status Bar The **status bar**, located at the bottom of the window above the Windows taskbar, presents information about the presentation, the progress of current tasks, and the status of certain commands and keys; it also provides controls for viewing the presentation. As you type text or perform certain tasks, various indicators and buttons may appear on the status bar.

The left side of the status bar in Figure 1–5 shows the current slide number followed by the total number of slides in the presentation. The right side of the status bar includes buttons and controls you can use to change the view of a slide and adjust the size of the displayed slide.

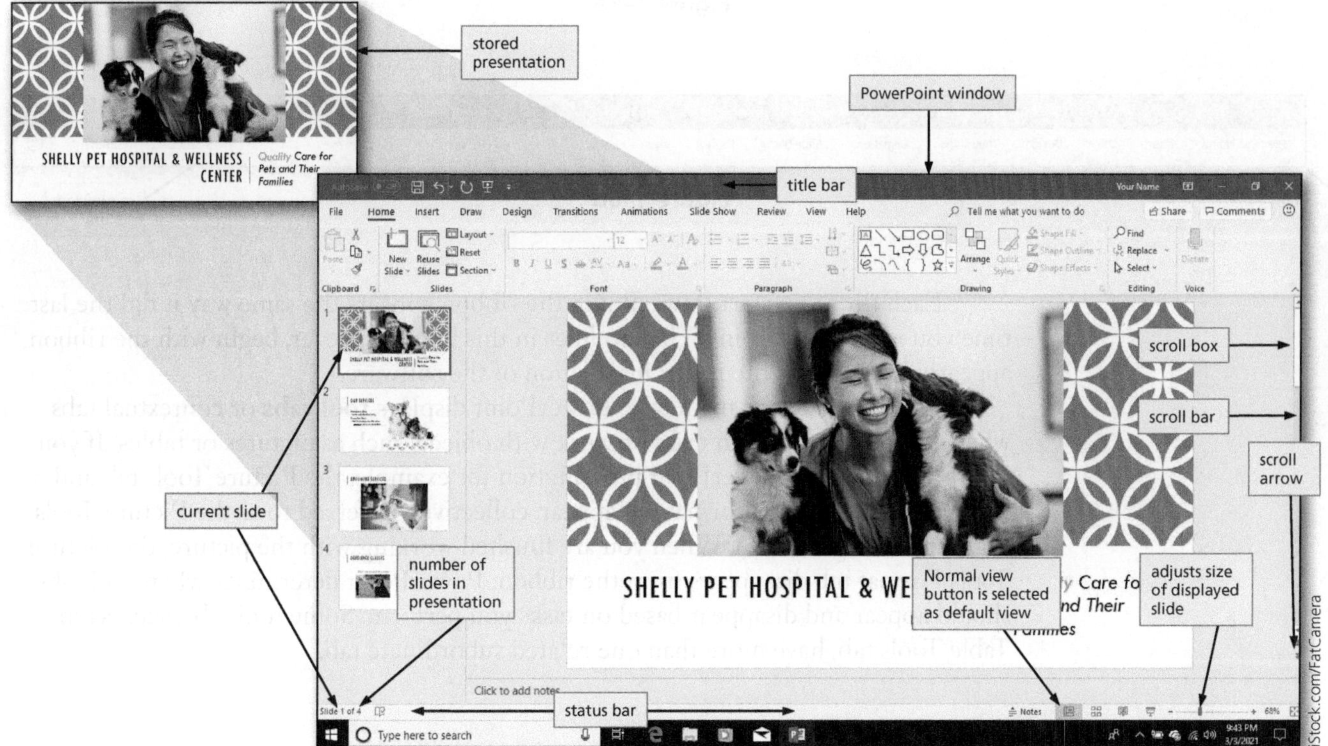

Figure 1–5

Ribbon The **ribbon**, located near the top of the PowerPoint window below the title bar, is the control center in PowerPoint (Figure 1–6a). The ribbon provides easy, central access to the tasks you perform while creating a presentation. The ribbon consists of tabs (pages) of grouped command buttons that you click to interact with PowerPoint. Each **tab** contains a collection of groups, and each **group** contains related command buttons and boxes.

When you start PowerPoint, the ribbon initially displays several main tabs, also called default or top-level tabs. The **Home tab**, also called the primary tab, contains the more frequently used commands. The ribbon tab currently displayed is called the **active tab**.

To display more of the slide in the window, some users prefer to minimize the ribbon, which hides the groups on the ribbon and displays only the main tabs (Figure 1–6b). To minimize the ribbon, click the 'Collapse the Ribbon' button or click the 'Ribbon Display Options' button and then click Show Tabs on the menu. To use commands on a minimized ribbon, click the tab that you wish to expand. To expand the ribbon, double-click a tab, click the 'Pin the Ribbon' button on an expanded tab, or click the 'Ribbon Display Options' button and then click 'Show Tabs and Commands' on the menu.

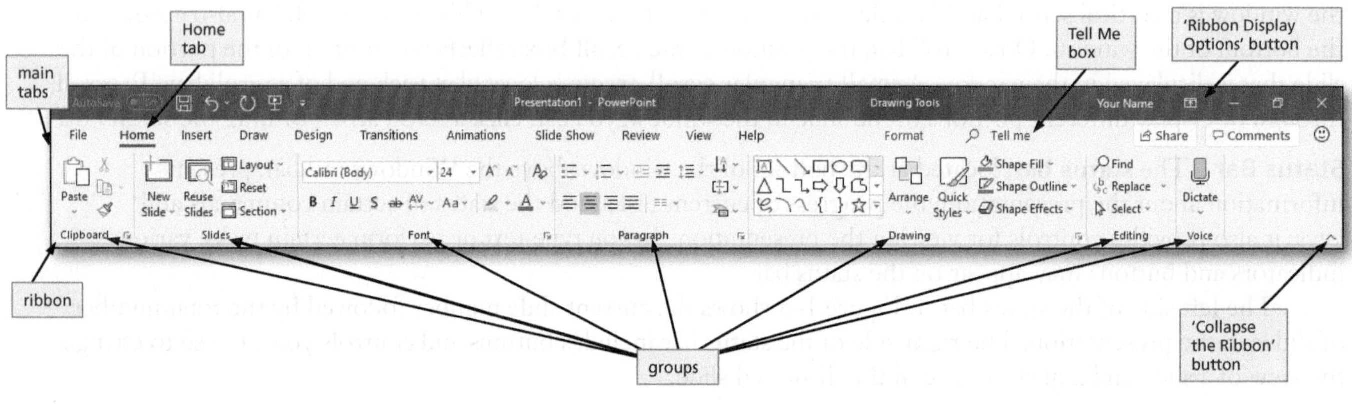

Figure 1–6a

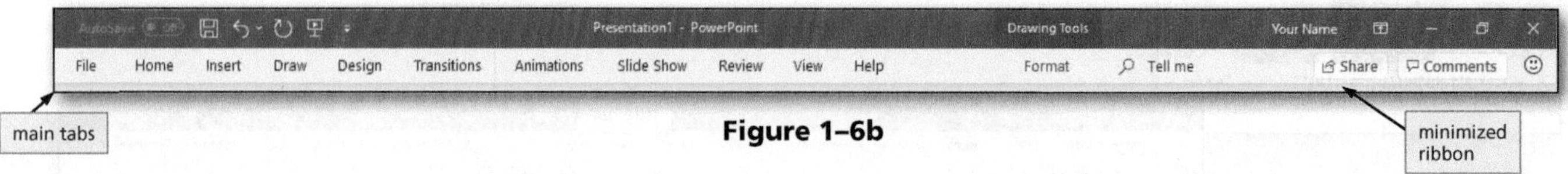

Figure 1–6b

Each time you start PowerPoint, the ribbon appears the same way it did the last time you used PowerPoint. The modules in this book, however, begin with the ribbon appearing as it did at the initial installation of the software.

In addition to the main tabs, PowerPoint displays **tool tabs** or contextual tabs when you perform certain tasks or work with objects such as pictures or tables. If you insert a picture in a PowerPoint presentation for example, the Picture Tools tab and its related subordinate Format tab appear, collectively referred to as the Picture Tools Format tab (Figure 1–7). When you are finished working with the picture, the Picture Tools Format tab disappears from the ribbon. PowerPoint determines when tool tabs should appear and disappear based on tasks you perform. Some tool tabs, such as the Table Tools tab, have more than one related subordinate tab.

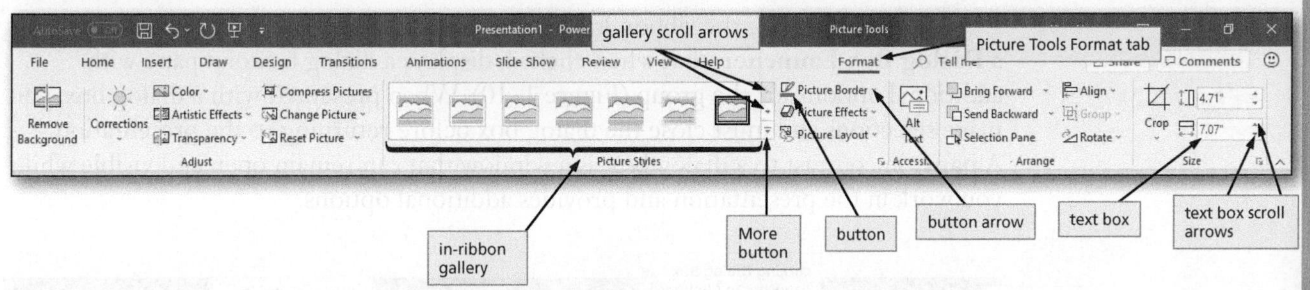

Figure 1–7

Groups on the ribbon include buttons, boxes (text boxes, check boxes, etc.), and galleries (Figure 1–8). A **gallery** is a collection of choices, often graphical, arranged in a grid or in a list that you can browse through before making a selection. You can scroll through choices in an in-ribbon gallery by clicking the gallery's scroll arrows. Or, you can click a gallery's More button to view more gallery options on the screen at a time.

Some buttons and boxes have arrows that, when clicked, also display a gallery; others always cause a gallery to be displayed when clicked. Most galleries support **Live Preview**, a feature that allows you to point to a gallery choice and see its effect in the presentation without actually selecting the choice.

Figure 1–8

Some commands on the ribbon display an image to help you remember their function. When you point to a command on the ribbon, all or part of the command glows in a shade of gray, and a ScreenTip appears on the screen. A **ScreenTip** is a label that appears when you point to a button or object that provides the name of the command, its purpose, available keyboard shortcut(s), and sometimes instructions for how to obtain help about the command (Figure 1–9).

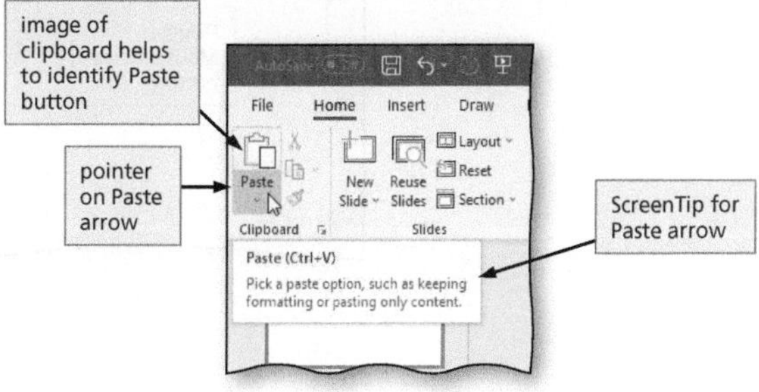

Figure 1–9

Some groups on the ribbon have a small arrow in the lower-right corner, called a **Dialog Box Launcher**, that when clicked, displays a dialog box or a pane with additional options for the group (Figure 1–10). When presented with a dialog box, you make selections and must close the dialog box before returning to the presentation. A **pane**, in contrast to a dialog box, is a window that can remain open and visible while you work in the presentation and provides additional options.

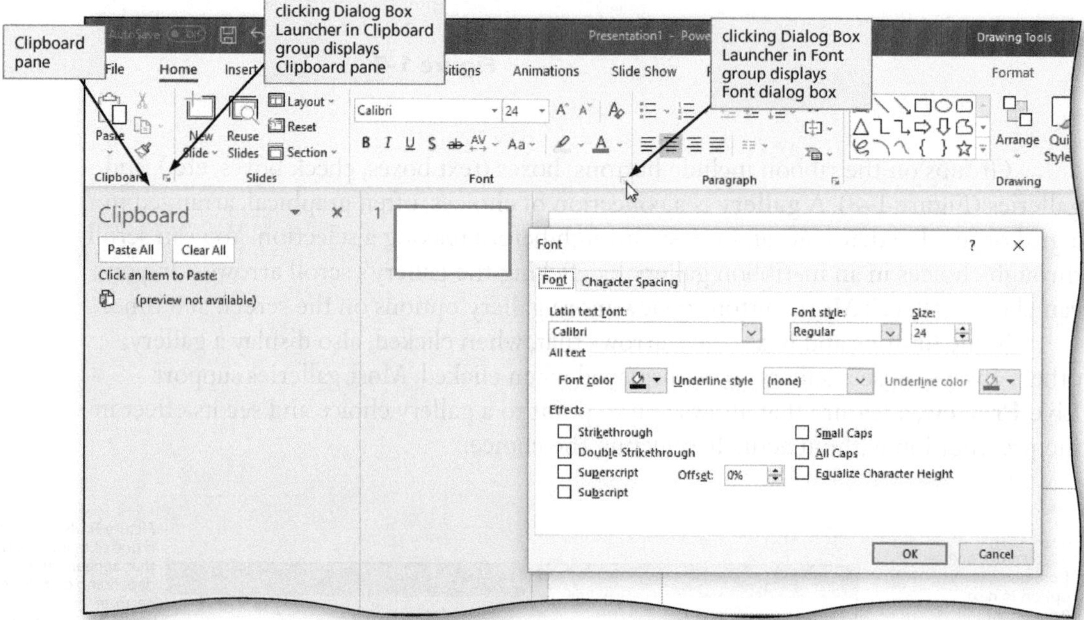

Figure 1–10

Tell Me Box The **Tell Me box**, which appears to the right of the tabs on the ribbon, is a type of search box used to find a command, perform specific tasks in PowerPoint, or access the PowerPoint Help system (Figure 1–11). As you type in the Tell Me box, the word-wheeling feature displays search results that are refined as you type. For example, if you want to center text in a slide, you can type "center" in the Tell Me box and then select the appropriate command.

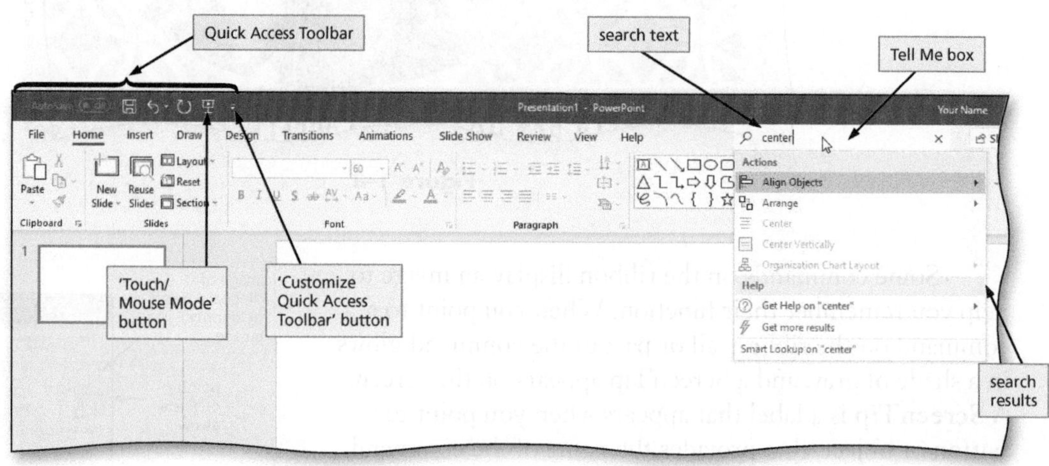

Figure 1–11

Quick Access Toolbar The **Quick Access Toolbar**, located initially (by default) above the ribbon at the left edge of the title bar, provides convenient one-click access to frequently used commands (shown in Figure 1–11). The commands on the Quick Access Toolbar always are available, regardless of the task you are performing. The Touch/Mouse Mode button on the Quick Access Toolbar allows you to switch between Touch mode and Mouse mode. If you primarily are using touch gestures, Touch mode will add more space between commands on menus and on the ribbon so that they are easier to tap. While touch gestures are convenient ways to interact with PowerPoint, not all features are supported when you are using Touch mode. If you are using a mouse, Mouse mode will not add the extra space between buttons and commands.

You can add other commands to or delete commands from the Quick Access Toolbar so that it contains the commands you use most often. To do this, click the 'Customize Quick Access Toolbar' button on the Quick Access Toolbar and then select the commands you want to add or remove. As you add commands to the Quick Access Toolbar, its length may interfere with the document title on the title bar. For this reason, PowerPoint provides an option of displaying the Quick Access Toolbar below the ribbon on the Quick Access Toolbar menu.

Each time you start PowerPoint, the Quick Access Toolbar appears the same way it did the last time you used PowerPoint. The modules in this book, however, begin with the Quick Access Toolbar appearing as it did at the initial installation of the software.

Mini Toolbar and Shortcut Menus The **Mini toolbar** is a small toolbar that appears next to selected text and contains the most frequently used text formatting commands such as bold, italic, font color, and font size. If you do not use the Mini toolbar, it disappears from the screen. The buttons, arrows, and boxes on the Mini toolbar vary, depending on whether you are using Touch mode or Mouse mode. To use the Mini toolbar, move the pointer into the Mini toolbar.

All commands on the Mini toolbar also exist on the ribbon. The purpose of the Mini toolbar is to minimize hand or mouse movement. For example, if you want to use a command that currently is not displayed on the active tab, you can use the command on the Mini toolbar instead of switching to a different tab to use the command.

A **shortcut menu**, which appears when you right-click an object, is a list of frequently used commands that relate to the right-clicked object. When you right-click selected text, for example, a shortcut menu appears with commands related to text. If you right-click an item in the window, PowerPoint displays both the Mini toolbar and a shortcut menu (Figure 1–12).

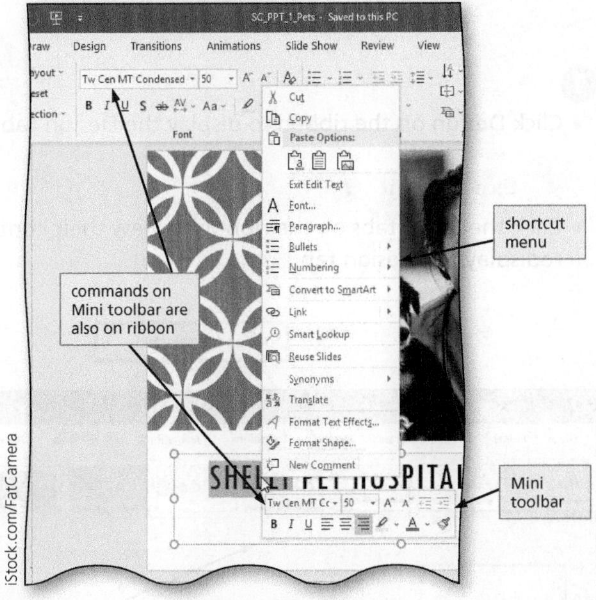

Figure 1–12

KeyTips If you prefer using the keyboard instead of the mouse, you can press ALT on the keyboard to display **KeyTips**, or keyboard code labels, for certain commands (Figure 1–13). To select a command using the keyboard, press the letter or number displayed in the KeyTip, which may cause additional KeyTips related to the selected command to appear. For example, to select the Bold button on the Home tab, press ALT, then press H, and then press. To remove KeyTips from the screen, press ALT or ESC until all KeyTips disappear, or click anywhere in the PowerPoint window.

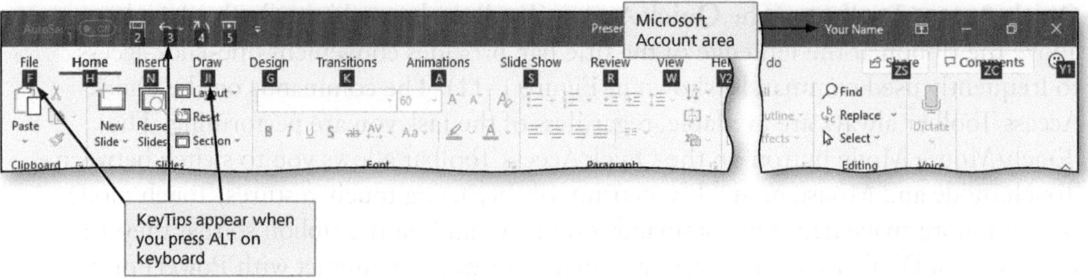

Figure 1–13

Microsoft Account Area In the Microsoft Account Area (shown in Figure 1–13), you can use the Sign in link to sign in to your Microsoft account. Once signed in, you will see your account information.

To Display a Different Tab on the Ribbon

When you start PowerPoint, the ribbon displays ten main tabs: File, Home, Insert, Design, Transitions, Animations, Slide Show, Review, View, and Help. The tab currently displayed is the active tab. To display a different tab on the ribbon, you click the tab. The following step displays the Design tab, that is, makes it the active tab. ***Why?*** *You are going to change the slide design, so you need to switch tabs to access options for completing this task.*

1

- Click Design on the ribbon to display the Design tab (Figure 1–14).

 **Experiment**

- Click the other tabs on the ribbon to view their contents. When you are finished, click Design on the ribbon to redisplay the Design tab.

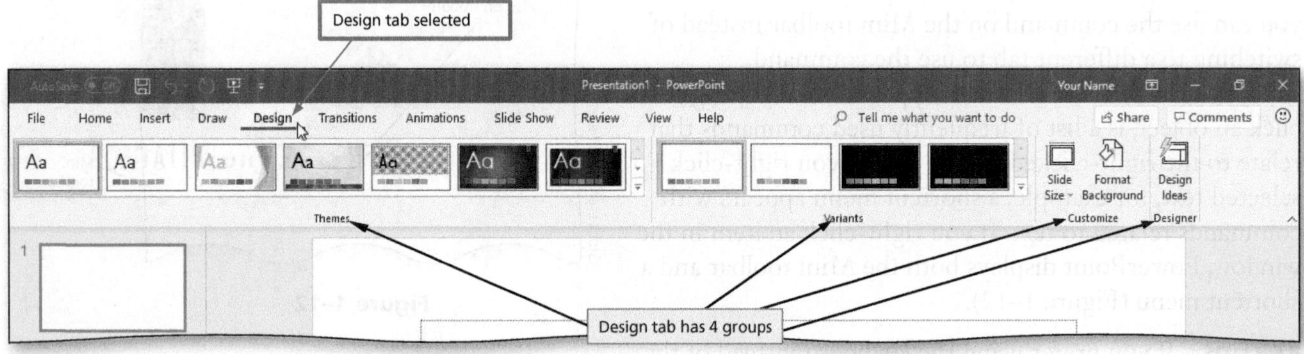

Figure 1–14

Other Ways

1. Press ALT, press letter corresponding to tab to display
2. Press ALT, press LEFT ARROW or RIGHT ARROW until desired tab is displayed

Creating a Title Slide

You easily can give the slides in a presentation a professional and integrated appearance by using a theme. A **theme** is a predefined design with coordinating colors, fonts, and graphical effects such as shadows and reflections that can be applied to presentations to give them a consistent, professional look. Themes are also sometimes called templates. Several themes are available when you start PowerPoint, each with a specific name. You also can add or change a theme while you are creating slides. Using one of the formatted themes makes creating a professional-looking presentation easier and quicker than using the Blank Presentation template, where you would need to make all design decisions.

When you open a new presentation, the default Title Slide layout appears. The purpose of this layout is to introduce the presentation to the audience. PowerPoint includes other standard layouts for each of the themes. The slide layouts are set up in **landscape orientation**, where the slide width is greater than its height. In landscape orientation, the slide size is preset to 10 inches wide and 7.5 inches high when printed on a standard sheet of paper measuring 11 inches wide and 8.5 inches high.

Placeholders are boxes with borders that are displayed when you create a new slide. Most layouts have both a title text placeholder and at least one content placeholder. Depending on the particular slide layout selected, title and subtitle placeholders are displayed for the slide title and subtitle; a content text placeholder is displayed for text, art, or a table, chart, picture, graphic, or movie. The title slide has two text placeholders where you can type the main heading, or title, of a new slide and the subtitle.

With the exception of the Blank slide layout, PowerPoint assumes every new slide has a title. To make creating a presentation easier, any text you type after a new slide appears becomes title text in the title text placeholder. The following steps change the theme and then create the title slide for this presentation.

BTW

Customizing a Slide Layout

PowerPoint provides a wide variety of slide layouts for each theme, but you can customize the layouts to make your deck unique. Display the View tab, click Slide Master (View tab | Master Views group), select the thumbnail below the slide master in the left pane that you would like to customize, and then make the desired modifications.

CONSIDER THIS

How do I choose the words for the slide?

All presentations should follow the 7 x 7 rule, which states that each slide should have a maximum of seven paragraphs, and each paragraph should have a maximum of seven words. In most cases, you should use the fewest words possible. PowerPoint designers must choose their words carefully and, in turn, help viewers read the slides easily.

Avoid line wraps. Your audience's eyes want to stop at the end of a line. Thus, you must plan your words carefully or adjust the font size so that each point displays on only one line.

To Choose a Presentation Theme

As you begin creating a new PowerPoint presentation, you can either start with no design elements by choosing Blank Presentation or you can select one of the available professionally designed themes. A theme provides consistency in design and color throughout the entire presentation by setting the color scheme, font set, and layout of a presentation. This collection of formatting choices includes a set of colors (the Theme Colors group), a set of heading and content text fonts (the Theme Fonts group), and a set of lines and fill effects (the Theme Effects group). These groups allow you to choose and change the appearance of all the slides or individual slides in your presentation. At any time while creating the slide deck, you may decide to switch the theme so that the slides have a totally different appearance. The following steps change the theme for this presentation from the Office Theme to the Parcel theme. ***Why?*** *The title slide will have text and a picture, so you want to select a theme, like Parcel, with a background that attracts attention but does not distract from the picture.*

1

- With the Design tab displaying, point to the More button (Design tab | Themes group) (Figure 1–15).

Q&A Why does a gray border display around the first theme thumbnail?
The gray border indicates the current theme. PowerPoint applied the default Office Theme when you chose the Blank Presentation theme.

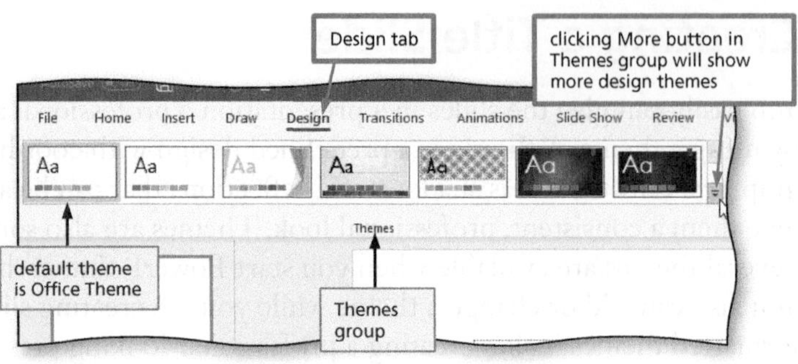

Figure 1–15

2

- Click the More button (Design tab | Themes group) to expand the gallery, which shows more theme gallery options. If necessary, scroll down to the bottom of the gallery and then point to the Parcel thumbnail to see a preview of that theme on Slide 1 (Figure 1–16).

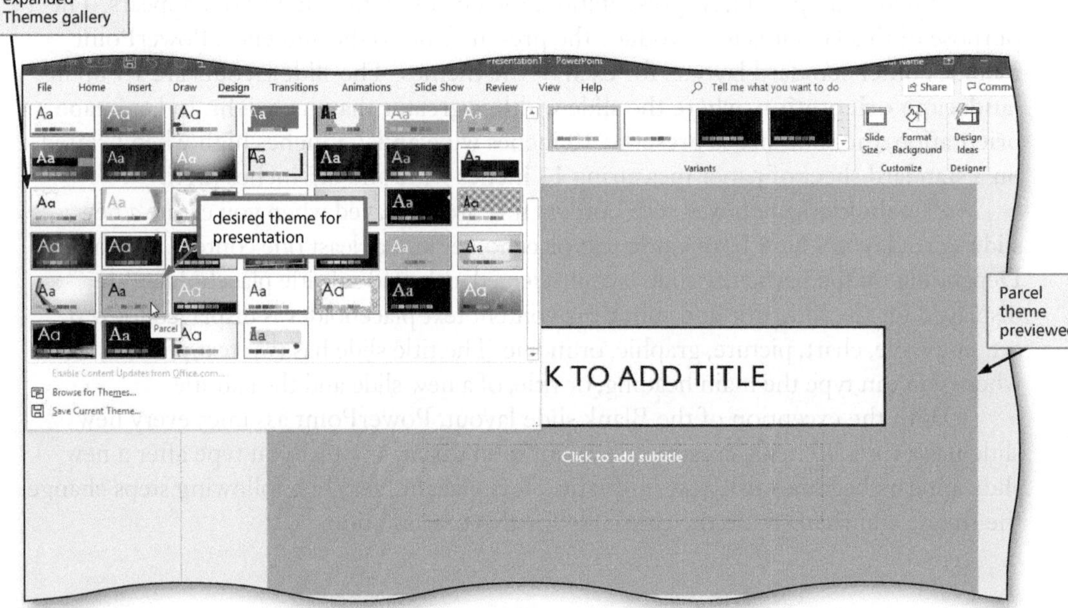

Figure 1–16

Experiment

- Point to various themes in the Themes gallery and watch the designs change on Slide 1.

Q&A Are the themes displayed in a specific order?
No. Your themes might be in a different order than shown here.

How can I determine the theme names?
If you point to a theme, a ScreenTip with the theme's name appears on the screen.

3

- Click the Parcel theme to apply this theme to the presentation (Figure 1–17).

Q&A If I decide at some future time that this design does not fit the theme of my presentation, can I apply a different design?
Yes. You can repeat these steps at any time while creating your presentation.

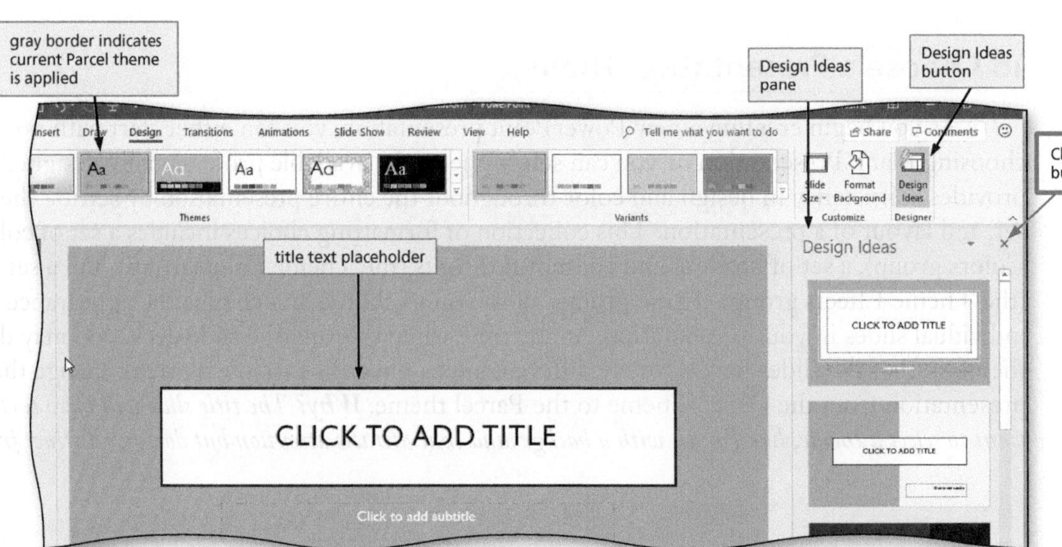

Figure 1–17

4

- **If the Design Ideas pane is displayed, click the Close button to close this pane.**

What is the Design Ideas pane?
PowerPoint generates suggestions automatically for arranging pictures, charts, tables, and other content on slides. You can scroll through these ideas and click one that meets your needs. PowerPoint then will arrange your slide content.

If I close the Design Ideas pane, can I reopen it?
Yes. Click the Design Ideas button (Design tab | Designer group) to open the pane.

To Enter the Presentation Title

The presentation title for Project 1 is Shelly Pet Hospital & Wellness Center. ***Why?*** *The presentation focuses on this business and the services offered.* The following steps create the slide show's title.

1

- **Click Home on the ribbon to display the Home tab.**
- **Click the label, 'Click to add title', located inside the title text placeholder to select the placeholder (Figure 1–18).**

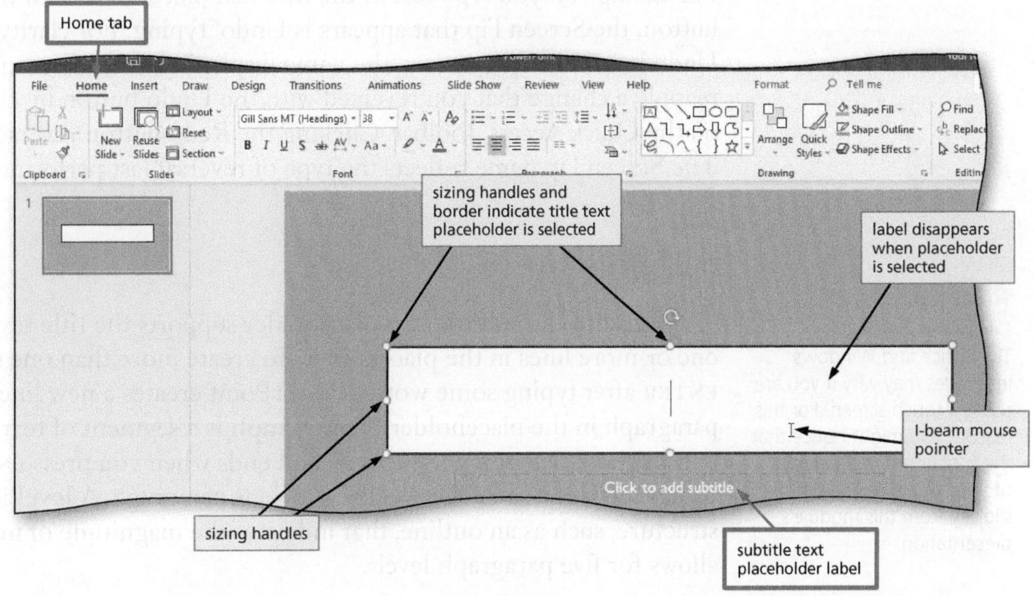

Figure 1–18

2

- **Type `Shelly Pet Hospital & Wellness Center` in the title text placeholder. Do not press ENTER (Figure 1–19).**

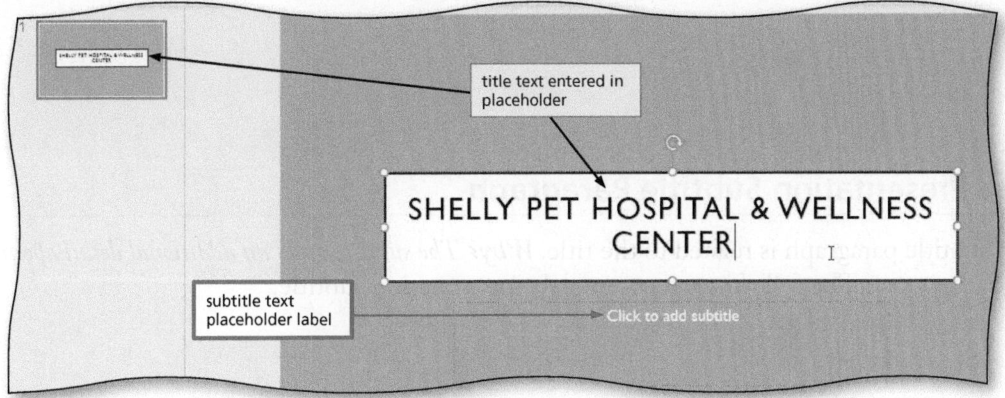

Figure 1–19

Q&A

Why does the text display with all capital letters despite the fact that I am typing uppercase and lowercase letters?
Some PowerPoint themes use All Caps for titles or subtitles as part of the design theme. This theme automatically converts lowercase letters to uppercase letters.

Correcting a Mistake When Typing

If you type the wrong letter, press BACKSPACE to erase all the characters back to and including the one that is incorrect. If you mistakenly press ENTER after typing the title and the insertion point is on the new line, simply press BACKSPACE to return the insertion point to the right of the last letter in the word, Center.

By default, PowerPoint allows you to reverse up to the last 20 changes by clicking the Undo button on the Quick Access Toolbar. The ScreenTip that appears when you point to the Undo button changes to indicate the type of change just made. For example, if you type text in the title text placeholder and then point to the Undo button, the ScreenTip that appears is Undo Typing. For clarity, when referencing the Undo button in this project, the name displaying in the ScreenTip is used. You can reapply a change that you reversed with the Undo button by clicking the Redo button on the Quick Access Toolbar. Clicking the Redo button reverses the last undo action. The ScreenTip name reflects the type of reversal last performed.

BTW
Touch Screen Differences
The Office and Windows interfaces may vary if you are using a touch screen. For this reason, you might notice that the function or appearance of your touch screen differs slightly from this module's presentation.

Paragraphs

Text in the subtitle text placeholder supports the title text. It can appear on one or more lines in the placeholder. To create more than one subtitle line, you press ENTER after typing some words. PowerPoint creates a new line, which is the second paragraph in the placeholder. A **paragraph** is a segment of text with the same format that begins when you press ENTER and ends when you press ENTER again. This new paragraph is the same level as the previous paragraph. A **level** is a position within a structure, such as an outline, that indicates the magnitude of importance. PowerPoint allows for five paragraph levels.

CONSIDER THIS

How do you use the touch keyboard with a touch screen?
To display the on-screen keyboard, tap the Touch Keyboard button on the Windows taskbar. When finished using the touch keyboard, tap the × button on the touch keyboard to close the keyboard.

To Enter the Presentation Subtitle Paragraph

The first subtitle paragraph is related to the title. ***Why?*** *The subtitle gives an additional detail about the Center's approach to pet care.* The following steps enter the presentation subtitle.

1

- Click the label, 'Click to add subtitle', located inside the subtitle text placeholder to select the placeholder (Figure 1–20).

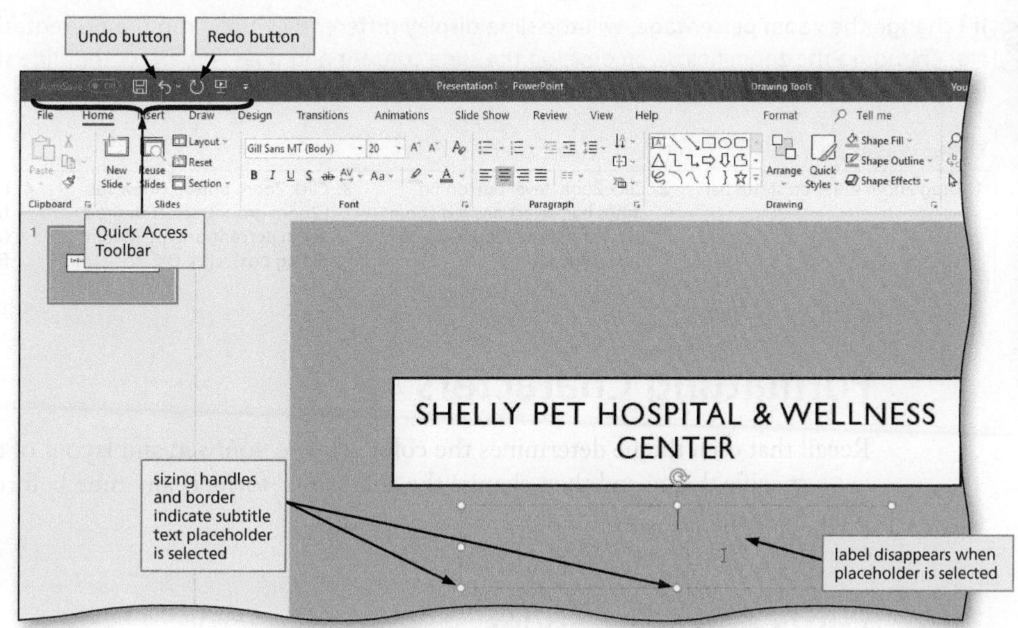

Figure 1–20

2

- Type **`Quality Care for Pets and Their Families`** but do not press ENTER (Figure 1–21).

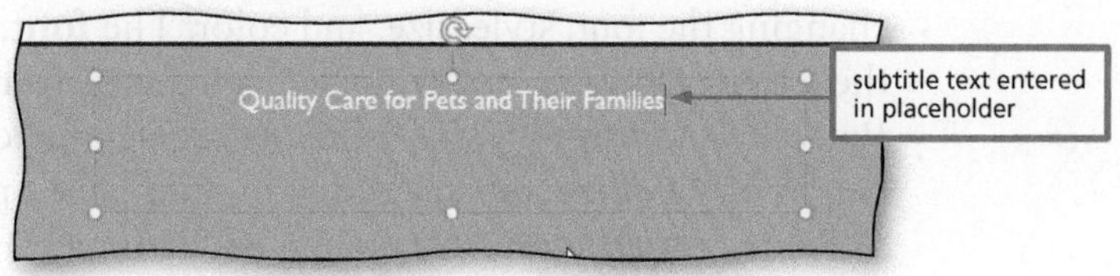

Figure 1–21

To Zoom a Slide

You can **zoom** the view of the slide on the screen so that the text or other content is enlarged or shrunk. When you zoom in, you get a close-up view of your slide; when you zoom out, you see more of the slide at a reduced size. You will be modifying the text and other slide components as you create the presentation, so you can enlarge the slide on the screen. ***Why?*** *Zooming the slide can help you see slide elements more clearly so that you can position them precisely where desired.* The following step changes the zoom to 90 percent.

1

- Click the Zoom In or Zoom Out button as many times as necessary until the Zoom button on the status bar displays 90% on its face (Figure 1–22).

Experiment

- Repeatedly click the Zoom In and Zoom Out buttons on the status bar and watch the size of the slide change in the Slide pane.

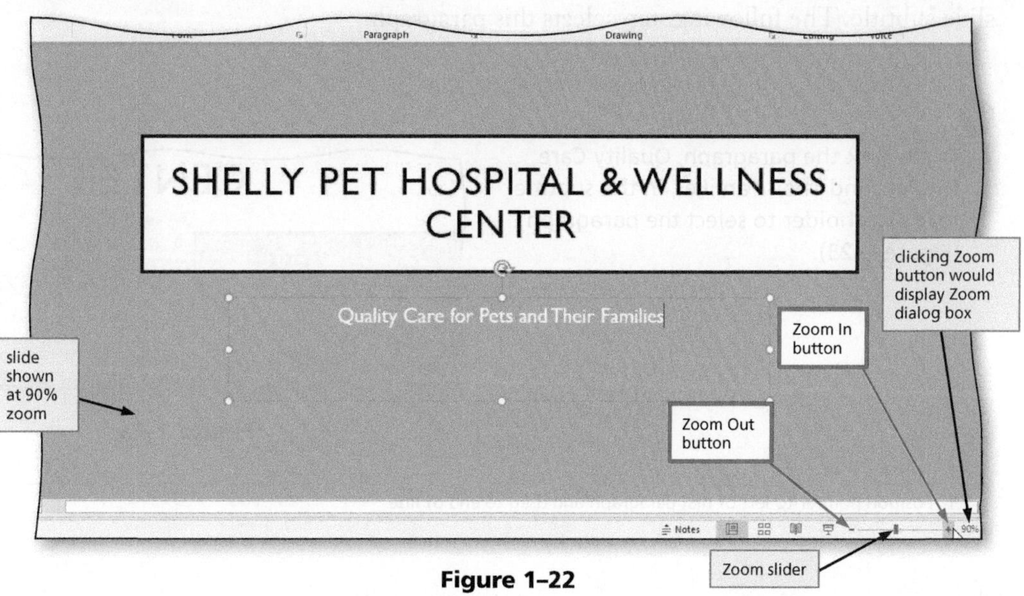

Figure 1–22

Q&A If I change the zoom percentage, will the slide display differently when I run the presentation?
No. Changing the zoom helps you develop the slide content and does not affect the slide show.

Other Ways

1. Drag Zoom slider on status bar
2. Click Zoom level button on status bar, select desired zoom percent or type (Zoom dialog box), click OK
3. Click Zoom button (View tab | Zoom group), select desired zoom percent or type (Zoom dialog box), click OK
4. For touch screens: Pinch two fingers together in Slide pane (zoom out) or stretch two fingers apart (zoom in)

Formatting Characters

Recall that each theme determines the color scheme, font set, and layout of a presentation. You can use a specific theme and then change the characters' formats any time before, during, or after you type the text.

Fonts and Font Styles

Characters that appear on the screen are a specific shape and size. Examples of how you can modify the appearance, or **formatting**, of these typed characters on the screen and in print include changing the font, style, size, and color. The **font**, or typeface, defines the appearance and shape of the letters, numbers, and special characters. A **font style** indicates how the characters are formatted. PowerPoint's text font styles include regular, italic, bold, and bold italic. **Font size** specifies the height of the characters measured in units called points. A **point** is 1/72 of an inch in height. Thus, a character with a font size of 36 is 36/72 (or 1/2) of an inch in height. **Font color** defines the hue of the characters.

This presentation uses the Parcel document theme, which has particular font styles and font sizes. The Parcel document theme default title text font is named Gill Sans MT. It has no special effects, and its size is 38 point. The Parcel default subtitle text font also is Gill Sans MT with a font size of 20 point.

To Select a Paragraph

You can use many techniques to format characters. When you want to apply the same formats to multiple words or paragraphs, it is helpful to select these words. ***Why?*** *It is efficient to select the desired text and then make the desired changes to all the characters simultaneously.* The first formatting change you will make will apply to the title slide subtitle. The following step selects this paragraph.

- Triple-click the paragraph, Quality Care for Pets and Their Families, in the subtitle text placeholder to select the paragraph (Figure 1–23).

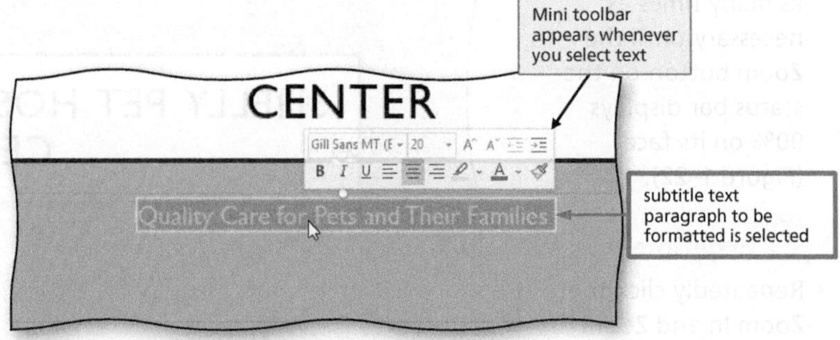

Figure 1–23

Other Ways

1. Position pointer to left of first paragraph and drag to end of line

To Italicize Text

Different font styles often are used on slides. ***Why?*** *These style changes make the words more appealing to the reader and emphasize particular text.* **Italic** text has a slanted appearance. Used sparingly, it draws the readers' eyes to these characters. The following step adds emphasis to the line of the subtitle text by changing regular text to italic text.

- With the subtitle text still selected, click the Italic button on the Mini toolbar to italicize that text on the slide (Figure 1–24).

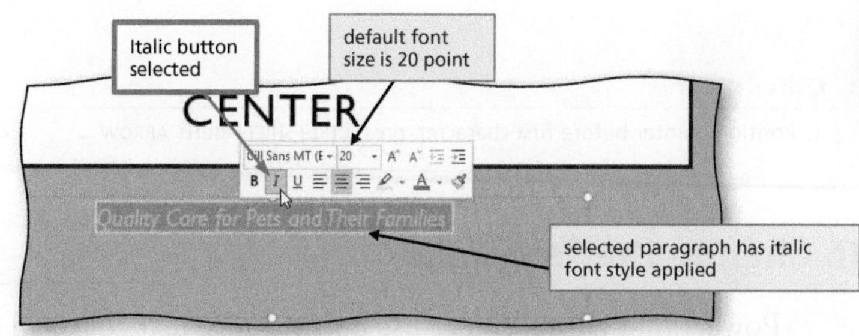

Figure 1–24

Q&A If I change my mind and decide not to italicize the text, how can I remove this style?
Immediately click the Undo button on the Quick Access Toolbar, click the Italic button a second time, or press CTRL+Z.

Other Ways

1. Right-click selected text, click Italic button on Mini toolbar near shortcut menu
2. Select text, click Italic button (Home tab | Font group)
3. Click Font dialog box launcher (Home tab | Font group), click Font tab (Font dialog box), click Italic in Font style list, click OK
4. Select text, press CTRL+I

To Increase Font Size

Why? *To add emphasis, you increase the font size for the subtitle text.* The 'Increase Font Size' button on the Mini toolbar increases the font size in preset increments. The following step uses this button to increase the font size.

- With the text, Quality Care for Pets and Their Families, selected, click the 'Increase Font Size' button on the Mini toolbar three times to increase the font size of the selected text from 20 to 32 point (Figure 1–25).

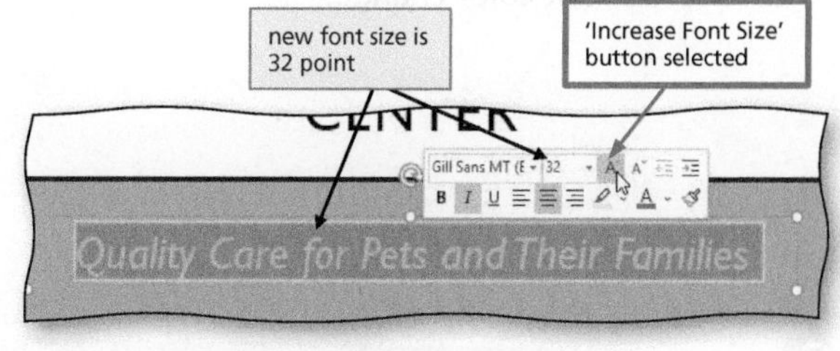

Figure 1–25

Q&A If the Mini toolbar disappears from the screen, how can I display it again?
Right-click the selected text, and the Mini toolbar should appear below a shortcut menu.

Other Ways

1. Click Font Size arrow on Mini toolbar, click desired font size in Font Size gallery
2. Click 'Increase Font Size' button (Home tab | Font group)
3. Click Font Size arrow (Home tab | Font group), click desired font size in Font size gallery
4. Press CTRL+SHIFT+>

To Select a Word

PowerPoint designers use many techniques to emphasize words and characters on a slide. To accentuate the word, Quality, on your slide, you want to increase the font size and change the font color to green for this word in the title text. To make these changes, you should begin by selecting the word, Quality. ***Why?*** *You could perform these actions separately, but it is more efficient to select the word and then change the font attributes.* The following step selects a word.

- Position the pointer somewhere in the word to be selected (in this case, in the word, Quality).
- Double-click the word to select it (Figure 1–26).

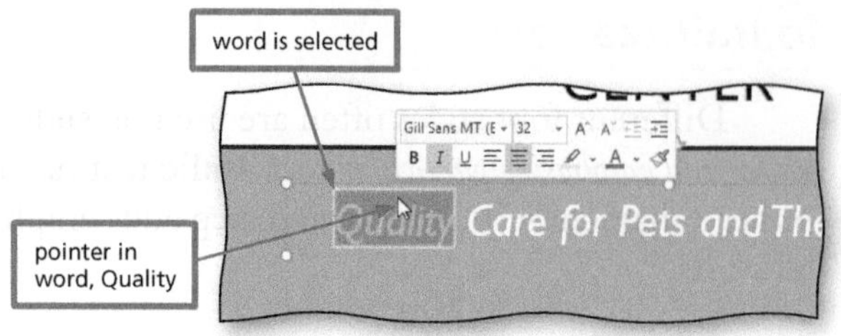

Figure 1–26

Other Ways

1. Position pointer before first character, press CTRL+SHIFT+RIGHT ARROW
2. Position pointer before first character, drag right to select word

To Change the Text Color

PowerPoint allows you to use one or more text colors in a presentation. You decide to change the color of the word you selected, Quality. ***Why?*** *The color, green, adds subtle emphasis to this word in your title slide text.* The following steps add emphasis to this word by changing the font color from white to green.

- With the word, Quality, selected, click the Font Color arrow on the Mini toolbar to display the Font Color gallery, which includes Theme Colors and Standard Colors (Figure 1–27).

Experiment

- Point to various colors in the gallery and watch the word's font color change.

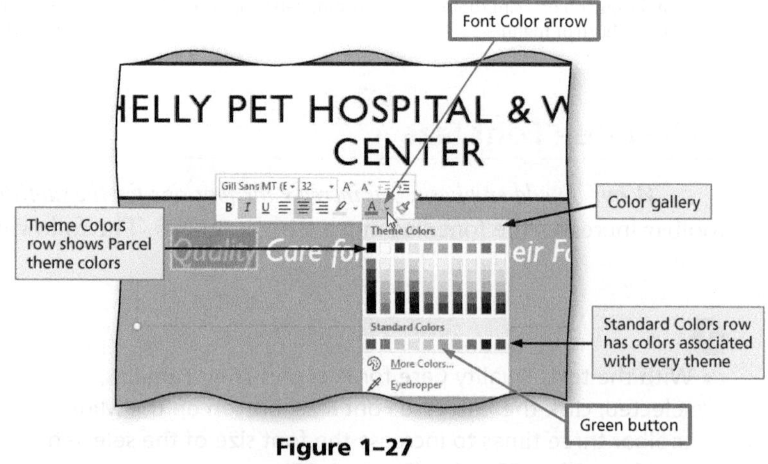

Figure 1–27

- Click Green in the Standard Colors row on the Mini toolbar (sixth color from left) to change the font color to Green (Figure 1–28).

Q&A What is the difference between the colors shown in the Theme Colors area and the Standard Colors?
The 10 colors in the top row of the Theme Colors area are two text, two background, and six accent colors in the Parcel theme; the five colors in each column under the top row display different transparencies. The Standard Colors are available in every document theme.

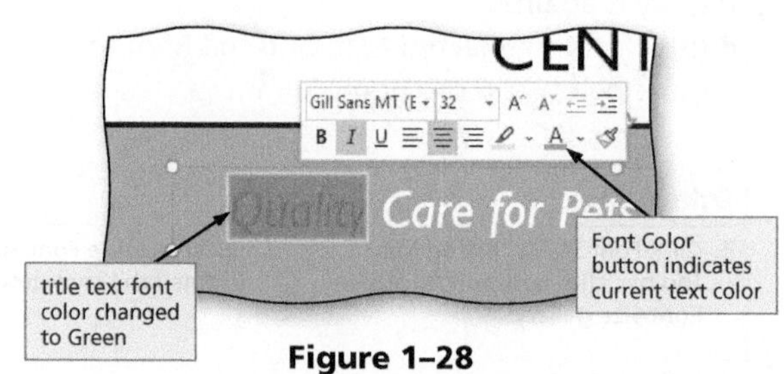

Figure 1–28

- Click outside the selected area to deselect the word.

Other Ways

1. Right-click selected text, click Font on shortcut menu, click Font Color button, click desired color
2. Click Font Color arrow (Home tab | Font group), click desired color

To Zoom a Slide

You have modified the subtitle text on Slide 1, so you now can zoom out to see more of the slide. The following step changes the zoom to 70 percent.

1. Click the Zoom Out button as many times as necessary until the Zoom button on the status bar displays 70% on its face (Figure 1–29).

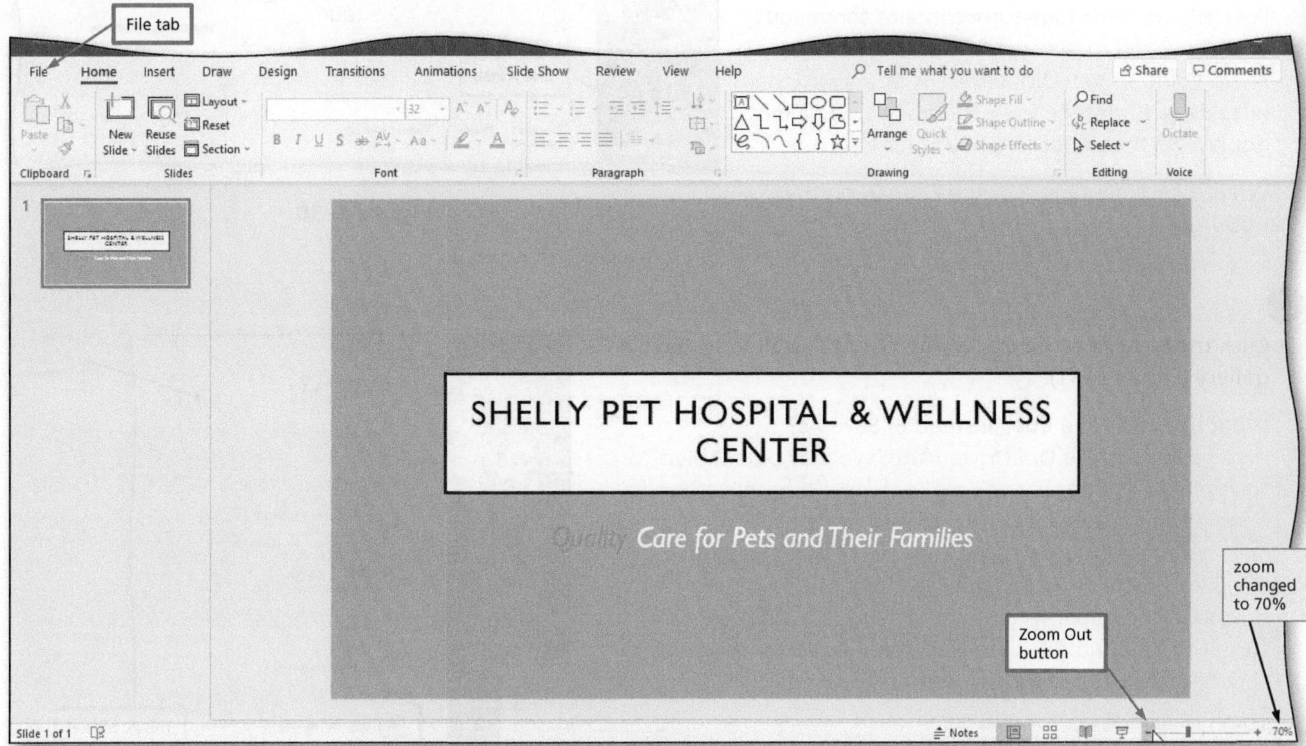

Figure 1–29

To Save a Presentation for the First Time

While you are building slides in a presentation, the computer or device stores it in memory. When you **save** a presentation, it is stored permanently on a storage medium such as a hard disk, USB flash drive, or online using a cloud storage service such as OneDrive so that you can retrieve it later. Once information is saved, it is referred to as a **file**. A **file name** is a unique, descriptive name assigned to a file when it is saved.

When saving a presentation, you must decide which storage medium to use:

- If you always work on the same computer and have no need to transport your projects to a different location, then your computer's hard drive will suffice as a storage location. It is a good idea, however, to save a backup copy of your projects on a separate medium in case the file becomes corrupted or the computer's hard drive fails. The documents created in this book are saved to the computer's hard drive.
- If you plan to work on your documents in various locations or on multiple computers or mobile devices, then you should save your documents on a portable medium, such as a USB flash drive. Alternatively, you can save your documents to an online cloud storage service such as OneDrive.

BTW

Organizing Files and Folders

You should organize and store files in folders so that you easily can find the files later. For example, if you are taking an introductory technology class called CIS 101, a good practice would be to save all PowerPoint files in a PowerPoint folder in a CIS 101 folder.

The following steps save a presentation in the Documents library on your computer's hard drive using the file name, Pet Hospital. ***Why?*** *You have performed many tasks while creating this project and do not want to risk losing the work completed thus far. Accordingly, you should save the presentation.*

1

- Click File on the ribbon (shown in Figure 1–29) to display Backstage view (Figure 1–30).

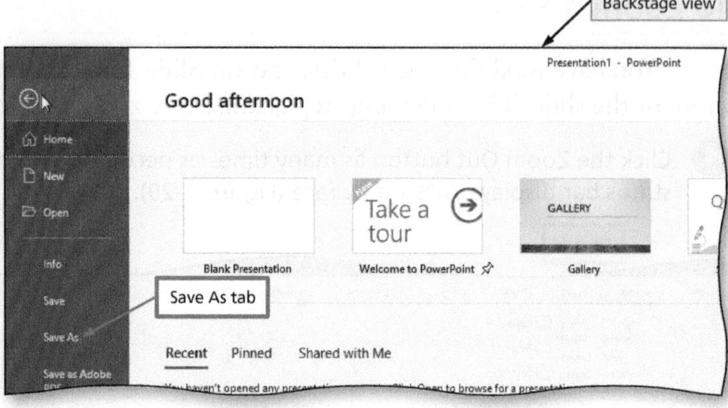

Figure 1–30

Q&A What is the purpose of the File tab on the ribbon, and what is Backstage view?
The File tab opens Backstage view in PowerPoint. **Backstage view** contains commands that allow you to manage files and options for PowerPoint. As you click different tabs along the left side of Backstage view, the associated gallery displays on the right side of Backstage view.

What if I accidentally click the File tab on the ribbon?
Click the Back button in Backstage view to return to the document window.

2

- Click the Save As tab in Backstage view to display the Save As gallery (Figure 1–31).

Q&A What if I see Save a Copy instead of Save As?
If you are saving to OneDrive, AutoSave may be enabled to save your changes as you make them. When AutoSave is enabled, you see Save a Copy instead of Save As. You can use Save a Copy in place of Save As, or, to disable AutoSave, click the Back button in Backstage view, click the AutoSave On button in the upper-left corner of the PowerPoint window to turn it to Off, and return to Backstage view where you can click Save As to save your changes manually.

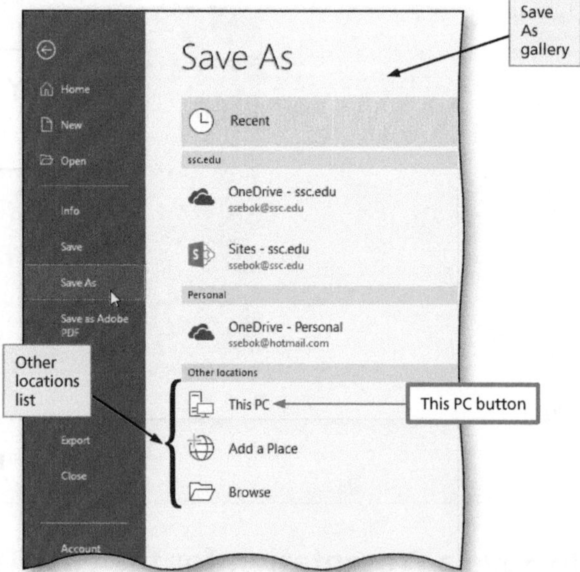

Figure 1–31

3

- Click This PC in the Other locations list to display the default save location on the computer or mobile device (Figure 1–32).

Q&A Can I type the file name below the default save location that displays in the Save As gallery?
If you want to save the file in the default location, you can type the file name in the text box below the default save location and then click the Save button to the right of the default save location. These steps show how to change to a different location on This PC.

What if I wanted to save to OneDrive instead?
You would click OneDrive in the Save As gallery, or if AutoSave is enabled, click Save a Copy to save to OneDrive.

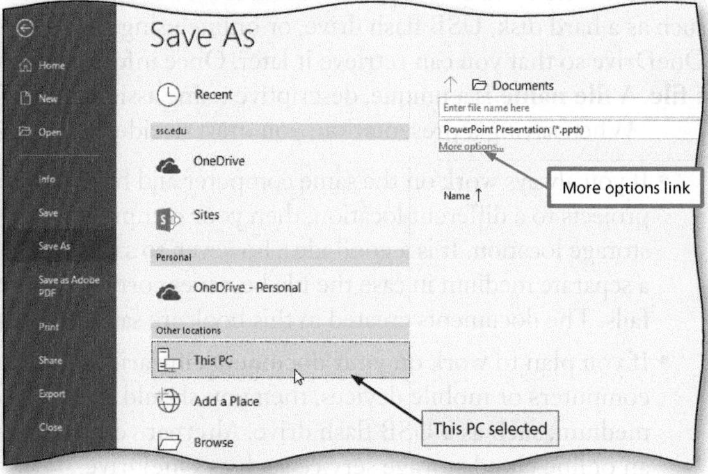

Figure 1–32

4

- Click the More options link to display the Save As dialog box.
- If necessary, click Documents in the Navigation pane to select the Documents library as the save location.
- Type `Pet Hospital` in the File name box to specify the file name for the presentation (Figure 1–33).

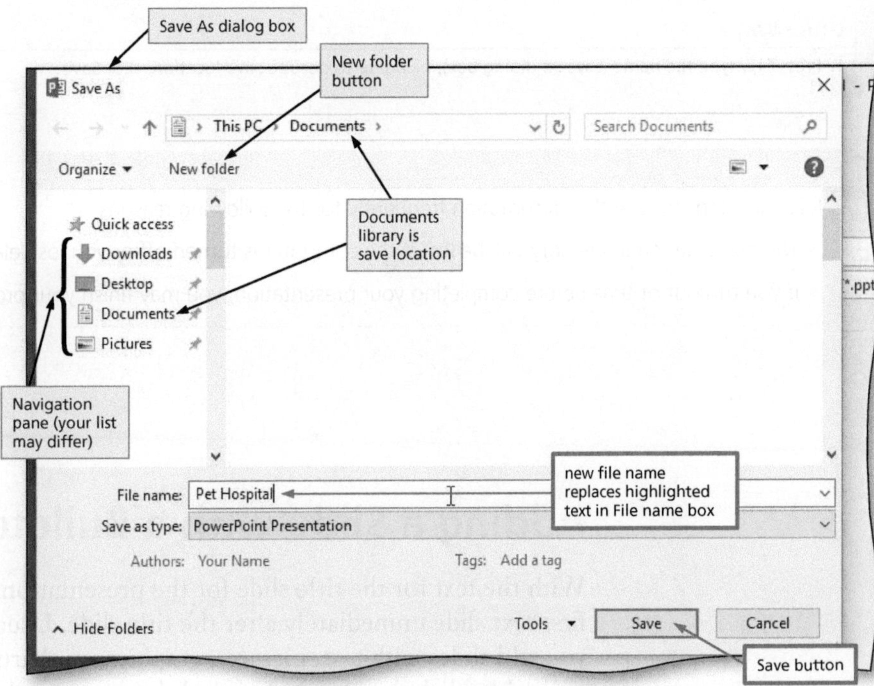

Figure 1–33

Q&A Why did the words from the title text placeholder, Shelly Pet Hospital & Wellness Center, display as the default file name in the Save As dialog box?
Words from the presentation title text placeholder are displayed as the default file name. Because the suggested file name is selected in the File Name box, you do not need to delete it; as soon as you begin typing, the new file name replaces the selected text.

Do I have to save to the Documents library?
No. You can save to any device, default folder, or a different folder. You also can create your own folders by clicking the New folder button shown in Figure 1–33. To save to a different location, navigate to that location in the Navigation pane instead of clicking Documents.

What characters can I use in a file name?
The only invalid characters are the backslash (\), slash (/), colon (:), asterisk (*), question mark (?), quotation mark ("), less than symbol (<), greater than symbol (>), and vertical bar (|).

Why is my list of files, folders, and drives arranged and named differently from those shown in the figure?
Your computer or mobile device's configuration determines how the list of files and folders is displayed and how drives are named. You can change the save location by clicking links in the Navigation pane.

5

- Click the Save button to save the presentation with the file name, Pet Hospital, to the default save location (Figure 1–34).

Q&A How do I know that PowerPoint saved the presentation?
While PowerPoint is saving your file, it briefly displays a message on the status bar indicating the amount of the file saved. When the presentation appears after saving, the new file name will be displayed in the title bar.

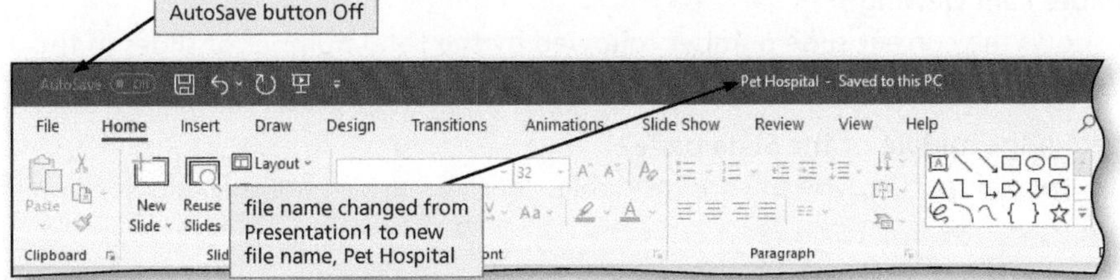

Figure 1–34

BTW
File Type
Depending on your Windows settings, the file type .pptx may be displayed on the title bar immediately to the right of the file name after you save the file. The file type .pptx identifies a PowerPoint document.

Other Ways

1. Press F12, type file name (Save As dialog box), navigate to desired save location, click Save

CONSIDER THIS

It is important to save the presentation frequently for the following reasons:

- The presentation in memory will be lost if the computer is turned off or you lose electrical power while PowerPoint is open.
- If you run out of time before completing your presentation, you may finish your project at a future time without starting over.

Adding a Slide with a Bulleted List

With the text for the title slide for the presentation created, the next step is to add the first text slide immediately after the title slide. Usually, when you create a presentation, you add slides with text, pictures, graphics, or charts. Some placeholders allow you to double-click the placeholder and then access other objects, such as videos, charts, diagrams, and organization charts. You can change the layout for a slide at any time during the creation of a presentation.

To Add a New Title and Content Slide

When you add a new slide, PowerPoint uses the Title and Content slide layout. This layout provides a title placeholder and a content area for text, art, charts, and other graphics. A vertical scroll bar appears in the Slide pane when you add the second slide. ***Why?*** *The scroll bar allows you to move from slide to slide easily.* A small thumbnail image of this slide also appears in the Slides tab. The following step adds a new slide with the Title and Content slide layout.

- Click the New Slide button (Home tab | Slides group) to insert a new slide with the Title and Content layout (Figure 1–35).

Q&A

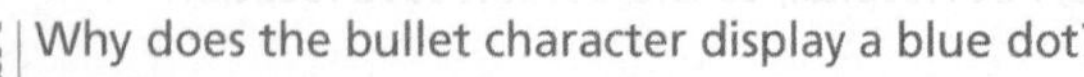

Why does the bullet character display a blue dot?
The Parcel document theme determines the bullet characters. Each paragraph level has an associated bullet character.

I clicked the New Slide arrow instead of the New Slide button. What should I do?
Click the Title and Content slide thumbnail in the Parcel layout gallery.

How do I know which slide number I am viewing?
The left edge of the status bar shows the current slide number followed by the total number of slides in the document. In addition, the slide number is displayed to the left of the slide thumbnail.

What are those six icons grouped in the middle of the Slide pane?
You can click one of the icons to insert a specific type of content: table, chart, SmartArt graphic, pictures, online pictures, or video.

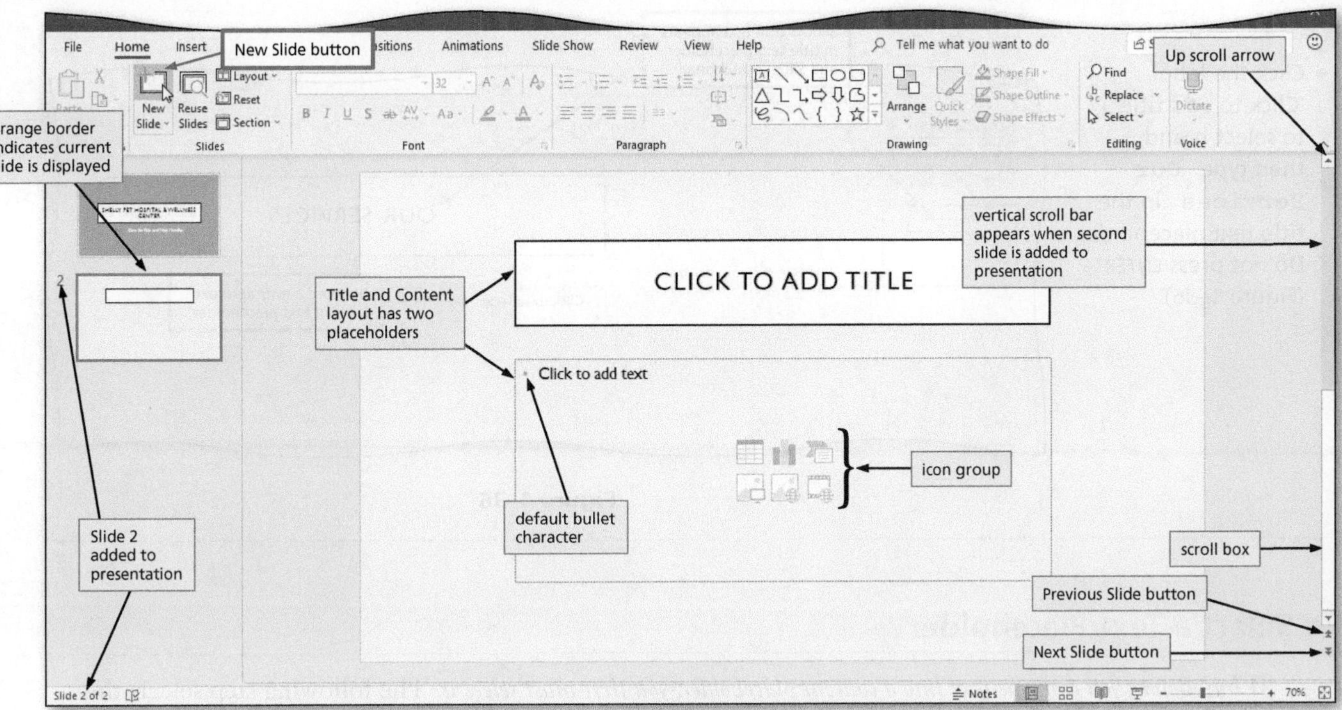

Figure 1–35

Other Ways

1. Click New Slide button (Insert tab | Slides group)
2. Press CTRL+M

Creating a Multilevel Bulleted List

The information in the Slide 2 text placeholder is presented in a bulleted list with three levels. A **bulleted list** is a series of paragraphs, each of which may be preceded by a bullet character, such as a dot, arrow, or checkmark. Most themes display a bullet character at the start of a paragraph by default. Some slides show more than one level of bulleted text, called a **multilevel bulleted list**. In a multilevel bulleted list, a lower-level paragraph is a subset of a higher-level paragraph. It usually contains information that supports the topic in the paragraph immediately above it.

Looking back at Figure 1–1b, you can see that two of the Slide 2 paragraphs appear at the same level, called the first level: Emergency Care, and Preventive Care. Beginning with the second level, each paragraph indents to the right of the preceding level and is pushed down to a lower level. For example, if you increase the indent of a first-level paragraph, it becomes a second-level paragraph. The second and fourth paragraphs on Slide 2 are second-level paragraphs. The last paragraph, One-third of dogs and cats are overweight, is a third-level paragraph.

Creating a text slide with a multilevel bulleted list requires several steps. Initially, you enter a slide title in the title text placeholder. Next, you select the content text placeholder. Then, you type the text for the multilevel bulleted list, increasing and decreasing the indents as needed. The next several sections enter the slide title and slide text with a multilevel bulleted list.

To Enter a Slide Title

PowerPoint assumes every new slide has a title. ***Why?*** *The audience members read the title and then can begin to focus their attention on the information being presented on that slide.* The title for Slide 2 is Our Services. The following step enters this title.

- Click the label, 'Click to add title', to select it and then type `Our Services` in the title text placeholder. Do not press ENTER (Figure 1–36).

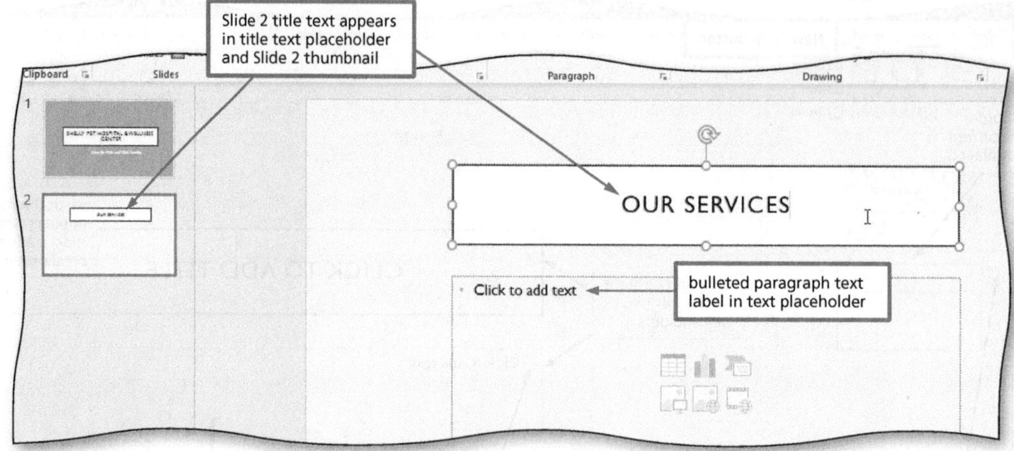

Figure 1–36

To Select a Text Placeholder

Why? Before you can type text into a content placeholder, you first must select it. The following step selects the text placeholder on Slide 2.

- Click the label, 'Click to add text', to select the content placeholder (Figure 1–37).

Q&A Why does my pointer have a different shape?
If you move the pointer away from the bullet, it will change shape.

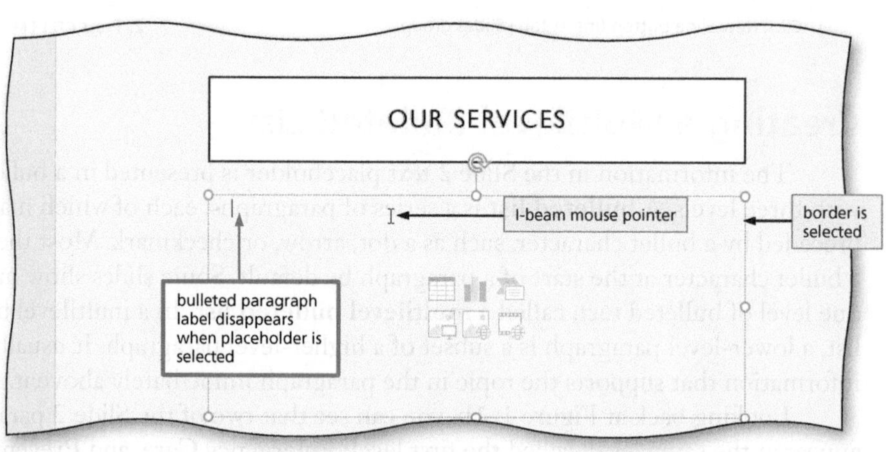

Figure 1–37

Other Ways
1. Press CTRL+ENTER

To Type a Multilevel Bulleted List

The content placeholder provides an area for the text characters. When you click inside a placeholder, you then can type or paste text. As discussed previously, a bulleted list is a list of paragraphs, each of which is preceded by a bullet. A paragraph is a segment of text ended by pressing ENTER. The theme determines the bullets for each level. ***Why?*** *The bullet variations are determined by the specific paragraph levels, and they generally vary in size, shape, and color.*

The content text placeholder is selected, so the next step is to type the multilevel bulleted list that consists of six paragraphs, as shown in Figure 1–1b. When you create a lower-level paragraph, you **demote** text (increase the list level); when you create a higher-level paragraph you **promote** text (decrease the list level). The following steps create a multilevel bulleted list consisting of three levels.

- Type **Emergency Care** and then press ENTER (Figure 1–38).

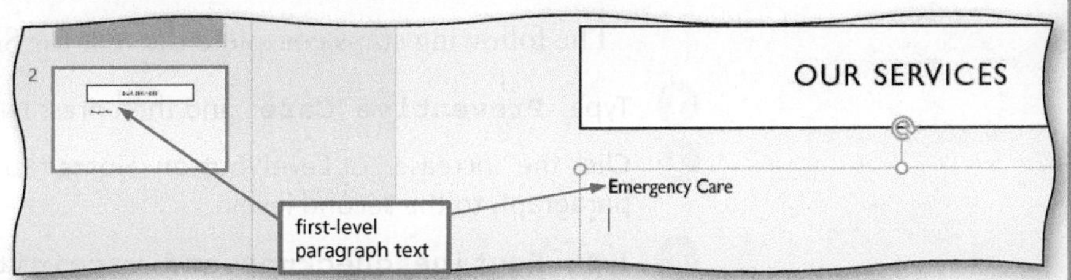

Figure 1–38

- Click the 'Increase List Level' button (Home tab | Paragraph group) to indent the second paragraph below the first and create a second-level paragraph (Figure 1–39).

Q&A Why does the bullet for this paragraph have a different size?
A different bullet is assigned to each paragraph level.

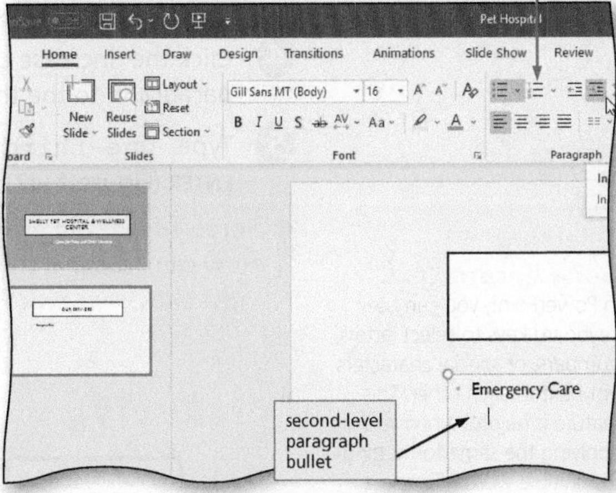

Figure 1–39

- Type **X-rays and laboratory testing** and then press ENTER (Figure 1–40).

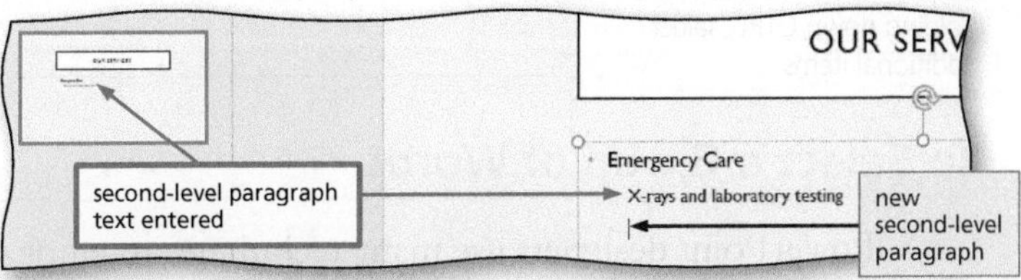

Figure 1–40

4

- Click the 'Decrease List Level' button (Home tab | Paragraph group) so that the second-level paragraph becomes a first-level paragraph (Figure 1–41).

Q&A Can I delete bullets on a slide?
Yes. If you do not want bullets to display in a particular paragraph, click the Bullets button (Home tab | Paragraph group) to toggle them off, or right-click the paragraph and then click the Bullets button on the shortcut menu.

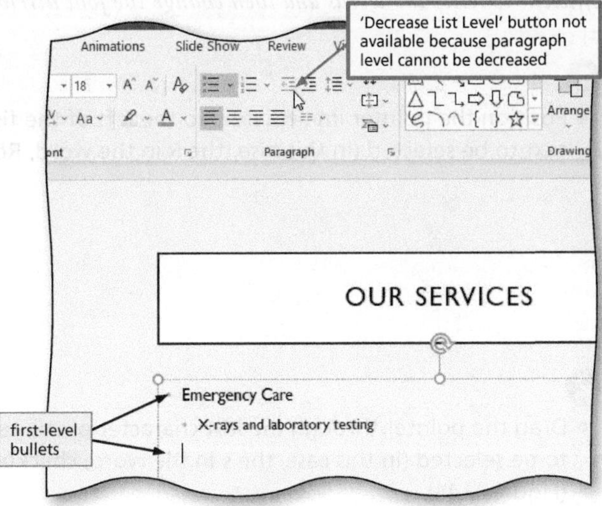

Figure 1–41

Other Ways

1. Press TAB to increase list level; press SHIFT+TAB to decrease list level

To Type the Remaining Text

The following steps complete the text for Slide 2.

1. Type **Preventive Care** and then press ENTER.
2. Click the 'Increase List Level' button (Home tab | Paragraph group) to demote the paragraph to the second level.
3. Type **Routine checkups and vaccinitions** and then press ENTER to add a new paragraph at the same level as the previous paragraph. **Note: In this step, the word, vaccinations, has been misspelled intentionally as vaccinitions to illustrate the use of PowerPoint's spell check feature.** Your slides may contain different misspelled words, depending upon the accuracy of your typing.
4. Click the 'Increase List Level' button (Home tab | Paragraph group) to demote the paragraph to the third level.
5. Type **One-third of dogs and cats are overweight** but do not press ENTER (Figure 1–42).

Q&A I pressed ENTER in error, and now a new bullet appears after the last entry on this slide. How can I remove this extra bullet?
Press BACKSPACE twice.

BTW
Selecting Nonadjacent Text
In PowerPoint, you can use keyboard keys to select letters, numbers, or special characters not next to each other. This feature is helpful when you are applying the same formatting to multiple words. To select nonadjacent text, select the first item, such as a word or paragraph, and then press and hold down CTRL. While holding down CTRL, select additional items.

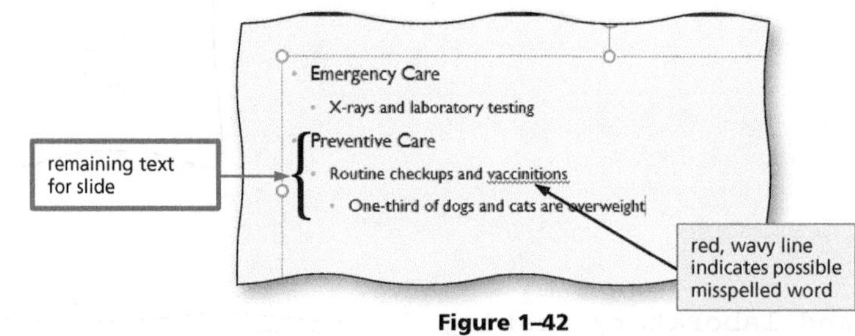

Figure 1–42

To Select a Group of Words

PowerPoint designers use many techniques to emphasize words and characters on a slide. To highlight the availability of regular examinations, you want to bold and increase the font size of the words, Routine checkups, in the body text. The following steps select two words. ***Why?*** *You could perform these actions separately, but it is more efficient to select the words and then change the font attributes.*

- Position the pointer immediately to the left of the first character of the text to be selected (in this case, the R in the word, Routine) (Figure 1–43).

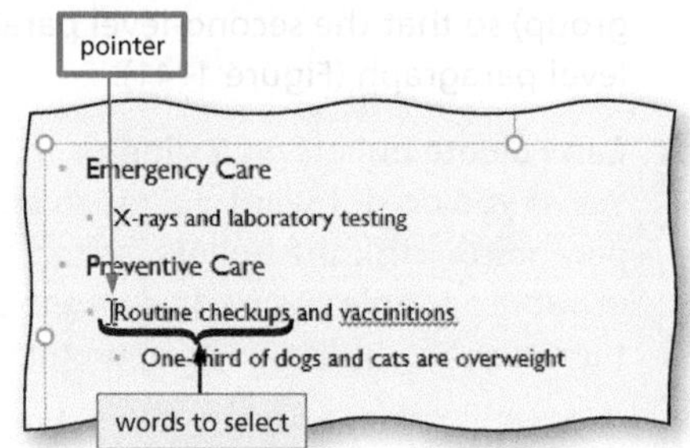

Figure 1–43

2

- Drag the pointer through the last character of the text to be selected (in this case, the s in the word, checkups) (Figure 1–44).

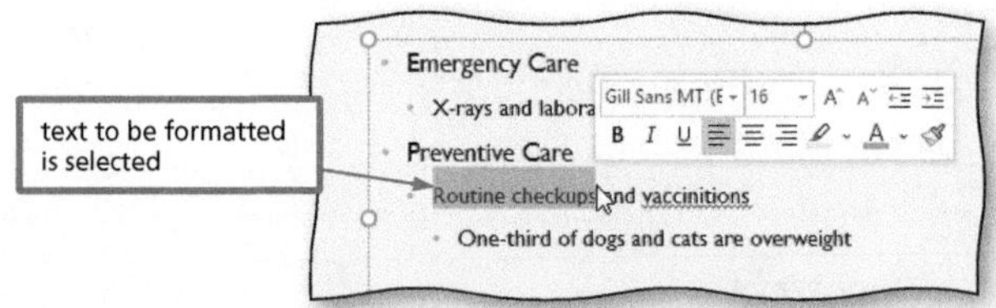

Figure 1–44

Other Ways

1. Press CTRL+SHIFT+RIGHT ARROW repeatedly until desired words are selected

To Bold Text

Why? To add more emphasis to the fact that the Center provides standard services, you want to bold the words, Routine checkups. **Bold** characters display somewhat thicker and darker than those that display in a regular font style. Clicking the Bold button on the Mini toolbar is an efficient method of bolding text. The following step bolds this text.

- With the words, Routine checkups, selected, click the Bold button on the Mini toolbar to bold the two words (Figure 1–45).

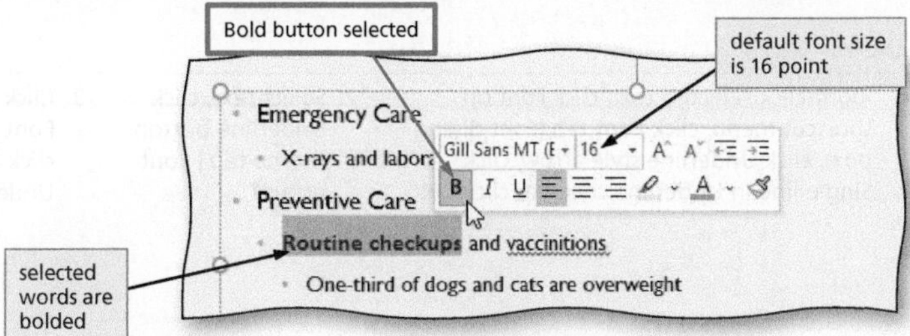

Figure 1–45

Other Ways

1. Right-click selected text, click Font on shortcut menu, click Font tab (Font dialog box), click Bold in Font style list, click OK
2. Select text, click Bold button (Home tab | Font group)
3. Click Font dialog box launcher (Home tab | Font group), click Font tab (Font dialog box), click Bold in Font style list, click OK
4. Select text, press CTRL+B

To Increase Font Size

The following steps increase the font size from 16 to 18 point. *Why? To add emphasis, you increase the font size for the words, Routine checkups.*

1. With the words, Routine checkups, still selected, click the 'Increase Font Size' button on the Mini toolbar once (Figure 1–46).
2. Click outside the selected area to deselect the two words.

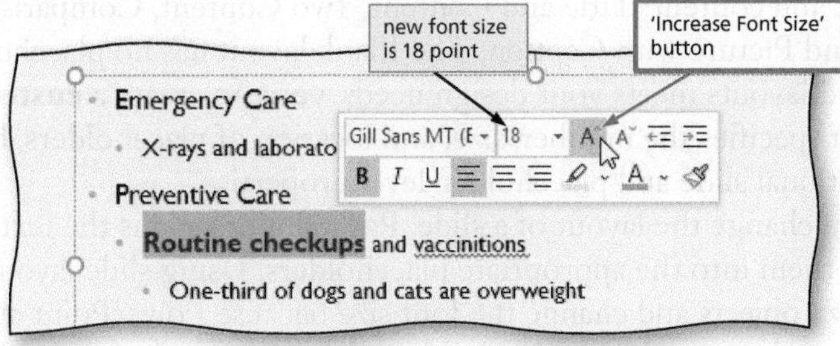

Figure 1–46

To Underline Text

Why? Underlined characters draw the audience's attention to that area of the slide and emphasize important information. Clicking the Underline button on the Mini toolbar is an efficient method of underlining text. To add more emphasis to the fact that many dogs and cats are overweight, you want to bold the words, One-third. The following steps underline this text.

- Select the words, One-third on the slide.
- Click the Underline button on the Mini toolbar to underline the two words (Figure 1–47).

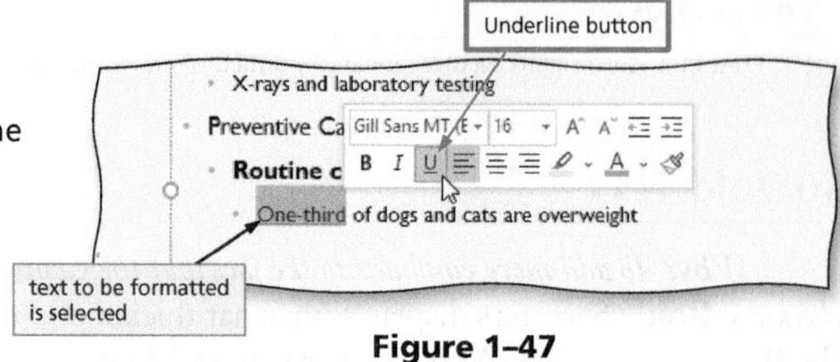

Figure 1–47

Other Ways

1. Right-click selected text, click Font on shortcut menu, click Font tab (Font dialog box), click Underline style arrow, click Single line in Underline style list, click OK	2. Select text, click Underline button (Home tab | Font group)	3. Click Font dialog box launcher (Home tab | Font group), click Font tab (Font dialog box), click Underline style arrow, click Single line in Underline style list, click OK	4. Select text, press CTRL+U

Adding Slides, Changing Slide Layouts, and Changing the Theme

Slide 3 in Figure 1–1c contains two pictures: one dog shaking its paw and a group of dogs in an obedience class. Slide 4 in Figure 1–1d contains a picture of a veterinarian cleaning a dog's ear and does not contain a bulleted list. When you add a new slide, PowerPoint applies the Title and Content layout. This layout and the Title Slide layout for Slide 1 are the default styles. A **layout** specifies the arrangement of placeholders on a slide. These placeholders are arranged in various configurations and can contain text, such as the slide title or a bulleted list, or they can contain content, such as SmartArt graphics, pictures, charts, tables, and shapes. The placement of the text in relationship to content depends on the slide layout. You can specify a particular slide layout when you add a new slide to a presentation or after you have created the slide.

Using the **layout gallery**, you can choose a slide layout. The nine layouts in this gallery have a variety of placeholders to define text and content positioning and formatting. Three layouts are for text: Title Slide, Section Header, and Title Only. Five are for text and content: Title and Content, Two Content, Comparison, Content with Caption, and Picture with Caption. The Blank layout has no placeholders. If none of these standard layouts meets your design needs, you can create a **custom layout**. A custom layout specifies the number, size, and location of placeholders, background content, and optional slide and placeholder-level properties.

When you change the layout of a slide, PowerPoint retains the text and objects and repositions them into the appropriate placeholders. Using slide layouts eliminates the need to resize objects and change the font size because PowerPoint automatically sizes the objects and text to fit the placeholders. At any time when creating the slide content, you can change the theme and variant to give the presentation a different look and feel.

To Add a New Slide and Enter a Slide Title and Headings

The text on Slide 3 in Figure 1–1c consists of a title and two headings. The appropriate layout for this slide is named Comparison. ***Why?*** *The Comparison layout has two headings and two text placeholders adjacent to each other, so an audience member easily can compare and contrast the items shown side by side.* The following steps add Slide 3 to the presentation with the Comparison layout and then enter the title and heading text for this slide.

1

- Click the New Slide arrow in the Slides group to display the Parcel layout gallery (Figure 1–48).

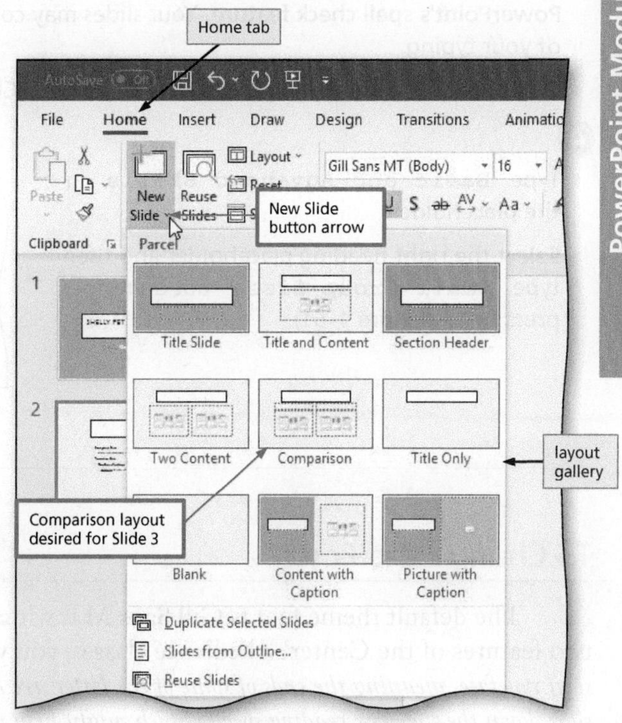

Figure 1–48

2

- Click Comparison to add Slide 3 and apply that layout (Figure 1–49).

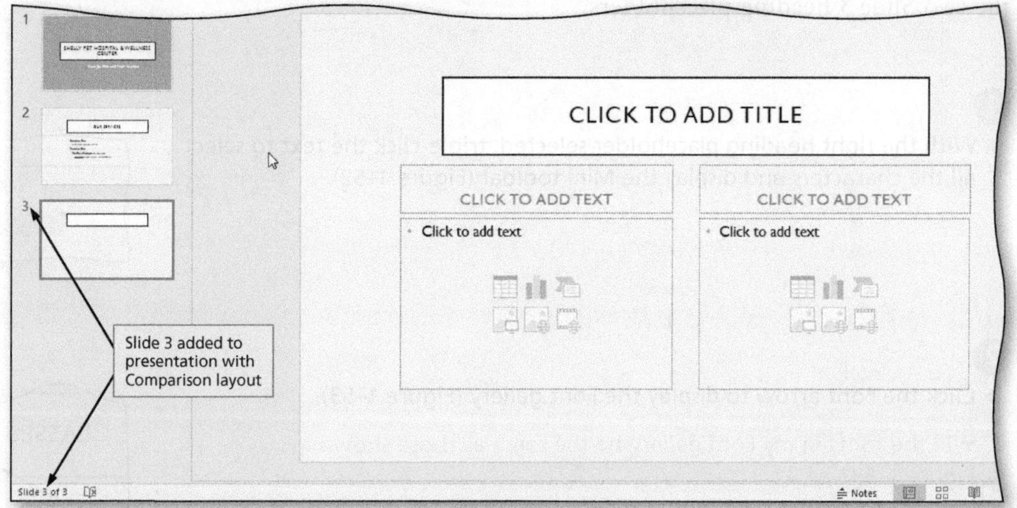

Figure 1–49

3

- Type **`Obedeince Classes`** in the title text placeholder. **Note: In this step, the word, Obedience, has been misspelled intentionally as Obedeince to illustrate the use of**

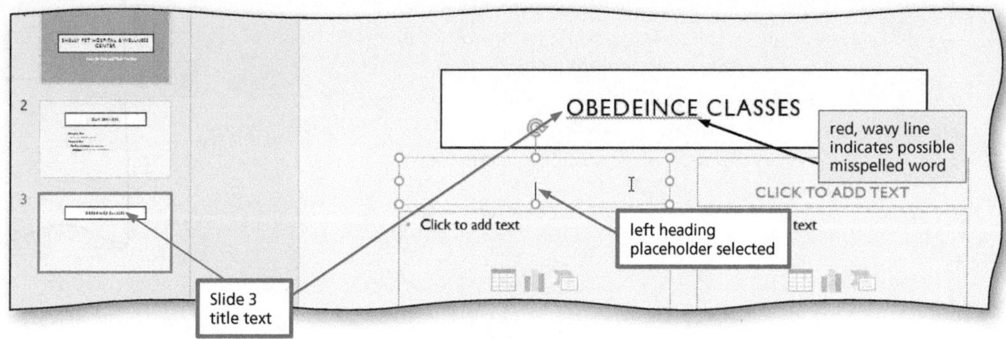

Figure 1–50

PowerPoint's spell check feature. Your slides may contain different misspelled words, depending upon the accuracy of your typing.

- Click the left heading placeholder with the label, 'Click to add text', to select this placeholder (Figure 1–50).

- Type **Basic and Advanced Skills** in the placeholder.
- Select the right heading placeholder and then type **Small Group Sizes** but do not press ENTER (Figure 1–51).

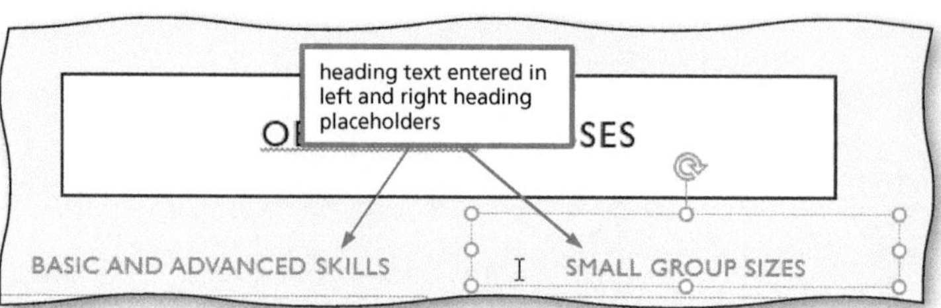

Figure 1–51

To Change the Font

The default theme font is Gill Sans MT, which is shown in the Font box. To draw more attention to the two features of the Center's obedience classes, you want to change the font to Cambria. ***Why?*** *Cambria is a serif typeface, meaning the ends of some of the letter are adorned with small decorations, called serifs. These adornments slow down the viewer's reading speed, which might help them retain the information they saw.* To change the font, you must select the text you want to format. Earlier in this module you selected a paragraph and then formatted the characters, and you follow the same procedure to change the font. The following steps change the text font in the two Slide 3 heading placeholders.

- With the right heading placeholder selected, triple-click the text to select all the characters and display the Mini toolbar (Figure 1–52).

Figure 1–52

- Click the Font arrow to display the Font gallery (Figure 1–53).

Q&A Will the fonts in my Font gallery be the same as those shown in Figure 1–53?

Your list of available fonts may differ, depending on what fonts you have installed and the type of printer you are using.

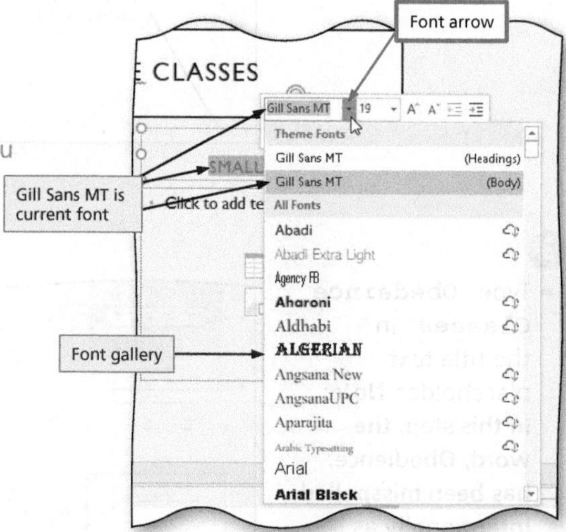

Figure 1–53

3

- Scroll through the Font gallery and then point to Cambria (or a similar font) to display a live preview of the title text in the Cambria font (Figure 1–54).

Experiment

- Point to various fonts in the Font gallery and watch the subtitle text font change in the slide.
- Click Cambria (or a similar font) to change the font of the selected text to Cambria.

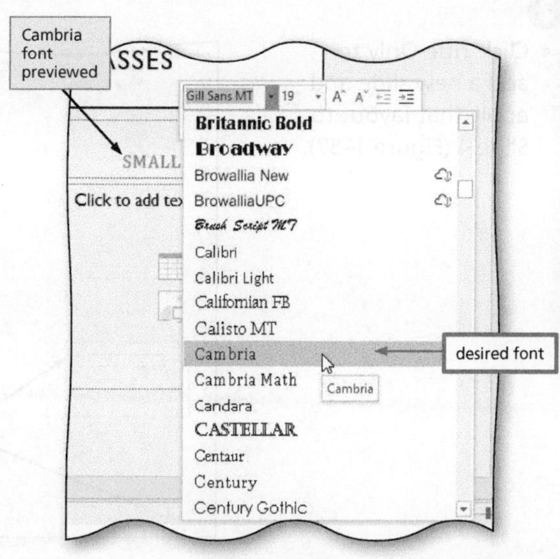

Figure 1–54

4

- Select all the words, Basic and Advanced Skills, in the left placeholder to display the Mini toolbar.
- Click the Font arrow to display the Font gallery. Note that Cambria is now displayed under Recently Used Fonts.
- Click Cambria (or a similar font) to change the font of the selected text to Cambria (Figure 1–55).

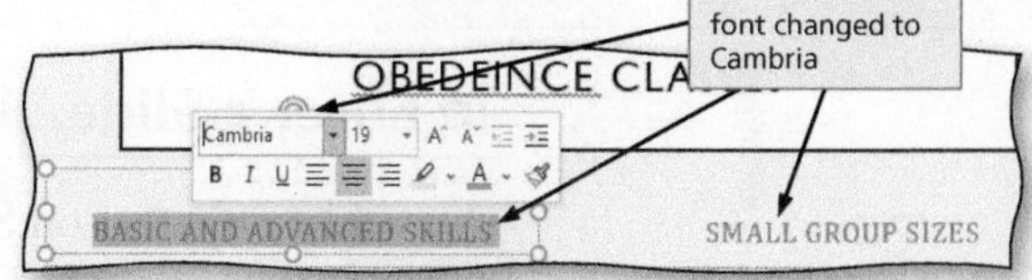

Figure 1–55

Other Ways

1. Click Font arrow (Home tab | Font group), click desired font in Font gallery
2. Right-click selected text, click Font on shortcut menu (Font dialog box), click Font tab, select desired font in Font list, click OK
3. Click Font dialog box launcher (Home tab | Font group), click Font tab (Font dialog box), select desired font in Font list, click OK
4. Press CTRL+SHIFT+F, click Font tab (Font dialog box), select desired font in the Font list, click OK
5. Right-click selected text, click Font arrow on Mini toolbar, select desired font

To Add a Slide with the Title Only Layout

The following steps add Slide 4 to the presentation with the Title Only slide layout style. ***Why?*** *The only text on the slide is the title, and the majority of the slide content is the picture.*

1

- If necessary, click Home on the ribbon to display the Home tab.
- Click the New Slide arrow (Home tab | Slides group) to display the Parcel layout gallery (Figure 1–56).

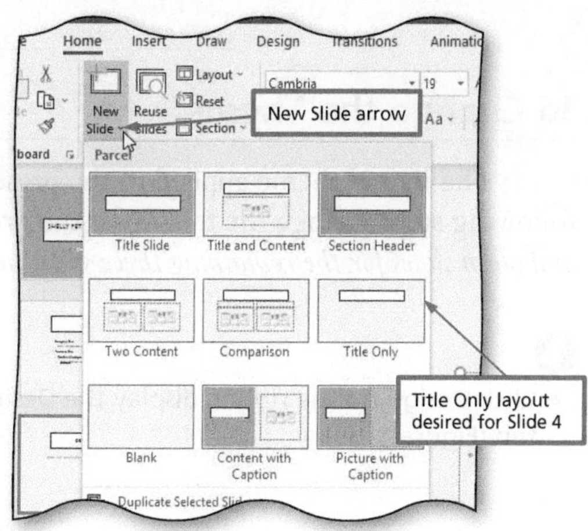

Figure 1–56

- Click Title Only to add a new slide and apply that layout to Slide 4 (Figure 1–57).

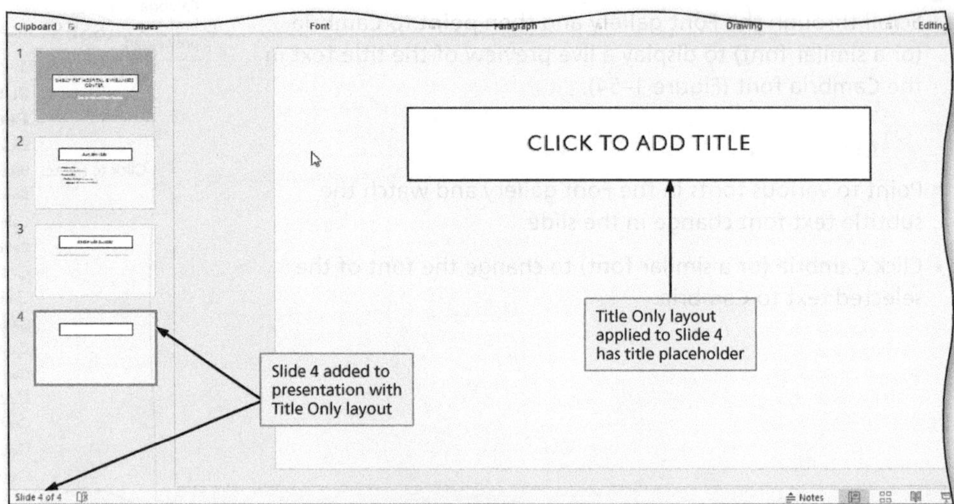

Figure 1–57

To Enter a Slide Title

The only text on Slide 4 is the title. The following step enters the title text for this slide. Because you have made several modifications to the presentation since you last saved it. Thus, you should save it again and then saves the presentation.

1 Type `Grooming Facilities` as the title text but do not press ENTER (Figure1–58).

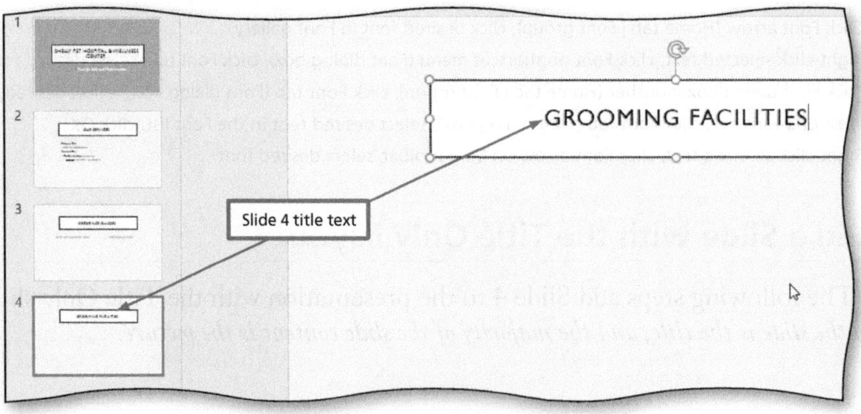

Figure 1–58

To Change the Theme

The Parcel theme applied to the presentation is simple and does not have many design elements. The following steps change the theme for the presentation. ***Why?*** *You want a lively design to call attention to the title slide and plain slides for the remaining three slides in the presentation.*

- Click Design on the ribbon display the Design tab (Figure 1–59).

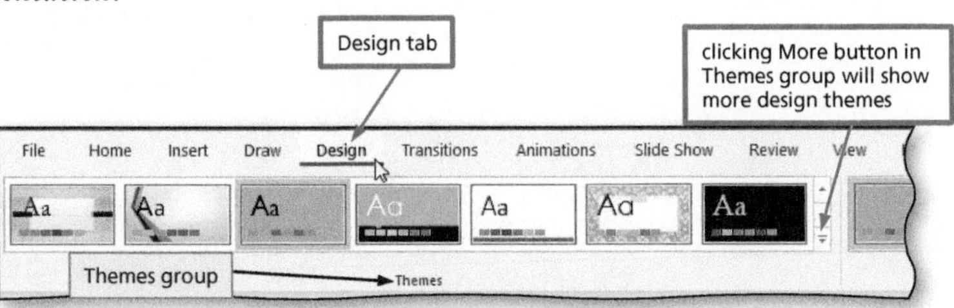

Figure 1–59

2

- Click the More button (Design tab | Themes group) to expand the Themes gallery. If necessary scroll down to view the Integral theme thumbnail.
- Point to the Integral theme to see a preview of that theme on Slide 4 (Figure 1–60).

Experiment

- Point to various document themes in the Themes gallery and watch the colors and fonts change on Slide 4.

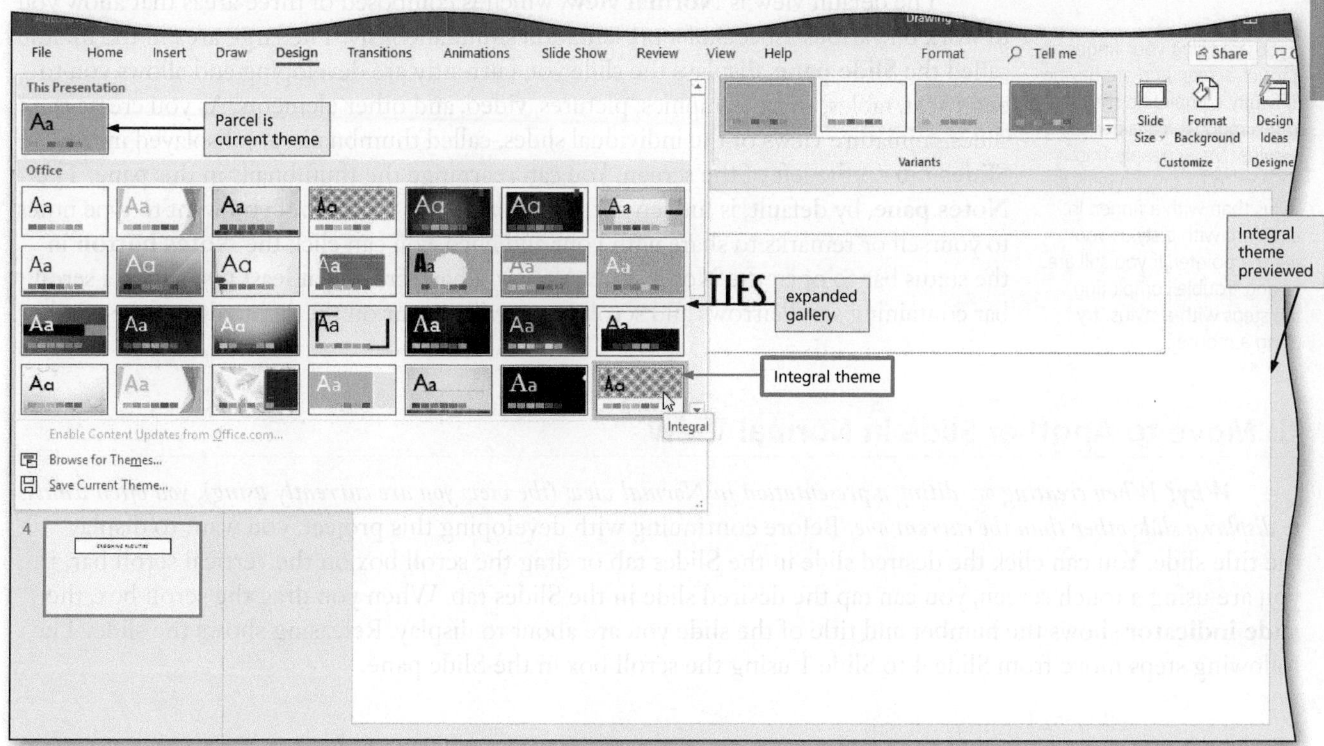

Figure 1–60

3

- Click the Integral theme to apply this theme to all four slides.
- If the Design Ideas pane is displayed, close it (Figure 1–61).

Figure 1–61

BTW
Pointer
If you are using a touch screen, the pointer may not appear on the screen as you perform touch gestures. The pointer will reappear when you begin using the mouse.

BTW
Touch Screen
If you are using your finger on a touch screen and are having difficulty completing the steps in this module, consider using a stylus. Many people find it easier to be precise with a stylus than with a finger. In addition, with a stylus you see the pointer. If you still are having trouble completing the steps with a stylus, try using a mouse.

PowerPoint Views

The PowerPoint window display varies depending on the view. A **view** is the mode in which the presentation appears on the screen. You will use some views when you are developing slides and others when you are delivering your presentation. When creating a presentation, you most likely will use Normal, Slide Sorter, Notes Pane, and Outline views. When presenting your slides to an audience, you most likely will use Slide Sorter, Presenter, and Reading views.

The default view is **Normal view**, which is composed of three areas that allow you to work on various aspects of a presentation simultaneously. The large area in the middle, called the **Slide pane**, displays the slide you currently are developing and allows you to enter text, tables, charts, graphics, pictures, video, and other elements. As you create the slides, miniature views of the individual slides, called thumbnails, are displayed in the **Slides tab** on the left of the screen. You can rearrange the thumbnails in this pane. The **Notes pane**, by default, is hidden at the bottom of the window. If you want to type notes to yourself or remarks to share with your audience, you can click the **Notes button** in the status bar to open the Notes pane. After you have created at least two slides, a scroll bar containing scroll arrows and scroll boxes will appear on the right edge of the window.

To Move to Another Slide in Normal View

Why? *When creating or editing a presentation in Normal view (the view you are currently using), you often want to display a slide other than the current one.* Before continuing with developing this project, you want to display the title slide. You can click the desired slide in the Slides tab or drag the scroll box on the vertical scroll bar; if you are using a touch screen, you can tap the desired slide in the Slides tab. When you drag the scroll box, the **slide indicator** shows the number and title of the slide you are about to display. Releasing shows the slide. The following steps move from Slide 4 to Slide 1 using the scroll box in the Slide pane.

- With Slide 4 displayed, position the pointer on the scroll box.
- Press and hold down the mouse button so that Slide: 4 of 4 Grooming Facilities appears in the slide indicator (Figure 1–62).

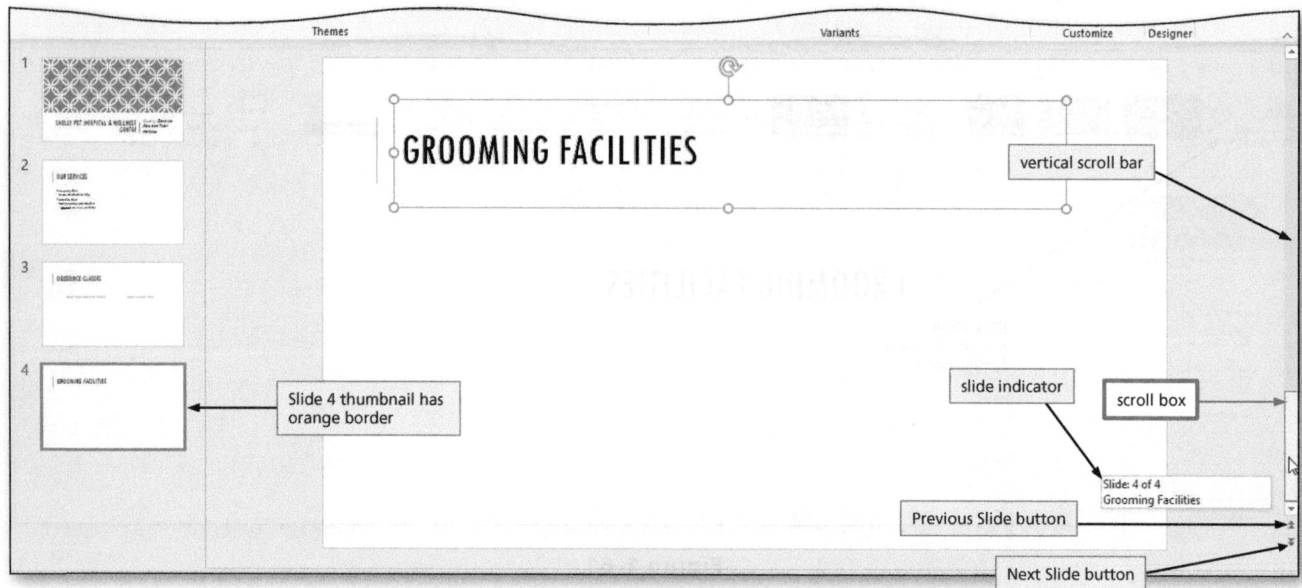

Figure 1–62

2

- Drag the scroll box up the vertical scroll bar until Slide: 1 of 4 Shelly Pet Hospital & Wellness ... appears in the slide indicator (Figure 1–63).

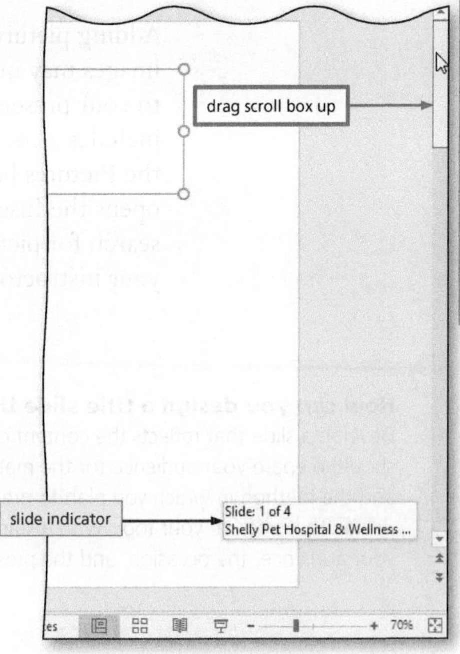

Figure 1–63

3

- Release so that Slide 1 appears in the Slide pane and the Slide 1 thumbnail has an orange border in the Slides tab (Figure 1–64).

Figure 1–64

Other Ways

1. Click Next Slide button or Previous Slide button to move forward or back one slide
2. Click slide in Slides tab
3. Press PAGE DOWN or PAGE UP to move forward or back one slide

Inserting, Resizing, and Moving Pictures

Adding pictures can help increase the visual and audio appeal of many slides. These images may include photographs, pictures, and other artwork. You can add pictures to your presentation in two ways. One way is by selecting one of the slide layouts that includes a content placeholder with a Pictures button. A second method is by clicking the Pictures button in the Images group on the Insert tab. Clicking the Pictures button opens the Insert Picture dialog box. The **Insert Picture dialog box** allows you to search for picture files that are stored on your computer or a storage device. Contact your instructor if you need the pictures used in the following steps.

CONSIDER THIS

How can you design a title slide that holds your audience's attention?

Develop a slide that reflects the content of your presentation but does so in a thought-provoking way. A title, at the very least, should prepare your audience for the material they are about to see and hear. Look for ways to focus attention on your theme and the method in which you plan to present this theme. A unique photograph or graphic can help generate interest. You may decide to introduce your topic with a startling fact, a rhetorical question, or a quotation. The device you choose depends upon your audience, the occasion, and the presentation's purpose.

To Insert a Picture into a Slide without a Content Placeholder

Slide 1 uses the Title Slide layout, which has two placeholders for text but none for graphical content. You want to place a graphic on Slide 1. ***Why?*** *It is likely that your viewers will see an image on this slide before they read any text, so you want to include a picture to create interest in the presentation and introduce your audience to the topic.* For this presentation, you will insert a photograph of two dogs and a veterinarian. Later in this module, you will resize and position the picture in an appropriate location. The following steps add a picture to Slide 1.

Note: To complete this assignment, you will be required to use the Data Files. Please contact your instructor for information about accessing the Data Files.

- With Slide 1 displayed, click Insert on the ribbon to display the Insert tab (Figure 1–65).

Figure 1–65

- Click the Pictures button (Insert tab | Images group) to display the Insert Picture dialog box.

Q&A | What should I do if no pictures are displayed when I click the Pictures button?
You may need to click the Online Pictures button instead of the Pictures button.

- Navigate to the PowerPoint1 folder. If necessary, scroll down and then click the picture called Support_PPT_1_PuppyLove.jpg, which is located in the Data Files (Figure 1–66).

Q&A Why do I see only a list of file names and not thumbnails of the pictures in my folder?
Your view is different from the view shown in Figure 1–66.

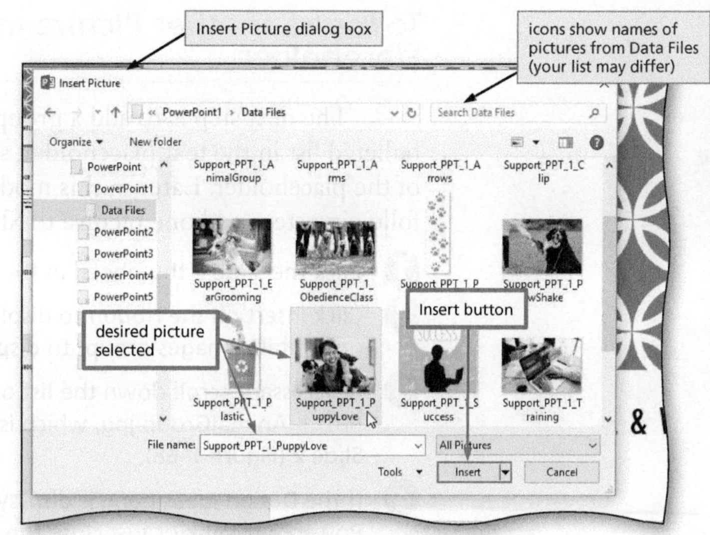

Figure 1–66

3

- Click the Insert button (Insert Picture dialog box) to insert the picture into Slide 1 (Figure 1–67).

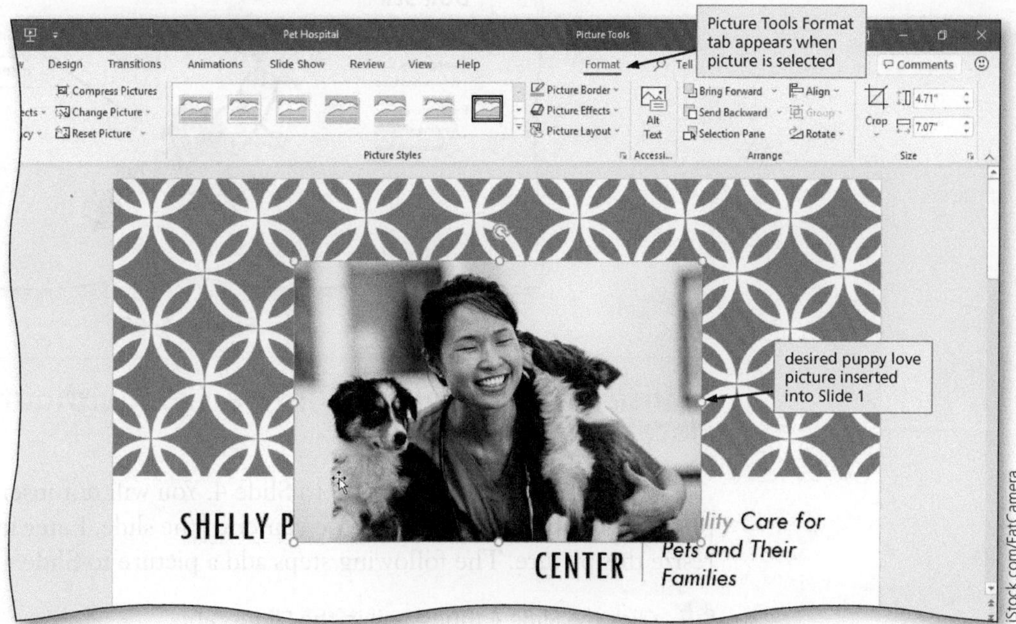

Figure 1–67

iStock.com/FatCamera

Q&A Can I double-click the picture or file name instead of selecting it and clicking the Insert button?
Yes. Either method inserts the picture.

Why is this picture displayed in this location on the slide?
The slide layout does not have a content placeholder, so PowerPoint inserts the file in an area of the slide. You will move and resize the picture later in this module.

What is the Alt Text shown at the bottom of the picture?
Alternative text (Alt text) descriptions help sight-impaired people who use screen readers understand the content of pictures.

4

- If the Design Ideas pane is displayed, click the 'Stop suggesting ideas until I restart PowerPoint' link or just close the pane.

Q&A Why is my picture a different size from the one shown in Figure1–1b?
The clip was inserted into the slide and not into a content placeholder. You will resize the picture later in this module.

To Insert another Picture into a Slide without a Content Placeholder

The next step is to add a group of animals picture to Slide 2. This slide has a bulleted list in the text placeholder, so the icon group does not display in the center of the placeholder. Later in this module, you will resize this inserted picture. The following steps add one picture to Slide 2.

1. Click the Slide 2 thumbnail in the Slides tab to display Slide 2.
2. Click Insert on the ribbon to display the Insert tab and then click the Pictures button (Insert tab | Images group) to display the Insert Picture dialog box.
3. If necessary, scroll down the list of files and then open the picture called Support_PPT_1_AnimalGroup.jpg, which is located in the Data Files, to insert the picture into Slide 2 (Figure 1–68).
4. If the Design Ideas pane is displayed, click the 'Stop suggesting ideas until I restart PowerPoint' link or just close the pane.

Figure 1–68

To Insert Another Picture into a Slide without a Content Placeholder

Next, you will add a picture to Slide 4. You will not insert this file into a content placeholder, so it will display in the center of the slide. Later in this module, you will resize this picture. The following steps add a picture to Slide 4.

1. Click the Slide 4 thumbnail in the Slides tab.
2. Display the Insert tab, click the Pictures button, and then insert the Support_PPT_1_EarGrooming.jpg file into Slide 4 (Figure 1–69).
3. If the Design Ideas pane is displayed, click the 'Stop suggesting ideas until I restart PowerPoint' link or just close the pane.

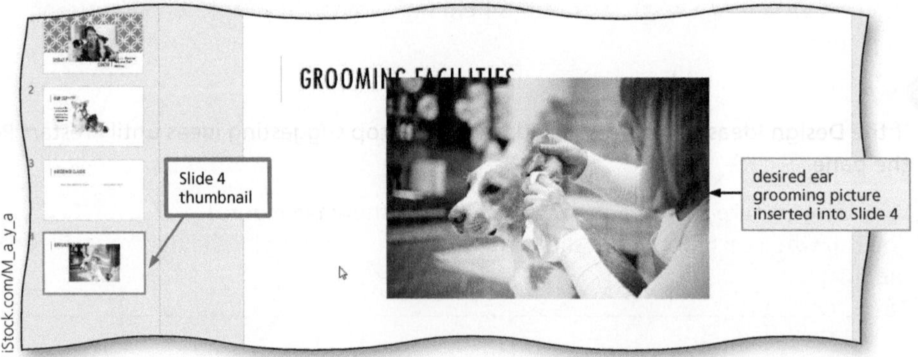

Figure 1–69

To Insert a Picture into a Content Placeholder

Slide 3 uses the Comparison layout, which has a content placeholder below each of the two headings. You desire to insert pictures into both content placeholders. ***Why?*** *You want to display two images showing that individual and group training classes are available.* The following steps insert a picture of a dog shaking his paw into the left content placeholder and a group of dogs into the right content placeholder on Slide 3.

- Click the Slide 3 thumbnail in the Slides tab to display Slide 3 (Figure 1–70).

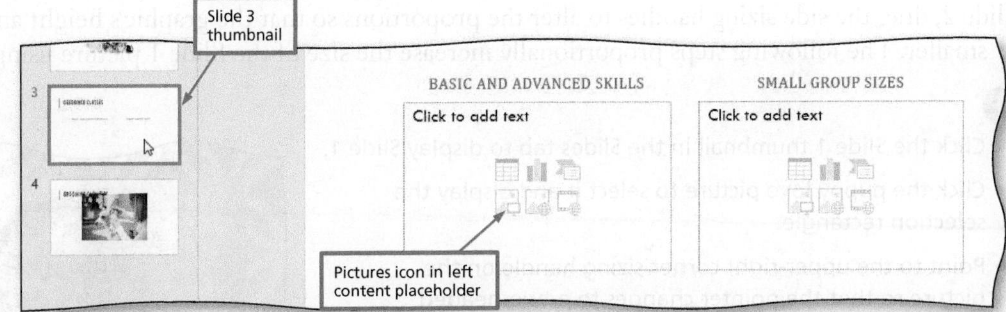

Figure 1–70

- Click the Pictures icon in the left content placeholder to select that placeholder and to open the Insert Picture dialog box.
- If necessary, scroll down the list of files, click Support_PPT_1_PawShake.jpg to select the file, and then double-click to insert the picture into the left content placeholder (Figure 1–71).

Q&A Do I need to select the file name before double-clicking to insert the picture?

No. You just can double-click the file name.

iStock.com/FatCamera

Figure 1–71

- Click the Pictures icon in the right content placeholder to select that placeholder and to open the Insert Picture dialog box.
- If necessary, scroll down the list to display the Support_PPT_1_ObedienceClass.jpg file name and then insert this picture into the right content placeholder (Figure 1–72).

desired animal group picture inserted into right content placeholder

SKILLS

SMALL GROUP SIZES

iStock.com/Highwaystarz-Photography

Figure 1–72

Resizing Photos and Illustrations

Sometimes it is necessary to change the size of pictures. **Resizing** includes enlarging or reducing the size of a graphic. You can resize these images using a variety of techniques. One method involves changing the size of a picture by specifying exact dimensions in a dialog box or in the Height and Width boxes in the Size group on the Picture Tools Format tab. Another method involves sliding or dragging one of the graphic's sizing handles to the desired location. A selected graphic appears surrounded by a **selection rectangle** which has small circles, called **sizing handles** or move handles, at each corner and middle location.

BTW

Microsoft Clip Organizer

Previous versions of Microsoft Office stored photos, pictures, animations, videos, and other media in the Clip Organizer. Office has replaced this feature with the Insert Pictures dialog box, which is displayed when you click Online Pictures (Insert tab | Images group). You then can search for and insert files.

To Proportionally Resize Pictures

Why? On Slides 1, 2, and 4, the picture sizes are too small to display aesthetically on the slides. At times it is important to maintain the proportions of a picture, such as when a person is featured prominently. To change the size of a picture and keep the width and height in proportion to each other, drag the corner sizing handles to view how the image will look on the slide. Using these corner handles maintains the graphic's original proportions. If, however, the proportions do not need to be maintained precisely, as with the paw prints picture you will insert in Slide 2, drag the side sizing handles to alter the proportions so that the graphic's height and width become larger or smaller. The following steps proportionally increase the size of the Slide 1 picture using a corner sizing handle.

1

- Click the Slide 1 thumbnail in the Slides tab to display Slide 1.
- Click the puppy love picture to select it and display the selection rectangle.
- Point to the upper-right corner sizing handle on the picture so that the pointer changes to a two-headed arrow (Figure 1–73).

Q&A I am using a touch screen and do not see a two-headed arrow when I press and hold the lower-right sizing handle. Why?
Touch screens may not display pointers; you can just press and slide sizing handles to resize.

Figure 1–73

- Drag the sizing handle diagonally toward the upper-right corner of the slide until the upper-right sizing handle or the crosshair is positioned approximately as shown in Figure 1–74.

Q&A What if the picture is not the same size as the one shown in Figure 1–74?
Repeat Steps 1 and 2.

Can I drag any corner sizing handle diagonally inward toward the opposite corner to resize the picture?
Yes.

Figure 1–74

- Release to resize the picture.
- View the Height and Width boxes (Picture Tools Format tab | Size group) to verify that the picture size is approximately 5.21" x 7.81".

Q&A What if I want to return the picture to its original size and start again?
With the picture selected, click the Reset Picture arrow (Picture Tools Format tab | Adjust group) and then click Reset Picture & Size in the Reset Picture gallery.

Can I resize the picture to exact measurements?
Yes. Click the Height and Width arrows (Picture Tools Format tab | Size group) to adjust the picture size.

To Resize the Picture on Slide 2

The animal group picture on Slide 2 also can be increased to fit much of the white space on the right side of the slide. To maintain the proportions of the original picture, drag one of the corner sizing handles. The following steps use a corner sizing handle to resize this picture.

1. Display Slide 2 and then click the picture to select it.
2. Drag any corner sizing handle on the picture diagonally outward until the picture is resized approximately as shown in Figure 1–75. The picture size should be approximately 5.22" x 8.05".

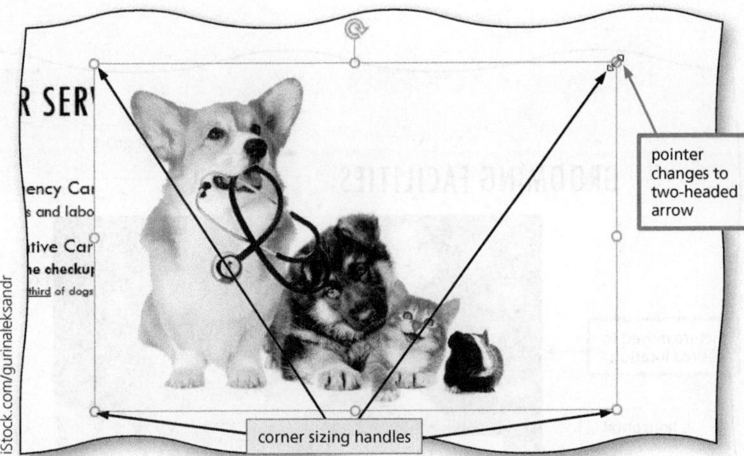

Figure 1–75

To Resize the Picture on Slide 4

The picture on Slide 4 can be increased to fit much of the white space on the slide. You want to maintain the proportion of the groomer and dog in this picture, so you will drag one of the corner sizing handles. The following steps resize this picture using a corner sizing handle.

1. Display Slide 4 and then click the picture to select it.
2. Drag any corner sizing handle on the picture diagonally outward until the picture is resized approximately as shown in Figure 1–76. The picture size should be approximately 5.49" x 8.24".

Figure 1–76

To Move Pictures

Why? *After you insert a picture on a slide, you might want to reposition it.* The picture on Slide 1 could be moved to the center of the blue area of the slide, the animal picture on Slide 2 could be moved to the right side of the slide, and the picture on Slide 4 could be positioned in the center of the slide. PowerPoint displays **smart guides** automatically when a picture, shape, or other object is moved and is close to lining up with another slide element. These layout guides, which display as dashed red lines, help you align slide elements vertically and horizontally. They display when aligning to the left, right, top, bottom, and middle of placeholders and other objects on a slide. For example, a smart guide will display to help you align the right or left edge of a picture in relation to a text placeholder or to another picture. The following steps center the picture on Slide 4 and move the pictures on Slides 2 and 1.

- If necessary, click the picture on Slide 4 to select it.
- With the four-headed arrow displaying, drag the picture downward until the vertical smart guide is displayed through the center of the picture and the horizontal smart guide is displayed along the bottom of the slide, as shown in Figure 1–77, and then release.
- If necessary, select the picture and then use the ARROW keys to position it precisely as shown in Figure 1–77.

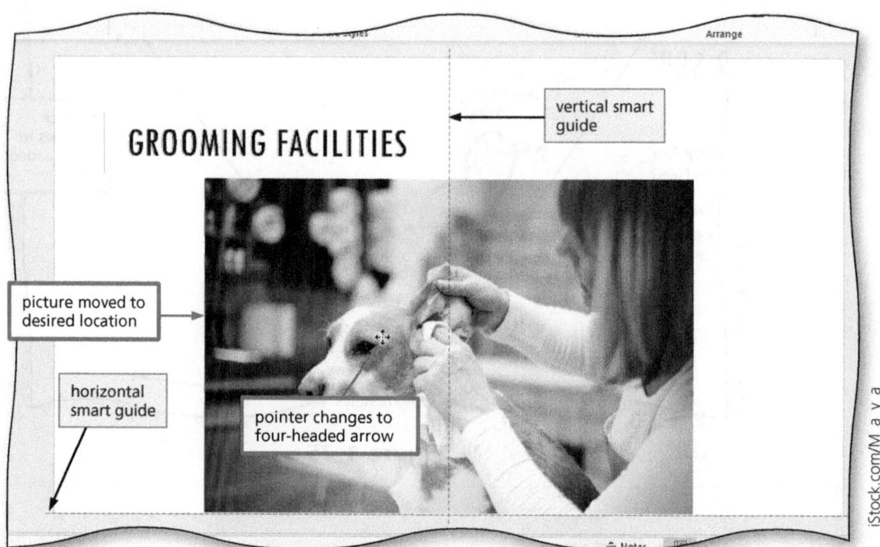

Figure 1–77

Q&A The picture still is not located exactly where I want it to display. What can I do to align the image?
Press CTRL while you press the ARROW keys. This key combination moves the picture in smaller increments than when you press only an ARROW key.

- Display Slide 2 and then click the picture to select it.
- Drag the picture until the vertical smart guide is displayed on the right side of the picture and the horizontal smart guide is displayed through the center of the picture (Figure 1–78).

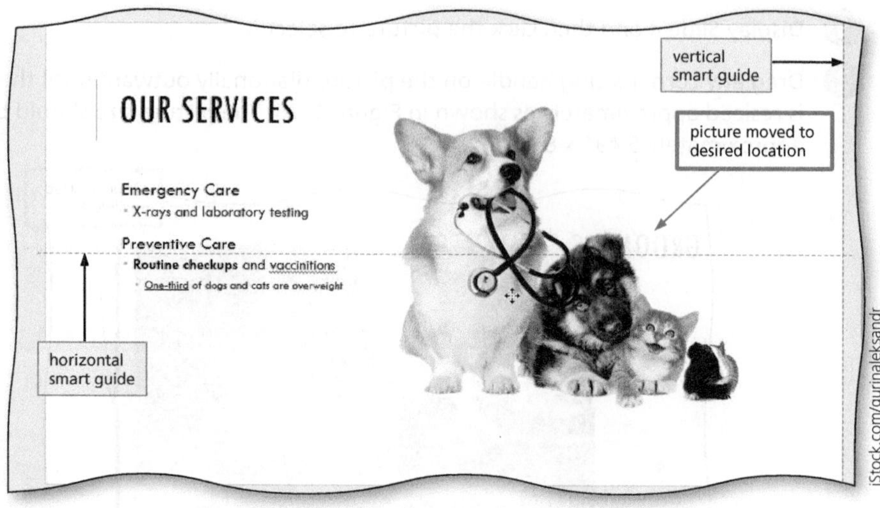

Figure 1–78

3

- Display Slide 1 and then click the picture to select it.
- Drag the picture upward and to the left until the vertical smart guide is displayed through the center of the picture and the horizontal smart guide is displayed along the top of the slide (Figure 1–79).

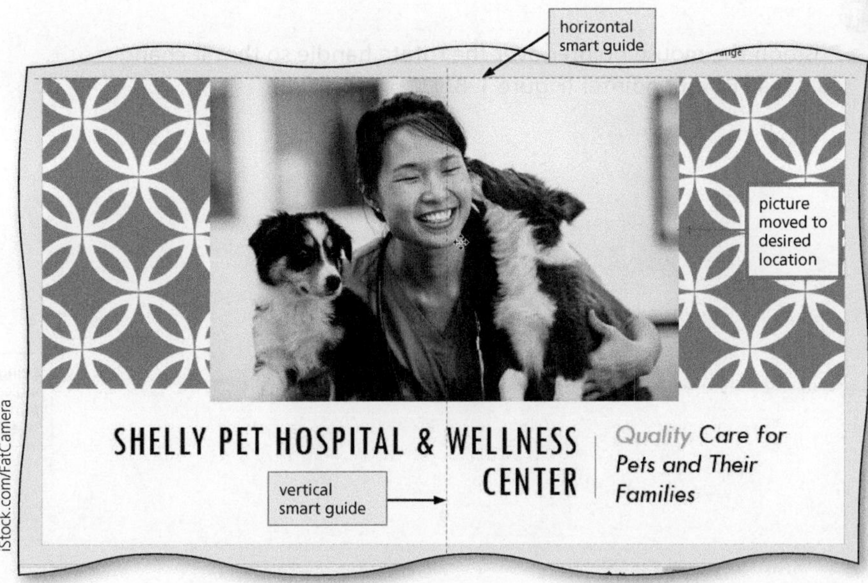

Figure 1–79

To Insert Another Picture into a Slide without a Content Placeholder

The next step is to add a picture of paw prints to Slide 2 to fill the space below the animal group picture. Later in this module, you will rotate and resize this inserted picture. The following steps add another picture to Slide 2.

BTW
Wrapping Text around a Photo
PowerPoint does not allow you to wrap text around a picture or other graphics, such as tables, shapes, and charts. This feature, however, is available in Word.

1. Display Slide 2, display the Insert tab, and then click the Pictures button (Insert tab | Images group) to display the Insert Picture dialog box.
2. If necessary, scroll down the list of files and then open the picture called Support_PPT_1_PawPrints.jpg, which is located in the Data Files, to insert the picture into Slide 2 (Figure 1–80).
3. If the Design Ideas pane is displayed, click the 'Stop suggesting ideas until I restart PowerPoint' link or just close the pane.

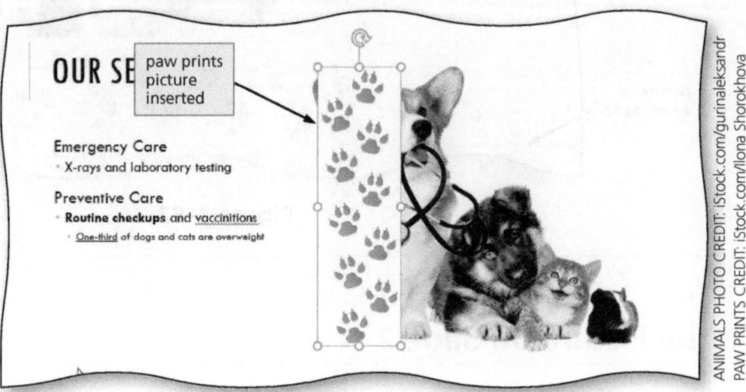

Figure 1–80

To Rotate a Picture

Why? The paw prints picture is vertical, and you want to display it at the bottom edge of the slide. Dragging the **rotate handle** above a selected object allows you to rotate an object in any direction. The following steps rotate the picture.

- Position the mouse pointer over the rotate handle so that it changes to a Free Rotate pointer (Figure 1–81).

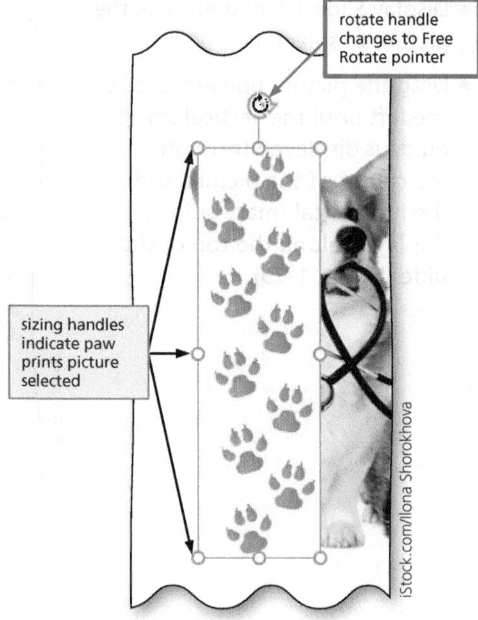

Figure 1–81

- Drag the rotate handle clockwise and then move the picture so that the vertical smart guide is the vertical smart guide is displayed through the center of the picture and the horizontal smart guide is displayed along the bottom of the slide, as shown in Figure 1–82.

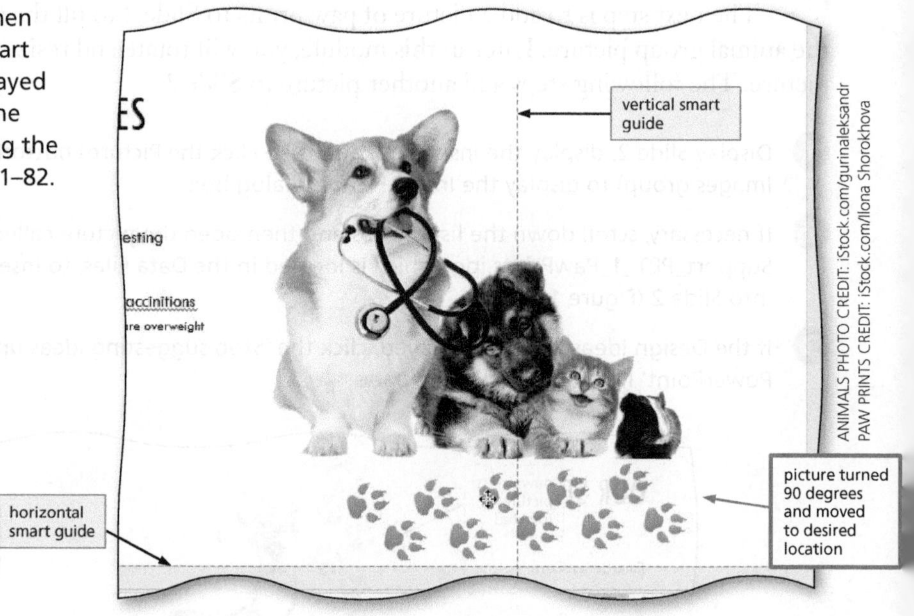

Figure 1–82

To Nonproportionally Resize the Picture on Slide 2

Why? *The width of the paw prints picture in Slide 2 is not as wide as the animal group picture, and the height is covering the kitten's paws. For aesthetic reasons, you want the paw prints and the animal group pictures to be the same width and not overlap.* The length of the paw prints picture can be increased slightly and the width can be decreased slightly without negatively distorting the original image. You can change the length and width of a picture by dragging the sizing handles on the sides of the image. The following steps resize the length and width of the paw prints picture using sizing handles along the sides of the image.

- With the paw prints picture selected and the selection rectangle is displayed, point to the middle sizing handle on the top edge of the picture so that the pointer changes to a two-headed arrow (Figure 1–83).

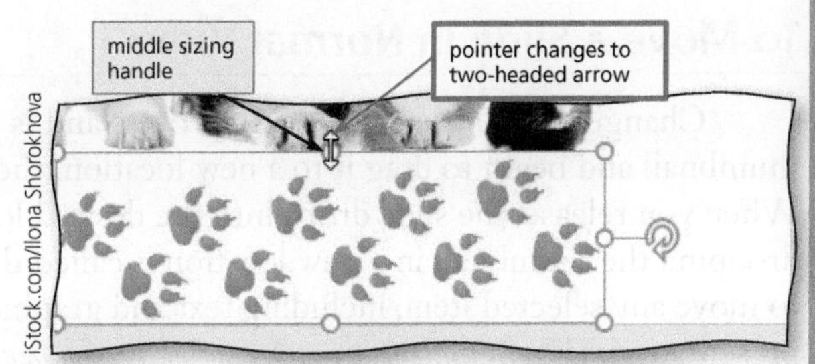

Figure 1–83

- Drag the sizing handle inward until the horizontal smart guide is displayed and the sizing handle or crosshair is positioned as shown in Figure 1–84. The approximate picture size should be 4.8" x 1.14".

Q&A What if the picture is not the same size as the one shown in Figure 1–84?
Repeat Steps 1 and 2.

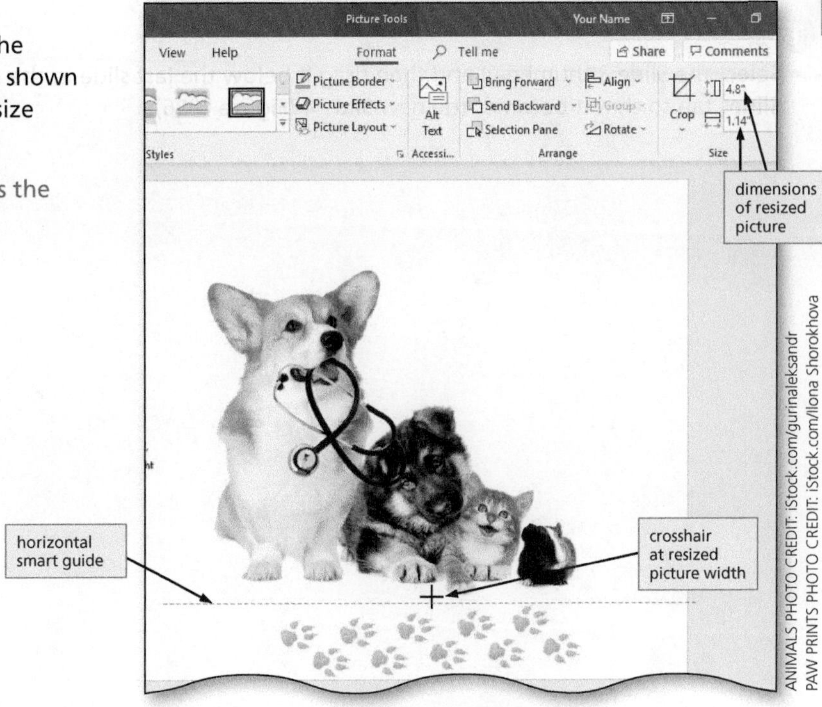

Figure 1–84

- Release to resize the picture.
- Drag the left sizing handle outward until the vertical smart guide is displayed beside the left side of the paw print picture and the sizing handle or crosshair is positioned as shown in Figure 1–85.
- Release to resize the picture. The approximate picture size should be 6.43" x 1.14".
- Click outside the picture to deselect it.

Q&A Can I move the picture in small increments?
Yes. To move or nudge the picture in very small increments, hold down CTRL with the picture selected while pressing the ARROW keys. You cannot perform this action using a touch screen.

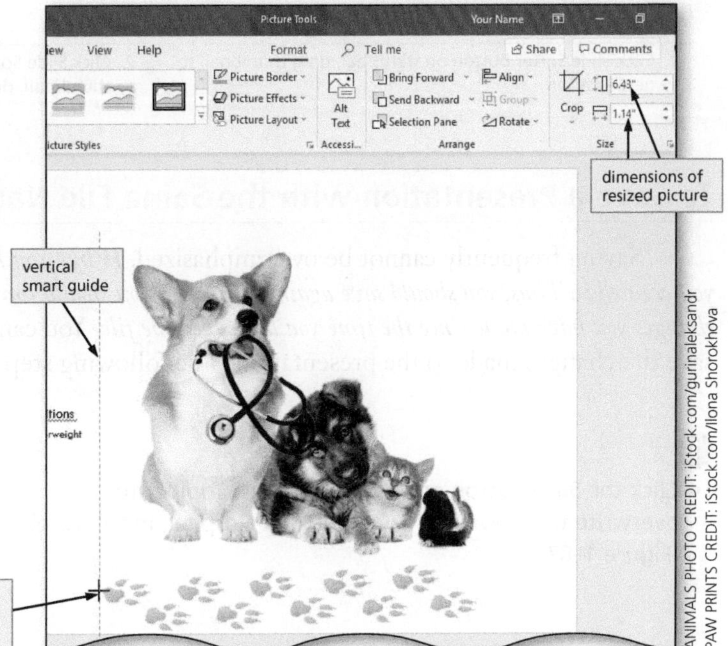

Figure 1–85

To Move a Slide in Normal View

Changing slide order is an easy process and is best performed in the Slides tab. When you click the thumbnail and begin to drag it to a new location, the remaining thumbnails realign to show the new sequence. When you release, the slide drops into the desired location. Hence, this process of sliding or dragging and then dropping the thumbnail in a new location is called **drag and drop**. You can use the drag-and-drop method to move any selected item, including text and graphics. The following step moves Slide 3 to the end of the presentation. ***Why?*** *Audience members often remember the final material they see and hear in a presentation, and you want to promote the Center's grooming services more than the obedience classes.*

- Select the Slide 3 thumbnail and then drag it below the last slide in the Slides tab so that it becomes the new Slide 4 (Figure 1–86).

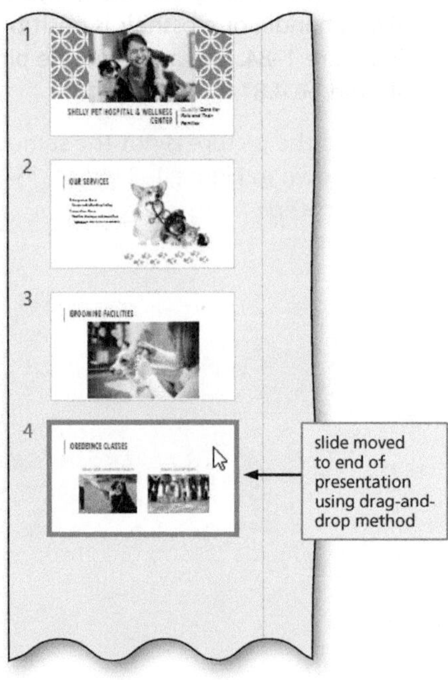

Figure 1–86

Other Ways

1. Click Slide Sorter button on status bar, drag thumbnail to new location
2. Click Slide Sorter button (View tab | Presentation Views group), click slide thumbnail, drag thumbnail to new location

To Save a Presentation with the Same File Name

Saving frequently cannot be overemphasized. ***Why?*** *You have made modifications to the file (presentation) since you created it. Thus, you should save again. Similarly, you should continue saving files frequently so that you do not lose the changes you have made since the time you last saved the file.* You can use the same file name, such as Pet Hospital, to save the changes made to the presentation. The following step saves a file again with the same file name.

- Click the Save button on the Quick Access Toolbar to overwrite the previously saved file (Pet Hospital, in this case) (Figure 1–87).

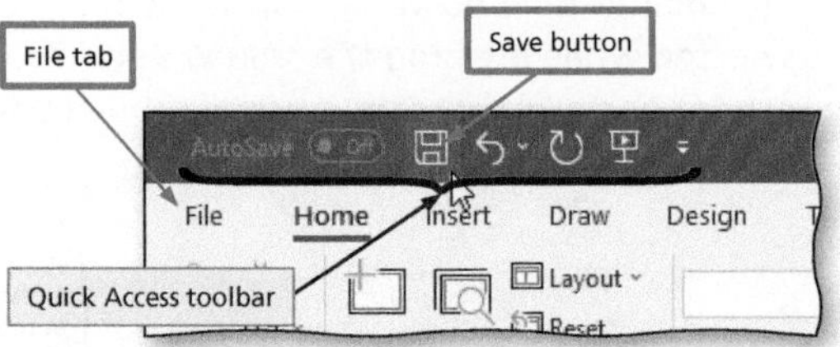

Figure 1–87

Other Ways

1. Press CTRL+S
2. Press SHIFT+F12

To Close a File Using Backstage View

Sometimes, you may want to close an Office file, such as a PowerPoint presentation, entirely and start over with a new file. You also may want to close a file when you are done working with it. ***Why?*** *You should close a file when you are done working with it so that you do not make inadvertent changes to it.* The following steps close the current active PowerPoint file, that is, the Pet Hospital presentation, without exiting PowerPoint.

- Click File on the ribbon to open Backstage view (Figure 1–88).

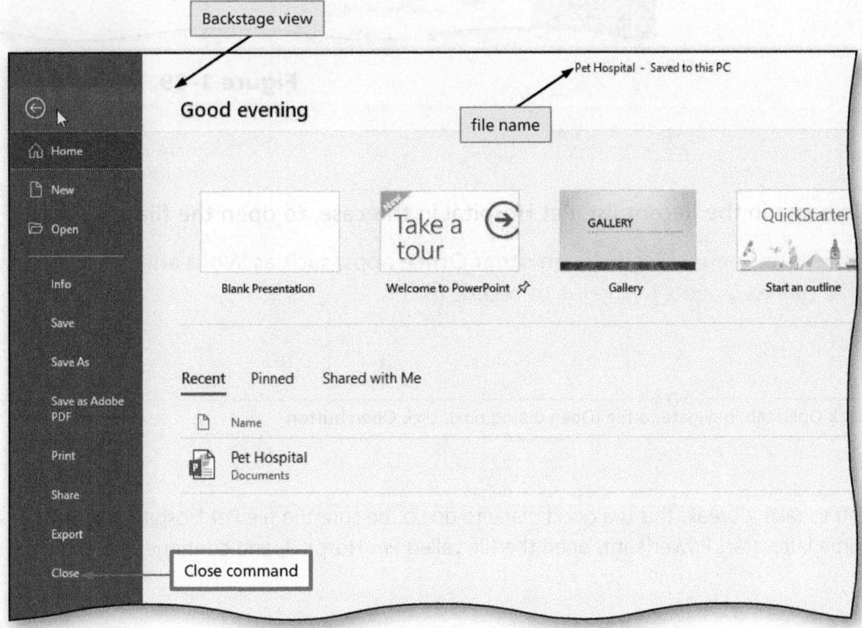

Figure 1–88

2

- Click Close in Backstage view to close the open file (Pet Hospital, in this case) without closing PowerPoint.

Q&A What if PowerPoint displays a dialog box about saving?
Click the Save button if you want to save the changes, click the Don't Save button if you want to ignore the changes since the last time you saved, and click Cancel if you do not want to close the presentation.

Other Ways

1. Press CTRL+F4

To Open a Recent File Using Backstage View

You sometimes need to open a file that you recently modified. ***Why?*** *You may have more changes to make, such as adding more content or correcting errors.* Backstage view allows you to access recent files easily. The following steps reopen the Pet Hospital file just closed.

BTW

Welcome Back!

If you are designing a slide in your deck other than Slide 1 and then save and close the document, PowerPoint's Welcome back! feature allows you to continue where you left off at the last save when you open the document. You may need to adjust the zoom if you are working at a different level than the default setting.

- Click File on the ribbon to open Backstage view.
- If necessary, click the Open tab in Backstage view to display the Open screen (Figure 1–89).

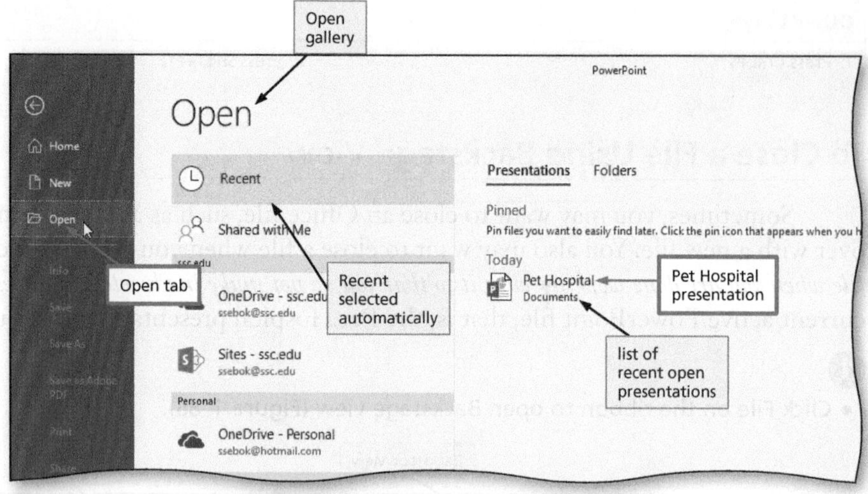

Figure 1–89

- Click the desired file name in the Recent list, Pet Hospital in this case, to open the file.

Q&A Can I use Backstage view to open a recent file in other Office apps, such as Word and Excel?
Yes, as long as the file name appears in the list of recent files.

Other Ways

1. Click File on ribbon, click Open tab, navigate to file (Open dialog box), click Open button

Break Point: If you wish to take a break, this is a good place to do so. Be sure the file Pet Hospital file is saved and then you can exit PowerPoint. To resume later, start PowerPoint, open the file called Pet Hospital, and continue following the steps from this location forward.

Making Changes to Slide Text Content

After creating slides in a presentation, you may find that you want to make changes to the text. Changes may be required because a slide contains an error, the scope of the presentation shifts, or the style is inconsistent. This section explains the types of changes that commonly occur when creating a presentation.

You generally make three types of changes to text in a presentation: additions, replacements, and deletions.

- Additions are necessary when you omit text from a slide and need to add it later. You may need to insert text in the form of a sentence, word, or single character. For example, you may want to add the presenter's middle name on the title slide.
- Replacements are needed when you want to revise the text in a presentation. For example, you may want to substitute the word, *their*, for the word, *there*.
- Deletions are required when text on a slide is incorrect or no longer is relevant to the presentation. For example, a slide may look cluttered. Therefore, you may want to remove one of the bulleted paragraphs to add more space.

Editing text in PowerPoint basically is the same as editing text in a word processing program. The following sections illustrate the most common changes made to text in a presentation.

Replacing Text in an Existing Slide

When you need to correct a word or phrase, you can replace the text by selecting the text to be replaced and then typing the new text. As soon as you press any key on the keyboard, the selected text is deleted and the new text is displayed.

PowerPoint inserts text to the left of the insertion point. The text to the right of the insertion point moves to the right (and shifts downward if necessary) to accommodate the added text.

BTW

Turning Off the Mini Toolbar

If you do not want the Mini toolbar to appear, click File on the ribbon to open Backstage view, click Options in Backstage view, if necessary click General (Options dialog box), remove the check mark from the 'Show Mini Toolbar on selection' check box, and then click OK.

Deleting Text

You can delete text using one of many methods. One is to use BACKSPACE to remove text just typed. The second is to position the insertion point to the left of the text you want to delete and then press DELETE. The third method is to drag through the text you want to delete and then click the Cut button on the Mini toolbar, DELETE or BACKSPACE, or press CTRL+X. Use the third method when deleting large sections of text.

To Delete Text in a Placeholder

Why? *The Center offers many services as part of its wellness program, so changing the word reinforces this concept.* The following steps change Facilities to Services in the Slide 3 title.

- Select Slide 3 and then position the pointer immediately to the right of the last character of the text to be selected in the title text placeholder (in this case, the s in the word, Facilities).
- Drag the pointer through the first character of the text to be selected (in this case, the F in the word, Facilities) (Figure 1–90).

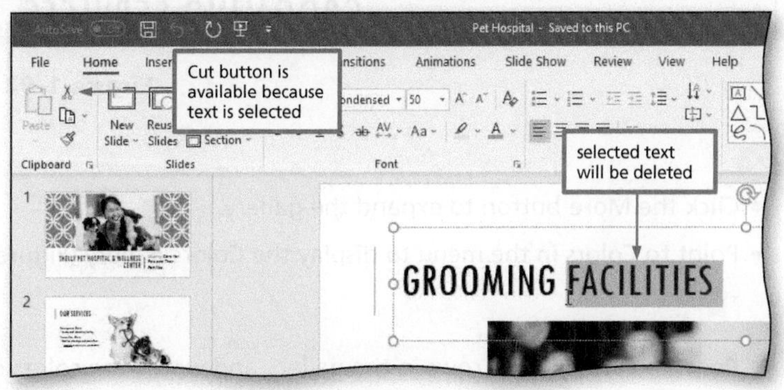

Figure 1–90

Q&A Can I drag from left to right or right to left?
Yes. Either direction will select the letters.

Could I also have selected the word, Facilities, by double-clicking it?
Yes. Either method works to select a word.

- Press DELETE to delete the selected text.
- Type **Services** as the second word in the title text placeholder (Figure 1–91).

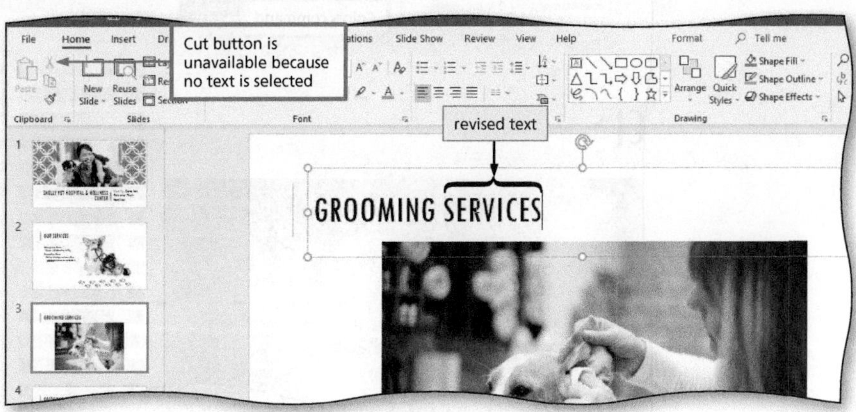

Figure 1–91

Q&A Could I have typed these words while the word, Facilities, was selected without cutting the text first?
Yes. Either method works to replace words.

Other Ways

1. Right-click selected text, click Cut on shortcut menu
2. Select text, press DELETE or BACKSPACE
3. Select text, press CTRL+X

To Change the Theme Colors

Every theme has 10 standard colors: two for text, two for backgrounds, and six for accents. The following steps change the theme colors for the Pet Hospital slides. ***Why?*** *You can change the look of your presentation and add variety by applying the colors from one theme to another theme.*

- Display the Design tab and then point to the More button in the Variants group (Design tab | Variants group) (Figure 1–92).

Figure 1–92

- Click the More button to expand the gallery.
- Point to Colors in the menu to display the Colors gallery (Figure 1–93).

Experiment

- Point to various color rows in the gallery and watch the colors change on Slide 3.

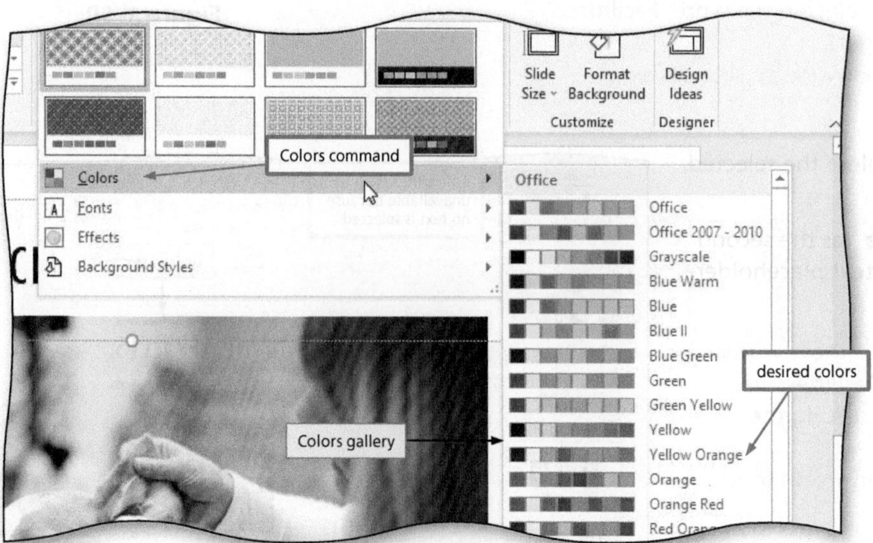

Figure 1–93

3

- Click Yellow Orange in the gallery to change the slides' theme colors (Figure 1–94).

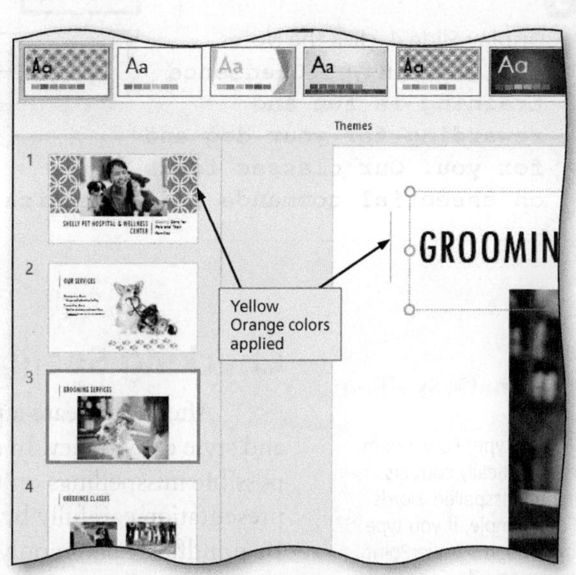

Figure 1–94

To Add Notes

Why? *As you create slides, you may find material you want to state verbally and do not want to include on the slide.* After adding these comments, you can print a set of speaker notes that will print below a small image of the slide. You can type and format comments in the Notes pane as you work in Normal view and then print this information as **notes pages**. Charts, tables, and pictures added to the Notes pane also print on these pages. The Notes pane is hidden until you click the Notes button on the status bar to open the pane. If you want to close the Notes pane, click the Notes button again. The following steps add text to the Notes pane on Slides 3 and 4.

BTW
Formatting Notes Pane Text
You can format text in the Notes pane in the same manner you format text on a slide. To add emphasis, for example, you can italicize key words or change the font color and size.

1

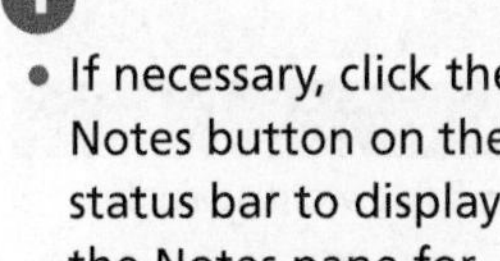

- If necessary, click the Notes button on the status bar to display the Notes pane for Slide 3 (Figure 1–95).

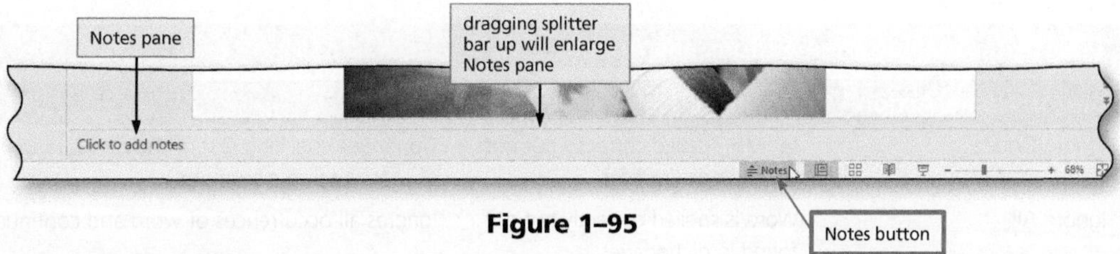

Figure 1–95

Q&A Why might I need to click the Notes button?
By default, the Notes pane is closed when you begin a new presentation. Once you display the Notes pane for any slide, the Notes pane will remain open unless you click the Notes button to close it.

2

- Click the Notes pane and then type `We offer quality dog and cat grooming services performed by our experienced pet stylist. We will pamper your pet with a bath, nail trimming, and ear cleaning. Services vary in price based on the animal's breed and size.` (Figure 1–96).

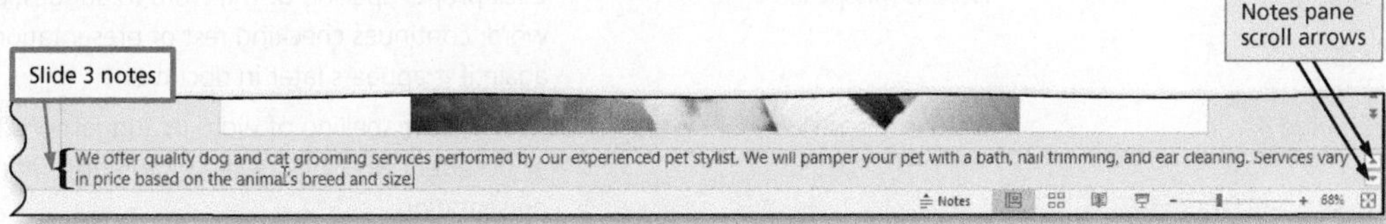

Figure 1–96

Q&A What if I cannot see all the lines I typed?
You can drag the splitter bar up to enlarge the Notes pane. Clicking the Notes pane scroll arrows or swiping up or down on the Notes pane allows you to view the entire text.

• Display Slide 4, click the Notes pane, and then type **Obedience training is fun and rewarding for your dog and for you. Our classes focus on essential commands and socialization.** (Figure 1–97).

Figure 1–97

BTW
Automatic Spelling Correction
As you type, PowerPoint automatically corrects some misspelled words. For example, if you type overwieght, PowerPoint automatically corrects the misspelling and displays the word, overweight, when you press SPACEBAR or type a punctuation mark. To see a complete list of automatically corrected words, click File on the ribbon to open Backstage view, click the Options tab, click Proofing in the left pane (PowerPoint Options dialog box), click AutoCorrect Options, and then scroll through the list near the bottom of the dialog box.

Checking Spelling

After you create a presentation, you should check it visually for spelling errors and style consistency. In addition, you can use PowerPoint's Spelling tool to identify possible misspellings on the slides and in the notes. You should proofread your presentation carefully by pointing to each word and saying it aloud as you point to it. Be mindful of commonly misused words such as its and it's, through and though, and to and too.

PowerPoint checks the entire presentation for spelling mistakes using a standard dictionary contained in the Microsoft Office group. This dictionary is shared with the other Microsoft Office applications such as Word and Excel. A custom dictionary is available if you want to add special words such as proper names, cities, and acronyms. When checking a presentation for spelling errors, PowerPoint opens the standard dictionary and the custom dictionary file, if one exists. When a word appears in the Spelling pane, you can perform one of several actions, as described in Table 1–1.

The standard dictionary contains commonly used English words. It does not, however, contain many proper names, abbreviations, technical terms, poetic contractions, or antiquated terms. PowerPoint treats words not found in the dictionaries as misspellings.

Table 1–1 Spelling Pane Buttons and Actions

Button Name/Action	When to Use	Action
Ignore Once	Word is spelled correctly but not found in dictionaries	Continues checking rest of the presentation but will flag word again if it appears later in document
Ignore All	Word is spelled correctly but not found in dictionaries	Ignores all occurrences of word and continues checking rest of presentation
Add	Add word to custom dictionary	Opens custom dictionary, adds word, and continues checking rest of presentation
Change	Word is misspelled	Click proper spelling of the word in Suggestions list; PowerPoint corrects word, continues checking rest of presentation, but will flag that word again if it appears later in document
Change All	Word is misspelled	Click proper spelling of word in Suggestions list; PowerPoint changes all occurrences of misspelled word and continues checking rest of presentation
Listen to the pronunciation	To hear the pronunciation of a word	Click audio speaker icon next to the properly spelled word near bottom of Spelling pane
View synonyms	See some synonyms for the correctly spelled word	View bullet list of synonyms below correctly spelled word near the bottom of Spelling pane
Close	Stop spelling checker	Closes spelling checker and returns to PowerPoint window

To Check Spelling

Why? Although PowerPoint's spelling checker is a valuable tool, it is not infallible. You should not rely on the spelling checker to catch all your mistakes. The following steps check the spelling on all slides in the Pet Hospital presentation.

- Click Review on the ribbon to display the Review tab.
- Click the Spelling button (Review tab | Proofing group) to start the spelling checker and display the Spelling pane (Figure 1–98).

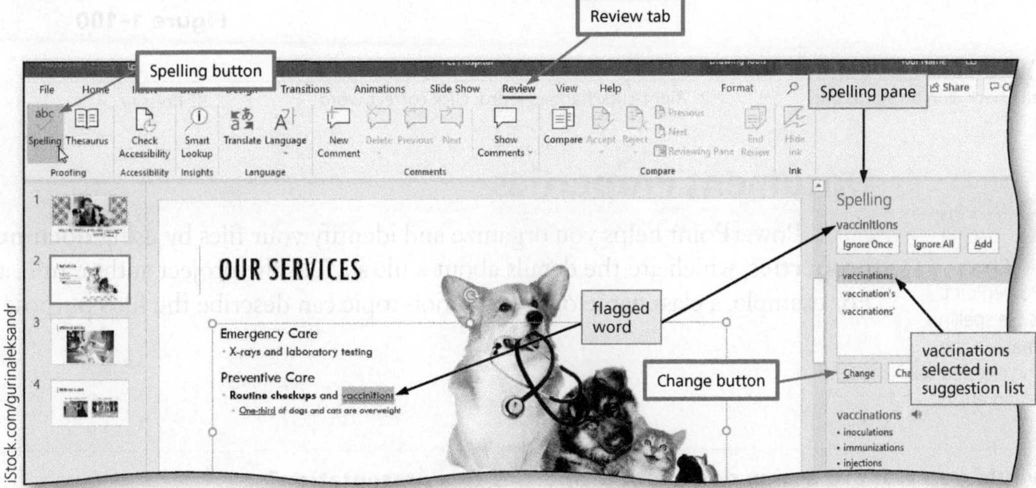

Figure 1–98

2

- With the word, vaccinitions, selected in the slide and in the Spelling pane, click the Change button (Spelling pane) to replace the misspelled flagged word, vaccinitions, with the selected correctly spelled word, vaccinations.

Q&A

Could I have clicked the Change All button instead of the Change button?
Yes. When you click the Change All button, you change the current and future occurrences of the misspelled word. The misspelled word, Obedeince, appears only once in the presentation, so clicking the Change or the Change All button in this instance produces identical results.

Occasionally a correctly spelled word is flagged as a possible misspelled word. Why?
Your custom dictionary does not contain the word, so it is seen as spelled incorrectly. You can add this word to a custom dictionary to prevent the spelling checker from flagging it as a mistake.

3

- Continue checking all flagged words in the presentation.
- When Slide 4 is displayed, replace the misspelled word, Obedeince, with the word, Obedience (Figure 1–99).

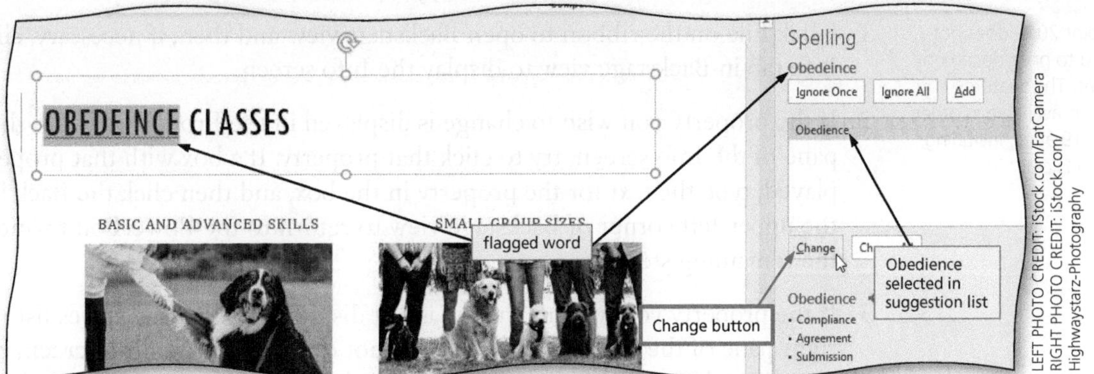

Figure 1–99

4

- Continue the spell check.
- When the Microsoft PowerPoint dialog box appears, click OK (Microsoft PowerPoint dialog box) to close the spelling checker and return to the slide where a possible misspelled word appeared (Figure 1–100).

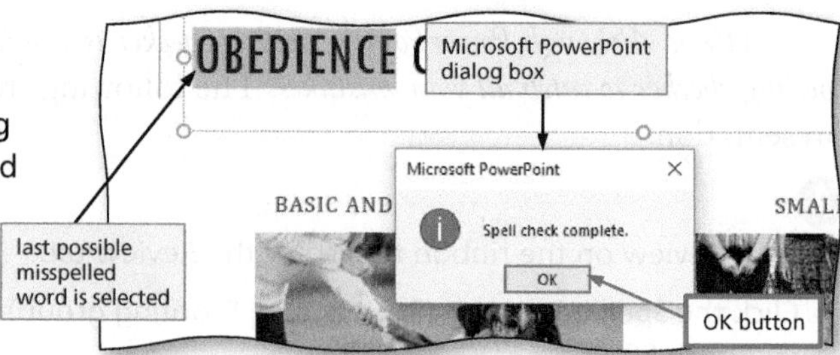

Figure 1–100

Other Ways

1. Click Spell Check icon on status bar
2. Right-click flagged word, click correct word
3. Press F7

BTW
Detecting Spelling Errors
The x in the Spell Check icon indicates PowerPoint detected a possible spelling error. A check mark in the icon indicates the entered text contains no spelling errors.

Document Properties

PowerPoint helps you organize and identify your files by using **document properties**, which are the details about a file such as the project author, title, and subject. For example, a class name or presentation topic can describe the file's purpose or content.

CONSIDER THIS

Why would you want to assign document properties to a presentation?
Document properties are valuable for a variety of reasons:

- Users can save time locating a particular file because they can view a file's document properties without opening the presentation.
- By creating consistent properties for files having similar content, users can better organize their presentations.
- Some organizations require PowerPoint users to add document properties so that other employees can view details about these files.

The more common document properties are standard and automatically updated properties. **Standard properties** are associated with all Microsoft Office files and include author, title, and subject. **Automatically updated properties** include file system properties, such as the date you create or change a file, and statistics, such as the file size.

BTW
Printing Document Properties
PowerPoint 2019 does not allow you to print document properties. This feature, however, is available in other Office 2019 apps, including Word and Excel.

To Change Document Properties

To change document properties, you would follow these steps.

1. Click File on the ribbon to open Backstage view and then, if necessary, click the Info tab in Backstage view to display the Info screen.
2. If the property you wish to change is displayed in the Properties list in the right pane of the Info screen, try to click that property. If a box with that property is displayed, type the text for the property in the box, and then click the Back button in the upper-left corner of Backstage view to return to the PowerPoint window. Skip the remaining steps.
3. If the property you wish to change is not displayed in the Properties list in the right pane of the Info screen or you cannot change it in the Info screen, click the Properties button in the right pane to display the Properties menu, and then click Advanced Properties on the Properties menu to display the Summary tab in the Properties dialog box.

Q&A Why are some of the document properties in my Document Information Panel already filled in?

The person who installed Office 2019 on your computer or network may have set or customized the properties.

4. Type the desired text in the appropriate property boxes.
5. Click OK (Properties dialog box) to close the dialog box
6. Click the Back button in the upper-left corner of Backstage view to return to the PowerPoint presentation window.

Changing Views

You have been using **Normal view** to create and edit your slides. Once you complete your slides in projects, you can review the final products by displaying each slide in **Slide Show view**, which occupies the full computer screen, to view how the slides will display in an actual presentation before an audience.

PowerPoint has other views to help review a presentation for content, organization, and overall appearance. **Slide Sorter view** allows you to look at several slides at one time. **Reading view** is similar to Slide Show view because each slide displays individually, but the slides do not fill the entire screen. Using this view, you easily can progress through the slides forward or backward with simple controls at the bottom of the window. Switching between Slide Sorter, Reading, and Normal views helps you review your presentation, assess whether the slides have an attractive design and adequate content, and make sure they are organized for the most impact. After reviewing the slides, you can change the view to Normal so that you may continue working on the presentation.

To Change Views

Why? *You have made several modifications to the slides, so you should check for balance and consistency.* The following steps change the view from Normal view to Slide Sorter view, then Reading view, and back to Normal view.

- Display Slide 1 and then click the Slide Sorter view button on the right side of the status bar to display the presentation in Slide Sorter view (Figure 1–101).

Q&A Why does a colored border display around Slide 1?

It is the current slide in the Slides tab.

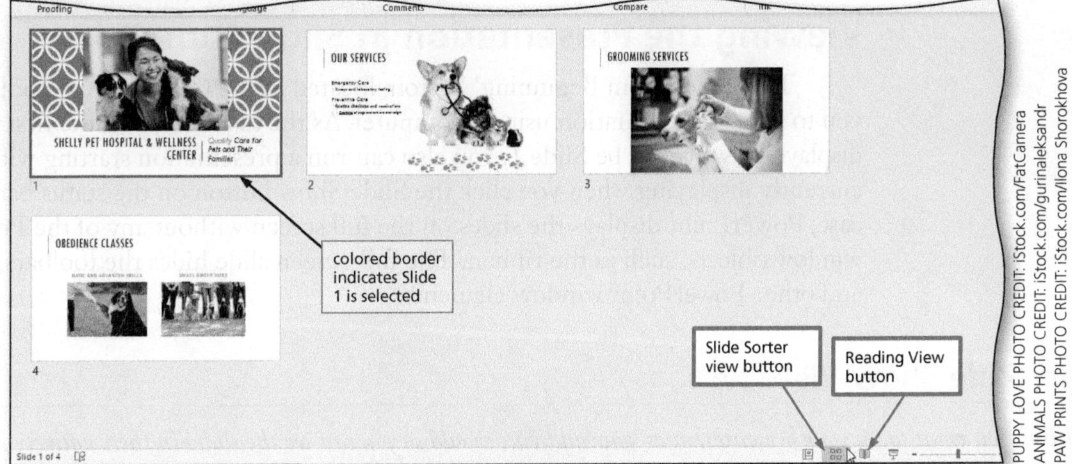

Figure 1–101

- Click the Reading View button on the right side of the status bar to display Slide 1 of the presentation in Reading view (Figure 1–102).

Figure 1–102

- Click the Next button three times to advance through the presentation.
- Click the Previous button two times to display Slide 2.
- Click the Menu button to display commonly used commands (Figure 1–103).

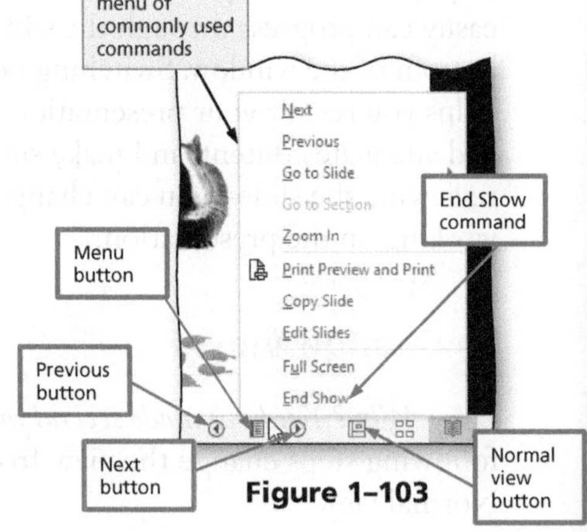

Figure 1–103

- Click End Show to return to Slide Sorter view, which is the view you were using before Reading view.
- Click the Normal view button to display the presentation in Normal view.

Viewing the Presentation in Slide Show View

The 'Start From Beginning' button, located in the Quick Access Toolbar, allows you to show a presentation using a computer. As the name implies, the first slide to be displayed always will be Slide 1. You also can run a presentation starting with the slide currently displaying when you click the Slide Show button on the status bar. In either case, PowerPoint displays the slides on the full screen without any of the PowerPoint window objects, such as the ribbon. The full-screen slide hides the toolbars, menus, and other PowerPoint window elements.

To Start Slide Show View

***Why?** You want to see your presentation as your audience would so you can see the slides in their entirety and view any transitions or other effects added to the slides.* When making a presentation, you use Slide Show view to display slides so that they fill the entire screen. This is the view you use to show your presentation to an audience. You can start Slide Show view from Normal view or Slide Sorter view. Slide Show view begins when you click the 'Start From Beginning' button or the Slide Show button. The following steps start Slide Show view starting with Slide 1.

1

- Point to the 'Start From Beginning' button on the Quick Access Toolbar (Figure 1–104).

Q&A What would have displayed if I had clicked the Slide Show button instead of the 'Start From Beginning' button?
When you click the Slide Show button to start the presentation, PowerPoint begins the show with the currently displayed slide, which in this case is Slide 1. If, however, a different slide had been displaying, the slide show would have begun with that slide.

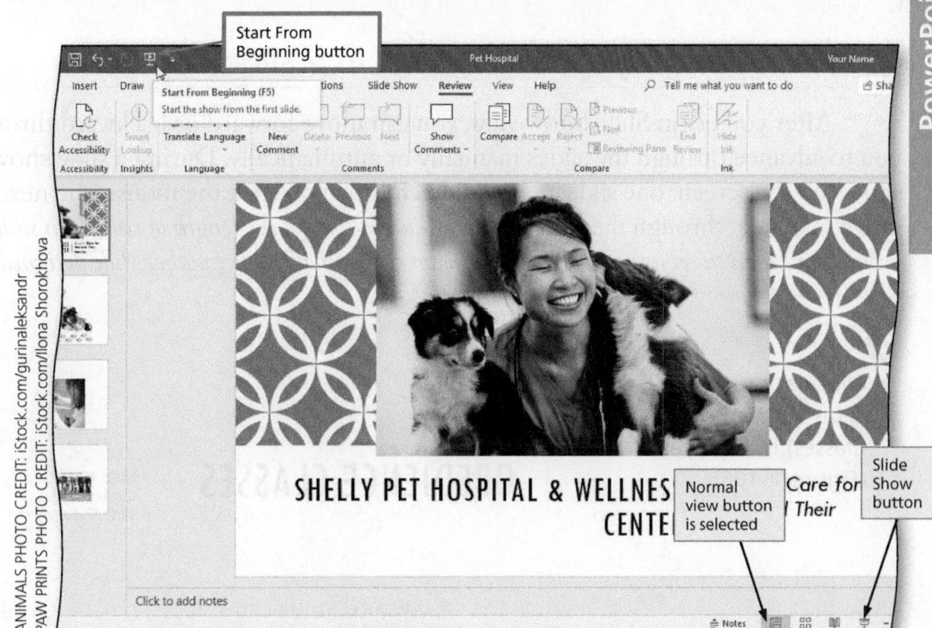

Figure 1–104

2

- Click the 'Start From Beginning' button to display the title slide (Figure 1–105). The screen goes dark, then Slide 1 displays in the entire window.

Q&A Where is the PowerPoint window?
When you run a slide show, the PowerPoint window is hidden. It will reappear once you end your slide show.

I see a small toolbar in the lower-left corner of my slide. What is this toolbar?
You may see the Slide Show toolbar when you begin running a slide show and then move the pointer or click. The buttons on this toolbar allow you to navigate to the next slide or the previous slide, to mark up the current slide, or to change the current display. If you do not see the toolbar, hover the mouse near the lower-left corner of the screen.

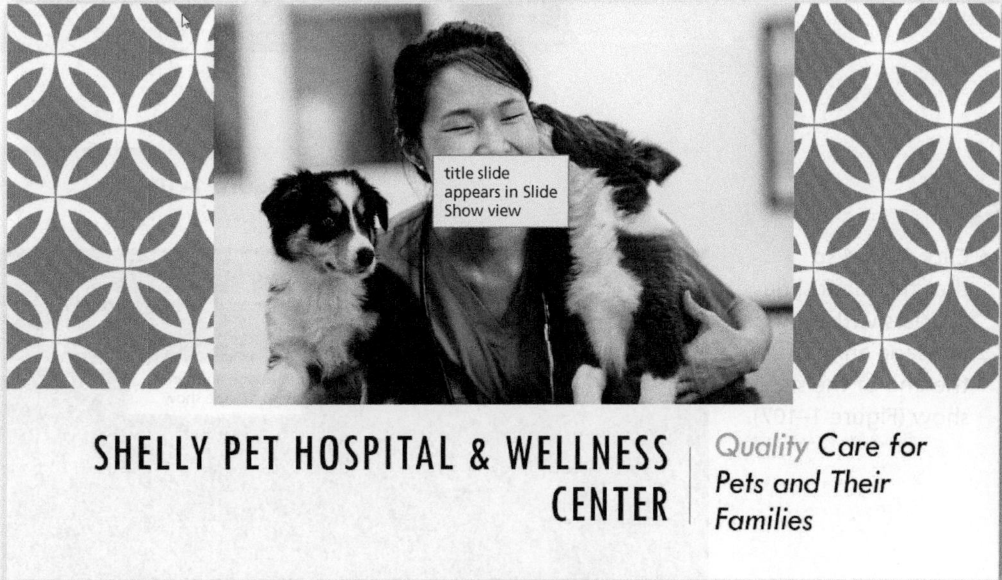

Figure 1–105

Other Ways

1. Display Slide 1, click Slide Show button on status bar
2. Click 'Start From Beginning' button (Slide Show tab | Start Slide Show group)
3. Press F5

To Move Manually through Slides in a Slide Show

After you begin Slide Show view, you can move forward or backward through the slides. PowerPoint allows you to advance through the slides manually or automatically. During a slide show, each slide in the presentation shows on the screen, one slide at a time. Each time you click the mouse, the next slide appears. The following steps move manually through the slides. ***Why?*** *You can control the length of time each slide is displayed and change the preset order if you need to review a slide already shown or jump ahead to another slide designed to display later in the presentation.*

1

- Click each slide until Slide 4 (Obedience Classes) is displayed (Figure 1–106).

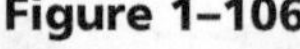

Figure 1–106

LEFT PHOTO CREDIT: iStock.com/FatCamera
RIGHT PHOTO CREDIT: iStock.com/Highwaystarz-Photography

2

- Click Slide 4 so that the black slide appears with a message announcing the end of the slide show (Figure 1–107).

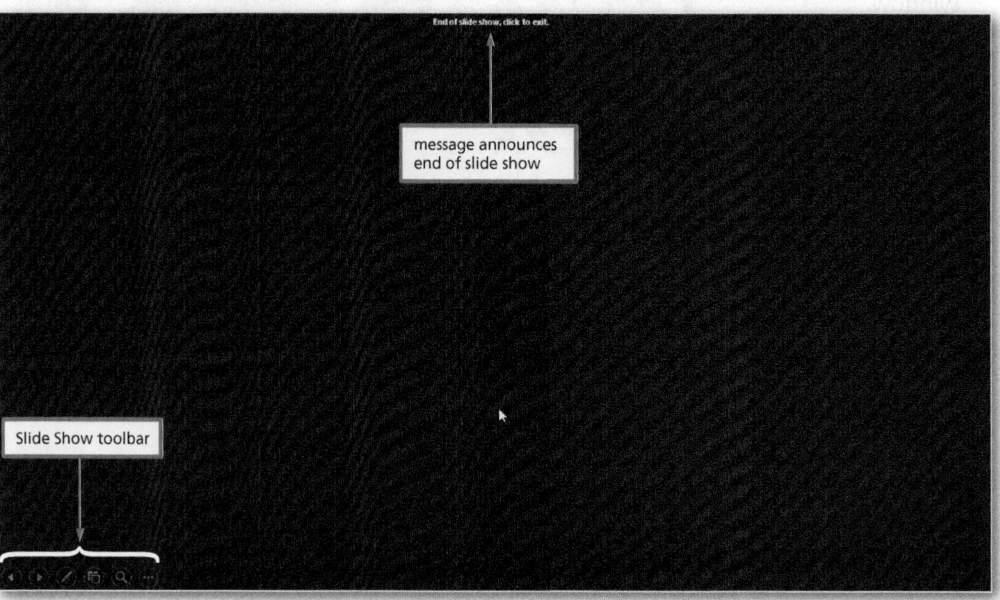

Figure 1–107

- Click the black slide to return to Normal view in the PowerPoint window.

Other Ways

1. Press PAGE DOWN to advance one slide at a time, or press PAGE UP to go back one slide at a time
2. Press RIGHT ARROW or DOWN ARROW to advance one slide at a time, or press LEFT ARROW or UP ARROW to go back one slide at a time
3. If Slide Show toolbar is displayed, click Next Slide or Previous Slide button on toolbar

Saving and Printing Files

While you are creating a presentation, the computer or mobile device stores it in memory. When you save a presentation, the computer or mobile device places it on a storage medium, such as a hard disk, solid state drive (SSD), USB flash drive, or cloud storage. The storage medium can be permanent in your computer, may be portable where you remove it from your computer, or may be on a web server you access through a network or the Internet.

To Save a File with a Different File Name

You might want to save a file with a different file name or to a different location. ***Why?*** *You might start a homework assignment with a data file and then save it with a final file name for submission to your instructor, saving it to a different location designated by your instructor.* The following steps save the Pet Hospital file with a different file name.

1. Click File on the ribbon to open Backstage view.
2. Click Save As in Backstage view to display the Save As screen.
3. Type `SC_PPT_1_Pets` in the File name box, replacing the existing file name.

Q&A What are all those characters in the file name in this project?
Some companies require certain rules be followed when creating file names; others allow you to choose your own. The file names in this book do not use spaces and all begin with SC (for Shelly Cashman) and PPT (for PowerPoint) followed by the module number and then a descriptor of the file contents, and use underscores instead of spaces so that they work with SAM, if you are using that platform as well.

4. Click the Save button to save the presentation with the new name.

BTW
Conserving Ink and Toner
If you want to conserve ink or toner, you can instruct PowerPoint to print draft quality documents by clicking File on the ribbon to open Backstage view, clicking Options in Backstage view to display the PowerPoint Options dialog box, clicking Advanced in the left pane (PowerPoint Options dialog box), scrolling to the Print area in the right pane, verifying there is no check mark in the High quality check box, and then clicking OK. Then, use Backstage view to print the document as usual.

To Print Full Page Slides

With the presentation opened, you may want to print it. ***Why?*** *Because you want to see how the slide will appear on paper, you want to print a hard copy on a printer.* The following steps print a hard copy of the contents of the presentation.

- Click File on the ribbon to open Backstage view.
- Click the Print tab in Backstage view to display the Print screen and a preview of Slide 1 (Figure 1–108).

Q&A What if I decide not to print the presentation at this time?
Click the Back button in the upper-left corner of Backstage view to return to the document window.

Why does the preview of my slide appear in black and white?
Your printer determines how the preview appears. If your printer is not capable of printing color images, the preview will appear in black and white.

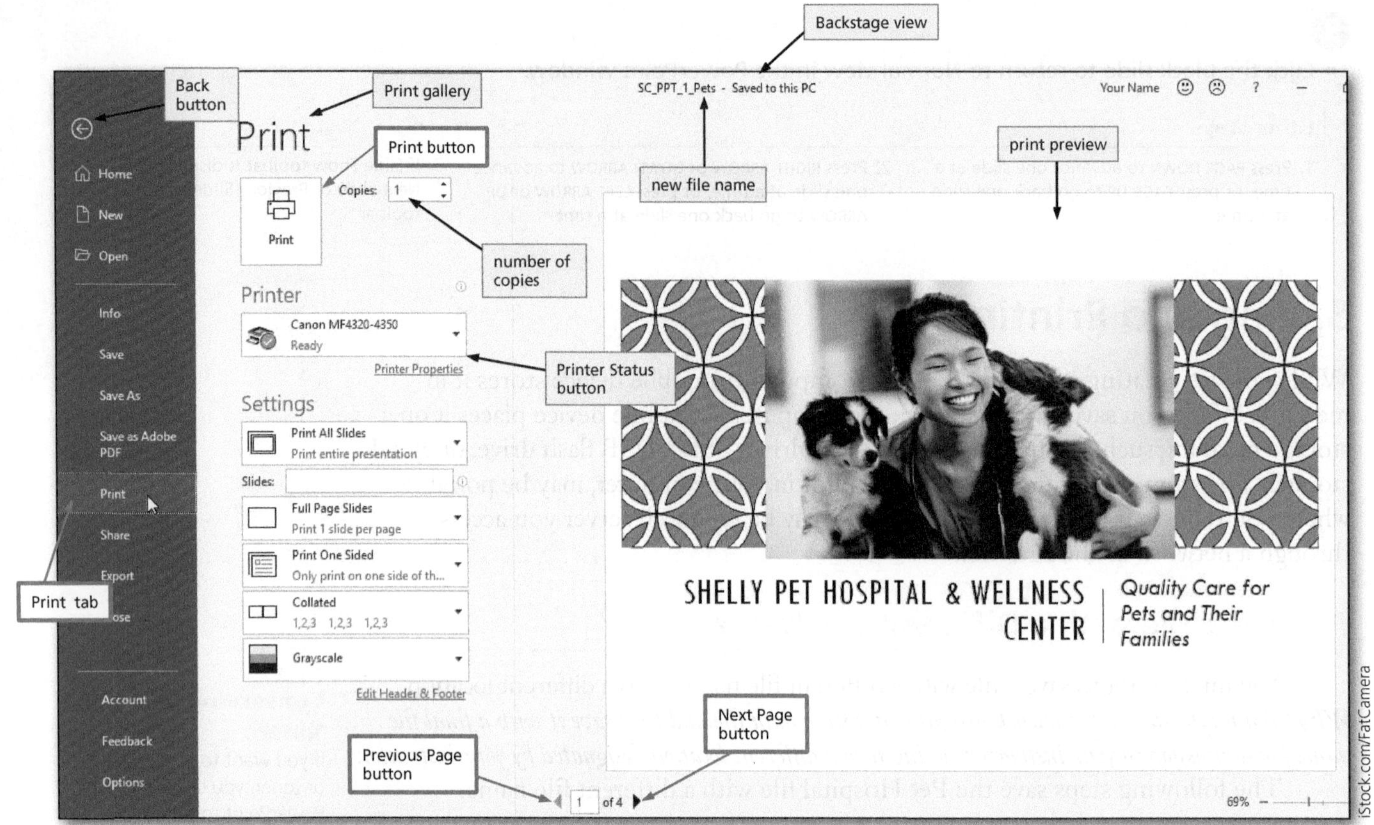

Figure 1–108

2

- Click the Next Page button to display Slide 2.

Q&A Do I need to change the display before I print?
No. You can print all the slides with any slide displaying in the preview window.

- Verify that the selected printer will print a hard copy of the presentation. If necessary, click the Printer Status button to display a list of available printer options and then click the desired printer to change the currently selected printer.

Q&A How can I print multiple copies of my presentation?
Increase the number in the Copies box in the Print screen.

3

- Click the Print button in the Print screen to print the presentation on the currently selected printer.
- When the printer stops, retrieve the hard copies (Figure 1–109).

Q&A What if I want to create a PDF of my presentation instead of printing a hard copy?
You would click the Printer Status button in the Print screen and then select Adobe PDF, which would create a PDF file.

Do I have to wait until my presentation is complete to print it?
No, you can print a presentation at any time while you are creating it.

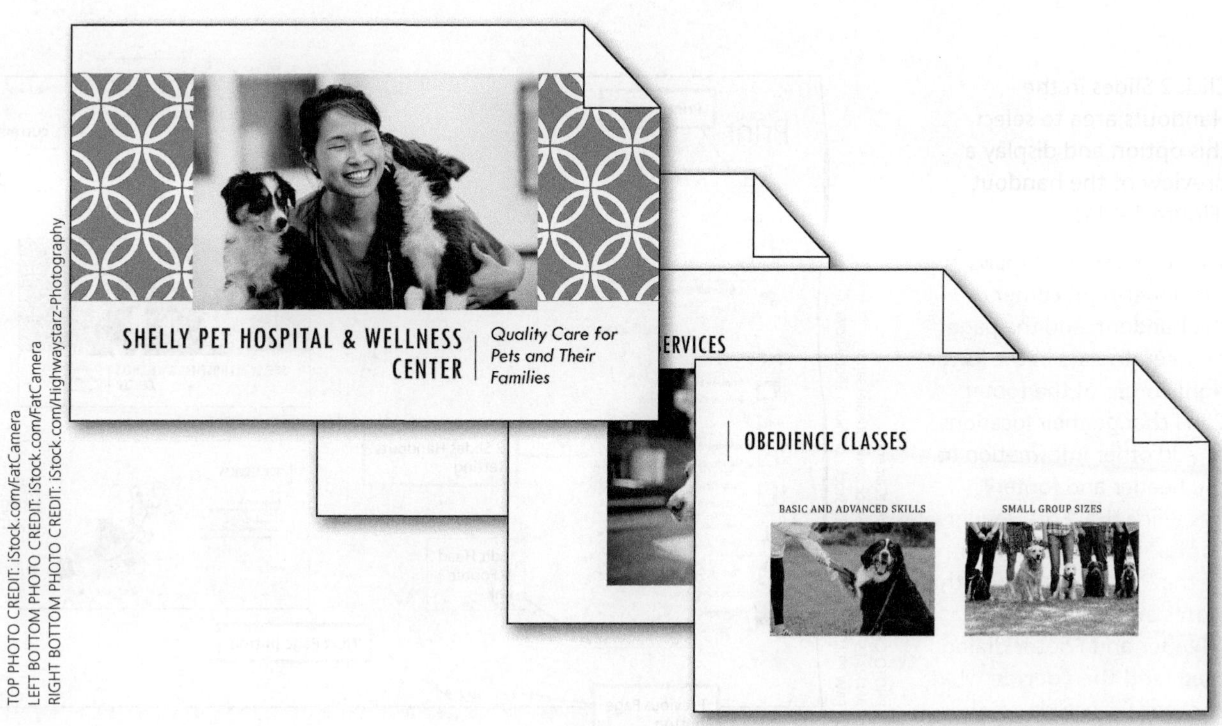

Figure 1–109

Other Ways

1. Press CTRL+P

To Preview and Print a Handout

Printing handouts is useful for reviewing a presentation. You can analyze several slides displayed simultaneously on one page. Additionally, many businesses distribute handouts of the slide show before or after a presentation so attendees can refer to a copy. Each page of the handout can contain reduced images of one, two, three, four, six, or nine slides. The three-slides-per-page handout includes lines beside each slide so that your audience can write notes conveniently. The following steps preview and print a presentation handout with two slides per page. ***Why?*** *Two of the slides are predominantly pictures, so your audience does not need full pages of those images. The five bulleted paragraphs on Slide 2 can be read easily on one-half of a sheet of paper.*

BTW
Printing Background Images
If you do not use a color printer, background images display on the screen but may not display in the printouts. Graphics are displayed depending upon the settings in the Print gallery. For example, the background will print if Color is specified whereas it will not with a Grayscale or Pure Black and White setting.

1

- If necessary, click File on the ribbon to open Backstage view and then click the Print tab.
- Click 'Full Page Slides' in the Settings area to display the Full Page Slides gallery (Figure 1–110).

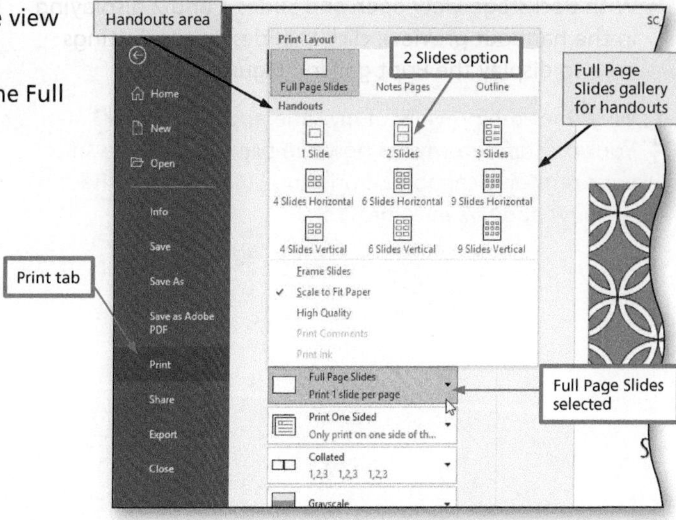

Figure 1–110

- Click 2 Slides in the Handouts area to select this option and display a preview of the handout (Figure 1–111).

Q&A The current date displays in the upper-right corner of the handout, and the page number displays in the lower-right corner of the footer. Can I change their locations or add other information to the header and footer?

Yes. Click the 'Edit Header & Footer' link at the bottom of the Print screen, click the Notes and Handouts tab (Header and Footer dialog box), and then decide what content to include on the handout page.

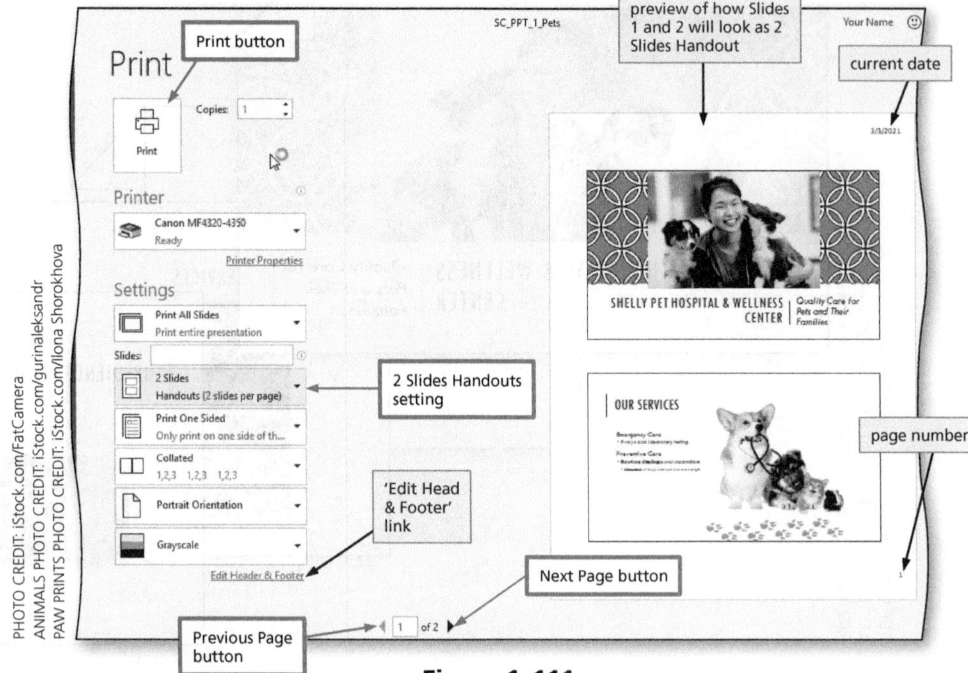

PHOTO CREDIT: iStock.com/FatCamera
ANIMALS PHOTO CREDIT: iStock.com/gurinaleksandr
PAW PRINTS PHOTO CREDIT: iStock.com/Ilona Shorokhova

Figure 1–111

- Click the Next Page and Previous Page buttons to display previews of the two pages in the handout.
- Click the Print button in the Print screen to print the handout.
- When the printer stops, retrieve the printed handout.

BTW

Distributing Slides

Instead of printing and distributing a hard copy of PowerPoint slides, you can distribute the slides electronically. Options include sending the slides via email; posting it on cloud storage (such as OneDrive) and sharing the link with others; posting it on social media, a blog, or other website; and sharing a link associated with an online location of the slides. You also can create and share a PDF or XPS image of the slides, so that users can view the file in Acrobat Reader or XPS Viewer instead of in PowerPoint.

To Print Speaker Notes

Why? *Comments added to slides in the Notes pane give the speaker information that supplements the text on the slide.* Notes will print with a small image of the slide at the top and the comments below the slide. The following steps print the speaker notes.

- With Backstage view open and Slides 1 and 2 displaying in the handout preview, click '2 Slides' in the Settings area to display the Print gallery (Figure 1–112).

Q&A Why does the preview of my slide appear in color?

Your printer determines how the preview appears. If your printer is capable of printing color images, the preview appears in color.

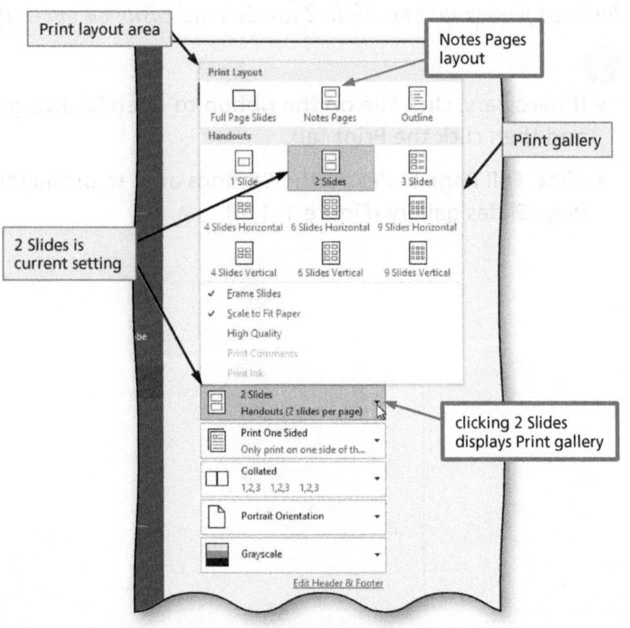

Figure 1–112

2

- Click Notes Pages in the Print Layout area to select this option and then click the Next Page button two times to display a preview of Slide 3 and notes in a handout (Figure 1–113).

Q&A Can I preview other slides now?
Yes. Click the Next Page button or the Previous Page button to preview the other slides.

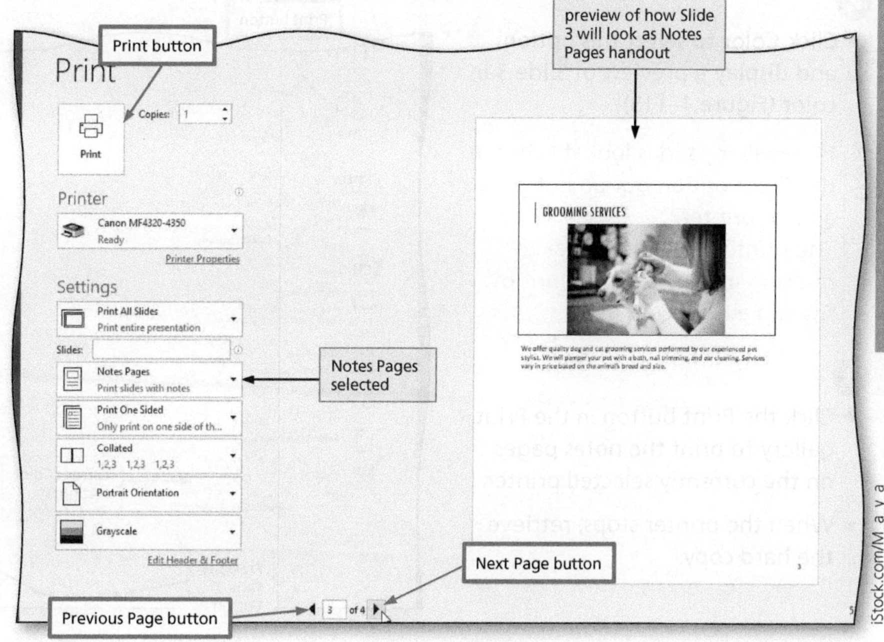

Figure 1–113

3

- Click the Print button in the Print gallery to print the notes pages on the currently selected printer.
- When the printer stops, retrieve the hard copy.

To Change the Print Color

Some printers are capable of printing in color, black and white, or grayscale. Grayscale, as the name implies, prints all objects on the page in black, white, and shades of gray. You can specify the print color by changing the setting in Backstage view. The following steps print the speaker notes in color. ***Why?*** *You want to distribute colorful handouts to audience members.*

BTW
Using Grayscale Setting
If you do not have a color printer or do not require a color printout, choosing Grayscale will print all pages in shades of gray. In grayscale, objects such as charts and tables will appear crisper and cleaner than if you chose the Color option on a non-color printer.

1

- With Backstage view open and Slide 3 displaying in the handout preview, click Grayscale in the Settings area to display the Color gallery (Figure 1–114).

Q&A How does the handout appear in Pure Black and White?
No shades of gray will print when the Pure Black and White setting is selected.

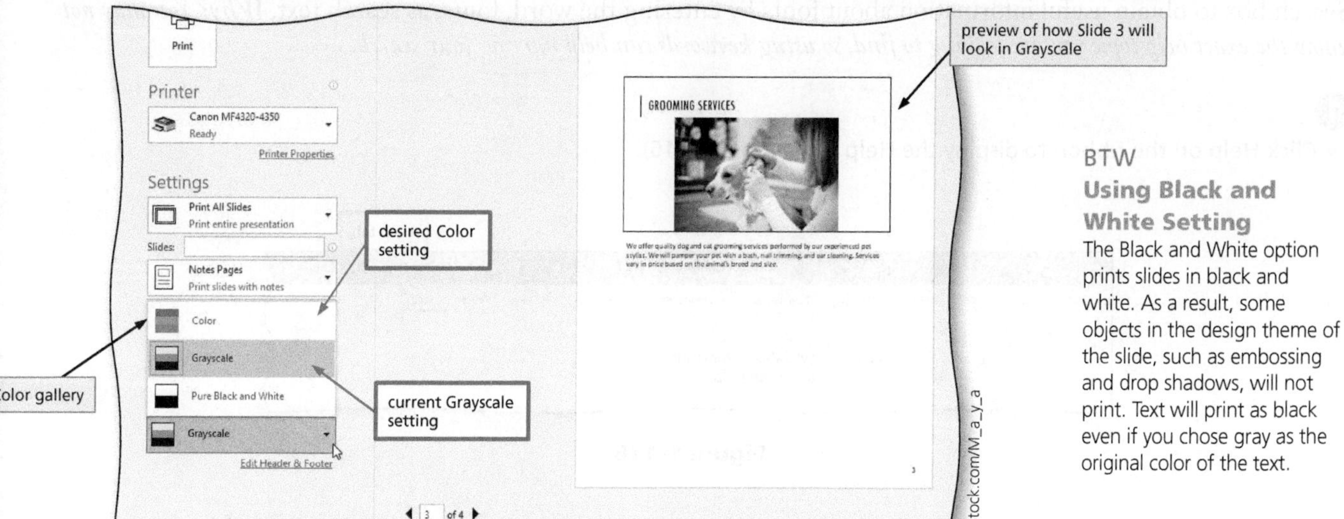

Figure 1–114

BTW
Using Black and White Setting
The Black and White option prints slides in black and white. As a result, some objects in the design theme of the slide, such as embossing and drop shadows, will not print. Text will print as black even if you chose gray as the original color of the text.

- Click Color to select this option and display a preview of Slide 3 in color (Figure 1–115).

Q&A How will my slides look if I choose the Color option but do not have a color printer?

The printout will be similar to printing in grayscale, but not of the same quality.

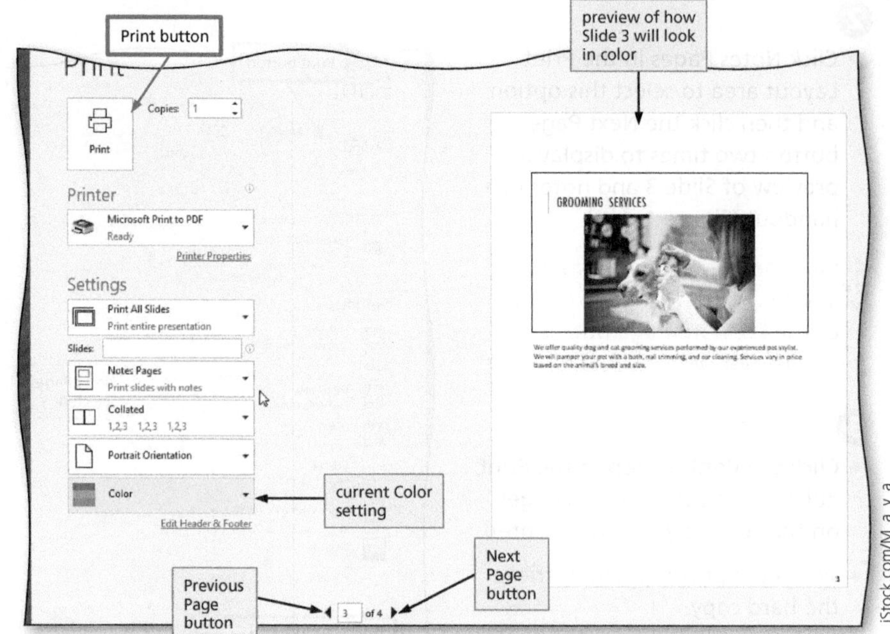

Figure 1–115

- Click the Print button in the Print gallery to print the notes pages on the currently selected printer.
- When the printer stops, retrieve the hard copy.

Using PowerPoint Help

At any time while you are using PowerPoint, you can use Office Help to display information about all topics associated with this app. Help is presented in a window that has browser-style navigation buttons. Once an Office app's Help window is open, several methods exist for navigating Help. You can search for help by using the Help pane or the Tell me box.

To Obtain Help Using the Search Box

Assume for the following example that you want to know more about fonts. The following steps use the Search box to obtain useful information about fonts by entering the word, fonts, as search text. ***Why?*** *You may not know the exact help topic you are looking to find, so using keywords can help narrow your search.*

1

- Click Help on the ribbon to display the Help tab (Figure 1–116).

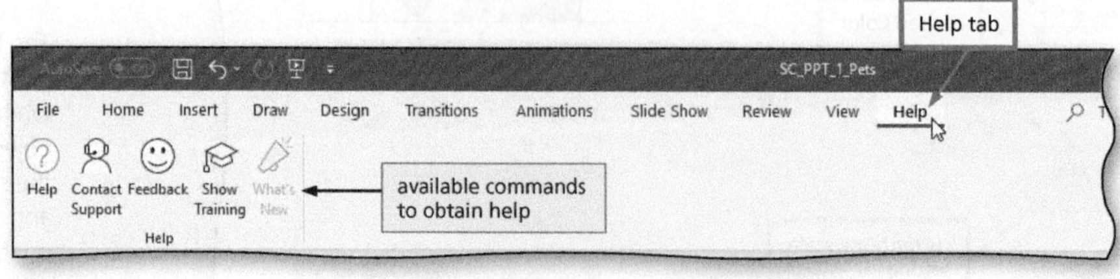

Figure 1–116

- Click the Help button (Help group) to display the Help pane (Figure 1–117).

Figure 1–117

- Type **fonts** in the Search help box at the top of the Help pane to enter the search text and display search suggestions (Figure 1–118).

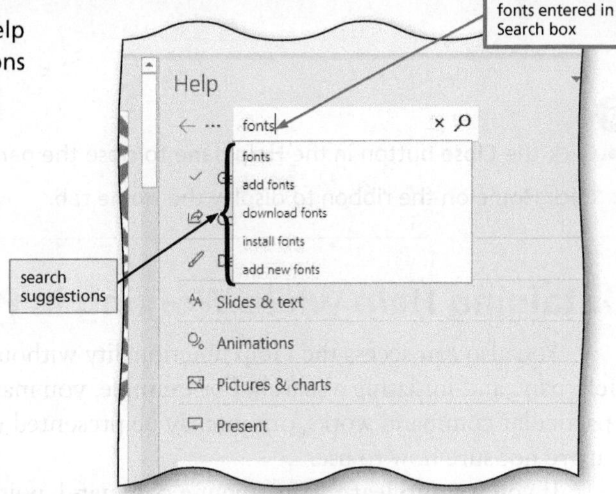

Figure 1–118

- Press ENTER to display the search results (Figure 1–119).

Q&A Why do my search results differ?
If you do not have an Internet connection, your results will reflect only the content of the Help files on your computer. When searching for help online, results also can change as content is added, deleted, and updated on the online Help webpages maintained by Microsoft.

Why were my search results not very helpful?
When initiating a search, be sure to check the spelling of the search text; also, keep your search specific to return the most accurate results.

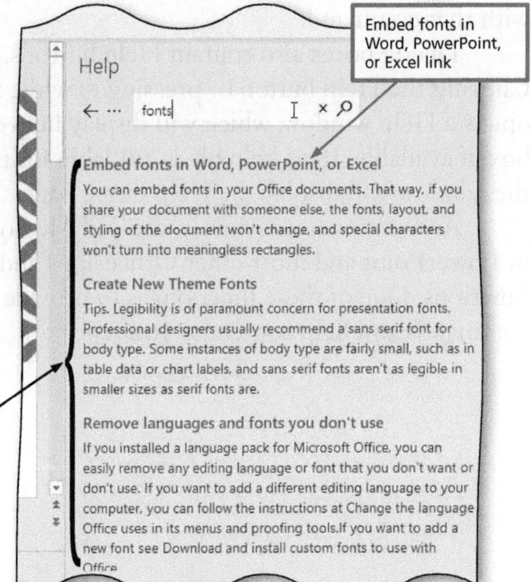

Figure 1–119

- Click 'Embed fonts in Word, PowerPoint, or Excel', or a similar link to display the Help information associated with the selected topic (Figure 1–120).

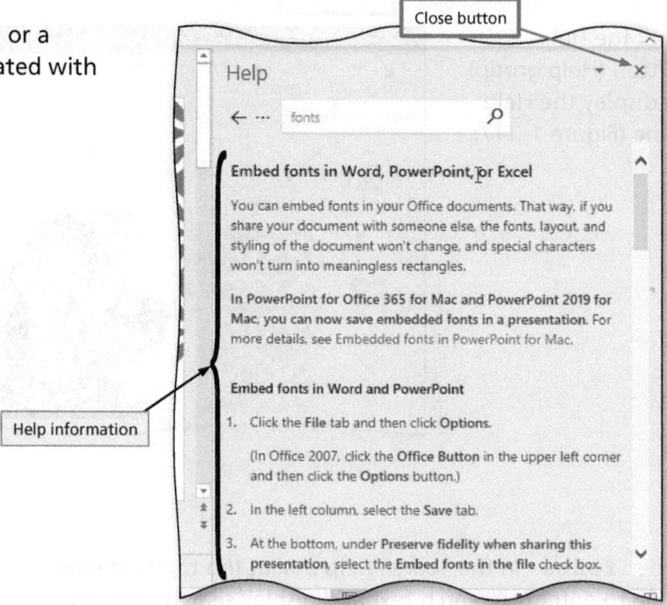

Figure 1–120

- Click the Close button in the Help pane to close the pane.
- Click Home on the ribbon to display the Home tab.

Obtaining Help while Working in PowerPoint

You also can access the Help functionality without first opening the Help pane and initiating a search. For example, you may be unsure about how a particular command works, or you may be presented with a dialog box that you are not sure how to use.

If you want to learn more about a command, point to its button and wait for the ScreenTip to appear, as shown in Figure 1–121. If the Help icon and 'Tell me more' link appear in the ScreenTip, click the 'Tell me more' link (or press F1 while pointing to the button) to open the Help window associated with that command.

Dialog boxes also contain Help buttons, as shown in Figure 1–122. Clicking the Help button or pressing F1 while the dialog box is displayed opens a Help window, which will display help contents specific to that dialog box, if available. If no help file is available for that particular dialog box, then the window will display the Help home page.

As mentioned previously, the Tell Me box is integrated into the ribbon in PowerPoint and most other Office apps and can perform a variety of functions. One of these functions is to provide easy access to commands and help content as you type.

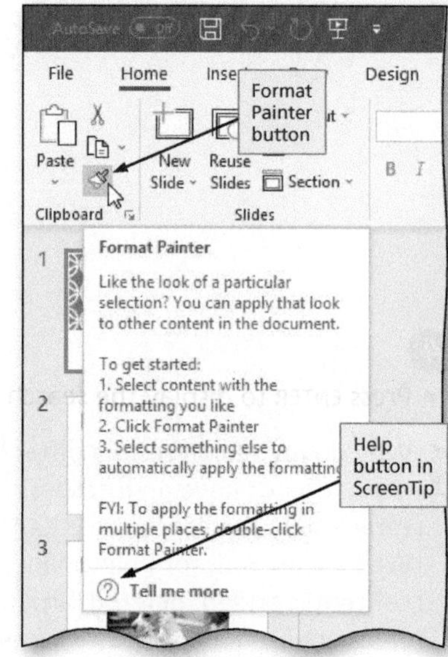

Figure 1–121

Figure 1–122

To Obtain Help Using the Tell Me Box

If you are having trouble finding a command in PowerPoint, you can use the Tell Me box to search for the function you are trying to perform. As you type, the Tell Me box will suggest commands that match the search text you are entering. ***Why?*** *You can use the Tell Me box to access commands quickly that you otherwise may be unable to find on the ribbon.* The following steps find information about borders.

1

- Type **border** in the Tell Me box and watch the search results appear.
- Point to Border Style to display a submenu displaying the various border designs (Figure 1–123).

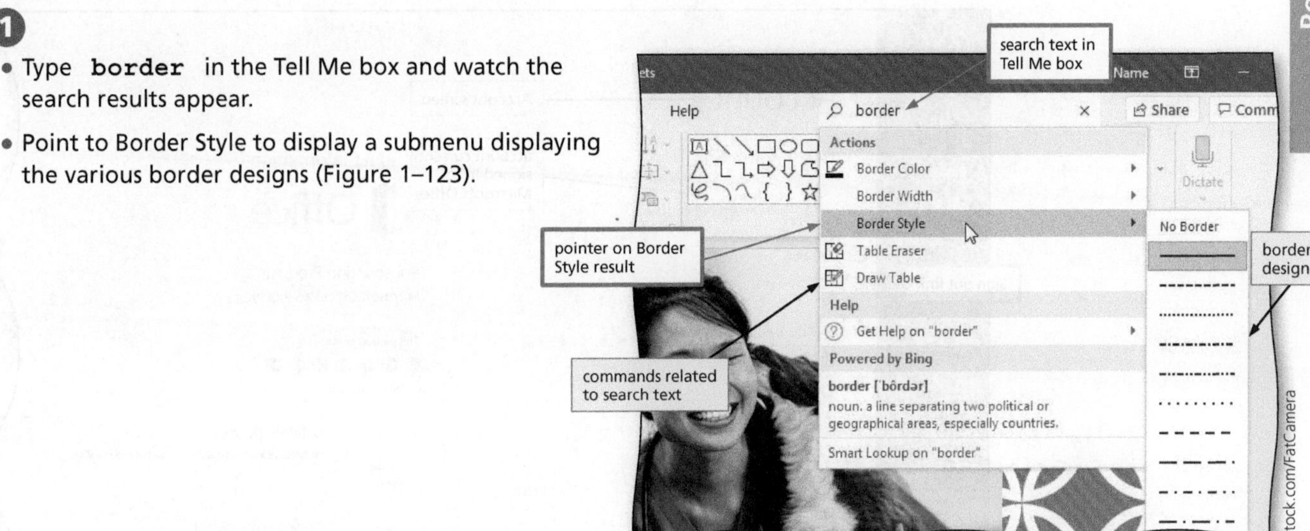

Figure 1–123

To Sign Out of a Microsoft Account

If you are using a public computer or otherwise wish to sign out of your Microsoft account, you should sign out of the account from the Accounts screen in Backstage view. Signing out of the account is the safest way to make sure that nobody else can access online files or settings stored in your Microsoft account. ***Why?*** *For security reasons, you should sign out of your Microsoft account when you are finished using a public or shared computer. Staying signed in to your Microsoft account might enable others to access your files.*

The following steps sign out of a Microsoft account from PowerPoint. If you do not wish to sign out of your Microsoft account, read these steps without performing them.

1. Click File on the ribbon to open Backstage view.
2. Click the Account tab to display the Account screen (Figure 1–124).
3. Click the Sign out link, which displays the Remove Account dialog box. If a Can't remove Windows accounts dialog box appears instead of the Remove Account dialog box, click OK and skip the remaining steps.

Q&A Why does a Can't remove Windows accounts dialog box appear?
If you signed in to Windows using your Microsoft account, then you also must sign out from Windows, rather than signing out from within PowerPoint. When you are finished using Windows, be sure to sign out at that time.

4. Click the Yes button (Remove Account dialog box) to sign out of your Microsoft account on this computer.

Q&A Should I sign out of Windows after removing my Microsoft account?
When you are finished using the computer, you should sign out of Windows for maximum security.

5. Click the Back button in the upper-left corner of Backstage view to return to the presentation.

6. sam Click the Close button to close the presentation and PowerPoint. If you are prompted to save changes, click Yes to save any changes made to the file since the last save.

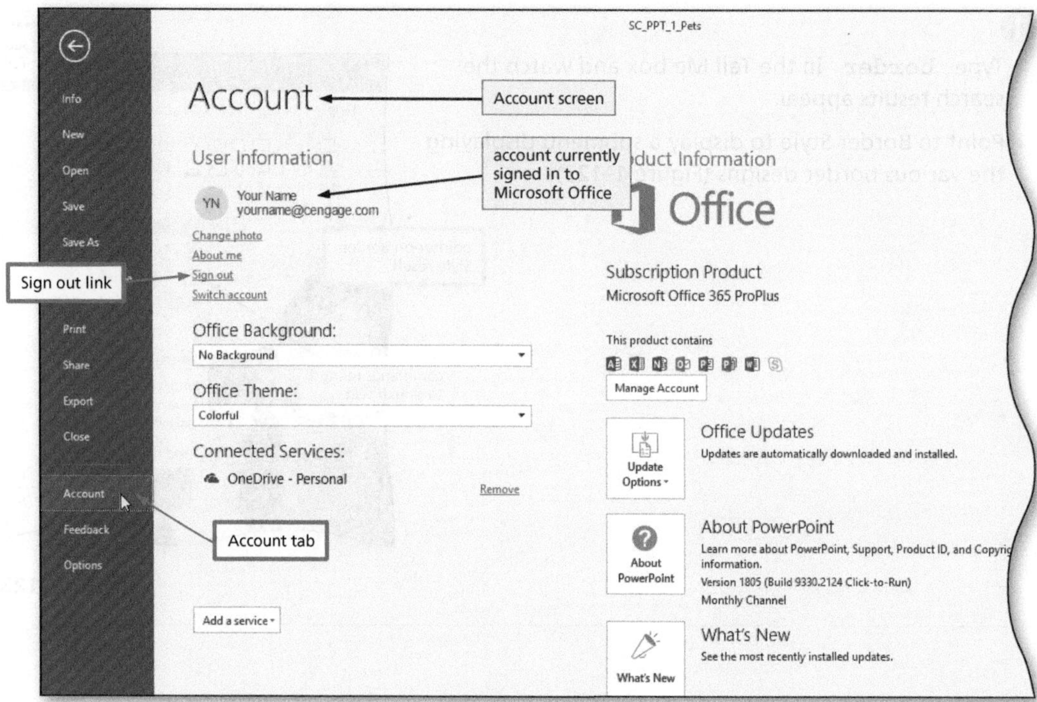

Figure 1–124

Summary

In this module, you learned how to use PowerPoint to create and enhance a presentation. Topics covered included starting PowerPoint, applying and changing a presentation theme and theme colors, creating a title slide and text slides with a multilevel bulleted list, inserting pictures and then resizing and moving them on a slide, formatting and editing text, adding notes, printing the presentation, and reviewing the presentation in several views.

CONSIDER THIS: PLAN AHEAD

What decisions do you need to make when creating your next presentation?

Use these guidelines as you complete the assignments in this module and create your own slide show decks outside of this class.

1. Determine the content you want to include on your slides.
2. Determine which theme is appropriate.
3. Identify the slide layouts that best communicate your message.
4. Format various text elements to emphasize important points.
    a) Select appropriate font sizes.
    b) Emphasize important words with bold, italic, or underlined type and color.
5. Locate graphical elements, such as pictures, that reinforce your message.
    a) Size and position them aesthetically on slides.
6. Determine a storage location for the presentation.
7. Determine the best method for distributing the presentation.

Apply Your Knowledge

Reinforce the skills and apply the concepts you learned in this module.

Modifying Character Formats and Paragraph Levels and Inserting and Moving a Picture

Note: To complete this assignment, you will be required to use the Data Files. Please contact your instructor for information about accessing the Data Files.

Instructions: Start PowerPoint. Open the presentation called SC_PPT_1-1.pptx, which is located in the Data Files. The presentation you open contains two unformatted slides. The Assistant Director of Student Affairs at your school has asked you to help her develop a presentation for incoming freshmen on the topic of how to be successful in college. She has started her preparation by creating two unformatted slides. You open her document and then modify the theme and colors, indent the paragraphs, insert, resize and move a picture, and format the text so the slides look like Figure 1–125.

Perform the following tasks:

1. Change the document theme to Ion. Change the theme colors to Blue.
2. On the title slide, use your name in place of Student Name and then italicize and underline your name.
   If requested by your instructor, change your first name to your grandmother's first name on the title slide.
3. Increase the title text font size to 60 point, change the font to Georgia, and then bold this text.
4. Insert the picture named Support_PPT_1_Success.jpg. Resize and position the picture using the smart guides to align the center of the image on the right side of the slide and the lower edge with the bottom of the subtitle text placeholder, as shown in Figure 1–125a.
5. On Slide 2, increase the indent of the second and third paragraphs to second-level paragraphs and the fourth paragraph to a third-level paragraph. Then combine paragraphs six and seven (Study group and Study routine) to read, `Join a study group and develop a study routine`, as shown in Figure 1–125b. Increase the indent of this paragraph to second level.
6. On Slide 2, type `Online classes pose special challenges. Be certain you can meet the technology requirements and stay connected with your instructors.` in the Notes pane.
7. Click the 'Start From Beginning' button to start the show from the first slide. Then click to display the second slide and again to end the presentation.
8. Save the file with the file name, `SC_PPT_1_Success`, and submit the revised presentation (shown in Figure 1–125) in the format specified by your instructor.
9. In Step 5, you combined two paragraphs and added text. How did this action improve the slide content?

Continued >

Apply Your Knowledge *continued*

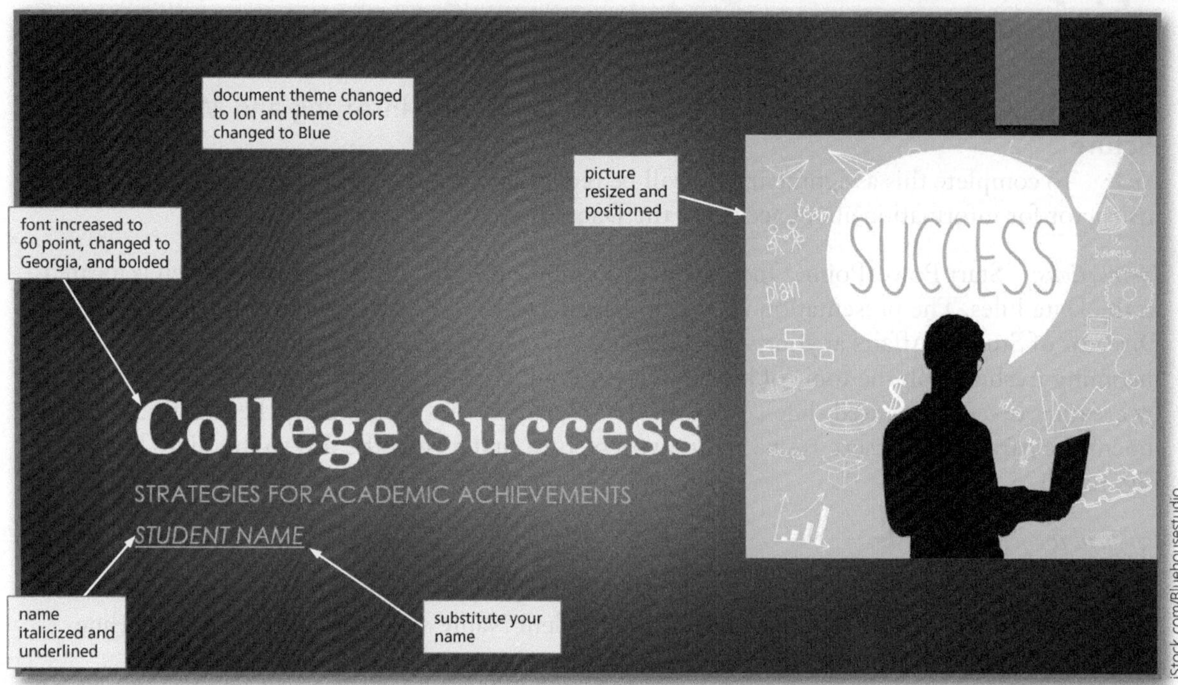

(a) Slide 1 (Title Slide with a Picture)

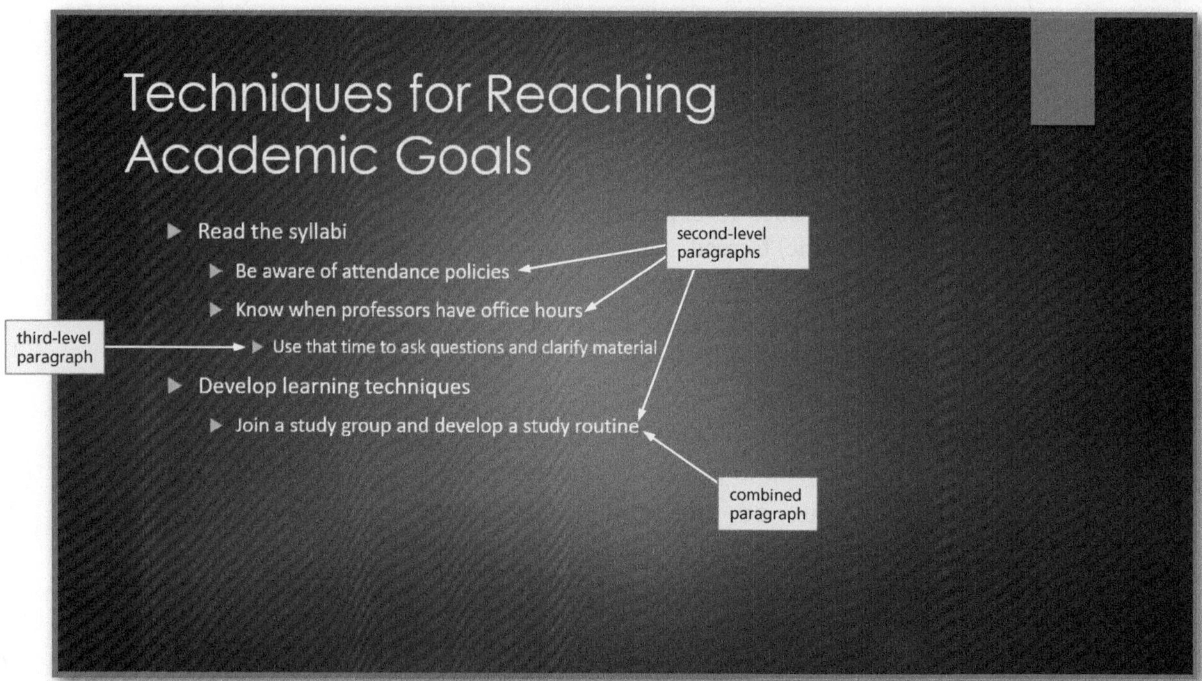

(b) Slide 2 (Multilevel Bulleted List)

Figure 1–125

Extend Your Knowledge

Extend the skills you learned in this module and experiment with new skills. You may need to use Help to complete the assignment.

Changing the Slide Theme, Layout, and Text

Note: To complete this assignment, you will be required to use the Data Files. Please contact your instructor for information about accessing the Data Files.

Instructions: Start PowerPoint. Open the presentation called SC_PPT_1-2.pptx, which is located in the Data Files. Slide 1 is shown in Figure 1–126. The Digital Marketing Consultant for your company is planning a presentation for senior managers on methods of increasing employees' workplace productivity. She has developed three slides to accompany her speech, and she has asked you to insert appropriate pictures, choose a theme, and format these slides.

Perform the following tasks:

1. Change the document theme to Parallax and the theme colors to Red.
2. On Slide 1, format the text using techniques you learned in this module, such as changing the font size and color and bolding, italicizing, and underlining words.
3. Replace the text, Student Name, with your name.
   If requested by your instructor, replace your last name on Slide 1 with the name of your hometown.
4. Delete the bullet preceding your name because, in most cases, a bullet is displayed as the first character in a list consisting of several paragraphs, not just one line of text. To delete the bullet, position the insertion point in the paragraph and then click the Bullets button (Home tab | Paragraph group).
5. Resize the picture and move it to an appropriate area on the slide.
6. On Slide 2, add bullets to the three paragraphs below the left heading placeholder. To add bullets, select the paragraphs and then click the Bullets button (Home tab | Paragraph group). Insert the picture called Support_PPT_1_Training.jpg, which is located in the Data Files, in the right content placeholder. Resize this picture and then move it to an appropriate area on the slide.
7. On Slide 3, add bullets to the five paragraphs below the left heading placeholder. Insert the picture called Support_PPT_1_Wheels.jpg, which is located in the Data Files, in the right content placeholder. Rotate and resize this picture and then move it to an appropriate area on the slide.
8. Duplicate the title slide. To duplicate this slide, select it, click the New Slide arrow (Home tab | Slides group) to display the layout gallery, and then click 'Duplicate Selected Slides' in the layout gallery.
9. Move the new slide to the end of the presentation. Change the subtitle text to **`Tap your employees' talents`** and then underline this text. Insert the two pictures, Support_PPT_1_Training.jpg and Support_PPT_1_Wheels.jpg, and then size and move all three pictures to appropriate places on the slide.
10. Click the 'Start From Beginning' button to start the show from the first slide. Then click to display each slide and again to end the presentation.
11. Save the file with the file name, **`SC_PPT_1_Productivity_Sample_Solution`**, and submit the revised presentation in the format specified by your instructor.
12. How did you determine the appropriate size and location of the three pictures on the duplicated slide?

Continued >

Extend Your Knowledge *continued*

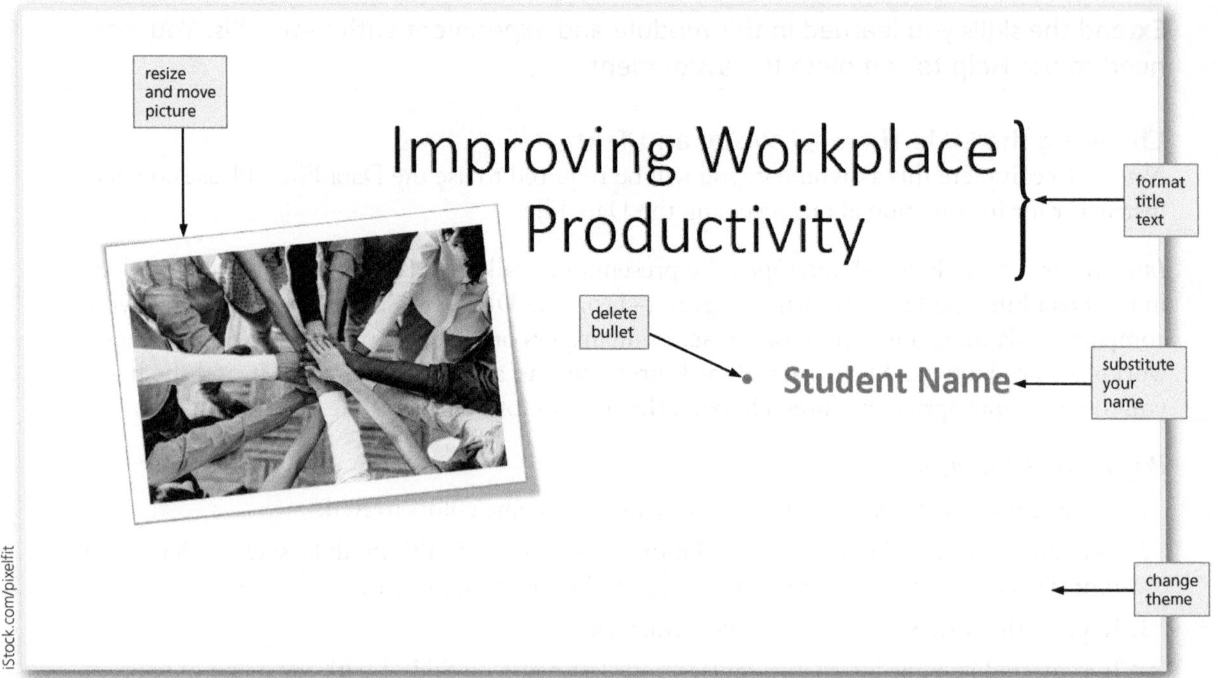

Figure 1–126

Expand Your World

Create a solution that uses cloud and web technologies by learning and investigating on your own from general guidance.

Modifying and Exporting a Presentation

Note: To complete this assignment, you will be required to use the Data Files. Please contact your instructor for information about accessing the Data Files.

Instructions: Start PowerPoint. Open the presentation called SC_PPT_1-3.pptx, which is located in the Data Files. The presentation you open contains one title slide promoting going green in the office. The Environmental Health Specialist at your company has instituted several environmentally friendly practices, and he is planning to give a talk announcing these changes. You are part of a committee to publicize the event and want to share the title slide you developed with some of the participants. You have decided to store the file on OneDrive. You are going to modify the slide you have created, shown in Figure 1–127, and save it to OneDrive.

Perform the following tasks:

1. Insert the pictures called Support_PPT_1_Clip.png and Support_PPT_1_Plastic.jpg, which are located in the Data Files. Size and then move them to the areas indicated in Figure 1–127. Use the smart guides to help you position the pictures.

   If requested to do so by your instructor, change the words, Boston, MA, to the town and state where you were born.

2. Export the file to your OneDrive account.
3. Save the file with the file name, `SC_PPT_1_Green`, and submit the presentation in the format specified by your instructor.
4. When would you save one of your files for school or your job to OneDrive? Do you think using OneDrive enhances collaboration efforts? Why?

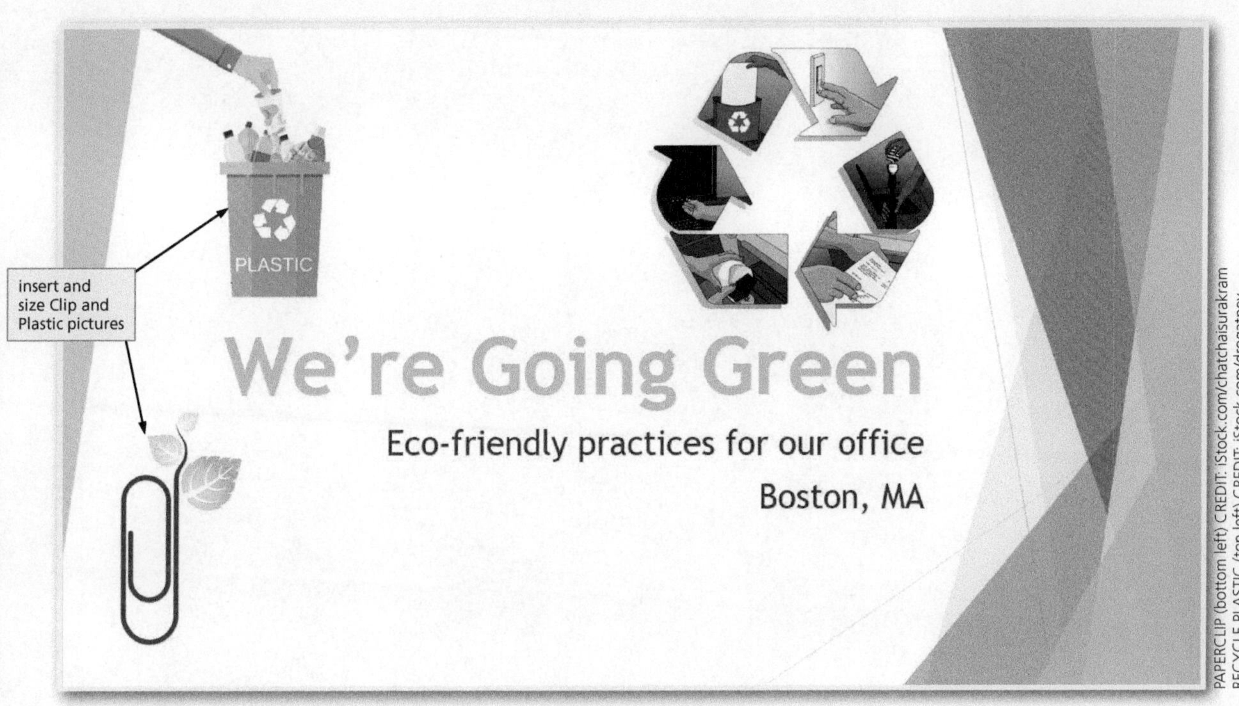

PAPERCLIP (bottom left) CREDIT: iStock.com/chatchaisurakram
RECYCLE PLASTIC (top left) CREDIT: iStock.com/drogatnev
RECYCLE IDEAS (top right) CREDIT: iStock.com/Kayann

Figure 1–127

In the Lab

Apply your creative thinking and problem-solving skills to design and implement a solution.

Design and Create a Presentation about Business Programs

Part 1: Your school is expanding the courses offered in the School of Business, and the department chair has asked you to help promote the program. She informs you that the classes emphasize creative and critical-thinking skills by combining material from the modern business world, liberal arts and sciences, environmental design, and engineering. Graduates possess technical skills that prepare them for success in their careers. Internships at local businesses provide real-work experience. Use the concepts and techniques presented in this module to prepare a presentation with a minimum of four slides that showcase the School of Business program. Research business programs at local schools for additional information about specific classes, tuition costs, admission requirements, and graduation rates. Select a suitable theme, and include a title slide and bulleted lists. Review and revise your presentation as needed. Submit your assignment in the format specified by your instructor.

Part 2: You made several decisions while creating the presentation in this assignment: what theme to use, where to place text, how to format the text (font, font size, paragraph alignment, bulleted paragraphs, italics, bold, underline, color). What was the rationale behind each of these decisions? When you reviewed the slides, what further revisions did you make and why? Where would you recommend showing this slide show?